29th EDITION
GUNS ILLUSTRATED®
1997

Edited by Harold A. Murtz
and the Editors of Gun Digest

DBI BOOKS
a division of Krause Publications, Inc.

STAFF

GUNS ILLUSTRATED

EDITOR
Harold A. Murtz

SENIOR STAFF EDITOR
Ray Ordorica

ASSOCIATE EDITOR
Robert S.L. Anderson

PRODUCTION MANAGER
John L. Duoba

EDITORIAL/PRODUCTION ASSOCIATE
Laura M. Mielzynski

ASSISTANT TO THE EDITOR
Lilo Anderson

ELECTRONIC PUBLISHING DIRECTOR
Sheldon L. Factor

ELECTRONIC PUBLISHING MANAGER
Nancy J. Mellem

ELECTRONIC PUBLISHING ASSOCIATE
Larry Levine

GRAPHIC DESIGN
John L. Duoba
Bill Limbaugh

MANAGING EDITOR
Pamela J. Johnson

PUBLISHER
Charles T. Hartigan

About Our Covers

Born in the opening days of World War II, the M-1 Carbine had a long service life in many armies. Some swore at it, others swore by it, and the little gun performed duties it wasn't designed to do. It turned out to be a darned good gun.

Center stage on our covers is the M-1A1 version of the Carbine, with the side-folding paratrooper stock, fifteen-shot magazine, later lever-type safety, and fully adjustable rear sight. With the stock folded, the gun could be carried in a canvas scabbard strapped to the trooper's leg. This stock is not as sturdy as the full wood type, but it does have its advantages. The M-1 Carbine at the rear has a number of early-issue features that are interesting, most notably the simple L-shaped flip rear sight. It gives only 200- and 300-yard settings for elevation, and needed to be drifted left or right for windage. In addition, there is no bayonet mount, and it has the cross-bolt safety.

See page 47 for Chuck Karwan's story, "The Much Maligned M-1 Carbine."

Carbines shown are from the editor's collection; accessories courtesy Robert Seccombe and Ray Ordorica.

Photo by John Hanusin.

Copyright © MCMXCIV by Krause Publications, Inc., 700 E. State St., Iola, WI 54990. All rights reserved. Printed in the United States of America.

No part of this publication may be reproduced, stored in a retrieval system, or transmitted in any form or by any means electronic, mechanical, photocopying, recording, or otherwise, without the prior written permission of the publisher.

The views and opinions contained herein are those of the authors. The editor and publisher disclaim all responsibility for the accuracy or correctness of the authors' views.

Manuscripts, contributions and inquiries, including first class return postage, should be sent to the GUNS ILLUSTRATED Editorial Offices, 4092 Commercial Ave., Northbrook, IL 60062. All materials received will receive reasonable care, but we will not be responsible for their safe return. Material accepted is subject to our requirements for editing and revisions. Author payment covers all rights and title to the accepted material, including photos, drawings and other illustrations. Payment is at our current rates.

CAUTION: Technical data presented here, particularly technical data on handloading and on firearms adjustment and alteration, inevitably reflects individual experience with particular equipment and components under specific circumstances the reader cannot duplicate exactly. Such data presentations therefore should be used for guidance only and with caution. Krause Publications, Inc. accepts no responsibility for results obtained using this data.

Arms and Armour Press, London, G.B. exclusive licensees and distributor in Britain and Europe, India and Pakistan. Book Services International, Sandton, Transvaal, exclusive distributor in South Africa and Zimbabwe. Forrester Books N.Z. Limited, Auckland, exclusive distributors in New Zealand.

ISBN 0-87349-182-3 Library of Congress Catalog #69-11342

CONTENTS

FEATURES

Kel-Tec and Kahr: The Mini-Nines Are Here!
by Wiley Clapp 4

The "Gas Trap" M-1 Rifles
by Billy Pyle 10

Our Most Lethal Military Rifle?
by C. Rodney James 15

Accuracy Rx for Your 22
by Jim Gosnell 20

The Poor Man's Race Gun
by Don Fisher 26

Gerlich's Taper-Bore Guns
by Konrad F. Schreier, Jr. 32

My Pair of Winchester Model 54s
by David A. Webb 38

Redefining the Pocket Pistol: Glock's Subcompact G26/G27
by Chuck Karwan 43

The Much Maligned M-1 Carbine: WWII's Best Non-Rifle Shoulder Arm
by Chuck Karwan 47

A Smith & Wesson 357/44
by Paul S. Scarlata 55

A Rigby Revival
by Jerry Horgesheimer 59

H&R's 999 Sportsman Lives!
by Gary M. Brown 65

The Baker Shotguns
by Don Hardin and Daryl Hallquist 69

Shoot That Three-Barrel Gun
by Dick Eades 76

A Decade of Change: The Blackpowder Revolution
by Joe Byers 82

Catalog Preview: What's New & Interesting
by Harold A. Murtz 87

DEPARTMENTS

GUNDEX® 90

Handguns
- Semi-Automatics 99
- Competition 129
- Double-Action Revolvers 138
- Single-Action Revolvers 147
- Miscellaneous 152

Rifles—Centerfire
- Semi-Automatics 157
- Lever & Slide Actions 162
- Bolt Actions 167
- Single Shots 183
- Drillings, Combos, Double Rifles 188

Rifles—Rimfire
- Semi-Automatics 190
- Lever & Slide Actions 193
- Bolt Actions & Single Shots 194
- Competition Centerfires & Rimfires 199

Shotguns
- Semi-Automatics 206
- Slide Actions 211
- Over/Unders 215
- Side-by-Sides 226
- Bolt Actions & Single Shots 230
- Military & Police 234

Blackpowder Guns
- Single Shot Pistols 237
- Revolvers 239
- Muskets & Rifles 244
- Shotguns 260

Airguns
- Handguns 262
- Long Guns 269

Scopes & Mounts 281

Scope Mounts 291

Arms Associations 295

Directory of the Arms Trade 297
- Product Directory 298
- Manufacturers' Directory 313

The P11 (left) and K9 fit easily inside this shooter's slightly larger-than-average hands, but both carry more muscle than most small "pocket" guns.

Kel-Tec and Kahr
THE MINI-NINES ARE HERE!

by WILEY CLAPP

The Kel-Tec P11 (top) and Kahr K9 are the smallest pistols ever built for the 9mm Parabellum cartridge, and both are very well suited to concealed carry.

THE 9MM LUGER cartridge has been with us for all of this troubled century. It persists because of its many virtues, which are counterbalanced by only a few vices. Principal among the vices is the somewhat less than ideal terminal ballistic performance for combat purposes. More to the point of this discussion, however, is the major virtue of the round—it's a tiny little thing. High-capacity magazines were not in use when DWM adapted their Luger pistol to the 9mm Parabellum cartridge, but a double column of those little 9mms was a major feature of the first *commercially successful* handgun originally designed for the round. The Browning Hi-Power was the gun and that double-wide magazine has been copied ever since. In time, the compact dimensions of the 9mm round contributed heavily to the so-called "Wondernine Wars" where nearly every pistol maker in the world found ways to stuff more and more rounds of 9mm ammo into full-sized police and military pistols. The popularity of the guns drove the ammo makers to redoubled efforts to make a little cartridge shoot much bigger.

But we are now at a point where capacity is moot for all but police and military sales. There's a new law which mandates civilian magazine capacity at no more than ten rounds. It has produced a design trend toward smaller pistols for civilians with their newly won right to carry a concealed firearm on their persons. After all, why put up with a bulky, large pistol with a high-capacity magazine blocked at ten rounds? The little 9mm round, beneficiary of soundly engineered modern ammunition with high-performance expanding bullets, is an ideal size for a new generation of scaled-down 9mm handguns. From the major handgun makers, there are already several fine new models, like Sigarms' P239, Glock's Model 26 and S&W's 3913 series, but this story is all about two exciting newcomers. The guns at hand are Kel-Tec's P11 and Kahr Arms' K9.

Both pistols are completely original designs rather than modified versions of other guns. Both are smaller than anything we have seen before in 9mm, with the Kel-Tec a trifle smaller than the Kahr. Over the many years that 9mm semi-autos have been designed and manufactured around the world, there have been efforts to build ever smaller ones by dispensing with the locked-breech, short-recoil method of operation. The most recent one was the ill-fated Detonics Pocket Nine, a blowback pistol that failed miserably. The 9mm ammunition operates at significant pressures, and doing away with the somewhat bulky locking parts may produce a more compact mechanism, but a completely unworkable one. If it's a full-service 9mm pistol, capable of handling any normal commercial load, you need the locked-breech design. Both of these pistols use the best ever developed, John Browning's tilting barrel system, but they do so in an exceedingly small package.

Full-time, everyday carrying guns have to be small. If they are not, human nature kicks in and the gun becomes a part-time, some-days gun. The reason for carrying a handgun is

SPECIFICATIONS

Kahr K9		Kel-Tec P11
3.5	Barrel Length (in.)	3.1
6.0	Overall Length (in.)	5.6
25	Weight (oz.)	14
7+1	Capacity	10+1
$595	Price	$300

Better make that mini-mini-nines, because these two recent designs are intended for concealed carry and backup

to win the fight we hope never presents itself, and as the cliche holds, the first rule of winning a gunfight is to have a gun. The point is simply that, for all but a few shooters, the defensive handgun has to be small enough to be habitually carried. It also follows that the chosen piece should also be powerful enough to deliver multiple hits, each of which stands a reasonable chance of terminating the action. For many years, this was the province of snub-nosed 38 Special revolvers and sometimes 380 ACPs. The 380 is still popular, but when you can have a full 9mm pistol of the same size and weight envelope, the advantage is overwhelmingly the 9mm's. For the first time, we have viable 9mm pistols no larger than 380s or snubbie 38 Special revolvers. It's a distinct breakthrough in gun making technology, driven by a perceived need in the shooting marketplace. All of the forgoing brings us around to the point where we can begin to examine a pair of fine new handgun designs.

Let's look at the Kel-Tec pistol first. It is the smaller and lighter of the two pistols, weighing just 14 ounces and running to 5.6 inches in overall length, with a 3.1-inch barrel. The three major components of the pistol's structure are the slide, receiver and grip. They're made from investment-cast steel, machined aluminum alloy and moulded polymer, respectively. The means of combining the receiver and grip is ingenious, and I'll bet we see the idea copied in the future. In normal gun terminology, the receiver is the entire lower half of the gun, as well as that portion of the arm where Federal law requires the placement of a serial number. Technically, that's true of the Kel-Tec, but the aluminum "receiver" is actually a machined alloy block mounted in the center of a moulded polymer grip. Held in place in the grip with three pins, the receiver provides the cam surface necessary to lock and unlock the pistol's Browning-style lockup. It also serves to position the ejector, plus trigger, drawbar, hammer and related pins that constitute the gun's lockwork. The hammer spring is anchored inside the lower rear corner of the polymer grip.

In the slide, which features a wide ejection port into which the squared barrel breech indexes, there's a conventional inertial firing pin and spring. There's also a more-or-less typical extractor. The pistol's barrel is a very short 3.1 inches, including

Shooter Walt Kesteloot tries some deliberate shooting with the P11, and despite the short grip he found it comfortable to fire.

The Kel-Tec sights are drift-adjustable for windage and have the popular three dots for reference. They're also made of polymer.

George Kelgren's P11 design features a polymer grip housing an aluminum receiver, topped with a cast steel barrel and slide. Grips are checkered panels; trigger is also polymer.

The P11 is quick and easy to field-strip. The part in the center is the slide release/lock, which is removed with a cartridge rim.

the chamber, and it has a reduced diameter section near the muzzle to permit the rear of the barrel to tilt downward for unlocking, extraction, etc. Most of this pistol's features, except for the unique receiver/grip configuration, are seen in many other guns. But the trigger is completely different. It's double-action-only, where trigger pressure first raises, then releases the hammer. Unlike most firing systems which have a hammer, the Kel-Tec's is different. Here, the hammer has no spur (it can't be cocked, so a spur is superfluous), and the mass of the hammer is centered on the pivot hole and shaft. The idea is to strike the firing pin and fire the pistol with speed, as opposed to weight. It's kind of like

(Top) Clapp delivers a fast double-tap with the Kahr K9 and Hornady Vector ammunition. Note the distance between bullet traces and shots on target. (Bottom) With the lighter and slower trigger of the P11, bullet traces and on-target hits are further apart.

SHOOTING RESULTS

Gun	Factory Load	Velocity (fps)	Group (in.)
Kahr K9	Hornady 147-gr. HP/XTP	875	3.67
Kel-Tec P11		867	4.22
Kahr K9	Speer 147-gr. Gold Dot	866	2.99
Kel-Tec P11		859	3.45
Kahr K9	Hornady 124-gr. FMJ/FP	1022	3.44
Kel-Tec P11		1004	3.89
Kahr K9	Remington 124-gr. Golden Saber	998	3.99
Kel-Tec P11		971	3.56
Kahr K9	Pro Load 115-gr. JHP	1044	3.07
Kel-Tec P11		1037	3.55
Kahr K9	CCI Lawman 115-gr. JHP	1011	3.36
Kel-Tec P11		1024	3.23

Accuracy results are for a ten-shot group fired from a braced sitting position on a shooting bench. Chronograph results produced by an Oehler Model 35P chronograph with skyscreens placed approximately 12 feet from the muzzle.

driving a nail with a single clean, fast strike of a lightweight hammer, as opposed to clubbing it in with a sledge.

The result of all the special engineering and innovative design is an uncommonly appealing little gun. Kel-Tec magazines are of the double-column variety and hold ten rounds. Because of their similarity at the upper end to those of Smith & Wesson, the shooter can also use the full range of S&W Third Generation double-column 9mm magazines—12-, 14-, 15- and 20-shot varieties. Despite this 10+1 capacity, the Kel-Tec P11 remains a small gun. The grip is small enough that there's room for only two fingers on the butt. Ergonomics are quite good despite the diminutive size. In my hand, the pistol feels rather like a thick PPK, and that's a pretty comfortable feel. There are no sharp corners or edges to abrade the shooter's hands or gear. Shooter amenities include a panel of checkering on either side of the grip and moulded-in grooves on the four corners of the grip section. The sights, triple-dot in the shooter's aspect, are plastic, with a small amount of windage adjustment available via drifting of the rear sight. The manual supplied with the gun shows a sight kit with several heights of both front and rear sights to adjust for a particular shooter's hold for a given load. All things considered, this seems to be a very nicely worked out handgun with a very strong appeal in the police backup and concealed carry markets.

That's also the intended market for the other pistol under consideration, the Kahr K9. This gun is 6 inches long with a 3.5-inch barrel. All steel, it weighs 25 ounces. K9 magazines take a single row of seven 9mm cartridges, making for an eight-shot pistol with the chamber loaded. It's remarkably slim for a 9mm, something like $8/10$-inch thick across the receiver. Most of the design features of the pistol are pretty much conventional, with the receiver a CNC-finished casting and the slide cut from bar stock. The breech locking system is modified Browning (like the majority of today's service pistols), and the square breech indexes into the wide ejection port when the slide is closed and locked into battery.

Like the Kel-Tec, the Kahr K9 is a double-action-only pistol. But unlike its contemporary mini-9mm, the Kahr works on the basis of a retractable striker in the slide, rather than a hammer and firing pin. In its handling, the K9 is something like a Glock, Sigma or S&W Third Generation DAO, because slide movement is required to set the trigger for a short, sweet trigger pull. This requires the shooter to understand that he has to execute a Tap-Rack-Bang immediate action drill in the event of a failure to fire. When the shooter presses the trigger of the K9, a portion of the cocking cam presses upward to move a safety block out of the path of the striker, and then pulls the striker from the half-cocked position to a fully withdrawn (cocked) position. A slight further movement to the rear will release the striker and fire the gun. It's simple and straightforward, with no need for external, manually applied safeties and/or decocking levers. As a plus, the trigger system requires only some 7 to 8 pounds of pressure—and it is really smooth.

Examining the disassembled pistol and its internal surfaces provides insight into the ingenuity that went into designing the gun. It's obvious the designers wanted to build a compact but rugged pistol, because there are no flimsy parts anywhere in sight. The barrel unlocks downward by means of a sturdy cross pin working in a kidney-shaped cam slot in the lower barrel lug. The barrel includes an integral feed ramp offset to the left. That's done to gain some room inside the receiver for the forward extensions of the trigger bar and related parts. Unlike many contemporary semi-autos, the K9 does not use the grips to cover and retain in place various bars and springs. Removing the grips—special rubber ones made by Hogue with an attractive pebbled surface—reveals a clean receiver. The K9 seems to be a sturdy and straightforward, all-steel handgun designed and built with high quality and durability in mind.

With the basic nature of the two pistols thus defined, we can begin to make some comparisons, then proceed to shooting side by side. Both guns have their strengths. In size, the P11 is shorter than the K9 by almost 1/2-inch, as well as being a whopping 11 ounces lighter. That makes the Kel-Tec considerably easier to pack around in purse or pocket everyday. It would also seem to be better for the law enforcement officer who uses it as a second, possibly even third, gun. Further theoretical advantage goes to the P11 on the basis of the 10+1 magazine capacity, as opposed to 7+1. And if the shooter happens to be carrying a Third Generation S&W as his primary service pistol, he can use his regular magazines to re-charge his P11 in the unlikely event the action gets that intense.

But that doesn't take into consideration a couple of other factors in favor of the Kahr K9. For one thing, the K9 has a butt section long enough for most shooters to get a full hand on, while the P11 can only take two fingers. The K9 is about twenty percent thinner than the Kel-Tec, which can be critically important in some concealment scenarios. And, although the K9 tested was on the heavy side at 25 ounces, the company will soon market an alloy-receiver version of the pistol weighing less than 19 ounces, which is much closer to the weight of the polymer-gripped Kel-Tec P11. Still, on the basis of a simple physical comparison, the better buy would seem to be the Kel-Tec, which also enjoys a markedly lower price tag.

I could not complete a description and analysis of the two guns without a serious amount of time at the range. I have been shooting early samples of both pistols for several months and have come to some inter-

The smoother trigger action of the K9 makes DAO shooting easy. The gun showed very adequate accuracy for its intended use.

The K9's sights are also drift-adjustable for windage, but use the bar-dot highlights. These sights are made of steel.

(Right) Except for the Hogue rubber grips, the Kahr K9 is all steel. An alloy-frame version will be offered soon to cut weight.

The field-stripped K9 shows good basic design and care in manufacture. The breech locking system is modified Browning.

The Kahr K9 is a small but hand-filling 9mm Parabellum pistol, and there's room for three fingers on the butt.

esting conclusions. Shooting the two mini*est* mini-nines, let me look at both reliability and shootability.

Let's begin with plain functional reliability. My sample Kahr K9, when properly lubricated and fed a diet of good modern ammunition, simply does not fail. In about 700-800 rounds, I have yet to experience any stoppages of any sort. I cannot make so positive a statement about the Kel-Tec, but I believe some of the things I did observe might facilitate a comparison. In the first 100 rounds of shooting with a cleaned and lubricated new pistol, I had seven failures. Three of them were failures to fire, i.e. lightly dented primer, but no boom. Second strikes usually set the round off. Since that initial session, the condition has yet to repeat itself, even with more of the same ammunition from the same lot. I can only conclude the firing mechanism needs to wear in a bit before it becomes totally reliable. The other type of malfunction noted in the first hundred rounds was a failure to chamber, where the round stops on the feed ramp without any indication it was caught on anything. It was as though the slide was not moving back into battery forcefully.

The condition seemed to lessen as more shots were fired in subsequent shooting exercises. Finally, we noted a spot on the top barrel flat where shooting had produced obvious signs of dragging, i.e. a shiny polished mark. It occurred where the slide comes back over the barrel in the rearward movement of the action parts. Lubrication of this spot helped a little, but a careful light stoning to polish the offending surface has eliminated the problem. Having seen two other P11s with exactly the same condition, I believe it is worthy of mention to prospective buyers. I would have to consider this to be a flaw worthy of the company's close attention.

Shootability of the two pistols was also a matter we investigated in some depth. Both have DAO triggers systems, but they are quite different. The P11 has a hammer and firing pin system, matched to a trigger that raises and releases the hammer with every full cycle pull of the trigger. Every pull of the trigger must be through the trigger's full arc. It's a simple and easy mechanism to shoot, right up until you begin to shoot full speed in combat shooting drills. I found it remarkably easy to short-stroke the trigger if I wasn't careful to allow it to go forward to the reset point. All shooting schools teach the combat shooter to deliver a pair of shots to each target. It's called the "controlled pair" or "hammer," and a really good shooter can do it in very short order. Trying for maximum speed in hammers produced short strokes of the trigger with disturbing frequency. This should not be viewed as criticism of the pistol, but rather an admonition to learn to manage the intricacies of the gun thoroughly, particularly when you contemplate carrying it defensively.

The Kahr K9 pistol, as we have already discussed, has a DAO trigger system that's more like the widely used Glock. The movement of the slide to the rear when the pistol fires serves to partially cock the striker for the next shot. It has what some call "short trigger reset," and the same exercises that caused me to short-stroke the P11 trigger were immeasurably easier with the K9. This pistol has an amazingly short, smooth, light DAO pull. You can even see the difference between the two systems in the adjacent photos. Using Hornady Vector ammo, which leaves a visible bullet trace when you fire, we took comparison photos of me shooting the two pistols. With the K9, a pair of shots produced traces very close to each other, which is a function of the speed with which I was able to fire the gun. The traces are materially farther apart with the P11, and part of that would also have to be attributable to the gun's lighter weight, which means it recoils farther from the line of sight and takes longer to bring back on target. Muzzle flip is pretty sharp and recoil is pretty snappy in a 14-ounce 9mm pistol you are holding with two fingers. I also did some basic target shooting, slow fire from a bench to see what the accuracy potential of the two guns was. In general, the accuracy was all that you could reasonably expect and certainly enough gun intended for close-range personal defense. When shooting for accuracy, I also checked velocities by means of Dr. Oehler's Model 35P chronograph. Not surprisingly, the bullets just don't seem to zip out of a shorty barrel like they do from a full-sized Beretta or the like.

The major point to understand is that these two pistols are the first of what may become a definite handgun type—the miniaturized 9mm pistol. There may be some movement toward small pistols in other calibers, but the 9mm cartridge looks just about perfect for the size. With modern ammunition like Gold Dot, Hydra-Shok, Golden Saber, et. al., the 9mm cartridge is much more of a performer than it was even just a few years ago. Both of these guns appear to be viable choices for personal defense, within the framework of deficiencies noted. The Kel-Tec P11 is shorter, lighter, less costly and has a higher capacity. The Kahr K9 is thinner, longer, heavier, more costly and holds fewer cartridges. Beyond any doubt, the Kahr is more accurate and reliable and is much easier to shoot. As we say in Nevada...."pick 'em."

IN MARCH OF 1932, the Adjutant General ordered Springfield Armory to begin production of eighty experimental 30-caliber semi-automatic rifles. These would be designated the "U.S. Semiautomatic Rifle, Caliber .30 TIE2." Based upon much prior research and development by John Garand and a modest budget of $80,000, the rifle that was to revolutionize conventional warfare had its humble beginning. This new rifle would, of course, establish precedents for all other nations to follow.

The Semiautomatic Rifle Board had initially recommended that the new rifle be in caliber 276. Chief of Staff of the Army at this time was General Douglas MacArthur, who disapproved the 276 caliber and directed that the rifle be made in 30-caliber. This would make all the cartridges interchangeable with the M1903s, M1918 BARs, and water- and air-cooled 30-caliber machine guns of the time.

The TIE2 rifles, or "Model Shop Rifles" as they were called, would be built on a semi-production basis. John Garand would personally supervise their manufacture. These first eighty rifles would take over two years for completion. During this production period a new designation would evolve. On August 3, 1933 the TIE2 would become the "U.S. Semi-automatic Rifle, Caliber .30 M1."

The Model Shop

Art Tuttle, the troubleshooter on the M-1 rifle project, explains that the Model Shop functioned as follows: "Herein are produced prototypes or mock-ups; basic ideas in plastic or wood called 'concepts', with no serial numbers. Example: Picture Mr. Garand and one or two model makers working on something in a 'keep-out' room. When this prototype was ready, a functionable model was then fabricated, part by hand and part by machinery in the Tool Room. This was still a product of the Model Shop, *not* the Tool Room, and it was sent to the Research Test Branch.

"Now, if this experimental model passed the Research and Development preliminary tests, a small group of pilot models would be made in the Tool Room; and pilot models will be subject to extensive testing.

"Then, with various corrections sustained, these pilot model guns functioned satisfactorily. Thus, the 'first eighty' were made by semi-production semi-Tool Room methods. This was still a Model Shop project under Mr. Garand's loving care. These initial guns were now serial numbered 1 through 80.

"There was no fine line or division between Model Shop and Tool Room activity. As soon as the model makers came up with a satisfactory component, the tool boys took over for tool design to produce the part with total interchangeability in mind.

"In general, model makers worked in wood, plastic, and steel to hand-fashion workable components. The toolmakers' job was to 'tool-up' for semi and limited production of the components. After testing and possible redesign by the model makers, parts would be changed and the toolmakers would alter their equipment accordingly.

"The model makers' concern was workability of components; toolmakers' concern was interchangeability of those pieces. Model Shop prototypes used the facilities of the Tool Room yet these early rifles were *not* a Tool Room product!"

Production of these early rifles would be completed in May of 1934 and service field testing would commence soon after. Seventy-five rifles would be dispatched to the field—twenty-five to the calvary and fifty to the infantry.

In August, 1934 the field testing was to be suspended and the rifles returned to the Armory Model Shop for inspection and possible design changes. Tolerances of various parts were modified, such as rebending the operating rod, new cam angle for the bolt in the handle of the operating rod, reworking the receiver ribs, etc.

In May 1935 after all eighty rifles had been reworked, the field testing resumed. Recommendations, changes,

The "Gas Trap" M-1 Rifles

and improvements would continue until October, 1935. With the testing finally completed, the new prototype was recommended and approved for standardization. Total unit cost per rifle was $1817.80.

Changes and improvements in the M-1 rifle would continue throughout its service life. The most frequent changes would occur in the production rifles of the late 1930s. Most of the newly designed and improved components would by added to the Model Shop guns in an effort to keep them up to the current standards of manufacture. The majority of the first eighty rifles would go through several major rebuilds in the early 1940s in preparation for service in World War II.

The word "Semiauto" in the official rifle designation and stamped on the receiver would be deleted beginning with M-1 serial number 81. There were no other markings on these receivers other than the serial number and nomenclature. Most of the individual parts were marked with the rifle's serial number on these earlier guns.

New Production Begins

The new rifle was officially adopted and approved for standardization on January 9, 1936. Now came the enormous set up for manufacture. First the ordnance drawings with acceptable tolerances had to be completed. Purchase of machines, equipment, and fixtures to convert raw materials into a newly-designed firearm had to be made. All of this was complicated and painstakingly slow. Bids, proposals, conversions—anything related to government acquisition takes a tremendous amount of time. Over a year and a half passed before the first M-1 came off the assembly line in July of 1937.

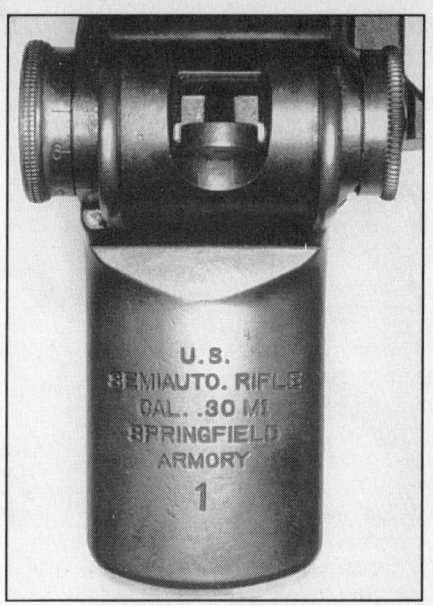

Early-production Garand rifles were different in many respects from the regular examples so often seen.

by BILLY PYLE

(Right) Receiver heel markings of M-1 serial number 1 (top) includes the word "semiauto," but this was deleted on later-production guns. The unnumbered receiver was one of a number of extras made early in the program. Both early guns are at the Springfield Armory National Historic Site.

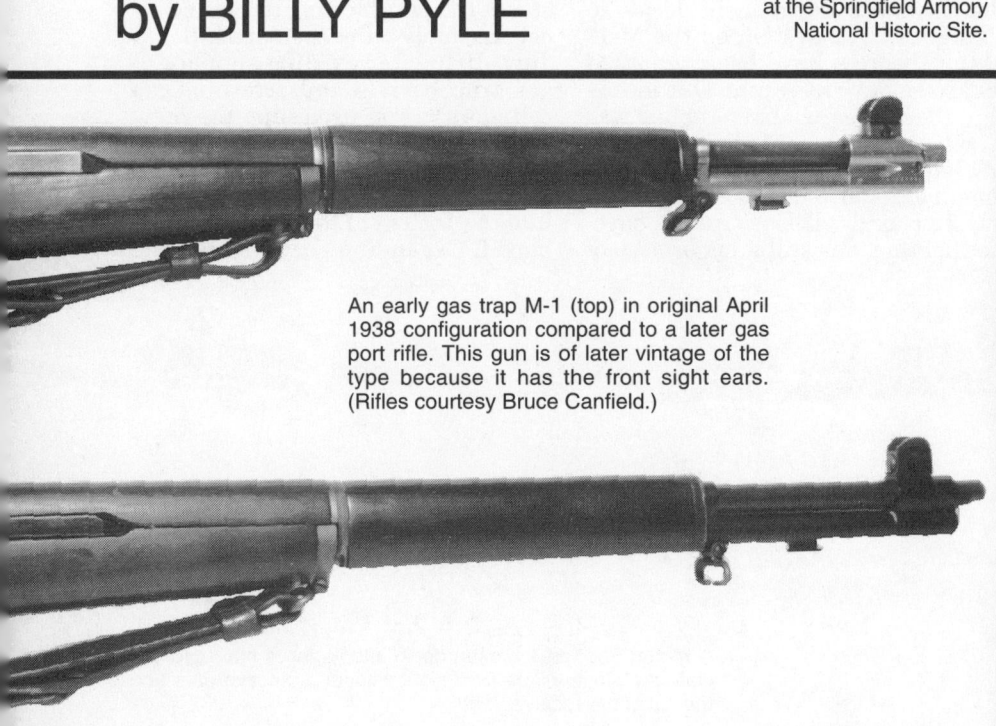

An early gas trap M-1 (top) in original April 1938 configuration compared to a later gas port rifle. This gun is of later vintage of the type because it has the front sight ears. (Rifles courtesy Bruce Canfield.)

The John C. Garand display at the Springfield Armory National Historic Site featured six of his rifles. Remodeling has since changed this layout. (Photo by Roy Arnold.)

This was serial number 81 which is now displayed in the museum at Springfield Armory National Historic Site.

Our discussion is limited to the first production of M-1s which are considerably different from the more commonly known examples of World War II. These are unofficially referred to as "gas trap" rifles to differentiate them from the later "gas port" rifles that superseded them. Officially the Army calls the "gas trap" gas cylinder assembly the "screw-on type" and the later version the "spline-type."

Gas trap production M-1s go from serial number 81 into the early 50,000 serial number range. Each part of the rifle generally has its respective piece mark or ordnance drawing number individually stamped on that component, including the stock and handguards. As time progressed, numbering of the parts gradually decreased to where only the major components such as the barrel, bolt, receiver, trigger housing, operating rod were marked with the drawing numbers.

The most striking and noticeable difference in the early M-1s is the gas cylinder assembly which screws on to the end of the 22-inch barrel, and is held in place by the bottom of the front sight in a single spline. The "gas trap" between the end of the barrel and the removable muzzle plug allows sufficient quantities of escaping gas from fired cartridges to impinge upon the face of the operating rod piston and cycle the rifle semi-automatically.

Why then in October of 1939 did the Ordnance Department decide to change the gas system on the M-1? Many theories have been proposed and some have relevance. One idea is that the single front barrel spline was a weak attachment for the long M1905 bayonet, which had an overall length of 20.5875 inches and a weight of 1.12 pounds. This is true, as bayonet fighting was still a major area of importance for the infantry soldier.

Another theory holds that the gas cylinder was hard to clean and patches could get caught in the trap between the muzzle plug and the cylinder, causing the rifle to improperly cycle. This is a remote possibility at best.

The real reason for the gas cylinder change was that on one occasion when the rifle was hot, while undergoing firing tests by troubleshooter Art Tuttle, the screw holding the muzzle plug in place loosened and came out, allowing the plug to rise out of position. The next fired round struck the plug blowing the gas cylinder assembly off of the barrel. So, in July, 1940 after existing supplies of gas trap barrels and screw-on gas cylinders were used up, the new "spline-type" gas cylinder assembly became standardized. It utilized a small hole called a gas port drilled into the bottom of the longer 24-inch barrel. Expanding gases behind the

A Model Shop M-1 broken down into its three main groups. Note the single-blade front sight without protective ears and the cut of the receiver legs.

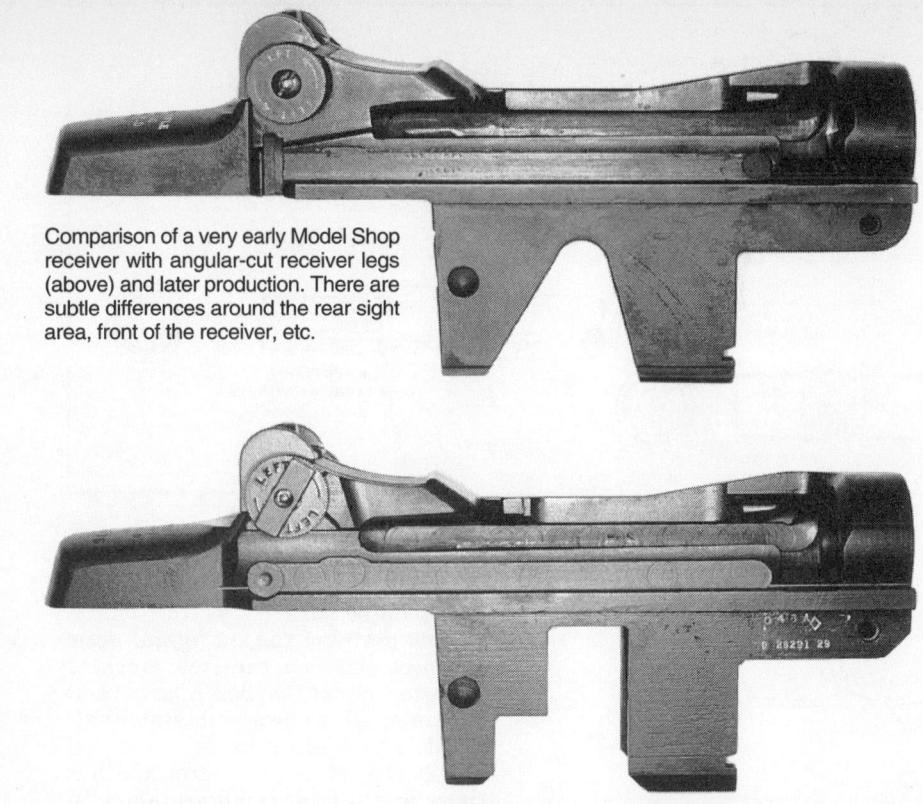

Comparison of a very early Model Shop receiver with angular-cut receiver legs (above) and later production. There are subtle differences around the rear sight area, front of the receiver, etc.

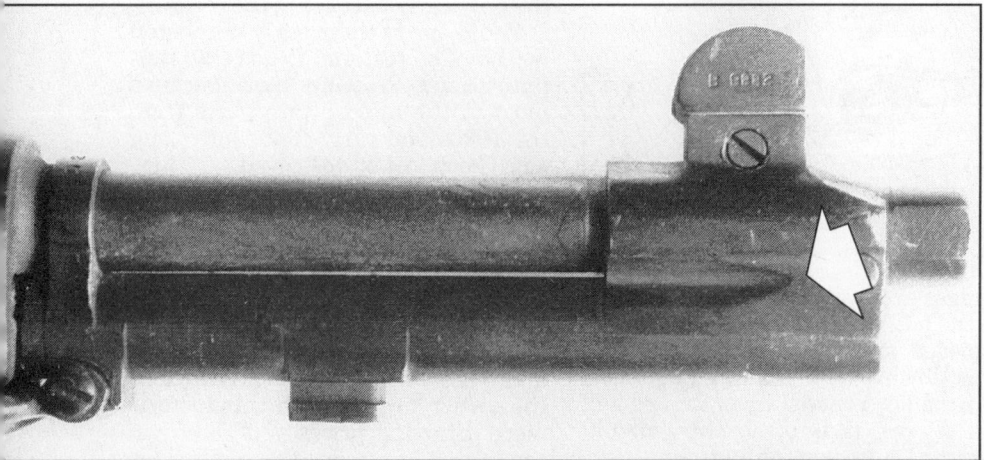

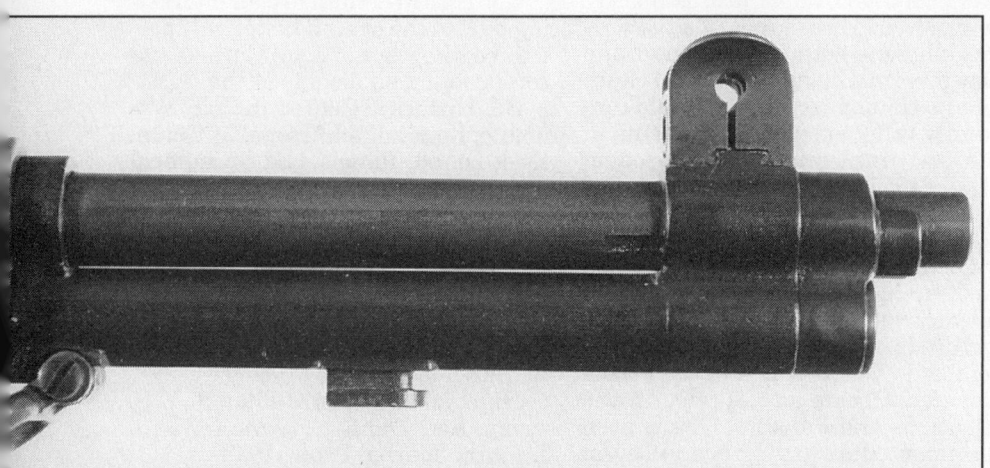

This early production screw-on gas cylinder assembly (above) has vertical sight ears and spear-pointed flutes. The later spline-type cylinder (below) superseded the gas trap unit in mid-1940.

fired bullet entered the gas cylinder through the gas port and cycled the rifle the same way that the "gas trap" system did.

Gas trap M-1s were eventually cycled through the arsenal overhaul process and the early serial numbered receivers were rebuilt with the newer type system. Most gas trap guns met this fate. The few that survived have become very expensive collector pieces.

There were other major differences between the gas trap and spline-type rifles. The early rifles had a solid buttplate, while the later guns had a trap door that opened to allow the stowage of cleaning equipment in two wells inside the buttstock.

Early operating-rod springs were made of a keystone-shaped cross section wire that has a square appearance. The follower rod also had a keystone-shaped compensating or "buffer spring" added to give the operating rod an extra forward boost from the recoil cycle. Keystone springs were sluggish and tended to bind inside the operating rod tube. The Wallace-Barnes Co. came out with a far superior round wire spring and keystone springs became history.

In addition, the front sight went from a single blade to one with parallel protective "ears" or "wings" on each side. A problem soon developed as trainees were mistaking the vertical ears with the actual sight blade when sighting. This situation was corrected by flaring the vertical ears out on each side.

Much has been made about some of the small problems that developed with the early-production rifles. As with any new system, bugs had to be worked out in manufacture and operation of the M-1. These were soon accommodated.

The most persistent and over-stated situation was a minor problem referred to as the "seventh round stoppage." On occasion, on *some* rifles, the eight-round clip would fail to feed on the seventh round; that one would rise up and jam in the receiver causing a stoppage.

What was the cause of the infamous "seventh round stoppage?" During receiver manufacture, the drill making the barrel hole came down too far and nicked the top corner of the inside vertical receiver guide rib on the gun's right side. This happened on comparatively few receivers. Was John Garand consulted? Yes. His response, since this condition never occurred on any of the Model Shop M-1s was: "Follow the machine drawings

These drawings illustrate the differences between the early gas trap cylinder and later design with three barrel splines and the valve assembly.

(Below) The seventh-round stoppage was caused by inadvertently machining off the top corner of the inside guide rib in the receiver. The problem was quickly corrected. (Drawings by Springfield Armory.)

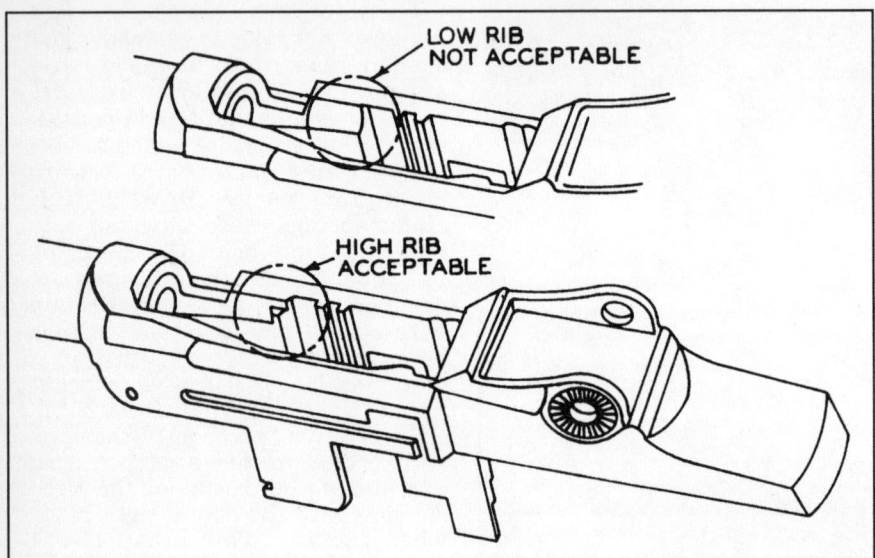

and stay within the tolerances and there won't be any problems." A stop was installed to limit the drilling depth of the barrel hole and this short-lived minor malfunction was soon forgotten.

As these early receivers were cycled through periodic overhaul, the inside receiver guide ribs were built up with weld and machined before the rifles were assembled into new arsenal "rebuilt" M-1s. An original gas trap M-1 will not have the receiver guide ribs built up with weld.

The eight cartridges in the spring-steel clip are staggered in such a manner when loaded that the top round can be loaded either on the left or the right. The rifle will fire the loaded clip either way.

The cartridges are normally loaded with the top round on the right. This allows the shooter to press the clip down and seat it into the receiver using the right thumb, with the palm of the right hand holding back the operating rod handle. If the cartridges are loaded with the top round to the left, the sharp edge of the clip is exposed and the shooter will press this down in the loading sequence. After a few repetitions of this he will get a sore thumb, so clips should always loaded top round right.

Other minor everyday manufacturing "glitches" would occur in M-1 rifle production and would just as quickly be resolved. These kinds of situations are inherent with production of any new firearm. Changes in manufacture and machining techniques would constantly bring about improvements in the M-1 until production ceased in May of 1957, making way for the newly adopted M-14 rifle in 7.62mm NATO caliber.

Of the slightly more than 50,000 gas trap M-1s produced, only a handful survive in their original as-manufactured specifications. Many did see combat in World War II in the Pacific Theater. Others saw service in the Aleutians and Panama. One is even documented as having been used in the Battle of the Bulge. Most were cycled through arsenal overhaul and emerged with the newer gas system and updated parts.

How many of these original guns actually exist on the free market? Thus far, about two dozen have been documented as original and unaltered. There are a lot of low serial numbered M-1s still around, but these are in later configuration with the only early part being the receiver.

Could one of these early numbered receivers be restored to gas trap configuration? Probably not, because most of the appropriate parts from the 1930s and early 1940s have long since been lost or destroyed.

Can an original gas trap M-1 rifle be purchased? They do become available on occasion as long-time M-1 collectors liquidate their prized trophies. What will the cost be? Prices will vary depending on condition, wear, appearance, provenance, serial number range and whether or not you can convince the owner to part with this historic piece. Starting prices generally will commence in the low five digit range and steadily progress upward, possibly as high as $40,000 or more!

Gas trap M-1 rifles are an interesting part of the overall historical spectrum of the work of John Garand and can be found on display at the Buffalo Bill Historical Center, in Cody Wyoming, Rock Island Arsenal Museum, Rock Island, Illinois, and Springfield Armory National Historic Site, Springfield, Massachusetts.

References

Article excerpted from the forthcoming Collector Grade Publications *The "Gas Trap M1 Rifles" 1932-1940* by Billy Pyle

Hatcher, Maj. Gen. Jullian S., U.S. Army, Ret. *The Book of the Garand.* Infantry Journal Press, 1938

by C. RODNEY JAMES

Our Most Lethal Military Rifle?

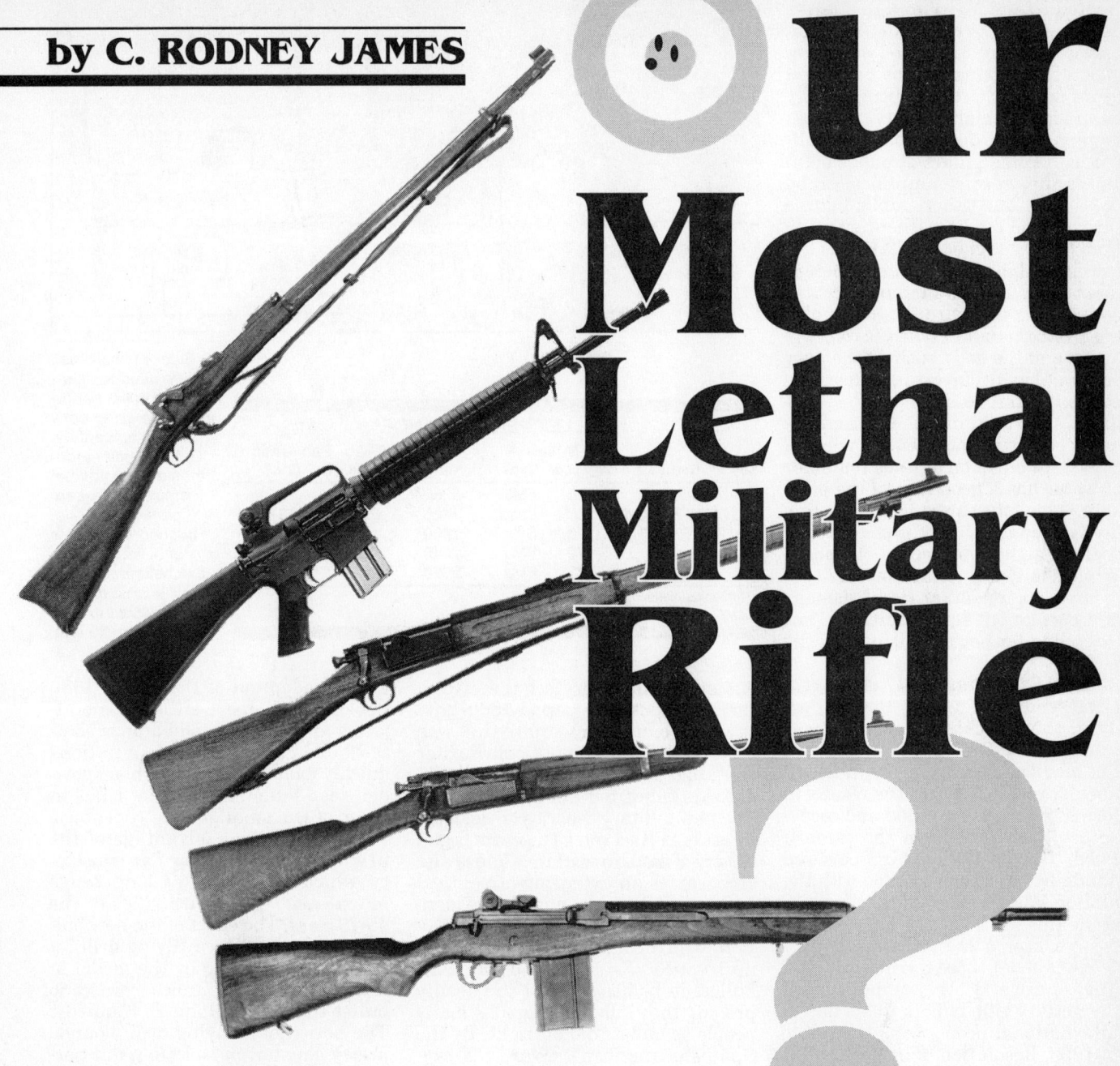

If you think it's one of the newer designs, guess again!

IT'S THE M-16 right? Maybe it's the M-14 or the M-1; the 03/A3 Springfield because of its accuracy? Forget the 30-40 Krag! That leaves the 45-70 Trapdoor Springfield. Whaaat?! You have to be kidding.

We hear the term "lethality" bandied about a lot these days, particularly by our friends, the gun grabbers. They have decided they know what's best for America and that is to get those nasty "assault" rifles out of our hands because they're so *lethal*. In point of fact, aside from their firepower, the civilian model M-16 and AK-47 rifles are rather modest in their lethality compared to earlier rifles issued by the U.S. military.

In medical terms, "lethality" is the effect of a particular bullet on a body. According to Dr. Martin Fackler, the leading wound ballistics expert in the country, bullet lethality is an easily understood concept. Lethality is determined by answering two questions: How big is the hole it produces? How deep is this hole? Bigger and deeper holes are more likely to intersect with vital organs, cause greater loss of blood, and result in death.

What about high velocity? In the 1960s, reports of horrendous wounds created by the M-16 and, to a lesser degree, AK-47 rifles in Vietnam began pouring in. The wounding effects were genuine, but presented by an ignorant press as being wholly an artifact of high velocity. As often happens, misinformation and half-truths become pillars of public opinion as they receive amplification by politicians and other public figures through the media without scrutiny from the researcher. In the case of the velocity/lethality controversy, there is *some* truth to the wounding effects of hydrostatic or hydraulic shock of a high velocity bullet *when* it contacts an area of the body such as the liver or cranial vault. Liver tissue has poor elasticity and brain tissue behaves like a semi-fluid in a sealed container. Anyone who has seen the effect of a 3000 fps bullet on a closed container of water has a good idea of the pressure-wave effect produced. *But*, this does not apply to other types of tissue with a higher degree of elasticity. While a large, instantaneous cavity is created, the resultant tissue damage of a permanent sort is minimal, not extending far beyond the path of the bullet.

The 7.62x39mm AK-47 rifle (actually a semi-auto) used by Patrick Purdy in the "Stockton Massacre" was examined by Dr. Fackler along with the medical data from the incident. Fackler concluded that the results in terms of killed, wounded and recovered would have been the same if Purdy had used a medium-powered handgun.[1] In a conversation with the author, Fackler allowed the possibility of the same result had Purdy's weapon been a 22 rimfire rifle.

What about those terrible wounds? The controversy over wounds caused by military rifle bullets was a flap of international proportions beginning in 1899. Resolution, if one can call it that, was the Hague Convention's ban on the "Dum Dum" bullet, a standard metal-jacketed 303 British military round with 1 millimeter of exposed lead point—demanding all rifle bullets have a full metal jacket. This was declared more "humane" and approved in the Hague Conventions of the period, which were among the first attempts to create "rules of war."

Rules are made to be broken, so it seems, and cynicism in international politics has always been with us. Mixed with this cynicism was the hard reality of caring for one's own troops by equipping them with weapons sufficient to protect them from their enemies. The period 1860-1905 saw a revolution in warfare that was both technical and political. Earlier wars had been decided primarily by one side killing more of the other side. The new military theories of visionaries such as Karl von Clausewitz began the era of modern warfare. Clausewitz saw war as an extension of political pressure. Advances in medicine identified microbes as the source of infection, which could be countered with antiseptics. X-rays could pinpoint bullets in bodies without the deadly probing that killed perhaps as many people as bullets did outright. By the Spanish-American War, X-ray-equipped, state-of-the-art hospital ships (circa 1898) were treating casualties within hours after they had come off the line in the Battle of Santiago.

A demand for good medical treatment of wounded soldiers had become part of civilized society. This concern also meant that winning a war against a civilized power no longer depended on creating fatalities so much as creating *casualties* on the other side, thereby bringing about an increased *economic* hardship in terms of money and manpower for their care.

The era of the small-bore high-velocity military rifle began with the French adoption of the Model 1886 Lebel, which used either a metal-jacketed bullet or a solid bronze boat-tail bullet. Other European nations quickly followed, giving up blackpowder, lead-bullet, single shot rifles in favor of the smaller bore repeaters. The most obvious advantage of the new weapons was their flat trajectory which made hits at long range much easier than with rifles of the 45-70 class. The effect of the new bullets was much like a "flying drill," a metaphor picked up by the media in reference to the Mannlicher-Carcano bullet that killed John F. Kennedy. The notion of a "flying drill" sounds pretty sinister, in isolation, but perhaps less so compared to "flying potato masher" or "flying sledge hammer" which would be a good metaphor for the 45-70, whose large soft bullet expands to deliver a heavy, bone-crushing, tissue-smashing blow.

Dr. Louis La Garde, later Commandant and Professor of Surgery at the U.S. Army Medical School, served in the Indian Campaigns and the Spanish-American War. He treated battle casualties from old and new rifles and later conducted extensive studies in wound ballistics.[2] By his assessment, the old Springfield was far more lethal than the 30-caliber high-velocity rifle. The heavy lead bullet ex-

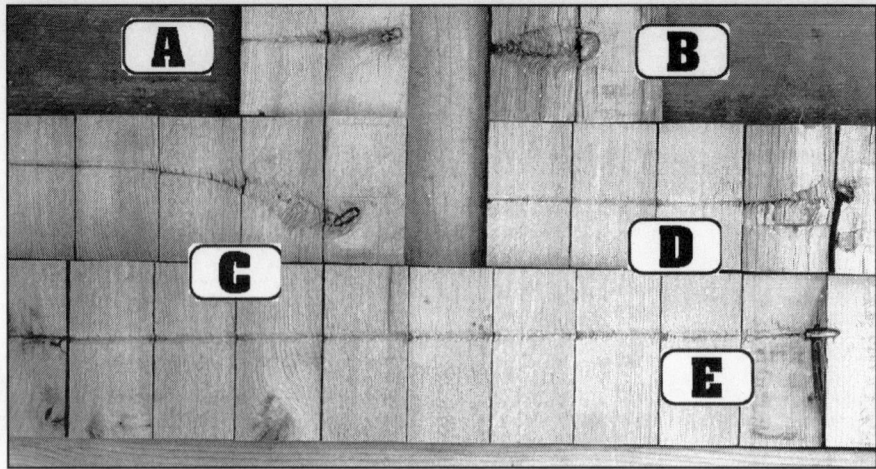

Blocks of solid oak were used to determine bullet performance in the early part of the century. Oak is much harder than a body and not comparable except perhaps to bone, but certain aspects of bullet behavior can be learned from such a test. All shots were fired from 50 feet.

BULLET PERFORMANCE

Key	Cartridge	Bullet Wgt.Grs.	Bullet Type	MV (fps)	ME (ft.lbs.)	Penetration (ins.)
A	223 Rem.	55	FMJ	3250	1325	5.5
B	45-70 Govt.[1]	500	Lead	1425	2255	3.6
C	7.62x39[2]	122	SC	2400	1560	12.6
D	30-06	172	FMJ	2640	2660	12.4
E	7x57 Mauser	173	FMJ	2296	2025	29.3

[1]1898 smokeless load
[2]Steel core

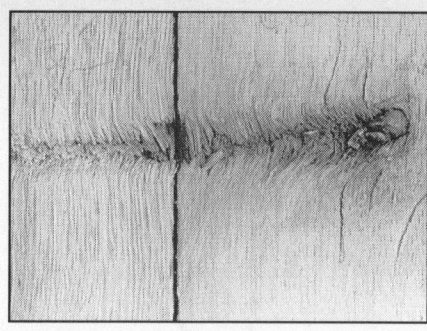
The 223 Remington bullet flipped over in the oak block and was going base first when it stopped. Fragments litter the bullet's path.

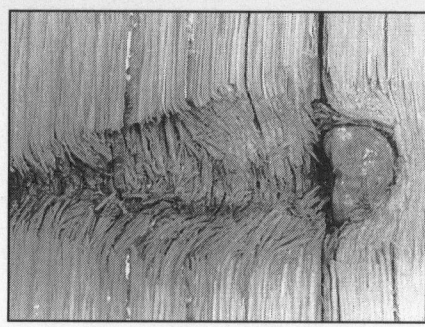
The massive 45-70 expanded rapidly in the oak, pulping a permanent cavity 1.8 inches in diameter, rapidly delivering all its energy. The bullet expanded to .9-inch.

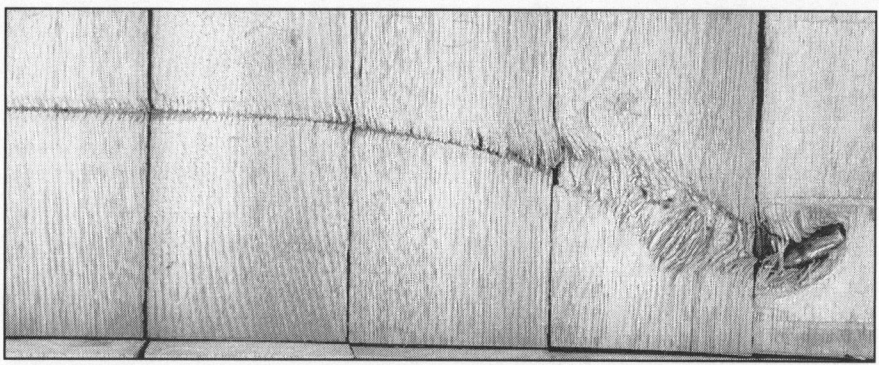
The 7.62x39mm Russian bullet penetrated 8.5 inches of oak before beginning its flip. In soft tissue this bullet travels about 10 inches before losing stability in this manner. The wound of a stable bullet is of the "flying drill" type, comparable to a handgun bullet of the same caliber.

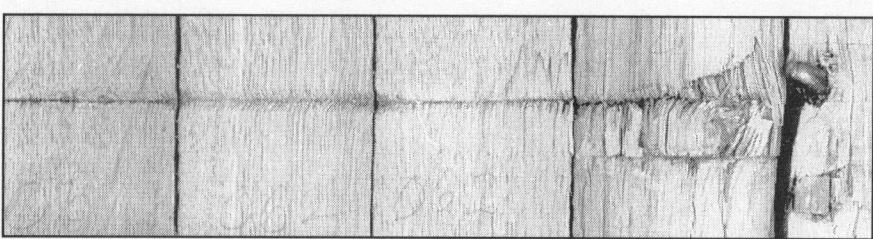
A 30-06 military round behaves much like the Russian, maintaining stability for about the first 10.5 inches of penetration.

A round-nosed 7mm Mauser remained stable throughout its entire passage through the oak. JFK assassination buffs should note the relatively pristine condition of the fired bullet after passing through more than two feet of solid hardwood.

Left to right: 45-70-500, 30-40 Krag (220 grains), 30-06 (150 grains), 7.62x39mm, 223 Remington.

panded and fragmented leaving these fragments in the wound. The bullet's large size made not only a larger wound, but often carried clothing, bits of equipment, coins, parts of watches, keys and similar items into wounds it made. The weight of the 45 (500 grains) retained lethal energy to distances well past the lethal range of the lighter Krag (220 grains) and 7mm Mauser (172 grains) rifles used in the Spanish-American War.

The first generation of 6mm to 8mm military rifles used round-nosed bullets with a full metal jacket of bronze or copper-nickel alloy—just what the geopoliticians ordered. Their flat trajectory and lower recoil made it easier to train the troops who used them. The "explosive" effects on liver tissue and crania out to 400 yards were apparent to all, but in actual combat the bullets proved a great disappointment. Unless a bone was struck, "flying drill" bullets made neat holes leaving clean wounds that healed quickly unless they became infected. In wars against "savage peoples" in Africa, the Philippines, and the Indian subcontinent, spear-throwing, machete-wielding warriors full of adrenalin absorbed bullet after bullet as they charged terrified British and American troops armed with 303 Enfield and 30-40 Krag rifles. Most of these attackers succumbed to their wounds, but only after stabbing and hacking a number of troops to death.

The British sought improved stopping power with their softpoint "Dum Dum" bullet, the use of which brought great criticism from other European nations with smaller colonial holdings, less power, less money and an envious hatred of all things British. A full account of how the politics of warfare forced the British to abandon their use of softpoint and hollowpoint bullets is in the excellent article by Colin Greenwood in the 1980 *Gun Digest*.[3]

The Hague Convention banned the use of expanding, poisonous and exploding bullets. The Germans, however, hit upon the discovery that their "spitzer," (pointed bullet) in addition to having less drag than the round-nose style, created a more severe wound. This design, with its long tapering point, had a heavy end and a light end and when the bullet lost stability by striking a body, the heavy rear would flip over the front causing the bullet to make a larger hole—often exiting base first as it tumbled. Soon, nearly everyone was using the spitzer bullet. The flip-over was improved by the British who filled the pointed end with aluminum and the rear with lead. Later, the Russians simply left an air cavity in the front.

The Vietnam era saw the latest improvement in the spitzer bullet that gave it much the same effect as an expanding type. By the simple expedient of increasing velocity, as in the case of the 7.62x39mm AK-47 and the 223 (5.56x45mm) M-16 bullets, greater instability on impact was achieved. The 55-grain M-16 bullet with a muzzle velocity of over 3000 fps would often break in half at the cannelure in the middle and the two halves would shred in the body creating a more massive wound. Even more deadly was the 7.62x51mm (308) NATO bullet made by the West German government which featured a very thin steel jacket, fifty percent thinner than the U.S. version, which would shred in a body causing an even more massive wound by virtue of its greater size and weight. Velocity was critical to achieving these effects. Once velocity dropped below 2500 fps, lethality decreased to handgun level with equivalent-caliber jacketed bullets.

The U.S. was slow to follow the European nations in adopting the flat-shooting metal-jacketed bullet. America's most recent conflict at that time had been with Native Americans in the West, which did not finally end until 1890. The 45-caliber Springfield rifle, designed by Erskine S. Allin, was an effective weapon that evolved out of the American Civil War—the first conflict that saw long-range sniping with rifles capable of a high degree of accuracy. Experiences with the 450 Whitworth and similar sniper rifles capable of picking off a man at a half-mile were not lost on the military, and late in the war plans began to create a long-range rifle capable of Whitworth performance to be placed in the hands of the individual soldier. The 405- and later 500-grain soft lead bullets were capable of accurate shooting to 1000 yards. Its high retention of energy made the 500-grain bullet capable of killing at ranges in excess of 3500 yards—well beyond that of any assault rifle bullet or even a 30-caliber 150- to 178-grain jacketed bullet. Volley fire from massed infantry or from a 45-70 Gatling gun could rain death on exposed cavalry or infantry in open trenches two miles away. One feature of the war in the West was the destruction of the Native American's primary food source, the bison. A 45-70 could often do this in a single shot. It was equally capable of shooting

All dressed up and nobody to fight: The U.S. Army Rifle Team of 1887. These experts with the 45 Government were capable of deadly accuracy at long range, but never got much of a chance to demonstrate their skills in battle.

through a horse, breaking both shoulders in the process. If that horse was going full bore with a Native American aboard, the rider was likely to be killed or seriously injured in the process.

Politics and history have more influence in shaping the image of people and things, including rifles and ammunition, than any personal merits or lack thereof. The Allin Trapdoor Springfield was of a simple and rugged design, continually improved upon from 1866 until its discontinuance in 1893. It was in the hands of National Guard troops into the 1920s. During its use it figured in no major wars or battles. Political enemies of the rifle constantly denigrated its obsolete design and slow rate of fire. Soldiers equipped with it, which included the author's grandfather, had no love for the vicious recoil delivered by the 500-grain long-range bullets. Spanish-American War veteran Charles Johnson Post allowed as how the rifle could knock down *two* men—the one hit by the bullet and the one behind the rifle. "You jammed a cartridge in," he wrote, "snapped the butt of the Springfield hard against your shoulder—for the recoil was like a hurled brick—and pulled the trigger." The blackpowder ammunition was a decided handicap. "The first blast of smoke obscured everything, and from that one on, we fired at where we remembered the distant Spanish trenches had been....The Spaniards instantly turned all they had into our cloud of smoke, including their Maxim machine guns." In five minutes of combat to cover an artillery withdrawal on San Juan Hill, two companies suffered twenty percent casualties.[4]

Perhaps the most remembered event in the Allin rifle's history was a disaster. This was the Battle of the Little Bighorn, where it was cited as a major contributing factor in Custer's defeat, owing to the jamming of the Springfield carbines his troops carried. Contemporary accounts that dirty guns and poor-quality, dirty ammunition were responsible have since come under the scrutiny of historians and archaeologists. Freed from the politics of the day, they have reassessed the battle in light of all the known facts, plus new information garnered from archaeological digs of the battlefield. Based on thousands of recovered cartridge cases, the incidence of jammed carbines was perhaps three percent. The cause very likely was not dirt, but its opposite—cleaning.[5,6] Standard practice at the time was to issue ammunition on an as-needed basis. This was fired in practice, carried on garrison duty and used in battle, often after long exposure to the elements. Sweat and salts used in tanning leather cartridge belts contributed to corrosion on the soft copper cartridges of the day. The customary practice was to polish metal parts with whatever was at hand. Charcoal on the ends of burned campfire sticks was a favorite for shining cartridges. As the heads lost metal they became thinner, weaker and more prone to swell and tear as the Springfield extractor attempted to yank fired cases free of the chamber. The best thinking on the Custer disaster is that it resulted from a combination of effective firepower on

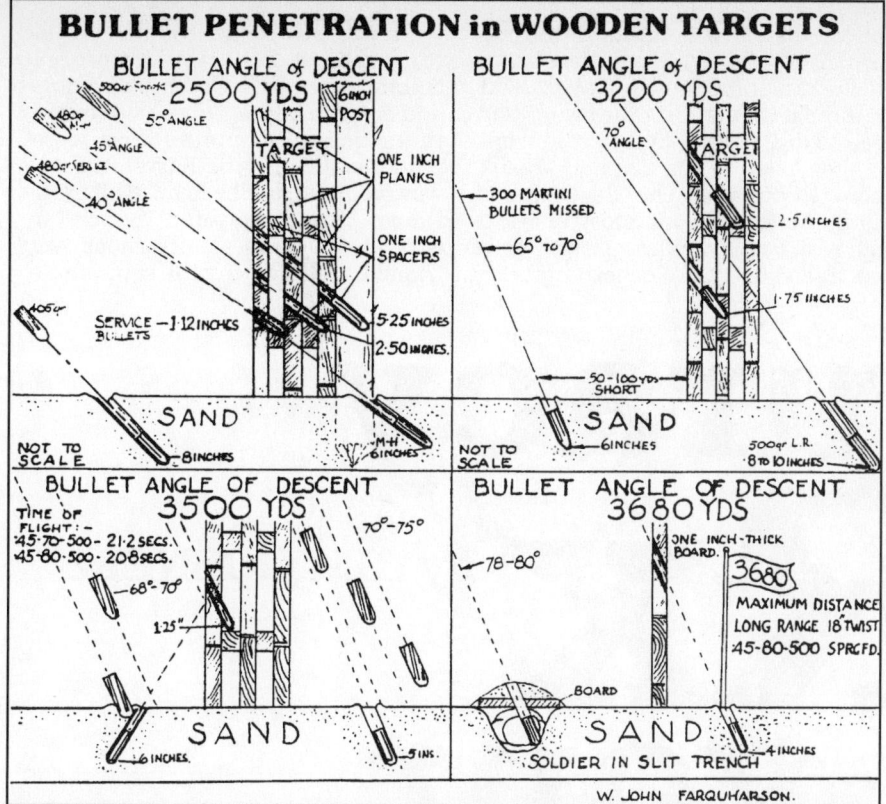

Results of long-range penetration studies made by the Springfield Armory in 1879 led to the adoption of the 500-grain bullet. The 300-grain Martini bullets, the nearest contender, failed to travel over 3200 yards. The experimental 45-80-500 test rifle was capable of punching through a 1-inch pine board at an incredible 3680 yards! Illus. by W. John Farquharson, from *.45-70 at Two Miles*; courtesy *Rifle* magazine.

the part of the Sioux, and panic in the ranks early in the battle with men bunching together in small isolated groups, which made easy pickings for their fearless foes.[7]

As warfare continued to evolve, new factors came into the military equation. The use of thick-walled, blockhouse fortifications was effective in stopping the heavy though soft 45-70, while proving ineffective against the deep penetration of jacketed bullets. The use of metal armor in trench fortifications and on vehicles hastened the obsolescence of the 45. Armor was countered with armor-piercing ammunition which made the 30-caliber even more of a flying drill, but enhanced the soldier's ability to inflict casualties against a protected enemy.

The notion of firepower—a combination of magazine capacity and rate of fire—looms large in the minds of firearms prohibitionists who equate this to an individual's ability to kill vast numbers in a few seconds. While this is true in theory, the reality of firing a spray of unaimed bullets is mostly misses. There is no better example of this than the one offered in the video production *Deadly Weapons*, where a Rambo-style burst from an M-60 machine gun is fired from the hip, cutting a path of dust puffs across a hillside where five man-targets are placed. After the dust has settled the shooter examines the targets to find one has been nicked—the equivalent of a flesh wound in the side. Firepower does have its applications. Spraying an area keeps enemy heads down and from returning fire. This is a useful tactic in assaulting an objective or in shooting one's way out of a tight situation and making a successful escape. Firepower has its down side in the amount of ammunition an individual can carry. Thus, the assault rifle exchanges decreased lethality for the greater firepower of lighter, less powerful ammunition. The notion of the great lethality of full-automatic fire dates from World War I, when open spaces between trenches were swept by sustained machinegun fire from a number of guns working in concert to cover one another with fields of fire. These were heavy guns served by four- or five-man crews, one of whom acted as gunner while the others pumped water to cool the barrel, fed belts of ammunition, carried ammunition up from a storage bunker, helped to clear jams and did whatever else was required to keep the gun firing. This is hardly the equivalent of one man firing an AK-47.

Lethality of a particular firearm thus becomes more and more governed by the circumstances of the individual situation. Inflicting casualties against those protected by armor will only be accomplished with armor-piercing ammunition that has enough energy to penetrate that particular armor. Whole American units equipped with 45-70 Springfields using blackpowder ammunition were pulled from the line because the smoke readily indicated their positions to Spanish troops.

It could be said the most lethal small arm would be a 50-caliber Browning super-sniper rifle, telescope equipped, weighing about 35 pounds and capable of hitting man-sized targets at 2000 yards. That is until the user of such a rifle found himself in an unexpected close encounter with an enemy carrying a 38 snubby who could empty the entire contents of that gun into the brisket of the sniper before he could bring the weapon off his shoulder.

Our modern assault rifles are therefore compromises designed to meet the greatest number of combat shooting situations *reasonably* well without really meeting any one of them *really* well. There will always be some other gun that is more accurate, more powerful, more maneuverable, more lethal or perhaps more appropriate to the situation than the one you are holding. ●

[1] Fackler, Martin, John A. Malinowski, Stephen W. Hoxie, and Alexander Jason. "Wounding Effects of the AK-47 Rifle Used by Patrick Purdey in the Stockton, California Schoolyard Shooting of January 17, 1989." *American Journal of Forensic Medicine and Pathology* 11(3) (1990), pp. 185-189.

[2] La Garde, Louis A. *Gunshot Injuries*. 2nd Rev. Ed. New York: Wm. Wood and Co., 1916.

[3] Greenwood, Colin. "The Political Factors." *Gun Digest* (1980), pp. 161-168.

[4] Post, Charles Johnson. *The Little War of Private Post*. Boston: Little Brown and Co., 1960.

[5] Shockley, Philip M. *The Trapdoor Springfield in the Service*. Aledo, Ill.: World-Wide Gun Report, Inc., 1958.

[6] Scott, Douglas D. and Richard A. Fox, Jr. *Archaeological Insights into the Custer Battle: An Assessment of the 1984 Field Season*. Norman and London: University of Oklahoma Press, 1987.

[7] Fox, Richard Allen, Jr. *Archaeology, History and Custer's Last Battle*. Norman and London: University of Oklahoma Press, 1993.

RECENTLY A FRIEND saw a Winchester Model 52 in the paper for sale and called to see if it was still available. It was and he rushed over to have a look. What he found was a rifle in fairly good condition and an owner wanting to unload it because he "could never get any accuracy out of it." The action was dirty and had accumulated a fair amount of crud, and the barrel was full of unburned powder. My friend spied a few boxes of cheap ammo on the shelf and inquired if that is what the owner had been using. It was, and that is what he shot in all of his 22s and wasn't about to change. The negotiations began. Making a long story short, a note with Ben Franklin's picture on it was traded for the Winchester 52.

On the way home, the new owner stopped off at the local gun store and bought some CCI Green Tag ammo and scope mounts. After cleaning up the action and running a couple of patches through the barrel, a scope was mounted and he headed off to the range. This gun printed ½-inch targets at 50 yards all afternoon. My friend is still wearing the same smile!

Accuracy Rx for your 22

by JIM GOSNELL

There's probably a lot more accuracy lurking in your rimfire sporter than you think. With patience you can easily get it to shoot like an expensive target gun.

In general, 22 Long Rifle accuracy is accepted as what a particular gun will do with standard ammunition. Most folks I know watch for the sales on ammo and when a good deal shows up, they head down to the store and buy a "brick" or two to keep them in supply. If they can dance some cans around on the range or knock off an occasional squirrel, they are happy. The average pop can measures $2^1/_2$ x $5^3/_4$ inches and, put in perspective, that's a big target, often giving the shooter a false sense of accuracy. To get better accuracy, the kind that you are proud enough to show off, the overall opinion is that one must put down some big bucks and purchase target ammunition. It's most unfortunate that the majority of people accept mediocrity as the inherent norm of the 22.

There are those who do go so far as to test various brands of ammo to find out which one their gun prefers. For the most part, 22s are very particular about their ammo diet. What is an accurate round for one gun might resemble a shotshell pattern in another gun. Using the right ammunition is considered the only way to improve accuracy in the 22, since you can't reload for it and you have no control over the powder and bullet in the round. This is the method that I have used for years. Another answer is to spend a bunch of money with the gunsmith, but that's pretty much out of the question for most of us. After all, you're not trying to win the Olympics, just hit what you are aiming at.

There is hope, however, for those wishing to dot the i on that can rather than just hit it. I would like to be able to say that this is a result of great advancements in technology, but I can't.

Very serious target shooters have long been using some "accurizing" methods with expensive target ammo to shave that extra .010-inch off their groups. These folks know that variations in the chamber can and will lead to variations in group size. It follows, then, that if those variations can be held to an absolute minimum, then groups should shrink. These shooters measure the rim thickness of each round and segregate them in lots of the same thickness. The 22 cartridge headspaces on the rim, and if all of the shells are of the same thickness then the firing pin falls the same distance each shot and, in theory and fact, ignition is much more uniform.

Rifles used in author's accuracy tests, left to right: Browning BPR 22 WMR, Ruger 77/22, Remington 541-T, Marlin 39A, Winchester Model 61, and Ruger 10/22.

An electronic scale such as this one from RCBS is indispensable for weighing cartridges. The two rim thickness gauges under the scale are from Bald Eagle, the one on the left for WMRs, the other for Long Rifles. The sorting block is from Sinclair and was most useful when making the final cut by weighing measured cases.

I don't mind telling you that I was shocked at the variations in rim thickness within one box of ammunition. I actually found one box that had rims measuring from .038- to .046-inch! Another surprise came when I pulled some bullets and found the priming mixture slopped up on the inside of the shell. What it boils down to is poor quality control, and we have to do the clean up. Some ammo companies want you to believe that you have to pay high prices for quality ammo, but as a result of this test, I have found this not to be so.

So, how do you go about measuring

29th EDITION, 1997 **21**

the rim thickness? There are a few different devices on the market, but I've been using a gauge made by Bald Eagle Precision Machine Co. It is simple and very accurate. It consists of a machined aluminum block with a dial indicator that reads to .001-inch. Simply put a shell in the slot on the block and read the rim thickness. To avoid trying to remember the thickness of the first shell, I set the gauge on zero with that shell in the unit and then separate the shells with plus or minus variations from there. A series of plastic margarine tubs comes in very handy for this. I have found it is easy to do a few bricks of ammo with this method in an evening while watching TV. Three is about my limit for one evening. However, before you start all of this measuring, first find out which ammo your rifle likes.

What you can expect is an improvement of up to twenty-five percent in group size. Read that again I said up to twenty-five percent, not that you definitely will get that kind of improvement. Some rifles and some ammo will show those kind of gains, and others will be less, but in most cases you will still be way ahead. Chances are that the biggest gains will be found in boxes of shells with the greatest variations in thickness.

The idea here is to have each round for a particular group measure the same. You may have one tub of shells with rims measuring .040-inch and another with .044-inch rims, and they will most likely give you closely matched groups. Keep in mind that you aslo have to keep the action clean. Dirt build-up on the chamber and bolt face can defeat what you are trying to accomplish with the rim measuring. Outers' Crud Cutter works wonders in that department and makes short work of an otherwise lengthy task.

The next method of reducing variations is to weigh each shell and group them in lots of the same weight. Here again, I was in for a rude awakening. It is not uncommon to find variations within a lot of ammo of ±0.3-grain, but I have come across differences as much as 4.5 grains from lightest to heaviest! Needless to say, that stuff was near worthless when it came to hitting anything.

The electronic scale is a real boon to the handloader and is the only way to complete this process of weighing with out ending up being fitted for a straitjacket. A few years ago, these devices were a luxury and the cost was high. Now there are several on the market that are very reasonable and extremely accurate. I use the RCBS and PACT scales regularly and find them to be of the finest quality.

When weighing shells for consistency, I weigh the first one and set the scale at zero with the shell on it. That shell is then kept as a reference

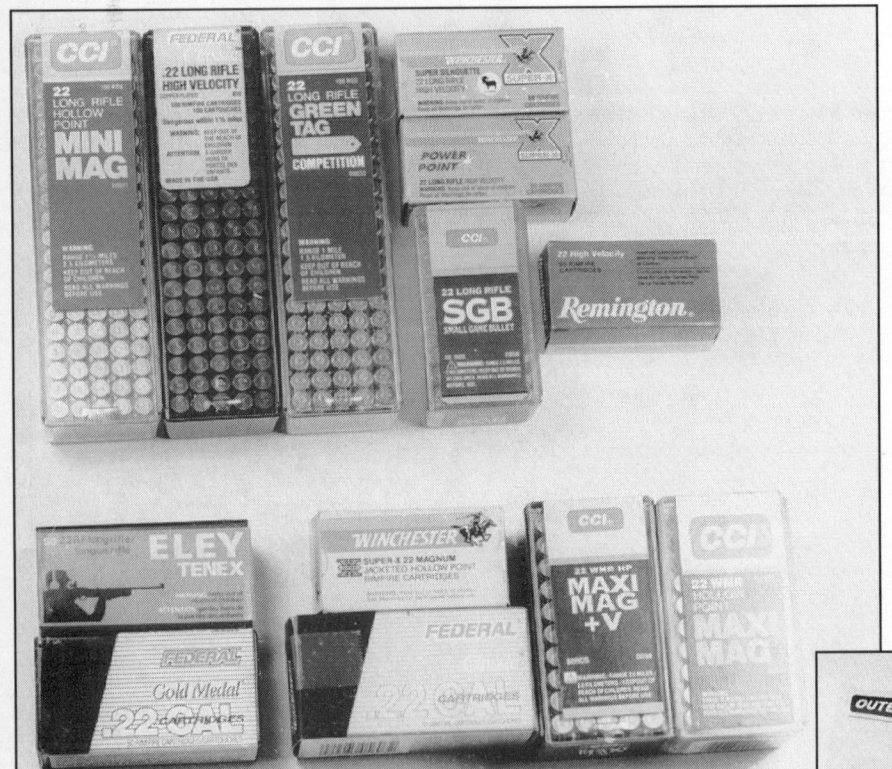

A variety of ammunition was used for this experiment. Target-grade ammo was used to try to determine if author's rifles were capable of shooting well enough to expect a difference. All were. CCI Green Tag is reasonably priced competition ammo and benefited from the measuring and weighing. Winchester Power Point and CCI SGB are hunting rounds that shoot well right from the box, especially the latter.

This target was shot with the Remington 541-T. The upper left target is unsorted CCI Green Tag. The lower left was shot with weighed shells and the upper right with measured shells. The lower right target was shot with rounds that were measured and then weighed to obtain maximum consistency. The process works!

weight and the additional shells are sorted by variance to $1/10$-grain weight difference. To put this in perspective, $1/10$-grain is $1/70,000$-pound. Accuracy gains can be significant with this method as well, but the measuring seems to show the best results.

Now, if you really want to see some serious shrinkage in your groups, combine the two methods. I recently reviewed a Volquartsen Mossad rifle, a conversion of the Ruger 10/22, and tried this method with the ammo that it had the most trouble with. Groups at 50 yards shrank in size from $3/4$-inch to $1/3$-inch! I was impressed. The Mossad is capable of groups in the neighborhood of .13-inch at that distance with the right ammo, but like other guns, it is picky about its diet.

To find out just how much this can be applied to the average 22 rifle, I thought it would be interesting to try weighing and measuring several brands of ammo and trying it in some different guns. Our editor suggested that I shoot some used "average" rifles to make the test as close to reality as possible and I had to agree. I wanted to use a bolt action, a semi-auto, a pump, and a lever action, so I ran down to my favorite gun shop to see what they had. Not much. There was some real junk, and the few that I considered using would not accept a scope. I was not about to tap the receiver on borrowed guns, and the scope is necessary, in my opinion, to ensure consistent shot placement. Seems people don't trade off their 22s of any value on a regular basis. Calls to all of the other gun shops in the area produced the same results. Charlie, owner of Charlie's Sporting goods, took pity on me. He searched his personal collection and came up with a beautiful Winchester Model 61 pump action. I have a Ruger 10/22 and a Ruger 77/22 so it was a start. In desperation, I contacted Remington and Marlin and they were most helpful. Remington supplied a Model 541-T bolt action and Marlin sent a Model 39-A lever gun. The Remington, Marlin, Winchester and Ruger 10/22 would be the main players in this test.

Trying to keep everything as equal as possible, I wanted to use the same type of scope on each gun. Four scopes is asking a bit much, so I borrowed two Weaver V-16s and Warne rings and mounts for each gun. The Weaver V-16 is the best value in scopes I have seen in a long time. The optics are absolutely outstanding, and the adjustable objective goes down to 10 yards! If it did not have Weaver printed on the side, I would have sworn that it was one of the high-dollar brands. This high-power scope makes quite a difference in groups. I tried getting the same results with a couple of lower power scopes, and my groups opened up considerably. The Warne rings and mounts are some of the strongest and easy to mount available, and I use them on many of my other rifles. Their system allowed me to switch scopes from gun to gun without much hassle.

For ammo, I wanted to use what is available in most stores. Winchester Power-Point is one that is not only widely available, but it's proving to be consistently accurate in most guns. CCI is available just about everywhere, and I used their Mini-Mag and a brick of the Green Tag, which is reasonably priced target-grade ammo. Federal Classic is

The Volquartsen Mossad, a highly modified Ruger 10/22, was used to verify gains in accuracy using the measuring and weighing process. This rifle is capable of near record-book accuracy and is a pure joy to shoot.

another readily available brand, so it joined the ranks. I spent the better part of a week's worth of evenings measuring and weighing ammo and had everything sorted out and ready to go. Wanting to find out how this affected magnum ammo as well, I pulled out my Browning BPR 22 WMR and sorted out some ammo for it as well.

You will also notice the CCI SGB (Small Game Bullet) listed on the nearby table. My original intent was not to include this round as CCI was already well represented, but I measured some out after all the other weighing and measuring had been done. I was pleasantly surprised to find a variation of ±.001-inch in the first box, and thinking it to be that one box in a million, I measured a few more boxes only to find the same results. This is as good or better than target-grade ammo, so my next step was to start weighing. Here again, I found unbelievable consistency, ±0.1 grains! I decided to give this stuff the acid test, so I set all of the sorted SGB aside and only shot straight from the box SGBs. The results speak for themselves; this is accurate ammunition. It is also high-speed ammunition; normally the lower speed target ammo turns in the best accuracy. Now, if CCI can maintain this kind of quality control on a regular round, why can't we expect the same from all of the 22 ammo makers?

I first mounted the Weavers on my 10/22 and the Remington 541. The Winchester and Browning guns have grooved receivers, and the Warne rings were perfect for that situation. All of the shooting was done using a Bench Master Rifle Rest to get the best consistency. When it comes to rifle testing, it is hard to beat this device.

My 10/22 has always taken a shine to the Winchester Power-Point and CCI Green Tag ammo. The Power-Point is a hollowpoint hunting round that shoots incredibly well, and the Green Tag is standard-velocity target fodder. Each group of ammo was shot in five-shot groups, and the average of three groups is recorded in the accompanying table. The Remington 541-T proved to be the most accurate of the test guns, but that was not a surprise to me. The only thing I did to it was adjust the trigger from 5 pounds to 2. A real surprise was the Winchester 61, which shot under ½-inch with the CCI SGB. I would have not believed it had I not seen it myself. The Marlin was a good shoot-

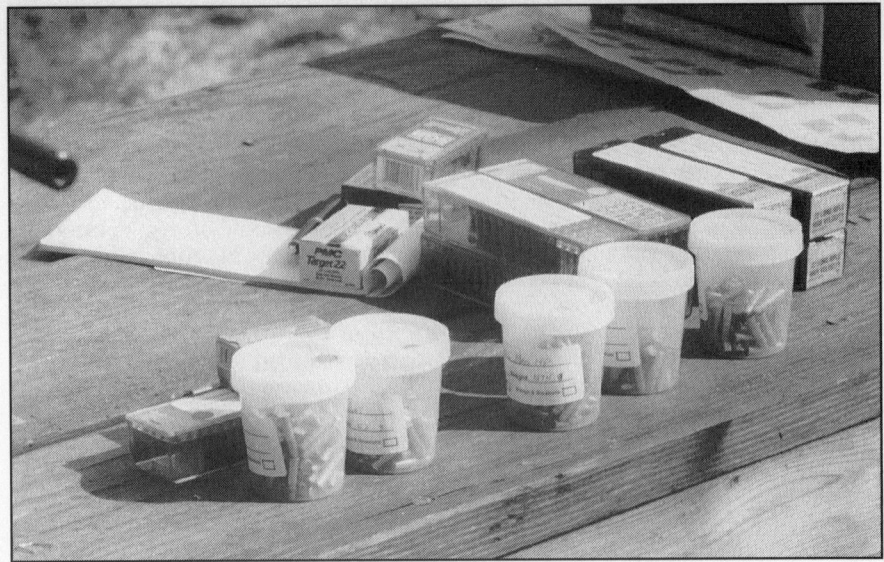

Author put his sorted ammo in plastic containers and marked them as to rim thickness, weight, or both. He had over twenty of them at the beginning of the test.

22 Rimfire Accuracy Results

Load/Rifle	OB (ins.)	M (ins.)	W (ins.)	M&W (ins.)
Winchester Power-Point				
Ruger 10/22	0.98	0.82	0.86	0.72
Remington 541-T	0.78	0.65	0.70	0.55
Winchester Model 61	0.95	0.76	0.88	0.74
Marlin 39-A	0.92	0.84	0.89	0.80
CCI Green Tag				
Ruger 10/22	0.77	0.68	0.72	0.51
Remington 541-T	0.65	0.58	0.62	0.47
Winchester Model 61	0.87	0.84	0.81	0.80
Marlin 39-A	0.72	0.67	0.69	0.65
Federal Classic				
Ruger 10/22	1.30	1.10	1.25	1.00
Remington 541-T	0.97	0.89	0.92	0.85
Winchester Model 61	1.00	0.93	0.96	0.91
Marlin 39-A	0.88	0.82	0.84	0.80
CCI SGB				
Ruger 10/22	0.61			
Remington 541-T	0.42			
Winchester Model 61	0.46			
Marlin 39-A	0.60			
Winchester HP 22 WMR				
Browning BPR	1.55	1.20	1.35	1.12
CCI Maxi Mag				
Browning BPR	1.10	0.90	0.95	0.87
Federal Classic				
Browning BPR	1.25	1.10	1.18	0.95
Winchester Power-Point				
Volquartsen Mossad 10/22	0.45	0.32	0.35	0.28
CCI SGB				
Volquartsen Mossad 10/22	0.23			
Fiocchi Match				
Volquartsen Mossad 10/22	0.14			
Eley Ten-X				
Volquartsen Mossad 10/22	0.155			
Federal Ultra Match				
Volquartsen Mossad 10/22	0.145			

All targets shot at 50 yards
Average of three five-shot groups
OB = Out of Box
M = Measured
W = Weighted
M&W = Measured & Weighed

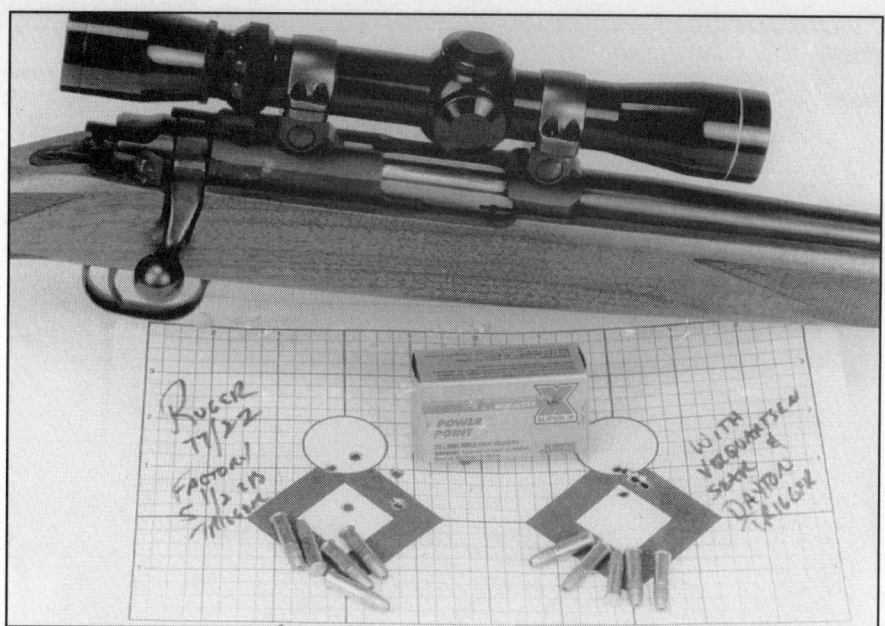

Before and after 50-yard target shot with Winchester Power-Point ammo from the Ruger 77/22. The group on the right was fired after the sear and trigger were replaced, showing these simple modifications do help.

Author used a Bench Master rifle rest for sure and consistent shot placement, and PACT Professional chronograph just to keep tabs on things.

er as well and most pleasant to shoot. The Micro-Groove barrel has always been accurate in the 22.

The ammo test proved to be most interesting. With most of the test guns, measuring the rim thickness and sorting the shells for consistency provided a considerable gain in accuracy. The weighing also showed improvement, but not to the same degree. When the shells were first measured and then sorted by weight, the accuracy gain was significant. I have experimented with many other types and brands of 22 ammo, and it almost always works. I say almost because, with some of the expensive target ammo, I'm not a good enough shooter to see major improvement.

The Browning BPR 22 WMR has never been a super accurate gun, just average. It did, however, benefit from the measuring and weighing of cartridges. I would imagine that more significant results can be expected out of some of the bolt-action WMR guns.

Aside from measuring and weighing ammo, there are a number of accuracy "enhancers" that work for the very popular Ruger 10/22 and 77/22. Some of the parts are available through Brownells and involve a "drop-in" hammer or sear. Installation is fairly simple, and these items generally reduce and improve the trigger pull, thus giving the shooter better control. I have used these things on numerous occasions and always get excellent results.

Dayton Triaster makes a trigger replacement for the 77/22 that will reduce the pull to 1½ pounds from the 5-pound factory trigger. I put one in my 77/22 and, wouldn't you know it, had some difficulty with the fit. It turned out to be a bit wide for my gun, and I spent about an hour with some stones honing it to fit. A call to the company assured me that this was not the norm, and they said that if anyone had trouble they should call. They guarantee their work.

Another nice item for the 77/22 is a replacement sear from Volquartsen. This will also reduce the pull to 1½ pounds. I first shot groups using the Dayton Traister trigger and then put the old trigger back and installed Volquartsen's sear. Using a 2-7x Leupold scope, groups at 50 yards went from 1¾ inches to just under an inch. With both units installed the trigger pull dropped to less than 1 pound, so I left the factory sear spring and adjusted the trigger screw. Now I have a very crisp break at 1¼ pounds, and I have managed a couple of groups measuring .65-inch with that gun. Next I intend to mount a Weaver V-16 on it and really dial it in.

Probably the easiest and least expensive improvement for accuracy is to maintain your gun. First of all, do not use a cleaning rod on your bore. If you must, make sure it is a coated, one-piece rod. The best answer is some fishing line with a loop tied in the end. Use dry patches to remove residue and then apply a light coating of something like Break-Free. Pay close attention to the bolt face and the inside of the receiver. Dirt build-up in there can cause the groups to grow. An old toothbrush and some Outers Crud Cutter can make short work of that. Go easy on the lube. Brownells Action Lube Plus is ideal for this purpose.

So, after all of this, is it worth it? Depends on your point of view. If you are happy just knocking cans around and don't show anybody your targets, maybe not. If you have a certain pride in your achievements and like hitting what you are aiming at, then the answer is yes. By sorting ammo and/or replacing some parts in your rifle (mostly Rugers), you can make some noticeable improvements in the accuracy department without having to dig too deep into your pockets. Who knows, you might even want to show off some of your targets!

The Poor Man's Race Gun

For this project, Fisher used a Colt Model 1991, but a 45 like this Norinco serves very well if you can find one. They're made of good materials, and the quality is excellent.

MY EDITOR CALLED called to ask if I would be interested in writing an article that would give budding handgunners an idea of what they'd have to spend to get into formal competition. My first question was what type of competition did he have in mind for the race gun? Next was what kind of a figure did he have in mind for the cost of the gun? IPSC shooting being one of the most popular types of competition, and the semi-auto the action of choice, we decided to build a gun around a new Colt 1991A1 45. The final cost of the completed gun was to be around $1000 to $1200, including the cost of the new pistol. With the price of a Colt Model 1991 around $350 in my area at this time, that leaves $650 to $850 for the work needed to build "The Poor Man's Race Gun," with many options available.

I decided to approach the subject from the point of view that the reader has little or no idea of what a race gun is all about. All he or she knows is that an interest to start shooting in competition has developed and the mind is willing to listen and learn. For this reason, I think it's best to first explain what you need in a competition gun and the best way to get your money's worth.

The main thing the race gun needs to be is totally reliable. Anything less will just not do. Nothing will destroy the competitive desire faster than shooting in a match and having the gun malfunction the first time out. All the practice in the world will not help you if the gun refuses to run each and every time you pull the trigger.

Fisher's personal IPSC Limited Class 45 has seen a lot of use and has well-worn bluing, but it'll still shoot under 3/4-inch at 50 yards from a Ransom Rest!

Speaking of pulling that trigger, this is the one area of the race gun that can help the new shooter get the best out of the money spent on all other work done to the gun. There is no way anyone can expect to shoot well if the trigger is not right. With the lawsuit-happy world we live in today, all the gunmakers build their guns with heavy trigger pulls that have a lot of sear engagement. You can expect to

26 GUNS ILLUSTRATED

You don't have to spend a million bucks to build a competitive gun for IPSC shooting. Here's how one custom gunsmith and top shooter does it.

by DON FISHER

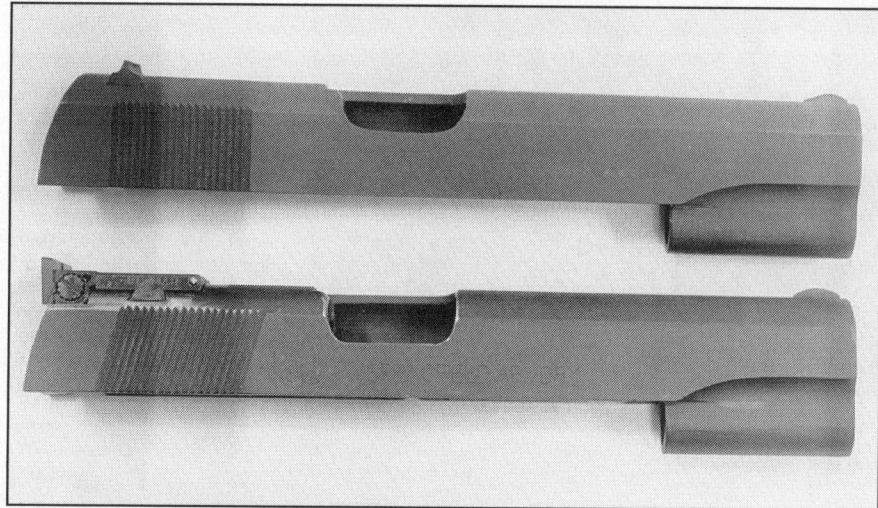

For reliability, the ejection port should be opened up from the stock dimensions (top). This helps the empty brass to fully exit the gun and prevent a stovepipe jam.

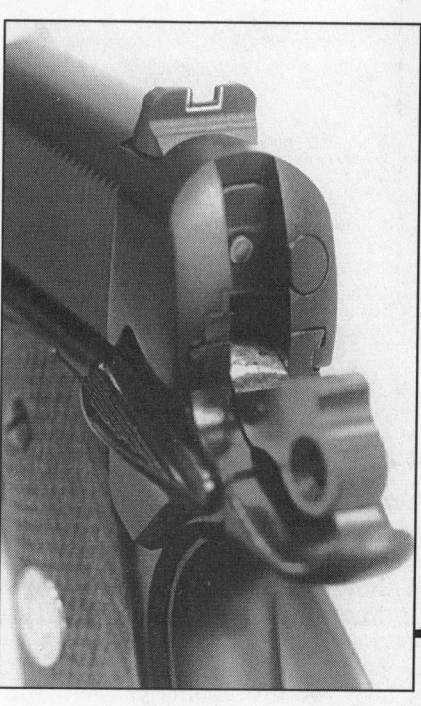

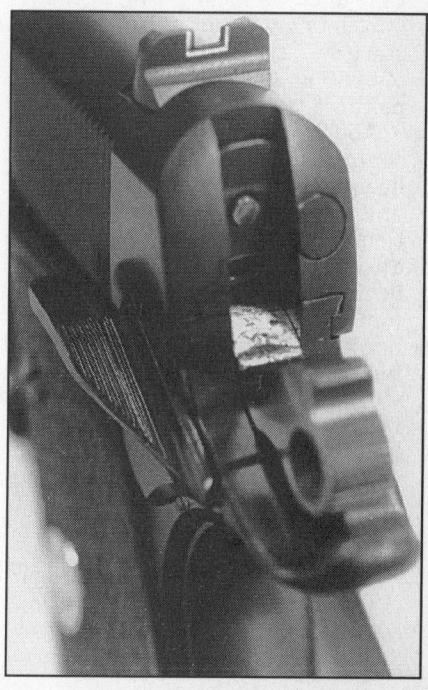

The thumb safety must be large enough for quick and sure acquisition, and the factory unit (top) just isn't up to the job. An extended safety (below) also gives the shooter a secure place to rest his thumb while shooting.

find a pull of no less than 6 pounds on a factory gun, and that is not what you want if you hope to do well in your first try at having fun with IPSC-style shooting. For a shooter new to this type of shooting, I recommend a trigger pull of $3\frac{1}{2}$ to 4 pounds. As you get used to shooting a gun from a holster you may want to lower that figure to help on the longer shots. The top shooters today commonly go down to about two pounds, but not until they can handle the gun safely with a heavier trigger. Lightening the trigger pull is something that can always be done later with little or no added expense, so don't get yourself in trouble by asking for a trigger that is too light before you're ready.

Next in line of importance is a good set of sights. The factory sights that come on a Colt 1991 are a lot better than what you got a few years ago, but they still could be better. My recommendation is to go with a set of Bo-Mar adjustable sights. Here we have to decide how you want to spend that money you have saved up. The factory sights will do for awhile, but you will probably want to get adjustable sights at some point; especially if the point of impact is not where the sights are aligned. If the factory sights shoot to point of aim, this could be a good place to save some money and get the cost of the gun into the price range you want. Adjustable sights can always be added later for a comparatively small cash outlay.

The next thing I recommend is that the gun be as accurate as possible. While a lot of people will try to tell you that you don't need an accurate gun until you learn how to shoot better, how do you really know if you can shoot well if the gun isn't accurate to start with. The way I try to explain it is like this: Let's say the gun shoots groups of 4 inches at 25 yards in the hands of an expert shot. Let's also assume that as a new shooter you are capable of shooting a 3-inch group. That means that the combination of the gun and you will shoot groups as large as 7 inches (the sum of the 4 inches the gun shoots and the 3 inches that you shoot). You go out and practice and your groups start getting smaller each day. Then one day you shoot a 1-inch group at 25 yards and you have a problem. Did the gun shoot a 4-inch group while you shot a 3-incher in the other direction so that you ended up with a 1-inch group? You shot high as the

Fisher recommends Bo-Mar sights (right) over the factory units for better sight acquisition and to allow you to adjust point of impact.

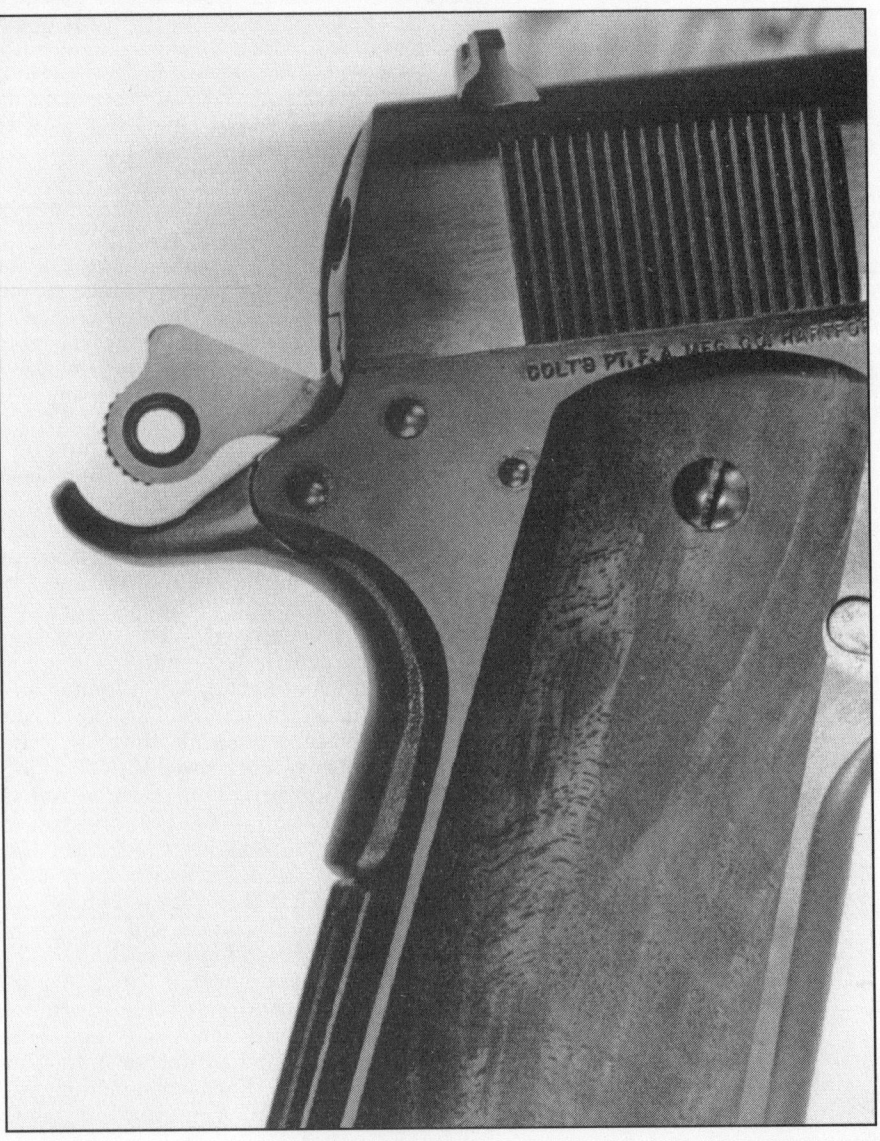

(Below) Two things here help to take hammer bite out of shooting a 45: the Commander hammer and the beavertail grip safety. The bigger safety also helps reduce felt recoil. Some shooters prefer smooth stocks over checkered or rubber types.

gun shot low and you accidentally hit what you were aiming at. How else can you explain a good group? On the other hand, if you have an accurate gun that shoots under an inch, anything over that is your fault and any time you shoot a good group you know that that was you also. *Now* you get direct feedback from every shot you fire, telling you how you're doing. Or as a customer once said to me, "I need an accurate gun a lot more than you do if I ever plan to beat you. I need all the help I can get just to catch up."

Now that we have the three basics that must be included in a good race gun, lets get down to building it. To start, lets try to come up with a cost of $650 or so to hit that $1,000 price point.

About eighteen years ago, before compensators were thought of, I designed a combination of features and work that I named my "Competition Package." It was designed to produce a good solid starting place to begin shooting and still give the customer a gun that will allow him or her to shoot up to their ability. Nothing will have to be changed later that will waste the customer's money, nor is there anything that is not going to help him. Nothing has been added just for the purpose of making extra profit. The following is a list of what you will get in the Competition Package for $575:

Enlarge Ejection Port
Extend Combat Safety
Adjust Trigger Pull

Bevel Magazine Well
Bob Hammer
Throat Barrel and Frame
Wolff Recoil Spring
Match Barrel Bushing
Metal Checkering on:
　Front Strap
　Mainspring Housing
　Front of Trigger Guard
Beavertail Safety
Adjust Extractor
Polish and Reblue
Testfiring (200 rounds)

I think it is a good idea to explain why each item is included in the package and how it will help the shooter to get the most enjoyment out of IPSC-style shooting. I also include the cost of each to let you know how your money can be best spent.

Enlarge Ejection Port: The ejection port needs to be opened up to let the brass out of the gun better. If brass comes back into the shooter's face or gets dented on ejection, the port needs to be opened up. This will also help to prevent brass from getting stuck in the port, a malfunction commonly called a "stovepipe" jam. **$25.00**

Extend Combat Safety: The safety that comes on the gun isn't large enough for reliable use when shooting from the holster. The safety has to be engaged when the gun is in the holster, and needs to be disengaged in a hurry and it's real easy to miss the small factory safety. A larger safety also gives the shooter a more secure place to rest the thumb of the shooting hand while firing. The factory safety is just too small to allow this practice. **$35.00**

Adjust Trigger Pull: This has already been covered, so let's just say that you will shoot a *lot* better with a smooth, light and creep-free pull. **$75.00**

Bevel Magazine Well: IPSC-style shooting requires that you reload the gun during a string of fire. By beveling the magazine well opening, it is a lot easier and faster to insert a new magazine. You would be surprised at how easy it is to miss the opening when the clock is running and people are watching! **$30.00**

Bob Hammer: see **Beavertail Grip Safety. $7.50**

Throat Barrel and Frame: The only thing this does is make it easier for the ammo in the magazine to find its way into the barrel chamber each and every time. The Colt 1911 pistol was designed for round-nosed ammo and it works fine. But for the best reliability with semi-wadcutter ammo and hollowpoints, this recontouring and polishing of the barrel opening and the frame will do wonders for the gun. **$25.00**

Wolff Recoil Spring: The factory spring works fine for factory ammo in the gun the way it comes from the factory, but if you intend to use this gun with reloads after it has been modified, it makes sense to use a recoil spring that is the right strength for the loads you will be using. There is no one spring that is best for all loads and conditions, so this is something that you may want to experiment with to find out what weight spring is best for you. Different springs will change the way the gun feels in your hand and may affect reliability as well, so try a few and see what you like. **$10.00**

Match Barrel Bushing: The factory barrel is made undersize so the gun can be assembled faster and so that parts interchange gun to gun. It's called mass production. The only problem with this is that it means that a certain amount of play results from the built-in tolerances of the manufacturing process. If all the play is eliminated, the front of the barrel will be in the exact same place in relation to the slide for every shot, and the accuracy of the gun will be greatly improved at a very reasonable cost. **$35.00**

Metal Checkering: The purpose of checkering is to give the shooter a better grip on the gun. You can't expect to shoot well if the gun slips in your hand, and checkering is the best way to prevent that slipping. I have found that 20 lines per inch (lpi) is the best.

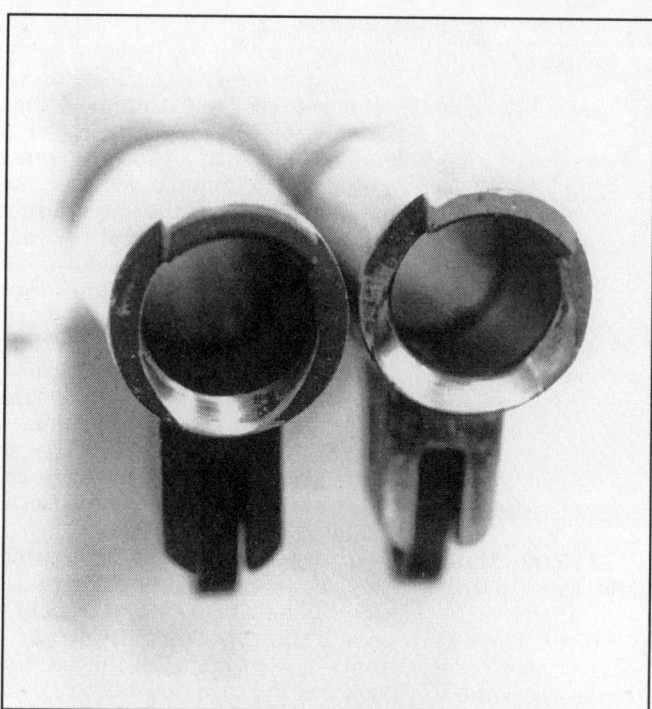

A throated barrel (right) has a wider, smoother opening and simply allows ammunition to feed more reliably. The frame feed ramp should also be altered. This is almost a necessity if you want to use semi-wadcutters and hollowpoints.

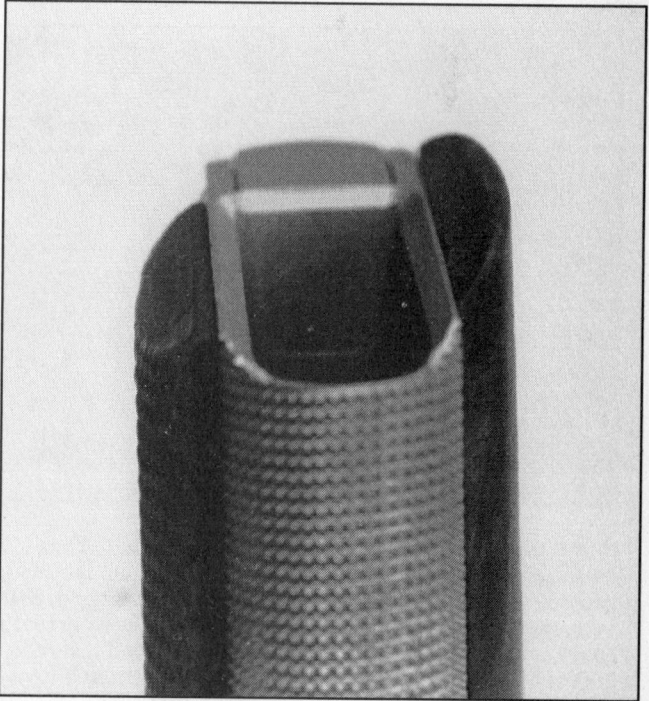

Since IPSC-style competition usually requires a reload during a string of fire, the magazine well needs to be beveled to make the job easier and quicker. Note how the right grip panel is longer to form a simple "funnel."

Checkering gives a better grip on the gun. Shown is 20 lpi checkering on just the mainspring housing (left) and extended onto the frame for an even more secure hold (right).

(Below) The trigger guard also gets attention. This is 20 lpi checkering, in addition to a recess cut at the top for the finger to rest, giving a better hold under recoil.

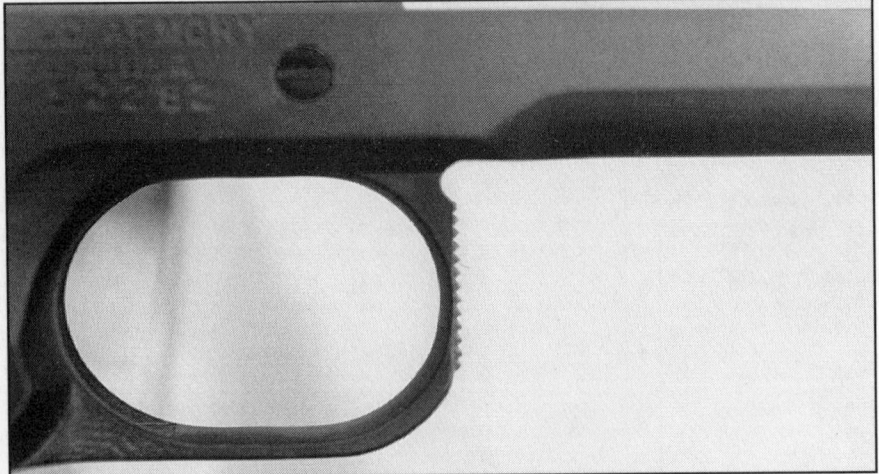

Some people like 30 lpi because it is easier on the hand, but it just doesn't provide as good a grip as 20 lpi does. If you aren't used to shooting a gun with checkering and you go out and shoot 500 rounds in one day, your hand is going to hurt. But if you work up to it slowly, your hand will get used to the 20 lpi checkering and you will really like it better than 30. Personally, I find 30 lpi to be too fine to really help much. Front Strap, **$125.00**; Mainspring Housing, **$40.00**; Front of Trigger Guard; **$40.00**.

Beavertail Grip Safety: The way to tell if someone shoots a Colt 45 a lot without a beavertail safety or without the hammer being bobbed is by the scar in the web of their hand. My hand has a permanent scar from years of shooting my guns before some brilliant soul came up the idea of the beavertail safety. Even with the hammer bobbed I still get hammer bite all the time. If you shoot with your thumb on top of the safety, as I do, you will still get hammer bite with a bobbed hammer, or even with a Commander-style hammer. A beavertail is the only sure cure for the problem. A second benefit is that it spreads out the downward thrust of the back of the gun over a larger area. When the gun recoils, this forces the grip safety down into the web of your hand, and the muzzle will tend to go up. A wider tang (read beavertail grip safety) will minimize this movement. This means that the gun is more pleasant to shoot and that the muzzle stays on target better. **$65.00**

Adjust Extractor: This procedure, along with opening the ejection port, will help to prevent a lot of problems. If the extractor is too loose, the empty case may slip off the extractor hook and the case may fail to extract, or at least fail to be ejected from the gun. If the extractor is too tight, the round coming up from the magazine may not rise up all the way and fail to feed into the chamber. If the brass

After accurizing, checkering, Bo-Mar sights, beavertail and extended safeties, bobbed hammer and smooth stocks, this gun turned in this excellent 25-yard, hand-held test target.

just clears the gun, the extractor may be too loose. If you can feel the slide hesitate when it is going shut, the extractor may be too tight. This is a very beneficial addition. **$10.00**

Polish and Reblue: Let's face it, you just spent a lot of money getting this gun built, so you don't want it to look like garbage, nor do you want it to rust where the finish has been removed. Rebluing will make the gun look better than new and provide excellent rust protection for years to come. **$65.00**

Testfiring, 200 rounds: This is the only way to tell if everything is correct. No matter who does the work, the gun needs to be shot to find out if it works the way it is supposed to work. And ten or twenty rounds isn't enough to really tell. Even if the gun is tested 200 rounds and it works every time, there is no guarantee that it will never malfunction. All it proves is that the gun runs with my ammo. I testfire all 45s with a 200-grain H&G #68 bullet loaded in well-used brass because this is what most shooters use. If you use hollowpoint bullets, it will be wise to testfire the gun with it and see if the gun will accept it. Included in the cost of the package, otherwise **$15.00** plus the cost of the ammo.

Some readers have probably noticed that I haven't included "Accurizing" in my Competition Package. The reason is that the package also makes for an excellent duty gun for a police officer. For those of you who don't already know it, most police departments don't provide the officer with a gun; he or she has to pay for the gun. Since a duty gun will seldom, if ever, be used at a range of over 10 yards, if in fact it is ever fired at all, very few officers are interested in spending the money to have a gun accurized. So while an accurized gun that will shoot under 2 inches at 50 yards is great for competition, a match barrel bushing will provide all the accuracy these folks need for self-defense. Accurizing a Colt semi-auto involves tightening the slide-to-frame fit and welding up and refitting the barrel to eliminate all play between the three parts. This forces the barrel to align with the sights the same way every time, which in turn allows the gun to place all the bullets in one ragged hole if the ammunition is of match quality and the shooter does his or her part. Accurize, **$150.00**; Accurize Deluxe, **$185.00**.

New sights have also not been included in the package for the same reason as the accurizing, and also because the selection of available sights is quite long. My recommendation for our gun is to use Bo-Mar adjustables. These give an excellent sight picture and allow you to get the point of impact exactly where you want it at the range at which you want to sight-in the gun. **$155.00**

Let's take a look at what we have: First there's $350 for the new Colt 45; the $575 cost of the Competition Package brings the price up to $925, a little under the lower limit. If we accurize the gun for $150 we will have an *excellent* competitive gun for $1,075. If we decide to go with the Bo-Mar sights at this time, that will add $155 for a total of $1,230, which is only $30 over the upper limit we set at the beginning of this project. Whether you go with the basic $925 version, the $1,075 combination, or the full $1230 treatment, you will have an excellent "Poor Man's Race Gun." It just depends on *your* idea of what *poor* is.

The German PzB-41 antitank gun with Gerlich tapered bore was first captured in North Africa in 1941. The cartridge in front of the gun is typical of the appearance of all Gerlich skirted, deformable-projectile ammunition, regardless of caliber.

Gerlich's TAPER-BORE

by KONRAD F. SCHREIER, JR.

ONE OF THE FIRST Nazi army "secret weapons" was used in North Africa in 1942. On May 15 in an engagement near Helfaya Pass—Hellfire Pass—the Desert Rats of the British 8th Army captured it. It was a unique little antitank gun with a 2.8/2.0cm (1.1/.79-inch) tapered bore, the *Panzerbuche*—antitank rifle—PzB-41, Model 1941.

The PzB-41 caused quite a stir in the free world press. Its ability to fire armor-piercing projectiles through most tank armor of the time was truly impressive.

The PzB-41 was a 500-pound weapon, or about half the weight of conventional 37mm (1.45-inch) antitank guns used widely at the time. It fired a skirted deformable 4-ounce projectile at a remarkable 4500 fps velocity, while a conventional 37mm antitank gun shot a 32-ounce projectile at about 2800 fps. Tests showed the German gun could punch holes in twice the thickness of armor a conventional 37mm antitank gun could. It went through 3 inches at 100 yards and 2 inches at 200 yards, and, like conventional 37mm antitank guns, it was considered effective up to 500 yards.

While the PzB-41 caused a great deal of interest and speculation in the press since it was a "Nazi secret weapon," British and U.S. Army ordnance people immediately recognized what it was: a Gerlich taper-bore gun. These ordnance people also knew the taper-bore barrel and deformable skirted projectile were based on those developed by Herman Gerlich in the 1930s.

However, the idea of attaining *very* high velocities using a gun with a tapered bore, firing deformable projectiles, actually dated back to the 1880s! U.S. Army Ordnance Department engineers had been familiar with the principle since that time and so had the British Army. It was an idea which had been a result of the ability of nitrocellulose "smokeless" gun powder to propel projectiles at velocities unattainable with old-time black gunpowder.

The first taper-bore gun system the Army Ordnance Department heard of was described in German inventor H.P. Hurst's 1888 U.S. patent for one. It was issued just as smokeless propellant was coming into wide use, and there is no record what, if any, actual experiments Hurst did.

In the 1890s another German inventor, Karl Puff of the armament center of Spandau, began experimenting with taper-bore guns firing deformable projectiles. He got a U.S. patent for his system in 1908, and the Army Ordnance Department's engineers were fully aware of his developments.

In 1908, the U.S. Army Ordnance Department fitted a standard Model 1903 Springfield with a .34/.30-inch taper-bore barrel to fire deformable projectiles, based on Puff's patent. While the rifle could fire at very high velocities, the deformable projectiles were erratic and lacked acceptable accuracy. In any case, the project was dropped since there was no military need for such a high-velocity rifle. This rifle is now in the collection of the Springfield Armory National Historic Site museum.

At the time World War I was ending, the U.S. Army had a requirement for high-velocity antiaircraft guns and began development. One experiment was with a 3.3/3.0-inch taper-bore

It is believed this is the Halger caliber 280 Ultra rifle Gerlich demonstrated in the U.S. in 1931-1932. It used a taper-rifled barrel on a standard Mauser sporting action with an American-style pistol grip stock.

The principle wasn't new, but this German inventor was the first to make it workable and effective

GUNS

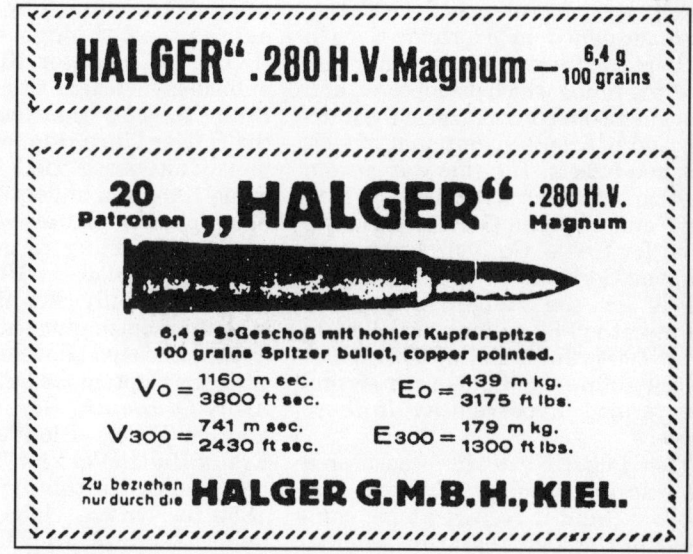

The label for a box of cartridges for the 280 Halger Ultra rifle, showing the extreme velocities claimed. The bullet was a conventional jacketed sporting design. The label dates from about 1930.

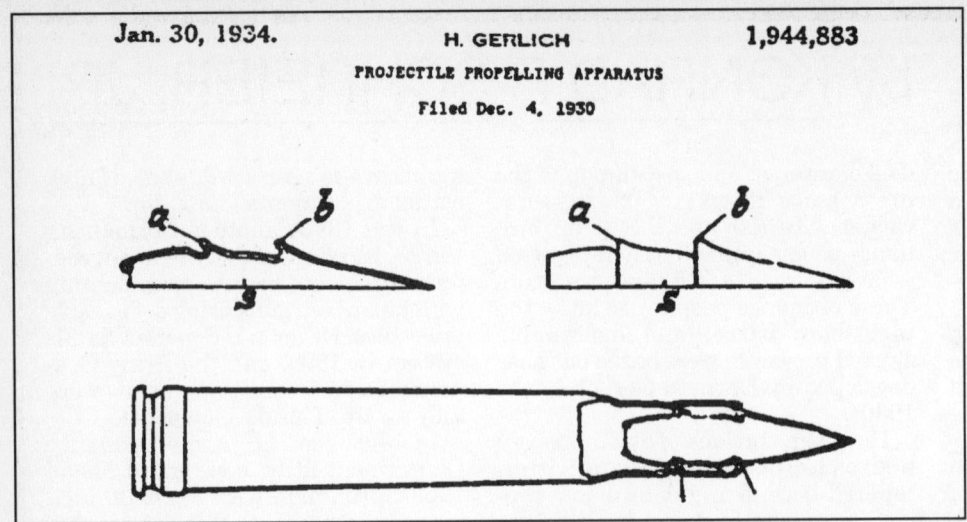

An early design drawing for Gerlich's first deformable-skirt bullet to be fired in tapered bores. The author has never seen an example of this round.

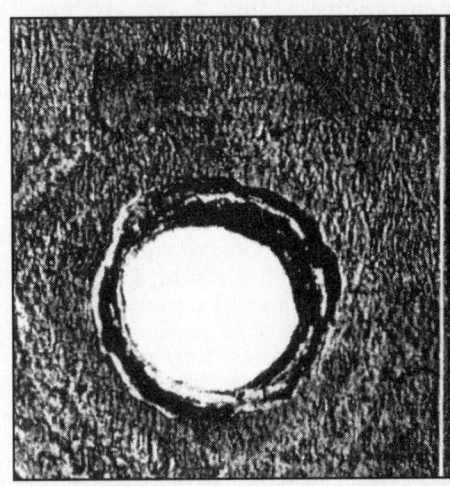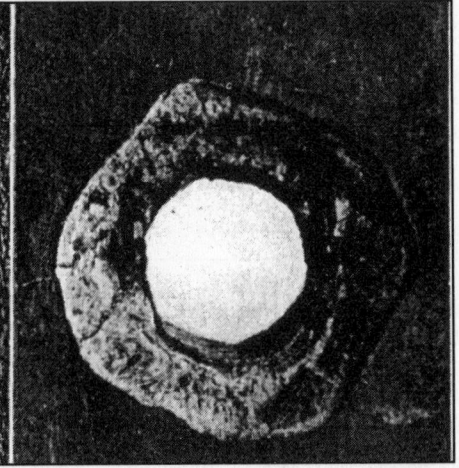

This hole in 5/16-inch armor plate was made by a Gerlich 280 Ultra rifle firing a bullet at about 3900 fps. This 1933 picture was one of the first published that showed the taper-bore gun's ability to punch holes in steel.

gun barrel firing deformable projectiles based on the system described in Puff's patent. While it did make a substantial increase in velocity, the problems of making the barrel and producing projectiles which performed consistently proved impossible to overcome and the project was eventually dropped.

During the 1920s, U.S. Army military attaches with embassies abroad reported a number of experiments were going on with taper-bore guns along the lines of Puff's. At the time, the increasing refinement of tanks was causing serious development of antitank guns firing their projectiles at higher and higher velocities, and the taper-bore gun firing deformable projectiles was a way of doing it.

Then, in the late 1920s, a new high-velocity sporting rifle called the Halger Ultra designed by Herman Gerlich appeared on the market. Its barrel had tapering rifling which disappeared into a short smooth bore section at the muzzle, and it fired conventional, if soft, jacketed bullets. The rifle was custom built on a Mauser action built by Halger G.m.b.H., Keil, Germany. Halger stood for Halbe, Gerlich's brother-in-law, and Gerlich.

Ads for the Halger Ultra rifle claimed the 280-caliber model could fire a 100-grain bullet at 3900 fps. A velocity of over 3000 feet-per-second was termed "hypervelocity" in those times.

The Halger Ultra rifle was offered for sale in Germany, England and the U.S., and it received wide comment in the sporting arms publications. However, both the rifle and its ammunition were very expensive, and, although it was on the market until the late 1930s only a few hundred were ever sold.

In the May-June 1930 issue of *Army Ordnance* magazine, an American publication read by military ordnance people throughout the world, "H. Gerlich, engineer, Kiel, Germany" published an article titled "Increasing Bullet Speeds" that described what the Halger Ultra rifle could do. It primarily discussed the 280 model and firing 100-grain bullets at velocities of 3900 fps. The text also described the projectile's ability to penetrate 5/16-inch armor plate at 100 yards, and this claim really caught the interest of ordnance engineers working on antitank weapon development.

In the September-October issue of *Army Ordnance,* Gerlich published another article titled "An Advanced Era of Bullet Velocity." In this story he discussed attaining velocities of 4850 fps with a Halger Ultra rifle using standard propellants, and as much as 5800 fps when using "special propellants." He also described and illustrated the effect of these hypervelocity projectiles on armor plate. An editorial note in the magazine stated the press had "garbled" their stories on what Gerlich claimed.

While many firearms authorities questioned Gerlich's 1931 claims, the U.S. Army Ordnance Department did not. They had access to Gerlich's recent patent application and knew he was working on taper-bore guns firing skirted deformable bullets, and that with this system it was entirely possible that he was achieving the hypervelocities he claimed.

While Gerlich was traveling in Germany, England and America in 1931-1932, demonstrating and selling Halger custom rifles, another article appeared in the March-April 1932 issue of *Army Ordnance*. It was written by retired German army ordnance authority Lt. Gen. H. Rohne and titled "The Ballistic Efficiency of Guns, Has a Great Increase of Velocity and Range Been Attained?" It was supported by ballistic mathematics of the possibilities and it questioned Gerlich's hyperveloctiy claims.

In the March-April 1933 issue of

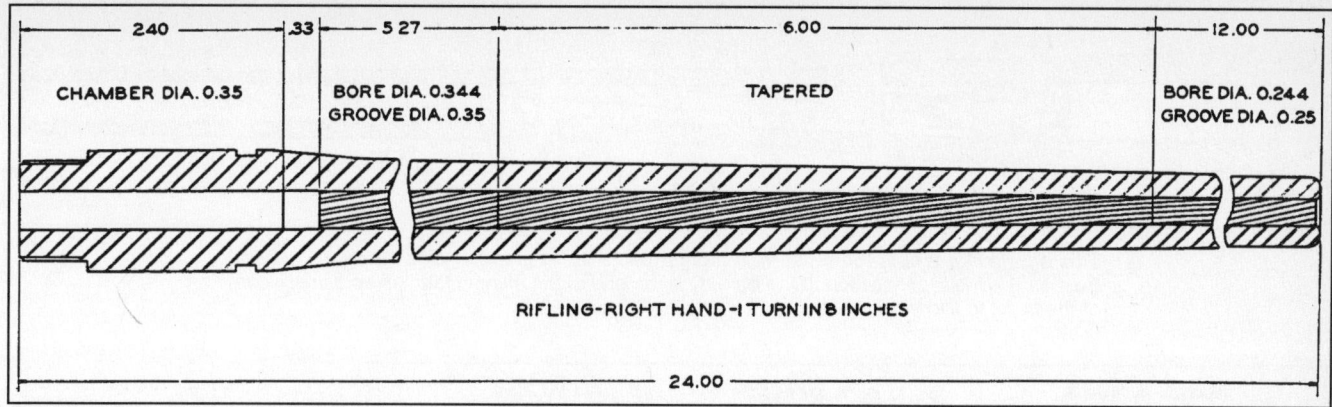

The U.S. Army's Gerlich .35/.25-inch taper-bore barrel designed and made by Springfield Armory about 1933. It was fitted to a pressure test gun fixture, and is typical of all Gerlich taper-bore barrels. Note the bore and groove dimensions.

Army Ordnance, U.S. Army Ordnance engineer Maj., later Col., Glen P. Wilhelm published the article "The Gerlich Rifle and Bullet," in which he not only discussed what Gerlich was doing but the history of taper-bore guns and what the U.S. Army was doing with them. He included drawings and information on the taper-bore barrel and skirted deformable projectiles that Army Ordnance was working on, following Gerlich's ideas and patents. Wilhelm indicated Gerlich's hypervelocity claims were completely possible.

Gerlich published his last article, "The Ballistic Efficiency of Guns," in *Army Ordnance* for January-February 1933. It discusses his hypervelocity gun system and its armor-piercing potential, and answers some of the criticisms Gen. Rhone made in his 1932 article. In the same issue, Maj. Wilhelm published "Armor vs. Bullets," which included comments on a hypervelocity gun's potential. This ended the magazine's articles on both Gerlich guns and armor piercing weapons for many years, in no small part because the U.S. Army classified the subject as "Confidential" and would not allow more to be published.

The September 1, 1934 edition of the *London Times* newspaper reported Gerlich's "sudden death." This obituary had neither the customary dates of birth and death nor the cause of his death. At the time, a rumor circulated in the U.S. Army Ordnance Department that he had been murdered by the Nazis because he was freely handing out information on the antitank potential of his gun system, and they wished to keep the development of an antitank "secret weapon" for their rearmament program.

However, the five U.S. patents awarded to Gerlich disclosed his developments, and Army Ordnance had received full information on them. The patents were:

- No. 1,944,883, filed December 4, 1930 and issued January 30, 1934, which claimed taper-bore rifle barrels and skirted deformable jacketed rifle bullets;
- No. 1,994,884, filed March 6, 1931 and issued January 30, 1934, which claimed impractical plastic-coated, deformable bullets for tapered rifle bores;
- No. 1,994,885, filed December 4, 1931 and issued January 30, 1934, which claimed mildly skirted deformable projectiles to be fired in taper-bore guns;
- No. 2,003,185, filed September 7, 1933 and issued May 28, 1935, which claimed the designs for special machine tools for making rifled taper-bore barrels;
- No. 2,110,264, filed October 29, 1935 and issued to his widow Franka Gerlich March 8, 1938, which claimed designs for radically skirted and other deformable projectiles for firing in taper-bore guns.

In addition, in the mid-1930s information was published on a high-velocity taper-bore shotgun Gerlich had developed but it was never patented. It was somewhat impractical due to the high chamber pressures developed, and no shotguns of the type are known to have been built. It is, however, worth nothing that a shotgun choke involves the slight tapering of the end section of its bore.

The five Gerlich patents mentioned above were the basis for the taper-bore guns and deformable projectiles of German World War II "Gerlich" antitank guns. And, obviously, the world's ordnance people knew about them before the war.

Springfield Armory made two .30/.24-inch Gerlich taper-bore barrels in 1932-1933, and Frankford Arsenal made skirted deformable projectiles to be fired in them. The accuracy proved to be poor and the armor penetration very limited due to the small test fixture gun, and no special weapon for them was made.

In the late 1930s the U.S. Army was very interested in improved antitank weapons, and in 1939 it again did some development work and testing of the Gerlich system. One variation developed by noted gun authority James V. Howe, author of *The Modern Gunsmith,* described it in the 1941 edition of this book. While Gerlich's deformable skirted projectile had two skirts, Howe designed one with only one skirt and used a fiber bushing to stabilize the projectile. Howe's bullet worked as desired, but it was deemed impossible to mass produce for military use. Howe's projectile did, however, anticipate the successful discarding-sabot, armor-piercing projectiles used in World War II.

Other U.S. Army Gerlich system tests were in calibers .30/.22-inch and .656/.50-inch. Firing was done with pressure test gun fixtures, and velocities up to 5000 fps were recorded, but accuracy was "very erratic." It is believed higher velocities may have been attained but the available measuring instruments were incapable of accurately recording them.

In Europe, another interesting Gerlich gun system development began in the late 1930s. Czechoslovakian arms engineer H.K. Janacek built and tested a 30- to 40-pound

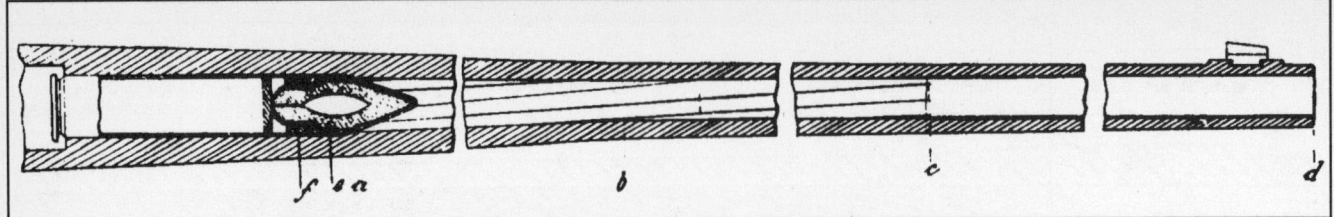

This drawing for a taper-bore rifle with a deformable bullet is from Puff's 1908 U.S. patent. Section B is the taper section of the bore, C is the end of the rifling. Note the void in the core of the bullet to allow deformation as it went down the bore.

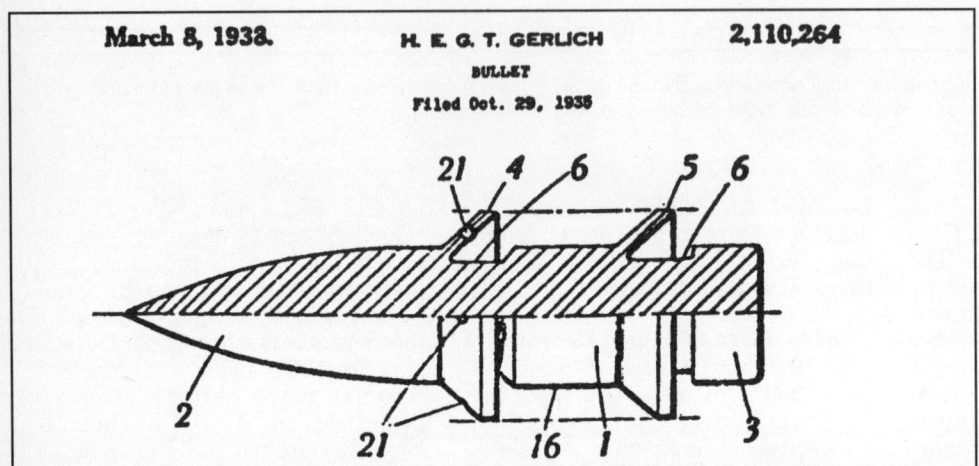

Patent drawing for a typical WWII Gerlich skirted, deformable projectile, designed about the time of Gerlich's death in 1934. Note the air vent holes (21) in the front skirt to allow uniform deformation.

experimental 15/11mm (.59/.43-inch) Gerlich-system taper-bore antitank rifle. When the Germans invaded his homeland, Janacek fled to England and was soon working in the armaments industry there. Though his Gerlich-system antitank rifle fell into German hands they never did anything more with it.

In England, in 1940, Janacek developed an interesting variation of the taper-bore gun and deformable projectile. This used a short, smooth, taper-bore adapter which screwed on the muzzle of a conventional rifled gun barrel. At the time the British were desperate for improved antitank guns, and they adopted this system as the "Littlejohn Adapter" for their standard 2-pounder (40mm, or 1.57-inch) tank and antitank gun. Although its use was always limited by short supplies of the special deformable-projectile ammunition, it proved effective and reasonably accurate, and it was available for issue at the end of World War II.

The U.S. Army tested but never adopted a Janacek Littlejohn Adapter for its standard 37mm tank/antitank gun. The British also tested it for larger-caliber tank/antitank guns but never adopted any of them. It was also tested for use on infantry rifles and 50-caliber weapons, but never adopted although the accuracy was adequate and the armor penetration was better than expected.

At the same time the Littlejohn Adapter was adopted by the British in 1940, the German army Waffenamt (Ordnance Department) was completing the development of its Gerlich taper-bore, deformable-projectile antitank guns. The 28/20 cm (1.1/.79-inch) PzB-41 went into production and this was the model captured by the British in 1941. Although its small projectile could penetrate tank armor, its light weight caused minimal damage. The conventional 5cm (2-inch) and 8.8cm (3.46-inch) antitank guns the Germans also used in North Africa were much more effective.

By 1942 the Germans had developed two larger Gerlich-system taper-bore antitank guns: the 4.2/2.8cm (1.65/1.1-inch) and the 7.5/5.5cm (2.95/2.2-inch), which mounted on conventional antitank gun carriages. Though both saw limited combat use, by 1943 they had been discarded because the Germans found it impossible to make the ammunition due to shortages of the special alloys the projectiles required, including the tungsten carbide armor penetrators. While both these guns could fire projectiles in the 4000-5000 fps range, their barrel life was less than 500 rounds.

What actually superseded the Gerlich taper-bore, skirted, deformable-projectile system was an equally effective design which fired a sabotted, lightweight projectile in conventional guns with the sabot falling off after the projectile left the gun muzzle. This system had been toyed with as far back as the 1800s, but the German army introduced it for modern tank and antitank guns in 1942.

In the U.S. Army, this system was adopted in 1943 as the Armor Piercing Discarding Sabot (APDS) projectile fired in High Velocity Armor Piercing (HVAP) ammunition. HVAP 3-inch and/or 76mm HVAP used in late World War II fired 3.95-pound armor penetrators at a muzzle velocity of about 3400 fps. Conventional armor-piercing projectiles for the same gun weighed 15.4 pounds and were fired at about 2600 fps. The HVAP round would penetrate about 50 percent more armor than the conventional armor-piercing projectile, and it could knock out the heavily armored German Panther and Tiger tanks at ranges of as much as 1000 to 1500 yards. HVAP ammunition is still used in tank guns today.

In recent years the APDS-type projectile has been successfully adapted to small arms ammunition. Remington's 30-06 Accelerator cartridge, which is fired in any conventional rifle of that caliber, fires a 55-grain projectile at about 4000 fps

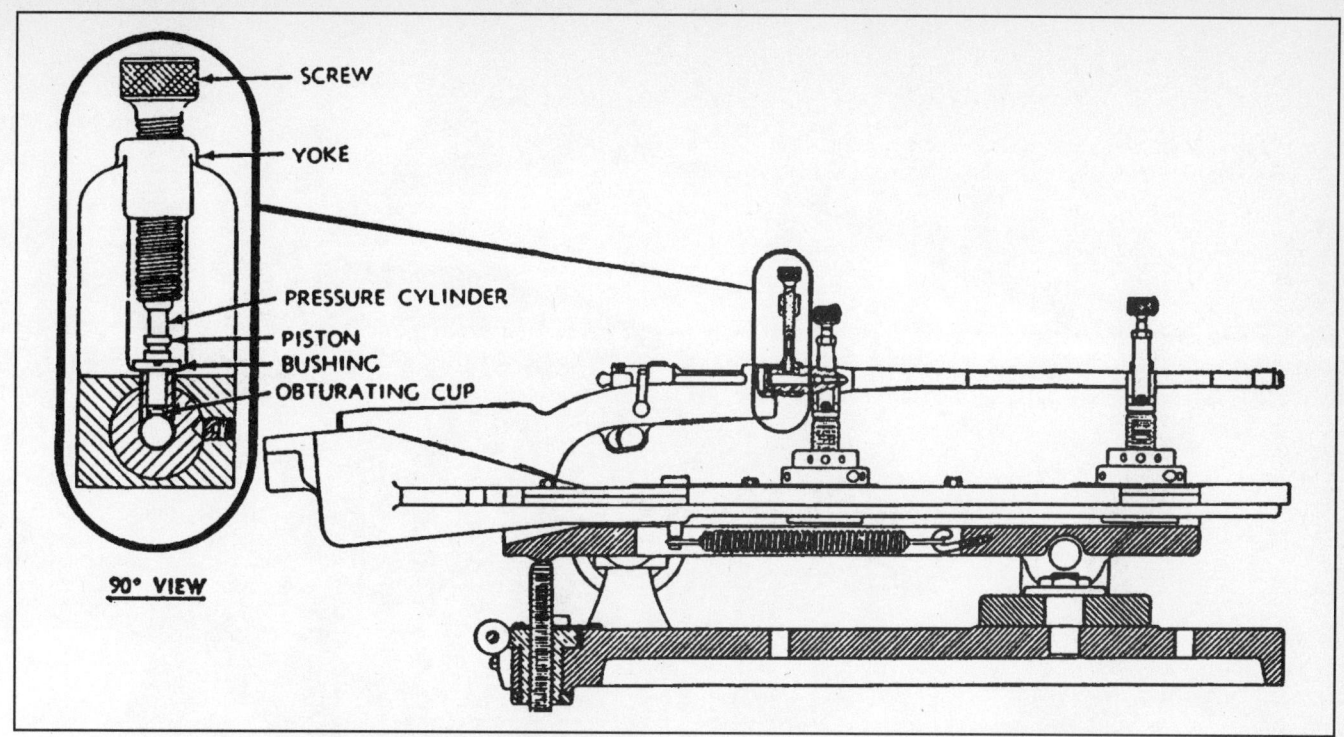

A typical U.S. Army Ordnance Dept. ammunition pressure test gun fixture of the type used to test Gerlich's taper-bore gun system. The chamber pressure of rifle-caliber, Gerlich-system ammunition was comparable to that of conventional ammo.

with acceptable accuracy. The U.S. Army Materiel Command's 50-caliber Sabbotted Light Armor Penetrator (SLAP) ammunition works on the same principle, and was used against hostile armor very effectively in the recent Operation Desert Storm.

In using 50-caliber SLAP ammunition in Operation Desert Storm, one effect common to all hypervelocity projectiles was observed: they glow in the dark. When fired at night they are heated by friction with the air in flight, and they appear to leave a light trail just like conventional tracer ammunition.

During World War II, the National Defense Research Council investigated the development of hypervelocity guns for the Army. In its 1942 report, "A Brief History of Tapered Bore Guns," their history was carefully described, and supporting documents were profuse. This report convinced the Army that, even though the Germans were using their Gerlich system taper-bore guns, they were not the best and simplest way of firing hypervelocity projectiles. First, the guns and deformable ammunition were difficult to manufacture. But, even more important, the taper-bore guns were incapable of firing conventional projectiles and their barrel life was short. The National Defense Research Council led the way in the development of our APDS-HVAP tank and antitank gun ammunition.

Despite the careful scientific consideration and rejection of the Gerlich taper-bore gun system for achieving hypervelocities, it is an idea which will not die.

In the late 1960s what was perhaps the ultimate taper-bore, gun-deformable projectile system was developed by ordnance engineer Russel S. Robinson: the "Salvo Squeezebore." This was a part of the U.S. Army's Project Salvo to develop weapons firing ammunition with multiple projectiles, from two to as many as six in each, to increase hit probability. Robinson first developed a taper-bore gun barrel which fired five caliber 30/.15-inch deformable projectiles per shot, and it worked. Then he enlarged the system to fire four caliber 50/.30-inch deformable projectiles at a shot. Although the system worked as designed, it was never adopted because it prevented arms firing it from using conventional ammunition.

In the 1970s, the U.S. Air Force experimented with a special barrel for its 20mm automatic aircraft cannon to fire a 4000 fps 20/10mm (.79/.39-inch) projectile in a deformable plastic jacket, which replaced the Gerlich deformable-skirt-type projectile. While armor penetration was excellent, the fact that the gun could not also fire conventional projectiles killed the project.

Although it would undoubtedly be much easier to produce tape-bore barrels and deformable projectiles with today's state-of-the-art materials and machine tools, the basic problems in the system still exist: Only the special deformable projectiles can be fired, and, for either military or sporting use, there are times when conventional projectiles will get the job done better. There are simpler and equally effective ways of achieving hypervelocities, such as the use of discarding-sabot, lightweight projectiles fired in conventional guns.

Target shooters, the original customers Gerlich seems to have had in mind when he developed his taper-bore, deformable-projectile system, have always been disappointed with it. They find accuracy is erratic because it is impossible to assure that the projectiles will deform identically for every shot. In fact, every test ever made of the system, military or civilian, has commented on the erratic accuracy. Gun designers and ordnance engineers have always agreed that while the Gerlich taper-bore hypervelocity gun firing deformable projectiles is one that looks very good in theory, it always fails to perform up to expectations in use. ●

MY PAIR OF WINCHESTER

The Model 70's predecessor came in a variety of styles and proved an excellent shooter.

MY VERY FIRST exposure to what I thought was a Model 54 Winchester actually was not. Guess maybe that statement needs a bit of an explanation. During the middle 1960s, I had become interested in competitive 30-caliber rifle shooting and shot in several matches using a borrowed '06 target rifle.

It turned out that the rifle loaned by a gunsmith friend was for sale. I knew I enjoyed the high-power rifle, as we call it, so it seemed the proper thing to do to purchase that Winchester target rifle.

I thought it to be a Model 54 because on the barrel it was so marked. However, a closer attention to detail showed the action was unmistakably Model 70. George Madis in *The Winchester Handbook* says some early Model 70 target rifles reportedly had Model 54 barrels installed on them. The serial number on mine was 3074. I had by happenstance obtained one of those early Model 70s.

This particular Model 70 was, within a few years, to be retired from the rigors of target shooting and another bolt-action target rifle was being built. However, as it turned out, not just one, but two, were obtained. While having a match rifle in 308 built on a Peruvian Mauser action, I happened to pay a visit to the gunsmith one day to follow its progress. There in the rack and for sale was a Model 54 bull barrel target rifle. Right then, that one was added to my stable.

The rifle has a serial number of 50945A. Some authorities writing about Winchester firearms indicate the last Model 54 rifle that rolled off

The author used his special-order Model 54, serial 50945A, for competitive shooting for a number of years. It certainly has a lot of checkering!

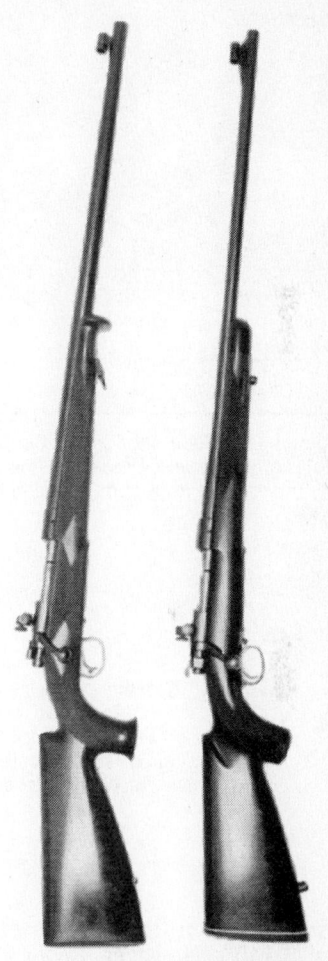

The Model 54 Target rifle (left) has a purpose-built stock that's quite attractive. The Model 70 target gun is an early example with Model 54 barrel.

MODEL 54s
by DAVID A. WEBB

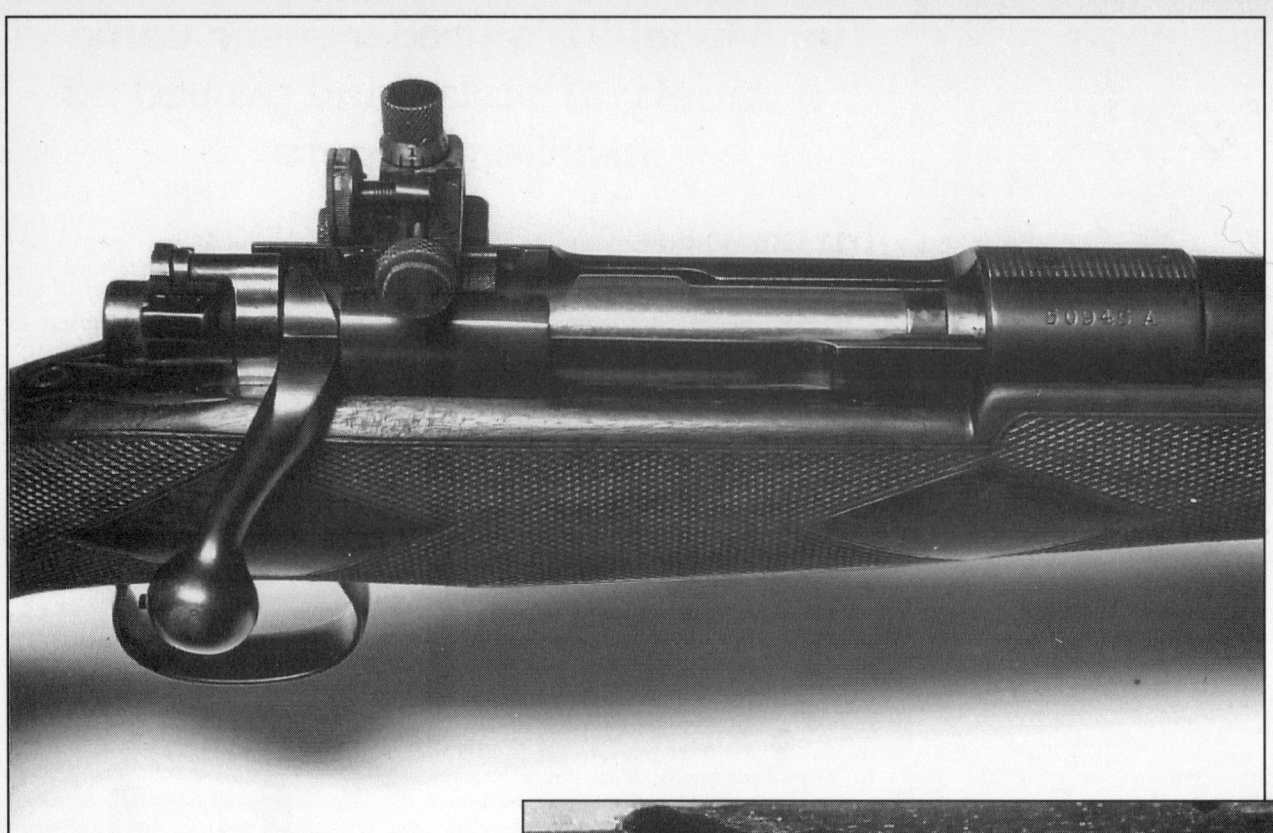

(Above) This close shot shows the bull-barreled Target Model 54 receiver. It was probably assembled from parts made in the late 1930s.

Closeup of the inspector's stamp (arrow) on the interior of the Target stock for Model 54 serial 50945A indicates it was made at Winchester's custom shop.

the production line was serial number 50145A. However, Roger C. Rule in *The Rifleman's Rifle* indicates there were 50,024 "standard" rifles manufactured from 1925 through 1941. Another 2005 rifles were produced as "specials" during this 16 years, making a total of 52,029 Model 54s produced. It can only be speculated that the bull-barreled target rifle with number 50945A was assembled from parts manufactured in the late 1930s. It probably was a "special" order rifle as the stock appears to be one that would have come from the Winchester custom shop.

Before discussing some additional details regarding the three Winchester rifles, I believe it is in order to discuss the Model 54, the forerunner to the Model 70. Today a number of collectors focus on the many variations of the pre-'64 Winchester Model 70s. There also has been some interest shown in the Winchester Model 54 rifles, although their models and variations were not nearly as numerous as occurred with the Model 70.

About the turn of the century, give or take a few years, the Winchester Repeating Arms Company tried twice to market centerfire bolt-action rifles. First they tried the Hotchkiss rifle, purchasing the patent rights in 1876 from Benjamin B. Hotchkiss. In the 1878 Ordnance Department trials, Winchester submitted several models. There were a total of twenty-eight rifles in the evaluation test and the Hotchkiss came in first. Ultimately, after several additional trials, Winchester was given a contract for 750 rifles. Later, a contract with China for 100,000 muskets was obtained; however, it evidently was never completed as the last Hotchkiss produced in 1899 had a serial number of 58,500. From parts on hand more rifles were assembled and the serial number 62,000 was passed.

Winchester's second entry was an unusual bolt-action design. Its Lee action operated by pulling the bolt upward and straight back. It was

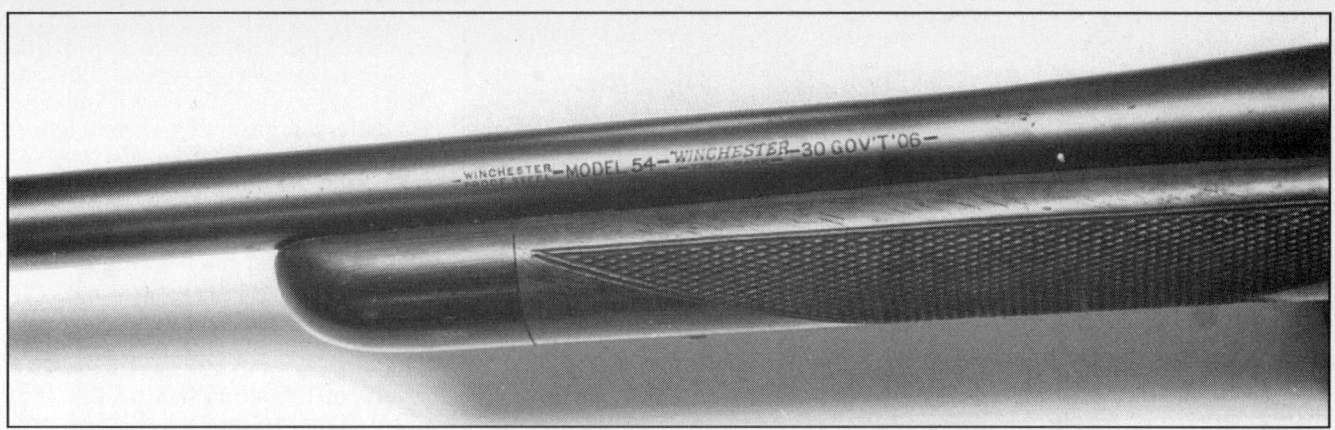

(Above) Webb's Model 70 heavy-barrel Target model with Model 54 barrel, serial 3074, was a product of the Winchester custom shop in 1937.

(Below) The top barrel is of the light sporter Model 54 Winchester, showing an assembly date of 1929; the bottom barrel indicates 1936 assembly of the bull-barrel target rifle.

thought the rapid rate of fire could gain acceptance by the American sportsman. Not so. There were only 20,000-odd Lee straight-pull rifles produced; of these only 1700 were sporting rifles; manufacturing ceased in 1902.

With these two lackluster attempts and a world war behind them, Winchester set about a new rifle design in the 1920s. Veterans were familiar with bolt-action rifles. The 1903 Springfield had a fine reputation, and at Eddystone Arsenal, at Remington and at Winchester the M1917 Enfield had been produced.

Remington Arms Company took advantage of their existing tooling for the M1917 Enfield and offered a new sporter rifle based on this action in 1921, designated the Remington Model 30. Winchester also thought about producing a rifle based on the M1917 action, but it had several characteristics Winchester engineers didn't like: the action was bulky and heavy; it cocked on closing; and had a very long striker fall. So Winchester started planning a new bolt-action rifle—Model 54 to be.

The Model 54 Winchester was produced for a relatively short period of time. The first rifles came off the New Haven production line in 1925, a group of sixteen, 30-06 target rifles. Reportedly, this batch of target rifles had no serial numbers assigned to them.

Over the next 16 years, ten different 54s with twenty-one different possible configurations were produced. There were ten chamberings, with the majority of rifles in 270 or 30-06. The 270 Winchester cartridge was first introduced in the Model 54.

Other cartridges for which the Model 54 was chambered included the 22 Hornet, 220 Swift, 250-3000 Savage, 257 Roberts, 7x57 Mauser, 30-30 WCF, 7.65 Belgian Mauser and 9x57 Mauser. The 22 Hornet chambering brought about an improvement in the Model 54. Initially, when the rifle was introduced, the lock time was quite slow. Alterations were made at the time the Hornet was introduced, and the lock time reduced substantially, thus increasing the accuracy potential of the rifle.

There were other improvements and modifications planned, but the rifle needed to be completely revamped. In late 1934, authorization was given by management to make the necessary changes and start planning for production of the new Model 70. It was just easier to issue a completely new model of the Winchester bolt rifle.

The Model 54 was not easy to mount a scope on—the bolt handle was too high and the Mauser-type safety did not allow for a scope.

Other complaints from early owners of the Model 54 included:
- The sheet-metal trigger guard and floorplate
- The trigger acting as a bolt-stop
- The absence of a gas port to allow gas to escape if case-head separation occurred
- A two-stage trigger

There were many positive design features of the Model 54 which led to the eventual success of the Model 70, because these features were retained in the new model Winchester bolt rifle:

The author's "pair" of Model 54s (from left): Model 70 with Model 54 barrel, Model 54 sporter, and Model 54 bull-barrel Target rifle.

- Receiver made as a single piece of machined steel properly heat-treated
- Dual locking lugs with the bolt handle serving as a safety lug
- The Mauser-type case extractor
- Excellent workmanship and a high standard of quality for finish

I did mention *three* rifles, right? Well, one is the Model 70, serial number 3074, with a Model 54 target barrel which is worthy of note on that basis, and because even today from benchrest at 100 yards it will group consistently between 1 to 1½ inches. Its pet handload in National Match brass uses Remington 9½M primers, 50 grains of Du Pont IMR4350 powder and the 180-grain Sierra boattail match bullet. That accuracy no longer holds out to 600 yards, but when one estimates the number of rounds gone down range through that Model 54 barrel, the retained accuracy speaks well for the quality of materials.

Then there is that bull barrel Model 54 rifle bought to replace Number 3074. It's been discussed.

What has not been discussed was my first Model 54, a 30-06 as well. It's a very light sporter—serial 32981A. Markings under the barrel indicate the rifle was probably assembled in 1929. It has a Lyman 48 receiver sight and will place, with a certain degree of reliability, five shots in a 1½- to 2-inch group at 100 yards. My 30-06 handload for hunting deer in the woods of western Pennsylvania starts with National Match brass and the Remington Magnum primers. The case is then charged with 49.0 grains of IMR4895 behind the 168-grain Sierra softpoint bullet. Accuracy of this M54 is also quite good considering the apparent amount of use that the rifle has had over the half-century-plus since it came off the production line.

Prior to World War II, rifles manufactured by Winchester had the last two digits of the year in which a barrel was produced and assembled with the action stamped on the underside of the barrel near the front receiver ring. My bull-barrel target M54 was put together in 1936.

Regardless of its collector interest, this target rifle was used for my competitive rifle shooting up until a few years ago. Other shooters often commented on the unusual design of the stock. The inspectors' stamp tells me the stock probably did come from Winchester's custom shop.

The NRA match course was the standard type of competition. During a year's time, I would attend six to eight matches firing over the 200-, 300- and 600-yard ranges. If I do my part, the rifle will consistently put its bullets into 1 MOA groups at each of those three target ranges. The load for this rifle consisted of 47.5 grains of IMR4895 in National Match cases primed with the Winchester WLR primer. At the 200- and 300-yard ranges, the 168-grain Hornady match bullet is the choice; while at 600 yards either the 180- or 190-grain Sierra match bullets buck the wind better.

My target Winchester rifles have fired their last shots in competitive matches. A least once a year they will be taken to the range and put through their paces, and they will be used on those occasions when the local Boy Scout troop asks for a demonstration concerning target shooting techniques. The featherweight Model 54 is still used to hunt deer-sized game when conditions are not right for using a scope-mounted rifle. These three bolt rifles have special places in my gun cabinet and each of my three sons will one day own one. ●

by CHUCK KARWAN

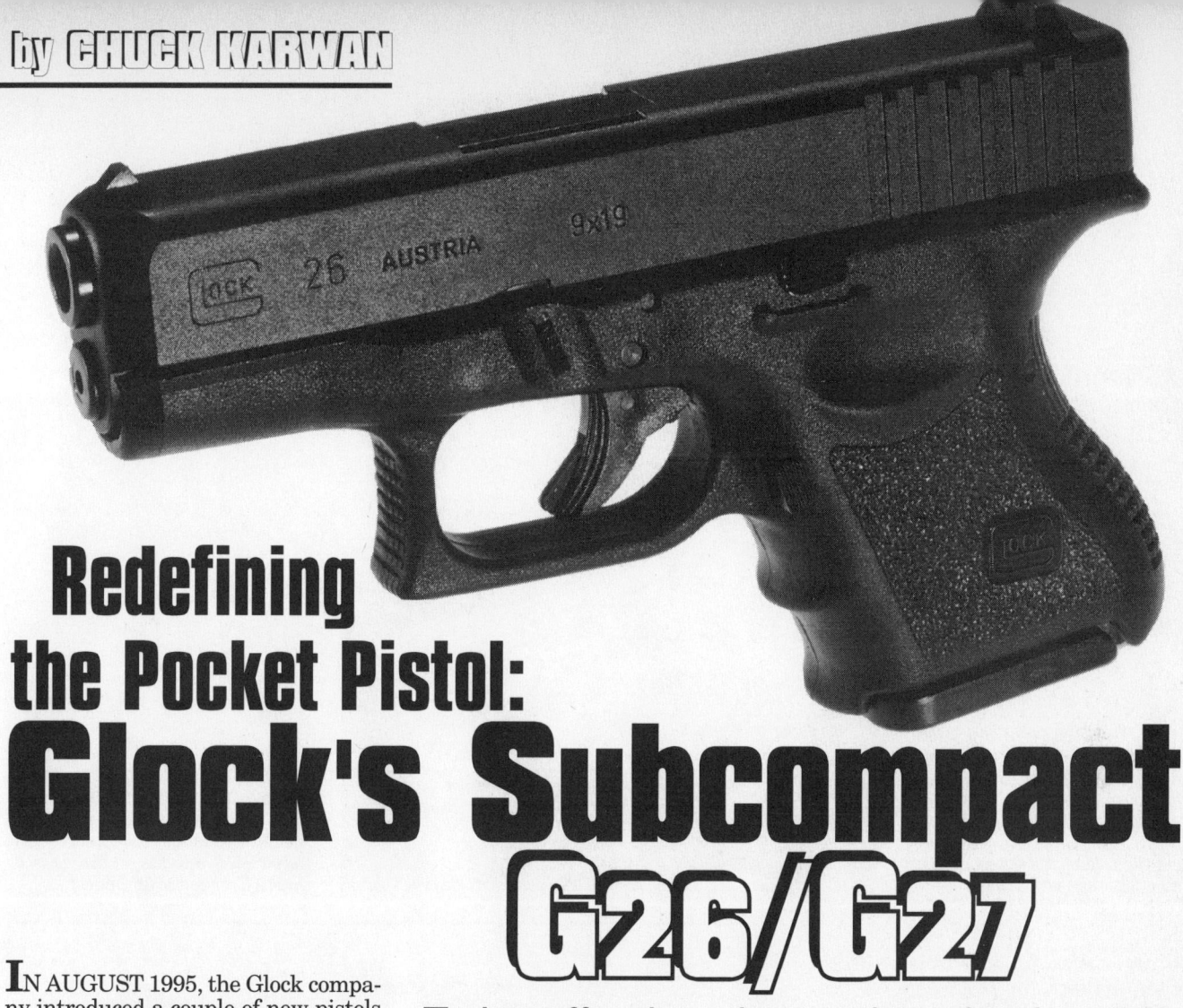

Redefining the Pocket Pistol:
Glock's Subcompact G26/G27

To be effective, the pocket pistol needs to be small and powerful, and these two Glocks score big on both points

IN AUGUST 1995, the Glock company introduced a couple of new pistols that have increased the performance envelope of concealment handguns to an incredible degree. Called the G26 in 9mm and the G27 in 40 S&W, Glock refers to them as their subcompact pistols.

For several decades the size standards for the smallest serious concealment handguns have been set by the S&W J-frame, 38 Special, 2-inch-barreled, five-shot revolvers, and the Walther PPK 380 ACP auto. By serious I mean powerful enough to be relatively effective at achieving incapacitation with good ammunition. Certainly there are smaller handguns, but they are usually chambered for the 22 Short, 22 LR, 22 WMR, 25 ACP, and the 32 ACP cartridges. These chamberings are far better than nothing, but their level of effectiveness for incapacitation is too low to suit many, if not most gun carriers. Indeed, even the 380 ACP and 38 Special using conventional ammunition fired from short barrels are considered by many shooters, including me, to be marginally effective at best.

The problem has always been one of size of the handgun versus its capabilities. Capabilities include not only the effectiveness of the chambering but also the number of rounds available and, to a lesser extent, the speed of firing and the practical accuracy of the gun. Good examples of that accuracy are the one- or two-shot derringers available that are chambered for such cartridges as 45 ACP or 45 Colt. Even though they are chambered for effective cartridges, they are slow to fire, only hold one or two rounds, and are accurate only at card-table or phone-booth ranges. Thus, even though these guns are small, easily concealed, and chambered for effective rounds, their limited capabilities make them unsatisfactory for most of us for use as a primary concealed weapon. Such guns are better employed in the backup gun role.

Now we have the new Glock subcompacts. They are about the same size in height and length as either the Walther PPK or the 2-inch S&W J-frame. They are slightly thicker than the Walther but thinner than the cylinder of the S&W. They are also about the same weight as steel-framed versions of either the S&W or the Walther.

When Gaston Glock designed these little beauties, he started with his compact G19 and G23 models in 9mm and 40 S&W. These are the compact versions of the full-size G17 and G22 pistols. To put things into perspective, the G19 and G23 compacts are incredibly capable handguns that had become the standards of their field for concealable handguns. As both guns have a magazine capacity as large as

Jake Karwan fires the G27 in 40 S&W, shown in full recoil. Though small and powerful, the gun is easy to shoot effectively.

(Right) The G26 9mm Glock (left) is about the same size and weight as the S&W M940 revolver and chambers the same cartridge. However, the Glock holds ten plus one rounds, while the S&W only holds five. Also, the Glock is much easier to shoot effectively.

(Below) The Glock G26/G27 (identical in size) are virtually the same height and length as a 2-inch-barreled S&W J frame, in this case a M640 Centennial 38 Special.

or larger than full-sized pistols from other makers, nothing else on the market could touch them for their same size and weight. However, while they can be concealed quite nicely, they are still too large for many concealed-carry situations, including ankle or pocket carry.

In simple terms, Mr. Glock took these already compact guns and trimmed an additional .55-inch off the length and .80-inch off the height. While it sounds simple, there was considerable engineering needed to get the resulting pistols to function properly. The most obvious indication of this is the unique recoil spring system developed for them. It is a telescoping dual spring setup with one spring inside of another. While this in itself is not new, the way that they telescope with both springs supplying force throughout the recoil cycle is new to the field of firearms, at least to my knowledge. This clever recoil spring system is credited with the remarkably low recoil impulse experienced when shooting these guns.

Looking at capacity first, thanks to their double-column magazines, the Glocks carry ten plus one in 9mm and nine plus one in 40 S&W, compared to only six plus one for the PPK and five for the S&W. Needless to say, the Glocks offer a huge improvement in this regard.

With regard to the effectiveness of their respective rounds, the 9mm Parabellum far outperforms the 38 Special or 380 ACP in any bullet weight, and the 40 S&W is even better. Indeed, in its best loadings it is one of the most effective handgun rounds available in normal-size handguns. Thus, the subcompact Glocks offer a quantum leap forward in capacity and cartridge effectiveness over the traditional 2-inch S&W or the PPK. Indeed, they are quite competitive in this regard with most full-sized 9mm and 40 S&W pistols made by other manufacturers.

I realized just how much this is

Jake Karwan demonstrates a good two-hand hold with the little G27. Even though it is a powerful cartridge in a small and lightweight pistol, it is not hard to control or uncomfortable to shoot, like many other small powerful handguns.

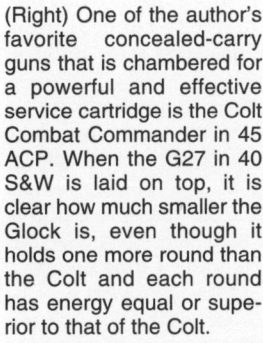

(Right) One of the author's favorite concealed-carry guns that is chambered for a powerful and effective service cartridge is the Colt Combat Commander in 45 ACP. When the G27 in 40 S&W is laid on top, it is clear how much smaller the Glock is, even though it holds one more round than the Colt and each round has energy equal or superior to that of the Colt.

true when I was visiting a sheriff's department on business. I noticed that their issue handgun was the S&W Model 1066 in 10mm. An inquiry revealed that their duty load was the same as the FBI's, or a 180-grain bullet at about 980 fps. I took great delight in showing them my 40 S&W Glock G27, and pointing out that even though it was over a pound lighter and much smaller than their S&Ws, it held the same number of rounds and was capable of delivering the same ballistics.

A similar situation developed when I attended a trade show in Wyoming that was visited by some patrolmen from the Wyoming Highway Patrol. These stalwart lads carried Beretta Model 96 pistols in 40 S&W. They were quite amazed to handle the G27 and find out that it shoots the same round as their duty pistol and holds only two rounds less, even though it is about 12 ounces lighter and much smaller.

Fortunately there are even more advantages. In general, small handguns are hard to shoot well. Certainly that is true of the 2-inch J-frame S&Ws. Practically everyone who has tried the subcompact Glocks has commented that they are nearly as easy to shoot well as their bigger brothers, even at ranges well beyond what would be the norm for a concealment gun. The very first day I had my hands on one of the little Glocks I was showing it to my friend Sgt. Larry Baird, a firearms instructor on the Portland, Oregon police department. We were on an indoor range in the department's basement. After warming up with a few rounds he engaged a couple of hostage targets he had set up at about ten yards. These are the type that has the bad guy hidden behind the hostage except for a bit of his upper torso and most of his head. He fired two shots at each as fast as he could, which is fast indeed. I estimate that he completed the exercise in under three seconds. A look at the targets showed that each had two well-centered hits to the head of the bad guy. I commented, "I bet you couldn't do that with a 2-inch Chief." He just smiled and said that I was right. After working with these guns I learned that a good shooter like Larry could take such head shots with them at 25 yards with complete confidence. These are certainly not just belly guns.

When one tries to shoot most small auto pistols quickly, particularly with a hasty grip on the gun, the top of the shooter's hand will often be hit with the pistol's slide. Not only does the shooter receive a painful though minor injury, the interference of his hand will often cause a malfunction that could be fatal in a real encounter. The Walther PPK is notorious for this, as are most other compact autos. The small Glocks have no such problem because their grips are based on those of their larger brothers, and the web of the shooter's hand is well protected from the slide.

When powerful cartridges are fired in small, light handguns there is always the worry of heavy recoil. I am admittedly a poor judge of such things, but I find that the G26 9mm is extremely easy to shoot with regard to recoil. The G27 40 has noticeably more kick but it is not uncomfortable at all, though shot recovery is slightly slower than with its 9mm brother. The consensus seems to be that the G26 9mm kicks less than even the G19 and that the G27 40 kicks no worse than the larger G23. It is quite clear that either kick significantly less than any of the 2-inch 38 Specials with hot loads, let alone the 2-inch 357s or 44 Specials.

The butt on the G26 and G27 is very short, allowing only two fingers of a normal-size hand to fit under the

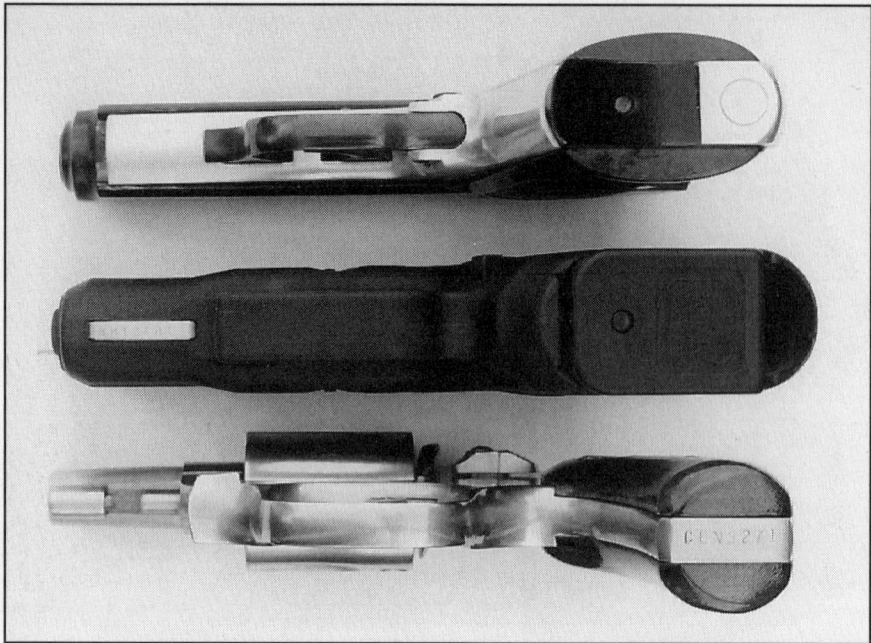

(Above) The Glock G26 is slightly thicker than the FEG R61 380 ACP on top, yet thinner than the cylinder of the S&W J-frame gun on the bottom.

A capacity comparison (from left) shows eleven rounds of 9mm (G26), ten rounds of 40 S&W (G27), seven 380 ACPs (Walther PPK), and five 38 Specials (S&W J frame).

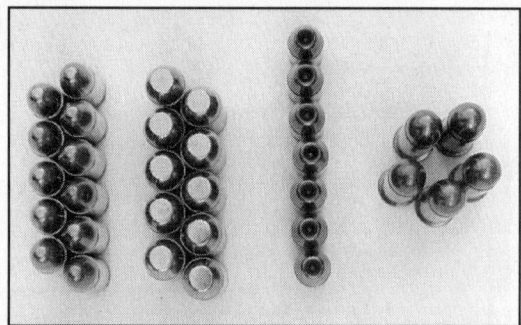

trigger guard. If you are used to handling one of the larger Glocks it does feel somewhat peculiar, but it has to be expected if the gun is to be small enough to be pocketable or used in an ankle holster. The grip that is left is adequate to control the gun and not hard to get used to. I find that by simply placing my little finger under the pistol's butt I can achieve a secure and comfortable grip on the gun.

A remarkably high percentage of people I have showed one of the little Glocks to have immediately commented that the grip was too short and that the gun would be better with a longer grip. Quite frankly I find that response to be nonsensical. If you want a small gun you automatically get a small grip. Interestingly, these same people do not typically make the same complaint about such guns as the S&W Chiefs Special or Walther PPK that have equally short grips. My standard response to this criticism of the small Glocks is simply to point out that Glock already had it covered by the G19 and G23. I also pointed out that the little Glocks will also accept any of the longer magazines of the other Glocks in the same chambering and function perfectly with them. Thus, if you want the grip of your G26 or G27 to be longer, just put in the longer magazine of the G19 or G23. When this is done, the magazine extends out the bottom enough to supply a place for the shooter's dangling fourth finger. Obviously, doing so will compromise the concealability of the gun, but if that is what you want the option is there.

The fact that these little Glocks can use the magazines of the larger guns make them particularly suitable for several applications. The most obvious is as a backup gun for a law enforcement officer carrying a larger Glock as his/her primary gun. When one of these is carried in such a role, the carrier has an ideal situation where his backup gun functions the same as his primary gun, has the same trigger pull, and can be reloaded from the same ammunition pouch carried for the primary gun. Clearly the new Glocks make terrific backup guns in general, but they are nearly perfect in that role when used in conjunction with a larger Glock in the same chambering.

The G26 and G27 also give law officers that are working the undercover scene capabilities that they never had before. For the first time they can be truly well armed while appearing not to be armed. As soon as these new guns were available I called a pal who works the gang scene, sometimes undercover, in one of our major cities. We got him the subcompact Glock and he immediately put it into use as a backup gun, off-duty gun, and as an undercover gun. At last report he was delighted.

Prior to the availability of the Glock subcompacts, I carried a Glock G23 40 S&W as my primary concealed-carry piece using an inside the waistband holster. When I was lightly clothed and could not carry the G23 I usually reverted to a Model 940 S&W Centennial in 9mm carried in my left front pocket. Once I got my hands on a G27, more often than not it became my primary concealment handgun carried either in a holster or in a pocket.

To be successful in pocketing the G26/G27 there is no question that you cannot be wearing tight trousers. However, fairly baggy trousers such as Dockers or full-cut jeans are popular these days and the little Glocks can be carried in them quite nicely. I tried to demonstrate this with a photo here, but it seemed silly because the picture didn't show anything.

Since the introduction of these subcompact Glocks some competition has surfaced, including the Kahr 9mm and the Kel-Tech P-11. The Kahr is thinner, but it holds fewer rounds and is heavier. The Kel-Tech is smaller, lighter, and holds the same number of rounds in 9mm but is not available in 40-caliber. Neither have the superb Glock two-stage trigger pull, nor its incredible simplicity and ease of maintenance. There is nothing yet on the market that can compete with the 40 G27 with regard to power, capacity, and size.

To say that I am enthusiastic about the G26/G27 is a gross understatement. These are incredibly capable guns for their size and weight, and they have all the endearing Glock qualities of extreme reliability, durability, simplicity and ruggedness, as well as shootability. At last check, Glock is in a back-order situation for these guns, but don't let that hold you back. The guns are worth the wait.

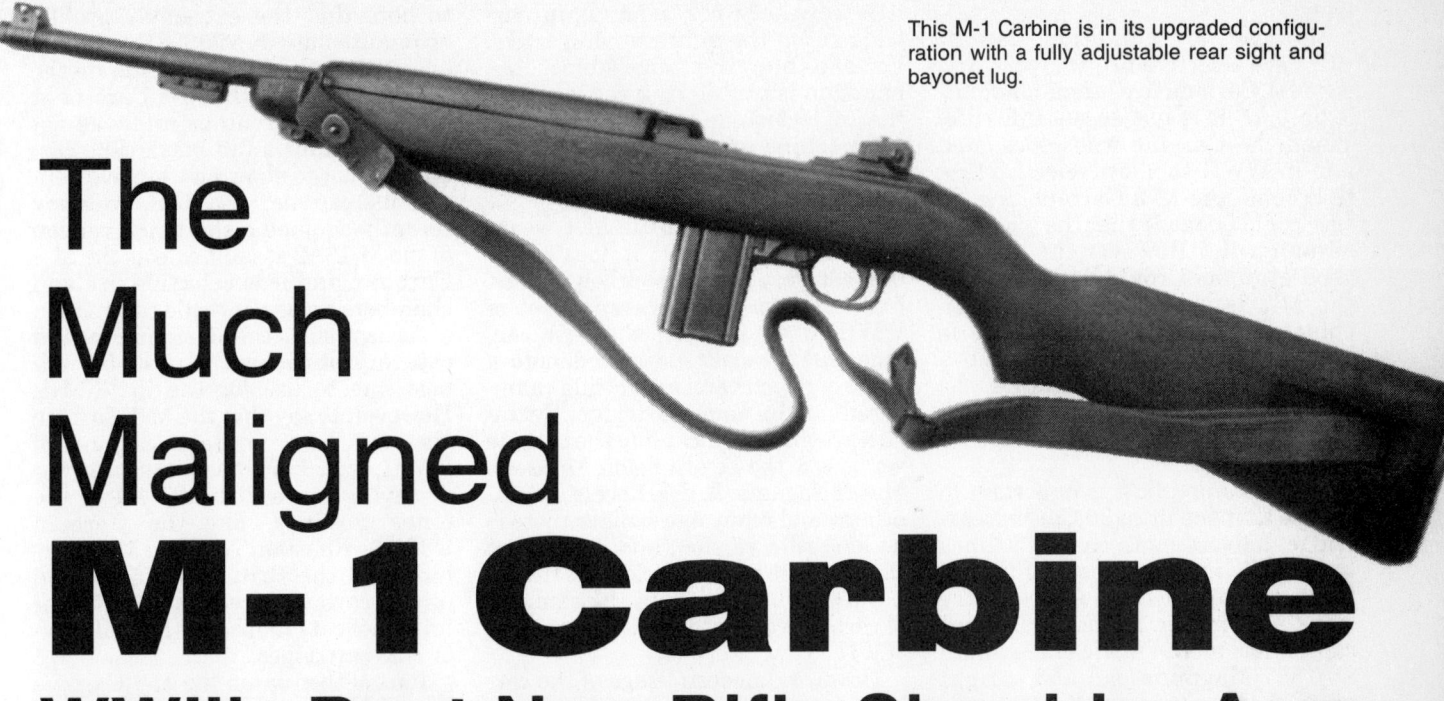

This M-1 Carbine is in its upgraded configuration with a fully adjustable rear sight and bayonet lug.

The Much Maligned M-1 Carbine

WWII's Best Non-Rifle Shoulder Arm

The handy little Carbine was called upon to do more than it was designed for and got "bad press" from inept users. It really is a good gun.

by CHUCK KARWAN

AMONG THE CURRENT crowd of gun writers there are few that have a good word to say about the little M-1 Carbine. This gun is usually portrayed as terribly inaccurate and so lacking in power that it is nearly worthless as a combat weapon. Reportedly, enemy soldiers would absorb fifteen of the little 110-grain 30-caliber bullets with nary a twitch and keep on charging. Most of these same writers will also tell you that a single 45 ACP bullet from an M1911A1 drops a bad guy hit with it nineteen times out of twenty.

The truth of the matter is that the M-1 Carbine is not nearly so bad; and the venerable M1911A1 isn't nearly that good. In my not so humble opinion, the M-1 Carbine was one of the premier weapons to come out of WWII, and it deserves a lot more credit than it has received. Indeed, I believe it to be the single best *non-rifle* individual shoulder weapon issued in the war. In addition, when the Carbine is fed modern ammunition with expanding bullets it becomes a formidable weapon that will outperform many of its most modern brethren inside 150 yards.

When one examines the small arms of WWII, many weapons stand out as the best of their breed. In heavy machineguns it was clearly the U.S. 50-caliber M2 Browning. Among water-cooled medium machineguns the title is shared by both the U.S. Browning M1917 and the British Vickers, both decorated veterans of WWI. For general purpose air-cooled machineguns it was the German MG42 and the U.S. Browning M1919A4/A6, though for vastly different reasons. In light machineguns few would argue with the British Bren being rated the best. Likewise few would question the M-1 Garand as the top battle rifle. Only a handful of true assault rifle models saw service in WWII, but the best was clearly the German Stg44. In the area of submachine guns there were many excellent designs, but several stand out, including the German MP40, the Italian Beretta Model 38/42 (my personal pick for the best), the Russian PPSh 41 and PPS 43, the Australian Owen and several others. Last but not least is the field of handguns, where three truly exemplary models stand above all others, the U.S. M1911A1, the German P38, and the Belgian Browning Hi-Power.

You will note that in spite of the grandiose claim in the title of this piece, the U.S. M-1 Carbine has not yet been mentioned. That is because it does not fit in any of the standard, accepted small-arms categories very well. Its cartridge is not nearly powerful enough to qualify it as a battle rifle round. Indeed, it is not as powerful as any of the standard intermediate-level assault rifle cartridges like the 7.92 Kurz, the 7.62x39mm, the 5.45x39mm or the 5.56mm NATO. However, at 955 foot pounds of muzzle energy, the 30 Carbine has only 90 foot pounds less muzzle energy than the Soviet AK74 5.45x39mm round. Thus, one could classify it as an underpowered assault-rifle cartridge.

However, by definition, assault rifles are selective-fire weapons and the M-1 Carbine fires semi-automatic only, so it is not an assault rifle. When the Carbine was redesigned late in WWII to allow selective fire, to become the M-2 Carbine, a good case could be made that the gun is an assault rifle. However, an equally good argument could be made that the M-2 is a selective-fire submachine gun, because its cartridge is ballistically not much more than a magnum pistol round. After all, the definition of a submachine gun is a full-automatic weapon that fires a pistol cartridge.

At the same time it is important to realize that the little 30 Carbine cartridge delivers more than 2.5 times the kinetic muzzle energy of typical 9mm Parabellum or 45 ACP military loads fired from a handgun. Ballistically it has more kinetic energy than any 357 Magnum load and is right up in there with many 44 Magnum loads when either of these are fired from a handgun. Though several revolvers and at least three auto pistols have been chambered for 30 Carbine, it is certainly not a handgun cartridge from the military perspective. For one thing the muzzle blast in a handgun is brutal. As a consequence the M-1 Carbine is certainly not a submachine gun and the M-2 Carbine probably does not fit that definition very well either.

Even though the little M-1 wears the "carbine" moniker, it does not fit that category very well either, at least from the military perspective of WWII. In that period, the term carbine was typically used to denote a short-barreled version of a rifle chambered for the same cartridge. Examples are myriad, including the carbine versions of the Lee-Enfields, Mausers, Mosin-Nagants, Krags, Lebels, Mannlichers, and many more. Since there is no long rifle version, and it does not chamber the same cartridge as the M-1 Garand, it does not fit the category of carbine very well as it was used in WWII.

However, modern usage of the carbine term includes just about any short-barreled, rifled shoulder arm that does not have full-automatic capability, even those chambered for pistol cartridges. It is also important to note that the extremely prolific semi-automatic Soviet SKS was specifically designated a carbine by the Soviets, and like the M-1 Carbine it had no rifle parentage and was not chambered for a full battle-rifle cartridge. Just to show how elusive definitions can be, the U.S. military recently adopted a shortened version of the M-16A2 assault rifle as the M-4 Carbine, and it is selective fire and chambers an assault-rifle cartridge.

As a result, the designation and category of *carbine* is probably the best one to use for the little M-1. However, to say that the M-1 Carbine was the best military carbine of WWII, which it was, is somewhat deceiving since virtually all of the other carbines, like the German G33/40, Russian Tokarev M40 carbine and the British No. 5 Enfield jungle carbine, are totally different breeds of cat chambered for full-power rifle cartridges.

Part of the reason the M-1 Carbine has picked up an undeservedly bad reputation is this difficulty in categorizing the gun. This, in turn, causes problems in deciding how it should or can be used, and what to compare it with. Too often the gun is criticized for not having the power or range of a battle rifle when it was never intended to be used in that role. It is a unique little gun that was designed specifically to bridge the gap between the rifle and the handgun and it does that job extremely well.

The M-1 Carbine was born in the opening days of WWII. It had become obvious that the complex nature of the modern army required many specialized personnel that were not combatants in the traditional sense. It was also clear that many of these people could not perform their jobs efficiently if they were required to carry a heavy and bulky combat rifle. At the same time, it was well recognized that if these people were issued a handgun as their personal weapon, few of them could use it effectively should the need arise. Thus, the requirement for a light and compact rifle evolved.

In June of 1940, the Secretary of War directed the Ordnance Depart-

A U.S. Marine helps refugees on Saipan move out of danger. Note that his Carbine has the grenade launcher attached.

ment to commence a program of development of a 5-pound shoulder firearm that would be an effective weapon up to 300 yards. The amazing thing is that the ammunition and the gun were developed, tested, and adopted by October of 1941. That is an incredible feat of ordnance engineering, particularly considering the excellence of the resulting firearm. By the end of 1942, about 100,000 guns had been produced and the numbers climbed at a phenomenal rate thereafter.

The M-1 Carbine was designed in a crash development program by Winchester to meet tough requirements. Winchester was not the only competitor in the trials, but its entry was head and shoulders above the competition and was the obvious winner. Contrary to popular belief, it was never intended for the Carbine to completely replace all the handguns in the military services. Indeed, it was intended to replace handguns for *some* personnel, and shoulder arms like submachine guns and rifles for others. There never was any intention for it to totally replace the pistols carried by pilots, machinegunners, tank crews, many MPs, and some others.

Most people are surprised to learn that the M-1 Carbine is the second most prolific military firearm in U.S. history with a total production of well over six million. The only U.S. firearm that beats it in total production is the M-16, which has been in production for some thirty years or so, to the tune of over seven million copies. Contrast that with the M-1 Carbine which was in military production for fewer than five years.

The Carbine was produced by ten primary contractors and over a thousand subcontractors that made minor components. By far the single biggest producer was the Inland Manufacturing Division of General Motors, located in Dayton, Ohio, which produced 2,642,097 Carbines of all types. Second in production was its developer, Winchester, with 818,059. It must be remembered that Winchester was also making M-1 Garands and doing other defense production at the same time. Other makers include Saginaw Steering Gear Division of General Motors, Underwood Elliot Fisher Co., National Postal Meter Co., Quality Hardware Machine Co., International Business Machine Corp., (IBM), Standard Products Co., Rock-ola Manufacturing Corp., and the John Pederson Co., which made only a very small quantity before the contract was taken over by Saginaw. You will note that Winchester was the only manufacturer that had any previous experience at making firearms.

The M-1 Carbine was officially adopted on October 23, 1941, as the "U.S. Carbine, Caliber .30 M1." Since there already was a "U.S. Rifle, Caliber .30 M1," the superb Garand, one would think that Ordnance could have come up with a more original nomenclature that would not be so confusing, particularly since they shot completely different 30-caliber cartridges. I can well remember a Special Forces unit I was in that ordered 30 M-1 Carbine ammunition and received 30 M-1 Garand (30-06) ammunition by mistake. One can only wonder how many times this happened during WWII, Korea, and Vietnam. Admittedly such a mix-up would be a much smaller problem for

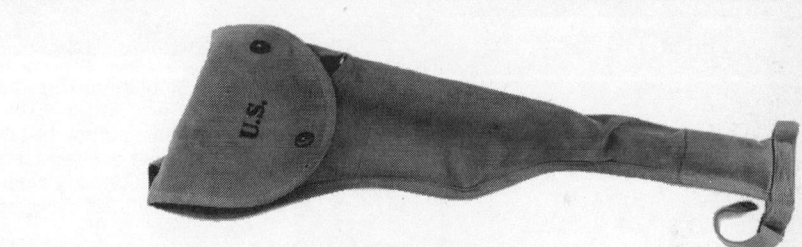

The M-1A1 Carbine was designed for use by paratroops, and had a left-folding stock to make it more compact. The case used to carry it for parachuting (above) fits onto the jumper's belt and attaches to his leg like a large pistol holster. The stock folds tight against the left side of the gun (below).

a unit that used both the Garand and the M-1 Carbine, but in my unit that was not the case.

Only a handful of M-1 Carbines were produced before the Japanese attack on Pearl Harbor on December 7, 1941. However, none were issued for service until August of 1942 when stocks of Carbines, magazines, and ammunition were high enough to support the normal attrition of combat. The first Carbines to see combat were with the U.S. forces that invaded North Africa in November '42. A folding-stock version, called the M-1A1 Carbine, and designed for paratroops was standardized in May '42 and first saw combat with the 82nd Airborne Division in the invasion of Sicily in July '43. In the Pacific Theater, some Carbines showed up in time for the latter days of the Solomon Islands campaign, but the first extensive use was by the Marines at Tarawa in November of '43. M-1 Carbines were also used extensively by Merrill's Marauders in early '44 when they became the first U.S. infantry unit to fight on mainland Asia in WWII.

It was not long after the issue of the M-1 Carbine began before it became common on all fronts, eventually becoming as numerous as the Garand even among front-line combat troops. While it was intended to be issued primarily to non-infantry support troops, it soon proved to be a superb close-range combat weapon with many advantages over other individual arms. It was far easier to use effectively than any handgun and had a much greater effective range. Both it and its ammunition were much lighter than any of the submachine guns in U.S. service, and it was much more accurate and had a greater effective range than any of them as well. It was lighter and handier than any of our military shotguns, had a much greater effective range, larger magazine capacity, and could be reloaded far quicker as well. Even compared to the enemy and Allied weapons, it was lighter and handier than any of their submachine guns except the machine pistols, yet possessed much greater accuracy, and a substantially greater effective range. Indeed, I would prefer the M-1 Carbine for combat use over any submachine gun except where noise suppression is needed. The 30 Carbine cartridge is very much supersonic and consequently difficult to make quiet.

Like all military weapons, the M-1 Carbine had its teething problems, but these were identified and corrected quickly. As soon as it was used in combat, a problem with the safety was identified. The original

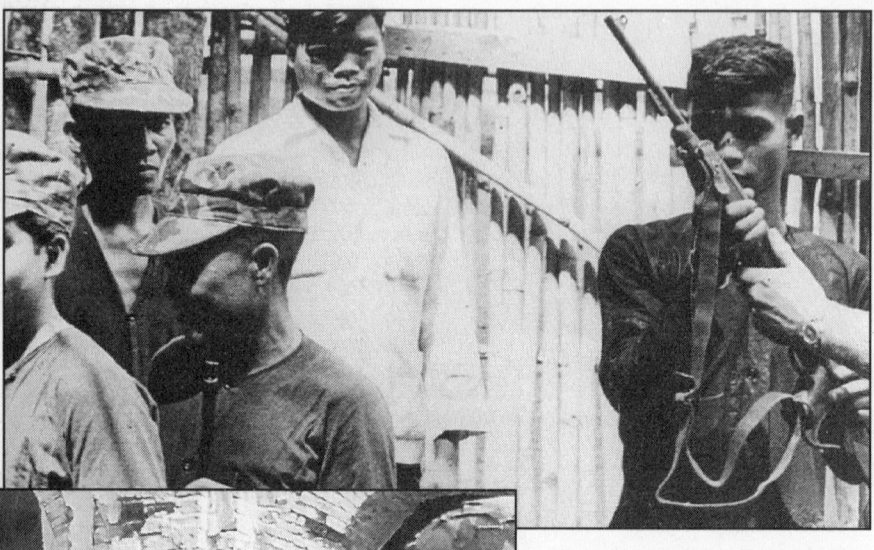

These Montagnard irregulars in Vietnam are shown here being issued folding-stock M-1A1 Carbines by their U.S. advisors. Carbines were a primary weapon for indigenous forces throughout the Vietnam war.

(Below) Two U.S. soldiers fire their M-1 Carbines in France during WWII. These early versions do not have bayonet lugs or adjustable sights.

(Above) South Korean troops shown here in Vietnam used many M-1 Carbines early in the Vietnam War, but later replaced them with M-16s.

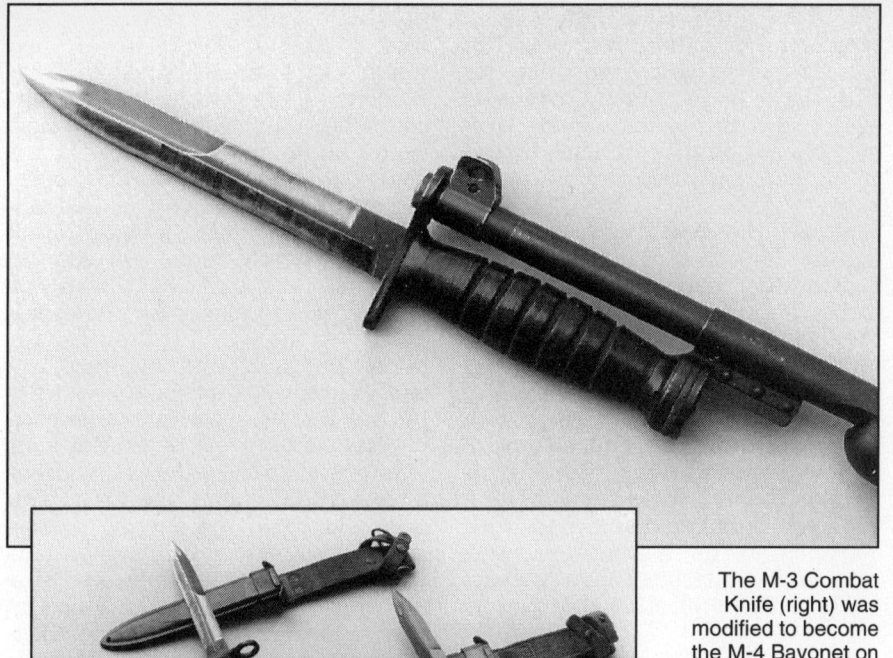

The M-3 Combat Knife (right) was modified to become the M-4 Bayonet on the left to fit a slightly modified M-1 Carbine (above).

style was of the cross-bolt type in front of the trigger guard, engaging when pushed to the right. Unfortunately the magazine catch was located right in front of the safety and it was of the cross-bolt style as well. All too often when a soldier would go to move the safety to the left to fire, he would instead accidentally push the magazine release and dump his magazine on the ground just when he most needed it. Steps were taken to change the operation of the safety and it was soon replaced with one that required a rotating movement. Since installation of the new safety required no modification of the weapon, they were supplied to units in the field so that guns that were already in service could be upgraded quite simply.

Similarly, all early-issue Carbines had an extremely simple L-shaped, two-position rear sight. Windage was achieved by moving the sight base laterally in the receiver's dovetail. The two sight legs offered the only elevation change, with one being set for up to 200 yards, the other for 300 yards. A far superior sight was developed that was adjustable from 100 to 300 yards using a ramp system, and adjustable for windage by a knob with click adjustments. These sights were also retrofitted to the older guns.

Both of these changes improved the M-1 Carbine, but others were more questionable. Troops that did not carry a rifle and bayonet during this early-war period were typically issued the M-3 combat knife. Since most of those troops had M-1 Carbines, someone had the bright idea that these people would be better armed if the M-3 knife could be fitted to the Carbine as a bayonet. Of course, this contradicts the intended purpose of the M-1 Carbine, and it ignores the fact that bayonets mounted on rifles have had questionable utility ever since the invention of repeating rifles, and especially so since the invention of semi-automatic rifles. Regardless, the M-3 knife was modified to include a muzzle ring on its cross guard and a catch on its butt, thereby becoming the M-4 bayonet. A new barrel band with a bayonet lug was designed for the Carbine that replaced the original band.

Even more questionable was a demand to allow the Carbine to fire rifle grenades. Such a grenade launcher and suitable blank cartridge were adopted, but the lightweight gun was never intended for such a role. Recoil is brutal and such use unduly stresses the gun, often breaking the stock. To use the launcher with the folding-stock M-1A1 required the stock to be folded and the gun held and fired upside down against the ground. There was a resultant high probability of breaking the pistol grip of the stock. Carbine users should stick to hand grenades and leave the rifle types to the Garands.

There is always a big clamor for full-automatic-fire capability from the troops in the field because they often have the misguided belief that it will make their fire more effective. In fact, from virtually all individual shoulder-fired weapons, fast aimed semi-automatic fire is demonstrably far more effective than automatic fire except at the closest ranges. The main problem is that the typically inadequately trained soldier, when given the option, will fire full automatic all the time whether or not it is appropriate. It is not commonly known, but the original development specifications for the Carbine included full-auto capability. This requirement was prophetically dropped because it was felt that such a light weapon would be difficult to control.

Because of the misguided demand from the field for a full-automatic Carbine, the Ordnance Department asked Winchester to develop a modified version of the gun that had selective fire capability. Once finalized it was adopted as the M-2 Carbine. Interestingly, the modifications were such that any M-1 Carbine could be converted to M-2 status via simple parts replacement. A thirty-shot magazine was designed and adopted for use in the M-2, and can also be used in the M-1 and other Carbine models. However, it was never as reliable as the original fifteen-shot magazine. Few M-2s saw actual combat before WWII's end. The same can be said for the M-3 Carbine which consisted of an M-2 equipped with an infrared night sight. All Carbine versions saw considerable action in the Korean War and many were used in Vietnam as well, though mostly by indigenous troops.

Shooting the M-2 Carbine on full automatic results in a rapidly climbing weapon if the burst exceeds a couple of rounds. It is only effective or useful in extremely close range work such as room or bunker clearing. To make the M-2 more controllable in full-automatic fire, a clamp-on muzzlebrake was developed. It does help keep the muzzle down, but it also greatly increases the muzzle blast effect to the shooter. You can't wear ear protection in combat so the brake was never popular.

In my opinion, the M-2 Carbine is the source of much of the bad reputation that the M-1/M-2 Carbines gained for being ineffective. After interviewing many veterans who used these guns in combat in three different wars, I am convinced that the vast majority of cases where enemy soldiers are reported to have absorbed an entire magazine of ammunition and kept coming, were actually cases where the soldier dumped a full magazine on full auto *in the general direction* and simply missed him. I am sure there was plenty of similar "spray and pray" activity with the semi-automatic Carbine as well, and with the same ineffectiveness blamed on the cartridge instead of on bad shooting, where it belonged.

Most of the controversy surrounding the Carbine is really around the 30 Carbine cartridge. Often overlooked by modern commentators is the fact that this was the only U.S. military cartridge made in WWII that was loaded with non-corrosive priming. Thus, a soldier armed with a Carbine had a tremendous advantage with regard to maintaining his weapon in good operating condition over his compatriots armed with Garands, BARs, Thompsons, etc., especially in a tropical environment.

There is no question that the 30 Carbine round is not nearly as effective as the 30-06. However, few would want to fire a 5.5-pound 30-06. Remember, the Carbine was intended to be a light, handy gun that would be far more effective than a pistol out to 300 yards and far easier to carry than a full-size rifle. The cartridge was designed to be an intermediate-powered round between the 30-06 and the 45 ACP. In terms of energy, it has about 2.5 times the energy of the 45 ACP fired from a pistol, but just over one-third the energy of the 30-06 fired from a rifle. Putting it in perspective, energy-wise it rests comfortably in 44 Magnum territory when the latter is fired from a revolver. Obviously, the 30 Carbine is no slouch in the energy department.

Of course, the effectiveness of a cartridge is not solely determined by its muzzle energy. However, that is a strong indicator of potential. The fully jacketed 110-grain round-nosed bullet generally drills a nice clean hole through whatever it hits. It is a rare human that could stop a 30 Carbine bullet regardless of the angle of fire. The good news is that this includes people wearing helmets and body armor that would easily turn a 45 ACP or 9mm Parabellum bullet. Unfortunately the trauma delivered to flesh is not high, but when it strikes bone, which will usually happen with a chest hit on a human, the resulting trauma is quite severe thanks to secondary missiles like bone fragments. It is probably impolite to point out that much the same is true for the full-metal-jacketed 30-06. The big difference is that the 30-06 can do it at much greater range or penetrate more substantial obstacles on the way to the target.

One report I gathered from an experienced Army surgeon in Vietnam indicated that many 30 Carbine wounds were indistinguishable from those types made by the 5.56mm, 7.62x39mm, or 7.62mm NATO rounds. Among the people I interviewed on the effectiveness of the 30 Carbine cartridge was one Marine who saw extensive action with the Carbine in the Pacific in WWII. He was quite emphatic that the gun and its little cartridge were plenty effective in the close-range combat that he experienced. He also stated that he greatly preferred the Carbine to the Garand for that type of fighting. Another experienced veteran was a Special Forces advisor in the early days of the Vietnam War. He had advised indigenous units armed almost com-

The M-2 Carbine is shown here with the easily attached muzzlebrake. Note the selector switch protruding above the stock and the thirty-round magazine developed for more sustained fire.

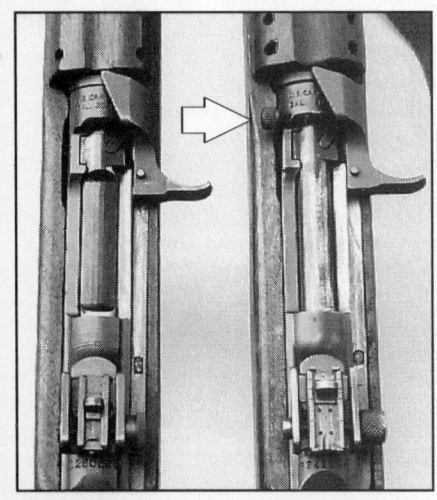
Comparison of the M-1 receiver (left) and the M-2. Other than the round bolt and the selector switch (arrow), they are identical in appearance.

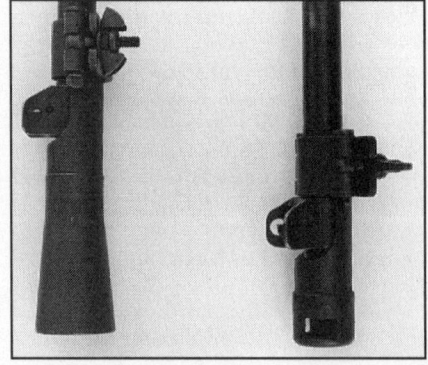
The accessory flash hider and muzzlebrake could be readily attached to any of the Carbine variations. The former was primarily intended for the M-3 Carbine with infrared sight, the latter for the M-2 Carbine to make it more controllable when fired full auto.

pletely with M-1 Carbines and had used the gun extensively himself in combat. He said the Carbines were quite effective at typical jungle warfare ranges, and that when the M16s arrived he did not find them to be significantly more effective than the old warhorse.

Probably the single most authoritative account on the effectiveness and value of the Carbine and its cartridge was written by Lt. Col. John George, who served as a company-grade officer in WWII with the famous 5307 Composite Unit, better known as Merrill's Marauders. The Marauders operated behind Japanese lines for an extended period with tremendous effect. George wrote of his combat experiences in a truly superb book titled *Shots Fired In Anger,* published by and available from the NRA. He was a gun crank and highly successful service rifle competitor before the war. Consequently, the book is written from the viewpoint of a person who is highly knowledgeable about guns. He had also seen a fair bit of action on Guadalcanal and had helped more than a few Japanese soldiers die for their country before he volunteered for Merrill's Marauders.

In the Marauders, then-Lt. George carried an M-1 Carbine as his primary weapon, but also had a scoped M1903 Springfield in the pack train for sniping and an M-1 Garand that he could trade for his M-1 Carbine if the need arose. In George's words, "The carbine turned out to be the ace weapon of the war, as far as I am concerned. It was light and handy, powerful, and reasonably accurate... The cartridge was powerful enough to penetrate several thicknesses of helmet, and to perforate the plates of the Japanese bullet-proof vest, which would only be dented by 45 auto slugs. It was flat shooting enough to have practical accuracy at more than two hundred yards... For many types of offensive fighting, such as sneak raids and infiltration tactics, it was often superior even to the M1 (Garand), penetration being the only point of difference."

George gives several accounts of M-1 Carbine use in the book. In one, he describes a chance encounter with a small Japanese patrol where he initiated the engagement with five fast shots from his Carbine. Several nearby Americans also engaged with their Carbines. It was over in seconds with six dead enemy soldiers, including a machinegunner, and no U.S. casualties. In the several other accounts of Carbine use there is a notable absence of enemy soldiers advancing with impunity through a hail of ineffective Carbine bullets.

Why is it that George and his fellow Marauders found the Carbine effective and so many others did not? It is all quite simple—they hit what they shot at. George makes a point in the book about the fact that they carefully zeroed their weapons and underwent marksmanship training and considerable practice before the Marauders were inserted into their area of operations. The simple fact is that a 30-caliber hole completely through the torso of just about anybody will take them out of action rather quickly. The idea that anyone could absorb a magazine full of Carbine bullets through the chest and keep coming is a myth born of bad shooting.

While a solid torso hit with a 30 Carbine bullet will neutralize most people, it may not instantly stop a determined attacker in some cases, particularly if he is hyped up on drugs. During the Philippine Insurrection there were more than a few instances where multiple hits from the 30-40 Krag, which is far more powerful than the Carbine, failed to stop charging Moros. There is no question it can happen even with arms far more powerful than the 30 Carbine. However, there are other things to consider. Today in modern combat pistolcraft we teach that if two shots to the chest do not bring down your antagonist, the shooter should immediately change his aiming point either to the head or the pelvic girdle. The former should result in a central nervous system hit that will result in immediate incapacitation or death, and the latter will reliably immobilize the attacker so that he can be neutralized with additional fire if necessary. This is exactly how the M-1 Carbine with military ammunition should be handled, and believe me when I say it is far easier to do with a Carbine than with any handgun.

It is popular in some circles to lament that "If only the Carbine had been chambered for a larger cartridge, what a great gun it would have been." I don't agree at all. First, a larger cartridge would have increased recoil, increased the weight of the ammunition, and likely increased the weight of the weapon. Yet, with the requirement of full-metal-jacketed bullets it is doubtful a larger cartridge would have been significantly more effective at all. For example, it is known that a non-expanding bullet shot from a 357 Magnum carbine tends to make clean 35-caliber holes through whatever is shot with it with little tissue damage. Also, the penetrating ability of a larger-diameter bullet against helmets and such is likely to be less than that of the 30 Carbine.

Knowing what we know today, the Carbine cartridge would likely have been more effective if the bullet had been made smaller. Something along the lines of a slightly shortened 221 Remington Fire Ball would have been the clear ticket, particularly if it had a bullet designed like the British 303 Mk 7, which would tumble reliably in flesh, or break up like the 5.56mm M-16 bullet often does.

Interestingly, in the early '60s Melvin Johnson, of WWII Johnson rifle and light machinegun fame, introduced a cartridge for the M-1 Carbine called the 5.7mm MMJ, or 22 Spitfire. It consisted of the 30 Carbine case necked down to take 22-caliber jacketed bullets of 40 to 50 grains, launched at 3000 fps (40 grain) or 2700 fps (50 grain). It outperforms the 221 Remington Fire Ball when fired from a 10-inch pistol. I strongly suspect it would have been a better manstopper than the original Carbine round.

Keep in mind that the main problem with the 30 Carbine cartridge stems from the military requirement for a full-metal-jacketed bullet. When the Carbine is fed modern expanding-bullet ammunition, as available from all the major manufacturers, the effectiveness picture changes considerably. With an expanding bullet the substantial energy of the cartridge is put to work. The bullet expands up to 50-caliber or even more, tissue damage is severe, and the bullet generally remains inside a man-size target rather than whistling through. Out to about 125 yards it produces a more severe wound than does the 5.56mm in its full-metal-jacket form.

One police unit I am familiar with has had quite a few shootings using the M-1 Carbine and jacketed softpoints. Quoting one of their more experienced officers, "We never had to shoot anyone twice." They found it to be extremely effective even against large and determined antagonists. Indeed, with soft-nose or hollowpoint ammunition, this is an extremely effective manstopper that equals or exceeds the performance of even the magnum handgun cartridges. It is far more effective than

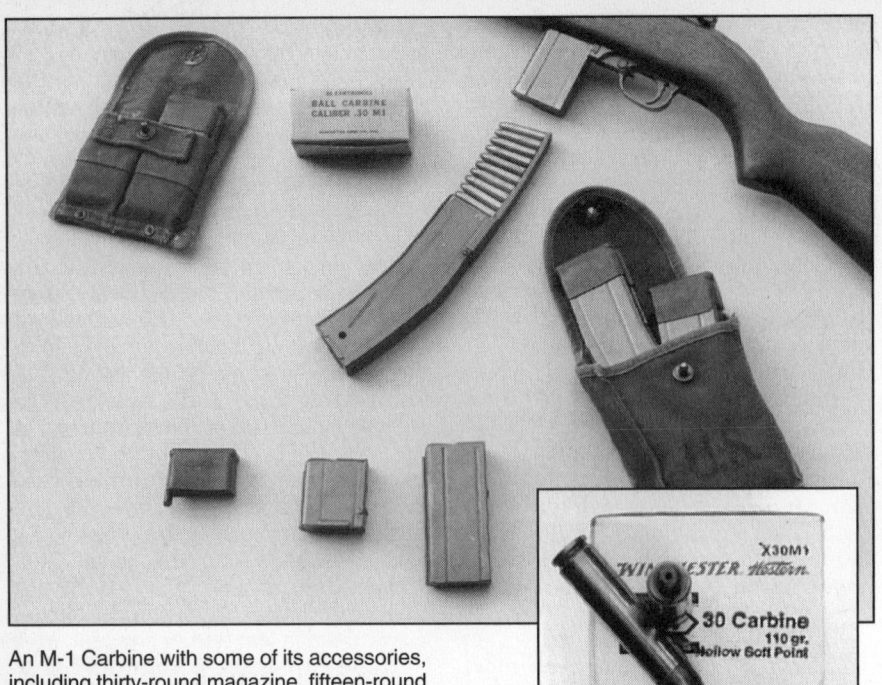

An M-1 Carbine with some of its accessories, including thirty-round magazine, fifteen-round magazine, commercial five-round magazine, magazine dust covers, two-pocket pouch for fifteen-round magazine, and four-pocket pouch for thirty-round mags.

When loaded with modern ammunition with expanding bullets, the M-1 Carbine becomes a formidable manstopper. The author favors the Winchester Hollow Soft Points shown here for their excellent accuracy, reliable feeding, and consistent bullet expansion.

any of the 9mm submachine guns that are currently so popular with police SWAT-type units, not to mention more accurate and as light as the lightest. With good expanding-bullet ammunition (I like Winchester's Hollow Soft Point the best), the M-1 Carbine makes a superb police support weapon and a great gun for home defense.

Once the Carbine began to see action in WWII and after a few bugs were worked out, it proved to be both rugged and reliable. As mentioned earlier, its non-corrosive ammunition was a major positive factor in keeping the gun working reliably when other guns were virtually ruined from rust in the bore, chamber, and gas system from firing corrosive ammunition.

I have fired many M-1 and M-2 Carbines and typically they will outshoot the average Model 94 Winchester 30-30. I have found it is not uncommon for them to surpass *service grade* Garand rifles out to about 200 yards. I expect a good tight Carbine in nice shape with high-quality ammunition to shoot 3-inch or better groups at 100 yards. Sometimes they will do considerably better. A friend once had a Carbine that would shoot groups just over an inch at 100 yards. Needless to say he was delighted. However, once he disassembled it for cleaning and reassembled it, groups went out to 2.5 inches. That was how we discovered that the bedding is critical to accuracy.

That the 30 Carbine cartridge is capable of excellent accuracy is easily proven with a T/C Contender. Likewise I have achieved fantastic accuracy with the Ruger Blackhawk revolver in that chambering. While it is no benchrest rifle, the Carbine and its cartridge are capable of more than adequate combat accuracy, and it will easily outshoot virtually any submachine gun.

The M-1 Carbine saw extensive use in WWII by U.S. troops and by the Free French units as well. These French were almost completely equipped with U.S. gear, but they had M1903 and M1917 bolt-action rifles instead of M-1 Garands. They complained so vehemently about having bolt actions instead of Garands that the U.S. command agreed to supply them with a high percentage of Carbines since there were insufficient Garands available. M-1 Carbines were also supplied by submarine to guerrilla forces in the Philippines and via air drop to resistance forces in Europe. These irregular units prized the Carbine because its light weight, rapid fire, and high capacity made it ideal for their hit-and-run tactics.

In the post-WWII period M-1 Carbines were supplied in large quantities to our allies. It remained a primary weapon of the French well into the 1970s. Carbine use in Korea was extensive but the long ranges typical in Korea often put it at a great handicap. In the Korean conflict it was supplied to virtually all the UN forces, including the British, that didn't use other U.S. small arms. The British also used them in their guerrilla war in Malaya and many of their other post-WWII engagements.

M-1 and M-2 Carbines were used extensively in Vietnam, first by the French and then by the small-statured South Vietnamese, Cambodian, and Montagnard troops trained and equipped by U.S. Special Forces advisors. Naturally, the advisors themselves often chose the Carbine as their personal weapon as well. An unofficial variation consisting of an M-2 Carbine fitted into an M-1A1 folding stock was particularly popular. This required making a clearance cut in the stock for the M-2 selector switch. Though they gradually were replaced by M-16 rifles, M-1 Carbines remained in wide use in Vietnam right until the U.S. withdrawal and probably after. The Carbine was well thought of in Vietnam. Curiously, there was small demand for a more powerful or more effective weapon to replace it.

There is no doubt that the M-1 Carbine was an extremely important factor in the success of the U.S. forces in both WWII and Korea. It was and is a superb weapon that is far more effective and versatile than any of the other *non-rifle* personal weapons like the submachine gun. It wasn't until the introduction of truly light assault rifles like the M-16 that the Carbine entered obsolescence, but it is important to realize that it is nearly a pound lighter than even the lightweight M-16.

In summary, the M-1 Carbine is (be patient here) light, handy, versatile, reasonably accurate, easy to maintain, extremely reliable, durable, inexpensive, and quite effective with the right ammunition for defensive or offensive purposes out to at least 200 yards. Other than that it has very little going for it.

by PAUL S. SCARLATA
photos by James Walters

It's a 38/44 Wannabe that isn't in any books. The moral here? If you can't find an original Heavy Duty, build your own!

A SMITH & WESSON 357/44

Vince Scarlata's 357/44 is a hybrid of parts from the S&W Model 27, Model 37 and 38/44 revolvers. It has the traditional features with simple, fixed sights, plain grips and a lanyard ring. Handling is improved with the Tyler T-grip adapter.

IT IS AN accepted fact that certain physical and/or mental traits continually reappear among members of a family over the generations. I'm not certain if what I am about to discuss is pertinent to this, but I think it does make for a very intelligent sounding opening paragraph. Both my older brother Vincent and I experience uncontrollable urges to buy a certain type of firearm. Now, I haven't the vaguest idea why we share this unique tendency, because in general our shooting interests are very different. I enjoy collecting and shooting old military rifles and competing in IPSC and bowling pin matches with my handguns. Vince is a Skeet shooter and dove hunter, and is enthralled by the more arcane, alchemic mysteries of reloading. But the one passion we both share is our love of fixed-sight S&W revolvers! OKAY, I can hear the choruses of scorn being

The counterbored chambers of the Model 27 cylinder provide full support for the hot 357 Magnum cartridges. There's a lot of metal between the chambers, so handloads can be tailored for best power needs.

29th EDITION, 1997 **55**

Right side of the 357/44 shows the Brazilian crest and Model 37 markings. Visible are three of the five screws that gave these older S&Ws the "Five Screw" model name.

The long ejector rod meant for 44- and 45-caliber cartridges provides complete ejection of 38 and 357 cases, shown here on the original 38/44 gun.

thrown at us, and you'll tell me that "real" handgun aficionados are interested in IPSC race guns, super magnum hunting revolvers, high-capacity Wondernines, etc. Then you'll probably add that the only place you're likely to see a fixed-sight revolver anymore is in the night stand drawer of a person not enlightened enough to buy a semi-auto; or perhaps the holsters of some backward, impoverished rural police department. You'll end by telling me that with the proper therapy perhaps the two of us can overcome this strange affliction.

Laugh at us if you want, but there are a few facts you should understand first. Long before Abe Lincoln considered running for president the revolver had become the preferred handgun of the American military, law enforcement officers, and most civilians. The fixed-sight revolver provided folks with a simple defensive sidearm with sufficient accuracy to get the job done at the ranges it was most likely to be used at. It has a simplicity that bespeaks an inherent ruggedness and reliability. Because of this, Vince and I find them irresistible and between us have amassed an eclectic selection of older S&W models: 455 2nd Model Hand Ejector, 38 Victory Model, 32 Regulation Police, 45 Model 1917, 45 Model 37 Brazilian, early Military & Police, and many others. But the model that we both feel is the ultimate fixed-sight S&W has eluded us for years—the S&W 38/44 Heavy Duty (official factory name), also sometimes known as the Super Police revolver.

By the 1930s, most U.S. police agencies had switched from either the 32 or 44/45 revolver to one chambered for the 38 Special cartridge, whose standard "police" loading used a 158-grain lead bullet moving at a velocity of 850 fps for 200 foot pounds of energy at the muzzle. By the standards of the time this proved a satisfactory police cartridge and was to remain fairly popular, if not very effective, with police forces around the world well into the 1980s. In the United States, the 1920s and '30s were times of great social change and economic unrest with all the attendant social problems. Crime rates skyrocketed to unheard of levels and a new breed of criminal arose who was more ruthless, better armed, and more mobile then any of their predecessors. The newly popular automobile provided these criminals with the means to commit crimes, escape quickly, and elude pursuit. And since the auto bodies of the day were made from heavy-gauge steel, they often provided criminals with a kind of armored vehicle. It quickly became obvious that the 38 Special was sadly lacking in its ability to penetrate auto bodies or even to puncture tires! The first solution attempted was bigger bullets—the 38 Special was loaded with bullets up to 200 grains with a velocity of 730 fps for 236 foot pounds of energy. Known variously as the —Super Police" or "Highway Patrol" loads, they proved to be superior manstoppers, but were still not very effective against autos. In addition, recoil was too heavy to comfortably shoot in medium-frame revolvers, which tended to loosen up if fed a steady diet of them.

To provide a revolver capable of handling these heavier loads, S&W introduced the 38/44 Heavy Duty in

The home-built gun (bottom) compares favorably with an original 38/44. Other than different barrel lengths and the dull finish, there's little to tell the two apart.

1930. It was their large frame (later known as the N-frame) 44 Hand Ejector model rebarreled and chambered for the 38 Special. To help tame recoil, S&W equipped the 38/44 with an ejector rod shroud to increase muzzle weight, while additional weight was provided by the smaller-diameter 38-caliber chambers in the 44-sized cylinder. It was a large, holster-size gun most commonly seen with a 5-inch barrel, but 3½-, 4-, 6-, and 8¾-inchers were also made. Postwar guns were offered only with 4- and 5-inch barrels. The weight was around 40 ounces, depending upon barrel length.

Sights consisted of the usual rounded blade front and square groove in the topstrap for the rear. All in all, it was a rugged, no-frills, service-type revolver capable of handling the hottest 38 Special loads then produced. In 1931 S&W, in cooperation with Remington, developed a special high performance load to answer the demands of police agencies for a 38 Special capable of penetrating auto bodies. It was loaded with a 158-grain hardened lead or FMJ round-nose bullet moving at the then unheard of velocity of 1175 fps, for a muzzle energy of 460 foot pounds. This was only slightly less powerful than a 357 Magnum with the same bullet. Introduced by Remington as the ".38 S&W Special Hi-Speed," it and S&W's revolver were generally dubbed the 38/44. It was the high performance champion revolver cartridge of its day and retained its popularity even after S&W's introduction of the 357 Magnum in 1935. The S&W 38/44 was an instant hit with highway patrols, state troopers, and sheriff's departments, especially in rural areas and the Western states, and remained in production until 1941. In general, before the early 1950s the S&W 357 was considered a "deluxe" sportsman's revolver, while the 38/44 was a service gun.

Neither my brother nor I had managed to locate a 38/44 despite several years of looking. Being a less patient person than me Vince decided two years ago that it was time to take matters into his own hands. Actually it all began when he answered an advertisement for a S&W M37 Brazilian revolver, and in the bargaining process ended up with not only the revolver but a small box of M37 frames, cylinders, barrels, etc. In the interim he came across an original 5-inch S&W 38/44 barrel at a gun show. Since this was as close as he had come to a 38/44, he bought it and stored it away in his junk closet "...just in case." The following year he was offered some more S&W parts, one of which was the cylinder and crane from a 357 Model 27 Highway Patrolman. One day while, I assume, having nothing better to do he was sorting through these treasures and was struck with an idea: Why not build his own 38/44? He first pulled out the box of M37 parts and after a few hours of sorting, checking, and fitting had assembled all the pieces necessary to put together a complete N-frame with lockwork.

The 38/44 barrel required some fitting and the barrel shoulder shortened .015-inch to permit correct sight alignment, and still allow the 1/8th turn necessary to provide proper barrel/frame interference. Fitting the M27 cylinder proved to be the biggest chore of the whole exercise: the crane was slightly oversized for the M37 frame and had to be filed to fit. The Brazilian revolver was originally chambered for the 45 ACP cartridge, necessitating a short cylinder to provide clearance for the half-moon clips. Because of this, the cylinder retaining stud was too wide for use with the longer M27 cylinder, requiring some judicious filing to shorten it to the proper size. Once done, the 357 cylinder snapped into place like it had been there all the time. The cylinder-end of the barrel was shortened .009-inch with a Brownell's Revolver Chamfering Tool Kit cutter, and the barrel/cylinder gap set at a snug .005-inch. In addition, a special cutter provided in the Brownell's kit was used to recut the forcing cone at 11 degrees. Finally, the timing and alignment were checked and some careful polishing of the trigger mechanism finished the project to Vince's satisfaction.

When he was done, Vince had assembled a revolver that looked, for all practical purposes, just like a production S&W 38/44 Super Police, right down to the lanyard ring favored by so many state police departments. The only giveaway is the large Brazilian government crest adorning the sideplate on the right side of the frame. A unique aspect of the revolver is that the cylinder chambers have had the numbers 1 through 6 stamped on the outside.

Why, or by whom, this was done is a mystery to everyone we've shown it to.

Measuring and weighing Vince's "357/44" showed it to have the same dimensions as a factory revolver. And while he had tried to keep the gun looking as original as possible he made two small concessions to shootability when he installed a pair of larger post-war-style N-frame grips and a Tyler's T-Grip aluminum grip adapter.

Earlier this year I borrowed the 357/44 to test. I have to tell you that despite his claims that it was a fine shooting revolver, I had my doubts. It did not inspire confidence at first glance as he had never bothered to have it reblued after he finished building it. Vince preferred to keep it in the rough and use it as a knock-about gun for his walks in the woods, or to keep in the glove box of his pickup truck. As with most revolvers from this era the sights, while rugged and foolproof, were not the easiest to use: the front was a rounded blade that Vince had filed down a bit to zero-in the revolver, while the rear consisted of a rather shallow notch cut into the topstrap. The single-action trigger pull was very light and crisp, but the DA mode was stiff, and not made any better by the grooved trigger. I test fired the S&W on a cold, windy January afternoon, which I find preferable to a hot, humid, windless North Carolina August afternoon! Test ammo consisted of 38 Specials from Black Hills and Federal, in addition to some 357s supplied by Remington and the Hansen Cartridge Co. Despite my initial low opinion of this rough looking revolver, it lived up to Vince's claims and proved to be quite accurate when fired from my adjustable pistol rest at 50 feet. Six-shot groups with each type of cartridge provided the following results:

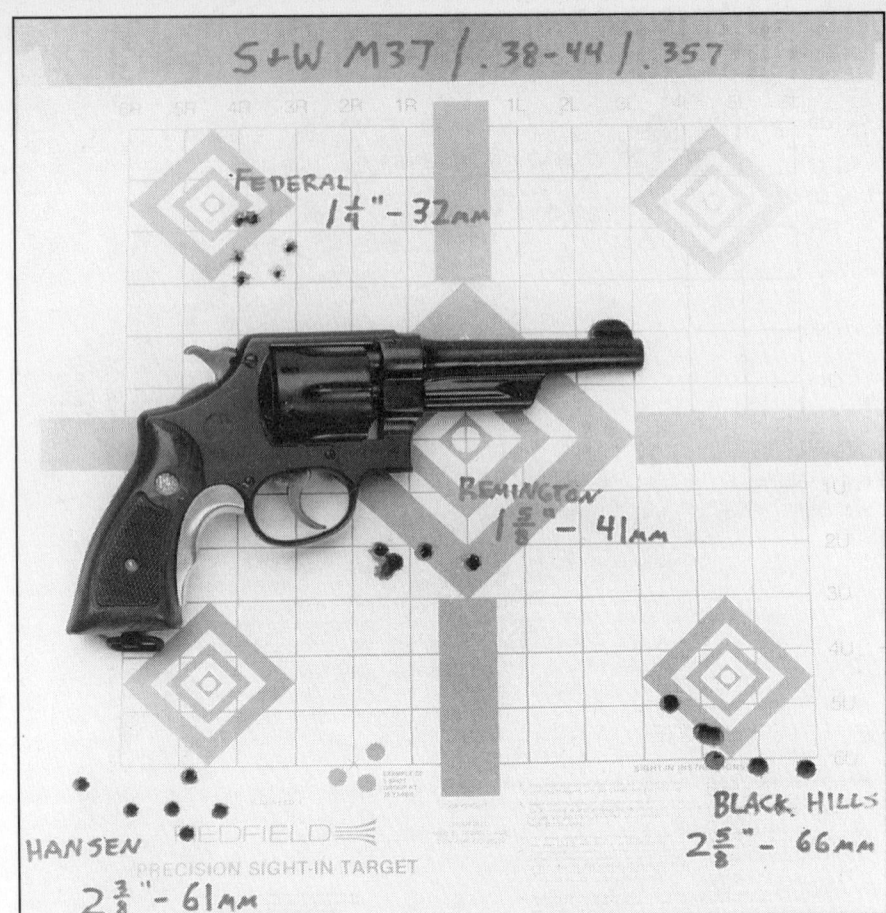

Accuracy with the 357/44 gun at 50 feet is quite good, especially with the Federal 38 Special, 158-grain LRN loads. For a self-defense gun, this is plenty accurate.

357/44 Accuracy Test

Load	Group Size (in.)
Remington 140 gr. JHP	1 5/8
Hansen 158 gr. JSP	2 3/8
Black Hills 148 gr. LWC	2 5/8
Federal 158 gr. LRN	1 1/4

Of the four, I found the Federal's performance especially surprising considering that old load is not known for either its accuracy or fight-stopping abilities.

OKAY, so it was accurate from a rest; now how about some fast off-hand DA shooting? I paced off 7 yards and set up a target stand with an IPSC-type target. Firing a series of rapid double taps, I put a cylinder full of each load downrange. Again, despite the poor sights, the old S&W proved to be a very natural pointer, and was quite controllable, even with the 357 ammo. While it tended to group a bit to the right (probably because of that doggone grooved trigger!), all twenty-four of my shots made a nice pattern in the A zone of the target. To lighten my car and improve gas mileage on the trip home, I decided to use up the rest of the ammo I had brought along. Accordingly, I set up a series of steel pepper popper targets at 10 yards and proceeded to have a bit of fun. In an attempt to be as "period conscious" as possible I fired the 357/44 one handed DA, which I'm sure would have met the approval of most 1930s police training officers. Here again, the S&W's natural pointing qualities came to the fore and it proved easy to consistently go six poppers for six rounds of ammo.

I found Vince's 357/44 a fitting example of the genre we both admire so much—no frills, accurate, reliable, and having an air of ruggedness about it. No doubt the original guns displayed the same qualities, which accounts for their popularity with police officers, soldiers, explorers, and civilians. But I could not abide such a fine handling handgun looking so shoddy. After repeated appeals to Vince's finer (?) sensibilities, he finally agreed to let me take it to my local gunsmith, Pat Linthicum of Randolph Shooters Supply, to be refinished. Pat has built, and rebuilt, a number of competition and carry guns for me over the years, and I felt he could do what needed to be done to repair this faded beauty's self esteem. In keeping with the Smith's intended purpose as a knock-about gun, Pat simply sandblasted and polished it, being careful not to mar the Brazilian crest, and then finished it off with a dull, matte blue. If anything, it now looks even more "practical" than before.

In the meanwhile, my opinion of the traditional fixed-sight revolver continues to grow. In spite of their plain-Jane image they are more than capable of performing their alloted task as defensive sidearms. And let's be honest about it—after that, anything else is just unnecessary fluff. ●

by **JERRY HORGESHEIMER**

A Rigby Revival

The 416 Rigby has an enviable and well-earned reputation for penetration and power.
Now it's available in an affordable domestic rifle

WHAT IS IT that stirs the blood of some of us at the mere mention of big bores? Maybe it's the scenes depicted by Hemingway and Ruark, or the escapades of Pondoro Taylor and Karamojo Bell, or maybe just the names of Holland & Holland, Westley Richards, and John Rigby. Whatever it is, this kind of excitement can arouse the hunter instinct in the most sedate armchair nimrod.

Big bores and British go together like salt and pepper. It was the British gunmakers who were supplying the firearms needs of the African market around the turn of the century. Of course, many of the ivory hunters of the time were either British or of British descent so it was only natural that these gunmakers would provide for their needs.

During the last century, big-bore blackpowder double rifles were the standard of the day. Then came cordite, the stick-like powder determined best for the tropical climates of Africa by the British army. It seems that the high temperatures of the tropics pushed pressures skyward, which could cause sticky or ruptured cases—not a good thing when facing a six-ton elephant at spitting distance. Cordite was deemed to be more stable than the new smokeless powders of the time.

With the introduction of the Mauser 98-type action, African rifles moved into the 20th century. It seems like new calibers were being introduced with the frequency of rabbits having litters. It was in 1911 that the London firm of John Rigby & Co. introduced the 416-caliber, a rimless sharp-shouldered, magnum-type big bore. This cartridge was to become one of the most popular to ever ride in an African big game hunter's cartridge belt.

The rimmed cartridge, better known as "flanged" in Great Britain and Africa, was traditionally used in double rifles. The extraction system on these rifles was designed for rimmed cases. Rimless and belted cases then were introduced for use in bolt-action guns (magazine rifles in British terminology). The 416 Rigby

29th EDITION, 1997 **59**

The Ruger Number 1 single shot rifle has a very strong falling-block action capable of handling heavy loads in big-bore cartridges. The scope is a Burris 1½-6x with Posi-Lock, which locks the reticle in place after sighting-in; a great feature, especially on big-bores.

The 416 Rigby cartridge dwarfs the 270 Winchester (middle) and the 22-250 Remington.

was designed for the Mauser Magnum action, rather than the classic double rifle. The famous Kynoch Cartridge Co. probably had more to do with the actual development than Rigby. Rigby established the requirements and some of the specifications for the cartridge and Kynoch took it from there, which was quite common procedure at the time for several famous British rifle makers.

This round was designed to drive a 410-grain softpoint or solid bullet at 2370 fps. That equates to a muzzle energy of 5115 foot pounds. Compare that to the 300-grain bullet from the 375 H&H Magnum at 2530 fps for 4263 foot pounds of energy. There is no question about the brute power of the 375, which, based on this comparative data, leaves absolutely no doubt about where the 416 stands.

The 416 Rigby case is big. Measuring 2.9 inches long, it is considerably longer than the 458 Winchester Magnum, which is 2.5 inches long. Although the 458 has a larger bullet diameter, the 416 has a better reputation for penetration and killing power. The reason is sectional density. This is a relative measure of the diameter of the bullet as compared to the weight. The actual formula uses the square of the diameter. Because the cross-sectional area of the 416 is smaller than the 458 but with the same weight behind it, it just naturally follows that penetration is going to be greater with the same bullet type and same velocity.

The 416 gained a great reputation in Africa for its outstanding effectiveness on the largest of game; namely elephant, rhino, and buffalo. No doubt, this was due in part to the steel-jacketed bullets Rigby originally supplied for this caliber. These full-patched bullets did not deform when plowing through bone and gristle, which means they maintained a relatively straight line into and through the animal. This is particularly important when carrying out a brain shot on an elephant. The bullet must travel through a couple of *feet* of honeycombed bone structure before reaching the brain. A bent bullet will often deviate from this line of sight by a considerable margin, resulting in a non-lethal hit and a major headache for the pachyderm.

Another reason for the popularity of this cartridge was the rifle itself. Rigby magazine rifles quickly gained a reputation for being completely reliable, and when dealing with Africa's Big Five, reliability can be a life and death matter. John Taylor, in his book *African Rifles and Cartridges*, had nothing but praise for both the Rigby rifle and the cartridge. To quote this famous elephant hunter, "It's tremendously popular thruout Africa, and deservedly so. It's a great killer. It's a perfect weapon for all-around use against heavy and dangerous game if you like a magazine rifle." John "Pondoro" Taylor also liked the 416 as lion medicine. Using soft-nose bullets, he said few others could "...crumple a charging lion" as reliably as this one did.

Many of the African ivory hunters, Taylor being no exception, preferred the double rifle because it was like carrying two guns in one, since there were two separate lock mechanisms, firing pins, barrels, etc. If a spring broke or a case got stuck in a chamber, the rifle could still be fired. Another advantage was that the second shot was available instantly by just slipping the trigger finger to the other trigger. Compare that to having to work a bolt, especially when looking up the trunk of a mad tusker intent on stomping you. Other advantages often expounded regarding the double rifle, even with 26-inch barrels, are a shorter overall length than the typical magazine rifle, usually better balance, and they're quicker to get into action.

The currently manufactured John Rigby 416 magazine rifles are based on either modified BRNO square-bridge magnum actions or Hartmann and Weiss actions. There are a

At 100 yards, groups fired from the bench averaged around 2 inches. Several were as tight as 1.3 inches, such as the one shown using the 400-grain A-Square Monolithic Solid.

Several powders were tested in the 416 Rigby cartridge, all with satisfactory results. More than a dozen manufacturers make bullets for this caliber, and dies are easily obtainable.

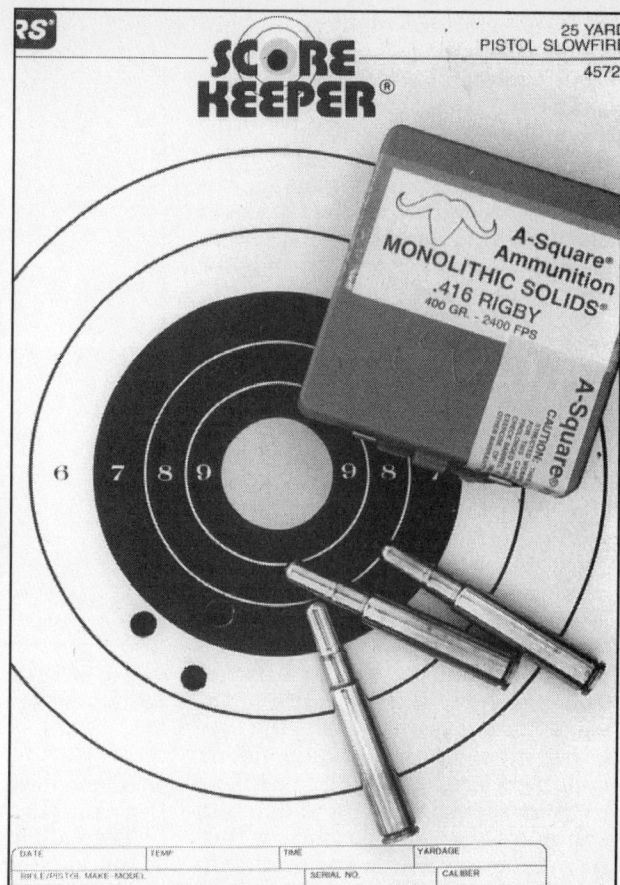

variety of options available but the base price is £6,000. In late 1995, that was equal to about $9000, which puts it out of reach for most of us.

For many years the only rifles available in 416 Rigby were the expensive British magazine rifles. Then in 1989 Ruger introduced this chambering in the Model 77 bolt rifle, followed in 1991 by the Number 1 single shot. Along with these introductions came factory 416 ammo from Federal. These two events have paved the way for this cartridge to become a permanent part of the present cadre of classic big game rounds. Ruger's Model 77 retails for around $1550 while the Number 1 goes for about $665. Additionally, several semi-custom rifles, like those made by A-Square and Dakota, are also fueling the Rigby fire, but are obviously considerably more expensive than the Rugers.

To those who have not tried them, the recoil of these big bore rifles may be a little intimidating. However, the 416 Rigby is considered to have relatively mild recoil compared to other large calibers producing a similar amount of energy. I found the Ruger Number 1 not unpleasant to shoot offhand, but again, it is all relative.

When collecting data for the accompanying tables, I would sometimes shoot forty or more rounds over a couple-hour period from a benchrest. However, by using the Bench Master shooting rest, much of the recoil was absorbed before it hit my shoulder. I am convinced you would have to be a masochist to shoot any kind of a really big bore rifle from the bench without some method of recoil absorption other than your body.

The Ruger Number 1 weighs just under ten pounds with the Burris 1½-6x Signature scope attached. This extra heft, over and above what

Table 1: 416 Rigby Ballistics

—Bullet—		Load	MV	Extr. Sprd.	Std. Dev.	3-shot Group
Wgt.Grs.	Type	(Grs./Powder)	(fps)	(fps)	(fps)	(ins.)
400	Federal Prem. Bear Claw SP	Factory	2336	3	2	2.6
410	Federal Prem. Solid	Factory	2285	29	14	1.3
400	A-Square Solid	Factory	2374	33	17	2.1
400	Barnes X	98.0/H450	2396	36	18	2.1
400	Barnes X	95.0/H4350	2538	16	8	1.9
400	Speer AGS	98.0/H4350	2543	16	8	2.9
400	Speer AGS	102.0/R22	2389	6	3	3.9
400	Speer AGS	104.0/R22	2430	25	12	4.4
350	Barnes X	100.0/H450	2532	47	26	1.3
350	Speer SP	98.0/H450	2417	52	27	1.5
350	Speer SP	102.0/H450	2518	49	26	1.5
350	Speer SP	96.0/H4350	2467	28	14	1.7
350	Speer SP	98.0/H4350	2537	15	8	2.1
300	Barnes X	104.0/H450	2653	19	9	2.3
300	Barnes X	99.0/H4350	2675	79	38	2.8

The Bear Claw softpoint is made by Trophy Bonded, Inc. and is available in Federal Premium ammunition.
The Speer 400 AGS is the African Grand Slam softpoint.
The Barnes X Bullet is a solid copper hollowpoint.
Velocity was measured 12 feet from the muzzle with an Oehler 35P chronograph.

a typical sporter-weight rifle might weigh, goes a long way toward reducing felt recoil. The 416 Rigby is not a caliber you would elect to shoot from the prone position, even with a rifle weighing ten pounds or more. However, when kneeling or standing, the recoil is readily absorbed without much pain. If the shooter is concentrating on a live target, seldom is the recoil felt anyway.

One caveat worth noting whenever shooting a high-powered rifle with a scope is to avoid "scope-eye." That half-moon indentation over the eyebrow is not the kind of scar you want to brag about to your hunting buddies; lion claw marks maybe, but allowing your scope to smack you in the face may be a little hard to live down. If you tend to crawl the stock, make sure the scope is mounted well forward. The Burris scope I used on the Ruger works okay for me but it is probably mounted too far back for some. Because of the position of the elevation and windage knobs, there is not much eye relief adjustment, and, therefore, it offers limited flexibility in fitting shooters of different statures. Other models made by Burris and other manufacturers may fit you better.

The Ruger Number 1 is a very strong falling block rifle not a lot different from the big-bore single shot British Farquharson used in Africa around the turn of the century. Many of the dangerous "big five" were dropped in their tracks with a single well-placed shot from these rifles. We have gotten away from the idea that a single shot rifle of any kind is appropriate, or even adequate. Granted, it is not as quick on a follow-up shot as a double, or even a magazine rifle, but carrying an extra round stuck between the fingers of the forward hand makes a surprisingly fast follow-up shot possible. I am convinced that if we all hunted with single shots, we would not only be better hunters, but less game would be wounded and lost.

The Ruger Number 1 has a massive receiver made to withstand virtually any modern cartridge. In fact, this rifle is designed to operate flawlessly with any type of factory round, be it rimless, rimmed, or belted magnum. Both the pistol grip and the forend are checkered, the wood is select American walnut, and the recoil pad is solid black rubber. A folding leaf rear sight is mounted on a quarter-rib while the front sight is a gold bead mounted on a dovetail blade. The tang safety is thumb oper-

Author with 416 Rigby at full recoil. The kick of this rifle is substantial but easily manageable by the average shooter.

ated and designed to engage both the sear and the internal hammer.

The ballistics of the 416 Rigby are going to be impressive regardless of the rifle you use with it. In fact, this caliber has developed such a reputation on dangerous game that there is almost something mystical about it. Maybe it is the long, slender 400-grain bullet with its great capacity for deep penetration that has won its name. Maybe it was the thick steel-jacketed bullets that Rigby was known for that endeared this caliber to the hearts and souls of those who staked their lives on its effectiveness. Whatever it was, it is not being lost on today's hunters, judging by its growing popularity, even in light of the many so-called modern magnums now available.

Currently, Federal Cartridge Co. offers several different bullets in this caliber in 400- and 410-grain weights; Trophy Bonded Bear Claw, Woodleigh Solid, and the Woodleigh Weldcore Soft Point. Each is designed for a special purpose. This variety of bullets provides the hunter with options, depending on the type of hunting he or she will be doing.

The A-Square Co. of Bedford, Kentucky, not only makes semi-custom rifles for the 416 Rigby cartridge, but it also produces ammunition in this caliber. This company offers what they call the Monolithic Solid, and two softpoints; the Dead Tough, a general purpose controlled expanding bullet, and the Lion Load, which is made for maximum destruction and less penetration. A-Square refers to these three loads as "The Triad" for a unique reason. They are designed to provide the same exterior ballistics so they can be used interchangeably with the same sight setting, keeping the point of impact the same.

Handloading for the 416 is made easier with the variety of bullets available. For this report, loads for three different bullet weights were tested for accuracy from the Ruger Number 1. Barnes offers the 300-, 325-, 350-, and 400-grain weights in their X Bullet, which is a solid copper hollowpoint that is unique in the industry. I have used this bullet on North American big game for a number of years and have come to rely on it for almost every hunting situation. It retains virtually 100 percent of its weight even when hitting heavy bone, expands uniformly across a wide spectrum of velocities, and has gained a reputation for deep penetration. That reputation has expanded over the past few years to include its use on most African game. Barnes also offers their more traditional softpoints and solids in this caliber.

Speer also offers several bullets for the handloader in 416 caliber, including a 400-grain tungsten core solid and 350- and 400-grain softpoints. More than a dozen other companies make 416 bullets for the handloader.

The three factory loads were tested in the 24-inch-barreled Ruger.

The 400- and 410-grain solid bullets by both A-Square and Federal penetrated 37½ inches of the phone books, two 1-gallon jugs of water, and kept on going.

When fired into water-soaked phone books, expansion of the two 400-grain bullets was quite impressive. Going through 24 inches, the Speer African Grand Slam shed about 15 percent of its weight and expanded to 73-caliber, while the Barnes X lost less than 1 percent, expanded to 80-caliber and went through a little over 26 inches.

The Federal Premium 400-grain Trophy Bonded Bear Claw softpoint was chronographed 12 feet in front of the muzzle at 2336 fps. This is virtually identical to the ballistics of the original Kynoch load developed 85 years ago. The original velocity of 2370 fps was probably clocked through a 26-inch barrel, and the Ruger's is only 24. If the instrumental velocity were corrected to muzzle velocity, another 20 or 30 fps could be added. The Federal Premium 410-grain solid had an instrumental velocity of 2285 fps, which, after adjustments, would be close to 2350 fps. The A-Square Monolithic Solid showed a velocity of 2374 fps before any adjustments. Note in the table that three-shot 100-yard groups measured from 1.3 to 2.6 inches, which is about average accuracy for an off-the-shelf, standard-weight big game rifle.

A variety of handloads were considered using the Hodgdon and Hornady reloading manuals. Generally, slower burning powders are recommended for the 416, so I used H450, H4350, and Reloder 22. The Barnes 400-grain X bullet and Speer 400-grain African Grand Slam softpoint were tested with several different powder charges. Velocities ranged from a low of 2389 fps to a high of

Table 2: 416 Rigby Penetration and Expansion

Wgt. Grs.	Bullet Type	Penetration (ins.)	Weight Retained (grs.)	Expanded Diameter (ins.)
400	Federal Prem. Trophy Bonded SP	20	356	.863
400	Speer African Grand Slam SP	24	337	.734
400	Barnes X	26½	397	.800
410	Federal Prem. Solid	36+	—	—
400	A-Square Monolithic Solid	36+	—	—
150	270 Winchester Power-Point	11½	67	.455

Test medium was water-soaked telephone books.

Although proving little, the effect of a 400-grain softpoint blowing up five 1-gallon milk jugs filled with water made an interesting sight. The concussion destroyed the sawhorse that held the jugs.

Five different bullets were tested in handloads in the big 416 Rigby cartridge. Velocities ranged from a low of 2285 fps to a high of 2675. The Barnes X has earned an excellent reputation.

2543 fps. No signs of excessive pressure appeared, even with the heavier load. The best group shot with any of the 400-grain loads was 1.9 inches, and that was with a charge of 95 grains of H4350 behind the big X bullet.

Typically, H4350 is a little more consistent in its burning rate than H450, causing less variation in shot-to-shot velocities, which promotes slightly better accuracy. However, the data in the nearby table do not generally bear this out. When shooting the 350-grain bullet, 100 grains of H450 behind the Barnes 350-grain X produced a group of only 1.3 inches. Notice that of the five loads tested in the 350-grain category, four were under 2 inches, and the one that was over two was barely so at 2.1 inches. It is obvious that the Ruger preferred the 350-grain bullet weight, at least from an accuracy standpoint.

Only two loads were tested with the relatively light 300-grain Barnes bullet. Velocities were impressive at 2653 and 2675, but accuracy dropped off somewhat at 2.3 and 2.8 inches. Accuracy with the factory loads varied from an impressive 1.3 inches from the Federal 410-grain solid to a high of 2.6 inches.

The 416 Rigby cartridge is considered a relatively flat shooter as far as big bores are concerned. For example, if the 400-grain softpoint bullet, with a muzzle velocity of 2400 fps, is sighted-in to hit 3 inches high at 100 yards, it crosses the line of sight at 200 yards, and is about 12 inches low at 300 yards. Even at 400 yards it is only about 36 inches low. Compare these numbers to the ballistics of a 180-grain 30-06 that leaves the muzzle at 2750 fps. If this cartridge is sighted to 3 inches high at 100 yards, it crosses the line of sight at about 235 yards, and is about 22 inches low at 400 yards. Certainly, there is some difference but not as much as one might expect.

To get an idea of the Rigby's deep penetration capabilities compared to other big bore calibers, a stack of water-soaked phone books was lined up and fired into using a couple of handloads and several factory rounds. These were compared to a 150-grain Winchester Power Point in 270-caliber. The table shows that typically the 416 softpoints penetrated about twice the distance of the 270 softpoint. Interestingly, the 416 solids went through all $36\frac{1}{2}$ inches of soggy paper, blew up two 1-gallon jugs full of water behind the phone books, and then went singing into the backstop. The 400-grain Barnes X bullet made it through $26\frac{1}{2}$ inches of tightly packed wet paper while the 400-grain Grand Slam was right behind it at 24 inches of penetration. This doesn't particularly prove anything, but water-logged phone books do seem to be a good test medium when there are no elephants available. And besides, it provides interesting information for speculation.

The 416 Rigby may not be the next whitetail or mule deer cartridge here in the states, but loaded wisely it could be handy on elk or moose. It may not pass the popularity of the 375 H&H in Africa, but based on its performance and growing popularity worldwide, it is certainly a contender for the all-round cartridge. At a ripe old age of 85 years, it is obviously not yet ready for retirement. •

My PERSONAL FASCINATION with top-break, self-ejecting revolvers began in 1949, when I was just six years old. Although I'd visited my grandparent's North Florida farm before, that was when I first became aware of "Grandma Brown's pistol." The revolver had been seized by Sheriff John Brown of Baker County, Florida (where, ironically, I presently reside) from a murder suspect during the early 1900s. The sheriff was my grandmother Iva Brown's father-in-law. He gave her the gun for self-protection due to my grandfather's frequent absences while helping to perfect the technique of budding, which revolutionized the state's early citrus industry.

Through Roy Jinks' excellent *History of Smith & Wesson*, I'd later learn that the gun in question was a Smith & Wesson Fourth Model 38 Double Action in caliber 38 S&W (Short not Special). Even back then the old revolver had about zero percent of its original bluing. I didn't know what proper "timing" meant during this period. I did know that if, on occasion, I didn't rotate the cylinder by hand until it clicked when at full cock, that fragments of lead would sting my hand upon firing. Not that I was given carte blanche to shoot the piece anytime I desired. I was more or less forbidden to do so by my mom and dad. Grandmas being grandmas, "Miss Iva" would often dip into her meager supply of 38 S&W ammo to indulge her favorite grandson—whenever my parents were gone for any appreciable amount of time. Per her wishes, everyone in the family knew that the old Smith & Wesson would someday by Gary's gun. As so often happens, though, the relic was nowhere to be

by GARY M. BROWN

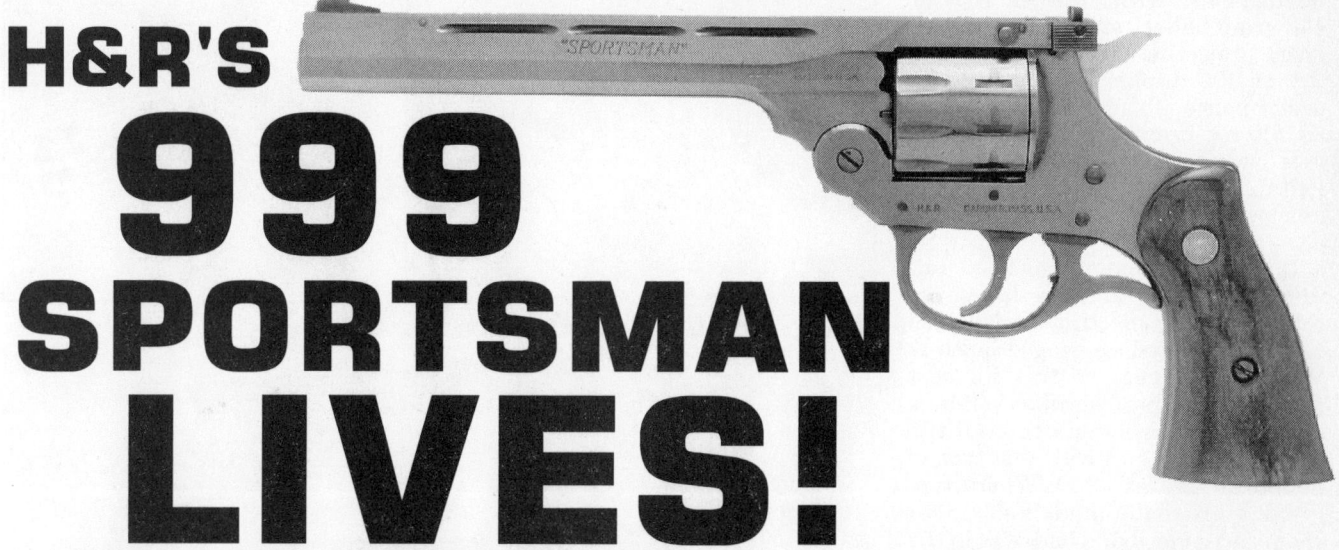

H&R'S 999 SPORTSMAN LIVES!

Born in the 1930s with an action style already outdated, the Triple Nine earned a reputation for reliability and accuracy and remains a good value today.

found upon her passing. I hope the person responsible for its disappearance has at least kept the thing. Its current worth is only about $50, but its sentimental value would make it nearly priceless to me.

The top-break, self-ejecting concept had been tested (briefly) by the U.S. Cavalry in the 1870s. The Schofield improved (better locking latch) S&W #3 was evaluated against the 1873 Colt Single Action Army (SAA). It was found lacking in two primary areas attributable to its action type. First, its truncated cylinder necessitated a shortened version of the current issue 45 Colt round for the SAA. Not only was the 45 S&W cartridge down-sized, but it was also downloaded, being charged with just 28 grains of blackpowder as opposed to the 40-grain loading of its competitor.

The second flaw was even more critical. The modified "King" simultaneous extraction/ejection system of the Schofields automatically spewed out all six rounds when the gun was opened, whether fired or not. The big revolver was also judged to be somewhat mechanically fragile when compared to the Colt. So the Schofield departed.

Certainly the most widespread usage of this revolver action type was by the British military. Starting in 1887 and continuing through 1939, Webley produced large-frame, heavy caliber top-break revolvers that evolved through succeeding "Marks" (I through VI). The vast majority of such pieces were produced in caliber 455 Webley. Known as the "Peacemaker of the British Empire," the historical significance of these arms relating to English heritage corresponds roughly to the effect that the Colt Single Action Army had on the early development of the United States. Following World War II, vast quantities of these 455s were altered to fire the 45 ACP cartridge secured in half-moon clips, and sold at giveaway prices. I bought a Mark VI many years ago and shot it quite a lot. Although they were never intended for my Webley, 45 ACP and 45 Auto Rim rounds performed perfectly in this arm. The 230-grain bullets produced a satisfying "kerplunk" upon striking any solid object. It was the first handgun I ever shot with

29th EDITION, 1997 **65**

real accuracy, which further reinforced my respect for guns with this type of action.

The 455s were joined in service by yet another top-break revolver in both spurred and "bobbed" hammer versions made by the Enfield Royal Small Arms Factory in caliber 38/200 British. Additionally, Smith & Wesson made thousands of Military & Police "Victory" hand-ejector (swing-out cylinder) revolvers for the British during World War II, in both 38/200 and 38 Special. The 38/200 was no more than the 38 S&W cartridge (loaded here with either a 145- or 146-grain bullet), stuffed with a 200-grain projectile. On paper, at least, the 38/200 duplicated the ballistic performance of the 455. The Enfield 38/200 top-breaks remained substitute standard sidearms in Great Britain long after its adoption of the fourteen-shot FN Browning Hi-Power.

Instead of becoming a famous military action type on these shores, the top-break, self-ejecting design was relegated to civilian usage. Smith & Wesson revolvers of this ilk cost much more than similar versions offered by other manufacturers. Still, S&W offered a gun with that type of action as late as 1940. Where top-break guns really made a name for themselves (good and bad) was in the pockets of common people wanting either inexpensive protection or inexpensive coercion. Some of the negative descriptive phrases used by their detractors included "Owl's Head," from the logo of the Iver Johnson Co., and the derisive catch-all term "Saturday Night Special."

In 1931, Harrington & Richardson, Inc. debuted the nine-shot, top-break, self-ejecting Sportsman No. 999. There was an earlier, similiar H&R revolver that held seven rounds. The nine-shot "Triple Nine" replaced the old model as part of an ongoing battle of cylinder capacity one-upmanship waged between H&R and I.J. While Iver Johnson did make some nine-shot guns, its primary claim to fame was the Sealed 8 line which featured cylinders that recessed the cartridge case heads.

The double-action Sportsman No. 999, capable of chambering 22 Short, Long or Long Rifle ammunition, appealed immediately to the budget-minded paper target shooters of the period. In 1933, as a concession to organized target competition, the single-action-only Sportsman No. 199 was introduced. The current scarcity

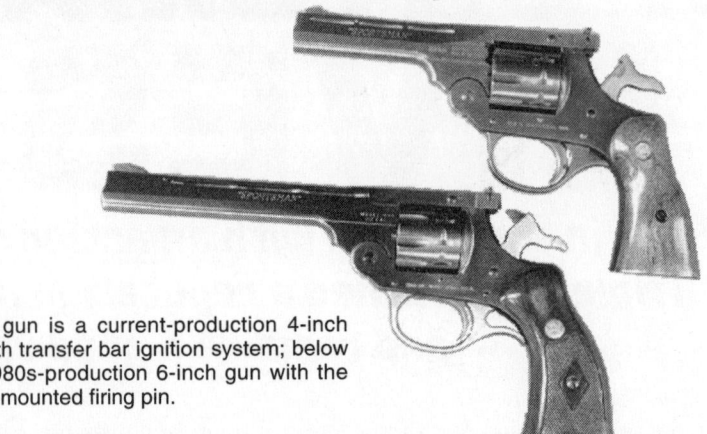

Bulging pockets and open buttons were of little concern to the author at age 8, here posing with Grandma Brown's top-break S&W. This gun led to Brown's fascination with top-breaks, including the H&Rs.

The author's as-new circa-1937 H&R No. 20 revolver is shown with post-war 38 S&W ammunition. Such centerfire H&Rs can be correctly regarded as "parents" of the M999 Sportsman series.

The top gun is a current-production 4-inch M999 with transfer bar ignition system; below it is a 1980s-production 6-inch gun with the hammer-mounted firing pin.

of this model indicates that few shooters were willing to sacrifice the versatility of the No. 999's double-action capability to purchase an identically priced No. 199. The inherent accuracy of both guns was due largely to their rigid one-piece barrels (with integral extensions), which were milled from solid steel.

Before we leave the target shooting theme, it should be noted that H&R briefly offered the Eureka No. 196 top-break revolver. This was, perhaps, the ultimate attempt to make a formal target pistol out of the basic Sportsman design. The 196 had a super-short cylinder, just long enough to house a 22 Long Rifle cartridge. Its barrel was elongated to the rear, thus lessening the jump of the bullet between cylinder and rifling. The No. 196 sold for about $6 more than either the 199 or 999. There were apparently few takers, and the pieces are considered true rarities today.

Where the No. 999 Sportsman actually excelled was in the holsters, packs and "kits" of hunters, trappers, campers, hikers, fishermen, etc. As a real-world utilitarian piece, the 6-inch barreled Triple Nine (the only barrel length offered for the gun until quite recently) quickly established a reputation for practical accuracy, and nearly flawless reliability of function.

The one positive aspect of top-break, self-ejecting revolvers was the design's rapid reloading capability. So long as all of the rounds had been fired (or if the shooter didn't care) there has never been a more rapid system for clearing a revolver prior

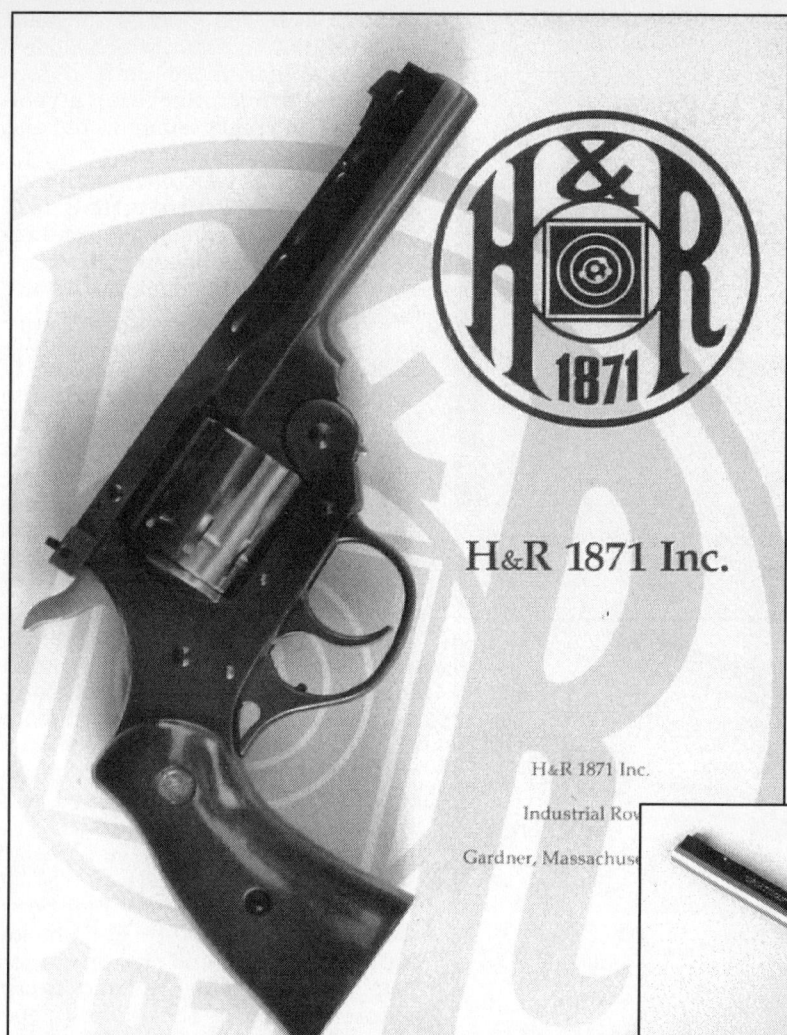

This current H&R 1871, Inc., 4-inch M999 features a "fluted" rib—neither ventilated nor solid—that makes manufacture cheaper and easier. It adds to the good looks of this neat revolver.

All three of these M999s have different features and make an interesting collection by themselves (from left): a 1966-vintage 6-incher with solid rib; a late 1970s/early 1980s 6-inch Sportsman with ventilated rib and hammer-mounted firing pin; current-production 4-inch Sportsman with smooth hardwood grips, fluted rib.

lovingly stored in a well oiled sock—ergo its current pristine condition. Unfortunately, the original cardboard box had been discarded. My interest in acquiring this gun was to duplicate (within reason) Grandma Brown's old pistol, in an as-new gun. According to an April, 1984 *American Rifleman* article, the revolver is a "Variation 10" version, produced between 1913 and 1937. A similar H&R is illustrated in the 1940 *Shooter's Bible* priced at $16.45 in either blue or nickel. According to the *'Rifleman* story, all blued No. 20s are scarce (nickel was the preferred finish), with blued 5-inch No. 20s being downright rare.

Second, is a nearly perfect Second Generation M-999 made in 1966. Like all Triple Nines, this gun features independently adjustable front (for elevation) and rear (for windage) sights. The 6-inch-tubed piece has a solid milled rib integral to the top of its barrel. It appears 1966 was the final year these guns were made with the solid rib. The 1967 *Shoot-*

to recharging. As the barrel latch is lifted, a hook and slide-type ratchet raises the extractor star. When properly manipulated, the assembly lifts *all* cases in the cylinder and flips them completely free of the gun. This procedure requires practice, lest one or more of the cases slip under the star, lodging there, thus effectively jamming the piece. One would think that the more rounds contained in the cylinder, the greater would be the likelihood that this malfunction will occur. The nine-shot Sportsman defies that logic and is seldom susceptible to this malady. Today, the self-ejecting feature is regarded as a plus. Combined with one or two HKS speedloaders, the Model 999 (as it is now known) provides a formidable self-defense package.

Let's take a quick look at some of my favorite revolvers, naturally all Harrington & Richardsons.

The first is the five-shot 38 S&W No. 20 Automatic Ejecting model. This 5-inch-barreled, blued revolver is in unfired condition. I bought this piece from the original owner about twenty years ago. It had been purchased just prior to the beginning of World War II for home protection, but had never been shot. It had been

er's Bible (printed in 1966) is the last to picture that rib style. Subsequently, M-999s were outfitted with true ventilated ribs. Whether or not such ribs were actually functional, dissipating heat waves created by extended shooting sessions, is a moot point. In this scribe's opinion, the vent rib Triple Nines are simply damned attractive! It is interesting to note that while the M-999 was updated in 1950 to Second Generation configuration (as illustrated by this gun), it was not pictured in its new, "modernized" form until the 1954 *Shooter's Bible*. The gun's rebounding hammer has a "fixed"

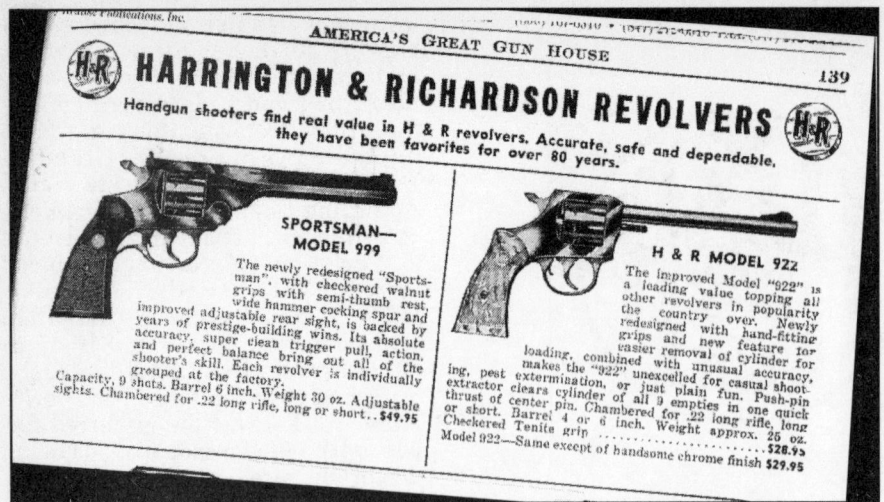

This ad from the 1954 *Shooter's Bible* listed the Sportsman Model 999 at $49.95 and billed it as a target gun. In the late '60s, the model was offered in satin chrome with the owner's name engraved on the barrel.

Author's favorite Triple Nine is the top gun with true ventilated rib. The solid rib (bottom) looks sturdier. Both guns are in as-new condition.

firing pin. Its action (both double and single) is crisp and smooth. Accuracy is excellent, with 25-yard groups averaging 2½ inches when using ammunition it likes. While collectible, it is your reporter's M-999 "shooter."

Number three is a fairly recent acquisition. This is a 6-inch Triple Nine with ventilated rib, absolutely new-unfired in its original box with all of its paperwork. The serial number places its production mid-way between the 1966 gun above, and the January 24, 1986 bankruptcy of the original H&R firm. Exactly when the "old" H&R switched over to a frame-mounted independent firing pin, activated by a transfer bar ignition system, is unclear. The late 1970s, early '80s gun shown still has a hammer-mounted, "fixed" firing pin. But, the transfer bar system was definitely used by the original H&R firm prior to going belly-up in 1986. This Sportsman was purchased quite recently at a cost substantially below suggested retail for the new H&R 1871 guns. It is, of course, my "collector" M-999.

H&R 1871, Inc. is a holding company/manufacturer, located in Gardner, MA, responsible for the current production of a limited number of firearms bearing the Harrington & Richardson name. While these weapons are virtually identical to the H&R guns made before the original firm went under, H&R 1871 assumes no responsibility for warranty work on those earlier pieces. New England Firearms is a wholly owned subsidiary of H&R 1871. The parent firm can be thought of as General Motors, with New England Firearms being analogous to its Chevrolet Motor Division.

The "old" 4-inch M-999 was first listed in the 1980 (printed 1979) *Shooter's Bible*, at $120, $5 below the 6-inch version. By 1982, the *'Bible* cataloged both lengths at $165. When last shown in the 1986 (printed 1985) *'Bible*, the two standard models sold for $215 each. The short barrel yields a lighter, handier gun, which is ideal for holster carry especially if constantly entering and exiting a vehicle. The 4-inch Sportsman would also be good for self-defense duty.

Which brings us to our fourth gun, a 4-inch M-999 of current H&R 1871 production. The ribs of these newly manufactured pieces are neither solid nor ventilated. Instead, they are fluted or grooved in the areas that were ventilated on most of the earlier guns. The original firm apparently used the fluting process just prior to its swan song. A long-time H&R employee states that there was a very pragmatic reason for this subtle change. Due to the 1100-degree hot-bluing process used by the "old" Harrington & Richardson, combined with a slight loss of structural integrity caused by the removal of metal necessary to create a true ventilated rib, considerable barrel warping had been experienced. Rather than simply returning to the unadorned plain rib, the current fluted effect was adopted. A pretty good compromise once the facts are known, but I still prefer those real ventilated ribs.

All current M-999s have transfer bar ignition systems. H&R 1871's Robin Sharpless proudly mentions the reintroduction of the "smoke cut," previously found only on earlier Triple Nines. This reverse taper counter-boring of the forcing cone allows for a bit of build-up of residue (wax, unburned powder grains, etc.) in the critical cylinder gap area.

As it came from the box, this new H&R's top-breaking action was fairly stiff. That's good, because it's designed to remain relatively tight over a lifetime of shooting. The trigger pull for both single and double action rivals that of my well-used 1966 gun, meaning it's quite good.

The fit and finish of current revolvers don't quite measure up to that of the old guns, but they're still very acceptable and pleasing. And to keep the price down as much as possible, the new grips are of smooth stained hardwood, rather than the checkered walnut of the past. No big deal, though, because these are usin' guns, not wall hangers.

I know that these H&Rs are not high-dollar collector items, but they do remind us that there is an alternative to the common double- and single-action revolver. The top-break design is interesting from an historical standpoint, and it's just plain fun to shoot. That's why I like and collect them.

●

WILLIAM H. BAKER is a name that appears and re-appears when we study the lineage of our classic American double shotguns. Yet, not enough is known about this inventive genius except that he must have been extremely restless.

Baker was born on Christmas in 1835 (about the time Colt was patenting his early pistols and Texas was emerging). What his role in the Civil War was is not known, except that he was granted a patent for a gun lock in 1863, so he must have been working on guns, or as a gun maker at that time in Marathon, New York. In 1875, while living in Lisle, New York, he was awarded a patent for a three-barreled gun that had two shot barrels and one rifle barrel. An ad in *Forest and Stream* of August, 1876 showed him as the maker of such a gun, but gave no notice of incorporation. The next year ads in the same magazine indicate W.H. Baker and Co. selling a new but very similar gun from Syracuse, New York. This gun sold from this address for a couple of years, but Baker was still on the move. In 1881 he was in business with boyhood friends, the Smith brothers in Syracuse. This company, the L.C. Smith Gun Co., was to last for sixty years and become one of the world's most respected gun producers. The legend on the gun stated "L.C. Smith, maker of the Baker Gun." But Baker moved to another gun operation. This pace of moving on an average of every two years was to continue until his death. He even served a stint as a cigar maker.

Baker's impact on the gun industry was probably greatest for his dependable gun fastening system. A sportsman in this period of our history had carried a gun through the "Great War" and had seen unreliable guns cost lives and had an aversion to them. A gun that had a good lockup was a step ahead of much of the competition in a critical marketplace.

After his short venture with what was to become the L.C. Smith Gun Co., Baker moved to Ithaca, New York. Here he joined his brother, as well as Leroy H. Smith and his brother-in-law, George Livermore, forming the W.H. Baker Co. After two years he left, leaving what was to become

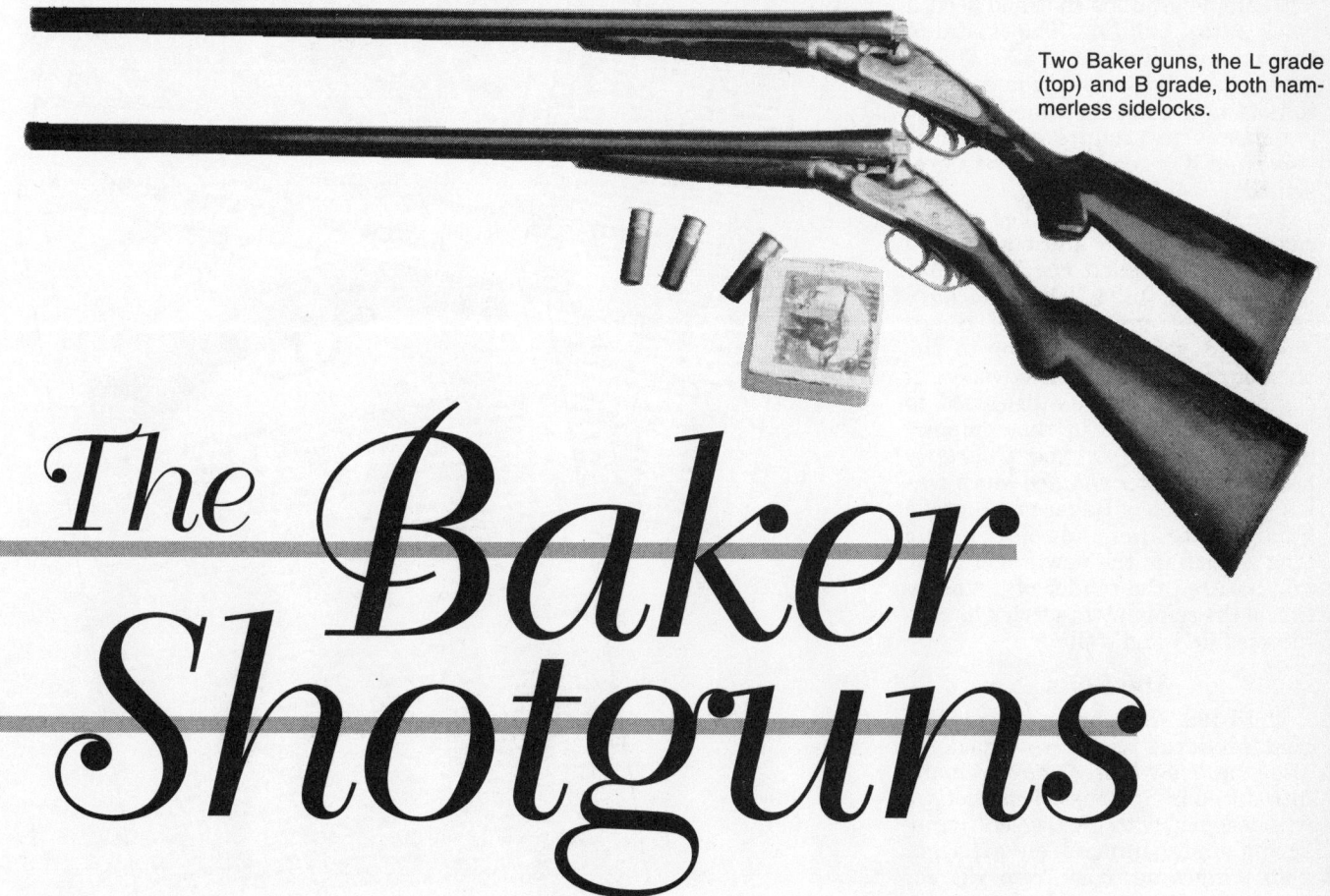

Two Baker guns, the L grade (top) and B grade, both hammerless sidelocks.

The Baker Shotguns

This company was one of the more prolific makers of double barrel shotguns, yet the guns are largely ignored by collectors.

by DON HARDIN and DARYL HALLQUIST

the Ithaca Gun Co. His brother Ellis, ten years his junior and a physician, had started a forging company back in Syracuse. W.H. joined up, and added a gun to the product line, forming Syracuse Forging and Gun Co. A fire ended this operation in 1889. The brothers moved to Batavia, New York where they started a new forging and gun works soon to be renamed The Baker Gun and Forging Co. Shortly after this new plant opened in 1889, William H. Baker died.

In a period of twenty years, Baker had founded three of the most prestigious gun companies in America. As fast as he moved, it is little wonder he didn't pause for a portrait.

Dr. Ellis Baker, an ardent sportsman, pushed forward with a new influx of capital on a building site with ample grounds that had been a brick school building. The capital of the company climbed to $200,000 to get them under way. It is interesting to note how easy it seemed to be to get money to produce shotguns at this time if a good design was presented.

The Baker Gun Co. worked hard at customer relations and began publishing a flyer called *The Baker Gun Quarterly* in 1894. The *Quarterly* extolled the advantages of Baker guns and gave suggestions to the shooter regarding the effectiveness of them. The paper was also used to introduce changes in the company offerings. In 1909, the *Quarterly* became the *Baker Gunner* which was a small catalog of Baker and Batavia guns. The testimonials often told of long shots from the new Baker guns, and assured the reader of the devotion of the company to serving its customers fairly and well.

The Guns

Until 1892, only hammer guns had been produced which were modeled after the "New Baker" gun originally introduced in Syracuse. This shotgun was designed with the triggers, mainspring and hammers on a trigger plate, allowing easy removal for repair or cleaning and adjustment. The gun was a good buy for the money at $25 with twist barrels, and $27.50 with better grade Damascus barrels. Around 250 guns per month were produced initially, and eventually production of 1000 per month was reached. In 1897, the hammer gun was modified as a bar-action sidelock with an extension rib on the barrels. This model can be identified by the Model 1897 marking engraved inside a diamond on the trigger guard. The price for this new model was the same as its predecessor. Offered in 10-, 12- and 16-gauge, this double was very popular. It differed from most hammer doubles by having good balance and its low hammers made mounting and firing the gun a smooth operation. The hammer doubles put the Baker Gun Company on the map.

The Baker Gunner was a quarterly catalog of Baker and Batavia guns, and included glowing testimonials from satisfied users.

The Baker Gun Co. took a big chance when they introduced hammerless doubles to their profitable line of hammer guns around 1892. The company chose a sidelock design, a decision that complicated the manufacturing process and required a larger number of skilled gunmakers. However, the addition probably as-

L.C. Smith's first gun-making venture was this sidelock double shotgun over a rifle barrel (a drilling) made on W.H. Baker's patent. It was offered in 10- and 12-gauge over 44-caliber centerfire.

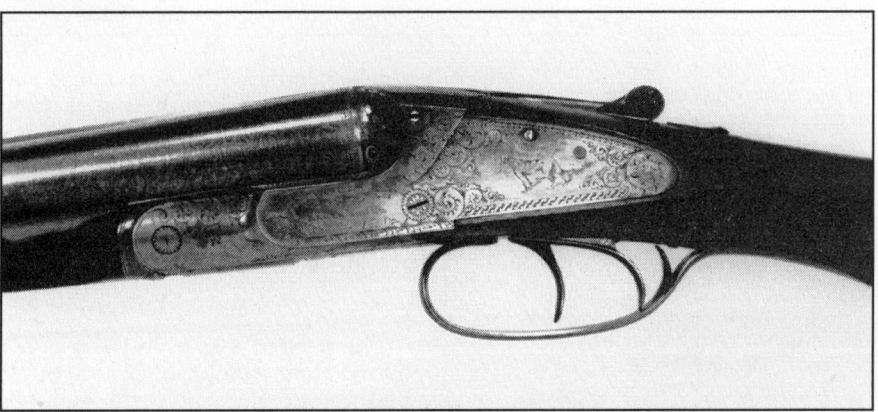

This early Paragon-grade Baker gun carries serial number 273. When introduced, this was their top-of-the line model. In 1909 it sold for $72.50.

The mid-grade Elite single barrel trap gun had a single trigger and shows mediocre engraving, although there's lots of it. It's a deep, slab-sided action.

sured the gun buying public that the Baker guns were keeping pace with the competition.

The shooting public at this time felt uneasy with the concept of a "hammerless" double as there was nothing to indicate if the gun was cocked. Baker advertisements exploited the design of their locks which blocked the firing pins when the safety was engaged. This new sidelock gun and the safety device were the invention of Frank Hollenbeck, a man of previous experience as a gunmaker.

The advertising of the new line emphasized a unique safety device that blocked the hammers instead of the triggers, which was the method used by the rest of the makers of hammerless doubles in this country. This system rendered the gun impossible to fire until a trigger was pulled, opening a hole in the device so that the hammers could strike the firing pins. The company claimed that this made having a safety on the gun unnecessary except "when you wish to make the gun as safe as not loaded—such as getting over a fence or into a boat or wagon.".

It is surprising that with those safety concerns the barrels were offered in laminated steels. That these barrels could be damaged with some of the newly available smokeless powders was the subject of articles in *Forest and Stream* as early as 1893.

In 1892-86, the company added a hammerless double shotgun known as the C grade to their offerings. This boxlock double was an indication the company recognized a need for a lower cost gun to compete with the imported high volume hardware trade guns. This gun was very similar in appearance to a gun made by the Syracuse Arms Co. Baker didn't seem to be satisfied with this gun and must have put it into production simply to meet the high demand for hammerless guns. In the November 1896 *Baker Gun Quarterly*, the company announced, "We find that there are some people to whom the question of price is of more importance than the question of safety....It is our aim to furnish whatever there is a demand for in the line of double barrel, breech loading shotguns, so we take pleasure in offering our new Batavia Hammerless gun." This statement, while not flattering to the new C-grade boxlock, was consistent with their claims and concern for safety.

The new sidelock hammerless was designated a Baker gun, while the boxlock model was called a Batavia Hammerless, indicating that the company felt that Baker guns were a superior product. The Batavia guns had no firing pin safety blocks as did the Bakers. This was also true of the lower-cost sidelock gun soon to be introduced.

In the latter part of the 1890s, management realized that there was a need for a lower priced sidelock sales leader if the company was to do well in a highly competitive marketplace.

Dissatisfaction with the management of the gun portion of the company led to the removal of Dr. Baker from the presidency and active connection with the company in 1898.

The L-grade guns were among the upper quality levels, as shown here by the wood and checkering. The action body shows almost complete engraving coverage, and the bottom (below) even has a nicely done dog with bird in the oval. Grades were not marked on the guns.

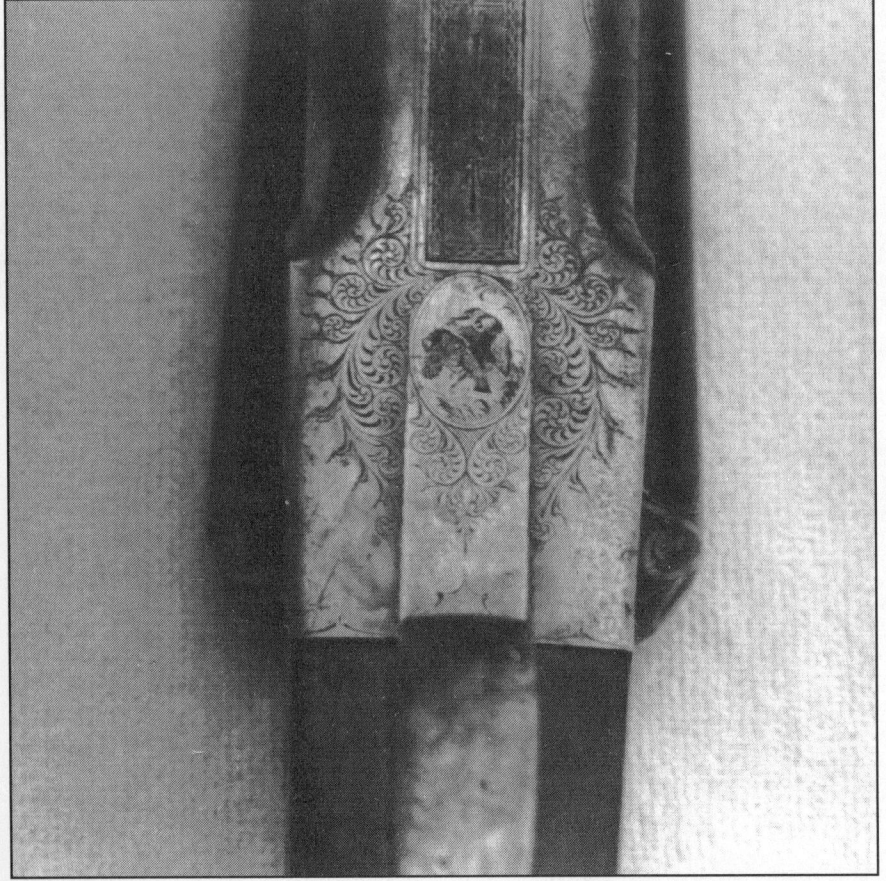

W.T. Mylcrane, the company secretary, ascended to the presidency and head of the business. Mylcrane soon fell ill and a Fredric M. Farwell was hired to run the plant. Farwell was a man of considerable success in business and an active sportsman. Later, in 1907, Farwell was to become president and would be instrumental in the adoption of single trigger and automatic ejector patents needed to stay current in the industry.

Around 1898 the company started production of the Batavia Leader, a sidelock gun with most parts very plain, but similar to the Baker-designated guns. The Batavia Leader was a compromise between the new leadership and those more conservative members who thought the new gun would hurt sales of the more expensive models.

The Baker Guns

The Baker hammerless shotgun, a back-action sidelock, locked up by bolting an extension rib and was equipped with the firing pin safety and rebounding locks. The sidelock action permitted a heavy frame and a lock simply designed, with the parts few in number and ample in size. The gun cocked via a cocking lever pivoted in the frame, raised by a bolt through the lug of the barrels. In 1909, the high-grade Baker guns were improved by adding a rotary-type bolt opposing the top rib extension in the direction of the locking. Cocking rollers were used to cock the automatic ejectors as well as the locks. The modified-action models were termed "Model Nineteen-Nine," and retained the firing pin safety feature.

At the time of introduction of the sidelock Baker guns, the grade designations were B, A, and Paragon in ascending order. All of the Baker doubles were mechanically the same, differing in quality of wood, embellishments and in the barrel steel.

The B grade was the lowest grade gun incorporating the firing pin safety, but was not of low quality. It was equipped with twist barrels of the best quality available, and all Baker guns were tested with nitro powder. The company claimed that the stocks were of imported walnut. Lockplates

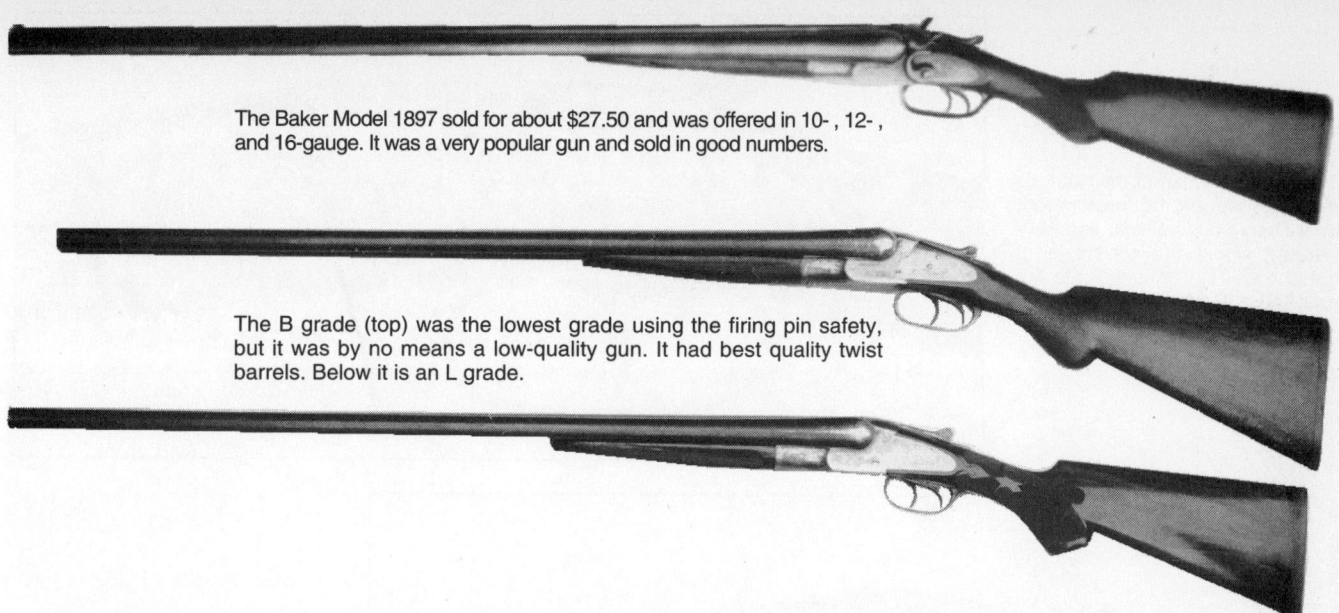

The Baker Model 1897 sold for about $27.50 and was offered in 10-, 12-, and 16-gauge. It was a very popular gun and sold in good numbers.

The B grade (top) was the lowest grade using the firing pin safety, but it was by no means a low-quality gun. It had best quality twist barrels. Below it is an L grade.

were engraved with a game scene and scroll work. The top lines, trigger guard and frame were also engraved. This gun was introduced sans ejectors for $35, and when last produced in 1909, sold for $41.50. It was offered in 10-, 12-, and 16-gauge.

The A-grade Baker was exactly the same as the B grade, except it had Damascus barrels. It was initially offered at $50 and was sold at $42.75 when removed from the Baker line in 1908. Earliest models of the B and A grade guns had engraving of about the same quantity as the Crown grade L.C. Smith. Later, the engraving on these Bakers were reduced to a level comparable to the 2E-grade Smith double, a gun made to sell for considerably more.

Similar to the A and B grades, but exhibiting better wood and engraving was the Paragon grade. It was introduced in 1894 and could only be ordered on a custom basis through a dealer or ordered directly from the Baker Gun Co. The Paragon was introduced at $60, and was probably the best gun bargain of the time. In 1909, the base price was $72.50. By 1909, ejectors had become standard equipment on most 12- and 16-gauge guns, and about half were furnished with Krupp Fluid Steel barrels. The demand for the Paragon at such a bargain price prompted lots of sales and requests for extras on the basic gun.

In 1897 a Pigeon grade gun was advertised in the *Baker Quarterly*. This straight-stocked model was to be equipped with fluid steel barrels and was to sell for $100. It is questionable if this gun was ever put into production as no other references to it have surfaced. In the 1890s and in the early 1900s, shotgun ammunition and materials were rapidly changing. Smokeless powder was replacing blackpowder shotshells and new steels become necessary to withstand greater and different pressures in shotgun barrels. To keep up with this trend, Baker Gun and Forging decided to offer its Paragon model with the option of steel barrels. In early 1903, the Special Paragon was announced. This gun could be had for $75 with Krupp steel or Whitworth Fluid Steel barrels. It sported a price tag of $200 and up, depending on the amount of engraving and special features ordered.

By 1904 two new guns had been added, the Baker Krupp and Deluxe, and the Special Paragon was deleted. This year also saw the introduction of an automatic ejector system for an additional $15-$25, depending on the grade of gun. The year 1905 saw the introduction of another new grade to be placed between the Krupp and Deluxe. This model had Holland steel barrels and a price tag of $150. I seriously doubt if there has ever been a better bargain available than a Baker gun in these grades at this time, unless it was Manhattan Island for $24 worth of beads.

The offerings became more complex by 1906. In the high grades the choices were: the regular Paragon, the Baker Krupp and the gun with Holland steel barrels and its Deluxe grade. Two lower grades were also introduced, the R and S. All of this was probably very confusing to the customer so Baker sought to simplify the grading system. The grades were renamed as follows: the original Paragon retained its name; the Krupp became the N grade; the Holland steel version became the L grade; and the Deluxe retained its name, although for a time was referred to as the H grade. All of these were special order guns and could be had with any reasonable features or dimension. For example, an L grade in the author's collection is ornately engraved and furnished with Whitworth steel barrels. A Deluxe grade in the collection sports the finest wood, finest Damascus barrels and 100 percent engraving coverage. A gun such as this could have been ordered with any choice of barrels and features that could drive the cost to the $1000 level. This would compare favorably with the most expensive offerings of the American gun producers of high reputation.

Many of the top grade Bakers were engraved by Frank A. Mason. He did beautiful work, particularly in laying out the engraving to enhance a game scene, rather than the crowding seen on many of the American high grade doubles of the time. The high grade Bakers were engraved to the request of the buyer, so identifying a specimen by its engraving is unlikely. Some scenes or a scroll pattern can be seen on separate guns in each grade.

The grades of the higher quality Bakers are hard to identify as they are not always marked. But, the 1909 Paragon, Expert, Deluxe, L, N, and older Paragons are in the 1-1200 serial number range, while A and B grade guns range from 1-7000. Obviously there is some overlap, but the amount and quality of engraving on Paragon and higher grades is lavish.

The R grade could be supplied with either Damascus or Krupp Fluid Steel barrels and with ejectors. This gun had

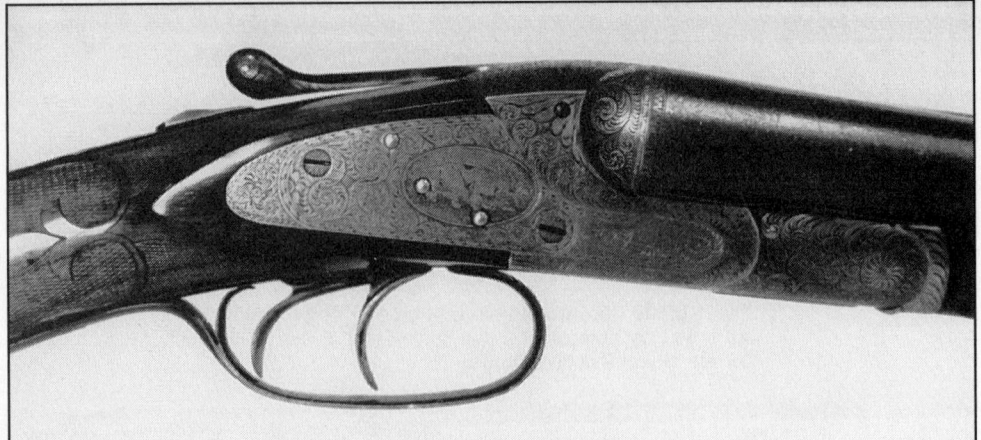

This Baker Deluxe in the author's collection sports the finest wood, best Damascus barrels, and 100-percent engraving coverage. It could easily be optioned into the four-figure level.

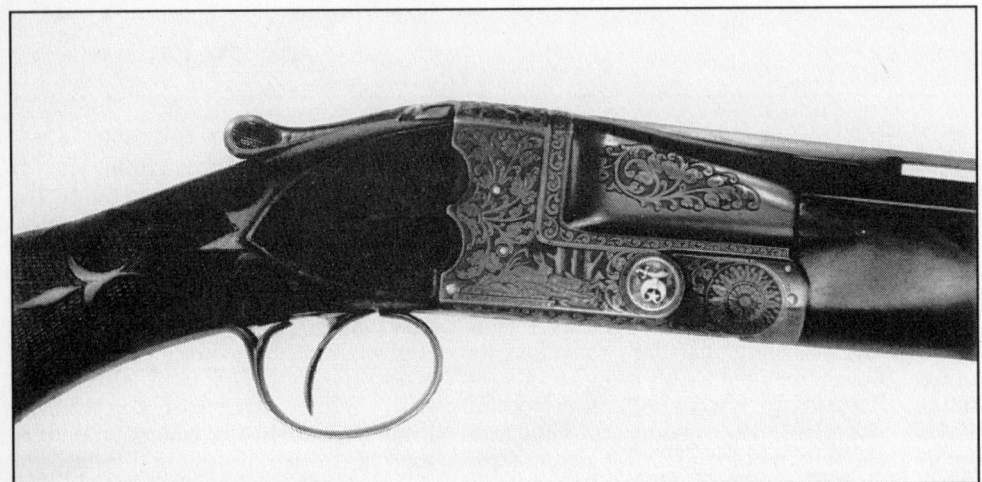

This transition model Superba single barrel trap gun has the early integral rib with a late receiver and ejector system. These were truly custom-made guns to the shooter's specifications.

simple scroll engraving and either a pointer or setter on each lockplate. It was priced at $48.75. The S grade was sold with "Homotensile" steel barrels and could be bought with ejectors for $35.50. As these were Baker guns instead of Batavias, they were equipped with the firing pin safety blocks. By 1908 the new R grade had replaced the old A grade in the Baker line. The old B grade was continued for another year.

Some of the early Paragon guns have caused confusion for collectors. They were often very elaborate and would have been a much higher grade if produced a few years later, when the Paragon was not the best gun in the Baker offerings.

The Baker doubles could be purchased with a single trigger, but this was not up to the standard of the rest of Baker engineering and was not easy for the shooter to use. The single trigger worked pretty well when set to fire the right barrel first, but would require a shift when set to fire the left barrel first. Very few Baker guns were equipped with this trigger.

Automatic ejectors could be retrofitted to higher grade guns if they were returned to the factory. The upgrading cost $10, the same as having them included in a new shotgun. A Paragon gun in the author's collection had ejectors added, which necessitated a different forend release than commonly used on Baker doubles.

In the 1909 *Baker Gunner*, a single barrel trap gun was announced which became available in 1910. The gun bolted via bars projecting from the standing breech into holes on each side of the barrel. The gun was fitted with a ventilated rib and was made completely to the specifications of the customer in terms of stock fit and engraving. It was offered in three grades: the Sterling at $80, the Elite at $125, and the Superba at $200. It was modified in 1915 by changing from an integral barrel to a more economical rib added later in the manufacturing process. The trap guns were custom built to the many whims and desires of a shooter for very little extra cost. Had the company kept making guns, the trap gun should have become a best seller.

The Batavia Guns

These lower-priced guns became the company's mainstay in terms of the number of sales. The first offering was the hammerless C grade, sold for only 2½ years (1896-1898). Many of this model were produced for and sold by Montgomery Ward and Co. after they were no longer identified as Batavia guns. The catalogs referred to this model as the Batavia Hammerless. This was the only boxlock gun that was to be produced.

None of the lower-cost guns were to have the firing pin safety devices and the wood was of a plain grade of European walnut. The barrels of the early models were of stub twist steel. Later, a cheaper model, the Batavia Special, was introduced with browned steel. These doubles were characterized by bright case-colors on the sidelocks which, although they lacked engraving, were attractive. These shotguns are the easiest to identify as they usually have the name of the grade prominently stamped on the lockplates. The Batavia Leader was the first of the lower cost sidelock shotguns.

A Batavia Damascus model was identical to the Batavia Leader except it was fitted with Damascus steel barrels while the Leader had

Production Data
Baker and Batavia Shotguns

	Years of Production	Original Cost	Serial # Range	Comments
Hammer Guns				
New Baker	1889-1897	$25.00 twist $29.50 Damascus	1-45,000	Trigger plate action; around 10,000 produced
1897 Model	1897-1916	$25.00 twist $29.50 Damascus	1-45,000	Sideplate action model
Hammerless Guns				
Baker Guns				
B	1897-1909	$35.00-41.50	1-7,000	1908 (new B grade replaced original B grade)
A	1897-1908	$42.75-47.75	1-7,000	
Paragon	1897-	$60.00 & up	1-1,200	
Pigeon	1897-1898	$100.00	1-1,200	Probably never made
R	1906-1916	$48.75	200,000+	Krupp steel or Damascus barrels
S	1906-1916	$35.50	200,000+	"Homotensile" steel
Krupp (N)	1904-1919	$75.00 & up	1-1,200	Also called Special Paragon (1903); called Holland steel grade (1905)
Expert (L)	1905-1919	$150 & up	1-1,200	
Deluxe (H)	1904-1919	$300 & up	1-1,200	
Black Beauty Special	1916-1919	$62.00	1-45,000	
Batavia Guns				
C grade	1896-1898	$27.73 twist $34.95 Damascus		Only Baker boxlock; many sold by Montgomery Ward
Batavia Leader	1903-1916	$25.00	75,000-156,000	With Damascus barrel, $3 more
Batavia Special	1906-1916	$21.75	75,000-161,000	
Batavia Damascus	1906-1916	$28.00	75,000-161,000	
Batavia Ejector	1908-1916	$35.00 twist $37.50 Damascus	75,000-161,000	Could be ordered with special steel
Batavia Brush Gun	1908-1916	$27.00 (with swivels) $24.00 (without swivels)	1-45,000	Short barrels, straight-grip stock
Black Beauty	1916-1919	$40.00	1-45,000	Replaced the Leader as sales leader in 1916
Trap Guns				
Sterling	1910-1919	$80.00		
Elite	1910-1919	$125.00		
Superba	1910-1919	$200.00		

twist steel tubes. The better Damascus barrels cost an additional $3. In 1908, the Batavia Ejector model was introduced. It was fitted with ejectors and a choice of fluid or Damascus barrels at $35 and $37.50 respectively.

The gun used a roller cocking design similar to the 1909 Paragons. An unusual offering for the time was added to the Batavia line in 1909 when the Batavia Brush gun was offered. This fast-handling model was equipped with 28-inch barrels, a straight grip stock, and open chokes, and was ahead of its time on the American market. The Brush gun was furnished with London Twist barrels and weighed in at only 6 pounds in 16-gauge. For an additional $3 the gun could be equipped with a sling strap and swivels, for a total cost of $27.

In 1915 and 1916, probably due to the effects of pump and autoloading shotguns on double barreled gun sales, both the Batavia and Baker model lines were redesignated. A double called the Black Beauty featuring a black oxide sideplate rather than bright case colors replaced the Leader. A Black Beauty Special was also offered, replacing the R and S grade Baker guns. These new models were equipped with steel barrels and were either not engraved or had very little line engraving.

After the World War, selling double guns had become more difficult. The company's offerings decreased and orders were being filled from parts in stock. In 1919, the gun portion of Baker Gun and Forging was sold to the H&D Folsom Co., which turned out a few of the lower grade guns from parts made in both Batavia and in the Folsom factory.

In sixteen years, the production had gone from 10,000 hammer guns per year to the point where production was no longer profitable. The forging business, however, was maintained and the company remained at the same location.

An admirer of fine guns can only wish that Paragon, Expert and Deluxe grade models had remained in production because they were truly fine American-made doubles. The Baker guns deserve the attention of the gun collector.

Many Baker guns are hard to identify, but we've learned a lot about them through research and collectors sharing their data. Hopefully, this article will shed some light on these interesting and varied double guns.●

Bibliography

Baker Quarterly, Vol. 1, #2, July, 1894

Baker Quarterly, Vol. 1, #6, February, 1896

Baker Quarterly, Vol. 2, #3, November, 1986

Baker Quarterly, Vol. 7, #4, May, 1903

Baker Quarterly, Vol. 10, #1, November, 1904

Baker Quarterly, Vol. 10, #4, February, 1906

Baker Gun Company Catalog, 1908

Baker Gunner No. 4, 1909

Baker Catalog No. 4, 1911

Baker Catalog, 1917

Baker Catalog, 1919

Hardin, Donald H., "Classic American Doubles," *American Rifleman*, November 1972.

Shanks, Kenneth, "W.H. Baker, Gunmaker of Distinction," *American Rifleman*, June 1968.

SHOOT THAT THREE-BARREL GUN

by DICK EADES

What looks like a keyhole above and between the barrels is part of a push-rod system that lifts the open rear sight as the barrel selector is pushed to one side. The rear sight is quite small and has a shallow notch.

THROUGHOUT THE COUNTRY, in closets, attics and other storage areas, rest thousands of old German drillings or three-barrel combination guns. They are too big to get lost and too pretty to throw away but many lie unused, rusting and collecting dust. Reason? Most are chambered for cartridges their owners never heard of. Unusual metric designations such as 7.62x51mmR may be marked on under-surfaces of the barrels, or the guns may be completely unmarked. Most were brought back as "war trophies" by troops returning from World War II.

By definition, a "drilling" is a three-barrel gun, carrying a double shotgun over a single rifle. Some drillings have a single shotshell barrel below two rifle barrels, which is an unusual arrangement. A seldom-seen type has a single shot barrel, a big game rifle barrel, and a smallbore barrel—a year-round combination. Other combination gun variations are not unheard of, including single shotguns over single rifles and four- or five-barrel shoulder guns. Although somewhat rare, there are a few guns that carry two rifle calibers and two shotgun barrels. The only five-barrel gun I have examined was a set of two 16-gauge shotgun barrels atop two large rifle barrels with a small-caliber rifle barrel inset between the four others. Most of the guns encountered in the United States will be the three-barreled variety.

There are many of these old German guns lying around not being used. They're interesting hunting tools that can be shot if you'll take the time to investigate them.

Developed in the last quarter of the 19th century, combination guns became quite popular in Germany. The primary reasons for their popularity were German laws which taxed ownership of hunting arms heavily. The tax was levied on the basis of a separate fee on each gun owned. Therefore, ownership of a combination rifle/shotgun cost only half of the tax for one of each of the two types. Another reason for the popularity of combination guns was the hunting style practiced in Germany. Most hunters there used established hunting towers to watch for game, and while sitting in the high tower, one was as apt to see a flock of grouse as a herd of deer, and he could use the same gun to take both types of game.

Many of these guns were masterpieces of the gunmaker's art, combining premium quality wood with elaborate, deep engraving on receivers and sidelocks. Gold and silver inlays were used on the better grade guns, as were built-in claw-type scope mounts on later models.

Most older drillings will be found with exposed hammers although a few hammerless examples may be encountered. Although hammerless actions were perfected much earlier, drillings made as late as the 1930s were usually made with exposed hammers. Even limited numbers of post-war drillings can be found with them.

The earliest examples of drillings usually have Damascus or twist-steel shotshell barrels. Fewer German guns will be seen with these than those originating in other countries. After development of fluid steel barrels, many were "damascened" or finished to *look* like Damascus steel. We recognize today that Damascus steel is inherently weak, but it was very highly regarded by earlier shooters who felt fluid steel barrels were a cheap substitute.

Most early drillings are found in 16-gauge, which is still a very popular shotgun gauge in Europe, and many of them are chambered for a shorter version of the shell than is

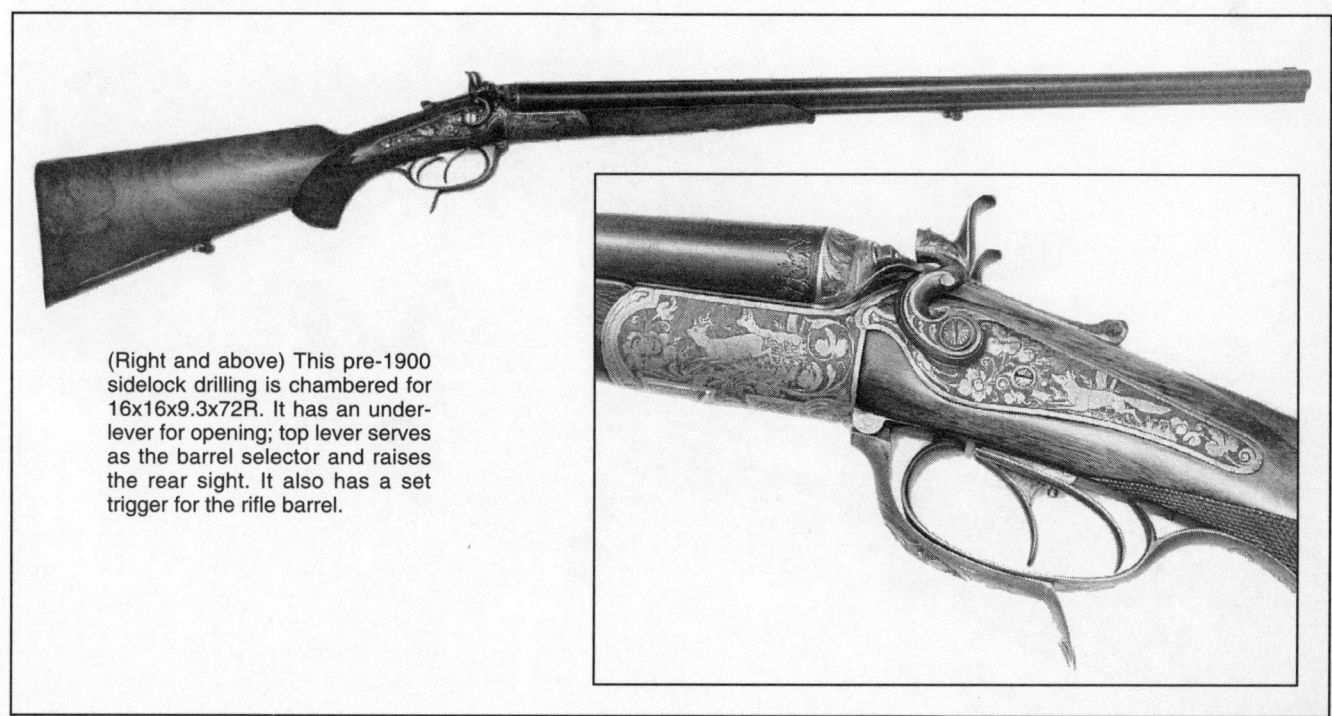

(Right and above) This pre-1900 sidelock drilling is chambered for 16x16x9.3x72R. It has an under-lever for opening; top lever serves as the barrel selector and raises the rear sight. It also has a set trigger for the rifle barrel.

currently available. Before firing *any* drilling, have the chamber length checked by a competent gunsmith. A modern, longer 16-gauge shell will seat in the older, short chambers but, upon firing, its crimp can't open enough to freely discharge the shot. This can result in dangerously high chamber pressure.

Drillings are encountered with various methods of opening the action for loading or unloading. Most break in a manner similar to a modern double-barreled shotgun, but the release mechanism may be quite different. Often, the top lever we are accustomed to seeing doesn't release the barrels but, instead, acts as a barrel selector to switch between the shotshell and rifle barrels. Many also use the top lever to raise a notched rear sight at the same time the rifle barrel is selected. Of this type, most use an underlever to unlock the barrels for loading. Some drillings, of course, have a top lever that does actually serve to open the barrel latch. On this type, the barrel selector is usually a sliding switch that looks like a safety on an American shotgun. The safety on this type gun is often a sliding button located on the left side of the stock, just below and to the rear of the receiver.

Decoration on these guns is usually quite elaborate. Game scenes as well as floral patterns frequently appear on the sideplates. Quality of this engraving can compare favorably with some of the best seen in this country, but I've also seen some amateurish jobs. Many of the actions and sidelocks are color case-hardened, and some will be seen with silvered actions and lockplates. Sling swivels are frequently part of the original equipment, as are cartridge "wells" holding a few rifle cartridges under a

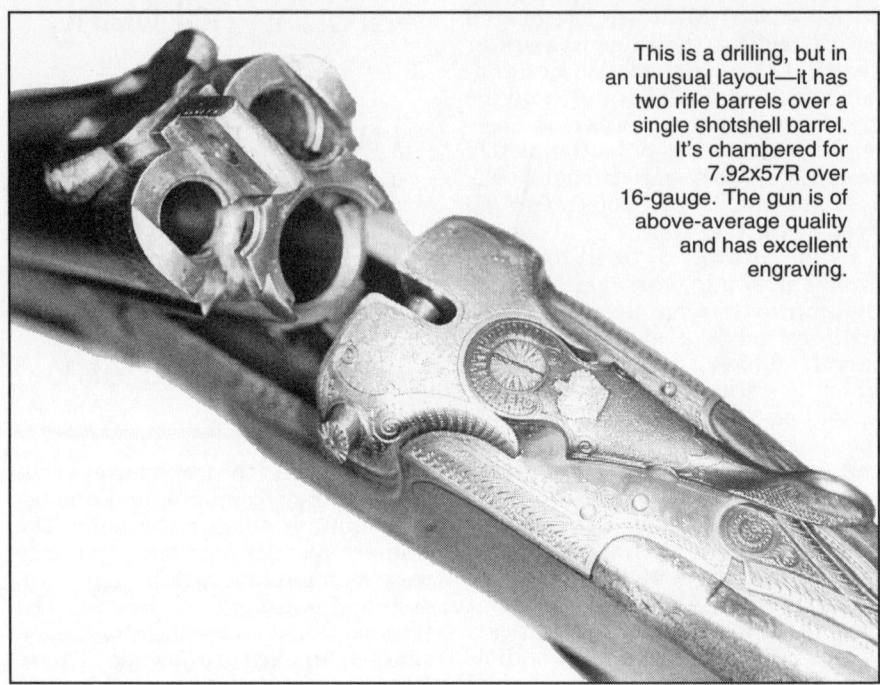

This is a drilling, but in an unusual layout—it has two rifle barrels over a single shotshell barrel. It's chambered for 7.92x57R over 16-gauge. The gun is of above-average quality and has excellent engraving.

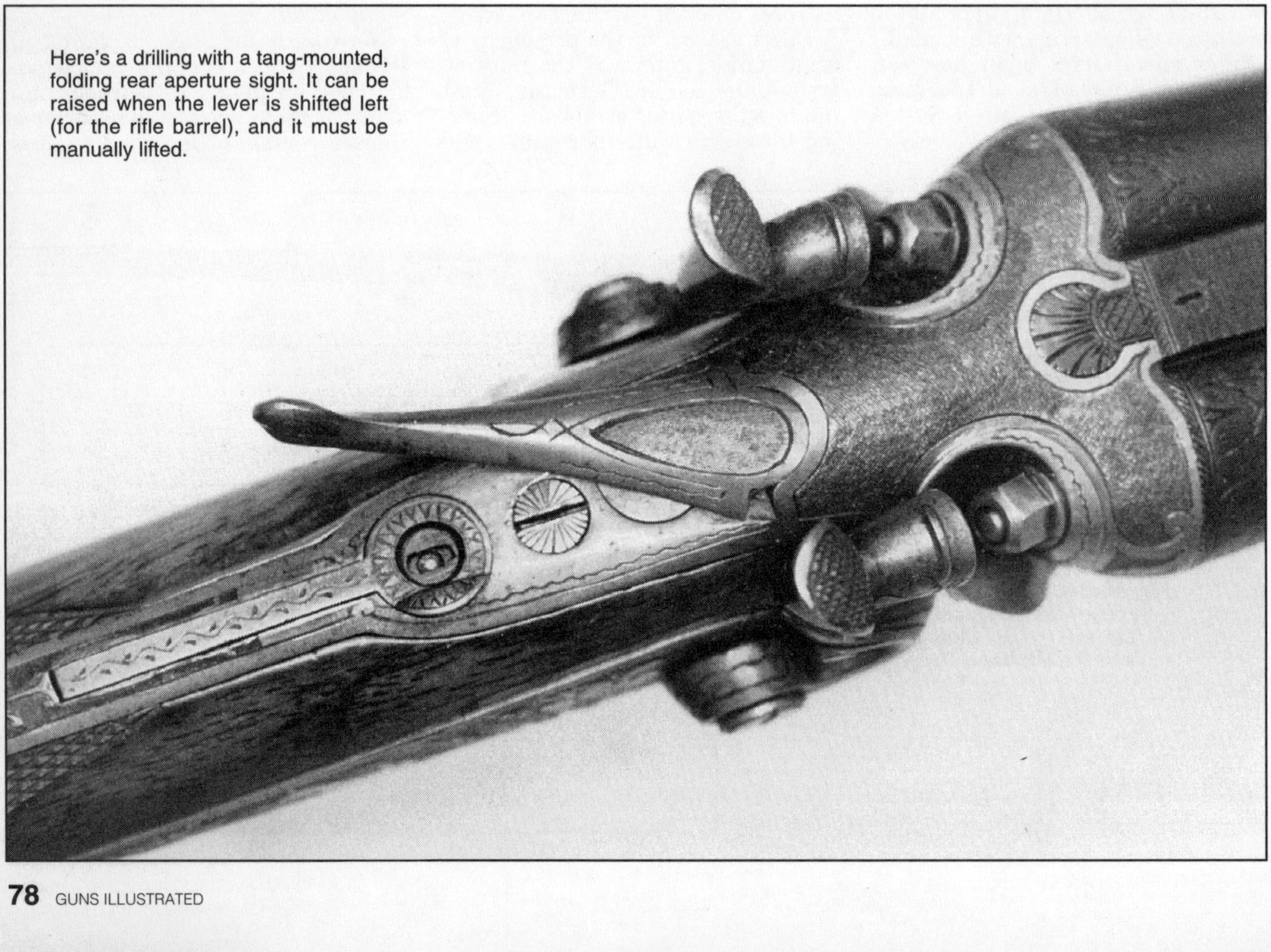

Here's a drilling with a tang-mounted, folding rear aperture sight. It can be raised when the lever is shifted left (for the rifle barrel), and it must be manually lifted.

spring loaded cover. These are usually found on the bottom of the buttstock, just forward of the buttplate, and these are sometimes nicely engraved and/or color hardened.

Premium wood, highly figured walnut with complex checkering patterns is the rule rather than the exception on drillings. A huge percentage will be seen with horn or engraved metal buttplates, although a few will lack a buttplate all together and have only a finely checkered wooden butt. Forend attaching plates usually carry some engraving and thinly slotted screws that are oriented so that the slots all point precisely fore and aft.

There's usually no problem determining whether or not the shotgun chambers will accommodate modern

Exposed hammer drillings are fairly common, like this pre-1900 example. It has an underlever for opening the action, top lever for barrel selection. This one is 16-gauge over 9.3x72R, and has less common scroll engraving.

Safety selectors were sometimes used, usually mounted on the left side of the gun. The tang-mounted slide selects rifle or shotshell barrel on this boxlock example.

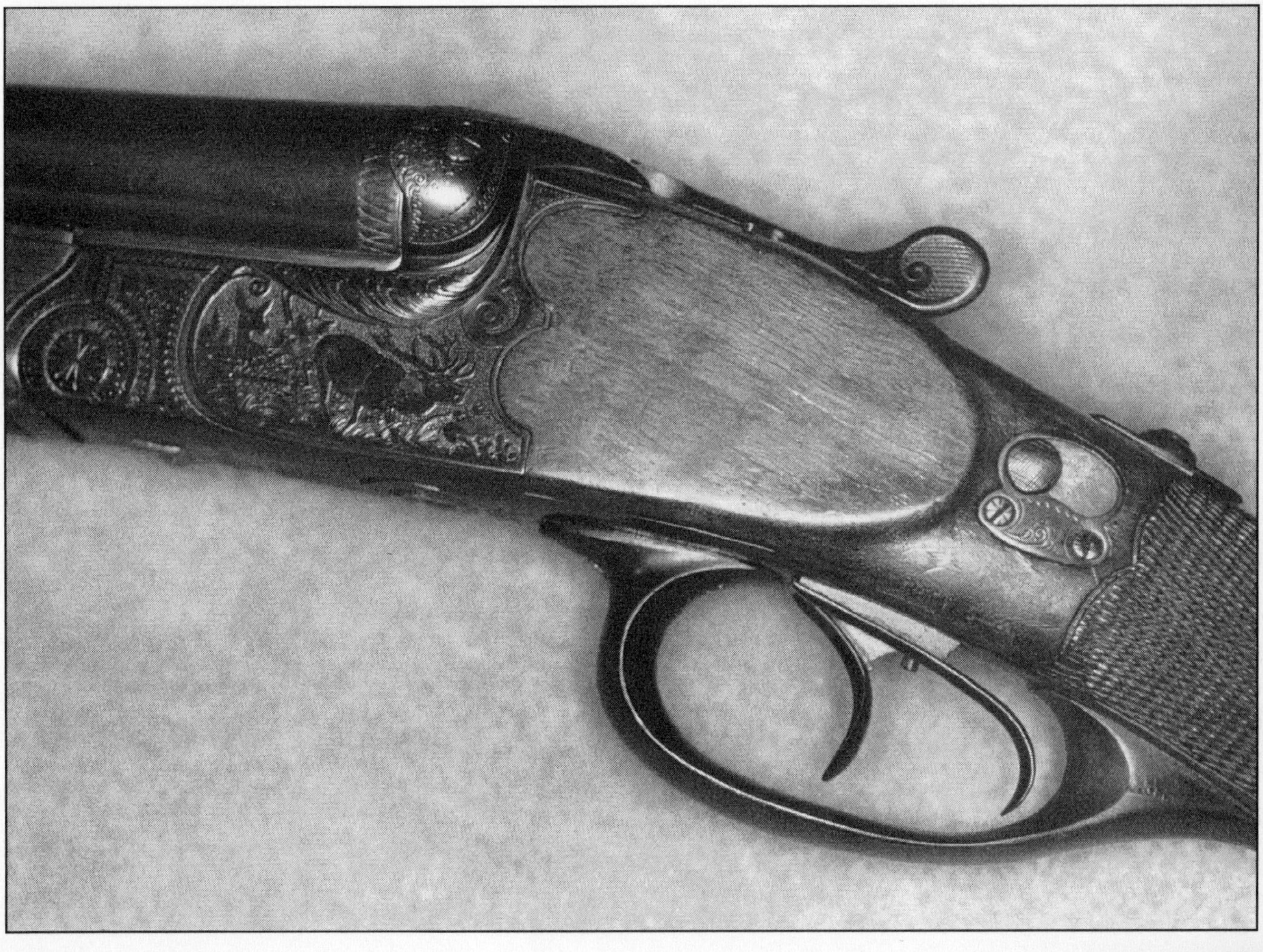

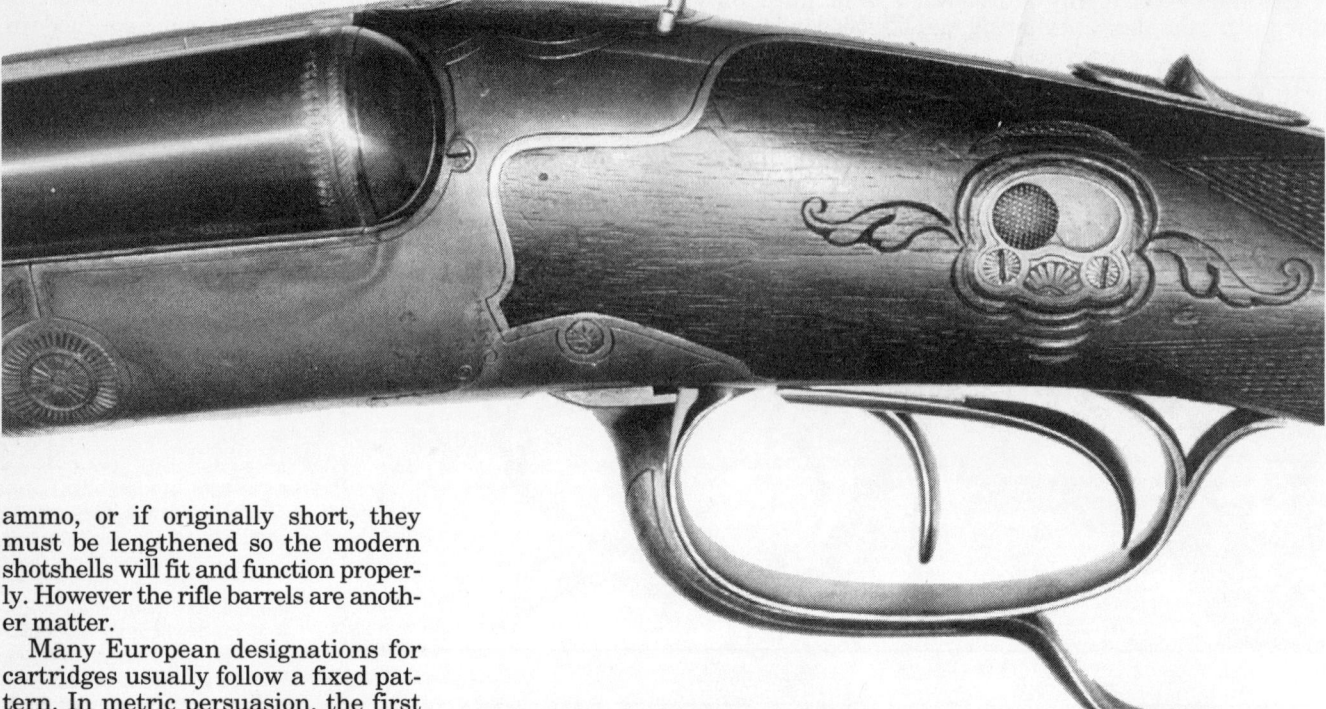

A hammerless drilling of unknown date. The lack of engraving would usually mark this as an inexpensive gun, but the wood-to-metal and metal-to-metal fit is superior. Note the cocking indicators on the top and the side safety.

ammo, or if originally short, they must be lengthened so the modern shotshells will fit and function properly. However the rifle barrels are another matter.

Many European designations for cartridges usually follow a fixed pattern. In metric persuasion, the first number commonly indicates nominal bore diameter of the rifle, and the second number is cartridge case length. Addition of the letter R to the name indicates a rimmed case. In the case of the 7.9x57, there were two different bullet diameters in common usage for rifles having differing groove diameters, but essentially the same cartridge name. Early "I" (for *Infanterie*) rifles utilized a round-nose bullet of .318-inch diameter, while later "IS" (for *Infanterie Spitzgeschoss*) rifles took a pointed bullet of .325-inch diameter. The larger "IS" bullets must not be used in "I"-bore rifles, or dangerous pressure can result.

Travel between the United States and Germany prior to World War II offered the opportunity for many rifle cartridges to migrate across the Atlantic. The 7.62x51mmR cartridge mentioned earlier carried a bullet of 7.62mm diameter in a case 51mm long. The case was rimmed, as indicated by the R suffix. This cartridge, as loaded in the United States is called the 30-30 Winchester, or 30 WCF. If you are fortunate enough to own a drilling so chambered, you can buy ammo at any sporting goods establishment.

Other common American calibers used in drillings often include the 5.6x35mmR (known here as the 22 Hornet), the 5.6x52mmR (or 22 Savage High Power), the 6.5x52mmR (or 25-35 Winchester), the 32-40 and the 7.62x63mm (30-06). Drillings were not generally chambered for rimless cartridges due to the difficulty in making an efficient extractor, but some will be encountered.

More modern U.S. cartridges are sometimes employed in late-vintage drillings. Post-war drillings have been chambered for most popular American cartridges, both rimmed and rimless. Krieghoff made a number of drillings featuring 12-gauge shotgun barrels and 30-06 rifle barrels immediately after the cessation of hostilities.

Probably the most popular caliber in the earlier drillings was the 9.3x72mmR. Nothing similar to this cartridge has ever been loaded in the United States. A few years ago, a drilling of this caliber was all but useless unless you wanted to go to the trouble and expense of having cartridge cases fabricated. Today, loaded ammo and components are offered by RWS and other European companies and are readily available in this country.

My first drilling was chambered for the 9.3x72mmR and I searched long and hard, without success, for ammunition. The late George Nonte, an old friend and prolific gun writer, came to my rescue. Although I watched him do it, I was never certain how it was possible. George formed some excellent 9.3x72mmR cases from commonly available military 30-06 brass. True, the rims were slightly thinner than those on a factory 9.3 case, but they worked quite well for years before new brass became available here. This was a complex swaging operation, requiring specialized dies not in common use, but, best of all, it worked. George was well versed in conversion of readily obtainable brass to those obsolete cases. If this sort of thing interests you, see if you can find a copy of either of his books, *Cartridge Conversions* or *The Home Guide to Cartridge Conversions*. Both were published by Stackpole and printings were large enough that copies may still be obtainable.

Many drillings will be encountered with unknown makers names or, worse yet, no makers name at all. They were apparently turned out by "cottage industry" gunsmiths who custom built them, using barrels they made or obtained from factories that built guns and/or parts for larg-

A deeply engraved cartridge box cover in the butt conceals recesses for four extra rifle rounds. This one hinges at the front, which is typical.

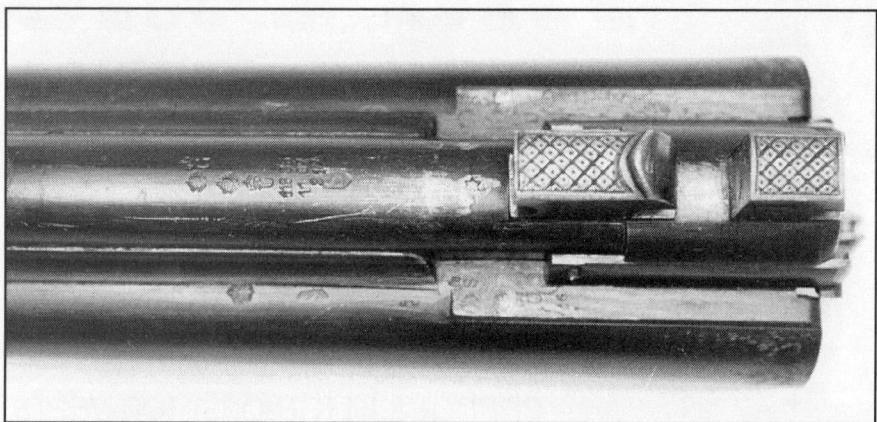

The underside of drilling barrels usually carry a multitude of markings. Some of them are required by the government, others denote caliber, actual bore diameter, date of manufacture.

er manufacturers. The caliber of many of these guns is not marked anywhere on them, and a chamber cast will be needed to determine what sort of fodder they need.

Drillings will be found in calibers varying from the relatively small 6.5x40mmR to the huge and powerful 10.25x69mmR and almost anything in between. Some may be found in English chamberings such as the 303 British, 360 Nitro Express, 400/350 Nitro Express or the 375 Flanged (rimmed) Nitro Express. English-caliber drillings were apparently made on special order for British customers who purchased the guns for use in Africa.

It almost may seem to our American developed tastes that some sort of contest was held to see who could build a drilling in the most obscure caliber. But, what seems obscure to us may be (or was) quite popular at the time and place of its origin. One very popular drilling caliber is the 9.3x74mmR, a powerful cartridge suitable for heavy game. It throws a 232-grain bullet at a muzzle velocity of 2600+ feet per second. This ammunition is available as loaded ammo or in component form from RWS or Norma. It is still in reasonably common use and combination guns so chambered are currently being manufactured.

Most drilling calibers are far more modest than the 9.3x74mmR. There is no really "dangerous" game found in Europe, although a few hog hunters may dispute that statement. Most drillings were meant for hunting in Central Europe, so immense power was not a requirement. The earlier mentioned 9.3x72mmR is probably typical of the ordinary drilling caliber. Present loadings of this 9.3 cartridge drive a 193-grain bullet at about 2000 fps. Not the thing for a charging lion, but it will do quite well on most short to mid-range deer hunting. A whole family of 9.3 rimmed cases, ranging from 48mm to 82mm in length have been used in drillings.

A different 9.3x72mm rimmed cartridge is occasionally found in some drillings. This one was developed by Sauer and is designated 9.3x72mmR Sauer. At a glance, the Sauer round looks much like the more common round, but it has a slight bottleneck and the cartridges will not interchange. Your chances of encountering a drilling in this caliber are not great, but if you meet a drilling made by Sauer it could happen. Although this cartridge is long out of production, brass can be formed from 9.3x74mmR cases, trimmed to length and fire-formed.

Another popular drilling cartridge is the 8x57mmJRS. The often-encountered 8x57mmJS was the standard German military cartridge used in the M98 Mauser. The JRS is simply a rimmed version of the same round. It is currently available from RWS and Norma, and is comparable to the 30-06. This is probably Europe's most popular, rimmed, medium-class cartridge today.

In whatever caliber, chances are you can either locate new ammunition or components, or convert some commonly available brass to the appropriate fodder for your drilling. If all else fails, there is always the possibility of rechambering your barrel to accommodate a readily available cartridge.

Start by checking the underside of the rifle barrel to determine if the caliber is marked. If so, check on availability of new ammo. If not, have a chamber cast made to determine what the rifle is intended to fire.

There's a certain panache that accompanies shooting or hunting with an old drilling. Wouldn't it be nice to go deer hunting and bag a few quail for the pot without changing guns?

A Decade The Black

Muzzle-loading has grown by leaps and bounds and has seen major changes in the past ten years. Here are highlights.

by JOE BYERS

TONY KNIGHT HAD an idea. If he built a muzzle-loading rifle that was based on function rather than tradition, would sportsmen buy it? Would they welcome a rifle that could take advantage of special muzzle-loading seasons?

In 1985, Knight introduced the MK-85, a radical new idea in blackpowder rifles. Engineered to be a serious hunting tool rather than a replica from the past, the "Knight Rifle" as it became known, featured in-line ignition, two safety devices, removable breech plug, synthetic stock, foam recoil pad, and an aluminum ramrod.

Knight's invention, like most technological changes, didn't catch on immediately. During that first year of introduction he built a couple each week in his garage. As the concept of a "modern muzzleloader" gained popularity, sales increased to about a thousand the next year and then grew ballistically. Today, almost any gun shop in America that sells muzzle-loading rifles is sure to have at least one Knight rifle on the rack.

"Tony Knight wasn't the first to build muzzleloaders of contemporary centerfire design," says blackpowder expert and author Toby Bridges. With more than a thousand blackpowder magazine articles and four books in circulation, Bridges is both a fan of the Knight rifle and well schooled in blackpowder and white smoke. "The British list a patent for the in-line ignition in 1810, but only a few were made because of manufacturing limitations," says Bridges. "In-line mechanics require very close tolerances which is why they weren't popular in the 1800s."

More recently, Bridges cites the Esophus Pacer, introduced in 1972, and the Michigan Arms Wolverine, two very modern rifles, but concepts that didn't last. Perhaps these designs were too far ahead of their time, and that's why they didn't capture the imagination of the American sportsman.

Tony Knight, on the other hand, designed a rifle that is safe, user friendly, reliable, and has the appear-

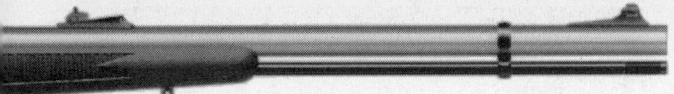
Remington Model 700 MLS.

# of Change
powder Revolution

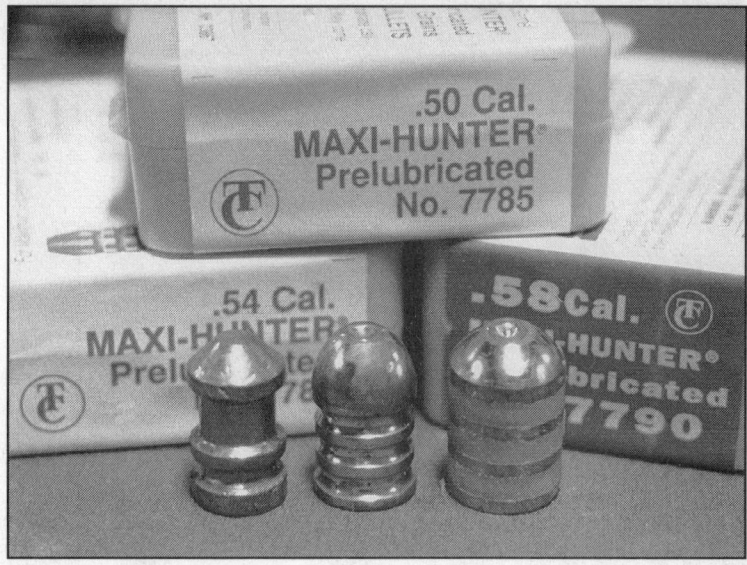

Over the last decade, the 50-caliber has proven to be the most popular, outselling the 54 by ten to one at T/C.

ance to which centerfire hunters can relate. Today, a host of contemporary rifles are available in a wide variety of stock designs, and other manufactures have joined the hunt.

"The biggest change in muzzleloading rifles in the past decade is the switch from patched round ball to bullets and sabots," says Tim Quinlin, National Sales Manager for Connecticut Valley Arms (CVA). "Along with that change came higher performance expectations. Muzzleloaders had been considered 50-yard guns, but today that range has doubled."

"The Knight rifle was a catalyst for change, and it triggered other innovation," says Quinlin. As a person whose profession is "what's happening" in blackpowder shooting as well as what's ahead, Quinlin highlighted a number of changing elements in recent years.

A major change has been the acceptability of a rifle scope for muzzleloaders. As hunters age, their ocular acuity decreases, but the scope helps keep their youthful efficiency and aids in identifying game. If you are shopping for a muzzleloader, don't be surprised if all but the most primitive rifles are drilled and tapped for scope mounting. At least three scope makers introduced scopes specifically designed for muzzleloaders this year.

The in-line ignition is also certainly on Quinlin's list of big changes. This system locates the nipple on the breech end of the barrel and sends a

Part of the new wave of gun designs include (from left): Modern Muzzleloading MK-85; CVA Apollo; Thompson/Center ThunderHawk; Thompson/Center Scout; and CVA Frontier. All but the Frontier are in-line ignition designs.

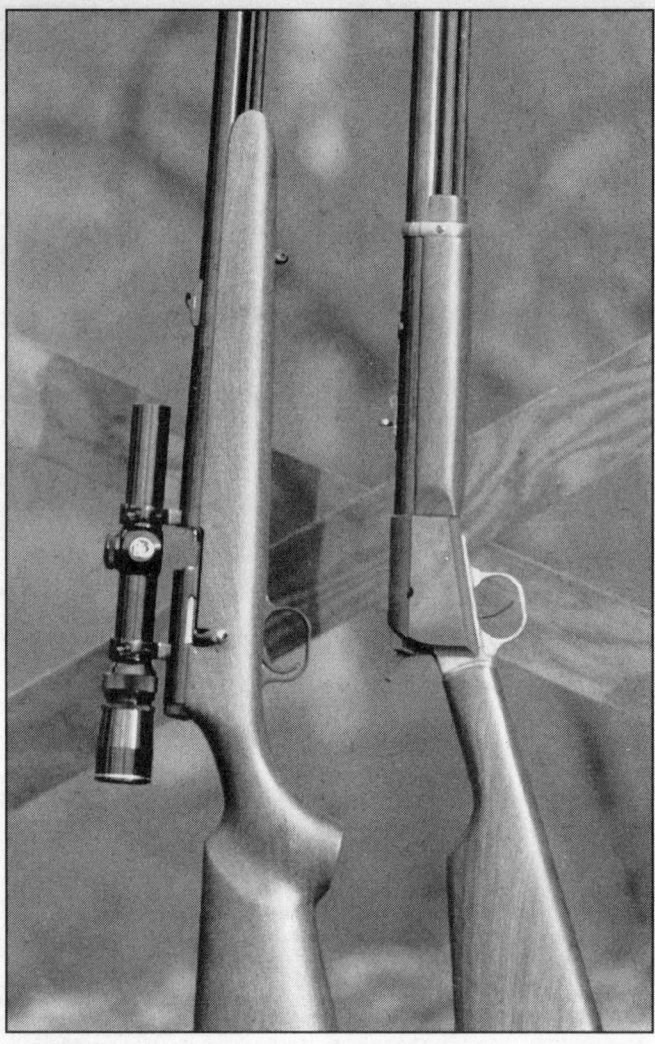

Tony Knight reinvented the muzzleloader with his MK-85 design. It has in-line ignition, laminated walnut or synthetic stock, Timney adjustable trigger, two safeties, modern scope, and construction of stainless as well as blued steel.

Two of Thompson/Center's in-line rifles are the ThunderHawk (left) and Scout, both very modern and extremely efficient. The Scout handles like a Western saddle gun.

spark directly to the powder charge, resulting in more consistent and complete combustion. He believes the primary advantage is providing the hunter with a gun that has the familiar shape and feel of a modern rifle.

In-lines have made synthetic stocks more popular, too. "As soon as you break from the traditional ranks, blackpowder rifles become hard-core hunting rifles," says Quinlin. "Recoil pads, cheekpieces and things that were almost forbidden ten years ago are now accepted."

If anyone thinks the in-line system isn't popular, bear in mind that Remington now offers two versions of their extremely popular centerfire Model 700 rifle as a muzzleloader. Called the Model 700 ML (blued) and Model 700 MLS (stainless), these are sure to become hits with the centerfire shooters who want to double their deer season.

In addition, these guns come with synthetic stocks, recoil pads and everything else that makes a gun "non-traditional." You can bet that if Remington has jumped on the bandwagon there's something to this modern approach to an old sport.

A more subtle change over the years was the move to faster twist barrels. This year, about sixty percent of CVA rifles will come with barrels that have a 1:32-inch twist. Faster twist barrels are needed for accuracy with conical bullets, and all manufacturers offer them.

Synthetic ramrods have nearly become standard equipment, preventing swelling and breakage, two ailments that can render a frontloader useless. Shooters are opting for a synthetic rod where ten years ago they thought it would ruin the look of a Hawken.

Today, most muzzle-loading accessories are designed for function and are of modern materials to make them more usable. CVA's 4-in-1 loader is an excellent example that combines bullet starter, palm saver, preloader and capping device in a single unit. Had Davy Crockett had access to today's polymers, he'd probably have developed the same thing.

A major change has also occurred in the methods for cleaning the guns. In blackpowder, we forgot what we once knew, "rediscovering" all-natural products to cut down on fouling. By using natural products you can shoot longer between cleaning, perhaps until the end of the season. As an example of this shift, CVA's old bore cleaner sells at ten percent of what it once did.

Thompson/Center's Wonderlube is an all-natural product that has been tested to allow 1000 shots between cleaning, and, most recently, T/C is offering lubes with a pine scent.

Finally, tests have proven the inefficiency of the patched round ball. A conical has almost double the down-

The conical delivers greater downrange energy than the patched round ball and has been a major change in muzzle-loading hunting. That translates into more meat in the freezer.

(Above) Jim Smith with his record book non-typical deer rack. Using up-to-date muzzle-loading equipment, like the Thompson/Center Hawken, helped him bag this twenty-seven-point monster.

Blackpowder shooters have rediscovered natural lubricants and bore cleaners. T/C's #13 Bore Cleaner is non-toxic and, the label says, "FDA Food Grade Rated." Best of all, the "new" compounds work!

range energy at 75 yards. Prelubricated conicals and sabotted bullets have emerged as the tools of the modern hunter.

As the concept of a "modern muzzleloader" began to catch on, other companies began to adapt their technology to meet the growing need. Thompson/Center introduced the ThunderHawk and now has the Fire Hawk, "a new in-line ignition muzzleloading rifle with the look and feel of a modern bolt-action, centerfire rifle."

The T/C Scout carbine and pistol are another recent introduction and the only actions combining a hammer/lock design, with in-line ignition. The fire hole in the nipple of these rifles is oversize, putting plenty of spark into the powder charge. To fire the rifle, cock the hammer and pull the trigger.

Traditions, as the name would imply, introduced several models of in-line rifles but continues quality production of the Hawken, Pennsylvania rifle, Henry Match rifle and others. As with T/C, CVA and other makers, sidelock ignition hasn't changed, but barrel and stocks have. Stainless barrels, scope mounts, and a general shortening has occurred. Sportsmen have learned that the shorter carbine models shoot favorably with the heavier models with longer barrels.

Gary "Doc" White introduced the White Muzzleloading System in 1968. As a gunsmith, he matched elongated bullets with precise barrel design to produce a rifle with superior accuracy that became the W-Series rifles. White bullets are made to .001-inch of tolerance earning them the title "SuperSlug." To meet the needs of traditionalists, G-Series rifles were developed that offer a double safety and improved ignition, yet retain the sidelock design.

Extended range, very accurate muzzleloaders, like the ones above, have enticed another group of shooters into their fold. Since muzzleloaders are legal for most state shotgun seasons for deer, frontloaders can pick up an extra 50 yards of shooting range over shotgun technology.

The fall of 1992 saw two new records set for blackpowder deer. David Wilson's giant Saskatchewan whitetail scored $193^{2}/_{8}$, besting the old record by six points. About the same time, Jim Smith tagged the monstrous non-typical "Browntown Buck" that scored $249^{7}/_{8}$, with a total of twenty-seven antler points.

Although each deer fell to men who had searched promising places to hunt, Wilson's buck was made possible by the evolution of contemporary frontloading gear. Wilson spends the entire fall hunting deer in Canada and is as passionate a whitetail hunter as breathes air. He wanted a muzzle-loading rifle that offered the maximum range and accuracy, and

29th EDITION, 1997 **85**

An interesting and innovative change for muzzleloaders is the use of sabots holding jacketed bullets to add to hunting effectiveness. Toby Bridges took this big 10-point Nebraska whitetail with a Knight MK-85, 100 grains of Pyrodex and a 260-grain jacketed hollowpoint pistol bullet in a sabot.

selected a newcomer on the muzzle-loading scene. Next to Tony Knight's introduction of the MK-85, Gonic Arms has perhaps the most innovative of recent introductions and was the reason Wilson selected a Gonic for his world record quest.

Unlike most muzzleloaders, Gonic rifles shoot "true caliber" bullets. That is, a 50-caliber rifle shoots a 50-caliber bullet and gains added chamber pressure in the process. Fred Rodney, founder of Gonic Arms, had been a part of Thompson/Center's muzzle-loading rifle production team from their inception and used his experience to patent his concept of a "magnum muzzleloader."

Gonic rifles feature a false muzzle and tapered rifling in the muzzle that allows a conical bullet to be consistently loaded. When you seat a bullet in a Gonic rifle, you literally inscribe the conical on the way down. As a result, loads of up to 150 grains of FFg are possible, producing impressive downrange energy, and this helped Wilson tag his record buck at a range in excess of 100 yards.

Smith's huge non-typical buck chased a doe from a national park sanctuary during Virginia's special blackpowder season and came toward the patient hunter. Using a Thompson/Center Hawken, Smith made his first shot count, and upon walking up to the buck he could hardly believe his eyes.

A significant boost to blackpowder shooting has been generated by the National Muzzleloading Rifle Association. The "other" NRA fights for the rights of muzzle-loading shooters in addition to working for increased hunting opportunities. With chapters in all fifty states, the NMRA has helped to give frontloading direction throughout the 1980s and into 1990s.

The "Longhunter Society" was officially established to provide a "book" for muzzle-loading hunters to enter their game and functions, much as the Boone & Crockett and Pope and Young organizations.

Whereas most states have adopted regulations allowing contemporary muzzle-loading equipment, one state holds firm. To hunt in Pennsylvania, one must use a flintlock rifle and patched round ball.

Jim Cullers owns the Fort Chambers Gun Shop (blackpowder only) in Chambersburg, Pennsylvania, and finds that his customers are about evenly split over the flintlock-only policy. Those in favor want to keep the seasons very traditional, while the other half want to enjoy the late hunting season with a rifle that has a more consistent ignition. Of course, allowing percussion rifles to be used in hunting seasons does not prohibit others from using flintlock rifles, but to date, this rationale has not gained a majority view with the game department.

A segment of blackpowder hunting that is very popular with many of Cullers' customers is reenacting. With Gettysburg, Antietam, and other famous Civil War battlefields receiving increased tourist attention, many men and women enjoy reliving historic battles and giving visitors a taste of realistic Civil War life.

Perhaps the best way to predict the future of blackpowder is to compare it to a similar revolution that occurred in the archery industry in the 1970s. In some ways, the compound bow and the modern muzzleloader are similar. Each broke with "traditional" tackle formats and was controversial at first. Both went through a legislative alert, when elected officials worried about taking the sport out of the challenge. Also, once the compound bow became established as the tool of choice by sportsmen, a host of spin-off accessories developed, a phenomenon happening in muzzle-loading today.

For the near future, look for more hunters to become increasingly involved in the sport. As seasons offer more hunting opportunities and muzzle-loading rifle prices remain modest, virtually every hunter in America may want to own one. As demand increases, expect early models to gain value as collector items. Finally, like archery, look for sportsmen who mature in the sport to look back toward traditional rifles. Once hunters become confident and successful with their contemporary frontloaders, it's only natural to go the other way toward where it all began. After we have tamed the in-line system and gotten the bugs out of frontloading, we may be standing in line at gun shops to examine the hottest thing in blackpowder—the flintlock. ●

CATALOG PREVIEW

What's New & Interesting

Here's a quick look at some of the new firearms you'll find in the Complete Compact Catalog

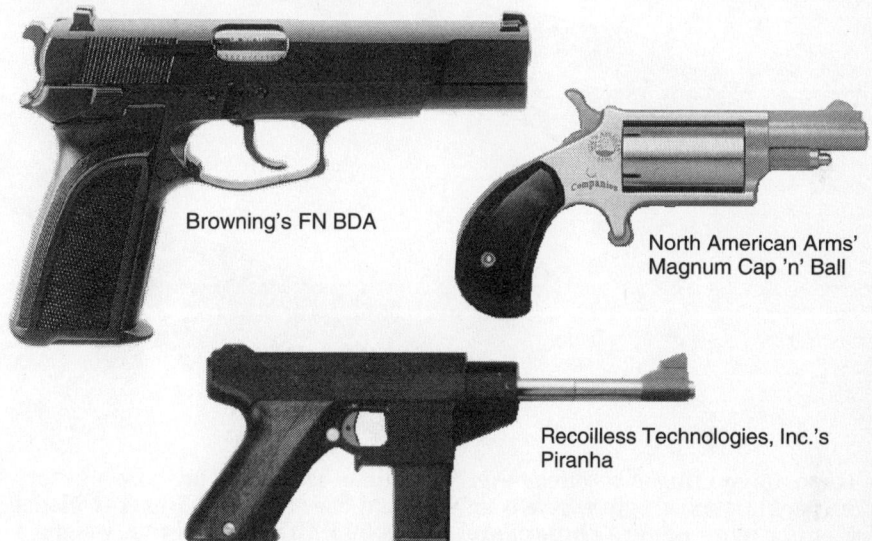

Browning's FN BDA

North American Arms' Magnum Cap 'n' Ball

Recoilless Technologies, Inc.'s Piranha

EACH YEAR, THE editors spend hundreds of man-hours assembling the catalog sections of GUNS ILLUSTRATED, bringing the reader the latest information on new products, keeping up with ever-changing prices, and tracking down new photos from the manufacturers.

In the course of putting all this data together, we see a lot of interesting guns, some of which stick in our minds as being particularly noteworthy. Here we give you an idea of what to notice in the vast expanse of the catalog, a few firearms that caught our eyes.

Handguns

It's amazing how many clones of the 1911-pattern 45s there are. **Brolin Arms** seems to be underway now with theirs, which is especially innovative. They make 45 autos for many tastes, from the nearly bone-stock Legend L45 and the Patriot Series P45C Comp to the Pro Series Pro-Stock and Pro-Comp competition guns. They're made in the U.S. and quality looks excellent. **KBI, Inc.** is importing a 1911 clone made in the Philippines by Armscor that looks competitive.

Browning, who nearly always has something new, this year introduces the FN BDA and BDAO, which are essentially Hi-Power variants in 9mm Parabellum. The Buck Mark family is also growing, with the addition of the new Buck Mark Bullseye that has a 7¼-inch barrel with three machined flutes on each side, Pro Target sights and special grips.

Colt is debuting variations on existing themes: a stainless Model 1991 A1, the Combat Target Model 1911-pattern, the 22 Target with bull barrel, and an Anaconda revolver with scope, mount and rings all covered in Realtree camouflage.

You can read about 'em up front, but the new **Glock** mini-guns, the Models 26 and 27 in 9mm Parabellum and 40 S&W respectively are definitely worth looking at if you're even considering carrying a handgun on your person. They're very compact, extemely reliable and nearly indestructible.

Not everyone is an old hand at handgunning, so **Harrington & Richardson** now has an entry-level revolver that's actually a beginner's package. The Model 929 Sidekick is a nine-shot 22 LR that comes with a lockable storage case, Uncle Mike's nylon holster, and a trial-size package of Tetra gun oil and grease.

For the more esoteric shooter, **Heckler & Koch** now has a Compact version of the USP pistol in 40 S&W, and the Mark 23, a civilian version of the SOCOM military handgun in 45 ACP.

For blackpowder fun shooting, **North American Arms** has adapted their jewel-like Mini-Revolvers to be front-loaders—percussion cap 'n' ball versions of the little stainless rimfires. These should be lots of fun for the charcoal-burning crowd.

Another newcomer, and an interesting one, is the 9mm Parabellum **Piranha** autoloader, said to be recoilless by the maker. With no kick this might be a very good trainer gun.

by HAROLD A. MURTZ

Ruger's Model 96/22 Magnum

Remington's Model 700 ML

Kongsberg's Thumbhole Sporter

Barrett's Model 95

Handgun hunting is becoming ever more popular, and shooters have been asking for more power. **Thompson/Center** has answered the call with the Encore, a very beefy single shot pistol that will fire just about anything you'd care to hang onto. Like 30-06.

The Longer Guns

There are a few new items at **Browning** you should look for, one of which is the BPCR (Black Powder Cartridge Rifle, see the 1995 GUNS ILLUSTRATED, page 58) Model 1885 in 45-70 and 40-65 chamberings that's fully outfitted for that game. The A-Bolt II line is growing with the A-Bolt II Eclipse, featuring a laminated thumbhole stock.

Kongsberg is a Norwegian-made bolt-action rifle that's new to these shores, and it should appeal to hunters who want something a little different. **Marlin** is now back in the bolt-action rifle business with their MR-7. In 270 or 30-06 for now, this is a good-looking rifle with all the best features. The really big-bore shooters should check out the **Barrett** Model 95, a 50 BMG bolt gun that weighs a petite 22 pounds. **Weatherby** rifles are now made in the U.S., and they have a new iteration called the Accumark with fluted stainless barrel and H-S Precision stock with special bedding. It's a powerful, long-range hunting rifle, pure and simple.

There are a few new developments for blackpowder shooters that you should look at. A new name in the business is **Peifer Rifle Co.** They offer the TS93 in 45- or 50-caliber, in four types—styling all their own, but attractive. Be sure to take a good look at the **Remington** Model 700 ML, a muzzle-loading version of the famous Model 700 centerfire rifle. Except for the ramrod hanging beneath the barrel you'd swear this was a standard M700.

Ruger fans are sure to shine on the new lever-action rifles, the Model 96, in 22 LR and 44 Magnum. Both versions use Ruger's detachable rotary magazines. They're nicely executed rifles that should sell like hotcakes. And speaking of lever guns, **USRAC/Winchester** now has a Trapper version of the Model 9422, with $16\frac{1}{2}$-inch barrel and handy $33\frac{1}{8}$-inch overall length.

The Shotguns

Scattergunners will be interested to see the Browning Gold Sporting Clays 12-gauge autoloader, and the Model 802 ES Sporting Clays over/under, more proof that the Clays sport is continuing to grow. So is the slug gun business, and **Savage** has jumped on this wagon with the Model 210F, a rifled bolt action based on their Model 110 rifle.

These are just a few of the new and neat guns we ran across while compiling this even-bigger-than-last-year's catalog section. The lifeblood of the industry is enticing shooters to buy new products, so sit back, browse through these pages and pick out a new addition to your battery. We hope you enjoy the selection.

THE COMPLETE COMPACT CATALOG

GUNDEX®	90-98
Semi-Automatic Handguns	99-129
Competition Handguns	129-137
Double-Action Revolvers	138-147
Single-Action Revolvers	147-152
Miscellaneous Handguns	152-156
Centerfire Rifles—Semi-Automatic	157-162
Centerfire Rifles—Lever & Slide	162-166
Centerfire Rifles—Bolt Action	167-183
Centerfire Rifles—Single Shot	183-187
Drillings, Combination Guns, Double Rifles	188-189
Rimfire Rifles—Semi-Automatic	190-192
Rimfire Rifles—Lever & Slide	193-194
Rimfire Rifles—Bolt Actions & Single Shots	194-199
Competition Rifles—Centerfire & Rimfire	199-206
Shotguns—Semi-Automatic	206-210
Shotguns—Slide Actions	211-214
Shotguns—Over/Unders	215-225
Shotguns—Side By Sides	226-230
Shotguns—Bolt Actions & Single Shots	230-234
Shotguns—Military & Police	234-236
Blackpowder Single Shot Pistols	237-239
Blackpowder Revolvers	239-243
Blackpowder Muskets & Rifles	244-260
Blackpowder Shotguns	260-262
Air Guns—Handguns	262-269
Air Guns—Long Guns	269-280
Scopes & Mounts	281-290
Scope Mounts	291-294
Arms Associations	295-296
Directory of the Arms Trade	297
Product Directory	298
Manufacturers' Directory	313

GUNDEX®

A listing of all the guns in the catalog, by name and model, alphabetically and numerically.

A

A-Square Caesar Bolt-Action Rifle, 168
A-Square Hamilcar Bolt-Action Rifle, 168
A-Square Hannibal Bolt-Action Rifle, 168
A.H. Fox CE Grade Side-by-Side Shotgun, 227
A.H. Fox DE Grade Side-by-Side Shotgun, 227
A.H. Fox Exhibition Grade Side-by-Side Shotgun, 227
A.H. Fox FE Grade Side-by-Side Shotgun, 227
A.H. Fox Side-by-Side Shotgun, 227
A.H. Fox XE Grade Side-by-Side Shotgun, 227
AA Arms AP9 Mini Pistol, 99
AA Arms AP9 Mini/5 Pistol, 99
AA Arms AP9 Pistol, 99
AA Arms AP9 Target Pistol, 99
AA Arms AR9 Autoloading Rifle, 157
AAO Model 2000 50-Caliber Rifle, 167
Accu-Tek Model AT-9SS Pistol, 99
Accu-Tek Model AT-32B Pistol, 99
Accu-Tek Model AT-32SS Pistol, 99
Accu-Tek Model AT-40SS Pistol, 99
Accu-Tek Model AT-45SS Pistol, 99
Accu-Tek Model AT-380B Pistol, 99
Accu-Tek Model AT-380SS Pistol, 99
Accu-Tek Model HC-380SS Pistol, 99
Air Arms TX 200 Air Rifle, 269
Airrow Model A6 Air Pistol, 262
Airrow Model A-8S1P Stealth Air Gun, 269
Airrow Model A-8SRB Stealth Air Gun, 270
American Arms Army 1860 Percussion Revolver, 239
American Arms Aussie Pistol, 99
American Arms Brittany Side-by-Side Shotgun, 225
American Arms Escort Pistol, 100
American Arms Gentry Double Shotgun, 226
American Arms Model P-98 Pistol, 100
American Arms Model PK22 Pistol, 100
American Arms Regulator DLX Single Action Revolver, 147
American Arms Regulator Single Action Revolver, 147
American Arms Silver I Over/Under Shotgun, 215
American Arms Silver II Over/Under Shotgun, 215
American Arms Silver Sporting Over/Under Shotgun, 215
American Arms Silver Upland Lite Over/Under Shotgun, 215
American Arms TS-OU 12 Shotgun, 215
American Arms TS/SS 12 Double Shotgun, 226
American Arms WS/OU 12 Shotgun, 215
American Arms WT/OU 10 Shotgun, 215
American Arms/Franchi Black Magic 48/AL Shotgun, 206
American Derringer Model 1, 152
American Derringer Model 4 Alaskan Survival Derringer, 153
American Derringer Model 4 Derringer, 153
American Derringer Model 6 Derringer, 153
American Derringer Model 7 Ultra Lightweight Derringer, 153
American Derringer Model 10 Lightweight Derringer, 153
American Derringer Model DA 38 Model Derringer, 153
American Derringer Model Lady Derringer, 153
American Derringer Model Texas Commemorative Derringer, 153
American Frontier 1851 Navy Conversion Revolver, 148
American Frontier 1851 Navy Richards & Mason Conversion Revolver, 148
American Frontier 1871-1872 Open-Top Revolver, 147
American Frontier 1871-1872 Pocket Model Revolver, 147
American Frontier Pocket Richards & Mason Navy Revolver, 147
American Frontier Remington New Model Revolver, 147
American Frontier Richards 1860 Army Revolver, 148
AMT 45 ACP Hardballer Long Slide Pistol, 100
AMT 45 ACP Hardballer Pistol, 100
AMT Automag II Pistol, 100
AMT Automag III Pistol, 100
AMT Automag IV Pistol, 100
AMT Back UP Double Action Only Pistol, 101
AMT Back UP II Pistol, 101
AMT Bolt-Action Rifle, 167
AMT Magnum Hunter, 190
Anics A-101 Air Pistol, 262
Anics A-101 Magnum Air Pistol, 262
Anics A-201 Air Revolver, 263
Anschutz 54.18MS E Silhouette Rifle, 200
Anschutz 54.18MS REP Deluxe Silhouette Rifle, 200
Anschutz 54.18MS Standard Silhouette Rifle, 200
Anschutz 64-MS Left Silhouette Rifle, 199
Anschutz 64-MSR Silhouette Rifle, 199
Anschutz 1416D Classic Rifle, 194

Anschutz 1416D Deluxe Rifle, 194
Anschutz 1516D Classic Rifle, 194
Anschutz 1516D Deluxe Rifle, 194
Anschutz 1700D Custom Rifle, 331, 194
Anschutz 1808D-RT Super Running Target Rifle, 200
Anschutz 1827B Biathlon Rifle, 199
Anschutz 1827BT Fortner Biathlon Rifle, 199
Anschutz 1903 Match Rifle, 200
Anschutz 1907 ISU Standard Match Rifle, 200
Anschutz 1910 Super Match Rifle, 200
Anschutz 1911 Prone Match Rifle, 200
Anschutz 1913 Super Match Rifle, 200
Anschutz 2002 Match Air Rifle, 270
Anschutz 2002D-RT Running Target Air Rifle, 270
Anschutz Achiever Bolt-Action Rifle, 194
Anschutz Achiever ST Super Target Rifle, 199
Anschutz BR-50 Benchrest Rifle, 199
Anschutz Exemplar Bolt-Action Pistol, 153
Anschutz Super Match Model 2007 ISU Standard Rifle, 200
Anschutz Super Match Model 2013 Rifle, 200
Argentine Hi-Power Detective Model Pistol, 101
Argentine Hi-Power Pistol, 101
Arizaga Model 31 Double Shotgun, 226
ArmaLite AR-10(T) Target Model Rifle, 201
ArmaLite AR-10A4 Autoloading Rifle, 157
ArmaLite M15A2 Post Ban Golden Eagle Rifle, 157
ArmaLite M15A2 Post Ban Heavy Barrel Rifle, 157
ArmaLite M15A2 Post Ban M4C Carbine, 157
ArmaLite M15A4 Post Ban M4A1C Carbine, 157
Armoury Army 1860 Percussion Revolver, 239
Armoury R140 Hawken Rifle, 244
Armscor M014P Standard Rifle, 194
Armscor M-12Y Youth Rifle, 195
Armscor M-14Y Youth Rifle, 194
Armscor M-20C Auto Carbine, 190
Armscor M-20P Standard Rifle, 190
Armscor M-30 Field Pump Shotgun, 211
Armscor M-30 Security Shotgun, 234
Armscor M-30 Special Purpose Shotgun, 234
Armscor M-30D Special Purpose Shotgun, 234
Armscor M-30R6 Security Shotgun, 234
Armscor M-30R8 Security Shotgun, 234
Armscor M-30SAS Special Purpose Shotgun, 234
Armscor M-200DC Revolver, 138
Armscor M-1400S Classic Bolt-Action Rifle, 194
Armscor M-1400SC Super Classic Rifle, 195
Armscor M-1500S Classic Rifle, 195
Armscor M-1500SC Super Classic Rifle, 195
Armscor M-1600 Auto Rifle, 190
Armscor M-1800S Classic Bolt-Action Rifle, 167
Armscor M-1800SC Super Classic Rifle, 167
Armscor M-1911-A1P Pistol, 100
Armscor M-2000S Classic Auto Rifle, 190
Armscor M-2000SC Super Classic Rifle, 190
Armscor Model AK22 Auto Rifle, 190
Armsport 1050 Series Double Shotgun, 226
Armsport 1863 Sharps Carbine, 244
Armsport 1863 Sharps Rifle, 244
Armsport 1866 Sharps Carbine, 183
Armsport 1866 Sharps Rifle, 183
Armsport 2700 Series Over/Under Shotgun, 215
Armsport 2730/2731 Over/Under Shotgun, 215
Armsport 2733/2735 Over/Under Shotgun, 215
Armsport 2741 Over/Under Shotgun, 215
Armsport 2742 Sporting Clays Over/Under Shotgun, 215
Armsport 2744 Sporting Clays Over/Under Shotgun, 215
Armsport 2750 Sporting Clays Over/Under Shotgun, 215
Armsport 2751 Sporting Clays Over/Under Shotgun, 215
Armsport Army 1860 Percussion Revolver, 239
Army 1851 Percussion Revolver, 240
Army 1860 Percussion Revolver, 239
Arnold Arms African Synthetic Rifle, 168
Arnold Arms African Trophy Rifle, 168
Arnold Arms Alaskan Bush Rifle, 167
Arnold Arms Alaskan Trophy Rifle, 167
Arnold Arms Grand African Rifle, 168
Arnold Arms Grand Alaskan Rifle, 167
Arnold Arms High Country Mountain Rifle, 167
Arnold Arms Safari Rifle, 168
Arnold Arms Serengeti Synthetic Rifle, 168
Arrieta Sidelock Double Shotguns, 226
Arrieta Sidelock Model 557 Double Shotgun, 226
Arrieta Sidelock Model 570 Double Shotgun, 226
Arrieta Sidelock Model 578 Double Shotgun, 226
Arrieta Sidelock Model 600 Imperial Double Shotgun, 226
Arrieta Sidelock Model 601 Imperial Tiro Double Shotgun, 226
Arrieta Sidelock Model 801 Double Shotgun, 226
Arrieta Sidelock Model 802 Double Shotgun, 226

Arrietta Sidelock Model 803 Double Shotgun, 226
Arrietta Sidelock Model 871 Double Shotgun, 226
Arrietta Sidelock Model 872 Double Shotgun, 226
Arrietta Sidelock Model 873 Double Shotgun, 226
Arrietta Sidelock Model 874 Double Shotgun, 226
Arrietta Sidelock Model 875 Double Shotgun, 226
ARS Hunting Master AR6 Air Rifle, 270
ARS/Career 707 Air Rifle, 270
ARS/Farco CO_2 Air Shotgun, 270
ARS/Farco CO_2 Stainless Steel Air Rifle, 270
ARS/Farco FP Survival Air Rifle, 270
ARS/King Hunting Master 900 Air Rifle, 270
ARS/King Hunting Master AR Air Rifle, 270
ARS/Magnum 6 Air Rifle, 271
ARS/QB77 Deluxe Air Rifle, 271
Astra A-70 Pistol, 101
Astra A-75 Decocker Pistol, 101
Astra A-100 Pistol, 101
Auto-Ordnance 27 A-1 Thompson, 157
Auto-Ordnance 45ACP General Model Pistol, 102
Auto-Ordnance 1911A1 Competition Model Pistol, 102
Auto-Ordnance 1911A1 Competition Model Pistol, 129
Auto-Ordnance 1911A1 Pistol, 102
Auto-Ordnance Thompson M1, 157
Auto-Ordnance ZG-51 Pit Bull Pistol, 102
AyA Boxlock Shotgun, 226
AyA Model 1 Double Shotgun, 227
AyA Model 2 Double Shotgun, 227
AyA Model 4 Deluxe Double Shotgun, 226
AyA Model 4 Double Shotgun, 226
AyA Model 53 Double Shotgun, 227
AyA Model 56 Double Shotgun, 227
AyA Model 931 Double Shotgun, 226
AyA Model XXV Double Shotgun, 226
AyA Model XXV Double Shotgun, 227
AyA Sidelock Double Shotguns, 227

B

Baby Bretton Model Fairplay Over/Under Shotgun, 215
Baby Bretton Over/Under Shotgun, 215
Baby Bretton Spring Deluxe Over/Under Shotgun, 215
Baby Bretton Spring Standard Over/Under Shotgun, 215
Baby Dragoon 1848 Percussion Revolver, 240
Baby Eagle Auto Pistol, 102
Baer 1911 Bullseye Wadcutter Pistol, 130
Baer 1911 Concept I Pistol, 102
Baer 1911 Concept III Pistol, 102
Baer 1911 Concept IV Pistol, 102
Baer 1911 Concept V Pistol, 102
Baer 1911 Concept VI Pistol, 102
Baer 1911 Concept VII Pistol, 102
Baer 1911 Concept VIII Pistol, 102
Baer 1911 Concept IX Pistol, 102
Baer 1911 Concept X Pistol, 102
Baer 1911 Custom Carry Pistol, 103
Baer 1911 National Match Hardball Pistol, 130
Baer 1911 Premier II Pistol, 102
Baer 1911 Prowler III Pistol, 102
Baer 1911 S.R.P. Pistol, 103
Baer 1911 Target Master Pistol, 130
Baer 1911 Ultimate Master Combat Pistol, 129
Baer 1911 Ultimate Master Steel Special Pistol, 129
Baer Lightweight 22 Pistol, 103
Baikal IJ-18 Single Barrel Shotgun, 230
Baikal IJ-18EM Single Barrel Shotgun, 230
Baikal IJ-18M Single Barrel Shotgun, 230
Baikal IJ-27 EIC Over/Under Shotgun, 215
Baikal IJ-27 Over/Under Shotgun, 215
Baikal IJ-27EM Over/Under Shotgun, 215
Baikal IJ-27M Over/Under Shotgun, 215
Baikal IJ-43 Double Shotgun, 227
Baikal IJ-43EM Double Shotgun, 227
Baikal IJ-43M Double Shotgun, 227
Baikal IJ-70 Pistol, 103
Baikal IJ-70HC Pistol, 103
Baikal TOZ-34P Over/Under Shotgun, 216
Barrett Model 82A-1 Autoloading Rifle, 158
Barrett Model 95 Bolt-Action Rifle, 168
Beeman Bearcub Air Rifle, 271
Beeman Crow Magnum Air Rifle, 271
Beeman HW70A Air Pistol, 264
Beeman Kodiak Air Rifle, 272
Beeman Mako Air Rifle, 272
Beeman Mako FT Air Rifle, 272
Beeman P1 Magnum Air Pistol, 263
Beeman P2 Match Air Pistol, 263
Beeman R1 Air Rifle, 272
Beeman R1 Carbine, 272
Beeman R1 Laser Air Rifle, 272
Beeman R1-AW Carbine, 272

Beeman R6 Air Rifle, 272
Beeman R7 Air Rifle, 272
Beeman R8 Air Rifle, 272
Beeman R9 Air Rifle, 272
Beeman R11 Air Rifle, 273
Beeman RX-1 Gas-Spring Magnum Air Rifle, 273
Beeman S1 Magnum Air Rifle, 273
Beeman Super 12 Air Rifle, 273
Beeman/Feinwerkbau 65 MKII Air Pistol, 263
Beeman/Feinwerkbau 102 Air Pistol, 263
Beeman/Feinwerkbau 300-S Mini-Match Air Rifle, 271
Beeman/Feinwerkbau 300-S Running Target Air Rifle, 271
Beeman/Feinwerkbau 300-S Series Match Air Rifle, 271
Beeman/Feinwerkbau 601 Air Rifle, 271
Beeman/Feinwerkbau 602 Air Rifle, 271
Beeman/Feinwerkbau C55 CO_2 Rapid Fire Pistol, 263
Beeman/Feinwerkbau C60 CO_2 Air Rifle, 271
Beeman/Feinwerkbau C-60 Running Target Air Rifle, 271
Beeman/Feinwerkbau C-62 CO_2 Air Rifle, 271
Beeman/Feinwerkbau Mini C60 Air Rifle, 271
Beeman/Feinwerkbau P30 Match Air Pistol, 263
Beeman/HW97 Air Rifle, 272
Beeman/Webley Hurricane Air Pistol, 264
Beeman/Webley Nemesis Air Pistol, 264
Beeman/Webley Tempest Air Pistol, 264
Benelli Black Eagle Competition Auto Shotgun, 206
Benelli Executive Series Type I Shotgun, 207
Benelli Executive Series Type II Shotgun, 207
Benelli Executive Series Type III Shotgun, 207
Benelli M1 Sporting Special Auto Shotgun, 207
Benelli M1 Super 90 Defense Shotgun, 235
Benelli M1 Super 90 Field Auto Shotgun, 207
Benelli M1 Super 90 Shotgun, 235
Benelli M1 Super 90 Tactical Shotgun, 235
Benelli M3 Super 90 Pump/Auto Shotgun, 235
Benelli Montefeltro Super 90 Shotgun, 207
Benelli MP 90S Match Pistol, 130
Benelli MP 95E Match Pistol, 130
Benelli Super Black Eagle Shotgun, 207
Benelli Super Black Eagle Slug Gun, 207
Benjamin Sheridan CO_2 Air Rifles, 273
Benjamin Sheridan CO_2 Pellet Pistols, 264
Benjamin Sheridan E17 Pellet Pistol, 264
Benjamin Sheridan E20 Pellet Pistol, 264
Benjamin Sheridan E22 Pellet Pistol, 264
Benjamin Sheridan EB17 Pellet Pistol, 264
Benjamin Sheridan EB20 Pellet Pistol, 264
Benjamin Sheridan EB22 Pellet Pistol, 264
Benjamin Sheridan FB9 Air Rifle, 273
Benjamin Sheridan G392 Air Rifle, 273
Benjamin Sheridan G397 Air Rifle, 273
Benjamin Sheridan H17 Pellet Pistol, 264
Benjamin Sheridan H20 Pellet Pistol, 264
Benjamin Sheridan H22 Pellet Pistol, 264
Benjamin Sheridan HB17 Pellet Pistol, 264
Benjamin Sheridan HB20 Pellet Pistol, 264
Benjamin Sheridan HB22 Pellet Pistol, 264
Benjamin Sheridan Model 392 (Pump-up) Air Rifles, 273
Benjamin Sheridan Model 397 (Pump-up) Air Rifles, 273
Benjamin Sheridan Model 397C (Pump-up) Carbine, 273
Benjamin Sheridan Model S392 (Pump-up) Air Rifles, 273
Benjamin Sheridan Model S397 (Pump-up) Air Rifles, 273
Benjamin Sheridan Pneumatic (Pump-up) Air Rifles, 273
Benjamin Sheridan Pneumatic Pellet Pistols, 264
Beretta 390 Gold Mallard Auto Shotgun, 207
Beretta 390 Silver Mallard Auto Shotgun, 207
Beretta 390 Slug Shotgun, 207
Beretta 390 Sport Skeet Shotgun, 208
Beretta 390 Sport Sporting Shotgun, 208
Beretta 390 Sport Trap Shotgun, 208
Beretta 390 Super Skeet Shotgun, 208
Beretta 390 Super Trap Shotgun, 208
Beretta 390 Waterfowl/Turkey Auto Shotgun, 207
Beretta 682 Continental Course Sporting Over/Under Shotgun, 216
Beretta 682 Gold Skeet Over/Under Shotgun, 216
Beretta 682 Gold Sporting Over/Under Shotgun, 216
Beretta 682 Gold Trap Over/Under Shotgun, 216
Beretta 682 Onyx Sporting Over/Under Shotgun, 216
Beretta 682 Super Skeet Over/Under Shotgun, 216
Beretta 682 Super Trap Over/Under Shotgun, 216
Beretta 686 Essential Over/Under Shotgun, 216
Beretta 686 Field Over/Under Shotgun, 217
Beretta 686 Silver Perdiz Skeet Over/Under Shotgun, 216
Beretta 686 Silver Pigeon Sporting Shotgun, 216
Beretta 686 Silver Pigeon Field Over/Under Shotgun, 217
Beretta 686 Silver Pigeon Field Set Over/Under Shotgun, 217
Beretta 686EL Gold Perdiz Over/Under Shotgun, 217
Beretta 687 Diamond Pigeon EELL Sporter Shotgun, 216
Beretta 687 EELL Diamond Pigeon Skeet Over/Under Shotgun, 216
Beretta 687 EELL Diamond Pigeon Trap Over/Under Shotgun, 216

Beretta 687 Silver Pigeon Sporting Combo Shotgun, 216
Beretta 687 Silver Pigeon Sporting Shotgun, 216
Beretta 687EELL Diamond Pigeon Field Combo Over/Under Shotgun, 217
Beretta 687EELL Diamond Pigeon Field Over/Under Shotgun, 217
Beretta 687EL Gold Pigeon Field Over/Under Shotgun, 217
Beretta 687EL Gold Pigeon Sporting Shotgun, 216
Beretta 687L Silver Piegeon Field Over/Under Shotgun, 217
Beretta 687L Silver Pigeon Sporting Shotgun, 216
Beretta A-303 Auto Shotgun, 207
Beretta A-303 Sporting Clays Shotgun, 207
Beretta A-303 Upland Model Shotgun, 207
Beretta A-303 Youth Gun, 207
Beretta ASE Gold Sporting Clays, Over/Under Shotgun, 216
Beretta Express SSO6 Gold O/U Double Rifle, 188
Beretta Express SSO6 O/U Double Rifle, 188
Beretta Express SSO O/U Double Rifle, 188
Beretta Model 21 Bobcat Pistol, 104
Beretta Model 80 Cheetah Series Pistol, 103
Beretta Model 84 Cheetah Pistol, 103
Beretta Model 85 Cheetah Pistol, 103
Beretta Model 86 Cheetah Pistol, 103
Beretta Model 89 Gold Standard Pistol, 130
Beretta Model 92D Centurion Pistol, 104
Beretta Model 92D Pistol, 104
Beretta Model 92F Stainless Pistol, 103
Beretta Model 92FD Centurion Pistol, 104
Beretta Model 92FS Pistol, 103
Beretta Model 96 Centurion Pistol, 104
Beretta Model 96 Pistol, 104
Beretta Model 96D Centurion Pistol, 104
Beretta Model 96D Pistol, 104
Beretta Model 452 Sidelock Shotgun, 227
Beretta Model 452EELL Sidelock Shotgun, 227
Beretta Model 455 SxS Express Rifle, 188
Beretta Model 950 Jeffire Pistol, 104
Beretta Model 1201FP3 Auto Shotgun, 235
Beretta Model 3032 Tomcat Pistol, 104
Beretta Model 8000/8040 Pistol, 104
Beretta Model 8000D Pistol, 104
Beretta Model 8040D Pistol, 104
Beretta Model Bernardelli PO18 DA Pistol, 104
Beretta Model SO5 Over/Under Shotgun, 216
Beretta Model SO6 Over/Under Shotgun, 216
Beretta Model SO6EELL Over/Under Shotgun, 216
Beretta Model SO9 Over/Under Shotgun, 216
Beretta Model Ultralight Onyx Over/Under Shotgun, 216
Beretta Onyx 686 Silver Pigeon Sporting Over/Under Shotgun, 216
Beretta Onyx Sporting Over/Under Shotgun, 216
Beretta Over/Under Field Shotguns, 217
Beretta Pintail Auto Shotgun, 208
Beretta Series 682 Gold Skeet, Trap Over/Under Shotguns, 216
Beretta Sporting Clays Over/Under Shotgun, 216
Bernardelli Model 69 Target Pistol, 130
Bernardelli Model AMR Pistol, 105
Bernardelli Model USA Pistol, 105
Bernardelli P. One DA Pistol, 105
Bernardelli P. One Practical VB Pistol, 105
Bernardelli PO18 Compact DA Pistol, 104
Bersa Series 95 Pistol, 105
Bersa Thunder 9 Pistol, 105
Bersa Thunder 22 Pistol, 105
Bersa Thunder 380 Pistol, 105
BF Single Shot Pistol, 130
Blaser R93 Bolt-Action Rifle, 169
Blaser R93 Deluxe Bolt-Action Rifle, 169
Blaser R93 Safari Bolt-Action Rifle, 169
Blaser R93 Safari Deluxe Bolt-Action Rifle, 169
Blaser R93 Safari Super Deluxe Bolt-Action Rifle, 169
Blaser R93 Super Deluxe Bolt-Action Rifle, 169
Bostonian Percussion Rifle, 244
BRNO Tau-7 CO_2 Match Pistol, 264
BRNO Tau-200 Air Rifle, 273
BRNO Tau-200 Junior Match Air Rifle, 273
BRNO ZKM 611 Auto Rifle, 190
BRNO ZKM 621 Auto Rifle, 190
Brolin Legend L45 Standard Pistol, 105
Brolin Legend L45C Compact Pistol, 105
Brolin P45C Compact Carrycomp Pistol, 106
Brolin Patriot P45 Standard Carrycomp Pistol, 106
Brolin Pro-Comp Competition Pistol, 131
Brolin Pro-Stock Competition Pistol, 131
Brown Model Single Shot Rifle, 183
Browning 425 Golden Clays Over/Under Shotgun, 218
Browning 425 Sporting Clays Over/Under Shotgun, 218
Browning 425 WSSF Over/Under Shotgun, 218
Browning A-Bolt Hunter Shotgun, 230
Browning A-Bolt II Composite Stalker Rifle, 169
Browning A-Bolt II Eclipse Rifle, 170
Browning A-Bolt II Gold Medallion Rifle, 169
Browning A-Bolt II Hunter Rifle, 169
Browning A-Bolt II Left Hand Rifle, 169

Browning A-Bolt II Medallion Rifle, 169
Browning A-Bolt II Micro Medallion Rifle, 169
Browning A-Bolt II Rifle, 169
Browning A-Bolt II Short Action Composite Rifle, 169
Browning A-Bolt II Short Action Hunter Rifle, 169
Browning A-Bolt II Short Action Medallion Rifle, 169
Browning A-Bolt II Short Action Rifle, 169
Browning A-Bolt II Stainless Stalker Rifle, 169
Browning A-Bolt II Varmint Rifle, 169
Browning A-Bolt Shotgun, 230
Browning A-Bolt Stalker Shotgun, 230
Browning Auto-5 Light 12 Auto Shotgun, 208
Browning Auto-5 Light 20 Auto Shotgun, 208
Browning Auto-5 Magnum 12 Shotgun, 209
Browning Auto-5 Magnum 20 Shotgun, 209
Browning Auto-5 Stalker Shotgun, 208
Browning Auto-22 Grade VI Rifle, 190
Browning Auto-22 Rifle, 190
Browning BAR Mark II Safari Magnum Rifle, 158
Browning BAR Mark II Safari Semi-Auto Rifle, 158
Browning BDA-380 DA Pistol, 106
Browning BDM DA Pistol, 106
Browning BL-22 Lever-Action Rifle, 193
Browning BPS Buck Special, Pump Shotgun, 211
Browning BPS Game Gun Deer Special Pump Shotgun, 211
Browning BPS Game Gun Turkey Special Pump Shotgun, 211
Browning BPS Ladies and Youth Model Pump Shotgun, 211
Browning BPS Pigeon Grade Pump Shotgun, 211
Browning BPS Pump Shotgun, 211
Browning BPS Stalker Pump Shotgun, 211
Browning BT-100 Grade I Trap Shotgun, 231
Browning BT-100 Trap Shotgun, 231
Browning Buck Mark 22 Pistol, 107
Browning Buck Mark Bullseye Pistol, 131
Browning Buck Mark Field 5.5 Pistol, 131
Browning Buck Mark Plus Pistol, 107
Browning Buck Mark Silhouette Pistol, 131
Browning Buck Mark Target 5.5 Gold Pistol, 131
Browning Buck Mark Target 5.5 Nickel Pistol, 131
Browning Buck Mark Target 5.5 Pistol, 131
Browning Buck Mark Unlimited Match Pistol, 131
Browning Buck Mark Varmint Pistol, 107
Browning Capitan Hi-Power Pistol, 106
Browning Citori Grade I Hunting Over/Under Shotgun, 217
Browning Citori Grade I Lightning Over/Under Shotgun, 217
Browning Citori Grade III Lightning Over/Under Shotgun, 217
Browning Citori Grade VI Lightning Over/Under Shotgun, 217
Browning Citori Gran Lightning Over/Under Shotgun, 217
Browning Citori Over/Under Shotgun, 217
Browning Citori Over/Under Skeet Special Over/Under Shotgun, 217
Browning Citori Special Trap Golden Clays Over/Under Shotgun, 217
Browning Citori Special Trap Grade I Over/Under Shotgun, 217
Browning Citori Special Trap Grade III Over/Under Shotgun, 217
Browning Citori Ultra Golden Clays Over/Under Shotgun, 217
Browning Citori Ultra Sporter Shotgun, 217
Browning Euro-Bolt II Rifle, 169
Browning FN BDA/BDAO Pistol, 106
Browning Gold 10 Auto Shotgun, 208
Browning Gold 10 Stalker Auto Shotgun, 208
Browning Gold Hunter Auto Shotgun, 208
Browning Gold Sporting Clays Auto Shotgun, 208
Browning Hi-Power 40 S&W Mark III Pistol, 106
Browning Hi-Power HP-Practical Pistol, 106
Browning Hi-Power Mark III Pistol, 106
Browning Hi-Power Pistol, 106
Browning Light Sporting 802 ES Over/Under Shotgun, 217
Browning Lightning BLR Lever-Action Rifle, 162
Browning Lightning BLR Long Action Rifle, 162
Browning Lightning Sporting Clays Over/Under Shotgun, 217
Browning Micro Buck Mark Pistol, 107
Browning Micro Buck Mark Plus Pistol, 106
Browning Micro Citori Lightning Over/Under Shotgun, 217
Browning Micro Recoiless Trap Shotgun, 230
Browning Model 1885 BPCR Rifle, 184
Browning Model 1885 High Wall Single Shot Rifle, 184
Browning Model 1885 Low Wall Rifle, 184
Browning Recoiless Trap Shotgun, 230
Browning Special Sporting Clays Over/Under Shotgun, 217
Browning Superlight Citori Grade I Over/Under Shotgun, 217
Browning Superlight Citori Grade III Over/Under Shotgun, 217

GUNDEX

Browning Superlight Citori Grade VI Over/Under Shotgun, 217
Browning Superlight Citori Over/Under Shotgun, 217
Bryco Model 38 Pistol, 107
Bryco Model 48 Pistol, 107
Bryco Model 59 Pistol, 107
BSA 240 Magnum Air Pistol, 265
BSA Supersport MK II Air Rifle, 274
BSA Supersport MK II Carbine, 274
Bushmaster M17S Bullpup Rifle, 158
Bushmaster Shorty XM-15 E2S Carbine, 158
Bushmaster Shorty XM-15 E2S Dissipator Carbine, 158
Bushmaster XM-15 E2S Target Model Rifle, 201
Bushmaster XM-15 E2S V-Match Rifle, 201

C

C.S. Richmond 1863 Musket, 255
Cabanas Espronceda IV Bolt-Action Rifle, 195
Cabanas Laser Rifle, 195
Cabanas Leyre Bolt-Action Rifle, 195
Cabanas Master Bolt-Action Rifle, 195
Cabanas Mini 82 Youth Bolt-Action Rifle, 195
Cabanas Model R83 Bolt-Action Rifle, 195
Cabanas Pony Youth Bolt-Action Rifle, 195
Cabanas Varmint Bolt-Action Rifle, 195
Cabela's 1858 Henry Replica, 162
Cabela's 1860 Henry Replica, 162
Cabela's 1866 Winchester Replica, 162
Cabela's 1873 Winchester Replica, 162
Cabela's Army 1860 Percussion Revolver, 239
Cabela's Blackpowder Shotgun, 260
Cabela's Blue Ridge Carbine, 244
Cabela's Blue Ridge Rifle, 244
Cabela's Cattleman's Carbine, 162
Cabela's Paterson Revolver, 240
Cabela's Red River Rifle, 244
Cabela's Rolling Block Muzzleloader Carbine, 244
Cabela's Rolling Block Muzzleloader, 244
Cabela's Sharps Sporting Rifle, 184
Cabela's Sharps Sporting Rifle, 244
Cabela's Sporterized Hawken Hunter Carbine, 244
Cabela's Sporterized Hawken Hunter Rifle, 244
Cabela's Traditional Hawken Rifle, 244
Calico Liberty 50 Carbine, 158
Calico Liberty 100 Carbine, 158
Calico M-110 Pistol, 107
Century Centurion 14 Sporter Rifle, 170
Century Centurion Over/Under Shotgun, 218
Century Custom Sporting Rifle, 170
Century Deluxe Custom Sporter Rifle, 170
Century Enfield Sporter #4 Rifle, 170
Century FEG P9R Pistol, 107
Century FEG P9RK Pistol, 107
Century Gun Dist. Model 100 Single Action Revolver, 148
Century International FAL Sporter Rifle, 158
Century International M-14 Semi-Auto Rifle, 159
Century Swedish Sporter #38 Rifle, 170
Century Tiger Dragunov Rifle, 159
Charles Daly Deluxe Over/Under Shotgun, 219
Charles Daly Field Grade Over/Under Shotgun, 219
Chipmunk Single Shot Rifle, 195
Churchill Turkey Auto Shotgun, 209
Churchill Windsor IV Over/Under Shotgun, 218
Churchill Windsor Sporting Clays Over/Under Shotgun, 218
Cimarron 1866 Winchester Replicas, 163
Cimarron 1873 30" Express Rifle, 163
Cimarron 1873 Frontier Six Shooter Revolver, 148
Cimarron 1873 Saddle Ring Carbine, 163
Cimarron 1873 Short Rifle, 163
Cimarron 1873 Sporting Rifle, 163
Cimarron New Thunderer Revolver, 148
Cimarron Rough Rider Artillery Model Single Action Revolver, 148
Cimarron U.S. Cavalry Model Single Action Revolver, 148
Colt 10mm Delta Elite Pistol, 108
Colt 38 SF-VI Revolver, 138
Colt 1847 Walker Percussion Revolver, 240
Colt 1849 Pocket Dragoon Percussion Revolver, 240
Colt 1851 Navy Percussion Revolver, 240
Colt 1860 Army Percussion Revolver, 240
Colt 1860 Army Police Percussion Revolver, 239
Colt 1860 Cavalry Model Percussion Revolver, 240
Colt 1861 Navy Percussion Revolver, 240
Colt 1862 Pocket Police Trapper Model Percussion Revolver, 241
Colt Anaconda Revolver, 138
Colt Combat Commander Pistol, 108
Colt Combat Elite MK IV/Series 80 Pistol, 108
Colt Combat Target Model Pistol, 109
Colt Delta Gold Cup Pistol, 131
Colt Double Eagle MK II/Series 90 Combat Comm. Pistol, 108
Colt Double Eagle MK II/Series 90 DA Pistol, 108
Colt Double Eagle Officer's ACP Pistol, 108
Colt Gold Cup National Match MK IV/Series 80 Pistol, 131
Colt Government Model 380 Pistol, 108
Colt Government Model MK IV/Series 80 Pistol, 108
Colt King Cobra Revolver, 138
Colt Lightweight Commander MK IV/Series 80 Pistol, 108
Colt Match Target Competition HBAR II Rifle, 201
Colt Match Target Competition HBAR Rifle, 201
Colt Match Target HBAR Rifle, 201
Colt Match Target Lightweight Rifle, 159
Colt Match Target Model Rifle, 201
Colt Model 1861 Musket, 244
Colt Model 1991 A1 Commander Pistol, 108
Colt Model 1991 A1 Compact Pistol, 108
Colt Model 1991 A1 Pistol, 108
Colt Mustang 380 Pistol, 109
Colt Mustang Plus II Pistol, 109
Colt Mustang Pocketlite Pistol, 109
Colt Officer's ACP MK IV/SEries 80 Pistol, 109
Colt Python Revolver, 138
Colt Single Action Army Revolver, 148
Colt Third Model Dragoon Percussion Revolver, 241
Colt's 22 Automatic Pistol, 107
Colt's 22 Target Pistol, 107
Competitor Single Shot Pistol, 131
Confederate Navy 1851 Percussion Revolver, 241
Connecticut Valley Classics Classic Field Grade I Over/Under Shotgun, 218
Connecticut Valley Classics Classic Field Grade II Over/Under Shotgun, 218
Connecticut Valley Classics Classic Field Grade III Over/Under Shotgun, 218
Connecticut Valley Classics Classic Field Over/Under Shotgun, 218
Connecticut Valley Classics Classic Field Waterfowler Over/Under Shotgun, 218
Connecticut Valley Classics Classic Flyer Over/Under Shotgun, 218
Connecticut Valley Classics Classic Skeet Over/Under Shotgun, 218
Connecticut Valley Classics Classic Sporter Over/Under Shotgun, 218
Connecticut Valley Classics Sporter Grade I Over/Under Shotgun, 218
Connecticut Valley Classics Sporter Grade II Over/Under Shotgun, 218
Connecticut Valley Classics Sporter Grade III Over/Under Shotgun, 218
Connecticut Valley Classics Women's Classic Sporter Over/Under Shotgun, 218
Cook & Brother Confederate Carbine, 245
Cook & Brother Confederate Rifle, 245
Coonan 357 Magnum Classic Model Pistol, 109
Coonan 357 Magnum Pistol, 109
Coonan Compact Cadet 357 Magnum Pistol, 109
Cooper Arms Model 21 Varmint Extreme Rifle, 170
Cooper Arms Model 22 Pro Varmint Extreme Rifle, 170
Cooper Arms Model 36 BR-50 Rifle, 201
Cooper Arms Model 36 Classic Sporter Rifle, 195
Cooper Arms Model 36 Custom Classic Rifle, 195
Cooper Arms Model 36 Featherweight Rifle, 195
Cooper Arms Model 36 Montana Trailblazer Rifle, 195
Cooper Arms Model 40 Centerfire Sporter Rifle, 171
Copperhead Black Fang Air Pistol, 265
Copperhead Black Fire Air Rifle, 274
Copperhead Black Lightning Air Rifle, 274
Copperhead Black Serpent Air Rifle, 274
Copperhead Black Venom Air Pistol, 265
Crosman Auto Air II Air Pistol, 265
Crosman Model 66 Powermaster Air Rifle, 274
Crosman Model 66RT Powermaster Air Rifle, 274
Crosman Model 357 Air Pistol, 265
Crosman Model 664SB Powermaster Air Rifle, 274
Crosman Model 664X Powermaster Air Rifle, 274
Crosman Model 760 Pumpmaster Air Rifle, 274
Crosman Model 760SB Pumpmaster Air Rifle, 274
Crosman Model 782 Black Diamond Air Rifle, 274
Crosman Model 795 Spring Master Air Rifle, 274
Crosman Model 1008 Repeat Air Pistol, 265
Crosman Model 1008SB Air Pistol, 265
Crosman Model 1077 Repeatair Air Rifle, 274
Crosman Model 1077SB Silver Series Air Rifle, 274
Crosman Model 1322 Air Pistol, 265
Crosman Model 1357 Air Pistol, 265
Crosman Model 1377 Air Pistol, 265
Crosman Model 1395 Backpacker Air Rifle, 274
Crosman Model 2100 Classic Air Rifle, 275
Crosman Model 2100SB Classic Air Rifle, 275
Crosman Model 2200 Magnum Air Rifle, 275
Crucelegui Hermanos Model 140 Double Shotgun, 228
Cumberland Mountain Blackpowder Rifle, 245
Cumberland Mountain Plateau Rifle, 184
CVA Apollo Brown Bear Rifle, 245
CVA Apollo Classic Rifle, 245
CVA Apollo Comet Rifle, 245
CVA Apollo Dominator Rifle, 245
CVA Apollo Shadow Rifle, 245
CVA Bobcat Hunter Rifle, 245
CVA Bobcat Rifle, 245
CVA Buckmaster Rifle, 245
CVA Classic Turkey Double Shotgun, 260
CVA Express Rifle, 246
CVA Frontier Hunter Carbine, 246
CVA Grey Wolf Rifle, 247
CVA Hawken Pistol, 237
CVA Hawken Rifle, 246
CVA Kentucky Rifle, 246
CVA Lynx Rifle, 246
CVA Plainshunter Rifle, 246
CVA Plainsman Rifle, 246
CVA Silver Wolf Rifle, 247
CVA St. Louis Hawken Classic Rifle, 246
CVA Staghorn Rifle, 245
CVA Timber Wolf Rifle, 247
CVA Trapper Percussion Shotgun, 261
CVA Varmint Rifle, 247
CVA Wolf Series Rifles, 247
CZ 75 Auto Pistol, 109
CZ 75 Compact Pistol, 109
CZ 75 Semi-Compact Pistol, 109
CZ 83 DA Pistol, 109
CZ 85 Auto Pistol, 109
CZ 85 Combat Pistol, 109
CZ 100 Auto Pistol, 110
CZ 527 Bolt-Action Rifle, 171
CZ 550 Bolt-Action Rifle, 171
CZ 602 Bolt-Action Rifle, 171
CZ ZKM-452 Deluxe Bolt-Action Rifle, 195

D

D-Max Sidewinder Revolver, 149
Daewoo DH40 Fastfire Pistol, 110
Daewoo DH 380 Pistol, 110
Daewoo DP51 Fastfire Pistol, 110
Daewoo DP51C Pistol, 110
Daewoo DP51S Pistol, 110
Daewoo DP52 Pistol, 110
Daewoo DP 380 Pistol, 110
Daewoo DR200 Autoloading Rifle, 159
Daewoo DR300 Autoloading Rifle, 159
Daisy 1938 Red Ryder Classic Air Rifle, 275
Daisy Model 840 Air Gun, 275
Daisy Model 91 Match Air Pistol, 266
Daisy Model 225 American Legend Air Rifle, 275
Daisy Model 288 Air Pistol, 265
Daisy Model 500 Raven Air Pistol, 266
Daisy Model 990 Dual-Power Air Rifle, 276
Daisy Model 1894 BB Rifle, 275
Daisy/Power Line 44 Revolver, 266
Daisy/Power Line 45 Air Pistol, 266
Daisy/Power Line 93 Air Pistol, 266
Daisy/Power Line 400 BB Pistol, 266
Daisy/Power Line 717 Pellet Pistol, 267
Daisy/Power Line 747 Pellet Pistol, 267
Daisy/Power Line 753 Target Rifle, 275
Daisy/Power Line 853 Air Rifle, 275
Daisy/Power Line 856 Pump-up Air Gun, 275
Daisy/Power Line 880 Pump-up Air Gun, 276
Daisy/Power Line 920 Air Rifle, 276
Daisy/Power Line 922 Air Rifle, 276
Daisy/Power Line 970 Air Rifle, 276
Daisy/Power Line 1140 Pellet Pistol, 267
Daisy/Power Line 1150 Pellet Rifle, 276
Daisy/Power Line 1170 Pellet Rifle, 276
Daisy/Power Line 1700 Air Pistol, 267
Daisy/Power Line 2001 Air Rifle, 276
Daisy/Power Line 2002 Pellet Rifle, 276
Daisy/Power Line CO_2 1200 Air Pistol, 267
Daisy/Power Line Eagle 7856 Pump-up Air Rifle, 276
Daisy/Power Line Match 777 Pellet Pistol, 266
Daisy/Youth Line 95 Air Rifle, 275
Daisy/Youth Line 105 Air Rifle, 275
Daisy/Youth Line 111 Air Rifle, 275
Dakota 22 Sporter Bolt-Action Rifle, 195
Dakota 76 Classic Bolt-Action Rifle, 171
Dakota 76 Safari Bolt-Action Rifle, 171
Dakota 76 Short Action Rifle, 171
Dakota 76 Varmint Rifle, 171
Dakota 416 Rigby African Rifle, 171
Dakota Single Shot Rifle, 184
Davis Big-Bore Derringers, 153
Davis D-Series Derringers, 153
Davis Derringers, 153
Davis Long-Bore Derringers, 153
Davis P-32 Pistol, 110
Davis P-380 Pistol, 110
Desert Eagle Magnum Pistol, 111
Desert Industries Double Deuce Pistol, 111
Desert Industries G-90 Single Shot Rifle, 184
Desert Industries Two Bit Special Pistol, 111
Desert Industries War Eagle Pistol, 111
Dixie 1863 Springfield Musket, 248
Dixie 1874 Sharps Blackpowder Silhouette Rifle, 184
Dixie 1874 Sharps Lightweight Hunter/Target Rifle, 184
Dixie Deerslayer Rifle, 247
Dixie Delux Cub Rifle, 247

Dixie English Matchlock Musket, 247
Dixie Engraved 1873 Rifle, 163
Dixie Inline Carbine, 247
Dixie Magnum Percussion Shotgun, 261
Dixie Pennsylvania Pistol, 237
Dixie Screw Barrel Pistol, 237
Dixie Sharps New Model 1859 Military Rifle, 247
Dixie Squirrel Rifle, 248
Dixie Tennessee Mountain Rifle, 248
Dixie U.S. Model 1816 Flintlock Musket, 248
Dixie U.S. Model 1861 Springfield, 248
Dixie Wyatt Earp Revolver, 241

E

E.A.A. Big Bore Bounty Hunter Single Action Revolver, 149
E.A.A. European Ladies Model Pistol, 110
E.A.A. European Model Pistol, 110
E.A.A. Standard Grade Revolver, 138
E.A.A. Witness DA Pistol, 111
E.A.A. Witness Gold Team Auto Pistol, 132
E.A.A. Witness Silver Team Auto Pistol, 132
E.A.A./Sabatti Model 1822 Auto Rifle, 191
E.A.A./Weihrauch HW 60 Target Rifle, 202
E.A.A./Weihrauch HW 660 Match Rifle, 202
Eagle Arms M4A1C Carbine, 159
Eagle Arms M4C Carbine, 159
Eagle Arms M15A2 Golden Eagle Rifle, 202
Eagle Arms M15A2 Post-Ban Heavy Barrel Rifle, 159
EMF 1860 Henry Rifle, 163
EMF 1863 Sharps Military Carbine, 248
EMF 1866 Yellowboy Lever-Action Rifles, 163
EMF 1894 Target Bisley Revolver, 149
EMF Army 1860 Percussion Revolver, 239
EMF Dakota 1875 Outlaw Revolver, 149
EMF Dakota 1890 Police Revolver, 149
EMF Dakota New Model Single Action Revolvers, 149
EMF Hartford Artillery Revolver, 149
EMF Hartford Cavalry Revolver, 149
EMF Hartford Pinkerton Revolver, 149
EMF Hartford Single Action Revolvers, 149
EMF Model 73 Lever-Action Rifle, 163
EMF Sharps Carbine, 184
EMF Sharps Rifle, 184
Erma EM1 Carbine, 190
Erma ER Match Revolver, 132
Erma ER-777 Sporting Revolver, 138
Erma ESP 85A Match Pistol, 132
Erma ESP Junior Match Pistol, 132
Erma KGP68 Pistol, 110
Erma SR-100 Precision Rifle, 202
Euroarms 1861 Springfield, Rifle, 248
Euroarms Army 1860 Percussion Revolver, 239
Euroarms Buffalo Carbine, 248
Euroarms Volunteer Target Rifle, 248

F

Famas Semi-Auto Air Rifle, 276
FAS 601 Match Pistol, 132
FAS 603 Match Pistol, 132
FAS 607 Match Pistol, 132
FEG B9R Pistol, 111
FEG FP9 Pistol, 112
FEG GKK-40C Pistol, 112
FEG GKK-45C Pistol, 112
FEG P9R Pistol, 112
FEG PJK-9HP Pistol, 112
FEG SMC-22 Pistol, 112
FEG SMC-380 Pistol, 112
FEG SMC-918 Pistol, 112
Auguste Francotte Bolt-Action Rifles, 172
Auguste Francotte Boxlock Double Shotgun, 227
Auguste Francotte Boxlock Mountain Double Rifle, 188
Auguste Francotte Boxlock Mountain Rifle, 188
Auguste Francotte Sidelock Double Rifles, 188
Auguste Francotte Sidelock Double Shotgun, 227
Auguste Francotte Sidelock Mountain Rifle, 188
Freedom Arms Casull Model 252 Silhouette Revolver, 132
Freedom Arms Casull Model 252 Varmint Revolver, 133
Freedom Arms Field Grade Single Action Revolver, 149
Freedom Arms Model 353 Field Grade Revolver, 149
Freedom Arms Model 353 Premier Grade Revolver, 149
Freedom Arms Model 353 Revolver, 149
Freedom Arms Model 353 Silhouette Revolver, 149
Freedom Arms Model 555 Revolver, 149
Freedom Arms Premier Single Action Revolver, 149
French-Style Dueling Pistol, 237

G

GAL Compact Pistol, 112
Garbi Model 100 Side-By-Side Shotgun, 227
Garbi Model 101 Side-by-Side Shotgun, 228
Garbi Model 103A Side-By-Side Shotgun, 227
Garbi Model 103B Side-By-Side Shotgun, 227
Garbi Model 200 Side-by-Side Shotgun, 228
GAT Air Pistol, 267
GAT Air Rifle, 276
Gaucher GN1 Silhouette Pistol, 154
Gaucher GP Silhouette Pistol, 133
Gaucher GP Silhouette Pistol, 154
Glock 17 Pistol, 112
Glock 17L Competition Pistol, 133
Glock 17L Pistol, 112
Glock 19 Pistol, 112
Glock 20 10mm Pistol, 113
Glock 21 Pistol, 113
Glock 22 Pistol, 113
Glock 23 Pistol, 113
Glock 24 Competition Model Pistol, 133
Glock 26 Pistol, 113
Glock 27 Pistol, 113
Golan Auto Pistol, 113
Gonic GA-87 M/L Rifle, 249
Gonic GA-93 Magnum M/L Rifle, 249
Griswold & Gunnison Percussion Revolver, 241

H

Hammerli 480K Match Air Pistol, 267
Hammerli 480 Match Air Pistol, 267
Hammerli Model 160 Free Pistol, 133
Hammerli Model 162 Free Pistol, 133
Hammerli Model 208s Pistol, 133
Hammerli Model 280 Target Pistol, 133
Hammerli Model 451 Match Air Rifle, 277
Harper's Ferry 1803 Flintlock Rifle, 249
Harper's Ferry 1806 Pistol, 237
Harrington & Richardson 929 NTA Trapper Edition Revolver, 139
Harrington & Richardson 929 Sidekick Revolver, 139
Harrington & Richardson 939 Premier Revolver, 139
Harrington & Richardson 949 Western Revolver, 139
Harrington & Richardson American Revolvers, 139
Harrington & Richardson SB2-980 Ultra Slug Shotgun, 231
Harrington & Richardson Sportsman 999 Revolver, 139
Harrington & Richardson Tamer Shotgun, 231
Harrington & Richardson Topper Deluxe Model 098 Shotgun, 231
Harrington & Richardson Topper Deluxe Rifled Slug Shotgun, 231
Harrington & Richardson Topper Junior Classic Shotgun, 231
Harrington & Richardson Topper Junior Model 098 Shotgun, 231
Harrington & Richardson Topper Model 098 Shotgun, 231
Harrington & Richardson Ultra Hunter Rifle, 185
Harrington & Richardson Ultra Varmint Rifle, 185
Harris Gunworks Antietam Sharps Rifle, 185
Harris Gunworks Classic Stainless Sporter Rifle, 172
Harris Gunworks Combo M-87 Series 50-Caliber Rifles, 202
Harris Gunworks Long Range Rifle, 203
Harris Gunworks M-86 Sniper Rifle, 202
Harris Gunworks M-87R Rifle, 202
Harris Gunworks M-89 Sniper Rifle, 203
Harris Gunworks M-92 Bullpup Rifle, 202
Harris Gunworks M-93SN Rifle, 202
Harris Gunworks National Match Rifle, 202
Harris Gunworks Signature Alaskan Rifle, 172
Harris Gunworks Signature Class Sporter Rifle, 172
Harris Gunworks Signature Jr. Long Range Pistol, 133
Harris Gunworks Signature Super Varminter Rifle, 172
Harris Gunworks Signature Titanium Mountain Rifle, 172
Harris Gunworks Talon Safari Rifle, 172
Harris Gunworks Talon Sporter Rifle, 172
Hartford Model 1851 Percussion Revolver, 241
Hatfield Mountain Rifle, 249
Hatfield Squirrel Rifle, 249
Hatfield Uplander Grade I Double Shotgun, 228
Hatfield Uplander Grade II Double Shotgun, 228
Hatfield Uplander Over/Under Shotgun, 219
Hawken Rifle, 249
Heckler & Koch Mark 23 Special Operations Pistol, 113
Heckler & Koch P7M8 Pistol, 114
Heckler & Koch PSG-1 Marksman Rifle, 203
Heckler & Koch USP 45 Pistol, 113
Heckler & Koch USP Pistol, 113
Heritage Rough Rider Revolver, 150
Heritage Sentry DA Revolver, 139
Heritage Stealth Pistol, 114
HHF Model 101 B 12 AT-DT Trap Combo Over/Under Shotgun, 219
HHF Model 101 B 12 ST Trap Over/Under Shotgun, 219
HHF Model 103 B 12 ST Over/Under Shotgun, 219
HHF Model 103 C 12 ST Over/Under Shotgun, 219
HHF Model 103 D 12 ST Over/Under Shotgun, 219
HHF Model 103 F 12 ST Over/Under Shotgun, 219
HHF Model 104 A 12 ST Over/Under Shotgun, 219
HHF Model 200 A 12 ST Side-by-Side Shotgun, 228
HHF Model 202 A 12 ST Side-by-Side Shotgun, 228
Hi-Point 9mm Carbine, 159
Hi-Point 9mm Pistol, 114
Hi-Point 40 S&W Pistol, 114
Hi-Point 45 Pistol, 114
Hi-Point Model 9mm Compact Pistol, 114
High Standard 10X Model Target Pistol, 134
High Standard Olympic Military Pistol, 134
High Standard Olympic Rapid Fire Pistol, 134
High Standard Supermatic Citation MS Pistol, 134
High Standard Supermatic Citation Pistol, 134
High Standard Supermatic Tournament Pistol, 134
High Standard Supermatic Trophy Pistol, 134
High Standard Victor 10X Target Pistol, 134
High Standard Victor Target Pistol, 134
HJS Antigua Derringer, 154
HJS Frontier Four Derringer, 154
HJS Lone Star Derringer, 154
Howa Lightning Bolt-Action Rifle, 172
Hungarian T-58 Pistol, 114

I

IBUS M17S 223 Bullpup Rifle, 160
Intratec CAT 9 Pistol, 114
Intratec CAT 45 Pistol, 114
Intratec Protec-22 Pistol, 114
Intratec Protec-25 Pistol, 114
Intratec Sport 22 Pistol, 114
Ithaca-Navy Hawken Rifle, 249

J

Jennings J-22 Pistol, 115
Jennings J-25 Pistol, 115

K

Kahr K9 DA Pistol, 115
Kareen MK II Pistol, 115
Kel-Tec P-11 Pistol, 115
Kemen KM-4 Extra Gold Over/Under Shotgun, 219
Kemen KM-4 Extra Luxe-A Over/Under Shotgun, 219
Kemen KM-4 Extra Luxe-B Over/Under Shotgun, 219
Kemen KM-4 Luxe-A Over/Under Shotgun, 219
Kemen KM-4 Over/Under Shotgun, 219
Kemen KM-4 Super Luxe Over/Under Shotgun, 219
Kentuckian Carbine, 250
Kentuckian Rifle, 250
Kentucky Flintlock Pistol, 237
Kentucky Flintlock Rifle, 250
Kentucky Percussion Pistol, 237
Kentucky Percussion Rifle, 250
Kimber Classic 45 Custom Pistol, 115
Kimber Classic 45 Custom Royal Pistol, 115
Kimber Classic 45 Gold Match Pistol, 115
Kimber Model 82C Classic Bolt-Action Rifle, 196
Kimber Model 82C Custom Match Bolt-Action Rifle, 196
Kimber Model 82C Stainless Classic Bolt-Action Rifle, 196
Kimber Model 82C SuperAmerica Bolt-Action Rifle, 196
Kimber Model 82C SVT Bolt-Action Rifle, 196
Kimber Model 82C Varmint Synthetic Bolt-Action Rifle, 196
Kimber Model 84C Classic Bolt-Action Rifle, 173
Kimber Model 84C Single Shot Varmint Rifle, 173
Kimber Model 84C SuperAmerica Rifle, 173
Kimber Model K770 Custom Rifle, 173
Kimber Model K770 SuperAmerica Rifle, 173
Knight BK-92 Black Knight Rifle, 250
Knight Hawkeye Pistol, 238
Knight LK-93 Wolverine Rifle, 250
Knight MK-85 Rifle, 250
Knight MK-95 Magnum Elite Rifle, 250
Kodiak MK. III Double Rifle, 251
Kongsberg Classic Rifle, 173
Kongsberg Thumbhole Sporter Rifle, 173
Krico Model 260 Auto Rifle, 191
Krico Model 300 Bolt-Action Rifles, 196
Krico Model 300 Deluxe Bolt-Action Rifle, 196
Krico Model 300 Stutzen Bolt-Action Rifle, 196
Krico Model 360 S2 Biathlon Rifle, 203
Krico Model 360S Biathlon Rifle, 203
Krico Model 400 Match Rifle, 203
Krico Model 500 Kricotronic Match Rifle, 203
Krico Model 600 Match Rifle, 203
Krico Model 600 Sniper Rifle, 203
Krico Model 700 Bolt-Action Rifle, 173
Krico Model 700 Deluxe Rifle, 173
Krico Model 700 Deluxe S Rifle, 173
Kriefhoff KS-5 Trap Shotgun, 232
Krieghoff K-80 Combo Shotgun, 219
Krieghoff K-80 International Skeet Over/Under Shotgun, 220
Krieghoff K-80 Over/Under Trap Shotgun, 219
Krieghoff K-80 Single Barrel Trap Shotgun, 232
Krieghoff K-80 Skeet Lightweight Over/Under Shotgun, 220
Krieghoff K-80 Skeet Over/Under Shotgun, 220
Krieghoff K-80 Skeet Special Over/Under Shotgun, 220

GUNDEX

Krieghoff K-80 Skeet Two-Barrel Set Over/Under Shotgun, 220
Krieghoff K-80 Sporting Clays Over/Under Shotgun, 220
Krieghoff K-80 Unsingle Shotgun, 219
Krieghoff K-80/RT Over/Under Shotguns, 220
Krieghoff KS-5 Special Shotgun, 232

L

L.A.R. Grizzly 44 Mag MK IV Pistol, 116
L.A.R. Grizzly 50 Big Boar Rifle, 174
L.A.R. Grizzly 50 Mark V Pistol, 116
L.A.R. Grizzly Win Mag MK I Pistol, 116
Laseraim Arms Series I Pistol, 116
Laseraim Arms Series II Pistol, 116
Laseraim Arms Series III Pistol, 116
Laurona Model 85 MS Super Pigeon Over/Under Shotgun, 220
Laurona Model 85 MS Super Trap Over/Under Shotgun, 220
Laurona Model 85S Super Skeet Over/Under Shotgun, 220
Laurona Silhouette 300 Sporting Clays Over/Under Shotgun, 220
Laurona Silhouette 300 Trap Over/Under Shotgun, 220
Laurona Silhouette 300 Ultra Magnum Over/Under Shotgun, 220
Laurona Super Model 83 MG Over/Under Shotgun, 220
Laurona Super Model 84S Super Trap Over/Under Shotgun, 220
Laurona Super Model 85 Super Game Over/Under Shotgun, 220
LeMat 18th Georgia Percussion Revolver, 241
LeMat Beauregard Percussion Revolver, 241
LeMat Cavalry Model Percussion Revolver, 241
LeMat Naval-Style Percussion Revolver, 241
LeMat Percussion Revolver, 241
LePage Percussion Dueling Pistol, 238
Ljutic LM-6 Super-Deluxe Combo Over/Under Shotgun, 220
Ljutic LM-6 Super-Deluxe Over/Under Shotgun, 220
Ljutic LT Super Deluxe Mono Gun Shotgun, 232
Ljutic Mono Gun Shotgun, 232
Llama III-A Small Frame Pistol, 117
Llama IX-C Large Frame Pistol, 116
Llama IX-D Compact Frame Pistol, 116
Llama Max-I Compensator Pistol, 117
Llama Max-I Pistol, 116
Llama Minimax Series Pistol, 117
London Armory 2-Band 1858 Enfield Rifle, 251
London Armory 3-Band 1853 Enfield Rifle, 251
London Armory 1861 Enfield Musketoon, 251
Lorcin L 9mm Pistol, 117
Lorcin L-22 Pistol, 117
Lorcin L-25 Pistol, 117
Lorcin L-32 Pistol, 117
Lorcin LT-25 Pistol, 117
Lorcin LT-32 Pistol, 117
Lorcin Over/Under Derringer, 154
Lyman Cougar In-Line Rifle, 251
Lyman Deerstalker Custom Carbine, 251
Lyman Deerstalker Rifle, 251
Lyman Great Plains Rifle, 251
Lyman Plains Pistol, 238
Lyman Trade Rifle, 251

M

Magnum Research Lone Eagle Single Shot Pistol, 154
Magtech Model 122.2 Bolt-Action Rifles, 196
Magtech Model 122.2R Bolt-Action Rifle, 196
Magtech Model 122.2S Bolt-Action Rifle, 196
Magtech Model 122.2T Bolt-Action Rifle, 196
Magtech Model 586.2-VR Pump Shotgun, 211
Magtech MT 586P Pump Shotgun, 235
Mandall/Cabanas Pistol, 154
Manurhin MR 73 Revolver, 139
Manurhin MR 73 Sport Revolver, 139
Manurhin MR 88 Revolver, 140
Manurhin MR 96 Revolver, 140
Marksman 28 International Air Rifle, 277
Marksman 40 International Air Rifle, 277
Marksman 55 Air Rifle, 277
Marksman 70T Air Rifle, 277
Marksman 1010 Repeater Air Pistol, 267
Marksman 1015 Special Edition Air Pistol, 268
Marksman 1710 Plainsman Air Rifle, 277
Marksman 1740 Air Rifle, 278
Marksman 1750 BB Biathlon Repeater Air Rifle, 278
Marksman 1780 Air Rifle, 278
Marksman 1790 Biathlon Trainer Air Rifle, 278
Marksman 1792 Competition Trainer Air Rifle, 278
Marksman Model 45 Air Rifle, 277
Marksman Model 60 Air Rifle, 277
Marlin Model 9 Camp Carbine, 160
Marlin Model 15YN "Little Buckaroo" Rifle, 197
Marlin Model 25MN Bolt-Action Rifle, 197
Marlin Model 25N Bolt-Action Repeater, 197

Marlin Model 30AS Lever-Action Carbine, 163
Marlin Model 39AS Golden Lever-Action Rifle, 193
Marlin Model 45 Carbine, 160
Marlin Model 55 Goose Gun Bolt Action Shotgun, 232
Marlin Model 60 Self-Loading Rifle, 191
Marlin Model 60SS Self-Loading Rifle, 191
Marlin Model 70PSS Stainless Self-Loading Rifle, 191
Marlin Model 336CS Lever-Action Carbine, 163
Marlin Model 444SS Lever-Action Sporter, 163
Marlin Model 512 Slugmaster Shotgun, 232
Marlin Model 880 Bolt-Action Rifle, 197
Marlin Model 880SQ Squirrel Rifle, 197
Marlin Model 880SS Stainless Steel Bolt-Action Rifle, 197
Marlin Model 881 Bolt-Action Rifle, 197
Marlin Model 882 Bolt-Action Rifle, 197
Marlin Model 882L Bolt-Action Rifle, 197
Marlin Model 882SS Bolt-Action Rifle, 197
Marlin Model 883 Bolt-Action Rifle, 197
Marlin Model 883SS Bolt-Action Rifle, 197
Marlin Model 922 Self-Loading Rifle, 191
Marlin Model 995SS Self-Loading Rifle, 191
Marlin Model 1894 Cowboy Rifle, 164
Marlin Model 1894CS Carbine, 164
Marlin Model 1894S Lever-Action Carbine, 164
Marlin Model 1895SS Lever-Action Rifle, 164
Marlin Model 2000L Target Rifle, 204
Marlin Model MR-7 Bolt-Action Rifle, 174
Marocchi Conquista Skeet Grade I Over/Under Shotgun, 221
Marocchi Conquista Skeet Grade II Over/Under Shotgun, 221
Marocchi Conquista Skeet Grade III Over/Under Shotgun, 221
Marocchi Conquista Skeet Over/Under Shotgun, 221
Marocchi Conquista Sporting Clays Grade I Over/Under Shotgun, 220
Marocchi Conquista Sporting Clays Grade II Over/Under Shotgun, 220
Marocchi Conquista Sporting Clays Grade III Over/Under Shotgun, 220
Marocchi Conquista Sporting Clays Over/Under Shotgun, 220
Marocchi Conquista Trap Grade I Over/Under Shotgun, 221
Marocchi Conquista Trap Grade II Over/Under Shotgun, 221
Marocchi Conquista Trap Grade III Over/Under Shotgun, 221
Marocchi Conquista Trap Over/Under Shotgun, 221
Marocchi Lady Sport Grade I Over/Under Shotgun, 221
Marocchi Lady Sport Grade II Over/Under Shotgun, 221
Marocchi Lady Sport Grade III Over/Under Shotgun, 221
Marocchi Lady Sport Over/Under Shotgun, 221
Mauser Model 96 Bolt-Action Rifle, 174
Maverick Model 88 Pump Shotgun, 212
Maverick Model 95 Bolt-Action Shotgun, 232
Maximum Single Shot Pistol, 154
Merkel Boxlock Double Rifles, 188
Merkel Drillings, 189
Merkel Model 8 Side-by-Side Shotgun, 228
Merkel Model 47E Side-by-Side Shotgun, 228
Merkel Model 47S Side-by-Side Shotgun, 228
Merkel Model 90K Drilling, 189
Merkel Model 90S Drilling, 189
Merkel Model 95K Drilling, 189
Merkel Model 95S Drilling, 189
Merkel Model 122 Side-by-Side Shotgun, 228
Merkel Model 140-1 Double Rifle, 188
Merkel Model 140-1.1 Double Rifle, 188
Merkel Model 147 Side-by-Side Shotgun, 228
Merkel Model 147E Side-by-Side Shotgun, 228
Merkel Model 147S Side-by-Side Shotgun, 228
Merkel Model 150-1 Double Rifle, 188
Merkel Model 150-1.1 Double Rifle, 188
Merkel Model 160 Side-by-Side Double Rifle, 188
Merkel Model 200 SC Sporting Clays Over/Under Shotgun, 221
Merkel Model 200E Over/Under Shotgun, 221
Merkel Model 200E Skeet Over/Under Shotgun, 221
Merkel Model 200E Trap Over/Under Shotgun, 221
Merkel Model 200ET Over/Under Shotgun, 221
Merkel Model 201ES Over/Under Shotgun, 221
Merkel Model 201ET Over/Under Shotgun, 221
Merkel Model 202E Over/Under Shotgun, 221
Merkel Model 203E Over/Under Shotgun, 221
Merkel Model 203ES Over/Under Shotgun, 221
Merkel Model 203ET Over/Under Shotgun, 221
Merkel Model 210E Combination Gun, 188
Merkel Model 211E Combination Gun, 188
Merkel Model 213E Combination Gun, 188
Merkel Model 221E Double Rifle, 188
Merkel Model 223E Double Rifle, 188
Merkel Model 247S Side-by-Side Shotgun, 228
Merkel Model 303E Over/Under Shotgun, 221
Merkel Model 313E Combination Gun, 188
Merkel Model 323E Double Rifle, 188
Merkel Model 347S Side-by-Side Shotgun, 228
Merkel Model 447S Side-by-Side Shotgun, 228

Merkel Model 2001 Over/Under Shotgun, 221
Merkel Over/Under Combination Guns, 188
Merkel Over/Under Double Rifles, 188
Mississippi 1841 Percussion Rifle, 260
Mitchell Arms 44 Magnum Pistol, 118
Mitchell Arms 45 Bullseye Pistol, 135
Mitchell Arms 45 Gold IPSC Limited Pistol, 135
Mitchell Arms 45 Gold Standard Model Pistol, 118
Mitchell Arms 45 Gold Tactical Model Pistol, 118
Mitchell Arms 45 Gold Wide Body Standard Pistol, 118
Mitchell Arms 45 Gold Wide Body Tactical Pistol, 118
Mitchell Arms Alpha Pistol, 117
Mitchell Arms Baron Pistol, 135
Mitchell Arms Gold Series Ambidextrous Auto Pistol, 118
Mitchell Arms Guardian Angel Pistol, 155
Mitchell Arms Jeff Cooper Commemorative Pistol, 118
Mitchell Arms Jeff Cooper Signature Auto Pistol, 118
Mitchell Arms LW9 Semi-Auto Carbine, 160
Mitchell Arms LW22 Semi-Auto Carbine, 191
Mitchell Arms Medalist Pistol, 134
Mitchell Arms Monarch II Pistol, 134
Mitchell Arms Monarch Pistol, 134
Mitchell Arms Sovereign Pistol, 135
Mitchell Arms Sportster Pistol, 135
Mitchell/Bernardelli Hemingway Lightweight Double Shotgun, 228
Mitchell/Bernardelli Las Palomas Double Shotgun, 228
Mitchell/Bernardelli Model 115 Over/Under Shotgun, 221
Mitchell/Bernardelli Model 115S Trap Skeet Over/Under Shotgun, 221
Mitchell/Bernardelli Model 192 MS Over/Under Shotgun, 221
Mitchell/Bernardelli Model 192 MS-MC Over/Under Shotgun, 221
Mitchell/Bernardelli Model 192 Waterfowl Over/Under Shotgun, 221
Mitchell/Bernardelli Model 220 MS Over/Under Shotgun, 221
Mitchell/Bernardelli Series Roma 3 Double Shotgun, 228
Mitchell/Bernardelli Series Roma 4 Double Shotgun, 228
Mitchell/Bernardelli Series Roma 6 Double Shotgun, 228
Mitchell/Bernardelli Series Roma 7 Double Shotgun, 228
Mitchell/Bernardelli Series Roma 7M Double Shotgun, 228
Mitchell/Bernardelli Series Roma 8M Double Shotgun, 228
Mitchell/Bernardelli Series Roma 9M Double Shotgun, 228
Mitchell/Bernardelli Series S. Uberto Double Shotgun, 228
Mitchell/Bernardelli Series S. Uberto F.S. Double Shotgun, 228
Model 1885 High Wall Rifle, 185
Morini 162E Match Air Pistol, 268
Morini Model 84E Free Pistol, 135
Mossberg American Field Model 835 Pump Shotgun, 212
Mossberg Model 500 Bantam Pump Shotgun, 212
Mossberg Model 500 Camo Combo Pump Shotgun, 212
Mossberg Model 500 Camo Pump Shotgun, 212
Mossberg Model 500 Cruiser Security Shotgun, 235
Mossberg Model 500 Ghost-Ring Shotgun, 236
Mossberg Model 500 Mariner Pump Shotgun, 236
Mossberg Model 500 Muzzleloader Combo Shotgun, 212
Mossberg Model 500 Persuader Security Shotgun, 235
Mossberg Model 500 Sporting Combo Pump Shotgun, 212
Mossberg Model 500 Sporting Pump Shotgun, 212
Mossberg Model 500 Trophy Slugster Pump Shotgun
Mossberg Model 500 Viking Pump Shotgun, 212
Mossberg Model 590 Ghost-Ring Shotgun, 236
Mossberg Model 590 Mariner Pump Shotgun, 236
Mossberg Model 590 Shotgun, 236
Mossberg Model 695 Slugster Shotgun, 233
Mossberg Model 695 Turkey Shotgun, 233
Mossberg Model 835 Crown Grade Ulti-Mag Pump Shotgun, 212
Mossberg Model 835 Viking Pump Shotgun, 212
Mossberg Model 9200 Bantam Shotgun, 209
Mossberg Model 9200 Camo Shotgun, 209
Mossberg Model 9200 Crown Grade Auto Shotgun, 209
Mossberg Model 9200 Crown Grade Trophy Auto Shotgun, 209
Mossberg Model 9200 Crown Grade Turkey Auto Shotgun, 209
Mossberg Model 9200 Persuader Auto Shotgun, 209
Mossberg Model 9200 USST Auto Shotgun, 209
Mossberg Model 9200 Viking Auto Shotgun, 209
Mossberg Model HS410 Shotgun, 235
Mossberg Turkey Model 500 Pump Shotgun, 212
Mountain Eagle Pistol, 118
Mowrey 1 N 30 Conical Rifle, 252
Mowrey Percussion Shotgun, 261
Mowrey Plains Rifle, 252
Mowrey Rocky Mountain Hunter Rifle, 252
Mowrey Silhouette Rifle, 252
Mowrey Squirrel Rifle, 252
J.P. Murray 1862-1864 Cavalry Carbine, 252

N

Navy 1861 Percussion Revolver, 239
Navy Arms 1777 Charleville Musket, 253
Navy Arms 1816 M.T. Wickham Musket, 253

Navy Arms 1859 Sharps Cavalry Carbine, 253
Navy Arms 1859 Sharps Infantry Rifle, 252
Navy Arms 1861 Springfield Rifle, 254
Navy Arms 1863 C.S. Richmond Rifle, 254
Navy Arms 1863 Springfield Rifle, 254
Navy Arms 1866 Yellowboy Carbine, 164
Navy Arms 1866 Yellowboy Rifle, 164
Navy Arms 1873 Single-Action Revolver, 150
Navy Arms 1873 Sporting Rifle, 164
Navy Arms 1873 Springfield Cavalry Carbine, 185
Navy Arms 1873 U.S. Artillery Model Revolver, 150
Navy Arms 1873 U.S. Cavalry Model Revolver, 150
Navy Arms 1873 Winchester-Style Carbine, 164
Navy Arms 1873 Winchester-Style Rifle, 164
Navy Arms 1874 Sharps Cavalry Carbine, 185
Navy Arms 1874 Sharps Infantry Rifle, 185
Navy Arms 1874 Sharps Sniper Rifle, 185
Navy Arms 1875 Schofield Revolver, 150
Navy Arms 1875 Schofield U.S. Cavalry Revolver, 150
Navy Arms 1875 Schofield Wells Fargo Revolver, 150
Navy Arms #2 Creedmoor Rifle, 185
Navy Arms Army 1860 Percussion Revolver, 239
Navy Arms Berdan 1859 Sharps Rifle, 252
Navy Arms Country Boy In-Line Rifle, 252
Navy Arms Deluxe 1858 Remington-Style Revolver, 241
Navy Arms Fowler Shotgun, 261
Navy Arms Hawken Hunter Carbine, 252
Navy Arms Hawken Hunter Rifle, 252
Navy Arms Henry Carbine, 164
Navy Arms Henry Trapper, 164
Navy Arms Iron Frame Henry, 164
Navy Arms Kodiak MK IV Drilling, 189
Navy Arms LePage Dueling Pistol, 238
Navy Arms Military Henry Rifle, 164
Navy Arms Mortimer Flintlock Rifle, 253
Navy Arms Mortimer Flintlock Shotgun, 261
Navy Arms Mortimer Match Flintlock Rifle, 253
Navy Arms Pennsylvania Long Rifle, 253
Navy Arms Rolling Block Buffalo Rifle, 185
Navy Arms Sharps Buffalo Rifle, 185
Navy Arms Sharps Plains Rifle, 185
Navy Arms Smith Artillery Carbine, 253
Navy Arms Smith Carbine, 253
Navy Arms Smith Cavalry Carbine, 253
Navy Arms Steel Shot Magnum Shotgun, 261
Navy Arms T&T Shotgun, 261
Navy Arms Tryon Creedmoor Target Model Rifle, 259
Navy Arms Volunteer Rifle, 253
Navy Arms Whitworth Military Target Rifle, 253
Navy Model 1851 Percussion Revolver, 241
New Advantage Arms Derringer, 155
New England Firearms Handi-Rifle, 186
New England Firearms Lady Ultra Revolver, 140
New England Firearms Standard Pardner Shotgun, 233
New England Firearms Standard Revolvers, 140
New England Firearms Survivor Rifle, 186
New England Firearms Survivor Shotgun, 233
New England Firearms Tracker II Slug Gun, 233
New England Firearms Tracker Slug Gun, 233
New England Firearms Turkey and Goose Gun, 233
New England Firearms Ultra Mag Revolver, 140
New England Firearms Ultra Revolver, 140
New Generation Snake Charmer Shotgun, 233
New Model 1858 Army Buffalo Percussion Revolver, 242
New Model 1858 Army Hartford Model Percussion Revolver, 242
New Model 1858 Army Percussion Revolver, 242
New Model 1858 Army Stainless Percussion Revolver, 242
New Model 1858 Army Target Model Percussion Revolver, 242
Norinco JW-15 Bolt-Action Rifle, 197
Norinco JW-27 Bolt-Action Rifle, 197
Norinco Model 22 ATD Rifle, 192
North American Arms Companion Magnum Percussion Revolver, 242
North American Arms Companion Percussion Revolver, 242
North American Black Widow Revolver, 150
North American Mini-Master Revolver, 150
North American Mini-Revolvers, 150
North American Munitions Model 1996 Pistol, 118

O

Olympic Arms PCR-1 Rifle, 160
Olympic Arms PCR-2 Rifle, 160
Olympic Arms PCR-3 Rifle, 160
Olympic Arms PCR-4 Rifle, 160
Olympic Arms PCR-5 Rifle, 160
Olympic Arms PCR-6 Rifle, 160
Olympic Arms PCR-Servicematch Rifle, 204

P

Para-Ordnance P12.45ER Pistol, 119
Para-Ordnance P12.45RR Pistol, 119
Para-Ordnance P13.45RR Pistol, 119
Para-Ordnance P14.45ER Pistol, 119
Para-Ordnance P14.45RR Pistol, 119
Para-Ordnance P16.40ER Pistol, 119
Para-Ordnance P-Series Pistols, 119
Pardini GP Rapid Fire Match Pistol, 135
Pardini GP Schuman Rapid Fire Match Pistol, 135
Pardini K50 Free Pistol, 135
Pardini K58 Match Air Pistol, 268
Pardini Model HP Target Pistol, 135
Pardini Model SP Target Pistol, 135
Parker Reproductions A-1 Special Side-by-Side Shotgun, 229
Parker Reproductions D Grade Side-by-Side Shotgun, 229
Parker Reproductions Side-by-Side Shotgun, 229
Pedersoli Mang Target Pistol, 238
Peifer Model TS-93 Pistol, 119
Pennsylvania Full-Stock Rifle, 254
Perazzi Mirage Special Skeet Over/Under Shotgun, 222
Perazzi MX8 Special Combo Over/Under Shotgun, 222
Perazzi MX8 Special Single Over/Under Shotgun, 222
Perazzi MX8 Special Skeet Over/Under Shotgun, 222
Perazzi MX8/20 Over/Under Shotgun, 222
Perazzi MX8/MX8 Special Trap Over/Under Shotgun, 222
Perazzi MX10 Over/Under Shotgun, 222
Perazzi MX12 Over/Under Shotgun, 222
Perazzi MX12C Over/Under Shotgun, 222
Perazzi MX20 Hunting Over/Under Shotgun, 222
Perazzi MX20C Hunting Over/Under Shotgun, 222
Perazzi MX28 Game Over/Under Shotgun, 222
Perazzi MX410 Game Over/Under Shotgun, 222
Perazzi Sporting Classic Over/Under Shotgun, 222
Perazzi TMX Special Single Trap Shotgun, 233
Phoenix Arms HP22 Pistol, 119
Phoenix Arms HP25 Pistol, 119
Phoenix Arms Model Raven Pistol, 119
Piotti Boss Over/Under Shotgun, 222
Piotti King Extra Side-by-Side Shotgun, 229
Piotti King No. 1 Side-by-Side Shotgun, 229
Piotti Lunik Side-by-Side Shotgun, 229
Piotti Piuma Side-by-Side Shotgun, 229
Piranha Auto Pistol, 119
Pocket Police 1862 Hartford Model Percussion Revolver, 242
Pocket Police 1862 Percussion Revolver, 242
Prairie River Arms PRA Bullpup Rifle, 254
Prairie River Arms PRA Classic Rifle, 254
PSA-25 Pistol, 119

Q

Queen Anne Flintlock Pistol, 238

R

Record Champion Repeater Pistol, 268
Record Jumbo Deluxe Air Pistol, 268
Remington 11-87 Premier Shotgun, 209
Remington 11-87 Premier Skeet Shotgun, 209
Remington 11-87 Premier Trap Shotgun, 209
Remington 11-87 Special Purpose Magnum Shotgun, 210
Remington 11-87 Special Purpose Magnum-Turkey Shotgun, 210
Remington 11-87 Special Purpose Synthetic Camo Shotgun, 210
Remington 11-87 Sporting Clays Shotgun, 209
Remington 11-87 SPS-Cantilever Shotgun, 210
Remington 11-87 SPS-Deer Shotgun, 210
Remington 11-87 SPS-T Camo Auto Shotgun, 210
Remington 11-96 Euro Ligthweight Auto Shotgun, 210
Remington 40-XB Rangemaster Target Rifle, 204
Remington 40-XBBR KS Target Rifle, 204
Remington 40-XC KS National Match Course Rifle, 204
Remington 40-XR KS Rimfire Position Rifle, 204
Remington 40-XR Rimfire Custom Sporter, 197
Remington 90T Super Single Shotgun, 233
Remington 396 Skeet Over/Under Shotgun, 222
Remington 396 Sporting Over/Under Shotgun, 222
Remington 541-T Bolt-Action Rifle, 198
Remington 541-T HB Bolt-Action Rifle, 198
Remington 552 BDL Speedmaster Rifle, 192
Remington 572 BDL Fieldmaster Pump Rifle, 193
Remington 700 APR African Plains Rifle, 175
Remington 700 AWR Alaskan Wilderness Rifle, 175
Remington 700 BDL DM Rifle, 175
Remington 700 BDL Left-Hand Rifle, 175
Remington 700 BDL SS DM Rifle, 175
Remington 700 BDL SS DM-B Rifle, 175
Remington 700 BDL SS Rifle, 175
Remington 700 Classic Rifle, 175
Remington 700 Custom KS Mountain Rifle, 175
Remington 700 LSS Rifle, 175
Remington 700 ML Rifle, 255
Remington 700 MLS Rifle, 255
Remington 700 MTN DM Rifle, 175
Remington 700 Safari Rifle, 175
Remington 700 Sendero Rifle, 175
Remington 700 Sendero SF Rifle, 175
Remington 870 Express Combo Shotgun, 213
Remington 870 Express HD Pump Shotgun, 213
Remington 870 Express Rifle-Sighted Deer Gun, 213
Remington 870 Express Shotgun, 213
Remington 870 Express Small Gauge Shotgun, 213
Remington 870 Express Synthetic Pump Shotgun, 213
Remington 870 Express Turkey Shotgun, 213
Remington 870 Express Youth Gun, 213
Remington 870 High Grade Shotguns, 213
Remington 870 Marine Magnum Pump Shotgun, 213
Remington 870 Special Purpose Synthetic Camo Shotgun, 213
Remington 870 SPS Cantilever Shotgun, 213
Remington 870 SPS-Deer Shotgun, 213
Remington 870 SPS-T Camo Pump Shotgun, 213
Remington 870 SPS-T Special Purpose Magnum Shotgun, 213
Remington 870 TC Trap Gun, 213
Remington 870 Wingmaster Pump Shotgun, 213
Remington 870D Pump Shotgun, 213
Remington 870F Pump Shotgun, 213
Remington 1100 20-Gauge Deer Gun Shotgun, 210
Remington 1100 LT-20 Auto Shotgun, 210
Remington 1100 LT-20 Skeet Shotgun, 210
Remington 1100 LT-20 Youth Shotgun, 210
Remington 1100 Special Field Shotgun, 210
Remington 1100 Sporting 28 Shotgun, 210
Remington 1100 Synthetic Shotgun, 210
Remington 7600 Slide-Action Carbine, 165
Remington 7600 Slide-Action Rifle, 165
Remington Model 522 Viper Auto Rifle, 192
Remington Model 7400 Auto Carbine, 161
Remington Model 7400 Auto Rifle, 161
Remington Model Seven Bolt-Action Rifle, 176
Remington Model Seven Custom KS Rifle, 176
Remington Model Seven Custom MS Rifle, 176
Remington Model Seven SS Rifle, 176
Remington Model Seven Youth Rifle, 176
Remington Peerless Over/Under Shotgun, 222
Remington SP-10 Magnum Auto Shotgun, 210
Remington SP-10 Magnum-Camo Auto Shotgun, 210
Rizzini Artemis Over/Under Shotgun, 223
Rizzini Aurum Over/Under Shotgun, 223
Rizzini S782 EMEL Over/Under Shotgun, 223
Rizzini S790 EMEL Over/Under Shotgun, 223
Rizzini S790 Sporting EL Over/Under Shotgun, 223
Rizzini S792 EMEL Over/Under Shotgun, 223
Rizzini Sidelock Side-by-Side Shotgun, 229
Rocky Mountain Arms Patriot Pistol, 119
Rogers & Spencer Burnished London Gray Percussion Revolver, 242
Rogers & Spencer Percussion Revolver, 242
Rogers & Spencer Target Model Percussion Revolver, 242
Rossi Lady Rossi Revolver, 140
Rossi Model 59 SA Pump Rifle, 193
Rossi Model 62 SA Pump Rifle, 193
Rossi Model 62 SAC Pump Carbine, 193
Rossi Model 65 Saddle-Ring Carbine, 165
Rossi Model 68 Revolver, 140
Rossi Model 68/2 Revolver, 140
Rossi Model 88 Stainless Revolver, 140
Rossi Model 92 Saddle-Ring Carbine, 165
Rossi Model 92 Short Carbine, 165
Rossi Model 515 Revolver, 140
Rossi Model 518 Revolver, 140
Rossi Model 720 Revolver, 141
Rossi Model 720C Revolver, 141
Rossi Model 851 Revolver, 141
Rossi Model 877 Revolver, 141
Rossi Model 971 Comp Gun Revolver, 141
Rossi Model 971 Revolver, 141
Rossi Model 971 VRC Revolver, 141
Rottweil Paragon Over/Under Shotgun, 223
RPM XL Hunter Single Shot Pistol, 155
RPM XL Silhouette Single Shot Pistol, 155
RPM XL Single Shot Pistol, 155
Ruger 10/22 Autoloading Carbine, 192
Ruger 10/22 Deluxe Sporter, 192
Ruger 10/22 DSP Deluxe Sporter, 192
Ruger 10/22 International Carbine, 192
Ruger 10/22 RB Autoloading Carbine, 192
Ruger 10/22RBI International Carbine, 192
Ruger 10/22T Target Rifle, 192
Ruger 22/45 Mark II Pistol, 120
Ruger 77/22 Hornet Bolt-Action Rifle, 177
Ruger 77/22 Rimfire Bolt-Action Rifle, 198
Ruger 77/22R Rimfire Bolt-Action Rifle, 198
Ruger 77/22RH Rifle, 177
Ruger 77/22RM Rimfire Bolt-Action Rifle, 198
Ruger 77/22RS Rimfire Bolt-Action Rifle, 198
Ruger 77/22RSH Rimfire Bolt-Action Rifle, 177
Ruger 77/22RSM Rimfire Bolt-Action Rifle, 198
Ruger 77/22VHZ Rimfire Bolt-Action Rifle, 177
Ruger Bisley Single Action Revolver, 151
Ruger Bisley Small Frame Revolver, 151
Ruger Blackhawk Revolver, 150
Ruger BN31 Single Action Revolver, 150
Ruger BN34X Single Action Revolver, 150
Ruger BN36 Single Action Revolver, 150

Ruger BN36X Single Action Revolver, 150
Ruger BN41 Single Action Revolver, 150
Ruger BN42 Single Action Revolver, 150
Ruger BN45 Single Action Revolver, 150
Ruger BP-7 Old Army Percussion Revolver, 243
Ruger BP-7F Old Army Percussion Revolver, 243
Ruger English Field Over/Under Shotgun, 222
Ruger GKBN34 Single Action Revolver, 150
Ruger GKBN36 Single Action Revolver, 150
Ruger GKBN44 Single Action Revolver, 150
Ruger GKBN45 Single Action Revolver, 150
Ruger GKS45N Single Action Revolver, 151
Ruger GKS47N Single Action Revolver, 151
Ruger GKS458N Single Action Revolver, 151
Ruger GP-100 Revolver, 141
Ruger GP-141 Revolver, 141
Ruger GP-160 Revolver, 141
Ruger GP-161 Revolver, 141
Ruger GPF-331 Revolver, 141
Ruger GPF-340 Revolver, 141
Ruger GPF-341 Revolver, 141
Ruger K10/22RB Autoloading Carbine, 192
Ruger K10/22RBI International Carbine, 192
Ruger K77/22 Varmint Rifle, 198
Ruger K77/22RMP Rimfire Bolt-Action Rifle, 198
Ruger K77/22RP Rimfire Bolt-Action Rifle, 198
Ruger K77/22RSMP Rimfire Bolt-Action Rifle, 198
Ruger K77/22RSP Rimfire Bolt-Action Rifle, 198
Ruger K77/22VBZ Varmint Rifle, 198
Ruger K77/22VMB Varmint Rifle, 198
Ruger K-Mini 14/5 Autoloading Rifle, 161
Ruger KBN34 Single Action Revolver, 150
Ruger KBN36 Single Action Revolver, 150
Ruger KBP-7 Old Army Percussion Revolver, 243
Ruger KBP-7F Old Army Percussion Revolver, 243
Ruger KGP-141 Revolver, 141
Ruger KGP-160 Revolver, 141
Ruger KGP-161 Revolver, 141
Ruger KGPF-330 Revolver, 141
Ruger KGPF-331 Revolver, 141
Ruger KGPF-340 Revolver, 141
Ruger KGPF-341 Revolver, 141
Ruger KM77VTMKII Rifle, 176
Ruger KMK4 Pistol, 120
Ruger KMK6 Pistol, 120
Ruger KMK-512 Bull Barrel Pistol, 135
Ruger KMK-678G Government Target Model Pistol, 135
Ruger KMK-678GC Pistol, 135
Ruger KP4 Pistol, 120
Ruger KP89 Pistol, 119
Ruger KP89D Decocker Pistol, 120
Ruger KP90 Safety Model Pistol, 120
Ruger KP94 Pistol, 120
Ruger KP94D Pistol, 120
Ruger KP94DAO Pistol, 120
Ruger KP512 Pistol, 120
Ruger KS45N Single Action Revolver, 151
Ruger KS47N Single Action Revolver, 151
Ruger KS411N Single Action Revolver, 151
Ruger KSP321XL Revolver, 142
Ruger KSP821L Revolver, 142
Ruger KSP-221 Revolver, 141
Ruger KSP-240 Revolver, 141
Ruger KSP-241 Revolver, 141
Ruger KSP-321 Revolver, 141
Ruger KSP-331 Revolver, 141
Ruger KSP-821 Revolver, 141
Ruger KSP-831 Revolver, 141
Ruger KSP-921 Revolver, 141
Ruger KSP-931 Revolver, 141
Ruger KSP-3231 Revolver, 141
Ruger M77 Mark II All-Weather Stainless Rifle, 176
Ruger M77 Mark II Express Rifle, 177
Ruger M77 Mark II Magnum Rifle, 176
Ruger M77 Mark II Rifle, 176
Ruger M77LRMKII Rifle, 176
Ruger M77MKII Rifle, 176
Ruger M77RL Ultra Light Rifle, 176
Ruger M77RLMKII Rifle, 176
Ruger M77RPMKII Rifle, 176
Ruger M77RSEXMKII Rifle, 177
Ruger M77RSI International Carbine, 176
Ruger M77RSIMKII Ruger, 176
Ruger M77RSMKII Rifle, 176
Ruger M77RSMMKII Rifle, 176
Ruger M77RSPMKII Rifle, 176
Ruger M77VT Target Rifle, 176
Ruger Mark II Bull Barrel Pistol, 135
Ruger Mark II Government Target Model Pistol, 135
Ruger Mark II Standard Pistol, 120
Ruger Mark II Target Model Pistol, 135
Ruger Mini Thirty Rifle, 161
Ruger Mini-14/5 Autoloading Rifle, 161
Ruger MK-4 Pistol, 120
Ruger MK-4B Compact Pistol, 121
Ruger MK-10 Bull Barrel Pistol, 135
Ruger MK-512 Bull Barrel Pistol, 135
Ruger MK-678 Target Model Pistol, 135

Ruger MK-678G Government Target Model Pistol, 135
Ruger MK6 Pistol, 120
Ruger Model 96/22 Lever-Action Rifle, 193
Ruger Model 96/22M Lever-Action Rifle, 193
Ruger Model 96/44 Lever-Action Rifle, 165
Ruger New Super Bearcat Single Action Revolver, 151
Ruger No. 1 RSI International Rifle, 186
Ruger No. 1A Light Sporter Rifle, 186
Ruger No. 1B Single Shot Rifle, 186
Ruger No. 1H Tropical Rifle, 186
Ruger No. 1S Medium Sporter Rifle, 186
Ruger No. 1V Special Varminter Rifle, 186
Ruger Old Army Percussion Revolver, 243
Ruger P89 Double-Action-Only Pistol, 120
Ruger P89 Pistol, 119
Ruger P89D Decocker Pistol, 120
Ruger P90 Decocker Pistol, 120
Ruger P90 Safety Model Pistol, 120
Ruger P93 Compact Pistol, 120
Ruger P94L Pistol, 120
Ruger P95 DAO Pistol, 120
Ruger P95 Pistol, 120
Ruger P95 Pistol, 120
Ruger P512 Pistol, 120
Ruger Red Label Over/Under Shotgun, 223
Ruger Redhawk Revolver, 142
Ruger S45N Single Action Revolver, 151
Ruger S47N Single Action Revolver, 151
Ruger S411N Single Action Revolver, 151
Ruger SBC4 Single Action Revolver, 151
Ruger SP101 Double-Action-Only Revolver, 142
Ruger SP101 Revolver, 141
Ruger Sporting Clays Over/Under Shotgun, 223
Ruger SSM Single-Six Ruger, 151
Ruger Stainless Government Competition Model 22 Pistol, 135
Ruger Super Blackhawk Revolver, 151
Ruger Super Redhawk Revolver, 142
Ruger Super Single-Six Convertible Revolver, 151
Ruger Vaquero Single Action Revolver, 151
Ruger Woodside Over/Under Shotgun, 223
Ruger Woodside Sporting Clays Over/Under Shotgun, 223
RWS Model 75S T01 Match Air Rifle, 278
RWS Model CA 100 Air Rifle, 278
RWS TX200 Magnum Air Rifle, 278
RWS TX200 SR Magnum Air Rifle, 278
RWS/Diana Model 5G Air Pistol, 268
RWS/Diana Model 6G Air Pistol, 269
RWS/Diana Model 6M Match Air Pistol, 268
RWS/Diana Model 24 Air Rifle, 278
RWS/Diana Model 24C Air Rifle, 278
RWS/Diana Model 34 Air Rifle, 278
RWS/Diana Model 34BC Air Rifle, 278
RWS/Diana Model 34N Air Rifle, 278
RWS/Diana Model 36 Air Rifle, 279
RWS/Diana Model 36 Carbine, 279
RWS/Diana Model 45 Air Rifle, 279
RWS/Diana Model 48 Air Rifle, 279
RWS/Diana Model 48B Air Rifle, 279
RWS/Diana Model 52 Air Rifle, 279
RWS/Diana Model 52 Deluxe Air Rifle, 279
RWS/Diana Model 54 Air King Air Rifle, 279
RWS/Diana Model 100 Match Air Rifle, 279

S

SA-85 Semi-Auto Rifle, 161
Sabatti Skeet Over/Under Shotgun, 223
Sabatti Sporting Clays Over/Under Shotgun, 223
Sabatti Trap Over/Under Shotgun, 223
Sabotti Over/Under Combination Gun, 189
Safari Arms Cohort Pistol, 121
Safari Arms Enforcer Pistol, 121
Safari Arms GI Safari Pistol, 121
Safari Arms Matchmaster Carrycomp I Pistol, 136
Safari Arms Matchmaster Pistol, 136
Sako Classic Bolt-Action Rifle, 177
Sako Fiberclass Sporter Rifle, 178
Sako Finnfire Bolt-Action Rifle, 198
Sako Hunter Left-Hand Rifle, 177
Sako Hunter Rifle, 177
Sako Lightweight Deluxe Rifle, 177
Sako Long-Range Hunting Rifle, 177
Sako Mannlicher-Style Carbine, 177
Sako Safari Grade Bolt-Action Rifle, 178
Sako Super Deluxe Sporter Rifle, 177
Sako TRG-21 Bolt-Action Rifle, 204
Sako TRG-S Bolt-Action Rifle, 178
Sako Varmint Heavy Barrel Rifle, 177
Sauer 90 Bolt-Action Rifle, 178
Sauer 202 Bolt-Action Rifle, 178
Sauer 202TR Target Rifle, 205
Sauer Drilling, 189
Savage 24F Predator O/U Combination Gun, 189
Savage 24F-20 Predator O/U Combination Gun, 189
Savage Mark I-G Bolt-Action Rifle, 199
Savage Mark I-GY Bolt-Action Rifle, 199
Savage Mark II-G Bolt-Action Rifle, 198

Savage Mark II-GL Bolt-Action Rifle, 198
Savage Mark II-GXP Bolt-Action Rifle, 198
Savage Mark II-GXP Package Gun, 198
Savage Mark II-GY Bolt-Action Rifle, 198
Savage Mark II-Y Bolt-Action Rifle, 198
Savage Model 64G Auto Rifle, 192
Savage Model 93G Magnum Bolt-Action Rifle, 199
Savage Model 99C Lever-Action Rifle, 165
Savage Model 99CE Centennial Edition Rifle, 165
Savage Model 110CY Ladies/Youth Rifle, 178
Savage Model 110FM Sierra Light Weight Rifle, 178
Savage Model 110FP Tactical Rifle, 178
Savage Model 110GCXP3 Package Gun, 179
Savage Model 110GXP3 Package Gun, 179
Savage Model 111 Classic Hunter Rifles, 179
Savage Model 111F Classic Hunter Rifle, 179
Savage Model 111FAK Express Rifle, 179
Savage Model 111FC Classic Hunter Rifle, 179
Savage Model 111FCXP3 Package Gun, 179
Savage Model 111FNS Classic Hunter Rifle, 179
Savage Model 111FXP3 Package Gun, 179
Savage Model 111G Classic Hunter Rifle, 179
Savage Model 111GC Classic Hunter Rifle, 179
Savage Model 111GNS Classic Hunter Rifle, 179
Savage Model 112 Varmint Rifles, 179
Savage Model 112BT Competition Grade Rifle, 205
Savage Model 112BT-S Competition Grade Rifle, 205
Savage Model 112BVSS Varmint Rifle, 179
Savage Model 112BVSS-S Varmint Rifle, 179
Savage Model 112FV Varmint Rifle, 179
Savage Model 112FVSS Varmint Rifle, 179
Savage Model 112FVSS-S Varmint Rifle, 179
Savage Model 114C Classic Rifle, 179
Savage Model 114CE Classic European Rifle, 179
Savage Model 116 Weather Warrior Rifles, 179
Savage Model 116FCS Weather Warrior Rifle, 179
Savage Model 116FCSAK Weather Warrior Rifle, 179
Savage Model 116FSAK Weather Warrior Rifle, 179
Savage Model 116FSK Kodiak Warrior Rifle, 179
Savage Model 116FSS Weather Warrior Rifle, 179
Savage Model 116SE Safari Express Rifle, 180
Savage Model 116US Ultra Stainless Rifle, 180
Savage Model 900B Biathlon Rifle, 205
Savage Model 900S Silhouette Rifle, 205
Savage Model 900TR Target Rifle, 205
Schuetzen Pistol Works Big Deuce Pistol, 121
Schuetzen Pistol Works Enforcer Carrycomp II Pistol, 121
Schuetzen Pistol Works Griffon Pistol, 121
Schuetzen Pistol Works Reliable 4-Star Pistol, 121
Schuetzen Pistol Works Reliable Pistol, 121
Schuetzen Pistol Works Renegade, 121
Second Model Brown Bess Carbine, 255
Second Model Brown Bess Musket, 255
Seecamp LWS 32 Pistol, 121
C. Sharps Arms 1875 Classic Sharps Rifle, 187
C. Sharps Arms New Model 1874 Old Reliable Rifle, 187
C. Sharps Arms New Model 1875 Business Rifle, 186
C. Sharps Arms New Model 1875 Carbine, Rifle, 186
C. Sharps Arms New Model 1875 Rifle, 186
C. Sharps Arms New Model 1875 Saddle Rifle, 186
C. Sharps Arms New Model 1875 Sporting Rifle, 186
C. Sharps Arms New Model 1875 Target & Long Range Rifle, 187
Sheriff Model 1851 Percussion Revolver, 243
Shiloh Sharps 1874 Business Rifle, 187
Shiloh Sharps 1874 Hartford Model Rifle, 187
Shiloh Sharps 1874 Long Range Express Rifle, 187
Shiloh Sharps 1874 Montana Roughrider, 187
Shiloh Sharps 1874 Saddle Rifle, 187
Shiloh Sharps 1874 Sporting Rifle No. 1, 187
Shiloh Sharps 1874 Sporting Rifle No. 3, 187
SIG P210-2 Pistol, 122
SIG P210-6 Pistol, 122
SIG Sauer P220 American Pistol, 122
SIG Sauer P225 DA Pistol, 122
SIG Sauer P226 DA Pistol, 122
SIG Sauer P228 DA Pistol, 122
SIG Sauer P229 DA Pistol, 122
SIG Sauer P230 DA Pistol, 122
SIG Sauer P230SL DA Pistol, 122
Silma Model 70 Over/Under Shotgun, 224
SKB Model 385 Side-by-Side Shotgun, 229
SKB Model 585 Over/Under Shotgun, 224
SKB Model 585 Skeet Over/Under Shotgun, 224
SKB Model 585 Skeet Set Over/Under Shotgun, 224
SKB Model 585 Sporting Clays Over/Under Shotgun, 224
SKB Model 585 Trap Over/Under Shotgun, 224
SKB Model 585 Two-Barrel Field Set Shotgun, 224
SKB Model 585 Waterfowler Over/Under Shotgun, 224
SKB Model 585 Youth Model Over/Under Shotgun, 224
SKB Model 785 Field Over/Under Shotgun, 224
SKB Model 785 Field Set Over/Under Shotgun, 224
SKB Model 785 Over/Under Shotgun, 224
SKB Model 785 Skeet Over/Under Shotgun, 224
SKB Model 785 Skeet Set Over/Under Shotgun, 224
SKB Model 785 Sporting Clays Over/Under Shotgun, 224
SKB Model 785 Sporting Clays Set Over/Under Shotgun, 224

SKB Model 785 Trap Combo Shotgun Over/Under Shotgun, 224
SKB Model 785 Trap Over/Under Shotgun, 224
Slavia Model 631 Air Rifle, 280
Smith & Wesson Model 10 M&P Heavy Barrel Revolver, 142
Smith & Wesson Model 10 M&P Revolver, 142
Smith & Wesson Model 13 H.B. M&P Revolver, 142
Smith & Wesson Model 14 Full Lug Revolver, 142
Smith & Wesson Model 15 Combat Masterpiece Revolver, 142
Smith & Wesson Model 17 K-22 Masterpiece Revolver, 143
Smith & Wesson Model 19 Combat Magnum Revolver, 143
Smith & Wesson Model 29 Revolver, 143
Smith & Wesson Model 36 Chiefs Special Revolver, 143
Smith & Wesson Model 36LS LadySmith Revolver, 143
Smith & Wesson Model 37 Airweight Revolver, 143
Smith & Wesson Model 38 Bodyguard Revolver, 144
Smith & Wesson Model 41 Target Pistol, 136
Smith & Wesson Model 49 Bodyguard Revolver, 144
Smith & Wesson Model 60 3" Full-Lug Revolver, 144
Smith & Wesson Model 60 Chiefs Special Revolver, 143
Smith & Wesson Model 60LS LadySmith Revolver, 143
Smith & Wesson Model 63 Kit Gun Revolver, 144
Smith & Wesson Model 64 M&P Revolver, 144
Smith & Wesson Model 65 H.B. M&P Revolver, 142
Smith & Wesson Model 65 Revolver, 142
Smith & Wesson Model 65LS LadySmith Revolver, 144
Smith & Wesson Model 66 Stainless Combat Magnum Revolver, 144
Smith & Wesson Model 67 Combat Masterpiece Revolver, 144
Smith & Wesson Model 410 DA Pistol, 123
Smith & Wesson Model 422 Pistol, 122
Smith & Wesson Model 442 Centennial Airweight Revolver, 145
Smith & Wesson Model 457 DA Pistol, 123
Smith & Wesson Model 586 Distinguished Combat Magnum Revolver, 144
Smith & Wesson Model 617 Full Lug Revolver, 144
Smith & Wesson Model 622 Pistol, 122
Smith & Wesson Model 622 VR Pistol, 123
Smith & Wesson Model 625 Revolver, 144
Smith & Wesson Model 629 Classic DX Revolver, 143
Smith & Wesson Model 629 Classic PowerPort Revolver, 143
Smith & Wesson Model 629 Classic Revolver, 143
Smith & Wesson Model 629 Revolver, 143
Smith & Wesson Model 637 Airweight Revolver, 143
Smith & Wesson Model 640 Centennial Revolver, 145
Smith & Wesson Model 642 Airweight Revolver, 145
Smith & Wesson Model 642LS LadySmith Revolver, 145
Smith & Wesson Model 649 Bodyguard Revolver, 144
Smith & Wesson Model 651 Revolver, 145
Smith & Wesson Model 657 Revolver, 145
Smith & Wesson Model 686 Distinguished Combat Magnum Revolver, 144
Smith & Wesson Model 686 Plus Revolver, 144
Smith & Wesson Model 908 Auto Pistol, 123
Smith & Wesson Model 909 DA Pistol, 123
Smith & Wesson Model 910 DA Pistol, 123
Smith & Wesson Model 940 Centennial Revolver, 145
Smith & Wesson Model 2206 Target Pistol, 123
Smith & Wesson Model 2213 Sportsman Pistol, 123
Smith & Wesson Model 2214 Sportsman Pistol, 123
Smith & Wesson Model 3913 DA Pistol, 123
Smith & Wesson Model 3913 LadySmith Pistol, 123
Smith & Wesson Model 3953 DA Pistol, 123
Smith & Wesson Model 4006 Pistol, 124
Smith & Wesson Model 4013 Pistol, 124
Smith & Wesson Model 4046 Pistol, 124
Smith & Wesson Model 4053 Pistol, 124
Smith & Wesson Model 4500 Series Pistols, 124
Smith & Wesson Model 4506 Pistol, 124
Smith & Wesson Model 4516 Pistol, 124
Smith & Wesson Model 4566 Pistol, 124
Smith & Wesson Model 4586 Pistol, 124
Smith & Wesson Model 5900 Series Pistol, 124
Smith & Wesson Model 5903 Pistol, 124
Smith & Wesson Model 5904 Pistol, 124
Smith & Wesson Model 5906 Pistol, 124
Smith & Wesson Model 5946 Pistol, 124
Smith & Wesson Model 6904 Pistol, 124
Smith & Wesson Model 6906 Pistol, 124
Smith & Wesson Model 6946 Pistol, 124
Smith & Wesson Sigma Series Pistols, 124
Smith & Wesson Sigma SW9C Pistol, 124
Smith & Wesson Sigma SW9F Pistol, 124
Smith & Wesson Sigma SW40C Pistol, 124
Smith & Wesson Sigma SW40F Pistol, 124
Smith & Wesson Sigma SW380 Pistol, 124
Snake Charmer II Shotgun, 234
Sphinx AT-380 Pistol, 125
Sphinx AT-2000C Competitor Pistol, 136
Sphinx AT-2000CS Competitor Pistol, 136
Sphinx AT-2000GM Grand Master Pistol, 136

Sphinx AT-2000GMS Grand Master Pistol, 136
Sphinx AT-2000H Pistol, 125
Sphinx AT-2000P Pistol, 125
Sphinx AT-2000PS Pistol, 125
Sphinx AT-2000S Pistol, 125
Spiller & Burr Percussion Revolver, 243
Springfield Inc. 1911A1 Basic Pistol, 125
Springfield Inc. 1911A1 Bullseye Wadcutter Pistol, 136
Springfield Inc. 1911A1 Champion Comp Pistol, 126
Springfield Inc. 1911A1 Champion Mil-Spec Pistol, 126
Springfield Inc. 1911A1 Compact Lightweight Pistol, 126
Springfield Inc. 1911A1 Compact Mil-Spec Pistol, 126
Springfield Inc. 1911A1 Competition Pistol, 136
Springfield Inc. 1911A1 Custom Carry Pistol, 125
Springfield Inc. 1911A1 Defender Pistol, 126
Springfield Inc. 1911A1 Factory Comp Pistol, 125
Springfield Inc. 1911A1 High Capacity Pistol, 125
Springfield Inc. 1911A1 Lightweight Pistol, 125
Springfield Inc. 1911A1 N.M. Hardball Pistol, 137
Springfield Inc. 1911A1 Pistol, 125
Springfield Inc. 1911A1 Standard Pistol, 125
Springfield Inc. 1911A1 Trophy Match Pistol, 136
Springfield Inc. Basic Competition Pistol, 136
Springfield Inc. Distinguished Limited Pistol, 136
Springfield Inc. Distinguished Pistol, 136
Springfield Inc. Expert Ltd. Pistol, 136
Springfield Inc. Expert Pistol, 136
Springfield Inc. M1A National Match Rifle, 161
Springfield Inc. M1A Rifle, 161
Springfield Inc. M1A Super Match Rifle, 161
Springfield Inc. M1A-A1 Bush Rifle, 161
Springfield Inc. M1A/M-21 Tactical Model Rifle, 205
Springfield Inc. M6 Scout Rifle/Shotgun, 189
Springfield Inc. N.R.A. PPC Pistol, 125
Springfield Inc. SAR-8 Sporter Rifle, 161
Springfield Inc. SAR-4800 Rifle, 161
Springfield Inc. V10 Ultra Compact Pistol, 126
Springfield Ind. M1A Super Match Rifle, 205
Star Firestar M45 Pistol, 126
Star Firestar Pistol, 126
Star Firestar Plus Pistol, 126
Star Ultrastar DA Pistol, 126
Steyr-Mannlicher SPG-T Rifle, 206
Steyr CO_2 Match 91 Air Rifle, 280
Steyr CO_2 Match Air Pistol, 269
Steyr CO_2 Match LP1 Air Pistol, 269
Steyr CO_2 Running Target Air Rifle, 280
Steyr LP5C Match Air Pistol, 269
Steyr-Mannlicher Luxus Model L Rifle, 180
Steyr-Mannlicher Luxus Model M Rifle, 180
Steyr-Mannlicher Luxus Model S Rifle, 180
Steyr-Mannlicher Match SPG-UIT Rifle, 206
Steyr-Mannlicher MIII Professional Rifle, 180
Steyr-Mannlicher SPG-CISM Rifle, 206
Steyr-Mannlicher Sporter Model L Rifle, 180
Steyr-Mannlicher Sporter Model M Rifle, 180
Steyr-Mannlicher Sporter Model S Rifle, 180
Steyr-Mannlicher Sporter Model S/T Rifle, 180
Steyr-Mannlicher Sporter Model SL Rifle, 180
Steyr-Mannlicher SSG-PI Rifle, 205
Steyr-Mannlicher SSG-PII Rifle, 205
Steyr-Mannlicher SSG-PIV Rifle, 205
Stoeger American Eagle Luger Pistol, 126
Stoeger Pro Series 95 Bull Barrel Pistol, 137
Stoeger Pro Series 95 Fluted Barrel Pistol, 137
Stoeger Pro Series 95 Vent Rib Pistol, 137
Stoeger/IGA Condor I Over/Under Shotgun, 224
Stoeger/IGA Condor II Over/Under Shotgun, 224
Stoeger/IGA Condor Supreme Over/Under Shotgun, 224
Stoeger/IGA English Stock Side-by-Side Shotgun, 229
Stoeger/IGA Ladies Side-by-Side Shotgun, 230
Stoeger/IGA Reuna Shotgun, 234
Stoeger/IGA Reuna Youth Shotgun, 234
Stoeger/IGA Uplander Coach Gun Side-by-Side Shotgun, 229
Stoeger/IGA Uplander Side-by-Side Shotgun, 229
Stoeger/IGA Youth Side-by-Side Shotgun, 230
Stone Mountain 1853 Enfield Musket, 255
Stone Mountain Arms Sheriff's Model Percussion Revolver, 240
Stone Mountain Silver Eagle Rifle, 255
Stoner SR-25 Carbine, 162
Stoner SR-25 Lightweight Match Rifle, 206
Stoner SR-25 Match Rifle, 206
Stoner SR-25 Sporter Rifle, 162
Sundance BOA Pistol, 127
Sundance Laser 25 Pistol, 127
Sundance Model A-25 Pistol, 127
Sundance Point Blank O/U Derringer, 155

T

Tactical Response TR-870 Border Patrol Model Shotgun, 236
Tactical Response TR-870 FBI Model Shotgun, 236
Tactical Response TR-870 K-9 Model Shotgun, 236

Tactical Response TR-870 Louis Awerbuck Model Shotgun, 236
Tactical Response TR-870 Military Model Shotgun, 236
Tactical Response TR-870 Patrol Model Shotgun, 236
Tactical Response TR-870 Practical Turkey Model Shotgun, 236
Tactical Response TR-870 Standard Model Shotgun, 236
Tactical Response TR-870 Urban Sniper Model Shotgun, 236
Tanner 50 Meter Free Rifle, 206
Tanner 300 Meter Free Rifle, 206
Tanner Standard UIT Rifle, 206
Tar-Hunt RSG-12 Matchless Model Shotgun, 234
Tar-Hunt RSG-12 Peerless Model Shotgun, 234
Tar-Hunt RSG-12 Professional Rifled Slug Gun, 234
Tar-Hunt RSG-12 Turkey Model Shotgun, 234
Taurus Model 44 Revolver, 145
Taurus Model 65 Revolver, 145
Taurus Model 66 Revolver, 145
Taurus Model 80 Standard Revolver, 145
Taurus Model 82 Heavy Barrel Revolver, 146
Taurus Model 83 Revolver, 146
Taurus Model 85 Revolver, 146
Taurus Model 85CH Revolver, 146
Taurus Model 94 Revolver, 146
Taurus Model 96 Revolver, 146
Taurus Model 431 Revolver, 146
Taurus Model 441 Revolver, 146
Taurus Model 605 Revolver, 146
Taurus Model 605CH Revolver, 146
Taurus Model 607 Revolver, 146
Taurus Model 608 Revolver, 146
Taurus Model 669 Revolver, 147
Taurus Model 689 Revolver, 147
Taurus Model 941 Revolver, 147
Taurus Model PT 22 Pistol, 127
Taurus Model PT 25 Pistol, 127
Taurus Model PT 58 Pistol, 127
Taurus Model PT 92AF Pistol, 127
Taurus Model PT 92AFC Pistol, 127
Taurus Model PT 99AF Pistol, 127
Taurus Model PT-908 Pistol, 128
Taurus Model PT-940 Pistol, 128
Taurus Model PT-945 Pistol, 128
Taurus PT 100 Pistol, 127
Taurus PT 101 Pistol, 127
Texas Armory Defender Derringer, 155
Texas Longhorn Arms "The Jezebel" Pistol, 155
Texas Longhorn Arms Cased Set, 152
Texas Longhorn Arms Grover's Improved No. Five Revolver, 151
Texas Longhorn Arms Right-hand Single Action Revolver, 151
Texas Longhorn Arms Sesquicentennial Model Revolver, 151
Texas Longhorn Arms Texas Border Special Revolver, 152
Texas Longhorn Arms West Texas Flat Top Target Revolver, 152
Texas Paterson 1836 Percussion Revolver, 243
The Judge Single Shot Pistol, 155
Thompson/Center Big Boar Rifle, 255
Thompson/Center Contender Carbine Youth Model, 187
Thompson/Center Contender Carbine, 187
Thompson/Center Contender Hunter Package, 156
Thompson/Center Contender Pistol, 156
Thompson/Center Encore Pistol, 156
Thompson/Center Fire Hawk Bantam, 255
Thompson/Center Fire Hawk Rifle, 255
Thompson/Center Grey Hawk Percussion Rifle, 256
Thompson/Center Hawken Rifle, 256
Thompson/Center Hawken Silver Elite Rifle, 256
Thompson/Center New Englander Rifle, 256
Thompson/Center New Englander Shotgun, 262
Thompson/Center Pennsylvania Hunter Carbine, 256
Thompson/Center Pennsylvania Hunter Rifle, 256
Thompson/Center Pennsylvania Match Rifle, 256
Thompson/Center Renegade Hunter Rifle, 256
Thompson/Center Renegade Rifle, 256
Thompson/Center Scout Carbine, 256
Thompson/Center Scout Pistol, 238
Thompson/Center Scout Rifle, 256
Thompson/Center Stainless Contender Carbine, 187
Thompson/Center Stainless Contender Pistol, 156
Thompson/Center Stainless Super 14 Contender Pistol, 156
Thompson/Center Stainless Super 16 Contender Pistol, 156
Thompson/Center Super 14 Contender Pistol, 137
Thompson/Center Super 16 Contender Pistol, 137
Thompson/Center Thunderhawk Carbine, 257
Thompson/Center Thunderhawk Shadow Rifle, 257
Tikka Continental Long Range Hunting Rifle, 180
Tikka Continental Varmint Rifle, 180
Tikka Model 512S Combination Gun, 189
Tikka Model 512S Double Rifle, 189
Tikka Model 512S Field Grade Over/Under Shotgun, 224

Tikka Model 512S Sporting Clays Over/Under Shotgun, 224
Tikka Whitetail Hunter Bolt-Action Rifle, 180
Tikka Whitetail Hunter Synthetic Rifle, 180
Traditions 1853 Three-Band Enfield Rifle, 258
Traditions 1861 U.S. Springfield Rifle, 259
Traditions Army 1860 Percussion Revolver, 239
Traditions Buckhunter In-Line Pistol, 239
Traditions Buckhunter Pro In-Line Rifle, 257
Traditions Buckhunter Pro Shotgun, 262
Traditions Buckskinner Carbine, 257
Traditions Buckskinner Pistol, 239
Traditions Deerhunter Composite Rifle, 258
Traditions Deerhunter Rifles, 257
Traditions Deerhunter Scout Rifle, 257
Traditions Hawken Woodsman Rifle, 258
Traditions In-Line Buckhunter Scout Rifle, 257
Traditions In-Line Buckhunter Series Rifles, 257
Traditions Kentucky Pistol, 239
Traditions Kentucky Rifle, 258
Traditions Pennsylvania Rifle, 258
Traditions Pioneer Pistol, 239
Traditions Pioneer Rifle, 258
Traditions Shenandoah Rifle, 258
Traditions Tennessee Rifle, 258
Traditions Trapper Pistol, 239
Traditions William Parker Pistol, 239
Tristar Model 311 Double Shotgun, 230
Tristar Model 311R Double Shotgun, 230
Tristar Model 333 Over/Under Shotgun, 225
Tristar Model 333D Over/Under Shotgun, 225
Tristar Model 333L Over/Under Shotgun, 225
Tristar Model 333SC Over/Under Shotgun, 225
Tristar Model 333SCL Over/Under Shotgun, 225
Tryon Trailblazer Rifle, 259

U

Uberti 1st Model Dragoon Percussion Revolver, 243
Uberti 2nd Model Dragoon Percussion Revolver, 243
Uberti 3rd Model Dragoon Percussion Revolver, 243
Uberti 1861 Navy Percussion Revolver, 240
Uberti 1862 Pocket Navy Percussion Revolver, 243
Uberti 1866 Sporting Carbine, 165
Uberti 1866 Sporting Rifle, 165
Uberti 1866 Yellowboy Carbine, 165
Uberti 1873 Buckhorn Single Action Revolver, 152
Uberti 1873 Cattleman Single Action Revolvers, 152
Uberti 1873 Cattlemen Bisley Revolver, 152
Uberti 1873 Sporting Carbine, 166
Uberti 1873 Sporting Rifle, 166
Uberti 1875 SA Army Outlaw Revolver, 152
Uberti 1890 Army Outlaw Revolver, 152
Uberti Army 1860 Percussion Revolver, 239
Uberti Henry Carbine, 166
Uberti Henry Rifle, 166
Uberti Henry Trapper, 166
Uberti Rolling Block Baby Carbine, 187
Uberti Rolling Block Target Pistol, 156
UFA Grand Teton Rifle, 259
UFA Teton Blackstone Rifle, 259
UFA Teton Rifle, 259
Ugartechea 10-Gauge Magnum Double Shotgun, 230
Ultra Light Arms Model 20 REB Hunter's Pistol, 156
Ultra Light Arms Model 20 RF Bolt-Action Rifle, 199
Ultra Light Arms Model 20 Rifle, 181

Ultra Light Arms Model 24 Left-Hand Rifle, 181
Ultra Light Arms Model 24 Rifle, 181
Ultra Light Arms Model 28 Rifle, 181
Ultra Light Arms Model 40 Rifle, 181
Ultra Light Arms Model 90 Muzzleloader Rifle, 259
Unique D.E.S. 32U Target Pistol, 137
Unique D.E.S. 69U Target Pistol, 137

V

Voere VEC-91 Lightning Bolt-Action Rifle, 181
Voere VEC-91BR Caseless Rifle, 181
Voere VEC-91HB Varmint Special Caseless Rifle, 181
Voere VEC-91SS Caseless Rifle, 181
Voere VEC-95CG Single Shot Pistol, 156
Voere VEC-RB Repeater Pistol, 156

W

Walker 1847 Hartford Model Percussion Revolver, 243
Walker 1847 Percussion Revolver, 243
Walther CPM-1 CO_2 Match Air Pistol, 269
Walther GSP Match Pistol, 137
Walther GSP-C Match Pistol, 137
Walther Model TPH Pistol, 128
Walther P88 Compact Pistol, 129
Walther P-5 Compact Pistol, 128
Walther P-5 Pistol, 128
Walther PP Pistol, 128
Walther PPK American Pistol, 128
Walther PPK/S American Pistol, 128
Weatherby Accumark Rifle, 182
Weatherby Athena Grade IV Over/Under Shotguns, 225
Weatherby Athena Grade V Field Over/Under Shotgun, 225
Weatherby Euromark Rifle, 182
Weatherby Lazermark V Rifle, 182
Weatherby Mark V Deluxe Bolt-Action Rifle, 181
Weatherby Mark V Eurosport Rifle, 181
Weatherby Mark V Sporter Bolt-Action Rifle, 181
Weatherby Mark V Stainless Rifle, 181
Weatherby Mark V Synthetic Rifle, 182
Weatherby Orion I Over/Under Shotgun, 225
Weatherby Orion II Classic Field Over/Under Shotgun, 225
Weatherby Orion II Classic Sporting Clays Over/Under Shotgun, 225
Weatherby Orion II Sporting Clays Over/Under Shotgun, 225
Weatherby Orion III Classic Field Over/Under Shotgun, 225
Weatherby Orion III Over/Under Shotgun, 225
Weatherby Orion Over/Under Shotgun, 225
Webley Patriot Air Rifle, 280
Wells Fargo 1848 Percussion Revolver, 240
Wesson & Harrington Buffalo Classic Rifle, 187
Whiscombe JW50 Air Rifle, 280
Whiscombe JW60 Air Rifle, 280
Whiscombe JW70 Air Rifle, 280
Whiscombe JW75 Air Rifle, 280
Whiscombe JW75 High Power Air Rifle, 280
Whiscombe JW Series Air Rifles, 280
White Shooting Systems Bison Rifle, 260
White Shooting Systems Super 91 Rifle, 259
White Shooting Systems Super Safari Rifle, 259

White Shooting Systems Tominator Shotgun, 262
White Shooting Systems White Lightning Rifle, 260
White Shooting Systems White Thunder Shotgun, 262
White Shooting Systems Whitetail Rifle, 260
Wichita Classic Rifle, 182
Wichita Classic Silhouette Pistol, 137
Wichita Silhouette Pistol, 137
Wichita Varmint Rifle, 182
Wildey Automatic Pistol, 129
Wilkinson "Linda" Pistol, 129
Wilkinson "Sherry" Pistol, 129
Wilkinson Terry Carbine, 162
Winchester 8-Shot Pistol Grip Pump Security Shotgun, 236
Winchester Model 12 Grade I Pump Shotgun, 214
Winchester Model 12 Grade IV Pump Station, 214
Winchester Model 12 Pump Shotgun, 214
Winchester Model 70 Classic Featherweight All-Terrain Rifle, 183
Winchester Model 70 Classic Featherweight Rifle, 183
Winchester Model 70 Classic Laredo Rifle, 183
Winchester Model 70 Classic SM Rifle, 182
Winchester Model 70 Classic Sporter Rifle, 182
Winchester Model 70 Classic Stainless Rifle, 182
Winchester Model 70 Classic Super Express Magnum Rifle, 183
Winchester Model 70 Classic Super Grade Rifle, 183
Winchester Model 70 Synthetic Heavy Varmint Rifle, 183
Winchester Model 94 Big Bore Side Eject Rifle, 166
Winchester Model 94 Legacy Rifle, 166
Winchester Model 94 Ranger Side Eject Lever-Action Rifle, 166
Winchester Model 94 Side Eject Lever-Action Rifle, 166
Winchester Model 94 Trapper Side Eject Carbine, 166
Winchester Model 94 Wrangler Side Eject Rifle, 166
Winchester Model 1300 Advantage Camo Deer Gun, 214
Winchester Model 1300 Black Shadow Deer Gun, 214
Winchester Model 1300 Black Shadow Field Gun, 214
Winchester Model 1300 Defender Field Combo Shotgun, 236
Winchester Model 1300 Defender Pump Shotgun, 236
Winchester Model 1300 Ladies/Youth Pump Shotgun, 214
Winchester Model 1300 Ranger Deer Gun, 214
Winchester Model 1300 Ranger Pump Gun Combo, 214
Winchester Model 1300 Ranger Pump Station, 214
Winchester Model 1300 Realtree Turkey Gun, 214
Winchester Model 1300 Stainless Marine Pump Shotgun, 236
Winchester Model 1300 Walnut Pump Shotgun, 214
Winchester Model 1895 High Grade Rifle, 166
Winchester Model 1895 Lever-Action Rifle, 166
Winchester Model 9422 High Grade Rifle, 194
Winchester Model 9422 Lever-Action Rifle, 193
Winchester Model 9422 Magnum Lever-Action Rifle, 194
Winchester Model 9422 Trapper, 194
Winchester Model Black Shadow Turkey Gun, 214
Winchester Ranger Rifle, 183

Z

Zouave Percussion Rifle, 424

HANDGUNS—AUTOLOADERS, SERVICE & SPORT

Includes models suitable for several forms of competition and other sporting purposes.

AA ARMS AP9 PISTOL
Caliber: 9mm Para., 10-shot magazine.
Barrel: 5".
Weight: 3.5 lbs. **Length:** 12" overall.
Stocks: Checkered black synthetic.
Sights: Post front adjustable for elevation, rear adjustable for windage.
Features: Ventilated barrel shroud; blue or electroless nickel finish. Made in U.S. by AA Arms.
Price: Blue $299.00
Price: Nickel $312.00
Price: AP9 Target (11" barrel) $399.00

ACCU-TEK MODEL AT-9SS AUTO PISTOL
Caliber: 9mm Para., 8-shot magazine.
Barrel: 3.2".
Weight: 28 oz. **Length:** 6.25" overall.
Stocks: Black checkered nylon.
Sights: Blade front, rear adjustable for windage; three-dot system.
Features: Stainless steel construction. Double action only. Firing pin block with no external safeties. Lifetime warranty. Introduced 1992. Made in U.S. by Accu-Tek.
Price: Satin stainless $317.00

Accu-Tek AT-45SS Auto Pistol
Same as the Model AT-9SS except chambered for 45 ACP, 6-shot magazine. Introduced 1995. Made in U.S. by Accu-Tek.
Price: Stainless steel $327.00

ACCU-TEK MODEL AT-380SS AUTO PISTOL
Caliber: 380 ACP, 5-shot magazine.
Barrel: 2.75".
Weight: 20 oz. **Length:** 5.6" overall.
Stocks: Grooved black composition.
Sights: Blade front, rear adjustable for windage.
Features: Stainless steel frame and slide. External hammer; manual thumb safety; firing pin block, trigger disconnect. Lifetime warranty. Introduced 1991. Made in U.S. by Accu-Tek.
Price: Satin stainless $191.00
Price: Black finish over steel (AT-380B) $196.00

Accu-Tek Model AT-32SS Auto Pistol
Same as the AT-380SS except chambered for 32 ACP. Introduced 1991.
Price: Satin stainless $185.00
Price: Black finish over steel (AT-32B) $190.00

ACCU-TEK MODEL HC-380SS AUTO PISTOL
Caliber: 380 ACP, 10-shot magazine.
Barrel: 2.75".
Weight: 28 oz. **Length:** 6" overall.
Stocks: Checkered black composition.
Sights: Blade front, rear adjustable for windage.
Features: External hammer; manual thumb safety with firing pin and trigger disconnect; bottom magazine release. Stainless finish. Introduced 1993. Made in U.S. by Accu-Tek.
Price: Satin stainless $243.00
Price: Black finish over stainless $248.00

AMERICAN ARMS AUSSIE PISTOL
Caliber: 9mm Para., 40 S&W, 10-shot magazine.
Barrel: 4 3/4".
Weight: 23 oz. **Length:** 7 7/8" overall.
Stocks: Integral; checkered polymer.
Sights: Blade front, rear adjustable for windage.
Features: Double action only. Polymer frame. Has five safeties—firing pin block; positive trigger safety; magazine safety; slide lock safety; loaded chamber indicator. Introduced 1996. From American Arms, Inc.
Price: $425.00

AA Arms AP9 Mini, AP9 Mini/5 Pistol
Similar to AP9 except scaled-down dimensions with 3" or 5" barrel.
Price: 3" barrel, blue $239.00
Price: 3" barrel, electroless nickel $259.00
Price: Mini/5, 5" barrel, blue $259.00
Price: Mini/5, 5" barrel, electroless nickel $279.00

Acc-Tek AT-9SS

Accu-Tek AT-40SS Auto Pistol
Same as the Model AT-9 except chambered for 40 S&W, 7-shot magazine. Introduced 1992.
Price: Stainless $317.00

Acc-Tek AT 380SS

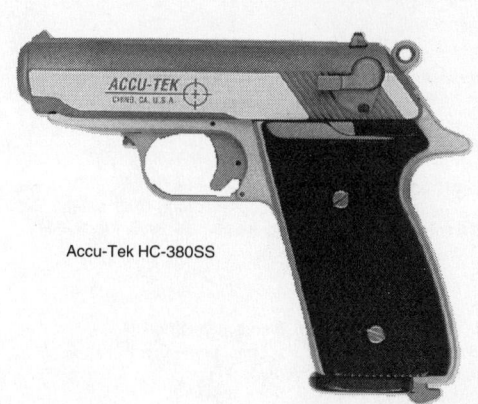
Accu-Tek HC-380SS

CAUTION: PRICES SHOWN ARE SUPPLIED BY THE MANUFACTURER OR IMPORTER. CHECK YOUR LOCAL GUN SHOP.

HANDGUNS—AUTOLOADERS, SERVICE & SPORT

American Arms Escort

AMERICAN ARMS ESCORT AUTO PISTOL
Caliber: 380 ACP, 7-shot magazine.
Barrel: 3⅜".
Weight: 19 oz. **Length:** 6⅛" overall.
Stocks: Soft polymer.
Sights: Blade front, rear adjustable for windage.
Features: Double-action-only trigger; stainless steel construction; chamber loaded indicator. Introduced 1995. From American Arms, Inc.
Price: $349.00

American Arms PK22

Armscor M-1911-A1P

AMT Automag II

AMERICAN ARMS MODEL PK22 DA AUTO PISTOL
Caliber: 22 LR, 8-shot magazine.
Barrel: 3.3".
Weight: 22 oz. **Length:** 6.3" overall.
Stocks: Checkered plastic.
Sights: Fixed.
Features: Double action. Polished blue finish. Slide-mounted safety. Made in the U.S. by American Arms, Inc.
Price: $199.00

AMERICAN ARMS MODEL P-98 AUTO PISTOL
Caliber: 22 LR, 8-shot magazine.
Barrel: 5".
Weight: 25 oz. **Length:** 8⅛" overall.
Stocks: Grooved black polymer.
Sights: Blade front, rear adjustable for windage.
Features: Double action with hammer-block safety, magazine disconnect safety. Alloy frame. Has external appearance of the Walther P-38 pistol. Introduced 1989. Made in U.S. by American Arms, Inc.
Price: $209.00

ARMSCOR M-1911-A1P AUTOLOADING PISTOL
Caliber: 45 ACP, 7- or 10-shot magazine.
Barrel: 5".
Weight: 38 oz. **Length:** 8¾" overall.
Stocks: Checkered.
Sights: Blade front, rear drift adjustable for windage; three-dot system.
Features: Skeletonized combat hammer and trigger; beavertail grip safety; extended slide release; oversize thumb safety; Parkerized finish. Introduced 1996. Imported from the Philippines by K.B.I., Inc.
Price: $399.99

AMT AUTOMAG II AUTO PISTOL
Caliber: 22 WMR, 9-shot magazine (7-shot with 3⅜" barrel).
Barrel: 3⅜", 4½", 6".
Weight: About 23 oz. **Length:** 9⅜" overall.
Stocks: Grooved carbon fiber.
Sights: Blade front, adjustable rear.
Features: Made of stainless steel. Gas-assisted action. Exposed hammer. Slide flats have brushed finish, rest is sandblast. Squared trigger guard. Introduced 1986. From AMT.
Price: $405.95

AMT AUTOMAG III PISTOL
Caliber: 30 Carbine, 8-shot magazine.
Barrel: 6⅜".
Weight: 43 oz. **Length:** 10½" overall.
Stocks: Carbon fiber.
Sights: Blade front, adjustable rear.
Features: Stainless steel construction. Hammer-drop safety. Slide flats have brushed finish, rest is sandblasted. Introduced 1989. From AMT.
Price: $469.79

AMT AUTOMAG IV PISTOL
Caliber: 45 Winchester Magnum, 6-shot magazine.
Barrel: 6.5".
Weight: 46 oz. **Length:** 10.5" overall.
Stocks: Carbon fiber.
Sights: Blade front, adjustable rear.
Features: Made of stainless steel with brushed finish. Introduced 1990. Made in U.S. by AMT.
Price: $699.99

AMT 45 ACP HARDBALLER
Caliber: 45 ACP.
Barrel: 5".
Weight: 39 oz. **Length:** 8½" overall.
Stocks: Wrap-around rubber.
Sights: Adjustable.
Features: Extended combat safety, serrated matte slide rib, loaded chamber indicator, long grip safety, beveled magazine well, adjustable target trigger. All stainless steel. From AMT.
Price: $549.95
Price: Government model (as above except no rib, fixed sights) $489.99

AMT 45 ACP HARDBALLER LONG SLIDE
Caliber: 45 ACP.
Barrel: 7". **Length:** 10½" overall.
Stocks: Wrap-around rubber.
Sights: Fully adjustable rear sight.
Features: Slide and barrel are 2" longer than the standard 45, giving less recoil, added velocity, longer sight radius. Has extended combat safety, serrated matte rib, loaded chamber indicator, wide adjustable trigger. From AMT.
Price: $595.99

HANDGUNS—AUTOLOADERS, SERVICE & SPORT

AMT BACK UP II AUTO PISTOL
Caliber: 380 ACP, 5-shot magazine.
Barrel: 2 1/2".
Weight: 18 oz. **Length:** 5" overall.
Stocks: Carbon fiber.
Sights: Fixed, open, recessed.
Features: Concealed hammer, blowback operation; manual and grip safeties. All stainless steel construction. Smallest domestically-produced pistol in 380. From AMT.
Price: $309.99

AMT Back Up Double Action Only Pistol
Similar to the standard Back Up except has double-action-only mechanism, enlarged trigger guard, slide is rounded ar rear. Has 5-shot magazine. Introduced 1992. From AMT.
Price: $329.99
Price: 9mm Para., 38 Super, 40 S&W, 45 ACP $449.99

AMT 45 ACP Backup

ARGENTINE HI-POWER 9MM AUTO PISTOL
Caliber: 9mm Para., 10-shot magazine.
Barrel: 4 21/32".
Weight: 32 oz. **Length:** 7 3/4" overall.
Stocks: Checkered walnut.
Sights: Blade front, adjustable rear.
Features: Produced in Argentina under F.N. Browning license. Introduced 1990. Imported by Century International Arms, Inc.
Price: About $299.95

Argentine Hi-Power Detective Model
Similar to the standard model except has 3.8" barrel, 6.9" overall length and weighs 33 oz. Grips are finger-groove, checkered soft rubber. Matte black finish. Introduced 1994. Imported by Century International Arms, Inc.
Price: About $310.00

Argentine Hi-Power

ASTRA A-70 AUTO PISTOL
Caliber: 9mm Para., 8-shot; 40 S&W, 7-shot magazine.
Barrel: 3.5".
Weight: 29.3 oz. **Length:** 6.5" overall.
Stocks: Checkered black plastic.
Sights: Blade front, rear adjustable for windage.
Features: All steel frame and slide. Checkered grip straps and trigger guard. Nickel or blue finish. Introduced 1992. Imported from Spain by European American Armory.
Price: Blue, 9mm Para. $360.00
Price: Blue, 40 S&W $360.00
Price: Nickel, 9mm Para. $385.00
Price: Nickel, 40 S&W $385.00
Price: Stainless steel, 9mm $450.00
Price: Stainless steel, 40 S&W $450.00

Astra A-75 Decocker Auto Pistol
Same as the A-70 except has decocker system, double or single action, different trigger, contoured pebble-grain grips. Introduced 1993. Imported from Spain by European American Armory.
Price: Blue, 9mm or 40 S&W $415.00
Price: Nickel, 9mm or 40 S&W $440.00
Price: Blue, 45 ACP $445.00
Price: Nickel, 45 ACP $460.00
Price: Stainless steel, 9mm, 40 S&W $495.00
Price: Featherweight (23.5 oz.), 9mm, blue $440.00

Astra A-75

> Consult our Directory pages for the location of firms mentioned.

ASTRA A-100 AUTO PISTOL
Caliber: 9mm Para., 10-shot; 40 S&W, 10-shot; 45 ACP, 9-shot magazine.
Barrel: 3.9".
Weight: 29 oz. **Length:** 7.1" overall.
Stocks: Checkered black plastic.
Sights: Blade front, interchangeable rear blades for elevation, screw adjustable for windage.
Features: Double action. Decocking lever permits lowering hammer onto locked firing pin. Automatic firing pin block. Side button magazine release. Introduced 1993. Imported from Spain by European American Armory.
Price: Blue, 9mm, 40 S&W, 45 ACP $450.00
Price: As above, nickel $475.00

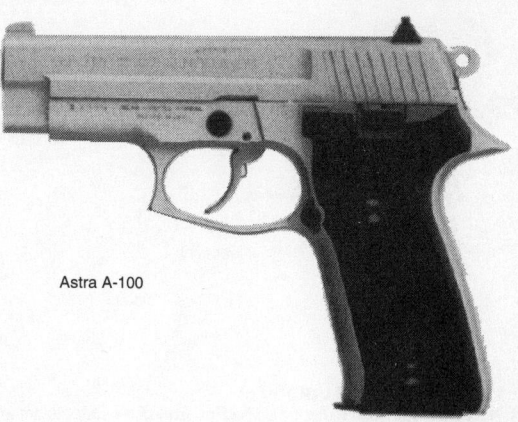

Astra A-100

HANDGUNS—AUTOLOADERS, SERVICE & SPORT

AUTO-ORDNANCE 1911A1 AUTOMATIC PISTOL
Caliber: 9mm Para., 38 Super, 9-shot; 10mm, 45 ACP, 7-shot magazine.
Barrel: 5".
Weight: 39 oz. **Length:** 8½" overall.
Stocks: Checkered plastic with medallion.
Sights: Blade front, rear adjustable for windage.
Features: Same specs as 1911A1 military guns—parts interchangeable. Frame and slide blued; each radius has non-glare finish. Made in U.S. by Auto-Ordnance Corp.
Price: 45 ACP, blue $397.50
Price: 45 ACP, Parkerized $389.95
Price: 45 ACP, satin nickel $425.95
Price: 9mm, 38 Super $435.00
Price: 10mm (has three-dot combat sights, rubber wrap-around grips) ..$435.00
Price: 45 ACP General Model (Commander style) $465.00
Price: Duo Tone (nickel frame, blue slide, three-dot sight system, textured black wrap-around grips) $435.00

Auto-Ordnance 1911A1 Competition Model
Similar to the standard Model 1911A1 except has barrel compensator. Commander hammer, flat mainspring housing, three-dot sight system, low-profile magazine funnel, Hi-Ride beavertail grip safety, full-length recoil spring guide system, black-textured rubber, wrap-around grips, and extended slide stop, safety and magazine catch. In 45 or 38 Super. Introduced 1994. Made in U.S. by Auto-Ordnance Corp.
Price: $635.00

Auto-Ordnance 1911A1

Auto-Ordnance ZG-51 Pit Bull Auto
Same as the 1911A1 except has 3½" barrel, weighs 36 oz. and has an over-all length of 7¼". Available in 45 ACP only; 7-shot magazine. Introduced 1989.
Price: $455.00

BABY EAGLE AUTO PISTOL
Caliber: 9mm Para., 40 S&W, 41 A.E.
Barrel: 4.37".
Weight: 35 oz. **Length:** 8.14" overall.
Stocks: High-impact black polymer.
Sights: Combat.
Features: Double-action mechanism; polygonal rifling; ambidextrous safety. Model 9mm F has frame-mounted safety on left side of pistol; Model 9mm FS has frame-mounted safety and 3.62" barrel. Introduced 1992. Imported by Magnum Research.
Price: 40 S&W, 41 A.E., 9mm (9mm F, 9mm FS), black finish $569.00
Price: Conversion kit, 9mm Para. to 41 A.E. $239.00
Price: 9mm FS, chrome finish $659.00
Price: 9mm FSS, matte black finish, frame-mounted safety, short grip, short barrel $569.00
Price: As above, chrome finish $659.00

Baby Eagle FS

Baer 1911 Concept III Auto Pistol
Same as the Concept I except has forged stainless frame with blued steel slide, Bo-Mar rear sight, 30 lpi checkering on front strap. Made in U.S. by Les Baer Custom, Inc.
Price: $1,500.00
Price: Concept IV (with Baer adjustable rear sight) $1,499.00
Price: Concept V (all stainless, Bo-Mar sight, checkered front strap) ..$1,598.00
Price: Concept VI (stainless, Baer adjustable sight, checkered front strap) $1,598.00

Baer 1911 Concept VII Auto Pistol
Same as the Concept I except reduced Commanche size with 4.25" barrel, weighs 27.5 oz., 7.75" overall. Blue finish, checkered front strap. Made in U.S. by Les Baer Custom, Inc.
Price: $1,480.00
Price: Concept VIII (stainless frame and slide, Baer adjustable rear sight) $1,598.00

Baer 1911 Concept IX Auto Pistol
Same as the Commanche Concept VII except has Baer lightweight forged aluminum frame, blued steel slide, Baer adjustable rear sight. Chambered for 45 ACP, 7-shot magazine. Made in U.S. by Les Baer Custom, Inc.
Price: $1,598.00
Price: Concept X (as above with stainless slide) $1,598.00

BAER 1911 CONCEPT I AUTO PISTOL
Caliber: 45 ACP, 7-shot magazine.
Barrel: 5".
Weight: 37 oz. **Length:** 8.5" overall.
Stocks: Checkered rosewood.
Sights: Baer dovetail front, Bo-Mar deluxe low-mount rear with hidden leaf.
Features: Baer forged steel frame, slide and barrel with Baer stainless bushing; slide fitted to frame; double serrated slide; Baer beavertail grip safety, checkered slide stop, tuned extractor, extended ejector, deluxe hammer and sear, match disconnector; lowered and flared ejection port; fitted recoil link; polished feed ramp, throated barrel; Baer fitted speed trigger, flat serrated mainspring housing. Blue finish. Made in U.S. by Les Baer Custom, Inc.
Price: $1,428.00
Price: Concept II (with Baer adjustable rear sight) $1,428.00

BAER 1911 PREMIER II AUTO PISTOL
Caliber: 45 ACP, 7- or 10-shot magazine.
Barrel: 5".
Weight: 37 oz. **Length:** 8.5" overall.
Stocks: Checkered rosewood, double diamond pattern.
Sights: Baer dovetailed front, low-mount Bo-Mar rear with hidden leaf.
Features: Baer NM forged steel frame and barrel with stainless bushing; slide fitted to frame; double serrated slide; lowered, flared ejection port; tuned, polished extractor; Baer extended ejector, checkered slide stop, aluminum speed trigger with 4-lb. pull, deluxe Commander hammer and sear, beavertail grip safety with pad, beveled magazine well, extended ambidextrous safety; flat mainspring housing; polished feed ramp and throated barrel; 30 lpi checkered front strap. Made in U.S. by Les Baer Custom, Inc.
Price: Blued $1,428.00
Price: Stainless $1,559.00
Price: 6" model, blued $1,690.00

Baer Premier II

Baer 1911 Prowler III Auto Pistol
Same as the Premier II except also has tapered cone stub weight and reverse recoil plug. Made in U.S. by Les Baer Custom, Inc.
Price: Standard size, blued $1,795.00

HANDGUNS—AUTOLOADERS, SERVICE & SPORT

Baer Custom Carry

BAER 1911 CUSTOM CARRY AUTO PISTOL
Caliber: 45 ACP, 7- or 10-shot magazine.
Barrel: 5".
Weight: 37 oz. **Length:** 8.5" overall.
Stocks: Checkered walnut.
Sights: Baer improved ramp-style dovetailed front, Novak low-mount rear.
Features: Baer forged NM frame, slide and barrel with stainless bushing; fitted slide to frame; double serrated slide (full-size only); Baer speed trigger with 4-lb. pull; Baer deluxe hammer and sear, tactical-style extended ambidextrous safety, beveled magazine well; polished feed ramp and throated barrel; tuned extractor; Baer extended ejector, checkered slide stop; lowered and flared ejection port, full-length recoil guide rod; recoil buff. Made in U.S. by Les Baer Custom, Inc.
Price: Standard size, blued $1,490.00
Price: Standard size, stainless $1,580.00
Price: Commanche size, blued $1,490.00
Price: Commanche size, stainless $1,580.00
Price: Commanche size, aluminum frame, blued slide $1,530.00
Price: Commanche size, aluminum frame, stainless slide $1,590.00

BAER LIGHTWEIGHT 22
Caliber: 22 LR.
Barrel: 5".
Weight: 25 oz. **Length:** 8.5" overall.
Stocks: Checkered walnut.
Sights: Blade front.
Features: Aluminum frame and slide. Baer beavertail grip safety with pad, checkered slide stop, deluxe hammer and sear, match disconnector, flat serrated mainspring housing, Baer fitted speed trigger, tuned extractor. Has total reliability tuning package, action job. Baer Ultra Coat finish. Introduced 1996. Made in U.S. by Les Baer Custom, Inc.
Price: Government model size, fixed sights $1,428.00
Price: Government model, Bo-Mar sights $1,498.00
Price: Commanche size, fixed sights $1,428.00

BAER 1911 S.R.P. PISTOL
Caliber: 45 ACP.
Barrel: 5".
Weight: 37 oz. **Length:** 8.5" overall.
Stocks: Checkered walnut.
Sights: Trijicon night sights.
Features: Similar to the F.B.I. contract gun except uses Baer forged steel frame. Has Baer match barrel with supported chamber, Wolff springs, complete tactical action job. All parts Mag-na-fluxed; deburred for tactical carry. Has Baer Ultra Coat finish. Tuned for reliability. Contact Baer for complete details. Introduced 1996. Made in U.S. by Les Baer Custom, Inc.
Price: Government or Commanche length $2,495.00

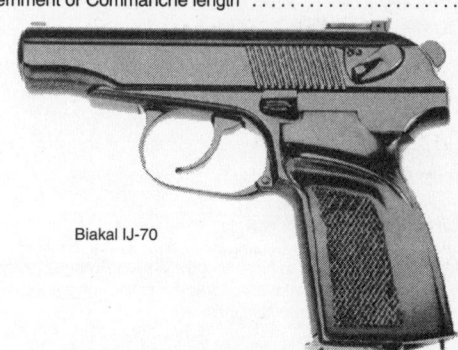
Biakal IJ-70

BAIKAL IJ-70 DA AUTO PISTOL
Caliber: 9x18mm Makarov, 8-shot magazine.
Barrel: 4".
Weight: 25 oz. **Length:** 6.25" overall.
Stocks: Checkered composition.
Sights: Blade front, rear adjustable for windage and elevation.
Features: Double action; all-steel construction; frame-mounted safety with decocker. Comes with two magazines, cleaning rod, universal tool. Introduced 1994. Imported from Russia by Century International Arms, K.B.I., Inc.
Price: 9x18mm, blue $199.00
Price: IJ-70HC, 9x18, 10-shot magazine, from K.B.I. $239.00
Price: As above, 380 ACP (K.B.I.) $249.00

BERETTA MODEL 80 CHEETAH SERIES DA PISTOLS
Caliber: 380 ACP, 10-shot magazine (M84); 8-shot (M85); 22 LR, 7-shot (M87), 22 LR, 8-shot (M89).
Barrel: 3.82".
Weight: About 23 oz. (M84/85); 20.8 oz. (M87). **Length:** 6.8" overall.
Stocks: Glossy black plastic (wood optional at extra cost).
Sights: Fixed front, drift-adjustable rear.
Features: Double action, quick takedown, convenient magazine release. Introduced 1977. Imported from Italy by Beretta U.S.A.
Price: Model 84 Cheetah, plastic grips $529.00
Price: Model 84 Cheetah, wood grips $557.00
Price: Model 84 Cheetah, wood grips, nickel finish $600.00
Price: Model 85 Cheetah, plastic grips, 8-shot $499.00
Price: Model 85 Cheetah, wood grips, 8-shot $530.00
Price: Model 85 Cheetah, wood grips, nickel, 8-shot $599.00
Price: Model 87 Cheetah wood, 22 LR, 7-shot $493.00

Beretta Model 86 Cheetah
Similar to the 380-caliber Model 85 except has tip-up barrel for first-round loading. Barrel length is 4.33", overall length of 7.33". Has 8-shot magazine, walnut grips. Introduced 1989.
Price: $514.00

BERETTA MODEL 92FS PISTOL
Caliber: 9mm Para., 10-shot magazine.
Barrel: 4.9".
Weight: 34 oz. **Length:** 8.5" overall.
Stocks: Checkered black plastic; wood optional at extra cost.
Sights: Blade front, rear adjustable for windage. Tritium night sights available.
Features: Double action. Extractor acts as chamber loaded indicator, squared trigger guard, grooved front- and backstraps, inertia firing pin. Matte finish. Introduced 1977. Made in U.S. and imported from Italy by Beretta U.S.A.
Price: With plastic grips $626.00
Price: With wood grips $647.00
Price: Tritium night sights, add $90.00

Manufacturers' addresses in the
Directory of the Arms Trade
page 313, this issue

Beretta Model 92FS

Beretta Model 92F Stainless Pistol
Same as the Model 92FS except has stainless steel barrel and slide, and frame of aluminum-zirconium alloy. Has three-dot sight system. Introduced 1992.
Price: $757.00
Price: For tritium sights, add $90.00

CAUTION: PRICES SHOWN ARE SUPPLIED BY THE MANUFACTURER OR IMPORTER. CHECK YOUR LOCAL GUNSHOP.

HANDGUNS—AUTOLOADERS, SERVICE & SPORT

Beretta Models 92FS/96 Centurion Pistols
Identical to the Model 92FS and 96F except uses shorter slide and barrel (4.3"). Tritium or three-dot sight systems. Plastic or wood grips. Available in 9mm or 40 S&W. Also available in D Models (double-action-only). Introduced 1992.
Price: Model 92FS Centurion, three-dot sights, plastic grips $626.00
Price: Model 92FS Centurion, wood grips $647.00
Price: Model 96 Centurion, three-dot sights, plastic grips $643.00
Price: Model 92D Centurion $586.00
Price: Model 96D Centurion $607.00
Price: For tritium sights, add $90.00

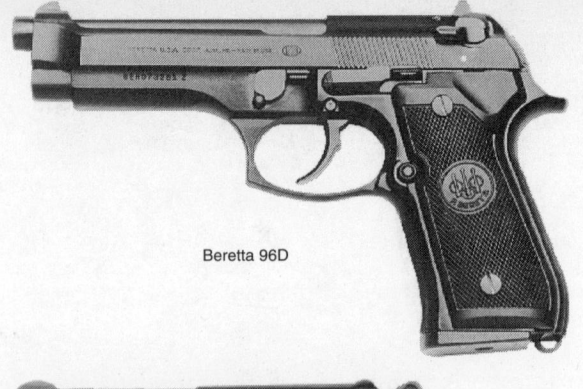
Beretta 96D

Beretta Model 96 Auto Pistol
Same as the Model 92F except chambered for 40 S&W. Ambidextrous safety mechanism with passive firing pin catch, slide safety/decocking lever, trigger bar disconnect. Has 10-shot magazine. Available with tritium or three-dot sights. Introduced 1992.
Price: Model 96, plastic grips $643.00
Price: Model 96D, double-action-only, three-dot sights $607.00
Price: For tritium sights, add $90.00

Beretta Model 92D Pistol
Same as the Model 92FS except double-action-only and has bobbed hammer, no external safety. Introduced 1992.
Price: With plastic grips, three-dot sights $586.00
Price: As above with tritium sights $676.00

Beretta 950 Jetfire

BERETTA MODEL 950 JETFIRE AUTO PISTOL
Caliber: 25 ACP, 8-shot.
Barrel: 2.4".
Weight: 9.9 oz. **Length:** 4.7" overall.
Stocks: Checkered black plastic or walnut.
Sights: Fixed.
Features: Single action, thumb safety; tip-up barrel for direct loading/unloading, cleaning. From Beretta U.S.A.
Price: Jetfire plastic, blue $187.00
Price: Jetfire plastic, nickel $221.00
Price: Jetfire wood, engraved $267.00
Price: Jetfire plastic, matte blue $159.00

Beretta Model 21 Bobcat Pistol
Similar to the Model 950 BS. Chambered for 22 LR or 25 ACP. Both double action. Has 2.4" barrel, 4.9" overall length; 7-round magazine on 22 cal.; 8 rounds in 25 ACP, 9.9 oz., available in nickel, matte, engraved or blue finish. Plastic or walnut grips. Introduced in 1985.
Price: Bobcat, 22-cal. $244.00
Price: Bobcat, nickel, 22-cal. $254.00
Price: Bobcat, 25-cal. $244.00
Price: Bobcat, nickel, 25-cal. $254.00
Price: Bobcat wood, engraved, 22 or 25 .... $294.00
Price: Bobcat plastic matte, 22 or 25 .... $194.00

Beretta M8000/8040 Cougar

BERETTA MODEL 8000/8040 COUGAR PISTOL
Caliber: 9mm Para., 10-shot, 40 S&W, 10-shot magazine.
Barrel: 3.6".
Weight: 33.5 oz. **Length:** 7" overall.
Stocks: Checkered plastic.
Sights: Blade front, rear drift adjustable for windage.
Features: Slide-mounted safety; rotating barrel; exposed hammer. Matte black Bruniton finish. Announced 1994. Imported from Italy by Beretta U.S.A.
Price: $699.00
Price: D models $663.00

BERETTA MODEL 3032 TOMCAT PISTOL
Caliber: 32 ACP, 7-shot magazine.
Barrel: 2.45".
Weight: 15 oz. **Length:** 5" overall.
Stocks: Checkered black plastic.
Sights: Blade front, drift-adjustable rear.
Features: Double action with exposed hammer; tip-up barrel for direct loading/unloading; thumb safety; polished or matte blue finish. Imported from Italy by Beretta U.S.A. Introduced 1996.
Price: Polished blue $299.00
Price: Matte blue $240.00

BERNARDELLI PO18 DA AUTO PISTOL
Caliber: 9mm Para., 10-shot magazine.
Barrel: 4.8".
Weight: 34.2 oz. **Length:** 8.23" overall.
Stocks: Checkered plastic; walnut optional.
Sights: Blade front, rear adjustable for windage and elevation; low profile, three-dot system.
Features: Manual thumb half-cock, magazine and auto-locking firing pin safeties. Thumb safety decocks hammer. Reversible magazine release. Imported from Italy by Mitchell Arms.
Price: Blue $505.00
Price: Chrome $568.00

Bernardelli PO18 Compact DA Auto Pistol
Similar to the PO18 except has 4" barrel, 7.44" overall length, 10-shot magazine. Weighs 31.7 oz. Imported from Italy by Mitchell Arms.
Price: Blue $552.00
Price: Chrome $600.00

Bernadelli PO18

HANDGUNS—AUTOLOADERS, SERVICE & SPORT

BERNARDELLI MODEL USA AUTO PISTOL
Caliber: 22 LR, 10-shot, 380 ACP, 7-shot magazine.
Barrel: 3.5".
Weight: 26.5 oz. **Length:** 6.5" overall.
Stocks: Checkered plastic with thumbrest.
Sights: Ramp front, white outline rear adjustable for windage and elevation.
Features: Hammer-block slide safety; loaded chamber indicator; dual recoil buffer springs; serrated trigger; inertia-type firing pin. Imported from Italy by Mitchell Arms.
Price: Blue, either caliber $387.00
Price: Chrome, either caliber $412.00
Price: Model AMR (6" barrel, target sights) $440.00

Bernadelli USA

BERNARDELLI P. ONE DA AUTO PISTOL
Caliber: 9mm Para., 16-shot, 40 S&W, 10-shot magazine.
Barrel: 4.8".
Weight: 34 oz. **Length:** 8.35" overall.
Stocks: Checkered black plastic.
Sights: Blade front, rear adjustable for windage and elevation; three dot system.
Features: Forged steel frame and slide; full-length slide rails; reversible magazine release; thumb safety/decocker; squared trigger guard. Introduced 1994. Imported from Italy by Mitchell Arms.
Price: 9mm Para., blue/black $530.00
Price: 9mm Para., chrome $580.00
Price: 40 S&W, blue/black $530.00
Price: 40 S&W, chrome $580.00

Bernardelli P. One Practical VB Pistol
Similar to the P. One except chambered for 9x21mm, two- or four-port compensator, straight trigger, micro-adjustable rear sight. Introduced 1994. Imported from Italy by Mitchell Arms.
Price: Blue/black, two-port compensator $1,425.00
Price: As above, four-port compensator $1,475.00
Price: Chrome, two-port compensator $1,498.00
Price: As above, four-port compensator $1,540.00
Price: Customized VB, four-plus-two-port compensator $2,150.00
Price: As above, chrome $2,200.00

BERSA THUNDER 9 AUTO PISTOL
Caliber: 9mm Para., 10-shot magazine.
Barrel: 4".
Weight: 30 oz. **Length:** 7 3/8" overall.
Stocks: Checkered black polymer.
Sights: Blade front, rear adjustable for windage and elevation; three-dot system.
Features: Double action. Ambidextrous safety, decocking levers and slide release; internal automatic firing pin safety; reversible extended magazine release; adjustable trigger stop; alloy frame. Link-free locked breech design. Matte blue finish. Introduced 1993. Imported from Argentina by Eagle Imports, Inc.
Price: Matte finish $474.95
Price: Satin nickel $524.95
Price Duo-Tone finish $491.95

Bersa Thunder 9

BERSA THUNDER 22 AUTO PISTOL
Caliber: 22 LR, 10-shot magazine.
Barrel: 3.5".
Weight: 24.2 oz. **Length:** 6.6" overall.
Stocks: Black polymer.
Sights: Blade front, notch rear adjustable for windage; three-dot system.
Features: Double action; firing pin and magazine safeties. Available in blue or nickel. Introduced 1995. Distributed by Eagle Imports, Inc.
Price: Blue $249.95
Price: Nickel $266.95

BERSA SERIES 95 AUTO PISTOL
Caliber: 380 ACP, 7-shot magazine.
Barrel: 3.5".
Weight: 22 oz. **Length:** 6.6" overall.
Stocks: Wrap-around textured rubber.
Sights: Blade front, rear adjustable for windage; three-dot system.
Features: Double action; firing pin and magazine safeties; combat-style trigger guard. Matte blue or satin nickel. Introduced 1992. Distributed by Eagle Imports, Inc.
Price: Matte blue $224.95
Price: Satin nickel $241.95

BERSA THUNDER 380 AUTO PISTOLS
Caliber: 380 ACP, 7-shot (Thunder 380), 10-shot magazine (Thunder 380 Plus).
Barrel: 3.5".
Weight: 25.75 oz. **Length:** 6.6" overall.
Stocks: Black rubber.
Sights: Blade front, notch rear adjustable for windage; three-dot system.
Features: Double action; firing pin and magazine safeties. Available in blue or nickel. Introduced 1995. Distributed by Eagle Imports, Inc.
Price: Thunder 380, 7-shot, deep blue finish $249.95
Price: As above, satin nickel $266.95
Price: Thunder 380 Plus, 10-shot, matte blue $316.95
Price: As above, satin nickel $349.95

BROLIN LEGEND L45 STANDARD PISTOL
Caliber: 45 ACP, 7-shot magazine.
Barrel: 5".
Weight: 36 oz. **Length:** 8.5" overall.
Stocks: Checkered walnut.
Sights: Orange ramp front, white outline rear.
Features: Throated match barrel; polished feed ramp; lowered and flared ejection port; beveled magazine well; flat top slide; flat mainspring housing; lightened aluminum match trigger; slotted Commander hammer; modified high-relief grip safety; matte blue finish. Introduced 1996. Made in U.S. by Brolin Arms.
Price: $449.00

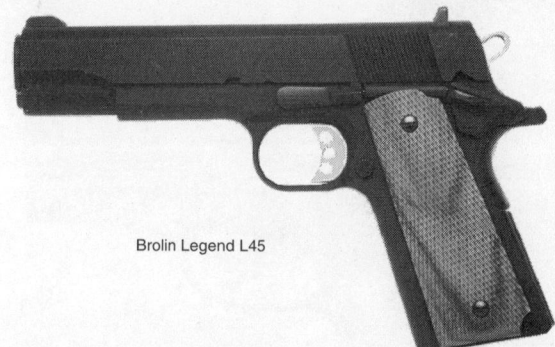
Brolin Legend L45

Brolin Legend L45C Compact Pistol
Similar to the L45 Standard pistol except has 4" barrel with conical lock up; overall length 7.5"; weighs 32 oz. Matte blue finish. Introduced 1996. Made in U.S. by Brolin Arms.
Price: $459.00

HANDGUNS—AUTOLOADERS, SERVICE & SPORT

BROLIN PATRIOT P45 STANDARD CARRY COMP
Caliber: 45 ACP, 7-shot magazine.
Barrel: 4".
Weight: 37 oz. **Length:** 8.5" overall.
Stocks: Checkered wood.
Sights: Orange ramp front, white outline rear.
Features: Dual-port compensator is integral with the throated match barrel; conical lock-up system; polished feed ramp; lowered and flared ejection port; beveled magazine well; flat-top slide; four-legged sear spring; serrated flat mainspring housing; high relief cut front strap; adjustable aluminum match trigger; beavertail grip safety; slotted Commander hammer. Introduced 1996. Made in U.S. by Brolin Arms.
Price: Blue or two-tone $649.00

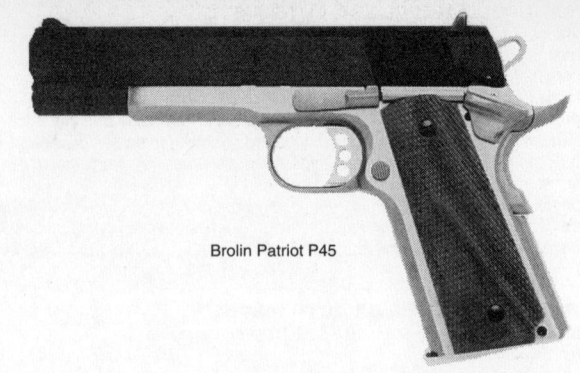

Brolin Patriot P45

Brolin P45C Compact Carry Comp
Similar to the P45 Standard Carry Comp except has 3.25" barrel with integral milled compensator; overall length 7.5"; weighs 33 oz. Introduced 1996. Made in U.S. by Brolin Arms.
Price: Blue or two-tone $679.00

BROWNING HI-POWER 9mm AUTOMATIC PISTOL
Caliber: 9mm Para., 40 S&W, 10-shot magazine.
Barrel: 4 21/32".
Weight: 32 oz. **Length:** 7 3/4" overall.
Stocks: Walnut, hand checkered, or black Polyamide.
Sights: 1/8" blade front; rear screw-adjustable for windage and elevation. Also available with fixed rear (drift-adjustable for windage).
Features: External hammer with half-cock and thumb safeties. A blow on the hammer cannot discharge a cartridge; cannot be fired with magazine removed. Fixed rear sight model available. Ambidextrous safety available only with matte finish, moulded grips. Imported from Belgium by Browning.
Price: Fixed sight model, walnut grips $584.75
Price: 9mm with rear sight adj. for w. and e., walnut grips ... $635.95
Price: Mark III, standard matte black finish, fixed sight, moulded grips, ambidextrous safety $550.75
Price: Silver chrome, adjustable sight, Pachmayr grips $650.95

Browning 40 S&W Hi-Power Mark III Pistol
Similar to the standard Hi-Power except chambered for 40 S&W, 10-shot magazine, weighs 35 oz., and has 4 3/4" barrel. Comes with matte blue finish, low profile front sight blade, drift-adjustable rear sight, ambidextrous safety, moulded polyamide grips with thumb rest. Introduced 1993. Imported from Belgium by Browning.
Price: Mark III $550.95

Browning Capitan Hi-Power Pistol
Similar to the standard Hi-Power except has adjustable tangent rear sight authentic to the early-production model. Also has Commander-style hammer. Checkered walnut grips, polished blue finish. Reintroduced 1993. Imported from Belgium by Browning.
Price: 9mm only $692.95

Browning Hi-Power HP-Practical Pistol
Similar to the standard Hi-Power except has silver-chromed frame with blued slide, wrap-around Pachmayr rubber grips, round-style serrated hammer and removable front sight, fixed rear (drift-adjustable for windage). Available in 9mm Para. or 40 S&W. Introduced 1991.
Price: $629.75
Price: With fully adjustable rear sight $681.95

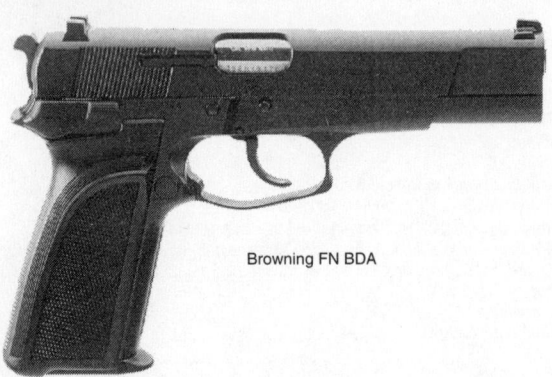

Browning FN BDA

BROWNING BDM DA AUTO PISTOL
Caliber: 9mm Para., 10-shot magazine.
Barrel: 4.73".
Weight: 31 oz. **Length:** 7.85" overall.
Stocks: Moulded black composition; checkered, with thumbrest on both sides.
Sights: Low profile removable blade front, rear screw adjustable for windage.
Features: Mode selector allows switching from DA pistol to "revolver" mode via a switch on the slide. Decocking lever/safety on the frame. Two redundant, passive, internal safety systems. All steel frame; matte black finish. Introduced 1991. Made in the U.S. From Browning.
Price: $612.95

BROWNING FN BDA/BDAO PISTOLS
Caliber: 9mm Para., 10-shot magazine.
Barrel: 4 5/8".
Weight: 31 oz. **Length:** 7 7/8" overall.
Stocks: Checkered, contoured composition.
Sights: Low profile three-dot system; blade front, rear adjustable for windage.
Features: All-steel slide and frame; tilt-barrel design; reversible magazine release; grooved front strap; matted blue finish; ambidextrous decocking lever on BDA. Available as DA or DAO. Introduced 1996. Imported from Belgium by Browning.
Price: Double action or double-action-only $612.95

Browning BDA 380

BROWNING BDA-380 DA AUTO PISTOL
Caliber: 380 ACP, 10-shot magazine.
Barrel: 3 13/16".
Weight: 23 oz. **Length:** 6 3/4" overall.
Stocks: Smooth walnut with inset Browning medallion.
Sights: Blade front, rear drift-adjustable for windage.
Features: Combination safety and decocking lever will automatically lower a cocked hammer to half-cock and can be operated by right- or left-hand shooters. Inertia firing pin. Introduced 1978. Imported from Italy by Browning.
Price: Blue $563.95
Price: Nickel $606.95

HANDGUNS—AUTOLOADERS, SERVICE & SPORT

Browning Micro Buck Mark Standard

Browning Buck Mark Varmint

BRYCO MODEL 48 AUTO PISTOLS
Caliber: 22 LR, 32 ACP, 380 ACP, 6-shot magazine.
Barrel: 4".
Weight: 19 oz. **Length:** 6.7" overall.
Stocks: Polished resin-impregnated wood.
Sights: Fixed.
Features: Safety locks sear and slide. Choice of satin nickel, bright chrome or black Teflon finishes. Announced 1988. From Jennings Firearms.
Price: 22 LR, 32 ACP, about $139.00
Price: 380 ACP, about $139.00

BRYCO MODEL 59 AUTO PISTOL
Caliber: 9mm Para., 10-shot magazine.
Barrel: 4".
Weight: 33 oz. **Length:** 6.5" overall.
Stocks: Black composition.
Sights: Blade front, fixed rear.
Features: Striker-fired action; manual thumb safety; polished blue finish. Comes with two magazines. Introduced 1994. From Jennings Firearms.
Price: About $169.00
Price: Model 58 (5.5" overall length, 30 oz.) $169.00

CENTURY FEG P9R PISTOL
Caliber: 9mm Para., 10-shot magazine.
Barrel: 4.6".
Weight: 35 oz. **Length:** 8" overall.
Stocks: Checkered walnut.
Sights: Blade front, rear drift adjustable for windage.
Features: Double action with hammer-drop safety. Polished blue finish. Comes with spare magazine. Imported from Hungary by Century International Arms.
Price: About $263.00
Price: Chrome finish, about $375.00

Century FEG P9RK Auto Pistol
Similar to the P9R except has 4.12" barrel, 7.5" overall length and weighs 33.6 oz. Checkered walnut grips, fixed sights, 10-shot magazine. Introduced 1994. Imported from Hungary by Century International Arms, Inc.
Price: About $290.00

COLT 22 AUTOMATIC PISTOL
Caliber: 22 LR, 10-shot magazine.
Barrel: 4.5".
Weight: 33 oz. **Length:** 8.62" overall.
Stocks: Textured black polymer.
Sights: Blade front, rear drift adjustable for windage.
Features: Stainless steel construction; ventilated barrel rib; single action mechanism; cocked striker indicator; push-button safety. Introduced 1994. Made in U.S. by Colt's Mfg. Co.
Price: $248.00

BROWNING BUCK MARK 22 PISTOL
Caliber: 22 LR, 10-shot magazine.
Barrel: 5 1/2".
Weight: 32 oz. **Length:** 9 1/2" overall.
Stocks: Black moulded composite with skip-line checkering.
Sights: Ramp front, Browning Pro Target rear adjustable for windage and elevation.
Features: All steel, matte blue finish or nickel, gold-colored trigger. Buck Mark Plus has laminated wood grips. Made in U.S. Introduced 1985. From Browning.
Price: Buck Mark, blue $256.95
Price: Buck Mark, nickel finish with contoured rubber stocks $301.95
Price: Buck Mark Plus $313.95

Browning Micro Buck Mark
Same as the standard Buck Mark and Buck Mark Plus except has 4" barrel. Available in blue or nickel. Has 16-click Pro Target rear sight. Introduced 1992.
Price: Blue $256.95
Price: Nickel $301.95
Price: Micro Buck Mark Plus $313.95

Browning Buck Mark Varmint
Same as the Buck Mark except has 9 7/8" heavy barrel with .900" diameter and full-length scope base (no open sights); walnut grips with optional forend, or finger-groove walnut. Overall length is 14", weighs 48 oz. Introduced 1987.
Price: $390.95

BRYCO MODEL 38 AUTO PISTOLS
Caliber: 22 LR, 32 ACP, 380 ACP, 6-shot magazine.
Barrel: 2.8".
Weight: 15 oz. **Length:** 5.3" overall.
Stocks: Polished resin-impregnated wood.
Sights: Fixed.
Features: Safety locks sear and slide. Choice of satin nickel, bright chrome or black Teflon finishes. Introduced 1988. From Jennings Firearms.
Price: 22 LR, 32 ACP, about $109.95
Price: 380 ACP, about $129.95

Calico M-110

CALICO M-110 AUTO PISTOL
Caliber: 22 LR, 100-shot magazine.
Barrel: 6".
Weight: 3.7 lbs. (loaded). **Length:** 17.9" overall.
Stocks: Moulded composition.
Sights: Adjustable post front, notch rear.
Features: Aluminum alloy frame; flash suppressor; pistol grip compartment; ambidextrous safety. Uses same helical-feed magazine as M-100 Carbine. Introduced 1986. Made in U.S. From Calico.
Price: $359.00

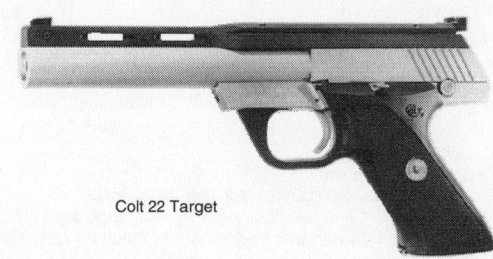

Colt 22 Target

Colt 22 Target Pistol
Similar to the Colt 22 pistol except has 6" bull barrel, full-length sighting rib with lightening cuts and mounting rail for optical sights; fully adjustable rear sight; removable sights; two-point factory adjusted trigger travel. Stainless steel frame. Introduced 1995. Made in U.S. by Colt's Mfg. Co.
Price: $377.00

CAUTION: PRICES SHOWN ARE SUPPLIED BY THE MANUFACTURER OR IMPORTER. CHECK YOUR LOCAL GUNSHOP.

HANDGUNS—AUTOLOADERS, SERVICE & SPORT

COLT COMBAT COMMANDER AUTO PISTOL
Caliber: 38 Super, 9-shot; 45 ACP, 8-shot.
Barrel: 4 1/4".
Weight: 36 oz. Length: 7 3/4" overall.
Stocks: Checkered rubber composite.
Sights: Fixed, glare-proofed blade front, square notch rear; three-dot system.
Features: Long trigger; arched housing; grip and thumb safeties.
Price: 45, blue $735.00
Price: 45, stainless $789.00
Price: 38 Super, stainless $789.00

Colt Lightweight Commander MK IV/Series 80
Same as Commander except high strength aluminum alloy frame, checkered rubber composite stocks, weighs 27 1/2 oz. 45 ACP only.
Price: Blue $735.00

COLT DOUBLE EAGLE MKII/SERIES 90 DA PISTOL
Caliber: 45 ACP, 8-shot magazine.
Barrel: 4 1/2", 5".
Weight: 39 oz. Length: 8 1/2" overall.
Stocks: Black checkered Xenoy thermoplastic.
Sights: Blade front, rear adjustable for windage. High profile three-dot system. Colt Accro adjustable sight optional.
Features: Made of stainless steel with matte finish. Checkered and curved extended trigger guard, wide steel trigger; decocking lever on left side; traditional magazine release; grooved frontstrap; beveled magazine well; extended grip guard; rounded, serrated combat-style hammer. Announced 1989.
Price: $727.00
Price: Combat Comm., 45, 4 1/2" bbl. $727.00

Colt Double Eagle Officer's ACP
Similar to the regular Double Eagle except 45 ACP only, 3 1/2" barrel, weighs 35 oz., 7 1/4" overall length. Has 5 1/4" sight radius. Introduced 1991.
Price: $727.00

COLT GOVERNMENT MODEL MK IV/SERIES 80
Caliber: 38 Super, 9-shot; 45 ACP, 8-shot magazine.
Barrel: 5".
Weight: 38 oz. Length: 8 1/2" overall.
Stocks: Black composite.
Sights: Ramp front, fixed square notch rear; three-dot system.
Features: Grip and thumb safeties and internal firing pin safety, long trigger.
Price: 45 ACP, blue $735.00
Price: 45 ACP, stainless $789.00
Price: 45 ACP, bright stainless $863.00
Price: 38 Super, blue $735.00
Price: 38 Super, stainless $789.00
Price: 38 Super, bright stainless $863.00

Colt 10mm Delta Elite
Similar to the Government Model except chambered for 10mm auto cartridge. Has three-dot high profile front and rear combat sights, checkered rubber composite stocks, internal firing pin safety, and new recoil spring/buffer system. Introduced 1987.
Price: Blue $807.00
Price: Stainless $860.00

Colt Combat Elite MK IV/Series 80
Similar to the Government Model except has stainless frame with ordnance steel slide and internal parts. High profile front, rear sights with three-dot system, extended grip safety, beveled magazine well, checkered rubber composite stocks. Introduced 1986.
Price: 45 ACP, STS/B $895.00
Price: 38 Super, STS/B $895.00

COLT MODEL 1991 A1 AUTO PISTOL
Caliber: 45 ACP, 7-shot magazine.
Barrel: 5".
Weight: 38 oz. Length: 8.5" overall.
Stocks: Checkered black composition.
Sights: Ramped blade front, fixed square notch rear, high profile.
Features: Parkerized finish. Continuation of serial number range used on original G.I. 1911 A1 guns. Comes with one magazine and moulded carrying case. Introduced 1991.
Price: $538.00
Price: Stainless $590.00

Colt Model 1991 A1 Compact Auto Pistol
Similar to the Model 1991 A1 except has 3 1/2" barrel. Overall length is 7", and gun is 3/8" shorter in height. Comes with one 6-shot magazine, moulded case. Introduced 1993.
Price: $538.00

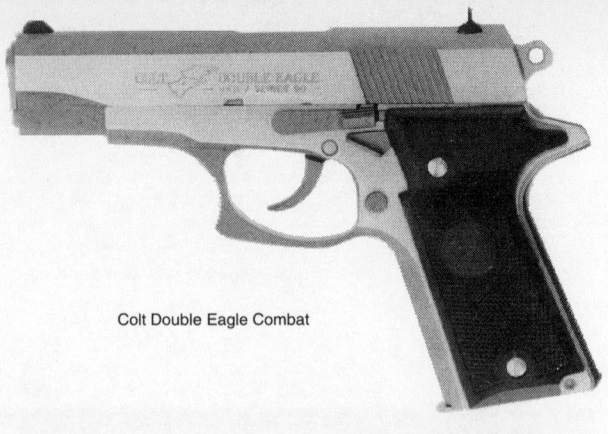

Colt Double Eagle Combat

Colt Government Model

Consult our Directory pages for the location of firms mentioned.

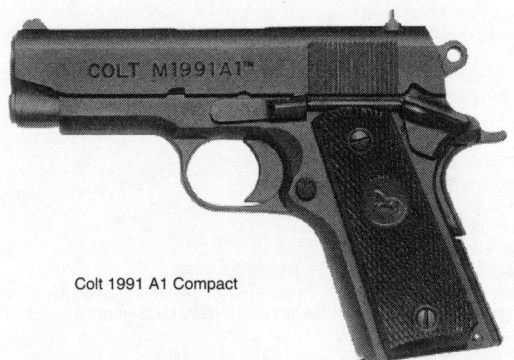

Colt 1991 A1 Compact

COLT GOVERNMENT MODEL 380
Caliber: 380 ACP, 7-shot magazine.
Barrel: 3 1/4".
Weight: 21 3/4 oz. Length: 6" overall.
Stocks: Checkered composition.
Sights: Ramp front, square notch rear, fixed.
Features: Scaled-down version of the 1911 A1 Colt G.M. Has thumb and internal firing pin safeties. Introduced 1983.
Price: Blue $462.00
Price: Stainless $493.00
Price: Pocketlite 380, blue $462.00

Colt Model 1991 A1 Commander Auto Pistol
Similar to the Model 1991 A1 except has 4 1/4" barrel. Parkerized finish. 7-shot magazine. Comes in moulded case. Introduced 1993.
Price: $538.00

HANDGUNS—AUTOLOADERS, SERVICE & SPORT

Colt Mustang 380, Mustang Pocketlite
Similar to the standard 380 Government Model. Mustang has steel frame (18.5 oz.), Pocketlite has aluminum alloy (12.5 oz.). Both are 1/2" shorter than 380 G.M., have 2 3/4" barrel. Introduced 1987.
- **Price:** Mustang 380, blue $462.00
- **Price:** As above, stainless $493.00
- **Price:** Mustang Pocketlite, blue $462.00
- **Price:** Mustang Pocketlite STS/N $493.00

Colt Mustang Plus II
Similar to the 380 Government Model except has the shorter barrel and slide of the Mustang. Introduced 1988.
- **Price:** Blue $462.00
- **Price:** Stainless $493.00

Colt Mustang 380

COLT OFFICER'S ACP MK IV/SERIES 80
Caliber: 45 ACP, 6-shot magazine.
Barrel: 3 1/2".
Weight: 34 oz. (steel frame); 24 oz. (alloy frame). **Length:** 7 1/4" overall.
Stocks: Checkered rubber composite.
Sights: Ramp blade front with white dot, square notch rear with two white dots.
Features: Trigger safety lock (thumb safety), grip safety, firing pin safety; long trigger; flat mainspring housing. Also available with lightweight alloy frame and in stainless steel. Introduced 1985.
- **Price:** Blue $735.00
- **Price:** L.W., blue finish $789.00
- **Price:** Stainless $735.00
- **Price:** Bright stainless $863.00

COLT COMBAT TARGET MODEL
Caliber: 45 ACP, 7-shot magazine.
Barrel: 5".
Weight: 39 oz. **Length:** 8 1/2" overall.
Stocks: Black composition.
Sights: Patridge-style front, Colt Accro adjustable rear.
Features: Steel target trigger with cut-out; flat-top slide; flared and lowered ejection port; beveled magazine well. Introduced 1996. Made in U.S. by Colt's Mfg. Co.
- **Price:** Matte blue $768.00
- **Price:** Matte stainless $820.00

COONAN 357 MAGNUM PISTOL
Caliber: 357 Mag., 7-shot magazine.
Barrel: 5".
Weight: 42 oz. **Length:** 8.3" overall.
Stocks: Smooth walnut.
Sights: Interchangeable ramp front, rear adjustable for windage.
Features: Stainless steel construction. Unique barrel hood improves accuracy and reliability. Linkless barrel. Many parts interchange with Colt autos. Has grip, hammer, half-cock safeties, extended slide latch. Made in U.S. by Coonan Arms, Inc.
- **Price:** 5" barrel $720.00
- **Price:** 6" barrel $755.00
- **Price:** With 6" compensated barrel $999.00
- **Price:** Classic model (Teflon black two-tone finish, 8-shot magazine, fully adjustable rear sight, integral compensated barrel) $1,400.00

Coonan Compact Cadet 357 Magnum Pistol
Similar to the 357 Magnum full-size gun except has 3.9" barrel, shorter frame, 6-shot magazine. Weight is 39 oz., overall length 7.8". Linkless bull barrel, full-length recoil spring guide rod, extended slide latch. Introduced 1993. Made in U.S. by Coonan Arms, Inc.
- **Price:** $841.00

Coonan 357 Magnum

CZ 75 AUTO PISTOL
Caliber: 9mm Para., 40 S&W, 10-shot magazine.
Barrel: 4.7".
Weight: 34.3 oz. **Length:** 8.1" overall.
Stocks: High impact checkered plastic.
Sights: Square post front, rear adjustable for windage; three-dot system.
Features: Single action/double action design; choice of black polymer, matte or high-polish blue finishes. All-steel frame. Imported from the Czech Republic by Magnum Research.
- **Price:** Black polymer finish $539.00
- **Price:** Nickel $569.00

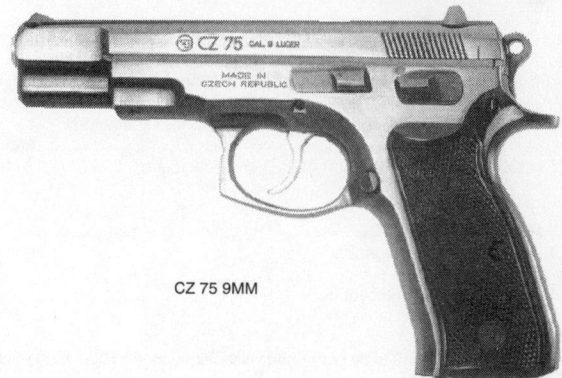

CZ 75 9MM

CZ 75 Compact Auto Pistol
Similar to the CZ 75 except has 10-shot magazine, 3.9" barrel and weighs 32 oz. Has removable front sight, non-glare ribbed slide top. Trigger guard is squared and serrated; combat hammer. Introduced 1993. Imported from the Czech Republic by Magnum Research.
- **Price:** Black polymer finish $539.00

CZ 75 Semi-Compact Auto Pistol
Uses the shorter slide and barrel of the CZ 75 Compact with the full-size frame of the standard CZ 75. Has 10-shot magazine; 9mm Para. only. Introduced 1994. Imported from the Czech Republic by Magnum Research.
- **Price:** Black polymer finish $519.00
- **Price:** Matte blue finish $539.00
- **Price:** High-polish blue finish $559.00

CZ 85 Auto Pistol
Same gun as the CZ 75 except has ambidextrous slide release and safety-levers; non-glare, ribbed slide top; squared, serrated trigger guard; trigger stop to prevent overtravel. Introduced 1986. Imported from the Czech Republic by Magnum Research.
- **Price:** Black polymer finish $549.00

CZ 85 Combat Auto Pistol
Same as the CZ 85 except has walnut grips, round combat hammer, fully adjustable rear sight, extended magazine release. Trigger parts coated with friction-free beryllium copper. Introduced 1992. Imported from the Czech Republic by Magnum Research.
- **Price:** Black polymer finish $649.00

CAUTION: PRICES SHOWN ARE SUPPLIED BY THE MANUFACTURER OR IMPORTER. CHECK YOUR LOCAL GUNSHOP.

HANDGUNS—AUTOLOADERS, SERVICE & SPORT

CZ 83 DOUBLE-ACTION PISTOL
Caliber: 32, 380 ACP, 10-shot magazine.
Barrel: 3.8".
Weight: 26.2 oz. **Length:** 6.8" overall.
Stocks: High impact checkered plastic.
Sights: Removable square post front, rear adjustable for windage; three-dot system.
Features: Single action/double action; ambidextrous magazine release and safety. Blue finish; non-glare ribbed slide top. Imported from the Czech Republic by Magnum Research.
Price: $409.00

CZ 83 380

CZ 100 AUTO PISTOL
Caliber: 9mm Para., 40 S&W, 10-shot magazine.
Barrel: 3.7".
Weight: 24 oz. **Length:** 6.9" overall.
Stocks: Grooved polymer.
Sights: Blade front with dot, white outline rear drift adjustable for windage.
Features: Double action only with firing pin block; polymer frame, steel slide; has laser sight mount. Introduced 1996. Imported from the Czech Republic by Magnum Research.
Price: $489.00

DAEWOO DP51 FASTFIRE AUTO PISTOL
Caliber: 9mm Para., 40 S&W, 10-shot magazine.
Barrel: 4.1".
Weight: 28.2 oz. **Length:** 7.5" overall.
Stocks: Checkered composition.
Sights: $1/8$" blade front, square notch rear drift adjustable for windage. Three dot system.
Features: Patented Fastfire mechanism. Ambidextrous manual safety and magazine catch, automatic firing pin block. Alloy frame, squared trigger guard. Matte black finish. Introduced 1991. Imported from South Korea by Kimber of America, distributed by Kimber and Nationwide Sports Dist.
Price: DP51 ....$400.00
Price: DH40 (40 S&W) $450.00

Daewoo DP51 Fastfire

Daewoo DP51C, DP51S Auto Pistols
Same as the DP51 except DP51C has 3.6" barrel, $1/4$" shorter grip frame, flat mainspring housing, and is 2 oz. lighter. Model DP51S has 3.6" barrel, same grip as standard DP51, weighs 27 oz. Introduced 1995. Imported from South Korea by Kimber of America, Inc., distributed by Kimber and Nationwide Sports Dist.
Price: DP51C $445.00
Price: DP51S $420.00

DAEWOO DP52, DH380 AUTO PISTOLS
Caliber: 22 LR, 10-shot magazine.
Barrel: 3.8".
Weight: 23 oz. **Length:** 6.7" overall.
Stocks: Checkered black composition with thumbrest.
Sights: $1/8$" blade front, rear drift adjustable for windage; three-dot system.
Features: All-steel construction with polished blue finish. Dual safety system with hammer block. Introduced 1994. Imported from South Korea by Kimber of America, distributed by Kimber and Nationwide Sports Distributors.
Price: $380.00
Price: DH380 (as above except 380 ACP, 7-shot magazine) $410.00

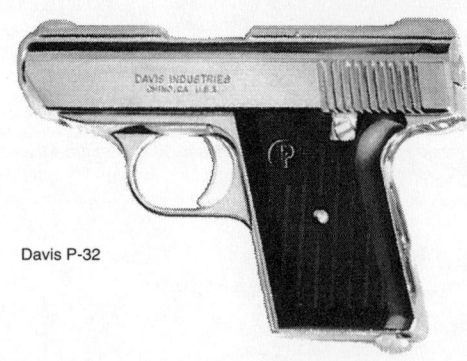
Davis P-32

DAVIS P-32 AUTO PISTOL
Caliber: 32 ACP, 6-shot magazine.
Barrel: 2.8".
Weight: 22 oz. **Length:** 5.4" overall.
Stocks: Laminated wood.
Sights: Fixed.
Features: Choice of black Teflon or chrome finish. Announced 1986. Made in U.S. by Davis Industries.
Price: $87.50

DAVIS P-380 AUTO PISTOL
Caliber: 32 ACP, 6-shot, 380 ACP, 5-shot magazine.
Barrel: 2.8".
Weight: 22 oz. **Length:** 5.4" overall.
Stocks: Black composition.
Sights: Fixed.
Features: Choice of chrome or black Teflon finish. Introduced 1991. Made in U.S. by Davis Industries.
Price: $98.00

E.A.A. EUROPEAN MODEL AUTO PISTOLS
Caliber: 32 ACP or 380 ACP, 7-shot magazine.
Barrel: 3.88".
Weight: 26 oz. **Length:** $7^{3}/_{8}$" overall.
Stocks: European hardwood.
Sights: Fixed blade front, rear drift-adjustable for windage.
Features: Chrome or blue finish; magazine, thumb and firing pin safeties; external hammer; safety-lever takedown. Imported from Italy by European American Armory.
Price: Blue $160.00
Price: Chrome $175.00
Price: Ladies Model $225.00

ERMA KGP68 AUTO PISTOL
Caliber: 32 ACP, 6-shot, 380 ACP, 5-shot.
Barrel: 4".
Weight: $22^{1}/_{2}$ oz. **Length:** $7^{3}/_{8}$" overall.
Stocks: Checkered plastic.
Sights: Fixed.
Features: Toggle action similar to original "Luger" pistol. Action stays open after last shot. Has magazine and sear disconnect safety systems. Imported from Germany by Mandall Shooting Supplies.
Price: $499.95

HANDGUNS—AUTOLOADERS, SERVICE & SPORT

Desert Eagle Magnum

DESERT EAGLE MAGNUM PISTOL
Caliber: 357 Mag., 9-shot; 44 Mag., 8-shot; 50 Magnum, 7-shot.
Barrel: 6", 10", interchangeable.
Weight: 357 Mag.—62 oz.; 41 Mag., 44 Mag.—69 oz.; 50 Mag.—72 oz.
Length: 10 1/4" overall (6" bbl.).
Stocks: Hogue rubber.
Sights: Blade on ramp front, combat-style rear. Adjustable available.
Features: Rotating three-lug bolt; ambidextrous safety; combat-style trigger guard; adjustable trigger optional. Military epoxy finish. Satin, bright nickel, hard chrome, polished and blued finishes available. Made in U.S. From Magnum Research, Inc.
Price: 357, 6" bbl., standard pistol $979.00
Price: 44 Mag., 6", standard pistol $999.00
Price: 50 Magnum, 6" bbl., standard pistol $1,049.00

DESERT INDUSTRIES WAR EAGLE PISTOL
Caliber: 380 ACP, 8- or 10-shot; 9mm Para., 14-shot; 10mm, 10-shot; 40 S&W, 10-shot; 45 ACP, 10-shot.
Barrel: 4".
Weight: 35.5 oz. **Length:** 7.5" overall.
Stocks: Rosewood.
Sights: Fixed.
Features: Double action; matte finish stainless steel; slide mounted ambidextrous safety. Announced 1986. From Desert Industries, Inc.
Price: $795.00
Price: 380 ACP $725.00

DESERT INDUSTRIES DOUBLE DEUCE, TWO BIT SPECIAL PISTOLS
Caliber: 22 LR, 6-shot; 25 ACP, 5-shot.
Barrel: 2 1/2".
Weight: 15 oz. **Length:** 5 1/2" overall.
Stocks: Rosewood.
Sights: Special order.
Features: Double action; stainless steel construction with matte finish; ambidextrous slide-mounted safety. From Desert Industries, Inc.
Price: 22 ....$399.95
Price: 25 (Two-Bit Special) $399.95

Desert Industries War Eagle

E.A.A. WITNESS DA AUTO PISTOL
Caliber: 9mm Para., 10-shot magazine; 38 Super, 40 S&W, 10-shot magazine; 45 ACP, 10-shot magazine.
Barrel: 4.50".
Weight: 35.33 oz. **Length:** 8.10" overall.
Stocks: Checkered rubber.
Sights: Undercut blade front, open rear adjustable for windage.
Features: Double-action trigger system; round trigger guard; frame-mounted safety. Introduced 1991. Imported from Italy by European American Armory.
Price: 9mm, blue $399.00
Price: 9mm, satin chrome $425.00
Price: 9mm Compact, blue, 10-shot $399.00
Price: As above, chrome $425.00
Price: 40 S&W, blue $425.00
Price: As above, chrome $450.00
Price: 40 S&W Compact, 8-shot, blue $425.00
Price: As above, chrome $450.00
Price: 45 ACP, blue $525.00
Price: As above, chrome $550.00
Price: 45 ACP Compact, 8-shot, blue $525.00
Price: As above, chrome $550.00
Price: 9mm/40 S&W Combo, blue, compact or full size ..$595.00
Price: 9mm or 40 S&W Carry Comp, blue $550.00

E.A.A. Witness

Manufacturers' addresses in the
Directory of the Arms Trade
page 313, this issue

FEG B9R AUTO PISTOL
Caliber: 380 ACP, 10-shot magazine.
Barrel: 4".
Weight: 25 oz. **Length:** 7" overall.
Stocks: Hand-checkered walnut.
Sights: Blade front, drift-adjustable rear.
Features: Hammer-drop safety; grooved backstrap; squared trigger guard. Comes with spare magazine. Introduced 1993. Imported from Hungary by Century International Arms.
Price: About $312.00

FEG B9R

HANDGUNS—AUTOLOADERS, SERVICE & SPORT

FEG FP9 AUTO PISTOL
Caliber: 9mm Para., 10-shot magazine.
Barrel: 5".
Weight: 35 oz. **Length:** 7.8" overall.
Stocks: Checkered walnut.
Sights: Blade front, windage-adjustable rear.
Features: Full-length ventilated rib. Polished blue finish. Comes with extra magazine. Introduced 1993. Imported from Hungary by Century International Arms.
Price: About $269.00

FEG GKK-45C DA AUTO PISTOL
Caliber: 45 ACP, 8-shot magazine.
Barrel: 4 1/8".
Weight: 36 oz. **Length:** 7 3/4" overall.
Stocks: Hand-checkered walnut.
Sights: Blade front, rear adjustable for windage; three-dot system.
Features: Combat-type trigger guard. Polished blue finish. Comes with two magazines, cleaning rod. Introduced 1995. Imported from Hungary by K.B.I., Inc.
Price: Blue $399.00
Price: GKK-40C (40 S&W, 9-shot magazine) $399.00

FEG PJK-9HP AUTO PISTOL
Caliber: 9mm Para., 10-shot magazine.
Barrel: 4.75".
Weight: 32 oz. **Length:** 8" overall.
Stocks: Hand-checkered walnut.
Sights: Blade front, rear adjustable for windage; three dot system.
Features: Single action; polished blue or hard chrome finish; rounded combat-style serrated hammer. Comes with two magazines and cleaning rod. Imported from Hungary by K.B.I., Inc.
Price: Blue $349.00
Price: Hard chrome $429.00

FEG GKK-45

FEG PJK-9HP

Consult our Directory pages for the location of firms mentioned.

FEG P9R AUTO PISTOL
Caliber: 9mm Para., 10-shot magazine.
Barrel: 4.6".
Weight: 35 oz. **Length:** 7.9" overall.
Stocks: Checkered walnut.
Sights: Blade front, rear adjustable for windage.
Features: Double-action mechanism; slide-mounted safety. All-Steel construction with polished blue finish. Comes with extra magazine. Introduced 1993. Imported from Hungary by Century International Arms.
Price: About $262.00

FEG SMC-380 AUTO PISTOL
Caliber: 380 ACP, 6-shot magazine.
Barrel: 3.5".
Weight: 18.5 oz. **Length:** 6.1" overall.
Stocks: Checkered composition with thumbrest.
Sights: Blade front, rear adjustable for windage.
Features: Patterned after the PPK pistol. Alloy frame, steel slide; double action. Blue finish. Comes with two magazines, cleaning rod. Imported from Hungary by K.B.I., Inc.
Price: $279.00

FEG SMC-22 DA AUTO PISTOL
Caliber: 22 LR, 8-shot magazine.
Barrel: 3.5".
Weight: 18.5 oz. **Length:** 6.12" overall.
Stocks: Checkered composition with thumbrest.
Sights: Blade front, rear adjustable for windage.
Features: Patterned after the PPK pistol. Alloy frame, steel slide; blue finish. Comes with two magazines, cleaning rod. Introduced 1994. Imported from Hungary by K.B.I., Inc.
Price: $279.00

FEG SMC-918 Auto Pistol
Same as the SMC-380 except chambered for 9x18 Makarov. Alloy frame, steel slide, blue finish. Comes with two magazines, cleaning rod. Introduced 1995. Imported from Hungary by K.B.I., Inc.
Price: $279.00

GAL COMPACT AUTO PISTOL
Caliber: 45 ACP, 8-shot magazine.
Barrel: 4.25".
Weight: 36 oz. **Length:** 7.75" overall.
Stocks: Rubberized wrap-around.
Sights: Low profile, fixed, three-dot system.
Features: Forged steel frame and slide; competition trigger, hammer, slide stop magazine release, beavertail grip safety; front and rear slide grooves; two-tone finish. Introduced 1996. Imported from Israel by J.O. Arms, Inc.
Price: $525.00

GLOCK 17 AUTO PISTOL
Caliber: 9mm Para., 10-shot magazine.
Barrel: 4.49".
Weight: 21.9 oz. (without magazine). **Length:** 7.28" overall.
Stocks: Black polymer.
Sights: Dot on front blade, white outline rear adjustable for windage.
Features: Polymer frame, steel slide; double-action trigger with "Safe Action" system; mechanical firing pin safety, drop safety; simple takedown without tools; locked breech, recoil operated action. Adopted by Austrian armed forces 1983. NATO approved 1984. Imported from Austria by Glock, Inc.
Price: With extra magazine, magazine loader, cleaning kit $606.00
Price: Model 17L (6" barrel) $790.00

Glock 19 Auto Pistol
Similar to the Glock 17 except has a 4" barrel, giving an overall length of 6.85" and weight of 20.99 oz. Magazine capacity is 10 rounds. Fixed or adjustable rear sight. Introduced 1988.
Price: $606.00

Glock 19

HANDGUNS—AUTOLOADERS, SERVICE & SPORT

Glock 21

Glock 20 10mm Auto Pistol
Similar to the Glock Model 17 except chambered for 10mm Automatic cartridge. Barrel length is 4.60", overall length is 7.59", and weight is 26.3 oz. (without magazine). Magazine capacity is 10 rounds. Fixed or adjustable rear sight. Comes with an extra magazine, magazine loader, cleaning rod and brush. Introduced 1990. Imported from Austria by Glock, Inc.
Price: $658.00

Glock 21 Auto Pistol
Similar to the Glock 17 except chambered for 45 ACP, 10-shot magazine. Overall length is 7.59", weight is 25.2 oz. (without magazine). Fixed or adjustable rear sight. Introduced 1991.
Price: $658.00

Glock 22 Auto Pistol
Similar to the Glock 17 except chambered for 40 S&W, 10-shot magazine. Overall length is 7.28", weight is 22.3 oz. (without magazine). Fixed or adjustable rear sight. Introduced 1990.
Price: $606.00

Glock 23 Auto Pistol
Similar to the Glock 19 except chambered for 40 S&W, 10-shot magazine. Overall length is 6.85", weight is 20.6 oz. (without magazine). Fixed or adjustable rear sight. Introduced 1990.
Price: $606.00

GLOCK 26, 27 AUTO PISTOLS
Caliber: 9mm Para. (M26), 10-shot magazine; 40 S&W (M27), 9-shot magazine.
Barrel: 3.47".
Weight: 21.75 oz. **Length:** 6.3" overall.
Stocks: Integral. Stippled polymer.
Sights: Dot on front blade, fixed or fully adjustable white outline rear.
Features: Subcompact size. Polymer frame, steel slide; double-action trigger with "Safe Action" system, three safeties. Matte black Tenifer finish. Hammer-forged barrel. Imported from Austria by Glock, Inc. Introduced 1996.
Price: Fixed sight $606.00
Price: Adjustable sight $634.00

GOLAN AUTO PISTOL
Caliber: 9mm Para., 40 S&W, 10-shot magazine.
Barrel: 3.9".
Weight: 34 oz. **Length:** 7" overall.
Stocks: Textured composition.
Sights: Fixed.
Features: Fully ambidextrous double/single action; forged steel slide, alloy frame; matte blue finish. Introduced 1994. Imported from Israel by J.O. Arms, Inc.
Price: $684.50

HECKLER & KOCH MARK 23 SPECIAL OPERATIONS PISTOL
Caliber: 45 ACP, 10-shot magazine.
Barrel: 5.87".
Weight: 43 oz. **Length:** 9.65" overall.
Stocks: Integral with frame; black polymer.
Sights: Blade front, rear drift adjustable for windage; three-dot.
Features: Polymer frame; double action; exposed hammer; short recoil, modified Browning action. Civilian version of the SOCOM pistol. Introduced 1996. Imported from Germany by Heckler & Koch, Inc.
Price: $1,995.00

HECKLER & KOCH USP AUTO PISTOL
Caliber: 9mm Para., 10-shot magazine, 40 S&W, 10-shot magazine.
Barrel: 4.25".
Weight: 28 oz. (USP40). **Length:** 6.9" overall.
Stocks: Non-slip stippled black polymer.
Sights: Blade front, rear adjustable for windage.
Features: New HK design with polymer frame, modified Browning action with recoil reduction system, single control lever. Special "hostile environment" finish on all metal parts. Available in SA/DA, DAO, left- and right-hand versions. Introduced 1993. Imported from Germany by Heckler & Koch, Inc.
Price: Right-hand $636.00
Price: Left-hand $656.00
Price: Stainless steel, right-hand $681.00
Price: Stainless steel, left-hand $701.00

Heckler & Koch USP 45 Auto Pistol
Similar to the 9mm and 40 S&W USP except chambered for 45 ACP, 10-shot magazine. Has 4.13" barrel, overall length of 7.87" and weighs 30.4 oz. Has adjustable three-dot sight system. Available in SA/DA, DAO, left- and right-hand versions. Introduced 1995. Imported from Germany by Heckler & Koch, Inc.
Price: Right-hand $696.00
Price: Left-hand $716.00
Price: Stainless steel right-hand $696.00
Price: Stainless steel left-hand $716.00

Glock 27 40 S&W

Heckler & Koch Mark 23

Heckler & Koch USP 45

HANDGUNS—AUTOLOADERS, SERVICE & SPORT

HECKLER & KOCH P7M8 AUTO PISTOL
Caliber: 9mm Para., 8-shot magazine.
Barrel: 4.13".
Weight: 29 oz. **Length:** 6.73" overall.
Stocks: Stippled black plastic.
Sights: Blade front, adjustable rear; three dot system.
Features: Unique "squeeze cocker" in frontstrap cocks the action. Gas-retarded action. Squared combat-type trigger guard. Blue finish. Compact size. Imported from Germany by Heckler & Koch, Inc.
Price: P7M8, blued $1,187.00

HERITAGE STEALTH AUTO PISTOL
Caliber: 9mm Para., 40 S&W, 10-shot magazine.
Barrel: 3.9".
Weight: 20.2 oz. **Length:** 6.3" overall.
Stocks: Black polymer; integral.
Sights: Blade front, rear drift adjustable for windage.
Features: Gas retarded blowback action; polymer frame, 17-4 stainless slide; frame mounted ambidextrous trigger safety, magazine safety. Introduced 1996. Made in U.S. by Heritage Mfg., Inc.
Price: $299.95

HI-POINT FIREARMS 40 S&W AUTO
Caliber: 40 S&W, 8-shot magazine.
Barrel: 4.5".
Weight: 39 oz. **Length:** 7.72" overall.
Stocks: Checkered acetal resin.
Sights: Fixed; low profile.
Features: Internal drop-safe mechansim; all aluminum frame. Introduced 1991. From MKS Supply, Inc.
Price: Matte black $148.95

HI-POINT FIREARMS 45 CALIBER PISTOL
Caliber: 45 ACP, 7-shot magazine.
Barrel: 4.5".
Weight: 39 oz. **Length:** 7.95" overall.
Stocks: Checkered acetal resin.
Sights: Fixed; low profile.
Features: Internal drop-safe mechanism; all aluminum frame. Introduced 1991. From MKS Supply, Inc.
Price: Matte black $148.95

HI-POINT FIREARMS MODEL 9MM COMPACT PISTOL
Caliber: 380 ACP, 9mm Para., 8-shot magazine.
Barrel: 3.5".
Weight: 29 oz. **Length:** 6.7" overall.
Stocks: Textured acetal plastic.
Sights: Combat-style fixed three-dot system; low profile.
Features: Single-action design; frame-mounted magazine release. Scratch-resistant matte finish. Introduced 1993. From MKS Supply, Inc.
Price: $124.95
Price: With polymer frame (29 oz.), non-slip grips $132.95
Price: 380 ACP $89.95

Intratec Cat 9

INTRATEC CAT 9 AUTO PISTOL
Caliber: 380 ACP, 9mm Para., 7-shot magazine.
Barrel: 3".
Weight: 21 oz. **Length:** 5.5" overall.
Stocks: Textured black polymer.
Sights: Fixed channel.
Features: Black polymer frame. Introduced 1993. Made in U.S. by Intratec.
Price: About $235.00

Heritage Stealth

Hi-Point 40 S&W

HI-POINT FIREARMS 9MM AUTO PISTOL
Caliber: 9mm Para., 9-shot magazine.
Barrel: 4.5".
Weight: 39 oz. **Length:** 7.72" overall.
Stocks: Textured acetal plastic.
Sights: Fixed, low profile.
Features: Single-action design. Scratch-resistant, non-glare blue finish. Introduced 1990. From MKS Supply, Inc.
Price: Matte black $139.95

HUNGARIAN T-58 AUTO PISTOL
Caliber: 7.62mm and 9mm Para., 8-shot magazine.
Barrel: 4.5".
Weight: 31 oz. **Length:** 7.68" overall.
Stocks: Grooved composition.
Sights: Blade front, rear adjustable for windage.
Features: Comes with both barrels and magazines. Thumb safety locks hammer. Blue finish. Imported by Century International Arms.
Price: About $187.00

INTRATEC CAT 45
Caliber: 40 S&W, 45 ACP; 6-shot magazine.
Barrel: 3.25".
Weight: 19 oz. **Length:** 6.35" overall.
Stocks: Moulded composition.
Sights: Fixed, channel.
Features: Black polymer frame. Introduced 1996. Made in U.S. by Intratec.
Price: $255.00

INTRATEC PROTEC-22, 25 AUTO PISTOLS
Caliber: 22 LR, 10-shot; 25 ACP, 8-shot magazine.
Barrel: 2 1/2".
Weight: 14 oz. **Length:** 5" overall.
Stocks: Wraparound composition in gray, black or driftwood color.
Sights: Fixed.
Features: Double-action only trigger mechanism. Choice of black, satin or TEC-KOTE finish. Announced 1991. Made in U.S. by Intratec.
Price: 22 or 25, black finish $112.00
Price: 22 or 25, satin or TEC-KOTE finish $117.00

INTRATEC SPORT 22 AUTO PISTOL
Caliber: 22 LR, 10-shot magazine.
Barrel: 4".
Weight: 28 oz. **Length:** 11 3/16" overall.
Stocks: Moulded composition.
Sights: Protected post front, adjustable for windage, rear adjustable elevation.
Features: Ambidextrous cocking knobs and safety. Matte black finish. Accepts any 10/22-type magazine. Introduced 1988. Made in U.S. by Intratec.
Price: $130.00

HANDGUNS—AUTOLOADERS, SERVICE & SPORT

Jennings J-25

JENNINGS J-22, J-25 AUTO PISTOLS
Caliber: 22 LR, 25 ACP, 6-shot magazine.
Barrel: 2 1/2".
Weight: 13 oz. (J-22). **Length:** 4 15/16" overall (J-22).
Stocks: Walnut on chrome or nickel models; grooved black Cycolac or resin-impregnated wood on Teflon model.
Sights: Fixed.
Features: Choice of bright chrome, satin nickel or black Teflon finish. Introduced 1981. From Jennings Firearms.
Price: J-22, about $79.95
Price: J-25, about $79.95

KAHR K9 DA AUTO PISTOL
Caliber: 9mm Para., 7-shot magazine.
Barrel: 3.5".
Weight: 25 oz. **Length:** 6" overall.
Stocks: Wrap-around textured soft polymer.
Sights: Blade front, rear drift adjustable for windage; bar-dot combat style.
Features: Trigger-cocking double-action mechanism with passive firing pin block. Made of 4140 ordnance steel with matte black finish. Introduced 1994. Made in U.S. by Kahr Arms.
Price: $595.00
Price: Matte black, night sights $692.00
Price: Matte nickel finish $678.00
Price: Nickel, night sights $775.00

Kahr K9

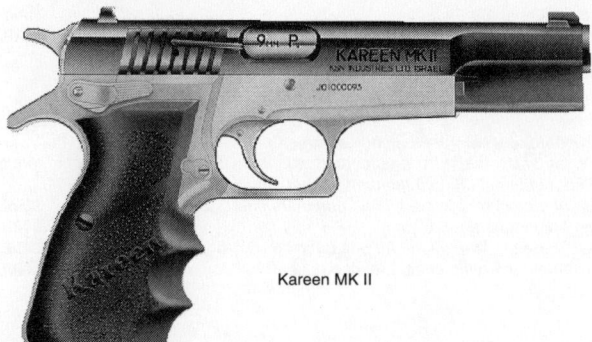
Kareen MK II

KAREEN MK II AUTO PISTOL
Caliber: 9mm Para., 10-shot magazine.
Barrel: 4.75".
Weight: 34 oz. **Length:** 7.85" overall.
Stocks: Textured composition.
Sights: Blade front, rear adjustable for windage.
Features: Single-action mechanism; ambidextrous external hammer safety; magazine safety; combat trigger guard. Two-tone finish. Introduced 1985. Imported from Israel by J.O. Arms & Ammunition.
Price: $425.00
Price: Kareem Mk II Compact 9mm (3.75" barrel, 30 oz., 6.75" overall length) $495.00

KEL-TEC P-11 AUTO PISTOL
Caliber: 9mm Para., 10-shot magazine.
Barrel: 3.1".
Weight: 14 oz. **Length:** 5.6" overall.
Stocks: Checkered black polymer.
Sights: Blade front, rear adjustable for windage.
Features: Ordnance steel slide, aluminum frame. Double-action-only trigger mechanism. Introduced 1995. Made in U.S. by Kel-Tec CNC Industries, Inc.
Price: Blue $309.00
Price: Stainless $407.00
Price: Parkerized $350.00

Kel-Tec P-11

Kimber Classic 45 Custom

KIMBER CLASSIC 45 CUSTOM AUTO PISTOL
Caliber: 45 ACP, 8-shot magazine.
Barrel: 5".
Weight: 38 oz. **Length:** 8.5" overall.
Stocks: Black synthetic.
Sights: McCormick dovetailed front, low combat rear.
Features: Uses Chip McCormick Corp. forged frame and slide, match-grade barrel, extended combat thumb safety, high beavertail grip safety, skeletonized lightweight composite trigger, skeletonized Commander-type hammer, elongated Commander ejector, and 8-shot magazine. Bead-blasted black oxide finish; flat mainspring housing; lowered and flared ejection port; serrated front and rear of slide; relief cut under trigger guard; Wolff spring set; beveled magazine well. Introduced 1995. Made in U.S. by Kimber of America, Inc.
Price: Custom $575.00
Price: Custom Stainless $650.00

Kimber Classic 45 Gold Match Auto Pistol
Same as the Custom Royal except also has Bo-Mar BMCS low-mount adjustable rear sight, fancy walnut grips, tighter tolerances. Comes with one 10-shot and one 8-shot magazine and factory proof target. Introduced 1995. Made in U.S. by Kimber of America, Inc.
Price: $925.00

Kimber Classic 45 Custom Royal Auto Pistol
Same as the Custom model except has checkered diamond-pattern walnut grips, long guide rod, polished blue finish, and comes with two 8-shot magazines. Introduced 1995. Made in U.S. by Kimber of America, Inc.
Price: $715.00

HANDGUNS—AUTOLOADERS, SERVICE & SPORT

L.A.R. GRIZZLY WIN MAG MK I PISTOL
Caliber: 357 Mag., 357/45, 10mm, 44 Mag., 45 Win. Mag., 45 ACP, 7-shot magazine.
Barrel: 5.4", 6.5".
Weight: 51 oz. **Length:** 10½" overall.
Stocks: Checkered rubber, non-slip combat-type.
Sights: Ramped blade front, fully adjustable rear.
Features: Uses basic Browning/Colt 1911A1 design; interchangeable calibers; beveled magazine well; combat-type flat, checkered rubber mainspring housing; lowered and back-chamfered ejection port; polished feed ramp; throated barrel; solid barrel bushings. Available in satin hard chrome, matte blue, Parkerized finishes. Introduced 1983. From L.A.R. Mfg., Inc.
Price: 45 Win. Mag. $1,000.00
Price: 357 Mag. $1,014.00
Price: Conversion units (357 Mag.) $248.00
Price: As above, 45 ACP, 10mm, 45 Win. Mag., 357/45 Win. Mag. $233.00

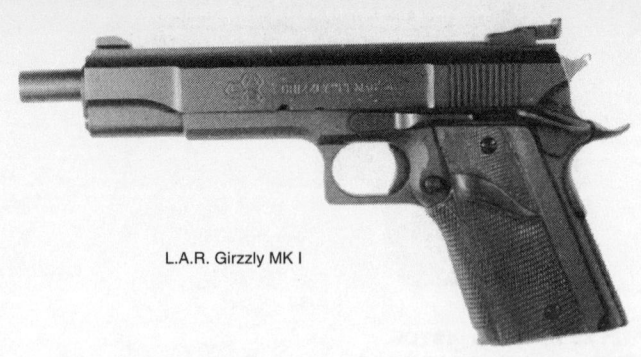
L.A.R. Girzzly MK I

L.A.R. Grizzly 50 Mark V Pistol
Similar to the Grizzly Win Mag Mark I except chambered for 50 Action Express with 6-shot magazine. Weight, empty, is 56 oz., overall length 10⅝". Choice of 5.4" or 6.5" barrel. Has same features as Mark I, IV pistols. Introduced 1993. From L.A.R. Mfg., Inc.
Price: $1,152.00

L.A.R. Grizzly 44 Mag MK IV
Similar to the Win Mag Mk I except chambered for 44 Magnum, has beavertail grip safety. Matte blue finish only. Has 5.4" or 6.5" barrel. Introduced 1991. From L.A.R. Mfg., Inc.
Price: $1,014.00

Laseraim Arms Series III Auto Pistol
Similar to the Series II except has 5" barrel only, with dual-port compensator; weighs 43 oz.; overall length is 7⅝". Choice of fixed or adjustable rear sight. Introduced 1994. Made in U.S. by Laseraim Technologies, Inc.
Price: Fixed sight $533.95
Price: Adjustable sight $559.95
Price: Fixed sight Dream Team Laseraim laser sight $629.95

LASERAIM ARMS SERIES I AUTO PISTOL
Caliber: 10mm Auto, 8-shot, 45 ACP, 7-shot magazine.
Barrel: 6", with compensator.
Weight: 46 oz. **Length:** 9.75" overall.
Stocks: Pebble-grained black composite.
Sights: Blade front, fully adjustable rear.
Features: Single action; barrel compensator; stainless steel construction; ambidextrous safety-levers; extended slide release; matte black Teflon finish; integral mount for laser sight. Introduced 1993. Made in U.S. by Laseraim Technologies, Inc.
Price: Standard, fixed sight $552.95
Price: Standard, Compact (4³⁄₈" barrel), fixed sight $552.95
Price: Adjustable sight $579.95
Price: Standard, fixed sight, Auto Illusion red dot sight system ..$649.95
Price: Standard, fixed sight, Laseraim Laser with Hotdot $694.95

Laseraim Arms Series II Auto Pistol
Similar to the Series I except without compensator, has matte stainless finish. Standard Series II has 5" barrel, weighs 43 oz., Compact has 3³⁄₈" barrel, weighs 37 oz. Blade front sight, rear adjustable for windage or fixed. Introduced 1993. Made in U.S. by Laseraim Technologies, Inc.
Price: Standard or Compact (3³⁄₈" barrel), fixed sight $399.95
Price: Adjustable sight, 5" only $429.95
Price: Standard, fixed sight, Auto Illusion red dot sight $499.95
Price: Standard, fixed sight, Laseraim Laser $499.95

LLAMA MAX-I AUTO PISTOLS
Caliber: 9mm Para., 9-shot, 45 ACP, 7-shot.
Barrel: 4¼" (Compact); 5⅛" (Government).
Weight: 34 oz. (Compact); 36 oz. (Government). **Length:** 7⅜" overall (Compact).
Stocks: Black rubber.
Sights: Blade front, rear adjustable for windage; three-dot system.
Features: Single-action trigger; skeletonized combat-style hammer; steel frame; extended manual and grip safeties. Introduced 1995. Imported from Spain by Import Sports, Inc.
Price: 9mm, 9-shot, Government model $349.95
Price: As above, Compact model $349.95
Price: 45 ACP, 7-shot, Government model $349.95
Price: As above, Duo-Tone finish $366.95
Price: As above, Compact model $382.95

Llama Max-I

LLAMA IX-C LARGE FRAME AUTO PISTOL
Caliber: 45 ACP, 10-shot.
Barrel: 5⅛".
Weight: 41 oz. **Length:** 8½" overall.
Stocks: Black rubber.
Sights: Blade front, rear adjustable for windage; three-dot system.
Features: Grip and manual safeties, ventilated rib. Imported from Spain by Import Sports, Inc.
Price: Matte finish $399.95

LLAMA IX-D COMPACT FRAME AUTO PISTOL
Caliber: 45 ACP, 10-shot.
Barrel: 4¼".
Weight: 39 oz.
Stocks: Black rubber.
Sights: Blade front, rear adjustable for windage; three-dot system.
Features: Scaled-down version of the Large Frame gun. Locked breech mechanism; manual and grip safeties. Introduced 1995. Imported from Spain by Import Sports, Inc.
Price: Matte finish $399.95

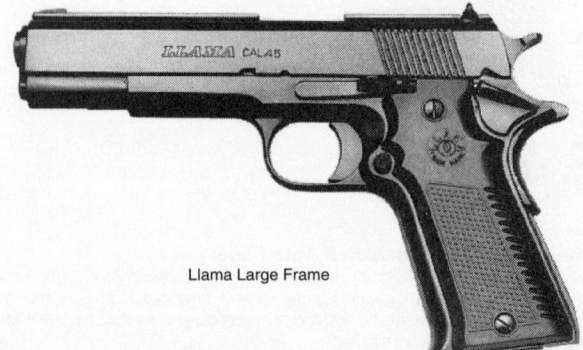
Llama Large Frame

HANDGUNS—AUTOLOADERS, SERVICE & SPORT

LLAMA III-A SMALL FRAME AUTO PISTOL
Caliber: 380 ACP.
Barrel: 3 11/16".
Weight: 23 oz. **Length:** 6 1/2" overall.
Stocks: Checkered polymer, thumbrest.
Sights: Fixed front, adjustable notch rear.
Features: Ventilated rib, manual and grip safeties. Imported from Spain by Import Sports, Inc.
Price: Blue $248.95
Price: Satin Chrome $291.95

LLAMA MAX-I COMPENSATOR
Caliber: 45 ACP, 7-, 10-shot magazine.
Barrel: 4 7/8" (without compensator, 6 1/3" with).
Weight: 42 oz. (7-shot). **Length:** 9 7/8" overall.
Stocks: Checkered rubber.
Sights: Dovetail blade front, fully adjustable rear.
Features: Extended beavertail grip safety, skeletonized combat hammer, extended slide release. Introduced 1996. Imported from Spain by Import Sports, Inc.
Price: 7-shot $491.95
Price: 10-shot $516.95

LORCIN L-22 AUTO PISTOL
Caliber: 22 LR, 9-shot magazine.
Barrel: 2.5".
Weight: 16 oz. **Length:** 5.25" overall.
Stocks: Black combat, or pink or pearl.
Sights: Fixed three-dot system.
Features: Available in chrome or black Teflon finish. Introduced 1989. From Lorcin Engineering.
Price: About $89.00

LORCIN L9MM AUTO PISTOL
Caliber: 9mm Para., 10-shot magazine.
Barrel: 4.5".
Weight: 31 oz. **Length:** 7.5" overall.
Stocks: Grooved black composition.
Sights: Fixed; three-dot system.
Features: Matte black finish; hooked trigger guard; grip safety. Introduced 1994. Made in U.S. by Lorcin Engineering.
Price: $159.00

LORCIN L-25, LT-25 AUTO PISTOLS
Caliber: 25 ACP, 7-shot magazine.
Barrel: 2.4".
Weight: 14.5 oz. **Length:** 4.8" overall.
Stocks: Smooth composition.
Sights: Fixed.
Features: Available in choice of finishes: chrome, black Teflon or camouflage. Introduced 1989. From Lorcin Engineering.
Price: L-25 .... $69.00
Price: LT-25 .... $79.00

LORCIN L-32, L-380 AUTO PISTOLS
Caliber: 32 ACP, 380 ACP, 7-shot magazine.
Barrel: 3.5".
Weight: 27 oz. **Length:** 6.6" overall.
Stocks: Grooved composition.
Sights: Fixed.
Features: Black Teflon or chrome finish with black grips. Introduced 1992. From Lorcin Engineering.
Price: L-32 32 ACP $89.00
Price: L-380 380 ACP $100.00

MITCHELL ARMS ALPHA AUTO PISTOL
Caliber: 45 ACP, 8- and 10-shot magazine.
Barrel: 5".
Weight: 41 oz. **Length:** 8.5" overall.
Stocks: Smooth polymer.
Sights: Interchangeable blade front, fully adjustable rear or drift adjustable rear.
Features: Interchangeable trigger modules permit double-action-only, single-action-only or SA/DA fire. Accepts any single-column, 8-shot 1911-style magazine. Frame-mounted decocker/safety; extended ambidextrous safety; extended slide latch; serrated combat hammer; beveled magazine well; heavy bull barrel (no bushing design); extended slide underlug; full-length recoil spring guide system. Introduced 1995. Made in U.S. From Mitchell Arms, Inc.
Price: Blue, fixed sight $695.00
Price: Blue, adjustable sight $725.00
Price: Stainless, fixed sight $725.00
Price: Stainless, adjustable sight $749.00

Llama Max-1 Compensator

LLAMA MINIMAX SERIES
Caliber: 9mm Para., 40 S&W, 45 ACP, 6-shot magazine.
Barrel: 3 1/2".
Weight: 35 oz. **Length:** 7 1/3" overall.
Stocks: Checkered rubber.
Sights: Three-dot combat.
Features: Single action, skeletonized combat-style hammer, extended slide release, cone-style barrel, flared ejection port. Introduced 1996. Imported from Spain by Import Sports, Inc.
Price: Blue $366.95
Price: Duo-Tone finish (45 only) $382.95
Price: Satin chrome $408.95
Price: Stainless steel finish $432.95

Lorcin L9MM

Lorcin L-25

Mitchell Arms Alpha

CAUTION: PRICES SHOWN ARE SUPPLIED BY THE MANUFACTURER OR IMPORTER. CHECK YOUR LOCAL GUNSHOP.

HANDGUNS—AUTOLOADERS, SERVICE & SPORT

MITCHELL GOLD SERIES AMBIDEXTROUS AUTO
Caliber: 9mm Para., 40 S&W.
Barrel: 4.4".
Weight: 33 oz. **Length:** NA.
Stocks: Checkered wood.
Sights: Dovetail blade front, drift-adjustable rear; three-dot system.
Features: Ambidextrous controls, including magazine release; chrome lined barrel; forged steel slide, aluminum frame. Announced 1996. Made in U.S. by Mitchell Arms.
Price: Black pearl $650.00
Price: Diamond $725.00
Price: Gold $795.00

Mitchell 45 Gold Tactical Model
Similar to the Standard model except fixed or adjustable sight; adjustable trigger; ambidextrous safety; extended slide stop; checkered walnut grips; skeleton hammer. Announced 1996. Made in U.S. by Mitchell Arms.
Price: With fixed sight $750.00
Price: With adjustable sight $775.00

Mitchell 45 Gold Wide Body Standard
Similar to the 45 Gold Standard except comes with 10-shot magazine; rear slide serrations only; satin-finished slide; walnut composite grips. Announced 1994. Made in U.S. by Mitchell Arms.
Price: $775.00

MITCHELL 45 GOLD STANDARD MODEL
Caliber: 45 ACP, 8-shot magazine.
Barrel: 5".
Weight: 32 oz. **Length:** 8.75" overall.
Stocks: Wrap-around rubber.
Sights: Blade front, fixed rear.
Features: Stainless steel with bright/satin finish; front and rear slide serrations; flat grooved mainspring housing; full-length mainspring guide rod; Commander hammer; beavertail grip safety. Announced 1994. Made in U.S. by Mitchell Arms.
Price: $675.00

MITCHELL ARMS SPORTSTER AUTO PISTOL
Caliber: 22 LR, 10-shot magazine.
Barrel: 4.5", 6.75".
Weight: 39 oz. (4.5" barrel). **Length:** 9" overall (4.5" barrel).
Stocks: Checkered black plastic.
Sights: Blade front, rear adjustable for windage.
Features: Military grip; standard trigger; push-button barrel takedown. Stainless steel or blue. Introduced 1992. From Mitchell Arms, Inc.
Price: $325.00

> Consult our Directory pages for the location of firms mentioned.

MITCHELL 44 MAGNUM AUTO PISTOL
Caliber: 44 Mag., 6-shot magazine.
Barrel: 5.5".
Weight: 46 oz. **Length:** NA.
Stocks: Checkered walnut.
Sights: Dovetail blade front, fully adjustable rear.
Features: Front and rear slide serrations; skeleton hammer. Announced 1996. Made in U.S. by Mitchell Arms.
Price: $1,190.00

Mitchell 45 Gold Tactical

Mitchell 45 Gold Wide Body Tactical
Similar to the 45 Gold Standard except 10-shot magazine; adjustable sight; ambidextrous safety; checkered mainspring housing; adjustable trigger; extended slide release; match barrel; skeleton Commander hammer; polished slide; black composite grips. Announced 1994. Made in U.S. by Mitchell Arms.
Price: $895.00

MITCHELL JEFF COOPER SIGNATURE AUTO
Caliber: 45 ACP, 8-shot magazine.
Barrel: 5" heavy match, no bushing.
Weight: 32 oz. **Length:** NA.
Stocks: Thin checkered composite.
Sights: Ramped front, fixed rear.
Features: Cooper's signature roll-marked on slide; slenderized frame; completely dehorned; short adjustable trigger; grooved arched mainspring housing; extended safety; military slide serrations; military guide rod; burn hammer. Announced 1996. Made in U.S. by Mitchell Arms.
Price: Satin black finish $795.00

Mitchell Jeff Cooper Commemorative Model
Similar to the Signature model except has polished frame; engraved signature; polished and gold-plated trigger; checkered walnut grips with medallion; gold-filled lettering. Limited edition gun comes with red and Marine gold lanyard with gold trim, certificate of authenticity, special case. Announced 1996. Made in U.S. by Mitchell Arms.
Price: $1,895.00

Mitchell Sportster

MOUNTAIN EAGLE AUTO PISTOL
Caliber: 22 LR, 10-shot magazine.
Barrel: 4.5", 6.5", 8".
Weight: 21 oz., 23 oz. **Length:** 10.6" overall (with 6.5" barrel).
Stocks: One-piece impact-resistant polymer in "conventional contour"; checkered panels.
Sights: Serrated ramp front with interchangeable blades, rear adjustable for windage and elevation; interchangeable blades.
Features: Injection moulded grip frame, alloy receiver; hybrid composite barrel replicates shape of the Desert Eagle pistol. Flat, smooth trigger. Introduced 1992. From Magnum Research.
Price: Mountain Eagle Compact $199.00
Price: Mountain Eagle Standard $239.00
Price: Mountain Eagle Target Edition (8" barrel) $279.00

NORTH AMERICAN MUNITIONS MODEL 1996
Caliber: 9mm Para., 9-shot magazine.
Barrel: 4.5".
Weight: 40 oz. **Length:** 8.38" overall.
Stocks: Black polycarbonate.
Sights: Blade front, adjustable rear; three-dot system.
Features: Gas-delayed blowback system; no external safeties; fixed 10-groove barrel. Introduced 1996. Made in U.S. From Intercontinental Munitions Distributors, Ltd.
Price: $275.00

Mountain Eagle Target

HANDGUNS—AUTOLOADERS, SERVICE & SPORT

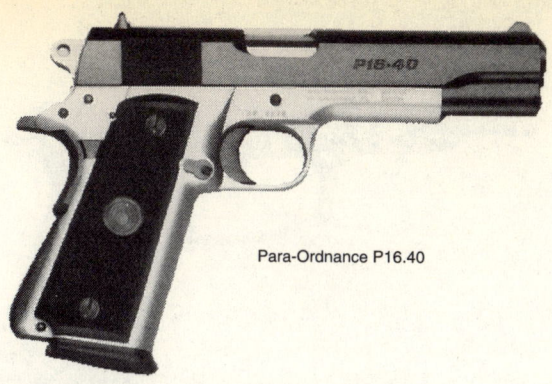

Para-Ordnance P16.40

PHOENIX ARMS MODEL RAVEN AUTO PISTOL
Caliber: 25 ACP, 6-shot magazine.
Barrel: 2⁷⁄₁₆".
Weight: 15 oz. **Length:** 4³⁄₄" overall.
Stocks: Ivory-colored or black slotted plastic.
Sights: Ramped front, fixed rear.
Features: Available in blue, nickel or chrome finish. Made in U.S. Available from Phoenix Arms.
Price: $79.00

PHOENIX ARMS HP22, HP25 AUTO PISTOLS
Caliber: 22 LR, 10-shot (HP22), 25 ACP, 10-shot (HP25).
Barrel: 3".
Weight: 20 oz. **Length:** 5¹⁄₂" overall.
Stocks: Checkered composition.
Sights: Blade front, adjustable rear.
Features: Single action; exposed hammer; manual hold-open; button magazine release. Available in satin nickel, polished blue finish. Introduced 1993. Made in U.S. by Phoenix Arms.
Price: $99.00

Piranha Pistol

PSA-25 Pistol

ROCKY MOUNTAIN ARMS PATRIOT PISTOL
Caliber: 223, 10-shot magazine.
Barrel: 7", with muzzle brake.
Weight: 5 lbs. **Length:** 20.5" overall.
Stocks: Black composition.
Sights: None furnished.
Features: Milled upper receiver with enhanced Weaver base; milled lower receiver from billet plate; machined aluminum National Match handguard. Finished in DuPont Teflon-S matte black or NATO green. Comes with black nylon case, one magazine. Introduced 1993. From Rocky Mountain Arms, Inc.
Price: With A-2 handle top .... $2,500.00 to $2,800.00
Price: Flat top model .... $3,000.00 to $3,500.00

PARA-ORDNANCE P-SERIES AUTO PISTOLS
Caliber: 40 S&W, 45 ACP, 10-shot magazine.
Barrel: 5".
Weight: 28 oz. (alloy frame). **Length:** 8.5" overall.
Stocks: Textured composition.
Sights: Blade front, rear adjustable for windage. High visibility three-dot system.
Features: Available with alloy, steel or stainless steel frame with black finish (silver or stainless gun). Steel and stainless steel frame guns weighs 38 oz. (P14.45), 35 oz. (P13.45), 33 oz. (P12.45). Grooved match trigger, rounded combat-style hammer. Beveled magazine well. Manual thumb, grip and firing pin lock safeties. Solid barrel bushing. Contact maker for full details. Introduced 1990. Made in Canada by Para-Ordnance.
Price: P14.45ER (steel frame) $750.00
Price: P14.45RR (alloy frame) $705.00
Price: P12.45RR (3¹⁄₂" bbl., 24 oz., alloy) $705.00
Price: P13.45RR (4¹⁄₄" barrel, 28 oz., alloy) $705.00
Price: P12.45ER (steel frame) $750.00
Price: P16.40ER (steel frame) $750.00

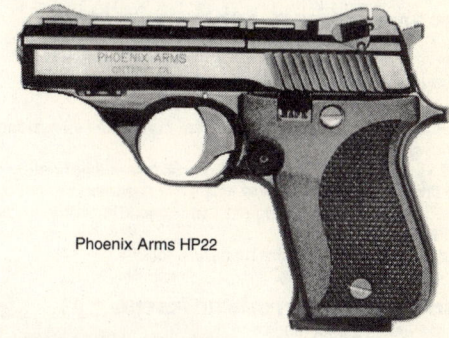

Phoenix Arms HP22

PIRANHA AUTOLOADING PISTOL
Caliber: 9mm Para., 9mm Largo, 30 Luger, 10-shot magazine.
Barrel: 4", 6", 8", 10", 16".
Weight: About 2.7 lbs. **Length:** 9" overall with 4" barrel.
Stocks: Smooth walnut.
Sights: Blade front, rear adjustable for windage.
Features: Nearly recoilless action; stainless steel construction; fires from closed bolt; change caliber by changing barrel. Introduced 1996. Made in U.S. by Recoillers Technologies, Inc.
Price: $600.00

> *Manufacturers' addresses in the*
> **Directory of the Arms Trade**
> *page 313, this issue*

PSA-25 AUTO PISTOL
Caliber: 25 ACP, 6-shot magazine.
Barrel: 2¹⁄₈".
Weight: 9.5 oz. **Length:** 4¹⁄₈" overall.
Stocks: Checkered black plastic.
Sights: Fixed.
Features: All steel construction with polished finish. Introduced 1984. Made in the U.S. by PSP.
Price: Black oxide $249.00
Price: Brushed satin chrome $301.00
Price: Featherweight $375.00

RUGER P89 AUTOMATIC PISTOL
Caliber: 9mm Para., 10-shot magazine.
Barrel: 4.50".
Weight: 32 oz. **Length:** 7.84" overall.
Stocks: Grooved black Xenoy composition.
Sights: Square post front, square notch rear adjustable for windage, both with white dot inserts.
Features: Double action with ambidextrous slide-mounted safety-levers. Slide is 4140 chrome-moly steel or 400-series stainless steel, frame is a lightweight aluminum alloy. Ambidextrous magazine release. Blue or stainless steel. Introduced 1986; stainless introduced 1990.
Price: P89, blue, with extra magazine and magazine loading tool, plastic case $410.00
Price: KP89, stainless, with extra magazine and magazine loading tool, plastic case $452.00

CAUTION: PRICES SHOWN ARE SUPPLIED BY THE MANUFACTURER OR IMPORTER. CHECK YOUR LOCAL GUNSHOP.

HANDGUNS—AUTOLOADERS, SERVICE & SPORT

Ruger P89D Decocker Automatic Pistol
Similar to the standard P89 except has ambidextrous decocking levers in place of the regular slide-mounted safety. The decocking levers move the firing pin inside the slide where the hammer can not reach it, while simultaneously blocking the firing pin from forward movement—allows shooter to decock a cocked pistol without manipulating the trigger. Conventional thumb decocking procedures are therefore unnecessary. Blue or stainless steel. Introduced 1990.
Price: P89D, blue with extra magazine and loader, plastic case $410.00
Price: KP89D, stainless, with extra magazine, plastic case $452.00

Ruger P89 Double-Action-Only Automatic Pistol
Same as the KP89 except operates only in the double-action mode. Has a spurless hammer, gripping grooves on each side of the rear of the slide; no external safety or decocking lever. An internal safety prevents forward movement of the firing pin unless the trigger is pulled. Available in 9mm Para., stainless steel only. Introduced 1991.
Price: With lockable case, extra magazine, magazine loading tool $452.00

RUGER P90 SAFETY MODEL AUTOMATIC PISTOL
Caliber: 45 ACP, 7-shot magazine.
Barrel: 4.50".
Weight: 33.5 oz. Length: 7.87" overall.
Stocks: Grooved black Xenoy composition.
Sights: Square post front, square notch rear adjustable for windage, both with white dot inserts.
Features: Double action with ambidextrous slide-mounted safety-levers which move the firing pin inside the slide where the hammer can not reach it, while simultaneously blocking the firing pin from forward movement. Stainless steel only. Introduced 1991.
Price: KP90 with plastic case, extra magazine, loader $488.65

RUGER P93 COMPACT AUTOMATIC PISTOL
Caliber: 9mm Para., 10-shot magazine.
Barrel: 3.9".
Weight: 31 oz. Length: 7.3" overall.
Stocks: Grooved black Xenoy composition.
Sights: Square post front, square notch rear adjustable for windage.
Features: Front of slide is crowned with a convex curve; slide has seven finger grooves; trigger guard bow is higher for a better grip; 400-series stainless slide, lightweight alloy frame. Decocker-only or DAO-only. Introduced 1993. Made in U.S. by Sturm, Ruger & Co.
Price: $520.00

Ruger KP94 Automatic Pistol
Sized midway between the full-size P-Series and the compact P93. Has 4.25" barrel, 7.5" overall length and weighs about 33 oz. KP94 is manual safety model; KP94DAO is double-action-only (both 9mm Para., 10-shot magazine); KP94D is decocker-only in 40 S&W with 10-shot magazine. Slide gripping grooves roll over top of slide. KP94 has ambidextrous safety-levers; KP94DAO has no external safety, full-cock hammer position or decocking lever; KP94D has ambidextrous decocking levers. Matte finish stainless slide, barrel, alloy frame. Introduced 1994. Made in U.S. by Sturm, Ruger & Co.
Price: KP94 (9mm), KP944 (40) $520.00
Price: KP94DAO (9mm), KP944DAO (40) $520.00
Price: KP94D (9mm), KP9440 (40 S&W) $520.00

Ruger P94L Automatic Pistol
Same as the KP94 except mounts a laser sight in a housing cast integrally with the frame. Allen-head screws control windage and elevation adjustments. Announced 1994. Made in U.S. by Sturm, Ruger & Co.
Price: For law enforcement only .... NA

Ruger KP89D

Ruger P90 Decocker Automatic Pistol
Similar to the P90 except has a manual decocking system. The ambidextrous decocking levers move the firing pin inside the slide where the hammer can not reach it, while simultaneously blocking the firing pin from forward movement—allows shooter to decock a cocked pistol without manipulating the trigger. Available only in stainless steel. Overall length 7.87", weighs 34 oz. Introduced 1991.
Price: P90D with lockable case, extra magazine, and magazine loading tool $488.65

Ruger P93 DAO

RUGER P95 AUTOMATIC PISTOL
Caliber: 9mm Para., 10-shot magazine.
Barrel: 3.9".
Weight: 27 oz. Length: 7.3" overall.
Stocks: Grooved; integral with frame.
Sights: Blade front, rear drift adjustable for windage; three-dot system.
Features: Moulded grip frame, stainless steel or chrome-moly slide. Suitable for +P+ ammunition. Decocker or DAO. Introduced 1996. Made in U.S. by Sturm, Ruger & Co. Comes with lockable plastic case, spare magazine, loading tool.
Price: P95 DAO double-action-only $343.00
Price: P95D decocker only $351.00

RUGER MARK II STANDARD AUTO PISTOL
Caliber: 22 LR, 10-shot magazine.
Barrel: 4³/₄" or 6".
Weight: 25 oz. (4³/₄" bbl.). Length: 8⁵/₁₆" (4³/₄" bbl.).
Stocks: Checkered plastic.
Sights: Fixed, wide blade front, square notch rear adjustable for windage.
Features: Updated design of the original Standard Auto. Has new bolt hold-open latch. 10-shot magazine, magazine catch, safety, trigger and new receiver contours. Introduced 1982.
Price: Blued (MK 4, MK 6) $252.00
Price: In stainless steel (KMK 4, KMK 6) $330.25

Ruger 22/45 Mark II Pistol
Similar to the other 22 Mark II autos except has grip frame of Zytel that matches the angle and magazine latch of the Model 1911 45 ACP pistol. Available in 4³/₄" standard and 5¹/₂" bull barrel. Introduced 1992.
Price: KP4 (4³/₄" barrel) $280.00
Price: KP512 (5¹/₂" bull barrel) $330.00
Price: P512 (5¹/₂" bull barrel, all blue) $237.50

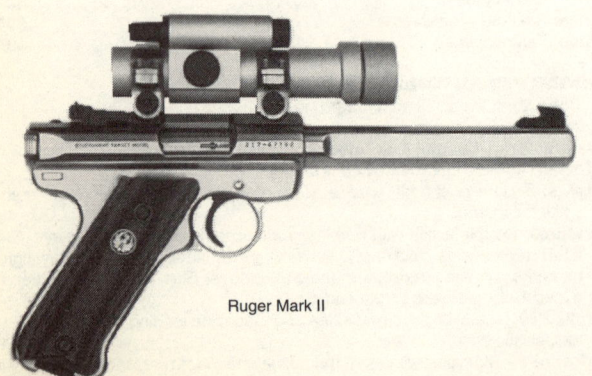
Ruger Mark II

HANDGUNS—AUTOLOADERS, SERVICE & SPORT

Ruger MK-4B Compact

Safari Arms Enforcer

Ruger MK-4B Compact Pistol
Similar to the Mark II Standard pistol except has 4" bull barrel, Patridge-type front sight, fully adjustable rear, and smooth laminated hardwood thumbrest stocks. Weighs 38 oz., overall length of $8^{3}/_{16}$". Comes with extra magazine, plastic case, lock. Introduced 1996. Made in U.S. by Sturm, Ruger & Co.
Price: $336.50

SAFARI ARMS COHORT PISTOL
Caliber: 45 ACP, 7-shot magazine.
Barrel: 3.8", 416 stainless.
Weight: 37 oz. **Length:** 8.5" overall.
Stocks: Smooth walnut with laser-etched black widow logo.
Sights: Ramped blade front, LPA adjustable rear.
Features: Combines the Enforcer model, slide and MatchMaster frame. Beavertail grip safety; extended thumb safety and slide release; Commander-style hammer. Throated, polished and tuned. Satin stainless finish. Introduced 1996. Made in U.S. by Safari Arms, Inc.
Price: $780.00

SAFARI ARMS ENFORCER PISTOL
Caliber: 45 ACP, 6-shot magazine.
Barrel: 3.8", stainless.
Weight: 36 oz. **Length:** 7.3" overall.
Stocks: Smooth walnut with etched black widow spider logo.
Sights: Ramped blade front, LPA adjustable rear.
Features: Extended safety, extended slide release; Commander-style hammer; beavertail grip safety; throated, polished, tuned. Parkerized matte black or satin stainless steel finishes. Made in U.S. by Safari Arms.
Price: $740.00

Schuetzen Pistol Works Enforcer Carrycomp II Pistol
Similar to the Enforcer except has Wil Schueman-designed hybrid compensator system. Introduced 1993. Made in U.S. by Safari Arms, Inc.
Price: 3.8" barrel $1,150.00
Price: 5" barrel $1,300.00

SCHUETZEN PISTOL WORKS BIG DEUCE PISTOL
Caliber: 45 ACP, 7-shot magazine.
Barrel: 6", 416 stainless steel.
Weight: 40.3 oz. **Length:** 9.5" overall.
Stocks: Smooth walnut.
Sights: Ramped blade front, LPA adjustable rear.
Features: Beavertail grip safety; extended thumb safety and slide release; Commander-style hammer. Throated, polished and tuned. Parkerized matte black slide with satin stainless steel frame. Introduced 1995. Made in U.S. by Safari Arms, Inc.
Price: $849.00

SCHUETZEN PISTOL WORKS GRIFFON PISTOL
Caliber: 45 ACP, 10-shot magazine.
Barrel: 5", 416 stainless steel.
Weight: 40.5 oz. **Length:** 8.5" overall.
Stocks: Smooth walnut.
Sights: Ramped blade front, LPA adjustable rear.
Features: 10+1 1911 enhanced 45. Beavertail grip safety; long aluminum trigger; full-length recoil spring guide; Commander-style hammer. Throated, polished and tuned. Grip size comparable to standard 1911. Satin stainless steel finish. Introduced 1996. Made in U.S. by Olympic Arms, Inc.
Price: $910.00

SCHUETZEN PISTOL WORKS RELIABLE PISTOL
Caliber: 45 ACP, 7-shot magazine.
Barrel: 5", 416 stainless steel.
Weight: 39 oz. **Length:** 8.5" overall.
Stocks: Checkered walnut.
Sights: Ramped blade front, LPA adjustable rear.
Features: Beavertail grip safety; long aluminum trigger; full-length recoil spring guide; Commander-style hammer. Throated, polished and tuned. Satin stainless steel finish. Introduced 1996. Made in U.S. by Safari Arms, Inc.
Price: $815.00

SCHUETZEN PISTOL WORKS RENEGADE
Caliber: 45 ACP, 7-shot magazine.
Barrel: 5", 416 stainless steel.
Weight: 39 oz. **Length:** 8.5" overall.
Stocks: Checkered walnut.
Sights: Ramped blade, LPA adjustable rear.
Features: True left-hand pistol. Beavertail grip safety; long aluminum trigger; full-length recoil spring guide; Commander-style hammer; satin stainless finish. Throated, polished and tuned. Introduced 1996. Made in U.S. by Safari Arms, Inc.
Price: $1,075.00

SAFARI ARMS GI SAFARI PISTOL
Caliber: 45 ACP, 7-shot magazine.
Barrel: 5", 416 stainless.
Weight: 39.9 oz. **Length:** 8.5" overall.
Stocks: Checkered walnut.
Sights: G.I.-style blade front, drift-adjustable rear.
Features: Beavertail grip safety; extended thumb safety and slide release; Commander-style hammer. Parkerized finish. Reintroduced 1996.
Price: $585.00

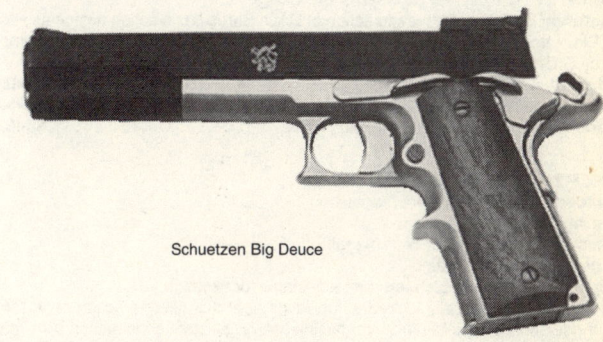

Schuetzen Big Deuce

Schuetzen Pistol Works Reliable 4-Star Pistol
Similar to the Reliable except has 4.5" barrel, 7.5" overall length, and weighs 35.7 oz. Introduced 1996. Made in U.S. by Safari Arms, Inc.
Price: $875.00

SEECAMP LWS 32 STAINLESS DA AUTO
Caliber: 32 ACP Win. Silvertip, 6-shot magazine.
Barrel: 2", integral with frame.
Weight: 10.5 oz. **Length:** $4^{1}/_{8}$" overall.
Stocks: Glass-filled nylon.
Sights: Smooth, no-snag, contoured slide and barrel top.
Features: Aircraft quality 17-4 PH stainless steel. Inertia-operated firing pin. Hammer fired double-action-only. Hammer automatically follows slide down to safety rest position after each shot—no manual safety needed. Magazine safety disconnector. Polished stainless. Introduced 1985. From L.W. Seecamp.
Price: $375.00

HANDGUNS—AUTOLOADERS, SERVICE & SPORT

SIG SAUER P220 "AMERICAN" AUTO PISTOL
Caliber: 38 Super, 45 ACP, (9-shot in 38 Super, 7 in 45).
Barrel: 4 3/8".
Weight: 28 1/4 oz. (9mm). **Length:** 7 3/4" overall.
Stocks: Checkered black plastic.
Sights: Blade front, drift adjustable rear for windage.
Features: Double action. Decocking lever permits lowering hammer onto locked firing pin. Squared combat-type trigger guard. Slide stays open after last shot. Imported from Germany by SIGARMS, Inc.
Price: "American," blue (side-button magazine release, 45 ACP only) . . . $805.00
Price: 45 ACP, blue, Siglite night sights $905.00
Price: K-Kote finish $850.00
Price: K-Kote, Siglite night sights $950.00

SIG SAUER P225 DA AUTO PISTOL
Caliber: 9mm Para., 8-shot magazine.
Barrel: 3.8".
Weight: 26 oz. **Length:** 7 3/32" overall.
Stocks: Checkered black plastic.
Sights: Blade front, rear adjustable for windage. Optional Siglite night sights.
Features: Double action. Decocking lever permits lowering hammer onto locked firing pin. Square combat-type trigger guard. Shortened, lightened version of P220. Imported from Germany by SIGARMS, Inc.
Price: Blue, SA/DA or DAO $780.00
Price: With Siglite night sights, blue, SA/DA or DAO $880.00
Price: K-Kote finish $850.00
Price: K-Kote with Siglite night sights $950.00

SIG Sauer P228 DA Auto Pistol
Similar to the P226 except has 3.86" barrel, with 7.08" overall length and 3.35" height. Chambered for 9mm Para. only, 10-shot magazine. Weight is 29.1 oz. with empty magazine. Introduced 1989. Imported from Germany by SIGARMS, Inc.
Price: Blue $825.00
Price: Blue, with Siglite night sights $925.00
Price: Blue, double-action-only $825.00
Price: Blue, double-action-only, Siglite night sights $975.00
Price: K-Kote finish $875.00
Price: K-Kote, Siglite night sights $975.00
Price: K-Kote, double-action-only $875.00
Price: K-Kote, double-action-only, Siglite night sights $975.00

SIG SAUER P230 DA AUTO PISTOL
Caliber: 32 ACP, 8-shot; 380 ACP, 7-shot.
Barrel: 3 3/4".
Weight: 16 oz. **Length:** 6 1/2" overall.
Stocks: Checkered black plastic.
Sights: Blade front, rear adjustable for windage.
Features: Double action/single action or DAO. Same basic action design as P220. Blowback operation, stationary barrel. Introduced 1977. Imported from Germany by SIGARMS, Inc.
Price: Blue $510.00
Price: In stainless steel (P230 SL) $595.00
Price: With stainless steel slide, blue frame $545.00

SIG P210-6 AUTO PISTOL
Caliber: 9mm Para., 8-shot magazine.
Barrel: 4 3/4".
Weight: 32 oz. **Length:** 8 1/2" overall.
Stocks: Checkered walnut.
Sights: Blade front, notch rear drift adjustable for windage.
Features: Mechanically locked, short-recoil operation; single action only; target trigger with adjustable stop; magazine safety; all-steel construction with matte blue finish. Optional 22 LR conversion kit consists of barrel, slide, recoil spring and magazine. Imported from Switzerland by SIGARMS, Inc.
Price: $2,300.00
Price: With 22LR conversion kit $2,900.00

SMITH & WESSON MODEL 422, 622 AUTO
Caliber: 22 LR, 10-shot magazine.
Barrel: 4 1/2", 6".
Weight: 22 oz. (4 1/2" bbl.). **Length:** 7 1/2" overall (4 1/2" bbl.).
Stocks: Checkered simulated woodgrain polymer.
Sights: Field—serrated ramp front, fixed rear; Target—serrated ramp front, adjustable rear.
Features: Aluminum frame, steel slide, brushed stainless steel or blue finish; internal hammer. Introduced 1987. Model 2206 introduced 1990.
Price: Blue, 4 1/2", 6", fixed sight $235.00
Price: As above, adjustable sight $290.00
Price: Stainless (Model 622), 4 1/2", 6", fixed sight $284.00
Price: As above, adjustable sight $337.00

SIG Sauer P228

SIG Sauer P226 DA Auto Pistol
Similar to the P220 pistol except has 4.4" barrel, and weighs 26 1/2 oz. 357 SIG or 9mm. Imported from Germany by SIGARMS, Inc.
Price: Blue $825.00
Price: With Siglite night sights $925.00
Price: Blue, double-action-only $825.00
Price: Blue, double-action-only, Siglite night sights $925.00
Price: K-Kote finish $875.00
Price: K-Kote, Siglite night sights $975.00
Price: K-Kote, double-action-only $875.00
Price: K-Kote, double-action-only, Siglite night sights $975.00

SIG Sauer P229 DA Auto Pistol
Similar to the P228 except chambered for 9mm Para., 40 S&W, 357 SIG. Has 3.86" barrel, 7.08" overall length and 3.35" height. Weight is 30.5 oz. Introduced 1991. Frame made in Germany, stainless steel slide assembly made in U.S.; pistol assembled in U.S. From SIGARMS, Inc.
Price: Blue $875.00
Price: With nickel slide $900.00
Price: Blue, double-action-only $875.00
Price: With Siglite night sights $975.00

SIG Sauer P230

SIG P-210-2 AUTO PISTOL
Caliber: 7.65mm or 9mm Para., 8-shot magazine.
Barrel: 4 3/4".
Weight: 31 3/4 oz. (9mm). **Length:** 8 1/2" overall.
Stocks: Checkered black composition.
Sights: Blade front, rear adjustable for windage.
Features: Lanyard loop; matte finish. Conversion unit for 22 LR available. Imported from Switzerland by Mandall Shooting Supplies.
Price: P-210-2 Service Pistol $3,500.00

Smith & Wesson Model 422

HANDGUNS—AUTOLOADERS, SERVICE & SPORT

Smith & Wesson Model 622 VR

Smith & Wesson Model 622 VR Auto
Similar to the Model 622 except 6" barrel only with ventilated rib, glass-beaded serrated sight line with revised ramped front sight; matte black trigger, barrel and extractor; revised trigger guard. Introduced 1996. Made in U.S. by Smith & Wesson.
Price: $310.00

Smith & Wesson Model 2213, 2214 Sportsman Auto
Similar to the Model 422 except has 3" barrel, 8-shot magazine; dovetail Patridge front sight with white dot, fixed rear with two white dots; matte blue finish, black composition grips with checkered panels. Overall length 6 1/8", weight 18 oz. Introduced 1990.
Price: $269.00
Price: Model 2213 (stainless steel) $314.00

Smith & Wesson Model 2206 Target Auto
Same as the Model 2206 except 6" barrel only; Millett Series 100 fully adjustable sight system; Patridge front sight; smooth contoured Herrett walnut target grips with thumbrest; serrated trigger with adjustable stop. Frame is bead-blasted along sighting plane, drilled and tapped for optics mount. Introduced 1994. Made in U.S. by Smith & Wesson.
Price: $433.00

Smith & Wesson Model 2206 Auto
Similar to the Model 422/622 except made entirely of stainless steel with non-reflective finish. Weight is 39 oz. Introduced 1990.
Price: With adjustable sight $385.00

Smith & Wesson Model 457

SMITH & WESSON MODEL 410 DA AUTO PISTOL
Caliber: 40 S&W, 10-shot magazine.
Barrel: 4".
Weight: 28.5 oz. **Length:** 7.5 oz.
Stocks: One-piece Xenoy, wrap-around with straight backstrap.
Sights: Post front, fixed rear; three-dot system.
Features: Aluminum alloy frame; blued carbon steel slide; traditional double action with left-side slide-mountd decocking lever. Introduced 1996. Made in U.S. by Smith & Wesson.
Price: $490.00

SMITH & WESSON MODEL 457 DA AUTO PISTOL
Caliber: 45 ACP, 7-shot magazine.
Barrel: 3 3/4".
Weight: 29 oz. **Length:** 7 1/4" overall.
Stocks: One-piece Xenoy, wrap-around with straight backstrap.
Sights: Post front, fixed rear, three-dot system.
Features: Aluminum alloy frame, matte blue carbon steel slide; bobbed hammer; smooth trigger. Introduced 1996. Made in U.S. by Smith & Wesson.
Price: $490.00

SMITH & WESSON MODEL 909, 910 DA AUTO PISTOLS
Caliber: 9mm Para., 10-shot magazine.
Barrel: 4".
Weight: 28 oz. **Length:** 7 3/8" overall.
Stocks: One-piece Xenoy, wrap-around with straight backstrap.
Sights: Post front with white dot, fixed two-dot rear.
Features: Alloy frame, blue carbon steel slide. Slide-mounted decocking lever. Introduced 1995.
Price: Model 910 ....$443.00
Price: Model 909 (9-shot magazine, curved backstrap, 27 oz.) $443.00

SMITH & WESSON MODEL 908 AUTO PISTOL
Caliber: 9mm Para., 8-shot magazine.
Barrel: 3 1/2".
Weight: 26 oz. **Length:** 6 13/16".
Stocks: One-piece Xenoy, wrap-around with straight backstrap.
Sights: Post front, fixed rear, three-dot system.
Features: Aluminum alloy frame, matte blue carbon steel slide; bobbed hammer; smooth trigger. Introduced 1996. Made in U.S. by Smith & Wesson.
Price: $443.00

SMITH & WESSON MODEL 3913 DOUBLE ACTION
Caliber: 9mm Para., 8-shot magazine.
Barrel: 3 1/2".
Weight: 26 oz. **Length:** 6 13/16" overall.
Stocks: One-piece Delrin wrap-around, textured surface.
Sights: Post front with white dot, Novak LoMount Carry with two dots, adjustable for windage.
Features: Aluminum alloy frame, stainless slide (M3913) or blue steel slide (M3914). Bobbed hammer with no half-cock notch; smooth .304" trigger with rounded edges. Straight backstrap. Extra magazine included. Introduced 1989.
Price: $622.00

Smith & Wesson Model 3913 LadySmith Auto
Similar to the standard Model 3913 except has frame that is upswept at the front, rounded trigger guard. Comes in frosted stainless steel with matching gray grips. Grips are ergonomically correct for a woman's hand. Novak LoMount Carry rear sight adjustable for windage, smooth edges for snag resistance. Extra magazine included. Introduced 1990.
Price: $640.00

Smith & Wesson Model 3953DA Pistol
Same as the Model 3913 except double-action-only. Model 3953 has stainless slide with alloy frame. Overall length 7"; weighs 25.5 oz. Extra magazine included. Introduced 1990.
Price: $622.00

Smith & Wesson Model 910

Smith & Wesson 3913 LadySmith

CAUTION: PRICES SHOWN ARE SUPPLIED BY THE MANUFACTURER OR IMPORTER. CHECK YOUR LOCAL GUNSHOP.

HANDGUNS—AUTOLOADERS, SERVICE & SPORT

SMITH & WESSON MODEL 4006 DA AUTO
Caliber: 40 S&W, 10-shot magazine.
Barrel: 4".
Weight: 38.5 oz. **Length:** 7⅞" overall.
Stocks: Xenoy wrap-around with checkered panels.
Sights: Replaceable post front with white dot, Novak LoMount Carry fixed rear with two white dots, or micro. click adjustable rear with two white dots.
Features: Stainless steel construction with non-reflective finish. Straight backstrap. Extra magazine included. Introduced 1990.
Price: With adjustable sights $775.00
Price: With fixed sight $745.00
Price: With fixed night sights $855.00

SMITH & WESSON MODEL 4013, 4053 AUTOS
Caliber: 40 S&W, 8-shot magazine.
Barrel: 3½".
Weight: 26 oz. **Length:** 7" overall.
Stocks: One-piece Xenoy wrap-around with straight backstrap.
Sights: Post front with white dot, fixed Novak LoMount Carry rear with two white dots.
Features: Model 4013 is traditional double action; Model 4053 is double-action-only; stainless slide on alloy frame. Introduced 1991.
Price: Model 4013 .... $722.00
Price: Model 4053 .... $722.00

SMITH & WESSON MODEL 4500 SERIES AUTOS
Caliber: 45 ACP, 7-shot (M4516), 8-shot magazine for M4506, 4566/4586.
Barrel: 3¾" (M4516), 5" (M4506).
Weight: 41 oz. (4506). **Length:** 7⅛" overall (4516).
Stocks: Xenoy one-piece wrap-around, arched or straight backstrap on M4506, straight only on M4516.
Sights: Post front with white dot, adjustable or fixed Novak LoMount Carry on M4506.
Features: M4506 has serrated hammer spur. Extra magazine included. Contact Smith & Wesson for complete data. Introduced 1989.
Price: Model 4506, fixed sight $774.00
Price: Model 4506, adjustable sight $806.00
Price: Model 4516, fixed sight $774.00
Price: Model 4566 (stainless, 4¼", traditional DA, ambidextrous safety, fixed sight) $774.00
Price: Model 4586 (stainless, 4¼", DA only) $774.00

SMITH & WESSON MODEL 5900 SERIES AUTO PISTOLS
Caliber: 9mm Para., 10-shot magazine.
Barrel: 4".
Weight: 28½ to 37½ oz. (fixed sight); 38 oz. (adjustable sight). **Length:** 7½" overall.
Stocks: Xenoy wrap-around with curved backstrap.
Sights: Post front with white dot, fixed or fully adjustable with two white dots.
Features: All stainless, stainless and alloy or carbon steel and alloy construction. Smooth .304" trigger, .260" serrated hammer. Extra magazine included. Introduced 1989.
Price: Model 5903 (stainless, alloy frame, traditional DA, fixed sight, ambidextrous safety) $690.00
Price: Model 5904 (blue, alloy frame, traditional DA, adjustable sight, ambidextrous safety) $642.00
Price: Model 5906 (stainless, traditional DA, adjustable sight, ambidextrous safety) $742.00
Price: As above, fixed sight $707.00
Price: With fixed night sights $817.00
Price: Model 5946 (as above, stainless frame and slide) $707.00

Smith & Wesson Model 6904/6906 Double-Action Autos
Similar to the Models 5904/5906 except with 3½" barrel, 10-shot magazine, fixed rear sight, .260" bobbed hammer. Extra magazine included. Introduced 1989.
Price: Model 6904, blue $614.00
Price: Model 6906, stainless $677.00
Price: Model 6906 with fixed night sights $788.00
Price: Model 6946 (stainless, DA only, fixed sights) $677.00

SMITH & WESSON SIGMA SW380 AUTO
Caliber: 380 ACP, 6-shot magazine.
Barrel: 3".
Weight: 14 oz. **Length:** 5.8" overall.
Stocks: Integral.
Sights: Fixed groove in the slide.
Features: Polymer frame; double-action-only trigger mechanism; grooved/serrated front and rear straps; two passive safeties. Introduced 1995. Made in U.S. by Smith & Wesson.
Price: $308.00

Smith & Wesson Model 4046 DA Pistol
Similar to the Model 4006 except is double-action-only. Has a semi-bobbed hammer, smooth trigger, 4" barrel; Novak LoMount Carry rear sight, post front with white dot. Overall length is 7½", weighs 28 oz. Extra magazine included. Introduced 1991.
Price: $745.00
Price: With fixed night sights $855.00

Smith & Wesson Model 4053

Smith & Wesson Model 4506

Smith & Wesson Sigma

SMITH & WESSON SIGMA SERIES PISTOLS
Caliber: 9mm Para., 40 S&W, 10-shot magazine.
Barrel: 4.5".
Weight: 26 oz. **Length:** 7.4" overall.
Stocks: Integral.
Sights: White dot front, fixed rear; three-dot system. Tritium night sights available.
Features: Ergonomic polymer frame; low barrel centerline; internal striker firing system; corrosion-resistant slide; Teflon-filled, electroless-nickel coated magazine. Introduced 1994. Made in U.S. by Smith & Wesson.
Price: Model SW9F (9mm Para.) $593.00
Price: Model SW40F (40 S&W) $593.00
Price: Model Compact, SW9C, SW 40C (4" bbl., 24.4 oz.) $593.00
Price: With fixed tritium night sights $697.00

HANDGUNS—AUTOLOADERS, SERVICE & SPORT

SPHINX AT-380 AUTO PISTOL
Caliber: 380 ACP, 10-shot magazine.
Barrel: 3.27".
Weight: 25 oz. **Length:** 6.03" overall.
Stocks: Checkered plastic.
Sights: Fixed.
Features: Double-action-only mechanism, Chamber loaded indicator; ambidextrous magazine release and slide latch. Introduced 1993. Imported from Switzerland by Sphinx USA, Inc.
Price: Two-tone $493.95
Price: Black finish $513.95
Price: Nickel/Palladium finish $564.95

SPHINX AT-2000S DOUBLE-ACTION PISTOL
Caliber: 9mm Para., 9x21mm, 40 S&W, 10-shot magazine.
Barrel: 4.53".
Weight: 36.3 oz. **Length:** 8.03" overall.
Stocks: Checkered neoprene.
Sights: Fixed, three-dot system.
Features: Double-action mechanism changeable to double-action-only. Stainless frame, blued slide. Ambidextrous safety, magazine release, slide latch. Introduced 1993. Imported from Switzerland by Sphinx USA, Inc.
Price: 9mm, two-tone $1,090.00
Price: 40 S&W, two-tone $1,120.00

Sphinx AT-2000P, AT-2000PS Auto Pistols
Same as the AT-2000S except AT-2000P has shortened frame, 3.74" barrel, 7.25" overall length, and weighs 34 oz. Model AT-2000PS has full-size frame. Both have stainless frame with blued slide. Introduced 1993. Imported from Switzerland by Sphinx USA, Inc.
Price: 9mm, two-tone $940.00
Price: 40 S&W, two-tone $980.00

Sphinx AT-2000H Auto Pistol
Similar to the AT-2000P except has shorter slide with 3.54" barrel, shorter frame, 10-shot magazine, with 7" overall length. Weight is 32.2 oz. Stainless frame with blued slide. Introduced 1993. Imported from Switzerland by Sphinx USA, Inc.
Price: 9mm, two-tone $940.00
Price: 40 S&W, two-tone $980.00

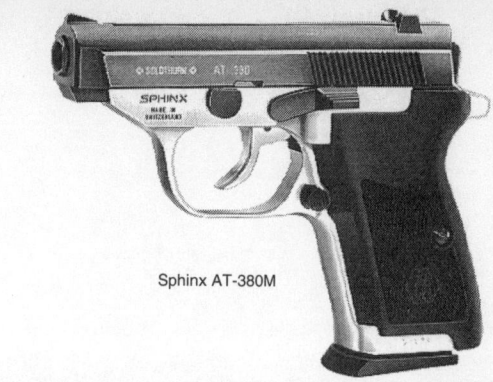
Sphinx AT-380M

Sphinx AT-2000P

Springfield Standard

SPRINGFIELD, INC. 1911A1 AUTO PISTOL
Caliber: 9mm Para., 9-shot; 38 Super, 9-shot; 45 ACP, 8-shot.
Barrel: 5".
Weight: 35.6 oz. **Length:** 8 5/8" overall.
Stocks: Checkered plastic or walnut.
Sights: Fixed three-dot system.
Features: Beveled magazine well; lowered and flared ejection port. All forged parts, including frame, barrel, slide. All new production. Introduced 1990. From Springfield, Inc.
Price: Basic, 45 ACP, Parkerized $476.00
Price: Standard, 45 ACP, blued $527.00
Price: Basic, 45 ACP, stainless $572.00
Price: Lightweight (28.6 oz., matte finish) $527.00
Price: Standard, 9mm, 38 Super, blued $557.00
Price: Standard, 9mm, stainless steel $587.00

Springfield, Inc. 1911A1 Custom Carry Gun
Similar to the standard 1911A1 except has fixed three-dot low profile sights, Videki speed trigger, match barrel and bushing; extended thumb safety, beavertail grip safety; beveled, polished magazine well, polished feed ramp and throated barrel; match Commander hammer and sear, tuned extractor; lowered and flared ejection port; recoil buffer system, full-length spring guide rod; walnut grips. Comes with two magazines with slam pads, plastic carrying case. Available in all popular calibers. Introduced 1992. From Springfield, Inc.
Price: $1,388.00

Springfield, Inc. 1911A1 Factory Comp
Similar to the standard 1911A1 except comes with bushing-type dual-port compensator, adjustable rear sight, extended thumb safety, Videki speed trigger, and beveled magazine well. Checkered walnut grips standard. Available in 38 Super or 45 ACP, blue only. Introduced 1992.
Price: 38 Super $947.00
Price: 45 ACP $984.00

Springfield, Inc. N.R.A. PPC Pistol
Specifically designed to comply with NRA rules for PPC competition. Has custom slide-to-frame fit; polished feed ramp; throated barrel; total internal honing; tuned extractor; recoil buffer system; fully checkered walnut grips; two fitted magazines; factory test target; custom carrying case. Introduced 1995. From Springfield, Inc.
Price: $1,632.00

Consult our Directory pages for the location of firms mentioned.

Springfield, Inc. 1911A1 High Capacity Pistol
Similar to the Standard 1911A1 except available in 45 ACP and 9mm with 10-shot magazine (45 ACP). Has Commander-style hammer, walnut grips, ambidextrous thumb safety, beveled magazine well, plastic carrying case. Introduced 1993. From Springfield, Inc.
Price: 45 ACP $622.00
Price: 9mm $638.00
Price: 45 ACP Factory Comp $964.00
Price: 45 ACP Comp Lightweight, matte finish $840.00
Price: 45 ACP Compact, blued $609.00
Price: As above, stainless steel $648.00

HANDGUNS—AUTOLOADERS, SERVICE & SPORT

Springfield Champion

Springfield, Inc. 1911A1 Champion Pistol
Similar to the standard 1911A1 except slide is 4.025". Has low-profile three-dot sight system. Comes with skeletonized hammer and walnut stocks. Available in 45 ACP only; blue or stainless. Introduced 1989.
Price: Blue $543.00
Price: Stainless $582.00
Price: Mil-Spec $476.00
Price: Champion Comp (single-port compensator) $871.00

Springfield, Inc. 1911A1 Compact Pistol
Similar to the Champion model except has a shortened frame height, 7.75" overall length. Magazine capacity is 7 shots. Has shortened hammer, checkered walnut grips. Available in 45 ACP only. Introduced 1989.
Price: Blued $543.00
Price: Stainless $582.00
Price: Compact Lightweight $543.00
Price: Mil-Spec $476.00

Springfield, Inc. V10 Ultra Compact Pistol
Similar to the 1911A1 Compact except has shorter slide, 3.5" barrel, recoil reducing compensator built into the barrel and slide. Beavertail grip safety, beveled magazine well, "hi-viz" combat sights, Videcki speed trigger, flared ejection port, stainless steel frame, blued slide, match grade barrel, walnut grips. Introduced 1996. From Springfield, Inc.
Price: V10 45 ACP $659.00
Price: Ultra Compact (no compensator), 45 ACP $569.00

Springfield, Inc. 1911A1 Defender Pistol
Similar to the 1911A1 Champion except has tapered cone dual-port compensator system, rubberized grips. Has reverse recoil plug, full-length recoil spring guide, serrated frontstrap, extended thumb safety, skeletonized hammer with modified grip safety to match and a Videki speed trigger. Bi-Tone finish. Introduced 1991.
Price: 45 ACP $993.00

STAR FIRESTAR AUTO PISTOL
Caliber: 9mm Para., 7-shot; 40 S&W, 6-shot.
Barrel: 3.39".
Weight: 30.35 oz. **Length:** 6.5" overall.
Stocks: Checkered rubber.
Sights: Blade front, fully adjustable rear; three-dot system.
Features: Low-profile, combat-style sights; ambidextrous safety. Available in blue or weather-resistant Starvel finish. Introduced 1990. Imported from Spain by Interarms.
Price: Blue, 9mm $450.00
Price: Starvel finish 9mm $450.00
Price: Blue, 40 S&W $465.00
Price: Starvel finish, 40 S&W $465.00

Star Firestar M45 Auto Pistol
Similar to the standard Firestar except chambered for 45 ACP with 6-shot magazine. Has 3.6" barrel, weighs 35 oz., 6.85" overall length. Reverse-taper Acculine barrel. Introduced 1992. Imported from Spain by Interarms.
Price: Blue $490.00
Price: Starvel finish $490.00

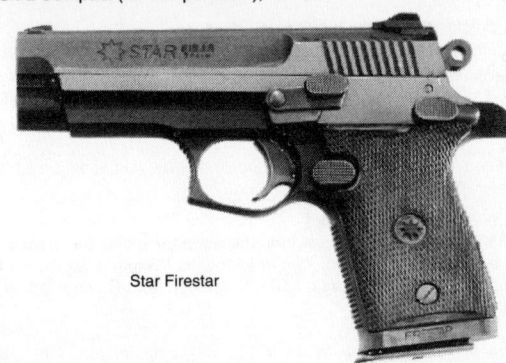

Star Firestar

Star Firestar Plus Auto Pistol
Same as the standard Firestar except has 10-shot magazine. Introduced 1994. Imported from Spain by Interarms.
Price: Blue, 9mm $460.00
Price: Starvel, 9mm $485.00

STAR ULTRASTAR DOUBLE-ACTION PISTOL
Caliber: 9mm Para., 9-shot magazine; 40 S&W, 8-shot.
Barrel: 3.57".
Weight: 26 oz. **Length:** 7" overall.
Stocks: Checkered black polymer.
Sights: Blade front, rear adjustable for windage; three-dot system.
Features: Polymer frame with inside steel slide rails; ambidextrous two-position safety (Safe and Decock). Introduced 1994. Imported from Spain by Interarms.
Price: $490.00

Star Firestar Plus

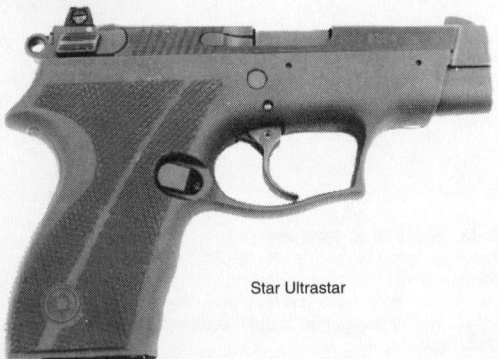

Star Ultrastar

Stoeger American Eagle Luger

STOEGER AMERICAN EAGLE LUGER
Caliber: 9mm Para., 7-shot magazine.
Barrel: 4", 6".
Weight: 32 oz. **Length:** 9.6" overall.
Stocks: Checkered walnut.
Sights: Blade front, fixed rear.
Features: Recreation of the American Eagle Luger pistol in stainless steel. Chamber loaded indicator. Introduced 1994. From Stoeger Industries.
Price: $695.00
Price: Navy Model, 6" barrel $695.00

HANDGUNS—AUTOLOADERS, SERVICE & SPORT

SUNDANCE MODEL A-25 AUTO PISTOL
Caliber: 25 ACP, 7-shot magazine.
Barrel: 2.5".
Weight: 16 oz. **Length:** 4⁷⁄₈" overall.
Stocks: Grooved black ABS or simulated smooth pearl; optional pink.
Sights: Fixed.
Features: Manual rotary safety; button magazine release. Bright chrome or black Teflon finish. Introduced 1989. Made in U.S. by Sundance Industries, Inc.
Price: $79.95

Sundance Laser 25

TAURUS MODEL PT 22/PT 25 AUTO PISTOLS
Caliber: 22 LR, 9-shot (PT 22); 25 ACP, 8-shot (PT 25).
Barrel: 2.75".
Weight: 12.3 oz. **Length:** 5.25" overall.
Stocks: Smooth Brazilian hardwood.
Sights: Blade front, fixed rear.
Features: Double action. Tip-up barrel for loading, cleaning. Blue or stainless. Introduced 1992. Made in U.S. by Taurus International.
Price: 22 LR or 25 ACP $187.00
Price: Nickel $195.00

TAURUS MODEL PT58 AUTO PISTOL
Caliber: 380 ACP, 10-shot magazine.
Barrel: 4.01".
Weight: 30 oz. **Length:** 7.2" overall.
Stocks: Brazilian hardwood.
Sights: Integral blade on slide front, notch rear adjustable for windage. Three-dot system.
Features: Double action with exposed hammer; inertia firing pin. Introduced 1988. Imported by Taurus International.
Price: Blue $429.00
Price: Stainless steel $470.00

TAURUS MODEL PT 92AF AUTO PISTOL
Caliber: 9mm Para., 10-shot magazine.
Barrel: 4.92".
Weight: 34 oz. **Length:** 8.54" overall.
Stocks: Brazilian hardwood.
Sights: Fixed notch rear. Three-dot sight system.
Features: Double action, exposed hammer, chamber loaded indicator, ambidextrous safety, inertia firing pin. Imported by Taurus International.
Price: Blue $479.00
Price: Blue, Deluxe Shooter's Pak (extra magazine, case) $477.00
Price: Stainless steel $493.00
Price: Stainless, Deluxe Shooter's Pak (extra magazine, case) $522.00

Taurus PT 99AF Auto Pistol
Similar to the PT-92 except has fully adjustable rear sight, smooth Brazilian walnut stocks and is available in stainless steel or polished blue. Introduced 1983.
Price: Blue $471.00
Price: Blue, Deluxe Shooter's Pak (extra magazine, case) $500.00
Price: Stainless steel $518.00
Price: Stainless, Deluxe Shooter's Pak (extra magazine, case) $546.00

Taurus PT 92AFC Compact Pistol
Similar to the PT-92 except has 4.25" barrel, 10-shot magazine, weighs 31 oz. and is 7.5" overall. Available in stainless steel or blue. Introduced 1991. Imported by Taurus International.
Price: Blue $449.00
Price: Stainless steel $493.00

Taurus PT 101 Auto Pistol
Same as the PT 100 except has micro-click rear sight adjustable for windage and elevation, three-dot combat-style. Introduced 1991.
Price: Blue $491.00
Price: Blue, Deluxe Shooter's Pak (extra magazine, case) $519.00
Price: Stainless $537.00
Price: Stainless, Deluxe Shooter's Pak (extra magazine, case) $565.00

SUNDANCE BOA AUTO PISTOL
Caliber: 25 ACP, 7-shot magazine.
Barrel: 2¹⁄₂".
Weight: 16 oz. **Length:** 4⁷⁄₈".
Stocks: Grooved ABS or smooth simulated pearl; optional pink.
Sights: Fixed.
Features: Patented grip safety, manual rotary safety; button magazine release; lifetime warranty. Bright chrome or black Teflon finish. Introduced 1991. Made in the U.S. by Sundance Industries, Inc.
Price: $95.00

SUNDANCE LASER 25 PISTOL
Caliber: 25 ACP, 7-shot magazine.
Barrel: 2¹⁄₂".
Weight: 18 oz. **Length:** 4⁷⁄₈" overall.
Stocks: Grooved black ABS.
Sights: Class IIIa laser, 670 NM, 5mW, and fixed open.
Features: Factory installed and sighted laser sight activated by squeezing the grip safety; manual rotary safety; button magazine release. Bright chrome or black finish. Introduced 1995. Made in U.S. by Sundance Industries, Inc.
Price: With laser $219.00
Price: Lady Laser (as above except different name, bright chrome only) .$219.00

Taurus PT 25

Taurus PT 92

Taurus PT 101

TAURUS PT 100 AUTO PISTOL
Caliber: 40 S&W, 10-shot magazine.
Barrel: 5".
Weight: 34 oz.
Stocks: Smooth Brazilian hardwood.
Sights: Fixed front, drift-adjustable rear. Three-dot combat.
Features: Double action, exposed hammer. Ambidextrous hammer-drop safety; inertia firing pin; chamber loaded indicator. Introduced 1991. Imported by Taurus International.
Price: Blue $469.00
Price: Blue, Deluxe Shooter's Pak (extra magazine, case) $497.00
Price: Stainless $514.00
Price: Stainless, Deluxe Shooter's Pak (extra magazine, case) $542.00

CAUTION: PRICES SHOWN ARE SUPPLIED BY THE MANUFACTURER OR IMPORTER. CHECK YOUR LOCAL GUNSHOP.

HANDGUNS—AUTOLOADERS, SERVICE & SPORT

TAURUS MODEL PT-908 AUTO PISTOL
Caliber: 9mm Para., 8-shot magazine.
Barrel: 3.8".
Weight: 30 oz. **Length:** 7.05" overall.
Stocks: Santoprene II.
Sights: Drift-adjustable front and rear; three-dot combat.
Features: Double action, exposed hammer; manual ambidextrous hammer-drop; inertia firing pin; chamber loaded indicator. Introduced 1993. Imported by Taurus International.
Price: Blue $435.00
Price: Stainless steel $473.00
Price: Blue, Deluxe Shooter's Pak $459.00
Price: Stainless, Deluxe Shooter's Pak $496.00

Taurus PT-940 Auto Pistol
Same as the PT-908 except chambered for 40 siW, 9-shot magazine. Introduced 1996. Imported by Taurus International.
Price: Blue $453.00
Price: Stainless $497.00
Price: Blue, Deluxe Shooter's Pak $476.00
Price: Stainless, Deluxe Shooter's Pack $520.00

TAURUS PT-945 AUTO PISTOL
Caliber: 45 ACP, 8-shot magazine.
Barrel: 4.25".
Weight: 29.5 oz. **Length:** 7.48" overall.
Stocks: Santoprene II.
Sights: Drift-adjustable front and rear; three-dot system.
Features: Double-action mechanism. Has manual ambidextrous hammer drop safety, intercept notch, firing pin block, chamber loaded indicator, last-shot hold-open. Introduced 1995. Imported by Taurus International.
Price: Blue $453.00
Price: Stainless $497.00
Price: Blue, Deluxe Shooter's Pak $476.00
Price: Stainless, Deluxe Shooter's Pak $520.00

WALTHER P-5 AUTO PISTOL
Caliber: 9mm.
Barrel: 3.6"
Weight: 28 oz. **Length:** 7" overall.
Stocks: Checkered polymer.
Sights: Blade front, adjustable rear.
Features: Uses the basic Walther P-38 double-action mechanism. Polished blue finish. Imported from Germany by Interarms.
Price: $900.00

WALTHER PP AUTO PISTOL
Caliber: 32 ACP, 380 ACP, 7-shot magazine.
Barrel: 3.86".
Weight: 23 1/2 oz. **Length:** 6.7" overall.
Stocks: Checkered plastic.
Sights: Fixed, white markings.
Features: Double action; manual safety blocks firing pin and drops hammer; chamber loaded indicator on 32 and 380; extra finger rest magazine provided. Imported from Germany by Interarms.
Price: 32 ....$999.00
Price: 380 ....$999.00
Price: Engraved models ....On Request

Manufacturers' addresses in the
Directory of the Arms Trade
page 313, this issue

WALTHER MODEL TPH AUTO PISTOL
Caliber: 22 LR, 25 ACP, 6-shot magazine.
Barrel: 2 1/4".
Weight: 14 oz. **Length:** 5 3/8" overall.
Stocks: Checkered black composition.
Sights: Blade front, rear drift-adjustable for windage.
Features: Made of stainless steel. Scaled-down version of the Walther PP/PPK series. Made in U.S. Introduced 1987. From Interarms.
Price: Blue or stainless steel, 22 or 25 ....$440.00

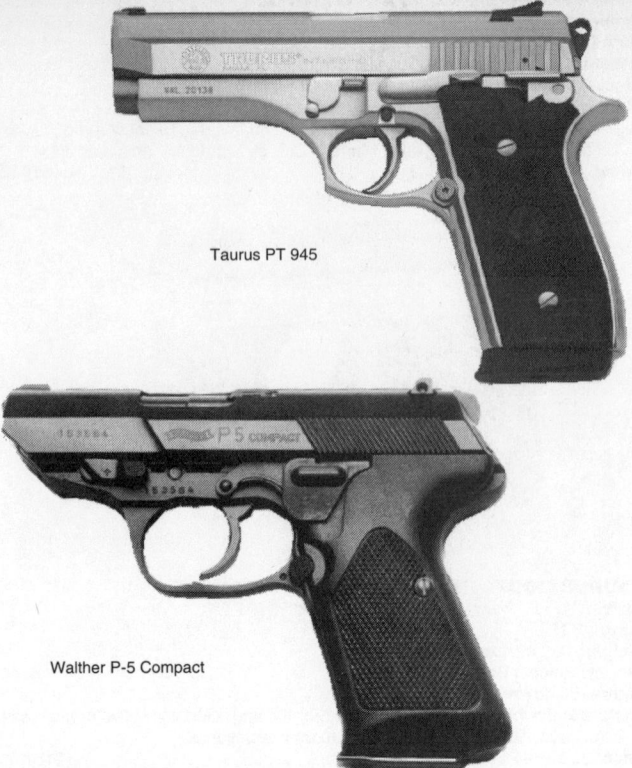

Taurus PT 945

Walther P-5 Compact

Walther P-5 Compact
Similar to the P-5 except has 3.2" barrel, weighs 26 oz., and has magazine release on left side of grip. Imported from Germany by Interarms.
Price: $900.00

Walther PPK/S American

Walther PPK American Auto Pistol
Similar to Walther PPK/S except weighs 21 oz., has 6-shot capacity. Made in the U.S. Introduced 1986.
Price: Stainless, 380 ACP only $540.00
Price: Blue, 380 ACP only $540.00

Walther TPH

Walther PPK/S American Auto Pistol
Similar to Walther PP except made entirely in the United States. Has 3.27" barrel with 6.1" length overall. Introduced 1980.
Price: 380 ACP only, blue $540.00
Price: As above, stainless $540.00

HANDGUNS—AUTOLOADERS, SERVICE & SPORT

WALTHER P88 COMPACT PISTOL
Caliber: 9mm Para., 10-shot magazine.
Barrel: 3.93".
Weight: 28 oz. **Length:** NA.
Stocks: Checkered black polymer.
Sights: Blade front, drift adjustable rear.
Features: Double action with ambidextrous decocking lever and magazine release; alloy frame; loaded chamber indicator; matte blue finish. Imported from Germany by Interarms.
Price: $900.00

Walther P88 Compact

WILDEY AUTOMATIC PISTOL
Caliber: 10mm Wildey Mag., 11mm Wildey Mag., 30 Wildey Mag., 357 Peterbuilt, 45 Win. Mag., 475 Wildey Mag., 7-shot magazine.
Barrel: 5", 6", 7", 8", 10", 12", 14" (45 Win. Mag.); 8", 10", 12", 14" (all other cals.). Interchangeable.
Weight: 64 oz. (5" barrel). **Length:** 11" overall (7" barrel).
Stocks: Hardwood.
Sights: Ramp front (interchangeable blades optional), fully adjustable rear. Scope base available.
Features: Gas-operated action. Made of stainless steel. Has three-lug rotary bolt. Double or single action. Polished and matte finish. Made in U.S. by Wildey, Inc.
Price: .... $1,175.00 to $1,495.00

WILKINSON "LINDA" AUTO PISTOL
Caliber: 9mm Para.
Barrel: 8 5/16".
Weight: 4 lbs., 13 oz. **Length:** 12 1/4" overall.
Stocks: Checkered black plastic pistol grip, walnut forend.
Sights: Protected blade front, aperture rear.
Features: Fires from closed bolt. Semi-auto only. Straight blowback action. Cross-bolt safety. Removable barrel. From Wilkinson Arms.
Price: $533.33

Wilkinson Sherry

WILKINSON "SHERRY" AUTO PISTOL
Caliber: 22 LR, 8-shot magazine.
Barrel: 2 1/8".
Weight: 9 1/4 oz. **Length:** 4 3/8" overall.
Stocks: Checkered black plastic.
Sights: Fixed, groove.
Features: Cross-bolt safety locks the sear into the hammer. Available in all blue finish or blue slide and trigger with gold frame. Introduced 1985.
Price: $195.00

HANDGUNS—COMPETITION HANDGUNS

Includes models suitable for several forms of competition and other sporting purposes.

AUTO-ORDNANCE 1911A1 COMPETITION MODEL
Caliber: 45 ACP.
Barrel: 5".
Weight: 42 oz. **Length:** 10" overall.
Stocks: Black textured rubber wrap-around.
Sights: Blade front, rear adjustable for windage; three-dot system.
Features: Machined compensator, combat Commander hammer; flat mainspring housing; low profile magazine funnel; metal form magazine bumper; high-ride beavertail grip safety; full-length recoil spring guide system; extended slide stop, safety and magazine catch; Videcki adjustable speed trigger; extended combat ejector. Introduced 1994. Made in U.S. by Auto-Ordnance Corp.
Price: $635.50

Auto-Ordnance Competition Model

Baer 1911 Ultimate Master

BAER 1911 ULTIMATE MASTER COMBAT PISTOL
Caliber: 45 ACP (others available), 10-shot magazine.
Barrel: 5"; Baer NM.
Weight: 37 oz. **Length:** 8.5" overall.
Stocks: Checkered rosewood.
Sights: Baer dovetail front, low-mount Bo-Mar rear with hidden leaf.
Features: Full-house competition gun. Baer forged NM blued steel frame and double serrated slide; Baer triple port, tapered cone compensator; fitted slide to frame; lowered, flared ejection port; Baer reverse recoil plug; full-length guide rod; recoil buff; beveled magazine well; Baer Commander hammer, sear; Baer extended ambidextrous safety, extended ejector, checkered slide stop, beavertail grip safety with pad, extended magazine release button; Baer speed trigger. Made in U.S. by Les Baer Custom, Inc.
Price: Compensated, open sights $1,996.00
Price: Uncompensated "Limited" Model $1,843.00
Price: Compensated, with Baer optics mount $2,360.00

Baer 1911 Ultimate Master "Steel Special" Pistol
Similar to the Ultimate Master except chambered for 38 Super with supported chamber (other calibers available), lighter slide, bushing-type compensator; two-piece guide rod. Designed for maximum 150 power factor. Comes without sights—scope and mount only. Hard chrome finish. Made in U.S. by Les Baer Custom, Inc.
Price: $2,670.00

CAUTION: PRICES SHOWN ARE SUPPLIED BY THE MANUFACTURER OR IMPORTER. CHECK YOUR LOCAL GUNSHOP.

HANDGUNS—COMPETITION HANDGUNS

Baer 1911 Bullseye Wadcutter

BAER 1911 NATIONAL MATCH HARDBALL PISTOL
Caliber: 45 ACP, 7-shot magazine.
Barrel: 5".
Weight: 37 oz. **Length:** 8.5" overall.
Stocks: Checkered walnut.
Sights: Baer dovetail front with undercut post, low-mount Bo-Mar rear with hidden leaf.
Features: Baer NM forged steel frame, double serrated slide and barrel with stainless bushing; slide fitted to frame; Baer match trigger with 4-lb. pull; polished feed ramp, throated barrel; checkered front strap, arched mainspring housing; Baer beveled magazine well; lowered, flared ejection port; tuned extractor; Baer extended ejector, checkered slide stop; recoil buff. Made in U.S. by Les Baer Custom, Inc.
Price: $1,180.00

Baer 1911 Target Master Pistol
Similar to the National Match Hardball except available in 45 ACP and other calibers, has Baer post-style dovetail front sight, flat serrated mainspring housing, standard trigger. Made in U.S. by Les Baer Custom, Inc.
Price: $1,263.00
Price: With 6" barrel $1,540.00

Baer 1911 Bullseye Wadcutter Pistol
Similar to the National Match Hardball except designed for wadcutter loads only. Has polished feed ramp and barrel throat; Bo-Mar rib on slide; full-length recoil rod; Baer speed trigger with 3½-lb. pull; Baer deluxe hammer and sear; Baer beavertail grip safety with pad; flat mainspring housing checkered 20 lpi. Blue finish; checkered walnut grips. Made in U.S. by Les Baer Custom, Inc.
Price: $1,347.00
Price: With 6" barrel $1,597.00

BENELLI MP95E MATCH PISTOL
Caliber: 22 LR, 9-shot magazine, or 32 S&W WC, 5-shot magazine.
Barrel: 4.33".
Weight: 38.8 oz. **Length:** 11.81" overall.
Stocks: Checkered walnut match type; anatomically shaped.
Sights: Match type. Blade front, click-adjustable rear for windage and elevation.
Features: Removable, trigger assembly. Special internal weight box on sub-frame below barrel. Cut for scope rails. Introduced 1993. Imported from Italy by European American Armory.
Price: Blue $550.00
Price: Chrome $599.00
Price: MP90S (competition version of MP95E), 22 LR $1,295.00
Price: As above, 32 S&W $1,495.00

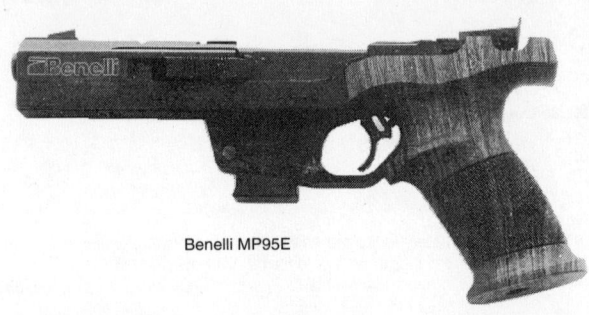

Benelli MP95E

BERNARDELLI MODEL 69 TARGET PISTOL
Caliber: 22 LR, 10-shot magazine.
Barrel: 5.9".
Weight: 38 oz. **Length:** 9" overall.
Stocks: Wrap-around, hand-checkered walnut with thumbrest.
Sights: Fully adjustable and interchangeable target type.
Features: Conforms to U.I.T. regulations. Has 7.1" sight radius, .27" wide grooved trigger. Manual thumb safety and magazine safety. Introduced 1987. Imported from Italy by Mitchell Arms.
Price: $612.00

Beretta Model 89

BERETTA MODEL 89 GOLD STANDARD PISTOL
Caliber: 22 LR, 8-shot magazine.
Barrel: 6"
Weight: 41 oz. **Length:** 9.5" overall.
Stocks: Target-type walnut with thumbrest.
Sights: Interchangeable blade front, fully adjustable rear.
Features: Single action target pistol. Matte black, Bruniton finish. Imported from Italy by Beretta U.S.A.
Price: $736.00

BF SINGLE SHOT PISTOL
Caliber: 22 LR, 357 Mag., 44 Mag., 7-30 Waters, 30-30 Win., 375 Win., 45-70; custom chamberings from 17 Rem. through 45-cal.
Barrel: 10", 10.75", 12", 15+".
Weight: 52 oz. **Length:** NA.
Stocks: Custom Herrett finger-groove grip and forend.
Sights: Undercut Patridge front, ½-MOA match-quality fully adjustable RPM Iron Sight rear; barrel or receiver mounting. Drilled and tapped for scope mounting.
Features: Rigid barrel/receiver; falling block action with short lock time; automatic ejection; air-gauged match barrels by Wilson or Douglas; matte black oxide finish standard, electroless nickel optional. Barrel has 11-degree recessed target crown. Introduced 1988. Made in U.S. by E.A. Brown Mfg.
Price: 10", no sights $499.95
Price: 10", RPM sights $564.95
Price: 10.75", no sights $529.95
Price: 10.75", RPM sights $594.95
Price: 12", no sights $562.95
Price: 12", RPM sights $643.75
Price: 15", no sights $592.95
Price: 15", RPM sights $675.00
Price: 10.75" Ultimate Silhouette (heavy barrel, special forend, RPM rear sight with hooded front, gold-plated trigger) $687.95

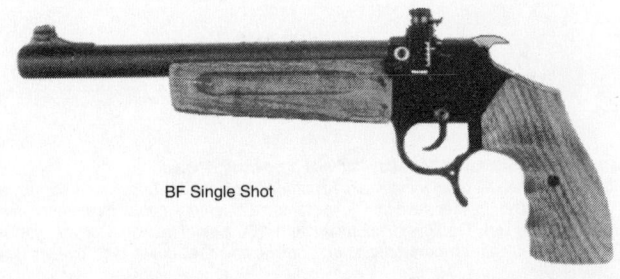

BF Single Shot

HANDGUNS—COMPETITION HANDGUNS

Browning Buck Mark Bullseye

BROWNING BUCK MARK SILHOUETTE
Caliber: 22 LR, 10-shot magazine.
Barrel: 9 7/8".
Weight: 53 oz. **Length:** 14" overall.
Stocks: Smooth walnut stocks and forend, or finger-groove walnut.
Sights: Post-type hooded front adjustable for blade width and height; Pro Target rear fully adjustable for windage and elevation.
Features: Heavy barrel with .900" diameter; 12 1/2" sight radius. Special sighting plane forms scope base. Introduced 1987. Made in U.S. From Browning.
Price: $434.95

Browning Buck Mark Unlimited Match
Same as the Buck Mark Silhouette except has 14" heavy barrel. Conforms to IHMSA 15" maximum sight radius rule. *Introduced 1991.
Price: $535.95

Browning Buck Mark Bullseye
Similar to the Buck Mark Silhouette except has 7 1/4" heavy barrel with three flutes per side; trigger is adjustable from 2 1/2 to 5 lbs.; specially designed rosewood target or three-finger-groove stocks with competition-style heel rest, or with contoured rubber grip. Overall length is 11 5/16", weighs 36 oz. Introduced 1996. Made in U.S. From Browning.
Price: With rubber stocks $376.95
Price: With rosewood stocks $484.95

Browning Buck Mark Target 5.5
Same as the Buck Mark Silhouette except has a 5 1/2" barrel with .900" diameter. Has hooded sights mounted on a scope base that accepts an optical or reflex sight. Rear sight is a Browning fully adjustable Pro Target, front sight is an adjustable post that customizes to different widths, and can be adjusted for height. Contoured walnut grips with thumbrest, or finger-groove walnut. Matte blue finish. Overall length is 9 5/8", weighs 35 1/2 oz. Has 10-shot magazine. Introduced 1990. From Browning.
Price: $411.95
Price: Target 5.5 Gold (as above with gold anodized frame and top rib) .$462.95
Price: Target 5.5 Nickel (as above with nickel frame and top rib) $462.95

Browning Buck Mark Target 5.5

Browning Buck Mark Field 5.5
Same as the Target 5.5 except has hoodless ramp-style front sight and low profile rear sight. Matte blue finish, contoured or finger-groove walnut stocks. Introduced 1991.
Price: $411.95

BROLIN PRO-STOCK COMPETITION PISTOL
Caliber: 45 ACP, 8-shot magazine.
Barrel: 5".
Weight: 37 oz. **Length:** 8.5" overall.
Stocks: Checkered with Brolin logo.
Sights: Ramp front, fully adjustable rear.
Features: Throated heavy match barrel; full-length recoil spring guide; polished feed ramp; lowered and flared ejection port; beveled magazine well; flat-top slide; serrated flat mainspring housing; high relief front strap cut; four-legged sear spring; adjustable match trigger; slotted Commander hammer; beavertail grip safety; ambidextrous thumb safety; front slide serrations. Introduced 1996. Made in U.S. by Brolin Arms.
Price: Blue $779.00
Price: Blue/stainless two-tone $799.00

Brolin Pro-Comp Competition Pistol
Similar to the Pro-Stock model except has integral milled DPC Comp on the heavy match barrel; barrel length 4", overall length 8.5"; weighs 37 oz.; 8-shot magazine. Introduced 1996. Made in U.S. by Brolin Arms.
Price: Blue $909.00
Price: Blue/stainless two-tone $929.00

COLT GOLD CUP NATIONAL MATCH MK IV/SERIES 80
Caliber: 45 ACP, 8-shot magazine.
Barrel: 5", with new design bushing.
Weight: 39 oz. **Length:** 8 1/2".
Stocks: Checkered rubber composite with silver-plated medallion.
Sights: Patridge-style front, Colt-Elliason rear adjustable for windage and elevation, sight radius 6 3/4".
Features: Arched or flat housing; wide, grooved trigger with adjustable stop; ribbed-top slide, hand fitted, with improved ejection port.
Price: Blue $937.00
Price: Stainless $1,003.00
Price: Bright stainless $1,073.00
Price: Delta Gold Cup (10mm, stainless) $1,027.00

Colt Gold Cup National Match

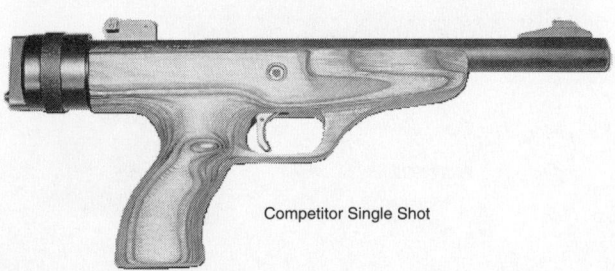
Competitor Single Shot

COMPETITOR SINGLE SHOT PISTOL
Caliber: 22 LR through 50 Action Express, including belted magnums.
Barrel: 14" standard; 10.5" silhouette; 16" optional.
Weight: About 59 oz. (14" bbl.). **Length:** 15.12" overall.
Stocks: Ambidextrous; synthetic (standard) or laminated or natural wood.
Sights: Ramp front, adjustable rear.
Features: Rotary canon-type action cocks on opening; cammed ejector; interchangeable barrels, ejectors. Adjustable single stage trigger, sliding thumb safety and trigger safety. Matte blue finish. Introduced 1988. From Competitor Corp., Inc.
Price: 14", standard calibers, synthetic grip $399.95
Price: Extra barrels, from $149.95

HANDGUNS—COMPETITION HANDGUNS

E.A.A. WITNESS GOLD TEAM AUTO
Caliber: 9mm Para., 9x21, 38 Super, 40 S&W, 45 ACP.
Barrel: 5.1".
Weight: 41.6 oz. **Length:** 9.6" overall.
Stocks: Checkered walnut, competition style.
Sights: Square post front, fully adjustable rear.
Features: Triple-chamber cone compensator; competition SA trigger; extended safety and magazine release; competition hammer; beveled magazine well; beavertail grip. Hand-fitted major components. Hard chrome finish. Match-grade barrel. From E.A.A. Custom Shop. Introduced 1992. From European American Armory.
Price: $2,195.00

E.A.A. Witness Gold Team

E.A.A. Witness Silver Team Auto
Similar to the Witness Gold Team except has double-chamber compensator, oval magazine release, black rubber grips, double-dip blue finish. Comes with Super Sight and drilled and tapped for scope mount. Built for the intermediate competition shooter. Introduced 1992. From European American Armory Custom Shop.
Price: 9mm Para., 9x21, 38 Super, 40 S&W, 45 ACP $975.00

ERMA ER MATCH REVOLVER
Caliber: 32 S&W Long, 6-shot.
Barrel: 6".
Weight: 47.3 oz. **Length:** 11.2" overall.
Stocks: Stippled walnut, adjustable match-type.
Sights: Blade front, micrometer rear adjustable for windage and elevation.
Features: Polished blue finish. Introduced 1989. Imported from Germany by Precision Sales International.
Price: 32 S&W Long $1,248.00

Erma ER Match Revolver

ERMA ESP 85A MATCH PISTOL
Caliber: 22 LR, 6-shot; 32 S&W, 6-shot magazine.
Barrel: 6".
Weight: 39 oz. **Length:** 10" overall.
Stocks: Match-type of stippled walnut; adjustable.
Sights: Interchangeable blade front, micrometer adjustable rear with interchangeable leaf.
Features: Five-way adjustable trigger; exposed hammer and separate firing pin block allow unlimited dry firing practice. Blue or matte chrome; right- or left-hand. Introduced 1989. Imported from Germany by Precision Sales International.
Price: 22 LR $1,695.00
Price: 22 LR, left-hand $1,735.00
Price: 22 LR, matte chrome $1,890.00
Price: 32 S&W $1,790.00
Price: 32 S&W, left-hand $1,830.00
Price: 32 S&W, matte chrome $2,095.00
Price: 32 S&W, matte chrome, left-hand $2,135.00

Erma ESP Junior Match Pistol
Similar to the ESP 85A Match except chambered only for 22 LR, blue finish only. Stippled non-adjustable walnut match grips (adjustable grips optional). Introduced 1995. Imported from Germany by Precision Sales International.
Price: $1,295.00

> Consult our Directory pages for the location of firms mentioned.

Erma ESP Junior Match

FAS 607 MATCH PISTOL
Caliber: 22 LR, 5-shot.
Barrel: 5.6".
Weight: 37 oz. **Length:** 11" overall.
Stocks: Walnut wrap-around; sizes small, medium, large or adjustable.
Sights: Match. Blade front, open notch rear fully adjustable for windage and elevation. Sight radius is 8.66".
Features: Line of sight is only 11/32" above centerline of bore; magazine is inserted from top; adjustable and removable trigger mechanism; single lever takedown. Full 5-year warranty. Imported from Italy by Nygord Precision Products.
Price: $1,175.00
Price: Model 603 (32 S&W) $1,175.00

FAS 601 Match Pistol
Similar to Model 607 except has different match stocks with adjustable palm shelf, 22 Short only for rapid fire shooting; weighs 40 oz., 5.6" bbl.; has gas ports through top of barrel and slide to reduce recoil; slightly different trigger and sear mechanisms. Imported from Italy by Nygord Precision Products.
Price: $1,250.00

FREEDOM ARMS CASULL MODEL 252 SILHOUETTE
Caliber: 22 LR, 5-shot cylinder.
Barrel: 9.95".
Weight: 63 oz. **Length:** NA
Stocks: Black micarta, western style.
Sights: 1/8" Patridge front, Iron Sight Gun Works silhouette rear, click adjustable for windage and elevation.
Features: Stainless steel. Built on the 454 Casull frame. Two-point firing pin, lightened hammer for fast lock time. Trigger pull is 3 to 5 lbs. with pre-set overtravel screw. Introduced 1991. From Freedom Arms.
Price: Silhouette Class $1,509.00
Price: Extra fitted 22 WMR cylinder $253.00

FAS 607 Match

HANDGUNS—COMPETITION HANDGUNS

Freedom Arms Casull Model 252 Varmint
Similar to the Silhouette Class revolver except has 7.5" barrel, weighs 59 oz., has black and green laminated hardwood grips, and comes with brass bead front sight, express shallow V rear sight with windage and elevation adjustments. Introduced 1991. From Freedom Arms.
Price: Varmint Class $1,454.00
Price: Extra fitted 22 WMR cylinder $253.00

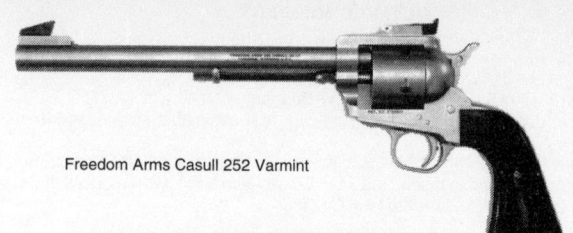
Freedom Arms Casull 252 Varmint

GAUCHER GP SILHOUETTE PISTOL
Caliber: 22 LR, single shot.
Barrel: 10".
Weight: 42.3 oz. **Length:** 15.5" overall.
Stocks: Stained hardwood.
Sights: Hooded post on ramp front, open rear adjustable for windage and elevation.
Features: Matte chrome barrel, blued bolt and sights. Other barrel lengths available on special order. Introduced 1991. Imported by Mandall Shooting Supplies.
Price: $425.00

Manufacturers' addresses in the **Directory of the Arms Trade** *page 313, this issue*

GLOCK 17L COMPETITION AUTO
Caliber: 9mm Para., 10-shot magazine.
Barrel: 6.02".
Weight: 23.3 oz. **Length:** 8.85" overall.
Stocks: Black polymer.
Sights: Blade front with white dot, fixed or adjustable rear.
Features: Polymer frame, steel slide; double-action trigger with "Safe Action" system; mechanical firing pin safety, drop safety; simple takedown without tools; locked breech, recoil operated action. Introduced 1989. Imported from Austria by Glock, Inc.
Price: $790.00

GLOCK 24 COMPETITION MODEL PISTOL
Caliber: 40 S&W, 10-shot magazine.
Barrel: 6.02".
Weight: 29.5 oz. **Length:** 8.85" overall.
Stocks: Black polymer.
Sights: Blade front with dot, white outline rear adjustable for windage.
Features: Long-slide competition model available as compensated or non-compensated gun. Factory-installed competition trigger; drop-free magazine. Introduced 1994. Imported from Austria by Glock, Inc.
Price: $790.00

Glock 24 Competition

HAMMERLI MODEL 160/162 FREE PISTOLS
Caliber: 22 LR, single shot.
Barrel: 11.30".
Weight: 46.94 oz. **Length:** 17.52" overall.
Stocks: Walnut; full match style with adjustable palm shelf. Stippled surfaces.
Sights: Changeable blade front, open, fully adjustable match rear.
Features: Model 160 has mechanical set trigger; Model 162 has electronic trigger; both fully adjustable with provisions for dry firing. Introduced 1993. Imported from Switzerland by Sigarms, Inc.
Price: Model 160, about $2,085.00
Price: Model 162, about $2,295.00

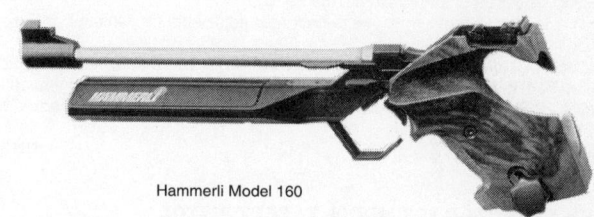
Hammerli Model 160

HAMMERLI MODEL 208s PISTOL
Caliber: 22 LR, 8-shot magazine.
Barrel: 5.9".
Weight: 37.5 oz. **Length:** 10" overall.
Stocks: Walnut, target-type with thumbrest.
Sights: Blade front, open fully adjustable rear.
Features: Adjustable trigger, including length; interchangeable rear sight elements. Imported from Switzerland by Sigarms, Inc.
Price: About $1,925.00

HARRIS GUNWORKS SIGNATURE JR. LONG RANGE PISTOL
Caliber: Any suitable caliber.
Barrel: To customer specs.
Weight: 5 lbs.
Stock: Gunworks fiberglass.
Sights: None furnished; comes with scope rings.
Features: Right- or left-hand benchrest action of titanium or stainless steel; single shot or repeater. Comes with bipod. Introduced 1992. Made in U.S. by Harris Gunworks, Inc.
Price: $2,400.00

HAMMERLI MODEL 280 TARGET PISTOL
Caliber: 22 LR, 6-shot; 32 S&W Long WC, 5-shot.
Barrel: 4.5".
Weight: 39.1 oz. (32). **Length:** 11.8" overall.
Stocks: Walnut match-type with stippling, adjustable palm shelf.
Sights: Match sights, micrometer adjustable; interchangeable elements.
Features: Has carbon-reinforced synthetic frame and bolt/barrel housing. Trigger is adjustable for pull weight, take-up weight, let-off, and length, and is interchangeable. Interchangeable metal or carbon fiber counterweights. Sight radius of 8.8". Comes with barrel weights, spare magazine, loading tool, cleaning rods. Introduced 1990. Imported from Sigarms, Inc.
Price: 22-cal., about $1,565.00
Price: 32-cal., about $1,765.00

Hammerli Model 280

CAUTION: PRICES SHOWN ARE SUPPLIED BY THE MANUFACTURER OR IMPORTER. CHECK YOUR LOCAL GUNSHOP.

HANDGUNS—COMPETITION HANDGUNS

HIGH STANDARD OLYMPIC MILITARY
Caliber: 22 Short, 5-shot magazine.
Barrel: 5.5" bull.
Weight: 44 oz. **Length:** 9.50" overall.
Stocks: Checkered hardwood with thumbrest.
Sights: Undercut ramp front, micro-click rear adjustable for windage and elevation.
Features: Removable barrel stabilizer; high strength aluminum slide, carbon steel frame; adjustable trigger and sear. Overall blue finish. Reintroduced 1994. Made in U.S. by High Standard Mfg. Co., Inc.
Price: $536.00

HIGH STANDARD OLYMPIC RAPID FIRE
Caliber: 22 Short, 5-shot magazine.
Barrel: 4".
Weight: 46 oz. **Length:** 11.5" overall.
Stocks: International-style stippled hardwood.
Sights: Undercut ramp front, fully adjustable rear.
Features: Integral muzzle brake and forward mounted compensator; trigger adjustable for weight of pull, travel; gold-plated trigger, slide stop, safety, magazine release; stippled front and backstraps; push-button barrel takedown. Introduced 1996. Made in U.S. by High Standard Mfg. Co.
Price: $1,995.00

HIGH STANDARD SUPERMATIC TOURNAMENT PISTOL
Caliber: 22 LR, 10-shot magazine.
Barrel: 5.5"; push-button takedown.
Weight: 43 oz. **Length:** 8.5" overall.
Stocks: Black rubber; ambidextrous.
Sights: Undercut ramp front, micro-click rear adjustable for windage and elevation.
Features: Slide-mounted rear sight. Blue finish. Reintroduced 1994. From High Standard Mfg. Co., Inc.
Price: $399.00

HIGH STANDARD SUPERMATIC TROPHY PISTOL
Caliber: 22 LR, 10-shot magazine.
Barrel: 5.5" or 7.25"; push-button takedown; drilled and tapped for scope mount.
Weight: 44 oz. **Length:** 9.5" overall.
Stocks: Checkered hardwood with thumbrest.
Sights: Undercut ramp front, micro-click rear adjustable for windage and elevation.
Features: Gold-plated trigger, slide lock, safety-lever and magazine release; stippled front grip and backstrap; adjustable trigger and sear. Barrel weights optional. A 22 Short version is available. Reintroduced 1994. From High Standard Mfg. Co., Inc.
Price: $516.00

HIGH STANDARD 10X MODEL TARGET PISTOL
Caliber: 22 LR, 10-shot magazine.
Barrel: 5.5"; push-button takedown.
Weight: 44 oz. **Length:** 9.5" overall.
Stocks: Checkered black epoxied walnut; ambidextrous.
Sights: Undercut ramp front, micro-click rear adjustable for windage and elevation.
Features: Hand built with select parts. Adjustable trigger and sear; Parkerized finish; stippled front grip and backstrap. Barrel weights optional. Comes with test target, extended warranty. Reintroduced 1994. From High Standard Mfg. Co., Inc.
Price: ....$869.00 to $1,095.00

MITCHELL ARMS MONARCH PISTOL
Caliber: 22 LR, 10-shot magazine.
Barrel: 5.5" bull, 7.25" fluted.
Weight: 44.5 oz. **Length:** 9.75" overall (5.5" barrel).
Stocks: Checkered walnut with thumbrest.
Sights: Undercut ramp front, click-adjsutable frame-mounted rear.
Features: Grip duplicates feel of military 45; positive action magazine latch; front and rear straps stippled. Trigger adjustable for pull, over-travel; gold-filled roll marks, gold-plated trigger, safety, magazine release; push-button barrel takedown. Introduced 1992. From Mitchell Arms, Inc.
Price: Stainless steel or blue $489.00

Mitchell Arms Monarch II Pistol
Same as the Monarch except has nickel-plated trigger, safety and magazine release, and has silver-filled roll marks. Available in satin finish stainless steel or blue. Introduced 1992. From Mitchell Arms, Inc.
Price: $498.00

High Standard Olympic Rapid Fire

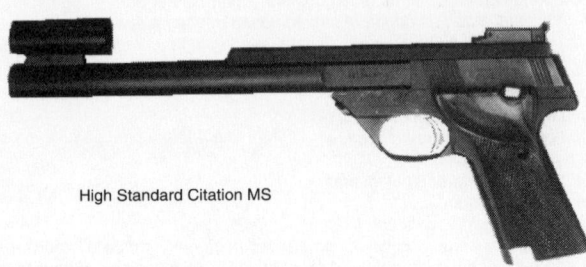

High Standard Citation MS

High Standard Supermatic Citation Pistol
Same as the Supermatic Trophy except has nickel-plated trigger, slide lock, safety lever, magazine release, and has slightly heavier trigger pull. Has stippled front-grip and backstrap, checkered hardwood thumbrest grips, adjustable trigger and sear. Matte blue finish. 5.5" barrel only. Conversion unit for 22 Short available. Reintroduced 1994. From High Standard Mfg. Co., Inc.
Price: $446.00
Price: With scope mount, rings, no sights $416.00

High Standard Supermatic Citation MS
Same as the Supermatic Citation except has 10" barrel and RPM sights. Introduced 1996. Made in U.S. by High Standard Mfg. Co., Inc.
Price: $695.00

HIGH STANDARD VICTOR TARGET PISTOL
Caliber: 22 LR, 10-shot magazine.
Barrel: 4.5" or 5.5"; push-button takedown.
Weight: 46 oz. **Length:** 9.5" overall.
Stocks: Checkered hardwood with thumbrest.
Sights: Undercut ramp front, micro-click rear adjustable for windage and elevation. Also available with scope mount, rings, no sights.
Features: Full-length aluminum vent rib (steel optional). Gold-plated trigger, slide lock, safety-lever and magazine release; stippled front grip and backstrap; adjustable trigger and sear. Comes with barrel weight. Blue or Parkerized finish. Reintroduced 1994. From High Standard Mfg. Co., Inc.
Price: $532.00
Price: Victor 10X $1,195.00
Price: With scope mount, rings, no sights $479.00

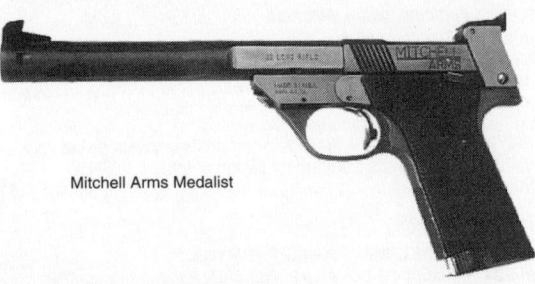

Mitchell Arms Medalist

MITCHELL ARMS MEDALIST AUTO PISTOL
Caliber: 22 Short, 22 LR, 10-shot magazine.
Barrel: 6.75" round tapered, with stabilizer.
Weight: 40 oz. **Length:** 11.25" overall.
Stocks: Checkered walnut with thumbrest.
Sights: Undercut ramp front, frame-mounted click adjustable square notch rear.
Features: Integral stabilizer with two removable weights. Trigger adjustable for pull and over-travel; blue finish or stainless or combo; stippled front and backstraps; push-button barrel takedown. Announced 1992. From Mitchell Arms.
Price: $599.00

HANDGUNS—COMPETITION HANDGUNS

MITCHELL ARMS BARON PISTOL
Caliber: 22 LR, 10-shot magazine.
Barrel: 5.5" bull.
Weight: 45 oz. Length: 10.25" overall.
Stocks: Checkered walnut.
Sights: Ramp front, slide-mounted square notch rear adjustable for windage and elevation.
Features: Military grip. Slide lock; smooth grip straps; push-button takedown; drilled and tapped for barrel weights. Introduced 1992. From Mitchell Arms, Inc.
Price: Stainless steel, blue or combo $395.00

MITCHELL ARMS SOVEREIGN AUTO PISTOL
Caliber: 22 LR, 10-shot magazine.
Barrel: 4.5" vent rib, 5.5" vent, dovetail or Weaver ribs.
Weight: 44 oz. Length: 9.75" overall.
Stocks: Military-type checkered walnut with thumbrest.
Sights: Blade front, fully adjustable rear mounted on rib.
Features: Push-button takedown for barrel interchangeability. Bright stainless steel combo or royal blue finish. Introduced 1994. Made in U.S. From Mitchell Arms.
Price: Vent rib, 4.5" barrel $595.00
Price: Dovetail rib, 5.5" barrel $595.00
Price: Weaver rib, 5.5" barrel $675.00

Mitchell Arms 45 Gold IPSC Limited Model
Similar to the Bullseye model except has hard-chromed frame; ghost-ring or adjustable sight; match trigger tuning; ambidextrous safety; fitted barrel and slide; extended magazine release; hex-head grip screws. Announced 1996. Made in U.S. by Mitchell Arms.
Price: $1,195.00

MORINI MODEL 84E FREE PISTOL
Caliber: 22 LR, single shot.
Barrel: 11.4".
Weight: 43.7 oz. Length: 19.4" overall.
Stocks: Adjustable match type with stippled surfaces.
Sights: Interchangeable blade front, match-type fully adjustable rear.
Features: Fully adjustable electronic trigger. Introduced 1995. Imported from Switzerland by Nygord Precision Products.
Price: $1,495.00

PARDINI K50 FREE PISTOL
Caliber: 22 LR, single shot.
Barrel: 9.8".
Weight: 34.6 oz. Length: 18.7" overall.
Stocks: Wrap-around walnut; adjustable match type.
Sights: Interchangeable post front, fully adjustable match open rear.
Features: Removable, adjustable match trigger. Barrel weights mount above the barrel. Introduced 1995. Imported from Italy by Nygord Precision Products.
Price: $995.00

Mitchell Arms Sovereign

MITCHELL ARMS 45 BULLSEYE MODEL
Caliber: 45 ACP, 8-shot magazine.
Barrel: 5", match.
Weight: 32 oz. Length: 8.75" overall.
Stocks: Checkered walnut.
Sights: Blade front, adjustable rear.
Features: Stainless steel construction; adjustable trigger; flat checkered mainspring housing; extended slide stop; front and rear slide serrations; checkered front strap; full-length guide rod; wadcutter recoil spring. Announced 1996. Made in U.S. by Mitchell Arms.
Price: $950.00

PARDINI GP RAPID FIRE MATCH PISTOL
Caliber: 22 Short, 5-shot magazine.
Barrel: 4.6".
Weight: 43.3 oz. Length: 11.6" overall.
Stocks: Wrap-around stippled walnut.
Sights: Interchangeable post front, fully adjustable match rear.
Features: Model GP Schuman has extended rear sight for longer sight radius. Introduced 1995. Imported from Italy by Nygord Precision Products.
Price: Model GP $995.00
Price: Model GP Schuman $1,395.00

PARDINI MODEL SP, HP TARGET PISTOLS
Caliber: 22 LR, 32 S&W, 5-shot magazine.
Barrel: 4.7".
Weight: 38.9 oz. Length: 11.6" overall.
Stocks: Adjustable; stippled walnut; match type.
Sights: Interchangeable blade front, interchangeable, fully adjustable rear.
Features: Fully adjustable match trigger. Introduced 1995. Imported from Italy by Nygord Precision Products.
Price: Model SP (22 LR) $950.00
Price: Model HP (32 S&W) $1,095.00

RUGER MARK II TARGET MODEL AUTO PISTOL
Caliber: 22 LR, 10-shot magazine.
Barrel: 6 7/8".
Weight: 42 oz. Length: 11 1/8" overall.
Stocks: Checkered hard plastic.
Sights: .125" blade front, micro-click rear, adjustable for windage and elevation. Sight radius 9 3/8".
Features: Introduced 1982.
Price: Blued (MK-678) $310.50
Price: Stainless (KMK-678) $389.00

Ruger Mark II Bull Barrel
Same gun as the Target Model except has 5 1/2" or 10" heavy barrel (10" meets all IHMSA regulations). Weight with 5 1/2" barrel is 42 oz., with 10" barrel, 51 oz.
Price: Blued (MK-512) $310.50
Price: Blued (MK-10) $294.50
Price: Stainless (KMK-10) $373.00
Price: Stainless (KMK-512) $389.00

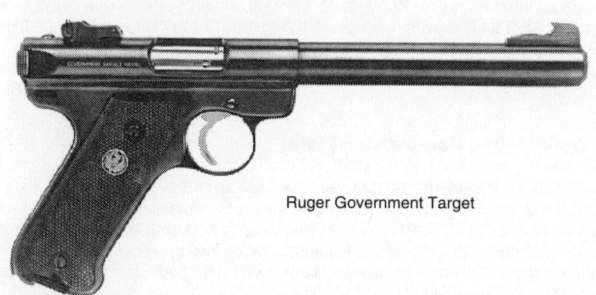

Ruger Government Target

Ruger Mark II Government Target Model
Same gun as the Mark II Target Model except has 6 7/8" barrel, higher sights and is roll marked "Government Target Model" on the right side of the receiver below the rear sight. Identical in all aspects to the military model used for training U.S. armed forces except for markings. Comes with factory test target. Introduced 1987.
Price: Blued (MK-678G) $356.50
Price: Stainless (KMK-678G) $427.25

Ruger Stainless Government Competition Model 22 Pistol
Similar to the Mark II Government Target Model stainless pistol except has 6 7/8" slab-sided barrel; the receiver top is drilled and tapped for a Ruger scope base adaptor of blued, chrome moly steel; comes with Ruger 1" stainless scope rings with integral bases for mounting a variety of optical sights; has checkered laminated grip panels with right-hand thumbrest. Has blued open sights with 9 1/4" radius. Overall length is 11 1/8", weight 45 oz. Introduced 1991.
Price: KMK-678GC $441.00

CAUTION: PRICES SHOWN ARE SUPPLIED BY THE MANUFACTURER OR IMPORTER. CHECK YOUR LOCAL GUNSHOP.

HANDGUNS—COMPETITION HANDGUNS

SMITH & WESSON MODEL 41 TARGET
Caliber: 22 LR, 10-shot clip.
Barrel: 5½", 7".
Weight: 44 oz. (5½" barrel). **Length:** 9" overall (5½" barrel).
Stocks: Checkered walnut with modified thumbrest, usable with either hand.
Sights: ⅛" Patridge on ramp base; micro-click rear adjustable for windage and elevation.
Features: ⅜" wide, grooved trigger; adjustable trigger stop.
Price: S&W Bright Blue, either barrel $753.00

SPHINX AT-2000C, CS COMPETITOR PISTOL
Caliber: 9mm Para., 9x21mm, 40 S&W, 10-shot.
Barrel: 5.31".
Weight: 40.56 oz. **Length:** 9.84" overall.
Stocks: Checkered neoprene.
Sights: Fully adjustable Bo-Mar or Tasco Pro-Point dot sight in Sphinx mount.
Features: Extended magazine release. Competition slide with dual-port compensated barrel. Two-tone finish only. Introduced 1993. Imported from Switzerland by Sphinx U.S.A., Inc.
Price: With Bo-Mar sights $1,902.00
Price: With Tasco Pro-Point and mount (AT-2000CS) $2,189.00

Sphinx AT-2000GM Grand Master Pistol
Similar to the AT-2000C except has single-action-only trigger mechanism, squared trigger guard, extended beavertail grip, safety and magazine release; notched competition slide for easier cocking. Two-tone finish only. Has dual-port compensated barrel. Available with fully adjustable Bo-Mar sights or Tasco Pro-Point and Sphinx mount. Introduced 1993. Imported from Switzerland by Sphinx U.S.A., Inc.
Price: With Bo-Mar sights (AT-2000GMS) $2,894.00
Price: With Tasco Pro-Point and mount (AT-2000GM) $2,972.00

SAFARI ARMS MATCHMASTER PISTOL
Caliber: 45 ACP, 7-shot magazine.
Barrel: 5", 6"; stainless steel.
Weight: 38 oz. **Length:** 8.5" overall.
Stocks: Smooth walnut with etched scorpion logo.
Sights: Ramped blade front, LPA adjustable rear.
Features: Beavertail grip safety, extended safety, extended slide release, Commander-style hammer; throated, polished, tuned. Finishes: Parkerized matte black, or satin stainless steel. Made in U.S. by Safari, Inc.
Price: 5" barrel $715.00
Price: 6" barrel $844.00

Smith & Wesson Model 41

Sphinx AT-2000c Competitor

Safari Arms Matchmaster Carrycomp I
Similar to the Matchmaster except has Wil Schueman-designed hybrid compensator system. Introduced 1993. Made in U.S. by Safari Arms, Inc.
Price: 3.8" barrel $1,150.00
Price: 5" barrel $1,300.00

SPRINGFIELD, INC. 1911A1 BULLSEYE WADCUTTER PISTOL
Caliber: 45 ACP.
Barrel: 5".
Weight: 45 oz. **Length:** 8.59" overall (5" barrel).
Stocks: Checkered walnut.
Sights: Bo-Mar rib with undercut blade front, fully adjustable rear.
Features: Built for wadcutter loads only. Has full-length recoil spring guide rod, fitted Videki speed trigger with 3.5-lb. pull; match Commander hammer and sear; beavertail grip safety; lowered and flared ejection port; tuned extractor; fitted slide to frame; recoil buffer system; beveled and polished magazine well; checkered front strap and steel mainspring housing (flat housing standard); polished and throated National Match barrel and bushing. Comes with two magazines with slam pads, plastic carrying case, test target. Introduced 1992. From Springfield, Inc.
Price: $1,665.00

Springfield, Inc. 1911A1 Trophy Match Pistol
Similar to the 1911A1 except factory accurized, Videki speed trigger, skeletonized hammer; has 4- to 5½-lb. trigger pull, click adjustable rear sight, match-grade barrel and bushing. Comes with checkered walnut grips. Introduced 1994. From Springfield, Inc.
Price: Blue $954.00
Price: Stainless steel $985.00

Springfield 1911A1 Trophy Match

Springfield, Inc. Basic Competition Pistol
Has low-mounted Bo-Mar adjustable rear sight, undercut blade front; match throated barrel and bushing; polished feed ramp; lowered and flared ejection port; fitted Videki speed trigger with tuned 3.5-lb. pull; fitted slide to frame; recoil buffer system; checkered walnut grips; serrated, arched mainspring housing. Comes with two magazines with slam pads, plastic carrying case. Introduced 1992. From Springfield, Inc.
Price: 45 ACP, blue, 5" only $1,439.00

Springfield, Inc. Expert Pistol
Similar to the Competition Pistol except has triple-chamber tapered cone compensator on match barrel with dovetailed front sight; lowered and flared ejection port; fully tuned for reliability; fitted slide to frame; extended ambidextrous thumb safety, extended magazine release button; beavertail grip safety; Pachmayr wrap-around grips. Comes with two magazines, plastic carrying case. Introduced 1992. From Springfield, Inc.
Price: 45 ACP, Duotone finish $1,915.00
Price: Expert Ltd. $1,804.00

Springfield, Inc. Competition Pistol
Similar to the 1911A1 Basic Competition Wadcutter Pistol except has brazed, serrated improved ramp front sight; Videki speed trigger with 3½-lb. pull; extended ambidextrous thumb safety; match Commander hammer and sear; serrated rear slide; Pachmayr flat mainspring housing; extended magazine release; beavertail grip safety; full-length recoil spring guide; Pachmayr wrap-around grips. Comes with two magazines with slam pads, plastic carrying case. Introduced 1992. From Springfield, Inc.
Price: 45 ACP, blue $1,598.00

Springfield, Inc. Distinguished Pistol
Has all the features of the 1911A1 Expert except is full-house pistol with deluxe Bo-Mar low-mounted adjustable rear sight; full-length recoil spring guide rod and recoil spring retainer; checkered frontstrap; S&A magazine well; walnut grips. Hard chrome finish. Comes with two magazines with slam pads, plastic carrying case. From Springfield, Inc.
Price: 45 ACP $2,717.00
Price: Distinguished Limited $2,606.00

HANDGUNS—COMPETITION HANDGUNS

Springfield, Inc. 1911A1 N.M. Hardball Pistol
Has Bo-Mar adjustable rear sight with undercut front blade; fitted match Videki trigger with 4-lb. pull; fitted slide to frame; throated National Match barrel and bushing, polished feed ramp; recoil buffer system; tuned extractor; Herrett walnut grips. Comes with two magazines, plastic carrying case, test target. Introduced 1992. From Springfield, Inc.
Price: 45 ACP, blue $1,485.00

STOEGER PRO SERIES 95 VENT RIB
Caliber: 22 LR, 10-shot magazine.
Barrel: 5 1/2".
Weight: 48 oz. **Length:** 9 5/8" overall.
Stocks: Pachmayr wrap-around checkered rubber.
Sights: Blade front, fully adjustable micro-click rear mounted on rib.
Features: Stainless steel construction; full-length ventilated rib; gold-plated trigger, slide lock, safety-lever and magazine release; adjustable trigger; interchangeable barrels. Introduced 1996. From Stoeger Ind.
Price: $565.00

Stoeger Pro Series 95 Bull Barrel
Similar to the Vent Rib model except has 5 1/2" bull barrel, rear sight mounted on slide bridge. Introduced 1996. From Stoeger Ind.
Price: $460.00

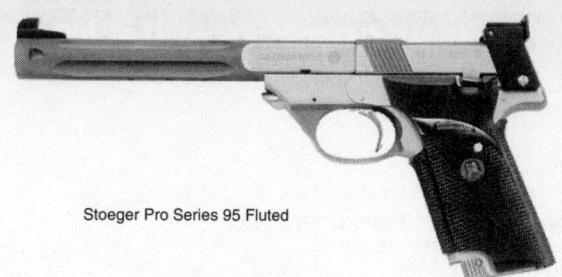

Stoeger Pro Series 95 Fluted

Stoeger Pro Series 95 Fluted Barrel
Similar to the Vent Rib model except has 7 1/2" heavy fluted barrel, rear sight mounted on slide bridge. Overall length 11 1/4", weighs 50 oz. Introduced 1996. From Stoeger Ind.
Price: $490.00

THOMPSON/CENTER SUPER 14 CONTENDER
Caliber: 22 LR, 222 Rem., 223 Rem., 7mm TCU, 7-30 Waters, 30-30 Win., 35 Rem., 357 Rem. Maximum, 44 Mag., 10mm Auto, 445 Super Mag., single shot.
Barrel: 14".
Weight: 45 oz. **Length:** 17 1/4" overall.
Stocks: T/C "Competitor Grip" (walnut and rubber).
Sights: Fully adjustable target-type.
Features: Break-open action with auto safety. Interchangeable barrels for both rimfire and centerfire calibers. Introduced 1978.
Price: Blued $473.80
Price: Stainless steel $504.70
Price: Extra barrels, blued $244.00
Price: Extra barrels, stainless steel $239.50

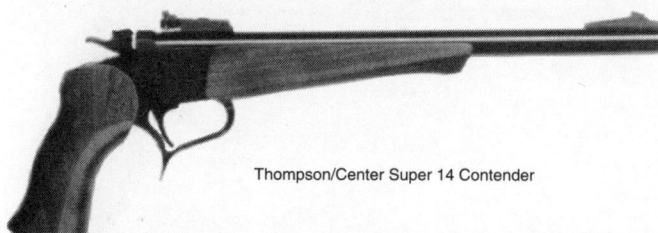

Thompson/Center Super 14 Contender

Thompson/Center Super 16 Contender
Same as the T/C Super 14 Contender except has 16 1/4" barrel. Rear sight can be mounted at mid-barrel position (10 3/4" radius) or moved to the rear (using scope mount position) for 14 3/4" radius. Overall length is 20 1/4". Comes with T/C Competitor Grip of walnut and rubber. Available in 22 LR, 22 WMR, 223 Rem., 7-30 Waters, 30-30 Win., 35 Rem., 44 Mag., 45-70 Gov't. Also available with 16" vent rib barrel with internal choke, caliber 45 Colt/410 shotshell.
Price: Blue $478.90
Price: Stainless steel $509.90
Price: 45-70 Gov't., blue $484.10
Price: As above, stainless steel $530.50
Price: Super 16 Vent Rib, blued $509.90
Price: As above, stainless steel $540.80
Price: Extra 16" barrel, blued $229.20
Price: As above, stainless steel $244.50
Price: Extra 45-70 barrel, blued $234.30
Price: As above, stainless steel $265.50
Price: Extra Super 16 vent rib barrel, blue $260.10
Price: As above, stainless steel $265.50

UNIQUE D.E.S. 32U TARGET PISTOL
Caliber: 32 S&W Long wadcutter.
Barrel: 5.9".
Weight: 40.2 oz.
Stocks: Anatomically shaped, adjustable stippled French walnut.
Sights: Blade front, micrometer click rear.
Features: Trigger adjustable for weight and position; dry firing mechanism; slide stop catch. Optional sleeve weights. Introduced 1990. Imported from France by Nygord Precision Products.
Price: Right-hand, about $1,350.00
Price: Left-hand, about $1,380.00

WALTHER GSP MATCH PISTOL
Caliber: 22 LR, 32 S&W Long (GSP-C), 5-shot magazine.
Barrel: 4.22".
Weight: 44.8 oz. (22 LR), 49.4 oz. (32). **Length:** 11.8" overall.
Stocks: Walnut.
Sights: Post front, match rear adjustable for windage and elevation.
Features: Available with either 2.2-lb. (1000 gm) or 3-lb. (1360 gm) trigger. Spare magazine, barrel weight, tools supplied. Imported from Germany by Nygord Precision Products.
Price: GSP, with case $1,495.00
Price: GSP-C, with case $1,595.00

WICHITA SILHOUETTE PISTOL
Caliber: 308 Win. F.L., 7mm IHMSA, 7mm-308.
Barrel: 14 15/16".
Weight: 4 1/2 lbs. **Length:** 21 3/8" overall.
Stock: American walnut with oil finish. Glass bedded.
Sights: Wichita Multi-Range sight system.
Features: Comes with left-hand action with right-hand grip. Round receiver and barrel. Fluted bolt, flat bolt handle. Wichita adjustable trigger. Introduced 1979. From Wichita Arms.
Price: Center grip stock $1,417.50
Price: As above except with Rear Position Stock and target-type Lightpull trigger $1,417.50

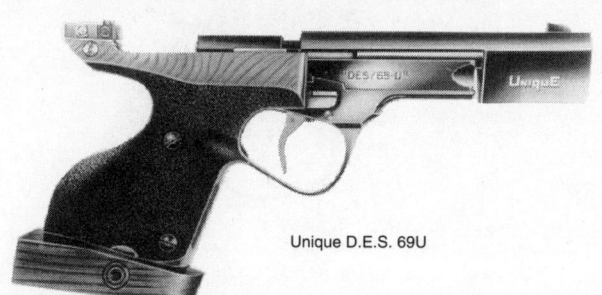

Unique D.E.S. 69U

UNIQUE D.E.S. 69U TARGET PISTOL
Caliber: 22 LR, 5-shot magazine.
Barrel: 5.91".
Weight: 35.3 oz. **Length:** 10.5" overall.
Stocks: French walnut target-style with thumbrest and adjustable shelf; hand-checkered panels.
Sights: Ramp front, micro. adjustable rear mounted on frame; 8.66" sight radius.
Features: Meets U.I.T. standards. Comes with 260-gram barrel weight; 100, 150, 350-gram weights available. Fully adjustable match trigger; dry-firing safety device. Imported from France by Nygord Precision Products.
Price: Right-hand, about $1,250.00
Price: Left-hand, about $1,290.00

WICHITA CLASSIC SILHOUETTE PISTOL
Caliber: All standard calibers with maximum overall length of 2.800".
Barrel: 11 1/4".
Weight: 3 lbs., 15 oz.
Stocks: AAA American walnut with oil finish, checkered grip.
Sights: Hooded post front, open adjustable rear.
Features: Three locking lug bolt, three gas ports; completely adjustable Wichita trigger. Introduced 1981. From Wichita Arms.
Price: $3,450.00

CAUTION: PRICES SHOWN ARE SUPPLIED BY THE MANUFACTURER OR IMPORTER. CHECK YOUR LOCAL GUNSHOP.

HANDGUNS—DOUBLE-ACTION REVOLVERS, SERVICE & SPORT

Includes models suitable for hunting and competitive courses for fire, both police and international.

Armscor M-200DC

ARMSCOR M-200DC REVOLVER
Caliber: 38 Spec., 6-shot cylinder.
Barrel: 2½", 4".
Weight: 22 oz. (2½" barrel). **Length:** 7³⁄₈" overall (2½" barrel).
Stocks: Checkered rubber.
Sights: Blade front, fixed notch rear.
Features: All-steel construction; floating firing pin, transfer bar ignition; shrouded ejector rod; blue finish. Reintroduced 1996. Imported from the Philippines by K.B.I., Inc.
Price: $199.99

COLT ANACONDA REVOLVER
Caliber: 44 Rem. Magnum, 45 Colt, 6-shot.
Barrel: 4", 6", 8".
Weight: 53 oz. (6" barrel). **Length:** 11⁵⁄₈" overall.
Stocks: TP combat style with finger grooves.
Sights: Red insert front, adjustable white outline rear.
Features: Stainless steel; full-length ejector rod housing; ventilated barrel rib; off-set bolt notches in cylinder; wide spur hammer. Introduced 1990.
Price: $612.00
Price: 45 Colt, 6", 8" barrel only $612.00
Price: With complete Realtree camouflage coverage $740.00
Price: As above with scope and mount $999.00

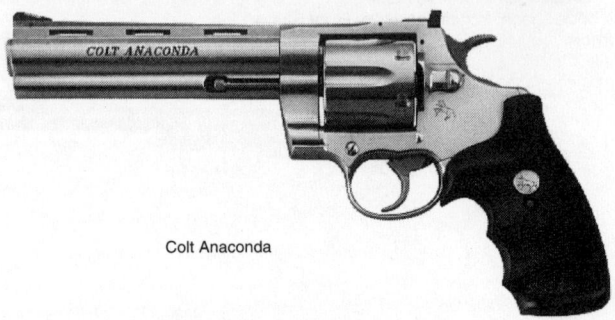

Colt Anaconda

COLT 38 SF-VI REVOLVER
Caliber: 38 Special, 6-shot.
Barrel: 2".
Weight: 21 oz. **Length:** 7" overall.
Stocks: Checkered black composition.
Sights: Ramp front, fixed rear.
Features: Has new lockwork. Made of stainless steel. Introduced 1995. From Colt's Mfg. Co.
Price: $408.00

COLT KING COBRA REVOLVER
Caliber: 357 Magnum, 6-shot.
Barrel: 4", 6".
Weight: 42 oz. (4" bbl.). **Length:** 9" overall (4" bbl.).
Stocks: TP combat style.
Sights: Red insert ramp front, adjustable white outline rear.
Features: Full-length contoured ejector rod housing, barrel rib. Introduced 1986.
Price: Stainless $455.00

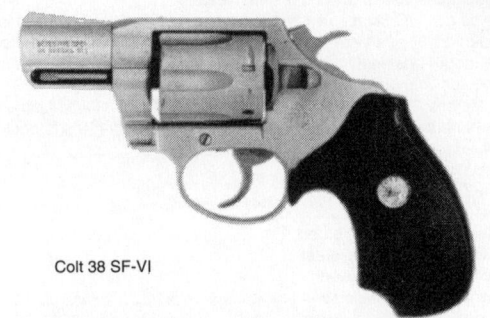

Colt 38 SF-VI

COLT PYTHON REVOLVER
Caliber: 357 Magnum (handles all 38 Spec.), 6-shot.
Barrel: 4", 6" or 8", with ventilated rib.
Weight: 38 oz. (4" bbl.). **Length:** 9¼" (4" bbl.).
Stocks: Hogue Monogrip (4"), TP combat style (6", 8").
Sights: ⅛" ramp front, adjustable notch rear.
Features: Ventilated rib; grooved, crisp trigger; swing-out cylinder; target hammer.
Price: Royal blue, 4", 6", 8" $815.00
Price: Stainless, 4", 6", 8" $904.00
Price: Bright stainless, 4", 6", 8" $935.00

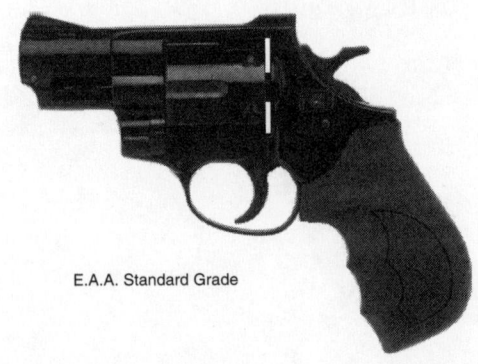

E.A.A. Standard Grade

E.A.A. STANDARD GRADE REVOLVERS
Caliber: 22 LR, 22 LR/22 WMR, 8-shot; 38 Spec., 6-shot; 357 magnum, 6-shot.
Barrel: 4", 6" (22 rimfire); 2", 4" (38 Spec.).
Weight: 38 oz. (22 rimfire, 4"). **Length:** 8.8" overall (4" bbl.).
Stocks: Rubber with finger grooves.
Sights: Blade front, fixed or adjustable on rimfires; fixed only on 32, 38.
Features: Swing-out cylinder; hammer block safety; blue finish. Introduced 1991. Imported from Germany by European American Armory.
Price: 38 Special 2" $180.00
Price: 38 Special, 4" $199.00
Price: 357 Magnum $199.00
Price: 22 LR, 6" $199.00
Price: 22 LR/22 WMR combo, 4" $200.00
Price: As above, 6" $200.00

ERMA ER-777 SPORTING REVOLVER
Caliber: 357 Mag., 6-shot.
Barrel: 5½".
Weight: 43.3 oz. **Length:** 9½" overall (4" barrel).
Stocks: Stippled walnut service-type.
Sights: Interchangeable blade front, micro-adjustable rear for windage and elevation.
Features: Polished blue finish. Adjustable trigger. Imported from Germany by Precision Sales Int'l. Introduced 1988.
Price: $1,019.00

HANDGUNS—DOUBLE-ACTION REVOLVERS, SERVICE & SPORT

HARRINGTON & RICHARDSON 939 PREMIER REVOLVER
Caliber: 22 LR, 9-shot cylinder.
Barrel: 6" heavy.
Weight: 36 oz. **Length:** NA.
Stocks: Walnut-finished hardwood.
Sights: Blade front, fully adjustable rear.
Features: Swing-out cylinder with plunger-type ejection; solid barrel rib; high-polish blue finish; double-action mechanism; Western-style grip. Introduced 1995. Made in U.S. by H&R 1871, Inc.
Price: $189.95

Harrington & Richardson 939

HARRINGTON & RICHARDSON SPORTSMAN 999 REVOLVER
Caliber: 22 Short, Long, Long Rifle, 9-shot.
Barrel: 4", 6".
Weight: 30 oz. (4" barrel). **Length:** 8.5" overall.
Stocks: Walnut-finished hardwood.
Sights: Blade front adjustable for elevation, rear adjustable for windage.
Features: Top-break loading; polished blue finish; automatic shell ejection. Reintroduced 1992. From H&R 1871, Inc.
Price: $279.95

Harrington & Richardson Sportsman 999

HARRINGTON & RICHARDSON 949 WESTERN REVOLVER
Caliber: 22 LR, 9-shot cylinder.
Barrel: $5^{1}/_{2}$", $7^{1}/_{2}$".
Weight: 36 oz. **Length:** NA.
Stocks: Walnut-stained hardwood.
Sights: Blade front, adjustable rear.
Features: Color case-hardened frame and backstrap, traditional loading gate and ejector rod. Introduced 1994. Made in U.S. by H&R 1871, Inc.
Price: About $189.95

HARRINGTON & RICHARDSON AMERICAN REVOLVERS
Caliber: 38 Spec., 5-shot.
Barrel: 2", 3".
Weight: 24 oz. **Length:** $7^{1}/_{8}$" overall.
Stocks: Pachmayr rubber.
Sights: Ramp front, fixed notch rear.
Features: Available in blue or nickel. Introduced 1996. Made in U.S. by Amtec 2000.
Price: ....NA

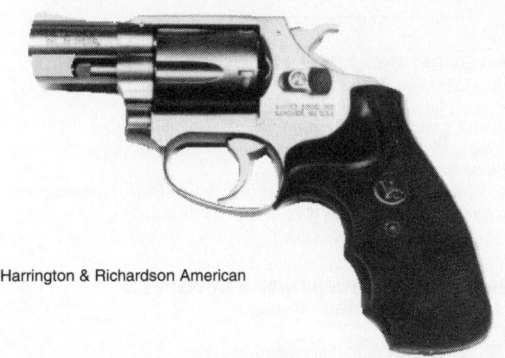
Harrington & Richardson American

HARRINGTON & RICHARDSON 929 SIDEKICK
Caliber: 22 LR, 9-shot cylinder.
Barrel: 4" heavy.
Weight: 30 oz. **Length:** NA.
Stocks: Cinnamon-color laminated wood.
Sights: Blade front, notch rear.
Features: Double action; swing-out cylinder, traditional loading gate; blued frame and barrel. Comes with lockable storage case, Uncle Mike's Sidekick holster. Introduced 1996. Made in U.S. by H&R 1871, Inc.
Price: $159.95
Price: NTA Trapper Edition, special rollmark, gray laminate grips $174.95

Manurhin MR73 Sport Revolver

Heritage Sentry

MANURHIN MR 73 SPORT REVOLVER
Caliber: 357 Magnum, 6-shot cylinder.
Barrel: 6".
Weight: 37 oz. **Length:** 11.1" overall.
Stocks: Checkered walnut.
Sights: Blade front, fully adjustable rear.
Features: Double action with adjustable trigger. High-polish blue finish, straw-colored hammer and trigger. Comes with extra sight. Introduced 1984. Imported from France by Century International Arms.
Price: About $1,500.00

HERITAGE SENTRY DOUBLE-ACTION REVOLVERS
Caliber: 38 Spec., 6-shot.
Barrel: 2".
Weight: 23 oz. **Length:** $6^{1}/_{4}$" overall (2" barrel).
Stocks: Checkered plastic.
Sights: Ramp front, fixed rear.
Features: Pull-pin-type ejection; serrated hammer and trigger. Polished blue or nickel finish. Introduced 1993. Made in U.S. by Heritage Mfg., Inc.
Price: ....$129.95 to $139.95

MANURHIN MR 73 REVOLVER
Caliber: 32 S&W, 38 Spec., 357 Mag.
Barrel: 3", 4", $5^{1}/_{4}$", $5^{3}/_{4}$", 6".
Weight: 38 oz. (6" barrel). **Length:** 11" overall (6" barrel).
Stocks: Checkered hardwood.
Sights: Blade front, fully adjustable rear.
Features: Polished bright blue finish; hammer-forged barrel. Imported from France by Sphinx U.S.A., Inc.
Price: Police model, 3" or 4" barrel $1,885.00
Price: Sport model, $5^{1}/_{4}$" or 6" barrel, undercut blade front sight $1,885.00
Price: 38 Spec. Match, $5^{3}/_{4}$" barrel, single action only $1,975.00
Price: 32 S&W Match, 6" barrel, single action only $1,975.00

HANDGUNS—DOUBLE-ACTION REVOLVERS, SERVICE & SPORT

Manurhin MR 96

MANURHIN MR 96 REVOLVER
Caliber: 357 Magnum, 6-shot.
Barrel: 3", 4", 5 1/4", 6".
Weight: 38.4 oz. **Length:** 8.8" overall.
Stocks: Checkered rubber.
Sights: Blade front, fully adjustable rear.
Features: Polished blue finish; removable sideplate holds action parts; separate barrel and shroud. Introduced 1996. Imported from France by Sphinx U.S.A., Inc.
Price: $857.95

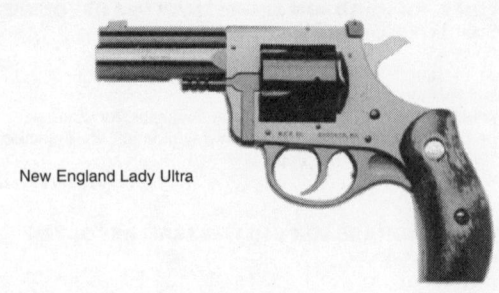

New England Lady Ultra

MANURHIN MR 88 REVOLVER
Caliber: 357 Magnum, 6-shot.
Barrel: 4", 5 1/4", 6".
Weight: 33.5 oz. **Length:** 8.1" overall.
Stocks: Checkered wood.
Sights: Blade front, fully adjustable rear.
Features: Stainless steel construction; hammer-forged barrel. Imported from France by Sphinx U.S.A., Inc.
Price: $877.95

> Consult our Directory pages for the location of firms mentioned.

NEW ENGLAND FIREARMS LADY ULTRA REVOLVER
Caliber: 32 H&R Mag., 5-shot.
Barrel: 3".
Weight: 31 oz. **Length:** 7.25" overall.
Stocks: Walnut-finished hardwood with NEF medallion.
Sights: Blade front, fully adjustable rear.
Features: Swing-out cylinder; polished blue finish. Comes with lockable storage case. Introduced 1992. From New England Firearms.
Price: $174.95

NEW ENGLAND FIREARMS ULTRA REVOLVER
Caliber: 22 LR, 9-shot; 22 WMR, 6-shot.
Barrel: 4", 6".
Weight: 36 oz. **Length:** 10 5/8" overall (6" barrel).
Stocks: Walnut-finished hardwood with NEF medallion.
Sights: Blade front, fully adjustable rear.
Features: Blue finish. Bull-style barrel with recessed muzzle, high "Lustre" blue/black finish. Introduced 1989. From New England Firearms.
Price: $174.95
Price: Ultra Mag 22 WMR $174.95

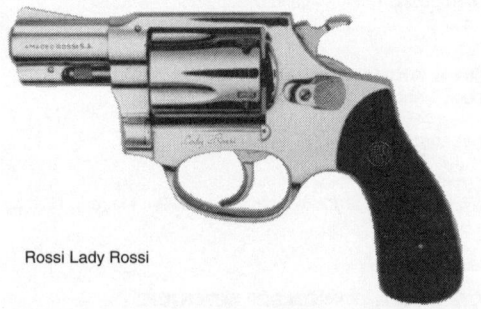

Rossi Lady Rossi

NEW ENGLAND FIREARMS STANDARD REVOLVERS
Caliber: 22 LR, 9-shot; 32 H&R Mag., 5-shot.
Barrel: 2 1/2", 4".
Weight: 26 oz. (22 LR, 2 1/2"). **Length:** 8 1/2" overall (4" bbl.).
Stocks: Walnut-finished American hardwood with NEF medallion.
Sights: Fixed.
Features: Choice of blue or nickel finish. Introduced 1988. From New England Firearms.
Price: 22 LR, 32 H&R Mag., blue $134.95
Price: 22 LR, 2 1/2", 4", nickel, 32 H&R Mag. 2 1/2" nickel $144.95

ROSSI LADY ROSSI REVOLVER
Caliber: 38 Spec., 5-shot.
Barrel: 2", 3".
Weight: 21 oz. **Length:** 6.5" overall (2" barrel).
Stocks: Smooth rosewood.
Sights: Fixed.
Features: High-polish stainless steel with "Lady Rossi" engraved on frame. Comes with velvet carry bag. Introduced 1995. Imported from Brazil by Interarms.
Price: $285.00

Rossi Model 518

ROSSI MODEL 68 REVOLVER
Caliber: 38 Spec.
Barrel: 2", 3".
Weight: 22 oz.
Stocks: Checkered wood and rubber.
Sights: Ramp front, low profile adjustable rear.
Features: All-steel frame, thumb latch operated swing-out cylinder. Introduced 1978. Imported from Brazil by Interarms.
Price: 38, blue, 3", wood or rubber grips $225.00
Price: M68/2 (2" barrel), wood or rubber grips $225.00
Price: 3", nickel $225.00

ROSSI MODEL 88 STAINLESS REVOLVER
Caliber: 38 Spec., 5-shot.
Barrel: 2", 3".
Weight: 22 oz. **Length:** 7.5" overall.
Stocks: Checkered wood, service-style, and rubber.
Sights: Ramp front, square notch rear drift adjustable for windage.
Features: All metal parts except springs are of 440 stainless steel; matte finish; small frame for concealability. Introduced 1983. Imported from Brazil by Interarms.
Price: 3" barrel, wood or rubber grips $255.00
Price: 2" barrel, wood or rubber grips $255.00

ROSSI MODEL 515, 518 REVOLVERS
Caliber: 22 LR (Model 518), 22 WMR (Model 515), 6-shot.
Barrel: 4".
Weight: 30 oz. **Length:** 9" overall.
Stocks: Checkered wood and finger-groove wrap-around rubber.
Sights: Blade front with red insert, rear adjustable for windage and elevation.
Features: Small frame; stainless steel construction; solid integral barrel rib. Introduced 1994. Imported from Brazil by Interarms.
Price: Model 518, 22 LR $255.00
Price: Model 515, 22 WMR $270.00

HANDGUNS—DOUBLE-ACTION REVOLVERS, SERVICE & SPORT

ROSSI MODEL 720 REVOLVER
Caliber: 44 Spec., 5-shot.
Barrel: 3".
Weight: 27.5 oz. **Length:** 8" overall.
Stocks: Checkered rubber, combat style.
Sights: Red insert front on ramp, fully adjustable rear.
Features: All stainless steel construction; solid barrel rib; full ejector rod shroud. Introduced 1992. Imported from Brazil by Interarms.
Price: $290.00
Price: Model 720C, spurless hammer, DA only $290.00

ROSSI MODEL 851 REVOLVER
Caliber: 38 Spec., 6-shot.
Barrel: 3" or 4".
Weight: 27.5 oz. (3" bbl.). **Length:** 8" overall (3" bbl.).
Stocks: Checkered Brazilian hardwood.
Sights: Blade front with red insert, rear adjustable for windage.
Features: Medium-size frame; stainless steel construction; ventilated barrel rib. Introduced 1991. Imported from Brazil by Interarms.
Price: $255.00

ROSSI MODEL 877 REVOLVER
Caliber: 357 Mag., 6-shot cylinder.
Barrel: 2".
Weight: 26 oz. **Length:** NA.
Stocks: Stippled synthetic.
Sights: Blade front, fixed groove rear.
Features: Stainless steel construction; fully enclosed ejector rod. Introduced 1996. Imported from Brazil by Interarms.
Price: $290.00

ROSSI MODEL 971 REVOLVER
Caliber: 357 Mag., 6-shot.
Barrel: 2$^1/_2$", 4", 6", heavy.
Weight: 36 oz. **Length:** 9" overall.
Stocks: Checkered Brazilian hardwood. Stainless models have checkered, contoured rubber.
Sights: Blade front, fully adjustable rear.
Features: Full-length ejector rod shroud; matted sight rib; target-type trigger, wide checkered hammer spur. Introduced 1988. Imported from Brazil by Interarms.
Price: 4", stainless $290.00
Price: 6", stainless $290.00
Price: 4", blue $255.00
Price: 2$^1/_2$", stainless $290.00

Rossi Model 877

Rossi Model 971 VRC

Rossi Model 971 VRC Revolver
Similar to the Model 971 except has Rossi's 8-port Vented Rib Compensator; checkered finger-groove rubber grips; stainless steel construction. Available with 2.5", 4", 6" barrel; weighs 30 oz. with 2$^5/_8$" barrel. Introduced 1996. Imported from Brazil by Interarms.
Price: $340.00

Rossi Model 971 Comp Gun
Same as the Model 971 stainless except has 3$^1/_4$" barrel with integral compensator. Overall length is 9", weighs 32 oz. Has red insert front sight, fully adjustable rear. Checkered, contoured rubber grips. Introduced 1993. Imported from Brazil by Interarms.
Price: $290.00

Manufacturers' addresses in the
Directory of the Arms Trade
page 313, this issue

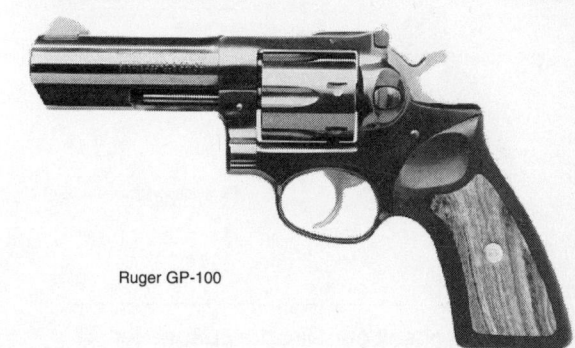
Ruger GP-100

RUGER GP-100 REVOLVERS
Caliber: 38 Spec., 357 Mag., 6-shot.
Barrel: 3", 3" heavy, 4", 4" heavy, 6", 6" heavy.
Weight: 3" barrel—35 oz., 3" heavy barrel—36 oz., 4" barrel—37 oz., 4" heavy barrel—38 oz.
Sights: Fixed; adjustable on 4" heavy, 6", 6" heavy barrels.
Stocks: Ruger Santoprene Cushioned Grip with Goncalo Alves inserts.
Features: Uses action and frame incorporating improvements and features of both the Security-Six and Redhawk revolvers. Full length and short ejector shroud. Satin blue and stainless steel. Available in high-gloss stainless steel finish. Introduced 1988.
Price: GP-141 (357, 4" heavy, adj. sights, blue) $440.00
Price: GP-160 (357, 6", adj. sights, blue) $440.00
Price: GP-161 (357, 6" heavy, adj. sights, blue) $440.00
Price: GPF-331 (357, 3" heavy), GPF-831 (38 Spec.) $423.00
Price: GPF-340 (357, 4"), GPF-840 (38 Spec.) $423.00
Price: GPF-341 (357, 4" heavy), GPF-841 (38 Spec.) $423.00
Price: KGP-141 (357, 4" heavy, adj. sights, stainless) $474.00
Price: KGP-160 (357, 6", adj. sights, stainless) $474.00
Price: KGP-161 (357, 6" heavy, adj. sights, stainless) $474.00
Price: KGPF-330 (357, 3", stainless), KGPF-830 (38 Spec.) $457.00
Price: KGPF-331 (357, 3" heavy, stainless), KGPF-831 (38 Spec.) ..$457.00
Price: KGPF-340 (357, 4", stainless), KGPF-840 (38 Spec.) $457.00
Price: KGPF-341 (357, 4" heavy, stainless), KGPF-841 (38 Spec.) ..$457.00

RUGER SP101 REVOLVERS
Caliber: 22 LR, 32 H&R Mag., 6-shot, 9mm Para., 38 Spec. +P, 357 Mag., 5-shot.
Barrel: 2$^1/_4$", 3$^1/_{16}$", 4".
Weight: 2$^1/_4$"—25 oz.; 3$^1/_{16}$"—27 oz.
Sights: Adjustable on 22, 32, fixed on others.
Stocks: Ruger Santoprene Cushioned Grip with Xenoy inserts.
Features: Incorporates improvements and features found in the GP-100 revolvers into a compact, small frame, double-action revolver. Full-length ejector shroud. Stainless steel only. Available with high-polish finish. Introduced 1988.
Price: KSP-821 (2$^1/_2$", 38 Spec.) $443.00
Price: KSP-831 (3$^1/_{16}$", 38 Spec.) $443.00
Price: KSP-221 (2$^1/_4$", 22 LR) $443.00
Price: KSP-240 (4", 22 LR) $443.00
Price: KSP-241 (4" heavy bbl., 22 LR) $443.00
Price: KSP-3231 (3$^1/_{16}$", 32 H&R) $443.00
Price: KSP-921 (2$^1/_4$", 9mm Para.) $443.00
Price: KSP-931 (3$^1/_{16}$", 9mm Para.) $443.00
Price: KSP-321 (2$^1/_4$", 357 Mag.) $443.00
Price: KSP-331 (3$^1/_{16}$", 357 Mag.) $443.00

HANDGUNS—DOUBLE-ACTION REVOLVERS, SERVICE & SPORT

Ruger SP101 DAO

Ruger SP101 Double-Action-Only Revolver
Similar to the standard SP101 except is double-action-only with no single-action sear notch. Has spurless hammer for snag-free handling, floating firing pin and Ruger's patented transfer bar safety system. Available with 2 1/4" barrel in 38 Special +P and 357 Magnum only. Weighs 25 1/2 oz., overall length 7.06". Natural brushed satin or high-polish stainless steel. Introduced 1993.
Price: KSP821L (38 Spec.), KSP321XL (357 Mag.) $443.00

RUGER REDHAWK
Caliber: 44 Rem. Mag., 6-shot.
Barrel: 5 1/2", 7 1/2".
Weight: About 54 oz. (7 1/2" bbl.). **Length:** 13" overall (7 1/2" barrel).
Stocks: Square butt Goncalo Alves.
Sights: Interchangeable Patridge-type front, rear adjustable for windage and elevation.
Features: Stainless steel, brushed satin finish, or blued ordnance steel. Has a 9 1/2" sight radius. Introduced 1979.
Price: Blued, 44 Mag., 5 1/2", 7 1/2" $490.00
Price: Blued, 44 Mag., 7 1/2", with scope mount, rings $527.00
Price: Stainless, 44 Mag., 5 1/2", 7 1/2" $547.00
Price: Stainless, 44 Mag., 7 1/2", with scope mount, rings $589.00

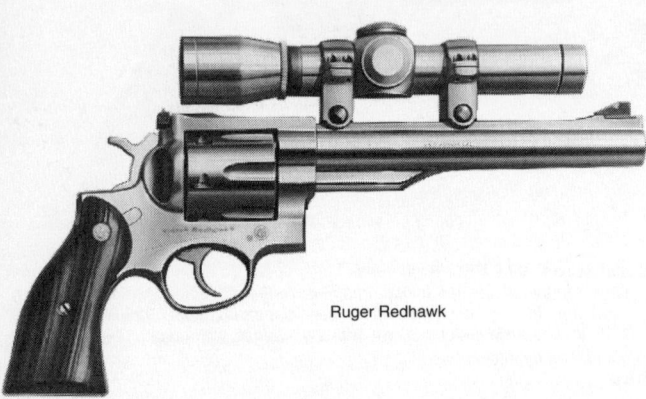

Ruger Redhawk

Ruger Super Redhawk Revolver
Similar to the standard Redhawk except has a heavy extended frame with the Ruger Integral Scope Mounting System on the wide topstrap. The wide hammer spur has been lowered for better scope clearance. Incorporates the mechanical design features and improvements of the GP-100. Choice of 7 1/2" or 9 1/2" barrel, both with ramp front sight base with Redhawk-style Interchangeable Insert sight blades, adjustable rear sight. Comes with Ruger "Cushioned Grip" panels of Santoprene with Goncalo Alves wood panels. Satin or high-polished stainless steel. Introduced 1987.
Price: KSRH-7 (7 1/2"), KSRH-9 (9 1/2") $589.00

SMITH & WESSON MODEL 10 M&P REVOLVER
Caliber: 38 Spec., 6-shot.
Barrel: 2", 4".
Weight: 30 oz. **Length:** 9 5/16" overall.
Stocks: Uncle Mike's Combat soft rubber; square butt. Wood optional.
Sights: Fixed, ramp front, square notch rear.
Price: Blue $383.00

Smith & Wesson Model 10 38 M&P Heavy Barrel
Same as regular M&P except has heavy 4" ribbed barrel with square butt grips. Weighs 33 1/2 oz.
Price: Blue $390.00

Smith & Wesson Model 65LS

SMITH & WESSON MODEL 13 H.B. M&P
Caliber: 357 Mag. and 38 Spec., 6-shot.
Barrel: 3" or 4".
Weight: 34 oz. **Length:** 9 5/16" overall (4" bbl.).
Stocks: Uncle Mike's Combat soft rubber; wood optional.
Sights: 1/8" serrated ramp front, fixed square notch rear.
Features: Heavy barrel, K-frame, square butt (4"), round butt (3").
Price: Blue $394.00
Price: Model 65, as above in stainless steel $427.00

Smith & Wesson Model 65 Revolver
Similiar to the Model 13 except made of stainless steel. Has Uncle Mike's Combat grips, smooth combat trigger, fixed notch rear sight. Made in U.S. by Smith & Wesson.
Price: 3" or 4" $427.00

> Consult our Directory pages for the location of firms mentioned.

SMITH & WESSON MODEL 14 FULL LUG REVOLVER
Caliber: 38 Spec., 6-shot.
Barrel: 6", full lug.
Weight: 47 oz. **Length:** 11 1/8" overall.
Stocks: Hogue soft rubber; wood optional.
Sights: Pinned Patridge front, adjustable micrometer click rear.
Features: Has .500" target hammer, .312" smooth combat trigger. Polished blue finish. Reintroduced 1991. Limited production.
Price: $465.00

Smith & Wesson Model 14

SMITH & WESSON MODEL 15 COMBAT MASTERPIECE
Caliber: 38 Spec., 6-shot.
Barrel: 4".
Weight: 32 oz. **Length:** 9 5/16" (4" bbl.).
Stocks: Uncle Mike's Combat soft rubber; wood optional.
Sights: Front, Baughman Quick Draw on ramp, micro-click rear adjustable for windage and elevation.
Price: Blued $419.00

HANDGUNS—DOUBLE-ACTION REVOLVERS, SERVICE & SPORT

Smith & Wesson Model 17

Smith & Wesson Model 19

Smith & Wesson Model 629 PowerPort

Smith & Wesson Model 37

Smith & Wesson Model 60LS

Smith & Wesson Model 60 Chiefs Special Stainless
 Same as Model 36 except 357 Magnum or 38 Special (only). All stainless construction, 2" bbl. and round butt only.
Price: Stainless steel $431.00

SMITH & WESSON MODEL 17 K-22 MASTERPIECE
Caliber: 22 LR, 10-shot cylinder.
Barrel: 6".
Weight: 42 oz. **Length:** 11 1/8" overall.
Stocks: Hogue rubber.
Sights: Pinned Patridge front, fully adjustable rear.
Features: Polished blue finish; smooth combat trigger; semi-target hammer. The 10-slot version of this model introduced 1996.
Price: $490.00

SMITH & WESSON MODEL 19 COMBAT MAGNUM
Caliber: 357 Mag. and 38 Spec., 6-shot.
Barrel: 2 1/2", 4", 6".
Weight: 36 oz. **Length:** 9 9/16" (4" bbl.).
Stocks: Uncle Mike's Combat soft rubber; wood optional.
Sights: Serrated ramp front 2 1/2" or 4" bbl., red ramp on 4", 6" bbl., micro-click rear adjustable for windage and elevation.
Price: S&W Bright Blue, adj. sights ....$416.00 to $430.00

SMITH & WESSON MODEL 29, 629 REVOLVERS
Caliber: 44 Magnum, 6-shot.
Barrel: 6", 8 3/8" (Model 29); 4", 6", 8 3/8" (Model 629).
Weight: 47 oz. (6" bbl.). **Length:** 11 3/8" overall (6" bbl.).
Stocks: Soft rubber; wood optional.
Sights: 1/8" red ramp front, micro-click rear, adjustable for windage and elevation.
Price: S&W Bright Blue, 6" $554.00
Price: S&W Bright Blue, 8 3/8" $566.00
Price: Model 629 (stainless steel), 4" $587.00
Price: Model 629, 6" $592.00
Price: Model 629, 8 3/8" barrel $606.00

Smith & Wesson Model 629 Classic Revolver
 Similar to the standard Model 629 except has full-lug 5", 6 1/2" or 8 3/8" barrel; chamfered front of cylinder; interchangable red ramp front sight with adjustable white outline rear; Hogue grips with S&W monogram; the frame is drilled and tapped for scope mounting. Factory accurizing and endurance packages. Overall length with 5" barrel is 10 1/2"; weighs 51 oz. Introduced 1990.
Price: Model 629 Classic (stainless), 5", 6 1/2" $629.00
Price: As above, 8 3/8" $650.00

Smith & Wesson Model 629 Classic DX Revolver
 Similar to the Model 629 Classic except offered only with 6 1/2" or 8 3/8" full-lug barrel; comes with five front sights: 50-yard red ramp; 50-yard black Patridge; 100-yard black Patridge with gold bead; 50-yard black ramp; and 50-yard black Patridge with white dot. Comes with Hogue combat-style round butt grip. Introduced 1991.
Price: Model 629 Classic DX, 6 1/2" $811.00
Price: As above, 8 3/8" $838.00

Smith & Wesson Model 629 Classic PowerPort Revolver
 Similar to the Model 629 Classic with 6 1/2" full-lug barrel except has PowerPort compensator. Introduced 1996. Made in U.S. by Smith & Wesson.
Price: 6 1/2" barrel only $629.00

SMITH & WESSON MODEL 36, 37 CHIEFS SPECIAL & AIRWEIGHT
Caliber: 38 Spec., 5-shot.
Barrel: 2".
Weight: 19 1/2 oz. (2" bbl.); 13 1/2 oz. (Airweight). **Length:** 6 1/2" (2" bbl. and round butt).
Stocks: Round butt soft rubber; wood optional.
Sights: Fixed, serrated ramp front, square notch rear.
Price: Blue, standard Model 36 ....$377.00
Price: Blue, Airweight Model 37, 2" only $412.00

Smith & Wesson Model 637 Airweight Revolver
 Similar to the Model 37 Airweight except has stainless steel barrel, cylinder and yoke; Uncle Mike's Boot Grip. Introduced 1996. Made in U.S. by Smith & Wesson.
Price: $428.00

Smith & Wesson Model 36LS, 60LS LadySmith
 Similar to the standard Model 36. Available with 2" barrel. Comes with smooth, contoured rosewood grips with the S&W monogram. Has a speedloader cutout. Comes in a fitted carry/storage case. Introduced 1989.
Price: Model 36LS $408.00
Price: Model 60LS (as above except in stainless) $461.00

CAUTION: PRICES SHOWN ARE SUPPLIED BY THE MANUFACTURER OR IMPORTER. CHECK YOUR LOCAL GUNSHOP.

HANDGUNS—DOUBLE-ACTION REVOLVERS, SERVICE & SPORT

Smith & Wesson Model 649

Smith & Wesson Model 63

SMITH & WESSON MODEL 65LS LADYSMITH
Caliber: 357 Magnum, 6-shot.
Barrel: 3".
Weight: 31 oz. **Length:** 7.94" overall.
Stocks: Rosewood, round butt.
Sights: Serrated ramp front, fixed notch rear.
Features: Stainless steel with frosted finish. Smooth combat trigger, service hammer, shrouded ejector rod. Comes with soft case. Introduced 1992.
Price: $461.00

SMITH & WESSON MODEL 66 STAINLESS COMBAT MAGNUM
Caliber: 357 Mag. and 38 Spec., 6-shot.
Barrel: 2½", 4", 6".
Weight: 36 oz. (4" barrel). **Length:** 9 9/16" overall.
Stocks: Soft rubber; wood optional.
Sights: Red ramp front, micro-click rear adjustable for windage and elevation.
Features: Satin finish stainless steel.
Price: 2½" $466.00
Price: 4", 6" $471.00

SMITH & WESSON MODEL 67 COMBAT MASTERPIECE
Caliber: 38 Special, 6-shot.
Barrel: 4".
Weight: 32 oz. **Length:** 9 5/16" overall.
Stocks: Soft rubber; wood optional.
Sights: Red ramp front, micro-click rear adjustable for windage and elevation.
Features: Stainless steel with satin finish. Smooth combat trigger, semi-target hammer. Introduced 1994.
Price: $467.00

SMITH & WESSON MODEL 586, 686 DISTINGUISHED COMBAT MAGNUMS
Caliber: 357 Magnum.
Barrel: 4", 6", full shroud.
Weight: 46 oz. (6"), 41 oz. (4").
Stocks: Soft rubber; wood optional.
Sights: Baughman red ramp front, four-position click-adjustable front, S&W micrometer click rear. Drilled and tapped for scope mount.
Features: Uses L-frame, but takes all K-frame grips. Full-length ejector rod shroud. Smooth combat-type trigger, semi-target type hammer. Trigger stop on 6" models. Also available in stainless as Model 686. Introduced 1981.
Price: Model 586, blue, 4", from $461.00
Price: Model 586, blue, 6" $466.00
Price: Model 686, 6", ported barrel $528.00
Price: Model 686, 8 3/8" $515.00
Price: Model 686, 2½" $481.00

Smith & Wesson Model 686 Magnum Plus Revolver
Similar to the Model 686 except has 7-shot cylinder, 2½", 4" or 6" barrel. Weighs 34½ oz., overall length 7½" (2½" barrel). Hogue rubber grips. Introduced 1996. Made in U.S. by Smith & Wesson.
Price: 2½" barrel $498.00
Price: 4" barrel $506.00
Price: 6" barrel $514.00

Smith & Wesson Model 60 3" Full-Lug Revolver
Similar to the Model 60 Chief's Special except has 3" full-lug barrel, adjustable micrometer click black blade rear sight; rubber Uncle Mike's Custom Grade Boot Grip. Overall length 7½"; weighs 24½ oz. Introduced 1991.
Price: $458.00

SMITH & WESSON MODEL 38 BODYGUARD
Caliber: 38 Spec., 5-shot.
Barrel: 2".
Weight: 14½ oz. **Length:** 6 5/16" overall.
Stocks: Soft rubber; wood optional.
Sights: Fixed serrated ramp front, square notch rear.
Features: Alloy frame; internal hammer.
Price: Blue $444.00
Price: Nickel $460.00

Smith & Wesson Model 49, 649 Bodyguard Revolvers
Same as Model 38 except steel construction, weighs 20½ oz.
Price: Blued, Model 49 ....$409.00
Price: Stainless, Model 649 ....$469.00

SMITH & WESSON MODEL 63 KIT GUN
Caliber: 22 LR, 6-shot.
Barrel: 2", 4".
Weight: 24 oz. (4" bbl.). **Length:** 8 3/8" (4" bbl. and round butt).
Stocks: Round butt soft rubber; wood optional.
Sights: Red ramp front, micro-click rear adjustable for windage and elevation.
Features: Stainless steel construction.
Price: 2" $458.00
Price: 4" $462.00

SMITH & WESSON MODEL 64 STAINLESS M&P
Caliber: 38 Spec., 6-shot.
Barrel: 2", 3", 4".
Weight: 34 oz. **Length:** 9 5/16" overall.
Stocks: Soft rubber; wood optional.
Sights: Fixed, 1/8" serrated ramp front, square notch rear.
Features: Satin finished stainless steel, square butt.
Price: 2" $415.00
Price: 3", 4" $423.00

SMITH & WESSON MODEL 617 FULL LUG REVOLVER
Caliber: 22 LR, 6-shot.
Barrel: 4", 6", 8 3/8".
Weight: 42 oz. (4" barrel). **Length:** NA.
Stocks: Soft rubber; wood optional.
Sights: Patridge front, adjustable rear. Drilled and tapped for scope mount.
Features: Stainless steel with satin finish; 4" has .312" smooth trigger, .375" semi-target hammer; 6" has either .312" combat or .400" serrated trigger, .375" semi-target or .500" target hammer; 8 3/8" with .400" serrated trigger, .500" target hammer. Introduced 1990.
Price: 4" $460.00
Price: 6", target hammer, combat trigger $490.00
Price: 8 3/8" $501.00

Smith & Wesson Model 625

SMITH & WESSON MODEL 625 REVOLVER
Caliber: 45 ACP, 6-shot.
Barrel: 5".
Weight: 46 oz. **Length:** 11.375" overall.
Stocks: Soft rubber; wood optional.
Sights: Patridge front on ramp, S&W micrometer click rear adjustable for windage and elevation.
Features: Stainless steel construction with .400" semi-target hammer, .312" smooth combat trigger; full lug barrel. Introduced 1989.
Price: $597.00

HANDGUNS—DOUBLE-ACTION REVOLVERS, SERVICE & SPORT

Smith & Wesson Model 442

Smith & Wesson Model 642

SMITH & WESSON MODEL 640 CENTENNIAL
Caliber: 357 Mag., 38 Spec., 5-shot.
Barrel: 2 1/8".
Weight: 25 oz. **Length:** 6 3/4" overall.
Stocks: Uncle Mike's Boot Grip.
Sights: Serrated ramp front, fixed notch rear.
Features: Stainless steel version of the original Model 40 but without the grip safety. Fully concealed hammer, snag-proof smooth edges. Introduced 1995 in 357 Magnum.
Price: $469.00
Price: Model 940 (9mm Para.) $474.00

Smith & Wesson Model 442 Centennial Airweight
Similar to the Model 640 Centennial except has alloy frame giving weight of 15.8 oz. Chambered for 38 Special, 2" carbon steel barrel; carbon steel cylinder; concealed hammer; Uncle Mike's Custom Grade Santoprene grips. Fixed square notch rear sight, serrated ramp front. Introduced 1993.
Price: Blue $427.00

Smith & Wesson Model 642 Airweight Revolver
Similar to the Model 442 Centennial Airweight except has stainless steel barrel, cylinder and yoke with matte finish; Uncle Mike's Boot Grip; weights 15.8 oz. Introduced 1996. Made in U.S. by Smith & Wesson.
Price: $442.00

Smith & Wesson Model 642LS LadySmith Revolver
Same as the Model 642 except has smooth combat wood grips, and comes with case; frosted matte finish. Introduced 1996. Made in U.S. by Smith & Wesson.
Price: $471.00

SMITH & WESSON MODEL 651 REVOLVER
Caliber: 22 WMR, 6-shot cylinder.
Barrel: 4".
Weight: 24 1/2 oz. **Length:** 8 11/16" overall.
Stocks: Soft rubber; wood optional.
Sights: Red ramp front, adjustable micrometer click rear.
Features: Stainless steel construction with semi-target hammer, smooth combat trigger. Reintroduced 1991. Limited production.
Price: $460.00

SMITH & WESSON MODEL 657 REVOLVER
Caliber: 41 Mag., 6-shot.
Barrel: 6".
Weight: 48 oz. **Length:** 11 3/8" overall.
Stocks: Soft rubber; wood optional.
Sights: Pinned 1/8" red ramp front, micro-click rear adjustable for windage and elevation.
Features: Stainless steel construction.
Price: $528.00

TAURUS MODEL 66 REVOLVER
Caliber: 357 Mag., 6-shot.
Barrel: 2.5", 4", 6".
Weight: 35 oz.(4" barrel).
Stocks: Soft black rubber.
Sights: Serrated ramp front, micro-click rear adjustable for windage and elevation. Red ramp front with white outline rear on stainlees models only.
Features: Wide target-type hammer spur, floating firing pin, heavy barrel with shrouded ejector rod. Introduced 1978. Imported by Taurus International.
Price: Blue, 2.5", 4", 6" $318.00
Price: Stainless, 2.5", 4", 6" $392.00

Taurus Model 65 Revolver
Same as the Model 66 except has fixed rear sight and ramp front. Available with 2.5" or 4" barrel only, round butt grip. Imported by Taurus International.
Price: Blue, 2.5", 4" $290.00
Price: Stainless, 2.5", 4" $357.00

TAURUS MODEL 80 STANDARD REVOLVER
Caliber: 38 Spec., 6-shot.
Barrel: 3" or 4".
Weight: 30 oz. (4" bbl.). **Length:** 9 1/4" overall (4" bbl.).
Stocks: Soft black rubber.
Sights: Serrated ramp front, square notch rear.
Features: Imported by Taurus International.
Price: Blue $252.00
Price: Stainless $299.00

Smith & Wesson Model 651

TAURUS MODEL 44 REVOLVER
Caliber: 44 Mag., 6-shot.
Barrel: 4", 6 1/2", 8 3/8".
Weight: 44 3/4 oz. (4" barrel). **Length:** NA.
Stocks: Soft black rubber.
Sights: Serrated ramp front, micro-click rear adjustable for windage and elevation.
Features: Heavy solid rib on 4", vent rib on 6 1/2", 8 3/8". Compensated barrel. Blued model has color case-hardened hammer and trigger. Introduced 1994. Imported by Taurus International.
Price: Blue, 4" $425.00
Price: Blue, 6 1/2", 8 3/8" $443.00
Price: Stainless, 4" $484.00
Price: Stainless, 6 1/2", 8 3/8" $504.00

Taurus Model 66

CAUTION: PRICES SHOWN ARE SUPPLIED BY THE MANUFACTURER OR IMPORTER. CHECK YOUR LOCAL GUNSHOP.

HANDGUNS—DOUBLE-ACTION REVOLVERS, SERVICE & SPORT

TAURUS MODEL 82 HEAVY BARREL REVOLVER
Caliber: 38 Spec., 6-shot.
Barrel: 3" or 4", heavy.
Weight: 34 oz. (4" bbl.). **Length:** 9 1/4" overall (4" bbl.).
Stocks: Soft black rubber.
Sights: Serrated ramp front, square notch rear.
Features: Imported by Taurus International.
Price: Blue $252.00
Price: Stainless $295.00

TAURUS MODEL 83 REVOLVER
Caliber: 38 Spec., 6-shot.
Barrel: 4" only, heavy.
Weight: 34 oz.
Stocks: Soft black rubber.
Sights: Ramp front, micro-click rear adjustable for windage and elevation.
Features: Blue or nickel finish. Introduced 1977. Imported by Taurus International.
Price: Blue $265.00
Price: Stainless $309.00

Taurus Model 85CH Revolver
Same as the Model 85 except has 2" barrel only and concealed hammer. Soft rubber boot grip. Introduced 1991. Imported by Taurus International.
Price: Blue $239.00
Price: Stainless $287.00

TAURUS MODEL 94 REVOLVER
Caliber: 22 LR, 9-shot cylinder.
Barrel: 3", 4", 5".
Weight: 25 oz.
Stocks: Soft black rubber.
Sights: Serrated ramp front, click-adjustable rear for windage and elevation.
Features: Floating firing pin, color case-hardened hammer and trigger. Introduced 1989. Imported by Taurus International.
Price: Blue $293.00
Price: Stainless $339.00

Taurus Model 82

TAURUS MODEL 85 REVOLVER
Caliber: 38 Spec., 5-shot.
Barrel: 2", 3".
Weight: 21 oz.
Stocks: Black rubber, boot grip.
Sights: Ramp front, square notch rear.
Features: Blue finish or stainless steel. Introduced 1980. Imported by Taurus International.
Price: Blue, 2", 3" $239.00
Price: Stainless steel $287.00

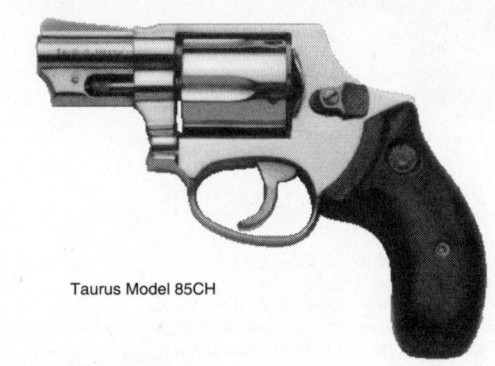

Taurus Model 85CH

> Consult our Directory pages for the location of firms mentioned.

TAURUS MODEL 96 REVOLVER
Caliber: 22 LR, 6-shot.
Barrel: 6".
Weight: 34 oz. **Length:** NA.
Stocks: Soft black rubber.
Sights: Patridge-type front, micrometer click rear adjustable for windage and elevation.
Features: Heavy solid barrel rib; target hammer; adjustable target trigger. Blue only. Imported by Taurus International.
Price: $358.00

TAURUS MODEL 441/431 REVOLVERS
Caliber: 44 Spec., 5-shot.
Barrel: 3", 4", 6".
Weight: 40.4 oz. (6" barrel). **Length:** NA.
Stocks: Soft black rubber.
Sights: Serrated ramp front, micrometer click rear adjustable for windage and elevation.
Features: Heavy barrel with solid rib and full-length ejector shroud. Introduced 1992. Imported by Taurus International.
Price: Model 441, Blue, 3", 4", 6" $298.00
Price: Model 441, Stainless, 3", 4", 6" $374.00
Price: Model 431 (fixed sights), blue, 2", 3", 4" ..$256.00
Price: Model 431 (fixed sights), stainless, 2", 3", 4" ..$350.00

TAURUS MODEL 607 REVOLVER
Caliber: 357 Mag., 7-shot.
Barrel: 4", 6 1/2".
Weight: 44 oz. **Length:** NA.
Stocks: Santoprene I with finger grooves.
Sights: Serrated ramp front, fully adjustable rear.
Features: Ventilated rib with built-in compensator on 6 1/2" barrel. Available in blue or stainless. Introduced 1995. Imported by Taurus international.
Price: Blue, 4" $425.00
Price: Blue, 6 1/2" $443.00
Price: Stainless, 4" $484.00
Price: Stainless, 6 1/2" $504.00

TAURUS MODEL 605 REVOLVER
Caliber: 357 Mag., 5-shot.
Barrel: 2 1/4", 3".
Weight: 24.5 oz. **Length:** NA.
Stocks: Finger-groove Santoprene I.
Sights: Serrated ramp front, fixed notch rear.
Features: Heavy, solid rib barrel; floating firing pin. Blue or stainless. Introduced 1995. Imported by Taurus International.
Price: Blue $262.00
Price: Stainless $312.00
Price: Model 605CH (concealed hammer) 2 1/4", blue ..$262.00
Price: Model 605CH, stainless, 2 1/4" $312.00

Taurus Model 607

Taurus Model 608 Revolver
Same as the Model 607 except has 8-shot cylinder. Introduced 1996. Imported by Taurus International.
Price: Blue, 4" $425.00
Price: Blue, 6 1/2" $443.00
Price: Stainless, 4" $484.00
Price: Stainless, 6 1/2" $504.00

HANDGUNS—DOUBLE-ACTION REVOLVERS, SERVICE & SPORT

TAURUS MODEL 669 REVOLVER
Caliber: 357 Mag., 6-shot.
Barrel: 4", 6".
Weight: 37 oz., (4" bbl.).
Stocks: Black rubber.
Sights: Serrated ramp front, micro-click rear adjustable for windage and elevation.
Features: Wide target-type hammer, floating firing pin, full-length barrel shroud. Introduced 1988. Imported by Taurus International.
Price: Blue, 4", 6" $327.00
Price: Blue, 4", 6" compensated $346.00
Price: Stainless, 4", 6" $401.00
Price: Stainless, 4", 6" compensated $421.00

Taurus Model 009

TAURUS MODEL 941 REVOLVER
Caliber: 22 WMR, 8-shot.
Barrel: 3", 4".
Weight: 27.5 oz. (4" barrel). **Length:** NA.
Stocks: Soft black rubber.
Sights: Serrated ramp front, rear adjustable for windage and elevation.
Features: Solid rib heavy barrel with full-length ejector rod shroud. Blue or stainless steel. Introduced 1992. Imported by Taurus International.
Price: Blue $315.00
Price: Stainless $366.00

Taurus Model 689 Revolver
Same as the Model 669 except has full-length ventilated barrel rib. Available in blue or stainless steel. Introduced 1990. From Taurus International.
Price: Blue, 4" or 6" $341.00
Price: Stainless, 4" or 6" $415.00

HANDGUNS—SINGLE-ACTION REVOLVERS
Both classic six-shooters and modern adaptations for hunting and sport.

AMERICAN ARMS REGULATOR SINGLE-ACTIONS
Caliber: 357 Mag. 44-40, 45 Colt.
Barrel: 4 3/4", 5 1/2", 7 1/2".
Weight: 32 oz. (4 3/4" barrel). **Length:** 8 1/6" overall (4 3/4" barrel).
Stocks: Smooth walnut.
Sights: Blade front, groove rear.
Features: Blued barrel and cylinder, brass trigger guard and backstrap. Introduced 1992. Imported from Italy by American Arms, Inc.
Price: Regulator, single cylinder $349.00
Price: Regulator, dual cylinder (44-40/44 Spec. or 45 Colt/45 ACP) ... $399.00
Price: Regulator DLX (all steel) $395.00

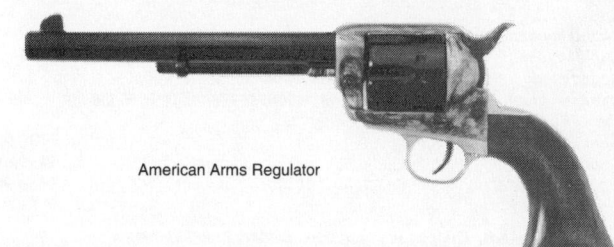
American Arms Regulator

American Frontier 1871-1872 Open-Top

AMERICAN FRONTIER POCKET RICHARDS & MASON NAVY
Caliber: 32, 5-shot cylinder.
Barrel: 4 3/4", 5 1/2".
Weight: NA. **Length:** NA.
Stocks: Varnished walnut.
Sights: Blade front, fixed rear.
Features: Shoots metallic-cartridge ammunition. Non-rebated cylinder; high-polish blue, silver-plated brass backstrap and trigger guard; ejector assembly; color case-hardened hammer and trigger. Introduced 1996. Imported from Italy by American Frontier Firearms Co.
Price: From $495.00

AMERICAN FRONTIER 1871-1872 OPEN-TOP REVOLVERS
Caliber: 38, 44.
Barrel: 4 3/4", 5 1/2", 7 1/2", 8" round.
Weight: NA. **Length:** NA.
Stocks: Varnished walnut.
Sights: Blade front, fixed rear.
Features: Reproduction of the early cartridge conversions from percussion. Made for metallic cartridges. High polish blued steel, silver-plated brass backstrap and trigger guard, color case-hardened hammer; straight non-rebated cylinder with naval engagement engraving; stamped with original patent dates. Does not have conversion breechplate. Introduced 1996. Imported from Italy by American Frontier Firearms Co.
Price: $795.00
Price: Tiffany model with Tiffany grips, silver and gold finish with engraving $995.00

AMERICAN FRONTIER 1871-1872 POCKET MODEL REVOLVER
Caliber: 32, 5-shot cylinder.
Barrel: 4 3/4", 5 1/2" round.
Weight: NA. **Length:** NA.
Stocks: Varnished walnut or Tiffany.
Sights: Blade front, fixed rear.
Features: Based on the 1862 Police percussion revolver converted to metallic cartridge. High polish blue finish with silver-plated brass backstrap and trigger guard, color case-hardened hammer. Introduced 1996. Imported from Italy by American Frontier Firearms Co.
Price: From $495.00

AMERICAN FRONTIER REMINGTON NEW MODEL REVOLVER
Caliber: 38, 44.
Barrel: 5 1/2", 7 1/2".
Weight: NA. **Length:** NA.
Stocks: Varnished walnut.
Sights: Blade front, fixed rear.
Features: Replica of the factory conversions by Remington between 1863 and 1875. High polish blue or silver finish with color case-hardened hammer; with or without ejector rod and loading gate. Introduced 1996. Imported from Italy by American Frontier Firearms Co.
Price: $695.00

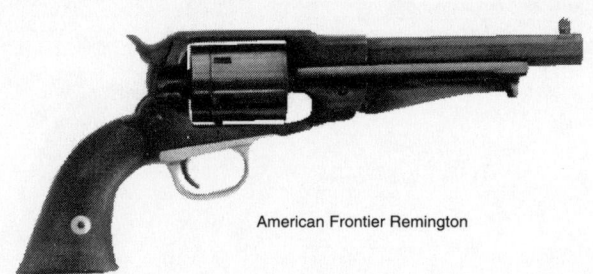
American Frontier Remington

CAUTION: PRICES SHOWN ARE SUPPLIED BY THE MANUFACTURER OR IMPORTER. CHECK YOUR LOCAL GUNSHOP.

HANDGUNS—SINGLE-ACTION REVOLVERS

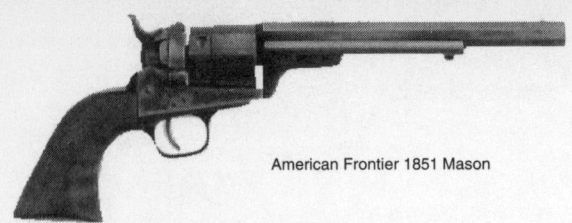
American Frontier 1851 Mason

American Frontier 1851 Navy Richards & Mason Conversion
Similar to the 1851 Navy Conversion except has Mason ejector assembly. Introduced 1996. Imported from Italy by American Frontier Firearms Co.
Price: $695.00

CENTURY GUN DIST. MODEL 100 SINGLE-ACTION
Caliber: 30-30, 375 Win., 444 Marlin, 45-70, 50-70.
Barrel: 6½" (standard), 8", 10", 12".
Weight: 6 lbs. (loaded). **Length:** 15" overall (8" bbl.).
Stocks: Smooth walnut.
Sights: Ramp front, Millett adjustable square notch rear.
Features: Highly polished high tensile strength manganese bronze frame, blue cylinder and barrel; coil spring trigger mechanism. Calibers other than 45-70 start at $2,000.00. Contact maker for full price information. Introduced 1975. Made in U.S. From Century Gun Dist., Inc.
Price: 6½" barrel, 45-70 ....$1,250.00

CIMARRON 1873 FRONTIER SIX SHOOTER
Caliber: 38 WCF, 357 Mag., 44 WCF, 44 Spec., 45 Colt.
Barrel: 4¾", 5½", 7½".
Weight: 39 oz. **Length:** 10" overall (4" barrel).
Stocks: Walnut.
Sights: Blade front, fixed or adjustable rear.
Features: Uses "old model" blackpowder frame with "Bullseye" ejector or New Model frame. Imported by Cimarron Arms.
Price: 4¾" barrel $439.95
Price: 5½" barrel $439.95
Price: 7½" barrel $439.95

CIMARRON U.S. CAVALRY MODEL SINGLE-ACTION
Caliber: 45 Colt
Barrel: 7½".
Weight: 42 oz. **Length:** 13½" overall.
Stocks: Walnut.
Sights: Fixed.
Features: Has "A.P. Casey" markings; "U.S." plus patent dates on frame, serial number on backstrap, trigger guard, frame and cylinder, "APC" cartouche on left grip; color case-hardened frame and hammer, rest charcoal blue. Exact copy of the original. Imported by Cimarron Arms.
Price: $469.00

Cimarron Rough Rider Artillery Model Single-Action
Similar to the U.S. Cavalry model except has 5½" barrel, weighs 39 oz., and is 11½" overall. U.S. markings and cartouche, case-hardened frame and hammer; 45 Colt only.
Price: $469.00

> *Manufacturers' addresses in the*
> **Directory of the Arms Trade**
> *page 313, this issue*

COLT SINGLE ACTION-ARMY REVOLVER
Caliber: 44-40, 45 Colt, 6-shot.
Barrel: 4¾", 5½", 7½".
Weight: 40 oz. (4¾" barrel). **Length:** 10¼" overall (4¾" barrel).
Stocks: Black Eagle composite.
Sights: Blade front, notch rear.
Features: Available in full nickel finish with nickel grip medallions, or Royal Blue with color case-hardened frame, gold grip medallions. Reintroduced 1992.
Price: $1,213.00

AMERICAN FRONTIER RICHARDS 1860 ARMY
Caliber: 38, 44.
Barrel: 4¾", 5½", 7½", round.
Weight: NA. **Length:** NA.
Stocks: Varnished walnut, Army size.
Sights: Blade front, fixed rear.
Features: Shoots metallic cartridge ammunition. Rebated cylinder; available with or without ejector assembly; high-polish blue including backstrap; silver-plated trigger guard; color case-hardened hammer and trigger. Introduced 1996. Imported from Italy by American Frontier Firearms Co.
Price: $695.00

AMERICAN FRONTIER 1851 NAVY CONVERSION
Caliber: 38, 44.
Barrel: 4¾", 5½", 7½", octagon.
Weight: NA. **Length:** NA.
Stocks: Varnished walnut, Navy size.
Sights: Blade front, fixed rear.
Features: Shoots metallic cartridge ammunition. Non-rebated cylinder; blued steel backstrap and trigger guard; color case-hardened hammer, trigger, ramrod, plunger; no ejector rod assembly. Introduced 1996. Imported from Italy by American Frontier Firearms Co.
Price: $695.00

Century Model 100

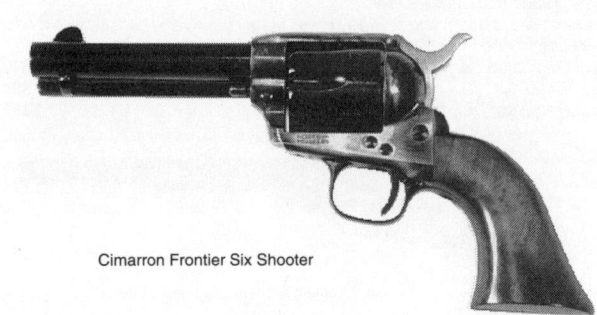
Cimarron Frontier Six Shooter

CIMARRON NEW THUNDERER REVOLVER
Caliber: 357 Mag., 44 WCF, 44 Spec., 45 Colt, 6-shot.
Barrel: 3½", 4¾", with ejector.
Weight: 38 oz. (3½" barrel). **Length:** NA.
Stocks: Hand-checkered walnut.
Sights: Blade front, notch rear.
Features: Thunderer grip; color case-hardened frame with balance blued, or nickel finish. Introduced 1993. Imported by Cimarron Arms.
Price: Color case-hardened $439.95
Price: Nickeled $559.95

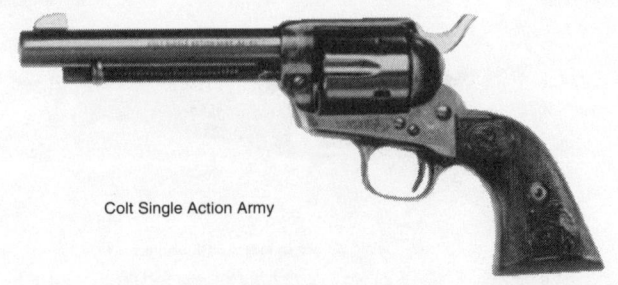
Colt Single Action Army

HANDGUNS—SINGLE-ACTION REVOLVERS

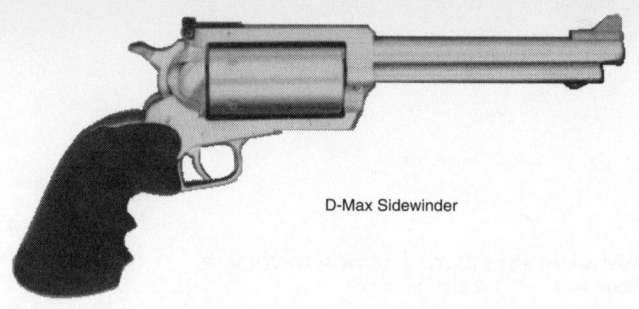

D-Max Sidewinder

D-MAX SIDEWINDER REVOLVER
Caliber: 45 Colt/410 shotshell, 6-shot.
Barrel: 6.5", 7.5".
Weight: 57 oz. (6.5"). **Length:** 14.1" (6.5" barrel).
Stocks: Hogue black rubber with finger grooves.
Sights: Blade on ramp front, fully adjustable rear.
Features: Stainless steel construction. Has removable choke for firing shotshells. Grooved, wide-spur hammer; transfer bar ignition; satin stainless finish. Introduced 1992. Made in U.S. by D-Max, Inc.
Price: $750.00

E.A.A. Big Bore Bounty Hunter

E.A.A. BIG BORE BOUNTY HUNTER SA REVOLVERS
Caliber: 357 Mag., 44 Mag., 45 Colt, 6-shot.
Barrel: 4½", 7½".
Weight: 2.5 lbs. **Length:** 11" overall (4⅝" barrel).
Stocks: Smooth walnut.
Sights: Blade front, grooved topstrap rear.
Features: Transfer bar safety; three position hammer; hammer forged barrel. Introduced 1992. Imported by European American Armory.
Price: Blue $299.00
Price: Color case-hardened frame $310.00

EMF HARTFORD SINGLE-ACTION REVOLVERS
Caliber: 22 LR, 357 Mag., 32-20, 38-40, 44-40, 44 Spec., 45 Colt.
Barrel: 4¾", 5½", 7½".
Weight: 45 oz. **Length:** 13" overall (7½" barrel).
Stocks: Smooth walnut.
Sights: Blade front, fixed rear.
Features: Identical to the original Colts with inspector cartouche on left grip, original patent dates and U.S. markings. All major parts serial numbered using original Colt-style lettering, numbering. Bullseye ejector head and color case-hardening on frame and hammer. Introduced 1990. From E.M.F.
Price: $600.00
Price: Cavalry or Artillery $655.00
Price: Nickel plated $725.00
Price: Engraved, nickel plated $840.00
Price: Pinkerton (bird's-head grip), 45 Colt, 4" barrel $680.00

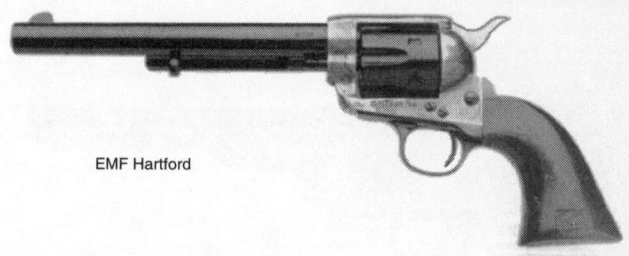

EMF Hartford

EMF 1894 Target Bisley Revolver
Similar to the Hartford single-action revolver except has special grip frame and trigger guard, wide spur hammer; available in 45 Colt only, 5½" or 7½" barrel. Introduced 1995. Imported by E.M.F.
Price: Blue $680.00
Price: Nickel $805.00

EMF DAKOTA 1875 OUTLAW REVOLVER
Caliber: 357 Mag., 44-40, 45 Colt.
Barrel: 7½".
Weight: 46 oz. **Length:** 13½" overall.
Stocks: Smooth walnut.
Sights: Blade front, fixed groove rear.
Features: Authentic copy of 1875 Remington with firing pin in hammer; color case-hardened frame, blue cylinder, barrel, steel backstrap and brass trigger guard. Also available in nickel, factory engraved. Imported by E.M.F.
Price: All calibers $465.00
Price: Nickel $550.00
Price: Engraved $600.00
Price: Engraved Nickel $710.00

EMF Dakota 1890 Police Revolver
Similar to the 1875 Outlaw except has 5½" barrel, weighs 40 oz., with 12½" overall length. Has lanyard ring in butt. No web under barrel. Calibers 357, 44-40, 45 Colt. Imported by E.M.F.
Price: All calibers $470.00
Price: Nickel $560.00
Price: Engraved $620.00
Price: Engraved nickel $725.00

EMF Dakota New Model Single-Action Revolvers
Similar to the standard Dakota except has color case-hardened forged steel frame, black nickel backstrap and trigger guard. Calibers 357 Mag., 44-40, 45 Colt only.
Price: $460.00
Price: Nickel $585.00

FREEDOM ARMS PREMIER SINGLE-ACTION REVOLVER
Caliber: 44 Mag., 454 Casull with 45 Colt, 45 ACP, 45 Win. Mag. optional cylinders, 5-shot.
Barrel: 4¾", 6", 7½", 10".
Weight: 50 oz. **Length:** 14" overall (7½" bbl.).
Stocks: Impregnated hardwood.
Sights: Blade front, notch or adjustable rear.
Features: All stainless steel construction; sliding bar safety system. Lifetime warranty. Made in U.S. by Freedom Arms, Inc.
Price: Field Grade (matte finish, Pachmayr grips), adjustable sights, 4¾", 6", 7½", 10" $1,301.00
Price: Field Grade, fixed sights, 4¾", 6", 7½", 10" $1,207.00
Price: Field Grade, 44 Rem. Mag., adjustable sights, all lengths $1,253.00
Price: Premier Grade 454 (brush finish, impregnated hardwood grips) adjustable sights, 4¾", 6", 7½", 10" $1,677.00
Price: Premier Grade, fixed sights, all barrel lengths $1,568.00
Price: Premier Grade, 44 Rem. Mag., adjustable sights, all lengths ...$1,627.00
Price: Fitted 45 ACP, 45 Colt or 45 Win. Mag cylinder, add $253.00

Freedom Arms Premier

Freedom Arms Model 353 Revolver
Similar to the Premier 454 Casull except chambered for 357 Magnum with 5-shot cylinder; 4¾", 6", 7½" or 9" barrel. Weighs 59 oz. with 7½" barrel. Field grade model has adjustable sights, matte finish, Pachmayr grips, 7½" or 10" barrel; Silhouette has 9" barrel, Patridge front sight, Iron Sight Gun Works Silhouette adjustable rear, Pachmayr grips, trigger over-travel adjustment screw. All stainless steel. Introduced 1992.
Price: Field Grade $1,253.00
Price: Premier Grade (brushed finish, impregnated hardwood grips, Premier Grade sights) $1,627.00
Price: Silhouette (9", 357 Mag., 10", 44 Mag.) $1,347.00

Freedom Arms Model 555 Revolver
Same as the 454 Casull except chambered for the 50 A.E. (Action Express) cartridge. Offered in Premier and Field Grades with adjustable sights, 4¾", 6", 7½" or 10" barrel. Introduced 1994. Made in U.S. by Freedom Arms, Inc.
Price: Premier Grade $1,677.00
Price: Field Grade $1,301.00

HANDGUNS—SINGLE-ACTION REVOLVERS

HERITAGE ROUGH RIDER REVOLVER
Caliber: 22 LR, 22 LR/22 WMR combo, 6-shot.
Barrel: 2³/₄", 3¹/₂", 4³/₄", 6¹/₂", 9".
Weight: 31 to 38 oz. **Length:** NA
Stocks: Exotic hardwood.
Sights: Blade front, fixed rear.
Features: Hammer block safety. High polish blue or nickel finish. Introduced 1993. Made in U.S. by Heritage Mfg., Inc.
Price: ....$109.95 to $169.95
Price: 2³/₄", 3¹/₂", 4³/₄" birdshead grip ....$129.95 to $149.95

Heritage Rough Rider

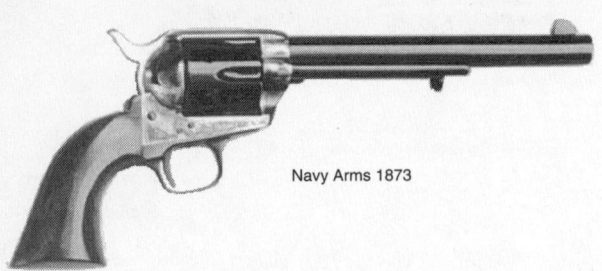
Navy Arms 1873

NAVY ARMS 1873 SINGLE-ACTION REVOLVER
Caliber: 44-40, 45 Colt, 6-shot cylinder.
Barrel: 3", 4³/₄", 5¹/₂", 7¹/₂".
Weight: 36 oz. **Length:** 10³/₄" overall (5¹/₂" barrel).
Stocks: Smooth walnut.
Sights: Blade front, groove in topstrap rear.
Features: Blue with color case-hardened frame, or nickel. Introduced 1991. Imported by Navy Arms.
Price: Blue $390.00
Price: Nickel $455.00
Price: 1873 U.S. Cavalry Model (7¹/₂", 45 Colt, arsenal markings) $480.00
Price: 1895 U.S. Artillery Model (as above, 5¹/₂" barrel) $480.00

> Consult our Directory pages for the location of firms mentioned.

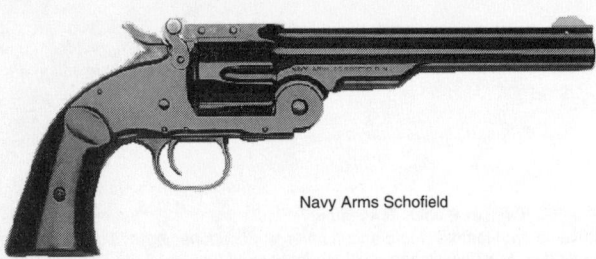
Navy Arms Schofield

NAVY ARMS 1875 SCHOFIELD REVOLVER
Caliber: 44-40, 44 S&W Spec., 45 Colt, 6-shot cylinder.
Barrel: 5", 7".
Weight: 39 oz. **Length:** 10³/₄" overall (5" barrel).
Stocks: Smooth walnut.
Sights: Blade front, notch rear.
Features: Replica of Smith & Wesson Model 3 Schofield. Single-action, top-break with automatic ejection. Polished blue finish. Introduced 1994. Imported by Navy Arms.
Price: Wells Fargo (5" barrel, Wells Fargo markings) $795.00
Price: U.S. Cavalry model (7" barrel, military markings) $795.00

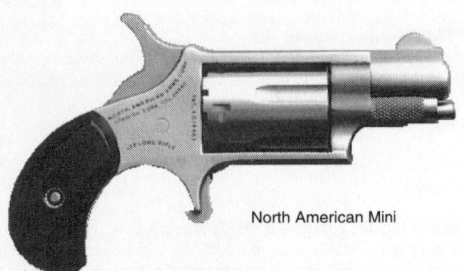
North American Mini

NORTH AMERICAN MINI-REVOLVERS
Caliber: 22 Short, 22 LR, 22 WMR, 5-shot.
Barrel: 1¹/₈", 1⁵/₈".
Weight: 4 to 6.6 oz. **Length:** 3⁵/₈" to 6¹/₈" overall.
Stocks: Laminated wood.
Sights: Blade front, notch fixed rear.
Features: All stainless steel construction. Polished satin and matte finish. Engraved models available. From North American Arms.
Price: 22 Short, 22 LR, 1¹/₈" bbl. $157.00
Price: 22 LR, 1⁵/₈" bbl. $157.00
Price: 22 WMR, 1⁵/₈" bbl. $178.00
Price: 22 WMR, 1¹/₈" or 1⁵/₈" bbl. with extra 22 LR cylinder $210.00

NORTH AMERICAN MINI-MASTER
Caliber: 22 LR, 22 WMR, 5-shot cylinder.
Barrel: 4".
Weight: 10.7 oz. **Length:** 7.75" overall.
Stocks: Checkered hard black rubber.
Sights: Blade front, white outline rear adjustable for elevation, or fixed.
Features: Heavy vent barrel; full-size grips. Non-fluted cylinder. Introduced 1989.
Price: Adjustable sight, 22 WMR or 22 LR $279.00
Price: As above with extra WMR/LR cylinder $317.00
Price: Fixed sight, 22 WMR or 22 LR $264.00
Price: As above with extra WMR/LR cylinder $302.00

North American Black Widow Revolver
Similar to the Mini-Master except has 2" heavy vent barrel. Built on the 22 WMR frame. Non-fluted cylinder, black rubber grips. Available with either Millett Low Profile fixed sights or Millett sight adjustable for elevation only. Overall length 5⁷/₈", weighs 8.8 oz. From North American Arms.
Price: Adjustable sight, 22 LR or 22 WMR $249.00
Price: As above with extra WMR/LR cylinder $285.00
Price: Fixed sight, 22 LR or 22 WMR $235.00
Price: As above with extra WMR/LR cylinder $270.00

Ruger Blackhawk

RUGER BLACKHAWK REVOLVER
Caliber: 30 Carbine, 357 Mag./38 Spec., 41 Mag., 45 Colt, 6-shot.
Barrel: 4⁵/₈" or 6¹/₂", either caliber; 7¹/₂" (30 Carbine, 45 Colt only).
Weight: 42 oz. (6¹/₂" bbl.). **Length:** 12¹/₄" overall (6¹/₂" bbl.).
Stocks: American walnut.
Sights: ¹/₈" ramp front, micro-click rear adjustable for windage and elevation.
Features: Ruger transfer bar safety system, independent firing pin, hardened chrome-moly steel frame, music wire springs throughout.
Price: Blue, 30 Carbine (7¹/₂" bbl.), BN31 ....$360.00
Price: Blue, 357 Mag. (4⁵/₈", 6¹/₂"), BN34, BN36 ....$360.00
Price: Blue, 357/9mm Convertible (4⁵/₈", 6¹/₂"), BN34X, BN36X $360.00
Price: Blue, 41 Mag., 45 Colt (4⁵/₈", 6¹/₂"), BN41, BN42, BN45 ......$360.00
Price: Stainless, 357 Mag. (4⁵/₈", 6¹/₂"), KBN34, KBN36 ....$443.00
Price: High-gloss stainless, 357 Mag. (4⁵/₈", 6¹/₂"), GKBN34, GKBN36 ..$443.00
Price: High-gloss stainless, 45 Colt (4⁵/₈", 7¹/₂"), GKBN44, GKBN45 ...$443.00

HANDGUNS—SINGLE-ACTION REVOLVERS

Ruger New Super Bearcat

RUGER SUPER SINGLE-SIX CONVERTIBLE
Caliber: 22 LR, 6-shot; 22 WMR in extra cylinder.
Barrel: 4⁵⁄₈", 5¹⁄₂", 6¹⁄₂", or 9¹⁄₂" (6-groove).
Weight: 34¹⁄₂ oz. (6¹⁄₂" bbl.). **Length:** 11¹³⁄₁₆" overall (6¹⁄₂" bbl.).
Stocks: Smooth American walnut.
Sights: Improved Patridge front on ramp, fully adjustable rear protected by integral frame ribs; or fixed sight.
Features: Ruger transfer bar safety system, gate-controlled loading, hardened chrome-moly steel frame, wide trigger, music wire springs throughout, independent firing pin.
Price: 4⁵⁄₈", 5¹⁄₂", 6¹⁄₂", 9¹⁄₂" barrel, blue, fixed or adjustable sight (5¹⁄₂", 6¹⁄₂") $313.00
Price: 5¹⁄₂", 6¹⁄₂" bbl. only, high-gloss stainless steel, fixed or adjustable sight $353.00

Ruger SSM Single-Six Revolver
Similar to the Super Single-Six revolver except chambered for 32 H&R Magnum (also handles 32 S&W and 32 S&W Long). Weighs about 34 oz. with 6¹⁄₂" barrel. Barrel lengths: 4⁵⁄₈", 5¹⁄₂", 6¹⁄₂", 9¹⁄₂". Introduced 1985.
Price: $313.00

Ruger Bisley Small Frame Revolver
Similar to the Single-Six except frame is styled after the classic Bisley "flat-top." Most mechanical parts are unchanged. Hammer is lower and smoothly curved with a deeply checkered spur. Trigger is strongly curved with a wide smooth surface. Longer grip frame designed with a hand-filling shape, and the trigger guard is a large oval. Adjustable dovetail rear sight; front sight base accepts interchangeable square blades of various heights and styles. Has an unfluted cylinder and roll engraving. Weighs about 41 oz. Chambered for 22 LR and 32 H&R Mag., 6¹⁄₂" barrel only. Introduced 1985.
Price: $360.00

Ruger Bisley Single-Action Revolver
Similar to standard Blackhawk except the hammer is lower with a smoothly curved, deeply checkered wide spur. The trigger is strongly curved with a wide smooth surface. Longer grip frame has a hand-filling shape. Adjustable rear sight, ramp-style front. Has an unfluted cylinder and roll engraving, adjustable sights. Chambered for 357, 41, 44 Mags. and 45 Colt; 7¹⁄₂" barrel; overall length of 13". Introduced 1985.
Price: $430.00

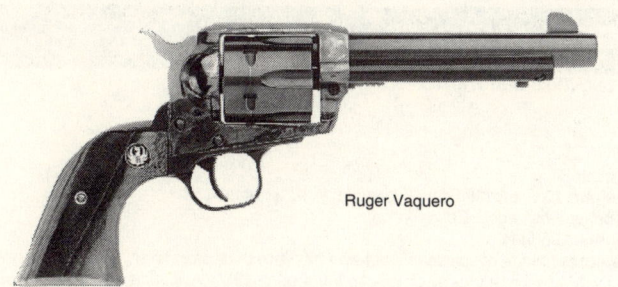
Ruger Vaquero

TEXAS LONGHORN ARMS RIGHT-HAND SINGLE-ACTION
Caliber: All centerfire pistol calibers.
Barrel: 4³⁄₄".
Weight: 40 oz. **Length:** 10¹⁄₄" overall.
Stocks: One-piece fancy walnut.
Sights: Blade front, grooved topstrap rear.
Features: Loading gate and ejector housing on left side of gun. Cylinder rotates to the left. All steel construction; color case-hardened frame; high polish blue; music wire coil springs. Lifetime guarantee to original owner. Introduced 1984. From Texas Longhorn Arms.
Price: South Texas Army Limited Edition—handmade, only 1,000 to be produced; "One of One Thousand" engraved on barrel $1,595.00

RUGER SUPER BLACKHAWK
Caliber: 44 Mag., 6-shot. Also fires 44 Spec.
Barrel: 4⁵⁄₈", 5¹⁄₂", 7¹⁄₂", 10¹⁄₂".
Weight: 48 oz. (7¹⁄₂" bbl.), 51 oz. (10¹⁄₂" bbl.). **Length:** 13³⁄₈" overall (7¹⁄₂" bbl.).
Stocks: American walnut.
Sights: ¹⁄₈" ramp front, micro-click rear adjustable for windage and elevation.
Features: Ruger transfer bar safety system, non-fluted cylinder, steel grip and cylinder frame, square back trigger guard, wide serrated trigger and wide spur hammer.
Price: Blue (S45N, S47N, S411N) $413.00
Price: Stainless (KS45N, KS47N, KS411N) $450.00
Price: High-gloss stainless (4⁵⁄₈", 5¹⁄₂", 7¹⁄₂"), GKS458N, GKS45N, GKS47N $450.00

RUGER NEW SUPER BEARCAT SINGLE-ACTION
Caliber: 22 LR, 6-shot.
Barrel: 4".
Weight: 23 oz. **Length:** 8⁷⁄₈" overall.
Stocks: Smooth rosewood with Ruger medallion.
Sights: Blade front, fixed notch rear.
Features: Reintroduction of the Ruger Super Bearcat with slightly lengthened frame, Ruger patented transfer bar safety system. Available in blue only. Introduced 1993. From Sturm, Ruger & Co.
Price: SBC4, blue $298.00

Ruger Bisley Single-Action

RUGER VAQUERO SINGLE-ACTION REVOLVER
Caliber: 44-40, 44 Mag., 45 Colt, 6-shot.
Barrel: 4⁵⁄₈", 5¹⁄₂", 7¹⁄₂".
Weight: 41 oz. **Length:** 13³⁄₈" overall (7¹⁄₂" barrel).
Stocks: Smooth rosewood with Ruger medallion.
Sights: Blade front, fixed notch rear.
Features: Uses Ruger's patented transfer bar safety system and loading gate interlock with classic styling. Blued model has color case-hardened finish on the frame, the rest polished and blued. Stainless model has high-gloss polish. Introduced 1993. From Sturm, Ruger & Co.
Price: BNV44 (4⁵⁄₈"), BNV445 (5¹⁄₂"), BNV45 (7¹⁄₂"), blue $434.00
Price: KBNV44 (4⁵⁄₈"), KBNV455 (5¹⁄₂"), KBNV45 (7¹⁄₂"), stainless $434.00

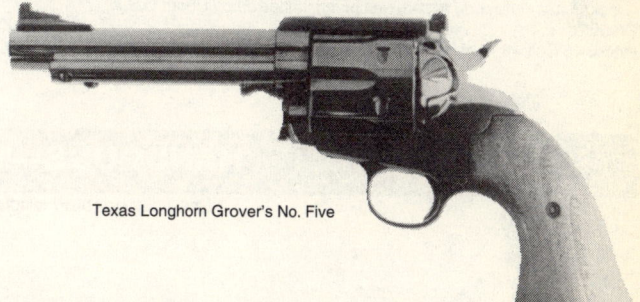
Texas Longhorn Grover's No. Five

TEXAS LONGHORN ARMS GROVER'S IMPROVED NO. FIVE
Caliber: 44 Mag., 6-shot.
Barrel: 5¹⁄₂".
Weight: 44 oz. **Length:** 11¹⁄₂" overall.
Stocks: Smooth walnut.
Sights: Square blade front on ramp, fully adjustable rear.
Features: Music wire coil spring action with double locking bolt; polished blue finish. Handmade in limited 1,200-gun production. Grip contour, straps, over-sized base pin, lever latch and lockwork identical copies of Elmer Keith design. Lifetime warranty to original owner. Introduced 1988.
Price: $1,195.00

Texas Longhorn Arms Sesquicentennial Model Revolver
Similar to the South Texas Army Model except has ³⁄₄-coverage Nimschke-style engraving, antique golden nickel plate finish, one-piece elephant ivory grips. Comes with handmade solid walnut presentation case, factory letter to owner. Limited edition of 150 units. Introduced 1986.
Price: $2,500.00

CAUTION: PRICES SHOWN ARE SUPPLIED BY THE MANUFACTURER OR IMPORTER. CHECK YOUR LOCAL GUNSHOP.

HANDGUNS—SINGLE-ACTION REVOLVERS

Texas Longhorn Arms Texas Border Special
Similar to the South Texas Army Limited Edition except has 4" barrel, bird's-head style grip. Same special features. Introduced 1984.
Price: $1,595.00

Texas Longhorn Arms West Texas Flat Top Target
Similar to the South Texas Army Limited Edition except choice of barrel length from 7½" through 15"; flat-top style frame; ⅛" contoured ramp front sight, old model steel micro-click rear adjustable for windage and elevation. Same special features. Introduced 1984.
Price: $1,595.00

Texas Longhorn Arms Cased Set
Set contains one each of the Texas Longhorn Right-Hand Single-Actions, all in the same caliber, same serial numbers (100, 200, 300, 400, 500, 600, 700, 800, 900). Ten sets to be made (#1000 donated to NRA museum). Comes in hand-tooled leather case. All other specs same as Limited Edition guns. Introduced 1984.
Price: $5,750.00
Price: With ¾-coverage "C-style" engraving $7,650.00

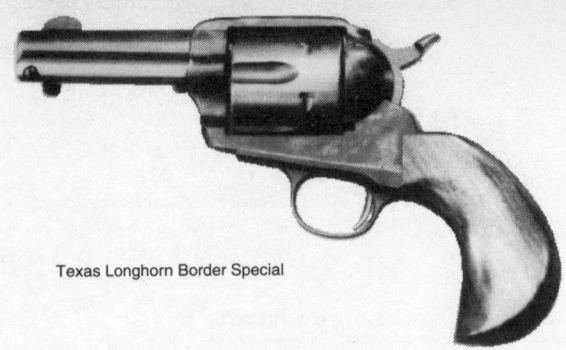
Texas Longhorn Border Special

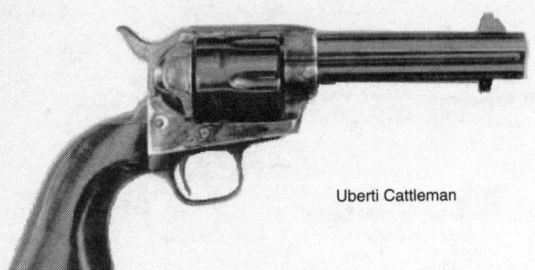
Uberti Cattleman

UBERTI 1873 CATTLEMAN SINGLE-ACTIONS
Caliber: 22 LR/22 WMR, 38 Spec., 357 Mag., 44 Spec., 44-40, 45 Colt/45 ACP, 6-shot.
Barrel: 4¾", 5½", 7½"; 44-40, 45 Colt also with 3", 3½", 4".
Weight: 38 oz. (5½" bbl.). **Length:** 10¾" overall (5½" bbl.).
Stocks: One-piece smooth walnut.
Sights: Blade front, groove rear; fully adjustable rear available.
Features: Steel or brass backstrap, trigger guard; color case-hardened frame, blued barrel, cylinder. Imported from Italy by Uberti U.S.A.
Price: Steel backstrap, trigger guard, fixed sights $435.00
Price: Brass backstrap, trigger guard, fixed sights $365.00
Price: Bisley model $435.00

Uberti 1873 Buckhorn Single-Action
A slightly larger version of the Cattleman revolver. Available in 44 Magnum or 44 Magnum/44-40 convertible, otherwise has same specs.
Price: Steel backstrap, trigger guard, fixed sights $410.00
Price: Convertible (two cylinders) $475.00

Uberti 1875 Army

UBERTI 1875 SA ARMY OUTLAW REVOLVER
Caliber: 357 Mag., 44-40, 45 Colt, 45 Colt/45 ACP convertible, 6-shot.
Barrel: 5½", 7½".
Weight: 44 oz. **Length:** 13¾" overall.
Stocks: Smooth walnut.
Sights: Blade front, notch rear.
Features: Replica of the 1875 Remington S.A. Army revolver. Brass trigger guard, color case-hardened frame, rest blued. Imported by Uberti U.S.A.
Price: $435.00
Price: 45 Colt/45 ACP convertible $475.00

UBERTI 1890 ARMY OUTLAW REVOLVER
Caliber: 357 Mag., 44-40, 45 Colt, 45 Colt/45 ACP convertible, 6-shot.
Barrel: 5½", 7½".
Weight: 37 oz. **Length:** 12½" overall.
Stocks: American walnut.
Sights: Blade front, groove rear.
Features: Replica of the 1890 Remington single-action. Brass trigger guard, rest is blued. Imported by Uberti U.S.A.
Price: $435.00
Price: 45 Colt/45 ACP convertible $475.00

HANDGUNS—MISCELLANEOUS
Specially adapted single-shot and multi-barrel arms.

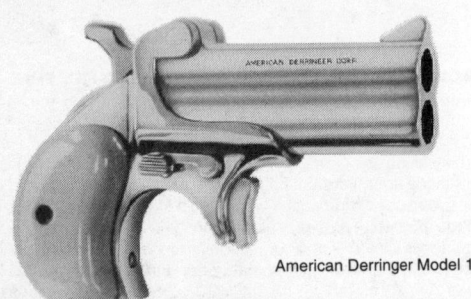
American Derringer Model 1

AMERICAN DERRINGER MODEL 1
Caliber: 22 LR, 22 WMR, 30 Carbine, 30 Luger, 30-30 Win., 32 H&R Mag., 32-20, 380 ACP, 38 Super, 38 Spec., 38 Spec. shotshell, 38 Spec. +P, 9mm Para., 357 Mag., 357 Mag./45/410, 357 Maximum, 10mm, 40 S&W, 41 Mag., 38-40, 44-40 Win., 44 Spec., 44 Mag., 45 Colt, 45 Win. Mag., 45 ACP, 45 Colt/410, 45-70 single shot.

Barrel: 3".
Weight: 15½ oz. (38 Spec.). **Length:** 4.82" overall.
Stocks: Rosewood, Zebra wood.
Sights: Blade front.
Features: Made of stainless steel with high-polish or satin finish. Two-shot capacity. Manual hammer block safety. Introduced 1980. Available in almost any pistol caliber. Contact the factory for complete list of available calibers and prices. From American Derringer Corp.
Price: 22 LR $245.00
Price: 38 Spec. $245.00
Price: 357 Maximum $265.00
Price: 357 Mag. $257.00
Price: 9mm, 380, ...$245.00
Price: 40 S&W $257.00
Price: 44 Spec., ...$320.00
Price: 44-40 Win., 45 Colt $320.00
Price: 30-30, 41, 44 Mags., 45 Win. Mag. ....$375.00 to $385.00
Price: 45-70, single shot $312.00
Price: 45 Colt, 410, 2½" $320.00
Price: 45 ACP, 10mm Auto $257.00

HANDGUNS—MISCELLANEOUS

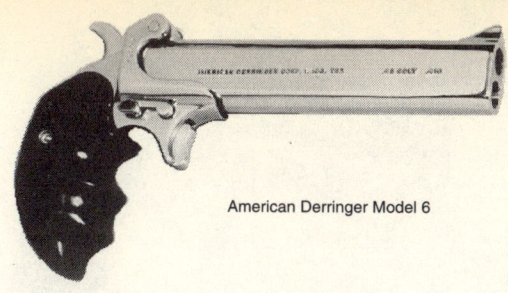
American Derringer Model 6

American Derringer Model 7 Ultra Lightweight
Similar to Model 1 except made of high strength aircraft aluminum. Weighs 7½ oz., 4.82" o.a.l., rosewood stocks. Available in 22 LR, 22 WMR, 32 H&R Mag., 380 ACP, 38 Spec., 44 Spec. Introduced 1986.
Price: 22 LR, WMR $240.00
Price: 38 Spec. $240.00
Price: 380 ACP $240.00
Price: 32 H&R Mag. $240.00
Price: 44 Spec. $500.00

American Derringer Lady Derringer
Same as the Model 1 except has tuned action, is fitted with scrimshawed synthetic ivory grips; chambered for 32 H&R Mag. and 38 Spec.; 357 Mag., 45 Colt. Deluxe Grade is highly polished; Deluxe Engraved is engraved in a pattern similar to that used on 1880s derringers. All come in a French fitted jewelry box. Introduced 1991.
Price: 32 H&R Mag. $280.00
Price: 357 Mag. $300.00
Price: 38 Spec. $200.00
Price: 45 Colt $345.00

ANSCHUTZ EXEMPLAR BOLT-ACTION PISTOL
Caliber: 22 LR, 5-shot; 22 Hornet, 5-shot.
Barrel: 10".
Weight: 3½ lbs. **Length:** 17" overall.
Stock: European walnut with stippled grip and forend.
Sights: Hooded front on ramp, open notch rear adjustable for windage and elevation.
Features: Uses Match 64 action with left-hand bolt; Anschutz #5091 two-stage trigger set at 9.85 oz. Receiver grooved for scope mounting; open sights easily removed. The 22 Hornet version uses Match 54 action with left-hand bolt, Anschutz #5099 two-stage trigger set at 19.6 oz. Introduced 1987. Imported from Germany by AcuSport Corp.
Price: 22 LR $580.75
Price: 22 LR, left-hand $473.14
Price: 22 Hornet (no sights, 10" bbl.) $1,009.89

DAVIS DERRINGERS
Caliber: 22 LR, 5-shot; 22 Hornet, 5-shot.
Barrel: 2.4".
Weight: 9.5 oz. **Length:** 4" overall.
Stocks: Laminated wood.
Sights: Blade front, fixed notch rear.
Features: Choice of black Teflon or chrome finish; spur trigger. Introduced 1986. Made in U.S. by Davis Industries.
Price: $75.00

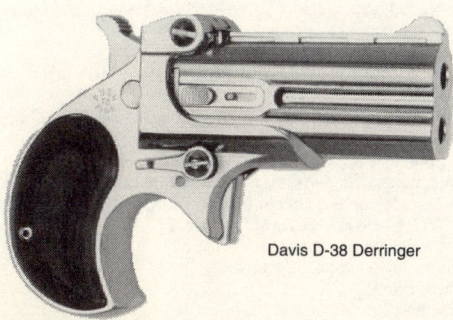
Davis D-38 Derringer

American Derringer Model 4
Similar to the Model 1 except has 4.1" barrel, overall length of 6", and weighs 16½ oz.; chambered for 357 Mag., 357 Maximum, 45-70, 3" 410-bore shotshells or 45 Colt or 44 Mag. Made of stainless steel. Manual hammer block safety. Introduced 1985.
Price: 3" 410/45 Colt $352.00
Price: 3" 410/45 Colt or 45-70 (Alaskan Survival model) $388.00
Price: 44 Mag. with oversize grips $422.00
Price: Alaskan Survival model (45-70 upper, 410 or 45 Colt lower) ...$388.00

American Derringer Model 6
Similar to the Model 1 except has 6" barrel chambered for 3" 410 shotshells or 22 WMR, 357 Mag., 45 ACP, 45 Colt; rosewood stocks; 8.2" o.a.l. and weighs 21 oz. Shoots either round for each barrel. Manual hammer block safety. Introduced 1986.
Price: 22 WMR $300.00
Price: 357 Mag. $300.00
Price: 45 Colt/410 ....$363.00
Price: 45 ACP $345.00

American Derringer Model 10 Lightweight
Similar to the Model 1 except frame is of aluminum, giving weight of 10 oz. Stainless barrels. Available in 38 Spec., 45 Colt or 45 ACP only. Matte gray finish. Introduced 1989.
Price: 45 Colt $320.00
Price: 45 ACP $257.00
Price: 38 Spec. $240.00

American Derringer Texas Commemorative
A Model 1 Derringer with solid brass frame, stainless steel barrel and rosewood grips. Available in 38 Spec., 44-40 Win., or 45 Colt. Introduced 1987.
Price: 38 Spec. $280.00
Price: 44-40 or 45 Colt $345.00

AMERICAN DERRINGER DA 38 MODEL
Caliber: 22 LR, 9mm Para., 38 Spec., 357 Mag., 40 S&W.
Barrel: 3".
Weight: 14.5 oz. **Length:** 4.8" overall.
Stocks: Rosewood, walnut or other hardwoods.
Sights: Fixed.
Features: Double-action only; two-shots. Manual safety. Made of satin-finished stainless steel and aluminum. Introduced 1989. From American Derringer Corp.
Price: 22 LR, 38 Spec. $300.00
Price: 9mm Para. $325.00
Price: 357 Mag., 40 S&W $350.00

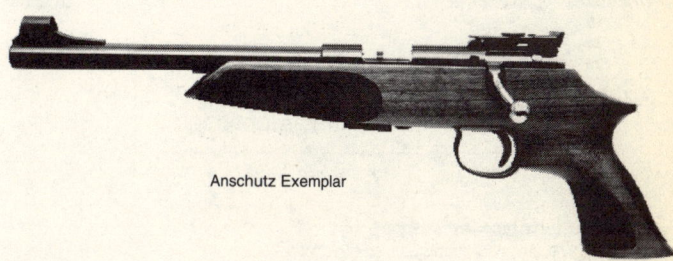
Anschutz Exemplar

DAVIS LONG-BORE DERRINGERS
Caliber: 22 WMR, 32 H&R Mag., 38 Spec., 9mm Para.
Barrel: 3.5".
Weight: 16 oz. **Length:** 5.4" overall.
Stocks: Textured black synthetic.
Sights: Fixed.
Features: Chrome or black teflon finish. Larger than Davis D-Series models. Introduced 1995. Made in U.S. by Davis Industries.
Price: $104.00
Price: Big-Bore models (same calibers, ¾" shorter barrels) $98.00

DAVIS D-SERIES DERRINGERS
Caliber: 22 WMR, 32 H&R, 38 Spec..
Barrel: 2.75".
Weight: 11.5 oz. **Length:** 4.65" overall.
Stocks: Textured black synthetic.
Sights: Blade front, fixed notch rear.
Features: Alloy frame, steel-lined barrels, steel breech block. Plunger-type safety with integral hammer block. Chrome or black Teflon finish. Introduced 1992. Made in U.S. by Davis Industries.
Price: $98.00

HANDGUNS—MISCELLANEOUS

HJS LONE STAR DERRINGER
Caliber: 380 ACP.
Barrel: 2".
Weight: 6 oz. **Length:** 3¹⁵/₁₆" overall.
Stocks: Brown plastic.
Sights: Groove.
Features: Stainless steel construction. Beryllium copper firing pin. Button-rifled barrel. Introduced 1993. Made in U.S. by HJS Arms, Inc.
Price: $185.00

HJS FRONTIER FOUR DERRINGER
Caliber: 22 LR.
Barrel: 2".
Weight: 5½ oz. **Length:** 3¹⁵/₁₆" overall.
Stocks: Brown plastic.
Sights: None.
Features: Four barrels fire with rotating firing pin. Stainless steel construction. Introduced 1993. Made in U.S. by HJS Arms, Inc.
Price: $165.00

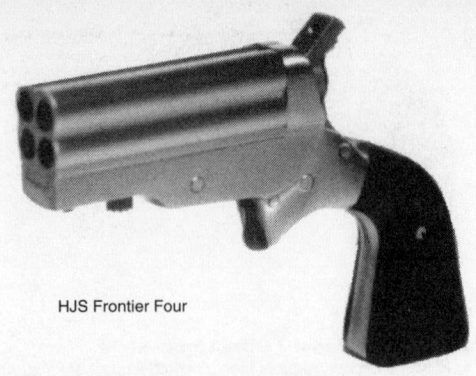
HJS Frontier Four

HJS Antigua Derringer
Same as the Frontier Four except blued barrel, brass frame, brass pivot pins. Brown plastic grips. Introduced 1994. Made in U.S. by HJS Arms, Inc.
Price: $180.00

GAUCHER GN1 SILHOUETTE PISTOL
Caliber: 22 LR, single shot.
Barrel: 10".
Weight: 2.4 lbs. **Length:** 15.5" overall.
Stocks: European hardwood.
Sights: Blade front, open adjustable rear.
Features: Bolt action, adjustable trigger. Introduced 1990. Imported from France by Mandall Shooting Supplies.
Price: About $525.00
Price: Model GP Silhouette $425.00

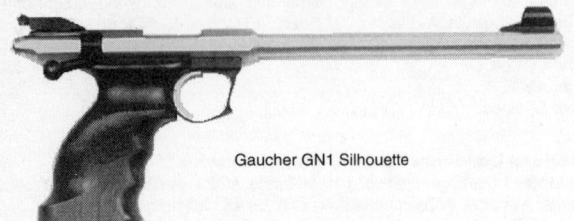
Gaucher GN1 Silhouette

MAGNUM RESEARCH LONE EAGLE SINGLE SHOT PISTOL
Caliber: 22 Hornet, 223, 22-250, 243, 7mm BR, 7mm-08, 30-30, 7.62x39, 308, 30-06, 357 Max., 35 Rem., 358 Win., 44 Mag., 444 Marlin.
Barrel: 14", interchangable.
Weight: 4lbs, 3 oz. to 4 lbs, 7 oz. **Length:** 15" overall.
Stocks: Ambidextrous.
Sights: None furnished; drilled and tapped for scope mounting and open sights. Open sights optional.
Features: Cannon-type rotating breech with spring-activated ejector. Ordnance steel with matte blue finish. Cross-bolt safety. External cocking lever on left side of gun. Introduced 1991. Available from Magnum Research, Inc.
Price: Complete pistol $408.00
Price: Barreled action only $289.00
Price: Scope base $14.00
Price: Adjustable open sights $35.00

LORCIN OVER/UNDER DERRINGER
Caliber: 38 Spec./357 Mag., 45 ACP.
Barrel: 3.5".
Weight: NA. **Length:** 6.5" overall.
Stocks: Black composition.
Sights: Blade front, fixed rear.
Features: Stainless steel construction. Rebounding hammer. Introduced 1996. Made in U.S. by Lorcin Engineering.
Price: $129.00

> Consult our Directory pages for the location of firms mentioned.

Magnum Research Lone Eagle

MANDALL/CABANAS PISTOL
Caliber: 177, pellet or round ball; single shot.
Barrel: 9".
Weight: 51 oz. **Length:** 19" overall.
Stock: Smooth wood with thumbrest.
Sights: Blade front on ramp, open adjustable rear.
Features: Fires round ball or pellets with 22 blank cartridge. Automatic safety; muzzlebrake. Imported from Mexico by Mandall Shooting Supplies.
Price: $139.95

MAXIMUM SINGLE SHOT PISTOL
Caliber: 22 LR, 22 Hornet, 22 BR, 22 PPC, 223 Rem., 22-250, 6mm BR, 6mm PPC, 243, 250 Savage, 6.5mm-35M, 270 MAX, 270 Win., 7mm TCU, 7mm BR, 7mm-35, 7mm INT-R, 7mm-08, 7mm Rocket, 7mm Super Mag., 30 Herrett, 30 Carbine, 30-30, 308 Win., 30x39, 32-20, 350 Rem. Mag., 357 Mag., 357 Maximum, 358 Win., 44 Mag., 454 Casull.
Barrel: 8¾", 10½", 14".
Weight: 61 oz. (10½" bbl.); 78 oz. (14" bbl.). **Length:** 15", 18½" overall (with 10½" and 14" bbl., respectively).
Stocks: Smooth walnut stocks and forend. Also available with 17° finger groove grip.
Sights: Ramp front, fully adjustable open rear.
Features: Falling block action; drilled and tapped for M.O.A. scope mounts; integral grip frame/receiver; adjustable trigger; Douglas barrel (interchangeable). Introduced 1983. Made in U.S. by M.O.A. Corp.
Price: Stainless receiver, blue barrel $653.00
Price: Stainless receiver, stainless barrel $711.00
Price: Extra blued barrel $164.00
Price: Extra stainless barrel $222.00
Price: Scope mount $52.00

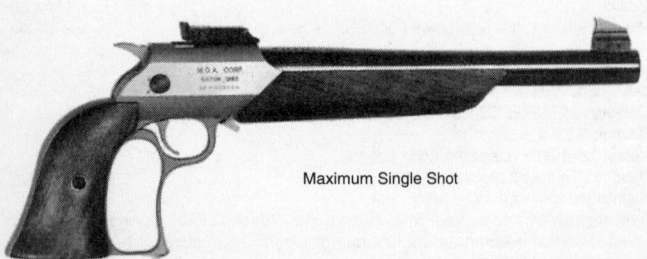
Maximum Single Shot

HANDGUNS—MISCELLANEOUS

MITCHELL ARMS GUARDIAN ANGEL PISTOL
Caliber: 22 LR, 22 WMR, 2-shot.
Barrel: 1 3/4".
Weight: 7 1/2 oz. **Length:** 4 3/4" overall.
Stocks: Checkered black synthetic.
Sights: Fixed channel.
Features: Uses a pre-loaded, drop-in 2-shot removable breechblock; double-action-only. Available in nickel, black nickel, satin steel, gold finishes. Deluxe comes in jewel box with angel charm. Introduced 1996. Made in U.S. by Mitchell Arms.
Price: ....$142.95 to $199.95

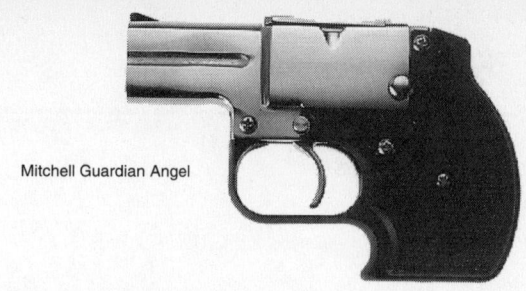
Mitchell Guardian Angel

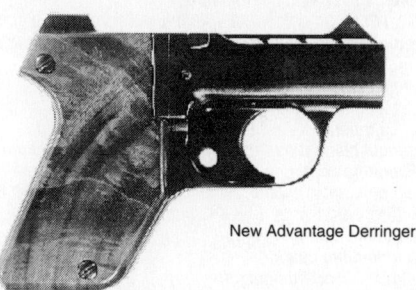
New Advantage Derringer

NEW ADVANTAGE ARMS DERRINGER
Caliber: 22 LR, 22 WMR, 4-shot.
Barrel: 2 1/2".
Weight: 15 oz. **Length:** 4 1/2" overall.
Stocks: Smooth walnut.
Sights: Fixed.
Features: Double-action mechanism, four barrels, revolving hammer with four firing pins. Rebounding hammer. Blue or stainless. Reintroduced 1989. From New Advantage Arms Corp.
Price: 22 LR, 22 WMR, blue, about $249.99
Price: As above, stainless, about $249.99

RPM XL SINGLE SHOT PISTOL
Caliber: 22 LR through 45-70.
Barrel: 8", 10 3/4", 12", 14".
Weight: About 60 oz. **Length:** NA.
Stocks: Smooth Goncalo Alves with thumb and heel rests.
Sights: Hooded front with interchangeable post, or Patridge; ISGW rear adjustable for windage and elevation.
Features: Barrel drilled and tapped for scope mount. Visible cocking indicator. Spring-loaded barrel lock, positive hammer-block safety. Trigger adjustable for weight of pull and over-travel. Contact maker for complete price list. Made in U.S. by RPM.
Price: Hunter model (stainless frame, 5/16" underlug, latch lever and positive extractor) $1,195.00
Price: Silhouette model (chrome-moly frame, blue or hard chrome finish) $857.50
Price: Extra barrel, 8" through 10 3/4" $287.50
Price: Muzzle brake $100.00

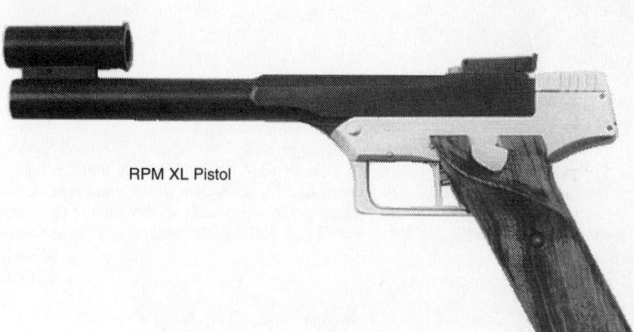
RPM XL Pistol

SUNDANCE POINT BLANK O/U DERRINGER
Caliber: 22 LR, 2-shot.
Barrel: 3".
Weight: 8 oz. **Length:** 4.6" overall.
Stocks: Grooved composition.
Sights: Blade front, fixed notch rear.
Features: Double-action trigger, push-bar safety, automatic chamber selection. Fully enclosed hammer. Matte black finish. Introduced 1994. Made in U.S. by Sundance Industries.
Price: $99.00

Sundance Point Blank

Texas Armory Defender

TEXAS ARMORY DEFENDER DERRINGER
Caliber: 9mm Para., 357 Mag., 44 Mag., 45 ACP, 45 Colt/410.
Barrel: 3".
Weight: 21 oz. **Length:** 5" overall.
Stocks: Smooth wood.
Sights: Blade front, fixed rear.
Features: Interchangeable barrels; retracting firing pins; rebounding hammer; cross-bolt safety; removable trigger guard; automatic extractor. Blasted finish stainless steel. Introduced 1993. Made in U.S. by Texas Armory.
Price: $310.00
Price: Extra barrel $100.00

TEXAS LONGHORN "THE JEZEBEL" PISTOL
Caliber: 22 Short, Long, Long Rifle, single shot.
Barrel: 6".
Weight: 15 oz. **Length:** 8" overall.
Stocks: One-piece fancy walnut grip (right- or left-hand), walnut forend.
Sights: Bead front, fixed rear.
Features: Handmade gun. Top-break action; all stainless steel; automatic hammer block safety; music wire coil springs. Barrel is half-round, half-octagon. Announced 1986. From Texas Longhorn Arms.
Price: About $250.00

THE JUDGE SINGLE SHOT PISTOL
Caliber: 22 Hornet, 22 K-Hornet, 218 Bee, 7-30 Waters, 30-30.
Barrel: 10" or 16.2".
Weight: NA. **Length:** NA.
Stocks: Walnut.
Sights: Bead on ramp front, open adjustable rear.
Features: Break-open design; made of 17-4 stainless steel. Also available as a kit. Introduced 1995. Made in U.S. by Cumberland Mountain Arms.
Price: ....NA

HANDGUNS—MISCELLANEOUS

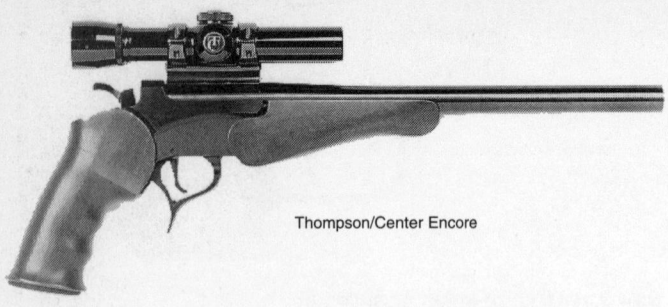
Thompson/Center Encore

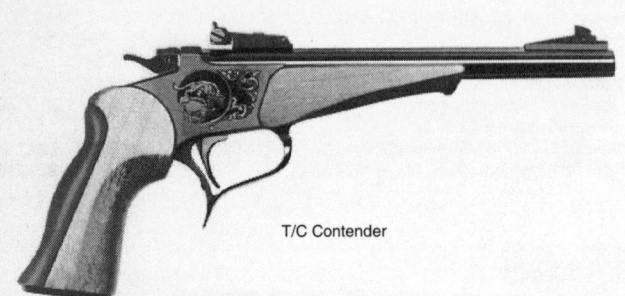
T/C Contender

THOMPSON/CENTER ENCORE PISTOL
Caliber: 22-250, 223, 7mm-08, 308, 30-06, single shot.
Barrel: 10", 15", tapered round.
Weight: NA **Length:** 19" overall with 10" barrel.
Stocks: American walnut with finger grooves, walnut forend.
Sights: Blade on ramp front, adjustable rear, or none.
Features: Interchangeable barrels; action opens by squeezing the trigger guard; drilled and tapped for scope mounting; blue finish. Announced 1996. Made in U.S. by Thompson/Center Arms.
Price: About $500.00

THOMPSON/CENTER CONTENDER
Caliber: 7mm TCU, 30-30 Win., 22 LR, 22 WMR, 22 Hornet, 223 Rem., 270 Ren, 7-30 Waters, 32-20 Win., 357 Mag., 357 Rem. Max., 44 Mag., 10mm Auto, 445 Super Mag., 45/410, single shot.
Barrel: 10", tapered octagon, bull barrel and vent. rib.
Weight: 43 oz. (10" bbl.). **Length:** 13 1/4" (10" bbl.).
Stocks: T/C "Competitor Grip." Right or left hand.
Sights: Under-cut blade ramp front, rear adjustable for windage and elevation.
Features: Break-open action with automatic safety. Single-action only. Interchangeable bbls., both caliber (rim & centerfire), and length. Drilled and tapped for scope. Engraved frame. See T/C catalog for exact barrel/caliber availability.
Price: Blued (rimfire cals.) $463.50
Price: Blued (centerfire cals.) $463.50
Price: Extra bbls. (standard octagon) $213.70
Price: 45/410, internal choke bbl. $218.90

Thompson/Center Stainless Contender
Same as the standard Contender except made of stainless steel with blued sights, black Rynite forend and ambidextrous finger-groove grip with a built-in rubber recoil cushion that has a sealed-in air pocket. Receiver has a different cougar etching. Available with 10" bull barrel in 22 LR, 22 LR Match, 22 Hornet, 223 Rem., 30-30 Win, 357 Mag., 44 Mag., 45 Colt/410. Introduced 1993.
Price: $494.40
Price: 45 Colt/410 ....$499.60
Price: With 22 LR match chamber $504.70

Thompson/Center Contender Hunter Package
Package contains the Contender pistol in 223, 7-30 Waters, 30-30, 375 Win., 357 Rem. Maximum, 35 Rem., 44 Mag. or 45-70 with 14" barrel with T/C's Muzzle Tamer, a 2.5x Recoil Proof Long Eye Relief scope with lighted reticle, q.d. sling swivels with a nylon carrying sling. Comes with a suede leather case with foam padding and fleece lining. Introduced 1990. From Thompson/Center Arms.
Price: Blued $798.00
Price: Stainless $829.00

Thompson/Center Stainless Super 14, Super 16 Contender
Same as the standard Super 14 and Super 16 except they are made of stainless steel with blued sights. Both models have black Rynite forend and finger-groove, ambidextrous grip with a built-in rubber recoil cushion that has a sealed-in air pocket. Receiver has a different cougar etching. Available in 22 LR, 22 LR Match, 22 Hornet, 223 Rem., 30-30 Win., 35 Rem. (Super 14), 45-70 (Super 16 only), 45 Colt/410. Introduced 1993.
Price: 14" bull barrel $504.70
Price: 16 1/4" bull barrel $509.90
Price: 45 Colt/410, 14" $535.60
Price: 45 Colt/410, 16" $530.50

UBERTI ROLLING BLOCK TARGET PISTOL
Caliber: 22 LR, 22 WMR, 22 Hornet, 357 Mag., 45 Colt, single shot.
Barrel: 9 7/8", half-round, half-octagon.
Weight: 44 oz. **Length:** 14" overall.
Stocks: Walnut grip and forend.
Sights: Blade front, fully adjustable rear.
Features: Replica of the 1871 rolling block target pistol. Brass trigger guard, color case-hardened frame, blue barrel. Imported by Uberti U.S.A.
Price: $410.00

Ultra Light Model 20

ULTRA LIGHT ARMS MODEL 20 REB HUNTER'S PISTOL
Caliber: 22-250 thru 308 Win. standard. Most silhouette calibers and others on request. 5-shot magazine.
Barrel: 14", Douglas No. 3.
Weight: 4 lbs.
Stock: Composite Kevlar, graphite reinforced. Du Pont Imron paint in green, brown, black and camo.
Sights: None furnished. Scope mount included.
Features: Timney adjustable trigger; two-position, three-function safety; benchrest quality action; matte or bright stock and metal finish; right- or left-hand action. Shipped in hard case. Introduced 1987. From Ultra Light Arms.
Price: $1,600.00

VOERE VEC-95CG SINGLE SHOT PISTOL
Caliber: 5.56mm, 6mm UCC caseless, single shot.
Barrel: 12", 14".
Weight: 3 lbs. **Length:** NA.
Stock: Black synthetic; center grip.
Sights: None furnished.
Features: Fires caseless ammunition via electronic ignition; two batteries in the grip last about 500 shots. Bolt action has two forward locking lugs. Tang safety. Drilled and tapped for scope mounting. Introduced 1995. Imported from Austria by JagerSport, Ltd.
Price: $1,495.00

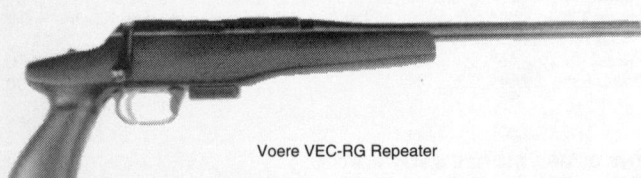
Voere VEC-RG Repeater

Voere VEC-RG Repeater pistol
Similar to the VEC-95CG except has rear grip stock and detachable 5-shot magazine. Available with 12" or 14" barrel. Introduced 1995. Imported from Austria by JagerSport, Ltd.
Price: $1,495.00

CENTERFIRE RIFLES—AUTOLOADERS

Both classic arms and recent designs in American-style repeaters for sport and field shooting.

AA ARMS AR9 SEMIAUTOMATIC RIFLE
Caliber: 9mm Para., 10-shot magazine.
Barrel: 16".
Weight: 6 lbs. Length: 31" overall.
Stock: Folding metal skeleton.
Sights: Post front adjustable for elevation, open rear for windage.
Features: Ventilated barrel shroud. Blue or electroless nickel finish. Made in U.S. by AA Arms, Inc.
Price: Blue $695.00

ARMALITE AR-10A4 RIFLE
Caliber: 308 Win., 10-slot magazine.
Barrel: 20" HBAR, 1:12" twist.
Weight: 9.75 lbs. Length: 41.5" overall.
Stock: Black composition.
Sights: Optional. Has Weaver-type rail.
Features: One-piece international-style flattop receiver; three-slot Picatinny rail gas system. Optional NM two-stage trigger; detachable carry handle with NM sight; detachable front sight assembly; scope mount; stainless barrel. Introduced 1995. Made in U.S. by ArmaLite, Inc.
Price: $1,325.00

ArmaLite M15A2 Heavy Barrel

ARMALITE M15A2 POST BAN HEAVY BARREL RIFLE
Caliber: 223, 10-shot magazine.
Barrel: 20" heavy, 1:9" twist.
Weight: 9.75 lbs. Length: 39.5" overall.
Stock: Black composition.
Sights: Elevation-adjustable front, E-2-style NM rear with 1/2-MOA adjustments.
Features: Upper and lower receivers have push-type pivot pin; hard-coat anodized; A2-style forward assist; M-16A2-type raised fence around magazine release button; recoil check brake. Introduced 1995. Made in U.S. by ArmaLite, Inc.
Price: $895.00

Manufacturers' addresses in the
Directory of the Arms Trade
page 313, this issue

ArmaLite M15A4 Post Ban M4A1C Carbine
Similar to the M15A2 Heavy Barrel rifle except has 16" heavy barrel with 1:9" twist; one-piece international-style flattop receiver with Picatinny (Weaver-type) rail including case deflector; detachable carry handle assembly; NM sights. Introduced 1995. Made in U.S. by ArmaLite, Inc.
Price: $935.00

ARMALITE M15A2 POST BAN GOLDEN EAGLE RIFLE
Caliber: 223, 10-shot magazine.
Barrel: 20", heavy premium stainless, 1:8" twist, 1.2" diameter.
Weight: 10.75 lbs. Length: 38.25" overall.
Stock: Black composition.
Sights: NM .050" front, NM rear with 1/4 MOA wandage, 1/2 MOA elevation.
Features: DCM approved; ArmaLite NM two-stage trigger; A2-style forward assist; hard-coat anodized receivers. Introduced 1995. Made in U.S. by ArmaLite, Inc.
Price: $1,200.00

ArmaLite M4C Carbine

ArmaLite M15A2 Post Ban M4C Carbine
Similar to the M15A2 Heavy Barrel rifle except has 16" heavy barrel with 1:9" twist. Weighs 8.25 lbs., overall length 35.4". Introduced 1996. Made in U.S. by ArmaLite, Inc.
Price: $870.00

Thompson M1

Auto-Ordnance Thompson M1
Similar to the Model 27 A-1 except is in the M-1 configuration with side cocking knob, horizontal forend, smooth unfinned barrel, sling swivels on butt and forend. Matte black finish. Introduced 1985.
Price: $772.50

AUTO-ORDNANCE 27 A-1 THOMPSON
Caliber: 45 ACP, 30-shot magazine.
Barrel: 16".
Weight: 11 1/2 lbs. Length: About 42" overall (Deluxe).
Stock: Walnut stock and vertical forend.
Sights: Blade front, open rear adjustable for windage.
Features: Recreation of Thompson Model 1927. Semi-auto only. Deluxe model has finned barrel, adjustable rear sight and compensator; Standard model has plain barrel and military sight. From Auto-Ordnance Corp.
Price: Deluxe $795.00
Price: 1927A1C Lightweight model $767.00

CAUTION: PRICES SHOWN ARE SUPPLIED BY THE MANUFACTURER OR IMPORTER. CHECK YOUR LOCAL GUN SHOP.

CENTERFIRE RIFLES—AUTOLOADERS

Barrett Model 82A-1

BARRETT MODEL 82A-1 SEMI-AUTOMATIC RIFLE
Caliber: 50 BMG, 10-shot detachable box magazine.
Barrel: 29".
Weight: 28.5 lbs. **Length:** 57" overall.
Stock: Composition with Sorbothane recoil pad.
Sights: Scope optional.
Features: Semi-automatic, recoil operated with recoiling barrel. Three-lug locking bolt; muzzlebrake. Self-leveling bipod. Fires same 50-cal. ammunition as the M2HB machinegun. Introduced 1985. From Barrett Firearms.
Price: From $6,800.00

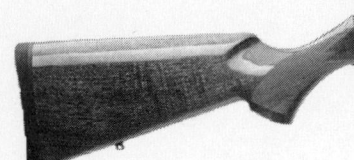

Browning Mark II Safari

BROWNING BAR MARK II SAFARI SEMI-AUTO RIFLE
Caliber: 243, 270, 30-06, 308.
Barrel: 22" round tapered.
Weight: 7 3/8 lbs. **Length:** 43" overall.
Stock: French walnut pistol grip stock and forend, hand checkered.
Sights: Gold bead on hooded ramp front, click adjustable rear, or no sights.
Features: Has new bolt release lever; removable trigger assembly with larger trigger guard; redesigned gas and buffer systems. Detachable 4-round box magazine. Scroll-engraved receiver is tapped for scope mounting. BOSS barrel vibration modulator and muzzlebrake system available only on models without sights. Mark II Safari introduced 1993. Imported from Belgium by Browning.
Price: Safari, with sights $729.95
Price: Safari, no sights $713.95
Price: Safari, no sights, BOSS $811.95

Browning BAR Mark II Safari Magnum Rifle
Same as the standard caliber model, except weighs 8 3/8 lbs., 45" overall, 24" bbl., 3-round mag. Cals. 7mm Mag., 300 Win. Mag., 338 Win. Mag. BOSS barrel vibration modulator and muzzlebrake system available only on models without sights. Introduced 1993.
Price: Safari, with sights $781.95
Price: Safari, no sights $765.95
Price: Safari, no sights, BOSS $863.95

BUSHMASTER SHORTY XM-15 E2S CARBINE
Caliber: 223, 30-shot magazine.
Barrel: 16", heavy; 1:9" twist.
Weight: 7.3 lbs. **Length:** 34.5" overall.
Stock: Fixed black composition.
Sights: Adjustable post front, adjustable aperture rear.
Features: Patterned after Colt M-16A2. Chrome-lined barrel with manganese phosphate finish. "Shorty" handguards. Has E-2 lower receiver with push-pin. Made in U.S. by Bushmaster Firearms Inc./Quality Parts Co.
Price: $730.00
Price: XM-15 E-2S Dissipator ("Dissipator" full-length handguard) $740.00

BUSHMASTER M17S BULLPUP RIFLE
Caliber: 223, 10-shot magazine.
Barrel: 21.5", heavy; 1:9" twist.
Weight: 8.2 lbs. **Length:** 30" overall.
Stock: Fiberglass-filled nylon.
Sights: Has 25-meter open emergency sights; designed for optics mounted to rail on carrying handle for Weaver-type rings.
Features: Gas-operated, short-stroke piston system; ambidextrous magazine release. Introduced 1993. Made in U.S. by Bushmaster Firearms, Inc./Quality Parts Co.
Price: $575.00

CALICO LIBERTY 50, 100 CARBINES
Caliber: 9mm Para.
Barrel: 16.1".
Weight: 7 lbs. **Length:** 34.5" overall.
Stock: Glass-filled, impact resistant polymer.
Sights: Adjustable front post, fixed notch and aperture flip rear.
Features: Helical feed magazine; ambidextrous, rotating sear/striker block safety; static cocking handle; retarded blowback action; aluminum alloy receiver. Introduced 1995. Made in U.S. by Calico.
Price: Liberty 50 ....$503.00
Price: Liberty 100 ....$517.00

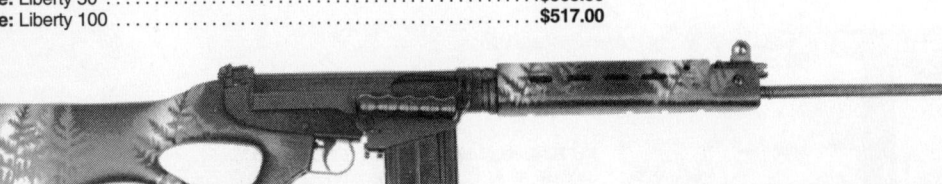

Calico Liberty 50

Century FAL Sporter

CENTURY INTERNATIONAL FAL SPORTER RIFLE
Caliber: 308 Win.
Barrel: 20.75".
Weight: 9 lbs., 13 oz. **Length:** 41.125" overall.
Stock: Bell & Carlson thumbhole sporter.
Sights: Protected post front, adjustable aperture rear.
Features: Matte blue finish; rubber butt pad. From Century International Arms.
Price: About $625.00

CENTERFIRE RIFLES—AUTOLOADERS

CENTURY INTERNATIONAL M-14 SEMI-AUTO RIFLE
Caliber: 308 Win., 10-shot magazine.
Barrel: 22".
Weight: 8.25 lbs. **Length:** 40.8" overall.
Stock: Walnut with rubber recoil pad.
Sights: Protected blade front, fully adjustable aperture rear.
Features: Gas-operated; forged receiver; Parkerized finish. Imported from China by Century International Arms.
Price: About $468.95

CENTURY TIGER DRAGUNOV RIFLE
Caliber: 7.62x54R, 5-shot magazine.
Barrel: 20.8".
Weight: 8.5 lbs. **Length:** 42.9" overall.
Stock: Thumbhole design of laminated European hardwood, black composition forend.
Sights: Blade front, open rear adjustable for elevation; comes with 4x rangefinding scope with sunshade, lighted reticle.
Features: Shortened version of Russian SVD sniper rifle. New manufacture. Blued metal. Quick-detachable scope mount. Comes with sling, cleaning kit, gas regulator tool, case. Imported from Russia by Century International Arms.
Price: About $1,350.00

Colt Match Target Lightweight

COLT MATCH TARGET LIGHTWEIGHT RIFLE
Caliber: 9mm Para., 223 Rem., 7.62x39mm, 5-shot magazine.
Barrel: 16".
Weight: 6.7 lbs. (223); 7.1 lbs. (9mm Para.). **Length:** 34.5" overall.
Stock: Composition stock, grip, forend.
Sights: Post front, rear adjustable for windage and elevation.
Features: 5-round detachable box magazine, flash suppressor, sling swivels. Forward bolt assist included. Introduced 1991.
Price: $987.00
Price: 7.62x39mm $987.00

Daewoo DR200

DAEWOO DR200 DR300 AUTOLOADING RIFLES
Caliber: 223 Rem., 7.62x39mm, 6-shot magazine.
Barrel: 18.3".
Weight: 9 lbs. **Length:** 39.2" overall.
Stock: Synthetic thumbhole style with rubber buttpad.
Sights: Post front in ring, aperture rear adjustable for windage and elevation.
Features: Forged aluminum receiver; bolt, bolt carrier, firing pin, piston and recoil spring contained in one assembly. Rotating bolt locking. Uses all AR-15 magazines. Introduced 1995. Imported from Korea by Kimber of America, Inc.
Price: DR200, 223 Rem. $535.00
Price: DR300, 7.62x39mm $750.00

Eagle Arms M15A2

Eagle Arms M4C Carbine
Collapsible carbine-type buttstock, 16" heavy carbine barrel. Has M15A2-style upper receiver; full front sight housing; M177-type flash supressor. Weighs about 7 lbs., 3 oz. Introduced 1989. Made in U.S. by Eagle Arms, Inc.
Price: $1,100.00
Price: M4A1C (as above except one-piece international-style upper receiver for scope mounting) $1,100.00

EAGLE ARMS M15A2 POST-BAN HEAVY BARREL RIFLE
Caliber: 223 Rem., 10-shot magazine.
Barrel: 20", premium, heavy; 1:9" twist.
Weight: 8 lbs., 2 oz. **Length:** 38 3/8" overall.
Stock: Black composition; weighted.
Sights: Elevation-adjustable front, E-2-style NM rear with 1/2-MOA adjustments, NM aperture.
Features: Upper and lower receivers have push-type pivot pin for easy takedown. Receivers hard coat anodized. A2-style forward assist mechanism. Integral raised M-16A2-type fence around magazine release button. Introduced 1995. Made in U.S. by Eagle Arms, Inc.
Price: $895.00

Hi-Point 9mm Carbine

HI-POINT 9mm CARBINE
Caliber: 9mm Para., 10-shot magazine.
Barrel: 16 1/2".
Weight: NA. **Length:** 31 1/2" overall.
Stock: Black polymer.
Sights: Protected post front, aperture rear. Integral scope mount.
Features: Grip-mounted magazine release. Parkerized or chrome finish. Sling swivels. Introduced 1996. Made in U.S. by MKS Supply, Inc.
Price: $169.00

CAUTION: PRICES SHOWN ARE SUPPLIED BY THE MANUFACTURER OR IMPORTER. CHECK YOUR LOCAL GUN SHOP.

CENTERFIRE RIFLES—AUTOLOADERS

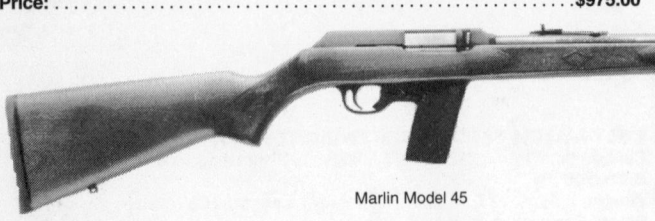

IBUS M17S Bullpup

IBUS M17S 223 BULLPUP RIFLE
Caliber: 223, 10-shot magazine.
Barrel: 21.5".
Weight: 8.2 lbs. **Length:** 30" overall.
Stock: Zytel glass-filled nylon.
Sights: None furnished. Comes with scope mount for Weaver-type rings.
Features: Gas-operated, short-stroke piston system. Ambidextrous magazine release. Introduced 1993. Made in U.S. by Bushmaster Firearms Inc./Quality Parts Co.
Price: $975.00

Marlin Model 45

Marlin Model 45 Carbine
Similar to the Model 9 except chambered for 45 ACP, 7-shot magazine. Introduced 1986.
Price: $424.40

MARLIN MODEL 9 CAMP CARBINE
Caliber: 9mm Para., 12-shot magazine.
Barrel: 16 1/2", Micro-Groove® rifling.
Weight: 6 3/4 lbs. **Length:** 35 1/2" overall.
Stock: Press-checkered walnut-finished Maine birch; rubber buttpad; Mar-Shield™ finish; swivel studs.
Sights: Ramp front with orange post, cutaway Wide-Scan™ hood, adjustable open rear.
Features: Manual bolt hold-open; Garand-type safety, magazine safety; loaded chamber indicator; receiver drilled, tapped for scope mounting. Introduced 1985.
Price: $424.40

Mitchell Arms LW9

MITCHELL ARMS LW9 SEMI-AUTO CARBINE
Caliber: 9mm Para., 10-shot magazine.
Barrel: 17".
Weight: 5 lbs. **Length:** 35" overall.
Stock: Black foam or fixed skeleton.
Sights: Protected post front, adjustable aperture rear.
Features: Blue finish; removable stock and barrel. Introduced 1996. Made in U.S. by Mitchell Arms.
Price: Skeleton stock $499.95
Price: Black foam stock $534.95

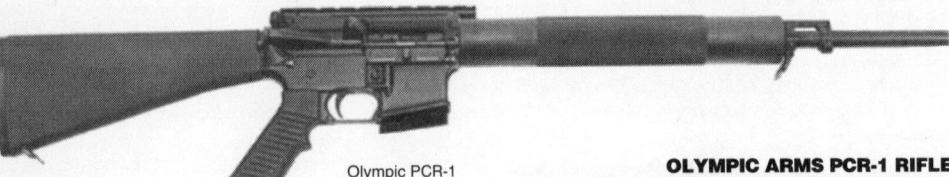

Olympic PCR-1

Olympic Arms PCR-2, PCR-3 Rifles
Similar to the PCR-1 except has 16" barrel, weighs 8 lbs., 2 oz.; has post front sight, fully adjustable aperture rear. Model PCR-3 has flattop upper receiver, cut-down front sight base. Introduced 1994. Made in U.S. by Olympic Arms, Inc.
Price: $1,025.00

OLYMPIC ARMS PCR-1 RIFLE
Caliber: 223, 10-shot magazine.
Barrel: 20", 24"; 416 stainless steel.
Weight: 10 lbs., 3 oz. **Length:** 38.25" overall with 20" barrel.
Stock: A2 stowaway grip and trapdoor butt.
Sights: None supplied; flattop upper receiver, cut-down front sight base.
Features: Based on the AR-15 rifle. Broach-cut, free-floating barrel with 1:8.5" or 1:10" twist. No bayonet lug. Crowned barrel; fluting available. Introduced 1994. Made in U.S. by Olympic Arms, Inc.
Price: $1,100.00

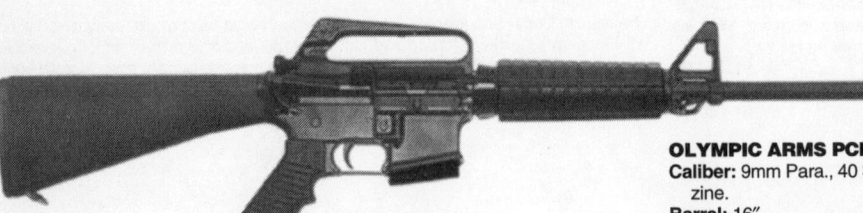

Olympic PCR-5

OLYMPIC ARMS PCR-4 RIFLE
Caliber: 223, 10-shot magazine.
Barrel: 20".
Weight: 8 lbs., 5 oz. **Length:** 38.25" overall.
Stock: A2 stowaway grip, trapdoor buttstock.
Sights: Post front, A1 rear adjustable for windage.
Features: Based on the AR-15 rifle. Barrel is button rifled with 1:9" twist. No bayonet lug. Introduced 1994. Made in U.S. by Olympic Arms, Inc.
Price: $810.00

OLYMPIC ARMS PCR-5, PCR-6 RIFLES
Caliber: 9mm Para., 40 S&W, 45 ACP, 223, 7.62x39mm (PCR-6), 10-shot magazine.
Barrel: 16".
Weight: 7 lbs. **Length:** 34.75" overall.
Stock: A2 stowaway grip, trapdoor buttstock.
Sights: Post front, A1 rear adjustable for windage.
Features: Based on the CAR-15. No bayonet lug. Button-cut rifling. Introduced 1994. Made in U.S. by Olympic Arms, Inc.
Price: 9mm Para., 40 S&W, 45 ACP $820.00
Price: 223 Rem. $775.00
Price: 7.62x39mm (PCR-6) $835.00

CENTERFIRE RIFLES—AUTOLOADERS

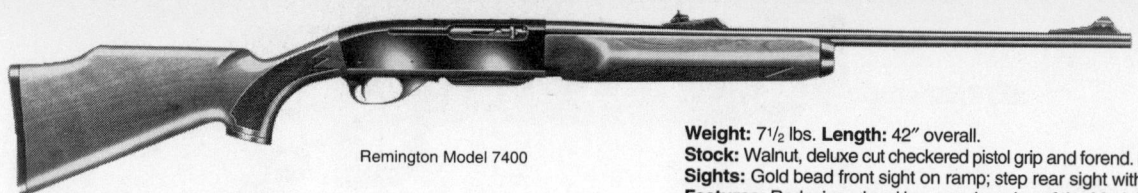

Remington Model 7400

REMINGTON MODEL 7400 AUTO RIFLE
Caliber: 243 Win., 270 Win., 280 Rem., 308 Win., 30-06, 4-shot magazine.
Barrel: 22" round tapered.
Weight: 7½ lbs. **Length:** 42" overall.
Stock: Walnut, deluxe cut checkered pistol grip and forend. Satin or high-gloss finish.
Sights: Gold bead front sight on ramp; step rear sight with windage adjustable.
Features: Redesigned and improved version of the Model 742. Positive cross-bolt safety. Receiver tapped for scope mount. Comes with green Remington hard case. Introduced 1981.
Price: About $573.00
Price: Carbine (18½" bbl., 30-06 only) $573.00

Ruger Mini-14/5

Ruger Mini Thirty Rifle
Similar to the Mini-14 Ranch Rifle except modified to chamber the 7.62x39 Russian service round. Weight is about 7 lbs., 3 oz. Has 6-groove barrel with 1:10" twist, Ruger Integral Scope Mount bases and folding peep rear sight. Detachable 5-shot staggered box magazine. Blued finish. Introduced 1987.
Price: Blue $556.00
Price: Stainless $609.00

RUGER MINI-14/5 AUTOLOADING RIFLE
Caliber: 223 Rem., 5-shot detachable box magazine.
Barrel: 18½". Rifling twist 1:9".
Weight: 6.4 lbs. **Length:** 37¼" overall.
Stock: American hardwood, steel reinforced.
Sights: Ramp front, fully adjustable rear.
Features: Fixed piston gas-operated, positive primary extraction. New buffer system, redesigned ejector system. Ruger S100RH scope rings included. 20-, 30-shot magazine available to police departments and government agencies only.
Price: Mini-14/5R, Ranch Rifle, blued, scope rings $556.00
Price: K-Mini-14/5R, Ranch Rifle, stainless, scope rings $609.00
Price: Mini-14/5, blued, no scope rings $516.00
Price: K-Mini-14/5, stainless, no scope rings $569.00

Springfield M1A

SA-85M SEMI-AUTO RIFLE
Caliber: 7.62x39mm, 6-shot magazine.
Barrel: 16.3".
Weight: 7.6 lbs. **Length:** 34.7" overall.
Stock: European hardwood; thumbhole design.
Sights: Post front, lpen adjustable rear.
Features: BATF-approved version of the Kalashnikov rifle. Gas operated. Black phosphate finish. Comes with one magazine, cleaning rod, cleaning/tool kit. Introduced 1995. Imported from Hungary by K.B.I., Inc.
Price: $399.00

SPRINGFIELD, INC. M1A RIFLE
Caliber: 7.62mm NATO (308), 5-, 10- or 20-shot box magazine.
Barrel: 25 1/16" with flash suppressor, 22" without suppressor.
Weight: 8¾ lbs. **Length:** 44¼" overall.
Stock: American walnut with walnut-colored heat-resistant fiberglass handguard. Matching walnut handguard available. Also available with fiberglass stock.
Sights: Military, square blade front, full click-adjustable aperture rear.
Features: Commercial equivalent of the U.S. M-14 service rifle with no provision for automatic firing. From Springfield, Inc.
Price: Standard M1A rifle, about $1,329.00
Price: National Match, about $1,670.00
Price: Super Match (heavy premium barrel), about $1,980.00
Price: M1A-A1 Bush Rifle, walnut stock, about $1,359.00

Springfield SAR-8

> Consult our Directory pages for the location of firms mentioned.

SPRINGFIELD, INC. SAR-4800 RIFLE
Caliber: 5.56, 7.62 NATO (308 Win.), 20-shot magazine.
Barrel: 21".
Weight: 9.5 lbs. **Length:** 43.3" overall.
Stock: Fiberglass forend, composite thunbhole butt.
Sights: Protected post front, adjustable peep rear.
Features: New production. Reintroduced 1995. From Springfield, Inc.
Price: $1,199.00

SPRINGFIELD, INC. SAR-8 SPORTER RIFLE
Caliber: 308 Win., 20-shot magazine.
Barrel: 18".
Weight: 8.7 lbs. **Length:** 40.3" overall.
Stock: Black composition, thumbhole buttstock.
Sights: Protected post front, rotary-style adjustable rear.
Features: Delayed roller-lock action; fluted chamber; matte black finish. Reintroduced 1995. From Springfield, Inc.
Price: $1,175.00

CAUTION: PRICES SHOWN ARE SUPPLIED BY THE MANUFACTURER OR IMPORTER. CHECK YOUR LOCAL GUN SHOP.

CENTERFIRE RIFLES—AUTOLOADERS

Stoner Sr-25 Sporter

STONER SR-25 SPORTER RIFLE
Caliber: 7.62 NATO, 10-shot steel magazine, 5-shot optional.
Barrel: 20″.
Weight: 8.75 lbs. **Length:** 40″ overall.
Stock: Black synthetic AR-15A2 design, AR-15A2-type synthetic round forend.
Sights: AR-15A2-style front adjustable for elevation, detachable rear is adjustable for windage.
Features: AR-15 trigger; AR-15-style seven-lug rotating bolt. Upper and lower receivers made of lightweight aircraft aluminum alloy. Quick-detachable carrying handle/rear sight assembly. Two-stage target trigger, shell deflector, bore guide, scope rings optional. Introduced 1993. Made in U.S. by Knight's Mfg. Co.
Price: $2,995.00

Stoner SR-25 Carbine
Similar to the SR-25 Sporter except has 16″ light/hunting contour barrel, weighs 7.75 lbs., 36″ overall. No sights furnished; has integral Weaver-style rail. Scope rings, iron sights optional. Introduced 1995. Made in U.S. by Knight's Mfg. Co.
Price: $2,995.00

WILKINSON TERRY CARBINE
Caliber: 9mm Para., 31-shot magazine.
Barrel: 16 3/16″.
Weight: 6 lbs., 3 oz. **Length:** 30″ overall.
Stock: Maple stock and forend.
Sights: Protected post front, aperture rear.
Features: Semi-automatic blowback action fires from a closed breech. Bolt-type safety and magazine catch. Ejection port has automatic trap door. Receiver equipped with dovetail for scope mounting. Made in U.S. From Wilkinson Arms.
Price: $636.29

CENTERFIRE RIFLES—LEVER & SLIDE

Both classic arms and recent designs in American-style repeaters for sport and field shooting.

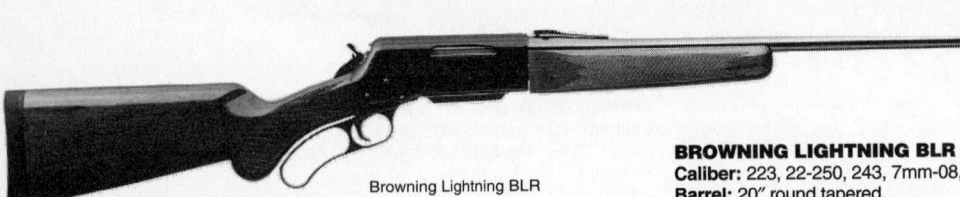
Browning Lightning BLR

Browning Lightning BLR Long Action
Similar to the standard Lightning BLR except has long action to accept 30-06, 270 and 7mm Rem. Mag. Barrel lengths are 22″ for 30-06 and 270, 24″ for 7mm Rem. Mag. Has six-lug rotary bolt; bolt and receiver are full-length fluted. Fold-down hammer at half-cock. Weighs about 7 lbs., overall length 42 7/8″ (22″ barrel). Introduced 1996.
Price: $608.95

CABELA'S CATTLEMAN'S CARBINE
Caliber: 44-40, 6-shot.
Barrel: 18″.
Weight: 4 lbs. **Length:** 34″ overall.
Stock: European walnut.
Sights: Blade front, notch rear.
Features: Revolving carbine. Color case-hardened frame, rest blued. Introduced 1994. Imported by Cabela's.
Price: $299.95

CABELA'S 1858 HENRY REPLICA
Caliber: 44-40, 13-shot magazine.
Barrel: 24 1/4″.
Weight: 9.5 lbs. **Length:** 43″ overall.
Stock: European walnut.
Sights: Bead front, open adjustable rear.
Features: Brass receiver and buttplate. Uses original Henry loading system. Faithful to the original rifle. Introduced 1994. Imported by Mitchell Arms, Inc.
Price: $649.95

CIMARRON 1860 HENRY REPLICA
Caliber: 44 WCF, 13-shot magazine.
Barrel: 24 1/4″ (rifle), 22″ (carbine).
Weight: 9 1/2 lbs. **Length:** 43″ overall (rifle).
Stock: European walnut.
Sights: Bead front, open adjustable rear.
Features: Brass receiver and buttplate. Uses original Henry loading system. Faithful to the original rifle. Introduced 1991. Imported by Cimarron Arms.
Price: $899.95

BROWNING LIGHTNING BLR LEVER-ACTION RIFLE
Caliber: 223, 22-250, 243, 7mm-08, 308 Win., 4-shot detachable magazine.
Barrel: 20″ round tapered.
Weight: 6 lbs., 8 oz. **Length:** 39 1/2″ overall.
Stock: Walnut. Checkered grip and forend, high-gloss finish.
Sights: Gold bead on ramp front; low profile square notch adjustable rear.
Features: Wide, grooved trigger; half-cock hammer safety; fold-down hammer. Receiver tapped for scope mount. Recoil pad installed. Introduced 1996. Imported from Japan by Browning.
Price: $576.95

CABELA'S 1866 WINCHESTER REPLICA
Caliber: 44-40, 13-shot.
Barrel: 24 1/4″.
Weight: 9 lbs. **Length:** 43″ overall.
Stock: European walnut.
Sights: Bead front, open adjustable rear.
Features: Solid brass receiver, buttplate, forend cap. Octagonal barrel. Faithful to the original Winchester `66 rifle. Introduced 1994. Imported by Cabela's.
Price: $499.95

Consult our Directory pages for the location of firms mentioned.

CABELA'S 1873 WINCHESTER REPLICA
Caliber: 44-40, 45 Colt, 13-shot.
Barrel: 24 1/4″, 30″.
Weight: 8.5 lbs. **Length:** 43 1/4″ overall.
Stock: European walnut.
Sights: Bead front, open adjustable rear; globe front, tang rear.
Features: Color case-hardened steel receiver. Faithful to the original Model 1873 rifle. Introduced 1994. Imported by Cabela's.
Price: With tang sight, globe front $639.95
Price: Sporting model, 30″ barrel, 44-40, 45 Colt $599.95
Price: With half-round/half-octagon barrel, half magazine $639.95

CENTERFIRE RIFLES—LEVER & SLIDE

CIMARRON 1866 WINCHESTER REPLICAS
Caliber: 22 LR, 22 WMR, 38 Spec., 44 WCF.
Barrel: 24¼" (rifle), 19" (carbine).
Weight: 9 lbs. **Length:** 43" overall (rifle).
Stock: European walnut.
Sights: Bead front, open adjustable rear.
Features: Solid brass receiver, buttplate, forend cap. Octagonal barrel. Faithful to the original Winchester `66 rifle. Introduced 1991. Imported by Cimarron Arms.
Price: Rifle $689.95
Price: Carbine $679.95

CIMARRON 1873 SHORT RIFLE
Caliber: 22 LR, 22 WMR, 357 Mag., 44-40, 45 Colt.
Barrel: 20" tapered octagon.
Weight: 7.5 lbs. **Length:** 39" overall.
Stock: Walnut.
Sights: Bead front, adjustable semi-buckhorn rear.
Features: Has half "button" magazine. Original-type markings, including caliber, on barrel and elevator and "Kings" patent. From Cimarron Arms.
Price: $899.95

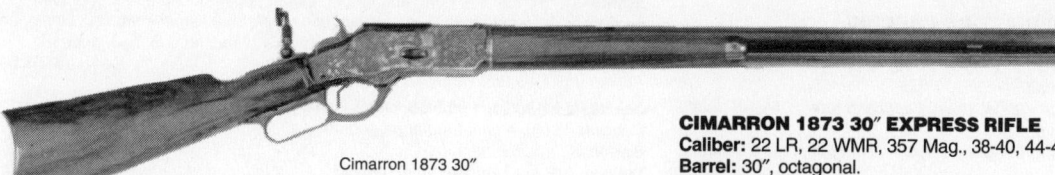
Cimarron 1873 30"

CIMARRON 1873 30" EXPRESS RIFLE
Caliber: 22 LR, 22 WMR, 357 Mag., 38-40, 44-40, 45 Colt.
Barrel: 30", octagonal.
Weight: 8½ lbs. **Length:** 48" overall.
Stock: Walnut.
Sights: Blade front, semi-buckhorn ramp rear. Tang sight optional.
Features: Color case-hardened frame; choice of modern blue-black or charcoal blue for other parts. Barrel marked "Kings Improvement." From Cimarron Arms.
Price: $949.95

Cimarron 1873 Sporting Rifle
Similar to the 1873 Express except has 24" barrel with half-magazine.
Price: $899.95
Price: 1873 Saddle Ring Carbine, 19" barrel $899.95

Dixie 1873

E.M.F. 1860 HENRY RIFLE
Caliber: 44-40 or 44 rimfire.
Barrel: 24.25".
Weight: About 9 lbs. **Length:** About 43.75" overall.
Stock: Oil-stained American walnut.
Sights: Blade front, rear adjustable for elevation.
Features: Reproduction of the original Henry rifle with brass frame and buttplate, rest blued. From E.M.F.
Price: Standard $1,100.00

DIXIE ENGRAVED 1873 RIFLE
Caliber: 44-40, 11-shot magazine.
Barrel: 20", round.
Weight: 7¾ lbs. **Length:** 39" overall.
Stock: Walnut.
Sights: Blade front, adjustable rear.
Features: Engraved and case-hardened frame. Duplicate of Winchester 1873. Made in Italy. From Dixie Gun Works.
Price: $1,250.00
Price: Plain, blued carbine $895.00

E.M.F. MODEL 73 LEVER-ACTION RIFLE
Caliber: 357 Mag., 44-40, 45 Colt.
Barrel: 24".
Weight: 8 lbs. **Length:** 43¼" overall.
Stock: European walnut.
Sights: Bead front, rear adjustable for windage and elevation.
Features: Color case-hardened frame (blue on carbine). Imported by E.M.F.
Price: Rifle $1,050.00
Price: Carbine, 19" barrel $1,020.00

E.M.F. 1866 YELLOWBOY LEVER ACTIONS
Caliber: 38 Spec., 44-40.
Barrel: 19" (carbine), 24" (rifle).
Weight: 9 lbs. **Length:** 43" overall (rifle).
Stock: European walnut.
Sights: Bead front, open adjustable rear.
Features: Solid brass frame, blued barrel, lever, hammer, buttplate. Imported from Italy by E.M.F.
Price: Rifle $848.00
Price: Carbine $825.00

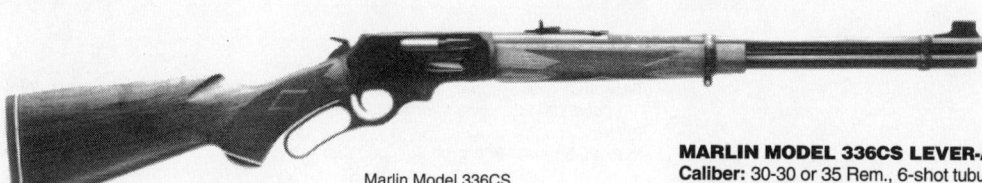
Marlin Model 336CS

Marlin Model 30AS Lever-Action Carbine
Same as the Marlin 336CS except has press-checkered, walnut-finished Maine birch pistol grip stock, 30-30 only, 6-shot. Hammer-block safety. Adjustable rear sight, brass bead front.
Price: $377.60

MARLIN MODEL 444SS LEVER-ACTION SPORTER
Caliber: 444 Marlin, 5-shot tubular magazine.
Barrel: 22" Micro-Groove®.
Weight: 7½ lbs. **Length:** 40½" overall.
Stock: Checkered American black walnut, capped pistol grip with white line spacers, rubber rifle buttpad. Mar-Shield® finish; swivel studs.

MARLIN MODEL 336CS LEVER-ACTION CARBINE
Caliber: 30-30 or 35 Rem., 6-shot tubular magazine.
Barrel: 20" Micro-Groove®.
Weight: 7 lbs. **Length:** 38½" overall.
Stock: Checkered American black walnut, capped pistol grip with white line spacers. Mar-Shield® finish; rubber buttpad; swivel studs.
Sights: Ramp front with Wide-Scan™ hood, semi-buckhorn folding rear adjustable for windage and elevation.
Features: Hammer-block safety. Receiver tapped for scope mount, offset hammer spur; top of receiver sand blasted to prevent glare.
Price: $443.50

Sights: Hooded ramp front, folding semi-buckhorn rear adjustable for windage and elevation.
Features: Hammer-block safety. Receiver tapped for scope mount; offset hammer spur.
Price: $522.60

CENTERFIRE RIFLES—LEVER & SLIDE

Marlin 1894 Cowboy

MARLIN MODEL 1894S LEVER-ACTION CARBINE
Caliber: 44 Spec./44 Mag., 10-shot tubular magazine.
Barrel: 20" Micro-Groove®.
Weight: 6 lbs. **Length:** 37½" overall.
Stock: Checkered American black walnut, straight grip and forend. Mar-Shield® finish. Rubber rifle buttpad; swivel studs.
Sights: Wide-Scan™ hooded ramp front, semi-buckhorn folding rear adjustable for windage and elevation.
Features: Hammer-block safety. Receiver tapped for scope mount, offset hammer spur, solid top receiver sand blasted to prevent glare.
Price: $459.35

MARLIN MODEL 1894 COWBOY
Caliber: 45 Colt, 10-shot magazine.
Barrel: 24" tapered octagon, deep cut rifling.
Weight: 7½ lbs. **Length:** 41½" overall.
Stock: Straight grip American black walnut with cut checkering, hard rubber buttplate, Mar-Shield® finish.
Sights: Marble carbine front, adjustable Marble semi-buckhorn rear.
Features: Squared finger lever; straight grip stock; blued steel forend tip. Designed for Cowboy Shooting events. Introduced 1996. Made in U.S. by Marlin.
Price: $668.00

MARLIN MODEL 1895SS LEVER-ACTION RIFLE
Caliber: 45-70, 4-shot tubular magazine.
Barrel: 22" round.
Weight: 7½ lbs. **Length:** 40½" overall.
Stock: Checkered American black walnut, full pistol grip. Mar-Shield® finish; rubber buttpad; quick detachable swivel studs.
Sights: Bead front with Wide-Scan™ hood, semi-buckhorn folding rear adjustable for windage and elevation.
Features: Hammer-block safety. Solid receiver tapped for scope mounts or receiver sights; offset hammer spur.
Price: $522.60

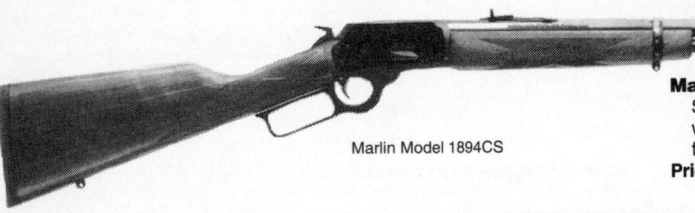
Marlin Model 1894CS

Marlin Model 1894CS Carbine
Similar to the standard Model 1894S except chambered for 38 Spec./357 Mag. with full-length 9-shot magazine, 18½" barrel, hammer-block safety, brass bead front sight. Introduced 1983.
Price: $459.35

Navy Arms Military Henry

NAVY ARMS MILITARY HENRY RIFLE
Caliber: 44-40, 12-shot magazine.
Barrel: 24¼".
Weight: 9 lbs., 4 oz.
Stock: European walnut.
Sights: Blade front, adjustable ladder-type rear.
Features: Brass frame, buttplate, rest blued. Recreation of the model used by cavalry units in the Civil War. Has full-length magazine tube, sling swivels; no forend. Imported from Italy by Navy Arms.
Price: $895.00

Navy Arms Henry Trapper
Similar to the Military Henry Rifle except has 16½" barrel, weighs 7½ lbs. Brass frame and buttplate, rest blued. Introduced 1991. Imported from Italy by Navy Arms.
Price: $875.00

NAVY ARMS 1866 YELLOWBOY RIFLE
Caliber: 44-40, 12-shot magazine.
Barrel: 24", full octagon.
Weight: 8½ lbs. **Length:** 42½" overall.
Stock: European walnut.

Navy Arms Henry Carbine
Similar to the Military Henry rifle except has 22" barrel, weighs 8 lbs., 12 oz., is 41" overall; no sling swivels. Caliber 44-40. Introduced 1992. Imported from Italy by Navy Arms.
Price: $875.00

Navy Arms Iron Frame Henry
Similar to the Military Henry Rifle except receiver is blued or color case-hardened steel. Imported by Navy Arms.
Price: $945.00

Sights: Blade front, adjustable ladder-type rear.
Features: Brass frame, forend tip, buttplate, blued barrel, lever, hammer. Introduced 1991. Imported from Italy by Navy Arms.
Price: $680.00
Price: Carbine, 19" barrel $670.00

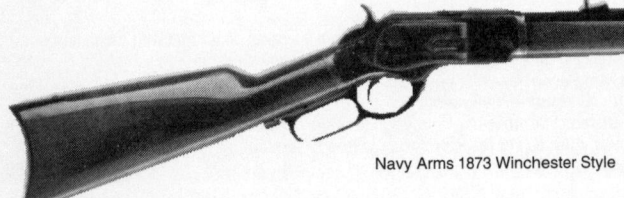
Navy Arms 1873 Winchester Style

Navy Arms 1873 Sporting Rifle
Similar to the 1873 Winchester-Style rifle except has checkered pistol grip stock, 30" octagonal barrel (24" available). Introduced 1992. Imported by Navy Arms.
Price: 30" barrel $960.00
Price: 24" barrel $930.00

NAVY ARMS 1873 WINCHESTER-STYLE RIFLE
Caliber: 44-40, 45 Colt, 12-shot magazine.
Barrel: 24".
Weight: 8¼ lbs. **Length:** 43" overall.
Stock: European walnut.
Sights: Blade front, buckhorn rear.
Features: Color case-hardened frame, rest blued. Full-octagon barrel. Imported by Navy Arms.
Price: $820.00
Price: Carbine, 19" barrel $800.00

CENTERFIRE RIFLES—LEVER & SLIDE

Remington 7600 Rifle

REMINGTON 7600 SLIDE ACTION
Caliber: 243, 270, 280, 30-06, 308.
Barrel: 22" round tapered.
Weight: 7½ lbs. **Length:** 42" overall.
Stock: Cut-checkered walnut pistol grip and forend, Monte Carlo with full cheek-piece. Satin or high-gloss finish.
Sights: Gold bead front sight on matted ramp, open step adjustable sporting rear.
Features: Redesigned and improved version of the Model 760. Detachable 4-shot clip. Cross-bolt safety. Receiver tapped for scope mount. Also available in high grade versions. Comes with green Remington hard case. Introduced 1981.
Price: About $540.00
Price: Carbine (18½" bbl., 30-06 only) $540.00

Rossi Model 92

Rossi Model 92 Short Carbine
Similar to the standard M92 except has 16" barrel, overall length of 33", in 38 Spec./357 Mag. only. Introduced 1986.
Price: $360.00

ROSSI MODEL 92 SADDLE-RING CARBINE
Caliber: 38 Spec./357 Mag., 44 Spec./44-40, 44 Mag., 45 Colt, 10-shot magazine.
Barrel: 20".
Weight: 5¾ lbs. **Length:** 37" overall.
Stock: Walnut.
Sights: Blade front, buckhorn rear.
Features: Recreation of the famous lever-action carbine. Handles 38 and 357 interchangeably. Introduced 1978. Imported by Interarms.
Price: $360.00
Price: 44 Spec./44 Mag. (Model 65) $360.00

Ruger Model 96/44

RUGER MODEL 96/44 LEVER-ACTION RIFLE
Caliber: 44 Mag., 4-shot rotary magazine.
Barrel: 18½".
Weight: 5⅞ lbs. **Length:** 37 5/16" overall.
Stock: American hardwood.
Sights: Gold bead front, folding leaf rear.
Features: Manual cross-bolt safety, visible cocking indicator; short-throw lever action; integral scope mount; blued finish. Introduced 1996. Made In U.S. by Sturm, Ruger & Co.
Price: $365.00

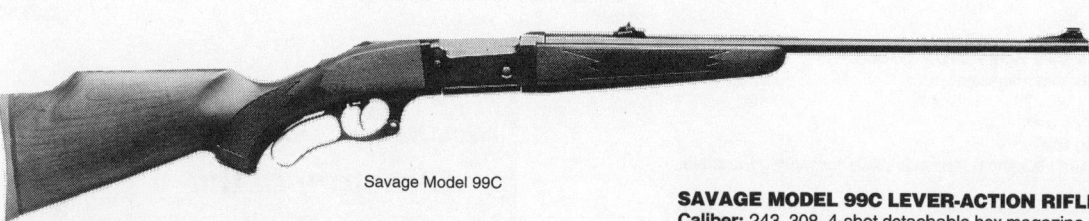

Savage Model 99C

Savage Model 99CE Centennial Edition
Similar to the Model 99C except chambered only for 300 Savage; serially numbered AS0001 through AS1000; gold-plated trigger and tang safety; fully engraved receiver with gold-plated figures; wrap-around forend checkering; nickel-plated swivel studs. Production of 1000 rifles. From Savage Arms. Introduced 1996.
Price: $1,660.00

SAVAGE MODEL 99C LEVER-ACTION RIFLE
Caliber: 243, 308, 4-shot detachable box magazine.
Barrel: 22".
Weight: 7¾ lbs. **Length:** 45½" overall.
Stock: American walnut; Monte Carlo comb; cut-checkered grip and forend.
Sights: Bead on blade front, open fully adjsutable rear. Drilled and tapped for scope mounts.
Features: Polished blue finish; solid red buttpad; swivel studs. From Savage Arms. Reintroduced 1996.
Price: $650.00

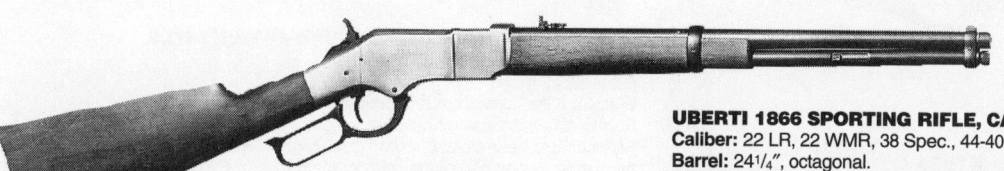

Uberti 1866 Sporting

UBERTI 1866 SPORTING RIFLE, CARBINE
Caliber: 22 LR, 22 WMR, 38 Spec., 44-40, 45 Colt.
Barrel: 24¼", octagonal.
Weight: 8.1 lbs. **Length:** 43¼" overall.
Stock: Walnut.
Sights: Blade front adjustable for windage, rear adjustable for elevation.
Features: Frame, buttplate, forend cap of polished brass, balance charcoal blued. Imported by Uberti USA Inc.
Price: $840.00
Price: Yellowboy Carbine (19" round bbl.) $760.00

CAUTION: PRICES SHOWN ARE SUPPLIED BY THE MANUFACTURER OR IMPORTER. CHECK YOUR LOCAL GUN SHOP.

CENTERFIRE RIFLES—LEVER & SLIDE

UBERTI 1873 SPORTING RIFLE, CARBINE
Caliber: 22 LR, 22 WMR, 38 Spec., 357 Mag., 44-40, 45 Colt.
Barrel: 24 1/4" half-octagon, 24 1/4", 30", octagonal.
Weight: 8.1 lbs. **Length:** 43 1/4" overall.
Stock: Walnut.
Sights: Blade front adjustable for windage, open rear adjustable for elevation.
Features: Color case-hardened frame, blued barrel, hammer, lever, buttplate, brass elevator. Also available with pistol grip stock ($100.00 extra). Imported from Italy by Uberti USA Inc.
Price: $970.00
Price: 1873 Carbine (19" round barrel) $920.00

UBERTI HENRY RIFLE
Caliber: 44-40, 45 Colt.
Barrel: 18 1/2", 22 1/4", 24 1/4", half-octagon.
Weight: 9.2 lbs. **Length:** 43 3/4" overall.
Stock: American walnut.
Sights: Blade front, rear adjustable for elevation.
Features: Frame, elevator, magazine follower, buttplate are brass, balance blue (also available in polished steel). Imported by Uberti USA Inc.
Price: $940.00
Price: Henry Carbine (22 1/4" bbl.) $950.00
Price: Henry Trapper (16", 18" bbl.) $950.00

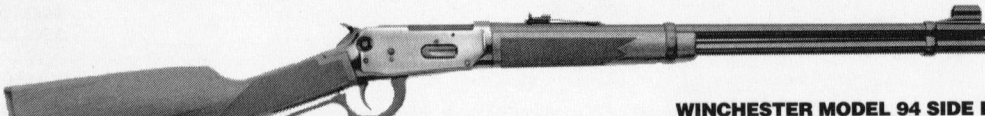
Winchester 94 Side Eject

Winchester Model 94 Ranger Side Eject Lever-Action Rifle
Same as Model 94 Side Eject except has 5-shot magazine, American hardwood stock and forend, post front sight. Specially inscribed with "1894-1994" on the receiver. Introduced 1985.
Price: $320.00
Price: With 4x32 Bushnell scope, mounts $376.00

Winchester Model 94 Wrangler Side Eject
Same as the Model 94 except has 16" barrel and large loop lever for large and/or gloved hands. Has 9-shot capacity (5-shot for 30-30), stainless steel claw extractor. Available in 30-30, 44 Magnum/44 Special. Specially inscribed with "1894-1994" on the receiver. Reintroduced 1992.
Price: 30-30 .... $384.00
Price: 44 Magnum/44 Special $404.00

WINCHESTER MODEL 94 SIDE EJECT LEVER-ACTION RIFLE
Caliber: 30-30 Win., 6-shot tubular magazine.
Barrel: 20".
Weight: 6 1/2 lbs. **Length:** 37 3/4" overall.
Stock: Straight grip walnut stock and forend.
Sights: Hooded blade front, semi-buckhorn rear. Drilled and tapped for scope mount. Post front sight on Trapper model.
Features: Solid frame, forged steel receiver; side ejection, exposed rebounding hammer with automatic trigger-activated transfer bar. Specially inscribed with "1894-1994" on the receiver. Introduced 1984.
Price: Checkered walnut $393.00
Price: No checkering, walnut $363.00
Price: With WinTuff laminated hardwood stock, 30-30 only $404.00

Winchester Model 94 Trapper Side Eject
Same as the Model 94 except has 16" barrel, 5-shot magazine in 30-30, 9-shot in 357 Mag., 44 Magnum/44 Special, 45 Colt. Has stainless steel claw extractor, saddle ring, hammer spur extension, walnut wood. Specially inscribed with "1894-1994" on the receiver.
Price: 30-30 .... $363.00
Price: 357 Mag., 44 Mag./44 Spec., 45 Colt $384.00

Winchester 94 Legacy

Winchester Model 94 Legacy
Similar to the Model 94 Side Eject except has half pistol grip walnut stock, checkered grip and forend. Chambered only for 30-30. Introduced 1995. Made in U.S. by U.S. Repeating Arms Co., Inc.
Price: $393.00

WINCHESTER MODEL 94 BIG BORE SIDE EJECT
Caliber: 307 Win., 356 Win., 6-shot magazine.
Barrel: 20".
Weight: 7 lbs. **Length:** 38 5/8" overall.
Stock: American walnut. Satin finish.
Sights: Hooded ramp front, semi-buckhorn rear adjustable for windage and elevation.
Features: All external metal parts have Winchester's deep blue finish. Rifling twist 1:12". Rubber recoil pad fitted to buttstock. Specially inscribed with "1894-1994" on the receiver. Introduced 1983. From U.S. Repeating Arms Co., Inc.
Price: $404.00

Manufacturers' addresses in the
Directory of the Arms Trade
page 313, this issue

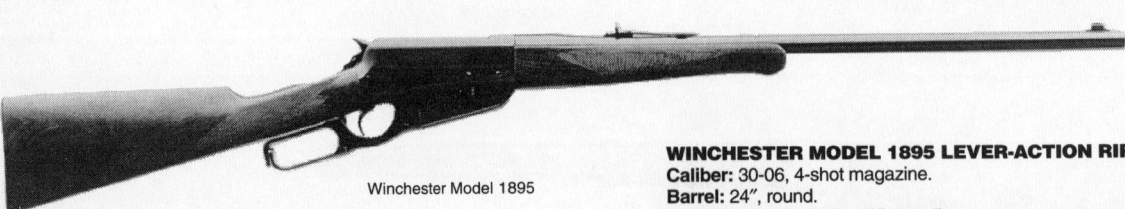
Winchester Model 1895

Winchester Model 1895 High Grade Rifle
Same as the Grade I except has silvered receiver with extensive engraving: right side shows two scenes portraying large big horn sheep; left side has bull elk and cow elk. Gold borders accent the scenes. Magazine and cocking lever also engraved. Has classic Winchester H-style checkering pattern on fancy grade American walnut. Only 4000 rifles made. Introduced 1995. From U.S. Repeating Arms Co., Inc.
Price: $1,360.00

WINCHESTER MODEL 1895 LEVER-ACTION RIFLE
Caliber: 30-06, 4-shot magazine.
Barrel: 24", round.
Weight: 8 lbs. **Length:** 42" overall.
Stock: American walnut.
Sights: Gold bead front, buckhorn rear adjustable for elevation.
Features: Recreation of the original Model 1895. Polished blue finish with Nimschke-style scroll engraving on receiver. Scalloped receiver, two-piece cocking lever, schnabel forend, straight-grip stock. Introduced 1995. Only 4000 rifles made. From U.S. Repeating Arms Co., Inc.
Price: Grade I $853.00

CENTERFIRE RIFLES—BOLT ACTION
Includes models for a wide variety of sporting and competitive purposes and uses.

AMT BOLT-ACTION RIFLE
Caliber: Single shot—22 Hornet, 222, 223, 22-250, 243 Win., 243 A, 22 PPC, 6mm PPC, 6.5x08, 7mm-08, 308; repeater—223, 22-250, 243 Win., 243 A, 6mm PPC, 25-06, 6.5x08, 270, 7mm-08, 308, 30-06, 7mm Rem. Mag; 300 Win. Mag., 338 Win. Mag., 375 H&H, 416 Rem; 458 Win. Mag., 416 Rigby, 7.62x39, 7x57.
Barrel: Up to 28", #3 contour.
Weight: About 8½ lbs.
Stock: Classic composite on Standard grade; McMillan or H-S Precision on Deluxe.
Sights: None furnished; drilled and tapped for scope mounting.
Features: Single shot uses cone breach action with post-64-type extractor, pre-64-type three-position safety; repeater has Mauser-type extractor and magazine, pre-64 three-position safety; plunger-type ejector; short, medium, long action, right- or left-handed. Introduced 1996. Made in U.S. by AMT. Deluxe has Mauser controlled feed action with plunger ejector, claw-type extractor; Standard uses push-feed post-64 Winchester-type action.
Price: Single shot $2,399.99
Price: Repeater Standard $1,109.99
Price: Repeater Deluxe $1,595.99

AAO MODEL 2000 50-CALIBER RIFLE
Caliber: 50 BMG, 5-shot magazine.
Barrel: 30"; 1:15" twist; muzzlebrake.
Weight: 24 lbs. **Length:** NA.
Stock: Cast alloy with gray anodized finish, Kick-Ease recoil pad.
Sights: None furnished. Drilled and tapped for scope base.
Features: Controlled feeding via rotating enclosed claw extractor; 90-degree bolt rotation; cone bolt face and barrel; trigger-mounted safety blocks sear; fully adjustable, detachable tripod. Introduced 1994. From American Arms & Ordnance.
Price: $4,000.00

Anschutz 1700D Custom

ANSCHUTZ 1700D CUSTOM RIFLE
Caliber: 22 Hornet, 5-shot clip; 222 Rem., 3-shot clip.
Barrel: 24".
Weight: 7½ lbs. **Length:** 43" overall.
Stock: Select European walnut.
Sights: Hooded ramp front, folding leaf rear; drilled and tapped for scope mounting.
Features: Adjustable single stage trigger. Stock has roll-over Monte Carlo cheekpiece, slim forend with Schnabel tip, Wundhammer palm swell on grip, rosewood grip cap with white diamond insert. Skip-line checkering on grip and forend. Introduced 1988. Imported from Germany by AcuSport.
Price: $1,297.56

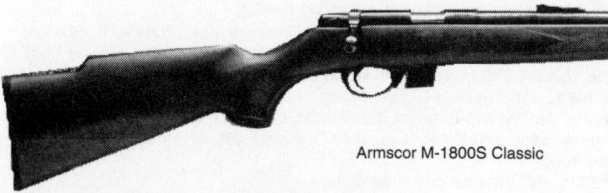
Armscor M-1800S Classic

ARMSCOR M-1800S CLASSIC BOLT-ACTION RIFLE
Caliber: 22 Hornet, 5-shot magazine.
Barrel: 22.6".
Weight: 6.6 lbs. **Length:** 41.25" overall.
Stock: Walnut-finished hardwood with Monte Carlo comb and checkpiece.
Sights: Ramped blade front, fully adjustable open rear.
Features: Receiver dovetailed for tip-off scope mount. Introduced 1996. Imported from the Philippines by K.B.I., Inc.
Price: $340.00

Armscor M-1800SC Super Classic Rifle
Similar to the M-1800S except has oil-finished American walnut stock with 18 lpi hand checkering; black hardwood grip cap and forend tip; highly polished barreled action; jewelled bolt; recoil pad; swivel studs. Imported from the Philippines by K.B.I., Inc.
Price: $430.00

ARNOLD ARMS ALASKAN BUSH RIFLE
Caliber: 223 to 338 Magnum.
Barrel: 22" to 26".
Weight: NA. **Length:** NA.
Stock: Synthetic; black, woodland or arctic camouflage.
Sights: Optional; drilled and tapped for scope mounting.
Features: Uses the Apollo action with controlled round feed or push feed; chrome-moly steel or stainless; one-piece bolt, handle, knob; cone head bolt and breech; three-position safety; fully adjustable trigger. Introduced 1996. Made in U.S. by Arnold Arms Co.
Price: Chrome-moly steel $2,995.00
Price: Stainless steel $3,145.00

Arnold Arms Alaskan Trophy Rifle
Similar to the Alaskan Bush rifle except chambered for 300 Magnums to 458 Win. Mag.; 24" to 26" barrel; Fibergrain or black synthetic stock, or AA English walnut; comes with barrel band on 375 H&H and larger; scope mount; iron sights. Introduced 1996. Made in U.S. by Arnold Arms Co.
Price: Chrome-moly steel $3,525.00
Price: Stainless steel $3,990.00
Price: Chrome-moly steel, walnut stock $5,140.00
Price: Stainless steel, walnut stock $5,299.00

> Consult our Directory pages for the location of firms mentioned.

Arnold Arms High Country Mountain Rifle
Simliar to the Alaskan Bush rifle except chambered for 257 to 338 Magnum; choice of AA English walnut or synthetic stock; scope mount only. Introduced 1996. Made in U.S. by Arnold Arms Co.
Price: Chrome-moly steel, synthetic stock $2,995.00
Price: Stainless steel, synthetic stock $3,170.00
Price: Chrome-moly steel, walnut stock $4,489.00
Price: Stainless steel, walnut stock $4,839.00

Arnold Arms Grand Alaskan Rifle
Similar to the Alaskan Bush rifle except has AAA fancy select or exhibition-grade English walnut; barrel band swivel; comes with iron sights and scope mount; 24" to 26" barrel; 300 Magnum to 458 Win. Mag. Introduced 1996. Made in U.S. by Arnold Arms Co.
Price: Chrome-moly steel, from $6,550.00
Price: Stainless steel, from $6,710.00

CENTERFIRE RIFLES—BOLT ACTION

ARNOLD ARMS SAFARI RIFLE
Caliber: 243 to 458 Win. Mag.
Barrel: 22" to 26".
Weight: NA. **Length:** NA.
Stock: Grade A and AA Fancy English walnut.
Sights: Optional; drilled and tapped for scope mounting.
Features: Uses the Apollo action with controlled or push round feed; one-piece bolt, handle, knob; cone head bolt and breech; three-position safety; fully adjustable trigger; chrome-moly steel in matte blue, polished, or bead blasted stainless. Introduced 1996. Made in U.S. by Arnold Arms Co.
Price: Grade A walnut, chrome-moly $4,435.00
Price: Grade A walnut, stainless steel $4,695.00
Price: Grade AA walnut, chrome-moly steel $4,690.00
Price: Grade AA walnut, stainless steel $4,840.00

Arnold Arms Grand African Rifle
Similar to the Safari rifle except has Exhibition Grade stock; polished blue chrome-moly steel or bead-blasted or teflon-coated stainless; barrel band; scope mount, express sights; calibers 338 Magnum to 458 Win. Mag.; 24" to 26" barrel. Introduced 1996. Made in U.S. by Arnold Arms Co.
Price: Chrome-moly steel $7,630.00
Price: Stainless steel $7,780.00

A-SQUARE CAESAR BOLT-ACTION RIFLE
Caliber: 7mm Rem. Mag., 7mm STW, 30-06, 300 Win. Mag., 300 H&H, 300 Wea. Mag., 8mm Rem. Mag., 338 Win. Mag., 340 Wea. Mag., 338 A-Square, 9.3x62, 9.3x64, 375 Wea. Mag., 375 H&H, 375 JRS, 375 A-Square, 416 Hoffman, 416 Rem. Mag., 416 Taylor, 404 Jeffery, 425 Express, 458 Win. Mag., 458 Lott, 450 Ackley, 460 Short A-Square, 470 Capstick, 495 A-Square.
Barrel: 20" to 26" (no-cost customer option).
Weight: 8 1/2 to 11 lbs.
Stock: Claro walnut with hand-rubbed oil finish; classic style with A-Square Coil-Chek® features for reduced recoil; flush detachable swivels. Customer choice of length of pull.
Sights: Choice of three-leaf express, forward or normal-mount scope, or combination (at extra cost).
Features: Matte non-reflective blue, double cross-bolts, steel and fiberglass reinforcement of wood from tang to forend tip; three-position positive safety; three-way adjustable trigger; expanded magazine capacity. Right- or left-hand. Introduced 1984. Made in U.S. by A-Square Co., Inc.
Price: Walnut stock $2,995.00
Price: Synthetic stock $3,345.00

Arnold Arms African Trophy Rifle
Similar to the Safari rifle except has AAA Extra Fancy English walnut stock with wrap-around checkering; matte blue chrome-moly or polished or bead blasted stainless steel; scope mount standard or optional Express sights. Introduced 1996. Made in U.S. by Arnold Arms Co.
Price: Blued chrome-moly steel $6,098.00
Price: Stainless steel $6,255.00

Arnold Arms Serengeti Synthetic Rifle
Similar to the Safari except has Fibergrain synthetic stock in classic or Monte Carlo style; traditional checkering pattern or stipple finish; polished or matte blue or bead-blast stainless finish; chambered for 243 to 300 Magnum. Introduced 1996. Made in U.S. by Arnold Arms Co.
Price: Chrome-moly steel $2,995.00
Price: Stainless steel $3,170.00

Arnold Arms African Synthetic Rifle
Similar to the Safari except has Fibergrain synthetic stock with or without cheekpiece and traditional checkering pattern, or stipple finish; standard iron sights or Express folding leaf optional; chambered for 338 Magnum to 458 Win. Mag.; 24" to 26" barrel. Introduced 1996. Made in U.S. by Arnold Arms Co.
Price: Chrome-moly steel $2,995.00
Price: Stainless steel $3,170.00

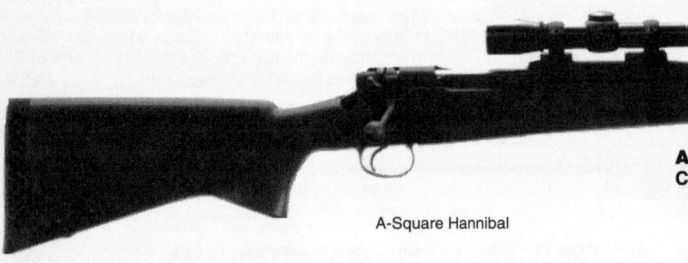
A-Square Hannibal

A-Square Hamilcar Bolt-Action Rifle
Similar to the A-Square Hannibal rifle except chambered for 25-06, 6.5x55, 270 Win., 7x57, 280 Rem., 30-06, 338-06, 9.3x62, 257 Wea. Mag., 264 Win. Mag., 270 Wea. Mag., 7mm Rem. Mag., 7mm Wea. Mag., 7mm STW, 300 Win. Mag., 300 Wea. Mag. Weighs 8-8 1/2 lbs. Introduced 1994. From A-Square Co., Inc.
Price: $2,995.00

A-SQUARE HANNIBAL BOLT-ACTION RIFLE
Caliber: 7mm Rem. Mag., 7mm STW, 30-06, 300 Win. Mag., 300 H&H, 300 Wea. Mag., 8mm Rem. Mag., 338 Win. Mag., 340 Wea. Mag., 338 A-Square Mag., 9.3x62, 9.3x64, 375 H&H, 375 Wea. Mag., 375 JRS, 375 A-Square Mag., 378 Wea. Mag., 416 Taylor, 416 Rem. Mag., 416 Hoffman, 416 Rigby, 416 Wea. Mag., 404 Jeffery, 425 Express, 458 Win. Mag., 458 Lott, 450 Ackley, 460 Short A-Square Mag., 460 Wea. Mag., 470 Capstick, 495 A-Square Mag., 500 A-Square Mag.
Barrel: 20" to 26" (no-cost customer option).
Weight: 9 to 11 3/4 lbs.
Stock: Claro walnut with hand-rubbed oil finish; classic style with A-Square Coil-Chek® features for reduced recoil; flush detachable swivels. Customer choice of length of pull. Available with synthetic stock.
Sights: Choice of three-leaf express, forward or normal-mount scope, or combination (at extra cost).
Features: Matte non-reflective blue, double cross-bolts, steel and fiberglass reinforcement of wood from tang to forend tip; Mauser-style claw extractor; expanded magazine capacity; two-position safety; three-way target trigger. Right-hand only. Introduced 1983. Made in U.S. by A-Square Co., Inc.
Price: Walnut stock $2,995.00
Price: Synthetic stock $3,345.00

Barrett Model 95

BARRETT MODEL 95 BOLT-ACTION RIFLE
Caliber: 50 BMG, 5-shot magazine.
Barrel: 29".
Weight: 22 lbs. **Length:** 45" overall.
Stock: Sorbothane recoil pad.
Sights: Scope optional.
Features: Updated version of the Model 90. Bolt-action, bullpup design. Disassembles without tools; extendable bipod legs; match-grade barrel; high efficiency muzzlebrake. Introduced 1995. From Barrett Firearms Mfg., Inc.
Price: From $4,700.00

CENTERFIRE RIFLES—BOLT ACTION

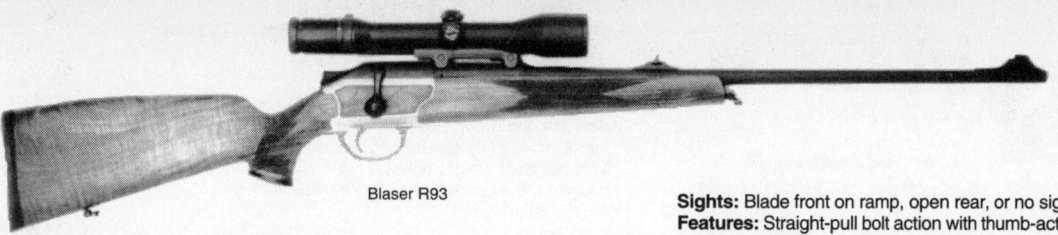
Blaser R93

BLASER R93 BOLT-ACTION RIFLE
Caliber: 222, 243, 6.5x55, 270, 7x57, 308, 30-06, 7mm Rem. Mag., 300 Win. Mag., 300 Wea. Mag., 338 Win. Mag., 375 H&H, 416 Rem. Mag., 3-shot magazine.
Barrel: 22" (standard calibers), 24" (magnum calibers).
Weight: 6.5 to 7.5 lbs. **Length:** 40" overall (22" barrel).
Stock: Two-piece European walnut.
Sights: Blade front on ramp, open rear, or no sights.
Features: Straight-pull bolt action with thumb-activated safety slide/cocking mechanism. Interchangeable barrels and bolt heads. Introduced 1994. Imported from Germany by Autumn Sales, Inc.
Price: Standard $2,800.00
Price: Deluxe (better wood, engraving) $3,100.00
Price: Super Deluxe (best wood, gold animal inlays) $3,500.00
Price: Safari, standard grade, 375 H&H, 416 Rem. Mag. $3,300.00
Price: Safari Deluxe $3,600.00
Price: Safari Super Deluxe $4,000.00

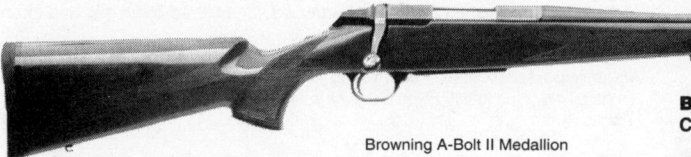
Browning A-Bolt II Medallion

Browning A-Bolt II Left Hand
Same as the Medallion model A-Bolt except has left-hand action and is available only in 270, 30-06, 7mm Rem. Mag., 375 H&H. BOSS barrel vibration modulator and muzzlebrake system not available in 375 H&H. Introduced 1987.
Price: $734.95
Price: With BOSS $832.95
Price: 375 H&H, with sights $846.95

Browning A-Bolt II Gold Medallion
Similar to the standard A-Bolt except has select walnut stock with brass spacers between rubber recoil pad and between the rosewood grip cap and forend tip; gold-filled barrel inscription; palm-swell pistol grip, Monte Carlo comb, 22 lpi checkering with double borders; engraved receiver flats. In 270, 30-06, 7mm Rem. Mag. only. Introduced 1988.
Price: $949.95
Price: For BOSS, add $98.00

Browning A-Bolt II Composite Stalker
Similar to the A-Bolt II Hunter except has black graphite-fiberglass stock with textured finish. Matte blue finish on all exposed metal surfaces. Available in 223, 22-250, 243, 7mm-08, 308, 30-06, 270, 280, 25-06, 7mm Rem. Mag., 300 Win. Mag., 338 Win. Mag. BOSS barrel vibration modulator and muzzlebrake system offered in all calibers. Introduced 1994.
Price: No sights $624.95
Price: No sights, BOSS $722.95

Browning A-Bolt II Stainless Stalker
Similar to the Hunter model A-Bolt except receiver and barrel are made of stainless steel; the rest of the exposed metal surfaces are finished with a durable matte silver-gray. Graphite-fiberglass composite textured stock. No sights are furnished. Available in 223, 22-250, 243, 308, 7mm-08, 270, 30-06, 7mm Rem. Mag., 375 H&H. Introduced 1987.
Price: $786.95
Price: With BOSS $884.95
Price: Left-hand, no sights $811.95
Price: With BOSS $909.95
Price: 375 H&H, with sights $895.95
Price: 375 H&H, left-hand, with sights $923.95

BROWNING A-BOLT II RIFLE
Caliber: 25-06, 270, 30-06, 280, 7mm Rem. Mag., 300 Win. Mag., 338 Win. Mag., 375 H&H Mag.
Barrel: 22" medium sporter weight with recessed muzzle; 26" on mag. cals.
Weight: 6 1/2 to 7 1/2 lbs. **Length:** 44 3/4" overall (magnum and standard); 41 3/4" (short action).
Stock: Classic style American walnut; recoil pad standard on magnum calibers.
Features: Short-throw (60°) fluted bolt, three locking lugs, plunger-type ejector; adjustable trigger is grooved and gold-plated. Hinged floorplate, detachable box magazine (4 rounds std. cals., 3 for magnums). Slide tang safety. Medallion has glossy stock finish, rosewood grip and forend caps, high polish blue. BOSS barrel vibration modulator and muzzlebrake system not available in 375 H&H. Introduced 1985. Imported from Japan by Browning.
Price: Medallion, no sights $706.95
Price: Hunter, no sights $605.95
Price: Hunter, with sights $681.95
Price: Medallion, 375 H&H Mag., with sights $818.95
Price: For BOSS add $98.00

Browning A-Bolt II Short Action
Similar to the standard A-Bolt except has short action for 223, 22-250, 243, 257 Roberts, 7mm-08, 284 Win., 308 chamberings. Available in Hunter or Medallion grades. Weighs 6 1/2 lbs. Other specs essentially the same. BOSS barrel vibration modulator and muzzlebrake system optional. Introduced 1985.
Price: Medallion, no sights $706.95
Price: Hunter, no sights $605.95
Price: Hunter, with sights $681.95
Price: Composite, no sights $624.95
Price: For BOSS, add $98.00

Browning A-Bolt II Micro Medallion
Similar to the standard A-Bolt except is a scaled-down version. Comes with 20" barrel, shortened length of pull (13 5/16"); three-shot magazine capacity; weighs 6 lbs., 1 oz. Available in 22 Hornet, 243, 308, 7mm-08, 257 Roberts, 223, 22-250. BOSS feature not available for this model. Introduced 1988.
Price: No sights $706.95

Browning A-Bolt II Varmint Rifle
Same as the A-Bolt II Hunter except has heavy varmint/target barrel, laminated wood stock with special dimensions, flat forend and palm swell grip. Chambered only for 223, 22-250, 308. Comes with BOSS barrel vibration modulator and muzzlebrake system. Introduced 1994.
Price: With BOSS, gloss or matte finish $939.95

Browning Euro Bolt

Browning Euro-Bolt II Rifle
Similar to the A-Bolt II Hunter except has satin-finished walnut stock with Continental-style cheekpiece, palm-swell grip and schnabel forend, rounded bolt shroud and Mannlicher-style flattened bolt handle. Available in 30-06 and 270 with 22" barrel, 7mm Rem. Mag. with 26" barrel. Weighs about 6 lbs., 11 oz. BOSS barrel vibration modulator and muzzlebrake system optional. Introduced 1993.
Price: $823.95
Price: For BOSS, add $98.00

CENTERFIRE RIFLES—BOLT ACTION

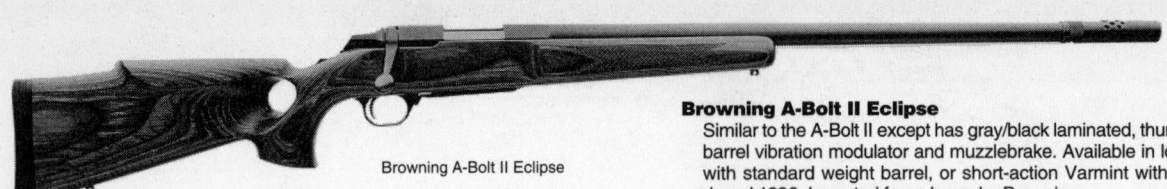
Browning A-Bolt II Eclipse

Browning A-Bolt II Eclipse
Similar to the A-Bolt II except has gray/black laminated, thumbhole stock, BOSS barrel vibration modulator and muzzlebrake. Available in long and short action with standard weight barrel, or short-action Varmint with heavy barrel. Introduced 1996. Imported from Japan by Browning.
Price: Standard barrel $1,024.95
Price: Varmint $1,054.95

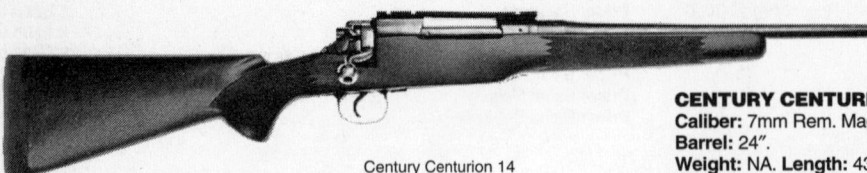
Century Centurion 14

CENTURY CENTURION 14 SPORTER
Caliber: 7mm Rem. Mag., 300 Win. Mag., 5-shot magazine.
Barrel: 24".
Weight: NA. Length: 43.3" overall.
Stock: Walnut-finished European hardwood. Checkered pistol grip and forend. Monte Carlo comb.
Sights: None furnished.
Features: Uses modified Pattern 14 Enfield action. Drilled and tapped; scope base mounted. Blue finish. From Century International Arms.
Price: About $275.00

CENTURY DELUXE CUSTOM SPORTER
Caliber: 243, 270, 308, 30-06.
Barrel: 24".
Weight: NA. Length: 44" overall.
Stock: Black synthetic.
Sights: None furnished. Scope base installed.
Features: Mauser 98 action; bent bolt handle for scope use; low-swing safety; matte black finish; blind magazine. Introduced 1992. From Century International Arms.
Price: About $288.00

CENTURY ENFIELD SPORTER #4
Caliber: 303 British, 10-shot magazine.
Barrel: 25.2".
Weight: 8 lbs., 5 oz. Length: 44.5" overall.
Stock: Beechwood with checkered pistol grip and forend, Monte Carlo comb.
Sights: Blade front, adjustable aperture rear.
Features: Uses Lee-Enfield action; blue finish. Trigger pinned to receiver. Introduced 1987. From Century International Arms.
Price: About $156.00

Century Custom Sporting Rifle

CENTURY CUSTOM SPORTING RIFLE
Caliber: 308, 7.62x39mm.
Barrel: 22".
Weight: 6.7 lbs. Length: 43.75".
Stock: Walnut-finished hardwood.
Sights: None furnished; comes with two-piece Weaver-type base.
Features: Uses small ring Model 98 action; low-swing safety; blue finish. Introduced 1994. From Century International Arms.
Price: About $275.00

CENTURY SWEDISH SPORTER #38
Caliber: 6.5x55 Swede, 5-shot magazine.
Barrel: 24".
Weight: NA. Length: 44.1" overall.
Stock: Walnut-finished European hardwood with checkered pistol grip and forend; Monte Carlo comb.
Sights: Blade front, adjustable rear.
Features: Uses M38 Swedish Mauser action; comes with Holden Ironsighter see-through scope mount. Introduced 1987. From Century International Arms.
Price: About $237.50

Cooper Model 22 PV

COOPER ARMS MODEL 22 PRO VARMINT EXTREME
Caliber: 22-250, 220 Swift, 243, 25-06, 6mm PPC, 308, single shot.
Barrel: 26"; stainless steel match grade, straight taper; free-floated.
Weight: NA. Length: NA.
Stock: AAA Claro walnut, oil finish, 22 lpi wrap-around borderless ribbon checkering, beaded cheekpiece, steel grip cap, flared varminter forend, Pachmayr pad.
Sights: None furnished; drilled and tapped for scope mounting.
Features: Uses a three front locking lug system. Available with sterling silver inlaid medallion, skeleton grip cap, and French walnut. Introduced 1995. Made in U.S. by Cooper Arms.
Price: $1,785.00
Price: Benchrest model with Jewell trigger $2,140.00
Price: Black Jack model (McMillan synthetic stock) $1,575.00

COOPER ARMS MODEL 21 VARMINT EXTREME RIFLE
Caliber: 17 Rem., 17 Mach IV, 221 Fireball, 222, 222 Rem. Mag., 223, 22 PPC, single shot.
Barrel: 23.75"; stainless steel, with competition step crown; free-floated.
Weight: NA. Length: NA.
Stock: AAA Claro walnut with flared oval forend, ambidextrous palm swell, 22 lpi checkering, oil finish, Pachmayr buttpad.
Sights: None furnished; drilled and tapped for scope mounting.
Features: Action has three mid-bolt locking lugs; adjustable trigger; glass bedded; swivel studs. Introduced 1994. Made in U.S. by Cooper Arms.
Price: $1,675.00
Price: Benchrest with Jewell trigger $2,140.00
Price: Classic model $1,675.00
Price: Custom Classic $1,960.00

CENTERFIRE RIFLES—BOLT ACTION

COOPER ARMS MODEL 40 CENTERFIRE SPORTER
Caliber: 22 Hornet, 22 K-Hornet, 5-shot magazine.
Barrel: 23".
Weight: 7 lbs. **Length:** 42 1/2" overall.
Stock: AAA Claro walnut with 22 lpi borderless wrap-around ribbon checkering, oil finish, steel grip cap, Pachmayr pad.
Sights: None furnished.
Features: Action has three mid-bolt locking lugs, 45-degree bolt rotation; fully adjustable trigger; swivel studs. Pachmayr butt pad. Introduced 1994. Made in U.S. by Cooper Arms.
Price: Classic $1,825.00
Price: Custom Classic (AAA Claro walnut, Monte Carlo beaded cheekpiece, oil finish) $2,025.00

CZ 550 BOLT-ACTION RIFLE
Caliber: 243, 308 (4-shot detachable magazine), 308, 270, 30-06, 7mm Rem. Mag., 300 Win. Mag. (5-shot internal magazine).
Barrel: 23.6".
Weight: 7.2 lbs. **Length:** 44.7" overall.
Stock: Walnut with high comb; checkered grip and forend.
Sights: None furnished; drilled and tapped for Remington 700-style bases.
Features: Polished blue finish. Introduced 1995. Imported from the Czech Republic by Magnum Research.
Price: . . . . $649.00 to $679.00
Price: Full Stock $849.00

CZ 527

CZ 527 BOLT-ACTION RIFLE
Caliber: 22 Hornet, 222 Rem., 223 Rem., detachable 5-shot magazine.
Barrel: 23 1/2"; standard or heavy barrel.
Weight: 6 lbs., 1 oz. **Length:** 42 1/2" overall.
Stock: European walnut with Monte Carlo.
Sights: Hooded front, open adjustable rear.
Features: Improved mini-Mauser action with non-rotating claw extractor; grooved receiver. Imported from the Czech Republic by Magnum Research.
Price: Standard $629.00

CZ ZKK 602

CZ ZKK 602 BOLT-ACTION RIFLES
Caliber: 7x57, 30-06, 270 (M600); 243, 308 (M601); 375 H&H, 416 Rigby, 416 Rem., 458 Win. Mag. (M602), 5-shot magazine.
Barrel: 25".
Weight: 7 lbs., 3 oz. to 9 lbs., 9 oz. **Length:** 43" overall.
Stock: Classic-style checkered walnut.
Sights: Hooded ramp front, open folding leaf adjustable rear.
Features: Improved Mauser action with controlled feed, claw extractor; safety blocks trigger and locks bolt; sling swivels. Imported from the Czech Republic by Magnum Research.
Price: $799.00

Dakota 76 Classic

DAKOTA 76 CLASSIC BOLT-ACTION RIFLE
Caliber: 257 Roberts, 270, 280, 30-06, 7mm Rem. Mag., 338 Win. Mag., 300 Win. Mag., 375 H&H, 458 Win. Mag.
Barrel: 23".
Weight: 7 1/2 lbs. **Length:** 43 1/2" overall.
Stock: Medium fancy grade walnut in classic style. Checkered pistol grip and forend; solid buttpad.
Sights: None furnished; drilled and tapped for scope mounts.
Features: Has many features of the original Model 70 Winchester. One-piece rail trigger guard assembly; steel grip cap. Model 70-style trigger. Many options available. Left-hand rifle available at same price. Introduced 1988. From Dakota Arms, Inc.
Price: $2,500.00

Dakota 76 Short Action Rifles
A scaled-down version of the standard Model 76. Standard chamberings are 22-250, 243, 6mm Rem., 250-3000, 7mm-08, 308, others on special order. Short Classic Grade has 21" barrel; Alpine Grade is lighter (6 1/2 lbs.), has a blind magazine and slimmer stock. Introduced 1989.
Price: Short Classic $2,300.00

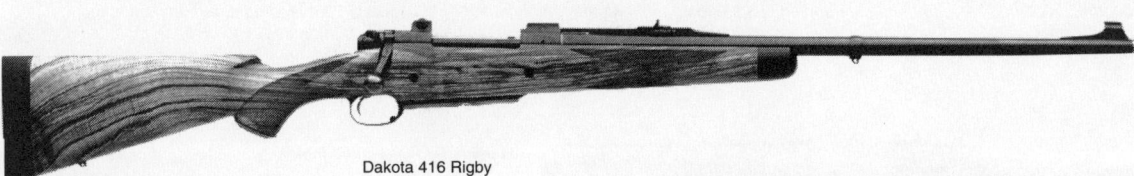
Dakota 416 Rigby

Dakota 416 Rigby African
Similar to the 76 Safari except chambered for 404 Jeffery, 416 Rigby, 416 Dakota, 450 Dakota, 4-round magazine, select wood, two stock cross-bolts. Has 24" barrel, weight of 9-10 lbs. Ramp front sight, standing leaf rear. Introduced 1989.
Price: $3,750.00

Dakota 76 Varmint Rifle
Similar to the Dakota 76 except is a single shot with heavy barrel contour and special stock dimensions for varmint shooting. Chambered for 17 Rem., 22 BR, 222 Rem., 22-250, 220 Swift, 223, 6mm BR, 6mm PPC. Introduced 1994. Made in U.S. by Dakota Arms, Inc.
Price: $2,300.00

DAKOTA 76 SAFARI BOLT-ACTION RIFLE
Caliber: 270 Win., 7x57, 280, 30-06, 7mm Dakota, 7mm Rem. Mag., 300 Dakota, 300 Win. Mag., 330 Dakota, 338 Win. Mag., 375 Dakota, 458 Win. Mag., 300 H&H, 375 H&H, 416 Rem.
Barrel: 23".
Weight: 8 1/2 lbs. **Length:** 43 1/2" overall.
Stock: XXX fancy walnut with ebony forend tip; point-pattern with wrap-around forend checkering.
Sights: Ramp front, standing leaf rear.
Features: Has many features of the original Model 70 Winchester. Barrel band front swivel, inletted rear. Cheekpiece with shadow line. Steel grip cap. Introduced 1988. From Dakota Arms, Inc.
Price: Wood stock $3,300.00

CENTERFIRE RIFLES—BOLT ACTION

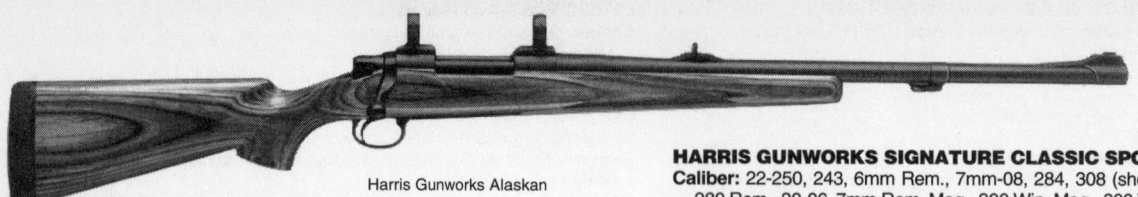

Harris Gunworks Alaskan

AUGUSTE FRANCOTTE BOLT-ACTION RIFLES
Caliber: 243, 270, 7x64, 30-06, 308, 300 Win. Mag., 338, 7mm Rem. Mag., 375 H&H, 458 Win. Mag.; others on request.
Barrel: 23 1/2" to 26 1/2".
Weight: 8 to 10 lbs.
Stock: Fancy European walnut. To customer specs.
Sights: To customer specs.
Features: Basically a custom gun, Francotte offers many options. Imported from Belgium by Armes de Chasse.
Price: From about (no engraving) .... $10,600.00 to $14,800.00

Harris Gunworks Signature Super Varminter
Similar to the Classic Sporter except has heavy contoured barrel, adjustable trigger, field bipod and special hand-bedded fiberglass stock. Chambered for 223, 22-250, 220 Swift, 243, 6mm Rem., 25-06, 7mm-08, 7mm BR, 308, 350 Rem. Mag. Comes with 1" rings and bases. Introduced 1989.
Price: $2,600.00

HARRIS GUNWORKS SIGNATURE CLASSIC SPORTER
Caliber: 22-250, 243, 6mm Rem., 7mm-08, 284, 308 (short action); 25-06, 270, 280 Rem., 30-06, 7mm Rem. Mag., 300 Win. Mag., 300 Wea. (long action); 338 Win. Mag., 340 Wea., 375 H&H (magnum action).
Barrel: 22", 24", 26".
Weight: 7 lbs. (short action).
Stock: Fiberglass in green, beige, brown or black. Recoil pad and 1" swivels installed. Length of pull up to 14 1/4".
Sights: None furnished. Comes with 1" rings and bases.
Features: Uses right- or left-hand action with matte black finish. Trigger pull set at 3 lbs. Four-round magazine for standard calibers; three for magnums. Aluminum floorplate. Wood stock optional. Introduced 1987. From Harris Gunworks, Inc.
Price: $2,600.00

Harris Gunworks Signature Alaskan
Similar to the Classic Sporter except has match-grade barrel with single leaf rear sight, barrel band front, 1" detachable rings and mounts, steel floorplate, electroless nickel finish. Has wood Monte Carlo stock with cheekpiece, palm-swell grip, solid buttpad. Chambered for 270, 280 Rem., 30-06, 7mm Rem. Mag., 300 Win. Mag., 300 Wea., 358 Win., 340 Wea., 375 H&H. Introduced 1989.
Price: $3,300.00

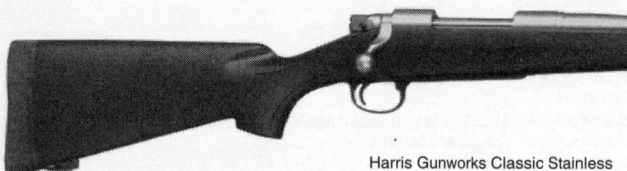

Harris Gunworks Classic Stainless

Harris Gunworks Signature Titanium Mountain Rifle
Similar to the Classic Sporter except action made of titanium alloy, barrel of chrome-moly steel. Stock is of graphite reinforced fiberglass. Weight is 5 1/2 lbs. Chambered for 270, 280 Rem., 30-06, 7mm Rem. Mag., 300 Win. Mag. Fiberglass stock optional. Introduced 1989.
Price: $3,200.00

HARRIS GUNWORKS TALON SAFARI RIFLE
Caliber: 300 Win. Mag., 300 Wea. Mag., 300 Phoenix, 338 Win. Mag., 30/378, 338 Lapua, 300 H&H, 340 Wea. Mag., 375 H&H, 404 Jeffery, 416 Rem. Mag., 458 Win. Mag. (Safari Magnum); 378 Wea. Mag., 416 Rigby, 416 Wea. Mag., 460 Wea. Mag. (Safari Super Magnum).
Barrel: 24".
Weight: About 9-10 lbs. **Length:** 43" overall.
Stock: Gunworks fiberglass Safari.
Sights: Barrel band front ramp, multi-leaf express rear.
Features: Uses Harris Gunworks Safari action. Has quick detachable 1" scope mounts, positive locking steel floorplate, barrel band sling swivel. Match-grade barrel. Matte black finish standard. Introduced 1989. From Harris Gunworks, Inc.
Price: Talon Safari Magnum $3,500.00
Price: Talon Safari Super Magnum $3,600.00

Harris Gunworks Classic Stainless Sporter
Similar to the Classic Sporter except barrel and action made of stainless steel. Same calibers, in addition to 416 Rem. Mag. Comes with fiberglass stock, right- or left-hand action in natural stainless, glass bead or black chrome sulfide finishes. Introduced 1990. From Harris Gunworks, Inc.
Price: $2,600.00

> Consult our Directory pages for the location of firms mentioned.

HARRIS GUNWORKS TALON SPORTER RIFLE
Caliber: 22-250, 243, 6mm Rem., 6mm BR, 7mm BR, 7mm-08, 25-06, 270, 280 Rem., 284, 308, 30-06, 350 Rem. Mag. (Long Action); 7mm Rem. Mag., 7mm STW, 300 Win. Mag., 300 Wea. Mag., 300 H&H, 338 Win. Mag., 340 Wea. Mag., 375 H&H, 416 Rem. Mag.
Barrel: 24" (standard).
Weight: About 7 1/2 lbs. **Length:** NA.
Stock: Choice of walnut or fiberglass.
Sights: None furnished; comes with rings and bases. Open sights optional.
Features: Uses pre-'64 Model 70-type action with cone breech, controlled feed, claw extractor and three-position safety. Barrel and action are of stainless steel; chrome-moly optional. Introduced 1991. From Harris Gunworks, Inc.
Price: $2,600.00

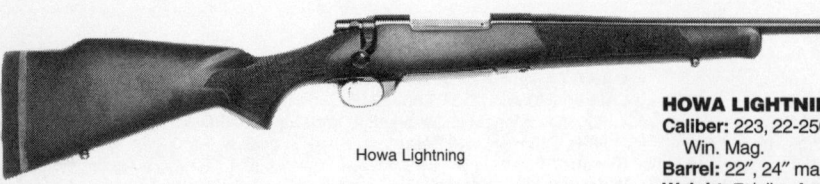

Howa Lightning

HOWA LIGHTNING BOLT-ACTION RIFLE
Caliber: 223, 22-250, 243, 270, 308, 30-06, 7mm Rem. Mag., 300 Win. Mag., 338 Win. Mag.
Barrel: 22", 24" magnum calibers.
Weight: 7 1/2 lbs. **Length:** 42" overall (22" barrel).
Stock: Black Bell & Carlson Carbelite composite with Monte Carlo comb; checkered grip and forend.
Sights: None furnished. Drilled and tapped for scope mounting.
Features: Sliding thumb safety; hinged floorplate; polished blue/black finish. Introduced 1993. From Interarms.
Price: Standard calibers $425.00
Price: Magnum calibers $425.00

CENTERFIRE RIFLES—BOLT ACTION

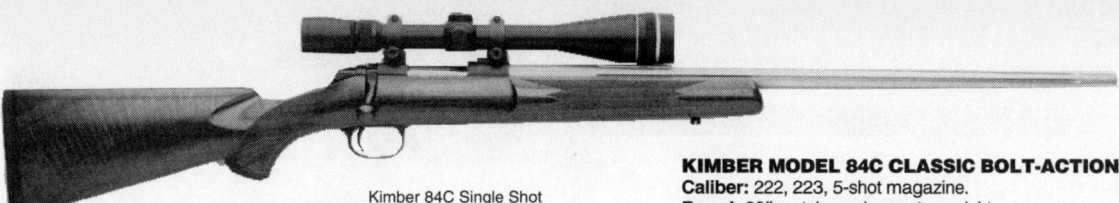
Kimber 84C Single Shot

Kimber Model 84C Single Shot Varmint
Similar to the Model 84C except is a single shot chambered only for 17 Rem. and 223 Rem.; 25" fluted match-grade stainless barrel with target crown; and has varmint-profile stock with wide forend. Introduced 1996. Made in U.S. by Kimber of America, Inc.
Price: $999.00

KIMBER MODEL 84C CLASSIC BOLT-ACTION RIFLE
Caliber: 222, 223, 5-shot magazine.
Barrel: 22" match-grade sporter weight.
Weight: 6 3/4 lbs. **Length:** 40 1/2" overall.
Stock: Select A Claro walnut.
Sights: None furnished; drilled and tapped for Warne, Leupold or Millett scope mounts.
Features: Controlled round feed with Mauser-style extractor; pillar-bedded action; free-floating barrel; fully adjustable trigger; steel floorplate and trigger guard. Reintroduced 1996. Made in U.S. by Kimber of America, Inc.
Price: $1,145.00

Kimber Model 84C SuperAmerica
Similar to the Model 84C Classic except has AAA Claro walnut stock with beaded checkpiece, ebony forend tip, wrap-around 22 lpi checkering, and black rubber butt pad. Chambered for 17 Rem., 222 Rem., 223 Rem. Reintroduced 1996. Made in U.S. by Kimber of America, Inc.
Price: $1,595.00

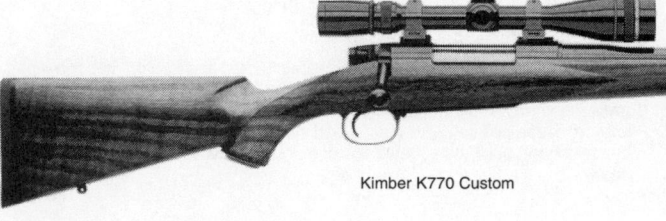
Kimber K770 Custom

Kimber Model K770 SuperAmerica Bolt-Action Rifle
Similar to the K770 Custom except has AAA Fancy Claro walnut stock with beaded checkpiece, ebony forend tip, and wrap-around hand-cut 22 lpi checkering. Introduced 1996.
Price: $1,260.00

KIMBER MODEL K770 CUSTOM RIFLE
Caliber: 270 Win., 30-06.
Barrel: 24" match grade, sporter weight.
Weight: About 7 1/2 lbs. **Length:** 43" overall.
Stock: Classic-style select Claro walnut, hand-cut panel checkering, solid rubber recoil pad, blued steel grip cap.
Sights: None furnished; drilled and tapped for Warne, Leupold or Millett scope mounts.
Features: Bolt locks into barrel breach; 60° bolt throw; pillar bedding; free-gloated barrel; hinged floorplate. Introduced 1996. Made in U.S. by Kimber of America, Inc.
Price: $745.00

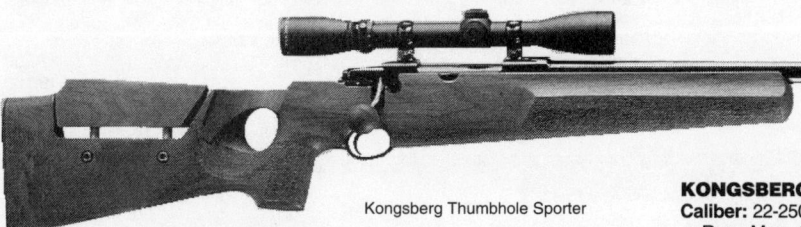
Kongsberg Thumbhole Sporter

KONGSBERG THUMBHOLE SPORTER RIFLE
Caliber: 22-250, 308 Win., 4-shot magazine.
Barrel: 23" heavy barrel (.750" muzzle).
Weight: About 8 1/2 lbs. **Length:** NA.
Stock: Oil-finished American walnut with stippled thumbhole grip, wide stippled forend, cheekpiece fully adjustable for height.
Sights: None furnished. Receiver dovetailed for scope mounting, and is drilled and tapped.
Features: Large bolt knob; rotary magazine; adjustable trigger; three-position safety; 60° bolt throw; claw extractor. Introduced 1993. Imported from Norway by Kongsberg America L.L.C.
Price: Right-hand $1,580.00
Price: Left-hand $1,718.00

KONGSBERG CLASSIC RIFLE
Caliber: 22-250, 243, 6.5x55, 270 Win., 30-06, 308 Win., 4-shot magazine; 7mm Rem. Mag., 300 Win. Mag., 338 Win. Mag., 3-shot magazine.
Barrel: 23" in standard calibers, 26" for magnums.
Weight: About 7 1/2 lbs. **Length:** 44" overall (23" barrel).
Stock: Oil-finished European walnut with straight fluted comb; 18 lpi checkering; rubber buttpad.
Sights: Hooded blade front, open adjustable rear. Receiver dovetailed for Weaver-type scope mount, and drilled and tapped.
Features: Rotary magazine; adjustable trigger; three-position safety; 60° bolt throw; claw extractor. Introduced 1993. Imported from Norway by Kingsberg America L.L.C.
Price: Right-hand, standard calibers $995.00
Price: Right-hand, magnum calibers $1,109.00
Price: Left-hand, standard calibers $1,133.00
Price: Left-hand, magnum calibers $1,245.00

Krico Model 700

KRICO MODEL 700 BOLT-ACTION RIFLES
Caliber: 17 Rem., 222, 222 Rem. Mag., 223, 5.6x50 Mag., 243, 308, 5.6x57 RWS, 22-250, 6.5x55, 6.5x57, 7x57, 270, 7x64, 30-06, 9.3x62, 6.5x68, 7mm Rem. Mag., 300 Win. Mag., 8x68S, 7.5 Swiss, 9.3x64, 6x62 Freres.
Barrel: 23.6" (std. cals.); 25.5" (mag. cals.).
Weight: 7 lbs. **Length:** 43.3" overall (23.6" bbl.).
Stock: European walnut, Bavarian cheekpiece.
Sights: Blade on ramp front, open adjustable rear.
Features: Removable box magazine; sliding safety. Drilled and tapped for scope mounting. Imported from Germany by Mandall Shooting Supplies.
Price: Model 700 ....$995.00
Price: Model 700 Deluxe S $1,495.00
Price: Model 700 Deluxe $1,025.00
Price: Model 700 Stutzen (full stock) $1,249.00

CENTERFIRE RIFLES—BOLT ACTION

L.A.R. Grizzly 50

L.A.R. GRIZZLY 50 BIG BOAR RIFLE
Caliber: 50 BMG, single shot.
Barrel: 36".
Weight: 28.4 lbs. **Length:** 45.5" overall.
Stock: Integral. Ventilated rubber recoil pad.
Sights: None furnished; scope mount.
Features: Bolt-action bullpup design; thumb safety. All-steel construction. Introduced 1994. Made in U.S. by L.A.R. Mfg., Inc.
Price: $2,570.00

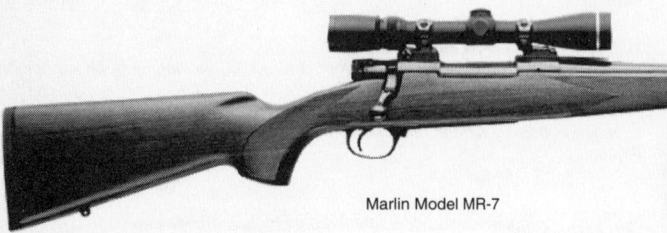
Marlin Model MR-7

MARLIN MODEL MR-7 BOLT-ACTION RIFLE
Caliber: 270, 30-06, 4-shot detachable box magazine.
Barrel: 22"; six-groove rifling.
Weight: 7 1/2 lbs. **Length:** 43" overall.
Stock: American black walnut with cut-checkered grip and forend, rubber buttpad, Mar-Shield® finish.
Sights: Bead on ramp front, adjustable rear, or no sights.
Features: Three-position safety; shrouded striker; red cocking indicator; adjustable 3-6 lb. trigger; quick-detachable swivel studs. Introduced 1996. Made in U.S. by Marlin.
Price: $610.90

MAUSER MODEL 96 BOLT-ACTION RIFLE
Caliber: 270, 30-06, 5-shot magazine.
Barrel: 22".
Weight: About 6.25 lbs. **Length:** 42" overall.
Stock: European walnut with checkered grip and forend.
Sights: None furnished; drilled and tapped for Remington 700 scope mounts.
Features: "Slide-bolt" straight-pull action with 16 locking lugs; tang mounted three-position safety; quick detachable sling swivels. Introduced 1996. Imported from Germany by GSI, Inc.
Price: ....$NA

REMINGTON 700 ADL BOLT-ACTION RIFLE
Caliber: 243, 270, 308, 30-06 and 7mm Rem. Mag.
Barrel: 22" or 24" round tapered.
Weight: 7 lbs. **Length:** 41 1/2" to 43 1/2" overall.
Stock: Walnut. Satin-finished pistol grip stock with fine-line cut checkering, Monte Carlo.
Sights: Gold bead ramp front; removable, step-adjustable rear with windage screw.
Features: Side safety, receiver tapped for scope mounts.
Price: About $472.00
Price: 7mm Rem. Mag., about $499.00

Remington 700 ADL Synthetic

Remington 700 BDL Bolt-Action Rifle
Same as the 700 ADL except chambered for 222, 223 (short action, 24" barrel), 22-250, 25-06, 6mm Rem. (short action, 22" barrel), 243, 270, 7mm-08, 280, 300 Savage, 30-06, 308; skip-line checkering; black forend tip and grip cap with white line spacers. Matted receiver top, quick-release floorplate. Hooded ramp front sight; q.d. swivels.
Price: About $576.00
Also available in 17 Rem., 7mm Rem. Mag., 300 Win. Mag. (long action, 24" barrel), 338 Win. Mag., 35 Whelen (long action, 22" barrel). Overall length 44 1/2", weight about 7 1/2 lbs.
Price: About $603.00
Price: Custom Grade, about $2,507.00

Remington 700 ADL Synthetic
Similar to the 700 ADL except has a fiberglass-reinforced synthetic stock with straight comb, raised cheekpiece, positive checkering, and black rubber buttpad. Metal has matte finish. Available in 243, 270, 308, 30-06 with 22" barrel, 7mm Rem. Mag. with 24" barrel. Introduced 1996.
Price: $412.00
Price: 7mm Rem. Mag. $439.00

Remington 700 VLS Varmint Laminated Stock
Similar to the 700 BDL except has 26" heavy barrel without sights, brown laminated stock with forend tip, grip cap, rubber buttpad. Available in 222 Rem., 223 Rem., 22-250, 243, 308. Polished blue finish. Introduced 1995.
Price: $609.00

Remington 700 VS SF Rifle
Similar to the Model 700 Varmint Synthetic except has satin-finish stainless barreled action with 26" fluted barrel, spherical concave muzzle crown. Chambered for 223, 220 Swift, 22-250, 308. Introduced 1994.
Price: $826.00

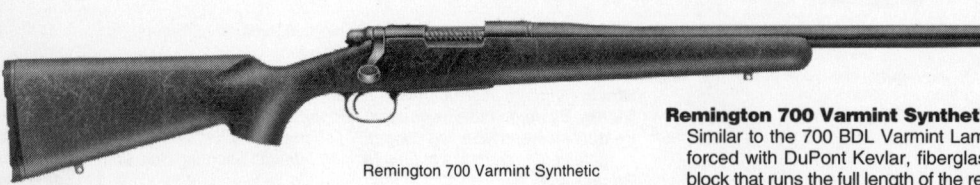
Remington 700 Varmint Synthetic

Remington 700 Varmint Synthetic Rifle
Similar to the 700 BDL Varmint Laminated except has composite stock reinforced with DuPont Kevlar, fiberglass and graphite. Has aluminum bedding block that runs the full length of the receiver. Free-floating 26" barrel. Metal has black matte finish; stock has textured black and gray finish and swivel studs. Available in 220 Swift, 223, 22-250, 308. Introduced 1992.
Price: $686.00

CENTERFIRE RIFLES—BOLT ACTION

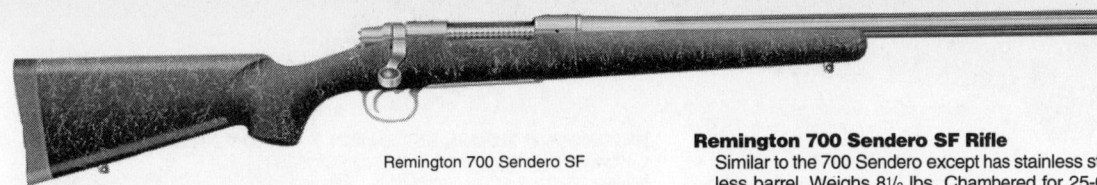
Remington 700 Sendero SF

Remington 700 Sendero Rifle
Similar to the Model 700 Varmint Synthetic except has long action for magnum calibers. Has 26" heavy varmint barrel with spherical concave crown. Chambered for 25-06, 270, 7mm Rem. Mag., 300 Win. Mag. Introduced 1994.
Price: 25-06, 270 ....$686.00
Price: 7mm Rem. Mag., 300 Win. Mag. $713.00

Remington 700 Custom KS Mountain Rifle
Similar to the 700 BDL except custom finished with Kevlar reinforced resin synthetic stock. Available in both left- and right-hand versions. Chambered for 270 Win., 280 Rem., 30-06, 7mm Rem. Mag., 300 Win. Mag., 300 Wea. Mag., 35 Whelen, 338 Win. Mag., 8mm Rem. Mag., 375 H&H, all with 24" barrel only. Weighs 6 lbs., 6 oz. Introduced 1986.
Price: Right-hand $1,089.00
Price: Left-hand $1,156.00
Price: Stainless $1,241.00

Remington 700 BDL SS DM Rifle
Same as the 700 BDL SS except has detachable box magazine. Barrel, receiver and bolt made of #416 stainless steel; black synthetic stock. Available in 243, 25-06, 270, 280, 7mm-08, 308, 30-06, 7mm Rem. Mag., 300 Win. Mag., 300 Wea. Mag., 338 Win. Mag. Introduced 1995.
Price: Standard calibers $676.00
Price: Magnum calibers $702.00

Remington 700 Sendero SF Rifle
Similar to the 700 Sendero except has stainless steel action and 26" fluted stainless barrel. Weighs 8½ lbs. Chambered for 25-06, 7mm Rem. Mag. and 300 Win. Mag. Introduced 1996.
Price: 25-06 ....$826.00
Price: 7mm Rem. Mag., 300 Win. Mag $853.00

Remington 700 BDL SS Rifle
Similar to the 700 BDL rifle except has hinged floorplate, 24" standard weight barrel in all calibers; magnum calibers have magnum-contour barrel. No sights supplied, but comes drilled and tapped. Has corrosion-resistant follower and fire control, stainless BDL-style barreled action with fine matte finish. Synthetic stock has straight comb and cheekpiece, textured finish, positive checkering, plated swivel studs. Calibers—270, 30-06; magnums—7mm Rem. Mag., 300 Win. Mag. Weighs 6¾-7 lbs. Introduced 1993.
Price: Standard calibers, about $623.00
Price: Magnum calibers, about $649.00

Remington 700 BDL Left Hand
Same as 700 BDL except mirror-image left-hand action, stock. Available in 270, 30-06 only.
Price: About $603.00
Price: 7mm Rem. Mag. $629.00

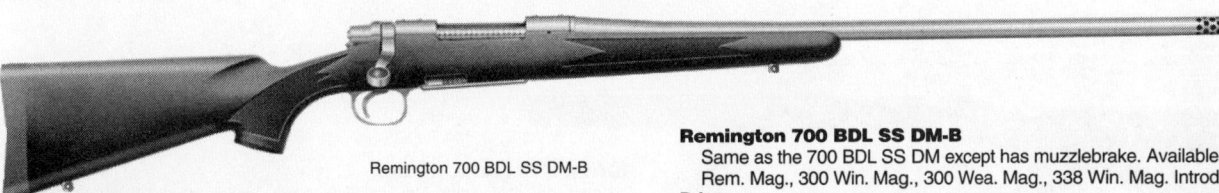
Remington 700 BDL SS DM-B

Remington 700 Safari
Similar to the 700 BDL except custom finished and tuned. In 8mm Rem. Mag., 375 H&H, 416 Rem. Mag. or 458 Win. Mag. calibers only with heavy barrel. Hand checkered, oil-finished stock in classic or Monte Carlo style with recoil pad installed. Delivery time is about 5 months.
Price: About $1,093.00
Price: Classic stock, left-hand $1,160.00
Price: Safari Custom KS (Kevlar stock), right-hand $1,258.00
Price: As above, left-hand $1,326.00

Remington 700 BDL SS DM-B
Same as the 700 BDL SS DM except has muzzlebrake. Available only in 7mm Rem. Mag., 300 Win. Mag., 300 Wea. Mag., 338 Win. Mag. Introduced 1996.
Price: $762.00

Remington 700 APR African Plains Rifle
Similar to the Model 700 BDL except has magnum receiver and specially contoured 26" Custom Shop barrel with satin finish, laminated wood stock with raised cheekpiece, satin finish, black buttpad, 20 lpi cut checkering. Chambered for 7mm Rem. Mag., 300 Win. Mag., 300 Wea. Mag., 338 Win. Mag., 375 H&H. Introduced 1994.
Price: $1,466.00

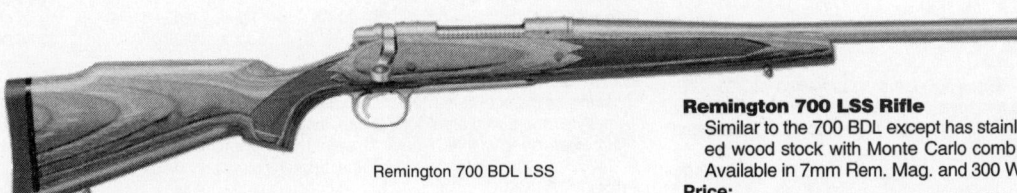
Remington 700 BDL LSS

Remington 700 BDL DM Rifle
Same as the 700 BDL except has detachable box magazine (4-shot, standard calibers, 3-shot for magnums). Has glossy stock finish, open sights, recoil pad, sling swivels. Right-hand action calibers: 6mm, 243, 25-06, 270, 280, 7mm-08, 30-06, 308, 7mm Rem. Mag., 300 Win. Mag., 338 Win. Mag.; left-hand calibers: 270, 30-06, 7mm Rem. Mag., 300 Win. Mag. Introduced 1995.
Price: Right-hand, standard calibers $628.00
Price: Left-hand, standard calibers $656.00
Price: Right-hand, magnum calibers $656.00
Price: Left-hand, magnum calibers $682.00

Remington 700 AWR Alaskan Wilderness Rifle
Similar to the Model 700 BDL except has stainless barreled action with satin blue finish; special 24" Custom Shop barrel profile; matte gray stock of fiberglass and graphite, reinforced with DuPont Kevlar, straight comb with raised cheekpiece, magnum-grade black rubber recoil pad. Chambered for 7mm Rem. Mag., 300 Win. Mag., 300 Wea. Mag., 338 Win. Mag., 375 H&H. Introduced 1994.
Price: $1,318.00

Remington 700 LSS Rifle
Similar to the 700 BDL except has stainless steel barreled action, gray laminated wood stock with Monte Carlo comb and cheekpiece. No sights furnished. Available in 7mm Rem. Mag. and 300 Win. Mag. Introduced 1996.
Price: $676.00

REMINGTON 700 CLASSIC RIFLE
Caliber: 375 H&H Mag.
Barrel: 24".
Weight: About 7¾ lbs. **Length:** 44½" overall.
Stock: American walnut, 20 lpi checkering on pistol grip and forend. Classic styling. Satin finish.
Sights: None furnished. Receiver drilled and tapped for scope mounting.
Features: A "classic" version of the M700 ADL with straight comb stock. Fitted with rubber recoil pad. Sling swivel studs installed. Hinged floorplate. Limited production in 1996 only.
Price: About $623.00

Remington 700 MTN DM Rifle
Similar to the 700 BDL except weighs 6¾ lbs., has a 22" tapered barrel. Redesigned pistol grip, straight comb, contoured cheekpiece, hand-rubbed oil stock finish, deep cut checkering, hinged floorplate and magazine follower, two-position thumb safety. Chambered for 243, 270 Win., 7mm-08, 25-06, 280 Rem., 30-06, 4-shot detachable box magazine. Overall length is 42½". Introduced 1995.
Price: About $629.00

CENTERFIRE RIFLES—BOLT ACTION

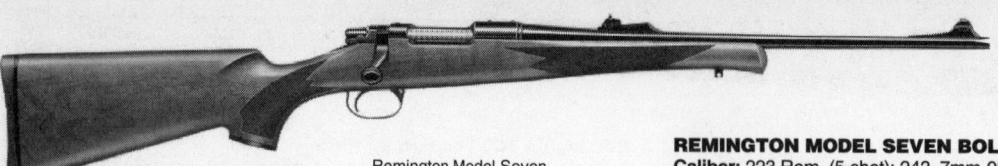
Remington Model Seven

Remington Model Seven Youth Rifle
Similar to the Model Seven except has hardwood stock with 12³/₁₆" length of pull and chambered for 243, 7mm-08. Introduced 1993.
Price: About $465.00

Remington Model Seven Custom MS Rifle
Similar to the Model Seven except has full-length Mannlicher-style stock of laminated wood with straight comb, solid black recoil pad, black steel forend tip, cut checkering, gloss finish. Barrel length 20", weighs 6³/₄ lbs. Available in 222 Rem., 223, 22-250, 243, 6mm Rem., 7mm-08 Rem., 308, 350 Rem. Mag. Calibers 250 Savage, 257 Roberts, 35 Rem. available on special order. Polished blue finish. Introduced 1993. From Remington Custom Shop.
Price: About $1,093.00

REMINGTON MODEL SEVEN BOLT-ACTION RIFLE
Caliber: 223 Rem. (5-shot); 243, 7mm-08, 308 (4-shot).
Barrel: 18¹/₂".
Weight: 6¹/₄ lbs. **Length:** 37¹/₂" overall.
Stock: Walnut, with modified schnabel forend. Cut checkering.
Sights: Ramp front, adjustable open rear.
Features: Short-action design; silent side safety; free-floated barrel except for single pressure point at forend tip. Introduced 1983.
Price: About $569.00

Remington Model Seven Custom KS
Similar to the standard Model Seven except has custom finished stock of lightweight Kevlar aramid fiber and chambered for 223 Rem., 7mm-08, 308, 35 Rem. and 350 Rem. Mag. Barrel length is 20", weighs 5³/₄ lbs. Comes with iron sights and is drilled and tapped for scope mounting. Special order through Remington Custom Shop. Introduced 1987.
Price: $1,089.00

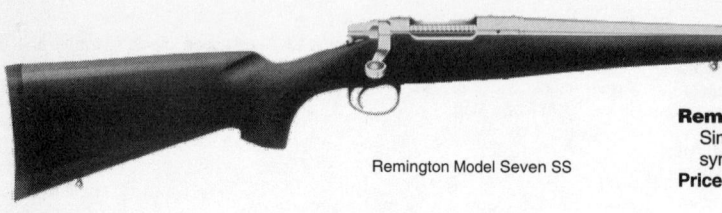
Remington Model Seven SS

Remington Model Seven SS
Similar to the Model Seven except has stainless steel barreled action and black synthetic stock, 20" barrel. Chambered for 243, 7mm-08, 308. Introduced 1994.
Price: About $623.00

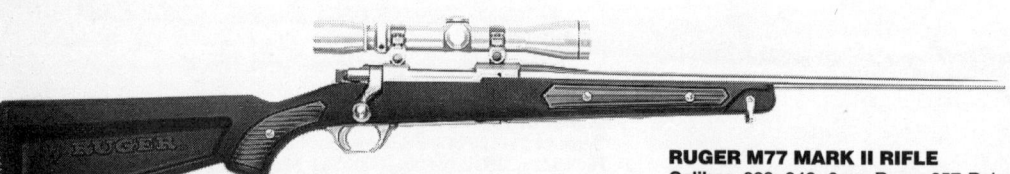
Ruger M77 All-Weather

Ruger M77 Mark II All-Weather Stainless Rifle
Similar to the wood-stock M77 Mark II except all metal parts are of stainless steel, and has an injection-moulded, glass-fiber-reinforced Du Pont Zytel stock. Chambered for 223, 243, 270, 308, 30-06, 7mm Rem. Mag., 300 Win. Mag., 338 Win. Mag. Has the fixed-blade-type ejector, three-position safety, and new trigger guard with patented floorplate latch. Comes with integral Scope Base Receiver and 1" Ruger scope rings, built-in sling swivel loops. Introduced 1990.
Price: KM77RPMKII $574.00
Price: KM77RSPMKII, open sights $635.00

Ruger M77RL Ultra Light
Similar to the standard M77 except weighs only 6 lbs., chambered for 223, 243, 308, 270, 30-06, 257; barrel tapped for target scope blocks; has 20" Ultra Light barrel. Overall length 40". Ruger's steel 1" scope rings supplied. Introduced 1983.
Price: M77RLMKII $610.00

RUGER M77 MARK II RIFLE
Caliber: 223, 243, 6mm Rem., 257 Roberts, 25-06, 6.5x55 Swedish, 270, 280 Rem., 308, 30-06, 7mm Rem. Mag., 300 Win. Mag., 338 Win. Mag., 4-shot magazine.
Barrel: 20", 22"; 24" (magnums).
Weight: About 7 lbs. **Length:** 39³/₄" overall.
Stock: Hand-checkered American walnut; swivel studs, rubber butt pad.
Sights: None furnished. Receiver has Ruger integral scope mount base, comes with Ruger 1" rings. Some models have iron sights.
Features: Short action with new trigger and three-position safety. New trigger guard with redesigned floorplate latch. Left-hand model available. Introduced 1989.
Price: M77RMKII (no sights) $574.00
Price: M77RSMKII (open sights) $635.00
Price: M77LRMKII (left-hand, 270, 30-06, 7mm Rem. Mag., 300 Win. Mag.) $574.00

Ruger M77RSI International Carbine
Same as the standard Model 77 except has 18¹/₂" barrel, full-length International-style stock, with steel forend cap, loop-type steel sling swivels. Integral-base receiver, open sights, Ruger 1" steel rings. Improved front sight. Available in 243, 270, 308, 30-06. Weighs 7 lbs. Length overall is 38³/₈".
Price: M77RSIMKII $642.00

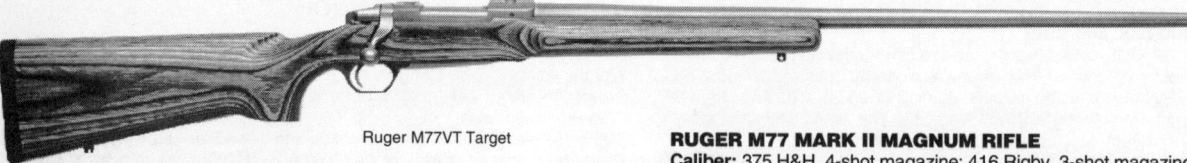
Ruger M77VT Target

RUGER M77VT TARGET RIFLE
Caliber: 22 PPC, 22-250, 220 Swift, 223, 243, 6mm PPC, 25-06, 308.
Barrel: 26" heavy stainless steel with target gray finish.
Weight: Approx. 9.25 lbs. **Length:** Approx. 44" overall.
Stock: Laminated American hardwood with beavertail forend, steel swivel studs; no checkering or grip cap.
Sights: Integral scope mount bases in receiver.
Features: Ruger diagonal bedding system. Ruger steel 1" scope rings supplied. Fully adjustable trigger. Steel floorplate and trigger guard. New version introduced 1992.
Price: KM77VTMKII $684.00

RUGER M77 MARK II MAGNUM RIFLE
Caliber: 375 H&H, 4-shot magazine; 416 Rigby, 3-shot magazine.
Barrel: 26", with integral steel rib; hammer forged.
Weight: 9.25 lbs. (375); 10.25 lbs. (416, 458). **Length:** 40.5" overall.
Stock: Circassian walnut with hand-cut checkering, swivel studs, steel grip cap, rubber butt pad.
Sights: Ramp front, two leaf express on serrated integral steel rib. Rib also serves as base for front scope ring.
Features: Uses an enlarged Mark II action with three-position safety, stainless bolt, steel trigger guard and hinged steel floorplate. Controlled feed. Introduced 1989.
Price: M77RSMMKII $1,550.00

CENTERFIRE RIFLES—BOLT ACTION

Ruger 77/22 Hornet

RUGER 77/22 HORNET BOLT-ACTION RIFLE
Caliber: 22 Hornet, 6-shot rotary magazine.
Barrel: 20".
Weight: About 6 lbs. **Length:** 39 3/4" overall.
Stock: Checkered American walnut, black rubber buttpad.
Sights: Brass bead front, open adjustable rear; also available without sights.
Features: Same basic features as the rimfire model except has slightly lengthened receiver. Uses Ruger rotary magazine. Three-position safety. Comes with 1" Ruger scope rings. Introduced 1994.
Price: 77/22RH (rings only) $489.00
Price: 77/22RSH (with sights) $499.00
Price: K77/22VHZ Varmint, laminated stock, no sights $535.00

Manufacturers' addresses in the
Directory of the Arms Trade
page 313, this issue

RUGER M77 MARK II EXPRESS RIFLE
Caliber: 270, 30-06, 7mm Rem. Mag., 300 Win. Mag., 4-shot magazine.
Barrel: 22", with integral steel rib; barrel-mounted front swivel stud; hammer forged.
Weight: 7.5 lbs. **Length:** 42.125" overall.
Stock: Hand-checkered medium quality French walnut with steel grip cap, black rubber butt pad, swivel studs.
Sights: Ramp front, V-notch two-leaf express rear adjustable for windage mounted on rib.
Features: Mark II action with three-position safety, stainless steel bolt, steel trigger guard, hinged steel floorplate. Introduced 1991.
Price: M77RSEXMKII $1,550.00

Sako Long-Range Rifle

Sako Long-Range Hunting Rifle
Similar to the long action Hunter model except has 26" fluted barrel and is chambered for 25-06, 270 Win., 7mm Rem. Mag., 300 Win. Mag. Introduced 1996. Imported from Finland by Stoeger.
Price: 25-06 .... $1,275.00
Price: 7mm Rem. Mag., 300 Win. Mag $1,290.00

Sako Mannlicher-Style Carbine
Same as the Hunter except has full "Mannlicher" style stock, 18 1/2" barrel, weighs 7 1/2 lbs., chambered for 243, 25-06, 270, 308 and 30-06, 7mm Rem. Mag., 300 Win. Mag., 338 Win. Mag., 375 H&H. Introduced 1977. From Stoeger.
Price: 243, 308 .... $1,275.00
Price: 270, 30-06 .... $1,310.00
Price: 338 Win. Mag. $1,335.00
Price: 375 H&H $1,350.00

Sako Super Deluxe Sporter
Similar to Hunter except has select European walnut with high-gloss finish and deep-cut oak leaf carving. Metal has super high polish, deep blue finish. Special order only.
Price: $3,100.00

Sako Classic Bolt Action
Similar to the Hunter except has classic-style stock with straight comb. Has 21 3/4" barrel, weighs 6 lbs. Matte finish wood. Introduced 1993. Imported from Finland by Stoeger.
Price: 243 .... $1,050.00
Price: 270, 30-06 .... $1,085.00
Price: 7mm Rem. Mag. $1,100.00

SAKO HUNTER RIFLE
Caliber: 17 Rem., 222, 223 (short action); 22-250, 243, 7mm-08, 308 (medium action); 25-06, 270, 270 Wea. Mag., 7mm Wea. Mag., 30-06, 7mm Rem. Mag., 300 Win. Mag., 338 Win. Mag., 340 Wea. Mag., 375 H&H Mag., 300 Wea. Mag., 416 Rem. Mag. (long action).
Barrel: 22" to 24" depending on caliber.
Weight: 5 3/4 lbs. (short); 6 1/4 lbs. (med.); 7 1/4 lbs. (long).
Stock: Hand-checkered European walnut.
Sights: None furnished.
Features: Adjustable trigger, hinged floorplate. Imported from Finland by Stoeger.
Price: 17 Rem., 222, 223 .... $1,050.00
Price: 22-250, 243, 308, 7mm-08 .... $1,050.00
Price: Long action cals. (except magnums) $1,085.00
Price: Magnum cals. $1,100.00
Price: 375 H&H, 416 Rem. Mag., from $1,120.00
Price: 300 Wea. $1,120.00

Sako Varmint Heavy Barrel
Same as Hunter except has heavy varmint barrel, beavertail forend; available in 17 Rem., 222, 223 (short action), 22 PPC, 6mm PPC (single shot), 22-250, 243, 308, 7mm-08 (medium action). Weight from 8 1/4 to 8 1/2 lbs., 5-shot magazine capacity.
Price: 17 Rem., 222, 223 (short action) $1,240.00
Price: 22-250, 243, 308 (medium action) $1,240.00
Price: 22 PPC, 6mm PPC (single shot) $1,475.00

Sako Hunter Left-Hand Rifle
Same gun as the Sako Hunter except has left-hand action, stock with dull finish. Available in medium, long and magnum actions. Introduced 1987.
Price: Standard calibers, 22-250 to 7mm-08 .... $1,135.00
Price: Magnum calibers $1,180.00
Price: 375 H&H, 416 Rem. Mag. $1,200.00
Price: Long action, 25-06, 270, 280, 30-06 .... $1,165.00

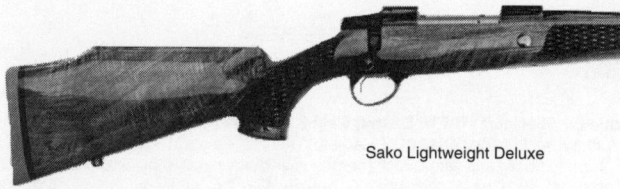
Sako Lightweight Deluxe

Sako Lightweight Deluxe
Same action as Hunter except has select wood, rosewood pistol grip cap and forend tip. Fine checkering on top surfaces of integral dovetail bases, bolt sleeve, bolt handle root and bolt knob. Vent. recoil pad, skip-line checkering, mirror finish bluing.
Price: 17 Rem., 222, 223, 22-250, 243, 308, 7mm-08 .... $1,475.00
Price: 25-06, 270, 280 Rem., 30-06 .... $1,510.00
Price: 7mm Rem. Mag., 300 Win. Mag., 338 Win. Mag. $1,525.00
Price: 300 Wea., 375 H&H, 416 Rem. Mag. $1,545.00

CAUTION: PRICES SHOWN ARE SUPPLIED BY THE MANUFACTURER OR IMPORTER. CHECK YOUR LOCAL GUNSHOP.

CENTERFIRE RIFLES—BOLT ACTION

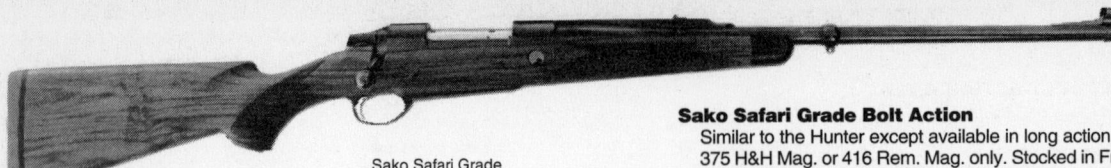
Sako Safari Grade

Sako Fiberclass Sporter
Similar to the Hunter except has a black fiberglass stock in the classic style, with wrinkle finish, rubber buttpad. Barrel length is 23", weight 7 lbs., 2 oz. Introduced 1985.
Price: 25-06, 270, 280 Rem., 30-06 ....$1,385.00
Price: 7mm Rem. Mag., 300 Win. Mag., 338 Win. Mag. $1,405.00
Price: 375 H&H, 416 Rem. Mag. $1,425.00

Sako Safari Grade Bolt Action
Similar to the Hunter except available in long action, calibers 338 Win. Mag. or 375 H&H Mag. or 416 Rem. Mag. only. Stocked in French walnut, checkered 20 lpi, solid rubber buttpad; grip cap and forend tip; quarter-rib "express" rear sight, hooded ramp front. Front sling swivel band-mounted on barrel.
Price: $2,765.00

Sako TRG-S

SAKO TRG-S BOLT-ACTION RIFLE
Caliber: 243, 7mm-08, 270, 6.5x55, 30-06, 7mm Rem. Mag., 300 Win. Mag., 338 Win. Mag., 270 Wea. Mag., 7mm Wea. Mag., 340 Wea. Mag., 375 H&H, 416 Rem. Mag., 5-shot magazine (4-shot for 375 H&H).
Barrel: 22", 24" (magnum calibers).
Weight: 7.75 lbs. **Length:** 45.5" overall.
Stock: Reinforced polyurethane with Monte Carlo comb.
Sights: None furnished.
Features: Resistance-free bolt with 60-degree lift. Recoil pad adjustable for length. Free-floating barrel, detachable magazine, fully adjustable trigger. Matte blue metal. Introduced 1993. Imported from Finland by Stoeger.
Price: 243, 7mm-08, 270, 30-06 ....$790.00
Price: Magnum calibers $830.00

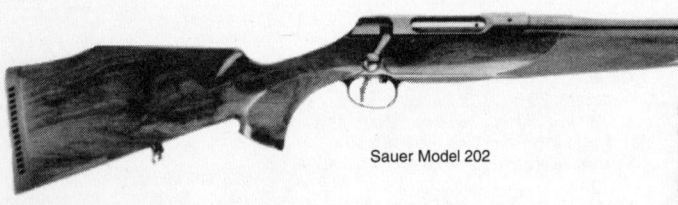
Sauer Model 202

SAUER 202 BOLT-ACTION RIFLE
Caliber: Standard—243, 270 Win., 308 Win., 30-06; magnum—7mm Rem. Mag., 300 Win. Mag., 375 H&H.
Barrel: 23.6" (standard), 26" (magnum).
Weight: 7.7 lbs. (standard) **Length:** 44.3" overall (23.6" barrel).
Stock: Select American Claro walnut with high-gloss epoxy finish, rosewood grip and forend caps; 22 lpi checkering.
Sights: None furnished; drilled and tapped for scope mounting.
Features: Short 60° bolt throw; detachable box magazine; six-lug bolt; quick-change barrel; tapered bore; adjustable two-stage trigger; firing pin cocking indicator. Introduced 1994. Imported from Germany by SIGARMS, Inc.
Price: Standard or magnum $900.00

SAUER 90 BOLT-ACTION RIFLE
Caliber: 243, 25-06, 270 Win., 308 Win., 30-06, 7mm Rem. Mag., 300 Win. Mag., 300 Wea. Mag., 375 H&H.
Barrel: 23.6" (standard calibers); 26" (magnums).
Weight: About 7.5 lbs. **Length:** 42.5" overall (23.6" barrel).
Stock: Select American Claro walnut with high-gloss epoxy finish, rosewood grip and forend caps; 22 lpi checkering.
Sights: None furnished; drilled and tapped for scope mounting.
Features: Three cam-actuated locking lugs on center of bolt; internal extractor; 65° bolt throw; detachable box magazine; tang safety; loaded chamber indicator; cocking indicator; adjustable trigger. Introduced 1986. Imported from Germany by SIGARMS, Inc.
Price: Standard or magnum $1,300.00

> Consult our Directory pages for the location of firms mentioned.

SAVAGE MODEL 110FP TACTICAL RIFLE
Caliber: 223, 25-06, 308, 30-06, 300 Win. Mag., 7mm Rem. Mag., 4-shot magazine.
Barrel: 24", heavy; recessed target muzzle.
Weight: 8 1/2 lbs. **Length:** 45.5" overall.
Stock: Black graphite/fiberglass composition; positive checkering.
Sights: None furnished. Receiver drilled and tapped for scope mounting.
Features: Pillar-bedded stock. Black matte finish on all metal parts. Double swivel studs on the forend for sling and/or bipod mount. Right or left-hand. Introduced 1990. From Savage Arms, Inc.
Price: $429.00

SAVAGE MODEL 110CY LADIES/YOUTH RIFLE
Caliber: 223, 243, 270, 300 Sav., 308, 5-shot magazine.
Barrel: 22".
Weight: About 6.5 lbs. **Length:** 42.5" overall.
Stock: Walnut-stained hardwood with high comb, cut checkering.
Sights: Ramp front, fully adjustable rear.
Features: Length of pull is 12.5", with red rubber buttpad. Drilled and tapped for scope mounting. Uses standard Model 110 barreled action. Introduced 1991. Made in U.S. by Savage Arms, Inc.
Price: $358.00

Savage 110 FM Sierra

Savage Model 110 FM Sierra Light Weight Rifle
Similar to the Model 110CY Ladies/Youth rifle except has 20" barrel, black graphite/fiberglass filled stock, comes with black nylon sling and quick detachable swivels. Overall length 41 1/2", weighs 6 1/4 lbs. Available in 243, 270, 308, 30-06. No sights furnished; drilled and tapped for scope mounting. Made in U.S. by Savage Arms, Inc. Introduced 1996.
Price: $410.00

CENTERFIRE RIFLES—BOLT ACTION

Savage Model 111FXP3, 111FCXP3 Package Guns
Similar to the Model 110 Series Package Guns except with lightweight, black graphite/fiberglass composite stock with non-glare finish, positive checkering. Same calibers as Model 110 rifles, plus 338 Win. Mag. Model 111FXP3 has fixed top-loading magazine; Model 111FCXP3 has detachable box. Both come with mounted 3-9x32 scope, quick-detachable swivels, sling. Introduced 1994. Made in U.S. by Savage Arms, Inc.
Price: Model 111FXP3, right- or left-hand $447.00
Price: Model 111FCXP3, right- or left-hand $489.00

SAVAGE MODEL 110GXP3, 110GCXP3 PACKAGE GUNS
Caliber: 223, 22-250, 243, 250 Savage, 25-06, 270, 300 Sav., 30-06, 308, 7mm Rem. Mag., 7mm-08, 300 Win. Mag. (Model 110GXP3); 270, 30-06, 7mm Rem. Mag., 300 Win. Mag. (Model 110GCXP3).
Barrel: 22" (standard calibers), 24" (magnum calibers).
Weight: 7.25-7.5 lbs. **Length:** 43.5" overall (22" barrel).
Stock: Monte Carlo-style hardwood with walnut finish, rubber buttpad, swivel studs.
Sights: None furnished.
Features: Model 110GXP3 has fixed, top-loading magazine, Model 110GCXP3 has detachable box magazine. Rifles come with a factory-mounted and bore-sighted 3-9x32 scope, rings and bases, quick-detachable swivels, sling. Left-hand models available in all calibers. Introduced 1991 (GXP3); 1994 (GCXP3). Made in U.S. by Savage Arms, Inc.
Price: Model 110GXP3, right- or left-hand $418.00
Price: Model 110GCXP3, right- or left-hand $482.00

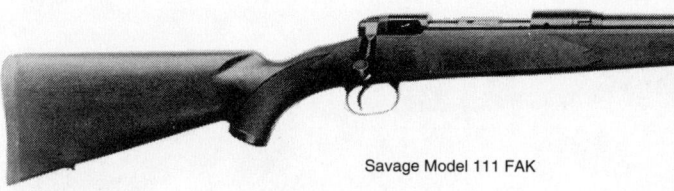

Savage Model 111 FAK

SAVAGE MODEL 111 CLASSIC HUNTER RIFLES
Caliber: 223, 22-250, 243, 250 Sav., 25-06, 270, 300 Sav., 30-06, 308, 7mm Rem. Mag., 7mm-08, 300 Win. Mag., 338 Win. Mag. (Models 111G, GL, GNS, F, FL, FNS); 270, 30-06, 7mm Rem. Mag., 300 Win. Mag. (Models 111GC, GLC, FC, FLC).
Barrel: 22", 24" (magnum calibers).
Weight: 6.3 to 7 lbs. **Length:** 43.5" overall (22" barrel).
Stock: Walnut-finished hardwood (M111G, GC); graphite/fiberglass filled composite.
Sights: Ramp front, open fully adjustable rear; drilled and tapped for scope mounting.
Features: Three-position top tang safety, double front locking lugs, free-floated button-rifled barrel. Comes with trigger lock, target, ear puffs. Introduced 1994. Made in U.S. by Savage Arms, Inc.
Price: Model 111FC (detachable magazine, composite stock, right- or left-hand) $418.00
Price: Model 111F (top-loading magazine, composite stock, right- or left-hand) $376.00
Price: Model 111FNS (as above, no sights, right-hand only) $372.00
Price: Model 111G (wood stock, top-loading magazine, right- or left-hand) $358.00
Price: Model 111GC (as above, detachable magazine) $407.00
Price: Model 111GNS (wood stock, top-loading magzine, no sights, right-hand only) $353.00
Price: Model 111FAK Express (blued, composite stock, top loading magazine, Adjustable Muzzle Brake) $450.00

SAVAGE MODEL 112 VARMINT RIFLES
Caliber: 22-250, 223, 5-shot magazine.
Barrel: 26" heavy.
Weight: 8.8 lbs. **Length:** 47.5" overall.
Stock: Black graphite/fiberglass filled composite with positive checkering.
Sights: None furnished; drilled and tapped for scope mounting.
Features: Pillar-bedded stock. Blued barrel with recessed target-style muzzle. Double front swivel studs for attaching bipod. Introduced 1991. Made in U.S. by Savage Arms, Inc.
Price: Model 112FV $400.00
Price: Model 112FVSS (cals. 223, 22-250, 25-06, 7mm Rem. Mag., 300 Win. Mag., stainless barrel, bolt handle, trigger guard) $510.00
Price: Model 112FVSS-S (as above, single shot) $500.00
Price: Model 112BVSS (heavy-prone laminated stock with high comb, Wund-hammer swell, fluted stainless barrel, bolt handle, trigger guard) $535.00
Price: Model 112BVSS-S (as above, single shot) $535.00

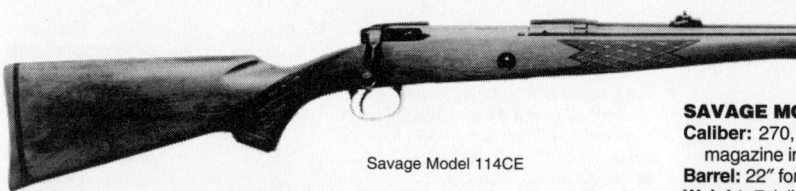

Savage Model 114CE

Savage Model 114CE Classic European
Similar to the Model 114C except the oil-finished walnut stock has a schnabel forend tip, cheekpiece and skip-line checkering; bead on blade front sight, fully adjustable open rear; solid red buttpad. Chambered for 270, 30-06, 7mm Rem. Mag., 300 Win. Mag. Introduced 1996. Made in U.S. by Savage Arms, Inc.
Price: $600.00

SAVAGE MODEL 114C CLASSIC RIFLE
Caliber: 270, 30-06, 7mm Rem. Mag., 300 Win. Mag.; 4-shot detachable box magazine in standard calibers, 3-shot for magnums.
Barrel: 22" for standard calibers, 24" for magnums.
Weight: 7 1/8 lbs. **Length:** 45 1/2" overall.
Stock: Oil-finished American walnut; checkered grip and forend.
Sights: None furnished; drilled and tapped for scope mounting.
Features: High polish blue on barrel, receiver and bolt handle; Savage logo laser-etched on bolt body; push-button magazine release. Made in U.S. by Savage Arms, Inc. Introduced 1996.
Price: $525.00

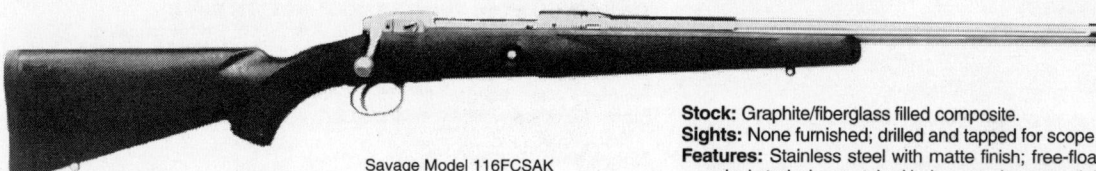

Savage Model 116FCSAK

SAVAGE MODEL 116 WEATHER WARRIORS
Caliber: 223, 243, 270, 30-06, 7mm Rem. Mag., 300 Win. Mag., 338 Win. Mag. (Model 116FSS); 270, 30-06, 7mm Rem. Mag., 300 Win. Mag. (Models 116FCSAK, 116FCS); 270, 30-06, 7mm Rem. Mag., 300 Win. Mag., 338 Win. Mag. (Models 116FSAK, 116FSK).
Barrel: 22", 24" for 7mm Rem. Mag., 300 Win. Mag., 338 Win. Mag. (M116FSS only).
Weight: 6.25 to 6.5 lbs. **Length:** 43.5" overall (22" barrel).
Stock: Graphite/fiberglass filled composite.
Sights: None furnished; drilled and tapped for scope mounting.
Features: Stainless steel with matte finish; free-floated barrel; quick-detachable swivel studs; laser-etched bolt; scope bases and rings. Left-hand models available in all models, calibers at same price. Models 116FCS, 116FSS introduced 1991; Model 116FSK introduced 1993; Model 116FCSAK, 116FSAK introduced 1994. Made in U.S. by Savage Arms, Inc.
Price: Model 116FSS (top-loading magazine) $491.00
Price: Model 116FCS (detachable box magazine) $554.00
Price: Model 116FCSAK (as above with Savage Adjustable Muzzle Brake system) $644.00
Price: Model 116FSAK (top-loading magazine, Savage Adjustable Muzzle Brake system) $581.00
Price: Model 116FSK Kodiak (as above with 22" Shock-Suppressor barrel) $554.00

CAUTION: PRICES SHOWN ARE SUPPLIED BY THE MANUFACTURER OR IMPORTER. CHECK YOUR LOCAL GUNSHOP.

CENTERFIRE RIFLES—BOLT ACTION

Savage Model 116SE

Savage Model 116US Ultra Stainless Rifle
Similar to the Model 116SE except chambered for 270, 30-06, 7mm Rem. Mag., 300 Win. Mag.; stock has high-gloss finish; no open sights. Stainless steel barreled action with satin finish. Introduced 1995. Made in U.S. by Savage Arms, Inc.
Price: $700.00

SAVAGE MODEL 116SE SAFARI EXPRESS RIFLE
Caliber: 300 Win. Mag., 338 Win. Mag., 425 Express, 458 Win. Mag.
Barrel: 24".
Weight: 8.5 lbs. **Length:** 45.5" overall.
Stock: Classic-style select walnut with ebony forend tip, deluxe cut checkering. Two cross bolts; internally vented recoil pad.
Sights: Bead on ramp front, three-leaf express rear.
Features: Controlled-round feed design; adjustable muzzlebrake; one-piece barrel band stud. Satin-finished stainless steel barreled action. Introduced 1994. Made in U.S. by Savage Arms, Inc.
Price: $900.00

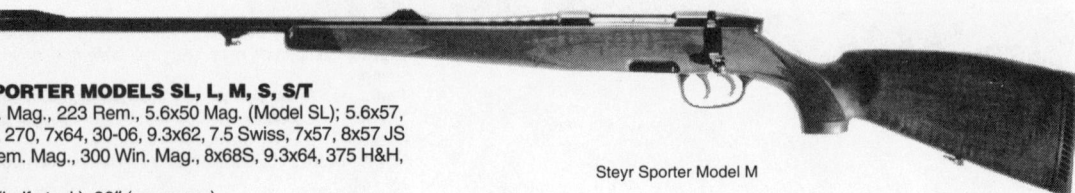

Steyr Sporter Model M

STEYR-MANNLICHER SPORTER MODELS SL, L, M, S, S/T
Caliber: 222 Rem., 222 Rem. Mag., 223 Rem., 5.6x50 Mag. (Model SL); 5.6x57, 243, 308 (Model L); 6.5x57, 270, 7x64, 30-06, 9.3x62, 7.5 Swiss, 7x57, 8x57 JS (Model M); 6.5x68, 7mm Rem. Mag., 300 Win. Mag., 8x68S, 9.3x64, 375 H&H, 458 Win. Mag. (Model S).
Barrel: 20" (full-stock), 23.6" (half-stock), 26" (magnums).
Weight: 6.8 to 7.5 lbs. **Length:** 39" (full-stock), 43" (half-stock).
Stock: Hand-checkered European walnut. Full Mannlicher or standard half-stock with Monte Carlo comb and rubber recoil pad.
Sights: Ramp front, open adjustable rear.
Features: Choice of single- or double-set triggers. Detachable 5-shot rotary magazine. Drilled and tapped for scope mounting. Model M actions available in left-hand models; S (magnum) actions available in half-stock only. Imported by GSI, Inc.
Price: Models SL, L, M, half-stock $2,023.00
Price: As above, full-stock, 20" barrel $2,179.00
Price: Models SL, L Varmint, 26" heavy barrel $2,179.00
Price: Model M left-hand, half-stock (270, 30-06, 7x64) $2,179.00
Price: As above, full-stock (270, 7x57, 7x64, 30-06) $2,335.00
Price: Model S Magnum $2,179.00
Price: Model S/T, 26" heavy barrel (375 H&H, 9.3x64, 458 Win. Mag.) $2,335.00

Steyr-Mannlicher MIII Professional Rifle
Similar to the Sporter series except has black ABS Cycolac half-stock, 23.6" barrel, no sights. Available in 270, 30-06, 7x64, single trigger or optional double-set. Weighs about 7 lbs., 5 oz. Introduced 1994. Imported by GSI, Inc.
Price: $995.00
Price: With stipple-checkered walnut stock $1,125.00

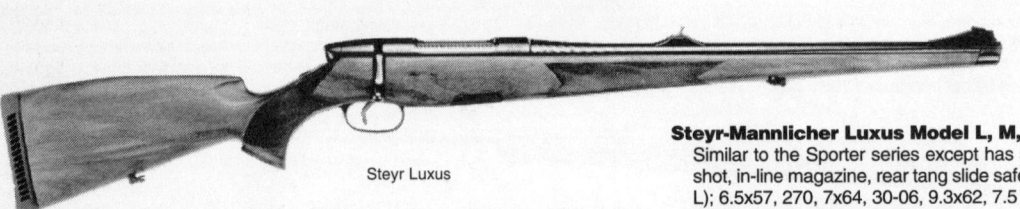

Steyr Luxus

Steyr-Mannlicher Luxus Model L, M, S
Similar to the Sporter series except has single set trigger, detachable steel 3-shot, in-line magazine, rear tang slide safety. Calibers: 5.6x57, 243, 308 (Model L); 6.5x57, 270, 7x64, 30-06, 9.3x62, 7.5 Swiss (Model M); 6.5x68, 7mm Rem. Mag., 300 Win. Mag., 8x68S (Model S). S (magnum) calibers available in half-stock only. Imported by GSI, Inc.
Price: Model L, M, half-stock $2,648.00
Price: As above, full-stock $2,804.00
Price: Model S (magnum) $2,804.00

Tikka Whitetail Hunter

Tikka Whitetail Hunter Synthetic Rifle
Similar to the Whitetail Hunter except has black synthetic stock; calibers 223, 308, 25-06, 270 Win., 30-06, 7mm Rem. Mag., 300 Win. Mag., 338 Win. Mag. Introduced 1996. Imported from Finland by Stoeger.
Price: Standard calibers $559.00
Price: Magnum calibers $589.00

Tikka Continental Varmint Rifle
Similar to the standard Tikka rifle except has 26" heavy barrel, extra-wide forend. Chambered for 22-250, 223, 308. Reintroduced 1996. Made in Finland by Sako. Imported by Stoeger.
Price: $644.00

TIKKA WHITETAIL HUNTER BOLT-ACTION RIFLE
Caliber: 22-250, 223, 243, 25-06, 270, 308, 30-06, 7mm Rem. Mag., 300 Win. Mag., 338 Win. Mag.
Barrel: 22 1/2" (std. cals.), 24 1/2" (magnum cals.).
Weight: 7 1/8 lbs. **Length:** 43" overall (std. cals.).
Stock: European walnut with Monte Carlo comb, rubber buttpad, checkered grip and forend.
Sights: None furnished.
Features: Detachable four-shot magazine (standard calibers), three-shot in magnums. Receiver dovetailed for scope mounting. Reintroduced 1996. Imported from Finland by Stoeger Industries.
Price: Standard calibers $559.00
Price: Magnum calibers $589.00

Tikka Continental Long Range Hunting Rifle
Similar to the Whitetail Hunter except has 26" heavy barrel. Available in 25-06, 270 Win., 7mm Rem. Mag., 300 Win. Mag. Introduced 1996. Imported from Finland by Stoeger.
Price: 25-06, 270 Win. $644.00
Price: 7 Rem. Mag., 300 Win. Mag. $674.00

CENTERFIRE RIFLES—BOLT ACTION

Ultra Light Model 20

ULTRA LIGHT ARMS MODEL 20 RIFLE
Caliber: 17 Rem., 22 Hornet, 222 Rem., 223 Rem. (Model 20S); 22-250, 6mm Rem., 243, 257 Roberts, 7x57, 7x57 Ackley, 7mm-08, 284 Win., 308 Savage. Improved and other calibers on request.
Barrel: 22" Douglas Premium No. 1 contour.
Weight: 4½ lbs. **Length:** 41½" overall.
Stock: Composite Kevlar, graphite reinforced. DuPont imron paint colors—green, black, brown and camo options. Choice of length of pull.
Sights: None furnished. Scope mount included.
Features: Timney adjustable trigger; two-position three-function safety. Benchrest quality action. Matte or bright stock and metal finish. 3" magazine length. Shipped in a hard case. From Ultra Light Arms, Inc.
Price: Right-hand $2,400.00
Price: Model 20 Left Hand (left-hand action and stock) $2,500.00
Price: Model 24 (25-06, 270, 280 Rem., 30-06, 3³⁄₈" magazine length) $2,500.00
Price: Model 24 Left Hand (left-hand action and stock) $2,600.00

Ultra Light Arms Model 28, Model 40 Rifles
Similar to the Model 20 except in 264, 7mm Rem. Mag., 300 Win. Mag., 338 Win. Mag. (Model 28), 300 Wea. Mag., 416 Rigby (Model 40). Both use 24" Douglas Premium No. 2 contour barrel. Weighs 5½ lbs., 45" overall length. KDF or ULA recoil arrestor built in. Any custom feature available on any ULA product can be incorporated.
Price: Right-hand, Model 28 or 40 ....$2,900.00
Price: Left-hand, Model 28 or 40 ....$3,000.00

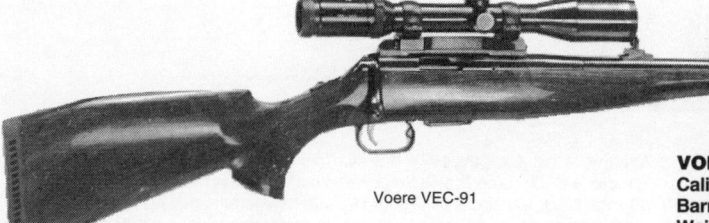
Voere VEC-91

VOERE VEC-91 LIGHTNING BOLT-ACTION RIFLE
Caliber: 5.56 UCC (223-cal.), 6mm UCC caseless, 5-shot magazine.
Barrel: 20".
Weight: 6 lbs. **Length:** 39" overall.
Stock: European walnut with cheekpiece, checkered grip and schnabel forend.
Sights: Blade on ramp front, open adjustable rear.
Features: Fires caseless ammunition via electric ignition; two batteries housed in the pistol grip last for about 5000 shots. Trigger is adjustable from 5 oz. to 7 lbs. Bolt action has twin forward locking lugs. Top tang safety. Drilled and tapped for scope mounting. Ammunition available from importer. Introduced 1991. Imported from Austria by JagerSport, Ltd.
Price: About $1,995.00

Voere VEC-91BR Caseless Rifle
Similar to the VEC-91 except has heavy 20" barrel, synthetic benchrest stock, and is a single shot. Drilled and tapped for scope mounting. Introduced 1995. Imported from Austria by JagerSport, Ltd.
Price: $1,995.00

Voere VEC-91HB Varmint Special Caseless Rifle
Similar to the VEC-91 except has 22" heavy sporter barrel, black synthetic or laminated wood stock. Drilled and tapped for scope mounts. Introduced 1995. Imported from Austria by JagerSport, Ltd.
Price: $1,695.00

Voere VEC-91SS Caseless Rifle
Similar to the VEC-91 except has synthetic stock with straight comb, matte-finished metal. Drilled and tapped for scope mounting. No open sights furnished. Introduced 1995. Imported from Austria by JagerSport, Ltd.
Price: 5.56mm UCC or 6mm UCC $1,495.00

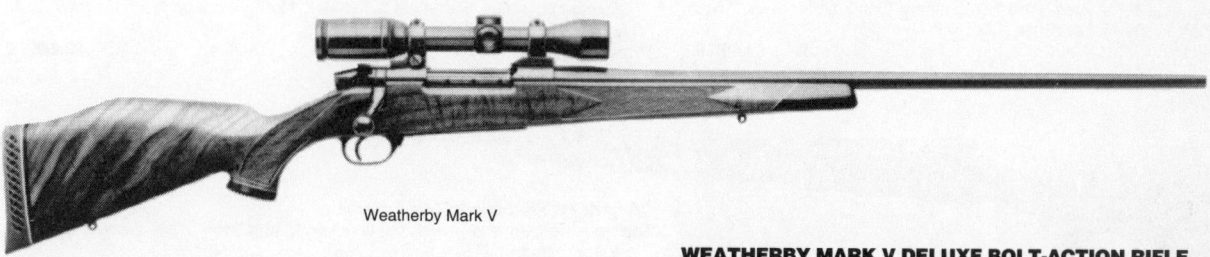
Weatherby Mark V

WEATHERBY MARK V DELUXE BOLT-ACTION RIFLE
Caliber: All Weatherby cals., plus 22-250, 30-06, 460 Wea. Mag.
Barrel: 24" or 26" round tapered.
Weight: 6½-10½ lbs. **Length:** 43¼"-46½" overall.
Stock: Walnut, Monte Carlo with cheekpiece, high luster finish, checkered pistol grip and forend, recoil pad.
Sights: Optional (extra).
Features: Cocking indicator, adjustable trigger, hinged floorplate, thumb safety, quick detachable sling swivels.
Price: 240, 257, 270, 7mm Wea. Mag., 26" $1,399.00
Price: 300 Wea. Mag., left-hand available, 340 Wea. Mag., right-hand, 26" $1,399.00
Price: 378 Wea. Mag., 26" $1,475.00
Price: 416 Wea. Mag., 26" $1,534.00
Price: 460 Wea. Mag., 26" $1,892.00

> Consult our Directory pages for the location of firms mentioned.

Weatherby Mark V Sporter Rifle
Same as the Mark V Deluxe without the embellishments. Metal has low-luster blue, stock is Claro walnut with high-gloss epoxy finish, Monte Carlo comb, recoil pad. Introduced 1993.
Price: 257 270, 7mm, 300, 340 Wea. Mags., 26" $899.00
Price: 375 H&H, 24" $899.00
Price: 7mm Rem. Mag., 300 Win. Mag., 338 Win. Mag., 24", ...$899.00

Weatherby Mark V Eurosport Rifle
Similar to the Mark V except has raised-comb Monte Carlo stock with hand-rubbed satin oil finish, low-luster blue metal. No grip cap or forend tip. Right-hand only. Introduced 1995. Made in U.S. From Weatherby.
Price: 257, 270, 7mm, 300, 340 Wea. Mags., 26" barrel $899.00
Price: 7mm Rem. Mag., 300, 338 Win. Mags., 24" barrel $899.00
Price: 375 H&H, 24" barrel $899.00

Weatherby Mark V Stainless Rifle
Similar to the Mark V except made of 400-series stainless steel. Has lightweight injection-moulded synthetic stock with raised Monte Carlo comb, checkered grip and forend, custom floorplate release. Right-hand only. Introduced 1995. Made in U.S. From Weatherby.
Price: 257, 270, 7mm, 300, 340 Wea. Mags. $999.00
Price: 7mm Rem. Mag., 300, 338 Win. Mags., 24" barrel $999.00
Price: 375 H&H, 24" barrel $999.00

CENTERFIRE RIFLES—BOLT ACTION

Weatherby Mark V Synthetic

Weatherby Euromark Rifle
Similar to the Mark V except has raised-comb Monte Carlo stock with hand-rubbed oil finish, fine-line hand-cut checkering, ebony grip and forend tips. All metal has low-luster blue. Right-hand only. Uses Mark V action. Introduced 1995. Made in U.S. From Weatherby.
Price: 257, 270, 7mm Wea. Mags., 26" barrel $1,449.00
Price: 300, 340 Wea. Mags, 26" barrel $1,449.00
Price: 416 Wea. Mag., 26" barrel $1,449.00

Weatherby Mark V Synthetic Rifle
Similar to the Mark V except has synthetic stock with raised Monte Carlo comb, dual-taper checkered forend. Low-luster blued metal. Weighs 7½ lbs. Uses Mark V action. Right-hand only. Introduced 1995. Made in U.S. From Weatherby.
Price: 257, 270, 7mm, 300, 340 Wea. Mags., 26" barrel $749.00
Price: 7mm Rem. Mag., 300, 338 Win. Mags., 24" barrel $749.00
Price: 375 H&H, 24" barrel $749.00

Weatherby Lazermark V Rifle
Same as standard Mark V except stock has extensive laser carving under cheekpiece on butt, pistol grip and forend. Introduced 1981.
Price: 240, 257, 270, 7mm Wea. Mag., 300, 340, right-hand, 26" $1,499.00
Price: 378 Wea. Mag., 26" $1,594.00
Price: 416 Wea. Mag., 26" $1,644.00
Price: 460 Wea. Mag., 26" $2,037.00

Weatherby Accumark

WEATHERBY ACCUMARK RIFLE
Caliber: 257, 270, 7mm, 300, 340 Wea. Mags., 7mm Rem. Mag., 300 Win. Mag.
Barrel: 26".
Weight: 8 lbs. Length: 46⅝" overall.
Stock: H-S Precision Pro-Series synthetic with aluminum bedding plate.
Sights: None furnished. Drilled and tapped for scope mounting.
Features: Uses Mark V action with heavy-contour stainless barrel with flutes, muzzle diameter of .705". Action coated with black oxide. Introduced 1996. Made in U.S. From Weatherby.
Price: $1,199.00

WICHITA CLASSIC RIFLE
Caliber: 17-222, 17-222 Mag., 222 Rem., 222 Rem. Mag., 223 Rem., 6x47; other calibers on special order.
Barrel: 21⅛".
Weight: 8 lbs. Length: 41" overall.
Stock: AAA Fancy American walnut. Hand-rubbed and checkered (20 lpi). Hand-inletted, glass bedded, steel grip cap. Pachmayr rubber recoil pad.
Sights: None. Drilled and tapped for scope mounting.
Features: Available as single shot only. Octagonal barrel and Wichita action, right- or left-hand. Checkered bolt handle. Bolt is hand-fitted, lapped and jeweled. Adjustable trigger is set at 2 lbs. Side thumb safety. Firing pin fall is 3/16". Non-glare blue finish. From Wichita Arms.
Price: Single shot $3,495.00

WICHITA VARMINT RIFLE
Caliber: 222 Rem., 222 Rem. Mag., 223 Rem., 22 PPC, 6mm PPC, 22-250, 243, 6mm Rem., 308 Win.; other calibers on special order.
Barrel: 20⅛".
Weight: 9 lbs. Length: 40⅛" overall.
Stock: AAA Fancy American walnut. Hand-rubbed finish, hand checkered, 20 lpi pattern. Hand-inletted, glass bedded, steel grip cap. Pachmayr rubber recoil pad.
Sights: None. Drilled and tapped for scope mounts.
Features: Right- or left-hand Wichita action with three locking lugs. Available as a single shot only. Checkered bolt handle. Bolt is hand fitted, lapped and jeweled. Side thumb safety. Firing pin fall is 3/16". Non-glare blue finish. From Wichita Arms.
Price: Single shot $2,695.00

Winchester Model 70 Classic

WINCHESTER MODEL 70 CLASSIC SPORTER
Caliber: 25-06, 270 Win., 270 Wea., 30-06, 264 Win. Mag., 7mm Rem. Mag., 300 Win. Mag., 300 Wea. Mag., 338 Win. Mag., 3-shot magazine; 5-shot for 25-06, 270 Win., 30-06.
Barrel: 24", 26" for magnums.
Weight: 7¾ lbs. Length: 44¾" overall.
Stock: American walnut with cut checkering and satin finish. Classic style with straight comb.
Sights: Optional hooded ramp front, adjustable folding leaf rear. Drilled and tapped for scope mounting.
Features: Uses pre-64-type action with controlled round feeding. Three-position safety, stainless steel magazine follower; rubber buttpad; epoxy bedded receiver recoil lug. BOSS barrel vibration modulator and muzzlebrake system optional. From U.S. Repeating Arms Co.
Price: With sights $651.00
Price: Without sights $613.00
Price: With BOSS (25-06, 264 Win. Mag., 270 Win., 270 Wea. Mag., 30-06, 7mm Rem. Mag., 300 Win. Mag., 300 Wea. Mag., 338 Win. Mag.) ...$728.00

Winchester Model 70 Classic SM
Same as the Model 70 Sporter except has pre-64 controlled feed action, black composite, graphite-impregnated stock and matte-finished metal. Available in 270, 30-06, 7mm Rem. Mag., 300 Win. Mag., 338 Win. Mag., 375 H&H. Weighs about 7.8 lbs. BOSS barrel vibration modulator and muzzlebrake system optional. Introduced 1994.
Price: $620.00
Price: 375 H&H, with sights $672.00
Price: With BOSS (270, 30-06, 7mm Rem. Mag., 300 Win. Mag., 338 Win. Mag.) $735.00

Winchester Model 70 Classic Stainless Rifle
Same as the Model 70 Classic Sporter except has stainless steel barrel and pre-64-style action with controlled round feeding and matte gray finish, black composite stock impregnated with fiberglass and graphite, contoured rubber recoil pad. Available in 22-250, 243, 308, 270, 30-06, 7mm Rem. Mag., 300 Win. Mag., 300 Wea. Mag., 338 Win. Mag., 375 H&H Mag. (24" barrel), 3- or 5-shot magazine. Weighs 6.75 lbs. BOSS barrel vibration modulator and muzzle-brake system optional. Introduced 1994.
Price: Without sights $672.00
Price: 375 H&H Mag., with sights $724.00
Price: With BOSS $788.00

CENTERFIRE RIFLES—BOLT ACTION

Winchester Model 70 Synthetic Heavy Varmint Rifle
Similar to the Model 70 Classic Sporter except has fiberglass/graphite stock, 26" heavy stainless steel barrel, blued receiver. Weighs about 10¾ lbs. Available in 220 Swift, 223, 22-250, 243, 308. Uses full-length Pillar Plus Accu Block bedding system. Introduced 1993.
Price: $746.00

WINCHESTER MODEL 70 CLASSIC SUPER EXPRESS MAGNUM
Caliber: 375 H&H Mag., 416 Rem. Mag., 458 Win. Mag., 3-shot magazine.
Barrel: 24" (375, 416), 22" (458).
Weight: 8¼ to 8½ lbs.
Stock: American walnut with Monte Carlo cheekpiece. Wrap-around checkering and finish.
Sights: Hooded ramp front, open rear.
Features: Controlled round feeding. Two steel cross bolts in stock for added strength. Front sling swivel stud mounted on barrel. Contoured rubber buttpad. From U.S. Repeating Arms Co.
Price: $865.00

Winchester Model 70 Classic Featherweight
Same as the Model 70 Classic except has claw controlled-round feeding system; action is bedded in a standard-grade walnut stock. Available in 22-250, 243, 308, 7mm-08, 270 Win., 280 Rem., 30-06. Drilled and tapped for scope mounts. Weighs 7.25 lbs. Introduced 1992.
Price: $620.00
Price: With BOSS $735.00

Winchester Model 70 Classic Featherweight All-Terrain
Similar to the Model 70 Classic Featherweight except has black, fiberglass/graphite stock in same style as the Classic Featherweight, barreled action made of stainless steel. Calibers 270 Win., 30-06, 7mm Rem. Mag., 300 Win. Mag. Introduced 1996.
Price: $672.00
Price: With BOSS $788.00

Winchester Model 70 Super Grade Classic

WINCHESTER RANGER RIFLE
Caliber: 223, 243, 270, 30-06.
Barrel: 22".
Weight: 7¾ lbs. **Length:** 42" overall.
Stock: Stained hardwood.
Sights: Hooded blade front, adjustable open rear.
Features: Three-position safety; push feed bolt with recessed-style bolt face; polished blue finish; drilled and tapped for scope mounting. Introduced 1985. From U.S. Repeating Arms Co.
Price: $482.00
Price: Ranger Ladies/Youth, 243, 308 only, scaled-down stock $482.00

WINCHESTER MODEL 70 CLASSIC SUPER GRADE
Caliber: 270, 30-06, 5-shot magazine; 7mm Rem. Mag., 300 Win. Mag., 338 Win. Mag., 3-shot magazine.
Barrel: 24", 26" for magnums.
Weight: About 7¾ lbs. to 8 lbs. **Length:** 44½" overall (24" bbl.)
Stock: Walnut with straight comb, sculptured cheekpiece, wrap-around cut checkering, tapered forend, solid rubber buttpad.
Sights: None furnished; comes with scope bases and rings.
Features: Controlled round feeding with stainless steel claw extractor, bolt guide rail, three-position safety; all steel bottom metal, hinged floorplate, stainless magazine follower. BOSS barrel vibration modulator and muzzlebrake system optional. Introduced 1994. From U.S. Repeating Arms Co.
Price: $840.00
Price: With BOSS system $956.00

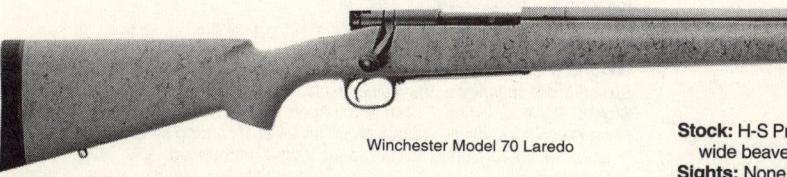
Winchester Model 70 Laredo

WINCHESTER MODEL 70 CLASSIC LAREDO
Caliber: 7mm Rem. Mag., 300 Win. Mag., 3-shot magazine.
Barrel: 26" heavy; 1:10" (300), 1:9.5" (7mm).
Weight: 9½ lbs. **Length:** 46¾" overall.
Stock: H-S Precision gray, synthetic with "Pillar Plus Accu-Block" bedding system, wide beavertail forend.
Sights: None furnished; drilled and topped for scope mounting.
Features: Pre-64-style, controlled round action with claw extractor, receiver-mounted blade ejector; matte blue finish. Introduced 1996. Made in U.S. by U.S. Repeating Arms Co.
Price: $764.00
Price: With BOSS $879.00

CENTERFIRE RIFLES—SINGLE SHOT

Classic and modern designs for sporting and competitive use.

Brown Model One

BROWN MODEL ONE SINGLE SHOT RIFLE
Caliber: 22 LR, 357 Mag., 44 Mag., 7-30 Waters, 30-30 Win., 375 Win., 45-70; custom chamberings from 17 Rem. through 45-caliber available.
Barrel: 22" or custom, bull or tapered.
Weight: 6 lbs. **Length:** NA.
Stock: Smooth walnut; custom takedown design by Woodsmith. Palm swell for right- or left-hand; rubber butt pad.
Sights: Optional. Drilled and tapped for scope mounting.
Features: Rigid barrel/receiver; falling block action with short lock time, automatic case ejection; air-gauged barrels by Wilson and Douglas. Muzzle has 11-degree target crown. Matte black oxide finish standard, polished and electroless nickel optional. Introduced 1988. Made in U.S. by E.A. Brown Mfg.
Price: $750.00

ARMSPORT 1866 SHARPS RIFLE, CARBINE
Caliber: 45-70.
Barrel: 28", round or octagonal.
Weight: 8.10 lbs. **Length:** 46" overall.
Stock: Walnut.
Sights: Blade front, folding adjustable rear. Tang sight set optionally available.
Features: Replica of the 1866 Sharps. Color case-hardened frame, rest blued. Imported by Armsport.
Price: $860.00
Price: With octagonal barrel $880.00
Price: Carbine, 22" round barrel $830.00

CENTERFIRE RIFLES—SINGLE SHOT

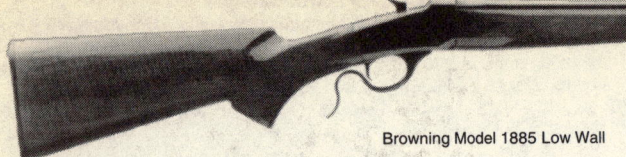

Browning Model 1885 Low Wall

BROWNING MODEL 1885 HIGH WALL SINGLE SHOT RIFLE
Caliber: 22-250, 30-06, 270, 7mm Rem. Mag., 45-70.
Barrel: 28".
Weight: About 8 1/2 lbs. **Length:** 43 1/2" overall.
Stock: Walnut with straight grip, schnabel forend.
Sights: None furnished; drilled and tapped for scope mounting.
Features: Replica of J.M. Browning's high-wall falling block rifle. Octagon barrel with recessed muzzle. Imported from Japan by Browning. Introduced 1985.
Price: $939.95

Browning Model 1885 BPCR Rifle
Similar to the 1885 High Wall rifle except the ejector system and shell deflector have been removed; chambered only for 40-65 and 45-70; color case-hardened full-tang receiver, lever, buttplate and grip cap; matte blue 30" part octagon, part round barrel. The Vernier tang sight has indexed elevation, is screw adjustable windage, and has three peep diameters. The hooded front sight has a built-in spirit level and comes with sight interchangeable inserts. Adjustable trigger. Overall length 46 1/8", weighs about 11 lbs. Introduced 1996. Imported from Japan by Browning.
Price: $1,664.95

Browning Model 1885 Low Wall Rifle
Similar to the Model 1885 High Wall except has trimmer receiver, thinner 24" octagonal barrel. Forend is mounted to the receiver. Adjustable trigger. Walnut pistol grip stock, trim schnabel forend with high-gloss finish. Available in 22 Hornet, 223 Rem., 243 Win. Overall length 39 1/2", weighs 6 lbs., 4 oz. Rifling twist rates: 1:16" (22 Hornet); 1:12" (223); 1:10" (243). Polished blue finish. Introduced 1995. Imported from Japan by Browning.
Price: $939.95

CABELA'S SHARPS SPORTING RIFLE
Caliber: 45-70.
Barrel: 32", tapered octagon.
Weight: 9 lbs. **Length:** 47 1/4" overall.
Stock: Checkered walnut.
Sights: Blade front, open adjustable rear.
Features: Color case-hardened receiver and hammer, rest blued. Introduced 1995. Imported by Cabela's.
Price: $749.95

CUMBERLAND MOUNTAIN PLATEAU RIFLE
Caliber: 40-65, 45-70.
Barrel: Up to 32"; round.
Weight: About 10 1/2 lbs. (32" barrel). **Length:** 48" overall (32" barrel).
Stock: American walnut.
Sights: Marble's bead front, Marble's open rear.
Features: Falling block action with underlever. Blued barrel and receiver. Stock has lacquer finish, crescent buttplate. Introduced 1995. Made in U.S. by Cumberland Mountain Arms, Inc.
Price: $1,085.00

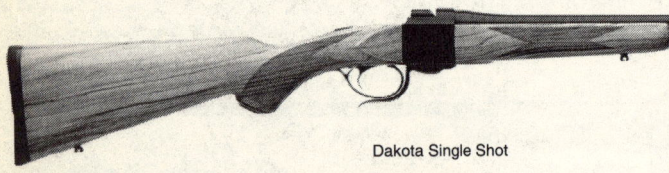

Dakota Single Shot

DESERT INDUSTRIES G-90 SINGLE SHOT RIFLE
Caliber: 22-250, 220 Swift, 223, 6mm, 243, 25-06, 257 Roberts, 270 Win., 270 Wea. Mag., 280, 7x57, 7mm Rem. Mag., 30-06, 300 Win. Mag., 300 Wea. Mag., 338 Win. Mag., 375 H&H, 45-70, 458 Win. Mag.
Barrel: 20", 22", 24", 26"; light, medium, heavy.
Weight: About 7.5 lbs.
Stock: Walnut.
Sights: None furnished. Drilled and tapped for scope mounting.
Features: Cylindrical falling block action. All steel construction. Blue finish. Announced 1990. From Desert Industries, Inc.
Price: $795.00

DAKOTA SINGLE SHOT RIFLE
Caliber: Most rimmed and rimless commercial calibers.
Barrel: 23".
Weight: 6 lbs. **Length:** 39 1/2" overall.
Stock: Medium fancy grade walnut in classic style. Checkered grip and forend.
Sights: None furnished. Drilled and tapped for scope mounting.
Features: Falling block action with under-lever. Top tang safety. Removable trigger plate for conversion to single set trigger. Introduced 1990. Made in U.S. by Dakota Arms.
Price: $2,500.00
Price: Barreled action $1,850.00
Price: Action only $1,500.00

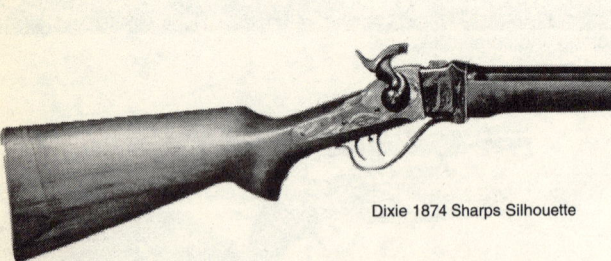

Dixie 1874 Sharps Silhouette

Dixie 1874 Sharps Lightweight Hunter/Target Rifle
Same as the Dixie 1874 Sharps Blackpowder Silhouette model except has a straight-grip buttstock with military-style buttplate. Based on the 1874 military model. Introduced 1995. Imported from Italy by Dixie Gun Works.
Price: $895.00

DIXIE 1874 SHARPS BLACKPOWDER SILHOUETTE RIFLE
Caliber: 45-70.
Barrel: 30"; tapered octagon; blued; 1:18" twist.
Weight: 10 lbs., 3 oz. **Length:** 47 1/2" overall.
Stock: Oiled walnut.
Sights: Blade front, ladder-type hunting rear.
Features: Replica of the Sharps #1 Sporter. Shotgun-style butt with checkered metal buttplate; color case-hardened receiver, hammer, lever and buttplate. Tang is drilled and tapped for tang sight. Double-set triggers. Meets standards for NRA blackpowder cartridge matches. Introduced 1995. Imported from Italy by Dixie Gun Works.
Price: $895.00

E.M.F. SHARPS RIFLE
Caliber: 45-70.
Barrel: 28", octagon.
Weight: 10 3/4 lbs. **Length:** NA.
Stock: Oiled walnut.
Sights: Blade front, flip-up open rear.

Features: Replica of the 1874 Sharps Sporting rifle. Color case-hardened lock; double-set trigger; blue finish. Imported by E.M.F.
Price: $950.00
Price: With browned finish $1,000.00
Price: Carbine (round 22" barrel, barrel band) $860.00

CENTERFIRE RIFLES—SINGLE SHOT

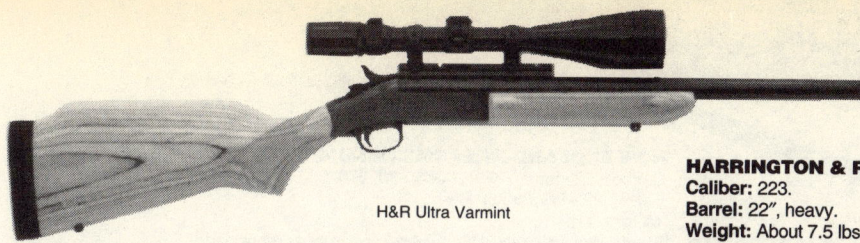
H&R Ultra Varmint

Harrington & Richardson Ultra Hunter Rifle
Similar to the Ultra Varmint rifle except chambered for 25-06 with 26" barrel, or 308 Win. and 357 Rem. Mag. with 22" barrel. Stock and forend are of cinnamon-colored laminate; hand-checkered grip and forend. Introduced 1995. Made in U.S. by H&R 1871, Inc.
Price: $249.95
Price: Rocky Mountain Elk Foundation Commemorative (35 Whelen 26" barrel) $269.95

MODEL 1885 HIGH WALL RIFLE
Caliber: 30-40 Krag, 32-40, 38-55, 40-65 WCF, 45-70.
Barrel: 26" (30-40), 28" all others. Douglas Premium #3 tapered octagon.
Weight: NA. **Length:** NA.
Stock: Premium American black walnut.
Sights: Marble's standard ivory bead front, #66 long blade top rear with reversible notch and elevator.
Features: Recreation of early octagon top, thick-wall High Wall with Coil spring action. Tang drilled, tapped for High Wall tang sight. Receiver, lever, hammer and breechblock color case-hardened. Introduced 1991. Available from Montana Armory, Inc.
Price: $1,095.00

HARRINGTON & RICHARDSON ULTRA VARMINT RIFLE
Caliber: 223.
Barrel: 22", heavy.
Weight: About 7.5 lbs. **Length:** NA.
Stock: Hand-checkered laminated birch with Monte Carlo comb.
Sights: None furnished. Drilled and tapped for scope mounting.
Features: Break-open action with side-lever release, positive ejection. Comes with scope mount. Blued receiver and barrel. Swivel studs. Introduced 1993. From H&R 1871, Inc.
Price: $249.95

HARRIS GUNWORKS ANTIETAM SHARPS RIFLE
Caliber: 40-65, 45-75.
Barrel: 30", 32", octagon or round, hand-lapped stainless or chromemoly.
Weight: 11.25 lbs. **Length:** 47" overall.
Stock: Choice of straight grip, pistol grip or Creedmoor with schnabel forend; pewter tip optional. Standard wood is A Fancy; higher grades available.
Sights: Montana Vintage Arms #111 Low Profile Spirit Level front, #108 mid-range tang rear with windage adjustments.
Features: Recreation of the 1874 Sharps sidehammer. Action is color case-hardened, barrel satin black. Chrome-moly barrel optionally blued. Optional sights include #112 Spirit Level Globe front with windage, #107 Long Range rear with windage. Introduced 1994. Made in U.S. by Harris Gunworks.
Price: $2,000.00

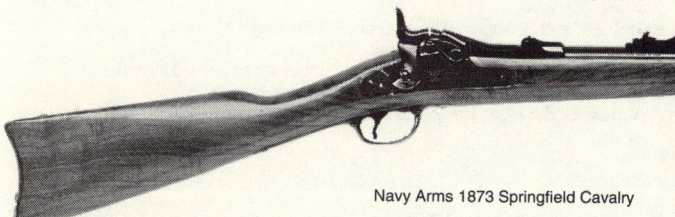
Navy Arms 1873 Springfield Cavalry

NAVY ARMS 1874 SHARPS CAVALRY CARBINE
Caliber: 45-70.
Barrel: 22".
Weight: 7lbs., 12 oz. **Length:** 39" overall.
Stock: Walnut.
Sights: Blade front, military ladder-type rear.
Features: Replica of the 1874 Sharps miltary carbine. Color case-hardened receiver and furniture. Imported by Navy Arms.
Price: $935.00

NAVY ARMS 1873 SPRINGFIELD CAVALRY CARBINE
Caliber: 45-70.
Barrel: 22".
Weight: 7 lbs. **Length:** 40 1/2" overall.
Stock: Walnut.
Sights: Blade front, military ladder rear.
Features: Blued lockplate and barrel; color case-hardened breechblock; saddle ring with bar. Replica of 7th Cavalry gun. Imported by Navy Arms.
Price: ....NA

Navy Arms 1874 Sharps Sniper Rifle
Similar to the Navy Arms Sharps Carbine except has 30" barrel, double-set triggers; weighs 8 lbs., 8 oz., overall length 46 3/4". Introduced 1984. Imported by Navy Arms.
Price: $1,115.00
Price: 1874 Sharps Infantry Rifle (three-band) $1,060.00

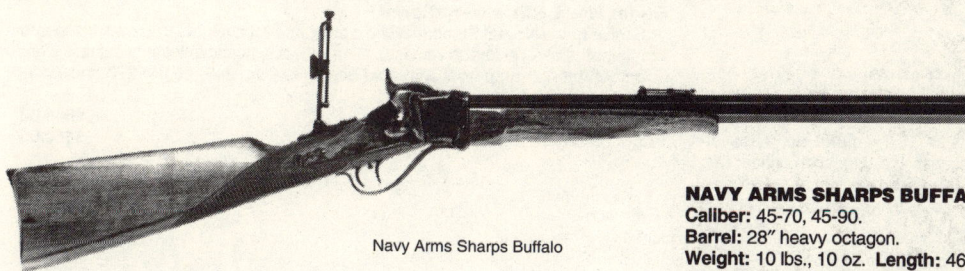
Navy Arms Sharps Buffalo

Navy Arms Sharps Plains Rifle
Similar to the Sharps Buffalo rifle except has 32" medium-weight barrel, weighs 9 lbs., 8 oz., and is 49" overall. Imported by Navy Arms.
Price: $1,050.00

NAVY ARMS SHARPS BUFFALO RIFLE
Caliber: 45-70, 45-90.
Barrel: 28" heavy octagon.
Weight: 10 lbs., 10 oz. **Length:** 46" overall.
Stock: Walnut; checkered grip and forend.
Sights: Blade front, ladder rear; tang sight optional.
Features: Color case-hardened receiver, blued barrel; double-set triggers. Imported by Navy Arms.
Price: $1,080.00

Navy Arms #2 Creedmoor Rifle
Similar to the Navy Arms Buffalo Rifle except has 30" tapered octagon barrel, checkered full-pistol grip stock, blade front sight, open adjustable rear sight and Creedmoor tang sight. Imported by Navy Arms.
Price: $875.00

NAVY ARMS ROLLING BLOCK BUFFALO RIFLE
Caliber: 45-70.
Barrel: 26", 30".
Stocks: Walnut.
Sights: Blade front, adjustable rear.
Features: Reproduction of classic rolling block action. Available with full-octagon or half-octagon-half-round barrel. Color case-hardened action. From Navy Arms.
Price: $650.00

CENTERFIRE RIFLES—SINGLE SHOT

New England Firearms Survivor

NEW ENGLAND FIREARMS SURVIVOR RIFLE
Caliber: 223, 357 Mag., single shot.
Barrel: 22".
Weight: 6 lbs. **Length:** 36" overall.
Stock: Black polymer, thumbhole design.
Sights: Blade front, fully adjustable open rear.
Features: Receiver drilled and tapped for scope mounting. Stock and forend have storage compartments for ammo, etc.; comes with integral swivels and black nylon sling. Introduced 1996. Made in U.S. by New England Firearms.
Price: Blue $219.95
Price: Electroless nickel $234.95

NEW ENGLAND FIREARMS HANDI-RIFLE
Caliber: 22 Hornet, 223, 243, 30-30, 270, 280 Rem., 30-06, 44 Mag., 45-70.
Barrel: 22", 26" for 280 Rem..
Weight: 7 lbs.
Stock: Walnut-finished hardwood; black rubber recoil pad.
Sights: Ramp front, folding rear (22 Hornet, 30-30, 45-70). Drilled and tapped for scope mount; 223, 243, 270, 280, 30-06 have no open sights, come with scope mounts.
Features: Break-open action with side-lever release. The 223, 243, 270 and 30-06 have recoil pad and Monte Carlo stock for shooting with scope. Swivel studs on all models. Blue finish. Introduced 1989. From New England Firearms.
Price: $214.95

Ruger No. 1B

Ruger No. 1A Light Sporter
Similar to the No. 1B Standard Rifle except has lightweight 22" barrel, Alexander Henry-style forend, adjustable folding leaf rear sight on quarter-rib, dovetailed ramp front with gold bead. Calibers 243, 30-06, 270 and 7x57. Weighs about 7 1/4 lbs.
Price: No. 1A $665.00
Price: Barreled action $450.00

Ruger No. 1S Medium Sporter
Similar to the No. 1B Standard Rifle except has Alexander Henry-style forend, adjustable folding leaf rear sight on quarter-rib, ramp front sight base and dovetail-type gold bead front sight. Calibers 218 Bee, 7mm Rem. Mag., 338 Win. Mag., 300 Win. Mag. with 26" barrel, 45-70 with 22" barrel. Weighs about 7 1/2 lbs. In 45-70.
Price: No. 1S $665.00
Price: Barreled action $440.00

RUGER NO. 1B SINGLE SHOT
Caliber: 218 Bee, 22 Hornet, 220 Swift, 22-250, 223, 243, 6mm Rem., 25-06, 257 Roberts, 270, 280, 30-06, 7mm Rem. Mag., 300 Win. Mag., 338 Win. Mag., 270 Wea., 300 Wea.
Barrel: 26" round tapered with quarter-rib; with Ruger 1" rings.
Weight: 8 lbs. **Length:** 43 3/8" overall.
Stock: Walnut, two-piece, checkered p.g. and semi-beavertail forend.
Sights: None, 1" scope rings supplied for integral mounts.
Features: Under-lever, hammerless falling block design has auto ejector, top tang safety.
Price: $665.00
Price: Barreled action $450.00

Ruger No. 1H Tropical Rifle
Similar to the No. 1B Standard Rifle except has Alexander Henry forend, adjustable folding leaf rear sight on quarter-rib, ramp front with dovetail gold bead, 24" heavy barrel. Calibers 375 H&H, 404 Jeffery, 416 Rem. Mag. (weighs about 8 1/4 lbs.), 416 Rigby, and 458 Win. Mag. (weighs about 9 lbs.).
Price: No. 1H $665.00
Price: Barreled action $440.00

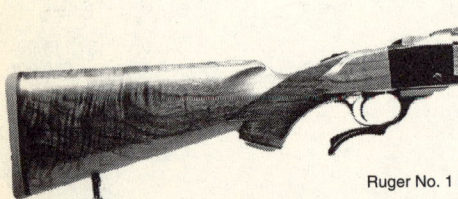

Ruger No. 1 RSI

Ruger No. 1V Special Varminter
Similar to the No. 1B Standard Rifle except has 24" heavy barrel. Semi-beavertail forend, barrel tapped for target scope block, with 1" Ruger scope rings. Calibers 22 PPC, 22-250, 220 Swift, 223, 6mm PPC, 25-06. Weight about 9 lbs.
Price: No. 1V $665.00
Price: Barreled action $440.00

Ruger No. 1 RSI International
Similar to the No. 1B Standard Rifle except has lightweight 20" barrel, full-length International-style forend with loop sling swivel, adjustable folding leaf rear sight on quarter-rib, ramp front with gold bead. Calibers 243, 30-06, 270 and 7x57. Weight is about 7 1/4 lbs.
Price: No. 1 RSI $668.00
Price: Barreled action $450.00

C. Sharps 1875 Sporting

C. SHARPS ARMS NEW MODEL 1875 RIFLE
Caliber: 22LR, 32-40 & 38-55 Ballard, 38-56 WCF, 40-65 WCF, 40-90 3 1/4", 40-90 2 5/8", 40-70 2 1/10", 40-70 2 1/2", 40-70 2 1/4", 40-50 1 11/16", 40-50 1 7/8", 45-90, 45-70, 45-100, 45-110, 45-120. Also available on special order only in 50-70, 50-90, 50-140.
Barrel: 24", 26", 30" (standard), 32", 34" optional.
Weight: 8-12 lbs.
Stocks: Walnut, straight grip, shotgun butt with checkered steel buttplate.
Sights: Silver blade front, Rocky Mountain buckhorn rear.
Features: Recreation of the 1875 Sharps rifle. Production guns will have case colored receiver. Available in Custom Sporting and Target versions upon request. Announced 1986. From C. Sharps Arms Co. and Montana Armory, Inc.
Price: 1875 Carbine (24" tapered round bbl.) $725.00
Price: 1875 Saddle Rifle (26" tapered oct. bbl.) $825.00
Price: 1875 Sporting Rifle (30" tapered oct. bbl.) $850.00
Price: 1875 Business Rifle (28" tapered round bbl.) .. $775.00

CENTERFIRE RIFLES—SINGLE SHOT

C. Sharps Arms 1875 Classic Sharps
Similar to the New Model 1875 Sporting Rifle except has 26", 28" or 30" full octagon barrel, crescent buttplate with toe plate, Hartford-style forend with cast German silver nose cap. Blade front sight, Rocky Mountain buckhorn rear. Weighs 10 lbs. Introduced 1987. From C. Sharps Arms Co. and Montana Armory, Inc.
Price: $1,075.00

C. Sharps Arms New Model 1875 Target & Long Range
Similar to the New Model 1875 except available in all listed calibers except 22 LR; 34" tapered octagon barrel; globe with post front sight, Long Range Vernier tang sight with windage adjustments. Pistol grip stock with cheek rest; checkered steel buttplate. Introduced 1991. From C. Sharps Arms Co. and Montana Armory, Inc.
Price: $1,165.00

SHARPS 1874 OLD RELIABLE
Caliber: 45-70.
Barrel: 28", octagonal.
Weight: 9 1/4 lbs. **Length:** 46" overall.
Stock: Checkered walnut.
Sights: Blade front, adjustable rear.
Features: Double set triggers on rifle. Color case-hardened receiver and buttplate, blued barrel. Imported from Italy by E.M.F.
Price: Rifle or carbine $950.00
Price: Military rifle, carbine $860.00
Price: Sporting rifle $860.00

Shiloh Sharps 1874 Montana Roughrider
Similar to the No. 1 Sporting Rifle except available with 30" full or half-octagon barrel; standard supreme or semi-fancy wood, shotgun, pistol grip or military-style butt. Weight about 8 1/2 lbs. Calibers 30-40, 40-50x1 11/16" BN, 40-70x2 1/10" BN, 45-70x2 1/10" ST. Globe front and tang sight optional.
Price: Standard supreme $1,044.00
Price: Semi-fancy $1,154.00

C. SHARPS ARMS NEW MODEL 1874 OLD RELIABLE
Caliber: 40-50, 40-70, 40-90, 45-70, 45-90, 45-100, 45-110, 45-120, 50-70, 50-90, 50-140.
Barrel: 26", 28", 30" tapered octagon.
Weight: About 10 lbs. **Length:** NA.
Stock: American black walnut; shotgun butt with checkered steel buttplate; straight grip, heavy forend with schnabel tip.
Sights: Blade front, buckhorn rear. Drilled and tapped for tang sight.
Features: Recreation of the Model 1874 Old Reliable Sharps Sporting Rifle. Double set triggers. Reintroduced 1991. Made in U.S. by C. Sharps Arms. Available from Montana Armory, Inc.
Price: $995.00

SHILOH SHARPS 1874 LONG RANGE EXPRESS
Caliber: 40-50 BN, 40-70 BN, 40-90 BN, 45-70 ST, 45-90 ST, 45-110 ST, 50-70 ST, 50-90 ST, 50-110 ST, 32-40, 38-55, 40-70 ST, 40-90 ST.
Barrel: 34" tapered octagon.
Weight: 10 1/2 lbs. **Length:** 51" overall.
Stock: Oil-finished semi-fancy walnut with pistol grip, shotgun-style butt, traditional cheek rest, schnabel forend.
Sights: Globe front, sporting tang rear.
Features: Recreation of the Model 1874 Sharps rifle. Double set triggers. Made in U.S. by Shiloh Rifle Mfg. Co.
Price: $1,174.00
Price: Sporting Rifle No. 1 (similar to above except with 30" bbl., blade front, buckhorn rear sight) $1,148.00
Price: Sporting Rifle No. 3 (similar to No. 1 except straight-grip stock, standard wood) $1,044.00
Price: 1874 Hartford model $1,214.00

Shiloh Sharps 1874 Business Rifle
Similar to No. 3 Rifle except has 28" heavy round barrel, military-style buttstock and steel buttplate. Weight about 9 1/2 lbs. Calibers 40-50 BN, 40-70 BN, 40-90 BN, 45-70 ST, 45-90 ST, 50-70 ST, 50-100 ST, 32-40, 38-55, 40-70 ST, 40-90 ST.
Price: $1,050.00
Price: 1874 Saddle Rifle (similar to Carbine except has 26" octagon barrel, semi-fancy shotgun butt) $1,102.00

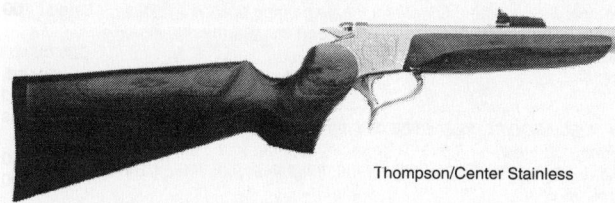
Thompson/Center Stainless

Thompson/Center Stainless Contender Carbine
Same as the blued Contender Carbine except made of stainless steel with blued sights. Available with walnut or Rynite stock and forend. Chambered for 22 LR, 22 Hornet, 223 Rem., 7-30 Waters, 30-30 Win., 410-bore. Youth model has walnut buttstock with 12" pull length. Introduced 1993.
Price: Rynite stock, forend $509.90

Manufacturers' addresses in the
Directory of the Arms Trade
page 313, this issue

UBERTI ROLLING BLOCK BABY CARBINE
Caliber: 22 LR, 22 WMR, 22 Hornet, 357 Mag., single shot.
Barrel: 22".
Weight: 4.8 lbs. **Length:** 35 1/2" overall.
Stock: Walnut stock and forend.
Sights: Blade front, fully adjustable open rear.
Features: Resembles Remington New Model No. 4 carbine. Brass trigger guard and buttplate; color case-hardened frame, blued barrel. Imported by Uberti USA Inc.
Price: $490.00

THOMPSON/CENTER CONTENDER CARBINE
Caliber: 22 LR, 22 Hornet, 223 Rem., 7mm T.C.U., 7x30 Waters, 30-30 Win., 357 Rem. Maximum, 35 Rem., 44 Mag., 410, single shot.
Barrel: 21".
Weight: 5 lbs., 2 oz. **Length:** 35" overall.
Stock: Checkered American walnut with rubber buttpad. Also with Rynite stock and forend.
Sights: Blade front, open adjustable rear.
Features: Uses the T/C Contender action. Eleven interchangeable barrels available, all with sights, drilled and tapped for scope mounting. Introduced 1985. Offered as a complete Carbine only.
Price: Rifle calibers $515.00
Price: Extra barrels, rifle calibers, each $234.30
Price: 410 shotgun $535.60
Price: Extra 410 barrel $260.10

Thompson/Center Contender Carbine Youth Model
Same as the standard Contender Carbine except has 16 1/4" barrel, shorter buttstock with 12" length of pull. Comes with fully adjustable open sights. Overall length is 29", weight about 4 lbs., 9 oz. Available in 22 LR, 22 WMR, 223 Rem., 7x30 Waters, 30-30, 35 Rem., 44 Mag. Also available with 16 1/4", rifled vent. rib barrel chambered for 45/410.
Price: $479.00
Price: Extra barrels $234.30
Price: Extra 45/410 barrel $260.10
Price: Extra 45-70 barrel $234.30

WESSON & HARRINGTON BUFFALO CLASSIC RIFLE
Caliber: 45-70.
Barrel: 32" heavy.
Weight: 9 lbs. **Length:** 52" overall.
Stock: American black walnut.
Sights: None furnished; drilled and tapped for peep sight; barrel dovetailed for front sight.
Features: Color case-hardened Handi-Rifle action with exposed hammer; color case-hardened crescent buttplate; 19th century checkering pattern. Introduced 1995. Made in U.S. by H&R 1871, Inc.
Price: About $349.95

DRILLINGS, COMBINATION GUNS, DOUBLE RIFLES

Designs for sporting and utility purposes worldwide.

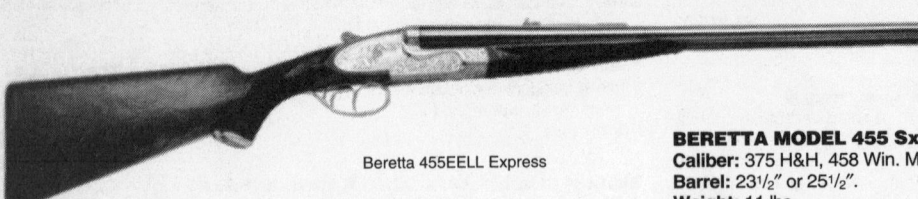

Beretta 455EELL Express

BERETTA EXPRESS SSO O/U DOUBLE RIFLES
Caliber: 375 H&H, 458 Win. Mag., 9.3x74R.
Barrel: 25.5″.
Weight: 11 lbs.
Stock: European walnut with hand-checkered grip and forend.
Sights: Blade front on ramp, open V-notch rear.
Features: Sidelock action with color case-hardened receiver (gold inlays on SSO6 Gold). Ejectors, double triggers, recoil pad. Introduced 1990. Imported from Italy by Beretta U.S.A.
Price: SSO6 .... $21,000.00
Price: SSO6 Gold $23,500.00

AUGUSTE FRANCOTTE BOXLOCK DOUBLE RIFLE
Caliber: 243, 270, 30-06, 7x64, 7x65R, 8x57JRS, 9.3x74R, 375 H&H, 470 N.E.; other calibers on request.
Barrel: 23.5″ to 26″.
Weight: NA. **Length:** NA.
Stock: Deluxe European walnut to customer specs; pistol grip or straight grip with Francotte cheekpiece; checkered butt; oil finish.
Sights: Bead front on long ramp, quarter-rib with fixed V rear.
Features: Side-by-side barrels; Anson & Deeley boxlock action with double triggers (front hinged), manual safety, floating firing pins and gas vent safety screws. Splinter or beavertail forend. English scroll engraving; coin finish or color case-hardening. Many options available. Made to customer specs. Imported from Belgium by Armes de Chasse.
Price: From about (no engraving) $16,500.00

AUGUSTE FRANCOTTE SIDELOCK DOUBLE RIFLES
Caliber: 243, 7x64, 7x65R, 8x57JRS, 270, 30-06, 9.3x74R, 375 H&H, 470 N.E.; others on request.
Barrel: 23½″ to 26″.
Weight: 7.61 lbs. (medium calibers), 11.1 lbs. (mag. calibers).
Stock: Fancy European walnut; dimensions to customer specs. Straight or pistol grip style. Checkered butt, oil finish.
Sights: Bead on ramp front, leaf rear on quarter-rib; to customer specs.
Features: Custom made to customer's specs. Special extractor for rimless cartridges; back-action sidelocks; double trigger with hinged front trigger. Automatic or free safety. Wide range of options available. Imported from Belgium by Armes de Chasse.
Price: From about (no engraving) .... $30,000.00 to $36,000

> Consult our Directory pages for the location of firms mentioned.

MERKEL OVER/UNDER COMBINATION GUNS
Caliber/Gauge: 12, 16, 20 (2¾″ chamber) over 22 Hornet, 5.6x50R, 5.6x52R, 222 Rem., 243 Win., 6.5x55, 6.5x57R, 7x57R, 7x65R, 308 Win., 30-06, 8x57JRS, 9.3x74R, 375 H&H.
Barrel: 25.6″.
Weight: About 7.6 lbs. **Length:** NA.
Stock: Oil-finished walnut; pistol grip, cheekpiece.
Sights: Bead front, fixed rear.
Features: Kersten double cross-bolt lock; scroll-engraved, color case-hardened receiver; Blitz action; double triggers. Imported from Germany by GSI.
Price: Model 210E $6,195.00
Price: Model 211E (silver-grayed receivcer, fine hunting scene engraving) $6,995.00
Price: Model 213E (sidelock action, English-style, large scroll Arabesque engraving) $13,595.00
Price: Model 313E (as above, medium-scroll engraving) $20,695.00

BERETTA MODEL 455 SxS EXPRESS RIFLE
Caliber: 375 H&H, 458 Win. Mag., 470 NE, 500 NE 3″, 416 Rigby.
Barrel: 23½″ or 25½″.
Weight: 11 lbs.
Stock: European walnut with hand-checkered grip and forend.
Sights: Blade front, folding leaf V-notch rear.
Features: Sidelock action with easily removable sideplates; color case-hardened finish (455), custom big game or floral motif engraving (455EELL). Double triggers, recoil pad. Introduced 1990. Imported from Italy by Beretta U.S.A.
Price: Model 455 .... $36,000.00
Price: Model 455EELL $47,000.00

AUGUSTE FRANCOTTE BOXLOCK MOUNTAIN RIFLE
Caliber: 5.6x57R, 5.6x65R, 6.5x57R, 7x57R, 7x65R.
Barrel: 24.5″.
Weight: NA. **Length:** NA.
Stock: Deluxe walnut to customer specifications.
Sights: Ramp front, quarter-rib fixed rear.
Features: Anson & Deeley boxlock action; many options available. Made to customer specifications. Imported from Belgium by Armes de Chasse.
Price: From about (no engraving) $15,000.00

AUGUSTE FRANCOTTE SIDELOCK MOUNTAIN RIFLE
Caliber: Rimmed calibers from 5mm to 9mm.
Barrel: 23″ to 26″; chopper lump.
Weight: NA. **Length:** NA.
Stock: Deluxe walnut to customer specifications.
Sights: Ramp front, quarter-rib fixed rear.
Features: True Holland & Holland system; many options available. Made to customer specifications. Imported from Belgium by Armes de Chasse.
Price: From about (no engraving) $28,000.00

MERKEL MODEL 160 SIDE-BY-SIDE DOUBLE RIFLE
Caliber: 22 Hornet, 5.6x50R Mag., 5.6x52R, 222 Rem., 243 Win., 6.5x55, 6.5x57R, 7x57R, 7x65R, 308, 30-06, 8x57JRS, 9.3x74R, 375 H&H.
Barrel: 25.6″.
Weight: About 7.7 lbs, depending upon caliber. **Length:** NA.
Stock: Oil-finished walnut with pistol grip, cheekpiece.
Sights: Blade front on ramp, fixed rear.
Features: Sidelock action. Double barrel locking lug with Greener cross-bolt; fine engraved hunting scenes on sideplates; Holland & Holland ejectors; double triggers. Imported from Germany by GSI.
Price: From $10,995.00

Merkel Boxlock Double Rifles
Similar to the Model 160 double rifle except with Anson & Deely boxlock action with cocking indicators, double triggers, engraved color case-hardened receiver. Introduced 1995. Imported from Germany by GSI.
Price: Model 140-1 .... $4,995.00
Price: Model 140-1.1 (engraved silver-gray receiver) $5,595.00
Price: Model 150-1 (false sideplates, silver-gray receiver, Arabesque engraving) $5,995.00
Price: Model 150-1.1 (as above with English Arabesque engraving) ... $6,995.00

MERKEL OVER/UNDER DOUBLE RIFLES
Caliber: 22 Hornet, 5.6x50R Mag., 5.6x52R, 222 Rem., 243 Win., 6.5x55, 6.5x57R, 7x57R, 7x65R, 308, 30-06, 8x57JRS, 9.3x74R.
Barrel: 25.6″.
Weight: About 7.7 lbs, depending upon caliber. **Length:** NA.
Stock: Oil-finished walnut with pistol grip, cheekpiece.
Sights: Blade front, fixed rear.
Features: Kersten double cross-bolt lock; scroll-engraved, case-hardened receiver; Blitz action with double triggers. Imported from Germany by GSI.
Price: Model 221 E (silver-grayed receiver finish, hunting scene engraving) $9,995.00
Price: Model 223E (sidelock action, English-style large-scroll Arabesque engraving) $16,295.00
Price: Model 323E (as above with medium-scroll engraving) $24,595.00

DRILLINGS, COMBINATION GUNS, DOUBLE RIFLES

MERKEL DRILLINGS
Caliber/Gauge: 12, 20, 3" chambers, 16, 2¾" chambers; 22 Hornet, 5.6x50R Mag., 5.6x52R, 222 Rem., 243 Win., 6.5x55, 6.5x57R, 7x57R, 7x65R, 308, 30-06, 8x57JRS, 9.3x74R, 375 H&H.
Barrel: 25.6".
Weight: 7.9 to 8.4 lbs. depending upon caliber. **Length:** NA.
Stock: Oil-finished walnut with pistol grip; cheekpiece on 12-, 16-gauge.
Sights: Blade front, fixed rear.
Features: Double barrel locking lug with Greener cross-bolt; scroll-engraved, case-hardened receiver; automatic trigger safety; Blitz action; double triggers. Imported from Germany by GSI.
Price: Model 90S (selective sear safety) $5,995.00
Price: Model 90K (manually cocked rifle system) $6,495.00
Price: Model 95S (selective sear safety) $7,195.00
Price: Model 95K (manually cocked rifle system) $7,695.00

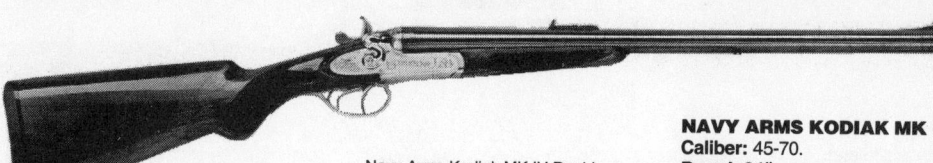

Navy Arms Kodiak MK IV Double

NAVY ARMS KODIAK MK IV DOUBLE RIFLE
Caliber: 45-70.
Barrel: 24".
Weight: 10 lbs., 3 oz. **Length:** 39¾" overall.
Stock: Checkered European walnut.
Sights: Bead front, folding leaf express rear.
Features: Blued, semi-regulated barrels; color case-hardened receiver and hammers; double triggers. Replica of Colt double rifle 1879-1885. Introduced 1996. Imported by Navy Arms.
Price: $3,125.00
Price: Engraved satin-finished receiver, browned barrels $4,000.00

SABATTI OVER/UNDER COMBINATION GUN
Caliber/Gauge: 12, 3" over 223 Rem.
Barrel: 25" (Imp. Mod.).
Weight: 8 lbs.
Stock: Checkered European walnut.
Sights: Bead on ramp front, fixed rear.
Features: Double triggers; blued, engraved receiver; automatic safety. Introduced 1996. Imported from Italy by K.B.I., Inc.
Price: $879.00

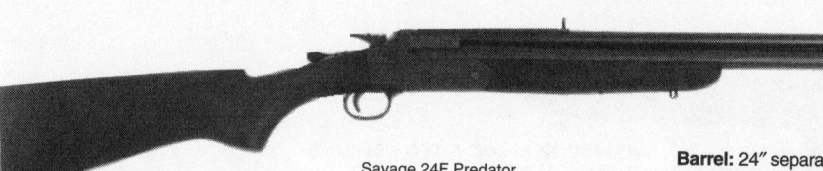

Savage 24F Predator

SAVAGE 24F PREDATOR O/U COMBINATION GUN
Caliber/Gauge: 22 Hornet, 223, 30-30 over 12 (24F-12) or 22 LR, 22 Hornet, 223, 30-30 over 20-ga. (24F-20); 3" chambers.
Action: Takedown, low rebounding visible hammer. Single trigger, barrel selector spur on hammer.
Barrel: 24" separated barrels; 12-ga. has Full, Mod., Imp. Cyl. choke tubes, 20-ga. has fixed Mod. choke.
Weight: 8 lbs. **Length:** 40½" overall.
Stock: Black Rynite composition.
Sights: Ramp front, rear open adjustable for elevation. Grooved for tip-off scope mount.
Features: Removable butt cap for storage and accessories. Introduced 1989.
Price: 24F-12 ....$400.00
Price: 24F-20 ....$400.00

SAUER DRILLING
Caliber/Gauge: 12, 2¾" chambers/243, 6.5x57R, 7x57R, 7x65R, 30-06, 9.3x74R; 16, 2¾" chambers/6.5x57R, 7x57R, 7x65R, 30-06.
Barrel: 25".
Weight: 7.5 lbs. **Length:** 46" overall.
Stock: Fancy French walnut with checkered grip and forend, hog-back comb, sculptured cheekpiece, hand-rubbed oil finish.
Sights: Bead front, automatic pop-up rifle rear.
Features: Greener boxlock cross-bolt action with double underlugs, Greener side safety; separate rifle cartridge extractor. Side-by-side shotgun barrels over rifle barrel. Nitride-coated, hand-engraved receiver available with English Arabesque or relief game animal scene engraving. Lux has profuse relief-engraved game scenes, extra-fancy stump wood. Imported from Germany by SIGARMS, Inc.
Price: Standard $4,600.00
Price: Lux $6,100.00

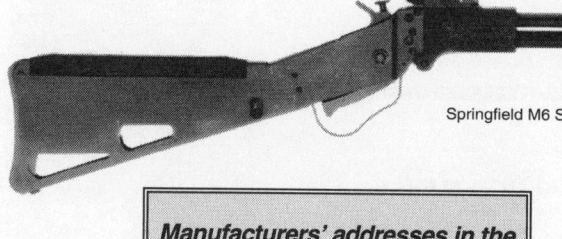

Springfield M6 Scout

SPRINGFIELD, INC. M6 SCOUT RIFLE/SHOTGUN
Caliber/Gauge: 22 LR or 22 Hornet over 410-bore.
Barrel: 18.25".
Weight: 4 lbs. **Length:** 32" overall.
Stock: Folding detachable with storage for 15 22 LR, four 410 shells.
Sights: Blade front, military aperture for 22; V-notch for 410.
Features: All-metal construction. Designed for quick disassembly and minimum maintenance. Folds for compact storage. Introduced 1982; reintroduced 1996. Imported from the Czech Republic by Springfield, Inc.
Price: Parkerized $160.00
Price: Stainless steel $190.00

Manufacturers' addresses in the
Directory of the Arms Trade
page 313, this issue

TIKKA MODEL 512S DOUBLE RIFLE
Caliber: 300, 30-06, 9.3x74R.
Barrel: 24".
Weight: 8⅝ lbs.
Stock: American walnut with Monte Carlo style.
Sights: Ramp front, adjustable open rear.
Features: Barrel selector mounted in trigger. Cocking indicators in tang. Recoil pad. Valmet scope mounts available. Introduced 1980. Imported from Italy by Stoeger.
Price: With ejectors $1,800.00

TIKKA MODEL 512S COMBINATION GUN
Caliber/Gauge: 12 over 222, 308, 30-06.
Barrel: 24" (Imp. Mod.).
Weight: 7⅝ lbs.
Stock: American walnut, with recoil pad. Monte Carlo style. Standard measurements 14"x1⅗"x2"x2⅗".
Sights: Blade front, flip-up-type open rear.
Features: Barrel selector on trigger. Hand-checkered stock and forend. Barrels are screw-adjustable to change bullet point of impact. Barrels are interchangeable. Introduced 1980. Imported from Italy by Stoeger.
Price: $1,400.00
Price: Extra barrels, from $775.00

CAUTION: PRICES SHOWN ARE SUPPLIED BY THE MANUFACTURER OR IMPORTER. CHECK YOUR LOCAL GUNSHOP.

RIMFIRE RIFLES—AUTOLOADERS

Designs for hunting, utility and sporting purposes, including training for competition.

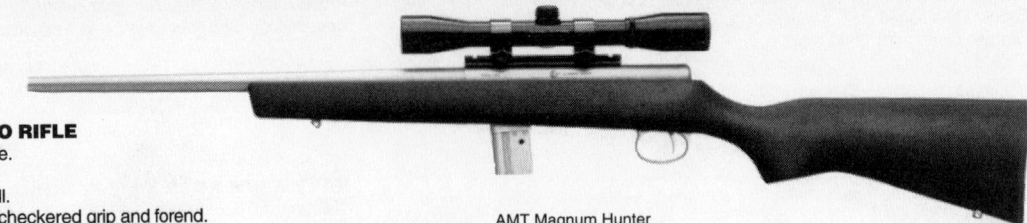

AMT Magnum Hunter

AMT MAGNUM HUNTER AUTO RIFLE
Caliber: 22 WMR, 10-shot magazine.
Barrel: 20".
Weight: 6 lbs. **Length:** 40½" overall.
Stock: Black fiberglass-filled nylon; checkered grip and forend.
Sights: None furnished; drilled and tapped for Weaver mount.
Features: Stainless steel construction. Free-floating target-weight barrel. Introduced 1995. Made in U.S. by AMT.
Price: $549.99

Armscor M-20P Standard Rifle
Similar to the M-20C except has 20.75" barrel, walnut-finished hardwood stock with Monte Carlo comb. Introduced 1990. Imported from the Philippines by K.B.I., Inc.
Price: $119.00

ARMSCOR MODEL AK22 AUTO RIFLE
Caliber: 22 LR, 10-shot magazine.
Barrel: 18.5".
Weight: 7.5 lbs. **Length:** 38" overall.
Stock: Plain mahogany.
Sights: Adjustable post front, leaf rear adjustable for elevation.
Features: Resembles the AK-47. Matte black finish. Introduced 1987. Imported from the Philippines by K.B.I., Inc.
Price: About $189.00

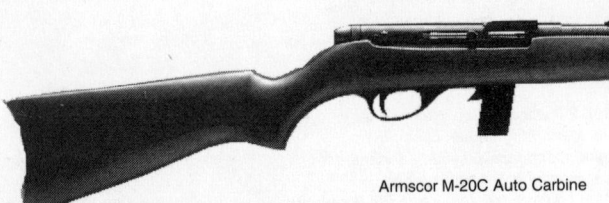

Armscor M-20C Auto Carbine

Armscor M-2000S Classic Auto Rifle
Similar to the M-20C except has 20.75" barrel; hand-checkered stock has Monte Carlo comb and cheekpiece; fully adjustable rear sight. Introduced 1990. Imported from the Philippines by K.B.I., Inc.
Price: $320.00

Armscor M-2000SC Super Classic Rifle
Similar to the M-2000S except has oil-finished American walnut stock with 18 lpi hand checkering; black hardwood grip cap and forend tip; highly polished barreled action; jewelled bolt; recoil pad; swivel studs. Imported from the Philippines by K.B.I., Inc.
Price: $320.00

ARMSCOR M-20C AUTO CARBINE
Caliber: 22 LR, 10-shot magazine.
Barrel: 18.25".
Weight: 6.5 lbs. **Length:** 38" overall.
Stock: Walnut-finished mahogany.
Sights: Hooded front, rear adjustable for elevation.
Features: Receiver grooved for scope mounting. Blued finish. Introduced 1990. Imported from the Philippines by Ruko Products.
Price: $139.99

ARMSCOR M-1600 AUTO RIFLE
Caliber: 22 LR, 10-shot magazine.
Barrel: 18.25".
Weight: 6.2 lbs. **Length:** 38.5" overall.
Stock: Black finished mahogany.
Sights: Post front, aperture rear.
Features: Resembles Colt AR-15. Matte black finish. Introduced 1987. Imported from the Philippines by K.B.I., Inc.
Price: About $175.00

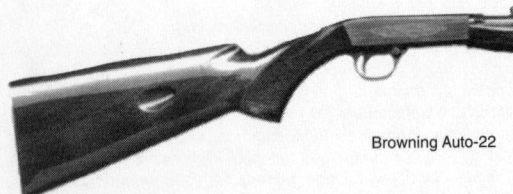

Browning Auto-22

Browning Auto-22 Grade VI
Same as the Grade I Auto-22 except available with either grayed or blued receiver with extensive engraving with gold-plated animals: right side pictures a fox and squirrel in a woodland scene; left side shows a beagle chasing a rabbit. On top is a portrait of the beagle. Stock and forend are of high-grade walnut with a double-bordered cut checkering design. Introduced 1987.
Price: Grade VI, blue or gray receiver $819.00

ERMA EM1 CARBINE
Caliber: 22 LR, 10-shot magazine.
Barrel: 18".
Weight: 5.6 lbs. **Length:** 35.5" overall.
Stock: Polished beech or oiled walnut.
Sights: Blade front, fully adjustable aperture rear.
Features: Blowback action. Receiver grooved for scope mounting. Imported from Germany by Mandall Shooting Supplies.
Price: $499.95

BROWNING AUTO-22 RIFLE
Caliber: 22 LR, 11-shot.
Barrel: 19¼".
Weight: 4¾ lbs. **Length:** 37" overall.
Stock: Checkered select walnut with pistol grip and semi-beavertail forend.
Sights: Gold bead front, folding leaf rear.
Features: Engraved receiver with polished blue finish; cross-bolt safety; tubular magazine in buttstock; easy takedown for carrying or storage. Imported from Japan by Browning.
Price: Grade I $398.95

BRNO ZKM 611/621 AUTO RIFLE
Caliber: 22 WMR, 6-shot magazine.
Barrel: 20".
Weight: 6 lbs., 2 oz. **Length:** 37" overall.
Stock: Walnut; checkered grip and forend.
Sights: Blade front, open rear.
Features: Removable box magazine; polished blue finish; grooved receiver for scope mounting; sling swivels; thumbscrew takedown. Introduced 1995. Imported from the Czech Republic by Magnum Research.
Price: Model 611 .... $569.00
Price: Model 621 (beech stock) $499.00

RIMFIRE RIFLES—AUTOLOADERS

E.A.A./SABATTI MODEL 1822 AUTO RIFLE
Caliber: 22 LR, 10-shot magazine.
Barrel: 18½" round tapered; bull barrel on Heavy and Thumbhole Heavy models.
Weight: 5¼ lbs. (Sporter). **Length:** 37" overall.
Stock: Stained hardwood; Thumbhole model has one-piece stock.
Sights: Bead front, folding leaf rear adjustable for elevation on Sporter model. Heavy and Thumbhole models only dovetailed for scope mount.
Features: Cross-bolt safety. Blue finish. Lifetime warranty. Introduced 1993. Imported from Italy by European American Armory.
Price: Sporter $190.00
Price: Heavy $205.00
Price: Thumbhole Heavy $350.00

Krico Model 260

KRICO MODEL 260 AUTO RIFLE
Caliber: 22 LR, 5-shot magazine.
Barrel: 19.6".
Weight: 6.6 lbs. **Length:** 38.9" overall.
Stock: Beech.
Sights: Blade on ramp front, open adjustable rear.
Features: Receiver grooved for scope mounting. Sliding safety. Imported from Germany by Mandall Shooting Supplies.
Price: $700.00

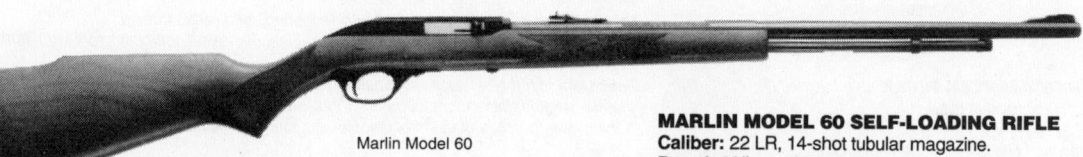
Marlin Model 60

MARLIN MODEL 60 SELF-LOADING RIFLE
Caliber: 22 LR, 14-shot tubular magazine.
Barrel: 22" round tapered.
Weight: About 5½ lbs. **Length:** 40½" overall.
Stock: Press-checkered, walnut-finished Maine birch with Monte Carlo, full pistol grip; Mar-Shieldr finish.
Sights: Ramp front, open adjustable rear.
Features: Matted receiver is grooved for scope mount. Manual bolt hold-open; automatic last-shot bolt hold-open.
Price: $158.40

Marlin Model 60SS Self-Loading Rifle
Same as the Model 60 except breech bolt, barrel and outer magazine tube are made of stainless steel; most other parts are either nickel-plated or coated to match the stainless finish. Monte Carlo stock is of black/gray Maine birch laminate, and has nickel-plated swivel studs, rubber butt pad. Introduced 1993.
Price: $244.20

MARLIN 70PSS STAINLESS RIFLE
Caliber: 22 LR, 7-shot magazine.
Barrel: 16¼" stainless steel, Micro-Groove® rifling.
Weight: 3¼ lbs. **Length:** 35¼" overall.
Stock: Black fiberglass-filled synthetic with abbreviated forend, nickel-plated swivel studs, moulded-in checkering.
Sights: Romp front with orange post, cutaway Wide Scan® hood; adjustable open rear. Receiver grooved for scope mounting.
Features: Takedown barrel; cross-bolt safety; manual bolt hold-open; last shot bolt hold-open; comes with padded carrying case. Introduced 1986. Made in U.S. by Marlin.
Price: $255.25

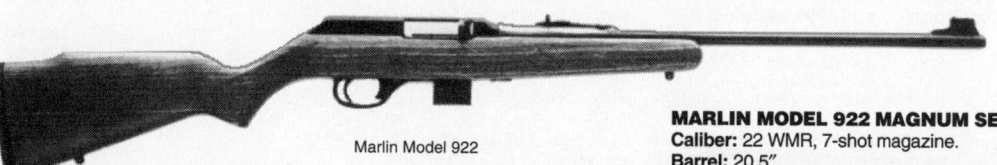
Marlin Model 922

MARLIN MODEL 922 MAGNUM SELF-LOADING RIFLE
Caliber: 22 WMR, 7-shot magazine.
Barrel: 20.5".
Weight: 6.5 lbs. **Length:** 39.75" overall.
Stock: Checkered American black walnut with Monte Carlo comb, swivel studs, rubber buttpad.
Sights: Ramp front with bead and removable Wide-Scan® hood, adjustable folding semi-buckhorn rear.
Features: Action based on the centerfire Model 9 Carbine. Receiver drilled and tapped for scope mounting. Automatic last-shot bolt hold open; magazine safety. Introduced 1993.
Price: $410.75

MARLIN MODEL 995SS SELF-LOADING RIFLE
Caliber: 22 LR, 7-shot clip magazine.
Barrel: 18" Micro-Groove®; stainless steel.
Weight: 5 lbs. **Length:** 37" overall.
Stock: Black fiberglass-filled synthetic with nickel-plated swivel studs, moulded-in checkering.
Sights: Ramp front with orange post and cut-away Wide-Scan® hood; screw-adjustable open rear.
Features: Stainless steel breechbolt and barrel. Receiver grooved for scope mount; bolt hold-open device; cross-bolt safety. Introduced 1979.
Price: $237.60

Mitchell Arms LW-22

MITCHELL ARMS LW22 SEMI-AUTO CARBINE
Caliber: 22 LR, 10-shot magazine.
Barrel: 17".
Weight: 3.25 lbs. **Length:** 35" overall.
Stock: Black foam or fixed skeleton.
Sights: Protected post front, adjustable aperture rear.
Features: Blue finish; removable stock and barrel. Introduced 1996. Made in U.S. by Mitchell Arms.
Price: Skeleton stock $274.95
Price: Black foam stock $304.95

RIMFIRE RIFLES—AUTOLOADERS

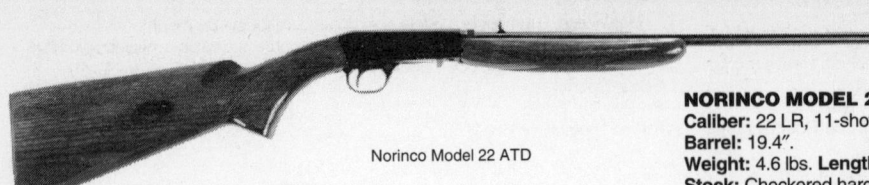
Norinco Model 22 ATD

NORINCO MODEL 22 ATD RIFLE
Caliber: 22 LR, 11-shot magazine.
Barrel: 19.4".
Weight: 4.6 lbs. **Length:** 36.6" overall.
Stock: Checkered hardwood.
Sights: Blade front, open adjustable rear.
Features: Browning-design takedown action for storage, transport. Cross-bolt safety. Tube magazine loads through buttplate. Blue finish with engraved receiver. Introduced 1987. Imported from China by Interarms.
Price: $150.00

Remington 522 Viper

REMINGTON MODEL 522 VIPER AUTOLOADING RIFLE
Caliber: 22 LR, 10-shot magazine.
Barrel: 20".
Weight: 4 5/8 lbs. **Length:** 40" overall.
Stock: Black synthetic with positive checkering, beavertail forend.
Sights: Bead on ramp front, fully adjustable open rear. Integral grooved rail for scope mounting.
Features: Synthetic stock and receiver with overall matte black finish. Has magazine safety, cocking indicator; manual and last-shot hold-open; trigger mechanism has primary and secondary sears; integral ejection port shield. Introduced 1993.
Price: $165.00

REMINGTON 552 BDL SPEEDMASTER RIFLE
Caliber: 22 S (20), L (17) or LR (15) tubular mag.
Barrel: 21" round tapered.
Weight: About 5 3/4 lbs. **Length:** 40" overall.
Stock: Walnut. Checkered grip and forend.
Sights: Bead front, step open rear adjustable for windage and elevation.
Features: Positive cross-bolt safety, receiver grooved for tip-off mount.
Price: About $340.00

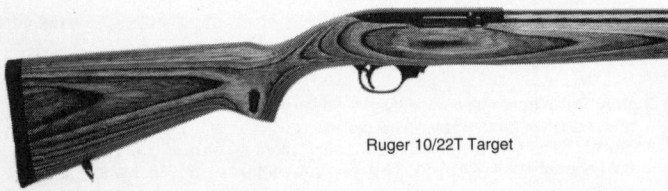
Ruger 10/22T Target

RUGER 10/22 AUTOLOADING CARBINE
Caliber: 22 LR, 10-shot rotary magazine.
Barrel: 18 1/2" round tapered.
Weight: 5 lbs. **Length:** 37 1/4" overall.
Stock: American hardwood with pistol grip and bbl. band.
Sights: Brass bead front, folding leaf rear adjustable for elevation.
Features: Detachable rotary magazine fits flush into stock, cross-bolt safety, receiver tapped and grooved for scope blocks or tip-off mount. Scope base adaptor furnished with each rifle.
Price: Model 10/22 RB (blue) $213.00
Price: Model K10/22RB (bright finish stainless barrel) $255.00

Ruger 10/22T Target Rifle
Similar to the 10/22 except has 20" heavy, hammer-forged barrel with tight chamber dimensions, improved trigger pull, laminated hardwood stock dimensioned for optical sights. No iron sights supplied. Introduced 1996. Made in U.S. by Sturm, Ruger & Co.
Price: $392.50

Ruger 10/22 International

Ruger 10/22 International Carbine
Similar to the Ruger 10/22 Carbine except has full-length International stock of American hardwood, checkered grip and forend; comes with rubber buttpad, sling swivels. Reintroduced 1994.
Price: Blue (10/22RBI) $262.00
Price: Stainless (K10/22RBI) $282.00

Ruger 10/22 Deluxe Sporter
Same as 10/22 Carbine except walnut stock with hand checkered pistol grip and forend; straight buttplate, no barrel band, has sling swivels.
Price: Model 10/22 DSP $274.00

Savage Model 64G

SAVAGE MODEL 64G AUTO RIFLE
Caliber: 22 LR, 10-shot magazine.
Barrel: 20".
Weight: 5 1/2 lbs. **Length:** 40" overall.
Stock: Walnut-finished hardwood with Monte Carlo-type comb, checkered grip and forend.
Sights: Bead front, open adjustable rear. Receiver grooved for scope mounting.
Features: Thumb-operated rotating safety. Blue finish. Side ejection, bolt hold-open device. Introduced 1990. Made in Canada, from Savage Arms.
Price: $123.00
Price: Model 64GXP Package Gun includes 4x15 scope and mounts $129.00

RIMFIRE RIFLES—LEVER & SLIDE ACTION

Classic and modern models for sport and utility, including training.

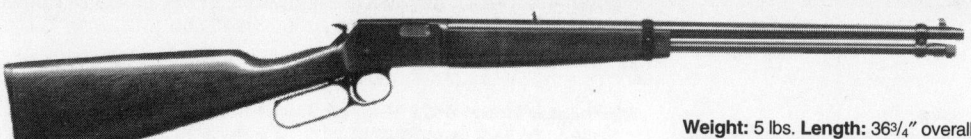
Browning BL-22

BROWNING BL-22 LEVER-ACTION RIFLE
Caliber: 22 S (22), L (17) or LR (15), tubular magazine.
Barrel: 20" round tapered.
Weight: 5 lbs. **Length:** 36 3/4" overall.
Stock: Walnut, two-piece straight grip Western style.
Sights: Bead post front, folding-leaf rear.
Features: Short throw lever, half-cock safety, receiver grooved for tip-off scope mounts. Imported from Japan by Browning.
Price: Grade I $345.95
Price: Grade II (engraved receiver, checkered grip and forend) $395.95

Marlin Model 39AS

MARLIN MODEL 39AS GOLDEN LEVER-ACTION RIFLE
Caliber: 22 S (26), L (21), LR (19), tubular magazine.
Barrel: 24" Micro-Groove®.
Weight: 6 1/2 lbs. **Length:** 40" overall.
Stock: Checkered American black walnut with white line spacers at pistol grip cap and buttplate; Mar-Shield® finish. Swivel studs; rubber buttpad.
Sights: Bead ramp front with detachable Wide-Scan™ hood, folding rear semi-buckhorn adjustable for windage and elevation.
Features: Hammer-block safety; rebounding hammer. Takedown action, receiver tapped for scope mount (supplied), offset hammer spur; gold-plated steel trigger.
Price: $444.80

REMINGTON 572 BDL FIELDMASTER PUMP RIFLE
Caliber: 22 S (20), L (17) or LR (14), tubular magazine.
Barrel: 21" round tapered.
Weight: 5 1/2 lbs. **Length:** 42" overall.
Stock: Walnut with checkered pistol grip and slide handle.
Sights: Blade ramp front; sliding ramp rear adjustable for windage and elevation.
Features: Cross-bolt safety; removing inner magazine tube converts rifle to single shot; receiver grooved for tip-off scope mount.
Price: About $353.00

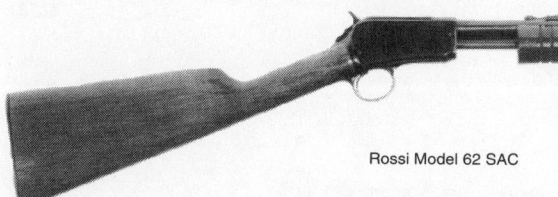
Rossi Model 62 SAC

ROSSI MODEL 62 SA PUMP RIFLE
Caliber: 22 LR, 22 WMR.
Barrel: 23", round or octagonal.
Weight: 5 3/4 lbs. **Length:** 39 1/4" overall.
Stock: Walnut, straight grip, grooved forend.
Sights: Fixed front, adjustable rear.
Features: Capacity 20 Short, 16 Long or 14 Long Rifle. Quick takedown. Imported from Brazil by Interarms.
Price: Blue $240.00
Price: Nickel $250.00
Price: Blue, with octagonal barrel $250.00
Price: 22 WMR, as Model 59 .... $280.00

Rossi Model 62 SAC Carbine
Same as standard model except 22 LR, has 16 1/4" barrel. Magazine holds slightly fewer cartridges.
Price: Blue $240.00
Price: Nickel $250.00

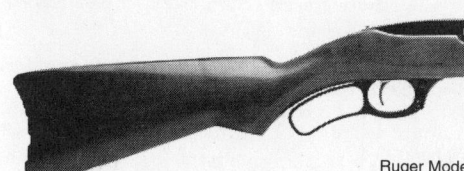
Ruger Model 96/22

RUGER MODEL 96/22 LEVER-ACTION RIFLE
Caliber: 22 LR, 10-shot rotary, magazine; 22 WMR, 9-shot rotary magazine.
Barrel: 18 1/2".
Weight: 5 1/4 lbs. **Length:** 37 1/4" overall.
Stock: American hardwood.
Sights: Gold bead front, folding leaf rear.
Features: Cross-bolt safety, visible cocking indicator; short-throw lever action. Screw-on dovetail scope base. Introduced 1996. Made in U.S. by Sturm, Ruger & Co.
Price: 96/22 (22 LR) $327.50
Price: 96/22M (22 WMR) $345.00

Winchester 9422 High Grade

WINCHESTER MODEL 9422 LEVER-ACTION RIFLE
Caliber: 22 S (21), L (17), LR (15), tubular magazine.
Barrel: 20 1/2".
Weight: 6 1/4 lbs. **Length:** 37 1/8" overall.
Stock: American walnut, two-piece, straight grip (no pistol grip).
Sights: Hooded ramp front, adjustable semi-buckhorn rear.
Features: Side ejection, receiver grooved for scope mounting, takedown action. From U.S. Repeating Arms Co.
Price: Walnut $407.00
Price: With WinTuff laminated stock $407.00

CAUTION: PRICES SHOWN ARE SUPPLIED BY THE MANUFACTURER OR IMPORTER. CHECK YOUR LOCAL GUNSHOP.

RIMFIRE RIFLES—LEVER & SLIDE ACTION

Winchester Model 9422 Trapper

Winchester Model 9422 Trapper
Similar to the Model 9422 with walnut stock except has 16½" barrel, overall length of 33⅛", weighs 5½ lbs. Magazine holds 15 Shorts, 12 Longs, 11 Long Rifles. Introduced 1996.
Price: $407.00

Winchester Model 9422 High Grade Rifle
Same as the standard Model 9422 except has high grade walnut with gloss finish, blued and engraved receiver with a coonhound on the right side, a racoon profile on the left, both framed with detailed Nimschke-style scrollwork. Chambered only for 22 LR. Introduced 1995. From U.S. Repeating Arms Co., Inc.
Price: $489.00

Winchester Model 9422 Magnum Lever-Action Rifle
Same as the 9422 except chambered for 22 WMR cartridge, has 11-round mag. capacity.
Price: Walnut $424.00
Price: With WinCam green stock $424.00
Price: With WinTuff brown laminated stock $424.00

RIMFIRE RIFLES—BOLT ACTIONS & SINGLE SHOTS

Includes models for a variety of sports, utility and competitive shooting.

Anschutz Achiever

ANSCHUTZ ACHIEVER BOLT-ACTION RIFLE
Caliber: 22 LR, 5-shot clip, single shot adaptor.
Barrel: 19½".
Weight: 5 lbs. Length: 35½" to 36⅔" overall.
Stock: Walnut-finished hardwood with adjustable buttplate, vented forend, stippled pistol grip. Length of pull adjustable from 11⅞" to 13".
Sights: Hooded front, open rear adjustable for windage and elevation.
Features: Uses Mark 2000-type action with adjustable two-stage trigger. Receiver grooved for scope mounting. Designed for training in junior rifle clubs and for starting young shooters. Introduced 1987. Imported from Germany by AcuSport Corp.
Price: $372.60

ANSCHUTZ 1710D CUSTOM RIFLE
Caliber: 22 LR, 5-shot clip.
Barrel: 24¼".
Weight: 7⅜ lbs. Length: 42½" overall.
Stock: Select European walnut.
Sights: Hooded ramp front, folding leaf rear; drilled and tapped for scope mounting.
Features: Match 54 action with adjustable single-stage trigger; roll-over Monte Carlo cheekpiece, slim forend with schnabel tip, Wundhammer palm swell on pistol grip, rosewood grip cap with white diamond insert; skip-line checkering on grip and forend. Introduced 1988. Imported from Germany by AcuSport Corp.
Price: $1,161.64

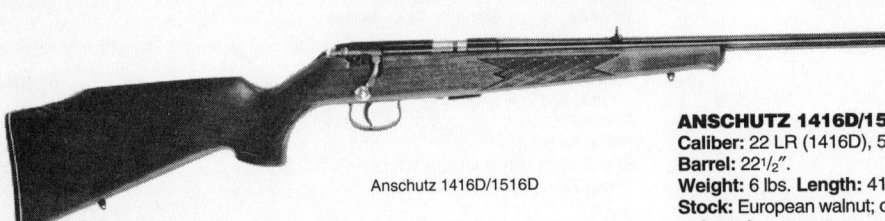
Anschutz 1416D/1516D

ANSCHUTZ 1416D/1516D CLASSIC RIFLES
Caliber: 22 LR (1416D), 5-shot clip; 22 WMR (1516D), 4-shot clip.
Barrel: 22½".
Weight: 6 lbs. Length: 41" overall.
Stock: European walnut; classic style with straight comb, checkered pistol grip and forend.
Sights: Hooded ramp front, folding leaf rear.
Features: Uses Match 64 action. Adjustable single stage trigger. Receiver grooved for scope mounting. Imported from Germany by AcuSport Corp.
Price: 1416D, 22 LR $604.72
Price: 1516D, 22 WMR $633.58
Price: 1416D Classic left-hand $633.58

Anschutz 1416D/1516D Deluxe Rifles
Similar to the Classic models except have European walnut stocks with roll-over Monte Carlo cheekpiece, slim forend with schnabel tip, fine cut checkering on grip and forend. Introduced 1988. Imported from Germany by AcuSport Corp.
Price: 1416D (22 LR) $673.11
Price: 1516D (22 WMR) $693.78

Armscor M-14P

ARMSCOR M-1400S CLASSIC BOLT-ACTION RIFLE
Caliber: 22 LR, 10-shot magazine.
Barrel: 22⅝".
Weight: 6.7 lbs. Length: 41.25" overall.
Stock: Walnut-finished mahogany.
Sights: Bead front, rear adjustable for elevation.
Features: Receiver grooved for scope mounting. Blued finish. Introduced 1987. Imported from the Philippines by K.B.I., Inc.
Price: $190.00

Armscor M-14P Standard Rifle
Similar to the M-1400S except has short walnut-finished hardwood stock for small shooters. Introduced 1987. Imported from the Philippines by K.B.I., Inc.
Price: $119.00
Price: M-14Y Youth (17.5" barrel) $119.00

RIMFIRE RIFLES—BOLT ACTIONS & SINGLE SHOTS

Armscor M-1400SC Super Classic Rifle
Similar to the M-1400S except has oil-finished American walnut stock with 18 lpi hand checkering; black hardwood grip cap and forend tip; highly polished barreled action; jewelled bolt; recoil pad; swivel studs. Imported from the Philippines by K.B.I., Inc.
Price: $340.00

Armscor M-12Y Youth Rifle
Similar to the M-1400S except has 17.5" barrel, and is a single shot. Weight is 4.1 lbs., overall length 34.4". Imported from the Philippines by K.B.I., Inc.
Price: $99.00

CABANAS LASER RIFLE
Caliber: 177.
Barrel: 19".
Weight: 6 lbs., 12 oz. **Length:** 42" overall.
Stock: Target-type thumbhole.
Sights: Blade front, open fully adjustable rear.
Features: Fires round ball or pellets with 22 blank cartridge. Imported from Mexico by Mandall Shooting Supplies.
Price: $159.95

Cabanas Espronceda IV Bolt-Action Rifle
Similar to the Leyre model except has full sporter stock, 18 3/4" barrel, 40" overall length, weighs 5 1/2 lbs.
Price: $134.95

> Consult our Directory pages for the location of firms mentioned.

CHIPMUNK SINGLE SHOT RIFLE
Caliber: 22, S, L, LR, single shot.
Barrel: 16 1/8".
Weight: About 2 1/2 lbs. **Length:** 30" overall.
Stocks: American walnut, or camouflage.
Sights: Post on ramp front, peep rear adjustable for windage and elevation.
Features: Drilled and tapped for scope mounting using special Chipmunk base ($9.95). Made in U.S. Introduced 1982. From Oregon Arms.
Price: Standard $174.95
Price: Deluxe (better wood, checkering) $225.00

Armscor M-1500SC Super Classic Rifle
Similar to the M-1500S except has oil-finished American walnut stock with 18 lpi hand checkering; black hardwood grip cap and forend tip; highly polished barreled action; jewelled bolt; recoil pad; swivel studs. Imported from the Philippines by K.B.I., Inc.
Price: $350.00

Armscor M-1500S Classic Rifle
Similar to the Model 1400S except chambered for 22 WMR. Has 22.6" barrel, double lug bolt, checkered stock, weighs 6.5 lbs. Introduced 1987.
Price: About $210.00

CABANAS MASTER BOLT-ACTION RIFLE
Caliber: 177, round ball or pellet; single shot.
Barrel: 19 1/2".
Weight: 8 lbs. **Length:** 45 1/2" overall.
Stocks: Walnut target-type with Monte Carlo.
Sights: Blade front, fully adjustable rear.
Features: Fires round ball or pellet with 22-cal. blank cartridge. Bolt action. Imported from Mexico by Mandall Shooting Supplies. Introduced 1984.
Price: $189.95
Price: Varmint model (has 21 1/2" barrel, 4 1/2 lbs., 41" overall length, varmint-type stock) $119.95

Cabanas Leyre Bolt-Action Rifle
Similar to Master model except 44" overall, has sport/target stock.
Price: $149.95
Price: Model R83 (17" barrel, hardwood stock, 40" o.a.l.) $79.95
Price: Mini 82 Youth (16 1/2" barrel, 33" overall length, 3 1/2 lbs.) $69.95
Price: Pony Youth (16" barrel, 34" overall length, 3.2 lbs.) $69.95

COOPER ARMS MODEL 36 CLASSIC SPORTER RIFLE
Caliber: 22 LR, 5-shot magazine.
Barrel: 22 3/4".
Weight: 7 lbs. **Length:** 42 1/2" overall.
Stock: AAA Claro walnut with 22 lpi checkering, oil finish.
Sights: None furnished.
Features: Action has three mid-bolt locking lugs, 45-degree bolt rotation; fully adjustable single stage match trigger; swivel studs. Pachmayr butt pad. Introduced 1991. Made in U.S. by Cooper Arms.
Price: $1,675.00
Price: Custom Classic (AAA Claro walnut, Monte Carlo beaded cheekpiece, oil finish) $1,960.00
Price: Model 36 Featherweight (black synthetic stock, 6.5 lbs.) $1,740.00
Price: Model 36 Montana Trailblazer (lighter weight, sporter barrel profile) $1,475.00

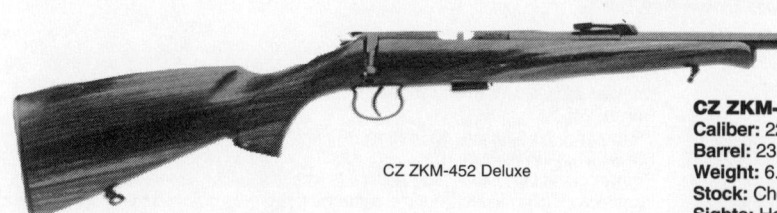

CZ ZKM-452 Deluxe

CZ ZKM-452 DELUXE BOLT-ACTION RIFLE
Caliber: 22 LR, 22 WMR, detachable 6- or 10-shot magazine.
Barrel: 23.6".
Weight: 6.9 lbs. **Length:** 43.5" overall.
Stock: Checkered walnut.
Sights: Hooded bead front, open rear adjustable for windage and elevation.
Features: Dual claw extractors, safety locks firing pin. Blue finish; grooved receiver; oiled stock; sling swivels. Introduced 1992. Imported from the Czech Republic by Magnum Research.
Price: 22 LR, 10-shot, standard $299.00
Price: 22 LR, 10-shot, Lux $329.00
Price: 22 WMR, 6-shot, standard $379.00
Price: 22 WMR, 6-shot, Lux $399.00

Dakota 22 Sporter

DAKOTA 22 SPORTER BOLT-ACTION RIFLE
Caliber: 22 LR, 5-shot magazine.
Barrel: 22" Premium.
Weight: About 6.5 lbs. **Length:** 42 1/2" overall.
Stock: Claro or English walnut in classic design; 13.6" length of pull. Point panel hand checkering. Swivel studs. Black buttpad.
Sights: None furnished.
Features: Combines features of Winchester 52 and Dakota 76 rifles. Full-sized receiver; rear locking lug and bolt machined from bar stock. Trigger and striker-blocking safety; Model 70-style trigger. Introduced 1992. From Dakota Arms, Inc.
Price: $1,500.00

RIMFIRE RIFLES—BOLT ACTIONS & SINGLE SHOTS

Kimber Model 82C Classic

Kimber Model 82C Custom Match Bolt-Action Rifle
Same as the Model 82C Classic except has high grade stock of AA French walnut with black ebony forend tip, full coverage 22 lpi borderless checkering, steel Neidner (uncheckered) buttplate, and satin rust blue finish. Reintroduced 1995. Made in U.S. by Kimber of America, Inc.
Price: $2,075.00

Kimber Model 82C Varmint Synthetic Bolt-Action Rifle
Similar to the Model 82C Classic except has a synthetic stock with a slightly larger forend to accommodate the medium/heavy barrel profile. Has fluted, 20" stainless steel match-grade barrel. Weighs about 7 1/2 lbs. Matte blue action. Introduced 1996. Made in U.S. by Kimber of America, Inc.
Price: $885.00

KIMBER MODEL 82C CLASSIC BOLT-ACTION RIFLE
Caliber: 22 LR, 4-shot magazine (10-shot available).
Barrel: 22", premium air-gauged, free-floated.
Weight: 6.5 lbs. **Length:** 40.5" overall.
Stock: Classic style of Claro walnut; 13.5" length of pull; hand-checkered; red rubber buttpad; polished steel grip cap.
Sights: None furnished; drilled and tapped for Warne, Leupold or Millett scope mounts (optionally available from factory).
Features: Action uses aluminum pillar bedding for consistent accuracy; single-set trigger with 2.5-lb. pull is fully adjustable. Reintroduced 1994. Made in U.S. by Kimber of America, Inc.
Price: $785.00

Kimber Model 82C SuperAmerica Bolt-Action Rifle
Similar to the Model 82C Classic except has AAA fancy grade Claro walnut with beaded cheekpiece, ebony forend tip; hand-checkered 22 lpi patterns with wrap-around coverage; black rubber buttpad. Reintroduced 1994. Made in U.S. by Kimber of America, Inc.
Price: $1,326.00

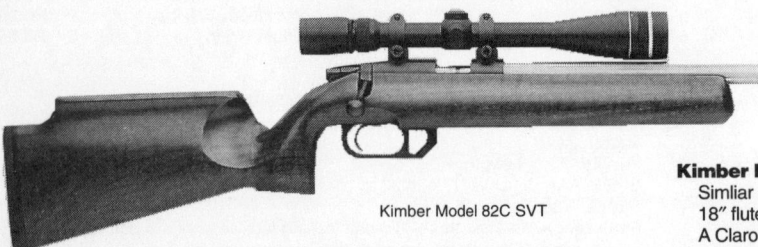
Kimber Model 82C SVT

Kimber Model 82C Stainless Classic Bolt-Action Rifle
Similar to the Model 82C except has a match-grade stainless steel barrel and matte-finished receiver. Introduced 1996. Made in U.S. by Kimber of America, Inc.
Price: $899.00

Kimber Model 82C SVT Bolt-Action Rifle
Simliar to the Model 82C except has an offhand high comb target-style stock; 18" fluted, stainless steel, target weight, match-grade barrel; single shot action; A Claro walnut; weighs 7 1/2 lbs. Designed for off-hand plinking, varmint shooting and competition. Introduced 1996. Made in U.S. by Kimber of America, Inc.
Price: $785.00

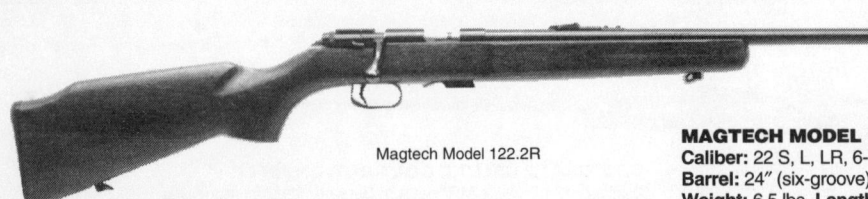
Magtech Model 122.2R

KRICO MODEL 300 BOLT-ACTION RIFLE
Caliber: 22 LR, 22 WMR, 22 Hornet.
Barrel: 19.6" (22 RF), 23.6" (Hornet).
Weight: 6.3 lbs. **Length:** 38.5" overall (22 RF).
Stock: Walnut-stained beech.
Sights: Blade on ramp front, open adjustable rear.
Features: Double triggers, sliding safety. Checkered grip and forend. Imported from Germany by Mandall Shooting Supplies.
Price: Model 300 Standard $700.00
Price: Model 300 Deluxe $795.00
Price: Model 300 Stutzen (walnut full-length stock) $825.00
Price: Model 300 SA (walnut Monte Carlo stock) $750.00

MAGTECH MODEL 122.2 BOLT-ACTION RIFLE
Caliber: 22 S, L, LR, 6- and 10-shot magazines.
Barrel: 24" (six-groove).
Weight: 6.5 lbs. **Length:** 43" overall.
Stock: Brazilian hardwood.
Sights: Blade front, open rear adjustable for windage and elevation.
Features: Sliding safety; double extractors; receiver grooved for scope mount. Introduced 1994. Imported from Brazil by Magtech Recreational Products, Inc.
Price: Model 122.2S (no sights) $139.95
Price: Model 122.2R (open sights) $149.95
Price: Model 122.2T (ramp front, micro-type open rear) $169.95

Marlin Model 15YN

MARLIN MODEL 15YN "LITTLE BUCKAROO"
Caliber: 22 S, L, LR, single shot.
Barrel: 16 1/4" Micro-Groove®.
Weight: 4 1/4 lbs. **Length:** 33 1/4" overall.
Stock: One-piece walnut-finished, press-checkered Maine birch with Monte Carlo; Mar-Shield® finish.
Sights: Ramp front, adjustable open rear.
Features: Beginner's rifle with thumb safety, easy-load feed throat, red cocking indicator. Receiver grooved for scope mounting. Introduced 1989.
Price: $171.80

RIMFIRE RIFLES—BOLT ACTIONS & SINGLE SHOTS

Marlin Model 880

Marlin Model 880 Bolt-Action Rifle
Caliber: 22 LR; 7-shot clip magazine.
Barrel: 22" Micro-Groove®.
Weight: 5½ lbs. **Length:** 41".
Stock: Checkered Monte Carlo American black walnut with checkered pistol grip and forend. Rubber buttpad, swivel studs. Mar-Shield® finish.
Sights: Wide-Scan™ ramp front, folding semi-buckhorn rear adjustable for windage and elevation.
Features: Receiver grooved for scope mount. Introduced 1989.
Price: $240.25

Marlin Model 880SS Stainless Steel Bolt-Action Rifle
Same as the Model 880 except barrel, receiver, front breech bolt, striker knob, trigger stud, cartridge lifter stud and outer magazine tube are made of stainless steel. Most other parts are nickel-plated to match the stainless finish. Has black fiberglass-filled AKZO synthetic stock with moulded-in checkering, stainless steel swivel studs. Introduced 1994. Made in U.S. by Marlin Firearms Co.
Price: $256.65

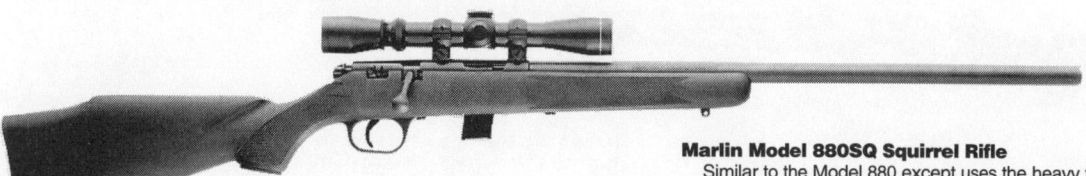
Marlin Model 880SQ

Marlin Model 880SQ Squirrel Rifle
Similar to the Model 880 except uses the heavy target barrel of Marlin's Model 2000L target rifle. Black synthetic stock with moulded-in checkering; double bedding screws; matte blue finish. Comes without sights, but has plugged dovetail for a rear sight, filled screw holes for front; receiver grooved for scope mount. Weighs 7 lbs. Introduced 1996. Made in U.S. by Marlin.
Price: $263.85

Marlin Model 25N Bolt-Action Repeater
Similar to Marlin 880, except walnut-finished pistol grip stock, adjustable open rear sight, ramp front.
Price: $173.30

Marlin Model 25MN Bolt-Action Rifle
Similar to the Model 25N except chambered for 22 WMR. Has 7-shot clip magazine, 22" Micro-Groove® barrel, checkered walnut-finished Maine birch stock. Introduced 1989.
Price: $198.20

Marlin Model 882SS Bolt-Action Rifle
Same as the Marlin Model 882 except has stainless steel front breech bolt, barrel, receiver and bolt knob. All other parts are either stainless steel or nickel-plated. Has black Monte Carlo stock of fiberglass-filled polycarbonate with moulded-in checkering, nickel-plated swivel studs. Introduced 1995. Made in U.S. by Marlin Firearms Co.
Price: $282.65

> *Manufacturers' addresses in the*
> # Directory of the Arms Trade
> *page 313, this issue*

Marlin Model 881 Bolt-Action Rifle
Same as the Marlin 880 except tubular magazine, holds 17 Long Rifle cartridges. Weighs 6 lbs.
Price: $250.25

Marlin Model 882 Bolt-Action Rifle
Same as the Marlin 880 except 22 WMR cal. only with 7-shot clip magazine; weight about 6 lbs. Comes with swivel studs.
Price: $264.90
Price: Model 882L (laminated hardwood stock) $280.85

Marlin Model 883 Bolt-Action Rifle
Same as Marlin 882 except tubular magazine holds 12 rounds of 22 WMR ammunition.
Price: $274.60

Marlin Model 883SS Bolt-Action Rifle
Same as the Model 883 except front breech bolt, striker knob, trigger stud, cartridge lifter stud and outer magazine tube are of stainless steel; other parts are nickel-plated. Has two-tone brown laminated Monte Carlo stock with swivel studs, rubber butt pad. Introduced 1993.
Price: $292.35

Norinco JW-27

Norinco JW-27 Bolt-Action Rifle
Caliber: 22 LR, 5-shot magazine.
Barrel: 22.75".
Weight: 5 lbs., 14 oz. **Length:** 41.75" overall.
Stock: Walnut-finished hardwood with checkered grip and forend.
Sights: Dovetailed bead on blade front, fully adjustable rear.
Features: Receiver grooved for scope mounting. Blued finish. Introduced 1992. Imported from China by Century International Arms.
Price: About $106.95

NORINCO JW-15 BOLT-ACTION RIFLE
Caliber: 22 LR, 5-shot detachable magazine.
Barrel: 24".
Weight: 5 lbs., 12 oz. **Length:** 41¾" overall.
Stock: Walnut-stained hardwood.
Sights: Hooded blade front, open rear drift adjustable for windage.
Features: Polished blue finish; sling swivels; wing-type safety. Introduced 1991. Imported by Interarms.
Price: About $109.00

REMINGTON 40-XR RIMFIRE CUSTOM SPORTER
Caliber: 22 LR.
Barrel: 24".
Weight: 10 lbs. **Length:** 42½" overall.
Stock: Full-sized walnut, checkered pistol grip and forend.
Sights: None furnished; drilled and tapped for scope mounting.
Features: Custom Shop gun. Duplicates Model 700 centerfire rifle.
Price: Grade I $2,507.00

RIMFIRE RIFLES—BOLT ACTIONS & SINGLE SHOTS

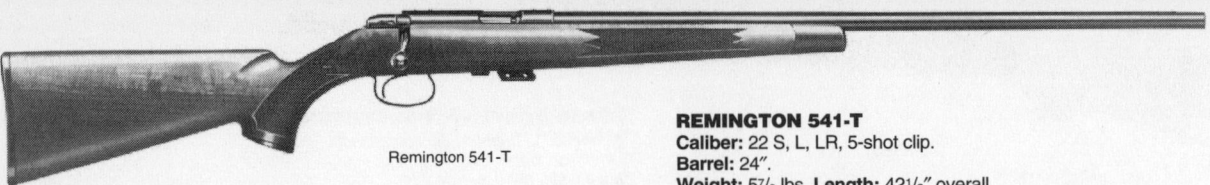
Remington 541-T

Remington 541-T HB Bolt-Action Rifle
Similar to the 541-T except has a heavy target-type barrel without sights. Receiver is drilled and tapped for scope mounting. American walnut stock with straight comb, satin finish, cut checkering, black checkered buttplate, black grip cap and forend tip. Weight is about 6½ lbs. Introduced 1993.
Price: $481.00

REMINGTON 541-T
Caliber: 22 S, L, LR, 5-shot clip.
Barrel: 24".
Weight: 5⅞ lbs. **Length:** 42½" overall.
Stock: Walnut, cut-checkered pistol grip and forend. Satin finish.
Sights: None. Drilled and tapped for scope mounts.
Features: Clip repeater. Thumb safety. Reintroduced 1986.
Price: About $455.00

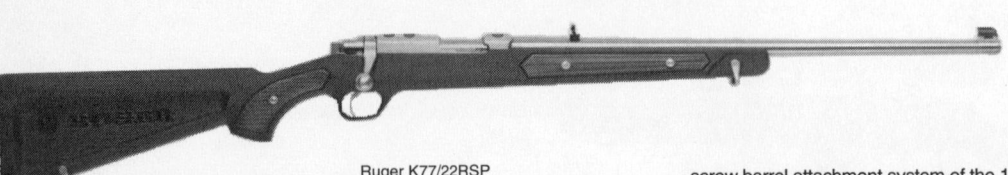
Ruger K77/22RSP

RUGER 77/22 RIMFIRE BOLT-ACTION RIFLE
Caliber: 22 LR, 10-shot rotary magazine; 22 WMR, 9-shot rotary magazine.
Barrel: 20".
Weight: About 5¾ lbs. **Length:** 39¾" overall.
Stock: Checkered American walnut or injection-moulded fiberglass-reinforced DuPont Zytel with Xenoy inserts in forend and grip, stainless sling swivels.
Sights: Brass bead front, adjustable folding leaf rear or plain barrel with 1" Ruger rings.
Features: Mauser-type action uses Ruger's 10-shot rotary magazine. Three-position safety, simplified bolt stop, patented bolt locking system. Uses the dual-screw barrel attachment system of the 10/22 rifle. Integral scope mounting system with 1" Ruger rings. Blued model introduced in 1983. Stainless steel model and blued model with the synthetic stock introduced in 1989.
Price: 77/22R (no sights, rings, walnut stock) $473.00
Price: 77/22RS (open sights, rings, walnut stock) $481.00
Price: K77/22RP (stainless, no sights, rings, synthetic stock) $473.00
Price: K77/22RSP (stainless, open sights, rings, synthetic stock) $481.00
Price: 77/22RM (22 WMR, blue, walnut stock) $473.00
Price: K77/22RSMP (22 WMR, stainless, open sights, rings, synthetic stock) $481.00
Price: K77/22RMP (22 WMR, stainless, synthetic stock) $473.00
Price: 77/22RSM (22 WMR, blue, open sights, rings, walnut stock) $481.00

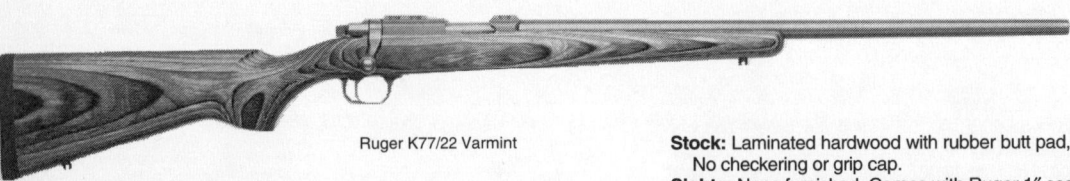
Ruger K77/22 Varmint

RUGER K77/22 VARMINT RIFLE
Caliber: 22 LR, 10-shot, 22 WMR, 9-shot detachable rotary magazine.
Barrel: 24", heavy.
Weight: 7.25 lbs. **Length:** 43.25" overall.
Stock: Laminated hardwood with rubber butt pad, quick-detachable swivel studs. No checkering or grip cap.
Sights: None furnished. Comes with Ruger 1" scope rings.
Features: Made of stainless steel with target gray finish. Three-position safety, dual extractors. Stock has wide, flat forend. Introduced 1993.
Price: K77/22VBZ, 22 LR $499.00
Price: K77/22VMB, 22 WMR $499.00

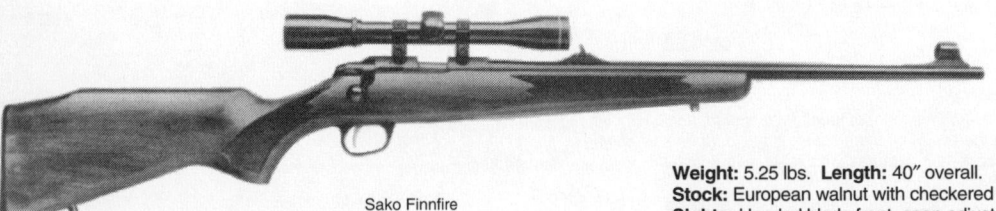
Sako Finnfire

SAKO FINNFIRE BOLT-ACTION RIFLE
Caliber: 22 LR, 5-shot magazine.
Barrel: 22".
Weight: 5.25 lbs. **Length:** 40" overall.
Stock: European walnut with checkered grip and forend.
Sights: Hooded blade front, open adjustable rear.
Features: Adjustable single-stage trigger; has 50-degree bolt lift. Introduced 1994. Imported from Finland by Stoeger Industries.
Price: $732.00
Price: With heavy barrel $815.00

Savage Mark II-GPX

SAVAGE MARK II-G BOLT-ACTION RIFLE
Caliber: 22 LR, 10-shot magazine.
Barrel: 20½".
Weight: 5½ lbs. **Length:** 39½" overall.
Stock: Walnut-finished hardwood with Monte Carlo-type comb, checkered grip and forend.
Sights: Bead front, open adjustable rear. Receiver grooved for scope mounting.
Features: Thumb-operated rotating safety. Blue finish. Introduced 1990. Made in Canada, from Savage Arms.
Price: $126.00
Price: Mark II-GY (youth), 19" barrel, 37" overall, 5 lbs. $126.00
Price: Mark II-GL, left-hand $126.00
Price: Mark II-Y (youth) left-hand $126.00
Price: Mark II-GXP includes 4x15 scope and mount $131.00
Price: Mark II-GXP Package Gun (comes with 4x15 scope) $131.00

RIMFIRE RIFLES—BOLT ACTIONS & SINGLE SHOTS

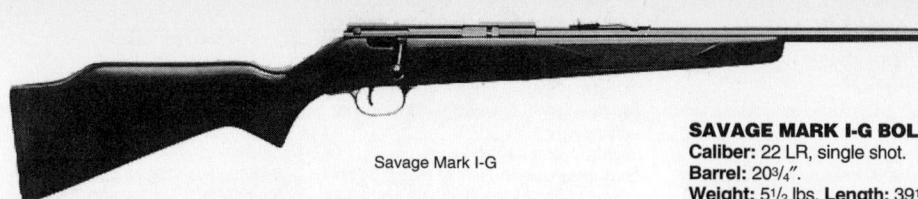
Savage Mark I-G

SAVAGE MODEL 93G MAGNUM BOLT-ACTION RIFLE
Caliber: 22 WMR, 5-shot magazine.
Barrel: 20 3/4".
Weight: 5 3/4 lbs. **Length:** 39 1/2" overall.
Stock: Walnut-finished hardwood with Monte Carlo-type comb, checkered grip and forend.
Sights: Bead front, adjustable open rear. Receiver grooved for scope mount.
Features: Thumb-operated rotary safety. Blue finish. Introduced 1994. Made in Canada, from Savage Arms.
Price: About $145.00

SAVAGE MARK I-G BOLT-ACTION RIFLE
Caliber: 22 LR, single shot.
Barrel: 20 3/4".
Weight: 5 1/2 lbs. **Length:** 39 1/2" overall.
Stock: Walnut-finished hardwood with Monte Carlo-type comb, checkered grip and forend.
Sights: Bead front, open adjustable rear. Receiver grooved for scope mounting.
Features: Thumb-operated rotating safety. Blue finish. Rifled or smooth bore. Introduced 1990. Made in Canada, from Savage Arms.
Price: Mark I, rifled or smooth bore $119.00
Price: Mark I-GY (Youth), 19" barrel, 37" overall, 5 lbs. $119.00

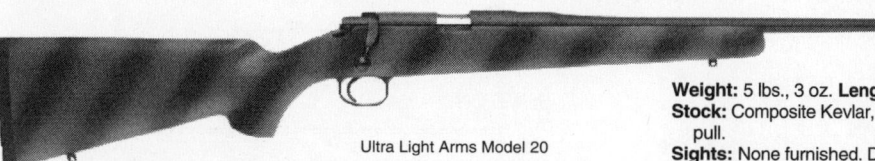
Ultra Light Arms Model 20

ULTRA LIGHT ARMS MODEL 20 RF BOLT-ACTION RIFLE
Caliber: 22 LR, single shot or 5-shot repeater.
Barrel: 22" Douglas Premium, #1 contour.
Weight: 5 lbs., 3 oz. **Length:** 41 1/2" overall.
Stock: Composite Kevlar, graphite reinforced. DuPont Imron paint; 13 1/2" length of pull.
Sights: None furnished. Drilled and tapped for scope mounting.
Features: Available as either single shot or repeater with 5-shot removable magazine. Comes with scope mounts. Introduced 1993. Made in U.S. by Ultra Light Arms, Inc.
Price: $800.00

COMPETITION RIFLES—CENTERFIRE & RIMFIRE

Includes models for classic American and ISU target competition and other sporting and competitive shooting.

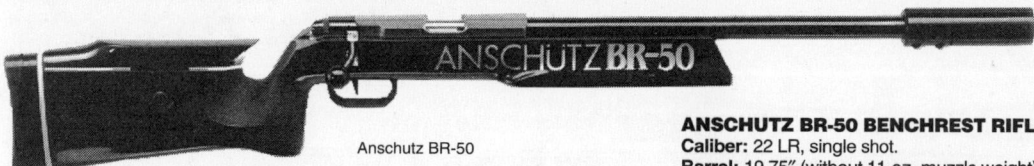
Anschutz BR-50

ANSCHUTZ BR-50 BENCHREST RIFLE
Caliber: 22 LR, single shot.
Barrel: 19.75" (without 11-oz. muzzle weight).
Weight: About 11 lbs. **Length:** 37.75" to 42.5" overall.
Stock: Benchrest style of European hardwood with stippled grip. Cheekpiece vertically adjustable to 1". Stock length adjustable via spacers and buttplate. Finished with glossy blue-black paint.
Sights: None furnished. Receiver grooved for mounts, barrel drilled and tapped for target mounts.
Features: Uses the Anschutz 2013 target action, #5018 two-stage adjustable target trigger factory set at 3.9 oz. Introduced 1994. Imported from Germany by Accuracy International, Champion's Choice, Champion Shooter's Supply, Gunsmithing, Inc.
Price: $2,304.00

ANSCHUTZ ACHIEVER ST SUPER TARGET RIFLE
Caliber: 22 LR, single shot.
Barrel: 22", .75" diameter.
Weight: About 6.5 lbs. **Length:** 38.75" to 39.75" overall.
Stock: Walnut-finished European hardwood with hand-stippled panels on grip and forend; 13.5" accessory rail on forend.
Sights: Optional. Receiver grooved for scope mounting.
Features: Designed for the advanced junior shooter with adjustable length of pull from 13.25" to 14.25" via removable butt spacers. Two-stage #5066 adjustable trigger factory set at 2.6 lbs. Introduced 1994. Imported from Germany by Accuracy International, Champion's Choice, Champion Shooter's Supply, Gunsmithing, Inc.
Price: $329.95
Price: Sight Set A $142.75

ANSCHUTZ 64-MSR, 64-MS LEFT SILHOUETTE RIFLE
Caliber: 22 LR, 5-shot magazine.
Barrel: 21 1/2", medium heavy; 7/8" diameter.
Weight: 8 lbs. **Length:** 39.5" overall.
Stock: Walnut-finished hardwood, silhouette-type.
Sights: None furnished. Receiver drilled and tapped for scope mounting.
Features: Uses Match 64 action. Designed for metallic silhouette competition. Stock has stippled checkering, contoured thumb groove with Wundhammer swell. Two-stage #5091 trigger. Slide safety locks sear and bolt. Introduced 1980. Imported from Germany by AcuSport Corp., Accuracy International, Champion's Choice, Champion Shooter's Supply, Gunsmithing, Inc.
Price: 64-MS $783.70
Price: 64-MS Left ....NA

ANSCHUTZ 1827B BIATHLON RIFLE
Caliber: 22 LR, 5-shot magazine.
Barrel: 21 1/2".
Weight: 8 1/2 lbs. with sights. **Length:** 42 1/2" overall.
Stock: European walnut with cheekpiece, stippled pistol grip and forend.
Sights: Optional globe front specially designed for Biathlon shooting, micrometer rear with hinged snow cap.
Features: Uses Super Match 54 action and nine-way adjustable trigger; adjustable wooden buttplate, Biathlon butthook, adjustable hand-stop rail. Introduced 1982. Imported from Germany by Accuracy International, Champion's Choice, Champion Shooter's Supply, Gunsmithing, Inc.
Price: Right-hand $1,537.80
Price: With laminated stock $1,593.60
Price: #6827 Sight Set $264.10

Anschutz 1827BT Fortner Biathlon Rifle
Similar to the Anschutz 1827B Biathlon rifle except uses Anschutz/Fortner system straight-pull bolt action. Introduced 1982. Imported from Germany by Accuracy International, Champion's Choice, Champion Shooter's Supply, Gunsmithing, Inc.
Price: Right-hand $2,312.90
Price: Right-hand, laminated stock $2,344.60
Price: Left-hand $2,542.80
Price: #6827 Sight Set $264.10

CAUTION: PRICES SHOWN ARE SUPPLIED BY THE MANUFACTURER OR IMPORTER. CHECK YOUR LOCAL GUNSHOP.

COMPETITION RIFLES—CENTERFIRE & RIMFIRE

ANSCHUTZ 1808D-RT SUPER RUNNING TARGET RIFLE
Caliber: 22 LR, single shot.
Barrel: 32½".
Weight: 9.4 lbs. **Length:** 50.5" overall.
Stock: European walnut. Heavy beavertail forend; adjustable cheekpiece and buttplate. Stippled grip and forend.
Sights: None furnished. Grooved for scope mounting.
Features: Designed for Running Target competition. Nine-way adjustable single-stage trigger, slide safety. Introduced 1991. Imported from Germany by Accuracy International, Champion's Choice, Champion Shooter's Supply, Gunsmithing, Inc.
Price: Right-hand $1,430.40

ANSCHUTZ 1911 PRONE MATCH RIFLE
Caliber: 22 LR, single shot.
Barrel: 27¼".
Weight: 11 lbs. **Length:** 46" overall.
Stock: Walnut-finished European hardwood; American prone style with Monte Carlo, cast-off cheekpiece, checkered pistol grip, beavertail forend with swivel rail and adjustable swivel, adjustable rubber buttplate.
Sights: None furnished. Receiver grooved for Anschutz sights (extra). Scope blocks.
Features: Two-stage #5018 trigger adjustable from 2.1 to 8.6 oz. Extremely fast lock time. Imported from Germany by Accuracy International, Champion's Choice, Champion Shooter's Supply, Gunsmithing, Inc.
Price: Right-hand, no sights $1,673.50

Anschutz 1907 ISU Standard Match Rifle
Same action as Model 1913 but with ⅞" diameter 26" barrel. Length is 44.5" overall, weighs 10 lbs. Choice of stock configurations. Vented forend. Designed for prone and position shooting ISU requirements; suitable for NRA matches. Imported from Germany by AcuSport Corp., Accuracy International, Champion's Choice, Champion Shooter's Supply, Gunsmithing, Inc.
Price: Right-hand, no sights, European hardwood stock $1,445.70
Price: With laminated hardwood stock $1,532.10
Price: Right-hand, no sights, walnut stock $1,500.80
Price: M1907-L (true left-hand action and stock) $1,516.90

ANSCHUTZ 1903 MATCH RIFLE
Caliber: 22 LR, single shot.
Barrel: 25", .75" diameter.
Weight: 8.6 lbs. **Length:** 43.75" overall.
Stock: Walnut-finished hardwood with adjustable cheekpiece; stippled grip and forend.
Sights: None furnished.
Features: Uses Anschutz Match 64 action and #5098 two-stage trigger. A medium weight rifle for intermediate and advanced Junior Match competition. Introduced 1987. Imported from Germany by AcuSport Corp., Accuracy International, Champion's Choice, Champion Shooter's Supply, Gunsmithing, Inc.
Price: Right-hand $829.60
Price: Left-hand $869.90

> *Manufacturers' addresses in the*
> **Directory of the Arms Trade**
> *page 313, this issue*

Anschutz 1913 Super Match Rifle
Same as the Model 1911 except European walnut International-type stock with adjustable cheekpiece, adjustable aluminum hook buttplate, adjustable hand stop, weighs 15.5 lbs., 46" overall. Imported from Germany by AcuSport Corp., Accuracy International, Champion's Choice, Champion Shooter's Supply, Gunsmithing, Inc.
Price: Right-hand, no sights $2,432.30
Price: M1913 left-hand $2,560.90

Anschutz 1910 Super Match Rifle
Similar to the Super Match 1913 rifle except has a stock of European hardwood with tapered forend and deep receiver area. Hand and palm rests not included. Uses Match 54 action. Adjustable hook buttplate and cheekpiece. Sights not included. Introduced 1982. Imported from Germany by Accuracy International, Champion's Choice, Champion Shooter's Supply, Gunsmithing, Inc.
Price: Right-hand $2,300.00

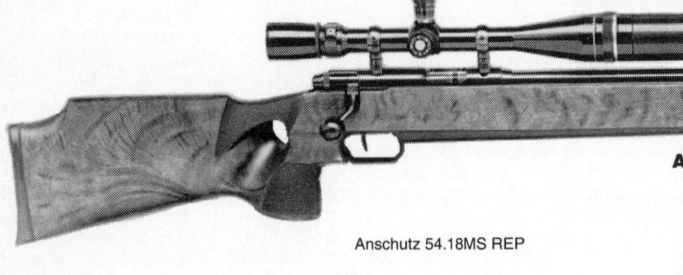
Anschutz 54.18MS REP

Anschutz 54.18MS REP Deluxe Silhouette Rifle
Same basic action and trigger specifications as the Anschutz 1913 Super Match but with removable 5-shot clip magazine, 22" barrel extendable to 30" using optional extension and weight set. Receiver drilled and tapped for scope mounting. Silhouette stock with thumbhole grip is of fiberglass with walnut wood Fibergrain finish. Introduced 1990. Imported from Germany by Accuracy International, Champion's Choice, Champion Shooter's Supply, Gunsmithing, Inc.
Price: 54.18MS REP Deluxe $1,237.80
Price: 54.18MS E single shot $1,154.70
Price: 54.18MS Standard with fiberglass stock ....$NA

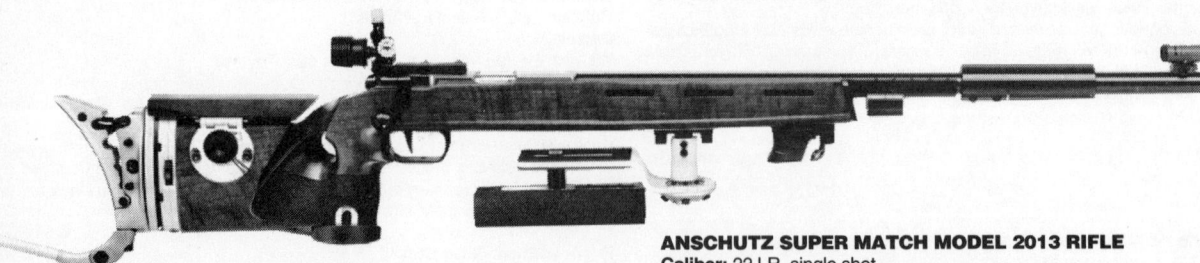
Anschutz 2013

Anschutz Super Match Model 2007 ISU Standard Rifle
Similar to the Model 2013 except has ISU Standard design. European walnut or blonde hardwood stock. Sights optional. Introduced 1992. Imported from Germany by Accuracy International, Champion's Choice, Champion Shooter's Supply, Gunsmithing, Inc.
Price: Right-hand, beech stock $1,975.00
Price: Left-hand, beech stock $2,102.00
Price: Right-hand, walnut stock $2,003.80

ANSCHUTZ SUPER MATCH MODEL 2013 RIFLE
Caliber: 22 LR, single shot.
Barrel: 19.75" (26" with tube installed).
Weight: 15.5 lbs. **Length:** 43" to 45.5" overall.
Stock: European walnut; target adjustable.
Sights: Optional. Uses #7020/20 sight set.
Features: Improved Super Match 54 action, #5018 trigger give fastest consistent lock time for a production target rifle. Barrel is micro-honed; trigger has nine points of adjustment, two stages. Slide safety. Comes with test target. Introduced 1992. Imported from Germany by Accuracy International, Champion's Choice, Champion Shooter's Supply, Gunsmithing, Inc.
Price: Right-hand $2,769.70
Price: Left-hand $2,899.20

COMPETITION RIFLES—CENTERFIRE & RIMFIRE

ArmaLite AR-10(T) Target

ARMALITE AR-10(T) TARGET MODEL
Caliber: 308, 10-shot magazine.
Barrel: 24" target weight with 1:10" twist.
Weight: 11 lbs. **Length:** 43.5" overall.
Stock: Black composition butt, fiberglass tubular forend.
Sights: Optional. Has one-piece international-style flattop receiver with Picatinny (Weaver-type) rail for scope mounting.
Features: Forged upper receiver with case deflector; receivers are hard-coat anodized. Optional detachable carry handle with NM sight; detachable front sight assembly; 30mm or 1" scope mount; stainless barrel. Introduced 1995. Made in U.S. by ArmaLite, Inc.
Price: $1,995.00

Bushmaster XM-15-E2S

BUSHMASTER XM-15 E2S V-MATCH RIFLE
Caliber: 223, 10-shot magazine.
Barrel: 20", 24", 26"; 1:9" twist; heavy.
Weight: 8.2 lbs. **Length:** 38.25" overall (20" barrel).
Stock: Black composition.
Sights: None furnished; comes with scope mount base installed.
Features: E2 lower receiver with push-pin-style takedown. Barrel is .950" outside diameter with counter-bored crown; upper receiver has brass deflector; free-floating steel handguard. Made in U.S. by Bushmaster Firearms Co./Quality Parts Co.
Price: 20" barrel $795.00
Price: 24" barrel $805.00
Price: 26" barrel $815.00

BUSHMASTER XM-15-E2S TARGET MODEL RIFLE
Caliber: 223, 10-shot magazine.
Barrel: 20", 24", 26"; 1:9" twist; heavy.
Weight: 8.1 lbs. **Length:** 38.25" overall (20" barrel).
Stock: Black composition.
Sights: Adjustable post front, adjustable aperture rear.
Features: Patterned after Colt M-16A2. Chrome-lined barrel with manganese phosphate exterior. Has E-2 lower receiver with push-pin. Made in U.S. by Bushmaster Firearms Co./Quality Parts Co.
Price: 20" match heavy barrel $740.00
Price: 24" match heavy barrel $750.00
Price: 26" match heavy barrel $760.00

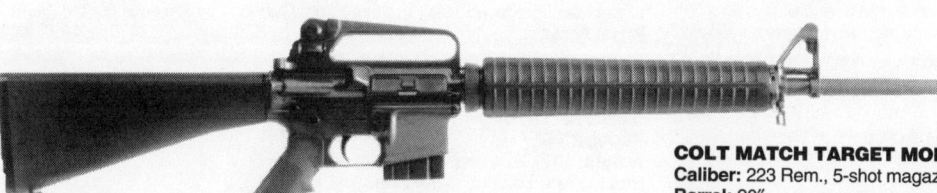

Colt Match Target HBAR

Colt Match Target HBAR Rifle
Similar to the Target Model except has heavy barrel, 800-meter rear sight adjustable for windage and elevation. Introduced 1991.
Price: $1,067.00

Colt Match Target Competition HBAR II Rifle
Similar to the Match Target Competition HBAR except has 16.1" barrel, weighs 7.1 lbs., overall length 34.5"; 1:9" twist barrel. Introduced 1995.
Price: $1,044.00

COLT MATCH TARGET MODEL RIFLE
Caliber: 223 Rem., 5-shot magazine.
Barrel: 20".
Weight: 7.5 lbs. **Length:** 39" overall.
Stock: Composition stock, grip, forend.
Sights: Post front, aperture rear adjustable for windage and elevation.
Features: Five-round detachable box magazine, standard-weight barrel, sling swivels. Has forward bolt assist. Military matte black finish. Model introduced 1991.
Price: $1,019.00

Colt Match Target Competition HBAR Rifle
Similar to the Sporter Target except has flat-top receiver with integral Weaver-type base for scope mounting. Counter-bored muzzle, 1:9" rifling twist. Introduced 1991.
Price: Model R6700 .... $1,073.00

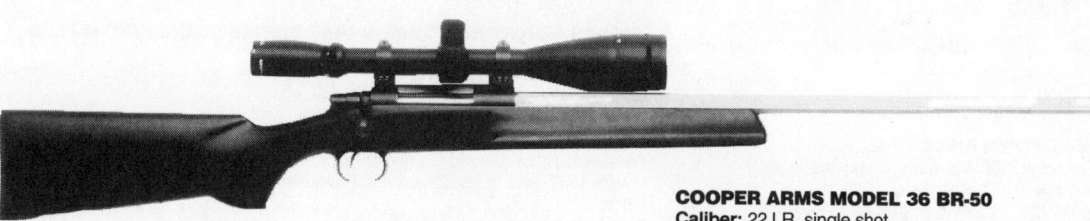

Cooper Model 36 BR-50

COOPER ARMS MODEL 36 BR-50
Caliber: 22 LR, single shot.
Barrel: 22", .860" straight.
Weight: 6.8 lbs. **Length:** 40.5" overall.
Stock: McMillan Benchrest.
Sights: None furnished.
Features: Action has three mid-bolt locking lugs; fully adjustable match grade trigger; stainless barrel. Introduced 1994. Made in U.S. by Cooper Arms.
Price: $1,850.00

CAUTION: PRICES SHOWN ARE SUPPLIED BY THE MANUFACTURER OR IMPORTER. CHECK YOUR LOCAL GUNSHOP.

COMPETITION RIFLES—CENTERFIRE & RIMFIRE

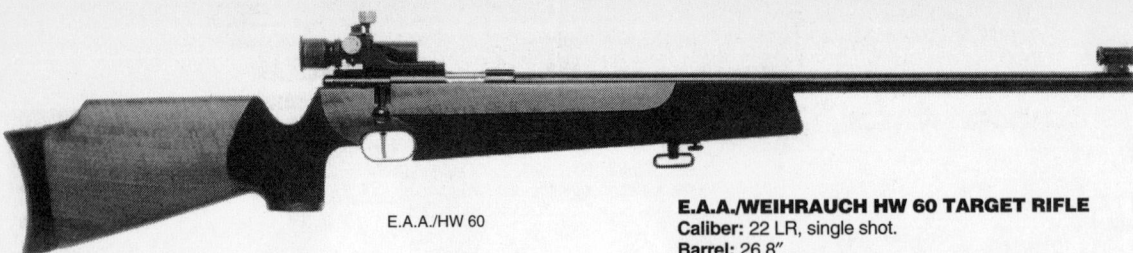
E.A.A./HW 60

E.A.A./WEIHRAUCH HW 60 TARGET RIFLE
Caliber: 22 LR, single shot.
Barrel: 26.8".
Weight: 10.8 lbs. **Length:** 45.7" overall.
Stock: Walnut with adjustable buttplate. Stippled pistol grip and forend. Rail with adjustable swivel.
Sights: Hooded ramp front, match-type aperture rear.
Features: Adjustable match trigger with push-button safety. Left-hand version also available. Introduced 1991. Imported from Germany by European American Armory.
Price: Right-hand $695.00
Price: Left-hand $875.00

E.A.A./HW 660 MATCH RIFLE
Caliber: 22 LR.
Barrel: 26".
Weight: 10.7 lbs. **Length:** 45.3" overall.
Stock: Match-type walnut with adjustable cheekpiece and buttplate.
Sights: Globe front, match aperture rear.
Features: Adjustable match trigger; stippled pistol grip and forend; forend accessory rail. Introduced 1991. Imported from Germany by European American Armory.
Price: About $874.95

Erma SR-100 Precision

ERMA SR-100 PRECISION RIFLE
Caliber: 308 Win. (10-shot), 300 Win. Mag. (8-shot), 338 Lapua Mag. (5-shot); detachable box magazine.
Barrel: 25.5" (308), 29.5" (300, 338).
Weight: 14.1 lbs. **Length:** 49.6" overall (25.5" barrel).
Stock: Thumbhole style of laminated wood with adjustable recoil pad and comb; aluminum forend rail for bipod or sling swivel.
Sights: None furnished.
Features: Interchangeable barrels; three-lug bolt locks into barrel; 60° bolt rotation; forged aluminum alloy receiver; fully adjustable match trigger; integral muzzlebrake. Inroduced 1996. Imported from Germany by Amtec 2000, Inc.
Price: About $8,000.00

EAGLE ARMS M15A2 GOLDEN EAGLE RIFLE
Caliber: 223 Rem.
Barrel: 20" extra-heavy NM; 1:8" twist.
Weight: 9 lbs., 10 oz. **Length:** 39 5/8" overall.
Stock: Black composition; weighted.
Sights: Elevation-adjustable NM extra-fine front with set screw, E2-style NM rear with 1/2-min. adjustments for windage and elevation; NM aperture.
Features: Upper and lower receivers have push-type pivot pin for easy takedown. Receivers hard coat anodized. Fence-type magazine release. Introduced 1989. Made in U.S. by Eagle Arms, Inc.
Price: $1,300.00

FINNISH LION STANDARD TARGET RIFLE
Caliber: 22 LR, single shot.
Barrel: 27 5/8".
Weight: 10 1/2 lbs. **Length:** 44 9/16" overall.
Stock: French walnut, target style.
Sights: Globe front, International micrometer rear.
Features: Optional accessories: palm rest, hook buttplate, forend stop and swivel assembly, buttplate extension, five front sight aperture inserts, three rear sight apertures, Allen wrench. Adjustable trigger. Imported from Finland by Mandall Shooting Supplies.
Price: Without sights $695.00
Price: Sight set $195.00

HARRIS GUNWORKS NATIONAL MATCH RIFLE
Caliber: 7mm-08, 308, 5-shot magazine.
Barrel: 24", stainless steel.
Weight: About 11 lbs. (std. bbl.). **Length:** 43" overall.
Stock: Fiberglass with adjustable buttplate.
Sights: Barrel band and Tompkins front; no rear sight furnished.
Features: Gunworks repeating action with clip slot, Canjar trigger. Match-grade barrel. Available in right-hand only. Fiberglass stock, sight installation, special machining and triggers optional. Introduced 1989. From Harris Gunworks, Inc.
Price: $2,600.00

Harris Gunworks M-86

HARRIS GUNWORKS COMBO M-87 SERIES 50-CALIBER RIFLES
Caliber: 50 BMG, single shot.
Barrel: 29, with muzzlebrake.
Weight: About 21 1/2 lbs. **Length:** 53" overall.
Stock: Gunworks fiberglass.
Sights: None furnished.
Features: Right-handed Gunworks stainless steel receiver, chrome-moly barrel with 1:15" twist. Introduced 1987. From Harris Gunworks, Inc.
Price: $3,735.00
Price: M87R 5-shot repeater $4,150.00
Price: M-87 (5-shot repeater) "Combo" $4,035.00
Price: M-92 Bullpup (shortened M-87 single shot with bullpup stock) ..$4,000.00
Price: M-93SN (10-shot repeater with folding stock, detachable magazine) $4,300.00

HARRIS GUNWORKS M-86 SNIPER RIFLE
Caliber: 308, 30-06, 4-shot magazine; 300 Win. Mag., 3-shot magazine.
Barrel: 24", Gunworks match-grade in heavy contour.
Weight: 11 1/4 lbs. (308), 11 1/2 lbs. (30-06, 300). **Length:** 43 1/2" overall.
Stock: Specially designed McHale fiberglass stock with textured grip and forend, recoil pad.
Sights: None furnished.
Features: Uses Gunworks repeating action. Comes with bipod. Matte black finish. Sling swivels. Introduced 1989. From Harris Gunworks, Inc.
Price: $2,700.00
Price: Takedown model $2,900.00

COMPETITION RIFLES—CENTERFIRE & RIMFIRE

Harris Gunworks Long Range

HARRIS GUNWORKS M-89 SNIPER RIFLE
Caliber: 308 Win., 5-shot magazine.
Barrel: 28" (with suppressor).
Weight: 15 lbs., 4 oz.
Stock: Fiberglass; adjustable for length; recoil pad.
Sights: None furnished. Drilled and tapped for scope mounting.
Features: Uses Gunworks repeating action. Comes with bipod. Introduced 1990. From Harris Gunworks, Inc.
Price: Standard (non-suppressed) $2,700.00

HARRIS GUNWORKS LONG RANGE RIFLE
Caliber: 300 Win. Mag., 7mm Rem. Mag., 300 Phoenix, 338 Lapua, single shot.
Barrel: 26", stainless steel, match-grade.
Weight: 14 lbs. **Length:** 46½" overall.
Stock: Fiberglass with adjustable buttplate and cheekpiece. Adjustable for length of pull, drop, cant and cast-off.
Sights: Barrel band and Tompkins front; no rear sight furnished.
Features: Uses Gunworks solid bottom single shot action and Canjar trigger. Barrel twist 1:12". Introduced 1989. From Harris Gunworks, Inc.
Price: $2,600.00

Heckler & Koch PSG-1

HECKLER & KOCH PSG-1 MARKSMAN RIFLE
Caliber: 308, 5- and 20-shot magazines.
Barrel: 25.6", heavy.
Weight: 17.8 lbs. **Length:** 47.5" overall.
Stock: Matte black high impact plastic, adjustable for length, pivoting butt cap, vertically-adjustable cheekpiece; target-type pistol grip with adjustable palm shelf.
Sights: Hendsoldt 6x42 scope.
Features: Uses HK-91 action with low-noise bolt closing device, special Marksman trigger group; special forend with T-way rail for sling swivel or tripod. Gun comes in special foam-fitted metal transport case with tripod, two 20-shot and two 5-shot magazines, tripod. Imported from Germany by Heckler & Koch, Inc. Introduced 1986.
Price: $10,497.00

KRICO MODEL 600 SNIPER RIFLE
Caliber: 222, 223, 22-250, 243, 308, 4-shot magazine.
Barrel: 23.6".
Weight: 9.2 lbs. **Length:** 45.2" overall.
Stock: European walnut with adjustable rubber buttplate.
Sights: None supplied; drilled and tapped for scope mounting.
Features: Match barrel with flash hider; large bolt knob; wide trigger shoe. Parkerized finish. Imported from Germany by Mandall Shooting Supplies.
Price: $2,645.00

KRICO MODEL 400 MATCH RIFLE
Caliber: 22 LR, 22 Hornet, 5-shot magazine.
Barrel: 23.2" (22 LR), 23.6" (22 Hornet).
Weight: 8.8 lbs. **Length:** 42.1" overall (22 RF).
Stock: European walnut, match type.
Sights: None furnished; receiver grooved for scope mounting.
Features: Heavy match barrel. Double-set or match trigger. Imported from Germany by Mandall Shooting Supplies.
Price: $950.00

Krico Model 360S Biathlon

KRICO MODEL 500 KRICOTRONIC MATCH RIFLE
Caliber: 22 LR, single shot.
Barrel: 23.6".
Weight: 9.4 lbs. **Length:** 42.1" overall.
Stock: European walnut, match type with adjustable butt.
Sights: Globe front, match micrometer aperture rear.
Features: Electronic ignition system for fastest possible lock time. Completely adjustable trigger. Barrel has tapered bore. Imported from Germany by Mandall Shooting Supplies.
Price: $3,950.00

KRICO MODEL 600 MATCH RIFLE
Caliber: 222, 223, 22-250, 243, 308, 5.6x50 Mag., 4-shot magazine.
Barrel: 23.6".
Weight: 8.8 lbs. **Length:** 43.3" overall.
Stock: Match stock of European walnut with cheekpiece.
Sights: None furnished; drilled and tapped for scope mounting.
Features: Match stock with vents in forend for cooling, rubber recoil pad, sling swivels. Imported from Germany by Mandall Shooting Supplies.
Price: $1,250.00

KRICO MODEL 360S BIATHLON RIFLE
Caliber: 22 LR, 5-shot magazine.
Barrel: 21.25".
Weight: 9.26 lbs. **Length:** 40.55" overall.
Stock: Walnut with high comb, adjustable buttplate.
Sights: Globe front, fully adjustable Diana 82 match peep rear.
Features: Straight-pull action with 17.6-oz. match trigger. Comes with five magazines (four stored in stock recess), muzzle/sight snow cap. Introduced 1991. Imported from Germany by Mandall Shooting Supplies.
Price: $1,695.00

KRICO MODEL 360 S2 BIATHLON RIFLE
Caliber: 22 LR, 5-shot magazine.
Barrel: 21.25".
Weight: 9 lbs., 15 oz. **Length:** 40.55" overall.
Stock: Biathlon design of black epoxy-finished walnut with pistol grip.
Sights: Globe front, fully adjustable Diana 82 match peep rear.
Features: Pistol grip-activated action. Comes with five magazines (four stored in stock recess), muzzle/sight snow cap. Introduced 1991. Imported from Germany by Mandall Shooting Supplies.
Price: $1,595.00

COMPETITION RIFLES—CENTERFIRE & RIMFIRE

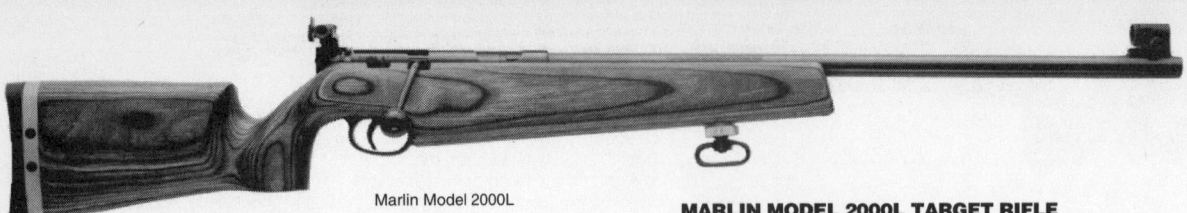
Marlin Model 2000L

OLYMPIC ARMS PCR-SERVICEMATCH RIFLE
Caliber: 223, 10-shot magazine.
Barrel: 20", broach-cut 416 stainless steel.
Weight: About 10 lbs. **Length:** 39.5" overall.
Stock: A2 stowaway grip and trapdoor buttstock.
Sights: Post front, E2-NM fully adjustable operture rear.
Features: Based on the AR-15. Conforms to all DCM standards. Free-floating 1:8.5" or 1:10" barrel; crowned barrel; no bayonet lug. Introduced 1996. Made in U.S. by Olympic Arms, Inc.
Price: $1,135.00

MARLIN MODEL 2000L TARGET RIFLE
Caliber: 22 LR, single shot.
Barrel: 22" heavy, Micro-Groove® rifling, match chamber, recessed muzzle.
Weight: 8 lbs. **Length:** 41" overall.
Stock: Laminated black/gray with ambidextrous pistol grip.
Sights: Hooded front with ten aperture inserts, fully adjustable target rear peep.
Features: Buttplate adjustable for length of pull, height and angle. Aluminum forend rail with stop and quick-detachable swivel. Two-stage target trigger; red cocking indicator. Five-shot adaptor kit available. Introduced 1991. From Marlin.
Price: $602.30

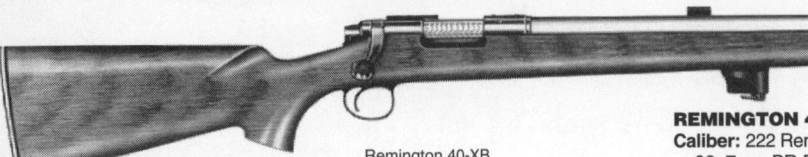
Remington 40-XB

REMINGTON 40-XBBR KS
Caliber: 22 BR Rem., 222 Rem., 222 Rem. Mag., 223, 6mmx47, 6mm BR Rem., 7.62 NATO (308 Win.).
Barrel: 20" (light varmint class), 24" (heavy varmint class).
Weight: 7 1/4 lbs. (light varmint class); 12 lbs. (heavy varmint class).
Length: 38" (20" bbl.), 42" (24" bbl.).
Stock: Kevlar.
Sights: None. Supplied with scope blocks.
Features: Unblued stainless steel barrel, trigger adjustable from 1 1/2 lbs. to 3 1/2 lbs. Special 2-oz. trigger at extra cost. Scope and mounts extra.
Price: With Kevlar stock $1,484.00
Price: Extra for 2-oz. trigger, about $168.00

REMINGTON 40-XB RANGEMASTER TARGET CENTERFIRE
Caliber: 222 Rem., 222 Rem. Mag., 223, 220 Swift, 22-250, 6mm Rem., 243, 25-06, 7mm BR Rem., 7mm Rem. Mag., 30-338 (30-7mm Rem. Mag.), 300 Win. Mag., 7.62 NATO (308 Win.), 30-06, single shot.
Barrel: 27 1/4".
Weight: 11 1/4 lbs. **Length:** 47" overall.
Stock: American walnut or Kevlar with high comb and beavertail forend stop. Rubber non-slip buttplate.
Sights: None. Scope blocks installed.
Features: Adjustable trigger. Stainless barrel and action. Receiver drilled and tapped for sights.
Price: Standard single shot, stainless steel barrel, about $1,333.00
Price: Repeater model $1,433.00
Price: Model 40-XB KS $1,504.00
Price: Repeater model (KS) $1,604.00
Price: Extra for 2-oz. trigger $168.00

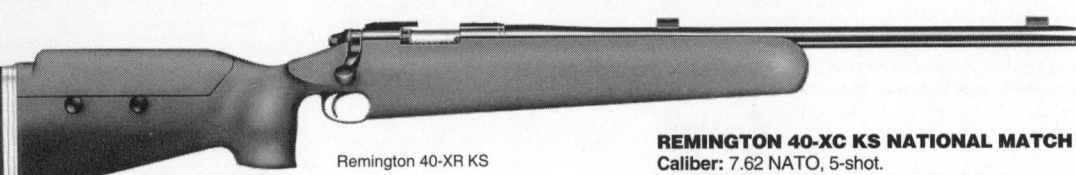
Remington 40-XR KS

REMINGTON 40-XR KS RIMFIRE POSITION RIFLE
Caliber: 22 LR, single shot.
Barrel: 24", heavy target.
Weight: 10 lbs. **Length:** 43" overall.
Stock: Kevlar. Position-style with front swivel block on forend guide rail.
Sights: Drilled and tapped. Furnished with scope blocks.
Features: Meets all ISU specifications. Deep forend, buttplate vertically adjustable, wide adjustable trigger.
Price: About $1,428.00

REMINGTON 40-XC KS NATIONAL MATCH COURSE RIFLE
Caliber: 7.62 NATO, 5-shot.
Barrel: 24", stainless steel.
Weight: 11 lbs. without sights. **Length:** 43 1/2" overall.
Stock: Kevlar, position-style, with palm swell, handstop.
Sights: None furnished.
Features: Designed to meet the needs of competitive shooters firing the national match courses. Position-style stock, top loading clip slot magazine, anti-bind bolt and receiver, stainless steel barrel and action. Meets all ISU Army Rifle specifications. Adjustable buttplate, adjustable trigger.
Price: About $1,484.00

Sako TRG-21

SAKO TRG-21 BOLT-ACTION RIFLE
Caliber: 308 Win., 10-shot magazine.
Barrel: 25.75".
Weight: 10.5 lbs. **Length:** 46.5" overall.
Stock: Reinforced polyurethane with fully adjustable cheekpiece and buttplate.
Sights: None furnished. Optional quick-detachable, one-piece scope mount base, 1" or 30mm rings.
Features: Resistance-free bolt, free-floating heavy stainless barrel, 60-degree bolt lift. Two-stage trigger is adjustable for length, pull, horizontal or vertical pitch. Introduced 1993. Imported from Finland by Stoeger.
Price: $4,265.00

COMPETITION RIFLES—CENTERFIRE & RIMFIRE

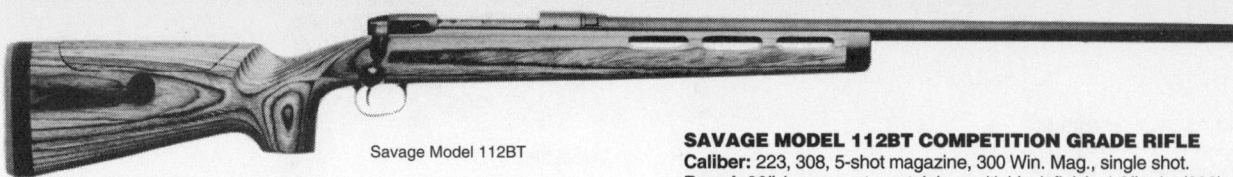
Savage Model 112BT

SAUER 202 TR TARGET RIFLE
Caliber: 6.5x55mm, 308 Win., 5-shot magazine.
Barrel: 26" or 28.5", heavy match target.
Weight: 12.1 lbs. **Length:** 44.5" overall.
Stock: One-piece true target type of laminated beechwood/epoxy; adjustable buttplate and cheekpiece.
Sights: Globe front, Sauer-Busk 200-600m diopter rear. Drilled and tapped for scope mounting.
Features: Interchangeable free-floating, hammer-forged barrel; two-stage adjustable trigger; vertical slide safety; 3 millisecond lock time; rail for swivel, bipod; right- or left-hand; Converts to 22 rimfire. Introduced 1994. Imported from Germany by SIGARMS, Inc.
Price: $1,900.00
Price: Spare Match-Target barrel $425.00

SAVAGE MODEL 112BT COMPETITION GRADE RIFLE
Caliber: 223, 308, 5-shot magazine, 300 Win. Mag., single shot.
Barrel: 26", heavy contour stainless with black finish; 1:9" twist (223), 1:10" (308).
Weight: 10.8 lbs. **Length:** 47.5" overall.
Stock: Laminated wood with straight comb, adjustable cheek rest, Wundhammer palm swell, ventilated forend. Recoil pad is adjustable for length of pull.
Sights: None furnished; drilled and tapped for scope mounting and aperture target-style sights. Recessed target-style muzzle has .812" diameter section for universal target sight base.
Features: Pillar-bedded stock, matte black alloy receiver. Bolt has black titanium nitride coating, large handle ball. Has alloy accessory rail on forend. Comes with safety gun lock, target and ear puffs. Introduced 1994. Made in U.S. by Savage Arms, Inc.
Price: $1,000.00
Price: 300 Win. Mag. (single shot 112BT-S) $1,000.00

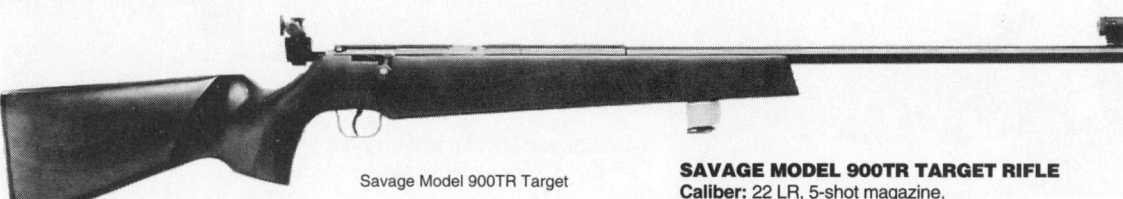
Savage Model 900TR Target

SAVAGE MODEL 900TR TARGET RIFLE
Caliber: 22 LR, 5-shot magazine.
Barrel: 25".
Weight: 8 lbs. **Length:** 43 5/8" overall.
Stock: Target-type, walnut-finished hardwood.
Sights: Target front with inserts, peep rear with 1/4-minute click adjustments.
Features: Comes with shooting rail and hand stop. Introduced 1991. Made in Canada, from Savage Arms.
Price: $415.00

SAVAGE MODEL 900B BIATHALON
Caliber: 22 LR, 5-shot magazine.
Barrel: 21".
Weight: 8 1/4 lbs. **Length:** 39 5/8" overall.
Stock: Natural finish hardwood with clip holder, carrying and shooting rails, butt hook, hand stop.
Sights: Target front with inserts, peep rear with 1/4-minute click adjustments.
Features: Biathlon-style rifle with snow cap muzzle protector. Comes with five magazines. Introduced 1991. Made in Canada, from Savage Arms.
Price: About $498.00

Savage Model 900S Silhouette Rifle
Similar to the Model 900B except has high-comb target-type stock of walnut-finished hardwood, one 5-shot magazine. Comes without sights, but receiver is drilled and tapped for scope base. Weighs about 8 lbs. Introduced 1992. Made in Canada, from Savage Arms.
Price: $346.00

Springfield M1A/M-21

Springfield, Inc. M1A/M-21 Tactical Model Rifle
Similar to the M1A Super Match except has special sniper stock with adjustable cheekpiece and rubber recoil pad. Weighs 11.2 lbs. From Springfield, Inc.
Price: $2,204.00

SPRINGFIELD, INC. M1A SUPER MATCH
Caliber: 308 Win.
Barrel: 22", heavy Douglas Premium or National Match.
Weight: About 10 lbs. **Length:** 44.31" overall.
Stock: Heavy walnut competition stock with longer pistol grip, contoured area behind the rear sight, thicker butt and forend, glass bedded.
Sights: National Match front and rear.
Features: Has figure-eight-style operating rod guide. Introduced 1987. From Springfield, Inc.
Price: About $2,050.00

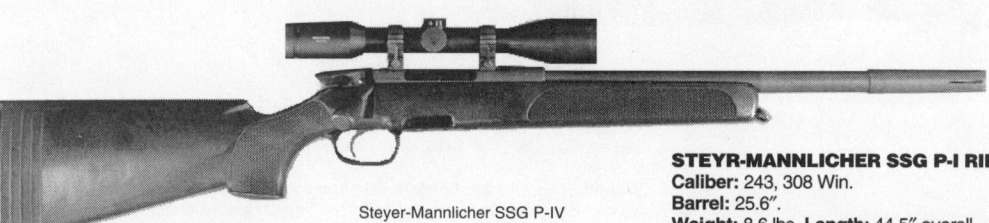
Steyer-Mannlicher SSG P-IV

Steyr-Mannlicher SSG P-IV Rifle
Similar to the SSG P-I except has 16.75" heavy barrel with flash hider. Available in 308 only. ABS Cycolac synthetic stock in green or black. Introduced 1992. Imported from Austria by GSI, Inc.
Price: $2,660.00

STEYR-MANNLICHER SSG P-I RIFLE
Caliber: 243, 308 Win.
Barrel: 25.6".
Weight: 8.6 lbs. **Length:** 44.5" overall.
Stock: ABS Cycolac synthetic half-stock. Removable spacers in butt adjusts length of pull from 12 3/4" to 14".
Sights: Hooded blade front, folding leaf rear.
Features: Parkerized finish. Choice of interchangeable single- or double-set triggers. Detachable 5-shot rotary magazine (10-shot optional). Receiver grooved for Steyr and Bock Quick Detach mounts. Imported from Austria by GSI, Inc.
Price: Synthetic half-stock $1,995.00
Price: SSG-PII (as above except has large bolt knob, heavy bbl., no sights, forend rail). $1,995.00

COMPETITION RIFLES—CENTERFIRE & RIMFIRE

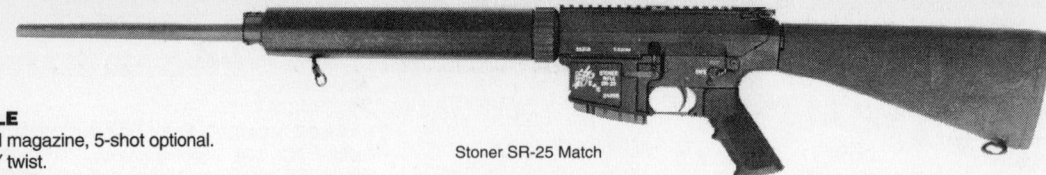
Stoner SR-25 Match

STONER SR-25 MATCH RIFLE
Caliber: 7.62 NATO, 10-shot steel magazine, 5-shot optional.
Barrel: 24" heavy match; 1:11.25" twist.
Weight: 10.75 lbs. **Length:** 44" overall.
Stock: Black synthetic AR-15A2 design. Full floating forend of Mil-spec synthetic attaches to upper receiver at a single point.
Sights: None furnished. Has integral Weaver-style rail. Rings and iron sights optional.
Features: Improved AR-15 trigger; AR-15-style seven-lug rotating bolt. Gas block rail mounts detachable front sight. Introduced 1993. Made in U.S. by Knight's Mfg. Co.
Price: $2,995.00
Price: SR-25 Lightweight Match (20" medium match target contour barrel, 9.5 lbs., 40" overall) $2,995.00

STEYR-MANNLICHER MATCH SPG-UIT RIFLE
Caliber: 308 Win.
Barrel: 25.5".
Weight: 10 lbs. **Length:** 44" overall.
Stock: Laminated and ventilated. Special UIT Match design.
Sights: Steyr globe front, Steyr peep rear.
Features: Double-pull trigger adjustable for let-off point, slack, weight of first-stage pull, release force and length; buttplate adjustable for height and length. Meets UIT specifications. Introduced 1992. Imported from Austria by GSI, Inc.
Price: $3,995.00
Price: SPG-CISM $4,295.00
Price: SPG-T $3,695.00

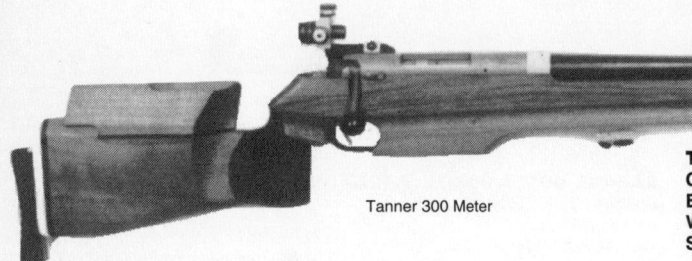
Tanner 300 Meter

TANNER STANDARD UIT RIFLE
Caliber: 308, 7.5mm Swiss, 10-shot.
Barrel: 25.9".
Weight: 10.5 lbs. **Length:** 40.6" overall.
Stock: Match style of seasoned nutwood with accessory rail; coarsely stippled pistol grip; high cheekpiece; vented forend.
Sights: Globe front with interchangeable inserts, Tanner micrometer-diopter rear with adjustable aperture.
Features: Two locking lug revolving bolt encloses case head. Trigger adjustable from 1/2 to 6 1/2 lbs.; match trigger optional. Comes with 300-meter test target. Imported from Switzerland by Mandall Shooting Supplies. Introduced 1984.
Price: About $4,700.00

TANNER 300 METER FREE RIFLE
Caliber: 308 Win., 7.5 Swiss, single shot.
Barrel: 27.58".
Weight: 15 lbs. **Length:** 45.3" overall.
Stock: Seasoned walnut, thumbhole style, with accessory rail, palm rest, adjustable hook butt.
Sights: Globe front with interchangeable inserts, Tanner-design micrometer-diopter rear with adjustable aperture.
Features: Three-lug revolving-lock bolt design; adjustable set trigger; short firing pin travel; supplied with 300-meter test target. Imported from Switzerland by Mandall Shooting Supplies. Introduced 1984.
Price: About $4,900.00

TANNER 50 METER FREE RIFLE
Caliber: 22 LR, single shot.
Barrel: 27.7".
Weight: 13.9 lbs. **Length:** 44.4" overall.
Stock: Seasoned walnut with palm rest, accessory rail, adjustable hook buttplate.
Sights: Globe front with interchangeable inserts, Tanner micrometer-diopter rear with adjustable aperture.
Features: Bolt action with externally adjustable set trigger. Supplied with 50-meter test target. Imported from Switzerland by Mandall Shooting Supplies. Introduced 1984.
Price: About $3,900.00

SHOTGUNS—AUTOLOADERS
Includes a wide variety of sporting guns and guns suitable for various competitions.

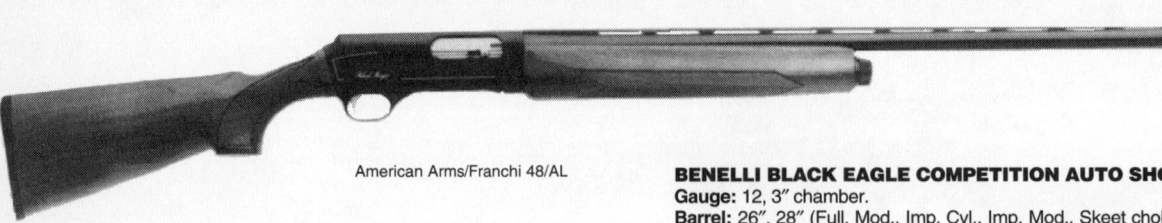
American Arms/Franchi 48/AL

AMERICAN ARMS/FRANCHI BLACK MAGIC 48/AL
Gauge: 12, 20 or 28, 2 3/4" chamber.
Barrel: 24", 26", 28" (Franchoke Imp. Cyl., Mod., Full choke tubes), 28 ga. has fixed Imp. Cyl. Vent. rib.
Weight: 5.2 lbs. (20-gauge). **Length:** NA
Stock: 14 1/4"x1 5/8"x2 1/2". Walnut with checkered grip and forend.
Features: Recoil-operated action. Chrome-lined bore; cross-bolt safety. Imported from Italy by American Arms, Inc.
Price: 12, 20 ....$649.00
Price: 28 ga. $725.00

BENELLI BLACK EAGLE COMPETITION AUTO SHOTGUN
Gauge: 12, 3" chamber.
Barrel: 26", 28" (Full, Mod., Imp. Cyl., Imp. Mod., Skeet choke tubes). Mid-bead sight.
Weight: 7.1 to 7.6 lbs. **Length:** 49 5/8" overall (26" barrel).
Stock: European walnut with high-gloss finish. Special competition stock comes with drop adjustment kit.
Features: Uses the Montefeltro rotating bolt inertia recoil operating system with a two-piece steel/aluminum etched receiver (bright on lower, blue upper). Drop adjustment kit allows the stock to be custom fitted without modifying the stock. Black lower receiver finish, blued upper. Introduced 1989. Imported from Italy by Heckler & Koch, Inc.
Price: $1,205.00

SHOTGUNS—AUTOLOADERS

Benelli Super Black Eagle

Benelli Super Black Eagle Slug Gun
Similar to the Benelli Super Black Eagle except has 24" E.R. Shaw Custom rifled barrel with 3" chamber, and comes with scope mount base. Uses the Montefeltro inertia recoil bolt system. Matte-finish receiver. Weight is 7.5 lbs., overall length 45.5". Wood or polymer stocks available. Introduced 1992. Imported from Italy by Heckler & Koch, Inc.
Price: $1,220.00
Price: With polymer stock $1,220.00

BENELLI M1 SUPER 90 FIELD AUTO SHOTGUN
Gauge: 12, 3" chamber.
Barrel: 21", 24", 26", 28" (choke tubes).
Weight: 7 lbs., 4 oz.
Stock: High impact polymer; wood on 26", 28".
Sights: Metal bead front.
Features: Sporting version of the military & police gun. Uses the rotating Montefeltro bolt system. Ventilated rib; blue finish. Comes with set of five choke tubes. Imported from Italy by Heckler & Koch, Inc.
Price: $884.00
Price: Wood stock version $900.00

BENELLI SUPER BLACK EAGLE SHOTGUN
Gauge: 12, 3 1/2" chamber.
Barrel: 24", 26", 28" (Imp. Cyl., Mod., Imp. Mod., Full choke tubes).
Weight: 7 lbs., 5 oz. **Length:** 49 5/8" overall (28" barrel).
Stock: European walnut with satin finish, or polymer. Adjustable for drop.
Sights: Bead front.
Features: Uses Montfeltro inertia recoil bolt system. Fires all 12-gauge shells from 2 3/4" to 3 1/2" magnums. Introduced 1991. Imported from Italy by Heckler & Koch, Inc.
Price: With 28" barrel $1,192.00
Price: With 24", 26" barrel, polymer stock $1,170.00

Benelli Executive Series Shotguns
Similar to the Black Eagle except has grayed steel lower receiver, hand-engraved and gold inlaid (Type III), and has highest grade of walnut stock with drop adjustment kit. Barrel lengths of 21", 24", 26", 28"; 3" chamber. **Special order only.** Introduced 1995. Imported from Italy by Heckler & Koch, Inc.
Price: Type I (about two-thirds engraving coverage) $4,550.00
Price: Type II (full coverage engraving) $5,200.00
Price: Type III (full coverage, gold inlays) $6,032.00

Benelli Montefeltro Super 90 20-Gauge Shotgun
Similar to the 12-gauge Montefeltro Super 90 except chambered for 3" 20-gauge, 24" or 26" barrel (choke tubes), weighs 5 lbs., 12 oz. Has drop-adjustable walnut stock with gloss finish, blued receiver. Overall length 47.5". Introduced 1993. Imported from Italy by Heckler & Koch, Inc.
Price: $905.00
Price: Limited Edition (26" barrel, special nickel-plated and engraved receiver inlaid with gold) $2,080.00

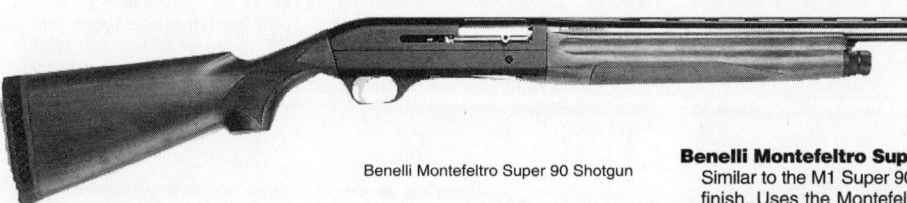

Benelli Montefeltro Super 90 Shotgun

BENELLI M1 SPORTING SPECIAL AUTO SHOTGUN
Gauge: 12, 3" chamber.
Barrel: 18.5" (Imp. Cyl. Mod., Full choke tubes).
Weight: 6 lbs., 8 oz. **Length:** 39.75" overall.
Stock: Sporting-style polymer with drop adjustment.
Sights: Ghost ring.
Features: Uses Montefeltro inertia recoil bolt system. Matte-finish receiver. Introduced 1993. Imported from Italy by Heckler & Koch, Inc.
Price: $905.00

Beretta A-303 Upland Model
Similar to the field A-303 except has straight English-style stock, 26" vent. rib barrel with Mobilchoke choke tubes, 3" chamber. Introduced 1989.
Price: $772.00

Benelli Montefeltro Super 90 Shotgun
Similar to the M1 Super 90 except has checkered walnut stock with high-gloss finish. Uses the Montefeltro rotating bolt system with a simple inertia recoil design. Full, Imp. Mod, Mod., Imp. Cyl. choke tubes. Weighs 7-7 1/2 lbs. Finish is matte black. Introduced 1987.
Price: 21", 24", 26", 28" $905.00
Price: Left-hand, 26", 28" $925.00
Price: 20-ga., Montefeltro Super 90, 24" 26", 5 3/4 lbs. $905.00

BERETTA A-303 AUTO SHOTGUN
Gauge: 20, 2 3/4" or 3" chamber.
Barrel: 24", 26", 28" Mobilchoke choke tubes.
Weight: About 6 1/2 lbs.
Stock: American walnut; hand-checkered grip and forend.
Features: Gas-operated action, alloy receiver, magazine cut-off, push-button safety. Mobilchoke models come with three interchangeable flush-mounted screw-in choke tubes. Imported from Italy by Beretta U.S.A. Introduced 1983.
Price: Mobilchoke, 20-ga. $772.00
Price: A-303 Youth Gun, 20-ga., 2 3/4" chamber, 24" barrel $772.00
Price: A-303 Sporting Clays with Mobilchoke, 20 gauge $822.00

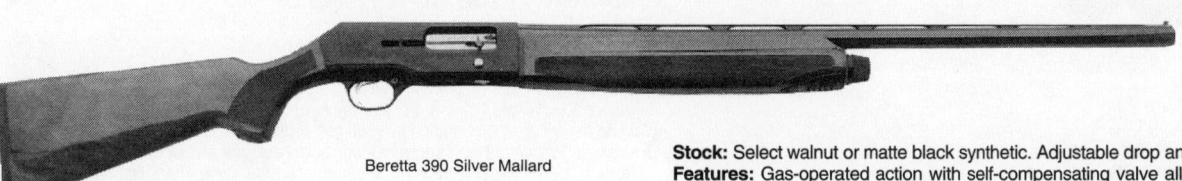

Beretta 390 Silver Mallard

BERETTA 390 SILVER MALLARD AUTO SHOTGUN
Gauge: 12, 3" chamber.
Barrel: 24", 26", 28", 30", Mobilchoke choke tubes.
Weight: 7.6 lbs.

Stock: Select walnut or matte black synthetic. Adjustable drop and cast.
Features: Gas-operated action with self-compensating valve allows shooting all loads without adjustment. Alloy receiver, reversible safety; chrome-plated bore; floating vent. rib. Matte-finish models for turkey/waterfowl and Deluxe with gold, engraving also available. Slug model available. Introduced 1992. Imported from Italy by Beretta U.S.A.
Price: Walnut or synthetic $822.00
Price: Waterfowl/Turkey (matte finish) $822.00
Price: Gold Mallard $987.00
Price: Slug model $822.00

CAUTION: PRICES SHOWN ARE SUPPLIED BY THE MANUFACTURER OR IMPORTER. CHECK YOUR LOCAL GUNSHOP.

SHOTGUNS—AUTOLOADERS

Beretta 390 Sport Trap/Skeet/Sporting Shotguns
Similar to the 390 Silver Mallard except has lower-contour, rounded receiver. Available with ported barrel. Trap has 30", 32" barrel (Full, Imp. Mod., Mod. choke tubes); Skeet has 26", 28" barrel (fixed Skeet); Sporting has 28", 30" (Full, Mod., Imp. Cyl., Skeet tubes). Introduced 1995. Imported from Italy by Beretta U.S.A.
Price: 390 Sport Trap $865.00
Price: As above, fixed Full choke $851.00
Price: 390 Sport Skeet $849.00
Price: 390 Sport Sporting $865.00
Price: Ported barrel, above models, add about $100.00

Beretta 390 Super Trap, Super Skeet Shotguns
Similar to the 390 Field except have adjustable-comb stocks that allow height adjustments via interchangeable comb inserts. Rounded recoil pad system allows adjustments for length of pull. Wide ventilated rib with orange front sight. Factory ported barrels in 28" (fixed Skeet), 30", 32" Trap (Mobilchoke tubes). Weighs 8.3 lbs. In 12-gauge only, with 3" chamber. Introduced 1993. Imported from Italy by Beretta U.S.A.
Price: 390 Super Trap $1,258.00
Price: 390 Super Skeet $1,199.00

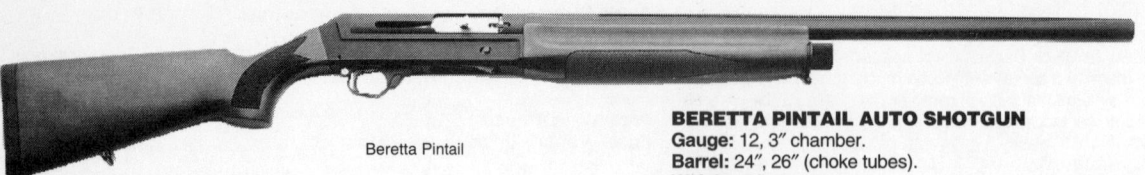

Beretta Pintail

BERETTA PINTAIL AUTO SHOTGUN
Gauge: 12, 3" chamber.
Barrel: 24", 26" (choke tubes).
Weight: 7 lbs.
Stock: Checkered walnut.
Features: Montefeltro-type short recoil action. Matte finish on wood and metal. Comes with sling swivels. Introduced 1993. Imported from Italy by Beretta U.S.A.
Price: $743.00

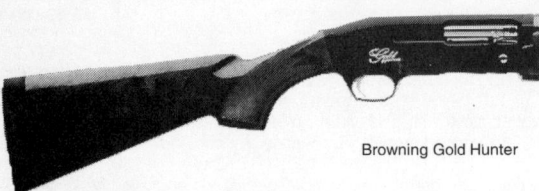

Browning Gold Hunter

Browning Gold Sporting Clays Auto
Similar to the Gold Hunter except 12-gauge only with 28" or 30" barrel; front and center beads on tapered ventilated rib; ported and back-bored Invector Plus barrel; 2³⁄₄" chamber; satin-finished stock with solid, radiused recoil pad with hard heel insert; non-glare black alloy receiver has "Sporting Clays" inscribed in gold. Introduced 1996. Imported from Japan by Browning.
Price: $759.95

BROWNING GOLD HUNTER AUTO SHOTGUN
Gauge: 12, 20, 3" chamber.
Barrel: 12-ga.—26", 28", 30", Invector Plus choke tubes; 20-ga.—26", 30", Invector choke tubes.
Weight: 7 lbs., 9 oz. (12-ga.), 6 lbs., 12 oz. (20-ga.) **Length:** 46¹⁄₄" overall (20-ga., 26" barrel).
Stock: 14"x1¹⁄₂"x2¹⁄₃"; select walnut with gloss finish; palm swell grip.
Features: Self-regulating, self-cleaning gas system shoots all loads; lightweight receiver with special non-glare deep black finish; large reversible safety button; large rounded trigger guard, gold trigger. The 20-gauge has slightly smaller dimensions; 12-gauge have back-bored barrels, Invector Plus tube system. Introduced 1994. Imported by Browning.
Price: 12- or 20-gauge $734.95
Price: Extra barrels $272.95

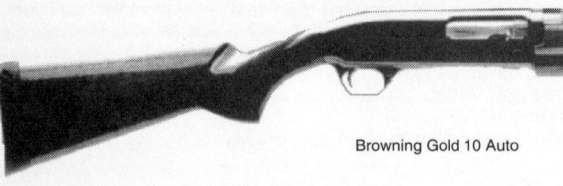

Browning Gold 10 Auto

Browning Gold 10 Stalker Auto Shotgun
Same as the standard Gold 10 except has non-glare metal finish and black graphite-fiberglass composite stock with dull finish and checkering. Introduced 1993. Imported by Browning.
Price: $1,007.95
Price: Extra barrel $261.95

BROWNING GOLD 10 AUTO SHOTGUN
Gauge: 10, 3¹⁄₂" chamber, 5-shot magazine.
Barrel: 26", 28", 30" (Imp. Cyl., Mod., Full standard Invector).
Weight: 10 lbs., 7 oz. (28" barrel).
Stock: 14³⁄₈"x1¹⁄₂"x2³⁄₈". Select walnut with gloss finish, cut checkering, recoil pad.
Features: Short-stroke, gas-operated action, cross-bolt safety. Forged steel receiver with polished blue finish. Introduced 1993. Imported by Browning.
Price: $1,007.95
Price: Extra barrel $261.95

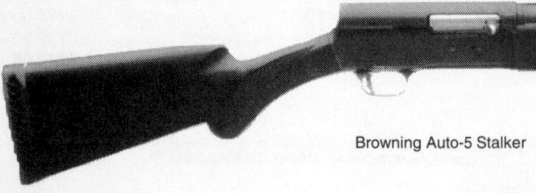

Browning Auto-5 Stalker

Browning Auto-5 Stalker
Similar to the Auto-5 Light and Magnum models except has matte blue metal finish and black graphite-fiberglass stock and forend. Stock is scratch and impact resistant and has checkered panels. Light Stalker has 2³⁄₄" chamber, 26" or 28" vent. rib barrel with Invector choke tubes, weighs 8 lbs., 1 oz. (26"). Magnum Stalker has 3" chamber, 28" or 30" back-bored vent. rib barrel with Invector choke tubes, weighs 8 lbs., 11 oz. (28"). Introduced 1992.
Price: Light Stalker $839.95
Price: Magnum Stalker $865.95

BROWNING AUTO-5 LIGHT 12 AND 20
Gauge: 12, 20, 5-shot; 3-shot plug furnished; 2³⁄₄" or 3" chamber.
Action: Recoil operated autoloader; takedown.
Barrel: 26", 28", 30" Invector (choke tube) barrel; also available with Light 20-ga. 28" (Mod.) or 26" (Imp. Cyl.) barrel.
Weight: 12-, 16-ga. 7¹⁄₄ lbs.; 20-ga. 6³⁄₈ lbs.
Stock: French walnut, hand checkered half-pistol grip and forend. 14¹⁄₄"x1⁵⁄₈"x2¹⁄₂".
Features: Receiver hand engraved with scroll designs and border. Double extractors, extra bbls. Interchangeable without factory fitting; mag. cut-off; cross-bolt safety. All models except Buck Special and game guns have back-bored barrels with Invector Plus choke tubes. Imported from Japan by Browning.
Price: Light 12, 20, vent. rib., Invector Plus $839.95
Price: Extra Invector barrel $307.95
Price: Light 12 Buck Special $828.95
Price: 12, 12 magnum barrel $307.95
Price: Light 12, Hunting, Invector Plus $839.95
Price: Buck Special barrel $269.95

SHOTGUNS—AUTOLOADERS

Browning Auto-5 Magnum 12
Same as standard Auto-5 except chambered for 3" magnum shells (also handles 2¾" magnum and 2¾" HV loads). 28" Mod., Full; 30" and 32" (Full) bbls. Back-bored barrel comes with Invector choke tubes. 14"x1⅝"x2½" stock. Recoil pad. Weighs 8¾ lbs.
Price: With back-bored barrel, Invector Plus $865.95
Price: Extra Invector Plus barrel $307.95

Browning Auto-5 Magnum 20
Same as Magnum 12 except 20-gauge, 26" or 28" barrel with Invector Plus choke tubes with back-bored barrels. With ventilated rib, weighs 7½ lbs.
Price: Invector Plus $865.95
Price: Extra Invector barrel $307.95

CHURCHILL TURKEY AUTOMATIC SHOTGUN
Gauge: 12, 3" chamber, 5-shot magazine.
Barrel: 25" (Mod., Full, Extra Full choke tubes).
Weight: 7 lbs. Length: NA.
Stock: Walnut with satin finish, hand checkering.
Features: Gas-operated action, magazine cut-off, non-glare metal finish. Gold-colored trigger. Introduced 1990. Imported by Ellett Bros.
Price: $569.95

> Consult our Directory pages for the location of firms mentioned.

Mossberg Model 9200

Mossberg Model 9200 Persuader
Similar to the Model 9200 Crown Grade except has black synthetic stock and forend, 18½" plain barrel with fixed Cyl. choke, swivel studs. Weighs 7 lbs. Made in U.S. by Mossberg. Introduced 1996.
Price: $390.00

Mossberg Model 9200 Viking
Similar to the Model 9200 Crown Grade except has black matte metal finish, moss-green synthetic stock and forend; 28" Accu-Choke vent. rib barrel with Mod. tube. Made in U.S. by Mossberg. Introduced 1996.
Price: $404.00

MOSSBERG MODEL 9200 CROWN GRADE AUTO SHOTGUN
Gauge: 12, 3" chamber.
Barrel: 24" (rifled bore), 24", 28" (Accu-Choke tubes); vent. rib.
Weight: About 7.5 lbs. Length: 48" overall (28" bbl.).
Stock: Walnut with high-gloss finish, cut checkering.
Features: Shoots all 2¾" or 3" loads without adjustment. Alloy receiver, ambidextrous top safety. Introduced 1992.
Price: 28", vent. rib $478.00
Price: Turkey, 24" vent. rib $478.00
Price: Trophy, 24" with scope base, rifled bore, Dual-Comb stock $500.00
Price: 24", rifle sights, rifled bore $478.00

Mossberg Model 9200 USST Autoloading Shotgun
Same as the Model 9200 Crown Grade except has "United States Shooting Team" custom engraved receiver. Comes with 26" vent. rib barrel with Accu-Choke tubes (including Skeet), cut-checkered walnut-finish stock and forend. Introduced 1993.
Price: $478.00

Mossberg 9200 Camo

Mossberg Model 9200 Bantam
Same as the Model 9200 Crown Grade except has 1" shorter stock, 22" vent. rib barrel with three Accu-Choke tubes. Made in U.S. by Mossberg. Introduced 1996.
Price: $478.00

Mossberg Model 9200 Camo Shotgun
Same as the Model 9200 Crown Grade except completely covered with Mossy Oak Tree Stand, Realtree AP gray or OFM camouflage finish. Available with 24" barrel with Accu-Choke tubes. Has synthetic stock and forend. Introduced 1993.
Price: Turkey, 24" vent. rib, Mossy Oak or Realtree finish $562.00
Price: 28" vent. rib, Accu-Chokes, OFM camo finish $463.00

Remington 11-87 Sporting Clays

REMINGTON 11-87 PREMIER SHOTGUN
Gauge: 12, 3" chamber.
Barrel: 26", 28", 30" Rem Choke tubes. Light Contour barrel.
Weight: About 8¼ lbs. Length: 46" overall (26" bbl.).
Stock: Walnut with satin or high-gloss finish; cut checkering; solid brown buttpad; no white spacers.
Sights: Bradley-type white-faced front, metal bead middle.
Features: Pressure compensating gas system allows shooting 2¾" or 3" loads interchangeably with no adjustments. Stainless magazine tube; redesigned feed latch, barrel support ring on operating bars; pinned forend. Introduced 1987.
Price: $670.00
Price: Left-hand $720.00
Price: Premier Cantilever Deer Barrel, sling, swivels, Monte Carlo stock $725.00

REMINGTON 11-87 SPORTING CLAYS
Gauge: 12, 2¾" chamber.
Barrel: 26", 28", vent. rib, Rem Choke (Skeet, Imp. Cyl., Mod., Full); Light Contour barrel. Medium height rib.
Weight: 7.5 lbs. Length: 46.5" overall (26" barrel).
Stock: 14³⁄₁₆"x1½"x2¼". Walnut, with cut checkering; sporting clays butt pad.
Features: Top of receiver, barrel and rib have matte finish; shortened magazine tube and forend; lengthened forcing cone; ivory bead front sight; competition trigger. Special no-wrench choke tubes marked on the outside. Comes in two-barrel fitted hard case. Introduced 1992.
Price: $732.00

Remington 11-87 Premier Trap
Similar to 11-87 Premier except trap dimension stock with straight or Monte Carlo combs; select walnut with satin finish and Tournament-grade cut checkering; 30" barrel with Rem Chokes (Trap Full, Trap Extra Full, Trap Super Full). Gas system set for 2¾" shells only. Introduced 1987.
Price: With Monte Carlo stock $725.00

Remington 11-87 Premier Skeet
Similar to 11-87 Premier except Skeet dimension stock with cut checkering, satin finish, two-piece buttplate; 26" barrel with Skeet or Rem Chokes (Skeet, Imp. Skeet). Gas system set for 2¾" shells only. Introduced 1987.
Price: $718.00

SHOTGUNS—AUTOLOADERS

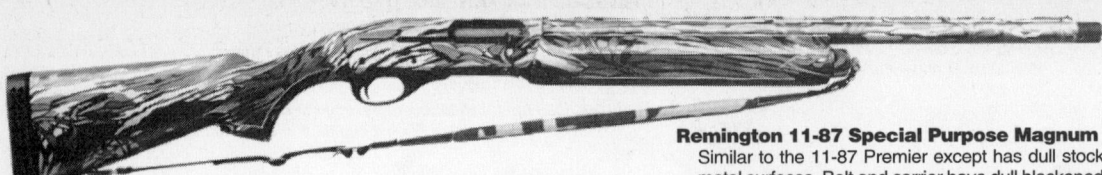
Remington 11-87 SPS-T Camo

Remington 11-87 SPS-T Camo Auto Shotgun
Similar to the 11-87 Special Purpose Magnum except with synthetic stock, 21" vent. rib barrel with Super-Full Turkey (.665" diameter with knurled extension) and Imp. Cyl. Rem Choke tubes. Completely covered with Mossy Oak Green Leaf camouflage. Bolt body, trigger guard and recoil pad are non-reflective black. Introduced 1993.
Price: $744.00

Remington 11-87 Special Purpose Synthetic Camo
Similar to the 11-87 Special Purpose Magnum except has synthetic stock and all metal (except bolt and trigger guard) and stock covered with Mossy Oak Bottomland camo finish. In 12-gauge only, 26", Rem Choke. Comes with camo sling, swivels. Introduced 1992.
Price: $730.00

Remington 11-87 Special Purpose Magnum
Similar to the 11-87 Premier except has dull stock finish, Parkerized exposed metal surfaces. Bolt and carrier have dull blackened coloring. Comes with 26" or 28" barrel with Rem Chokes, padded Cordura nylon sling and quick detachable swivels. Introduced 1987.
Price: $644.00
Price: With synthetic stock and forend (SPS) $644.00
Price: Magnum-Turkey with synthetic stock (SPS-T) $657.00

Remington 11-87 SPS-Deer Shotgun
Similar to the 11-87 Special Purpose Camo except has fully-rifled 21" barrel with rifle sights, black non-reflective, synthetic stock and forend, black carrying sling. Introduced 1993.
Price: $665.00

Remington 11-87 SPS Cantilever Shotgun
Similar to the 11-87 SPS except has fully rifled barrel; synthetic stock with Monte Carlo comb; cantilever scope mount deer barrel. Comes with sling and swivels. Introduced 1994.
Price: $725.00

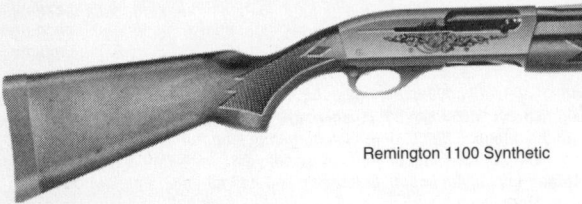
Remington 1100 Synthetic

Remington 1100 Synthetic
Similar to the 1100 LT magnum except in 12- or 20-gauage, and has black synthetic stock; vent. rib 28" barrel on 12-gauge, 26" on 20, both with Mod. Rem Choke tube. Weighs about 7½ lbs. Introduced 1996.
Price: $492.00

Remington 1100 20-Gauge Deer Gun
Same as 1100 except 20-ga. only, 21" barrel (Imp. Cyl.), rifle sights adjustable for windage and elevation; recoil pad with white spacer. Weighs 7¼ lbs.
Price: About $584.00

REMINGTON 1100 LT-20 AUTO
Gauge: 20.
Barrel: 25" (Full, Mod.), 26", 28" with Rem Chokes.
Weight: 7½ lbs.
Stock: 14"x1½"x2½". American walnut, checkered pistol grip and forend.
Features: Quickly interchangeable barrels. Matted receiver top with scroll work on both sides of receiver. Cross-bolt safety.
Price: With Rem Chokes, 20-ga. about $625.00
Price: Youth Gun LT-20 (21" Rem Choke) $625.00
Price: 20-ga., 3" magnum $625.00
Price: Skeet, 26", cut checkering, Rem. Choke $710.00

Remington 1100 Special Field
Similar to Standard Model 1100 except 12- and 20-ga. only, comes with 23" Rem Choke barrel. LT-20 version 6½ lbs.; has straight-grip stock, shorter forend, both with cut checkering. Comes with vent. rib only; matte finish receiver without engraving. Introduced 1983.
Price: 12- and 20-ga., 23" Rem Choke, about $625.00

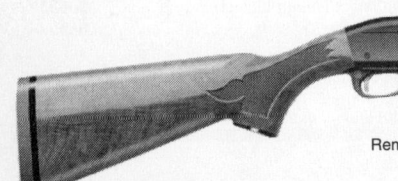
Remington 1100 Sporting 28

Remington 1100 Sporting 28
Similar to the 1100 LT-20 except in 28-gauge with 25" barrel; comes with Skeet, Imp. Cyl., Light Mod., Mod. Rem Choke tubes. Fancy walnut with gloss finish, Sporting rubber buttpad. Made in U.S. by Remington. Introduced 1996.
Price: $725.00

REMINGTON 11-96 EURO LIGHTWEIGHT AUTO SHOTGUN
Gauge: 12, 3" chamber.
Barrel: 26", 28", Rem Chokes.
Weight: 6⅞ lbs. (26" barrel). **Length:** 46" overall (26" barrel).
Stock: Semi-fancy Claro walnut with cut checkering; solid rubber butt pad.
Features: Pressure-compensating gas system allows shooting 2¾" or 3" loads interchangeably with no adjustments. Lightweight steel receiver with scroll-engraved panels; stainless steel magazine tube; 6mm ventilated rib on light contour barrel. Introduced 1996. Made in U.S. by Remington.
Price: $849.00

Remington SP-10 Magnum-Camo

Remington SP-10 Magnum-Camo Auto Shotgun
Similar to the SP-10 Magnum except buttstock, forend, receiver, barrel and magazine cap are covered with Mossy Oak Bottomland camo finish; bolt body and trigger guard have matte black finish. Comes with Extra-Full Turkey Rem Choke tube, 23" vent. rib barrel with mid-rib bead and Bradley-style front sight, swivel studs and quick-detachable swivels, and a non-slip Cordura carrying sling in the same camo pattern. Introduced 1993.
Price: $1,121.00

REMINGTON SP-10 MAGNUM AUTO SHOTGUN
Gauge: 10, 3½" chamber, 3-shot magazine.
Barrel: 26", 30" (Full and Mod. Rem Chokes).
Weight: 11 to 11¼ lbs. **Length:** 47½" overall (26" barrel).
Stock: Walnut with satin finish. Checkered grip and forend.
Sights: Metal bead front.
Features: Stainless steel gas system with moving cylinder; ⅜" ventilated rib. Receiver and barrel have matte finish. Brown recoil pad. Comes with padded Cordura nylon sling. Introduced 1989.
Price: $1,033.00

SHOTGUNS—SLIDE ACTIONS

Includes a wide variety of sporting guns and guns suitable for competitive shooting.

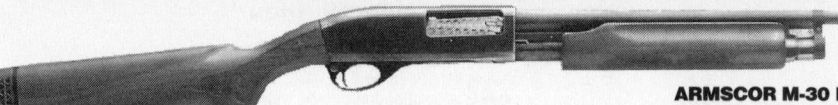

Armscor M-30 Field

ARMSCOR M-30 FIELD PUMP SHOTGUN
Gauge: 12, 3" chamber.
Barrel: 28" fixed Mod., or with Mod. and Full choke tubes.
Weight: 7.6 lbs.
Stock: Walnut-finished hardwood.
Features: Double action slide bars; blued steel receiver; damascened bolt. Introduced 1996. Imported from the Philippines by K.B.I., Inc.
Price: With fixed choke $209.00
Price: With choke tubes $259.00

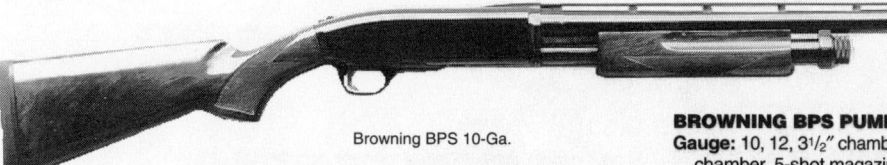

Browning BPS 10-Ga.

BROWNING BPS PUMP SHOTGUN
Gauge: 10, 12, 3½" chamber; 12 or 20, 3" chamber (2¾" in target guns), 28, 2¾" chamber, 5-shot magazine.
Barrel: 10-ga.—24" Buck Special, 28", 30", 32" Invector; 12-, 20- ga.—22", 24", 26", 28", 30", 32" (Imp. Cyl., Mod. or Full). Also available with Invector choke tubes, 12- or 20-ga.; Upland Special has 22" barrel with Invector tubes. BPS 3" and 3½" have back-bored barrel.
Weight: 7 lbs., 8 oz. (28" barrel). **Length:** 48¾" overall (28" barrel).
Stock: 14¼"x1½"x2½". Select walnut, semi-beavertail forend, full pistol grip stock.
Features: All 12-gauge 3" guns except Buck Special and game guns have back-bored barrels with Invector Plus choke tubes. Bottom feeding and ejection, receiver top safety, high post vent. rib. Double action bars eliminate binding. Vent. rib barrels only. All 12- and 20-gauge guns with 3" chamber available with fully engraved receiver flats at no extra cost. Each gauge has its own unique game scene. Introduced 1977. Imported from Japan by Browning.
Price: 10-ga., Hunting, Invector $671.95
Price: 12-ga., 3½" Mag., Hunting, Invector Plus $671.95
Price: 12-, 20-ga., Hunting, Invector Plus $534.95
Price: 12-, 20-ga., Upland Special, Invector Plus $534.95
Price: 10-ga. Buck Special $676.95
Price: 12-ga. Buck Special $519.95
Price: 28-ga., Hunting, Invector $534.95

Manufacturers' addresses in the
Directory of the Arms Trade
page 313, this issue

Browning BPS Game Gun Turkey Special
Similar to the standard BPS except has satin-finished walnut stock and dull-finished barrel and receiver. Receiver is drilled and tapped for scope mounting. Rifle-style stock dimensions and swivel studs. Has Extra-Full Turkey choke tube. Introduced 1992.
Price: $571.95

Browning BPS Pump Shotgun Ladies and Youth Model
Same as BPS Upland Special except 20-ga. only, 22" Invector barrel, stock has pistol grip with recoil pad. Length of pull is 13¼". Introduced 1986.
Price: $534.95

Browning BPS Pigeon Grade Pump Shotgun
Same as the standard BPS except has select high grade walnut stock and forend, and gold-trimmed receiver. Available in 12-gauge only with 26" or 28" vent. rib barrels. Introduced 1992.
Price: $713.95
Price: 10-gauge Waterfowl Model $860.95

Browning BPS Stalker

Browning BPS Stalker Pump Shotgun
Same gun as the standard BPS except all exposed metal parts have a matte blued finish and the stock has a durable black finish with a black recoil pad. Available in 10-ga. (3½") and 12-ga. with 3" or 3½" chamber, 22", 28", 30" barrel with Invector choke system. Introduced 1987.
Price: 12-ga., 3" chamber, Invector Plus $534.95
Price: 10-, 12-ga., 3½" chamber $671.95

Browning BPS Game Gun Deer Special
Similar to the standard BPS except has newly designed receiver/magazine tube/barrel mounting system to eliminate play, heavy 20.5" barrel with rifle-type sights with adjustable rear, solid receiver scope mount, "rifle" stock dimensions for scope or open sights, sling swivel studs. Gloss or matte finished wood with checkering, polished blue metal. Introduced 1992.
Price: $603.95

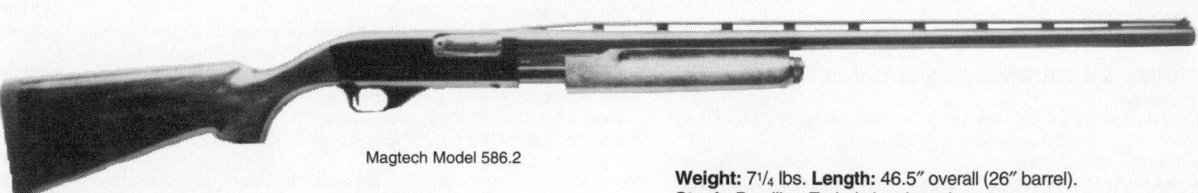

Magtech Model 586.2

MAGTECH MODEL 586.2-VR PUMP SHOTGUN
Gauge: 12, 3" chamber.
Barrel: 26", 28", choke tubes.
Weight: 7¼ lbs. **Length:** 46.5" overall (26" barrel).
Stock: Brazilian Embuia hardwood.
Features: Double action slide bars. Ventilated rib with bead front sight. Polished blue finish. Introduced 1995. Imported from Brazil by Magtech Recreational Products.
Price: About $255.00

CAUTION: PRICES SHOWN ARE SUPPLIED BY THE MANUFACTURER OR IMPORTER. CHECK YOUR LOCAL GUNSHOP.

SHOTGUNS—SLIDE ACTIONS

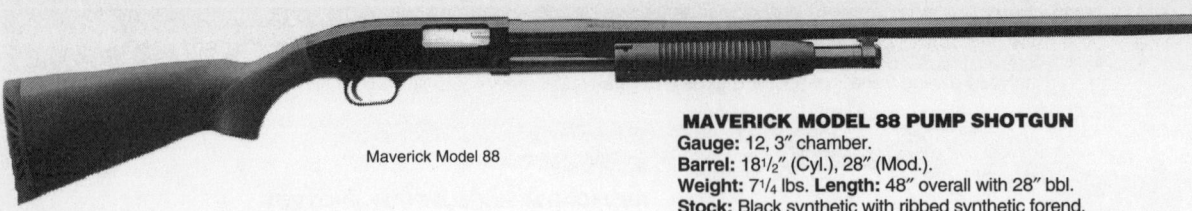

Maverick Model 88

MAVERICK MODEL 88 PUMP SHOTGUN
Gauge: 12, 3" chamber.
Barrel: 18 1/2" (Cyl.), 28" (Mod.).
Weight: 7 1/4 lbs. **Length:** 48" overall with 28" bbl.
Stock: Black synthetic with ribbed synthetic forend.
Sights: Bead front.
Features: Alloy receiver with blue finish; dual slide bars; cross-bolt safety in trigger guard; interchangeable barrels. Rubber recoil pad. Mossberg Cablelock included. Introduced 1989. From Maverick Arms, Inc.
Price: Model 88, synthetic stock, 28" Mod. $221.00
Price: Model 88, synthetic stock, 28" ACCU-TUBE, Mod. $235.00
Price: Model 88, synthetic stock, 24" with rifle sights $235.00

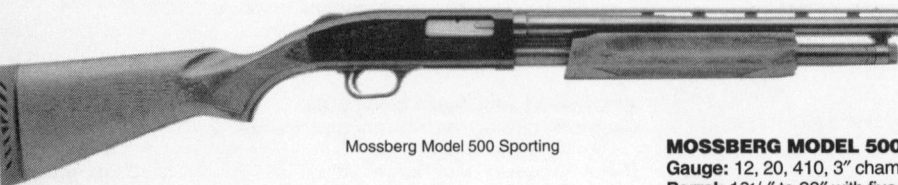

Mossberg Model 500 Sporting

Mossberg Model 500 Camo Pump
Same as the Model 500 Sporting Pump except 12-gauge only and entire gun is covered with special camouflage finish. Receiver drilled and tapped for scope mounting. Comes with quick detachable swivel studs, swivels, camouflage sling, Mossberg Cablelock.
Price: From about $296.00
Price: Camo Combo (as above with extra Slugster barrel), from about ..$379.00

Mossberg Turkey Model 500 Pump
Same as the Model 500 Sporting Pump except has overall OFM camo finish, Ghost-Ring sights, Accu-Choke barrel with Imp. Cyl., Mod., Full, Extra-Full lead shot choke tubes, 24" barrel, swivel studs, camo sling. Introduced 1992.
Price: $384.00

Mossberg Model 500 Muzzleloader Combo
Same as the Model 500 Sporting Pump except comes with 24" rifled bore, rifle-sighted Slugster barrel and 24" fully rifled 50-caliber muzzleloading barrel and ramrod. Uses #209 standard primer. Introduced 1992.
Price: $385.00

MOSSBERG MODEL 500 TROPHY SLUGSTER
Gauge: 12, 3" chamber.
Barrel: 24", rifled bore. Integral scope mount.
Weight: 7 1/4 lbs. **Length:** 44" overall.
Stock: 14" pull, 1 3/8" drop at heel. Walnut; Dual Comb design for proper eye positioning with or without scoped barrels. Recoil pad and swivel studs.
Features: Ambidextrous thumb safety, twin extractors, dual slide bars. Comes with scope mount. Mossberg Cablelock included. Introduced 1988.
Price: Rifled bore, with scope mount $354.00
Price: Cyl. bore, rifle sights $288.00
Price: Rifled bore, rifle sights $326.00
Price: With Marinecoat finish $415.00

MOSSBERG MODEL 500 SPORTING PUMP
Gauge: 12, 20, 410, 3" chamber.
Barrel: 18 1/2" to 28" with fixed or Accu-Choke, plain or vent. rib.
Weight: 6 1/4 lbs. (410), 7 1/4 lbs. (12). **Length:** 48" overall (28" barrel).
Stock: 14"x1 1/2"x2 1/2". Walnut-stained hardwood. Cut-checkered grip and forend.
Sights: White bead front, brass mid-bead.
Features: Ambidextrous thumb safety, twin extractors, disconnecting safety, dual action bars. Quiet Carry forend. Mossberg Cablelock included. From Mossberg.
Price: From about $281.00
Price: Sporting Combos (field barrel and Slugster barrel), from $312.00

Mossberg Model 500 Bantam Pump
Same as the Model 500 Sporting Pump except 20-gauge only, 22" vent. rib Accu-Choke barrel with Mod. choke tube; has 1" shorter stock, reduced length from pistol grip to trigger, reduced forend reach. Introduced 1992.
Price: $281.00

Mossberg Model 500 Viking
Similar to the Model 500 Sporting except in 12-gauge with 24" rifled bore, rifle sights or 28" vent. rib with Mod. Accu-Choke tube, or 20-gauge 26" vent. rib with Mod. Accu-Choke tube; moss-green synthetic stock and forend, matte metal finish. Made in U.S. by Mossberg. Introduced 1996.
Price: $266.00
Price: With rifled barrel $312.00

Mossberg American Field Model 835 Pump Shotgun
Same as the Model 835 Crown Grade except has walnut-stained hardwood stock and comes only with Modified choke tube, 28" barrel. Introduced 1992.
Price: $313.00

Mossberg Model 835 Viking
Similar to the Model 835 Crown Grade except has moss-green synthetic stock and forend, matte metal finish, 28" vent. rib Accu-Mag. barrel with Mod. tube. Made in U.S. by Mossberg. Introduced 1996.
Price: $301.00

Mossberg Model 835 Crown Grade

MOSSBERG MODEL 835 CROWN GRADE ULTI-MAG PUMP
Gauge: 12, 3 1/2" chamber.
Barrel: 24" rifled bore, 24", 28", Accu-Mag with four choke tubes for steel or lead shot.
Weight: 7 3/4 lbs. **Length:** 48 1/2" overall.
Stock: 14"x1 1/2"x2 1/2". Dual Comb. Cut-checkered walnut or camo synthetic; both have recoil pad.
Sights: White bead front, brass mid-bead.
Features: Shoots 2 3/4", 3" or 3 1/2" shells. Backbored barrel to reduce recoil, improve patterns. Ambidextrous thumb safety, twin extractors, dual slide bars. Mossberg Cablelock included. Introduced 1988.

Price: 28" vent. rib, Dual-Comb stock $412.00
Price: As above, standard stock $404.00
Price: 24" Trophy Slugster, rifled bore, scope base, Dual-Comb stock ..$369.00
Price: Combo, 24" rifled bore, rifle sights, 28" vent. rib, Accu-Mag choke tubes, Dual-Comb stock $384.00
Price: Combo, 24" Trophy Slugster rifled bore, 28" vent. rib, Accu-Mag Mod. tube, Dual-Comb stock $407.00
Price: Realtree or Mossy Oak Camo Turkey, 24" vent. rib, Accu-Mag Extra-Full tube, synthetic stock $493.00
Price: Realtree Camo, 28" vent. rib, Accu-Mag tubes, synthetic stock ..$493.00
Price: Realtree Camo Combo, 24" rifled bore, rifle sights, 24" vent. rib Accu-Mag choke tubes, synthetic stock, hard case $601.00
Price: OFM Camo, 28" vent. rib, Accu-Mag tubes, synthetic stock $441.00
Price: OFM Camo Combo, 24" rifled bore, rifle sights, 28" vent. rib, Accu-Mag tubes, synthetic stock $515.00

SHOTGUNS—SLIDE ACTIONS

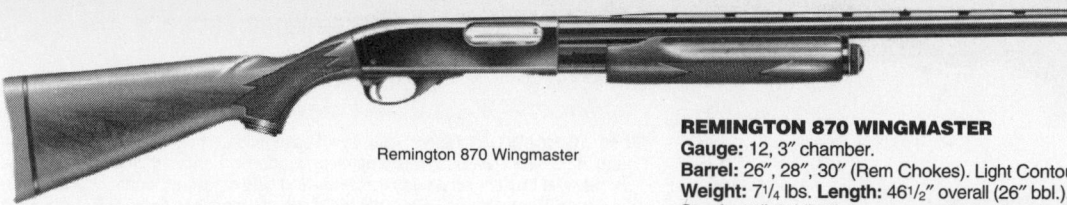
Remington 870 Wingmaster

Remington 870 Wingmaster
Gauge: 12, 3" chamber.
Barrel: 26", 28", 30" (Rem Chokes). Light Contour barrel.
Weight: 7 1/4 lbs. **Length:** 46 1/2" overall (26" bbl.).
Stock: 14"x2 1/2"x1". American walnut with satin or high-gloss finish, cut-checkered pistol grip and forend. Rubber buttpad.
Sights: Ivory bead front, metal mid-bead.
Features: Double action bars; cross-bolt safety; blue finish. Available in right- or left-hand style. Introduced 1986.
Price: $505.00
Price: LW-20 20-ga., vent. rib, 26", 28" (Rem Choke) $492.00
Price: Fully rifled Cantilever, 20" $585.00

Remington 870 Marine Magnum
Similar to the 870 Wingmaster except all metal is plated with electroless nickel and has black synthetic stock and forend. Has 18" plain barrel (Cyl.), bead front sight, 7-shot magazine. Introduced 1992.
Price: $500.00

Remington 870 TC Trap Gun
Similar to the 870 Wingmaster except has tournament-grade, satin-finished American walnut stock with straight or Monte Carlo comb, over-bored 30" vent. rib barrel with 2 3/4" chamber, over-bore-matched Rem Choke tubes. Made in U.S. by Remington. Reintroduced 1996.
Price: $632.00
Price: With Monte Carlo stock $647.00

Remington 870 SPS Cantilever Shotgun
Similar to the 870 SPS-Deer except has rifled barrel; synthetic stock with Monte Carlo comb; cantilever scope mount deer barrel. Comes with sling and swivels. Introduced 1994.
Price: With fully rifled barrel $483.00

Remington 870 SPS-Deer Shotgun
Has fully-rifled 20" barrel with rifle sights, black non-reflective, synthetic stock and forend, black carrying sling. Introduced 1993.
Price: $423.00

Remington 870 SPS-T Camo Pump Shotgun
Similar to the 870 Special Purpose Magnum except with synthetic stock, 21" vent. rib barrel with Super-Full Turkey (.665" diameter with knurled extension) and Imp. Cyl. Rem Choke tubes. Completely covered with Mossy Oak Green Leaf camouflage. Bolt body, trigger guard and recoil pad are non-reflective black. Introduced 1993.
Price: $497.00

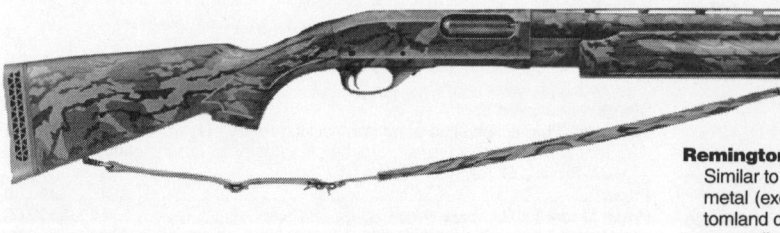
Remington 870 SPS Camo

Remington 870 SPS-T Special Purpose Magnum
Similar to the Model 870 except chambered only for 12-ga., 3" shells, 26" or 28" Rem Choke barrel. All exposed metal surfaces are finished in dull, non-reflective black. Black synthetic stock and forend. Comes with padded Cordura 2" wide sling, quick-detachable swivels. Chrome-lined bores. Dark recoil pad. Introduced 1985.
Price: $412.00

Remington 870 High Grades
Same as 870 except better walnut, hand checkering. Engraved receiver and barrel. Vent. rib. Stock dimensions to order.
Price: 870D, about $2,610.00
Price: 870F, about $5,377.00
Price: 870F with gold inlay, about $8,062.00

Remington 870 Express Rifle-Sighted Deer Gun
Same as the Model 870 Express except comes with 20" barrel with fixed Imp. Cyl. choke, open iron sights, Monte Carlo stock. Introduced 1991.
Price: $287.00
Price: With fully rifled barrel $325.00

Remington Model 870 Express Youth Gun
Same as the Model 870 Express except comes with 12 1/2" length of pull, 21" barrel with Mod. Rem Choke tube. Hardwood stock with low-luster finish. Introduced 1991.
Price: 20-ga. Express Youth (1" shorter stock) $292.00
Price: 20-ga. Express Youth Deer (rifle sights, fully rifled barrel) $325.00

Remington 870 Special Purpose Synthetic Camo
Similar to the 870 Special Purpose Magnum except has synthetic stock and all metal (except bolt and trigger guard) and stock covered with Mossy Oak Bottomland camo finish, In 12-gauge only, 26" vent. rib, Rem Choke. Comes with camo sling, swivels. Introduced 1992.
Price: $483.00

Remington 870 Express
Similar to the 870 Wingmaster except has a walnut-toned hardwood stock with solid, black recoil pad and pressed checkering on grip and forend. Outside metal surfaces have a black oxide finish. Comes with 26" or 28" vent. rib barrel with a Mod. Rem Choke tube. Introduced 1987.
Price: 12 or 20 .... $292.00
Price: Express Combo (with extra 20" Deer barrel), 12 or 20 .... $395.00
Price: Express 20-ga., 28" with Mod. Rem Choke tubes $292.00

Remington 870 Express Turkey
Same as the Model 870 Express except comes with 3" chamber, 21" vent. rib turkey barrel and Extra-Full Rem Choke Turkey tube; 12-ga. only. Introduced 1991.
Price: $305.00

Remington 870 Express Synthetic
Similar to the 870 Express with 26", 28" barrel except has synthetic stock and forend. Introduced 1994.
Price: $299.00

Remington 870 Express Small Gauge
Similar to the 870 Express except is scaled down for 28-gauge and 410-bore. Has 25" vent. rib barrel with fixed Mod. choke; solid black rubber buttpad. Reintroduced 1996.
Price: $307.00

Remington 870 Express HD

Remington 870 Express HD
Similar to the 870 Express except in 12-gauge only, 18" (Cyl.) barrel with bead front sight, synthetic stock and forend with non-reflective black finish and positive checkering. Introduced 1995.
Price: $292.00

SHOTGUNS—SLIDE ACTIONS

Winchester Model 12

WINCHESTER MODEL 12 PUMP SHOTGUN
Gauge: 20, 2¾" chamber, 5-shot magazine.
Barrel: 26" (Imp. Cyl.). Vent. rib.
Weight: 7 lbs. **Length:** 45" overall.
Stock: 14"x2½"x1½". Select walnut with satin finish. Checkered grip and forend.
Features: Grade I has plain blued receiver; production limited to 4000 guns. Grade IV receiver has engraved game scenes and gold highlights identical to traditional Grade IV, and is limited to 1000 guns. Introduced 1993. From U.S. Repeating Arms Co., Inc.
Price: Grade I $879.00
Price: Grade IV $1,431.00

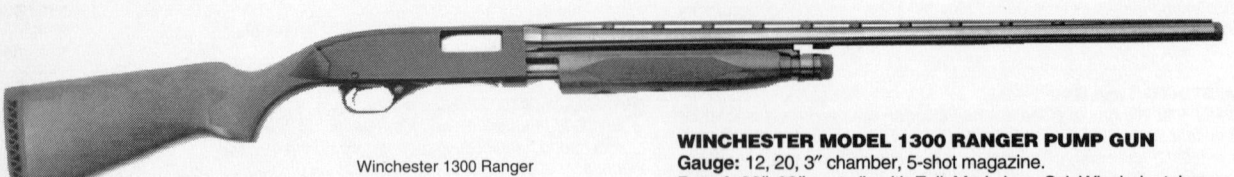

Winchester 1300 Ranger

Winchester Model 1300 Ranger Pump Gun Combo & Deer Gun
Similar to the standard Ranger except comes with two barrels: 22" (Cyl.) deer barrel with rifle-type sights and an interchangeable 28" vent. rib Winchoke barrel with Full, Mod. and Imp. Cyl. choke tubes. Drilled and tapped; comes with rings and bases. Available in 12- and 20-gauge 3" only, with recoil pad. Introduced 1983.
Price: Deer Combo with two barrels $379.00
Price: 12-ga., 22" rifled barrel $343.00
Price: 12-ga., 22" (Imp. Cyl., rifled sabot tubes) $404.00
Price: Combo 12-ga. with 18" (Cyl.) and 28" (Mod. tube) $393.00
Price: Rifled Deer Combo (22" rifled and 28" vent. rib barrels, 12 or 20-ga.) $404.00

Winchester Model 1300 Black Shadow Field Gun
Similar to the Model 1300 Walnut except has black composite stock and forend, matte black finish. Have vent. rib 26" or 28" barrel, 3" chamber, comes with Mod. Winchoke tube. Introduced 1995. From U.S. Repeating Arms Co., Inc.
Price: $296.00

WINCHESTER MODEL 1300 RANGER PUMP GUN
Gauge: 12, 20, 3" chamber, 5-shot magazine.
Barrel: 26", 28" vent. rib with Full, Mod., Imp. Cyl. Winchoke tubes.
Weight: 7 to 7¼ lbs. **Length:** 48⅝" to 50⅝" overall.
Stock: Walnut-finished hardwood with ribbed forend.
Sights: Metal bead front.
Features: Cross-bolt safety, black rubber recoil pad, twin action slide bars, front-locking rotating bolt. From U.S. Repeating Arms Co., Inc.
Price: Vent. rib barrel, Winchoke $309.00

WINCHESTER MODEL 1300 WALNUT PUMP
Gauge: 12, 20, 3" chamber, 5-shot capacity.
Barrel: 26", 28", vent. rib, with Full, Mod., Imp. Cyl. Winchoke tubes.
Weight: 6⅜ lbs. **Length:** 42⅝" overall.
Stock: American walnut, with deep cut checkering on pistol grip, traditional ribbed forend; high luster finish.
Sights: Metal bead front.
Features: Twin action slide bars; front-locking rotary bolt; roll-engraved receiver; blued, highly polished metal; cross-bolt safety with red indicator. Introduced 1984. From U.S. Repeating Arms Co., Inc.
Price: $340.00
Price: Model 1300 Ladies/Youth, 20-ga., 22" vent. rib $309.00

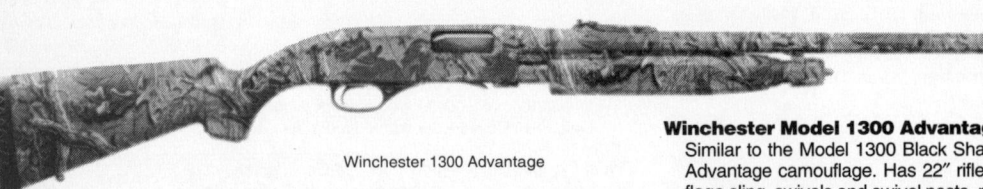

Winchester 1300 Advantage

Winchester Model 1300 Advantage Camo Deer Gun
Similar to the Model 1300 Black Shadow Deer Gun except has full coverage Advantage camouflage. Has 22" rifled or smoothbore barrel, padded camouflage sling, swivels and swivel posts, rifle sights. Receiver drilled and tapped for scope mounting. Introduced 1995. From U.S. Repeating Arms Co., Inc.
Price: Rifled bore $432.00
Price: Smoothbore $410.00

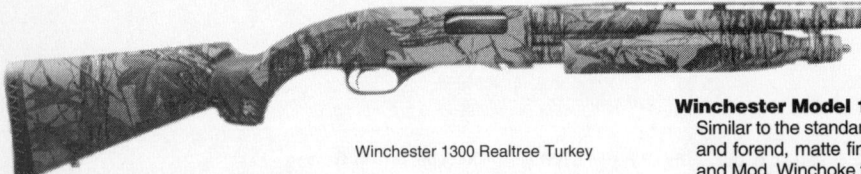

Winchester 1300 Realtree Turkey

Winchester Model 1300 Realtree® Turkey Gun
Similar to the standard Model 1300 except has synthetic Realtree® camo stock and forend, matte finished barrel and receiver, 22" barrel with Extra Full, Full and Mod. Winchoke tubes. Drilled and tapped for scope mounting. Comes with padded, adjustable sling. In 12-gauge only, 3" chamber; weighs about 7 lbs. Introduced 1994. From U.S. Repeating Arms Co., Inc.
Price: $370.00
Price: With full coverage All-Purpose Realtree® camo $432.00

Winchester Model 1300 Black Shadow Deer Gun
Similar to the Model 1300 Black Shadow Turkey Gun except has ramp-type front sight, fully adjustable rear, drilled and tapped for scope mounting. Black composite stock and forend, matte black metal. Smoothbore 22" barrel with one Imp. Cyl. Winchoke tube; 12-gauge only, 3" chamber. Weighs 7¼ lbs. Introduced 1994. From U.S. Repeating Arms Co., Inc.
Price: $296.00

Winchester Model 1300 Black Shadow Turkey Gun
Similar to the Model 1300 Realtree® Turkey except synthetic stock and forend are matte black, and all metal surfaces finished matte black. Drilled and tapped for scope mounting. In 12-gauge only, 3" chamber, 22" vent. rib barrel; comes with one Full Winchoke tube. Introduced 1994. From U.S. Repeating Arms Co., Inc.
Price: $296.00

SHOTGUNS—OVER/UNDERS
Includes a variety of game guns and guns for competitive shooting.

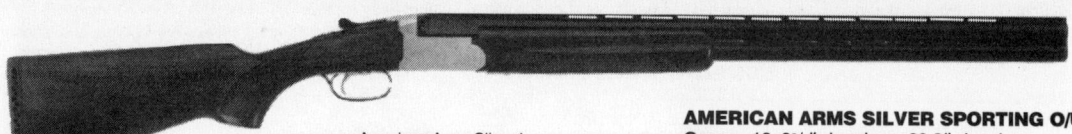
American Arms Silver I

AMERICAN ARMS SILVER I O/U
Gauge: 12, 20, 28, 410, 3" chamber (28 has 2 3/4").
Barrel: 26" (Imp. Cyl. & Mod., all gauges), 28" (Mod. & Full, 12, 20).
Weight: About 6 3/4 lbs.
Stock: 14 1/8"x1 3/8"x2 3/8". Checkered walnut.
Sights: Metal bead front.
Features: Boxlock action with scroll engraving, silver finish. Single selective trigger, extractors. Chrome-lined barrels. Manual safety. Rubber recoil pad. Introduced 1987. Imported from Italy by American Arms, Inc.
Price: 12- or 20-gauge $599.00
Price: 28 or 410 .... $625.00

American Arms Silver Upland Lite
Similar to the Silver I except weighs 6 lbs., 4 oz. (12-gauge), 5 lbs., 12 oz. (20-gauge). Single selective trigger, automatic selective ejectors. Franchoke tubes, vent. rib, engraved frame with antique silver finish. Introduced 1994. Imported by American Arms, Inc.
Price: 12- , 20-ga., 3" chambers, 26" $899.00

AMERICAN ARMS SILVER SPORTING O/U
Gauge: 12, 2 3/4" chambers, 20 3" chambers.
Barrel: 28", 30" (Skeet, Imp. Cyl., Mod., Full choke tubes).
Weight: 7 3/8 lbs. **Length:** 45 1/2" overall.
Stock: 14 3/8"x1 1/2"x2 3/8". Figured walnut, cut checkering; Sporting Clays quick-mount buttpad.
Sights: Target bead front.
Features: Boxlock action with single selective mechanical trigger, automatic selective ejectors; special broadway channeled rib; vented barrel rib; chrome bores. Chrome-nickel finish on frame, with engraving. Introduced 1990. Imported from Italy by American Arms, Inc.
Price: $899.00

American Arms Silver II Shotgun
Similar to the Silver I except 26" barrel (Imp. Cyl., Mod., Full choke tubes, 12- and 20-ga.), 28" (Imp. Cyl., Mod., Full choke tubes, 12-ga. only), 26" (Imp. Cyl. & Mod. fixed chokes, 28 and 410), automatic selective ejectors. Weight is about 6 lbs., 15 oz. (12-ga., 26").
Price: $699.00
Price: 28, 410 .... $725.00

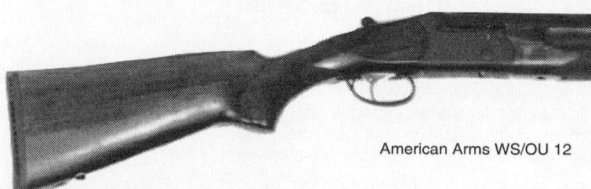
American Arms WS/OU 12

American Arms WT/OU 10 Shotgun
Similar to the WS/OU 12 except chambered for 10-gauge 3 1/2" shell, 26" (Full & Full, choke tubes) barrel. Single selective trigger, extractors. Non-reflective finish on wood and metal. Imported by American Arms, Inc.
Price: $950.00

AMERICAN ARMS WS/OU 12, TS/OU 12 SHOTGUNS
Gauge: 12, 3 1/2" chambers.
Barrel: WS/OU—28" (Imp. Cyl., Mod., Full choke tubes); TS/OU—24" (Imp. Cyl., Mod., Full choke tubes).
Weight: 6 lbs. 15 oz. **Length:** 46" overall.
Stock: 14 1/8"x1 1/8"x2 3/8". European walnut with cut checkering, black vented recoil pad, matte finish.
Features: Boxlock action with single selective trigger, automatic selective ejectors; chrome bores. Matte metal finish. Imported by American Arms, Inc.
Price: $725.00

ARMSPORT 2700 SERIES O/U
Gauge: 12, 20.
Barrel: 26" (Imp. Cyl. & Mod.); 28" (Mod. & Full); vent. rib.
Weight: 8 lbs.
Stock: European walnut, hand-checkered pistol grip and forend.
Features: Single selective trigger, automatic ejectors, engraved receiver. Imported by Armsport. Contact Armsport for complete list of models.
Price: M2733/2735 (Boss-type action, 12, 20, extractors) $790.00
Price: M2741 (as above with ejectors) $825.00
Price: M2730/2731 (as above with single trigger, screw-in chokes) $975.00
Price: M2742 Sporting Clays (12-ga., 28", choke tubes) $930.00
Price: M2744 Sporting Clays (20-ga., 26", choke tubes) $930.00
Price: M2750 Sporting Clays (12-ga., 28", choke tubes, sideplates) .. $1,050.00
Price: M2751 Sporting Clays (20-ga., 26", choke tubes, sideplates) .. $1,050.00

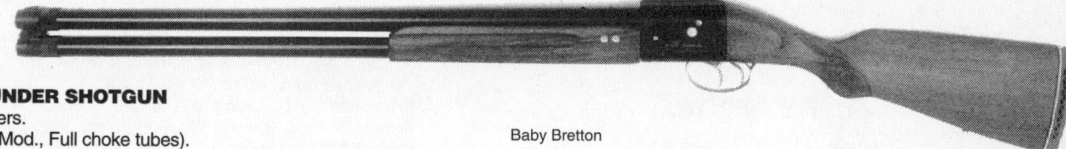
Baby Bretton

BABY BRETTON OVER/UNDER SHOTGUN
Gauge: 12 or 20, 2 3/4" chambers.
Barrel: 27 1/2" (Cyl., Imp. Cyl., Mod., Full choke tubes).
Weight: About 5 lbs.
Stock: Walnut, checkered pistol grip and forend, oil finish.
Features: Receiver slides open on two guide rods, is locked by a large thumb lever on the right side. Extractors only. Light alloy barrels. Imported from France by Mandall Shooting Supplies.
Price: Sprint Standard $895.00
Price: Sprint Deluxe $975.00
Price: Model Fairplay $1,025.00

BAIKAL IJ-27 OVER/UNDER SHOTGUN
Gauge: 12, 2 3/4" chambers.
Barrel: 28" (Mod. & Full).
Weight: 7 lbs.
Stock: Checkered walnut.
Features: Double triggers; extractors; blued receiver with engraving. Reintroduced 1994. Imported from Russia by K.B.I., Inc.
Price: $299.00
Price: IJ-27 EIC (single trigger, automatic ejectors) $339.00

BAIKAL IJ-27M OVER-UNDER SHOTGUN
Gauge: 12, 2 3/4" chambers.
Barrel: 28.5" (Mod. & Full).
Weight: 7.5 lbs. **Length:** 44.5" overall.
Stock: European hardwood.
Features: Engraved boxlock action with double triggers, extractors; chrome-lined barrels; sling swivels. Imported from Russia by Century International Arms.
Price: About $340.00
Price: IJ-27EM (selective automatic ejectors), about $365.00

CAUTION: PRICES SHOWN ARE SUPPLIED BY THE MANUFACTURER OR IMPORTER. CHECK YOUR LOCAL GUNSHOP.

SHOTGUNS—OVER/UNDERS

BAIKAL TOZ-34P OVER/UNDER SHOTGUN
Gauge: 12, 2¾" chambers.
Barrel: 28" (Full & Imp. Cyl.).
Weight: 7.5 lbs. **Length:** 44" overall.
Stock: European walnut.
Features: Engraved, blued receiver; cocking indicator; double triggers. Ventilated rib, ventilated rubber buttpad. Imported from Russia by Century International Arms.
Price: About $405.00
Price: With ejectors, about $475.00

BERETTA MODEL ULTRALIGHT ONYX O/U
Gauge: 12, 2¾" chambers.
Barrel: 26", 28", Mobilchoke choke tubes.
Weight: About 5 lbs., 13 oz.
Stock: Select American walnut with checkered grip and forend.
Features: Low-profile aluminum alloy receiver with titanium breech face insert. Silvered receiver with game scene engraving. Single selective trigger; automatic safety. Introduced 1992. Imported from Italy by Beretta U.S.A.
Price: $1,716.00

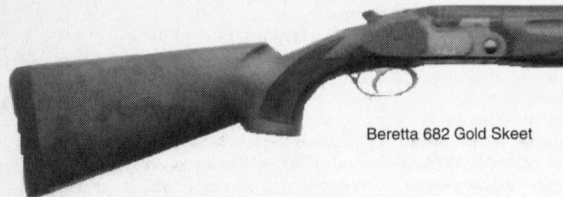
Beretta 682 Gold Skeet

BERETTA SERIES 682 GOLD SKEET, TRAP OVER/UNDERS
Gauge: 12, 2¾" chambers.
Barrel: Skeet—26" and 28"; trap—30" and 32", Imp. Mod. & Full and Mobilchoke; trap mono shotguns—32" and 34" Mobilchoke; trap top single guns—32" and 34" Full and Mobilchoke; trap combo sets—from 30" O/U, to 32" O/U, 34" top single.
Stock: Close-grained walnut, hand checkered.
Sights: White Bradley bead front sight and center bead.
Features: Receiver has Greystone gunmetal gray finish with gold accents. Trap Monte Carlo stock has deluxe trap recoil pad. Various grades available; contact Beretta U.S.A. for details. Imported from Italy by Beretta U.S.A.
Price: 682 Gold Skeet $2,731.00
Price: 682 Gold Trap $2,789.00
Price: 682 Gold Trap Top Combo .... $3,689.00 to $3,832.00
Price: 682 Gold Super Trap Top Combo $4,190.00
Price: 686 Silver Perdiz Skeet (28") $1,499.00
Price: 687 EELL Diamond Pigeon Trap $4,991.00
Price: 687 EELL Diamond Pigeon Skeet (4-bbl. set) $8,899.00
Price: 687 EELL Diamond Pigeon Trap Top Mono ...... $5,241.00 to $5,291.00
Price: 682 Super Skeet (adjustable comb and butt pads, bbl. porting) .. $3,006.00
Price: 682 Super Trap (adjustable comb and butt pad, barrel porting) .... $2,907.00 to $3,983.00
Price: ASE Gold Skeet $8,737.00
Price: ASE Gold Trap $8,815.00
Price: ASE Gold Trap Top Combo $10,287.00

BERETTA MODEL 686 ESSENTIAL O/U
Gauge: 12, 3" chambers.
Barrel: 26", 28", Mobilchoke tubes (Imp. Cyl., Mod., Full).
Weight: 6.7 lbs. **Length:** 45.7" overall (28" barrels).
Stock: 14.5"x2.2"x1.4". American walnut; radiused black buttplate.
Features: Matte finish on receiver and barrels; hard-chrome bores; low-profile receiver with dual conical locking lugs; single selective trigger, ejectors. Introduced 1994. Imported from Italy by Beretta U.S.A.
Price: $1,186.00

BERETTA ONYX SPORTING O/U SHOTGUN
Gauge: 12, 3" chambers.
Barrel: 28", 30" (Mobilchoke tubes).
Weight: 7.7 lbs.
Stock: Checkered American walnut.
Features: Intended for the beginning sporting clays shooter. Has wide, vented 12.5mm target rib, radiused recoil pad. Matte black finish on receiver and barrels. Introduced 1993. Imported from Italy by Beretta U.S.A.
Price: $1,499.00
Price: 686 Silver Pigeon Sporting (as above except coin silver receiver with scroll engraving; 12- or 20-ga.) $1,573.00

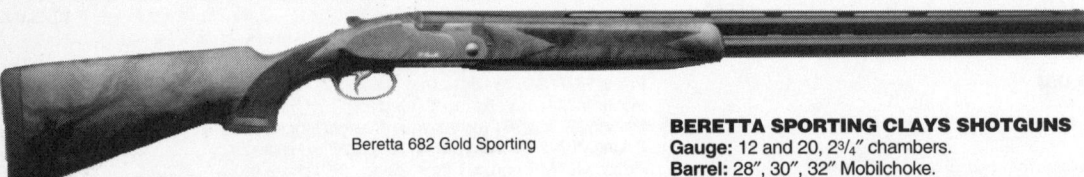
Beretta 682 Gold Sporting

Manufacturers' addresses in the
Directory of the Arms Trade
page 313, this issue

BERETTA SPORTING CLAYS SHOTGUNS
Gauge: 12 and 20, 2¾" chambers.
Barrel: 28", 30", 32" Mobilchoke.
Stock: Close-grained walnut.
Features: Equipped with Beretta Mobilchoke flush-mounted screw-in choke tube system. Dual-purpose O/U for hunting and Sporting Clays. 12- or 20-gauge, 28", 30" Mobilchoke tubes (four, Skeet, Imp. Cyl., Mod., Full). Wide 12.5mm top rib with 2.5mm center groove; 686 Onyx models have matte black receiver, 686 Silver Pigeon has silver receiver with scroll engraving; 687 Silver Pigeon Sporting has silver receiver, highly figured walnut; 687 EL Pigeon Sporting has game scene engraving with gold inlaid animals on full sideplate. Introduced 1994. Imported from Italy by Beretta U.S.A.
Price: 682 Gold Sporting, 28", 30", 32" (with case) $2,789.00
Price: 682 Gold Sporting, 28", 30", ported, adj. l.o.p. $2,999.00
Price: 682 Onyx Sporting $1,499.00
Price: 682 Continental Course Sporting, 2¾" chambers, 28" $2,431.00
Price: 686 Silver Pigeon Sporting $1,573.00
Price: 687L Silver Pigeon Sporting $2,354.00
Price: 687 Silver Pigeon Sporting (20 gauge) $2,354.00
Price: 687 Diamond Pigeon EELL Sporter (hand engraved sideplates, deluxe wood) $5,098.00
Price: 687 Silver Pigeon Sporting Combo, 28" and 30" $3,518.00
Price: ASE Gold Sporting Clay $8,815.00

Beretta 687EL Gold Pigeon Sporting O/U
Similar to the 687 Silver Pigeon Sporting except has sideplates with gold inlay game scene, vent. side and top ribs, bright orange front sight. Stock and forend are of high grade walnut with fine-line checkering. Available in 12-gauge only with 28" or 30" barrels and Mobilchoke tubes. Weight is 6 lbs., 13 oz. Introduced 1993. Imported from Italy by Beretta U.S.A.
Price: $3,320.00

BERETTA MODEL SO5, SO6, SO9 SHOTGUNS
Gauge: 12, 2¾" chambers.
Barrel: To customer specs.
Stock: To customer specs.
Features: SO5—Trap, Skeet and Sporting Clays models SO5; SO6—SO6 and SO6 EELL are field models. SO6 has a case-hardened or silver receiver with contour hand engraving. SO6 EELL has hand-engraved receiver in a fine floral or "fine English" pattern or game scene, with bas-relief chisel work and gold inlays. SO6 and SO6 EELL are available with sidelocks removable by hand. Imported from Italy by Beretta U.S.A.
Price: SO5 Trap, Skeet, Sporting $13,000.00
Price: SO6 Trap, Skeet, Sporting $17,500.00
Price: SO6 EELL Field, custom specs $28,000.00
Price: SO9 (12, 20, 28, 410, 26", 28", 30", any choke) $31,000.00

SHOTGUNS—OVER/UNDERS

Beretta 686 Silver Pigeon Field

BERETTA OVER/UNDER FIELD SHOTGUNS
Gauge: 12, 20, 28, and 410 bore, 2 3/4", 3" and 3 1/2" chambers.
Barrel: 26" and 28" (Mobilchoke tubes).
Stock: Close-grained walnut.
Features: Highly-figured, American walnut stocks and forends, and a unique, weather-resistant finish on barrels. The 686 Onyx bears a gold P. Beretta signature on each side of the receiver. Silver designates standard 686, 687 models with silver receivers; 686 Silver Pigeon has enhanced engraving pattern, schnabel forend; Gold indicates higher grade 686EL, 687EL models with full sideplates; Diamond is for 687EELL models with highest grade wood, engraving. Case provided with Gold and Diamond grades. Silver Gold, Diamond grades introduced 1994. Imported from Italy by Beretta U.S.A.
Price: 686 Onyx $1,473.00
Price: 686 Silver Pigeon two-bbl. set $2,259.00
Price: 686 Silver Pigeon $1,544.00
Price: 686EL Gold Perdiz (engraved sideplates, hard case) $1,999.00
Price: 687L Silver Pigeon $2,031.00
Price: 687EL Gold Pigeon (gold inlays, sideplates) $3,446.00
Price: 687EL Gold Pigeon, 410, 26", 28-ga., 28" $3,599.00
Price: 687EELL Diamond Pigeon (engraved sideplates) $4,999.00
Price: 687EELL Diamond Pigeon, 28-ga., 26" $4,999.00
Price: 687EELL Diamond Pigeon Combo, 20- and 28-ga., 26" $5,577.00

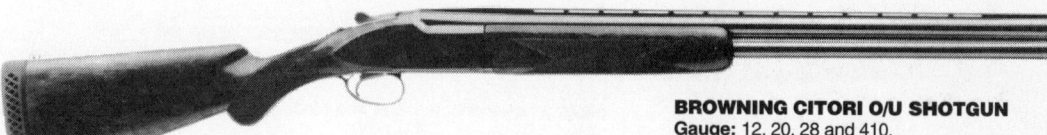
Browning Citori Gran Lightning

Browning Citori Special Trap Models
Similar to standard Citori except 12 gauge only; 30", 32" ported or non-ported (Invector Plus); Monte Carlo cheek piece (14 3/8"x1 3/8"x1 3/8"x2"); fitted with trap-style recoil pad; high post target rib, ventilated side ribs.
Price: Grade I, Invector Plus, ported bbls. $1,580.00
Price: Grade III, Invector Plus Ported $2,179.00
Price: Golden Clays $3,239.00
Price: Adjustable comb stock, add $210.00

Browning Superlight Citori Over/Under
Similar to the standard Citori except available in 12, 20 with 24", 26" or 28" Invector barrels, 28 or 410 with 26" barrels choked Imp. Cyl. & Mod. or 28" choked Mod. & Full. Has straight grip stock, Schnabel forend tip. Superlight 12 weighs 6 lbs., 9 oz. (26" barrels); Superlight 20, 5 lbs., 12 oz. (26" barrels). Introduced 1982.
Price: Grade I only, 28 or 410, Invector $1,439.00
Price: Grade III, Invector, 12 or 20 ....$2,000.00
Price: Grade III, 28 or 410, Invector $2,242.00
Price: Grade VI, Invector, 12 or 20 ....$2,919.00
Price: Grade VI, 28 or 410, Invector $3,145.00
Price: Grade I Invector, 12 or 20 ....$1,386.00
Price: Grade I Invector, Upland Special (24" bbls.), 12 or 20 .$1,386.00

BROWNING CITORI O/U SHOTGUN
Gauge: 12, 20, 28 and 410.
Barrel: 26", 28" in 28 and 410. Offered with Invector choke tubes. All 12- and 20-gauge models have back-bored barrels and Invector Plus choke system.
Weight: 6 lbs., 8 oz. (26" 410) to 7 lbs., 13 oz. (30" 12-ga.).
Length: 43" overall (26" bbl.).
Stock: Dense walnut, hand checkered, full pistol grip, beavertail forend. Field-type recoil pad on 12-ga. field guns and trap and Skeet models.
Sights: Medium raised beads, German nickel silver.
Features: Barrel selector integral with safety, automatic ejectors, three-piece takedown. Imported from Japan by Browning. Contact Browning for complete list of models and prices.
Price: Grade I, Hunting, Invector, 12 and 20 ....$1,134.00
Price: Grade I, Lightning, 28 and 410, Invector $1,418.00
Price: Grade III, Lightning, 28 and 410, Invector $2,242.00
Price: Grade VI, 28 and 410 Lightning, Invector $3,145.00
Price: Grade I, Lightning, Invector Plus, 12, 20 ....$1,376.00
Price: Grade I, Hunting, 28", 30" only, 3 1/2", Invector Plus .$1,418.00
Price: Grade III, Lightning, Invector, 12, 20 ....$2,000.00
Price: Grade VI, Lightning, Invector, 12, 20 ....$2,919.00
Price: Gran Lightning, 26", 28", Invector, 12 ,20 ....$1,869.00
Price: Gran Lightning, 28, 410 ....$1,969.00

Browning Lightning Sporting Clays
Similar to the Citori Lightning with rounded pistol grip and classic forend. Has high post tapered rib or lower hunting-style rib with 30" back-bored Invector Plus barrels, ported or non-ported, 3" chambers. Gloss stock finish, radiused recoil pad. Has "Lightning Sporting Clays Edition" engraved and gold filled on receiver. Introduced 1989.
Price: Low-rib, ported $1,490.00
Price: High-rib, ported $1,565.00
Price: Golden Clays, low rib, ported $3,203.00
Price: Golden Clays, high rib, ported $3,092.00
Price: Adjustable comb stock, all models, add $210.00

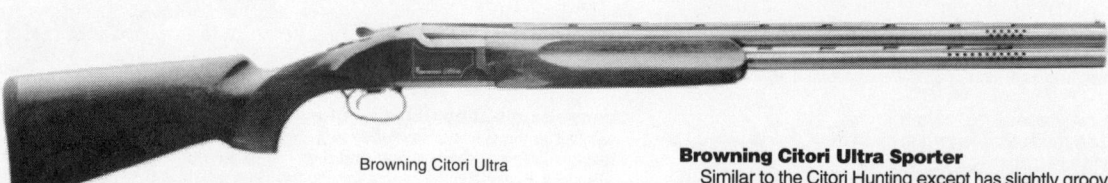
Browning Citori Ultra

Browning Micro Citori Lightning
Similar to the standard Citori 20-ga. Lightning except scaled down for smaller shooter. Comes with 24" Invector Plus back-bored barrels, 13 3/4" length of pull. Weighs about 6 lbs., 3 oz. Introduced 1991.
Price: Grade I $1,428.00

Browning Special Sporting Clays
Similar to the Citori Ultra Sporter except has full pistol grip stock with palm swell, gloss finish, 28", 30" or 32" barrels with back-bored Invector Plus chokes (ported or non-ported), high post tapered rib. Also available as 28" and 30" two-barrel set. Introduced 1989.
Price: With ported barrels $1,565.00
Price: As above, adjustable comb $1,775.00
Price: Golden Clays $3,203.00
Price: With adjustable comb stock $3,413.00

Browning Citori Ultra Sporter
Similar to the Citori Hunting except has slightly grooved, semi-beavertail forend, satin-finish stock, radiused rubber buttpad. Has three interchangeable trigger shoes, trigger has three length of pull adjustments. Ventilated rib tapers from 13mm to 10mm, 28" or 30" barrels (ported or non-ported) with Invector Plus choke tubes. Ventilated side ribs. Introduced 1989.
Price: With ported barrels, gray or blue receiver $1,722.00
Price: Golden Clays $3,203.00

Browning Citori O/U Special Skeet
Similar to standard Citori except 26", 28" barrels, ventilated side ribs, Invector choke tubes; stock dimensions of 14 3/8"x1 1/2"x2", fitted with Skeet-style recoil pad; conventional target rib and high post target rib.
Price: Grade I Invector, 12-, 20-ga., Invector Plus (high post rib) $1,586.00
Price: Grade I, 28 and 410 (high post rib) $1,549.00
Price: Grade III, 28, 410 (high post rib) $2,184.00
Price: Golden Clays $3,239.00
Price: Grade III, 12-ga. Invector Plus $2,179.00
Price: Adjustable comb stock, add $210.00

SHOTGUNS—OVER/UNDERS

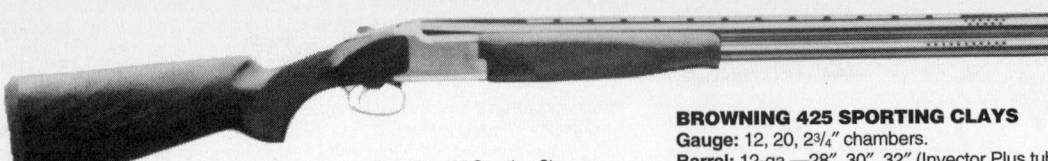
Browning 425 Sporting Clays

Browning 425 WSSF Shotgun
Similar to the 425 Sporting Clays except in 12-gauge only, has stock dimensions specifically tailored to women shooters (14¼"x1½"x1½"); top lever and takedown lever are easier to operate. Stock and forend have teal-colored finish with WSSF logo. Introduced 1995. Imported by Browning.
Price: $1,775.00

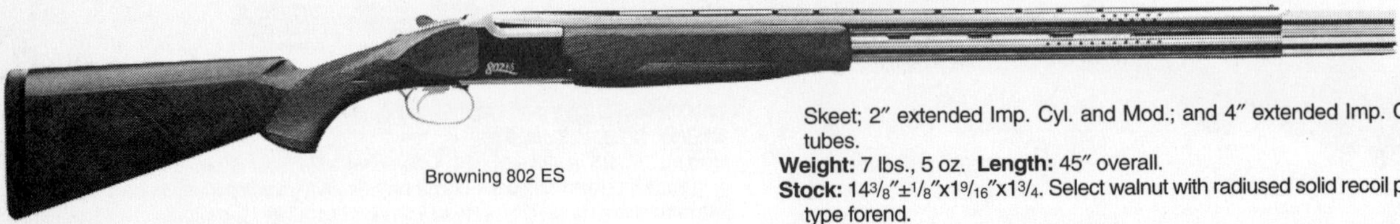

BROWNING 425 SPORTING CLAYS
Gauge: 12, 20, 2¾" chambers.
Barrel: 12-ga.—28", 30", 32" (Invector Plus tubes), back-bored; 20-ga.—28", 30" (Invector Plus tubes).
Weight: 7 lbs., 13 oz. (12-ga., 28").
Stock: 14¹³⁄₁₆" (±⅛")x1⁷⁄₁₆"x2³⁄₁₆" (12-ga.). Select walnut with gloss finish, cut checkering, schnabel forend.
Features: Grayed receiver with engraving, blued barrels. Barrels are ported on 12-gauge guns. Has low 10mm wide vent rib. Comes with three interchangeable trigger shoes to adjust length of pull. Introduced in U.S. 1993. Imported by Browning.
Price: Grade I, 12-, 20-ga., Invector Plus $1,775.00
Price: Golden Clays, 12-, 20-ga., Invector Plus $3,305.00
Price: Adjustable comb stock, add $210.00

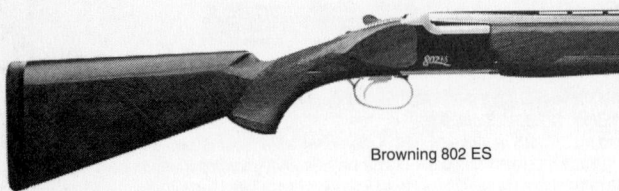
Browning 802 ES

BROWNING LIGHT SPORTING 802 ES O/U
Gauge: 12, 2¾" chambers.
Barrel: 28", back-bored Invector Plus. Comes with flush-mounted Imp. Cyl. and Skeet; 2" extended Imp. Cyl. and Mod.; and 4" extended Imp. Cyl. and Mod. tubes.
Weight: 7 lbs., 5 oz. **Length:** 45" overall.
Stock: 14³⁄₈"±⅛"x1⁹⁄₁₆"x1¾". Select walnut with radiused solid recoil pad, schnabel-type forend.
Features: Trigger adjustable for length of pull; narrow 6.2mm ventilated rib; ventilated barrel side rib; blued receiver. Introduced 1996. Imported from Japan from Browning.
Price: $1,880.00

CENTURY CENTURION OVER/UNDER SHOTGUN
Gauge: 12, 2¾" chambers.
Barrel: 28" (Mod. & Full).
Weight: 7.3 lbs. **Length:** 44.5" overall.
Stock: European walnut.
Features: Double triggers; extractors. Polished blue finish. Introduced 1993. Imported by Century International Arms.
Price: About $380.00

Churchill Windsor Sporting Clays Over/Under
Similar to the Windsor IV except 12-gauge only, with 28" or 30" barrels (choke tubes); barrels are ported, back-bored and have lengthened forcing cones; tapered ventilated rib, ventilated side rib; Sporting-style forend with finger grooves; select walnut stock with palm swell grip. Introduced 1995. Imported by Ellett Bros.
Price: $1,125.00

CHURCHILL WINDSOR IV OVER/UNDER SHOTGUN
Gauge: 12, 20, 3" chambers.
Barrel: 12 ga.—26", 28"; 20 ga.—26"; choke tubes.
Weight: About 7.5 lbs.
Stock: Walnut; rubber recoil pad.
Features: Automatic ejectors, single selective trigger; ventilated top and side ribs; silvered receiver. Introduced 1995. Imported by Ellett Bros.
Price: $932.00

> Consult our Directory pages for the location of firms mentioned.

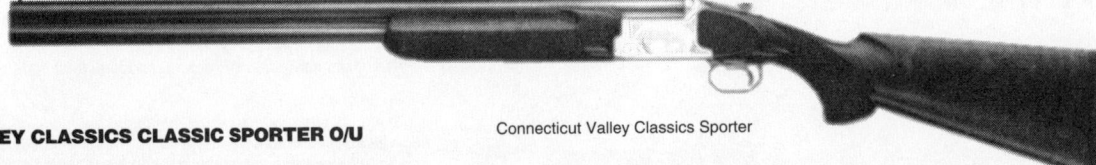
Connecticut Valley Classics Sporter

CONNECTICUT VALLEY CLASSICS CLASSIC SPORTER O/U
Gauge: 12, 3" chambers.
Barrel: 28", 30", 32" (Skeet, Imp. Cyl. Mod., Full CV choke tubes); elongated forcing cones.
Weight: 7¾ lbs. **Length:** 44⅞" overall (28" barrels).
Stock: 14½"x1½"x2⅛". AA grade semi-fancy American black walnut with 20 lpi hand-checkered grip and forend; hand rubbed oil finish.
Features: Receiver duplicates Classic Doubles M101 specifications. Stainless receiver with fine engraving. Bores and chambers suitable for steel shot. Optionally available are CV Plus (2⅜" tubes) choke tubes. Introduced 1993. Made in U.S. by Connecticut Valley Classics.
Price: Grade I $3,195.00
Price: Grade II, AAA fancy walnut, 22 lpi checkering, enhanced engraving $3,795.00
Price: Grade III, AAA select fancy walnut, 22 lpi Fleur de lis checkering, enhanced engraving, bird scenes, gold inlay, gold-plated trigger $4,195.00
Price: Women's Classic Sporter, 28" only, shorter stock, different stock dimensions $3,195.00

Connecticut Valley Classics Classic Skeet
Similar to the Classic Sporter except has 29" barrel with 9mm Skeet rib. AA American black or Claro walnut, 20 lpi checkering. Introduced 1995. Made in U.S. by Century International Arms.
Price: $3,195.00

Connecticut Valley Classics Classic Field O/U
Similar to the Classic Sporter except 27½" barrels with standard choke tubes, slightly different stock shape and dimensions for hunting. Over-bored barrels with lengthened forcing cones. Introduced 1995. Made in U.S. by Century International Arms.
Price: Grade I $3,195.00
Price: Grade II (see Sporter prices) $3,595.00
Price: Grade III $4,195.00

Connecticut Valley Classics Classic Flyer
Similar to the Classic Sporter except has AAA American black or Claro walnut, Premier Grade 22 lpi checkering, choice of standard or schnabel forend, special engraving pattern, gold inlay, gold-plated trigger, 11mm tapered top rib. Introduced 1995. Made in U.S. by Century International Arms.
Price: $3,995.00

Connecticut Valley Classics Classic Field Waterfowler
Similar to the Classic Sporter except with 30" barrel only, blued, non-reflective overall finish. Interchangeable CV choke tube system includes Skeet, Imp. Cyl., Mod. Full tubes. Introduced 1995. Made in U.S. by Connecticut Valley Classics.
Price: $2,995.00

SHOTGUNS—OVER/UNDERS

CHARLES DALY FIELD GRADE O/U
Gauge: 12 or 20, 3" chambers.
Barrel: 12- and 20- ga.—26" (Imp. Cyl. & Mod.), 12-ga.—28" (Mod. & Full).
Weight: 6 lbs., 15 oz. (12-ga.); 6 lbs., 10 oz. (20-ga.). **Length:** 43½" overall (26").
Stock: 14⅛"x1⅜"x2⅜". Walnut with cut-checkered grip and forend. Black, vent. rubber recoil pad. Semi-gloss finish.
Features: Boxlock action with manual safety; extractors; single selective trigger. Color case-hardened receiver with engraving. Introduced 1989. Imported from Europe by Outdoor Sports Headquarters.
Price: $545.00
Price: Sporting Clays model (12-ga., 30", choke tubes) $895.00

Charles Daly Deluxe Over/Under
Similar to the Field Grade except available in 12 and 20 gauge, has automatic selective ejectors, antique silver finish on frame, and has choke tubes for Imp. Cyl., Mod. and Full. Introduced 1989.
Price: $770.00

HATFIELD UPLANDER OVER/UNDER SHOTGUN
Gauge: 20, 28, 3" chambers.
Barrel: 26" (Imp. Cyl. & Mod.).
Weight: 5 lbs., 4 oz.
Stock: Straight English grip of special select XXX fancy walnut; hand-checkered grip and forend; hand-rubbed oil finish.
Features: Boxlock action with single selective trigger; half-coverage hand engraving; French gray finish. Comes with English-style oxblood leather luggage case with billiard felt interior. Special engraving, stock dimensions, metal finish available. Introduced 1994. From Hatfield Gun Co.
Price: Grade I $3,749.00

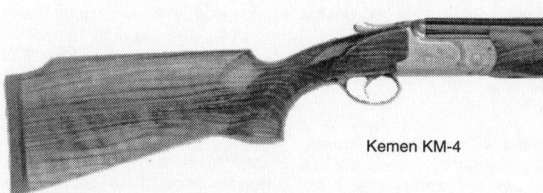
Kemen KM-4

HHF MODEL 101 B 12 ST TRAP O/U
Gauge: 12, 3" chambers.
Barrel: 30", fixed chokes or choke tubes; 16mm rib.
Weight: About 8 lbs.
Stock: Circassian walnut to trap dimensions; Monte Carlo comb, palm swell grip, recoil pad.
Features: Single selective trigger; manual safety; automatic ejectors or extractors. Many custom features available. Silvered frame with 50 percent engraving coverage. Introduced 1995. Imported from Turkey by Turkish Firearms Corp.
Price: With extractors $1,050.00
Price: With ejectors $1,680.00
Price: Model 101 B 12 AT-DT (trap combo, 32" barrels) $2,295.00

KEMEN OVER/UNDER SHOTGUNS
Gauge: 12, 2¾" or 3" chambers.
Barrel: 27⅝" (Hunting, Pigeon, Sporting Clays, Skeet), 30", 32" (Sporting Clays, Trap).
Weight: 7.25 to 8.5 lbs.
Stock: Dimensions to customer specs. High grade walnut.
Features: Drop-out trigger assembly; ventilated flat or step top rib, ventilated, solid or no side ribs. Low-profile receiver with black finish on Standard model, antique silver on sideplate models and all engraved, gold inlaid models. Barrels, forend, trigger parts interchangeable with Perazzi. Comes with hard case, accessory tools, spares. Introduced 1989. Imported from Spain by U.S.A. Sporting Clays.
Price: KM-4 Standard $6,179.00
Price: KM-4 Luxe-A (engraved scroll), Luxe-B (game scenes) $10,644.00
Price: KM-4 Super Luxe (engraved game scene) $12,064.00
Price: KM-4 Extra Luxe-A (scroll engraved sideplates) $13,960.00
Price: KM-4 Extra Luxe-B (game scene sideplates) $16,030.00
Price: KM-4 Extra Gold (inlays, game scene) $19,607.00

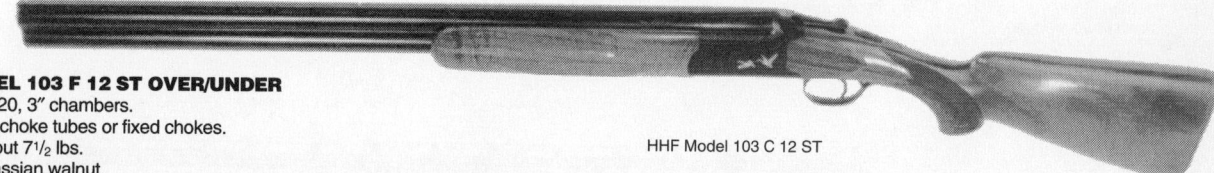
HHF Model 103 C 12 ST

HHF MODEL 103 F 12 ST OVER/UNDER
Gauge: 12, 20, 3" chambers.
Barrel: 28", choke tubes or fixed chokes.
Weight: About 7½ lbs.
Stock: Circassian walnut.
Features: Boxlock action with dummy sideplates. Single selective trigger; manual safety; extractors. Can be ordered with many custom options. Has 100 percent engraving coverage, inlaid animals on blackened sideplates. Introduced 1995. Imported from Turkey by Turkish Firearms Corp.
Price: With extractors $1,120.00
Price: With automatic ejectors $1,750.00
Price: Model 103 C 12 ST (black receiver, 50 percent engraving coverage, extractors) $1,050.00
Price: As above, ejectors $1,680.00
Price: Model 103 D 12 ST (standard boxlock with 80 percent engraving coverage, extractors) $1,050.00
Price: As above, ejectors $1,680.00
Price: Model 103 B 12 ST (double triggers, extractors, 80 percent engraving coverage, fixed chokes) $995.00
Price: As above, 28, 410 ....$1,550.00
Price: With choke tubes, extractors (12, 20) $1,050.00

HHF MODEL 104 A 12 ST OVER/UNDER
Gauge: 12, 3" chambers.
Barrel: 28", fixed chokes or choke tubes.
Weight: About 7½ lbs.
Stock: Circassian walnut, field dimensions.
Features: Boxlock action with manual safety, extractors, double triggers. Silvered, engraved receiver. Has 15 percent engraving coverage. Introduced 1995. Imported from Turkey by Turkish Firearms Corp.
Price: Fixed chokes, extractors $925.00
Price: As above, 28, 410 ....$1,295.00
Price: Choke tubes, ejectors (12, 20) $925.00

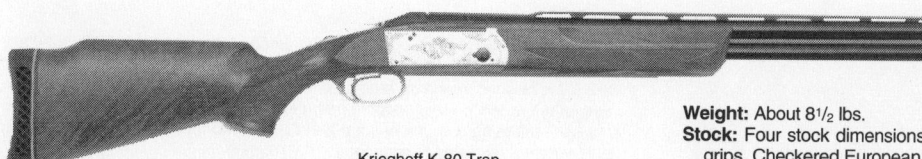
Krieghoff K-80 Trap

KRIEGHOFF K-80 O/U TRAP SHOTGUN
Gauge: 12, 2¾" chambers.
Barrel: 30", 32" (Imp. Mod. & Full or choke tubes).
Weight: About 8½ lbs.
Stock: Four stock dimensions or adjustable stock available; all have palm-swell grips. Checkered European walnut.
Features: Satin nickel receiver. Selective mechanical trigger, adjustable for position. Ventilated step rib. Introduced 1980. Imported from Germany by Krieghoff International, Inc.
Price: K-80 O/U (30", 32", Imp. Mod. & Full), from $7,100.00
Price: K-80 Unsingle (32", 34", Full), Standard, from $7,650.00
Price: K-80 Combo (two-barrel set), Standard, from $9,970.00

CAUTION: PRICES SHOWN ARE SUPPLIED BY THE MANUFACTURER OR IMPORTER. CHECK YOUR LOCAL GUNSHOP.

SHOTGUNS—OVER/UNDERS

Krieghoff K-80 Sporting Clays

KRIEGHOFF K-80 SKEET SHOTGUN
Gauge: 12, 2¾" chambers.
Barrel: 28" (Skeet & Skeet, optional Tula or choke tubes).
Weight: About 7¾ lbs.
Stock: American Skeet or straight Skeet stocks, with palm-swell grips. Walnut.
Features: Satin gray receiver finish. Selective mechanical trigger adjustable for position. Choice of ventilated 8mm parallel flat rib or ventilated 8-12mm tapered flat rib. Introduced 1980. Imported from Germany by Krieghoff International, Inc.
Price: Standard, Skeet chokes $6,650.00
Price: As above, Tula chokes $7,450.00
Price: Lightweight model (weighs 7 lbs.), Standard $6,650.00
Price: Two-Barrel Set (tube concept), 12-ga., Standard $11,305.00
Price: Skeet Special (28", tapered flat rib, Skeet & Skeet choke tubes) $7,300.00

Krieghoff K-80 Four-Barrel Skeet Set
Similar to the Standard Skeet except comes with barrels for 12, 20, 28, 410. Comes with fitted aluminum case.
Price: Standard grade $15,950.00

LAURONA SILHOUETTE 300 SPORTING CLAYS
Gauge: 12, 2¾" or 3" chambers.
Barrel: 28", 29" (Multichoke tubes, flush-type or knurled).
Weight: 7 lbs., 12 oz.
Stock: 14⅜"x1⅜"x2½". European walnut with full pistol grip, beavertail forend. Rubber buttpad.
Features: Selective single trigger, automatic selective ejectors. Introduced 1988. Imported from Spain by Galaxy Imports.
Price: $1,250.00
Price: Silhouette Ultra-Magnum, 3½" chambers $1,265.00

Laurona Silhouette 300 Trap
Same gun as the Silhouette 300 Sporting Clays except has 29" barrels, trap stock dimensions of 14⅜"x1⁷⁄₁₆"x1⅝", weighs 7 lbs., 15 oz. Available with flush or knurled Multichokes.
Price: $1,310.00

KRIEGHOFF K-80 SPORTING CLAYS O/U
Gauge: 12.
Barrel: 28", 30" or 32" with choke tubes.
Weight: About 8 lbs.
Stock: #3 Sporting stock designed for gun-down shooting.
Features: Choice of standard or lightweight receiver with satin nickel finish and classic scroll engraving. Selective mechanical trigger adjustable for position. Choice of tapered flat or 8mm parallel flat barrel rib. Free-floating barrels. Aluminum case. Imported from Germany by Krieghoff International, Inc.
Price: Standard grade with five choke tubes $7,850.00

Krieghoff K-80/RT Shotguns
Same as the standard K-80 shotguns except has a removable internally selective trigger mechanism. Can be considered an option on all K-80 guns of any configuration. Introduced 1990.
Price: RT (removable trigger) option on K-80 guns, add $1,000.00
Price: Extra pull trigger mechanisms $1,275.00

Krieghoff K-80 International Skeet
Similar to the Standard Skeet except has ½" ventilated Broadway-style rib, special Tula chokes with gas release holes at muzzle. International Skeet stock. Comes in fitted aluminum case.
Price: Standard grade $7,450.00

LAURONA SUPER MODEL OVER/UNDERS
Gauge: 12, 20, 2¾" or 3" chambers.
Barrel: 26", 28" (Multichoke), 29" (Multichokes and Full).
Weight: About 7 lbs.
Stock: European walnut. Dimensions may vary according to model. Full pistol grip.
Features: Boxlock action, silvered with engraving. Automatic selective ejectors; choke tubes available on most models; single selective or twin single triggers; black chrome barrels. Has 5-year warranty, including metal finish. Imported from Spain by Galaxy Imports.
Price: Model 83 MG, 12- or 20-ga. $1,215.00
Price: Model 84S Super Trap (fixed chokes) $1,340.00
Price: Model 85 Super Game, 12- or 20-ga. $1,215.00
Price: Model 85 MS Super Trap (Full/Multichoke) $1,390.00
Price: Model 85 MS Super Pigeon $1,370.00
Price: Model 85 S Super Skeet, 12-ga. $1,300.00

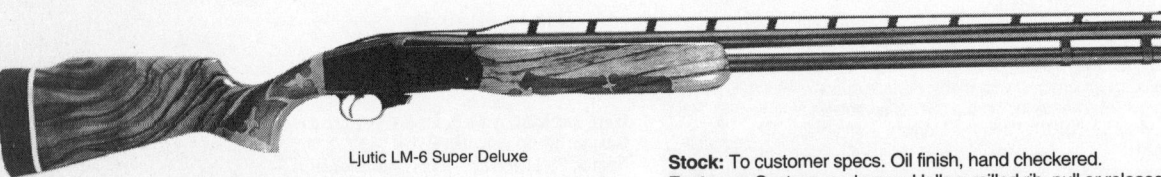
Ljutic LM-6 Super Deluxe

LJUTIC LM-6 SUPER DELUXE O/U SHOTGUN
Gauge: 12.
Barrel: 28" to 34", choked to customer specs for live birds, trap, International Trap.
Weight: To customer specs.
Stock: To customer specs. Oil finish, hand checkered.
Features: Custom-made gun. Hollow-milled rib, pull or release trigger, pushbutton opener in front of trigger guard. From Ljutic Industries.
Price: Super Deluxe LM-6 O/U $19,995.00
Price: Over/under Combo (interchangeable single barrel, two trigger guards, one for single trigger, one for doubles) $26,995.00
Price: Extra over/under barrel sets, 29"-32" $5,995.00

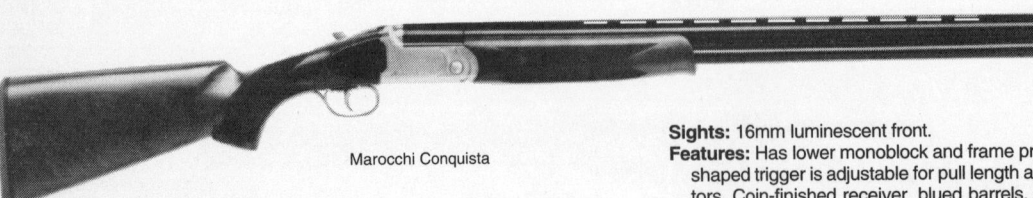
Marocchi Conquista

MAROCCHI CONQUISTA SPORTING CLAYS O/U SHOTGUNS
Gauge: 12, 2¾" chambers.
Barrel: 28", 30", 32" (Contrechoke tubes); 10mm concave vent. rib.
Weight: About 8 lbs.
Stock: 14½"-14⅞"x2³⁄₁₆"x1⁷⁄₁₆"; American walnut with checkered grip and forend; Sporting Clays butt pad.
Sights: 16mm luminescent front.
Features: Has lower monoblock and frame profile. Fast lock time. Ergonomically-shaped trigger is adjustable for pull length and weight. Automatic selective ejectors. Coin-finished receiver, blued barrels. Comes with five choke tubes, hard case, stock wrench. Also available as true left-hand model—opening lever operates from left to right; stock has left-hand cast. Introduced 1994. Imported from Italy by Precision Sales International.
Price: Grade I, right-hand $1,895.00
Price: Grade I, left-hand $1,945.00
Price: Grade II, right-hand $2,285.00
Price: Grade II, left-hand $2,335.00
Price: Grade III, right-hand, from $3,250.00
Price: Grade III, left-hand, from $3,350.00

SHOTGUNS—OVER/UNDERS

Marocchi Lady Sport O/U Shotgun
Ergonomically designed specifically for women shooters. Similar to the Conquista Sporting Clays model except has 28" or 30" barrels with five Contrechoke tubes, stock dimensions of 13 7/8"-14 1/4"x1 11/32"x2 9/32"; weighs about 7 1/2 lbs. Also available as left-hand model—opening lever operates from left to right; stock has left-hand cast. Also available with colored graphics finish on frame and opening lever. Introduced 1995. Imported from Italy by Precision Sales International.
- Price: Grade I, right-hand $1,945.00
- Price: Grade II, right-hand $2,335.00
- Price: Grade III, right-hand, from $3,350.00
- Price: Left-hand, add (all grades) $50.00
- Price: Colored graphics frame (Grade I only), add $50.00

Marocchi Conquista Trap Over/Under Shotgun
Similar to the Conquista Sporting Clays model except has 30" or 32" barrels choked Full & Full, stock dimensions of 14 1/2"-14 7/8"x1 11/16"x1 9/32"; weighs about 8 1/4 lbs. Introduced 1994. Imported from Italy by Precision Sales International.
- Price: Grade I, right-hand $1,895.00
- Price: Grade II, right-hand $2,285.00
- Price: Grade III, right-hand, from $3,250.00

Marocchi Conquista Skeet Over/Under Shotgun
Similar to the Conquista Sporting Clays except has 28" (Skeet & Skeet) barrels, stock dimensions of 14 3/8"-14 3/4"x2 3/16"x1 1/2". Weighs about 7 3/4 lbs. Introduced 1994. Imported from Italy by Precision Sales International.
- Price: Grade I, right-hand $1,895.00
- Price: Grade II, right-hand $2,285.00
- Price: Grade III, right-hand, from $3,250.00

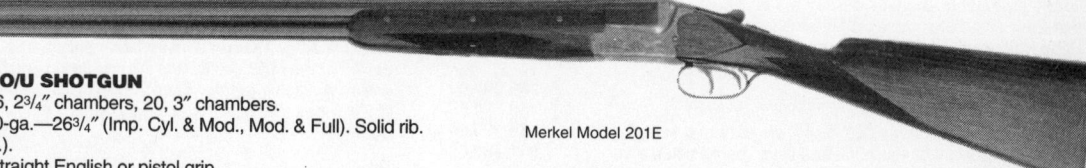

Merkel Model 201E

MERKEL MODEL 200E O/U SHOTGUN
Gauge: 12, 3" chambers, 16, 2 3/4" chambers, 20, 3" chambers.
Barrel: 12-, 16-ga.—28"; 20-ga.—26 3/4" (Imp. Cyl. & Mod., Mod. & Full). Solid rib.
Weight: About 7 lbs. (12-ga.).
Stock: Oil-finished walnut; straight English or pistol grip.
Features: Scroll engraved, color case-hardened receiver. Single selective or double triggers; ejectors. Imported from Germany by GSI.
- Price: Model 200E $3,395.00
- Price: Model 201E (as above except silver-grayed receiver with engraved hunting scenes, also 28-ga.) $4,895.00
- Price: Model 202E (as above except has false sideplates, fine hunting scenes with Arabesque engraving) $8,895.00

Merkel Model 200E Skeet, Trap Over/Unders
Similar to the Model 200E except in 12-gauge only with 2 3/4" chambers, tapered ventilated rib, competition stock with full pistol grip, half-coverage Arabesque engraving on silver-grayed receiver. Single selective trigger only. Model 200ES has 26 3/4" (Skeet & Skeet) barrels; Model 200ET has 30" (Full & Full) barrels. Imported from Germany by GSI.
- Price: Model 200ET $4,895.00
- Price: Model 201ES (full-coverage engraving) $7,495.00
- Price: Model 201ET (full-coverage engraving) $7,495.00
- Price: Model 203ES (sidelock action, Skeet) $12,950.00
- Price: Model 203ET (sidelock action, Trap) $12,950.00

Merkel Model 200 SC Sporting Clays O/U
Similar to the Model 200E except has 30" barrels with lengthened forcing cones, five Briley choke tubes. Kersten double cross-bolt lock, color case-hardened receiver, Blitz action; single selective trigger adjustable for length of pull. Select grade stock with competition recoil pad; tapered vent. rib. Comes with fitted luggage case. Introduced 1995. Imported from Germany by GSI.
- Price: $7,495.00
- Price: With fixed Imp. Cyl. and light mod. chokes $6,995.00

Merkel Model 203E, 303E Over/Under Shotguns
Similar to the Model 200E except with Holland & Holland-style sidelocks, both quick-detachable: Model 203E with cranked screw, 303E with integral retracting hook. Model 203E has coil spring ejectors; 303E H&H ejectors. Both have silver-grayed receiver with English-style Arabesque engraving—large scrolls on 203E, medium on 303E. Imported from Germany by GSI.
- Price: Model 203E $10,695.00
- Price: Model 303E $19,950.00

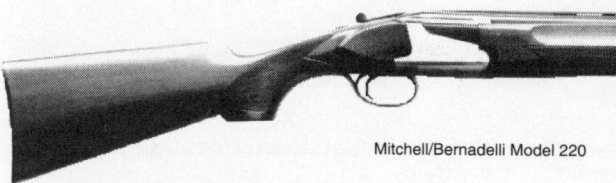

Mitchell/Bernadelli Model 220

Mitchell/Bernadelli Model 115 Over/Under Shotgun
Similar to the Model 192 except designed for competition shooting with thicker barrel walls, specially designed stock with anatomical grip. Leather-faced recoil pad and schnabel forend on Sporting Clays and Skeet guns. Concave top rib, ventilated middle rib. Imported from Italy by Mitchell Arms.
- Price: Model 115 S (inclined-plane locking, ejectors, selective or non-selective trigger, Multichoke standard on Sporting Clays) $2,895.00
- Price: Model 115 S Trap/Skeet $2,799.00

MITCHELL/BERNARDELLI MODEL 192 MS-MC O/U SHOTGUN
Gauge: 12, 2 3/4" chambers.
Barrel: 25 1/2" (Imp. Cyl. & Imp. Mod., Cyl. & Mod.), 26 3/4" (Imp. Cyl. & Imp. Mod., Mod. & Full), 28" (Mod. & Full), 29 1/2" (Imp. Mod. & Full); or with Multichoke tubes.
Weight: About 7 lbs.
Stock: 14"x1 3/8"x2 3/8". Hand-checkered European walnut. English or pistol grip style.
Features: Boxlock action; single selective trigger. Silvered, engraved action. Imported from Italy by Mitchell Arms.
- Price: With Multichokes $1,340.00
- Price: Model 192 Waterfowler (3 1/2" chambers, three Multichoke tubes) $1,460.00
- Price: Model 192 MS (Sporting Clays, non-selective or selective trigger) $2,140.00
- Price: Model 220 MS (similar to M192 except 20-ga., different frame) .. $1,490.00
- Price: Model 220 (20-ga., 3" chambers) $1,420.00

Mitchell/Bernadelli Model 220

Perazzi Mirage Special Four-Gauge Skeet
Similar to the Mirage Sporting model except has Skeet dimensions, interchangeable, adjustable four-position trigger assembly. Comes with four barrel sets in 12, 20, 28, 410, flat 5/16"x5/16" rib.
- Price: From $19,385.00

PERAZZI MIRAGE SPECIAL SPORTING O/U
Gauge: 12, 2 3/4" chambers.
Barrel: 28 3/8" (Imp. Mod. & Extra Full), 29 1/2" (choke tubes).
Weight: 7 lbs., 12 oz.
Stock: Special specifications.
Features: Has single selective trigger; flat 7/16"x5/16" vent. rib. Many options available. Imported from Italy by Perazzi U.S.A., Inc.
- Price: $9,160.00

CAUTION: PRICES SHOWN ARE SUPPLIED BY THE MANUFACTURER OR IMPORTER. CHECK YOUR LOCAL GUNSHOP.

SHOTGUNS—OVER/UNDERS

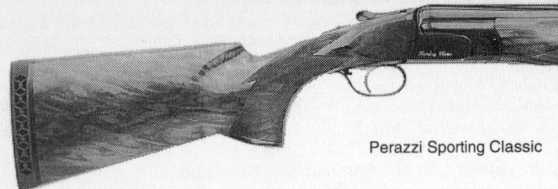

Perazzi Sporting Classic

PERAZZI MX8/MX8 SPECIAL TRAP, SKEET
Gauge: 12, 2³/₄" chambers.
Barrel: Trap—29¹/₂" (Imp. Mod. & Extra Full), 31¹/₂" (Full & Extra Full). Choke tubes optional. Skeet—27⁵/₈" (Skeet & Skeet).
Weight: About 8¹/₂ lbs. (Trap); 7 lbs., 15 oz. (Skeet).
Stock: Interchangeable and custom made to customer specs.
Features: Has detachable and interchangeable trigger group with flat V springs. Flat ⁷/₁₆" ventilated rib. Many options available. Imported from Italy by Perazzi U.S.A., Inc.
Price: From $8,090.00
Price: MX8 Special (adj. four-position trigger), from $8,570.00
Price: MX8 Special Single (32" or 34" single barrel, step rib), from $8,300.00
Price: MX8 Special Combo (o/u and single barrel sets), from $11,280.00

PERAZZI MX10 OVER/UNDER SHOTGUN
Gauge: 12, 2³/₄" chambers.
Barrel: 29.5", 31.5" (fixed chokes).
Weight: NA.
Stock: Walnut; cheekpiece adjustable for elevation and cast.
Features: Comes with six pattern adjustment rib inserts. Vent. side rib. Externally selective trigger. Available in single barrel, combo, over/under trap, Skeet, pigeon and sporting models. Introduced 1993. Imported from Italy by Perazzi U.S.A., Inc.
Price: From $10,300.00

PERAZZI MX28, MX410 GAME O/U SHOTGUNS
Gauge: 28, 2³/₄" chambers, 410, 3" chambers.
Barrel: 26" (Imp. Cyl. & Full).
Weight: NA.
Stock: To customer specifications.
Features: Made on scaled-down frames proportioned to the gauge. Introduced 1993. Imported from Italy by Perazzi U.S.A., Inc.
Price: From $16,170.00

Perazzi Sporting Classic O/U
Same as the Mirage Special Sporting except is deluxe version with select wood and engraving. Available with flush mount choke tubes, 29.5" barrels. Introduced 1993.
Price: From $10,200.00

Perazzi Mirage Special Skeet Over/Under
Similar to the MX8 Skeet except has adjustable four-position trigger, Skeet stock dimensions.
Price: From $8,570.00

Perazzi MX8/20 Over/Under Shotgun
Similar to the MX8 except has smaller frame and has a removable trigger mechanism. Available in trap, Skeet, sporting or game models with fixed chokes or choke tubes. Stock is made to customer specifications. Introduced 1993.
Price: From $8,090.00

PERAZZI MX12 HUNTING OVER/UNDER
Gauge: 12, 2³/₄" chambers.
Barrel: 26", 27⁵/₈", 28³/₈", 29¹/₂" (Mod. & Full); choke tubes available in 27⁵/₈", 29¹/₂" only (MX12C).
Weight: 7 lbs., 4 oz.
Stock: To customer specs; Interchangeable.
Features: Single selective trigger; coil springs used in action; schnabel forend tip. Imported from Italy by Perazzi U.S.A., Inc.
Price: From $8,090.00
Price: MX12C (with choke tubes), from $8,680.00

Perazzi MX20 Hunting Over/Under
Similar to the MX12 except 20-ga. frame size. Available in 20, 28, 410 with 2³/₄" or 3" chambers. 26" standard, and choked Mod. & Full. Weight is 6 lbs., 6 oz.
Price: From $8,090.00
Price: MX20C (as above, 20-ga. only, choke tubes), from $8,680.00

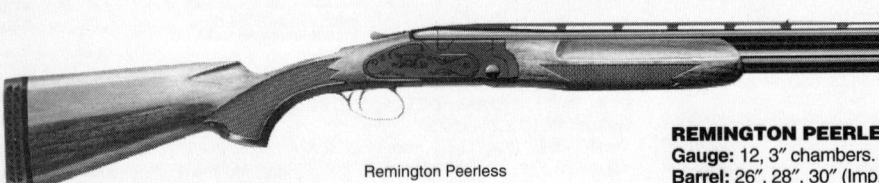

Remington Peerless

REMINGTON PEERLESS OVER/UNDER SHOTGUN
Gauge: 12, 3" chambers.
Barrel: 26", 28", 30" (Imp. Cyl., Mod., Full Rem Chokes).
Weight: 7¹/₄ lbs. (26" barrels). **Length:** 43" overall (26" barrels).
Stock: 14³/₁₆"x1¹/₂"x2¹/₄". American walnut with Imron gloss finish, cut-checkered grip and forend. Black, ventilated recoil pad.
Features: Boxlock action with removable sideplates. Gold-plated, single selective trigger, automatic safety, automatic ejectors. Fast lock time. Mid-rib bead, Bradley-type front. Polished blue finish with light scrollwork on sideplates, Remington logo on bottom of receiver. Introduced 1993.
Price: $1,225.00

PIOTTI BOSS OVER/UNDER SHOTGUN
Gauge: 12, 20.
Barrel: 26" to 32", chokes as specified.
Weight: 6.5 to 8 lbs.
Stock: Dimensions to customer specs. Best quality figured walnut.
Features: Essentially a custom-made gun with many options. Introduced 1993. Imported from Italy by Wm. Larkin Moore.
Price: From $36,600.00

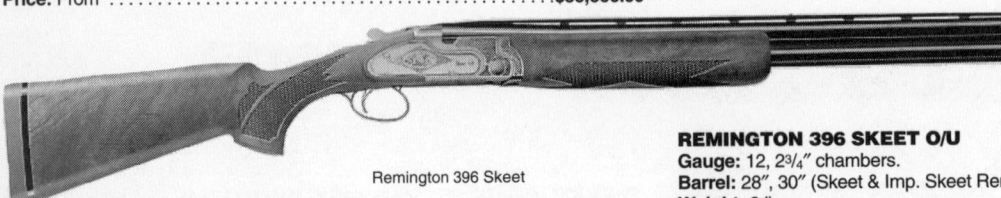

Remington 396 Skeet

Remington 396 Sporting O/U
Similar to the 396 Skeet except the 28", 30" barrels are factory ported, and come with Skeet, Imp. Skeet, Imp. Cyl. and Mod. Rem Choke tubes. Made in U.S. by Remington. Introduced 1996.
Price: $2,659.00

REMINGTON 396 SKEET O/U
Gauge: 12, 2³/₄" chambers.
Barrel: 28", 30" (Skeet & Imp. Skeet Rem. Choke tubes).
Weight: 8 lbs.
Stock: 14³/₁₆"x1¹/₂"x2¹/₄". Fancy, figured American walnut. Target-style forend, larger-radius comb, grip palm swell.
Features: Boxlock action with removable sideplates. Barrels have lengthened forcing cones; 10mm non-stepped, parallel rib; engraved receiver, sideplates, trigger guard, top lever, forend iron are finished with gray nitride. Made in U.S. by Remington. Introduced 1996.
Price: $2,526.00

SHOTGUNS—OVER/UNDERS

RIZZINI AURUM OVER/UNDER SHOTGUN
Gauge: 12, 16, 20, 28, 410.
Barrel: 26", 27½", Mod. & Full, Imp. Cyl. & Imp. Mod. choke tubes.
Weight: About 6.6 lbs.
Stock: 14"x1½"x2⅛".
Features: Boxlock action; single selective trigger; ejectors; profuse engraving on silvered receiver. Comes with fitted case. Introduced 1996. Imported from Italy by Wm. Larkin Moore & Co.
Price: From $1,875.00

Rizzini Artemis Over/Under Shotgun
Same as the Aurum model except has dummy sideplates with extensive game scene engraving. Fancy European walnut stock. Comes with fitted case. Introduced 1996. Imported from Italy by Wm. Larkin Moore & Co.
Price: From $2,120.00

RIZZINI S782 EMEL OVER/UNDER SHOTGUN
Gauge: 12, 2¾" chambers.
Barrel: 26", 27.5" (Imp. Cyl. & Imp. Mod.).
Weight: About 6.75 lbs.
Stock: 14"x1½"x2⅛". Extra fancy select walnut.
Features: Boxlock action with dummy sideplates; extensive engraving with gold inlaid game birds; silvered receiver; automatic ejectors; single selective trigger. Comes with Nizzoli leather case. Introduced 1996. Imported from Italy by Wm. Larkin Moore & Co.
Price: From $10,300.00

ROTTWEIL PARAGON OVER/UNDER
Gauge: 12, 2¾" chambers.
Barrel: 28", 30", five choke tubes.
Weight: 7 lbs.
Stock: 14½"x1½"x2½"; European walnut.

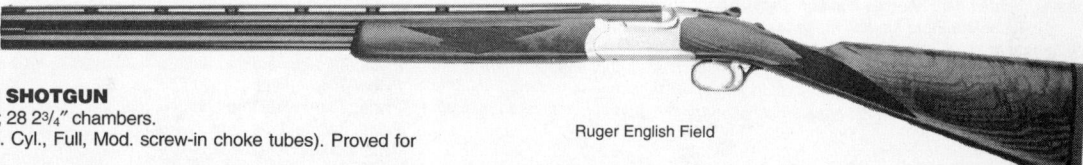
Ruger English Field

RUGER RED LABEL O/U SHOTGUN
Gauge: 12, 20, 3" chambers; 28 2¾" chambers.
Barrel: 26", 28" (Skeet, Imp. Cyl., Full, Mod. screw-in choke tubes). Proved for steel shot.
Weight: About 7 lbs. (20-ga.); 7½ lbs. (12-ga.). **Length:** 43" overall (26" barrels).
Stock: 14"x1½"x2½". Straight grain American walnut. Checkered pistol grip and forend, rubber butt pad.
Features: Choice of blue or stainless receiver. Single selective mechanical trigger, selective automatic ejectors; serrated free-floating vent. rib. Comes with two Skeet, one Imp. Cyl., one Mod., one Full choke tube and wrench. Made in U.S. by Sturm, Ruger & Co.
Price: Red Label with pistol grip stock $1,215.00
Price: English Field with straight-grip stock $1,215.00

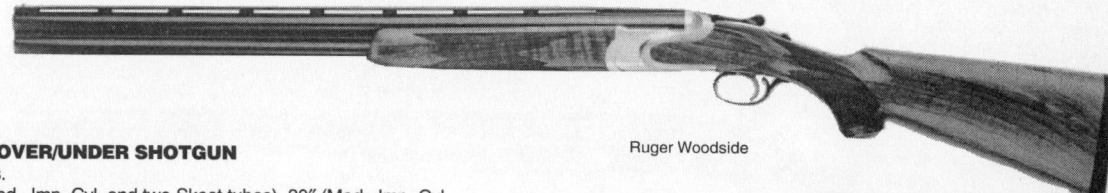
Ruger Woodside

RUGER WOODSIDE OVER/UNDER SHOTGUN
Gauge: 12, 3" chambers.
Barrel: 26", 28" (Full, Mod., Imp. Cyl. and two Skeet tubes), 30" (Mod., Imp. Cyl. and two Skeet tubes).
Weight: 7½ to 8 lbs.
Stock: 14⅛"x1½"x2½". Select Circassian walnut; pistol grip or straight English grip.
Features: Has a newly patented Ruger cocking mechanism for easier, smoother opening. Buttstock extends forward into action as two side panels. Single selective mechanical trigger, selective automatic ejectors; serrated free-floating rib; back-bored barrels with stainless steel choke tubes. Blued barrels, stainless steel receiver. Engraved action available. Introduced 1995. Made in U.S. by Sturm, Ruger & Co.
Price: $1,675.00
Price: Woodside Sporting Clays (30" barrels) $1,675.00

SABATTI SPORTING CLAYS OVER/UNDER SHOTGUN
Gauge: 12, 3" chambers.
Barrel: 28", five ICT choke tubes.
Weight: 7.3 lbs.
Stock: Checkered European walnut; solid rubber butt pad.
Features: Blued, engraved receiver; single selective trigger; automatic ejectors; automatic safety. Introduced 1996. Imported from italy by K.B.I., Inc.
Price: $809.00

Sabatti Trap O/U Shotgun
Similar to the Sporting Clays model except has 30" Imp. Mod. & Full barrels, trap stock dimensions; weighs 8 lbs.; 2¾" chambers. Introduced 1996. Imported from Italy by K.B.I., Inc.
Price: $819.00

RIZZINI S790 SPORTING EL OVER/UNDER
Gauge: 12, 2¾" chambers.
Barrel: 28", 29.5", Imp. Mod., Mod., Full choke tubes.
Weight: 8.1 lbs.
Stock: 14"x1½"x2". Extra-fancy select walnut.
Features: Boxlock action; automatic ejectors; single selective trigger; 10mm top rib. Comes with case. Introduced 1996. Imported from Italy by Wm. Larkin Moore & Co.
Price: $3,060.00

RIZZINI S790 EMEL OVER/UNDER SHOTGUN
Gauge: 20, 28, 410.
Barrel: 26", 27.5" (Imp. Cyl. & Imp. Mod.).
Weight: About 6 lbs.
Stock: 14"x1½"x2⅛". Extra-fancy select walnut.
Features: Boxlock action with profuse engraving; automatic ejectors; single selective trigger; silvered receiver. Comes with Nizzoli leather case. Introduced 1996. Imported from Italy by Wm. Larkin Moore & Co.
Price: From $8,750.00

Rizzini S792 EMEL Over/Under Shotgun
Similar to the S790 EMEL except has dummy sideplates with extensive engraving coverage. Comes with Nizzoli leather case. Introduced 1996. Imported from Italy by Wm. Larkin Moore & Co.
Price: From $8,750.00

Features: Boxlock action. Detachable trigger assembly; ejectors can be deactivated; convertible top lever for right- or left-hand use; trigger adjustable for position. Imported from Germany by Dynamit Nobel-RWS, Inc.
Price: $5,995.00

Ruger Sporting Clays O/U Shotgun
Similar to the Red Label except 30" back-bored barrels, stainless steel choke tubes. Weighs 7.75 lbs., overall length 47". Stock dimensions of 14⅛"x1½"x2½". Free-floating serrated vent. rib with brass front and mid-rib beads. No barrel side spacers. Comes with two Skeet, one Imp. Cyl., one Mod. choke tubes. Full and Extra-Full available at extra cost. 12 ga. introduced 1992, 20 ga. introduced 1994.
Price: 12 or 20 ....$1,349.00

Consult our Directory pages for the location of firms mentioned.

Sabatti Skeet O/U Shotgun
Simliar to the Sporting Clays model except 2¾" chambers, 26" Skeet 1 & Skeet 2 barrels; weighs 7 lbs. Introduced 1996. Imported from Italy by K.B.I., Inc.
Price: $799.00

SHOTGUNS—OVER/UNDERS

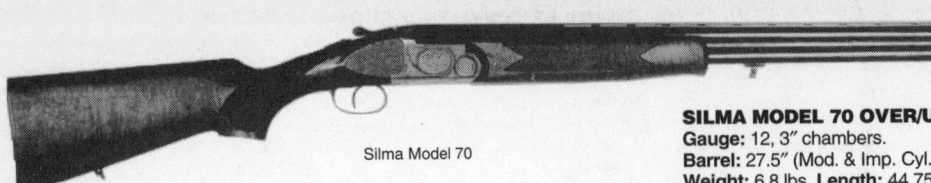
Silma Model 70

SILMA MODEL 70 OVER/UNDER SHOTGUN
Gauge: 12, 3" chambers.
Barrel: 27.5" (Mod. & Imp. Cyl.).
Weight: 6.8 lbs. **Length:** 44.75" overall.
Stock: European walnut.
Features: Engraved, blued boxlock action with single trigger; sling swivels. Introduced 1995. Imported from Italy by Century International Arms.
Price: About $540.00

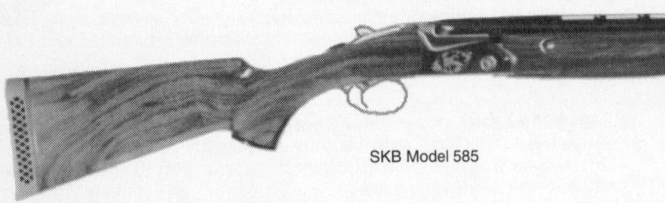
SKB Model 585

SKB Model 585 Waterfowler Shotgun
Similar to the Model 585 Field except 12-gauge only, 28" or 30" barrels with Imp. Cyl., Skeet 1, Mod. Inter-Choke tubes. Bead-blasted receiver with silver nitride finish; bead-blasted, blued barrels. Oil-finished stock and forend. Introduced 1995. Imported from Japan by G.U., Inc.
Price: $1,329.00

SKB Model 585 Youth Model Shotgun
Similar to the Field Model 585 except has 13$\frac{1}{2}$" length of pull. Available in 12-gauge with 26" or 28", or 20-gauge with 26" barrels. The 12-gauge has .755" bores, lengthened forcing cones and competition series choke tubes. Introduced 1994. Imported from Japan by G.U., Inc.
Price: $1,179.00

SKB MODEL 785 OVER/UNDER SHOTGUN
Gauge: 12, 20, 3"; 28, 2$\frac{3}{4}$"; 410, 3".
Barrel: 26", 28", 30", 32" (Inter-Choke tubes).
Weight: 6 lbs., 10 oz. to 8 lbs.
Stock: 14$\frac{1}{8}$"x1$\frac{1}{2}$"x2$\frac{3}{16}$" (Field). Hand-checkered American black walnut with high-gloss finish; semi-beavertail forend. Target stocks available in standard or Monte Carlo styles.
Sights: Metal bead front (Field), target style on Skeet, trap, Sporting Clays models.
Features: Boxlock action with Greener-style cross bolt; single selective chrome-plated trigger, chrome-plated selective ejectors; manual safety. Chrome-plated, over-size, back-bored barrels with lengthened forcing cones. Introduced 1995. Imported from Japan by G.U. Inc.

SKB MODEL 585 OVER/UNDER SHOTGUN
Gauge: 12 or 20, 3"; 28, 2$\frac{3}{4}$"; 410, 3".
Barrel: 12-ga.—26", 28", 30", 32", 34" (Inter-Choke tube); 20-ga.—26", 28" (Inter-Choke tube); 28—26", 28" (Inter-Choke tube); 410—26", 28" (Imp. Cyl. & Mod., Mod. & Full). Ventilated side ribs.
Weight: 6.6 to 8.5 lbs. **Length:** 43" to 51$\frac{3}{8}$" overall.
Stock: 14$\frac{1}{8}$"x1$\frac{1}{2}$"x2$\frac{3}{16}$". Hand checkered walnut with high-gloss finish. Target stocks available in standard and Monte Carlo.
Sights: Metal bead front (field), target style on Skeet, trap, Sporting Clays.
Features: Boxlock action; silver nitride finish with Field or Target pattern engraving; manual safety, automatic ejectors, single selective trigger. All 12-gauge barrels are back-bored, have lengthened forcing cones and longer choke tube system. Sporting Clays models in 12-gauge with 28" or 30" barrels available with optional $\frac{3}{8}$" step-up target-style rib, matte finish, nickel center bead, white front bead. Introduced 1992. Imported from Japan by G.U., Inc.
Price: Field $1,179.00
Price: Two-barrel Field Set, 12 & 20 .... $1,929.00
Price: Two-barrel Field Set, 20 & 28 or 28 & 410 .. $1,989.00
Price: Trap, Skeet $1,279.00
Price: Two-barrel trap combo $1,929.00
Price: Sporting Clays model .... $1,329.00 to $1,379.00
Price: Skeet Set (20, 28, 410) $2,999.00

Price: Field, 12 or 20 .... $1,899.00
Price: Field, 28 or 410 .... $1,949.00
Price: Field set, 12 and 20 .... $2,749.00
Price: Field set, 20 and 28 or 28 and 410 .... $2,819.00
Price: Sporting Clays, 12 or 20 .... $2,029.00
Price: Sporting Clays, 28 .... $2,079.00
Price: Sporting Clays set, 12 and 20 .... $2,889.00
Price: Skeet, 12 or 20 .... $1,949.00
Price: Skeet, 28 or 410 .... $1,999.00
Price: Skeet, three-barrel set, 20, 28, 410 .... $3,929.00
Price: Trap, standard or Monte Carlo $1,949.00
Price: Trap combo, standard or Monte Carlo ... $2,719.00

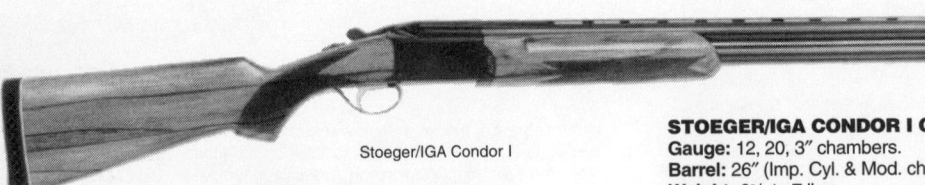
Stoeger/IGA Condor I

STOEGER/IGA CONDOR I OVER/UNDER SHOTGUN
Gauge: 12, 20, 3" chambers.
Barrel: 26" (Imp. Cyl. & Mod. choke tubes), 28" (Mod. & Full choke tubes).
Weight: 6$\frac{3}{4}$ to 7 lbs.
Stock: 14$\frac{1}{2}$"x1$\frac{1}{2}$"x2$\frac{1}{2}$". Oil-finished hardwood with checkered pistol grip and forend.
Features: Manual safety, single trigger, extractors only, ventilated top rib. Introduced 1983. Imported from Brazil by Stoeger Industries.
Price: With choke tubes $500.00
Price: Condor II (sames as Condor I except has double triggers, moulded buttplate) $415.00
Price: Condor Supreme (same as Condor I with single trigger, choke tubes, but with auto. ejectors), 12- or 20-ga., 26", 28" $599.00

Manufacturers' addresses in the
Directory of the Arms Trade
page 313, this issue

TIKKA MODEL 512S FIELD GRADE OVER/UNDER
Gauge: 12, 20, 3" chambers.
Barrel: 26", 28", with stainless steel screw-in chokes (Imp. Cyl, Mod., Imp. Mod., Full); 20-ga., 28" only.
Weight: About 7$\frac{1}{4}$ lbs.
Stock: American walnut. Standard dimensions—13$\frac{9}{10}$"x1$\frac{1}{2}$"x2$\frac{2}{5}$". Checkered pistol grip and forend.
Features: Free interchangeability of barrels, stocks and forends into double rifle model, combination gun, etc. Barrel selector in trigger; auto. top tang safety; barrel cocking indicators. Introduced 1980. Imported from Italy by Stoeger.
Price: Model 512S (ejectors), Field Grade $1,290.00
Price: Model 512S Sporting Clays, 12-ga., 28", choke tubes $1,325.00

SHOTGUNS—OVER/UNDERS

Tristar Model 333

Tristar Model 333SC Over/Under
Same as the Model 333 except has 11mm rib with target sight beads, elongated forcing cones, porter barrels, stainless extended Sporting choke tubes (Skeet, Imp. Cyl., Imp. Cyl., Mod.), Sporting Clays recoil pad. Introduced 1996. Imported from Turkey by Tristar Sporting Arms, Ltd.
Price: $899.95

TRISTAR MODEL 333 OVER/UNDER
Gauge: 12, 20, 3" chambers.
Barrel: 12 ga.—26", 28", 30"; 20 ga.—26", 28"; five choke tubes.
Weight: $7^{1}/_{2}$-$7^{3}/_{4}$ lbs. **Length:** 45" overall.
Stock: Hand-checkered fancy grade Turkish walnut; full pistol grip, semi-beavertail forend; black recoil pad.
Features: Boxlock action with slivered, hand-engraved receiver; automatic selective ejectors, mechanical single selective trigger; stainless steel firing pins; auto safety; hard chrome bores. Introduced 1995. Imported from Turkey by Tristar Sporting Arms, Ltd.
Price: $799.95

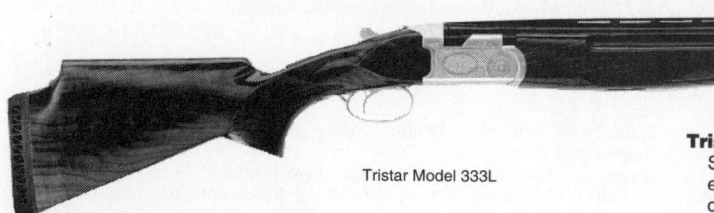

Tristar Model 333L

Tristar Model 333SCL Over/Under
Same as the Model 333SC except has special stock dimensions for female shooters: $13^{1}/_{2}$x$1^{1}/_{2}$"x3"x$^{1}/_{4}$". Introduced 1996. Imported from Turkey by Tristar Sporting Arms, Ltd.
Price: $899.95

Tristar Model 300 Over/Under
Similar to the Model 333 except has standard grade walnut, extractors, etched frame, double triggers, manual safety, plastic buttplate. Available in 12-ga. only with 26" (Imp. Cyl. & Mod.) or 28" (Mod. & Full) barrels. Introduced 1996. Imported from Turkey by Tristar Sporting Arms, Ltd.
Price: $429.95

Tristar Model 333L Over/Under
Same as the Model 333 except has special stock dimensions for female shooters: $13^{1}/_{2}$x$1^{1}/_{2}$"x3"x$^{1}/_{4}$". Available in 12-ga. with 26", 28" or 20 ga. 26", with five choke tubes. Introduced 1996. Imported from Turkey by Tristar Sporting Arms, Ltd.
Price: $799.95

Tristar Model 330 Over/Under
Similar to the Model 333 except has standard grade walnut, etched engraving, fixed chokes, extractors only. Introduced 1996. Imported from Turkey by Tristar Sporting Arms, Ltd.
Price: $549.00
Price: Model 330D (as above except with three choke tubes, ejectors) ..$689.00

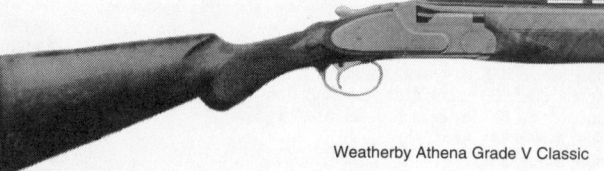

Weatherby Athena Grade V Classic

Weatherby Athena Grade V Classic Field O/U
Similar to the Athena Grade IV except has rounded pistol grip, slender forend, oil-finished Claro walnut stock with fine-line checkering, Old English recoil pad. Sideplate receiver has rose and scroll engraving. Available in 12-gauge, 26", 28", 30", 20-gauge, 26", 28", all with 3" chambers. Introduced 1993.
Price: $2,527.00

WEATHERBY ORION O/U SHOTGUNS
Gauge: 12, 20, 3" chambers.
Barrel: 12-gauge—26", 28", 30"; 20-gauge— 26", 30"; IMC Multi-Choke tubes.
Weight: $6^{1}/_{2}$ to 9 lbs.
Stock: American walnut, checkered grip and forend. Rubber recoil pad. Dimensions for Field and Skeet models, $14^{1}/_{4}$"x$1^{1}/_{2}$"x$2^{1}/_{2}$".
Features: Selective automatic ejectors, single selective mechanical trigger. Top tang safety, Greener cross bolt. Orion I has plain blued receiver, no engraving; Orion III has silver-gray receiver with engraving. Imported from Japan by Weatherby.
Price: Orion I, Field, 12, IMC, 26", 28", 30" $1,289.00
Price: Orion I, Field, 20, IMC, 26", 28" $1,289.00
Price: Orion III, Field, 12, IMC, 26", 28", 30" $1,626.00
Price: Orion III, Field, 20, IMC, 26", 28" $1,626.00

Weatherby Orion II Classic Sporting Clays O/U
Similar to the Orion II Sporting Clays except has rounded pistol grip, slender forend, high-gloss wood finish. Silver-gray nitride receiver has scroll engraving with clay pigeon monogram in gold-plate overlay. Stepped Broadway-style competition vent. rib, vent. side rib. Available in 12-gauge, 28", 30" with choke tubes. Introduced 1993.
Price: $1,460.00

WEATHERBY ATHENA GRADE IV O/U SHOTGUNS
Gauge: 12, 20, 3" chambers.
Action: Boxlock (simulated sidelock) top lever break-open. Selective auto ejectors, single selective trigger (selector inside trigger guard).
Barrel: 26", 28", IMC Multi-Choke tubes.
Weight: 12-ga., $7^{3}/_{8}$ lbs.; 20-ga. $6^{7}/_{8}$ lbs.
Stock: American walnut, checkered pistol grip and forend ($14^{1}/_{4}$"x$1^{1}/_{2}$"x$2^{1}/_{2}$").
Features: Mechanically operated trigger. Top tang safety, Greener cross bolt, fully engraved receiver, recoil pad installed. IMC models furnished with three interchangeable flush-fitting choke tubes. Imported from Japan by Weatherby. Introduced 1982.
Price: 12-ga., IMC, 26", 28" $2,200.00
Price: 20-ga., IMC, 26", 28" $2,200.00

Weatherby Orion II, III Classic Field O/Us
Similar to the Orion II, Orion III except with rounded pistol grip, slender forend, high gloss Claro walnut stock with fine-line checkering, Old English recoil pad. Sideplate receiver has rose and scroll engraving. Available in 12-gauge, 26", 28", 30" (IMC tubes), 20-gauge, 26", 28" (IMC tubes), 28-gauge, 26" (IMC tubes), 3" chambers. Introduced 1993.
Price: Orion II Classic Field $1,363.00
Price: Orion III Classic Field (12 and 20 only) $1,626.00

Weatherby Orion II Sporting Clays O/U
Similar to the Orion II Field except in 12-gauge only with $2^{3}/_{4}$" chambers, 28", 30" barrels with Imp. Cyl., Mod., Full chokes. High-gloss stock finish. Stock dimensions are $14^{1}/_{4}$"x$1^{1}/_{2}$"x$2^{1}/_{4}$"; weighs 7.5 to 8 lbs. Matte finish, competition center vent. rib, mid-barrel and enlarged front beads. Rounded recoil pad. Receiver finished in silver nitride with acid-etched, gold-plate clay pigeon monogram. Barrels have lengthened forcing cones. Introduced 1992.
Price: $1,460.00

SHOTGUNS—SIDE BY SIDES

Variety of models for utility and sporting use, including some competitive shooting.

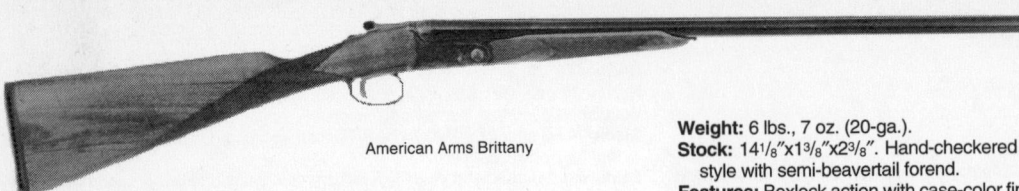

American Arms Brittany

AMERICAN ARMS BRITTANY SHOTGUN
Gauge: 12, 20, 3" chambers.
Barrel: 12-ga.—27"; 20-ga.—25" (Imp. Cyl., Mod., Full choke tubes).
Weight: 6 lbs., 7 oz. (20-ga.).
Stock: 14 1/8"x1 3/8"x2 3/8". Hand-checkered walnut with oil finish, straight English-style with semi-beavertail forend.
Features: Boxlock action with case-color finish, engraving; single selective trigger, automatic selective ejectors; rubber recoil pad. Introduced 1989. Imported from Spain by American Arms, Inc.
Price: $849.00

American Arms Gentry

AMERICAN ARMS GENTRY DOUBLE SHOTGUN
Gauge: 12, 20, 410, 3" chambers; 28 ga. 2 3/4" chambers.
Barrel: 26" (Imp. Cyl. & Mod., all gauges), 28" (Mod., & Full, 12 and 20 gauges).
Weight: 6 1/4 to 6 3/4 lbs.
Stock: 14 1/8"x1 3/8"x2 3/8". Hand-checkered walnut with semi-gloss finish.
Sights: Metal bead front.
Features: Boxlock action with English-style scroll engraving, color case-hardened finish. Double triggers, extractors. Independent floating firing pins. safety. Five-year warranty. Introduced 1987. Imported from Spain by American Arms, Inc.
Price: 12 or 20 ....$725.00
Price: 28 or 410 ....$757.00

AMERICAN ARMS TS/SS 12 DOUBLE
Gauge: 12, 3 1/2" chambers.
Barrel: 26", choke tubes; solid raised rib.
Weight: 7 lbs., 6 oz.
Stock: Walnut; cut-checked grip and forend.
Features: Non-reflective metal and wood finishes; boxlock action; single trigger; extractors. Imported by American Arms, Inc.
Price: $750.00

ARRIETA SIDELOCK DOUBLE SHOTGUNS
Gauge: 12, 16, 20, 28, 410.
Barrel: Length and chokes to customer specs.
Weight: To customer specs.
Stock: 14 1/2"x1 1/2"x2 1/2 (standard dimensions), or to customer specs. Straight English with checkered butt (standard), or pistol grip. Select European walnut with oil finish.
Features: Essentially a custom gun with myriad options. Holland & Holland-pattern hand-detachable sidelocks, selective automatic ejectors, double triggers (hinged front) standard. Some have self-opening action. Finish and engraving to customer specs. Imported from Spain by Wingshooting Adventures.
Price: Model 557, auto ejectors, from $2,750.00
Price: Model 570, auto ejectors, from $3,380.00
Price: Model 578, auto ejectors, from $3,740.00
Price: Model 600 Imperial, self-opening, from $4,990.00
Price: Model 601 Imperial Tiro, self-opening, from $5,750.00
Price: Model 801, from $7,950.00
Price: Model 802, from $7,950.00
Price: Model 803, from $5,850.00
Price: Model 871, auto ejectors, from $4,290.00
Price: Model 872, self-opening, from $9,790.00
Price: Model 873, self-opening, from $6,850.00
Price: Model 874, self-opening, from $7,950.00
Price: Model 875, self-opening, from $12,950.00

Manufacturers' addresses in the
Directory of the Arms Trade
page 313, this issue

ARMSPORT 1050 SERIES DOUBLE SHOTGUNS
Gauge: 12, 20, 410, 28, 3" chambers.
Barrel: 12-ga.—28" (Mod. & Full); 20-ga.—26" (Imp. & Mod.); 410—26" (Full & Full); 28-ga.—26" (Mod. & Full).
Weight: About 6 3/4 lbs.
Stock: European walnut.
Features: Chrome-lined barrels. Boxlock action with engraving. Imported from Italy by Armsport.
Price: 12, 20 ....$785.00
Price: 28, 410 ....$860.00

AYA Model XXV Boxlock

AYA BOXLOCK SHOTGUNS
Gauge: 12, 16, 20, 28, 410.
Barrel: 26", 27", 28", depending upon gauge.
Weight: 5 to 7 lbs.
Stock: European walnut.
Features: Anson & Deeley system with double locking lugs; chopper lump barrels; bushed firing pins; automatic safety and ejectors; articulated front trigger. Imported by Armes de Chasse.
Price: Model 931, self-opening, from $14,500.00
Price: Model XXV, 12 or 20 ....$3,000.00
Price: Model 4 Deluxe, 12, 16, 20, 28, 410 ....$3,000.00
Price: Model 4, 12, 16, 20, 28, 410 ....$1,700.00

ARIZAGA MODEL 31 DOUBLE SHOTGUN
Gauge: 12, 16, 20, 28, 410.
Barrel: 26", 28" (standard chokes).
Weight: 6 lbs., 9 oz. **Length:** 45" overall.
Stock: Straight English style or pistol grip.
Features: Boxlock action with double triggers; blued, engraved receiver. Imported by Mandall Shooting Supplies.
Price: $550.00

SHOTGUNS—SIDE BY SIDES

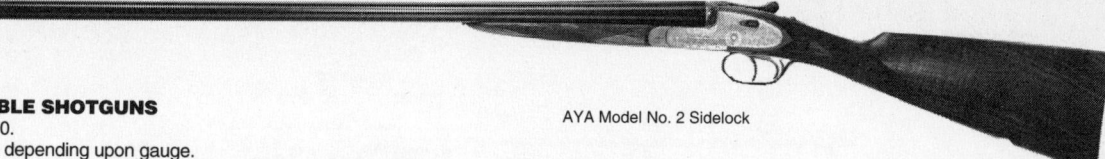

AYA Model No. 2 Sidelock

AYA SIDELOCK DOUBLE SHOTGUNS
Gauge: 12, 16, 20, 28, 410.
Barrel: 26", 27", 28", 29", depending upon gauge.
Weight: NA.
Stock: Figured European walnut; cut checkering; oil finish.
Features: Sidelock actions with double triggers (articulated front), automatic safety, automatic ejectors, cocking indicators, bushed firing pins, replaceable hinge pins, chopper lump barrels. Many options available. Imported by Armes de Chasse.
Price: Model 1, 12 or 20, exhibition-quality wood $6,600.00
Price: Model 2, 12, 16, 20, 28, 410 .... $3,200.00
Price: Model 53, 12, 16, 20 .... $5,000.00
Price: Model 56, 12 only $8,000.00
Price: Model XXV, 12 or 20, Churchill-type rib $4,000.00

BAIKAL IJ-43M DOUBLE SHOTGUN
Gauge: 12, 2 3/4" chambers.
Barrel: 28.5" (Mod. & Full).
Weight: NA. **Length:** 44.5" overall.
Stock: European hardwood.
Features: Blued boxlock action with double triggers, extractors, automatic safety; sling swivels. Chrome-lined bores. Imported from Russia by Century International Arms.
Price: About $255.00
Price: IJ-43EM (automatic ejectors), about $270.00

AUGUSTE FRANCOTTE BOXLOCK SHOTGUN
Gauge: 12, 16, 20, 28 and 410-bore, 2 3/4" or 3" chambers.
Barrel: 26" to 29", chokes to customer specs.
Weight: NA. **Length:** NA.
Stock: Deluxe European walnut to customer specs. Straight or pistol grip; checkered butt; oil finish; splinter or beavertail forend.
Sights: Bead front.
Features: Anson & Deeley boxlock action with double locks, double triggers (front hinged), manual or automatic safety, Holland & Holland ejectors. English scroll engraving, coin finish or color case-hardening. Custom made to customer's specs. Many options available. Imported from Belgium by Armes de Chasse.
Price: From about (no engraving) $16,500.00

BAIKAL IJ-43 DOUBLE SHOTGUN
Gauge: 12, 2 3/4" chambers.
Barrel: 20" (Cyl. & Cyl.), 28" (Mod. & Full).
Weight: About 6.75 lbs.
Stock: Checkered walnut.
Features: Double triggers; extractors; blued, engraved receiver. Reintroduced 1994. Imported from Russia by K.B.I., Inc.
Price: $249.00

BERETTA MODEL 452 SIDELOCK SHOTGUN
Gauge: 12, 2 3/4" or 3" chambers.
Barrel: 26", 28", 30", choked to customer specs.
Weight: 6 lbs., 13 oz.
Stock: Dimensions to customer specs. Highly figured walnut; Model 452 EELL has walnut briar.
Features: Full sidelock action with English-type double bolting; automatic selective ejectors, manual safety; double triggers, single or single non-selective trigger on request. Essentially custom made to specifications. Model 452 is coin finished without engraving; 452 EELL is fully engraved. Imported from Italy by Beretta U.S.A.
Price: 452 .... $22,500.00
Price: 452 EELL $31,000.00

AUGUSTE FRANCOTTE SIDELOCK SHOTGUN
Gauge: 12, 16, 20, 28 and 410-bore, 2 3/4" or 3" chambers.
Barrel: 26" to 29", chokes to customer specs.
Weight: NA. **Length:** NA.
Stock: Deluxe European walnut to customer specs. Straight or pistol grip; checkered butt; oil finish; splinter or beavertail forend.
Sights: Bead front.
Features: True Holland & Holland sidelock action with double locks, double triggers (front hinged), manual or automatic safety, Holland & Holland ejectors. English scroll engraving, coin finish or color case-hardening. Many options available. Imported from Belgium by Armes de Chasse.
Price: From about (no engraving) .... $20,000.00 to $25,000.00

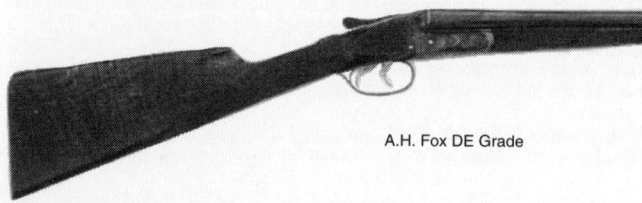

A.H. Fox DE Grade

A.H. FOX SIDE-BY-SIDE SHOTGUNS
Gauge: 16, 20, 28, 410.
Barrel: Length and chokes to customer specifications. Rust-blued Chromox or Krupp steel.
Weight: 5 1/2 to 6 3/4 lbs.
Stock: Dimensions to customer specifications. Hand-checkered Turkish Circassian walnut with hand-rubbed oil finish. Straight, semi- or full pistol grip; splinter, schnabel or beavertail forend; traditional pad, hard rubber buttplate or skeleton butt.
Features: Boxlock action with automatic ejectors; double or Fox single selective trigger. Scalloped, rebated and color case-hardened receiver; hand finished and hand-engraved. Grades differ in engraving, inlays, grade of wood, amount of hand finishing. Introduced 1993. Made in U.S. by Connecticut Shotgun Mfg.
Price: CE Grade $7,200.00
Price: XE Grade $8,500.00
Price: DE Grade $12,500.00
Price: FE Grade $17,500.00
Price: Exhibition Grade $25,000.000
Price: 28/410 CE Grade $8,200.00
Price: 28/410 XE Grade $9,700.00
Price: 28/410 DE Grade $13,800.00
Price: 28/410 FE Grade $14,700.00
Price: 28/410 Exhibition Grade $25,000.00

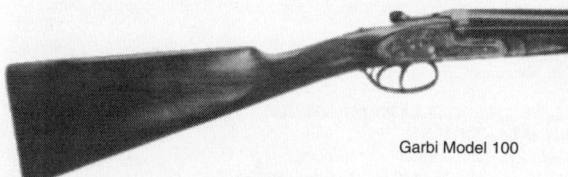

Garbi Model 100

Garbi Model 103A, B Side-by-Side
Similar to the Garbi Model 100 except has Purdey-type fine scroll and rosette engraving. Better overall quality than the Model 101. Model 103B has nickel-chrome steel barrels, H&H-type easy opening mechanism; other mechanical details remain the same. Imported from Spain by Wm. Larkin Moore.
Price: Model 103A, from $7,100.00
Price: Model 103B, from $9,800.00

GARBI MODEL 100 DOUBLE
Gauge: 12, 16, 20, 28.
Barrel: 26", 28", choked to customer specs.
Weight: 5 1/2 to 7 1/2 lbs.
Stock: 14 1/2"x2 1/4"x1 1/2". European walnut. Straight grip, checkered butt, classic forend.
Features: Sidelock action, automatic ejectors, double triggers standard. Color case-hardened action, coin finish optional. Single trigger; beavertail forend, etc. optional. Five other models are available. Imported from Spain by Wm. Larkin Moore.
Price: From $4,500.00

CAUTION: PRICES SHOWN ARE SUPPLIED BY THE MANUFACTURER OR IMPORTER. CHECK YOUR LOCAL GUNSHOP.

SHOTGUNS—SIDE BY SIDES

Garbi Model 101 Side-by-Side
Similar to the Garbi Model 100 except is hand engraved with scroll engraving, select walnut stock. Better overall quality than the Model 100. Imported from Spain by Wm. Larkin Moore.
Price: From $5,800.00

Garbi Model 200 Side-by-Side
Similar to the Garbi Model 100 except has heavy-duty locks, magnum proofed. Very fine Continental-style floral and scroll engraving, well figured walnut stock. Other mechanical features remain the same. Imported from Spain by Wm. Larkin Moore.
Price: $9,375.00

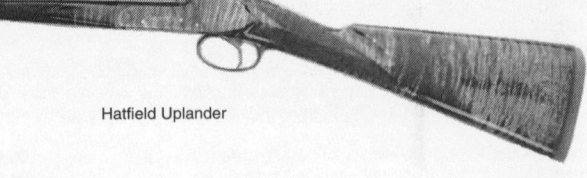
Hatfield Uplander

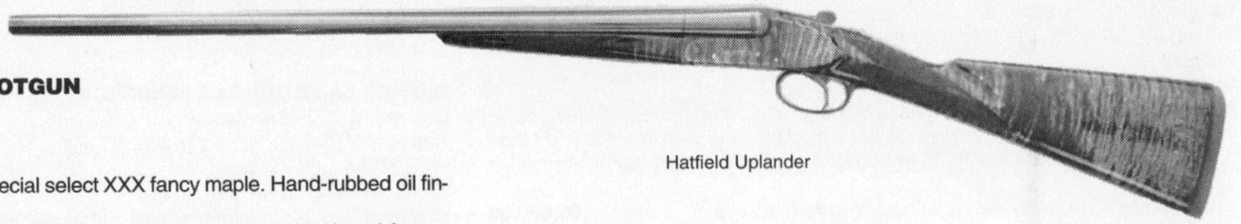

HATFIELD UPLANDER SHOTGUN
Gauge: 20, 3" chambers.
Barrel: 26" (Imp. Cyl. & Mod.).
Weight: 5¾ lbs.
Stock: Straight English style, special select XXX fancy maple. Hand-rubbed oil finish. Splinter forend.
Features: Double locking under-lug boxlock action; color case-hardened frame; single non-selective trigger. Grades differ in engraving, finish, gold work. Introduced 1988. From Hatfield.
Price: Grade I $2,249.00
Price: Grade II $2,995.00

CRUCELEGUI HERMANOS MODEL 150 DOUBLE
Gauge: 12, 16 or 20, 2¾" chambers.
Action: Greener triple cross bolt.
Barrel: 20", 26", 28", 30", 32" (Cyl. & Cyl., Full & Full, Mod. & Full, Mod. & Imp. Cyl., Imp. Cyl. & Full, Mod. & Mod.).
Weight: 5 to 7¼ lbs.
Stock: Hand-checkered walnut, beavertail forend.
Features: Double triggers; color case-hardened receiver; sling swivels; chrome-lined bores. Imported from Spain by Mandall Shooting Supplies.
Price: $450.00

HHF MODEL 200 A 12 ST SIDE-BY-SIDE
Gauge: 12, 3" chambers.
Barrel: 28", fixed chokes or choke tubes.
Weight: About 7½ lbs.
Stock: Circassian walnut, field dimensions.
Features: Boxlock action with single selective trigger, extractors, manual safety. Silvered receiver with 15 percent engraving coverage. Many options available. Introduced 1995. Imported from Turkey by Turkish Firearms Corp.
Price: Fixed chokes, extractors $1,050.00
Price: As above, 28, 410 ....$1,495.00
Price: Choke tubes, extractors $1,050.00
Price: Model 202 A 12 ST (double triggers, 30 percent engraving coverage $1,025.00
Price: As above, 28, 410 ....$1,495.00
Price: With extractors, choke tubes, 12, 20 ....$1,025.00

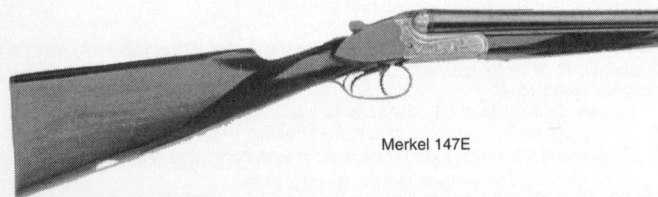
Merkel 147E

Merkel Model 47S, 147S Side-by-Sides
Similar to the Model 122 except with Holland & Holland-style sidelock action with cocking indicators, ejectors. Silver-grayed receiver and sideplates have Arabesque engraving, engraved border and screws (Model 47S), or fine hunting scene engraving (Model 147S). Imported from Germany by GSI.
Price: Model 47S $4,495.00
Price: Model 147S $5,595.00
Price: Model 247S (English-style engraving, large scrolls) $6,895.00
Price: Model 347S (English-style engraving, medium scrolls) $7,895.00
Price: Model 447S (English-style engraving, small scrolls) $8,995.00

MERKEL MODEL 8, 47E SIDE-BY-SIDE SHOTGUNS
Gauge: 12, 3" chambers, 16, 2¾" chambers, 20, 3" chambers.
Barrel: 12-, 16-ga.—28"; 20-ga.—26¾" (Imp. Cyl. & Mod., Mod. & Full).
Weight: About 6¾ lbs. (12-ga.).
Stock: Oil-finished walnut; straight English or pistol grip.
Features: Anson & Deeley-type boxlock action with single selective or double triggers, automatic safety, cocking indicators. Color case-hardened receiver with standard Arabesque engraving. Imported from Germany by GSI.
Price: Model 8 (extractors only) $1,395.00
Price: Model 47E (H&H ejectors) $1,795.00
Price: Model 147 (extractors, silver-grayed receiver with hunting scenes) $1,895.00
Price: Model 147E (as above with ejectors) $2,295.00
Price: Model 122 (as above with false sideplates, fine engraving) $3,795.00

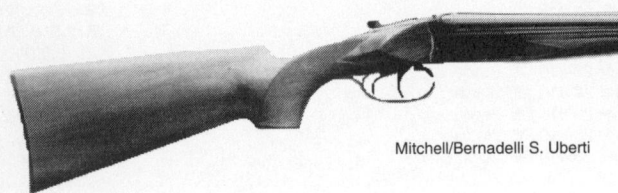
Mitchell/Bernadelli S. Uberti

Mitchell/Bernardelli Series Roma Shotguns
Similar to the Series S. Uberto models except with dummy sideplates to simulate sidelock action. In 12-, 16-, 20-, 28-gauge, 25½", 26¾", 28", 29" barrels. Straight English or pistol grip stock. Chrome-lined barrels, boxlock action, double triggers, ejectors, automatic safety. Checkered butt. Special choke combinations, barrel lengths available. Imported from Italy by Mitchell Arms.
Price: Roma 3, extractors, about $1,470.00
Price: Roma 4, about $1,800.00
Price: Roma 6, about $1,970.00
Price: Roma 7M, ejectors, about $2,750.00
Price: Roma 8M, ejectors, about $3,250.00
Price: Roma 9M, ejectors, about $3,850.00
Price: Las Palomas, 12, 20, about $3,350.00

MITCHELL/BERNARDELLI SERIES S. UBERTO DOUBLES
Gauge: 12, 20, 28, 2¾" or 3" chambers.
Barrel: 25⅝", 26¾", 28", 29½" (Mod. & Full).
Weight: 6 to 6½ lbs.
Stock: 14³⁄₁₆"x2³⁄₈"x1⁹⁄₁₆" standard dimensions. Select walnut with hand checkering.
Features: Anson & Deeley boxlock action with Purdey locks, choice of extractors or ejectors. Custom options available. Imported from Italy by Mitchell Arms.
Price: With ejectors $1,555.00
Price: With extractors $1,435.00
Price: F.S. model, ejectors $1,750.00

MITCHELL/BERNARDELLI HEMINGWAY LIGHTWEIGHT DOUBLES
Gauge: 12, 20, 2¾" or 3", 16, 2¾" chambers.
Barrel: 23½" to 28" (Cyl. & Imp. Cyl. to Mod. & Full).
Weight: 6¼ lbs.
Stock: Straight English grip of checkered European walnut.
Features: Silvered and engraved boxlock action. Folding front trigger on double-trigger models. Ejectors. Imported from Italy by Mitchell Arms.
Price: 12 or 20 ....$1,750.00
Price: With single trigger $1,800.00
Price: Deluxe, double trigger $1,900.00
Price: As above, single trigger $2,000.00

SHOTGUNS—SIDE BY SIDES

PARKER REPRODUCTIONS SIDE-BY-SIDE SHOTGUN
Gauge: 12, 16/20 combo, 20, 28, 2¾" and 3" chambers.
Barrel: 26" (Skeet 1 & 2, Imp. Cyl. & Mod.), 28" (Mod. & Full, 2¾" and 3", 12, 20, 28; Skeet 1 & 2, Imp. Cyl. & Mod., Mod. & Full 16-ga. only).
Weight: 6¾ lbs. (12-ga.)
Stock: Checkered (26 lpi) AAA fancy California English or Claro walnut, skeleton steel and checkered butt. Straight or pistol grip, splinter or beavertail forend.
Features: Exact reproduction of the original Parker—parts interchange. Double or single selective trigger, selective ejectors, hard-chromed bores, designed for steel shot. One, two or three (16-20, 20) barrel sets available. Hand-engraved snap caps included. Introduced 1984. Made by Winchester. Imported from Japan by Parker Division, Reagent Chemical.
Price: D Grade, one-barrel set ... $3,370.00
Price: Two-barrel set, same gauge ... $4,200.00
Price: Two-barrel set, 16/20 ... $4,870.00
Price: Three-barrel set, 16/20/20 ... $5,630.00
Price: A-1 Special two-barrel set ... $11,200.00
Price: A-1 Special three-barrel set ... $13,200.00

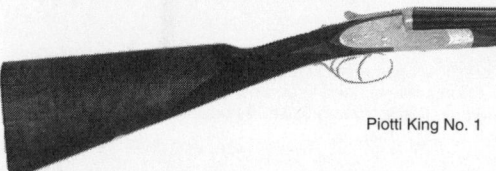
Piotti King No. 1

Piotti Lunik Side-by-Side
Similar to the Piotti King No. 1 except better overall quality. Has Renaissance-style large scroll engraving in relief, gold crown in top lever, gold name and gold crest in forend. Best quality Holland & Holland-pattern sidelock ejector double with chopper lump (demi-bloc) barrels. Other mechanical specifications remain the same. Imported from Italy by Wm. Larkin Moore.
Price: From ... $22,200.00

Piotti King Extra Side-by-Side
Similar to the Piotti King No. 1 except highest quality wood and metal work. Choice of either bulino game scene engraving or game scene engraving with gold inlays. Engraved and signed by a master engraver. Exhibition grade wood. Other mechanical specifications remain the same. Imported from Italy by Wm. Larkin Moore.
Price: From ... $26,500.00

RIZZINI SIDELOCK SIDE-BY-SIDE
Gauge: 12, 16, 20, 28, 410.
Barrel: 25" to 30" (12-, 16-, 20-ga.), 25" to 28" (28, 410). To customer specs. Chokes as specified.
Weight: 6½ lbs. to 8 lbs. (12-ga. to customer specs).
Stock: Dimensions to customer specs. Finely figured walnut; straight grip with checkered butt with classic splinter forend and hand-rubbed oil finish standard. Pistol grip, beavertail forend, satin luster finish optional.
Features: Holland & Holland pattern sidelock action, auto ejectors. Double triggers with front trigger hinged optional; non-selective single trigger standard. Coin finish standard. Top rib level, file cut standard; concave optional. Imported from Italy by Wm. Larkin Moore.
Price: 12-, 20-ga., from ... $43,700.00
Price: 28, 410 bore, from ... $48,700.00

PIOTTI KING NO. 1 SIDE-BY-SIDE
Gauge: 12, 16, 20, 28, 410.
Barrel: 25" to 30" (12-ga.), 25" to 28" (16, 20, 28, 410). To customer specs. Chokes as specified.
Weight: 6½ lbs. to 8 lbs. (12-ga. to customer specs.).
Stock: Dimensions to customer specs. Finely figured walnut; straight grip with checkered butt with classic splinter forend and hand-rubbed oil finish standard. Pistol grip, beavertail forend, satin luster finish optional.
Features: Holland & Holland pattern sidelock action, automatic ejectors. Double trigger with front trigger hinged standard; non-selective single trigger optional. Coin finish standard; color case-hardened optional. Top rib; level, file-cut standard; concave, ventilated optional. Very fine, full coverage scroll engraving with small floral bouquets, gold crown in top lever, name in gold, and gold crest in forend. Imported from Italy by Wm. Larkin Moore.
Price: From ... $20,600.00

PIOTTI PIUMA SIDE-BY-SIDE
Gauge: 12, 16, 20, 28, 410.
Barrel: 25" to 30" (12-ga.), 25" to 28" (16, 20, 28, 410).
Weight: 5½ to 6¼ lbs. (20-ga.).
Stock: Dimensions to customer specs. Straight grip stock with walnut checkered butt, classic splinter forend, hand-rubbed oil finish are standard; pistol grip, beavertail forend, satin luster finish optional.
Features: Anson & Deeley boxlock ejector double with chopper lump barrels. Level, file-cut rib, light scroll and rosette engraving, scalloped frame. Double triggers with hinged front standard, single non-selective optional. Coin finish standard, color case-hardened optional. Imported from Italy by Wm. Larkin Moore.
Price: From ... $11,800.00

> Consult our Directory pages for the location of firms mentioned.

SKB Model 385

SKB MODEL 385 SIDE-BY-SIDE
Gauge: 20, 3" chambers; 28, 2¾" chambers.
Barrel: 26" (Imp. Cyl., Mod., Skeet choke tubes).
Weight: 6¾ lbs. **Length:** 42½" overall.
Stock: 14⅛"x1½"x2½" American walnut with straight or pistol grip stock, semi-beavertail forend.
Features: Boxlock action. Silver nitrided receiver with engraving; solid barrel rib; single selective trigger, selective automatic ejectors, automatic safety. Introduced 1996. Imported from Japan by G.U. Inc.
Price: ... $1,695.00

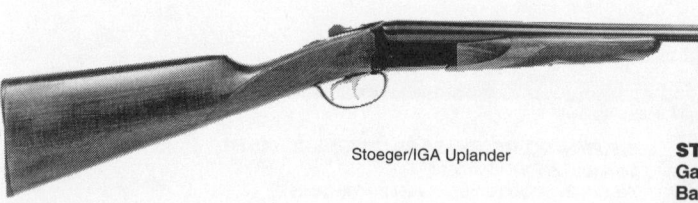
Stoeger/IGA Uplander

STOEGER/IGA UPLANDER SIDE-BY-SIDE SHOTGUN
Gauge: 12, 20, 28, 2¾" chambers; 410, 3" chambers.
Barrel: 26" (Full & Full, 410 only, Imp. Cyl. & Mod.), 28" (Mod. & Full).
Weight: 6¾ to 7 lbs.
Stock: 14½"x1½"x2½". Oil-finished hardwood. Checkered pistol grip and forend.
Features: Automatic safety, extractors only, solid matted barrel rib. Double triggers only. Introduced 1983. Imported from Brazil by Stoeger Industries.
Price: ... $398.00
Price: With choke tubes ... $442.00
Price: Coach Gun, 12, 20, 410, 20" bbls. ... $382.00
Price: Coach Gun, nickel finish, black stock ... $424.00
Price: Coach Gun, engraved stock ... $412.00

Stoeger/IGA English Stock Side-by-Side
Similar to the Uplander except in 410-bore only with 24" barrels (Mod. & Mod.), straight English stock and beavertail forend. Has automatic safety, extractors, double triggers. Intro 1996. Imported from Brazil by Stoeger.
Price: ... $398.00

CAUTION: PRICES SHOWN ARE SUPPLIED BY THE MANUFACTURER OR IMPORTER. CHECK YOUR LOCAL GUNSHOP.

SHOTGUNS—SIDE BY SIDES

Stoeger/IGA Youth Side-by-Side
Similar to the Uplander except in 410-bore with 24" barrels (Mod. & Full), 13" length of pull, ventilated recoil pad. Has double triggers, extractors, auto safety. Intro 1996. Imported from Brazil by Stoeger.
Price: $408.00

Stoeger/IGA Ladies Side-by-Side
Similar to the Uplander except in 20-ga. only with 24" barrels (Imp. Cyl. & Mod. choke tubes), 13" length of pull, ventilated rubber recoil pad. Has extractors, double triggers, automatic safety. Introduced 1996. Imported from Brazil by Stoeger.
Price: $450.00

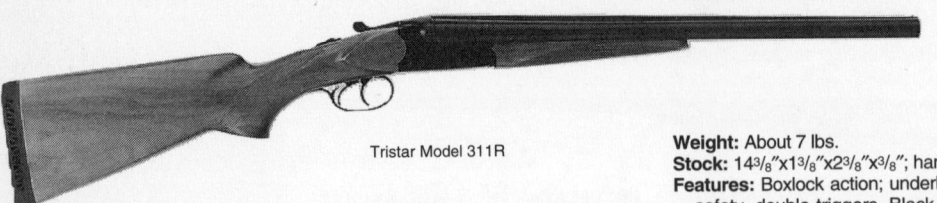
Tristar Model 311R

TRISTAR MODEL 311 DOUBLE
Gauge: 12, 20, 3" chambers.
Barrel: 26", 28", five choke tubes.
Weight: About 7 lbs.
Stock: 14 3/8"x1 3/8"x2 3/8"x3/8"; hand-checkered Turkish walnut; recoil pad.
Features: Boxlock action; underlug and Greener bolt lockup; extractors, manual safety, double triggers. Black chrome finish. Introduced 1996. Imported from Turkey by Tristar Sporting Arms, Ltd.
Price: $599.00
Price: Model 311R (20" Cyl. & Cyl. barrels) $429.00

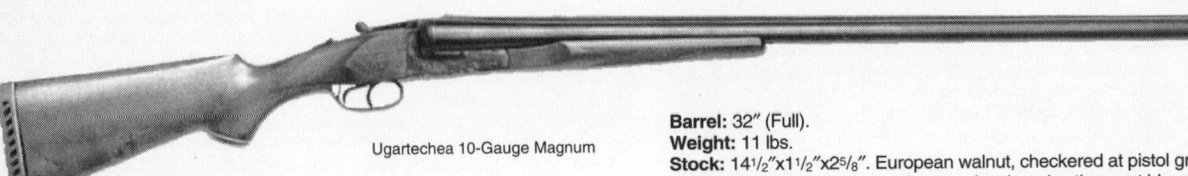
Ugartechea 10-Gauge Magnum

UGARTECHEA 10-GAUGE MAGNUM SHOTGUN
Gauge: 10, 3 1/2" chambers.
Action: Boxlock.
Barrel: 32" (Full).
Weight: 11 lbs.
Stock: 14 1/2"x1 1/2"x2 5/8". European walnut, checkered at pistol grip and forend.
Features: Double triggers; color case-hardened action, rest blued. Front and center metal beads on matted rib; ventilated rubber recoil pad. Forend release has positive Purdey-type mechanism. Imported from Spain by Mandall Shooting Supplies.
Price: $699.50

SHOTGUNS—BOLT ACTIONS & SINGLE SHOTS

Variety of designs for utility and sporting purposes, as well as for competitive shooting.

BAIKAL IJ-18 SINGLE BARREL SHOTGUN
Gauge: 12, 3" chamber.
Barrel: 28.5".
Weight: 6 lbs. Length: 44.5" overall.
Stock: European hardwood.
Features: Chrome-lined bore; extractor; cocking indicator; cross-bolt safety. Imported from Russia by Century International Arms.
Price: About $95.00
Price: IJ-18EM (automatic ejector), about $108.00

BAIKAL IJ-18M SHOTGUN
Gauge: 12, 16, 2 3/4", 20, 410, 3" chamber.
Barrel: 12, 20-ga.—26" (Imp. Cyl.), 410 (Full); 12, 20-ga.—28" (Full, Mod.).
Weight: 5.5 to 6 lbs.
Stock: Stained hardwood.
Features: External hammer with cocking indicator; trigger block safety; engraved, blued receiver. Reintroduced 1994. Imported from Russia by K.B.I., Inc.
Price: $69.00

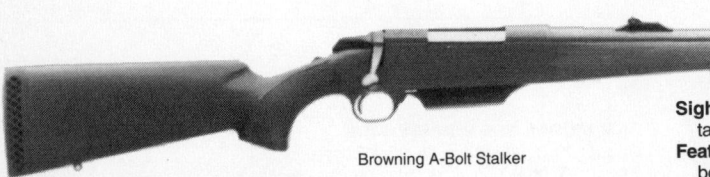
Browning A-Bolt Stalker

BROWNING A-BOLT SHOTGUN
Gauge: 12, 3" chamber, 2-shot detachable magazine.
Barrel: 22" (fully rifled), 23" (5" Invector choke tubes).
Weight: 7 lbs., 2 oz. Length: 44 3/4" overall.
Stock: 14"x 5/8"x 1/2". Walnut with satin finish on Hunter; Stalker has black graphite fiberglass composite. Swivel studs.
Sights: Blade front with red insert, open adjustable rear or none. Drilled and tapped for scope mounting.
Features: Uses same bolt system as A-Bolt rifle with 60° bolt throw; front-locking bolt with claw extractor; hinged floorplate. Matte finish on barrel and receiver. Introduced 1995. Imported by Browning.
Price: Hunter, rifled choke tube, open sights $828.95
Price: As above, no sights $804.95
Price: Hunter, rifled barrel, open sights $881.95
Price: As above, no sights $856.95
Price: Stalker, rifled, choke tube, open sights $744.95
Price: As above, no sights $719.95
Price: Stalker, rifled barrel, no sights $772.95

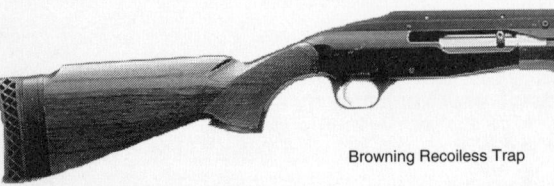
Browning Recoiless Trap

Browning Micro Recoilless Trap Shotgun
Same as the standard Recoilless Trap except has 27" barrel, weighs 8 lbs., 10 oz., and stock length of pull adjustable from 13" to 13 3/4", Overall length 47 5/8". Introduced 1993. Imported by Browning.
Price: $1,995.00

BROWNING RECOILLESS TRAP SHOTGUN
Gauge: 12, 2 3/4" chamber.
Barrel: Back-bored 30" (Invector Plus tubes).
Weight: 9 lbs., 1 oz. Length: 51 5/8" overall.
Stock: 14"-14 3/4"x1 3/8"-1 3/4"x1 1/8"-1 3/4". Select walnut with high gloss finish, cut checkering.
Features: Eliminates up to 72 percent of recoil. Mass of the inner mechansim (barrel, receiver and inner bolt) is driven forward when trigger is pulled, cancelling most recoil. Forend is used to cock action when the action is forward. Ventilated rib adjusts to move point of impact; drop at comb and length of pull adjustable. Introduced 1993. Imported by Browning.
Price: $1,995.00

SHOTGUNS—BOLT ACTIONS & SINGLE SHOTS

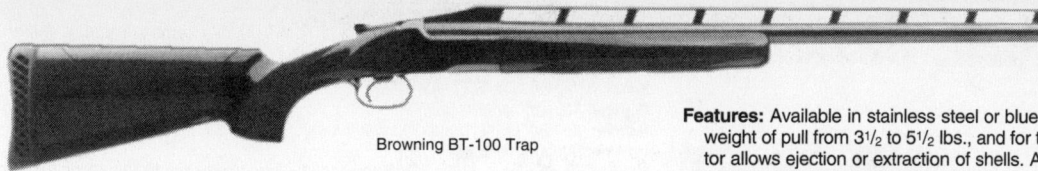

Browning BT-100 Trap

BROWNING BT-100 TRAP SHOTGUN
Gauge: 12, 2¾" chamber.
Barrel: 32", 34" (Invector Plus); back-bored; also with fixed Full choke.
Weight: 8 lbs., 9 oz. **Length:** 48½" overall (32" barrel).
Stock: 14⅜"x1 9/16"x1 7/16"x2" (Monte Carlo); 14⅜"x1¾"x1¼"x2⅛" (thumbhole). Walnut with high gloss finish; cut checkering. Wedge-shaped forend with finger groove.

Features: Available in stainless steel or blue. Has drop-out trigger adjustable for weight of pull from 3½ to 5½ lbs., and for three length postions; Ejector-Selector allows ejection or extraction of shells. Available with adjustable comb stock and thumbhole style. Introduced 1995. Imported from Japan by Browning.
Price: Grade I, blue, Monte Carlo, Invector Plus $1,995.00
Price: As above, fixed Full choke $1,948.00
Price: Stainless steel, Monte Carlo, Invector Plus $2,415.00
Price: As above, fixed Full choke $2,368.00
Price: Thumbhole stock, blue, Invector Plus $2,270.00
Price: Thumbhole stock, stainless, Invector Plus $2,690.00
Price: Adjustable comb stock, add $210.00
Price: Replacement trigger assembly $525.00

H&R SB2-980 Ultra Slug

HARRINGTON & RICHARDSON SB2-980 ULTRA SLUG
Gauge: 12, 20, 3" chamber.
Barrel: 22" (20 ga. Youth) 24", fully rifled.
Weight: 9 lbs. **Length:** NA.
Stock: Walnut-stained hardwood.
Sights: None furnished; comes with scope mount.
Features: Uses the H&R 10-gauge action with heavy-wall barrel. Monte Carlo stock has sling swivels; comes with black nylon sling. Introduced 1995. Made in U.S. by H&R 1871, Inc.
Price: $209.95

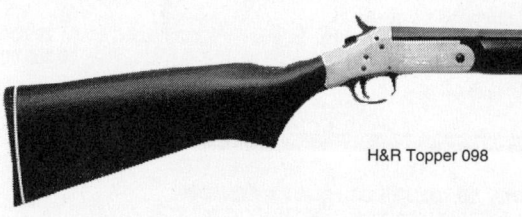

H&R Topper 098

HARRINGTON & RICHARDSON TOPPER MODEL 098
Gauge: 12, 16, 20, 28 (2¾"), 410, 3" chamber.
Barrel: 12 ga.—28" (Mod., Full); 16 ga.—28" (Mod.); 20 ga.—26" (Mod.); 28 ga.—26" (Mod.); 410 bore—26" (Full).
Weight: 5-6 lbs.
Stock: Black-finish hardwood with full pistol grip; semi-beavertail forend.
Sights: Gold bead front.
Features: Break-open action with side-lever release, automatic ejector. Satin nickel frame, blued barrel. Reintroduced 1992. From H&R 1871, Inc.
Price: $114.95
Price: Topper Junior 098 (as above except 22" barrel, 20-ga. (Mod.), 410-bore (Full), 12½" length of pull) $119.95

Harrington & Richardson Topper Junior Classic Shotgun
Similar to the Topper Junior 098 except available in 20-gauge (3", Mod.), 410-bore (Full) with 3" chamber; 28-gauge, 2¾" chamber (Mod.); all have 22" barrel. Stock is American black walnut with cut-checkered pistol grip and forend. Ventilated rubber recoil pad with white line spacers. Blued barrel, blued frame. Introduced 1992. From H&R 1871, Inc.
Price: $144.95

> Consult our Directory pages for the location of firms mentioned.

Harrington & Richardson Topper Deluxe Model 098
Similar to the standard Topper 098 except 12-gauge only with 3½" chamber, 28" barrel with choke tube (comes with Mod. tube, others optional). Satin nickel frame, blued barrel, black-finished wood. Introduced 1992. From H&R 1871, Inc.
Price: $134.95

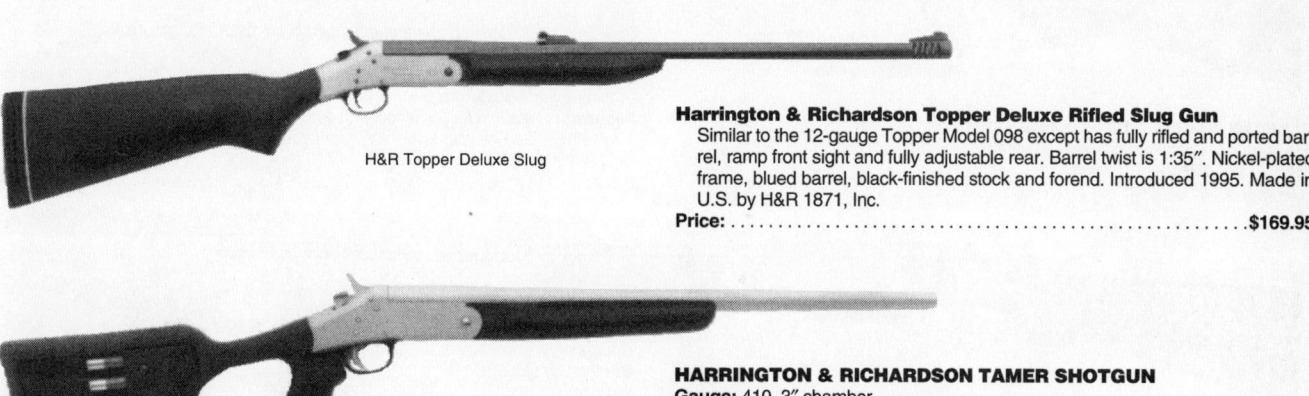

H&R Topper Deluxe Slug

Harrington & Richardson Topper Deluxe Rifled Slug Gun
Similar to the 12-gauge Topper Model 098 except has fully rifled and ported barrel, ramp front sight and fully adjustable rear. Barrel twist is 1:35". Nickel-plated frame, blued barrel, black-finished stock and forend. Introduced 1995. Made in U.S. by H&R 1871, Inc.
Price: $169.95

H&R Tamer

HARRINGTON & RICHARDSON TAMER SHOTGUN
Gauge: 410, 3" chamber.
Barrel: 19½" (Full).
Weight: 5-6 lbs. **Length:** 33" overall.
Stock: Thumbhole grip of high density black polymer.
Features: Uses H&R Topper action with matte electroless nickel finish. Stock holds four spare shotshells. Introduced 1994. From H&R 1871, Inc.
Price: $124.95

SHOTGUNS—BOLT ACTIONS & SINGLE SHOTS

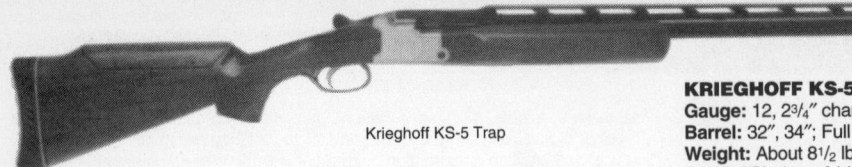
Krieghoff KS-5 Trap

KRIEGHOFF KS-5 TRAP GUN
Gauge: 12, 2¾" chamber.
Barrel: 32", 34"; Full choke or choke tubes.
Weight: About 8½ lbs.
Stock: Choice of high Monte Carlo (1½"), low Monte Carlo (1⅜") or factory adjustable stock. European walnut.
Features: Ventilated tapered step rib. Adjustable trigger or optional release trigger. Satin gray electroless nickel receiver. Comes with fitted aluminum case. Introduced 1988. Imported from Germany by Krieghoff International, Inc.
Price: Fixed choke, cased $3,575.00
Price: With choke tubes $3,975.00

Krieghoff KS-5 Special
Same as the KS-5 except the barrel has a fully adjustable rib and adjustable stock. Rib allows shooter to adjust point of impact from 50%/50% to nearly 90%/10%. Introduced 1990.
Price: $4,480.00

KRIEGHOFF K-80 SINGLE BARREL TRAP GUN
Gauge: 12, 2¾" chamber.
Barrel: 32" or 34" Unsingle; 34" Top Single. Fixed Full or choke tubes.
Weight: About 8¾ lbs.
Stock: Four stock dimensions or adjustable stock available. All hand-checkered European walnut.
Features: Satin nickel finish with K-80 logo. Selective mechanical trigger adjustable for finger position. Tapered step vent. rib. Adjustable point of impact on Unsingle.
Price: Standard grade full Unsingle $7,595.00
Price: Standard grade full Top Single combo (special order), from $9,595.00
Price: RT (removable trigger) option, add $1,000.00

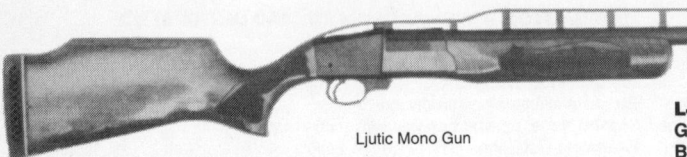
Ljutic Mono Gun

LJUTIC MONO GUN SINGLE BARREL
Gauge: 12 only.
Barrel: 34", choked to customer specs; hollow-milled rib, 35½" sight plane.
Weight: Approx. 9 lbs.
Stock: To customer specs. Oil finish, hand checkered.
Features: Totally custom made. Pull or release trigger; removable trigger guard contains trigger and hammer mechanism; Ljutic pushbutton opener on front of trigger guard. From Ljutic Industries.
Price: With standard, medium or Olympic rib, custom 32"-34" bbls. ...$4,795.00
Price: As above with screw-in choke barrel $5,000.00

Ljutic LTX Super Deluxe Mono Gun
Super Deluxe version of the standard Mono Gun with high quality wood, extra-fancy checkering pattern in 24 lpi, double recessed choking. Available in two weights: 8¼ lbs. or 8¾ lbs. Extra light 33" barrel; medium-height rib. Introduced 1984. From Ljutic Industries.
Price: $5,895.00
Price: With three screw-in choke tubes $6,095.00

Marlin Model 55

MARLIN MODEL 55 GOOSE GUN BOLT ACTION
Gauge: 12 only, 2¾" or 3" chamber.
Action: Bolt action, thumb safety, detachable two-shot clip. Red cocking indicator.
Barrel: 36" (Full).
Weight: 8 lbs. **Length:** 56¾" overall.
Stock: Walnut-finished hardwood, pistol grip, ventilated recoil pad. Swivel studs, MarShield® finish.
Features: Brass bead front sight, U-groove rear sight.
Price: $307.55

Marlin 512 Slugmaster

MARLIN MODEL 512 SLUGMASTER SHOTGUN
Gauge: 12, 3" chamber; 2-shot detachable box magazine.
Barrel: 21", rifled (1:28" twist).
Weight: 8 lbs. **Length:** 44¾" overall.
Stock: Walnut-finished, press-checkered Maine birch with Mar-Shield® finish, ventilated recoil pad.
Sights: Ramp front with brass bead and removable Wide-Scan™ hood, adjustable folding semi-buckhorn rear. Drilled and tapped for scope mounting.
Features: Uses Model 55 action with thumb safety. Designed for shooting saboted slugs. Comes with special Weaver scope mount. Introduced 1994. Made in U.S. by Marlin Firearms Co.
Price: $353.35

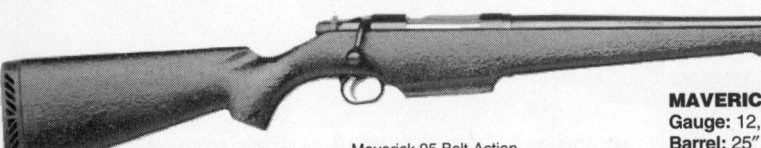
Maverick 95 Bolt-Action

MAVERICK MODEL 95 BOLT-ACTION SHOTGUN
Gauge: 12, 3" chamber, 2-shot magazine.
Barrel: 25" (Mod.).
Weight: 6.5 lbs.
Stock: Textured black synthetic.
Sights: Bead front.
Features: Full-length stock with integral magazine; ambidextrous rotating safety; twin extractors; rubber recoil pad. Blue finish. Introduced 1995. From Maverick Arms.
Price: $184.00

SHOTGUNS—BOLT ACTIONS & SINGLE SHOTS

Mossberg Model 695 Slugster

Mossberg Model 695 Turkey
Same as the Model 695 Slugster except has smoothbore 22" barrel with Extra-Full Turkey Accu-Choke tube, full OFM camouflage finish, fixed U-notch rear sight, bead front. Made in U.S. by Mossberg. Introduced 1996.
Price: $276.00

MOSSBERG MODEL 695 SLUGSTER
Gauge: 12, 3" chamber.
Barrel: 22"; fully rifled, ported.
Weight: 7$1/2$ lbs.
Stock: Black synthetic, with swivel studs and rubber recoil pad.
Sights: Blade front, folding rifle-style leaf rear. Comes with Weaver-style scope bases.
Features: Matte metal finish; rotating thumb safety; detachable 2-shot magazine. Mossberg Cablelock. Made in U.S. by Mossberg. Introduced 1996.
Price: $293.00

New England Turkey and Goose

NEW ENGLAND FIREARMS STANDARD PARDNER
Gauge: 12, 20, 410, 3" chamber; 16, 28, 2$3/4$" chamber.
Barrel: 12-ga.—28" (Full, Mod.), 32" (Full); 16-ga.—28" (Full), 32" (Full); 20-ga.—26" (Full, Mod.); 28-ga.—26" (Mod.); 410-bore—26" (Full).
Weight: 5-6 lbs. **Length:** 43" overall (28" barrel).
Stock: Walnut-finished hardwood with full pistol grip.
Sights: Bead front.
Features: Transfer bar ignition; break-open action with side-lever release. Introduced 1987. From New England Firearms.
Price: $99.95
Price: Youth model (20-, 28-ga., 410, 22" barrel, recoil pad) $109.95
Price: 12-ga., 32" (Full) $104.95

NEW ENGLAND FIREARMS SURVIVOR
Gauge: 12, 20, 410/45 Colt, 3" chamber.
Barrel: 22" (Mod.); 20" (410/45 Colt, rifled barrel, choke tube).
Weight: 6 lbs. **Length:** 36" overall.
Stock: Black polymer with thumbhole/pistol grip, sling swivels; beavertail forend.
Sights: Bead front.
Features: Buttplate removes to expose storage for extra ammunition; forend also holds extra ammunition. Black or nickel finish. Introduced 1993. From New England Firearms.
Price: Black $129.95
Price: Nickel $145.95
Price: 410/45 Colt, black $145.95
Price: 410/45 Colt, nickel $164.95

NEW ENGLAND FIREARMS TURKEY AND GOOSE GUN
Gauge: 10, 3$1/2$" chamber.
Barrel: 28" (Full), 32" (Mod.).
Weight: 9.5 lbs. **Length:** 44" overall.
Stock: American hardwood with walnut, or matte camo finish; ventilated rubber recoil pad.
Sights: Bead front.
Features: Break-open action with side-lever release; ejector. Matte finish on metal. Introduced 1992. From New England Firearms.
Price: Walnut-finish wood $149.95
Price: Camo finish, sling and swivels $159.95
Price: Camo finish, 32", sling and swivels $179.95
Price: Black matte finish, 24", Turkey Full choke tube, sling and swivels .$184.95

NEW ENGLAND FIREARMS TRACKER SLUG GUN
Gauge: 12, 20, 3" chamber.
Barrel: 24" (Cyl.).
Weight: 6 lbs. **Length:** 40" overall.
Stock: Walnut-finished hardwood with full pistol grip, recoil pad.
Sights: Blade front, fully adjustable rifle-type rear.
Features: Break-open action with side-lever release; blued barrel, color case-hardened frame. Introduced 1992. From New England Firearms.
Price: Tracker $129.95
Price: Tracker II (as above except fully rifled bore) $139.95

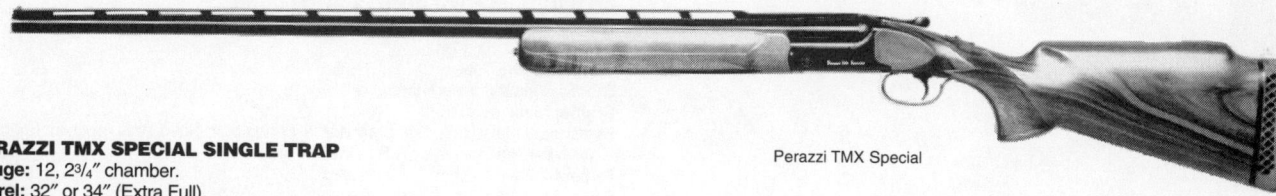
Perazzi TMX Special

PERAZZI TMX SPECIAL SINGLE TRAP
Gauge: 12, 2$3/4$" chamber.
Barrel: 32" or 34" (Extra Full).
Weight: 8 lbs., 6 oz.
Stock: To customer specs; interchangeable.
Features: Special high rib; adjustable four-position trigger. Also available with choke tubes. Imported from Italy by Perazzi U.S.A., Inc.
Price: From $6,590.00

SAVAGE MODEL 210F MASTER SHOT SLUG GUN
Gauge: 12, 3" chamber; 2-shot magazine.
Barrel: 24" 1:35" rifling twist.
Weight: 7$1/2$ lbs. **Length:** 43.5" overall.
Stock: Glass-filled polymer with positive checkering.
Features: Based on the Savage Model 110 action; 60° bolt lift; controlled round feed; comes with scope mount. Introduced 1996. Made in U.S. by Savage Arms.
Price: ....NA

REMINGTON 90-T SUPER SINGLE SHOTGUN
Gauge: 12, 2$3/4$" chamber.
Barrel: 30", 32", 34", fixed choke or Rem Choke tubes; ported or non-ported. Medium-high tapered, ventilated rib; white Bradley-type front bead, stainless center bead.
Weight: About 8$3/4$ lbs.
Stock: 14$3/8$"x1$3/8$" (or 1$1/2$" or 1$1/4$")x1$1/2$". Choice of drops at comb, pull length available plus or minus 1". Figured American walnut with low-luster finish, checkered 18 lpi; black vented rubber recoil pad. Cavity in forend and buttstock for added weight.
Features: Barrel is over-bored with elongated forcing cones. Removable sideplates can be ordered with engraving; drop-out trigger assembly. Metal has non-glare matte finish. Available with extra barrels in different lengths, chokes, extra trigger assemblies and sideplates, porting, stocks. Introduced 1990. From Remington.
Price: Depending on options $3,199.00
Price: With high post adjustable rib $3,992.00

CAUTION: PRICES SHOWN ARE SUPPLIED BY THE MANUFACTURER OR IMPORTER. CHECK YOUR LOCAL GUNSHOP.

SHOTGUNS—BOLT ACTIONS & SINGLE SHOTS

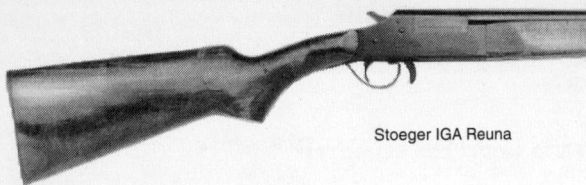

Stoeger IGA Reuna

SNAKE CHARMER II SHOTGUN
Gauge: 410, 3" chamber.
Barrel: 18 1/4".
Weight: About 3 1/2 lbs. **Length:** 28 5/8" overall.
Stock: ABS grade impact resistant plastic.
Features: Thumbhole-type stock holds four extra rounds. Stainless steel barrel and frame. Reintroduced 1989. From Sporting Arms Mfg., Inc.
Price: $149.00
Price: New Generation Snake Charmer (as above except with black carbon steel bbl.) $139.00

STOEGER/IGA REUNA SINGLE BARREL SHOTGUN
Gauge: 12, 2 3/4" chamber; 20, 410, 3" chamber.
Barrel: 12-ga.—26" (Imp. Cyl.), 28" (Full); 20-ga.—26" (Full); 410 bore—26" (Full).
Weight: 5 1/4 lbs.
Stock: 14"x1 1/2"x2 1/2". Brazilian hardwood.
Sights: Metal bead front.
Features: Exposed hammer with half-cock safety; extractor; blue finish. Introduced 1987. Imported from Brazil by Stoeger Industries.
Price: $120.00
Price: 12-, 20-ga., Full choke tube $142.00
Price: Youth model (20-ga., 410, 22" Full) $132.00

Tar-Hunt Bolt Action

TAR-HUNT RSG-12 PROFESSIONAL RIFLED SLUG GUN
Gauge: 12, 20, 2 3/4" chamber.
Barrel: 21 1/2"; fully rifled, with muzzlebrake.
Weight: 7 3/4 lbs. **Length:** 41 1/2" overall.
Stock: Matte black McMillan fiberglass with Pachmayr Decelerator pad.
Sights: None furnished; comes with Weaver-style bases and Burris Zee steel rings.
Features: Uses new rifle-style action with two locking lugs; two-position safety; single-stage, adjustable rifle trigger; muzzlebrake. Many options available. Right- and left-hand models at same prices. Introduced 1991. Made in U.S. by Tar-Hunt Custom Rifles, Inc.

Price: Professional model, right- or left hand $1,395.00
Price: Turkey model (smoothbore, black McMillan fiberglass stock, Remington Rem-Choke thread system), right- or left-hand $1,439.00
Price: Matchless model (400-grit gloss metal finish, McMillan Fibergrain or camouflage stock), right- or left-hand $1,783.50
Price: Peerless model NP-3 nickel/teflon metal finish, McMillan Fibergrain fiberglass stock), right- or left-hand $1,973.25

SHOTGUNS—MILITARY & POLICE

Designs for utility, suitable for and adaptable to competitions and other sporting purposes.

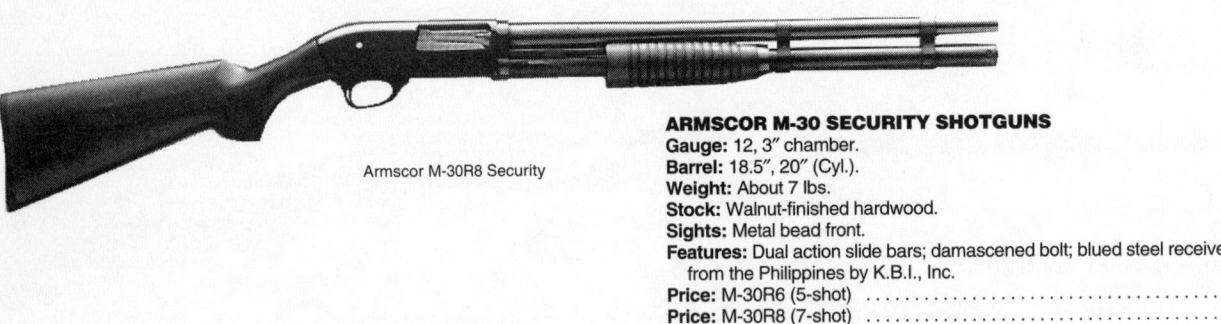

Armscor M-30R8 Security

ARMSCOR M-30 SECURITY SHOTGUNS
Gauge: 12, 3" chamber.
Barrel: 18.5", 20" (Cyl.).
Weight: About 7 lbs.
Stock: Walnut-finished hardwood.
Sights: Metal bead front.
Features: Dual action slide bars; damascened bolt; blued steel receiver. Imported from the Philippines by K.B.I., Inc.
Price: M-30R6 (5-shot) $199.00
Price: M-30R8 (7-shot) $210.00

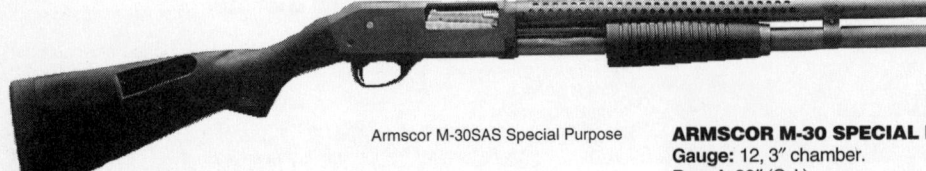

Armscor M-30SAS Special Purpose

ARMSCOR M-30 SPECIAL PURPOSE SHOTGUNS
Gauge: 12, 3" chamber.
Barrel: 20" (Cyl.).
Weight: 7.5 lbs.
Stock: Walnut-finished hardwood, or synthetic speedfeed.
Sights: Rifle sights on M-30DG, metal bead front on M-305AS.
Features: M-30DB has 7-shot magazine, polished blue receiver; M-305AS based on Special Air Services gun with 7-shot magazine, ventilated barrel shroud, Parkerized finish. Introduced 1996. Imported from the Philippines by K.B.I., Inc.
Price: M-30DG $249.00
Price: M-30SAS $279.00

Consult our Directory pages for the location of firms mentioned.

SHOTGUNS—MILITARY & POLICE

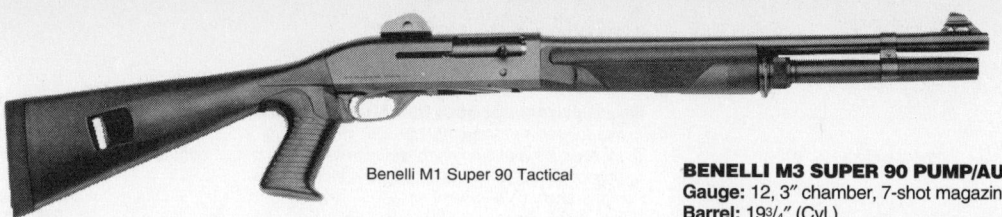
Benelli M1 Super 90 Tactical

Benelli M1 Super 90 Tactical Shotgun
Similar to the M1 Super 90 except has 18.5" barrel with Imp. Cyl., Mod., Full choke tubes, rifle sights of Ghost Ring system (tritium night sights optional), 5-shot magazine. In 12-gauge (3" chamber) only, matte-finish receiver. Overall length 39.75". Introduced 1993. Imported from Italy by Heckler & Koch, Inc.
Price: With rifle sights, standard stock $860.00
Price: As above, pistol grip stock $895.00
Price: With Ghost Rifle sights, standard stock $902.00
Price: As above, pistol grip stock $936.00

Benelli M1 Super 90 Defense Shotgun
Similar to the M1 Super 90 except has 18.5" barrel, rifle sights or Ghost Ring system (tritium night sights optional), 3-shot magazine with 2-shot extension. In 12-gauge (3" chamber) only, matte-finish receiver. Overall length 39$^{3}/_{4}$". Introduced 1993. Imported from Italy by Heckler & Koch, Inc.
Price: With rifle sights, pistol grip stock $851.00
Price: With Ghost Ring sights, pistol grip stock $892.00

BENELLI M3 SUPER 90 PUMP/AUTO SHOTGUN
Gauge: 12, 3" chamber, 7-shot magazine.
Barrel: 19$^{3}/_{4}$" (Cyl.).
Weight: 7 lbs., 8 oz. **Length:** 41" overall.
Stock: High-impact polymer with sling loop in side of butt; rubberized pistol grip on stock.
Sights: Post front, buckhorn rear adjustable for windage. Ghost ring system available.
Features: Combination pump/auto action. Alloy receiver with inertia recoil rotating locking lug bolt; matte finish; automatic shell release lever. Introduced 1989. Imported by Heckler & Koch, Inc.
Price: With standard stock $1,016.00
Price: With Ghost Ring sight system, standard stock $1,086.00

Benelli M1 Super 90
Similar to the M3 Super 90 except is semi-automatic only, has overall length of 39$^{3}/_{4}$" and weighs 6.5 lbs. Introduced 1986.
Price: Slug Gun with standard stock $819.00
Price: With pistol grip stock (Defense) $851.00
Price: With ghost ring sight system (standard stock) $860.00
Price: With ghost ring sight system, pistol grip stock (Defense) $892.00

Beretta Model 1201FP3

BERETTA MODEL 1201FP3 AUTO SHOTGUN
Gauge: 12, 3" chamber.
Barrel: 20" (Cyl.).
Weight: 6.3 lbs. **Length:** NA
Stock: Special strengthened technopolymer, matte black finish.
Stock: Fixed rifle type.
Features: Has 6-shot magazine. Introduced 1988. Imported from Italy by Beretta U.S.A.
Price: $715.00

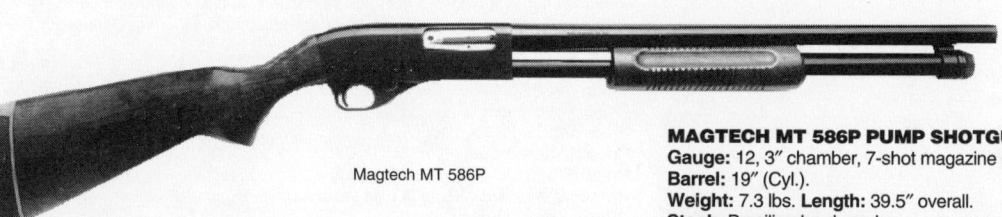
Magtech MT 586P

MAGTECH MT 586P PUMP SHOTGUN
Gauge: 12, 3" chamber, 7-shot magazine (8-shot with 2$^{3}/_{4}$" shells).
Barrel: 19" (Cyl.).
Weight: 7.3 lbs. **Length:** 39.5" overall.
Stock: Brazilian hardwood.
Sights: Bead front.
Features: Dual action slide bars, cross-bolt safety. Blue finish. Introduced 1991. Imported from Brazil by Magtech Recreational Products.
Price: About $219.00

Mossberg Model 500

Mossberg Model HS410 Shotgun
Similar to the Model 500 Security pump except chambered for 20 gauge or 410 with 3" chamber; has pistol grip forend, thick recoil pad, muzzlebrake and has special spreader choke on the 18.5" barrel. Overall length is 37.5", weight is 6.25 lbs. Blue finish; synthetic field stock. Mossberg Cablelock and video included. Introduced 1990.
Price: HS 410 ....$293.00

MOSSBERG MODEL 500 PERSUADER SECURITY SHOTGUNS
Gauge: 12, 20, 410, 3" chamber.
Barrel: 18$^{1}/_{2}$", 20" (Cyl.).
Weight: 7 lbs.
Stock: Walnut-finished hardwood or synthetic field.
Sights: Metal bead front.
Features: Available in 6- or 8-shot models. Top-mounted safety, double action slide bars, swivel studs, rubber recoil pad. Blue, Parkerized, Marinecote finishes. Mossberg Cablelock included. From Mossberg.
Price: 12- or 20-ga., 18$^{1}/_{2}$", blue, wood or synthetic stock, 6-shot $281.00
Price: As above, Parkerized finish, synthetic stock, 6-shot $315.00
Price: Cruiser, 12- or 20-ga., 18$^{1}/_{2}$", blue, pistol grip, heat shield $272.00
Price: As above, 410-bore $279.00
Price: 12-ga., 8-shot, blue, wood or synthetic stock $281.00
Price: As above with rifle sights $304.00
Price: 6- or 8-shot with Accu-Choke barrel $281.00

CAUTION: PRICES SHOWN ARE SUPPLIED BY THE MANUFACTURER OR IMPORTER. CHECK YOUR LOCAL GUNSHOP.

SHOTGUNS—MILITARY & POLICE

Mossberg Model 500 Mariner

Mossberg Model 500, 590 Mariner Pump
Similar to the Model 500 or 590 Security except all metal parts finished with Marinecote metal finish to resist rust and corrosion. Synthetic field stock; pistol grip kit included. Mossberg Cablelock included.
Price: 6-shot, 18½" barrel $403.00
Price: As above with Ghost-Ring sights $459.00
Price: 9-shot, 20" barrel $415.00
Price: As above with Ghost-Ring sights $471.00

Mossberg Model 590 Ghost-Ring

MOSSBERG MODEL 590 SHOTGUN
Gauge: 12, 3" chamber.
Barrel: 20" (Cyl.).
Weight: 7¼ lbs.
Stock: Synthetic field or Speedfeed.
Sights: Metal bead front.
Features: Top-mounted safety, double slide action bars. Comes with heat shield, bayonet lug, swivel studs, rubber recoil pad. Blue, Parkerized or Marinecote finish. Mossberg Cablelock included. From Mossberg.
Price: Blue, synthetic stock $329.00
Price: Parkerized, synthetic stock $379.00
Price: Blue, Speedfeed stock $362.00
Price: Parkerized, Speedfeed stock $412.00

Mossberg Model 500, 590 Ghost-Ring Shotguns
Similar to the Model 500 Security except has adjustable blade front, adjustable Ghost-Ring rear sight with protective "ears." Model 500 has 18.5" (Cyl.) barrel, 6-shot capacity; Model 590 has 20" (Cyl.) barrel, 9-shot capacity. Both have synthetic field stock. Mossberg Cablelock included. Introduced 1990. From Mossberg.
Price: Model 500, blue $331.00
Price: As above, Parkerized $384.00
Price: Model 590, blue $379.00
Price: As above, Parkerized $432.00
Price: Parkerized, Speedfeed stock $465.00
Price: Parkerized, synthetic stock, Accu-Choke barrel $454.00

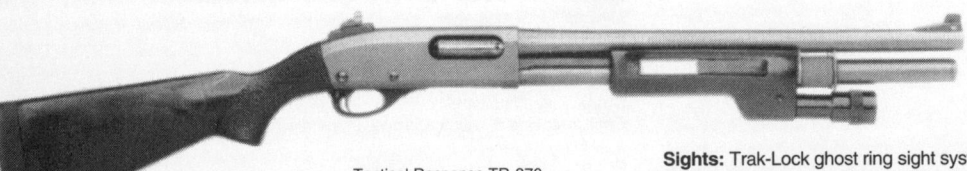

Tactical Response TR-870

Sights: Trak-Lock ghost ring sight system. Front sight has tritium insert.
Features: Highly modified Remington 870P with Parkerized finish. Comes with nylon three-way adjustable sling, high visibility non-binding follower, high performance magazine spring, Jumbo Head safety, and Side Saddle extended 6-shot shell carrier on left side of receiver. Introduced 1991. From Scattergun Technologies, Inc.
Price: Standard model $815.00
Price: FBI model $770.00
Price: Patrol model $595.00
Price: Border Patrol model $605.00
Price: Military model $690.00
Price: K-9 model (Rem. 11-87 action) $860.00
Price: Urban Sniper, Rem. 11-87 action $1,290.00
Price: Louis Awerbuck model $705.00
Price: Practical Turkey model $725.00

TACTICAL RESPONSE TR-870 STANDARD MODEL SHOTGUN
Gauge: 12, 3" chamber, 7-shot magazine.
Barrel: 18" (Cyl.).
Weight: 9 lbs. Length: 38" overall.
Stock: Fiberglass-filled polypropolene with non-snag recoil absorbing butt pad. Nylon tactical forend houses flashlight.

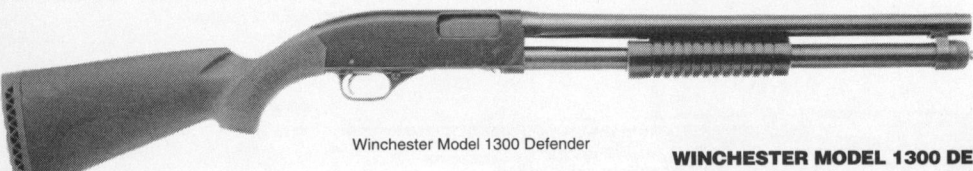

Winchester Model 1300 Defender

WINCHESTER MODEL 1300 DEFENDER PUMP GUN
Gauge: 12, 20, 3" chamber, 5- or 8-shot capacity.
Barrel: 18" (Cyl.).
Weight: 6¾ lbs. Length: 38⅝" overall.
Stock: Walnut-finished hardwood stock and ribbed forend, or synthetic; or pistol grip.
Sights: Metal bead front.
Features: Cross-bolt safety, front-locking rotary bolt, twin action slide bars. Black rubber buttpad. From U.S. Repeating Arms Co.
Price: 8-shot, wood or synthetic stock $290.00
Price: 5-shot, wood stock $290.00
Price: Defender Field Combo with pistol grip $393.00

Winchester Model 1300 Stainless Marine Pump Gun
Same as the Defender except has bright chrome finish, stainless steel barrel, rifle-type sights only. Phosphate coated receiver for corrosion resistance. Pistol grip optional.
Price: $460.00

Manufacturers' addresses in the
Directory of the Arms Trade
page 313, this issue

Winchester 8-Shot Pistol Grip Pump Security Shotguns
Same as regular Defender Pump but with pistol grip and forend of high-impact resistant ABS plastic with non-glare black finish. Introduced 1984.
Price: Pistol Grip Defender $290.00

BLACKPOWDER SINGLE SHOT PISTOLS—FLINT & PERCUSSION

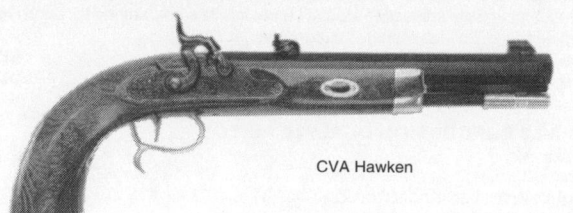
CVA Hawken

CVA HAWKEN PISTOL
Caliber: 50.
Barrel: 9 3/4"; 15/16" flats.
Weight: 50 oz. **Length:** 16 1/2" overall.
Stock: Select hardwood.
Sights: Beaded blade front, fully adjustable open rear.
Features: Color case-hardened lock, polished brass wedge plate, nose cap, ramrod thimble, trigger guard, grip cap. Imported by CVA.
Price: $149.95
Price: Kit $119.95
Price: With laminated stock $159.95

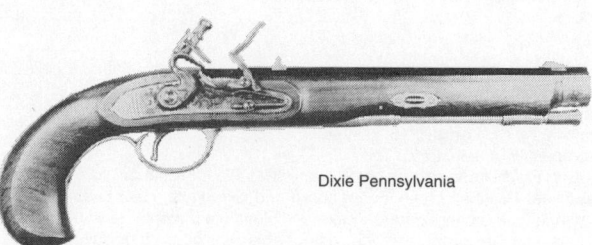
Dixie Pennsylvania

DIXIE PENNSYLVANIA PISTOL
Caliber: 44 (.430" round ball).
Barrel: 10" (7/8" octagon).
Weight: 2 1/2 lbs.
Stock: Walnut-stained hardwood.
Sights: Blade front, open rear drift-adjustable for windage; brass.
Features: Available in flint only. Brass trigger guard, thimbles, nosecap, wedgeplates; high-luster blue barrel. Imported from Italy by Dixie Gun Works.
Price: Finished $159.95
Price: Kit $119.95

Dixie Screw Barrel

DIXIE SCREW BARREL PISTOL
Caliber: .445".
Barrel: 2 1/2".
Weight: 8 oz. **Length:** 6 1/2" overall.
Stock: Walnut.
Features: Trigger folds down when hammer is cocked. Close copy of the originals once made in Belgium. Uses No. 11 percussion caps. From Dixie Gun Works.
Price: $99.95
Price: Kit $79.95

FRENCH-STYLE DUELING PISTOL
Caliber: 44.
Barrel: 10".
Weight: 35 oz. **Length:** 15 3/4" overall.
Stock: Carved walnut.
Sights: Fixed.
Features: Comes with velvet-lined case and accessories. Imported by Mandall Shooting Supplies.
Price: $295.00

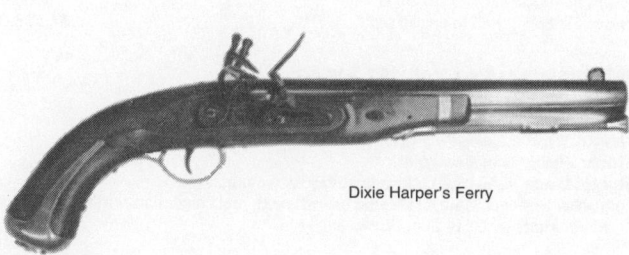
Dixie Harper's Ferry

HARPER'S FERRY 1806 PISTOL
Caliber: 58 (.570" round ball).
Barrel: 10".
Weight: 40 oz. **Length:** 16" overall.
Stock: Walnut.
Sights: Fixed.
Features: Case-hardened lock, brass-mounted browned barrel. Replica of the first U.S. Gov't.-made flintlock pistol. Imported by Navy Arms, Dixie Gun Works.
Price: ....$275.00 to $405.00
Price: Kit (Dixie) $199.95
Price: Cased set (Navy Arms) $335.00

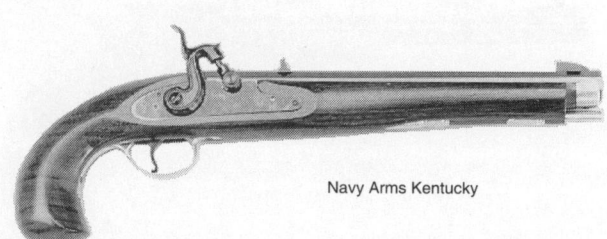
Navy Arms Kentucky

KENTUCKY FLINTLOCK PISTOL
Caliber: 44, 45.
Barrel: 10 1/8".
Weight: 32 oz. **Length:** 15 1/2" overall.
Stock: Walnut.
Sights: Fixed.
Features: Specifications, including caliber, weight and length may vary with importer. Case-hardened lock, blued barrel; available also as brass barrel flint Model 1821. Imported by Navy Arms (44 only), The Armoury.
Price: ....$145.00 to $225.00
Price: In kit form, from ....$90.00 to $112.00
Price: Single cased set (Navy Arms) $350.00
Price: Double cased set (Navy Arms) $580.00

Kentucky Percussion Pistol
Similar to flint version but percussion lock. Imported by The Armoury, Navy Arms, CVA (50-cal.).
Price: ....$129.95 to $250.00
Price: Steel barrel (Armoury) $179.00
Price: Single cased set (Navy Arms) $335.00
Price: Double cased set (Navy Arms) $550.00

CAUTION: PRICES SHOWN ARE SUPPLIED BY THE MANUFACTURER OR IMPORTER. CHECK YOUR LOCAL GUNSHOP.

BLACKPOWDER SINGLE SHOT PISTOLS—FLINT & PERCUSSION

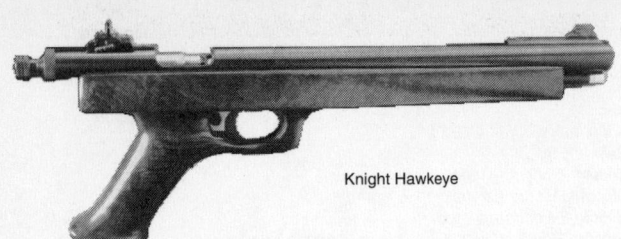
Knight Hawkeye

KNIGHT HAWKEYE PISTOL
Caliber: 50.
Barrel: 12", 1:20" twist.
Weight: 3 1/4 lbs. **Length:** 20" overall.
Stock: Black composite, autumn brown or shadow black laminate.
Sights: Bead front on ramp, open fully adjustable rear.
Features: In-line ignition design; patented double safety system; removable breech plug; fully adjustable trigger; receiver drilled and tapped for scope mounting. Made in U.S. by Modern Muzzle Loading, Inc.
Price: Blued $359.95
Price: Stainless $429.95

LE PAGE PERCUSSION DUELING PISTOL
Caliber: 44.
Barrel: 10", rifled.
Weight: 40 oz. **Length:** 16" overall.
Stock: Walnut, fluted butt.
Sights: Blade front, notch rear.
Features: Double-set triggers. Blued barrel; trigger guard and buttcap are polished silver. Imported by Dixie Gun Works.
Price: $425.00

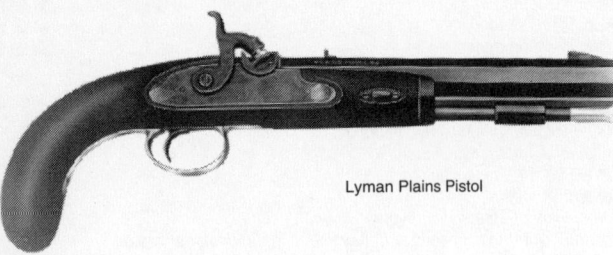
Lyman Plains Pistol

LYMAN PLAINS PISTOL
Caliber: 50 or 54.
Barrel: 8", 1:30" twist, both calibers.
Weight: 50 oz. **Length:** 15" overall.
Stock: Walnut half-stock.
Sights: Blade front, square notch rear adjustable for windage.
Features: Polished brass trigger guard and ramrod tip, color case-hardened coil spring lock, spring-loaded trigger, stainless steel nipple, blackened iron furniture. Hooked patent breech, detachable belt hook. Introduced 1981. From Lyman Products.
Price: Finished $224.95
Price: Kit $179.95

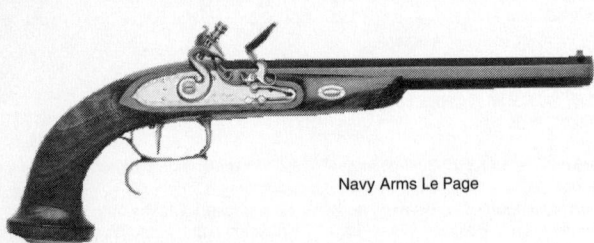
Navy Arms Le Page

NAVY ARMS LE PAGE DUELING PISTOL
Caliber: 44.
Barrel: 9", octagon, rifled.
Weight: 34 oz. **Length:** 15" overall.
Stock: European walnut.
Sights: Adjustable rear.
Features: Single-set trigger. Polished metal finish. From Navy Arms.
Price: Percussion $500.00
Price: Single cased set, percussion $775.00
Price: Double cased set, percussion $1,300.00
Price: Flintlock, rifled $625.00
Price: Flintlock, smoothbore (45-cal.) $625.00
Price: Flintlock, single cased set $900.00
Price: Flintlock, double cased set $1,575.00

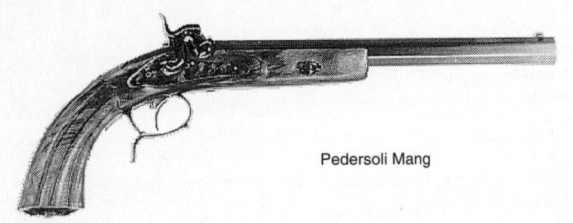
Pedersoli Mang

PEDERSOLI MANG TARGET PISTOL
Caliber: 38.
Barrel: 10.5", octagonal; 1:15" twist.
Weight: 2.5 lbs. **Length:** 17.25" overall.
Stock: Walnut with fluted grip.
Sights: Blade front, open rear adjustable for windage.
Features: Browned barrel, polished breech plug, rest color case-hardened. Imported from Italy by Dixie Gun Works.
Price: $749.00

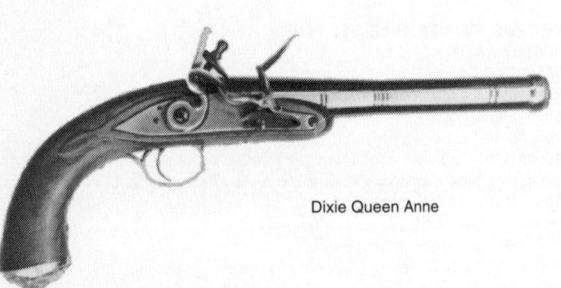
Dixie Queen Anne

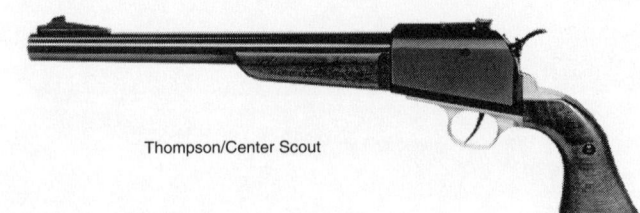
Thompson/Center Scout

THOMPSON/CENTER SCOUT PISTOL
Caliber: 45, 50 and 54.
Barrel: 12", interchangeable.
Weight: 4 lbs., 6 oz. **Length:** NA.
Stocks: American black walnut stocks and forend.
Sights: Blade on ramp front, fully adjustable Patridge rear.
Features: Patented in-line ignition system with special vented breech plug. Patented trigger mechanism consists of only two moving parts. Interchangeable barrels. Wide grooved hammer. Brass trigger guard assembly. Introduced 1990. From Thompson/Center.
Price: 45-, 50- or 54-cal. $350.00

QUEEN ANNE FLINTLOCK PISTOL
Caliber: 50 (.490" round ball).
Barrel: 7 1/2", smoothbore.
Stock: Walnut.
Sights: None.
Features: Browned steel barrel, fluted brass trigger guard, brass mask on butt. Lockplate left in the white. Made by Pedersoli in Italy. Introduced 1983. Imported by Dixie Gun Works.
Price: $189.95
Price: Kit $138.50

BLACKPOWDER SINGLE SHOT PISTOLS—FLINT & PERCUSSION

TRADITIONS BUCKHUNTER PRO IN-LINE PISTOL
Caliber: 50, 54.
Barrel: 10" round.
Weight: 48 oz. **Length:** 14" overall.
Stock: Smooth walnut or black epoxy coated grip and forend.
Sights: Beaded blade front, folding adjustable rear.
Features: Thumb safety; removable stainless steel breech plug; adjustable trigger, barrel drilled and tapped for scope mounting. From Traditions.
Price: With walnut grip $230.00
Price: Nickel with black grip $247.00

Traditions Buckhunter

TRADITIONS BUCKSKINNER PISTOL
Caliber: 50.
Barrel: 10" octagonal, 7/8" flats, 1:20" twist.
Weight: 40 oz. **Length:** 15" overall.
Stocks: Stained beech or laminated wood.
Sights: Blade front, fixed rear.
Features: Percussion ignition. Blackened furniture. Imported by Traditions.
Price: Beech stocks $165.00
Price: Laminated stocks $180.00

TRADITIONS KENTUCKY PISTOL
Caliber: 50.
Barrel: 10"; octagon with 7/8" flats; 1:20" twist.
Weight: 40 oz. **Length:** 15" overall.
Stock: Stained beech.
Sights: Blade front, fixed rear.
Features: Birds-head grip; brass thimbles; color case-hardened lock. Percussion only. Introduced 1995. From Traditions.
Price: Finished $142.00
Price: Kit $115.00

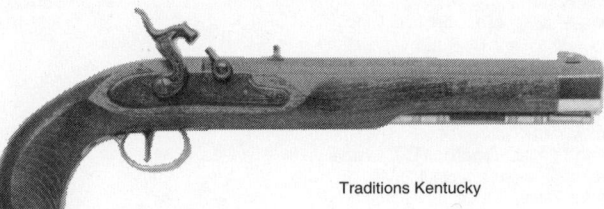
Traditions Kentucky

TRADITIONS PIONEER PISTOL
Caliber: 45.
Barrel: 9 5/8", 13/16" flats, 1:16" twist.
Weight: 31 oz. **Length:** 15" overall.
Stock: Beech.
Sights: Blade front, fixed rear.
Features: V-type mainspring. Single trigger. German silver furniture, blackened hardware. From Traditions.
Price: $157.00
Price: Kit $126.00

TRADITIONS TRAPPER PISTOL
Caliber: 50.
Barrel: 9 3/4", 7/8" flats, 1:20" twist.
Weight: 2 3/4 lbs. **Length:** 16" overall.
Stock: Beech.
Sights: Blade front, adjustable rear.
Features: Double-set triggers; brass buttcap, trigger guard, wedge plate, forend tip, thimble. From Traditions.
Price: Percission $190.00
Price: Flintlock $207.00
Price: Kit $148.00

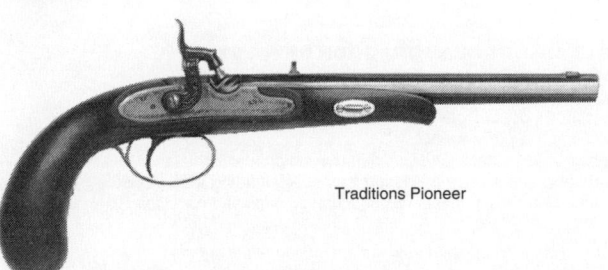
Traditions Pioneer

TRADITIONS WILLIAM PARKER PISTOL
Caliber: 50.
Barrel: 10 3/8", 15/16" flats; polished steel.
Weight: 37 oz. **Length:** 17 1/2" overall.
Stock: Walnut with checkered grip.
Sights: Brass blade front, fixed rear.
Features: Replica dueling pistol with 1:20" twist, hooked breech. Brass wedge plate, trigger guard, cap guard; separate ramrod. Double-set triggers. Polished steel barrel, lock. Imported by Traditions.
Price: $282.00

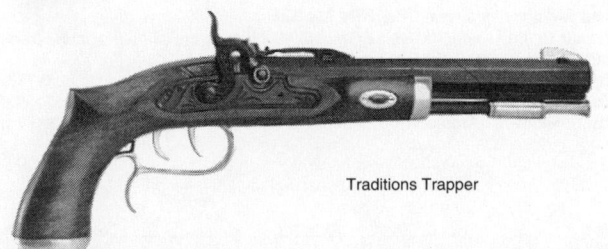
Traditions Trapper

BLACKPOWDER REVOLVERS

ARMY 1860 PERCUSSION REVOLVER
Caliber: 44, 6-shot.
Barrel: 8".
Weight: 40 oz. **Length:** 13 5/8" overall.
Stocks: Walnut.
Sights: Fixed.
Features: Engraved Navy scene on cylinder; brass trigger guard; case-hardened frame, loading lever and hammer. Some importers supply pistol cut for detachable shoulder stock, have accessory stock available. Imported by American Arms, Cabela's (1860 Lawman), E.M.F., Navy Arms, The Armoury, Cimarron, Dixie Gun Works (half-fluted cylinder, not roll engraved), Euroarms of America (brass or steel model), Armsport, Traditions (brass or steel), Uberti U.S.A. Inc.
Price: About ....$92.95 to $300.00
Price: Hartford model, steel frame, German silver trim, cartouches (E.M.F.) $215.00
Price: Single cased set (Navy Arms) $300.00

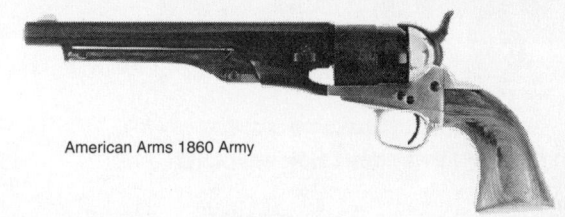
American Arms 1860 Army

Price: Double cased set (Navy Arms) $490.00
Price: 1861 Navy: Same as Army except 36-cal., 7 1/2" bbl., weighs 41 oz., cut for shoulder stock; round cylinder (fluted available), from CVA (brass frame, 44-cal.) ....$99.95 to $249.00
Price: Steel frame kit (E.M.F., Euroarms) ....$125.00 to $216.25
Price: Colt Army Police, fluted cyl., 5 1/2", 36-cal. (Cabela's) $124.95

CAUTION: PRICES SHOWN ARE SUPPLIED BY THE MANUFACTURER OR IMPORTER. CHECK YOUR LOCAL GUNSHOP.

BLACKPOWDER REVOLVERS

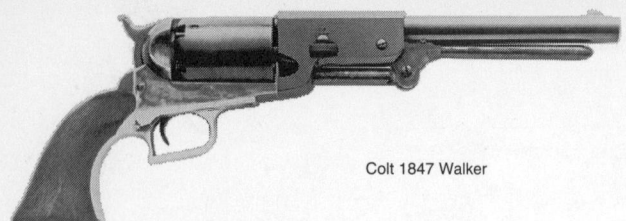
Colt 1847 Walker

COLT 1847 WALKER PERCUSSION REVOLVER
Caliber: 44.
Barrel: 9", 7 groove, right-hand twist.
Weight: 73 oz.
Stocks: One-piece walnut.
Sights: German silver front sight, hammer notch rear.
Features: Made in U.S. Faithful reproduction of the original gun, including markings. Color case-hardened frame, hammer, loading lever and plunger. Blue steel backstrap, brass square-back trigger guard. Blue barrel, cylinder, trigger and wedge. From Colt Blackpowder Arms Co.
Price: $442.50

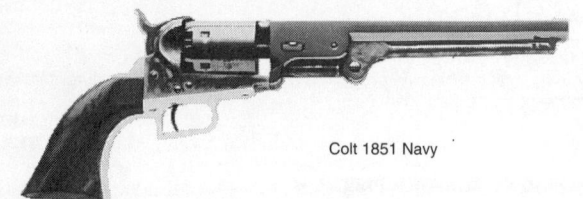
Colt 1851 Navy

COLT 1851 NAVY PERCUSSION REVOLVER
Caliber: 36.
Barrel: 7 1/2", octagonal, 7 groove left-hand twist.
Weight: 40 1/2 oz.
Stocks: One-piece oiled American walnut.
Sights: Brass pin front, hammer notch rear.
Features: Faithful reproduction of the original gun. Color case-hardened frame, loading lever, plunger, hammer and latch. Blue cylinder, trigger, barrel, screws, wedge. Silver-plated brass backstrap and square-back trigger guard. From Colt Blackpowder Arms Co.
Price: $427.50

Uberti 1861 Navy Percussion Revolver
Similar to 1851 Navy except has round 7 1/2" barrel, rounded trigger guard, German silver blade front sight, "creeping" loading lever. Available with fluted or round cylinder. Imported by Uberti USA Inc.
Price: Steel backstrap, trigger guard, cut for stock $300.00

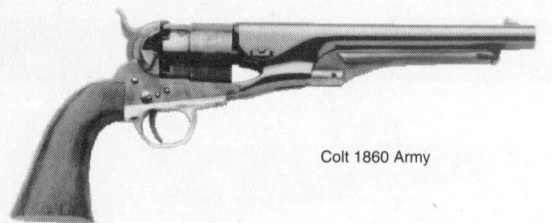
Colt 1860 Army

COLT 1861 NAVY PERCUSSION REVOLVER
Caliber: 36.
Barrel: 7 1/2".
Weight: 42 oz. **Length:** 13 1/8" overall.
Stocks: One-piece walnut.
Sights: Blade front, hammer notch rear.
Features: Color case-hardened frame, loading lever, plunger; blued barrel, backstrap, trigger guard; roll-engraved cylinder and barrel. From Colt Blackpowder Arms Co.
Price: $465.00

ARMY 1851 PERCUSSION REVOLVER
Caliber: 44, 6-shot.
Barrel: 7 1/2".
Weight: 45 oz. **Length:** 13" overall.
Stocks: Walnut finish.
Sights: Fixed.
Features: 44-caliber version of the 1851 Navy. Imported by The Armoury, Armsport.
Price: $129.00

BABY DRAGOON 1848, 1849 POCKET, WELLS FARGO
Caliber: 31.
Barrel: 3", 4", 5", 6"; seven-groove, RH twist.
Weight: About 21 oz.
Stocks: Varnished walnut.
Sights: Brass pin front, hammer notch rear.
Features: No loading lever on Baby Dragoon or Wells Fargo models. Unfluted cylinder with stagecoach holdup scene; cupped cylinder pin; no grease grooves; one safety pin on cylinder and slot in hammer face; straight (flat) mainspring. From Armsport, Dixie Gun Works, Uberti USA Inc., Cabela's.
Price: 6" barrel, with loading lever (Dixie Gun Works) $254.95
Price: 4" (Cabela's, Uberti USA Inc.) $169.95

CABELA'S PATERSON REVOLVER
Caliber: 36, 5-shot cylinder.
Barrel: 7 1/2".
Weight: 24 oz. **Length:** 11 1/2" overall.
Stocks: One-piece walnut.
Sights: Fixed.
Features: Recreation of the 1836 gun. Color case-hardened frame, steel backstrap; roll-engraved cylinder scene. Imported by Cabela's.
Price: $229.95

COLT 1849 POCKET DRAGOON REVOLVER
Caliber: 31.
Barrel: 4".
Weight: 24 oz. **Length:** 9 1/2" overall.
Stocks: One-piece walnut.
Sights: Fixed. Brass pin front, hammer notch rear.
Features: Color case-hardened frame. No loading lever. Unfluted cylinder with engraved scene. Exact reproduction of original. From Colt Blackpowder Arms Co.
Price: $390.00

Stone Mountain Arms Sheriff's Model
Similar to the Uberti 1861 Navy except has 5 1/2" barrel, brass or steel frame, semi-fluted cylinder. In 44-caliber only.
Price: Steel frame, finished $179.95
Price: Brass frame (Armsport) $155.00
Price: Steel frame (Armsport) $193.00

> Consult our Directory pages for the location of firms mentioned.

COLT 1860 ARMY PERCUSSION REVOLVER
Caliber: 44.
Barrel: 8", 7 groove, left-hand twist.
Weight: 42 oz.
Stocks: One-piece walnut.
Sights: German silver front sight, hammer notch rear.
Features: Steel backstrap cut for shoulder stock; brass trigger guard. Cylinder has Navy scene. Color case-hardened frame, hammer, loading lever. Reproduction of original gun with all original markings. From Colt Blackpowder Arms Co.
Price: $427.50

Colt 1860 "Cavalry Model" Percussion Revolver
Similar to the 1860 Army except has fluted cylinder. Color case-hardened frame, hammer, loading lever and plunger; blued barrel, backstrap and cylinder, brass trigger guard. Has four-screw frame cut for optional shoulder stock. From Colt Blackpowder Arms Co.
Price: $465.00

BLACKPOWDER REVOLVERS

Griswold & Gunnison

COLT THIRD MODEL DRAGOON
Caliber: 44.
Barrel: 7½".
Weight: 66 oz. **Length:** 13¾" overall.
Stocks: One-piece walnut.
Sights: Blade front, hammer notch rear.
Features: Color case-hardened frame, hammer, lever and plunger; round trigger guard; flat mainspring; hammer roller; rectangular bolt cuts. From Colt Blackpowder Arms Co.
Price: Three-screw frame with brass grip straps $487.50
Price: Four-screw frame with blued steel grip straps, shoulder stock cuts, dovetailed folding leaf rear sight $502.50

COLT 1862 POCKET POLICE "TRAPPER MODEL" REVOLVER
Caliber: 36.
Barrel: 3½".
Weight: 20 oz. **Length:** 8½" overall.
Stocks: One-piece walnut.
Sights: Blade front, hammer notch rear.
Features: Has separate 4⅝" brass ramrod. Color case-hardened frame and hammer; silver-plated backstrap and trigger guard; blued semi-fluted cylinder, blued barrel. From Colt Blackpowder Arms Co.
Price: $442.50

Manufacturers' addresses in the **Directory of the Arms Trade** *page 313, this issue*

DIXIE WYATT EARP REVOLVER
Caliber: 44.
Barrel: 12" octagon.
Weight: 46 oz. **Length:** 18" overall.
Stocks: Two-piece walnut.
Sights: Fixed.
Features: Highly polished brass frame, backstrap and trigger guard; blued barrel and cylinder; case-hardened hammer, trigger and loading lever. Navy-size shoulder stock ($45) will fit with minor fitting. From Dixie Gun Works.
Price: $130.00

GRISWOLD & GUNNISON PERCUSSION REVOLVER
Caliber: 36 or 44, 6-shot.
Barrel: 7½".
Weight: 44 oz. (36-cal.). **Length:** 13" overall.
Stocks: Walnut.
Sights: Fixed.
Features: Replica of famous Confederate pistol. Brass frame, backstrap and trigger guard; case-hardened loading lever; rebated cylinder (44-cal. only). Rounded Dragoon-type barrel. Imported by Navy Arms as Reb Model 1860.
Price: $115.00
Price: Kit $90.00
Price: Single cased set $235.00
Price: Double cased set $365.00

LE MAT REVOLVER
Caliber: 44/65.
Barrel: 6¾" (revolver); 4⅞" (single shot).
Weight: 3 lbs., 7 oz.
Stocks: Hand-checkered walnut.
Sights: Post front, hammer notch rear.
Features: Exact reproduction with all-steel construction; 44-cal. 9-shot cylinder, 65-cal. single barrel; color case-hardened hammer with selector; spur trigger guard; ring at butt; lever-type barrel release. From Navy Arms.
Price: Cavalry model (lanyard ring, spur trigger guard) $595.00
Price: Army model (round trigger guard, pin-type barrel release) $595.00
Price: Naval-style (thumb selector on hammer) $595.00
Price: Engraved 18th Georgia cased set $795.00
Price: Engraved Beauregard cased set $1,000.00

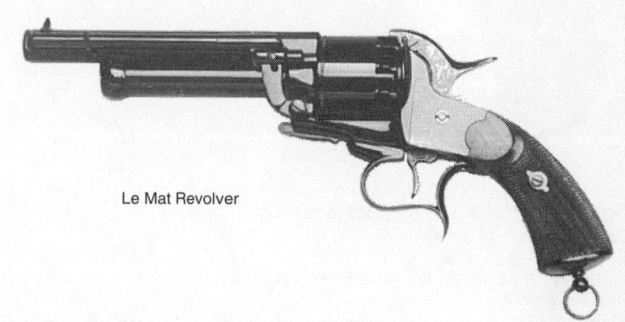
Le Mat Revolver

NAVY MODEL 1851 PERCUSSION REVOLVER
Caliber: 36, 44, 6-shot.
Barrel: 7½".
Weight: 44 oz. **Length:** 13" overall.
Stocks: Walnut finish.
Sights: Post front, hammer notch rear.
Features: Brass backstrap and trigger guard; some have 1st Model squareback trigger guard, engraved cylinder with navy battle scene; case-hardened frame, hammer, loading lever. Imported by American Arms, The Armoury, Cabela's, Navy Arms, E.M.F., Dixie Gun Works, Euroarms of America, Armsport, CVA (36-cal. only), Traditions (44 only), Uberti USA Inc., Stone Mountain Arms.
Price: Brass frame ....$99.95 to $280.00
Price: Steel frame ....$130.00 to $285.00
Price: Kit form ....$110.00 to $123.95
Price: Engraved model (Dixie Gun Works) $139.95
Price: Single cased set, steel frame (Navy Arms) $280.00
Price: Double cased set, steel frame (Navy Arms) $455.00
Price: Confederate Navy (Cabela's) $69.95
Price: Hartford model, steel frame, German silver trim, cartouche (E.M.F.) $190.00

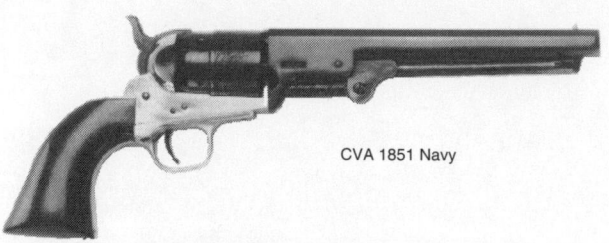
CVA 1851 Navy

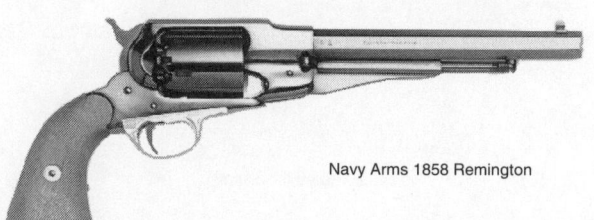
Navy Arms 1858 Remington

NAVY ARMS DELUXE 1858 REMINGTON-STYLE REVOLVER
Caliber: 44.
Barrel: 8".
Weight: 2 lbs., 13 oz.
Stocks: Smooth walnut.
Sights: Dovetailed blade front.
Features: First exact reproduction—correct in size and weight to the original, with progressive rifling; highly polished with blue finish, silver-plated trigger guard. From Navy Arms.
Price: Deluxe model $415.00

CAUTION: PRICES SHOWN ARE SUPPLIED BY THE MANUFACTURER OR IMPORTER. CHECK YOUR LOCAL GUNSHOP.

BLACKPOWDER REVOLVERS

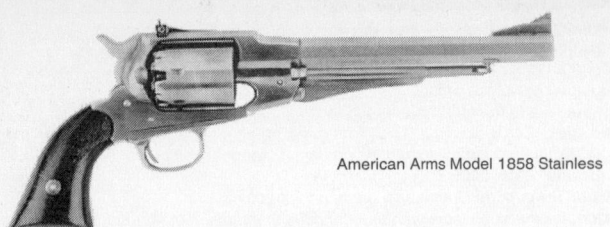
American Arms Model 1858 Stainless

NEW MODEL 1858 ARMY PERCUSSION REVOLVER
Caliber: 36 or 44, 6-shot.
Barrel: 6 1/2" or 8".
Weight: 38 oz. **Length:** 13 1/2" overall.
Stocks: Walnut.
Sights: Blade front, groove-in-frame rear.
Features: Replica of Remington Model 1858. Also available from some importers as Army Model Belt Revolver in 36-cal., a shortened and lightened version of the 44. Target Model (Uberti USA Inc., Navy Arms) has fully adjustable target rear sight, target front, 36 or 44. Imported by American Arms, Cabela's, Cimarron, CVA (as 1858 Army, steel or brass frame, 44 only), Dixie Gun Works, Navy Arms, The Armoury, E.M.F., Euroarms of America (engraved, stainless and plain), Armsport, Traditions (44 only), Uberti USA Inc. Stone Mountain Arms.
Price: Steel frame, about ....$99.95 to $280.00
Price: Steel frame kit (Euroarms, Navy Arms) ....$115.95 to $242.00
Price: Single cased set (Navy Arms) $290.00
Price: Double cased set (Navy Arms) $480.00
Price: Stainless steel Model 1858 (American Arms, Euroarms, Uberti USA Inc., Cabela's, Navy Arms, Armsport, Traditions) ....$169.95 to $380.00
Price: Target Model, adjustable rear sight (Cabela's, Euroarms, Uberti USA Inc., Navy Arms, Stone Mountain Arms) ....$95.95 to $399.00
Price: Brass frame (CVA, Cabela's, Traditions, Navy Arms) ...$79.95 to $212.95
Price: As above, kit (Dixie Gun Works, Navy Arms) ....$145.00 to $188.95
Price: Buffalo model, 44-cal. (Cabela's) $129.95
Price: Hartford model, steel frame, German silver trim, cartouche (E.M.F.) $215.00

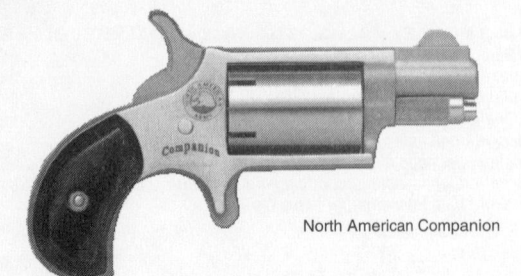
North American Companion

NORTH AMERICAN COMPANION PERCUSSION REVOLVER
Caliber: 22.
Barrel: 1 1/8".
Weight: 5.1 oz. **Length:** 4 5/10" overall.
Stocks: Laminated wood.
Sights: Blade front, notch fixed rear.
Features: All stainless steel construction. Uses standard #11 percussion caps. Comes with bullets, powder measure, bullet seater, leather clip holster, gun rag. Long Rifle or Magnum frame size. Introduced 1996. Made in U.S. by North American Arms.
Price: Long Rifle frame $160.00

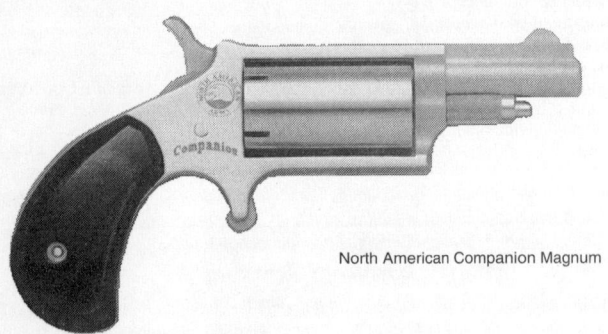
North American Companion Magnum

North American Magnum Companion Percussion Revolver
Similar to the Companion except has larger frame. Weighs 7.2 oz., has 1 5/8" barrel, measures 5 7/16" overall. Comes with bullets, powder measure, bullet seater, leather clip holster, gun rag. Introduced 1996. Made in U.S. by North American Arms.
Price: $180.00

POCKET POLICE 1862 PERCUSSION REVOLVER
Caliber: 36, 5-shot.
Barrel: 4 1/2", 5 1/2", 6 1/2", 7 1/2".
Weight: 26 oz. **Length:** 12" overall (6 1/2" bbl.).
Stocks: Walnut.
Sights: Fixed.
Features: Round tapered barrel; half-fluted and rebated cylinder; case-hardened frame, loading lever and hammer; silver or brass trigger guard and backstrap. Imported by CVA (7 1/2" only), Navy Arms (5 1/2" only), Uberti USA Inc. (5 1/2", 6 1/2" only).
Price: About ....$139.95 to $310.00
Price: Single cased set with accessories (Navy Arms) $365.00
Price: Hartford model, steel frame, German silver trim, cartouche (E.M.F.) $215.00

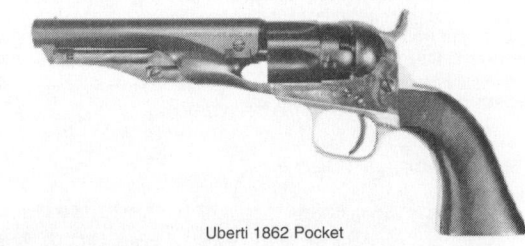
Uberti 1862 Pocket

> Consult our Directory pages for the location of firms mentioned.

ROGERS & SPENCER PERCUSSION REVOLVER
Caliber: 44.
Barrel: 7 1/2".
Weight: 47 oz. **Length:** 13 3/4" overall.
Stocks: Walnut.
Sights: Cone front, integral groove in frame for rear.
Features: Accurate reproduction of a Civil War design. Solid frame; extra large nipple cut-out on rear of cylinder; loading lever and cylinder easily removed for cleaning. From Euroarms of America (standard blue, engraved, burnished, target models), Navy Arms, Stone Mountain Arms.
Price: ....$160.00 to $289.00
Price: Nickel-plated $215.00
Price: Engraved (Euroarms) $287.00
Price: Kit version ....$245.00 to $252.00
Price: Target version (Euroarms, Navy Arms) ....$239.00 to $270.00
Price: Burnished London Gray (Euroarms, Navy Arms) .....$245.00 to $270.00

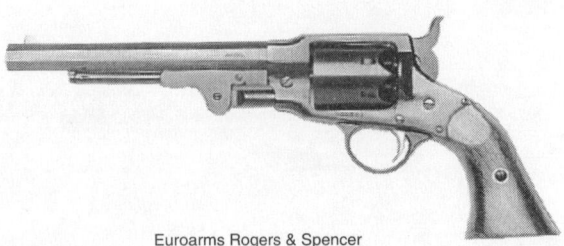
Euroarms Rogers & Spencer

BLACKPOWDER REVOLVERS

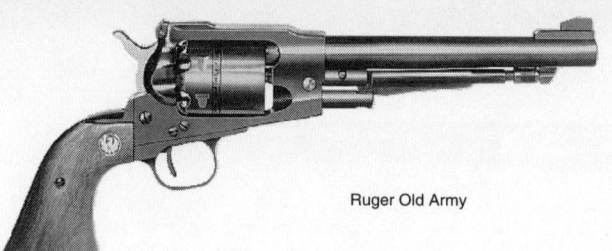
Ruger Old Army

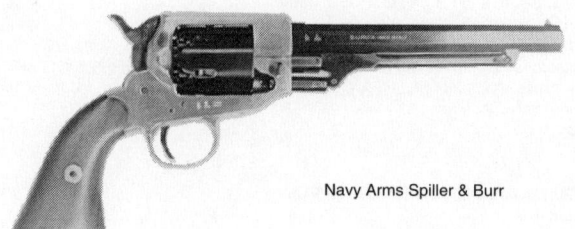
Navy Arms Spiller & Burr

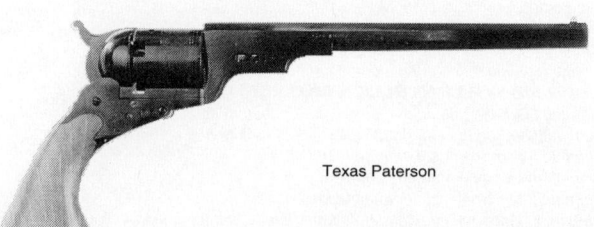
Texas Paterson

RUGER OLD ARMY PERCUSSION REVOLVER
Caliber: 45, 6-shot. Uses .457" dia. lead bullets.
Barrel: 7 1/2" (6-groove, 16" twist).
Weight: 46 oz. **Length:** 13 3/4" overall.
Stocks: Smooth walnut.
Sights: Ramp front, rear adjustable for windage and elevation; or fixed (groove).
Features: Stainless steel; standard size nipples, chrome-moly steel cylinder and frame, same lockwork as in original Super Blackhawk. Also available in stainless steel. Made in USA. From Sturm, Ruger & Co.
Price: Stainless steel (Model KBP-7) $465.00
Price: Blued steel (Model BP-7) $413.00
Price: Stainless steel, fixed sight (KBP-7F) $465.00
Price: Blued steel, fixed sight (BP-7F) $413.00

SHERIFF MODEL 1851 PERCUSSION REVOLVER
Caliber: 36, 44, 6-shot.
Barrel: 5".
Weight: 40 oz. **Length:** 10 1/2" overall.
Stocks: Walnut.
Sights: Fixed.
Features: Brass backstrap and trigger guard; engraved navy scene; case-hardened frame, hammer, loading lever. Imported by E.M.F., Stone Mountain Arms (5 1/2" barrel).
Price: Steel frame (E.M.F.) $172.00
Price: Brass frame (E.M.F.) $140.00
Price: Steel frame (Stone Mountain Arms) $159.95

SPILLER & BURR REVOLVER
Caliber: 36 (.375" round ball).
Barrel: 7", octagon.
Weight: 2 1/2 lbs. **Length:** 12 1/2" overall.
Stocks: Two-piece walnut.
Sights: Fixed.
Features: Reproduction of the C.S.A. revolver. Brass frame and trigger guard. Also available as a kit. From Cabela's, Dixie Gun Works, Navy Arms.
Price: ....$89.95 to $199.00
Price: Kit form $129.95
Price: Single cased set (Navy Arms) $270.00
Price: Double cased set (Navy Arms) $430.00

TEXAS PATERSON 1836 REVOLVER
Caliber: 36 (.375" round ball).
Barrel: 7 1/2".
Weight: 42 oz.
Stocks: One-piece walnut.
Sights: Fixed.
Features: Copy of Sam Colt's first commercially-made revolving pistol. Has no loading lever but comes with loading tool. From Dixie Gun Works, Navy Arms, Uberti USA Inc.
Price: About ....$325.00 to $395.00
Price: With loading lever (Uberti USA Inc.) $450.00
Price: Engraved (Navy Arms) $465.00

UBERTI 1862 POCKET NAVY PERCUSSION REVOLVER
Caliber: 36, 5-shot.
Barrel: 5 1/2", 6 1/2", octagonal, 7-groove, LH twist.
Weight: 27 oz. (5 1/2" barrel). **Length:** 10 1/2" overall (5 1/2" bbl.).
Stocks: One-piece varnished walnut.
Sights: Brass pin front, hammer notch rear.
Features: Rebated cylinder, hinged loading lever, brass or silver-plated backstrap and trigger guard, color-cased frame, hammer, loading lever, plunger and latch, rest blued. Has original-type markings. From Uberti USA Inc.
Price: With brass backstrap, trigger guard $310.00

UBERTI 1st MODEL DRAGOON
Caliber: 44.
Barrel: 7 1/2", part round, part octagon.
Weight: 64 oz.
Stocks: One-piece walnut.
Sights: German silver blade front, hammer notch rear.
Features: First model has oval bolt cuts in cylinder, square-back flared trigger guard, V-type mainspring, short trigger. Ranger and Indian scene roll-engraved on cylinder. Color case-hardened frame, loading lever, plunger and hammer; blue barrel, cylinder, trigger and wedge. Available with old-time charcoal blue or standard blue-black finish. Polished brass backstrap and trigger guard. From Uberti USA Inc.
Price: $325.00

Uberti 2nd Model Dragoon Revolver
Similar to the 1st Model except distinguished by rectangular bolt cuts in the cylinder.
Price: $325.00

Uberti 3rd Model Dragoon Revolver
Similar to the 2nd Model except for oval trigger guard, long trigger, modifications to the loading lever and latch. Imported by Uberti USA Inc.
Price: Military model (frame cut for shoulder stock, steel backstrap) $330.00
Price: Civilian (brass backstrap, trigger guard) $325.00

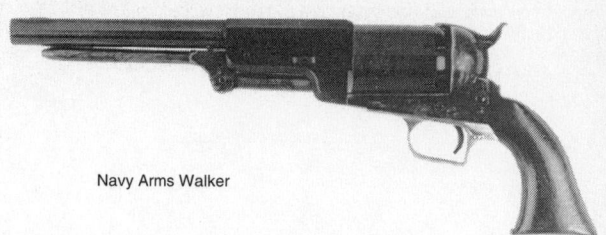
Navy Arms Walker

WALKER 1847 PERCUSSION REVOLVER
Caliber: 44, 6-shot.
Barrel: 9".
Weight: 84 oz. **Length:** 15 1/2" overall.
Stocks: Walnut.
Sights: Fixed.
Features: Case-hardened frame, loading lever and hammer; iron backstrap; brass trigger guard; engraved cylinder. Imported by Cabela's, CVA, Navy Arms, Dixie Gun Works, Uberti USA Inc., E.M.F., Cimarron, Traditions.
Price: About ....$225.00 to $360.00
Price: Single cased set (Navy Arms) $405.00
Price: Deluxe Walker with French fitted case (Navy Arms) $505.00
Price: Hartford model, steel frame, German silver trim, cartouche (E.M.F.) $295.00

CAUTION: PRICES SHOWN ARE SUPPLIED BY THE MANUFACTURER OR IMPORTER. CHECK YOUR LOCAL GUNSHOP.

BLACKPOWDER MUSKETS & RIFLES

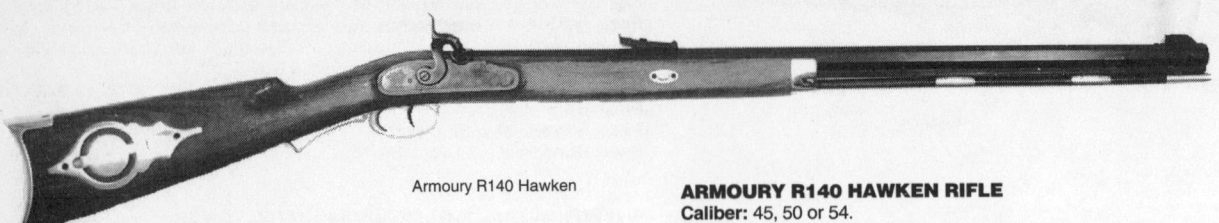

Armoury R140 Hawken

ARMSPORT 1863 SHARPS RIFLE, CARBINE
Caliber: 45, 54.
Barrel: 28", round.
Weight: 8.4 lbs. **Length:** 46" overall.
Stock: Walnut.
Sights: Blade front, folding adjustable rear. Tang sight set optionally available.
Features: Replica of the 1863 Sharps. Color case-hardened frame, rest blued. Imported by Armsport.
Price: $740.00
Price: Carbine, 54 caliber, 22" barrel $640.00

CABELA'S BLUE RIDGE RIFLE
Caliber: 32, 36, 45, 50, 54.
Barrel: 39", octagonal.
Weight: About 7 3/4 lbs. **Length:** 55" overall.
Stock: American black walnut.
Sights: Blade front, rear drift adjustable for windage.
Features: Color case-hardened lockplate and cock/hammer, brass trigger guard and buttplate, double set, double-phased triggers. From Cabela's.
Price: Percussion $299.95
Price: Flintlock $319.95
Price: Percussion carbine (28" barrel) $259.95

CABELA'S RED RIVER RIFLE
Caliber: 45, 50, 54, 58.
Barrel: NA.
Weight: About 7 lbs. **Length:** 45" overall.
Stock: Walnut-stained hardwood.
Sights: Blade front, adjustable buckhorn rear.
Features: Brass trigger guard, forend cap, thimbles; color case-hardened lock and hammer; rubber recoil pad. Introduced 1995. Imported by Cabela's.
Price: $119.95

CABELA'S SHARPS SPORTING RIFLE
Caliber: 45, 54.
Barrel: 31", octagonal.
Weight: About 10 lbs. **Length:** 49" overall.
Stock: American walnut with checkered grip and forend.
Sights: Blade front, ladder-type adjustable rear.
Features: Color case-hardened lock and buttplate. Adjustable double set, double-phased triggers. From Cabela's.
Price: $649.00

Manufacturers' addresses in the
Directory of the Arms Trade
page 313, this issue

ARMOURY R140 HAWKEN RIFLE
Caliber: 45, 50 or 54.
Barrel: 29".
Weight: 8 3/4 to 9 lbs. **Length:** 45 3/4" overall.
Stock: Walnut, with cheekpiece.
Sights: Dovetail front, fully adjustable rear.
Features: Octagon barrel, removable breech plug; double set triggers; blued barrel, brass stock fittings, color case-hardened percussion lock. From Armsport, The Armoury.
Price: ....$225.00 to $245.00

BOSTONIAN PERCUSSION RIFLE
Caliber: 45.
Barrel: 30", octagonal.
Weight: 7 1/4 lbs. **Length:** 46" overall.
Stock: Walnut.
Sights: Blade front, fixed notch rear.
Features: Color case-hardened lock, brass trigger guard, buttplate, patchbox. Imported from Italy by E.M.F.
Price: $285.00

CABELA'S ROLLING BLOCK MUZZLELOADER
Caliber: 50, 54.
Barrel: 26 1/2" octagonal; 1:32" (50), 1:48" (54) twist.
Weight: About 9 1/4 lbs. **Length:** 43 1/2" overall.
Stock: American walnut, rubber butt pad.
Sights: Blade front, adjustable buckhorn rear.
Features: Uses in-line ignition system, Brass trigger guard, color case-hardened hammer, block and buttplate; black-finished, engraved receiver; easily removable screw-in breech plug; black ramrod and thimble. From Cabela's.
Price: $289.95

Cabela's Rolling Block Muzzleloader Carbine
Similar to the rifle version except has 22 1/4" barrel, weighs 8 1/4 lbs. Has bead on ramp front sight, modern fully adjustable rear. From Cabela's.
Price: $269.95

CABELA'S TRADITIONAL HAWKEN
Caliber: 45, 50, 54, 58.
Barrel: 29".
Weight: About 9 lbs.
Stock: Walnut.
Sights: Blade front, open adjustable rear.
Features: Flintlock or percussion. Adjustable double-set triggers. Polished brass furniture, color case-hardened lock. Imported by Cabela's.
Price: Percussion, right-hand $159.95
Price: Percussion, left-hand $169.95
Price: Flintlock, right-hand $184.95

Cabela's Sporterized Hawken Hunter Rifle
Similar to the Traditional Hawken's except has more modern stock style with rubber recoil pad, blued furniture, sling swivels. Percussion only, in 45-, 50-, 54- or 58-caliber.
Price: Carbine or rifle, right-hand $179.95
Price: Carbine or rifle, left-hand $189.95

COLT MODEL 1861 MUSKET
Caliber: 58.
Barrel: 40".
Weight: 9 lbs., 3 oz. **Length:** 56" overall.
Stock: Oil-finished walnut.
Sights: Blade front, adjustable folding leaf rear.
Features: Made to original specifications and has authentic Civil War Colt markings. Bright-finished metal, blued nipple and rear sight. Bayonet and accessories available. From Colt Blackpowder Arms Co.
Price: $615.00

BLACKPOWDER MUSKETS & RIFLES

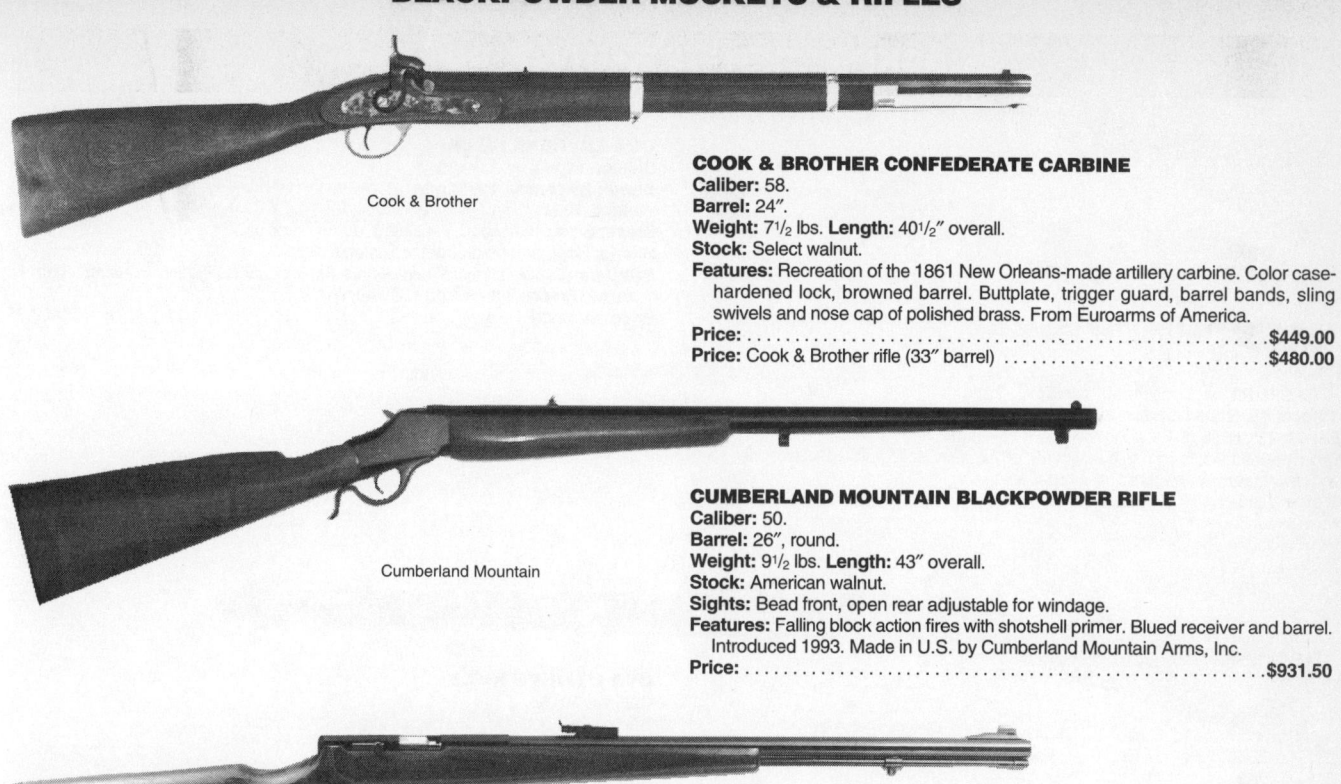
Cook & Brother

COOK & BROTHER CONFEDERATE CARBINE
Caliber: 58.
Barrel: 24".
Weight: 7 1/2 lbs. **Length:** 40 1/2" overall.
Stock: Select walnut.
Features: Recreation of the 1861 New Orleans-made artillery carbine. Color case-hardened lock, browned barrel. Buttplate, trigger guard, barrel bands, sling swivels and nose cap of polished brass. From Euroarms of America.
Price: $449.00
Price: Cook & Brother rifle (33" barrel) $480.00

Cumberland Mountain

CUMBERLAND MOUNTAIN BLACKPOWDER RIFLE
Caliber: 50.
Barrel: 26", round.
Weight: 9 1/2 lbs. **Length:** 43" overall.
Stock: American walnut.
Sights: Bead front, open rear adjustable for windage.
Features: Falling block action fires with shotshell primer. Blued receiver and barrel. Introduced 1993. Made in U.S. by Cumberland Mountain Arms, Inc.
Price: $931.50

CVA Apollo Classic

CVA APOLLO SHADOW, CLASSIC RIFLES
Caliber: 50, 54.
Barrel: 24"; round with octagon integral receiver; 1:32" twist.
Weight: 7-7 1/2 lbs. **Length:** 42" overall.
Stock: Synthetic Dura-Grip (Shadow); brown laminate with swivel studs (Classic); pistol grip, solid rubber buttpad.
Sights: Blade on ramp front, fully adjustable rear; drilled and tapped for scope mounting.
Features: In-line ignition, modern-style trigger with automatic safety; oversize trigger guard; synthetic ramrod. From CVA.
Price: Shadow $229.95
Price: Classic $259.95

CVA Buckmaster Rifle
Similar to the Apollo Comet except has Dura-Grip synthetic stock with Advantage camouflage pattern, and blued barrel and action. Introduced 1996. From CVA.
Price: $239.00

CVA Apollo Comet Rifle
Similar to the Apollo Shadow except stainless steel barrel and action, synthetic stock with matte black finish. Available in 50-caliber only. Introduced 1995. From CVA.
Price: $279.95

CVA Staghorn Rifle
Similar to the Apollo Comet except has blued barrel and action, and is available in 50, 54 caliber. Drilled and tapped receiver for scope mount or aperture sight. Introduced 1996.
Price: $179.00

CVA BOBCAT RIFLE
Caliber: 50 and 54.
Barrel: 26"; 1:48" twist.
Weight: 6 1/2 lbs. **Length:** 40" overall.
Stock: Dura-Grip synthetic.
Sights: Blade front, open rear.
Features: Oversize trigger guard; wood ramrod; matte black finish. Introduced 1995. From CVA.
Price: $99.95

CVA Apollo Dominator
Similar to the Apollo Shadow except has a Bell & Carlson synthetic thumbhole stock, stainless steel barrel and action, Williams micro adjustable rear sight, bead on blade front. Drilled and tapped for scope mounting. Introduced 1996. From CVA.
Price: $329.95

CVA Bobcat Hunter
Similar to the Bobcat except has black synthetic stock with checkered wrist and forend, drilled and tapped for scope mounting, engraved, blued lockplate and offset hammer, and has sporter adjustable rear sight. Available in 50- and 54-caliber. Introduced 1995. From CVA.
Price: $149.95

CVA Apollo Brown Bear
Similar to the CVA Classic except has select grade hardwood stock with oil finish, raised comb and cheekpiece; bead front sight, Williams Hunter rear; blued barrel, receiver; drilled and tapped for scope mounting. Introduced 1996. From CVA.
Price: $229.95

BLACKPOWDER MUSKETS & RIFLES

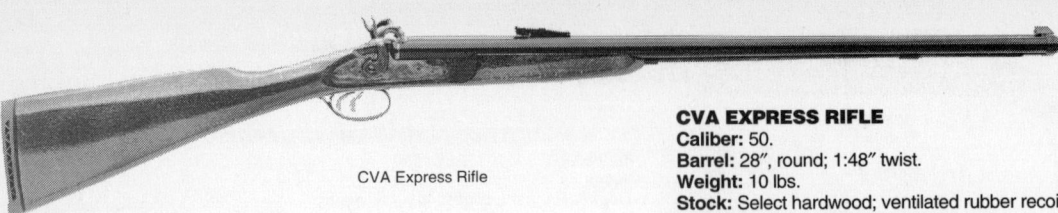

CVA Express Rifle

CVA EXPRESS RIFLE
Caliber: 50.
Barrel: 28", round; 1:48" twist.
Weight: 10 lbs.
Stock: Select hardwood; ventilated rubber recoil pad.
Sights: Bead and blade front, adjustable rear.
Features: Double rifle with twin percussion locks and triggers, adjustable barrels. Button breech. Introduced 1989. From CVA.
Price: Finished $429.95

CVA FRONTIER HUNTER CARBINE
Caliber: 50, 54.
Barrel: 24"; 15/16" flats; 1:32" twist.
Weight: 6 3/4 lbs. **Length:** 40" overall.
Stock: Laminated hardwood.
Sights: Bead front, Patridge-style click-adjustable rear.
Features: Offset hammer; black-chromed furniture; solid buttpad; barrel drilled and tapped for scope mounting. From CVA.
Price: $219.95

CVA St. Louis Hawken

CVA HAWKEN RIFLE
Caliber: 50, 54.
Barrel: 28", octagon; 15/16" across flats; 1:48" twist.
Weight: 8 lbs. **Length:** 44" overall.
Stock: Select hardwood.
Sights: Beaded blade front, fully adjustable open rear.
Features: Fully adjustable double-set triggers; synthetic ramrod (kits have wood); brass patch box, wedge plates, nosecap, thimbles, trigger guard and buttplate; blued barrel; color case-hardened, engraved lockplate. V-type mainspring. Button breech. Introduced 1981. From CVA.
Price: St. Louis Hawken, finished (50-, 54-cal.) $209.95
Price: As above, combo kit (50-, 54-cal. bbls.) $229.95
Price: Left-hand, percussion $234.95
Price: Flintlock, 50-cal. only $234.95
Price: Flintlock, left-hand $249.95
Price: Percussion kit (50-cal., blued, wood ramrod) $169.95
Price: St. Louis Hawken Classic (laminated stock) $249.95

CVA KENTUCKY RIFLE
Caliber: 50.
Barrel: 33 1/2", rifled, octagon; 7/8" flats.
Weight: 7 1/2 lbs. **Length:** 48" overall.
Stock: Select hardwood.
Sights: Brass Kentucky blade-type front, fixed open rear.
Features: Available in percussion only. Color case-hardened lockplate. Stainless steel nipple included. From CVA.
Price: Percussion $279.95
Price: Percussion kit $189.95

CVA Lynx

CVA LYNX RIFLE
Caliber: 50 and 54.
Barrel: 26", octagonal; 15/16" flats; 1:48" twist.
Weight: About 6 1/2 lbs. **Length:** 40" overall.
Stock: Dura-Grip synthetic.
Sights: Beaded blade front, rear adjustable for windage.
Features: Oversize trigger guard; color case-hardened lock, blued barrel, Realtree All Purpose® camo stock. Drilled and tapped for scope mounting. Synthetic ramrod. Introduced 1995. From CVA.
Price: $179.95

CVA PLAINSHUNTER RIFLE
Caliber: 50.
Barrel: 26", octagonal; 15/16" flats; 1:48" twist.
Weight: About 6 1/2 lbs. **Length:** 40" overall.
Stock: Select hardwood.
Sights: Brass blade front, semi-buckhorn rear.
Features: Brass nosecap, thimbles, wedge plates; wood ramrod. Introduced 1995. From CVA.
Price: $174.95

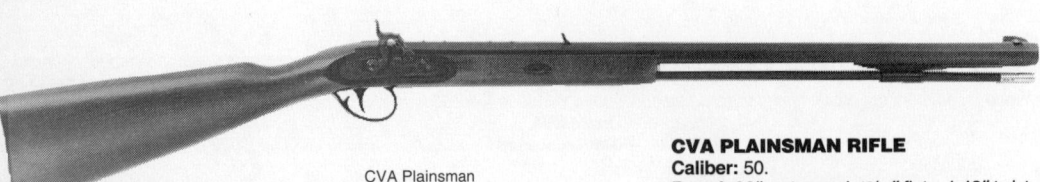

CVA Plainsman

CVA PLAINSMAN RIFLE
Caliber: 50.
Barrel: 26", octagonal; 15/16" flats; 1:48" twist.
Weight: 6 1/2 lbs. **Length:** 40" overall.
Stock: Stained hardwood.
Sights: Brass blade front, fixed rear.
Features: Oversize trigger guard; color case-hardened lock; wood ramrod; matte finish. Introduced 1995. From CVA.
Price: $159.95

BLACKPOWDER MUSKETS & RIFLES

CVA Timber Wolf

CVA VARMINT RIFLE
Caliber: 32.
Barrel: 24" octagonal; 7/8" flats; 1:48" rifling.
Weight: 6 3/4 lbs. **Length:** 40" overall.
Stock: Select hardwood.
Sights: Blade front, Patridge-style click adjustable rear.
Features: Brass trigger guard, nose cap, wedge plate, thimble and buttplate. Drilled and tapped for scope mounting. Color case-hardened lock. Single trigger. Aluminum ramrod. Imported by CVA.
Price: $219.95

CVA WOLF SERIES RIFLES
Caliber: 50, 54.
Barrel: 26" octagonal; 1:32: twist; 15/16" flats; blue finish.
Weight: 6 1/2 lbs. **Length:** 40" overall.
Stock: Tuff-Lite polymer—gray finish, solid buttplate (Grey Wolf); Realtree All Purpose® camo finish, solid buttplate (Timber Wolf); checkered grip.
Sights: Blade front on ramp, fully adjustable open rear; drilled and tapped for scope mounting.
Features: Oversize trigger guard; synthetic ramrod; offset hammer. From CVA.
Price: Grey Wolf $199.95
Price: Timber Wolf (50-cal. only) $229.95

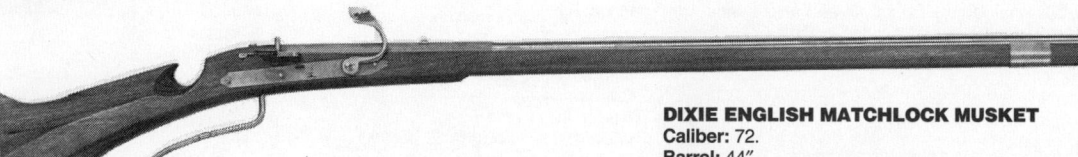

CVA Silver Wolf

CVA Silver Wolf Rifle
Similar to the Wolf Series except has 26" stainless steel barrel, nickeled lock, black Tufflite Dura-Grip synthetic stock. Introduced 1995. From CVA.
Price: $229.95

Dixie English Matchlock

DIXIE ENGLISH MATCHLOCK MUSKET
Caliber: 72.
Barrel: 44".
Weight: 8 lbs. **Length:** 57.75" overall.
Stock: Walnut with satin oil finish.
Sights: Blade front, open rear adjustable for windage.
Features: Replica of circa 1600-1680 English matchlock. Getz barrel with 11" octagonal area at rear, rest is round with cannon-type muzzle. All steel finished in the white. Imported by Dixie Gun Works.
Price: $895.00

DIXIE DELUX CUB RIFLE
Caliber: 40.
Barrel: 28".
Weight: 6 1/2 lbs.
Stock: Walnut.
Sights: Fixed.
Features: Short rifle for small game and beginning shooters. Brass patchbox and furniture. Flint or percussion. From Dixie Gun Works.
Price: Finished $335.00
Price: Kit $259.00
Price: Deerslayer (50-caliber) $350.00

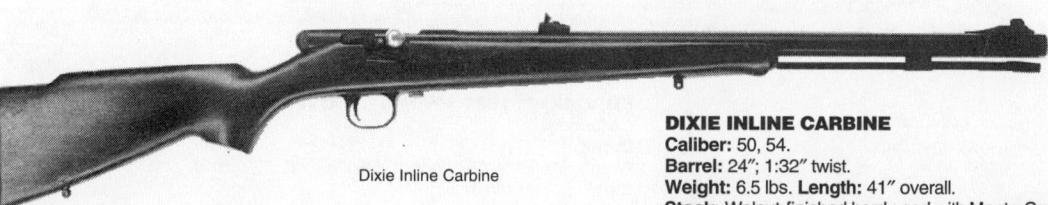

Dixie 1859 Sharps

DIXIE SHARPS NEW MODEL 1859 MILITARY RIFLE
Caliber: 54.
Barrel: 30", 6-groove; 1:48" twist.
Weight: 9 lbs. **Length:** 45 1/2" overall.
Stock: Oiled walnut.
Sights: Blade front, ladder-style rear.
Features: Blued barrel, color case-hardened barrel bands, receiver, hammer, nose cap, lever, patchbox cover and buttplate. Introduced 1995. Imported from Italy by Dixie Gun Works.
Price: $895.00

Dixie Inline Carbine

DIXIE INLINE CARBINE
Caliber: 50, 54.
Barrel: 24"; 1:32" twist.
Weight: 6.5 lbs. **Length:** 41" overall.
Stock: Walnut-finished hardwood with Monte Carlo comb.
Sights: Ramp front with red insert, open fully adjustable rear.
Features: Sliding "bolt" fully encloses cap and nipple. Fully adjustable trigger, automatic safety. Aluminum ramrod. Imported from Italy by Dixie Gun Works.
Price: $349.95

BLACKPOWDER MUSKETS & RIFLES

DIXIE TENNESSEE MOUNTAIN RIFLE
Caliber: 32 or 50.
Barrel: 41½", 6-groove rifling, brown finish. **Length:** 56" overall.
Stock: Walnut, oil finish; Kentucky-style.
Sights: Silver blade front, open buckhorn rear.
Features: Recreation of the original mountain rifles. Early Schultz lock, interchangeable flint or percussion with vent plug or drum and nipple. Tumbler has fly. Double-set triggers. All metal parts browned. From Dixie Gun Works.
Price: Flint or percussion, finished rifle, 50-cal. $575.00
Price: Kit, 50-cal. $495.00
Price: Left-hand model, flint or percussion $575.00
Price: Left-hand kit, flint or perc., 50-cal. $495.00
Price: Squirrel Rifle (as above except in 32-cal. with 13/16" barrel flats), flint or percussion $575.00
Price: Kit, 32-cal., flint or percussion $495.00

DIXIE 1863 SPRINGFIELD MUSKET
Caliber: 58 (.570" patched ball or .575" Minie).
Barrel: 50", rifled.
Stocks: Walnut stained.
Sights: Blade front, adjustable ladder-type rear.
Features: Bright-finish lock, barrel, furniture. Reproduction of the last of the regulation muzzleloaders. Imported from Japan by Dixie Gun Works.
Price: Finished $595.00
Price: Kit $525.00

Dixie Model 1816

DIXIE U.S. MODEL 1816 FLINTLOCK MUSKET
Caliber: 69.
Barrel: 42", smoothbore.
Weight: 9.75 lbs. **Length:** 56.5" overall.
Stock: Walnut with oil finish.
Sights: Blade front.
Features: All metal finished "National Armory Bright"; three barrel bands with springs; steel ramrod with button-shaped head. Imported by Dixie Gun Works.
Price: $725.00

DIXIE U.S. MODEL 1861 SPRINGFIELD
Caliber: 58.
Barrel: 40".
Weight: About 8 lbs. **Length:** 55 13/16" overall.
Stock: Oil-finished walnut.
Sights: Blade front, step adjustable rear.
Features: Exact recreation of original rifle. Sling swivels attached to trigger guard bow and middle barrel band. Lockplate marked "1861" with eagle motif and "U.S. Springfield" in front of hammer; "U.S." stamped on top of buttplate. From Dixie Gun Works.
Price: $595.00
Price: From Stone Mountain Arms $599.00
Price: Kit $525.00

E.M.F. 1863 SHARPS MILITARY CARBINE
Caliber: 54.
Barrel: 22", round.
Weight: 8 lbs. **Length:** 39" overall.
Stock: Oiled walnut.
Sights: Blade front, military ladder-type rear.
Features: Color case-hardened lock, rest blued. Imported by E.M.F.
Price: $860.00

> Consult our Directory pages for the location of firms mentioned.

Euroarms Volunteer

EUROARMS BUFFALO CARBINE
Caliber: 58.
Barrel: 26", round.
Weight: 7¾ lbs. **Length:** 42" overall.
Stock: Walnut.
Sights: Blade front, open adjustable rear.
Features: Shoots .575" round ball. Color case-hardened lock, blue hammer, barrel, trigger; brass furniture. Brass patchbox. Imported by Euroarms of America.
Price: $440.00

EUROARMS VOLUNTEER TARGET RIFLE
Caliber: .451.
Barrel: 33" (two-band), 36" (three-band).
Weight: 11 lbs. (two-band). **Length:** 48.75" overall (two-band).
Stock: European walnut with checkered wrist and forend.
Sights: Hooded bead front, adjustable rear with interchangeable leaves.
Features: Alexander Henry-type rifling with 1:20" twist. Color case-hardened hammer and lockplate, brass trigger guard and nose cap, rest blued. Imported by Euroarms of America.
Price: Two-band $720.00
Price: Three-band $773.00

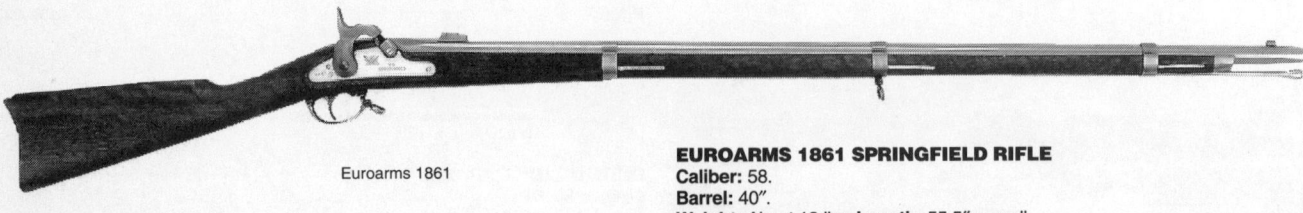
Euroarms 1861

EUROARMS 1861 SPRINGFIELD RIFLE
Caliber: 58.
Barrel: 40".
Weight: About 10 lbs. **Length:** 55.5" overall.
Stock: European walnut.
Sights: Blade front, three-leaf military rear.
Features: Reproduction of the original three-band rifle. Lockplate marked "1861" with eagle and "U.S. Springfield." Metal left in the white. Imported by Euroarms of America.
Price: $564.00

BLACKPOWDER MUSKETS & RIFLES

Gonic GA-87

Gonic GA-93 Magnum M/L Rifle
Similar to the GA-87 except has open bolt mechanism, single safety, 22" barrel and comes only in 50-caliber. Stock is black wrinkle-finish wood or gray or brown, standard or thumbhole laminate. **Partial listing shown.** Introduced 1993. From Gonic Arms, Inc.
Price: Black stock, blue, no sights $483.30
Price: As above, stainless $562.25
Price: Laminated stock, blue, no sights $554.25
Price: As above, stainless $650.65
Price: Black stock, blue, open sights $500.57
Price: As above, stainless $603.04
Price: Laminated stock, blue, open sights $595.24
Price: As above, stainless $691.44

GONIC GA-87 M/L RIFLE
Caliber: 45, 50
Barrel: 26".
Weight: 6 to 6$\frac{1}{2}$ lbs. **Length:** 43" overall (Carbine).
Stock: American walnut with checkered grip and forend, or laminated stock.
Sights: Optional bead front, open or peep rear adjustable for windage and elevation; drilled and tapped for scope bases (included).
Features: Closed-breech action with straight-line ignition. Modern trigger mechanism with ambidextrous safety. Satin blue finish on metal, satin stock finish. Introduced 1989. From Gonic Arms, Inc.
Price: Standard rifle, no sights $800.41
Price: As above, with sights, from $869.93
Price: Walnut stock, peep sight $800.41

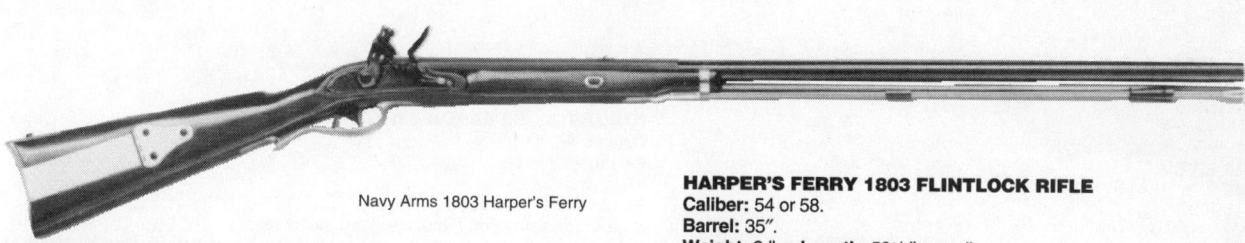
Navy Arms 1803 Harper's Ferry

HATFIELD MOUNTAIN RIFLE
Caliber: 50, 54.
Barrel: 32".
Weight: 8 lbs. **Length:** 49" overall.
Stock: Select American fancy maple. Half-stock with nose cap.
Sights: Silver blade front on brass base, fixed buckhorn rear.
Features: Traditional leaf spring and fly lock with extra-wide tumbler of 4140 steel. Slow rust brown metal finish. Double-set triggers. From Hatfield Gun Co.
Price: $950.00

HARPER'S FERRY 1803 FLINTLOCK RIFLE
Caliber: 54 or 58.
Barrel: 35".
Weight: 9 lbs. **Length:** 59$\frac{1}{2}$" overall.
Stock: Walnut with cheekpiece.
Sights: Brass blade front, fixed steel rear.
Features: Brass trigger guard, sideplate, buttplate; steel patch box. Imported by Euroarms of America, Navy Arms (54-cal. only), Cabela's, Stone Mountain Arms.
Price: .... $495.95 to $729.00
Price: 54-cal. (Navy Arms) $615.00

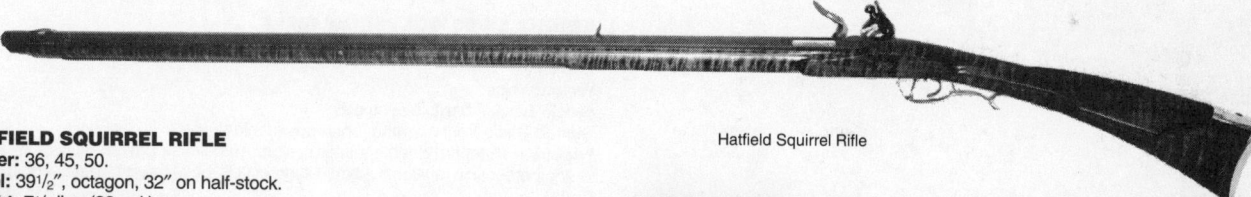
Hatfield Squirrel Rifle

HATFIELD SQUIRREL RIFLE
Caliber: 36, 45, 50.
Barrel: 39$\frac{1}{2}$", octagon, 32" on half-stock.
Weight: 7$\frac{1}{2}$ lbs. (32-cal.).
Stock: American fancy maple.
Sights: Silver blade front, buckhorn rear.
Features: Recreation of the traditional squirrel rifle. Available in flint or percussion with brass trigger guard and buttplate. From Hatfield Rifle Works. Introduced 1983.
Price: Full stock, percussion, Grade II $819.00
Price: As above, flintlock $819.00
Price: As above, Grade III, flint or percussion $969.00

HAWKEN RIFLE
Caliber: 45, 50, 54 or 58.
Barrel: 28", blued, 6-groove rifling.
Weight: 8$\frac{3}{4}$ lbs. **Length:** 44" overall.
Stock: Walnut with cheekpiece.
Sights: Blade front, fully adjustable rear.
Features: Coil mainspring, double-set triggers, polished brass furniture. From Armsport, Navy Arms, E.M.F.
Price: .... $220.00 to $345.00

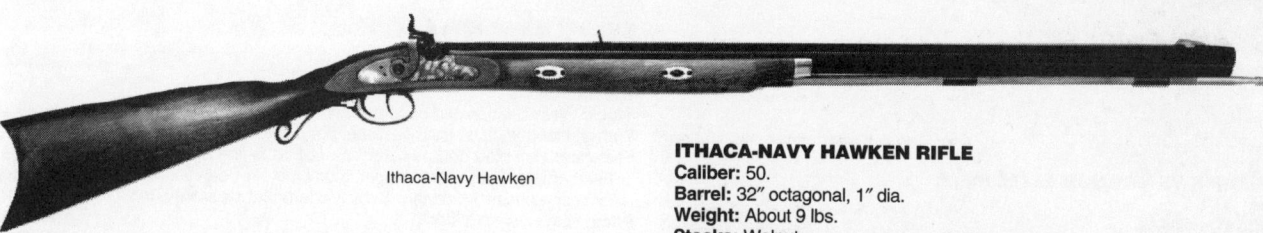
Ithaca-Navy Hawken

ITHACA-NAVY HAWKEN RIFLE
Caliber: 50.
Barrel: 32" octagonal, 1" dia.
Weight: About 9 lbs.
Stocks: Walnut.
Sights: Blade front, rear adjustable for windage.
Features: Hooked breech, 1$\frac{7}{8}$" throw percussion lock. Attached twin thimbles and under-rib. German silver barrel key inlays, Hawken-style toe and buttplates, lock bolt inlays, barrel wedges, entry thimble, trigger guard, ramrod and cleaning jag, nipple and nipple wrench. Introduced 1977. From Navy Arms.
Price: Complete, percussion $400.00

CAUTION: PRICES SHOWN ARE SUPPLIED BY THE MANUFACTURER OR IMPORTER. CHECK YOUR LOCAL GUNSHOP.

BLACKPOWDER MUSKETS & RIFLES

Navy Arms Kentucky

KENTUCKIAN RIFLE & CARBINE
Caliber: 44.
Barrel: 35" (Rifle), 27½" (Carbine).
Weight: 7 lbs. (Rifle), 5½ lbs. (Carbine). **Length:** 51" overall (Rifle), 43" (Carbine).
Stock: Walnut stain.
Sights: Brass blade front, steel V-ramp rear.
Features: Octagon barrel, case-hardened and engraved lockplates. Brass furniture. Imported by Dixie Gun Works.
Price: Rifle or carbine, flint, about $269.95
Price: As above, percussion, about $259.95

KENTUCKY FLINTLOCK RIFLE
Caliber: 44, 45, or 50.
Barrel: 35".
Weight: 7 lbs. **Length:** 50" overall.
Stock: Walnut stained, brass fittings.
Sights: Fixed.
Features: Available in carbine model also, 28" bbl. Some variations in detail, finish. Kits also available from some importers. Imported by Navy Arms, The Armoury.
Price: About . . . . $217.95 to $345.00
Price: Flintlock, 45 or 50-cal. (Navy Arms) $410.00

Kentucky Percussion Rifle
Similar to flintlock except percussion lock. Finish and features vary with importer. Imported by Navy Arms, The Armoury, CVA.
Price: About $259.95
Price: 45- or 50-cal. (Navy Arms) $400.00
Price: Kit, 50-cal. (CVA) $189.95

Knight BK-92 Black Knight

KNIGHT BK-92 BLACK KNIGHT RIFLE
Caliber: 50, 54.
Barrel: 24", blued.
Weight: 6½ lbs.
Stock: Black composition.
Sights: Blade front on ramp, open adjustable rear.
Features: Patented double safety system; removable breech plug for cleaning; adjustable Accu-Lite trigger; Green Mountain barrel; receiver drilled and tapped for scope bases. Made in U.S. by Modern Muzzleloading, Inc.
Price: With composition stock $399.95

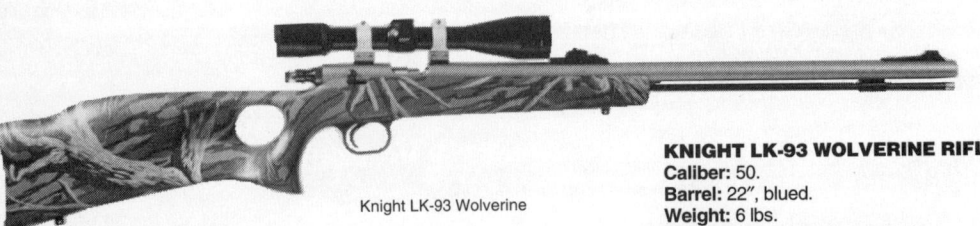
Knight LK-93 Wolverine

KNIGHT LK-93 WOLVERINE RIFLE
Caliber: 50.
Barrel: 22", blued.
Weight: 6 lbs.
Stock: Black Fiber-Lite synthetic.
Sights: Blade front on ramp, open adjustable rear.
Features: Patented double safety system; removable breech plug; Sure-Fire in-line percussion ignition system. Made in U.S. by Modern Muzzleloading, Inc.
Price: $319.95
Price: LK-93 Stainless $399.95
Price: LK-93 Thumbhole $409.95

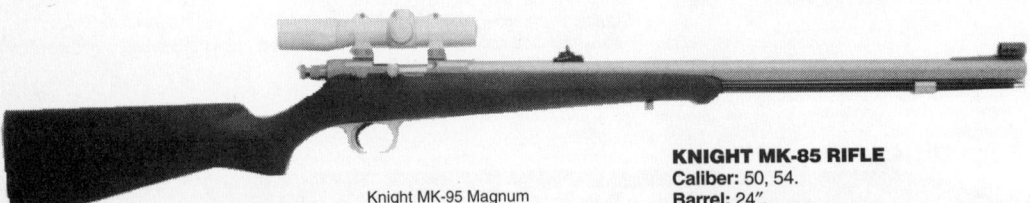
Knight MK-95 Magnum

KNIGHT MK-95 MAGNUM ELITE RIFLE
Caliber: 50, 54.
Barrel: 24", stainless.
Weight: 6¾ lbs.
Stock: Composition; black or Realtree All-Purpose camouflage.
Sights: Hooded blade front on ramp, open adjustable rear.
Features: Enclosed Posi-Fire ignition system uses large rifle primers; Timney Featherweight adjustable trigger; Green Mountain barrel; receiver drilled and tapped for scope bases. Made in U.S. by Modern Muzzleloading, Inc.
Price: Black composition stock $839.95

KNIGHT MK-85 RIFLE
Caliber: 50, 54.
Barrel: 24".
Weight: 6¾ lbs.
Stock: Walnut, laminated or composition.
Sights: Hooded blade front on ramp, open adjustable rear.
Features: Patented double safety; Sure-Fire in-line percussion ignition; Timney Featherweight adjustable trigger; aluminum ramrod; receiver drilled and tapped for scope bases. Made in U.S. by Modern Muzzleloading, Inc.
Price: Hunter, walnut stock $539.95
Price: Stalker, laminated or composition stock $679.95
Price: Predator (stainless steel), laminated or composition stock $759.95
Price: Knight Hawk, blued, composition thumbhole stock $779.95
Price: As above, stainless steel $869.95

BLACKPOWDER MUSKETS & RIFLES

Kodiak MK. III Double Rifle

KODIAK MK. III DOUBLE RIFLE
Caliber: 54x54, 58x58, 50x50.
Barrel: 28", 5-groove, 1:48" twist.
Weight: 9½ lbs. **Length:** 43¼" overall.
Stock: Czechoslovakian walnut, hand-checkered.
Sights: Adjustable bead front, adjustable open rear.
Features: Hooked breech allows interchangeability of barrels. Comes with sling, swivels, bullet mould and bullet starter. Engraved lockplates, top tang and trigger guard. Locks and top tang polished, rest browned. Introduced 1976. Imported from Italy by Navy Arms.
Price: 50-, 54-, 58-cal. SxS $775.00

LONDON ARMORY 3-BAND 1853 ENFIELD
Caliber: 58 (.577" Minie, .575" round ball, .580" maxi ball).
Barrel: 39".
Weight: 9½ lbs. **Length:** 54" overall.
Stock: European walnut.
Sights: Inverted "V" front, traditional Enfield folding ladder rear.
Features: Recreation of the famed London Armory Company Pattern 1853 Enfield Musket. One-piece walnut stock, brass buttplate, trigger guard and nose cap. Lockplate marked "London Armoury Co." and with a British crown. Blued Baddeley barrel bands. From Dixie Gun Works, Euroarms of America, Navy Arms.
Price: About ....$350.00 to $484.00
Price: Assembled kit (Dixie, Euroarms of America) ....$425.00 to $431.00

LONDON ARMORY 2-BAND 1858 ENFIELD
Caliber: .577" Minie, .575" round ball.
Barrel: 33".
Weight: 10 lbs. **Length:** 49" overall.
Stock: Walnut.
Sights: Folding leaf rear adjustable for elevation.
Features: Blued barrel, color case-hardened lock and hammer, polished brass buttplate, trigger guard, nosecap. From Navy Arms, Euroarms of America, Dixie Gun Works.
Price: ....$385.00 to $531.00

London Armory 1861

LONDON ARMORY 1861 ENFIELD MUSKETOON
Caliber: 58, Minie ball.
Barrel: 24", round.
Weight: 7-7½ lbs. **Length:** 40½" overall.
Stock: Walnut, with sling swivels.
Sights: Blade front, graduated military-leaf rear.
Features: Brass trigger guard, nose cap, buttplate; blued barrel, bands, lockplate, swivels. Imported by Euroarms of America, Navy Arms.
Price: ....$300.00 to $427.00
Price: Kit ....$365.00 to $373.00

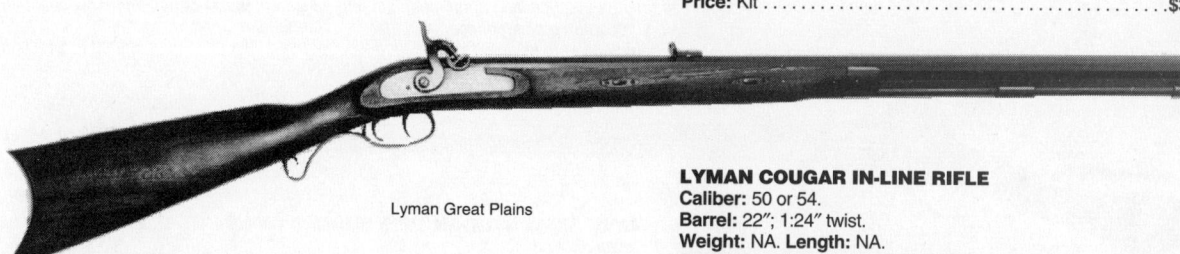

Lyman Great Plains

LYMAN COUGAR IN-LINE RIFLE
Caliber: 50 or 54.
Barrel: 22"; 1:24" twist.
Weight: NA. **Length:** NA.
Stock: Smooth walnut; swivel studs.
Sights: Bead on ramp front, folding adjustable rear. Drilled and tapped for Lyman 57WTR receiver sight and Weaver scope bases.
Features: Blued barrel and receiver. Has bolt safety notch and trigger safety. Rubber recoil pad. Delrin ramrod. Introduced 1996. From Lyman.
Price: $299.95

LYMAN GREAT PLAINS RIFLE
Caliber: 50- or 54-cal.
Barrel: 32", 1:66" twist.
Weight: 9 lbs.
Stock: Walnut.
Sights: Steel blade front, buckhorn rear adjustable for windage and elevation and fixed notch primitive sight included.
Features: Blued steel furniture. Stainless steel nipple. Coil spring lock, Hawken-style trigger guard and double-set triggers. Round thimbles recessed and sweated into rib. Steel wedge plates and toe plate. Introduced 1979. From Lyman.
Price: Percussion $416.95
Price: Flintlock $445.95
Price: Percussion kit $329.95
Price: Flintlock kit $359.95
Price: Left-hand percussion $416.95
Price: Left-hand flintlock $445.95

LYMAN TRADE RIFLE
Caliber: 50, 54.
Barrel: 28" octagon, 1:48" twist.
Weight: 8¾ lbs. **Length:** 45" overall.
Stock: European walnut.
Sights: Blade front, open rear adjustable for windage or optional fixed sights.
Features: Fast twist rifling for conical bullets. Polished brass furniture with blue steel parts, stainless steel nipple. Hook breech, single trigger, coil spring percussion lock. Steel barrel rib and ramrod ferrules. Introduced 1980. From Lyman.
Price: Percussion $299.95
Price: Flintlock $319.95

LYMAN DEERSTALKER RIFLE
Caliber: 50, 54.
Barrel: 24", octagonal; 1:48" rifling.
Weight: 7½ lbs.
Stock: Walnut with black rubber buttpad.
Sights: Lyman #37MA beaded front, fully adjustable fold-down Lyman #16A rear.
Features: Stock has less drop for quick sighting. All metal parts are blackened, with color case-hardened lock; single trigger. Comes with sling and swivels. Available in flint or percussion. Introduced 1990. From Lyman.
Price: 50- or 54-cal., percussion $299.95
Price: 50- or 54-cal., flintlock $319.95
Price: 50- or 54-cal., percussion, left-hand $299.95
Price: 50-cal., flintlock, left-hand $319.95

Lyman Deerstalker Custom Carbine
Similar to the Deerstalker rifle except in 50-caliber only with 21" stepped octagon barrel; 1:24" twist for optimum performance with conical projectiles. Comes with Lyman 37MA front sight, Lyman 16A folding rear. Weighs 6¾ lbs., measures 38½" overall. Percussion or flintlock. Comes with Delrin ramrod, modern sling and swivels. Introduced 1991.
Price: Percussion $309.95
Price: Percussion, left-hand $309.95

BLACKPOWDER MUSKETS & RIFLES

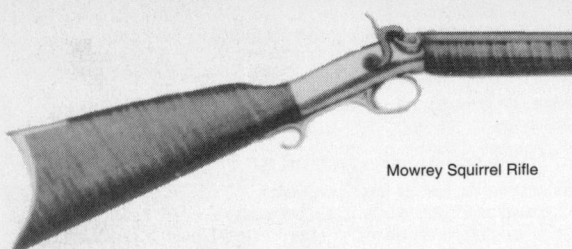

Mowrey Squirrel Rifle

MOWREY SQUIRREL RIFLE
Caliber: 32, 36 or 45.
Barrel: 28"; 13/1" flats; 1:66" twist.
Weight: About 7.5 lbs. **Length:** 43" overall.
Stock: Curly maple; crescent buttplate.
Sights: German silver blade front, semi-buckhorn rear.
Features: Brass or steel boxlock action; cut-rifled barrel. Steel rifles have browned finish, brass have browned barrel. Adjustable sear and trigger pull. Made in U.S. by Mowrey Gun Works.
Price: Brass or steel $350.00
Price: Kit $300.00

Mowrey Silhouette Rifle
Similar to the Squirrel Rifle except in 40-caliber with 32" barrel. Available in brass or steel frame.
Price: Brass frame $350.00
Price: Steel frame $350.00
Price: Kit, brass or steel $300.00

Mowrey Plains Rifle
Similar to the Squirrel Rifle except in 50- or 54-caliber with 32" barrel. Available in brass or steel frame.
Price: Brass frame $350.00
Price: Steel frame $350.00
Price: Rocky Mountain Hunter (as above except 28" bbl.), brass $350.00
Price: As above, steel frame $350.00
Price: All above in kit form $300.00

Mowrey 1 N 30 Conical Rifle
Similar to the Squirrel Rifle except in steel frame only, 45-, 50- or 54-caliber. Has special 1:24" twist barrel for conical- and sabot-style bullets. The 50- and 54-caliber barrels have 1" flats.
Price: $350.00
Price: Kit $300.00

Navy Arms J.P. Murray

J.P. MURRAY 1862-1864 CAVALRY CARBINE
Caliber: 58 (.577" Minie).
Barrel: 23".
Weight: 7 lbs., 9 oz. **Length:** 39" overall.
Stock: Walnut.
Sights: Blade front, rear drift adjustable for windage.
Features: Browned barrel, color case-hardened lock, blued swivel and band springs, polished brass buttplate, trigger guard, barrel bands. From Navy Arms, Euroarms of America.
Price: .... $405.00 to $440.00

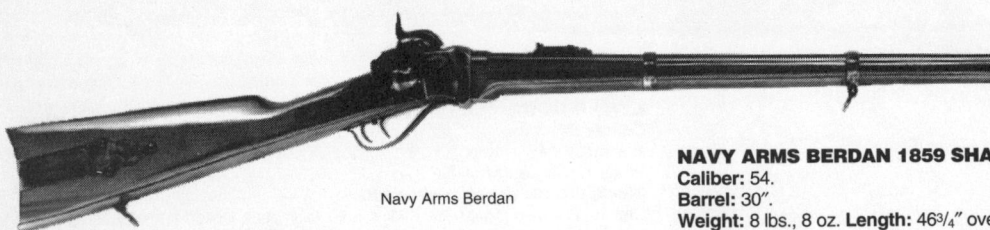

Navy Arms Berdan

NAVY ARMS BERDAN 1859 SHARPS RIFLE
Caliber: 54.
Barrel: 30".
Weight: 8 lbs., 8 oz. **Length:** 46 3/4" overall.
Stock: Walnut.
Sights: Blade front, folding military ladder-type rear.
Features: Replica of the Union sniper rifle used by Berdan's 1st and 2nd Sharpshooter regiments. Color case-hardened receiver, patch box, furniture. Double-set triggers. Imported by Navy Arms.
Price: $1,095.00
Price: 1859 Sharps Infantry Rifle (three-band) $1,030.00

NAVY ARMS HAWKEN HUNTER RIFLE/CARBINE
Caliber: 50, 54, 58.
Barrel: 22 1/2" or 28"; 1:48" twist.
Weight: 6 lbs., 12 oz. **Length:** 39" overall.
Stock: Walnut with cheekpiece.
Sights: Blade front, fully adjustable rear.
Features: Double-set triggers; all metal has matte black finish; rubber recoil pad; detachable sling swivels. Imported by Navy Arms.
Price: Rifle or Carbine $240.00

Navy Arms Country Boy

NAVY ARMS COUNTRY BOY IN-LINE RIFLE
Caliber: 50.
Barrel: 24".
Weight: 8 lbs. **Length:** 41" overall.
Stock: Black composition.
Sights: Bead front, fully adjustable open rear.
Features: Chrome-lined barrel; receiver drilled and tapped for scope mount; buttstock has trap containing takedown tool for nipple and breech plug removal. Introduced 1996. From Navy Arms.
Price: $175.00

BLACKPOWDER MUSKETS & RIFLES

Navy Arms Mortimer Match

NAVY ARMS MORTIMER FLINTLOCK RIFLE
Caliber: 54.
Barrel: 36".
Weight: 9 lbs. **Length:** 52 1/4" overall.
Stock: Checkered walnut.
Sights: Bead front, rear adjustable for windage.
Features: Waterproof pan, roller frizzen; sling swivels; browned barrel; external safety. Introduced 1991. Imported by Navy Arms.
Price: $780.00
Price: Mortimer Match Rifle (hooded globe front sight, fully adjustable target aperture rear, color case-hardened lock) $900.00

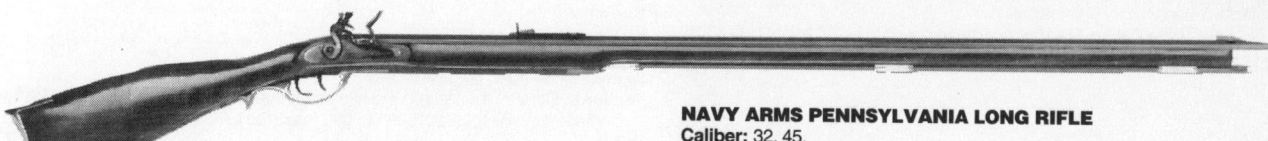
Navy Arms Pennsylvania

NAVY ARMS PENNSYLVANIA LONG RIFLE
Caliber: 32, 45.
Barrel: 40 1/2".
Weight: 7 1/2 lbs. **Length:** 56 1/2" overall.
Stock: Walnut.
Sights: Blade front, fully adjustable rear.
Features: Browned barrel, brass furniture, polished lock with double-set triggers. Imported by Navy Arms.
Price: Percussion $460.00
Price: Flintlock $475.00

Navy Arms Smith Carbine

NAVY ARMS SMITH CARBINE
Caliber: 50.
Barrel: 21 1/2".
Weight: 7 3/4 lbs. **Length:** 39" overall.
Stock: American walnut.
Sights: Brass blade front, folding ladder-type rear.
Features: Replica of the breech-loading Civil War carbine. Color case-hardened receiver, rest blued. Cavalry model has saddle ring and bar, Artillery model has sling swivels. Imported by Navy Arms.
Price: Cavalry model $600.00
Price: Artillery model $600.00

Navy Arms Whitworth

NAVY ARMS VOLUNTEER RIFLE
Caliber: .451".
Barrel: 32".
Weight: 9 1/2 lbs. **Length:** 49" overall.
Stock: Walnut, checkered wrist and forend.
Sights: Globe front, adjustable ladder-type rear.
Features: Recreation of the type of gun issued to volunteer regiments during the 1860s. Rigby-pattern rifling, patent breech, detented lock. Stock is glass bedded for accuracy. Imported by Navy Arms.
Price: $775.00

NAVY ARMS 1859 SHARPS CAVALRY CARBINE
Caliber: 54.
Barrel: 22".
Weight: 7 3/4 lbs. **Length:** 39" overall.
Stock: Walnut.
Sights: Blade front, military ladder-type rear.
Features: Color case-hardened action, blued barrel. Has saddle ring. Introduced 1991. Imported from Navy Arms.
Price: $885.00

NAVY ARMS WHITWORTH MILITARY TARGET RIFLE
Caliber: 45.
Barrel: 36".
Weight: 9 1/4 lbs. **Length:** 52 1/2" overall.
Stock: Walnut. Checkered at wrist and forend.
Sights: Hooded post front, open step-adjustable rear.
Features: Faithful reproduction of the Whitworth rifle, only bored for 45-cal. Trigger has a detented lock, capable of being adjusted very finely without risk of the sear nose catching on the half-cock bent and damaging both parts. Introduced 1978. Imported by Navy Arms.
Price: $835.00

NAVY ARMS 1777 CHARLEVILLE MUSKET
Caliber: 69.
Barrel: 44 5/8".
Weight: 10 lbs., 4 oz. **Length:** 59 3/4" overall.
Stock: Walnut.
Sights: Brass blade front.
Features: Exact copy of the musket used in the French Revolution. All steel is polished, in the white. Brass flashpan. Introduced 1991. Imported by Navy Arms.
Price: $810.00
Price: 1816 M.T. Wickham Musket $810.00

CAUTION: PRICES SHOWN ARE SUPPLIED BY THE MANUFACTURER OR IMPORTER. CHECK YOUR LOCAL GUNSHOP.

BLACKPOWDER MUSKETS & RIFLES

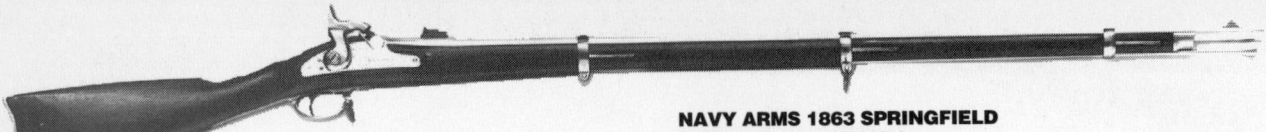
Navy Arms 1863

NAVY ARMS 1863 SPRINGFIELD
Caliber: 58, uses .575" Minie.
Barrel: 40", rifled.
Weight: 9 1/2 lbs. **Length:** 56" overall.
Stock: Walnut.
Sights: Open rear adjustable for elevation.
Features: Full-size three-band musket. Polished bright metal, including lock. From Navy Arms.
Price: Finished rifle $550.00

NAVY ARMS 1861 SPRINGFIELD RIFLE
Caliber: 58.
Barrel: 40".
Weight: 10 lbs., 4 oz. **Length:** 56" overall.
Stock: Walnut.
Sights: Blade front, military leaf rear.
Features: Steel barrel, lock and all furniture have polished bright finish. Has 1855-style hammer. Imported by Navy Arms.
Price: $550.00

NAVY ARMS 1863 C.S. RICHMOND RIFLE
Caliber: 58.
Barrel: 40".
Weight: 10 lbs. **Length:** NA.
Stock: Walnut.
Sights: Blade front, adjustable rear.
Features: Copy of the three-band rifle musket made at Richmond Armory for the Confederacy. All steel polished bright. Imported by Navy Arms.
Price: $550.00

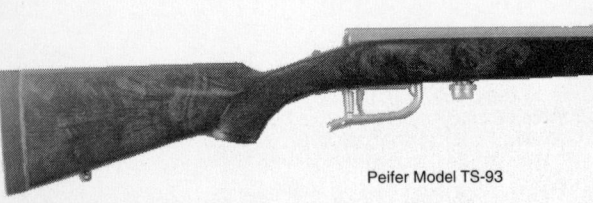
Peifer Model TS-93

PEIFER MODEL TS-93 RIFLE
Caliber: 45, 50.
Barrel: 24" Douglas premium; 1:20" twist in 45, 1:28" in 50.
Weight: 7 lbs. **Length:** 43 1/4" overall.
Stock: Bell & Carlson solid composite, with recoil pad, swivel studs.
Sights: Williams bead front on ramp, fully adjustable open rear. Drilled and tapped for Weaver scope mounts with dovetail for rear peep.
Features: In-line ignition uses #209 shotshell primer; extremely fast lock time; fully enclosed breech; adjustable trigger; automatic safety; removal primer holder. Blue or stainless. Made in U.S. by Peifer Rifle Co. Introduced 1996.
Price: Blue, black stock $663.00
Price: Blue, wood or camouflage composite stock, or stainless with black composite stock $728.75
Price: Stainless, wood or camouflage composite stock $795.00

PENNSYLVANIA FULL-STOCK RIFLE
Caliber: 45 or 50.
Barrel: 32" rifled, 15/16" dia.
Weight: 8 1/2 lbs.
Stock: Walnut.
Sights: Fixed.
Features: Available in flint or percussion. Blued lock and barrel, brass furniture. Offered complete or in kit form. From The Armoury.
Price: Flint $250.00
Price: Percussion $225.00

Prairie River Bullpup

PRAIRIE RIVER ARMS PRA BULLPUP RIFLE
Caliber: 50, 54.
Barrel: 28"; 1:28" twist.
Weight: 7 1/2 lbs. **Length:** 31 1/2" overall.
Stock: Hardwood or black all-weather.
Sights: Blade front, open adjustable rear.
Features: Bullpup design thumbhole stock. Patented internal percussion ignition system. Left-hand model available. Dovetailed for scope mount. Introduced 1995. Made in U.S. by Prairie River Arms.
Price: 4140 alloy barrel, hardwood stock $375.00
Price: As above, black stock $390.00
Price: Stainless barrel, hardwood stock $425.00
Price: As above, black stock $440.00

Prairie River Classic

PRAIRIE RIVER ARMS PRA CLASSIC RIFLE
Caliber: 50, 54.
Barrel: 26"; 1:28" twist.
Weight: 7 1/2 lbs. **Length:** 40 1/2" overall.
Stock: Hardwood or black all-weather.
Sights: Blade front, open adjustable rear.
Features: Patented internal percussion ignition system. Drilled and tapped for scope mount. Introduced 1995. Made in U.S. by Prairie River Arms, Ltd.
Price: 4140 alloy barrel, hardwood stock $375.00
Price: As above, stainless barrel $425.00
Price: 4140 alloy barrel, black all-weather stock $390.00
Price: As above, stainless barrel $440.00

BLACKPOWDER MUSKETS & RIFLES

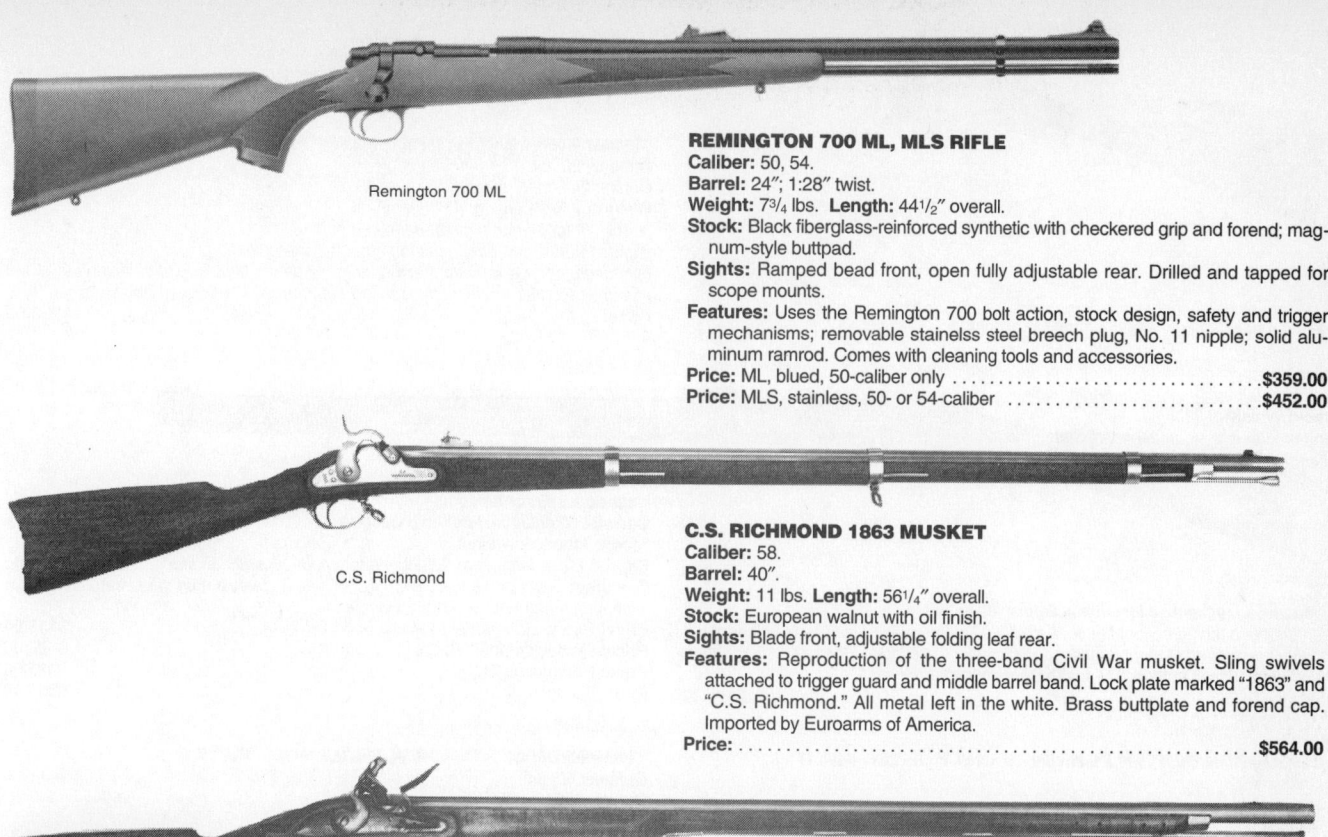

Remington 700 ML

C.S. Richmond

Navy Arms Brown Bess

REMINGTON 700 ML, MLS RIFLE
Caliber: 50, 54.
Barrel: 24"; 1:28" twist.
Weight: 7 3/4 lbs. **Length:** 44 1/2" overall.
Stock: Black fiberglass-reinforced synthetic with checkered grip and forend; magnum-style buttpad.
Sights: Ramped bead front, open fully adjustable rear. Drilled and tapped for scope mounts.
Features: Uses the Remington 700 bolt action, stock design, safety and trigger mechanisms; removable stainelss steel breech plug, No. 11 nipple; solid aluminum ramrod. Comes with cleaning tools and accessories.
Price: ML, blued, 50-caliber only $359.00
Price: MLS, stainless, 50- or 54-caliber $452.00

C.S. RICHMOND 1863 MUSKET
Caliber: 58.
Barrel: 40".
Weight: 11 lbs. **Length:** 56 1/4" overall.
Stock: European walnut with oil finish.
Sights: Blade front, adjustable folding leaf rear.
Features: Reproduction of the three-band Civil War musket. Sling swivels attached to trigger guard and middle barrel band. Lock plate marked "1863" and "C.S. Richmond." All metal left in the white. Brass buttplate and forend cap. Imported by Euroarms of America.
Price: $564.00

SECOND MODEL BROWN BESS MUSKET
Caliber: 75, uses .735" round ball.
Barrel: 42", smoothbore.
Weight: 9 1/2 lbs. **Length:** 59" overall.
Stock: Walnut (Navy); walnut-stained hardwood (Dixie).
Sights: Fixed.
Features: Polished barrel and lock with brass trigger guard and buttplate. Bayonet and scabbard available. From Navy Arms, Dixie Gun Works, Cabela's.
Price: Finished ....$475.00 to $850.00
Price: Kit (Dixie Gun Works, Navy Arms) ....$510.00 to $625.00
Price: Carbine (Navy Arms) $750.00

STONE MOUNTAIN 1853 ENFIELD MUSKET
Caliber: 58.
Barrel: 39".
Weight: About 9 lbs. **Length:** 54" overall.
Stock: Walnut.
Sights: Inverted V front, rear step adjustable for elevation.
Features: Three-band musket. Barrel, tang, breech plug are blued, color case-hardened lock, brass nose cap, trigger guard and buttplate. From Stone Mountain Arms.
Price: $550.00

THOMPSON/CENTER BIG BOAR RIFLE
Caliber: 58.
Barrel: 26" octagon; 1:48" twist.
Weight: 7 3/4 lbs. **Length:** 42 1/2" overall.
Stock: American black walnut; rubber buttpad; swivels.
Sights: Bead front, fullt adjustable open rear.
Features: Percussion lock; single trigger with wide bow trigger guard. Comes with soft leather sling. Introduced 1991. From Thompson/Center.
Price: $355.00

STONE MOUNTAIN SILVER EAGLE RIFLE
Caliber: 50.
Barrel: 26", octagonal; 15/16" flats; 1:48" twist.
Weight: About 6 1/2 lbs. **Length:** 40" overall.
Stock: Dura-Grip synthetic; checkered grip and forend.
Sights: Blade front, fixed rear.
Features: Weatherguard nickel finish on metal; oversize trigger guard. Introduced 1995. From Stone Mountain Arms.
Price: $139.95
Price: Silver Eagle Hunter (adjustable sight, drilled and tapped for scope mount, swivel studs, synthetic ramrod) $159.95

Thompson/Center Fire Hawk

THOMPSON/CENTER FIRE HAWK RIFLE
Caliber: 32, 50, 54, 58.
Barrel: 24"; 1:38" twist.
Weight: 7 lbs. **Length:** 41 3/4" overall.
Stock: American black walnut or black Rynite; Rynite thumbhole style; all with cheekpiece and swivel studs.
Sights: Ramp front with bead, adjustable leaf-style rear.
Features: In-line ignition with sliding thumb safety; free-floated barrel; exposed nipple; adjustable trigger. Available in blue or stainless. Comes with Weaver-style scope mount bases. Introduced 1995. Made in U.S. by Thompson/Center Arms.
Price: Blue, walnut stock, 32, 50, 54, 58 ....$365.00
Price: Stainless, walnut stock, 50, 54 ....$405.00
Price: Stainless, Rynite stock, 50, 54 ....$395.00
Price: Blue, thumbhole stock, 50, 54 ....$385.00
Price: Stainless, thumbhole stock, 50, 54 ....$425.00
Price: Bantam model with 13 1/4" pull, 21" barrel $365.00
Price: Blue, Advantage camo stock, 50, 54 ....$395.00

CAUTION: PRICES SHOWN ARE SUPPLIED BY THE MANUFACTURER OR IMPORTER. CHECK YOUR LOCAL GUNSHOP.

BLACKPOWDER MUSKETS & RIFLES

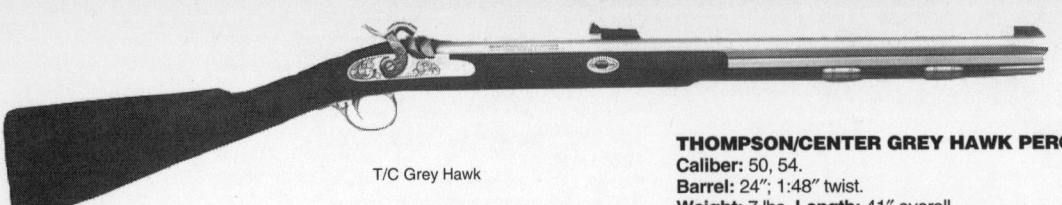

T/C Grey Hawk

THOMPSON/CENTER GREY HAWK PERCUSSION RIFLE
Caliber: 50, 54.
Barrel: 24"; 1:48" twist.
Weight: 7 lbs. **Length:** 41" overall.
Stock: Black Rynite with rubber recoil pad.
Sights: Bead front, fully adjustable open hunting rear.
Features: Stainless steel barrel, lock, hammer, trigger guard, thimbles; blued sights. Percussion only. Introduced 1993. From Thompson/Center Arms.
Price: $330.00

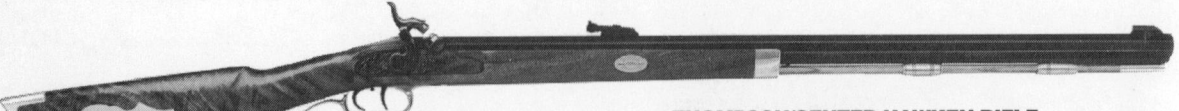

T/C Hawken

THOMPSON/CENTER HAWKEN RIFLE
Caliber: 45, 50 or 54.
Barrel: 28" octagon, hooked breech.
Stock: American walnut.
Sights: Blade front, rear adjustable for windage and elevation.
Features: Solid brass furniture, double-set triggers, button rifled barrel, coil-type mainspring. From Thompson/Center.
Price: Percussion model (45-, 50- or 54-cal.) $455.00
Price: Flintlock model (50-cal.) $425.00
Price: Percussion kit $315.00
Price: Flintlock kit $335.00

Thompson/Center Hawken Silver Elite Rifle
Similar to the 50-caliber Hawken except all metal is satin-finished stainless steel. Has semi-fancy American walnut stock without patchbox. Percussion only. Introduced 1996. Made in U.S. by Thompson/Center Arms.
Price: $495.00

THOMPSON/CENTER PENNSYLVANIA HUNTER RIFLE
Caliber: 50.
Barrel: 31", half-octagon, half-round.
Weight: About 7½ lbs. **Length:** 48" overall.
Stock: Black walnut.
Sights: Open, adjustable.
Features: Rifled 1:66" for round ball shooting. Available in flintlock or percussion. From Thompson/Center.
Price: Flintlock $375.00

THOMPSON/CENTER NEW ENGLANDER RIFLE
Caliber: 50, 54.
Barrel: 28", round.
Weight: 7 lbs., 15 oz.
Stock: American walnut or Rynite.
Sights: Open, adjustable.
Features: Color case-hardened percussion lock with engraving, rest blued. Also accepts 12-ga. shotgun barrel. Introduced 1987. From Thompson/Center.
Price: Right-hand model $310.00
Price: As above, Rynite stock $295.00
Price: Left-hand model $330.00
Price: Accessory 12-ga. barrel, right-hand $170.00

Thompson/Center Pennsylvania Hunter Carbine
Similar to the Pennsylvania Hunter except has 21" barrel, weighs 6.5 lbs., and has an overall length of 38". Designed for shooting patched round balls. Available in percussion or flintlock styles. Introduced 1992. From Thompson/Center.
Price: Percussion $340.00
Price: Flintlock $355.00

Thompson/Center Pennsylvania Match Rifle
Similar to the Pennsylvania Hunter except has a tang peep sight, globe front with Seven interchangeable inserts. Introduced 1996. Made in U.S. by Thompson/Center Arms.
Price: $400.00

Thompson/Center Renegade Hunter
Similar to standard Renegade except has single trigger in a large-bow shotgun-style trigger guard, no brass trim. Available in 50- or 54-caliber. Color case-hardened lock, rest blued. Introduced 1987. From Thompson/Center.
Price: $335.00

THOMPSON/CENTER RENEGADE RIFLE
Caliber: 50 and 54.
Barrel: 26", 1" across the flats.
Weight: 8 lbs.
Stock: American walnut.
Sights: Open hunting (Patridge) style, fully adjustable for windage and elevation.
Features: Coil spring lock, double-set triggers, blued steel trim. From Thompson/Center.
Price: Percussion model $360.00
Price: Flintlock model, 50-cal. only $370.00
Price: Percussion kit $275.00
Price: Left-hand percussion, 50- or 54-cal. $370.00

Thompson/Center Scout Rifle
Similar to the Scout Carbine except has 24" part octagon, part round barrel (round only on Rynite-stocked model), solid brass forend cap on walnut-stocked gun. Barrel twist is 1:38". Available in 50- and 54-caliber. Introduced 1995. Made in U.S. by Thompson/Center Arms.
Price: With walnut stock $435.00
Price: With Rynite stock $360.00

T/C Scout Rifle

THOMPSON/CENTER SCOUT CARBINE
Caliber: 50 and 54.
Barrel: 21", interchangeable, 1:38" twist.
Weight: 7 lbs., 4 oz. **Length:** 38⅝" overall.
Stocks: American black walnut stock and forend.
Sights: Bead front, adjustable semi-buckhorn rear.
Features: Patented in-line ignition system with special vented breech plug. Patented trigger mechanism consists of only two moving parts. Interchangeable barrels. Wide grooved hammer. Brass trigger guard assembly, brass barrel band and buttplate. Ramrod has blued hardware. Comes with quick detachable swivels and suede leather carrying sling. Drilled and tapped for standard scope mounts. Introduced 1990. From Thompson/Center.
Price: 50- or 54-cal. $425.00
Price: With black Rynite stock $350.00

BLACKPOWDER MUSKETS & RIFLES

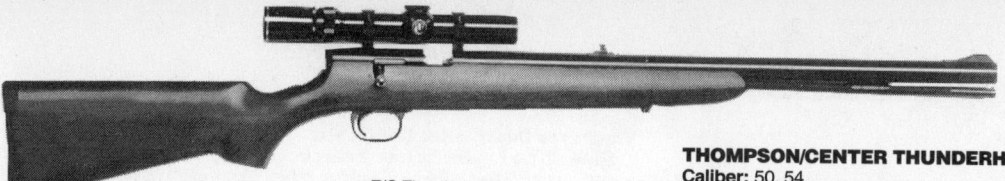

T/C Thunderhawk

THOMPSON/CENTER THUNDERHAWK CARBINE
Caliber: 50, 54.
Barrel: 21", 24"; 1:38" twist.
Weight: 6.75 lbs. **Length:** 38.75" overall.
Stock: American walnut or black Rynite with rubber recoil pad.
Sights: Bead on ramp front, adjustable leaf rear.
Features: Uses modern in-line ignition system, adjustable trigger. Knurled striker handle indicators for Safe and Fire. Black wood ramrod, Drilled and tapped for T/C scope mounts. Introduced 1993. From Thompson/Center Arms.
Price: Blue with walnut stock $315.00
Price: Stainless steel with Rynite stock $345.00
Price: Blue with Rynite stock $305.00

Thompson/Center ThunderHawk Shadow
Similar to the ThunderHawk except 24" barrel only, blued barrel and receiver, composite stock, polycarbonate adjustable rear sight. Available in 50- or 54-caliber. Introduced 1996. Made in U.S. by Thompson/Center Arms.
Price: $275.00

Traditions In-Line Buckhunter

TRADITIONS IN-LINE BUCKHUNTER SERIES RIFLES
Caliber: 50, 54.
Barrel: 24", round; 1:32" (50), 1:48" (54) twist.
Weight: 7 lbs., 6 oz. to 8 lbs. **Length:** 41" overall.
Stock: Beech, epoxy coated beech, laminated or fiberglass thumbhole; rubber recoil pad.
Sights: Beaded blade front, click adjustable rear. Drilled and tapped for scope mounting.
Features: Removable breech plug; PVC ramrod; sling swivels. Fifteen models available with blackened furniture, blued, C-nickel barrels, thumbhole stock. Introduced 1995. From Traditions.
Price: ....$222.00 to $345.00

Traditions Buckhunter In-Line Scout
Similar to the Buckhunter except has 22" C-Nickel barrel, 50-caliber only; 1:32" twist; black epoxied beech stock with 13" pull length. Introduced 1996. Imported by Traditions.
Price: $239.00

Traditions Buckhunter Pro In-Line

TRADITIONS BUCKHUNTER PRO IN-LINE RIFLES
Caliber: 50 (1:32" twist), 54 (1:48" twist).
Barrel: 24" tapered round.
Weight: 7 1/2 lbs. **Length:** 42" overall.
Stock: Beech, composite or laminated; thumbhole available in black Mossy Oak Treestand or Realtree® Advantage camouflage.
Sights: Beaded blade front, fully adjustable open rear. Drilled and tapped for scope mounting.
Features: In-line percussion ignition system; adjustable trigger; manual thumb safety; removable stainless steel breech plug. Seventeen models available. Introduced 1996. From Traditions.
Price: ....$222.00 to $406.00

TRADITIONS BUCKSKINNER CARBINE
Caliber: 50.
Barrel: 21", 15/16" flats, half octagon, half round; 1:20" or 1:66" twist.
Weight: 6 lbs. **Length:** 37" overall.
Stock: Beech or black laminated.
Sights: Beaded blade front, hunting-style open rear click adjustable for windage and elevation.
Features: Uses V-type mainspring, single trigger. Non-glare hardware. From Traditions.
Price: Flintlock $264.00
Price: Flintlock, laminated stock $336.00
Price: Percussion, 50 ....$236.00
Price: Percussion, laminated stock, 50 ....$305.00
Price: Percussion, left-hand $255.00

> Consult our Directory pages for the location of firms mentioned.

Traditions Deerhunter

TRADITIONS DEERHUNTER RIFLE SERIES
Caliber: 32, 50 or 54.
Barrel: 24", octagonal, 15/16" flats; 1:48" or 1:66" twist.
Weight: 6 lbs. **Length:** 40" overall.
Stock: Stained beech with rubber buttpad, sling swivels.
Sights: Blade front, fixed rear.
Features: Flint or percussion with color case-hardened lock. Hooked breech, oversized trigger guard, blackened furniture, PVC ramrod. All-Weather has epoxied beech stock and C-Nickel barrel. Drilled and tapped for scope mounting. Imported by Traditions, Inc.
Price: Percussion, 50 or 54, 1:48" twist $189.00
Price: Flintlock, 50-caliber only, 1:66" twist $198.00
Price: Percussion kit, 50 or 54 ....$153.00
Price: Flintlock, All-Weather, 50-cal. $166.00
Price: Percussion, All-Weather, 50 or 54 ....$198.00
Price: Small Game, 32-cal., percussion $189.00

Traditions Deerhunter Scout Rifle
Similar to the Deerhunter except in 32-caliber percussion only with 22" octagon barrel; 1:48" twist; weighs 5 lbs., 10 oz.; 36 1/2" overall length; beech stock; drilled and tapped for scope mounting; hooked breech; PVC ramrod. Introduced 1996. Imported by Traditions.
Price: $172.00

CAUTION: PRICES SHOWN ARE SUPPLIED BY THE MANUFACTURER OR IMPORTER. CHECK YOUR LOCAL GUNSHOP.

BLACKPOWDER MUSKETS & RIFLES

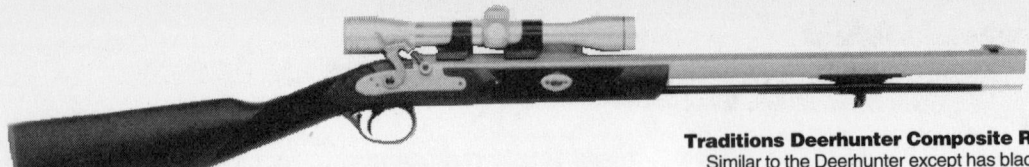

Traditions Deerhunter Composite

Traditions Deerhunter Composite Rifle
Similar to the Deerhunter except has black composite stock with checkered grip and forend. Blued barrel or C-Nickel finish, 50, 54 percussion, 50-caliber flintlock. Introduced 1996. Imported by Traditions.
Price: Blued, percussion $172.00
Price: C-Nickel barrel, 50-cal. percussion and flintlock, 54-cal. percussion $189.00

TRADITIONS HAWKEN WOODSMAN RIFLE
Caliber: 50 and 54.
Barrel: 28"; 15/16" flats.
Weight: 7 lbs., 11 oz. Length: 44 1/2" overall.
Stock: Walnut-stained hardwood.
Sights: Beaded blade front, hunting-style open rear adjustable for windage and elevation.
Features: Percussion only. Brass patchbox and furniture. Double triggers. From Traditions.
Price: 50 or 54 ....$247.00
Price: 50-cal., left-hand $264.00

TRADITIONS KENTUCKY RIFLE
Caliber: 50.
Barrel: 33 1/2"; 7/8" flats; 1:66" twist.
Weight: 7 lbs. Length: 49" overall.
Stock: Beech; inletted toe plate.
Sights: Blade front, fixed rear.
Features: Full-length, two-piece stock; brass furniture; color case-hardened lock. Introduced 1995. From Traditions.
Price: Finished $247.00
Price: Kit $198.00

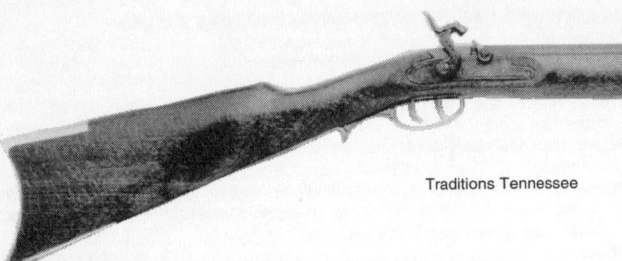

Traditions Tennessee

TRADITIONS TENNESSEE RIFLE
Caliber: 50.
Barrel: 24", octagon with 15/16" flats; 1:32" twist.
Weight: 6 lbs. Length: 40 1/2" overall.
Stock: Stained beech.
Sights: Blade front, fixed rear.
Features: One-piece stock has inletted brass furniture, cheekpiece; double-set trigger; V-type mainspring. Flint or percussion. Introduced 1995. From Traditions.
Price: Percussion $297.00
Price: Flintlock $313.00

TRADITIONS PENNSYLVANIA RIFLE
Caliber: 50.
Barrel: 40 1/4", 7/8" flats; 1:66" twist, octagon.
Weight: 9 lbs. Length: 57 1/2" overall.
Stock: Walnut.
Sights: Blade front, adjustable rear.
Features: Brass patchbox and ornamentation. Double-set triggers. From Traditions.
Price: Flintlock $506.00
Price: Percussion $496.00

TRADITIONS PIONEER RIFLE
Caliber: 50, 54.
Barrel: 28", 15/16" flats.
Weight: 7 lbs. Length: 44" overall.
Stock: Beech with pistol grip, recoil pad.
Sights: German silver blade front, buckhorn rear with elevation ramp.
Features: V-type mainspring, adjustable single trigger; blackened furniture; color case-hardened lock; large trigger guard. From Traditions.
Price: Percussion only, rifle $214.00

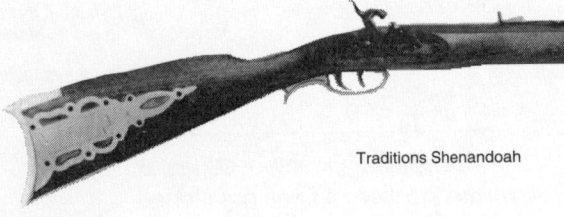

Traditions Shenandoah

TRADITIONS SHENANDOAH RIFLE
Caliber: 50.
Barrel: 33 1/2" octagon, 1:66" twist.
Weight: 7 lbs., 3 oz. Length: 49 1/2" overall.
Stock: Walnut.
Sights: Blade front, buckhorn rear.
Features: V-type mainspring; double-set trigger; solid brass buttplate, patchbox, nose cap, thimbles, rigger guard. Introduced 1996. From Traditions.
Price: Flintlock $366.00
Price: Percussion $348.00

Traditions Model 1853

TRADITIONS 1853 THREE-BAND ENFIELD
Caliber: 58.
Barrel: 39"; 1:48" twist.
Weight: 10 lbs. Length: 55" overall.
Stock: Walnut.
Sights: Military front, adjustable ladder-type rear.
Features: Color case-hardened lock; brass buttplate, trigger guard, nose cap. Has V-type mainspring; steel ramrod; sling swivels. Introduced 1995. From Traditions.
Price: $595.00

BLACKPOWDER MUSKETS & RIFLES

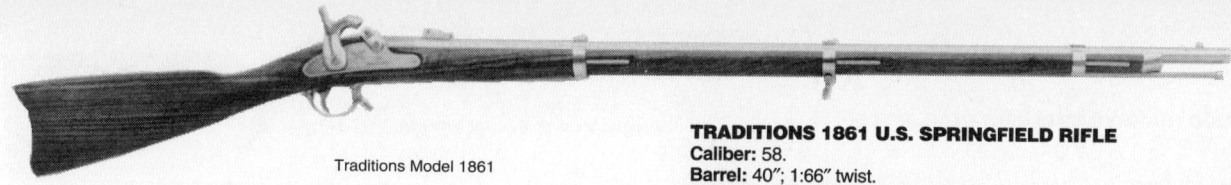

Traditions Model 1861

TRADITIONS 1861 U.S. SPRINGFIELD RIFLE
Caliber: 58.
Barrel: 40"; 1:66" twist.
Weight: 10 lbs. **Length:** 56" overall.
Stock: Walnut.
Sights: Military front, adjustable ladder-type rear.
Features: Full-length stock with white steel barrel, buttplate, ramrod, trigger guard, barrel bands, swivels, lockplate. Introduced 1995. From Traditions.
Price: $645.00

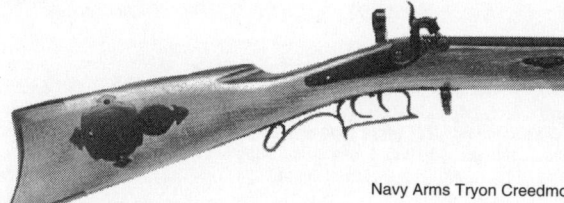

Navy Arms Tryon Creedmoor

TRYON TRAILBLAZER RIFLE
Caliber: 50, 54.
Barrel: 28", 30".
Weight: 9 lbs. **Length:** 48" overall.
Stock: European walnut with cheekpiece.
Sights: Blade front, semi-buckhorn rear.
Features: Reproduction of a rifle made by George Tryon about 1820. Double-set triggers, back action lock, hooked breech with long tang. From Armsport.
Price: About $825.00

Navy Arms Tryon Creedmoor Target Model
Similar to the standard Tryon rifle except 45-caliber only, 33" octagon barrel, globe front sight with inserts, fully adjustable match rear. Has double-set triggers, sling swivels. Imported by Navy Arms.
Price: $780.00

UFA Grand Teton Rifle
Similar to the Teton model except has 30" tapered octagon barrel in 45- or 50-caliber only. Available in blue or stainless steel with brushed or matte finish, brown or black laminated wood stock and forend. Weighs 9 lbs., overall length 46". Introduced 1994. Made in U.S. by UFA, Inc.
Price: $995.00
Price: With premium walnut or maple $1,145.00

UFA TETON RIFLE
Caliber: 45, 50, 12-bore (rifled, 72-cal.), 12-gauge.
Barrel: 26".
Weight: 8 lbs. **Length:** 42" overall.
Stock: Black or brown laminated wood; 1" recoil pad.
Sights: Marble's bead front, Marble's fully adjustable rear.
Features: Removable, interchangeable barrel; removable one-piece breech plug/nipple, hammer/trigger assembly; hammer blowback block; glass-bedded stock and forend. Introduced 1994. Made in U.S. by UFA, Inc.
Price: Stainless or blued $834.00
Price: With premium walnut or maple $984.00
Price: Extra barrels $165.00

UFA Teton Blackstone Rifle
Similar to the Teton model except in 50-caliber only, 26" barrel with shallow groove 1:26" rifling. Available only in stainless steel with matte finish. Has hardwood stock with black epoxy coating, 1" recoil pad. Weighs 7½ lbs., overall length 42". Introduced 1994. Made in U.S. by UFA, Inc.
Price: $534.00

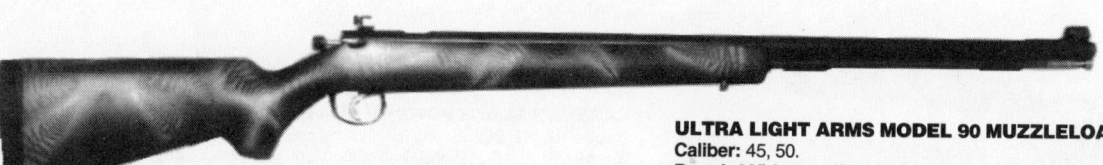

Ultra Light Model 90

ULTRA LIGHT ARMS MODEL 90 MUZZLELOADER
Caliber: 45, 50.
Barrel: 28", button rifled; 1:48" twist.
Weight: 6 lbs.
Stock: Kevlar/graphite, colors optional.
Sights: Hooded blade front on ramp, Williams aperture rear adjustable for windage and elevation.
Features: In-line ignition system with top loading port. Timney trigger; integral side safety. Comes with recoil pad, sling swivels and hard case. Introduced 1990. Made in U.S. by Ultra Light Arms.
Price: $950.00

White Shooting Systems Super 91

WHITE SHOOTING SYSTEMS SUPER 91 BLACKPOWDER RIFLE
Caliber: 41, 45 or 50.
Barrel: 26".
Weight: 7½ lbs. **Length:** 43.5" overall.
Stock: Black laminate or black composite; recoil pad, swivel studs.
Sights: Bead front on ramp, fully adjustable open rear.
Features: Insta-Fire straight-line ignition system; all stainless steel construction; side-swing safety; fully adjustable trigger; full barrel under-rib with two ramrod thimbles. Introduced 1991. Made in U.S. by White Shooting Systems, Inc.
Price: Blue, hardwood stock, 50-cal. $599.00
Price: Stainless $659.00
Price: Stainless, laminate stock $699.95

White Shooting Systems Super Safari Rifle
Same as the stainless Super 91 except has Mannlicher-style stock of black composite. Introduced 1993. From White Shooting Systems, Inc.
Price: $799.00

CAUTION: PRICES SHOWN ARE SUPPLIED BY THE MANUFACTURER OR IMPORTER. CHECK YOUR LOCAL GUNSHOP.

BLACKPOWDER MUSKETS & RIFLES

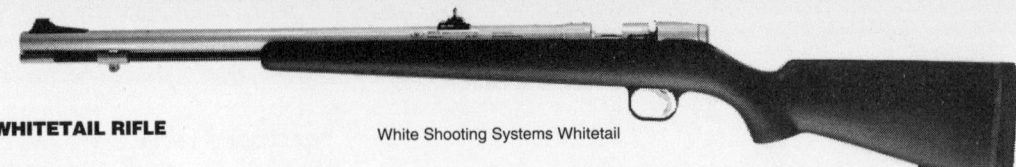

White Shooting Systems Whitetail

WHITE SHOOTING SYSTEMS WHITETAIL RIFLE
Caliber: 41, 45 or 50.
Barrel: 22".
Weight: 6.5 lbs. **Length:** 39.5" overall.
Stock: Black composite; classic style; recoil pad, swivel studs.
Sights: Bead front on ramp, fully adjustable open rear.
Features: Insta-Fire straight-line ignition; action and trigger safeties; adjustable trigger; stainless steel. Introduced 1992. Made in U.S. by White Shooting Systems, Inc.
Price: Blue, wood stock, bull bbl., 50-cal. $399.00
Price: Stainless, composite stock $499.00
Price: Stainless, laminate stock $549.00

> Consult our Directory pages for the location of firms mentioned.

White Shooting Systems Bison Blackpowder Rifle
Similar to the blued Whitetail model except in 54-caliber (1:28" twist) with 22" ball barrel. Uses Insta-Fire in-line percussion system, double safety. Adjustable sight, black-finished hardwood stock, matte blue metal finish, Delron ramrod, swivel studs. Drilled and tapped for scope mounting. Weighs 7 1/4 lbs. Introduced 1993. From White Shooting Systems, Inc.
Price: $399.95

White Shooting Systems White Lightning Rifle
Similar to the Whitetail stainless rifle except uses smaller action with cocking lever and secondary safety on right side, primary safety on the left. Available only in 50-caliber with 22" barrel. Weighs 6.4 lbs., 40" overall. Has black hardwood stock. Introduced 1995. From White Shooting Systems, Inc.
Price: $299.95

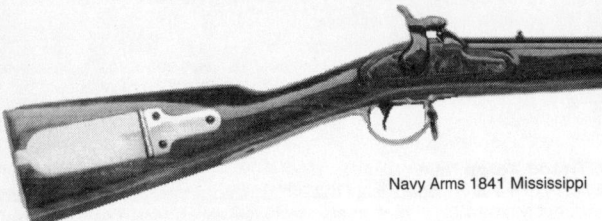

Navy Arms 1841 Mississippi

Mississippi 1841 Percussion Rifle
Similar to Zouave rifle but patterned after U.S. Model 1841. Imported by Dixie Gun Works, Euroarms of America, Navy Arms, Stone Mountain Arms.
Price: ....$430.00 to $487.00

ZOUAVE PERCUSSION RIFLE
Caliber: 58, 59.
Barrel: 32 1/2".
Weight: 9 1/2 lbs. **Length:** 48 1/2" overall.
Stock: Walnut finish, brass patchbox and buttplate.
Sights: Fixed front, rear adjustable for elevation.
Features: Color case-hardened lockplate, blued barrel. From Navy Arms, Dixie Gun Works, Euroarms of America (M1863), E.M.F., Cabela's.
Price: About ....$325.00 to $465.00
Price: Kit (Euroarms 58-cal. only) $331.00

BLACKPOWDER SHOTGUNS

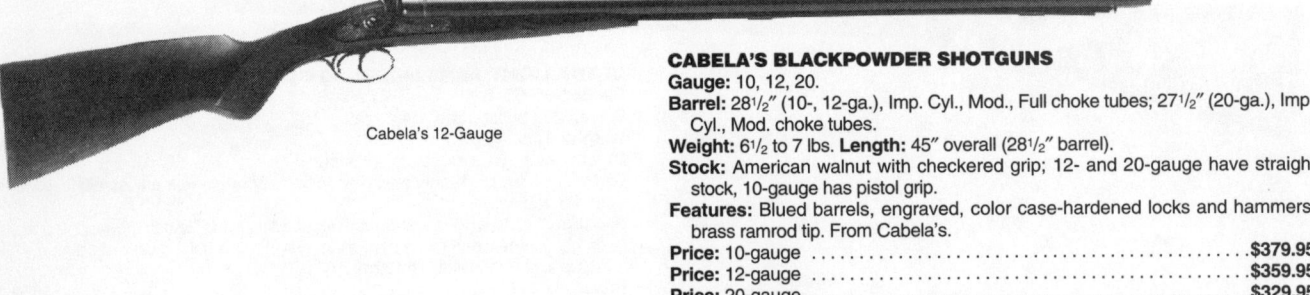

Cabela's 12-Gauge

CABELA'S BLACKPOWDER SHOTGUNS
Gauge: 10, 12, 20.
Barrel: 28 1/2" (10-, 12-ga.), Imp. Cyl., Mod., Full choke tubes; 27 1/2" (20-ga.), Imp. Cyl., Mod. choke tubes.
Weight: 6 1/2 to 7 lbs. **Length:** 45" overall (28 1/2" barrel).
Stock: American walnut with checkered grip; 12- and 20-gauge have straight stock, 10-gauge has pistol grip.
Features: Blued barrels, engraved, color case-hardened locks and hammers, brass ramrod tip. From Cabela's.
Price: 10-gauge $379.95
Price: 12-gauge $359.95
Price: 20-gauge $329.95

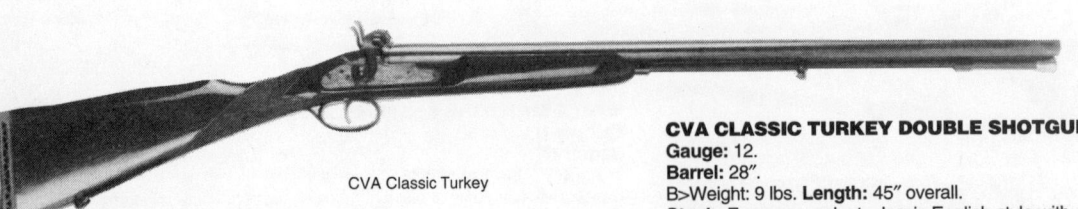

CVA Classic Turkey

CVA CLASSIC TURKEY DOUBLE SHOTGUN
Gauge: 12.
Barrel: 28".
B>**Weight:** 9 lbs. **Length:** 45" overall.
Stock: European walnut; classic English style with checkered straight grip, wrap-around forend with bottom screw attachment.
Sights: Bead front.
Features: Hinged double triggers; color case-hardened and engraved lockplates, trigger guard and tang. Polymer-coated fiberglass ramrod. Rubber recoil pad. Not suitable for steel shot. Introduced 1990. Imported by CVA.
Price: $429.95

BLACKPOWDER SHOTGUNS

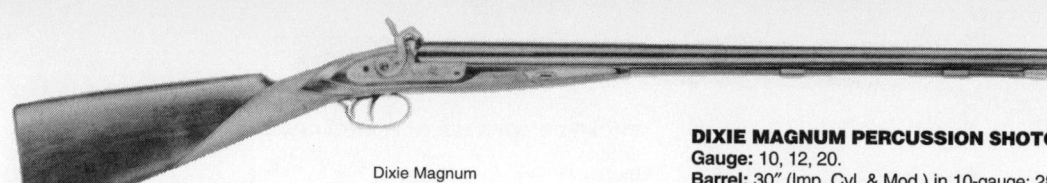
Dixie Magnum

DIXIE MAGNUM PERCUSSION SHOTGUN
Gauge: 10, 12, 20.
Barrel: 30″ (Imp. Cyl. & Mod.) in 10-gauge; 28″ in 12-gauge.
Weight: 6 1/4 lbs. **Length:** 45″ overall.
Stock: Hand-checkered walnut, 14″ pull.
Features: Double triggers; light hand engraving; case-hardened locks in 12-gauge, polished steel in 10-gauge; sling swivels. From Dixie Gun Works.
Price: Upland $449.00
Price: 12-ga. kit $375.00
Price: 20-ga. $495.00
Price: 10-ga. $495.00
Price: 10-ga. kit $375.00

CVA TRAPPER PERCUSSION
Gauge: 12.
Barrel: 28″.
Weight: 6 lbs. **Length:** 46″ overall.
Stock: English-style checkered straight grip of walnut-finished hardwood.
Sights: Brass bead front.
Features: Single blued barrel; color case-hardened lockplate and hammer; screw adjustable sear engagements, V-type mainspring; brass wedge plates; color case-hardened and engraved trigger guard and tang. From CVA.
Price: Finished $239.95

Mowrey Shotgun

MOWREY SHOTGUN
Gauge: 12, 28.
Barrel: 28″ (28-gauge, Cyl.); 32″ (12-gauge, Cyl.); octagonal.
Weight: About 8 lbs. **Length:** 48″ overall (32″ barrel).
Stock: Curly maple.
Sights: Bead front.
Features: Brass or steel frame; shotgun butt. Made in U.S. by Mowrey Gun Works.
Price: Finished $350.00
Price: Kit $300.00

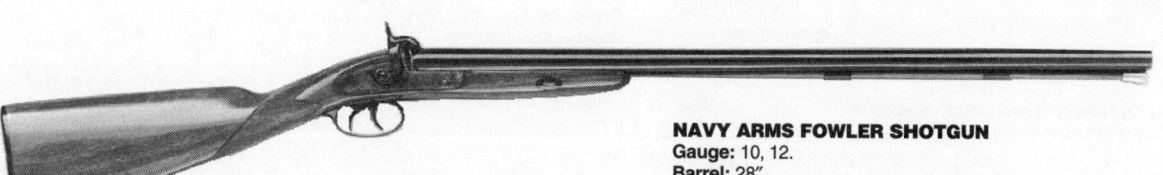
Navy Arms Fowler

NAVY ARMS FOWLER SHOTGUN
Gauge: 10, 12.
Barrel: 28″.
Weight: 7 lbs., 12 oz. **Length:** 45″ overall.
Stock: Walnut-stained hardwood.
Features: Color case-hardened lockplates and hammers; checkered stock. Imported by Navy Arms.
Price: $340.00

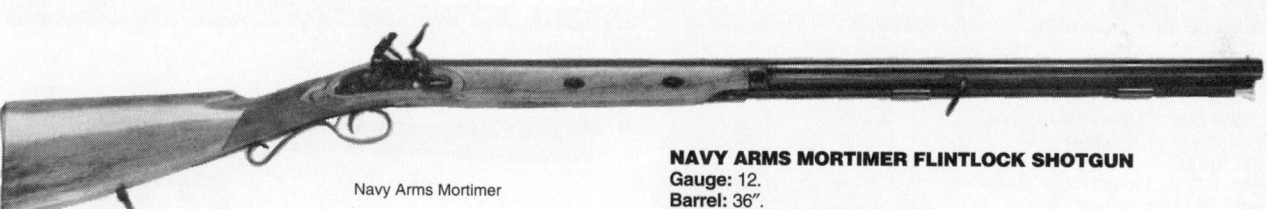
Navy Arms Mortimer

NAVY ARMS MORTIMER FLINTLOCK SHOTGUN
Gauge: 12.
Barrel: 36″.
Weight: 7 lbs. **Length:** 53″ overall.
Stock: Walnut, with cheekpiece.
Features: Waterproof pan, roller frizzen, external safety. Color case-hardened lock, rest blued. Imported by Navy Arms.
Price: $735.00

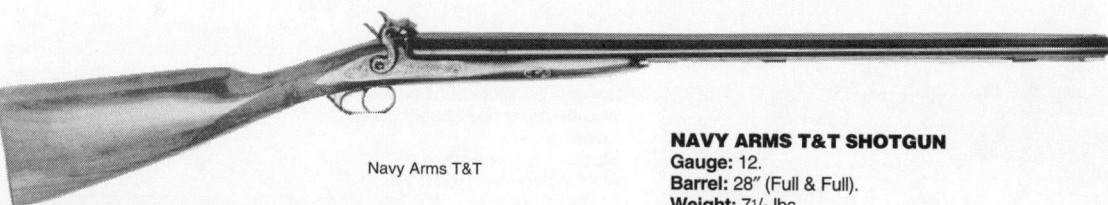
Navy Arms T&T

NAVY ARMS T&T SHOTGUN
Gauge: 12.
Barrel: 28″ (Full & Full).
Weight: 7 1/2 lbs.
Stock: Walnut.
Sights: Bead front.
Features: Color case-hardened locks, double triggers, blued steel furniture. From Navy Arms.
Price: $540.00

NAVY ARMS STEEL SHOT MAGNUM SHOTGUN
Gauge: 10.
Barrel: 28″ (Cyl. & Cyl.).
Weight: 7 lbs., 9 oz. **Length:** 45 1/2″ overall.
Stock: Walnut, with cheekpiece.
Features: Designed specifically for steel shot. Engraved, polished locks; sling swivels; blued barrels. Imported by Navy Arms.
Price: $560.00

CAUTION: PRICES SHOWN ARE SUPPLIED BY THE MANUFACTURER OR IMPORTER. CHECK YOUR LOCAL GUNSHOP.

BLACKPOWDER SHOTGUNS

T/C New Englander

THOMPSON/CENTER NEW ENGLANDER SHOTGUN
Gauge: 12.
Barrel: 28" (Imp. Cyl.), round.
Weight: 5 lbs., 2 oz.
Stock: Select American black walnut with straight grip.
Features: Percussion lock is color case-hardened, rest blued. Also accepts 26" round 50- and 54-cal. rifle barrel. Introduced 1986. From Thompson/Center.
Price: Right-hand $330.00

Traditions Buckhunter Pro

TRADITIONS BUCKHUNTER PRO SHOTGUN
Gauge: 12.
Barrel: 24"; choke tube.
Weight: 6 lbs., 4oz. **Length:** 43" overall.
Stock: Composite matte black, Mossy Oak Treestand or Advantage camouflage.
Features: In-line action with removable stainless steel breech plug; thumb safety; adjustable trigger; rubber buttpad. Introduced 1996. From Traditions.
Price: With black stock $313.00
Price: With camouflage stock $366.00

White Shooting Systems White Thunder

WHITE SHOOTING SYSTEMS WHITE THUNDER SHOTGUN
Gauge: 12.
Barrel: 26" (Imp. Cyl., Mod., Full choke tubes); ventilated rib.
Weight: About $5^{3}/_{4}$ lbs.
Stock: Black hardwood.
Features: InstaFire in-line ignition; double safeties; match-grade trigger; Delron ramrod. Introduced 1995. From White Shooting Systems, Inc.
Price: $459.95

White Shooting Systems "Tominator" Shotgun
Similar to the White Thunder except has Imp. Cyl., Mod., Full and Super Full Turkey choke tubes; black laminate stock. Introduced 1995. From White Shooting Systems, Inc.
Price: $549.95

AIRGUNS—HANDGUNS

AIRROW MODEL A6 AIR PISTOL
Caliber: #2512 10.75" arrow.
Barrel: 10.75".
Weight: 1.75 lbs. **Length:** 16.5" overall.
Power: CO_2 or compressed air.
Stocks: Checkered composition.
Sights: Bead front, fully adjustable Williams rear.
Features: Velocity to 375 fps. Pneumatic air trigger. Floating barrel. All aircraft aluminum and stainless steel construction; Mil-spec materials and finishes. Announced 1993. From Swivel Machine Works, Inc.
Price: About $597.00

Airrow Model A6

Anics A-101 Magnum

ANICS A-101 AIR PISTOL
Caliber: 177, 4.5mm, BB; 15-shot magazine.
Barrel: 4.5" steel smoothbore.
Weight: 35 oz. **Length:** 7" overall.
Power: CO_2
Stocks: Checkered plastic.
Sights: Blade front, fixed rear.
Features: Velocity to 460 fps. Semi-automatic action; double action only; cross-bolt safety; black and silver finish. Comes with two 15-shot magazines. Introduced 1996. Imported by Anics, Inc.
Price: With case, about $65.00

Anics A-101 Magnum Air Pistol
Similar to the A-101 except has 6" barrel with compensator, gives about 490 fps. Introduced 1996. Imported by Anics, Inc.
Price: With case, about $72.00

AIRGUNS—HANDGUNS

ANICS A-201 AIR REVOLVER
Caliber: 177, 4.5mm, BB; 36-shot cylinder.
Barrel: 4", 6" steel smoothbore.
Weight: 36 oz. **Length:** 9.75" overall.
Power: CO_2
Stocks: Checkered plastic.
Sights: Blade front, fully adjustable rear.
Features: Velocity about 425 fps. Fixed barrel; single/double action; rotating cylinder; manual cross-bolt safety; blue and silver finish. Introduced 1996. Imported by Anics, Inc.
Price: $75.00

BEEMAN P1 MAGNUM AIR PISTOL
Caliber: 177, 5mm, single shot.
Barrel: 8.4".
Weight: 2.5 lbs. **Length:** 11" overall.
Power: Top lever cocking; spring-piston.
Stocks: Checkered walnut.
Sights: Blade front, square notch rear with click micrometer adjustments for windage and elevation. Grooved for scope mounting.
Features: Dual power for 177 and 20-cal.: low setting gives 350-400 fps; high setting 500-600 fps. Rearward expanding mainspring simulates firearm recoil. All Colt 45 auto grips fit gun. Dry-firing feature for practice. Optional wooden shoulder stock. Introduced 1985. Imported by Beeman.
Price: 177, 5mm $405.00

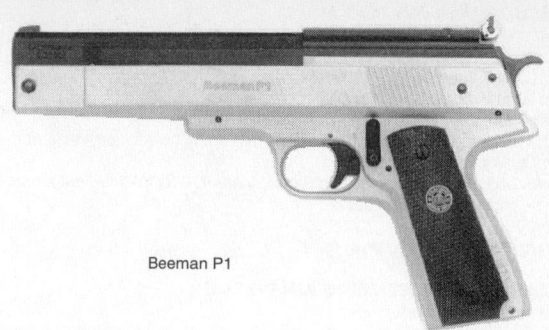
Beeman P1

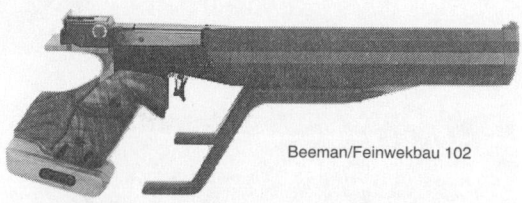
Beeman/Feinwekbau 102

BEEMAN/FEINWERKBAU 102 PISTOL
Caliber: 177, single shot.
Barrel: 10.1", 12-groove rifling.
Weight: 2.5 lbs. **Length:** 16.5" overall.
Power: Single-stroke pneumatic, underlever cocking.
Stocks: Stippled walnut with adjustable palm shelf.
Sights: Blade front, open rear adjustable for windage and elevation. Notch size adjustable for width. Interchangeable front blades.
Features: Velocity 460 fps. Fully adjustable trigger. Cocking effort 12 lbs. Introduced 1988. Imported by Beeman.
Price: Right-hand $1,530.00
Price: Left-hand $1,580.00

Beeman P2 Match Air Pistol
Similar to the Beeman P1 Magnum except shoots only 177 pellets; completely recoilless single-stroke pnuematic action. Weighs 2.2 lbs. Choice of thumbrest match grips or standard style. Introduced 1990.
Price: 177, 5mm, standard grip $435.00
Price: 177, match grip $465.00

BEEMAN/FEINWERKBAU 65 MKII AIR PISTOL
Caliber: 177, single shot.
Barrel: 6.1", removable bbl. wgt. available.
Weight: 42 oz. **Length:** 13.3" overall.
Power: Spring, sidelever cocking.
Stocks: Walnut, stippled thumbrest; adjustable or fixed.
Sights: Front, interchangeable post element system, open rear, click adjustable for windage and elevation and for sighting notch width. Scope mount available.
Features: New shorter barrel for better balance and control. Cocking effort 9 lbs. Two-stage trigger, four adjustments. Quiet firing, 525 fps. Programs instantly for recoil or recoilless operation. Permanently lubricated. Steel piston ring. Imported by Beeman.
Price: Right-hand $1,170.00
Price: Left-hand $1,220.00

BEEMAN/FWB P30 MATCH AIR PISTOL
Caliber: 177, single shot.
Barrel: $10^{5}/_{16}$", with muzzlebrake.
Weight: 2.4 lbs. **Length:** 16.5" overall.
Power: Pre-charged pneumatic.
Stocks: Stippled walnut; adjustable match type.
Sights: Undercut blade front, fully adjustable match rear.
Features: Velocity to 525 fps; up to 200 shots per CO_2 cartridge. Fully adjustable trigger; built-in muzzlebrake. Introduced 1995. Imported from Germany by Beeman.
Price: Right-hand $1,530.00
Price: Left-hand $1,580.00

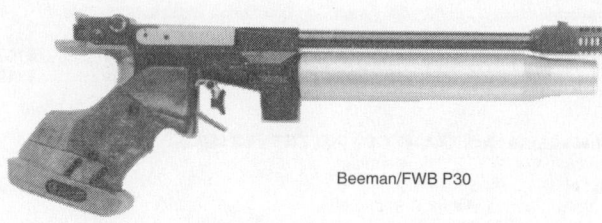
Beeman/FWB P30

Manufacturers' addresses in the
Directory of the Arms Trade
page 313, this issue

Beeman/FWB C55

BEEMAN/FWB C55 CO₂ RAPID FIRE PISTOL
Caliber: 177, single shot or 5-shot magazine.
Barrel: 7.3".
Weight: 2.5 lbs. **Length:** 15" overall.
Power: Special CO_2 cylinder.
Stocks: Anatomical, adjustable.
Sights: Interchangeable front, fully adjustable open micro-click rear with adjustable notch size.
Features: Velocity 510 fps. Has 11.75" sight radius. Built-in muzzlebrake. Introduced 1993. Imported by Beeman Precision Airguns.
Price: Right-hand $1,705.00
Price: Left-hand $1,755.00

CAUTION: PRICES SHOWN ARE SUPPLIED BY THE MANUFACTURER OR IMPORTER. CHECK YOUR LOCAL GUNSHOP.

AIRGUNS—HANDGUNS

BEEMAN HW70A AIR PISTOL
Caliber: 177, single shot.
Barrel: 6 1/4", rifled.
Weight: 38 oz. **Length:** 12 3/4" overall.
Power: Spring, barrel cocking.
Stocks: Plastic, with thumbrest.
Sights: Hooded post front, square notch rear adjustable for windage and elevation. Comes with scope base.
Features: Adjustable trigger, 24-lb. cocking effort, 410 fps MV; automatic barrel safety. Imported by Beeman.
Price: $215.00
Price: HW70S, black grip, silver finish $240.00

BEEMAN/WEBLEY NEMESIS AIR PISTOL
Caliber: 177, single shot.
Barrel: 7".
Weight: 2.2 lbs. **Length:** 9.8" overall.
Power: Single-stroke pneumatic.
Stocks: Checkered black composition.
Sights: Blade on ramp front, fully adjustable rear. Integral scope rail.
Features: Velocity to 400 fps. Adjustable two-stage trigger, manual safety. Recoilless action. Introduced 1995. Imported from England by Beeman.
Price: $190.00

BEEMAN/WEBLEY TEMPEST AIR PISTOL
Caliber: 177, 22, single shot.
Barrel: 6 7/8".
Weight: 32 oz. **Length:** 8.9" overall.
Power: Spring-piston, break barrel.
Stocks: Checkered black plastic with thumbrest.
Sights: Blade front, adjustable rear.
Features: Velocity to 500 fps (177), 400 fps (22). Aluminum frame; black epoxy finish; manual safety. Imported from England by Beeman.
Price: $200.00

Beeman/Webley Hurricane Air Pistol
Similar to the Tempest except has extended frame in the rear for a click-adjustable rear sight; hooded front sight; comes with scope mount. Imported from England by Beeman.
Price: $225.00

Beeman HW70A

Beeman/Webley Nemesis

Beeman/Webley Tempest

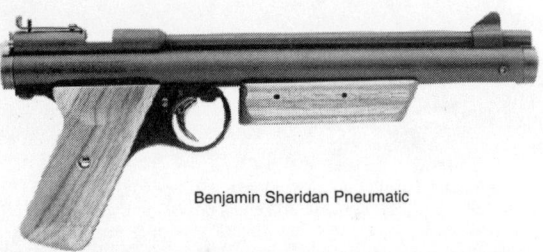
Benjamin Sheridan Pneumatic

Benjamin Sheridan CO$_2$

BRNO Tau-7 Match

BENJAMIN SHERIDAN PNEUMATIC PELLET PISTOLS
Caliber: 177, 20, 22, single shot.
Barrel: 9 3/8", rifled brass.
Weight: 38 oz. **Length:** 13 1/8" overall.
Power: Underlever pneumatic, hand pumped.
Stocks: Walnut stocks and pump handle.
Sights: High ramp front, fully adjustable notch rear.
Features: Velocity to 525 fps (variable). Bolt action with cross-bolt safety. Choice of black or nickel finish. Made in U.S. by Benjamin Sheridan Co.
Price: Black finish, HB17 (177), HB20 (20), HB22 (22), about $106.00
Price: Nickel finish, H17 (177), H20 (20), H22 (22), about $112.75

BENJAMIN SHERIDAN CO$_2$ PELLET PISTOLS
Caliber: 177, 20, 22, single shot.
Barrel: 6 3/8", rifled brass.
Weight: 29 oz. **Length:** 9.8" overall.
Power: 12-gram CO$_2$ cylinder.
Stocks: Walnut.
Sights: High ramp front, fully adjustable notch rear.
Features: Velocity to 500 fps. Turn-bolt action with cross-bolt safety. Gives about 40 shots per CO$_2$ cylinder. Black or nickel finish. Made in U.S. by Benjamin Sheridan Co.
Price: Black finish, EB17 (177), EB20 (20), EB22 (22), about $97.25
Price: Nickel finish, E17 (177), E20 (20), E22 (22), about $110.50

BRNO TAU-7 CO$_2$ MATCH PISTOL
Caliber: 177.
Barrel: 10.24".
Weight: 37 oz. **Length:** 15.75" overall.
Power: 12.5-gram CO$_2$ cartridge.
Stocks: Stippled hardwood with adjustable palm rest.
Sights: Blade front, open fully adjustable rear.
Features: Comes with extra seals and counterweight. Blue finish. Imported by Century International Arms, Great Lakes Airguns.
Price: About $326.50

AIRGUNS—HANDGUNS

BSA 240 MAGNUM AIR PISTOL
Caliber: 177, 22
Barrel: 5½", rifled.
Weight: 28 oz. **Length:** 8½" overall.
Power: Spring-air.
Stocks: Oil-finish hardwood.
Sights: Post front, fully adjustable rear.
Features: Velocity about 390 fps (177). Automatic safety; adjustable trigger; matte finish. Introduced 1996. Imported frmo England by Great Lakes Airguns.
Price: $224.75

COPPERHEAD BLACK VENOM PISTOL
Caliber: 177 pellets, BB, 17-shot magazine.
Barrel: 4.75" smoothbore.
Weight: 16 oz. **Length:** 10.8" overall.
Power: Spring.
Stocks: Checkered.
Sights: Blade front, adjustable rear.
Features: Velocity to 260 fps (BBs), 250 fps (pellets). Spring-fed magazine; cross-bolt safety. Introduced 1996. Made in U.S. by Crosman Corp.
Price: About $16.00

COPPERHEAD BLACK FANG PISTOL
Caliber: 177 BB, 17-shot magazine.
Barrel: 4.75" smoothbore.
Weight: 10 oz. **Length:** 10.8" overall.
Power: Spring.
Stocks: Checkered.
Sights: Blade front, fixed notch rear.
Features: Velocity to 240 fps. Spring-fed magazine; cross-bolt safety. Introduced 1996. Made in U.S. by Crosman Corp.
Price: About $14.00

BSA 240 Magnum

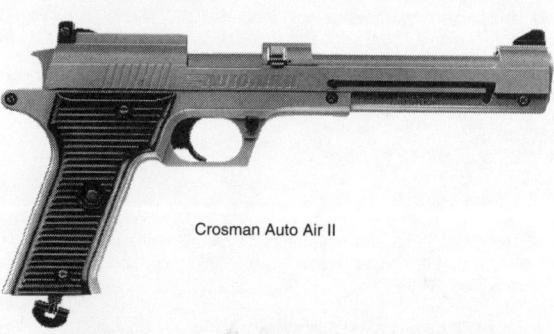
Crosman Auto Air II

Crosman Model 1008

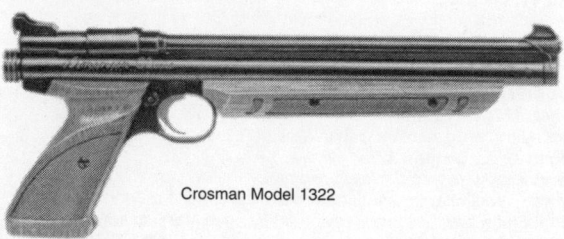
Crosman Model 1322

CROSMAN AUTO AIR II PISTOL
Caliber: BB, 17-shot magazine, 177 pellet, single shot.
Barrel: 8⅝" steel, smoothbore.
Weight: 13 oz. **Length:** 10¾" overall.
Power: CO_2 Powerlet.
Stocks: Grooved plastic.
Sights: Blade front, adjustable rear; highlighted system.
Features: Velocity to 480 fps (BBs), 430 fps (pellets). Semi-automatic action with BBs, single shot with pellets. Silvered finish. Introduced 1991. From Crosman.
Price: About $29.00

CROSMAN MODEL 357 AIR PISTOL
Caliber: 177, 6- and 10-shot pellet clips.
Barrel: 4" (Model 357-4), 6" (Model 357-6), rifled steel; 8" (Model 357-8), rifled brass.
Weight: 32 oz. (6"). **Length:** 11³⁄₈" overall (357-6).
Power: CO_2 Powerlet.
Stocks: Checkered wood-grain plastic.
Sights: Ramp front, fully adjustable rear.
Features: Average 430 fps (Model 357-6). Break-open barrel for easy loading. Single or double action. Vent. rib barrel. Wide, smooth trigger. Two cylinders come with each gun. Model 357-8 has matte gray finish, black grips. From Crosman.
Price: 4" or 6", about $46.50
Price: 8", about $53.25
Price: Model 1357 (same gun as above, except shoots BBs, has 6-shot clip), about $46.50

CROSMAN MODEL 1008 REPEAT AIR
Caliber: 177, 8-shot pellet clip
Barrel: 4.25", rifled steel.
Weight: 17 oz. **Length:** 8.625" overall.
Power: CO_2 Powerlet.
Stocks: Checkered plastic.
Sights: Post front, adjustable rear.
Features: Velocity about 430 fps. Break-open barrel for easy loading; single or double semi-automatic action; two 8-shot clips included. Optional carrying case available. Introduced 1992. From Crosman.
Price: About $45.00
Price: With case, about $55.00
Price: Model 1008SB (silver and black finish), about $47.00

CROSMAN MODEL 1322, 1377 AIR PISTOLS
Caliber: 177 (M1377), 22 (M1322), single shot.
Barrel: 8", rifled steel.
Weight: 39 oz. **Length:** 13⅝".
Power: Hand pumped.
Sights: Blade front, rear adjustable for windage and elevation.
Features: Moulded plastic grip, hand size pump forearm. Cross-bolt safety. Model 1377 also shoots BBs. From Crosman.
Price: About $53.00

DAISY MODEL 288 AIR PISTOL
Caliber: 177 pellets, 24-shot.
Barrel: Smoothbore steel.
Weight: .8 lb. **Length:** 12.1" overall.
Power: Single stroke spring-air.
Stocks: Moulded resin with checkering and thumbrest.
Sights: Blade and ramp front, open fixed rear.
Features: Velocity to 215 fps. Cross-bolt trigger block safety. Black finish. From Daisy Mfg. Co.
Price: About $26.00

AIRGUNS—HANDGUNS

DAISY MODEL 91 MATCH PISTOL
Caliber: 177, single shot.
Barrel: 10.25", rifled steel.
Weight: 2.5 lbs. **Length:** 16.5" overall.
Power: CO_2, 12-gram cylinder.
Stocks: Stippled hardwood; anatomically shaped and adjustable.
Sights: Blade and ramp front, changeable-width rear notch with full micrometer adjustments.
Features: Velocity to 476 fps. Gives 55 shots per cylinder. Fully adjustable trigger. Imported by Daisy Mfg. Co.
Price: About $670.00

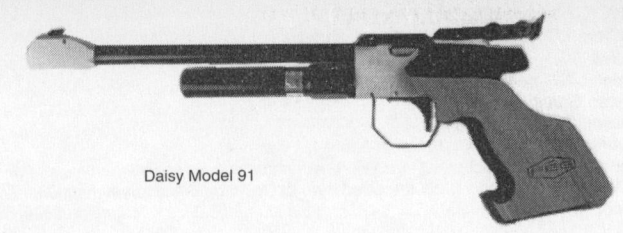
Daisy Model 91

Daisy Model 500

DAISY MODEL 500 RAVEN AIR PISTOL
Caliber: 177 pellets, single shot.
Barrel: Rifled steel.
Weight: 36 oz. **Length:** 8.5" overall.
Power: CO_2.
Stocks: Moulded plastic with checkering.
Sights: Blade front, fixed rear.
Features: Velocity up to 500 fps. Hammer-block safety. Resembles semi-auto centerfire pistol. Barrel tips up for loading. Introduced 1993. From Daisy Mfg. Co.
Price: About $65.00

DAISY/POWER LINE 44 REVOLVER
Caliber: 177 pellets, 6-shot.
Barrel: 6", rifled steel; interchangeable 4" and 8".
Weight: 2.7 lbs.
Power: CO_2.
Stocks: Moulded plastic with checkering.
Sights: Blade on ramp front, fully adjustable notch rear.
Features: Velocity up to 400 fps. Replica of 44 Magnum revolver. Has swingout cylinder and interchangeable barrels. Introduced 1987. From Daisy Mfg. Co.
Price: $70.00

DAISY/POWER LINE 45 AIR PISTOL
Caliber: 177, 13-shot clip.
Barrel: 5", rifled steel.
Weight: 1.25 lbs. **Length:** 8.5" overall.
Power: CO_2.
Stocks: Checkered plastic.
Sights: Fixed.
Features: Velocity 400 fps. Semi-automatic repeater with double-action trigger. Manually operated lever-type trigger block safety; magazine safety. Introduced 1990. From Daisy Mfg. Co.
Price: About $80.00
Price: Model 645 (nickel-chrome plated), about $85.00

Daisy/Power Line 45

DAISY/POWER LINE 93 PISTOL
Caliber: 177, BB, 15-shot clip.
Barrel: 5", steel.
Weight: 17 oz. **Length:** NA.
Power: CO_2.
Stocks: Checkered plastic.
Sights: Fixed.
Features: Velocity to 400 fps. Semi-automatic repeater. Manual lever-type trigger-block safety. Introduced 1991. From Daisy Mfg. Co.
Price: About $80.00
Price: Model 693 (nickel-chrome plated), about $85.00

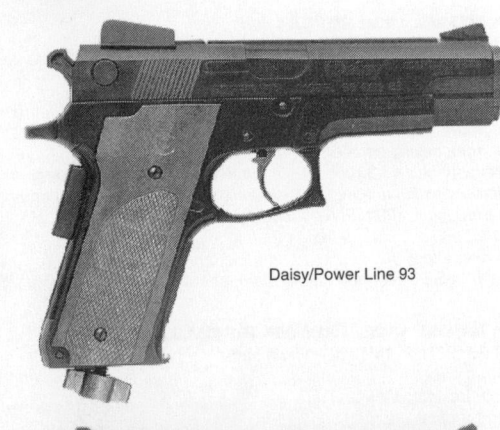
Daisy/Power Line 93

DAISY/POWER LINE 400 BB PISTOL
Caliber: BB, 20-shot magazine.
Barrel: Smoothbore steel.
Weight: 1.4 lbs. **Length:** 10.7" overall.
Power: 12-gram CO_2.
Stocks: Moulded black checkered plastic.
Sights: Blade front, fixed open rear.
Features: Velocity to 420 fps. Blowback slide cycles automatically on firing. Rotary trigger block safety. Introduced 1994. From Daisy Mfg. Co.
Price: About $83.00

DAISY/POWER LINE MATCH 777 PELLET PISTOL
Caliber: 177, single shot.
Barrel: 9.61" rifled steel by Lothar Walther.
Weight: 32 oz. **Length:** 13$1/2$" overall.
Power: Sidelever, single-pump pneumatic.
Stocks: Smooth hardwood, fully contoured with palm and thumbrest.
Sights: Blade and ramp front, match-grade open rear with adjustable width notch, micro. click adjustments.
Features: Adjustable trigger; manual cross-bolt safety. MV of 385 fps. Comes with cleaning kit, adjustment tool and pellets. From Daisy Mfg. Co.
Price: About $335.00

Daisy/Power Line 400

AIRGUNS—HANDGUNS

DAISY/POWER LINE 717 PELLET PISTOL
Caliber: 177, single shot.
Barrel: 9.61".
Weight: 2.8 lbs. **Length:** 13 1/2" overall.
Stocks: Moulded wood-grain plastic, with thumbrest.
Sights: Blade and ramp front, micro-adjustable notch rear.
Features: Single pump pneumatic pistol. Rifled steel barrel. Cross-bolt trigger block. Muzzle velocity 385 fps. From Daisy Mfg. Co. Introduced 1979.
Price: About $80.00

Daisy/Power Line 747 Pistol
Similar to the 717 pistol except has a 12-groove rifled steel barrel by Lothar Walther, and adjustable trigger pull weight. Velocity of 360 fps. Manual cross-bolt safety.
Price: About $160.00

Daisy/Power Line 717

Daisy/Power Line 1140

DAISY/POWER LINE 1140 PELLET PISTOL
Caliber: 177, single shot.
Barrel: Rifled steel.
Weight: 1.3 lbs. **Length:** 11.7" overall.
Power: Single-stroke barrel cocking.
Stocks: Checkered resin.
Sights: Hooded post front, open adjustable rear.
Features: Velocity to 325 fps. Made of black lightweight engineering resin. Introduced 1995. From Daisy.
Price: About $45.50

DAISY/POWER LINE CO_2 1200 PISTOL
Caliber: BB, 177.
Barrel: 10 1/2", smooth.
Weight: 1.6 lbs. **Length:** 11.1" overall.
Power: Daisy CO_2 cylinder.
Stocks: Contoured, checkered moulded wood-grain plastic.
Sights: Blade ramp front, fully adjustable square notch rear.
Features: 60-shot BB reservoir, gravity feed. Cross-bolt safety. Velocity of 420-450 fps for more than 100 shots. From Daisy Mfg. Co.
Price: About $37.50

Daisy/Power Line 1200

DAISY/POWER LINE 1700 AIR PISTOL
Caliber: 177 BB, 60-shot magazine.
Barrel: Smoothbore steel.
Weight: 1.4 lbs. **Length:** 11.2" overall.
Power: CO_2.
Stocks: Moulded checkered plastic.
Sights: Blade front, adjustable rear.
Features: Velocity to 420 fps. Cross-bolt trigger block safety; matte finish. Has 3/8" dovetail mount for scope or point sight. Introduced 1994. From Daisy Mfg. Co.
Price: About $40.00

"GAT" AIR PISTOL
Caliber: 177, single shot.
Barrel: 7 1/2" cocked, 9 1/2" extended.
Weight: 22 oz.
Power: Spring-piston.
Stocks: Cast checkered metal.
Sights: Fixed.
Features: Shoots pellets, corks or darts. Matte black finish. Imported from England by Stone Enterprises, Inc.
Price: $21.95

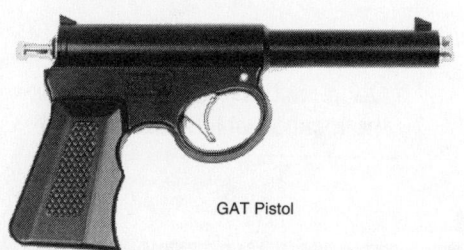

GAT Pistol

HAMMERLI 480 MATCH AIR PISTOL
Caliber: 177, single shot.
Barrel: 9.8".
Weight: 37 oz. **Length:** 16.5" overall.
Power: Air or CO_2.
Stocks: Walnut with 7-degree rake adjustment. Stippled grip area.
Sights: Undercut blade front, fully adjustable open match rear.
Features: Under-barrel cannister charges with air or CO_2 for power supply; gives 320 shots per filling. Trigger adjustable for position. Introduced 1994. Imported from Switzerland by Hammerli Pistols U.S.A.
Price: $1,325.00

Hammerli 480k Match Air Pistol
Similar to the 480 except has a short, detachable aluminum air cylinder for use only with compressed air; can be filled while on the gun or off; special adjustable barrel weights. Muzzle velocity of 470 fps, gives about 180 shots. Has stippled black composition grip with adjustable palm shelf and rake angle. Comes with air pressure gauge. Introduced 1996. Imported from Switzerland by SIGARMS, Inc.
Price: $1,155.00

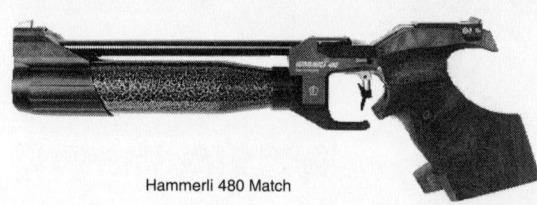

Hammerli 480 Match

MARKSMAN 1010 REPEATER PISTOL
Caliber: 177, 18-shot repeater.
Barrel: 2 1/2", smoothbore.
Weight: 24 oz. **Length:** 8 1/4" overall.
Power: Spring.
Features: Velocity to 200 fps. Thumb safety. Black finish. Uses BBs, darts or pellets. Repeats with BBs only. From Marksman Products.
Price: Matte black finish $25.50
Price: Model 1010X (as above except nickel-plated) $33.50

CAUTION: PRICES SHOWN ARE SUPPLIED BY THE MANUFACTURER OR IMPORTER. CHECK YOUR LOCAL GUNSHOP.

AIRGUNS—HANDGUNS

MARKSMAN 1015 SPECIAL EDITION AIR PISTOL
Caliber: 177, 24-shot repeater.
Barrel: 3.8", rifled.
Weight: 22 oz. **Length:** 10.3" overall.
Power: Spring-air.
Stocks: Checkered brown composition.
Sights: Fixed.
Features: Velocity about 230 fps. Skeletonized trigger, extended barrel with "ported compensator." Shoots BBs, pellets, darts or bolts. From Marksman Products.
Price: $31.75

Marksman 1015

MORINI 162E MATCH AIR PISTOL
Caliber: 177, single shot.
Barrel: 9.4".
Weight: 32 oz. **Length:** 16.1" overall.
Power: Pre-charged CO_2.
Stocks: Adjustable match type.
Sights: Interchangeable blade front, fully adjustable match-type rear.
Features: Power mechanism shuts down when pressure drops to a pre-set level. Adjustable electronic trigger. Introduced 1995. Imported from Switzerland by Nygord Precision Products.
Price: $950.00

PARDINI K58 MATCH AIR PISTOL
Caliber: 177, single shot.
Barrel: 9.0".
Weight: 37.7 oz. **Length:** 15.5" overall.
Power: Pre-charged compressed air; single-stroke cocking.
Stocks: Adjustable match type; stippled walnut.
Sights: Interchangeable post front, fully adjustable match rear.
Features: Fully adjustable trigger. Introduced 1995. Imported from Italy by Nygord Precision Products.
Price: $650.00
Price: K60 model (CO_2) $650.00

Record Champion Repeater

RECORD CHAMPION REPEATER PISTOL
Caliber: 177, 12-shot magazine.
Barrel: 7.6", rifled.
Weight: 2.8", rifled. **Length:** 10.2" overall.
Power: Spring-air.
Stocks: Oil-finished walnut.
Sights: Post front, fully adjustable rear.
Features: Velocity about 420 fps. Magazine loads through bottom of the grip. Full-length dovetail for scope mounting. Manual safety. Introduced 1996. Imported from Germany by Great Lakes Airguns.
Price: $161.50

RECORD JUMBO DELUXE AIR PISTOL
Caliber: 177, single shot.
Barrel: 6", rifled.
Weight: 1.9 lbs. **Length:** 7.25" overall.
Power: Spring-air, lateral cocking lever.
Stocks: Smooth walnut.
Sights: Blade front, fully adjustable open rear.
Features: Velocity to 322 fps. Thumb safety. Grip magazine compartment for extra pellet storage. Introduced 1983. Imported from Germany by Great Lakes Airguns.
Price: $121.34

Record Jumbo

Consult our Directory pages for the location of firms mentioned.

RWS/Diana Model 6M

RWS/Diana Model 5G

RWS/DIANA MODEL 5G AIR PISTOL
Caliber: 177, single shot.
Barrel: 7".
Weight: 2 3/4 lbs. **Length:** 15" overall.
Power: Spring-air, barrel cocking.
Stocks: Plastic, thumbrest design.
Sights: Tunnel front, micro-click open rear.
Features: Velocity of 450 fps. Adjustable two-stage trigger with automatic safety. Imported from Germany by Dynamit Nobel-RWS, Inc.
Price: $260.00

RWS/DIANA MODEL 6M MATCH AIR PISTOL
Caliber: 177, single shot.
Barrel: 7".
Weight: 3 lbs. **Length:** 15" overall.
Power: Spring-air, barrel cocking.
Stocks: Walnut-finished hardwood with thumbrest.
Sights: Adjustable front, micro. click open rear.
Features: Velocity of 410 fps. Recoilless double piston system, movable barrel shroud to protect from sight during cocking. Imported from Germany by Dynamit Nobel-RWS, Inc.
Price: Right-hand $585.00
Price: Left-hand $640.00

AIRGUNS—HANDGUNS

RWS/Diana Model 6G

RWS/Diana Model 6G Air Pistols
Similar to the Model 6M except does not have the movable barrel shroud. Has click micrometer rear sight, two-stage adjustable trigger, interchangeable tunnel front sight. Available in right- or left-hand models.
Price: Right-hand $450.00
Price: Left-hand $490.00

STEYR CO_2 MATCH LP1 PISTOL
Caliber: 177, single shot.
Barrel: 9".
Weight: 38.7 oz. **Length:** 15.3" overall.
Power: Pre-compressed CO_2 cylinders.
Stocks: Fully adjustable Morini match with palm shelf; stippled walnut.
Sights: Interchangeable blade in 4mm, 4.5mm or 5mm widths, fully adjustable open rear with interchangeable 3.5mm or 4mm leaves.
Features: Velocity about 500 fps. Adjustable trigger, adjustable sight radius from 12.4" to 13.2". Imported from Austria by Nygord Precision Products.
Price: About $1,095.00
Price: LP1C (compensated) $1,150.00

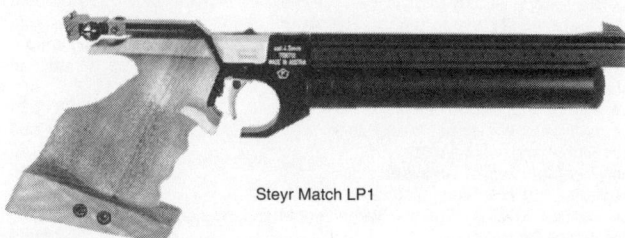
Steyr Match LP1

STEYR LP5 MATCH PISTOL
Caliber: 177, 5-shot magazine.
Barrel: NA.
Weight: 40.2 oz. **Length:** 13.39" overall.
Power: Pre-compressed CO_2 cylinders.
Stocks: Adjustable Morini match with palm shelf; stippled walnut.
Sights: Movable 2.5mm blade front; 2-3mm interchangeable in .2mm increments; fully adjustable open match rear.
Features: Velocity about 500 fps. Fully adjustable trigger; has dry-fire feature. Barrel and grip weights available. Introduced 1993. Imported from Austria by Nygord Precision Products.
Price: About $1,250.00

WALTHER CPM-1 CO_2 MATCH PISTOL
Caliber: 177, single shot.
Barrel: 8.66".
Weight: NA. **Length:** 15.1" overall.
Power: CO_2.
Stocks: Orthopaedic target type.
Sights: Undercut blade front, open match rear fully adjustable for windage and elevation.
Features: Adjustable velocity; matte finish. Introduced 1995. Imported from Germany by Nygord Precision Products.
Price: $950.00

STEYR LP 5C MATCH AIR PISTOL
Caliber: 177, 5-shot magazine.
Barrel: NA.
Weight: 40.7 oz. **Length:** 15.2" overall.
Power: Pre-charged air cylinder.
Stocks: Adjustable match type.
Sights: Interchangeable blade front, fully adjustable match rear.
Features: Adjustable sight radius; fully adjustable trigger. Has barrel compensator. Introduced 1995. Imported from Austria by Nygord Precision Products.
Price: $1,325.00

AIRGUNS—LONG GUNS

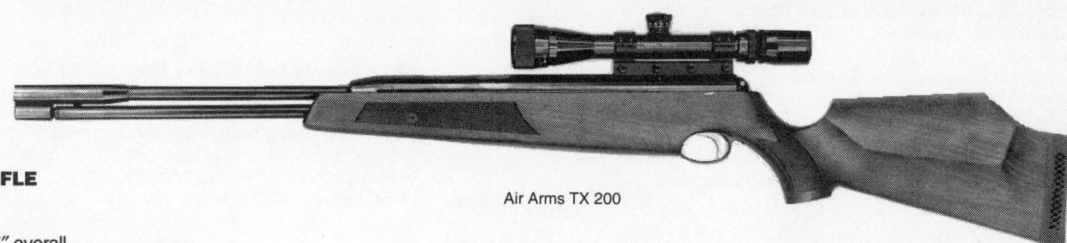
Air Arms TX 200

AIR ARMS TX 200 AIR RIFLE
Caliber: 177; single shot.
Barrel: 15.7".
Weight: 9.3 lbs. **Length:** 41.5" overall.
Power: Spring-air; underlever cocking.
Stock: Oil-finished hardwood; checkered grip and forend; rubber buttpad.
Sights: None furnished.
Features: Velocity about 900 fps. Automatic safety; adjustable two-stage trigger. Imported from England by Great Lakes Airguns.
Price: $489.81

Airrow A-8S1P

AIRROW MODEL A-8S1P STEALTH AIR GUN
Caliber: #2512 16" arrow.
Barrel: 16".
Weight: 4.4 lbs. **Length:** 30.1" overall.
Power: CO_2 or compressed air; variable power.
Stock: Telescoping CAR-15-type.
Sights: Scope rings only.
Features: Velocity to 650 fps with 260-grain arrow. Pneumatic air trigger. All aircraft aluminum and stainless steel construction. Mil-spec materials and finishes. Waterproof case. Introduced 1991. From Swivel Machine Works, Inc.
Price: About $1,699.00

AIRGUNS—LONG GUNS

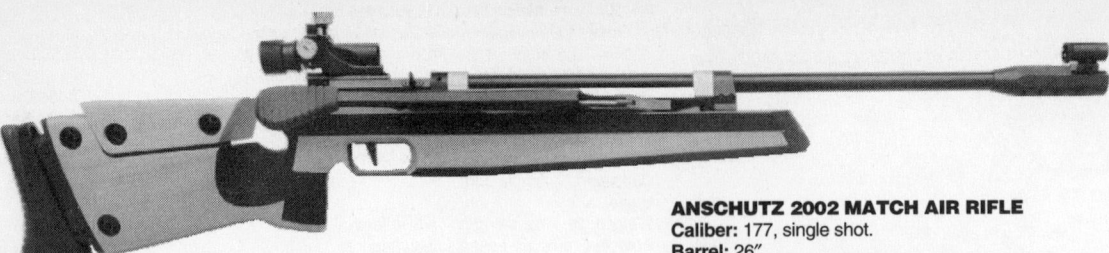

Anschutz 2002

ANSCHUTZ 2002 MATCH AIR RIFLE
Caliber: 177, single shot.
Barrel: 26".
Weight: 10 1/2 lbs. **Length:** 44.5" overall.
Stock: European walnut, blonde hardwood or colored laminated hardwood; stippled grip and forend.
Sights: Optional sight set #6834.
Features: Muzzle velocity 575 fps. Balance, weight match the 1907 ISU smallbore rifle. Uses #5021 match trigger. Recoil and vibration free. Fully adjustable cheekpiece and buttplate; accessory rail under forend. Introduced 1988. Imported from Germany by Gunsmithing, Inc., Champion's Choice, Champion Shooter's Supply, Accuracy International.
Price: Right-hand, blonde hardwood stock $1,212.20
Price: Left-hand, blonde hardwood stock $1,272.80
Price: Right-hand, walnut stock $1,261.40
Price: Right-hand, color laminated stock $1,291.60
Price: Left-hand, color laminated stock $1,355.30
Price: Model 2002D-RT Running Target, right-hand, no sights $1,419.20
Price: #6834 Sight Set $245.90

AIRROW MODEL A-8SRB STEALTH AIR GUN
Caliber: 177, 22, 25, 38, 9-shot.
Barrel: 19.7"; rifled.
Weight: 6 lbs. **Length:** 34" overall.
Power: CO_2 or compressed air; variable power.
Stock: Telescoping CAR-15-type.
Sights: Scope rings only.
Features: Velocity 1100 fps in all calibers. Pneumatic air trigger. All aircraft aluminum and stainless steel construction. Mil-spec materials and finishes. Introduced 1992. From Swivel Machine Works, Inc.
Price: About $2,299.00

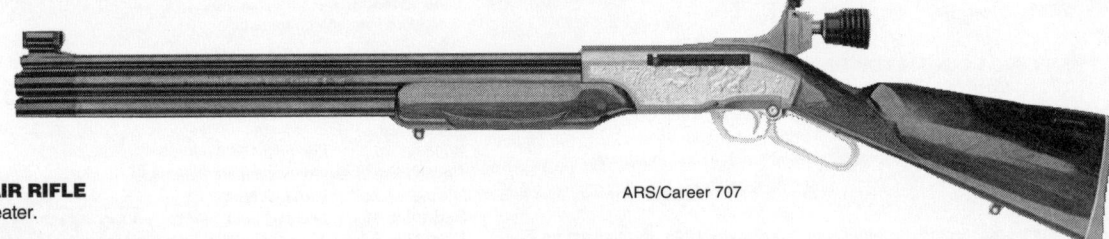

ARS/Career 707

ARS/CAREER 707 AIR RIFLE
Caliber: 22, 6-shot repeater.
Barrel: 23".
Weight: 7.75 lbs. **Length:** 40.5" overall.
Power: Pre-compressed air; variable power.
Stock: Indonesian walnut with checkered grip, gloss finish.
Sights: Hooded post front with interchangeable inserts, fully adjustable diopter rear.
Features: Velocity to 1000 fps. Lever-action with straight feed magazine; pressure gauge in lower front air reservoir; scope mounting rail included. Introduced 1996. Imported from the Philippines by Air Rifle Specialists.
Price: $580.00

ARS/FARCO CO_2 AIR SHOTGUN
Caliber: 51 (28-gauge).
Barrel: 30".
Weight: 7 lbs. **Length:** 48 1/2" overall.
Power: 10-oz. refillable CO_2 tank.
Stock: Hardwood.
Sights: Blade front, fixed rear.
Features: Gives over 100 ft. lbs. energy for taking small game. Imported from the Philippines by Air Rifle Specialists.
Price: $460.00

ARS/FARCO FP SURVIVAL AIR RIFLE
Caliber: 22, 25, single shot.
Barrel: 22 3/4".
Weight: 5 3/4 lbs. **Length:** 42 3/4" overall.
Power: Multi-pump foot pump.
Stock: Philippine hardwood.
Sights: Blade front, fixed rear.
Features: Velocity to 850 fps (22 or 25). Receiver grooved for scope mounting. Imported from the Philippines by Air Rifle Specialists.
Price: $295.00

ARS/Farco CO_2 Stainless Steel Air Rifle
Similar to the ARS/Farco CO_2 shotgun except in 22- or 25-caliber with 21 1/2" barrel; weighs 6 3/4 lbs., 42 1/2" overall; Philippine hardwood stock with stippled grip and forend; blade front sight, adjustable rear, grooved for scope mount. Uses 10-oz. refillable CO_2 cylinder. Made of stainless steel. Imported from the Philippines by Air Rifle Specialists.
Price: Including CO_2 cylinder $460.00

ARS/King Hunting Master

ARS/KING HUNTING MASTER AIR RIFLE
Caliber: 22, 5-shot repeater.
Barrel: 22 3/4".
Weight: 7 3/4 lbs. **Length:** 42" overall.
Power: Pre-compressed air from 3000 psi diving tank.
Stock: Indonesian walnut with checkered grip and forend; rubber buttpad.
Sights: Blade front, fully adjustable open rear. Receiver grooved for scope mounting.
Features: Velocity over 1000 fps with 32-grain pellet. High and low power switch for hunting or target velocities. Side lever cocks action and inserts pellet. Rotary magazine. Imported from Korea by Air Rifle Specialists.
Price: $580.00
Price: Hunting Master 900 (9mm, limited production) $1,000.00

ARS HUNTING MASTER AR6 AIR RIFLE
Caliber: 22, 6-shot repeater.
Barrel: 25 1/2".
Weight: 7 lbs. **Length:** 41 1/4" overall.
Power: Pre-compressed air from 3000 psi diving tank.
Stock: Indonesian walnut with checkered grip; rubber buttpad.
Sights: Blade front, adjustable peep rear.
Features: Velocity over 1000 fps with 32-grain pellet. Receiver grooved for scope mounting. Has 6-shot rotary magazine. Imported by Air Rifle Specialists.
Price: $580.00

AIRGUNS—LONG GUNS

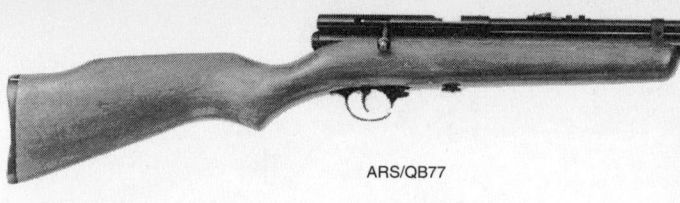
ARS/QB77

ARS/Magnum 6 Air Rifle
Similar to the King Hunting Master except is 6-shot repeater with 23¾" barrel, weighs 8¼ lbs. Stock is walnut-stained hardwood with checkered grip and forend; rubber buttpad. Velocity of 1000+ fps with 32-grain pellet. Imported from Korea by Air Rifle Specialists.
Price: $500.00

BEEMAN CROW MAGNUM AIR RIFLE
Caliber: 20, 22, 25, single shot.
Barrel: 16"; 10-groove rifling.
Weight: 8.5 lbs. **Length:** 46" overall.
Power: Gas-spring; adjustable power to 32 foot pounds muzzle energy. Barrel-cocking.
Stock: Classic-style hardwood; hand checkered.
Sights: For scope use only; built-in base and 1" rings included.
Features: Adjustable two-stage trigger. Automatic safety. Also available in 22-caliber on special order. Introduced 1992. Imported by Beeman.
Price: $1,220.00

ARS/QB77 DELUXE AIR RIFLE
Caliber: 177, 22, single shot.
Barrel: 21½".
Weight: 5½ lbs. **Length:** 40" overall.
Power: Two 12-oz. CO_2 cylinders.
Stock: Walnut-stained hardwood.
Sights: Blade front, adjustable rear.
Features: Velocity to 625 fps (22), 725 fps (177). Receiver grooved for scope mounting. Comes with bulk-fill valve. Imported by Air Rifle Specialists.
Price: $195.00

BEEMAN/FEINWERKBAU 300-S MINI-MATCH
Caliber: 177, single shot.
Barrel: 17⅛".
Weight: 8.8 lbs. **Length:** 40" overall.
Power: Spring-piston, single stroke sidelever cocking.
Stock: Walnut. Stippled grip, adjustable buttplate. Scaled-down for youthful or slightly built shooters.
Sights: Globe front with interchangeable inserts, micro. adjustable rear. Front and rear sights move as a single unit.
Features: Recoilless, vibration free. Grooved for scope mounts. Steel piston ring. Cocking effort about 9½ lbs. Barrel sleeve optional. Left-hand model available. Introduced 1978. Imported by Beeman.
Price: Right-hand $1,270.00
Price: Left-hand $1,370.00

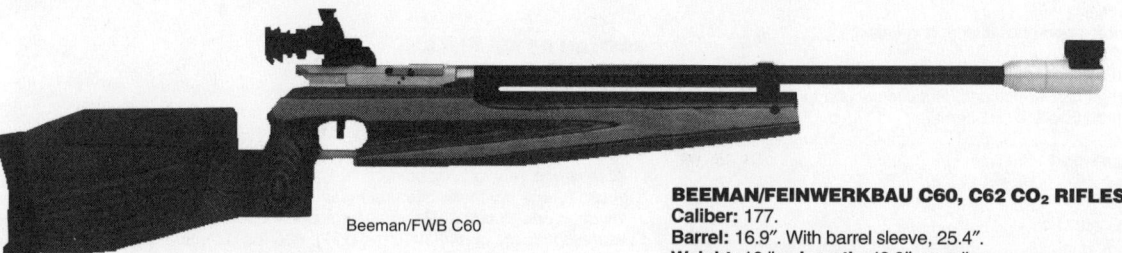
Beeman/FWB C60

BEEMAN BEARCUB AIR RIFLE
Caliber: 177, single shot.
Barrel: 13".
Weight: 7.2 lbs. **Length:** 37.8" overall.
Power: Spring-piston, barrel cocking.
Stock: Stained hardwood.
Sights: Hooded post front, open fully adjustable rear.
Features: Velocity to 915 fps. Polished blue finish; receiver dovetailed for scope mounting. Imported from England by Beeman Precision Airguns.
Price: $310.00

BEEMAN/FEINWERKBAU C60, C62 CO_2 RIFLES
Caliber: 177.
Barrel: 16.9". With barrel sleeve, 25.4".
Weight: 10 lbs. **Length:** 42.6" overall.
Stock: Laminated hardwood and hard rubber.
Sights: Tunnel front with interchangeable inserts, quick release micro. click match aperture rear.
Features: Similar features, performance as Beeman/FWB 601. Virtually no cocking effort. Right- or left-hand. Running target version available. Introduced 1987. Imported from Germany by Beeman.
Price: Right-hand, C62 ....$1,750.00
Price: Left-hand, C62 ....$1,900.00
Price: Running Target, right-hand, C60 ....$1,675.00
Price: Running Target, left-hand, C60 ....$1,825.00
Price: Mini C60, right-hand, C60 ....$1,675.00

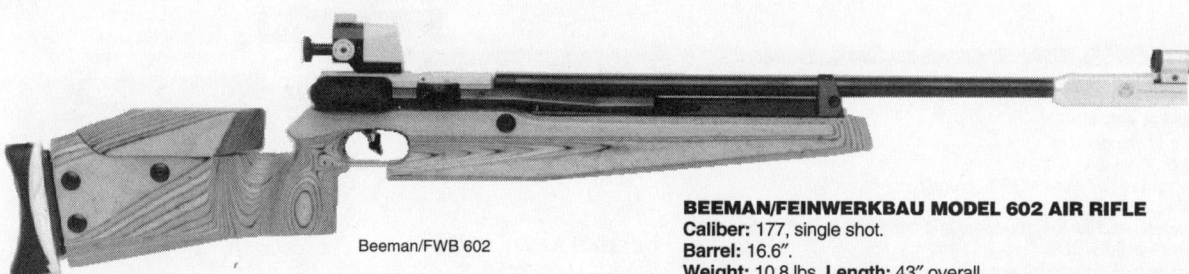
Beeman/FWB 602

BEEMAN/FEINWERKBAU 300-S SERIES MATCH RIFLE
Caliber: 177, single shot.
Barrel: 19.9", fixed solid with receiver.
Weight: Approx. 10 lbs. with optional bbl. sleeve. **Length:** 42.8" overall.
Power: Spring-piston, single stroke sidelever.
Stock: Match model—walnut, deep forend, adjustable buttplate.
Sights: Globe front with interchangeable inserts. Click micro. adjustable match aperture rear. Front and rear sights move as a single unit.
Features: Recoilless, vibration free. Five-way adjustable match trigger. Grooved for scope mounts. Permanent lubrication, steel piston ring. Cocking effort 9 lbs. Optional 10-oz. barrel sleeve. Available from Beeman.
Price: Right-hand $1,270.00
Price: Left-hand $1,370.00

BEEMAN/FEINWERKBAU MODEL 602 AIR RIFLE
Caliber: 177, single shot.
Barrel: 16.6".
Weight: 10.8 lbs. **Length:** 43" overall.
Power: Single stroke pneumatic.
Stock: Special laminated hardwoods and hard rubber for stability.
Sights: Tunnel front with interchangeable inserts, click micrometer match aperture rear.
Features: Recoilless action; double supported barrel; special, short rifled area frees pellet from barrel faster so shooter's motion has minimum effect on accuracy. Fully adjustable match trigger. Trigger and sights blocked when loading latch is open. Imported by Beeman.
Price: Right-hand $1,875.00
Price: Left-hand $2,035.00

Beeman/Feinwerkbau 601 Running Target
Similar to the standard Model 601. Has 16.9" barrel (33.7" with barrel sleeve); special match trigger, short loading gate which allows scope mounting. No sights—built for scope use only. Introduced 1987.
Price: Right-hand $1,750.00

CAUTION: PRICES SHOWN ARE SUPPLIED BY THE MANUFACTURER OR IMPORTER. CHECK YOUR LOCAL GUNSHOP.

AIRGUNS—LONG GUNS

Beeman/HW 97

BEEMAN/HW 97 AIR RIFLE
Caliber: 177, 20, single shot.
Barrel: 17.75".
Weight: 9.2 lbs. **Length:** 44.1" overall.
Power: Spring-piston, underlever cocking.
Stock: Walnut-stained beech; rubber buttpad.
Sights: None. Receiver grooved for scope mounting.
Features: Velocity 830 fps (177). Fixed barrel with fully opening, direct loading breech. Adjustable trigger. Introduced 1994. Imported by Beeman Precision Airguns.
Price: Right-hand only $535.00

BEEMAN KODIAK AIR RIFLE
Caliber: 25, single shot.
Barrel: 17.6".
Weight: 9 lbs. **Length:** 45.6" overall.
Power: Spring-piston, barrel cocking.
Stock: Stained hardwood.
Sights: Blade front, open fully adjustable rear.
Features: Velocity to 820 fps. Up to 30 foot pounds muzzle energy. Introduced 1993. Imported by Beeman.
Price: $595.00

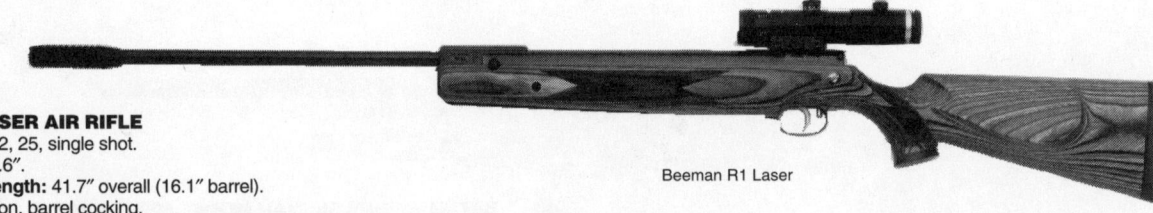
Beeman Mako

BEEMAN MAKO AIR RIFLE
Caliber: 177, single shot.
Barrel: 20", with compensator.
Weight: 7.3 lbs. **Length:** 38.5" overall.
Power: Pre-charged pneumatic.
Stock: Stained beech; Monte Carlo cheekpiece; checkered grip.
Sights: None furnished.
Features: Velocity to 930 fps. Gives over 50 shots per charge. Manual safety; brass trigger blade; vented rubber butt pad. Requires scuba tank for air. Introduced 1994. Imported from England by Beeman.
Price: $875.00
Price: Mako FT (thumbhole stock) $1,250.00

BEEMAN R1 CARBINE
Caliber: 177, 20, 22, 25, single shot.
Barrel: 16.1".
Weight: 8.6 lbs. **Length:** 41.7" overall.
Power: Spring-piston, barrel cocking.
Stock: Stained beech; Monte Carlo comb and checkpiece; cut checkered pistol grip; rubber buttpad.
Sights: Tunnel front with interchangeable inserts, open adjustable rear; receiver grooved for scope mounting.
Features: Velocity up to 1000 fps (177). Non-drying nylon piston and breech seals. Adjustable metal trigger. Machined steel receiver end cap and safety. Right- or left-hand stock. Imported by Beeman.
Price: 177, 20, 22, 25, right-hand $525.00
Price: As above, left-hand $575.00
Price: R1-AW (synthetic stock, nickel plating) $650.00

BEEMAN R1 AIR RIFLE
Caliber: 177, 20 or 22, single shot.
Barrel: 19.6", 12-groove rifling.
Weight: 8.5 lbs. **Length:** 45.2" overall.
Power: Spring-piston, barrel cocking.
Stock: Walnut-stained beech; cut-checkered pistol grip; Monte Carlo comb and cheekpiece; rubber buttpad.
Sights: Tunnel front with interchangeable inserts, open rear click-adjustable for windage and elevation. Grooved for scope mounting.
Features: Velocity of 940-1000 fps (177), 860 fps (20), 800 fps (22). Non-drying nylon piston and breech seals. Adjustable metal trigger. Milled steel safety. Right- or left-hand stock. Available with adjustable cheekpiece and buttplate at extra cost. Custom and Super Laser versions available. Imported by Beeman.
Price: Right-hand, 177, 20, 22 .... $525.00
Price: Left-hand, 177, 20, 22 .... $575.00

Beeman R1 Laser

BEEMAN R1 LASER AIR RIFLE
Caliber: 177, 20, 22, 25, single shot.
Barrel: 16.1" or 19.6".
Weight: 8.4 lbs. **Length:** 41.7" overall (16.1" barrel).
Power: Spring-piston, barrel cocking.
Stock: Laminated wood with Monte Carlo comb and cheekpiece; checkered pistol grip and forend; rubber buttpad.
Sights: Tunnel front with interchangeable inserts, open adjustable rear.
Features: Velocity up to 1150 fps (177). Special powerplant components. Built from the Beeman R1 rifle by Beeman.
Price: 177, 20, 22, 25 .... $995.00

BEEMAN R6 AIR RIFLE
Caliber: 177, single shot.
Barrel: NA.
Weight: 7.1 lbs. **Length:** 41.8" overall.
Power: Spring-piston, barrel cocking.
Stock: Stained hardwood.
Sights: Tunnel post front, open fully adjustable rear.
Features: Velocity to 815 fps. Two-stage Rekord adjustable trigger; receiver dovetailed for scope mounting; automatic safety. Introduced 1996. Imported from Germany by Beeman Precision Airguns.
Price: $325.00

BEEMAN R8 AIR RIFLE
Caliber: 177, single shot.
Barrel: 18.3".
Weight: 7.2 lbs. **Length:** 43.1" overall.
Power: Spring-piston, barrel cocking.
Stock: Walnut with Monte Carlo cheekpiece; checkered pistol grip.
Sights: Globe front, fully adjustable rear; interchangeable inserts.
Features: Velocity of 735 fps. Similar to the R1. Nylon piston and breech seals. Adjustable match-grade, two-stage, grooved metal trigger. Milled steel safety. Rubber buttpad. Imported by Beeman.
Price: $380.00

Beeman R7 Air Rifle
Similar to the R8 model except has lighter ambidextrous stock, match-grade trigger block; velocity of 680-700 fps; barrel length 17"; weighs 5.8 lbs. Milled steel safety. Imported by Beeman.
Price: 177 .... $325.00

AIRGUNS—LONG GUNS

BEEMAN R9 AIR RIFLE
Caliber: 177, 20, single shot.
Barrel: NA.
Weight: 7.3 lbs. **Length:** 43" overall.
Power: Spring-piston, barrel cocking.
Stock: Stained hardwood.
Sights: Tunnel post front, fully adjustable open rear.
Features: Velocity to 1000 fps (177), 800 fps (20). Adjustable Rekord trigger; automatic safety; receiver dovetailed for scope mounting. Introduced 1996. Imported from Germany by Beeman Precision Airguns.
Price: $335.00

BEEMAN SUPER 12 AIR RIFLE
Caliber: 22, 25, 12-shot magazine.
Barrel: 19", 12-groove rifling.
Weight: 7.8 lbs. **Length:** 41.7" overall.
Power: Pre-charged pneumatic; external air reservoir.
Stock: European walnut.
Sights: None furnished; drilled and tapped for scope mounting; scope mount included.
Features: Velocity to 850 fps (25-caliber). Adjustable power setting gives 30-70 shots per 400 cc air bottle. Requires scuba tank for air. Introduced 1995. Imported by Beeman.
Price: $1,675.00

Beeman R11

BEEMAN R11 AIR RIFLE
Caliber: 177, single shot.
Barrel: 19.6".
Weight: 8.8 lbs. **Length:** 47" overall.
Power: Spring-piston, barrel cocking.
Stock: Walnut-stained beech; adjustable buttplate and cheekpiece.
Sights: None furnished. Has dovetail for scope mounting.
Features: Velocity 910-940 fps. All-steel barrel sleeve. Imported by Beeman.
Price: $530.00

BEEMAN S1 MAGNUM AIR RIFLE
Caliber: 177, single shot.
Barrel: 19".
Weight: 7.1 lbs. **Length:** 45.5" overall.
Power: Spring-piston, barrel cocking.
Stock: Stained beech with Monte Carlo cheekpiece; checkered grip.
Sights: Hooded post front, fully adjustable micrometer click rear.
Features: Velocity to 900 fps. Automatic safety; receiver grooved for scope mounting; two-stage adjustable trigger; curved rubber buttpad. Introduced 1995. Imported by Beeman.
Price: $210.00

BEEMAN RX-1 GAS-SPRING MAGNUM AIR RIFLE
Caliber: 177, 20, 22, 25, single shot.
Barrel: 19.6", 12-groove rifling.
Weight: 8.8 lbs.
Power: Gas-spring piston air; single stroke barrel cocking.
Stock: Walnut-finished hardwood, hand checkered, with cheekpiece. Adjustable cheekpiece and buttplate.
Sights: Tunnel front, click-adjustable rear.
Features: Velocity adjustable to about 1200 fps. Uses special sealed chamber of air as a mainspring. Gas-spring cannot take a set. Introduced 1990. Imported by Beeman.
Price: 177, 20, 22 or 25 regular, right-hand $575.00
Price: 177, 20, 22, 25, left-hand $675.00

BENJAMIN SHERIDAN CO$_2$ AIR RIFLES
Caliber: 177, 20 or 22, single shot.
Barrel: 19 3/8", rifled brass.
Weight: 5 lbs. **Length:** 36 1/2" overall.
Power: 12-gram CO$_2$ cylinder.
Stock: American walnut with buttplate.
Sights: High ramp front, fully adjustable notch rear.
Features: Velocity to 680 fps (177). Bolt action with ambidextrous push-pull safety. Gives about 40 shots per cylinder. Black or nickel finish. Introduced 1991. Made in the U.S. by Benjamin Sheridan Co.
Price: Black finish, Model G397 (177), Model G392 (22), about $115.25
Price: Black finish, Model FB9 (20), about $124.50

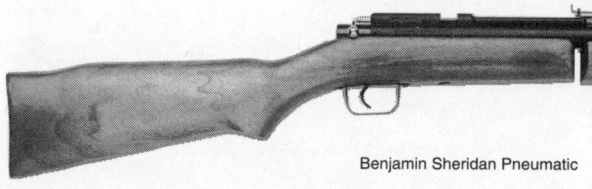
Benjamin Sheridan Pneumatic

Benjamin Sheridan 397C Pneumatic Carbine
Similar to the standard Model 397 except has 16 3/4" barrel, weighs 4 lbs., 3 oz. Velocity about 650 fps. Introduced 1995. Made in U.S. by Benjamin Sheridan Co.
Price: About $122.50

BENJAMIN SHERIDAN PNEUMATIC (PUMP-UP) AIR RIFLES
Caliber: 177 or 22, single shot.
Barrel: 19 3/8", rifled brass.
Weight: 5 1/2 lbs. **Length:** 36 1/4" overall.
Power: Underlever pneumatic, hand pumped.
Stock: American walnut stock and forend.
Sights: High ramp front, fully adjustable notch rear.
Features: Variable velocity to 800 fps. Bolt action with ambidextrous push-pull safety. Black or nickel finish. Introduced 1991. Made in the U.S. by Benjamin Sheridan Co.
Price: Black finish, Model 397 (177), Model 392 (22), about $126.50
Price: Nickel finish, Model S397 (177), Model S392 (22), about $135.25

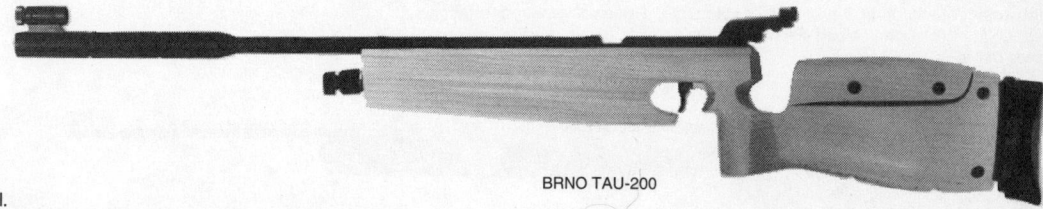
BRNO TAU-200

BRNO TAU-200 AIR RIFLE
Caliber: 177, single shot.
Barrel: 19", rifled.
Weight: 8 lbs. **Length:** 42" overall.
Power: 6-oz. CO$_2$ cartridge.
Stock: Wood match style with adjustable comb and buttplate.
Sights: Globe front with interchangeable inserts, fully adjustable open rear.
Features: Adjustable trigger. Comes with sling, extra seals, CO$_2$ cartridges, large CO$_2$ bottle, counterweight. Introduced 1993. Imported by Century International Arms, Great Lakes Airguns..
Price: About $423.25
Price: Junior Match (synthetic stock, 7 lbs.) $259.95

Consult our Directory pages for the location of firms mentioned.

AIRGUNS—LONG GUNS

BSA Supersport MK II

BSA SUPERSPORT MKII AIR RIFLE
Caliber: 177, single shot.
Barrel: 18".
Weight: 6.5 lbs. **Length:** 41" overall.
Power: Spring-air, barrel cocking.
Stock: Walnut-stained beech; rubber recoil pad.
Sights: Bead or blade front, fully adjsutable open rear.
Features: Velocity to 935 fps. Adjustable trigger; manual safety; receiver grooved for scope mounting. Imported from England by Great Lakes Airguns.
Price: $225.81
Price: Carbine, 14" barrel, 37" overall $252.97

COPPERHEAD BLACK FIRE RIFLE
Caliber: 177 BB only.
Barrel: 14" smoothbore steel.
Weight: 2 lbs., 7 oz. **Length:** 31½" overall.
Power: Pneumatic, hand pumped.
Stock: Textured plastic.
Sights: Blade front, open adjustable rear.
Features: Velocity to 437 fps. Introduced 1996. Made in U.S. by Crosman Corp.
Price: About $25.00

COPPERHEAD BLACK LIGHTNING RIFLE
Caliber: 177 BB, 15-shot magazine.
Barrel: 14" smoothbore.
Weight: 2 lbs. **Length:** 32" overall.
Power: Single-stroke pneumatic.
Stock: Textured plastic.
Sights: Bead front.
Features: Velocity to 350 fps. Cross-bolt safety. Introduced 1996. Made in U.S. by Crosman Corp.
Price: About $22.00

COPPERHEAD BLACK SERPENT RIFLE
Caliber: 177 pellets, 5-shot, on BB, 195-shot magazine.
Barrel: 19½" smoothbore steel.
Weight: 2 lbs., 14 oz. **Length:** 35⅞" overall.
Power: Pneumatic, single pump.
Stock: Textured plastic.
Sights: Blade front, open adjustable rear.
Features: Velocity to 405 fps. Introduced 1996. Made in U.S. by Crosman Corp.
Price: About $34.00

CROSMAN MODEL 66 POWERMASTER
Caliber: 177 (single shot pellet) or BB, 200-shot reservoir.
Barrel: 20", rifled steel.
Weight: 3 lbs. **Length:** 38½" overall.
Power: Pneumatic; hand pumped.
Stock: Wood-grained ABS plastic; checkered pistol grip and forend.
Sights: Ramp front, fully adjustable open rear.
Features: Velocity about 645 fps. Bolt action, cross-bolt safety. Introduced 1983. From Crosman.
Price: About $44.00
Price: Model 66RT (as above with Realtree® camo finish), about $50.00
Price: Model 664X (as above, with 4x scope) $55.00
Price: Model 664SB (as above with silver and black finish), about $57.00

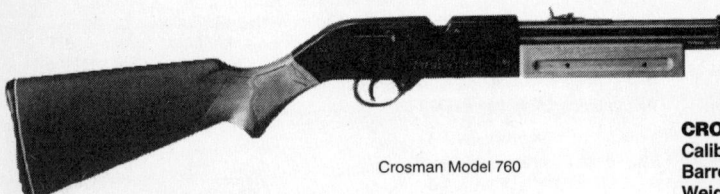

Crosman Model 760

CROSMAN MODEL 782 BLACK DIAMOND AIR RIFLE
Caliber: 177 pellets (5-shot clip) or BB (195-shot reservoir).
Barrel: 18", rifled steel.
Weight: 3 lbs.
Power: CO$_2$ Powerlet.
Stock: Wood-grained ABS plastic; checkered grip and forend.
Sights: Blade front, open adjustable rear.
Features: Velocity up to 595 fps (pellets), 650 fps (BB). Black finish with white diamonds. Introduced 1990. From Crosman.
Price: About $42.75

CROSMAN MODEL 1389 BACKPACKER RIFLE
Caliber: 177, single shot.
Barrel: 14", rifled steel.
Weight: 3 lbs. 3 oz. **Length:** 31" overall.
Power: Hand pumped, pneumatic.
Stock: Composition, skeletal type.
Sights: Blade front, rear adjustable for windage and elevation.
Features: Velocity to 560 fps. Detachable stock. Receiver grooved for scope mounting. Metal parts blued. From Crosman.
Price: About $54.75

CROSMAN MODEL 760 PUMPMASTER
Caliber: 177 pellets (single shot) or BB (200-shot reservoir).
Barrel: 19½", rifled steel.
Weight: 2 lbs., 12 oz. **Length:** 33.5" overall.
Power: Pneumatic, hand pumped.
Stock: Walnut-finished ABS plastic stock and forend
Features: Velocity to 590 fps (BBs, 10 pumps). Short stroke, power determined by number of strokes. Post front sight and adjustable rear sight. Cross-bolt safety. Introduced 1966. From Crosman.
Price: About $32.00
Price: Model 760SB (silver and black finish), about $45.25

CROSMAN MODEL 795 SPRING MASTER RIFLE
Caliber: 177, single shot.
Barrel: Rifled steel.
Weight: 4 lbs., 8 oz. **Length:** 42" overall.
Power: Spring-piston.
Stock: Black synthetic.
Sights: Hooded front, fully adjustable rear.
Features: Velocity about 550 fps. Introduced 1995. From Crosman.
Price: About $65.00

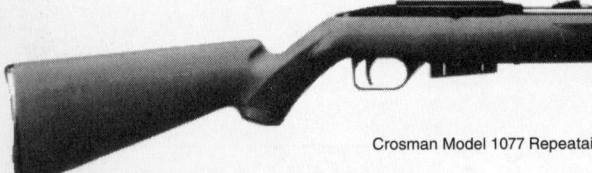

Crosman Model 1077 Repeatair

CROSMAN MODEL 1077 REPEATAIR RIFLE
Caliber: 177 pellets, 12-shot clip
Barrel: 20.3", rifled steel.
Weight: 3 lbs., 11 oz. **Length:** 38.8" overall.
Power: CO$_2$ Powerlet.
Stock: Textured synthetic.
Sights: Blade front, fully adjustable rear.
Features: Velocity 590 fps. Removable 12-shot clip. True semi-automatic action. Introduced 1993. From Crosman.
Price: About $62.75
Price: 1077SB Silver Series (black stock, silver bbl.) $65.00

AIRGUNS—LONG GUNS

CROSMAN MODEL 2100 CLASSIC AIR RIFLE
Caliber: 177 pellets (single shot), or BB (200-shot BB reservoir).
Barrel: 21", rifled.
Weight: 4 lbs., 13 oz. **Length:** 39¾" overall.
Power: Pump-up, pneumatic.
Stock: Wood-grained checkered ABS plastic.
Features: Three pumps give about 450 fps, 10 pumps about 755 fps (BBs). Cross-bolt safety; concealed reservoir holds over 200 BBs. From Crosman.
Price: About $58.50
Price: Model 2100SB (silver and black finish), about $60.25

CROSMAN MODEL 2200 MAGNUM AIR RIFLE
Caliber: 22, single shot.
Barrel: 19", rifled steel.
Weight: 4 lbs., 12 oz. **Length:** 39" overall.
Stock: Full-size, wood-grained ABS plastic with checkered grip and forend.
Sights: Ramp front, open step-adjustable rear.
Features: Variable pump power—three pumps give 395 fps, six pumps 530 fps, 10 pumps 595 fps (average). Full-size adult air rifle. Has white line spacers at pistol grip and buttplate. Introduced 1978. From Crosman.
Price: About $58.50

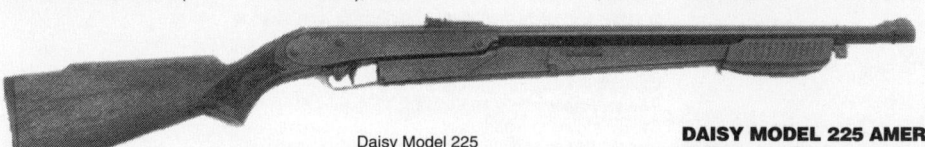
Daisy Model 225

DAISY/YOUTH LINE RIFLES

Model:	95	111	105
Caliber:	BB	BB	BB
Barrel:	18"	18"	13½"
Length:	35.2"	34.3"	29.8"
Power:	Spring	Spring	Spring
Capacity:	700	650	400
Price: About	$45.00	$35.00	$29.00

Features: Model 95 stock and forend are wood; 105 and 111 have plastic stocks. From Daisy Mfg. Co.

DAISY/POWER LINE 753 TARGET RIFLE
Caliber: 177, single shot.
Barrel: 20.9", Lothar Walther.
Weight: 6.4 lbs. **Length:** 39.75" overall.
Power: Recoilless pneumatic, single pump.
Stock: Walnut with adjustable cheekpiece and buttplate.
Sights: Globe front with interchangeable inserts, diopter rear with micro. click adjustments.
Features: Includes front sight reticle assortment, web shooting sling. From Daisy Mfg. Co.
Price: About $412.00

DAISY MODEL 225 AMERICAN LEGEND
Caliber: 177 BB, 650-shot magazine.
Barrel: Smoothbore steel.
Weight: 2.8 lbs. **Length:** 37.2" overall.
Power: Single-pump spring air.
Stock: Moulded woodgrain plastic.
Sights: Blade and ramp front, adjustable open rear.
Features: Velocity to 330 fps. Grooved pump handle; Monte Carlo-style stock with cheekpiece and checkered grip. Cross-bolt trigger block safety. Introduced 1994. From Daisy Mfg. Co.
Price: About $50.00

DAISY MODEL 1894 BB RIFLE
Caliber: BB, 40-shot magazine.
Barrel: 17.5". Round shroud.
Weight: 2.2 lbs. **Length:** 39.5" overall.
Power: Spring-air.
Stock: Moulded woodgrain plastic.
Sights: Blade on ramp front, adjustable open rear.
Features: Velocity 300 fps. Side loading port; sliding sear-block safety; die-cast receiver. Made in U.S. From Daisy Mfg. Co.
Price: $42.00

Daisy Red Ryder

DAISY 1938 RED RYDER CLASSIC
Caliber: BB, 650-shot repeating action.
Barrel: Smoothbore steel with shroud.

DAISY/POWER LINE 853
Caliber: 177 pellets.
Barrel: 20.9"; 12-groove rifling, high-grade solid steel by Lothar Walther™, precision crowned; bore size for precision match pellets.
Weight: 5.08 lbs. **Length:** 38.9" overall.
Power: Single-pump pneumatic.

Weight: 2.2 lbs. **Length:** 35.4" overall.
Stock: Walnut stock burned with Red Ryder lariat signature.
Sights: Post front, adjustable V-slot rear.
Features: Walnut forend. Saddle ring with leather thong. Lever cocking. Gravity feed. Controlled velocity. One of Daisy's most popular guns. From Daisy Mfg. Co.
Price: About $45.00

Stock: Full-length, select American hardwood, stained and finished; black buttplate with white spacers.
Sights: Globe front with four aperture inserts; precision micrometer adjustable rear peep sight mounted on a standard ⅜" dovetail receiver mount.
Features: Single shot. From Daisy Mfg. Co.
Price: About $245.00

Daisy Model 840

DAISY/POWER LINE 856 PUMP-UP AIRGUN
Caliber: 177 pellets (single shot) or BB (100-shot reservoir).
Barrel: Rifled steel with shroud.
Weight: 2.7 lbs. **Length:** 37.4" overall.
Power: Pneumatic pump-up.
Stock: Moulded wood-grain with Monte Carlo cheekpiece.
Sights: Ramp and blade front, open rear adjustable for elevation.
Features: Velocity from 315 fps (two pumps) to 650 fps (10 pumps). Shoots BBs or pellets. Heavy die-cast metal receiver. Cross-bolt trigger-block safety. Introduced 1984. From Daisy Mfg. Co.
Price: About $45.00

DAISY MODEL 840
Caliber: 177 pellet single shot; or BB 350-shot.
Barrel: 19", smoothbore, steel.
Weight: 2.7 lbs. **Length:** 36.8" overall.
Power: Pneumatic, single pump.
Stock: Moulded wood-grain stock and forend.
Sights: Ramp front, open, adjustable rear.
Features: Muzzle velocity 335 fps (BB), 300 fps (pellet). Steel buttplate; straight pull bolt action; cross-bolt safety. Forend forms pump lever. Introduced 1978. From Daisy Mfg. Co.
Price: About $40.00

AIRGUNS—LONG GUNS

DAISY/POWER LINE 880 PUMP-UP AIRGUN
Caliber: 177 pellets, BB.
Barrel: Rifled steel with shroud.
Weight: 4.5 lbs. **Length:** 37¾" overall.
Power: Pneumatic pump-up.
Stock: Wood-grain moulded plastic with Monte Carlo cheekpiece.
Sights: Ramp front, open rear adjustable for elevation.
Features: Crafted by Daisy. Variable power (velocity and range) increase with pump strokes. 10 strokes for maximum power. 100-shot BB magazine. Cross-bolt trigger safety. Positive cocking valve. From Daisy Mfg. Co.
Price: About $60.00

DAISY/POWER LINE 922
Caliber: 22, 5-shot clip.
Barrel: Rifled steel with shroud.
Weight: 4.5 lbs. **Length:** 37¾" overall.
Stock: Moulded wood-grained plastic with checkered pistol grip and forend, Monte Carlo cheekpiece.
Sights: Ramp front, fully adjustable open rear.
Features: Muzzle velocity from 270 fps (two pumps) to 530 fps (10 pumps). Straight-pull bolt action. Separate buttplate and grip cap with white spacers. Introduced 1978. From Daisy Mfg. Co.
Price: About $85.00
Price: Models 970/920 (same as Model 922 except with hardwood stock and forend), about $120.00

DAISY MODEL 990 DUAL-POWER AIR RIFLE
Caliber: 177 pellets (single shot) or BB (100-shot magazine).
Barrel: Rifled steel.
Weight: 4.1 lbs. **Length:** 37.4" overall.
Power: Pneumatic pump-up and 12-gram CO_2.
Stock: Moulded woodgrain.
Sights: Ramp and blade front, adjustable open rear.
Features: Velocity to 650 fps (BB), 630 fps (pellet). Choice of pump or CO_2 power. Shoots BBs or pellets. Heavy die-cast receiver dovetailed for scope mount. Cross-bolt trigger block safety. Introduced 1993. From Daisy Mfg. Co.
Price: About $70.00

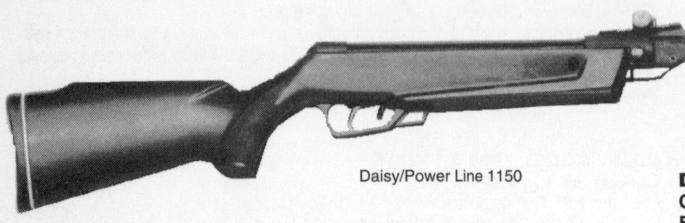
Daisy/Power Line 1150

DAISY/POWER LINE 1150 PELLET RIFLE
Caliber: 177, single shot.
Barrel: Rifled steel.
Weight: NA. **Length:** 37" overall.
Power: Spring-air, barrel cocking.
Stock: Black moulded plastic.
Sights: Blade on ramp front, micrometer adjustable open rear.
Features: Velocity to 600 fps. Introduced 1995. From Daisy Mfg. Co.
Price: About $90.00

DAISY/POWER LINE 1170 PELLET RIFLE
Caliber: 177, single shot.
Barrel: Rifled steel.
Weight: 5.5 lbs. **Length:** 42.5" overall.
Power: Spring-air, barrel cocking.
Stock: Hardwood.
Sights: Hooded post front, micrometer adjustable open rear.
Features: Velocity to 800 fps. Monte Carlo comb. Introduced 1995. From Daisy Mfg. Co.
Price: About $162.00

Daisy/Power Line 2001

Consult our Directory pages for the location of firms mentioned.

DAISY/POWER LINE 2001 AIR RIFLE
Caliber: 177 pellets, 35-shot helical magazine.
Barrel: Rifled steel.
Weight: 3.1 lbs. **Length:** 37.4" overall.
Power: CO_2.
Stock: Moulded woodgrain with Monte Carlo comb.
Sights: Ramp and blade front, fully adjustable open rear.
Features: Velocity to 625 fps. Bolt-action repeater with cross-bolt trigger block safety; checkered grip and forend; white buttplate spacer. Introduced 1994. From Daisy Mfg. Co.
Price: About $75.00

DAISY/POWER LINE EAGLE 7856 PUMP-UP AIRGUN
Caliber: 177 (pellets), BB, 100-shot BB magazine.
Barrel: Rifled steel with shroud.
Weight: 2¾ lbs. **Length:** 37.4" overall.
Power: Pneumatic pump-up.
Stock: Moulded wood-grain plastic.
Sights: Ramp and blade front, open rear adjustable for elevation.
Features: Velocity from 315 fps (two pumps) to 650 fps (10 pumps). Finger grooved forend. Cross-bolt trigger-block safety. Introduced 1985. From Daisy Mfg. Co.
Price: With 4x scope, about $60.00

DAISY/POWER LINE 2002 PELLET RIFLE
Caliber: 177, 35-shot magazine.
Barrel: Rifled steel.
Weight: 3.6 lbs. **Length:** 37.5" overall.
Power: 12-gram CO_2.
Stock: Moulded polymer.
Sights: Ramped blade front, open fully adjustable rear.
Features: Velocity to 630 fps. Continuous feed helical design Mag Clip. Cross-bolt trigger block safety. Introduced 1995. From Daisy Mfg. Co.
Price: About $82.50

FAMAS SEMI-AUTO AIR RIFLE
Caliber: 177, 10-shot magazine.
Barrel: 19.2".
Weight: About 8 lbs. **Length:** 29.8" overall.
Power: 12-gram CO_2.
Stock: Synthetic bullpup design.
Sights: Adjustable front, aperture rear.
Features: Velocity of 425 fps. Duplicates size, weight and feel of the centerfire MAS French military rifle in caliber 223. Introduced 1988. Imported from France by Century International Arms.
Price: About $275.00

"GAT" AIR RIFLE
Caliber: 177, single shot.
Barrel: 17¼" cocked, 23¼" extended.
Weight: 3 lbs.
Power: Spring-piston.
Stock: Composition.
Sights: Fixed.
Features: Velocity about 450 fps. Shoots pellets, darts, corks. Imported from England by Stone Enterprises, Inc.
Price: $34.95

AIRGUNS—LONG GUNS

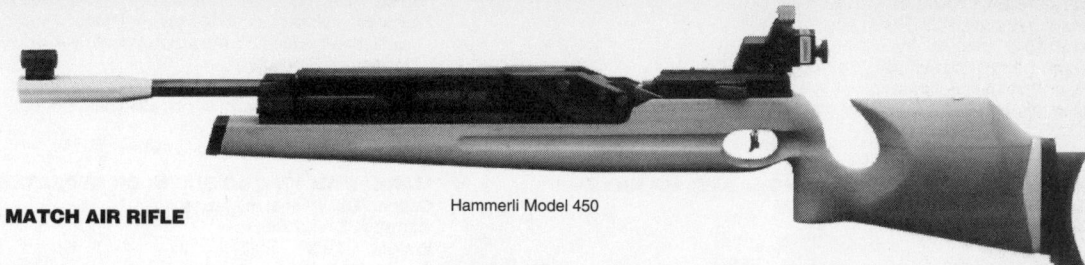
Hammerli Model 450

HAMMERLI MODEL 450 MATCH AIR RIFLE
Caliber: 177, single shot.
Barrel: 19.5".
Weight: 9.8 lbs. **Length:** 43.3" overall.
Power: Pneumatic.
Stock: Match style with stippled grip, rubber buttpad. Beach or walnut.
Sights: Match tunnel front, Hammerli diopter rear.
Features: Velocity about 560 fps. Removable sights; forend sling rail; adjustable trigger; adjustable comb. Introduced 1994. Imported from Switzerland by SIGARMS, Inc.
Price: Beech stock $1,355.00
Price: Walnut stock $1,395.00

MARKSMAN 28 INTERNATIONAL AIR RIFLE
Caliber: 177, single shot.
Barrel: 17".
Weight: 5 3/4 lbs.
Power: Spring-air, barrel cocking.
Stock: Hardwood.
Sights: Hooded front, adjustable rear.
Features: Velocity of 580-620 fps. Introduced 1989. Imported from Germany by Marksman Products.
Price: $220.00

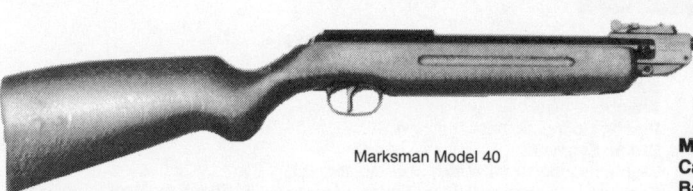
Marksman Model 40

MARKSMAN 40 INTERNATIONAL AIR RIFLE
Caliber: 177, single shot.
Barrel: 18 3/8".
Weight: 7 1/3 lbs.
Power: Spring-air, barrel cocking.
Stock: Hardwood.
Sights: Hooded front, adjustable rear.
Features: Velocity of 700-720 fps. Introduced 1989. Imported from Germany by Marksman Products.
Price: $245.00

MARKSMAN MODEL 60 AIR RIFLE
Caliber: 177, single shot.
Barrel: 18.5", rifled.
Weight: 8.9 lbs. **Length:** 44.75" overall.
Power: Spring-piston, underlever cocking.
Stock: Walnut-stained beech with Monte Carlo comb, hand-checkered pistol grip, rubber butt pad.
Sights: Blade front, open, micro. adjustable rear.
Features: Velocity of 810-840 fps. Automatic button safety on rear of receiver. Receiver grooved for scope mounting. Fully adjustable Rekord trigger. Introduced 1990. Imported from Germany by Marksman Products.
Price: $485.00
Price: Model 61 Carbine $485.00

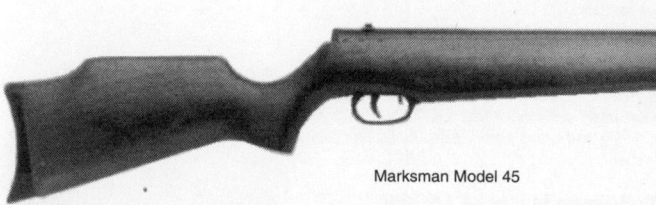
Marksman Model 45

MARKSMAN 70T AIR RIFLE
Caliber: 177, single shot.
Barrel: 19.75".
Weight: 8 lbs. **Length:** 45.5" overall.
Power: Spring-air, barrel cocking.
Stock: Stained hardwood with Monte Carlo cheekpiece, rubber buttpad, cut checkered pistol grip.
Sights: Hooded front, open fully adjustable rear.
Features: Velocity of 910-940 fps; adjustable Rekord trigger. Introduced 1988. Imported from Germany by Marksman Products.
Price: 177 .... $350.00

MARKSMAN MODEL 45 AIR RIFLE
Caliber: 177, single shot.
Barrel: 19.1".
Weight: 7.3 lbs. **Length:** 46.75" overall.
Power: Spring-air, barrel cocking.
Stock: Stained hardwood with Monte Carlo cheekpiece, butt pad.
Sights: Hooded front, fully adjustable micrometer rear.
Features: Velocity 900-930 fps. Adjustable trigger; automatic safety. Introduced 1993. Imported from Spain by Marksman Products.
Price: $189.00

Marksman 55 Air Rifle
Similar to the Model 70T except has uncheckered hardwood stock, no cheekpiece, plastic buttplate. Adjustable Rekord trigger. Overall length is 45.25", weight is 7 1/2 lbs. Available in 177-caliber only.
Price: $295.00

Marksman 1710

MARKSMAN 1710 PLAINSMAN AIR RIFLE
Caliber: BB, 20-shot repeater.
Barrel: Smoothbore steel with shroud.
Weight: 2.25 lbs. **Length:** 34" overall.
Power: Spring-air.
Stock: Stained hardwood.
Sights: Blade on ramp front, adjustable V-slot rear.
Features: Velocity about 275 fps. Positive feed; automatic safety. Introduced 1994. Made in U.S. From Marksman Products.
Price: $36.00

AIRGUNS—LONG GUNS

MARKSMAN 1740 AIR RIFLE
Caliber: 177 or 18-shot BB repeater.
Barrel: 15½", smoothbore.
Weight: 5 lbs., 1 oz. **Length:** 36½" overall.
Power: Spring, barrel cocking.
Stock: Moulded high-impact ABS plastic.
Sights: Ramp front, open rear adjustable for elevation.
Features: Velocity about 450 fps. Automatic safety; fixed front, adjustable rear sight; positive feed BB magazine; shoots 177-cal. BBs, pellets and darts. From Marksman Products.
Price: $50.00
Price: Model 1780 (deluxe sights, rifled barrel, shoots only pellets) $66.00

MARKSMAN 1792 COMPETITION TRAINER AIR RIFLE
Caliber: 177, single shot.
Barrel: 15", rifled.
Weight: 4.7 lbs.
Power: Spring-air, barrel cocking.
Stock: Synthetic.
Sights: Hooded front, match-style diopter rear.
Features: Velocity about 450 fps. Automatic safety. Introduced 1993. More economical version of the 1790 Biathlon Trainer. Made in U.S. From Marksman Products.
Price: $60.00

MARKSMAN 1750 BB BIATHLON REPEATER RIFLE
Caliber: BB, 18-shot magazine.
Barrel: 15", smoothbore.
Weight: 4.7 lbs.
Power: Spring-piston, barrel cocking.
Stock: Moulded composition.
Sights: Tunnel front, open adjustable rear.
Features: Velocity of 450 fps. Automatic safety. Positive Feed System loads a BB each time gun is cocked. Introduced 1990. From Marksman Products.
Price: $57.00

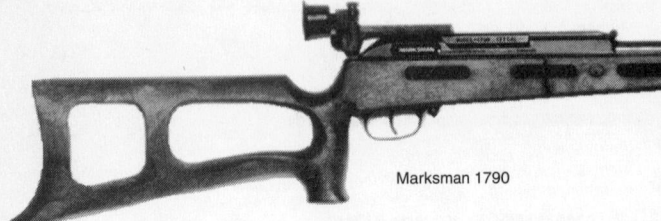
Marksman 1790

MARKSMAN 1790 BIATHLON TRAINER
Caliber: 177, single shot.
Barrel: 15", rifled.
Weight: 4.7 lbs.
Power: Spring-air, barrel cocking.
Stock: Synthetic.
Sights: Hooded front, match-style diopter rear.
Features: Velocity of 450 fps. Endorsed by the U.S. Shooting Team. Introduced 1989. From Marksman Products.
Price: $69.00

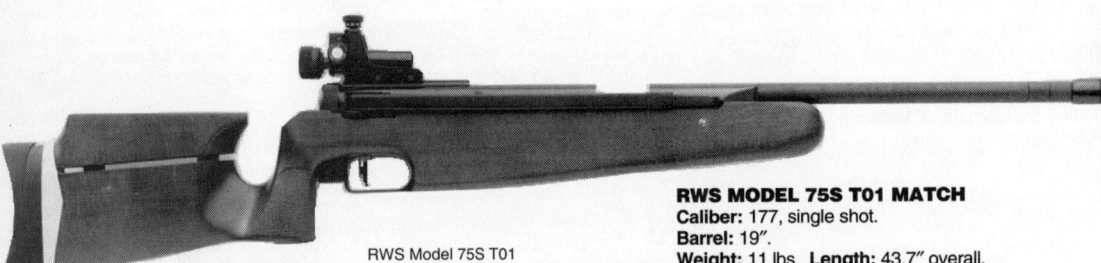
RWS Model 75S T01

RWS MODEL 75S T01 MATCH
Caliber: 177, single shot.
Barrel: 19".
Weight: 11 lbs. **Length:** 43.7" overall.
Power: Dual spring piston.
Stock: Oil-finished beech with stippled grip; adjustable cheekpiece, buttplate.
Sights: Globe front, fully adjustable match peep rear.
Features: Velocity of 580 fps. Fully adjustable trigger; recoilless action. Introduced 1990. Imported from Germany by Dynamit Nobel-RWS.
Price: $1,650.00

RWS/Diana Model 34 Air Rifle
Similar to the Model 24 except has 19" barrel, weighs 7.5 lbs. Gives velocity of 1000 fps (177), 800 fps (22). Adjustable trigger, synthetic seals. Comes with scope rail.
Price: 177 or 22 ....$285.00
Price: Model 34N (nickel-plated metal, black epoxy-coated wood stock) .$330.00
Price: Model 34BC (matte black metal, black stock, 4x32 scope, mounts) $485.00

RWS MODEL CA 100 AIR RIFLE
Caliber: 177, single shot.
Barrel: 22".
Weight: 11.4 lbs. **Length:** 44" overall.
Power: Compressed air; interchangeable cylinders.
Stock: Laminated hardwood with adjustable cheekpiece and buttplate.
Sights: Optional.
Features: Gives 250 shots per full charge. Double-sided power regulator. Introduced 1995. Imported from England by Dynamit Nobel-RWS, Inc.
Price: $2,100.00

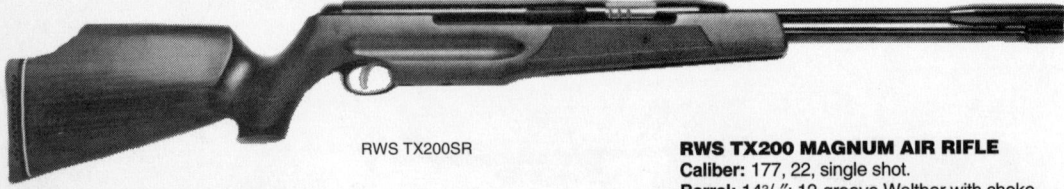
RWS TX200SR

RWS TX200 MAGNUM AIR RIFLE
Caliber: 177, 22, single shot.
Barrel: 14¾"; 12-groove Walther with choke.
Weight: 8½ lbs. **Length:** 42" overall.
Power: Spring-air, underlever cocking.
Stock: Beech or walnut (177 only) with Monte Carlo cheekpiece; checkered grip and forend; rubber recoil pad.
Sights: None furnished; scope rail.
Features: Adjustable two-stage match trigger; automatic safety; floating piston. Made by Air Arms. Introduced 1995. Imported from England by Dynamit Nobel-RWS, Inc.
Price: $560.00
Price: TX200SR (recoilless version of above, slightly different stock), from $660.00

RWS/DIANA MODEL 24 AIR RIFLE
Caliber: 177, 22, single shot.
Barrel: 17", rifled.
Weight: 6 lbs. **Length:** 42" overall.
Power: Spring-air, barrel cocking.
Stock: Beech.
Sights: Hooded front, adjustable rear.
Features: Velocity of 700 fps (177). Easy cocking effort; blue finish. Imported from Germany by Dynamit Nobel-RWS, Inc.
Price: $205.00
Price: Model 24C $205.00

AIRGUNS—LONG GUNS

RWS/DIANA MODEL 45 AIR RIFLE
Caliber: 177, single shot.
Weight: 8 lbs. **Length:** 45" overall.
Power: Spring-air, barrel cocking.
Stock: Walnut-finished hardwood with rubber recoil pad.
Sights: Globe front with interchangeable inserts, micro. click open rear with four-way blade.
Features: Velocity of 820 fps. Dovetail base for either micrometer peep sight or scope mounting. Automatic safety. Imported from Germany by Dynamit Nobel-RWS, Inc.
Price: $330.00

> Consult our Directory pages for the location of firms mentioned.

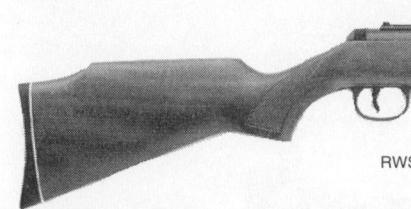
RWS/Diana Model 36

RWS/DIANA MODEL 36 AIR RIFLE
Caliber: 177, 22, single shot.
Barrel: 19", rifled.
Weight: 8 lbs. **Length:** 45" overall.
Power: Spring-air, barrel cocking.
Stock: Beech.
Sights: Hooded front (interchangeable inserts available), adjustable rear.
Features: Velocity of 1000 fps (177-cal.). Comes with scope mount; two-stage adjustable trigger. Imported from Germany by Dynamit Nobel-RWS, Inc.
Price: $415.00
Price: Model 36 Carbine (same as Model 36 except has 15" barrel) $415.00

RWS/Diana Model 52 Deluxe

RWS/DIANA MODEL 52 AIR RIFLE
Caliber: 177, 22, single shot.
Barrel: 17", rifled.
Weight: 8½ lbs. **Length:** 43" overall.
Power: Spring-air, sidelever cocking.
Stock: Beech, with Monte Carlo, cheekpiece, checkered grip and forend.
Sights: Ramp front, adjustable rear.
Features: Velocity of 1100 fps (177). Blue finish. Solid rubber buttpad. Imported from Germany by Dynamit Nobel-RWS, Inc.
Price: $535.00
Price: Model 52 Deluxe (select walnut stock, rosewood grip and forend caps, palm swell grip) $775.00
Price: Model 48B (as above except matte black metal, black stock) $535.00
Price: Model 48 (same as Model 52 except no Monte Carlo, cheekpiece or checkering) $530.00

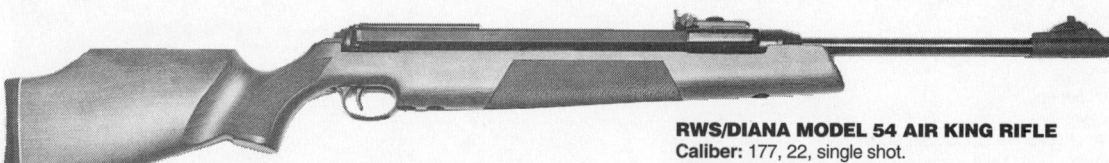
RWS/Diana Model 54 Air King

RWS/DIANA MODEL 54 AIR KING RIFLE
Caliber: 177, 22, single shot.
Barrel: 17".
Weight: 9 lbs. **Length:** 43" overall.
Power: Spring-air, sidelever cocking.
Stock: Walnut with Monte Carlo cheekpiece, checkered grip and forend.
Sights: Ramp front, fully adjustable rear.
Features: Velocity to 1000 fps (177), 900 fps (22). Totally recoilless system; floating action absorbs recoil. Imported from Germany by Dynamit Nobel-RWS, Inc.
Price: $750.00

RWS/Diana Model 100

RWS/DIANA MODEL 100 MATCH AIR RIFLE
Caliber: 177, single shot.
Barrel: 19".
Weight: 11 lbs. **Length:** 43" overall.
Power: Spring-air, sidelever cocking.
Stock: Walnut.
Sights: Tunnel front, fully adjustable match rear.
Features: Velocity of 580 fps. Single-stroke cocking; cheekpiece adjustable for height and length; recoilless operation. Cocking lever secured against rebound. Introduced 1990. Imported from Germany by Dynamit Nobel-RWS, Inc.
Price: Right-hand only $1,650.00

CAUTION: PRICES SHOWN ARE SUPPLIED BY THE MANUFACTURER OR IMPORTER. CHECK YOUR LOCAL GUNSHOP.

AIRGUNS—LONG GUNS

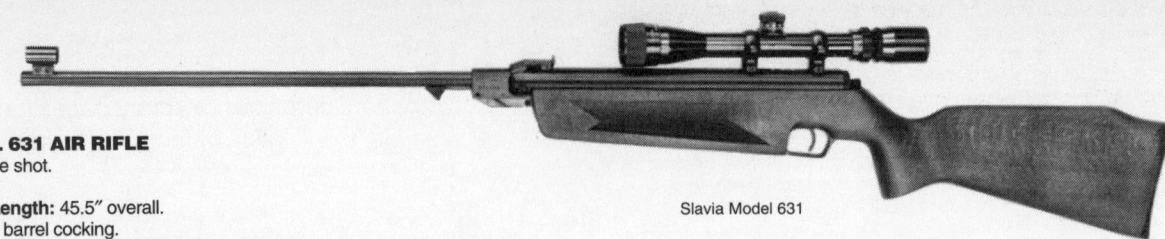
Slavia Model 631

SLAVIA MODEL 631 AIR RIFLE
Caliber: 177, single shot.
Barrel: 21".
Weight: 6.8 lbs. **Length:** 45.5" overall.
Power: Spring-air; barrel cocking.
Stock: Oil-finished European hardwood; checkered forend.
Sights: Hooded post front, fully adjustable open rear.
Features: Velocity to 630 fps. Adjustable two-stage trigger; receiver grooved for scope mounting; automatic safety. Introduced 1996. Imported from the Czech Republic by Great Lakes Airguns.
Price: $112.50

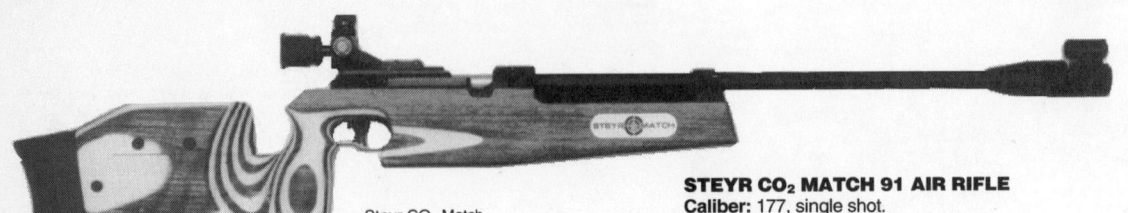
Steyr CO₂ Match

STEYR CO$_2$ MATCH 91 AIR RIFLE
Caliber: 177, single shot.
Barrel: 23.75", (13.75" rifled).
Weight: 10.5 lbs. **Length:** 51.7" overall.
Power: CO_2.
Stock: Match. Laminated wood. Adjustable buttplate and cheekpiece.
Sights: None furnished; comes with scope mount.
Features: Velocity 577 fps. CO_2 cylinders are refillable; about 320 shots per cylinder. Designed for 10-meter shooting. Introduced 1990. Imported from Austria by Nygord Precision Products.
Price: About $1,350.00
Price: Left-hand, about $1,400.00
Price: Running Target Rifle, right-hand, about $1,450.00
Price: As above, left-hand, about $1,425.00

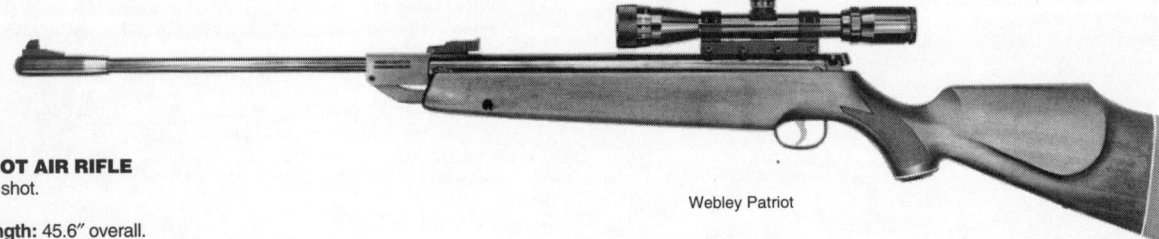
Webley Patriot

WEBLEY PATRIOT AIR RIFLE
Caliber: 22, single shot.
Barrel: 17.5".
Weight: 9 lbs. **Length:** 45.6" overall.
Power: Spring-air; barrel cocking.
Stock: Walnut-stained beech; checkered grip; rubber buttpad.
Sights: Post front, fully adjustable open rear.
Features: Velocity to 932 fps. Automatic safety; receiver grooved for scope mounting. Imported from England by Great Lakes Airguns.
Price: $497.72

Whiscombe JW70 FB

WHISCOMBE JW SERIES AIR RIFLES
Caliber: 177, 20, 22, 25, single shot.
Barrel: 17", Lothar Walther.
Weight: 9 lbs., 8 oz. **Length:** 39" overall.
Power: Dual spring-piston, multi-stroke; underlever cocking.
Stock: Walnut with adjustable buttplate.
Sights: None furnished; grooved scope rail.
Features: Velocity 660-890 fps (22-caliber, fixed barrel) depending upon model. Interchangeable barrels; automatic safety; muzzle weight; semi-floating action; twin opposed pistons with counter-wound springs; adjustable trigger. Introduced 1995. Imported from England by Pelaire Products.
Price: JW50, fixed barrel only $1,440.00
Price: JW60, fixed barrel only $1,495.00
Price: JW70, fixed barrel only $1,550.00
Price: JW75, fixed barrel only $1,575.00
Price: JW75 High Power, fixed barrel avail. $1,595.00

Manufacturers' addresses in the
Directory of the Arms Trade
page 313, this issue

SCOPES & MOUNTS

Maker and Model	Magn.	Field at 100 Yds. (feet)	Eye Relief (in.)	Length (in.)	Tube Dia. (in.)	W&E Adjust-ments	Weight (ozs.)	Price	Other Data
AAL OPTICS									
Micro-Dot Scopes[1]									[1]Brightness-adjustable fiber optic red dot reticle. Waterproof, nitrogen-filled one-piece tube tube. Tinted see-through lens covers and battery included. [2]Parallax adjustable. [3]Ultra Dot sights include rings, battery, polarized filter, and 5-year warranty. All models available in black or satin finish. [4]Illuminated red dot has eleven brightness settings. Shock-proof aluminum tube. [5]Fiber optic red dot has five brightness settings. Shock-proof polymer tube. From AAL Optics.
1.5-4.5x20 Rifle	1.5-4.5	80-26	3	9.8	1	Int.	10.5	$287.00	
2-7x32	2-7	54-18	3	11.0	1	Int.	12.1	299.00	
3-9x40	3-9	40-14	3	12.2	1	Int.	13.3	319.00	
4x-12x56[2]	4-12	30-10	3	14.3	1	Int.	18.3	409.00	
Ultra-Dot Sights[3]									
Ultra-Dot 25[4]	1	—	—	5.1	1	Int.	3.9	139.00	
Ultra-Dot 30[4]	1	—	—	5.1	30mm	Int.	4.0	149.00	
Ultra Dot Patriot[5]	1	—	—	5.1	1	Int.	2.9	119.00	
ADCO									[1]Multi-Color Dot system changes from red to green. [2]For airguns, paintball, rimfires. Uses common lithium wafer battery. [3]Comes with standard dovetail mount. [4]3/8" dovetail mount; poly body; adj. intensity diode. [5] Adj. dot size—5, 10, 15 MOA.
MiRAGE Ranger 1"	0	—	—	5.2	1	Int.	3.9	159.00	
MiRAGE Ranger 30mm	0	—	—	5.5	30mm	Int.	5.0	179.00	
MiRAGE Sportsman[1]	0	—	—	5.2	1	Int.	4.5	249.00	
MiRAGE Competitor[1]	0	—	—	5.5	30mm	Int.	5.5	269.00	
MiRAGE Trident[5]	0	—	—	6.0	30mm	Int.	6.5	499.00	
IMP Sight[2]	0	—	—	4.5	—	Int.	1.3	19.95	
Square Shooter[3]	0	—	—	5.0	—	Int.	5	129.00	
MiRAGE Eclipse[1]	0	—	—	5.5	30mm	Int.	5.5	249.00	
MiRAGE Champ Red Dot	0	—	—	4.5	—	Int.	2	39.95	
AIMPOINT									Illuminates red dot in field of view. Noparallax (dot does not need to be centered). Unlimited field of view and eye relief. On/off, adj. intensity. Dot covers 3" @ 100 yds. Mounts avail. for all sights and scopes. [1]Comes with 30mm rings, battery, lens cloth. [2]Requires 1" rings. Black or stainless finish. 3x scope attachment (for rifles only), $129.95. [3]Projects red dot of visible laser light onto target. Black finish (LSR-2B) or stainless (LSR-2S); or comes with rings and accessories. Optional toggle switch, $34.95. [4]Lithium battery life up to 15 hours. [5]Black finish (AP 5000-B) or stainless (AP 5000-S); avail. with regular 3-min. or 10-min. Mag Dot as B2 or S2. [6]For Beretta, Browning, Colt Gov't., Desert Eagle, Glock, Ruger, SIG-Sauer, S&W. [6]For Colt, S&W. From Aimpoint U.S.A.
Comp	0	—	—	4.6	30mm	Int.	4.3	308.00	
Series 5000[4]	0	—	—	5.75	30mm	Int.	5.8	277.00	
Series 3000 Universal[2]	0	—	—	5.5	1	Int.	5.5	232.00	
Series 5000/2x[1]	2	—	—	7	30mm	Int.	9	367.00	
Laserdot	—	—	—	3.5	1	Int.	4.0	319.95	
Autolaser[5]	—	—	—	3.75	1	Int.	4.3	351.00	
Revolver Laser[6]	—	—	—	3.5	1	Int.	3.6	339.00	
ARMSON O.E.G.									Shows red dot aiming point. No batteries needed. Standard model fits 1" ring mounts (not incl.). Other models available for many popular shotguns, para-military rifles and carbines. [1]Daylight Only Sight with 3/8" dovetail mount for 22s. Does not contain tritium. From Trijicon, Inc.
Standard	0	—	—	5 1/8	1	Int.	4.3	175.00	
22 DOS[1]	0	—	—	3 3/4	—	Int.	3.0	104.00	
22 Day/Night	0	—	—	3 3/4	—	Int.	3.0	146.00	
M16/AR-15	0	—	—	5 1/8	—	Int.	5.5	209.00	
Colt Pistol	0	—	—	3 3/4	—	Int.	3.0	209.00	
BAUSCH & LOMB									[1]Adj. objective, sunshade. [2]Also in matte and silver finish, $632.00. [3]Also in matte finish, $589.00. [4]Also in matte finish, $370.95; silver finish, $370.95. [5]Also in matte finish, $361.95. [6]50mm objective; matte finish, $453.95. [7]Also in matte finish, $430.95. [8]Also in silver finish, $321.95. [9]Also in matte finish, $432.95 Partial listing shown. Contact Bausch & Lomb Sports Optics Div. for details.
Elite 4000									
40-6244A[1]	6-24	18-4.5	3	16.9	1	Int.	20.2	702.00	
40-2104G[2]	2.5-10	41.5-10.8	3	13.5	1	Int.	16	606.00	
40-1636G[3]	1.5-6	61.8-16.1	3	12.8	1	Int.	15.4	565.00	
40-1040	10	10.5	3.6	13.8	1	Int.	22.1	1,745.00	
Elite 3000									
30-4124A[1]	4-12	26.9-9	3	13.2	1	Int.	15.0	421.95	
30-3940G[4]	3-9	33.8-11.5	3	12.6	1	Int.	13.0	348.95	
30-2732G[5]	2-7	44.6-12.7	3	11.6	1	Int.	12.0	342.95	
30-3950G[6]	3-9	31.5-10.5	3	15.7	1	Int.	19	434.95	
30-1545M[7]	1.5-4.5	63-20	3.3	12.5	1	Int.	13	434.95	
30-3955E	3-9	31.5-10.5	3	15.6	30mm	Int.	22	633.95	
Elite 3000 Handgun									
30-2028G[8]	2	23	9-26	8.4	1	Int.	6.9	301.95	
30-2632G[9]	2-6	10-4	20	9.0	1	Int.	10.0	413.95	
BEEMAN									All scopes have 5-point reticle, all glass, fully coated lenses. [1]Includes mount. [2]Also as 66RL with lighted color reticle, $355.00. [3]Also as SS-2L 3x with color 4pt. reticle. Imported by Beeman
Blue Ribbon SS-3[1]	1.5-4	42-25	3	5.8	7/8	Int.	8.5	300.00	
Blue Ribbon 66R[2]	2-7	62-16	3	11.4	1	Int.	14.9	315.00	
Blue Ribbon SS-2[1,3]	4	25	3.5	7.0	1.4	Int.	13.7	305.00	
Blue Ribbon 25 Pistol	2	19	10-24	9.1	1	Int.	7.4	155.00	
B-SQUARE									[1]Blue finish; stainless, $209.95. T-slot mount; cord or integral switch. [2]Blue finish; stainless, $259.95. T-slot mount; cord or integral switch. Uses common A76 batteries. [3]High intensity 635 beam, $349.95 (blue), $359.95 (stainless). Dimensions 1.1"x1.1"x.6". From B-Square.
BSL-1[1]	—	—	—	2.75	.75	Int.	2.25	199.95	
Mini-Laser[2,3]	—	—	—	1.1	—	Int.	2.9	239.95	
BURRIS									All scopes avail. in Plex reticle. Steel-on-steel click adjustments. [1]Dot reticle on some models. [2]Post crosshair reticle extra. [3]Matte satin finish. [4]Available with parallax adjustment (standard on 10x, 12x, 4-12x, 6-12x, 6-18x, 6x HBR and 3-12x Signature). [5]Silver matte finish extra. [6]Target knobs extra, standard on silhouette models, LER and XER with P.A., 6x HBR. [7]Sunshade avail. [8]Avail. with Fine Plex reticle. [9]Available with Heavy Plex reticle. [10]Available with Posi-Lock. [11]Available with Peep Plex reticle. [12]Also avail. for rimfires, airguns.
Fullfield									
1x LER[3]	1	51	4.5-20	8.8	1	Int.	7.9	278.00	
1 1/2x[9]	1.6	62	3.5-3.75	10 1/4	1	Int.	9.0	268.00	
2 1/2x[9]	2.5	55	3.5-3.75	10 1/4	1	Int.	9.0	282.00	
4x[1,2,3]	3.75	36	3.5-3.75	11 1/4	1	Int.	11.5	285.00	
6x[1,3]	5.8	23	3.5-3.75	13	1	Int.	12.0	312.00	
12x[1,4,6,7,8]	11.8	10.5	3.5-3.75	15	1	Int.	15	392.00	
1-4x XER[3]	1.0-3.8	53-15	4.25-30	8.8	1	Int.	10.3	342.00	
1 3/4-5x[1,2,9,10]	1.7-4.6	66-25	3.5-3.75	10 7/8	1	Int.	13	340.00	

CAUTION: PRICES SHOWN ARE SUPPLIED BY THE MANUFACTURER OR IMPORTER. CHECK YOUR LOCAL GUNSHOP.

HUNTING, TARGET & VARMINT SCOPES

Maker and Model	Magn.	Field at 100 Yds. (feet)	Eye Relief (in.)	Length (in.)	Tube Dia. (in.)	W&E Adjustments	Weight (ozs.)	Price	Other Data
Burris (cont.)									
2-7x[1,2,3]	2.5-6.8	47-18	3.5-3.75	12	1	Int.	14	364.00	
3-9x[1,2,3]	3.3-8.7	38-15	3.5-3.75	12 5/8	1	Int.	15	339.00	
3.5-10x50mm[3,5,10]	3.7-9.7	29.5-11	3.5-3.75	14	1	Int.	19	450.00	
4-12x[1,4,8,11]	4.4-11.8	27-10	3.5-3.75	15	1	Int.	18	458.00	
6-18x[1,3,4,6,7,8]	6.5-17.6	16-7	3.5-3.75	15.8	1	Int.	18.5	479.00	
Compact Scopes									
4x[4,5]	3.6	24	3 3/4-5	8 1/4	1	Int.	7.8	239.00	
6x[1,4]	5.5	17	3 3/4-5	9	1	Int.	8.2	254.00	
6x HBR[1,5,8]	6.0	13	4.5	11 1/4	1	Int.	13.0	329.00	
2-7x	2.5-6.9	32-14	3 3/4-5	12	1	Int.	10.5	327.00	
3-9x[5]	3.6-8.8	25-11	3 3/4-5	12 5/8	1	Int.	11.5	335.00	
4-12x[1,4,6]	4.5-11.6	19-8	3 3/4-4	15	1	Int.	15	442.00	LER=Long Eye Relief; IER=Intermediate Eye Relief; XER=Extra Eye Relief. Partial listing shown, contact maker for complete data. From Burris.
Signature Series									
1.5-6x[2,3,5,9,10]	1.7-5.8	70-20	3.5-4.0	10.8	1	Int.	13.0	429.00	
4x[3]	4.0	30	3.5-4.0	12 1/8	1	Int.	14	349.00	
6x[3]	6.0	20	3.5-4.0	12 1/8	1	Int.	14	358.00	
2-8x[3,5,11]	2.1-7.7	53-17	3.5-4.0	11.75	1	Int.	14	498.00	
3-9x[3,5,10]	3.3-8.8	36-14	3.5-4.0	12 7/8	1	Int.	15.5	509.00	
2 1/2-10x[3,5,10]	2.7-9.5	37-10.5	3.5-4.0	14	1	Int.	19.0	552.00	
3-12x[3,10]	3.3-11.7	34-9	3.5-4.0	14 1/4	1	Int.	21	612.00	
4-16x[1,3,5,6,8,10]	4.3-15.7	33-9	3.5-4.0	15.4	1	Int.	23.7	624.00	
6-24x[1,3,5,6,8,10]	6.6-23.8	17-6	3.5-4.0	16.0	1	Int.	22.7	664.00	
8-32x[8,10,12]	8.6-31.4	13-3.8	3.5-4.0	17	1	Int.	24	727.00	
Handgun									
1 1/2-4x LER[1,5,10]	1.6-3.	16-11	11-25	10 1/4	1	Int.	11	365.00	
2-7x LER[3,4,5,10]	2-6.5	21-7	7-27	9.5	1	Int.	12.6	358.00	
3-9x LER[4,5,10]	3.4-8.4	12-5	22-14	11	1	Int.	14	402.00	
1x LER[1]	1.1	27	10-24	8 3/4	1	Int.	6.8	228.00	
2x LER[4,5,6]	1.7	21	10-24	8 3/4	1	Int.	6.8	235.00	
3x LER[4,6]	2.7	17	10-20	8 7/8	1	Int.	6.8	252.00	
4x LER[1,4,5,6,10]	3.7	11	10-22	9 5/8	1	Int.	9.0	262.00	
7x IER[1,4,5,6]	6.5	6.5	10-16	11 1/4	1	Int.	10	329.00	
10x IER[1,4,6]	9.5	4	8-12	13 1/2	1	Int.	14	388.00	
Scout Scope									
1 1/2x XER[3,9]	1.5	22	7-18	9	1	Int.	7.3	238.00	
2 3/4x XER[3,9]	2.7	15	7-14	9 3/8	1	Int.	7.5	235.00	
BUSHNELL									
Trophy									
73-0130[1]	1	61	—	5.25	30mm	Int.	5.5	282.95	[1]45mm objective. [2]Wide angle; silver or matte finish, $297.95. [3]Also silver finish, $205.95. [4]Also silver finish, $267.95. [5]56mm objective. [6]Selective red L.E.D. dot for low light hunting. [7]Also silver finish, $65.95. [8]Adj. obj. [9]Variable intensity; interchangeable extra reticles (Dual Rings, Open Cross Hairs, Rising Dot) $128.95; fits Weaver-style base.
73-2545[1]	2.5-10	39-10	3	13.75	1	Int.	14	310.95	
73-1500[2]	1.75-5	68-23	3.5	10.8	1	Int.	12.3	258.95	
73-4124[2]	4-12	32-11	3	12.5	1	Int.	16.1	288.95	
73-3940	3-9	42-14	3	11.7	1	Int.	13.2	186.95	
73-6184	6-18	17.3-6	3	14.8	1	Int.	17.9	338.95	
HOLOsight[9]	1	—	—	6	—	Int.	8.7	599.95	
Trophy Handgun									
73-0232[3]	2	20	9-26	8.7	1	Int.	7.7	190.95	
73-2632[4]	2-6	21-7	9-26	9.1	1	Int.	9.6	252.95	
Banner Standard									
71-2520	2.5	44	3.6	10	1	Int.	7.5	84.95	
71-3956[5]	3-9	37-12	3.5	13.7	1	Int.	17.3	288.95	
Lite-Site									
71-3940[6]	3-9	36-13	3.1	12.8	1	Int.	15.5	368.95	
Sportview									
79-0004	4	31	4	11.7	1	Int.	11.2	92.95	
79-0039	3-9	38-13	3.5	10.75	1	Int.	11.2	109.95	
79-0412[8]	4-12	27-9	3.2	13.1	1	Int.	14.6	132.95	
79-0640	6	20.5	3	12.25	1	Int.	10.4	91.95	
79-1393[7]	3-9	35-12	3.5	11.75	1	Int.	10	66.95	
79-1545	1.5-4.5	69-24	3	10.7	1	Int.	8.6	88.95	
79-3145	3.5-10	36-13	3	12.75	1	Int.	13.9	145.95	
79-1403	4	29	4	11.75	1	Int.	9.2	53.95	
79-6184	6-18	19.1-6.8	3	14.5	1	Int.	15.9	159.95	
79-3938	3-9	42-14	3	12.7	1	Int.	12.5	105.95	
79-3720	3-7	23-11	2.6	11.3	.75	Int.	5.7	40.95	
Turkey & Brush									
73-1420	1.75-4	73-30	3.5	10.8	32mm	Int.	10.9	263.95	
CHARLES DALY									
4x32	4	28	3.25	11.75	1	Int.	9.5	70.00	Waterproof, fog-proof. [1]Shotgun scope. From Outdoor Sports Headquarters.
4x32[1]	4	16	6	8.8	1	Int.	9.2	90.00	
4x40 WA	4	36	3.25	13	1	Int.	11.5	98.00	
2-7x32 WA	2-7	56-17	3	11.5	1	Int.	12	125.00	
3-9x40	3-9	35-14	3	12.5	1	Int.	11.25	110.00	
3-9x40 WA	3-9	36-13	3	12.75	1	Int.	12.5	125.00	
4-12x40 WA	4-12	30-11	3	13.75	1	Int.	14.5	133.00	

HUNTING, TARGET & VARMINT SCOPES

Maker and Model	Magn.	Field at 100 Yds. (feet)	Eye Relief (in.)	Length (in.)	Tube Dia. (in.)	W&E Adjustments	Weight (ozs.)	Price	Other Data
DOCTER OPTIC									Matte black and matte silver finish available. All lenses multi-coated. Illuminated reticle avail., choice of reticles. Rail mount, aspherical lenses avail. Aspherical lens model, **$1,375.00**. Imported from Germany by Docter Optic Technologies, Inc.
Fixed Power									
4x32	4	31	3	10.7	26mm	Int.	10.0	898.00	
6x42	6	20	3	12.8	26mm	Int.	12.7	1,004.00	
8x56[1]	8	15	3	14.7	26mm	Int.	15.6	1,240.00	
Variables									
1-4x24	1-4	79.7-31.3	3	10.8	30mm	Int.	13	1,300.00	
1.2-5x32	1.2-5	65-25	3	11.6	30mm	Int.	15.4	1,345.00	
1.5-6x42	1.5-6	41.3-20.6	3	12.7	30mm	Int.	16.8	1,378.00	
2.5-10x48	2.5-10	36.6-12.4	3	13.7	30mm	Int.	18.6	1,378.00	
2-12x56	3-12	44.2-13.8	3	14.8	30mm	Int.	20.3	1,425.00	
FROM JENA									[1]Military scope with adjustable parallax. Fixed powers have 26mm tubes, variables have 30mm tubes. Some models avail. with steel tubes. All lenses multi-coated. Dust and water tight. From Jena, Europtik, Ltd.
4x36	4	39	3.5	11.6	26mm	Int.	14	695.00	
6x36	6	21	3.5	12	26mm	Int.	14	795.00	
6x42	6	21	3.5	13	26mm	Int.	15	860.00	
8x56	8	18	3.5	14.4	26mm	Int.	20	890.00	
1.5-6x42	1.5-6	61.7-23	3.5	12.6	30mm	Int.	17	975.00	
2-8x42	2-8	52-17	3.5	13.3	30mm	Int.	17	1,050.00	
2.5-10x56	2.5-10	40-13.6	3.5	15	30mm	Int.	21	1,195.00	
3-12x56	3-12	NA	NA	NA	30mm	Int.	NA	1,195.00	
4-16x56	4-16	NA	NA	NA	30mm	Int.	NA	1,225.00	
3-9x40	3-9	NA	NA	NA	1	Int.	NA	1,120.00	
2.5-10x46	2.5-10	NA	NA	NA	30mm	Int.	NA	1,150.00	
4-16x56[1]	4-16	NA	NA	NA	30mm	Int.	NA	1,695.00	
INTERAIMS									Intended for handguns. Comes with rings. Dot size less than 1½" @ 100 yds. Waterproof. Battery life 50-10,000 hours. Black or nickel finish. 2x booster, 1" or 30mm, **$139.00** Imported by Stoeger.
One V	0	—	—	4.5	1	Int.	4	159.95	
One V 30	0	—	—	4.5	30mm	Int.	4	176.95	
KAHLES									[1]Steel tube. [2]Ballistic cam system with military rangefinder. Waterproof, fogproof, nitrogen filled. Choice of reticles. Imported from Austria by Swarovski Optic NA.
K1.5-6x42-L	1.5-6	61-21	—	12.5	30mm	Int.	15.8	721.12	
K2.2-9x42-L	2.2-9	39.5-15	—	13.3	30mm	Int.	15.5	887.78	
K3-12x56-L	3-12	30-11	—	15.2	30mm	Int.	18	943.33	
KZF84-6[1,2]	6	23	—	12.5	1	Int.	17.6	1,245.00	
KZF84-10[1,2]	10	13	—	13.25	1	Int.	18	1,245.00	
KILHAM									Unlimited eye relief; internal click adjustments; crosshair reticle. Fits Thompson/Center rail mounts, for S&W K, N, Ruger Blackhawk, Super, Super Single-Six, Contender.
Hutson Handgunner II	1.7	8	—	5½	⅞	Int.	5.1	119.95	
Hutson Handgunner	3	8	10-12	6	⅞	Int.	5.3	119.95	
LASERAIM									[1]Red dot/laser combo; 300-yd. range; LA3XHD Hotdot has 500-yd. range **$249.00**; 4 MOA dot size, laser gives 2" dot size at 100 yds. [2]30mm obj. lens. [3]4 MOA dot at 100 yds.; fits Weaver base. [4]300-yd. range; 2" dot at 100 yds.; rechargeable Nicad battery. [5]1.5-mile range; 1" dot at 100 yds.; 20+ hrs. batt. life. [6]1.5-mile range; 1" dot at 100 yds.; rechargeable Nicad battery (comes with in-field charger); Black or satin finish. With mount, **$169.00**. [7]Laser projects 2" dot at 100 yds.; with rotary switch; with Hotdot **$237.00**; with Hotdot, touch switch **$357.00**. [8]For Glock 17-27; G1 Hotdot **$299.00**; price installed. [10]Fits std. Weaver base, no rings required; 6-MOA dot; seven brightness settings. All have w&e adj.; black or satin silver finish. From Laseraim Technologies, Inc.
LA3X Dualdot[1]	—	—	—	6	—	Int.	12	199.00	
LA5[3]	—	—	—	2	.75	Int.	1.2	236.00	
LA10 Hotdot[4]	—	—	—	3.87	.75	Int.	NA	396.00	
LA11 Hotdot[5]	—	—	—	2.75	.75	Int.	NA	292.00	
LA14	—	—	—	NA	NA	Int.	NA	314.00	
LA16 Hotdot Mighty Sight[6]	—	—	—	1.5	NA	Int.	1.5	169.00	
Red Dot Sights									
LA93 Illusion III[2]	—	—	—	6.0	—	Int.	5.0	139.00	
LA9750 Grand Illusion[10]	—	—	—	5.5	50mm	Int.	7.0	199.00	
Lasers									
MA3 Mini Aimer[7]	—	—	—	1.5	⅝	Int.	1.0	155.00	
G1 Laser[8]	—	—	—	1.5	—	Int.	2.0	289.00	
LASER DEVICES									Projects high intensity beam of laser light onto target as an aiming point. Adj. for w. & e. [1]Diode laser system. From Laser Devices, Inc.
He Ne FA-6	—	—	—	6.2	—	Int.	11	229.50	
He Ne FA-9	—	—	—	12	—	Int.	16	299.00	
He Ne FA-9P	—	—	—	9	—	Int.	14	299.00	
FA-4[1]	—	—	—	4.5	—	Int.	3.5	299.00	
LEUPOLD									Constantly centered reticles, choice of Duplex, tapered CPC, Leupold Dot, Crosshair and Dot. CPC and Dot reticles avail. [1]2x and 4x scopes have from 12"-24" of eye relief and are suitable for handguns, top ejection arms and muzzleloaders. [2]3x9 Compact, 6x Compact, 12x, 3x9, 3.5x10 and 6.5x20 come with adjustable objective. [3]Target scopes have 1-min. divisions with ¼-min. clicks, and adjustable objectives. 50-ft. Focus Adaptor available for indoor target ranges, **$53.60**. Sunshade available for all adjustable objective scopes, **$21.40-39.30**. [4]Also available in matte finish for about **$15.00** extra. [5]Silver finish about **$15.00** extra. [6]Matte finish. [7]Battery life 60 min.; dot size .625" @ 25 yds. Black matte finish Partial listing shown. **Contact Leupold for complete details.**
Vari-X III 3.5x10 STD Tactical	3.5-10	29.5-10.7	3.6-4.6	12.5	1	Int.	13.5	716.10	
M8-2X EER[1]	1.7	21.2	12-24	7.9	1	Int.	6.0	271.40	
M8-2X EER Silver[1]	1.7	21.2	12-24	7.9	1	Int.	6.0	292.90	
M8-4X EER[1]	3.7	9	12-24	8.4	1	Int.	7.0	367.90	
M8-4X EER Silver[1]	3.7	9	12-24	8.4	1	Int.	7.0	367.90	
Vari-X 2.5-8.0 EER	2.5-8.0	13-4.3	11.7-12	9.7	1	Int.	10.9	530.40	
M8-4X Compact	3.6	25.5	4.5	9.2	1	Int.	7.5	335.70	
Vari-X 2-7x Compact	2.5-6.6	41.7-16.5	5-3.7	9.9	1	Int.	8.5	421.40	
Vari-X 3-9x Compact	3.2-8.6	34-13.5	4.0-3.0	11-11.3	1	Int.	11.0	435.70	
Vari-X 6-18x40	6.7-17.1	14.5-6.6	4.7-3.7	13.4	1	Int.	14.0	821.40	
M8-4X	4.0	24	4.0	10.7	1	Int.	9.3	335.70	
M8-6X[6]	5.9	17.7	4.3	11.4	1	Int.	10.0	358.90	
M8-6x 42mm	6.0	17	4.5	12	1	Int.	11.3	444.60	
M8-12x A.O. Varmint	11.6	9.1	4.2	13.0	1	Int.	13.5	498.20	
BR-24X[3]	24.0	4.7	3.2	13.8	1	Int.	15.3	896.40	
BR-36X[3]	36.0	3.2	3.4	14.1	1	Int.	15.6	937.50	
Vari-X 3-9x Compact EFR A.O.	3.8-8.6	34.0-13.5	4.0-3.0	11.0	1	Int.	11	491.10	
Vari-X-II 1x4	1.6-4.2	70.5-28.5	4.3-3.8	9.2	1	Int.	9.0	360.70	
Vari-X-II 2x7[4]	2.5-6.6	42.5-17.8	4.9-3.8	11.0	1	Int.	10.5	391.10	
Vari-X-II 3x9[1,4,5]	3.3-8.6	32.3-14.0	4.1-3.7	12.3	1	Int.	13.5	394.60	
Vari-X-II 3-9x50mm[4]	3.3-8.6	32.3-14	4.7-3.7	12	1	Int.	13.6	501.80	
Vari-X-II 4-12 A.O. Matte	4.4-11.6	22.8-11.0	5.0-3.3	12.3	1	Int.	13.5	542.90	
M8-2.5x32 IER Scout	2.3	22	9-17	10.0	1	Int.	7.5	353.60	
Vari-X-III 1.5x5	1.5-4.5	66.0-23.0	5.3-3.7	9.4	1	Int.	9.5	551.80	

CAUTION: PRICES SHOWN ARE SUPPLIED BY THE MANUFACTURER OR IMPORTER. CHECK YOUR LOCAL GUNSHOP.

HUNTING, TARGET & VARMINT SCOPES

Maker and Model	Magn.	Field at 100 Yds. (feet)	Eye Relief (in.)	Length (in.)	Tube Dia. (in.)	W&E Adjustments	Weight (ozs.)	Price	Other Data
Leupold (cont.)									
Vari-X-III 1.75-6x 32	1.9-5.6	47-18	4.8-3.7	9.8	1	Int.	11	575.40	
Vari-X-III 2.5x8[4]	2.6-7.8	37.0-13.5	4.7-3.7	11.3	1	Int.	11.5	594.60	
Vari-X-III 3.5-10x50 A.O.	3.3-9.7	29.5-10.7	4.6-3.6	12.4	1	Int.	13.0	769.60	
Vari-X-III 3.5-10x50[2,4]	3.3-9.7	29.5-10.7	4.6-3.6	12.4	1	Int.	14.4	714.30	
Vari-X-III 4.5-14	4.7-13.7	20.8-7.4	5.0-3.7	12.4	1	Int.	14.5	691.10	
Vari-X-III 4.5-14x50	4.7-13.7	20.8-7.4	5.0-3.7	12.4	1	Int.	14.5	828.60	
Vari-X-III 6.5-20 A.O. Varmint	6.5-19.2	14.2-5.5	5.3-3.6	14.2	1	Int.	17.5	839.30	
Vari-X-III 6.5-20x Target EFR A.O.	6.5-19.2	—	5.3-3.6	14.2	1	Int.	16.5	812.50	
Mark 4 M3-6x	6	17.7	4.5	13.1	30mm	Int.	21	1,612.50	
Mark 4 M1-10x[6]	10	11.1	3.6	13 1/8	1	Int.	21	1,612.50	
Mark 4 M1-16x[6]	16	6.6	4.1	12 7/8	1	Int.	22	1,612.50	
Mark 4 M3-10x[6]	10	11.1	3.6	13 1/8	1	Int.	21	1,612.50	
Vari-X-III 6.5x20[2]	6.5-19.2	14.2-5.5	5.3-3.6	14.2	1	Int.	16.0	719.60	
Rimfire									
Vari-X-II 2-7x RF Special	3.6	25.5	4.5	9.2	1	Int.	7.5	421.40	
Shotgun									
M8 4x	3.7	9.0	12-24	8.4	1	Int.	6.0	357.10	
Vari-X-II 1x4	1.6-4.2	70.5-28.5	4.3-3.8	9.2	1	Int.	9.0	382.10	
Vari-X-II 2x7	2.5-6.6	42.5-17.8	4.9-3.8	11.0	1	Int.	9.0	412.50	
Laser									
LaserLight[7]	—	—	—	1.18	NA	Int.	.5	292.90	
LYMAN									Made under license from Lyman to Lyman's orig. specs. Blue steel. Three-point suspension rear mount with 1/4-min. click adj. Data listed are for 20x model. [1]Price approximate. Made in U.S. by Parsons Optical Mfg. Co.
Super TargetSpot[1]	10,12,15,20,25,30	5.5	2	24.3	.75	Int.	27.5	685.00	
McMILLAN									42mm obj. lens; 1/4-MOA clicks; nitrogen filled, fogproof, waterproof; etched duplex-type reticle. [1]Tactical Scope with external adj. knobs, military reticle; 60+ min. adj.
Vision Master 2.5-10x	2.5-10	14.2-4.4	4.3-3.3	13.3	30mm	Int.	17.0	1,250.00	
Vision Master Model I[1]	2.5-10	14.2-4.4	4.3-3.3	13.3	30mm	Int.	17.0	1,250.00	
MILLETT									Full coated lenses; parallax-free; three lenses; 30mm has 10-min. dot, 1-Inch has 3-min. dot. Black or silver finish. From Millett Sights.
Red Dot 1 Inch	1	36.65	—	NA	1	Int.	NA	189.95	
Red Dot 30mm	1	58	—	NA	30mm	Int.	NA	289.95	
MIRADOR									[1]Wide Angle scope. Multi-coated objective lens. Nitrogen filled; waterproof; shockproof. From Mirador Optical Corp.
RXW 4x40[1]	4	37	3.8	12.4	1	Int.	12	179.95	
RXW 1.5-5x20[1]	1.5-5	46-17.4	4.3	11.1	1	Int.	10	188.95	
RXW 3-9x40	3-9	43-14.5	3.1	12.9	1	Int.	13.4	251.95	
NIKON									Super multi-coated lenses and blackening of all internal metal parts for maximum light gathering capability; positive 1/4-MOA; fogproof; waterproof; shockproof; luster and matte finish. [1]Also available in matte silver finish. [2]Available in silver matte finish. From Nikon, Inc.
4x40[2]	4	26.7	3.5	11.7	1	Int.	11.7	284.00	
1.5-4.5x20	1.5-4.5	67.8-22.5	3.7-3.2	10.1	1	Int.	9.5	358.00	
1.5-4.5x24 EER	1.5-4.4	13.7-5.8	24-18	8.9	1	Int.	9.3	352.00	
2-7x32	2-7	46.7-13.7	3.9-3.3	11.3	1	Int.	11.3	367.00	
3-9x40[1]	3-9	33.8-11.3	3.6-3.2	12.5	1	Int.	12.5	371.00	
3.5-10x50	3.5-10	25.5-8.9	3.9-3.8	13.7	1	Int.	15.5	489.00	
4-12x40 A.O.	4-12	25.7-8.6	3.6-3.2	14	1	Int.	16.6	476.00	
4-12x50 A.O.	4-12	25.4-8.5	3.6-3.5	14.0	1	Int.	18.3	578.00	
6.5-20x44	6.5-19.4	16.2-5.4	3.5-3.1	14.8	1	Int.	19.6	591.00	
2x20 EER	2	22	26.4	8.1	1	Int.	6.3	213.00	
PARSONS									Adjustable for parallax, focus. Micrometer rear mount with 1/4-min. click adjustments. Price is approximate. Made in U.S. by Parsons Optical Mfg. Co.
Parsons Long Scope	6	10	2	28-34+	3/4	Ext.	13	475.00-525.00	
PENTAX									[1]Glossy finish; matte finish, $530.00; satin chrome, $550.00. [2]Glossy finish; matte finish, $560.00; satin chrome, $580.00. [3]Glossy finish; matte finish, $580.00; satin chrome, $600.00. [4]Glossy-XL finish; matte-XL finish, $720.00; satin chrome-XL finish, $740.00. [5]Glossy finish; matte finish, $770.00. [6]Glossy finish, Fine Plex; matte finish, Fine Plex, $810.00; dot reticle, add $10.00. [7]Glossy finish; matte finish, $504.00; satin chrome, $524.00. [8]Glossy finish; matte finish, $420.00; satin chrome $440.00. [9]Lightseeker II $624.00 glossy, $648.00 matte. [10]Lightseeker II $804.00 glossy, $828.00 matte. [11]Glossy finish; matte finish, $360.00. [12]Glossy finish; matte finish, $440.00. [13]Glossy finish; matte finish, $310.00; Mossy Oak, $330.00. [14]Glossy finish; satin chrome, $260.00. [15]Glossy finish; satin chrome, $380.00. [16]Glossy finish; satin chrome, $390.00. [17]Lightseeker II $836.00 glossy, $844.00 satin chrome. Imported by Pentax Corp.
Lightseeker 2-8x[1]	2-8	53-17	3-3.5	11.7	1	Int.	14.0	530.00	
Lightseeker 3-9x[2,9]	3-9	36-14	3-3.5	12.7	1	Int.	15.0	560.00	
Lightseeker 1.75-6x[7]	1.75-6	71-20	3.5-4	10.75	1	Int.	13.0	484.00	
Lightseeker 3.5-10x[3]	3.5-10	29.5-11	3-3.25	14.0	1	Int.	19.5	588.00	
Lightseeker 3-11x[4]	3-11	38.5-13	3-3.25	13.3	1	Int.	19	700.00	
Lightseeker 4-16x AO[5,10]	4-16	3-3.5	33-9	15.4	1	Int.	23.7	760.00	
Lightseeker 6-24 AO[6,17]	6-24	18-5.5	3-3.25	16	1	Int.	22.7	800.00	
3-9x[8]	3-9	38-14.7	3-3.25	13.0	1	Int.	15.0	400.00	
Shotgun									
Lightseeker Zero-X SG Plus[11]	0	51	4.5-15	8.9	1	Int.	7.9	340.00	
Lightseeker Zero-X/V SG Plus[12]	0-4	53.8-15	3.5-7	8.9	1	Int.	10.3	420.00	
Lightseeker 2.5x SG Plus[13]	2.5	55	3-3.5	10.0	1	Int.	9.0	346.00	
Pistol									
2x[14]	2	21	10-24	8.8	1	Int.	6.8	230.00	
1.5-4x[15]	1.5-4	16-11	11-25, 11-18	10.0	1	Int.	11.0	350.00	
2.5-7x[16]	2.5-7	12-7.5	11-28, 9-14	12.0	1	Int.	12.5	370.00	
RWS									Air gun scopes. All have Dyna-Plex reticle. Model 800 is for air pistols. [1]M450, 3-9x40mm, $200.00. Imported from Japan by Dynamit Nobel-RWS.
300	4	36	3.5	11 3/4	1	Int.	13.2	170.00	
400[1]	2-7	55-16	3.5	11 3/4	1	Int.	13.2	190.00	
450	3-9	43-14	3.5	12	1	Int.	14.3	215.00	
500	4	36	3.5	12 1/4	1	Int.	13.9	225.00	
550	2-7	55-16	3.5	12 3/4	1	Int.	14.3	235.00	
600	3-9	43-14	3.5	13	1	Int.	16.5	260.00	

HUNTING, TARGET & VARMINT SCOPES

Maker and Model	Magn.	Field at 100 Yds. (feet)	Eye Relief (in.)	Length (in.)	Tube Dia. (in.)	W&E Adjustments	Weight (ozs.)	Price	Other Data
REDFIELD									*Accutrac feature avail. on these scopes at extra cost. Traditionals have round lenses. 4-Plex reticle is standard. [1]Magnum proof. Specially designed for magnum and auto pistols. Uses Double Dovetail mounts. Also in nickel-plated finish, 2x, **$239.95**, 4x, **$239.95**, 2½-7x, **$322.95**, 2½-7x matte black, **$322.95**. [2]With matte finish **$619.95**. [3]Also available with matte finish at extra cost. [4]All Golden Five Star scopes come with Butler Creek flip-up lens covers. [5]56mm adj. objective; European #4 or 4-Plex reticle; comes with 30mm steel rings with Rotary Dovetail System. ¼-min. click adj. Also in matte finish, **$805.95**. [6]Also available nickel-plated **$363.95**. [7]With target knob, **$439.95**; black matte finish, **$493.95**; black matte with target knob, **$446.95**. [8]Black matte finish, **$400.95**. [9]Also avail. in black matte, **$246.95**. [10]Also avail. in black matte, **$462.95**; black matte with target knobs, **$480.95**; with Accu-Trac, black matte,**$512.95**. [11]Fine crosshair, black finish; **$681.95** dot reticle or black or fine crosshair and matte finish; **$737.95** with dot, matte; Quick-Zero target knobs, 1/8-MOA reticle, adj. obj. [12]Comes with rings, see-through lens covers, variable intensity, four dial-in sight patterns. Selected models shown. **Contact Redfield for full data.**
Ultimate Illuminator 3-9x	3.4-9.1	27-9	3-3.5	15.1	30mm	Int.	20.5	705.95	
Ultimate Illuminator 3-12x[5]	2.9-11.7	27-10.5	3-3½	15.4	30mm	Int.	23	805.95	
Widefield Illuminator 2-7x	2.0-6.8	56-17	3-3.5	11.7	1	Int.	13.5	539.95	
Widefield Illuminator 3-9x*[2]	2.9-8.7	38-13	3½	12¾	1	Int.	17	609.95	
Widefield Illuminator 3-10x	3-10.1	29-10.5	3-3.5	14.75	1	Int.	18.0	681.95	
Tracker 4x[3]	3.9	28.9	3½	11.02	1	Int.	9.8	187.95	
Tracker 6x[3]	6.2	18	3.5	12.4	1	Int.	11.1	217.95	
Tracker 8x	8.1	13.5	3.5	12.4	1	Int.	11.1	226.95	
Tracker 2-7x[3]	2.3-6.9	36.6-12.2	3½	12.20	1	Int.	11.6	239.95	
Tracker 3-9x[3]	3.0-9.0	34.4-11.3	3½	14.96	1	Int.	13.4	269.95	
Traditional 4x ¾"	4	24½	3½	9⅜	¾	Int.	—	229.95	
Traditional 2½x	2½	43	3½	10¼	1	Int.	8½	161.95	
Golden Five Star 4x[4]	4	28.5	3.75	11.3	1	Int.	9.75	259.95	
Golden Five Star 6x[4]	6	18	3.75	12.2	1	Int.	11.5	282.95	
Golden Five Star 2-7x[4]	2.4-7.4	42-14	3-3.75	11.25	1	Int.	12	333.95	
Golden Five Star 3-9x[4,6]	3.0-9.1	34-11	3-3.75	12.50	1	Int.	13	409.95	
Golden Five Star 3-9x 50mm[4]	3.0-9.1	36.0-11.5	3-3.5	12.8	1	Int.	16	440.95	
Golden Five Star 4-12x A.O.*[4,10]	3.9-11.4	27-9	3-3.75	13.8	1	Int.	16	505.95	
Golden Five Star 6-18x A.O.*[4,7]	6.1-18.1	18.6	3-3.75	14.3	1	Int.	18	483.95	
6-24x Varmint[11]	5.9-23.8	15-5.5	3-3.5	15.75	1	Int.	26	664.95	
I.E.R. 1-4x Shotgun	1.3-3.8	48-16	6	10.2	1	Int.	12	373.95	
Compact Scopes									
Golden Five Star Compact 2-7x	2.4-7.1	40-16	3-3.5	9.75	1	Int.	9.8	329.95	
Golden Five Star Compact 3-9x	3.3-9.1	32-11.25	3-3.5	10.7	1	Int.	10.5	346.95	
Golden Five Star Compact 4-12x	4.1-12.4	22.4-8.3	3-3.5	12	1	Int.	13	439.95	
Hunter									
3-9x	3-9	34.4-11.3	3.5	12.4	1	Int.	12.6	NA	
Handgun Scopes									
Golden Five Star 2x	2	24	9.5-20	7.88	1	Int.	6	223.95	
Golden Five Star 4x	4	75	13-19	8.63	1	Int.	6.1	223.95	
Golden Five Star 2½-7x	2½-7	11-3.75	11-26	9.4	1	Int.	9.3	303.95	
Widefield Low Profile Compact									
Widefield 4xLP Compact	3.7	33	3.5	9.35	1	Int.	10	303.95	
Widefield 3-9x LP Compact	3.3-9	37.0-13.7	3-3.5	10.20	1	Int.	13	387.95	
ESD[12]	—	14.9	—	5.25	30mm	Int.	6.0	NA	
Low Profile Scopes									
Widefield 2¾xLP	2¾	55½	3½	10½	1	Int.	8	283.95	
Widefield 4xLP	3.6	37½	3½	11½	1	Int.	10	317.95	
Widefield 6xLP	5.5	23	3½	12¾	1	Int.	11	340.95	
Widefield 1¾x-5xLP[8]	1¾-5	70-27	3½	10¾	1	Int.	11½	389.95	
Widefield 2x-7xLP*	2-7	49-19	3½	11¾	1	Int.	13	400.95	
Widefield 3x-9xLP*	3-9	39-15	3½	12½	1	Int.	14	445.95	
SCHMIDT & BENDER									All scopes have 30-yr. warranty, click adjustments, centered reticles, rotation indicators. [1]Glass reticle; steel or aluminum. Available in aluminum with mounting rail. [2]Aluminum only. [3]Aluminum tube. Choice of two bullet drop compensators, choice of two sunshades, two rangefinding reticles. From Schmidt & Bender, Inc.
Fixed									
4x36	4	30	3.25	11	1	Int.	14	725.00	
6x42	6	21	3.25	13	1	Int.	17	795.00	
8x56	8	16.5	3.25	14	1	Int.	22	915.00	
10x42	10	10.5	3.25	13	1	Int.	18	910.00	
Variables									
1.25-4x20[1]	1.25-4	96-16	3.25	10	30mm	Int.	15.5	980.00	
1.5-6x42[1]	1.5-6	60-19.5	3.25	12	30mm	Int.	19.7	1,073.00	
2.5-10x56[1]	2.5-10	37.5-12	3.25	14	30mm	Int.	24.6	1,298.00	
3-12x42[2]	3-12	34.5-11.5	3.25	13.5	30mm	Int.	19.0	1,222.00	
3-12x50[1]	3-12	33.3-12.6	3.25	13.5	30mm	Int.	22.9	1,262.00	
Police/Marksman									
Fixed									
6x42[3]	6	21	3.25	13.0	30mm	Int.	17.0	980.00	
10x42[3]	10	10.5	3.25	13.0	30mm	Int.	18	1,055.00	
Variables									
3-12x42[3]	3-12	34.5-11.5	3.25	13.5	30mm	Int.	NA	1,510.00	
3-12x50[3]	3-12	33.3-12.6	3.25	13.5	30mm	Int.	NA	1,550.00	
1.5-6x42[3]	1.5-6	60-19.5	3.25	12.0	30mm	Int.	NA	1,350.00	
SHEPHERD									[1]Also avail. as 310-P, 310-PE, **$524.25**. [2]Also avail. as 310-P1, 310-P2, 310-P3, 310-Pla, 310-PE1, 310-P22, 310-P22 Mag., 310-PE, **$524.95**. All have patented Dual Reticle system with rangefinder bullet drop compensation; multi-coated lenses, waterprooof, shockproof, nitrogen filled, matte finish. Varmint Shepherd Scope, Ltd.
3940-E	3-9	43.5-15	3.3	13	1	Int.	17	1,039.40	
310-2[1,2]	3-10	35.3-11.6	3-3.75	12.8	1	Int.	18	524.25	

CAUTION: PRICES SHOWN ARE SUPPLIED BY THE MANUFACTURER OR IMPORTER. CHECK YOUR LOCAL GUNSHOP.

HUNTING, TARGET & VARMINT SCOPES

Maker and Model	Magn.	Field at 100 Yds. (feet)	Eye Relief (in.)	Length (in.)	Tube Dia. (in.)	W&E Adjustments	Weight (ozs.)	Price	Other Data
SIGHTRON									[1]Black finish; also stainless. [2]3 MOA dot; also with 5 or 10 MOA dot. [3]Variable 3, 5, 10 MOA dot; black finish; also stainless. [4]Satin black; also stainless. Electronic Red Dot scopes come with ring mounts, front and rear extension tubes, polarizing filter, battery, haze filter caps, wrench. Rifle, pistol, shotgun scopes have aluminum tubes, Exac Trak adjustments. Lifetime warranty. From Sightron, Inc.
Electronic Red Dot									
S33-3[1,2]	1	58	—	5.15	33mm	Int.	5.43	279.99	
S33-30[3]	1	58	—	5.74	33mm	Int.	6.27	369.99	
Riflescopes									
Variables									
SII 1.56x42	1.5-6	51-16	3.8-4.0	11.8	1	Int.	15.35	377.99	
SII 39x42[4]	3-9	34-12	3.6-4.2	12.34	1	Int.	13.22	358.99	
Fixed									
SII 4x42	4	31	4.0	12.48	1	Int.	12.34	289.99	
SII 6x42[4]	6	20	4.0	12.48	1	Int.	12.34	289.99	
SII 8x42[4]	8	16	4.0	12.48	1	Int.	12.34	289.99	
Target									
SII 24x44	24	4	4.33	13.26	1	Int.	15.87	406.99	
SII 416x42	4-16	27-7	3.5-3.6	13.74	1	Int.	16.0	426.99	
SII 624-42	6-24	16-5	3.7-3.8	14.7	1	Int.	18.7	449.99	
Compact									
SII 4x32	4	25	4.5	9.72	1	Int.	9.34	247.99	
Shotgun									
SII 2.5x20SG	2.5	41	4.3	10.23	1	Int.	8.46	232.99	
Pistol									
SII 1x28P[1]	1	30	9.0-24.0	9.44	1	Int.	8.46	197.99	
SII 2x28P[1]	2	16-10	9.0-24.0	9.56	1	Int.	8.28	196.99	
SIMMONS									[1]Matte; also polished finish. [2]Silver; also black matte or polished. [3]Black matte finish. [4]Granite finish; black polish $216.95; silver $218.95; also with 50mm obj., black granite $336.95. [5]Camouflage. [6]Black polish. [7]With ring mounts. [8]Black polished; also black or silver matte. [9]Lighted reticle, Black Granite finish. [10]50mm obj.; black matte. [11]Black or silver matte. [12]75-yd. parallax; black or silver matte. [13]TV view. [14]Adj. obj. [15]V-TAC reticle in 1st focal plane; 4" sunshade; flat black. [16]Adj. objective; 4" sunshade; black matte. [17]Black Granite finish; 50-yd. parallax; ProDiamond reticle. [18]Octagon body; rings included; black matter or silver finish. [19]Black matte finish; also available in silver. **Only selected models shown.** Contact Simmons Outdoor Corp. for complete details.
AETEC									
2100[8]	2.8-10	44-14	5	11.9	1	Int.	15.5	349.95	
2104[16]	3.8-12	33-11	4	13.5	1	Int.	20.0	364.95	
V-TAC									
3006[15]	3-9	33-11	4.1-3.0	12 3/8	1	Int.	25.25	699.95	
44 Mag									
M-1044[11]	3-10	36.2-10.5	3.4-3.3	13.1	1	Int.	16.3	259.95	
M-1045	4-12	27-9	3	12.6	1	Int.	19.5	279.95	
M-1047	6.5-20	14-.5	2.6-3.4	12.8	1	Int.	19.5	289.95	
Prohunter									
7700[1]	2-7	58-17	3.25	11.6	1	Int.	12.4	169.95	
7710[2]	3-9	40-15	3	12.6	1	Int.	13.4	179.95	
7716	4-12	29.6-10.0	3	13.6	1	Int.	20	199.95	
7720	6-18	38-13	2.5	12.5	1	Int.	13.5	224.95	
7740[3]	6	34.1	3	12.6	1	Int.	9.5	144.95	
Prohunter Handgun									
7732[19]	2	21.5	10.5-26.4	7.8	1	Int.	5.75	179.95	
7738[19]	4	7	10.5-26.4	8.5	1	Int.	7.25	189.95	
7744[19]	2.5-7	11-4	15.7-19.7	9.3	1	Int.	9.0	229.95	
Whitetail Classic									
WTC9[9]	3	11.5	11-20	9.0	1	Int.	9.2	329.95	
WTC11	1.5-5	80-23.5	3.4-3.2	12.6	1	Int.	11.8	184.95	
WTC12	2.5-8	46.5-14.5	3.2-3	12.6	1	Int.	12.8	199.95	
WTC13	3.5-10	35-12	3.2-3	12.4	1	Int.	12.8	219.95	
WTC16	4	36.8	4	9.9	1	Int.	12	149.95	
WTC17	4-12	26-7.9	3	12.8	1	Int.	19.5	329.95	
Pro50									
8830[10]	2.5-10	30.5-11	3.2	12.75	1	Int.	13.0	169.95	
8800[10]	4-12	27-9	3.5	13.2	1	Int.	18.25	179.95	
8810[10]	6-18	17-5.8	3.6	13.2	1	Int.	18.25	199.95	
Master Red Dot									
51004[11]	1	40	—	5.25	30mm	Int.	4.8	269.95	
Deerfield									
21006	4	28	4	12.0	1	Int.	9.1	74.95	
21029	3-9	32-11	3.4	12.6	1	Int.	12.3	104.95	
21031	4-12	28-11	3-2.8	13.9	1	Int.	14.6	139.95	
Gold Medal Silhouette									
23002	6-20	17.4-5.4	3	14.5	1	Int.	18.3	529.95	
Gold Medal Handgun									
22002[6]	2.5-7	9.7-4.0	8.9-19.4	9.25	1	Int.	9.0	329.95	
22004[6]	2	3.9	8.6-19.5	7.3	1	Int.	7.4	229.95	
22006[6]	4	8.9	9.8-18.7	9	1	Int.	8.8	269.95	
Shotgun									
21005	2.5	29	4.6	7.1	1	Int.	7.2	99.95	
7789D	2	27	6	8.8	1	Int.	8.1	129.95	
7788	1	60	3.8	9.4	1	Int.	10.2	129.95	
7790D	4	16	5.5	8.8	1	Int.	9.2	139.95	
7791D	1.5-5	75-23	3.4	9.3	1	Int.	9.7	139.95	
WTC89D[17]	2	31	5.5	8.8	1	Int.	8.75	159.95	
Rimfire									
1022[7]	4	36	3.5	11.5	1	Int.	10	74.95	
Blackpowder									
BP0420M[18]	4	19.5	4	7.5	1	Int.	8.3	139.95	
BP2520M[12]	2.5	24	6	7.4	1	Int.	7.3	109.95	
BP420M[12]	4	19.5	4	7.5	1	Int.	8.3	109.95	
BP2732M[12]	2-7	57.7-16.6	3	11.6	1	Int.	12.4	129.95	

HUNTING, TARGET & VARMINT SCOPES

Maker and Model	Magn.	Field at 100 Yds. (feet)	Eye Relief (in.)	Length (in.)	Tube Dia. (in.)	W&E Adjust-ments	Weight (ozs.)	Price	Other Data
Simmons (cont.)									
Fireview									
21507[13]	4	34	3.3	12.8	1	Int.	9	89.95	
21513[13]	3-9	40-13	3.5-2.6	12.8	1	Int.	11.7	99.95	
Competition Air Gun									
21612[14]	4-12	25-9	3.1-2.9	13.1	1	Int.	15.8	179.95	
21618[14]	6-18	18-7	2.9-2.7	13.8	1	Int.	18.2	189.95	
STEINER									
Penetrator									
6x42	6	20.4	3.1	14.8	26mm	Int.	14	1,099.00	Waterproof, fogproof, nitrogen filled, accordion-type eye cup. [1]Heavy-duplex or European #4 reticle. Aluminum tubes; matte black finish. From Pioneer Research.
8x56	8	15	3.1	14.8	26mm	Int.	17	1,299.00	
Hunting Z									
1.5-5x20[1]	1.5-5	32-12	4.3	9.6	30mm	Int.	11.7	1,499.00	
2.5-8x36[1]	2.5-8	40-15	4	11.6	30mm	Int.	13.4	1,799.00	
3.5-10x50[1]	3.5-10	77-25	4	12.4	30mm	Int.	16.9	1,899.00	
SWAROVSKI HABICHT									
PH Series									
1.25-4x24[1]	1.25-4	86-27	4.5	10.6	30mm	Int.	15.9	987.78	All models offered in either steel or lightweight alloy tubes. Weights shown are for lightweight versions. Choice of nine constantly centered reticles. Eyepiece recoil mechanism and rubber ring shield to protect face. American-style plex reticle available in 2.2-9x42 and 3-12x56 traditional European scopes. [1]Alloy weighs 12.3 oz. [2]Alloy weighs 15.9 oz, [3]Alloy weighs 14.8 oz. [4]Alloy weighs 18.3 oz. [5]Alloy weighs 16.6 oz. Imported by Swarovski Optik North America Ltd.
1.5-6x42[2]	1.5-6	65.4-21	3.75	13	30mm	Int.	20.5	1,100.00	
2.5-10x42[3]	2.5-10	39.6-12.3	3.75	13.2	30mm	Int.	19.4	1,276.67	
2.5-10x56[4]	2.5-10	39.6-12.3	3.75	14.7	30mm	Int.	24.3	1,376.67	
3-12x50[5]	3-12	33-10.5	3.75	14.3	30mm	Int.	22.0	1,698.89	
6x42	6	23	3.25	12.6	1	Int.	17.9	921.11	
8x50	8	17	3.25	14.4	30mm	Int.	19.9	954.44	
8x56	8	17	3¼	14.4	30mm	Int.	23	998.89	
AL Series									
4x32A	4	30	3.2	11.5	1	Int.	10.8	554.44	
6x36A	6	21	3.2	11.9	1	Int.	11.5	610.00	
1.5-4.5x20A	1.5-4.5	75-25.8	3.5	9.53	1	Int.	10.6	656.56	
3-9x36	3-9	39-13.5	3.3	11.9	1	Int.	13	698.89	
SWIFT									
600 4x15	4	16.2	2.4	11	¾	Int.	4.7	24.00	All Swift scopes, with the exception of the 4x15, have Quadraplex reticles and are fogproof and waterproof. The 4x15 has crosshair reticle and is non-waterproof. [1]Available in black or silver finish—same price. [2]Comes with ring mounts, wrench, lens caps, extension tubes, filter, battery. From Swift Instruments.
601 3-7x20	3-7	25-12	3-2.9	11	1	Int.	5.6	53.00	
649 4-12x50	4-12	30-10	3-2.8	13.2	1	Int.	14.6	216.00	
650 4x32	4	29	3.5	12	1	Int.	9	80.00	
653 4x40WA[1]	4	35.5	3.75	12.25	1	Int.	12	98.00	
654 3-9x32	3-9	35.75-12.75	3	12.75	1	Int.	13.75	95.00	
656 3-9x40WA[1]	3-9	42.5-13.5	2.75	12.75	1	Int.	14	103.00	
657 6x40	6	18	3.75	13	1	Int.	10	99.50	
660 4x20	4	25	4	11.8	1	Int.	9	80.00	
664 4-12x40[1]	4-12	27-9	3-2.8	13.3	1	Int.	14.8	143.00	
665 1.5-4.5x21	1.5-4.5	69-24.5	3.5-3	10.9	1	Int.	9.6	98.00	
666 Shotgun 1x20	1	113	3.2	7.5	1	Int.	9.6	102.00	
667 Fire-Fly[2]	1	—	—	5.3	30mm	Int.	5	215.00	
668M 4x32	4	25	4	10	1	Int.	8.9	95.00	
Pistol Scopes									
661 4x32	4	90	10-22	9.2	1	Int.	9.5	115.00	
662 2.5x32	2.5	14.3	9-22	8.9	1	Int.	9.3	110.00	
663 2x20[1]	2	18.3	9-21	7.2	1	Int.	8.4	115.00	
TASCO									
Titan									
T1.56x42N	1.5-6	59-20	3.5	12	30mm	Int.	16.4	680.00	[1]Water, fog & shockproof; fully coated optics; ¼-min. click stops; haze filter caps; 30-day/limited lifetime warranty. [2]30/30 range finding reticle. [3]World Class Wide Angle; Supercon multi-coated optics; Opti-Centered® 30/30 range finding reticle; lifetime warranty. [4]⅓ greater zoom range. [5]Trajectory compensating scopes, Opti-Centered® stadia reticle. [6]Anodized finish. [7]True one-power scope. [8]Coated optics; crosshair reticle; ring mounts included to fit most 22, 10mm receivers. [9]Fits Remington 870, 1100, 11-87. [10]Electronic dot reticle with rheostat; coated optics; adj. for windage and elevation; waterproof, shockproof, fogproof; Lithium battery; 3x power booster avail.; matte black or matte aluminum finish; dot or T-3 reticle. [11]TV view. [12]Also matte aluminum finish. [13]Also with crosshair reticle. [14]Also 30/30 reticle. [15]Dot size 1.5" at 100 yds.; waterproof. [16]Also in stainless finish. [17]Black matte or stainless finish. [18]Also with stainless finish. [19]Also in matte black. [20]Available with 5-min. or 10-min. dot. [21]Available with 10, 15, 20-min. dot. [22]20mm; also 32mm. [23]20mm; black matte; also stainless steel; also 32mm. Contact Tasco for details on complete line.
T39x42N	3-9	37-13	3.5	12.5	30mm	Int.	16.8	645.00	
T312x52N	3-12	27-10	4.5	14	30mm	Int.	20.7	764.00	
Big Horn									
BH2.510x50	2.5-10	44-11	4	13.5	1	Int.	16	611.00	
BH4.518x50	4.5-18	30-7.3	4	13.5	1	Int.	16	679.00	
World Class									
WA4x40	4	36	3	13	1	Int.	11.5	135.00	
WA6x40	6	23	3	12.75	1	Int.	11.5	144.00	
WA13.5x20[1,3,10]	1-3.5	115-31	3.5	9.75	1	Int.	10.2	161.00	
WA1.75-5x20[1,3]	1.75-5	72-24	3	10⅝	1	Int.	10.0	152.00	
WA2.58x40[18]	2.5-8	44-14	3	11.75	1	Int.	14.25	178.00	
WA27x32[1,3,9]	2-7	56-17	3.25	11.5	1	Int.	12	161.00	
WA39x40[1,3,6,11,18]	3-9	43.5-15	3	12.75	1	Int.	13.0	199.00	
World Class Airgun									
AG4x40WA	4	36	3	13	1	Int.	14	374.00	
AG39x50WA	3-9	41-14	3	15	1	Int.	17.5	509.00	
World Class Electronic									
ERD39x40WA	3-9	41-14	3	12.75	1	Int.	16	323.00	
World Class Mag IV-44									
WC2510x44[6,19]	2.5-10	41-11	3.5	12.5	1	Int.	14.4	305.00	
World Class TS									
TS24x44[19]	24	4.5	3	14	1	Int.	17.9	407.00	
TS36x44[19]	36	3	3	14	1	Int.	17.9	441.00	
TS832x44[19]	8-24	11-3.5	3	14	1	Int.	19.5	492.00	
TS624x44[19]	6-24	15-4.5	3	14	1	Int.	18.5	475.00	

CAUTION: PRICES SHOWN ARE SUPPLIED BY THE MANUFACTURER OR IMPORTER. CHECK YOUR LOCAL GUNSHOP.

HUNTING, TARGET & VARMINT SCOPES

Maker and Model	Magn.	Field at 100 Yds. (feet)	Eye Relief (in.)	Length (in.)	Tube Dia. (in.)	W&E Adjustments	Weight (ozs.)	Price	Other Data
Tasco (cont.)									
World Class TR									
TR39x40WA	3-9	41-14	3	13.0	1	Int.	12.5	305.00	
World Class Pistol									
PWC2x22[12]	2	25	11-20	8.75	1	Int.	7.3	288.00	
PWC4x28[12]	4	8	12-19	9.45	1	Int.	7.9	340.00	
P1.254x28[12]	1.25-4	23-9	15-23	9.25	1	Int.	8.2	339.00	
Mag IV									
W312x40[1,2,4]	3-12	35-9	3	12.25	1	Int.	12	152.00	
W416x40[1,2,4,16,17]	4-16	26-7	3	14.25	1	Int.	15.6	203.00	
W624x40	6-24	17-4	3	15.25	1	Int.	16.8	255.00	
Golden Antler									
GA4x32TV	4	32	3	13	1	Int.	12.7	79.00	
GA4x40TV	4	32	3	12	1	Int.	12.5	85.00	
GA39x32TV[11]	3-9	39-13	3	—	1	Int.	12.2	102.00	
GA39x40TV	3-9	39-13	3	12.5	1	Int.	13	135.00	
GA39x40WA	3-9	41-15	3	12.75	1	Int.	13	152.00	
Silver Antler									
SA2.5x32	2.5	42	3¼	11	1	Int.	10	99.00	
SA4x40	4	32	3	12	1	Int.	12.5	85.00	
SA39x32	3-9	39-13	3	13.25	1	Int.	12.2	101.00	
SA39x40[12]	3-9	41-15	3	12.75	1	Int.	13	152.00	
SA39x40	3-9	39-13	3	12.5	1	Int.	13	135.00	
SA4x32[12]	4	32	3	13	1	Int.	12.7	79.00	
Pronghorn									
PH2.5x32	2.5	42	3.25	11	1	Int.	10	76.00	
PH4x32	4	32	3	12	1	Int.	12.5	61.00	
PH4x40	4	36	3	13	1	Int.	11.5	83.00	
PH6x40	6	20	3	12.5	1	Int.	11.5	90.00	
PH39x32	3-9	39-13	3	12	1	Int.	11	83.00	
PH39x40	3-9	39-13	3	13	1	Int.	12.1	110.00	
High Country									
HC416x40	4-16	26-7	3.25	14.25	1	Int.	15.6	254.00	
HC624x10	6-24	17-4	3	15.25	1	Int.	16.8	280.00	
HC39x40	3-9	41-15	3	12.75	1	Int.	13.0	195.00	
HC3.510x40	3.5-10	30-10.5	3	11.75	1	Int.	14.25	220.00	
Rubber Armored									
RC39x40A	3-9	35-12	3.25	12.5	1	Int.	14.3	255.00	
TR Scopes									
TR39x40WA	3-9	41-14	3	13	1	Int.	12.5	305.00	
TR416x40	4-16	26-7	3	14.25	1	Int.	16.8	373.00	
TR624x40	6-24	17-4	3	15.5	1	Int.	17.5	407.00	
Bantam									
S1.5-45x20[22]	1.5-4.5	69.5-23	4	10.25	1	Int.	10	NA	
S2.5x20[23]	2.5	22	6	7.5	1	Int.	7.5	NA	
Airgun									
AG4x20	4	20	2.5	10.75	.75	Int.	5	40.00	
AG4x40WA	4	36	3	13.0	1	Int.	14	373.00	
AG4x32N	4	30	3	—	1	Int.	12.25	144.00	
AG27x32	2-7	48-17	3	12.25	1	Int.	14	178.00	
AG37x20	3-7	24-11	3	11.5	1	Int.	6.5	73.00	
AG39x50WA	3-9	41-14	3	15	1	Int.	17.5	475.00	
Rimfire									
RF4x15[8]	4	22.5	2.5	11	.75	Int.	4	17.00	
RF4x32[19]	4	31	3	12.25	1	Int.	12.6	86.00	
RF37x20	3-7	24-11	2.5	11.5	.75	Int.	5.7	45.00	
P1.5x15	1.5	22.5	9.5-20.75	8.75	.75	Int.	3.25	37.00	
Propoint									
PDP2[10,12,20]	1	40	—	5	30mm	Int.	5	254.00	
PDP3[10,12,20]	1	52	—	5	30mm	Int.	5	367.00	
PDP4[17,21]	1	82	—	—	45mm	Int.	6.1	458.00	
PB1[13]	3	35	3	5.5	30mm	Int.	6.0	183.00	
PB3	2	30	—	1.25	30mm	Int.	2.6	214.00	
PDP3CMP	1	68	—	4.75	33mm	Int.	—	390.00	
PDP5	1	82	—	5.5	45mm	Int.	9.1	340.00	
World Class Plus									
WCP4x44	4	32	3¼	12.75	1	Int.	13.5	271.00	
WCP3.510x50[19]	3.5-10	30-10.5	3¾	13	1	Int.	17.1	407.00	
WCP6x44	6	21	3.25	12.75	1	Int.	13.6	288.00	
WCP39x44[1,17]	3-9	39-14	3.5	12.75	1	Int.	15.8	305.00	
LaserPoint LP2[15]	—	—	—	2	⅝	Int.	.75	374.00	
THOMPSON/CENTER RECOIL PROOF SCOPES									
Pistol Scopes									
8356[1]	2	22.1	10.5-26.4	7⅘	1	Int.	6.4	264.00	
8312[2]	2.5	15	9-21	7⅖	1	Int.	6.6	227.00	
8315[3]	2.5-7	15-5	8-21, 8-11	9¼	1	Int.	9.2	324.00	
8352[4]	4	22.1	10.5-26.4	7⅘	1	Int.	6.4	300.00	
8320[5]	2.5	15	9-21	7⅖	1	Int.	8.2	342.00	
8326[6]	2.5-7	15-5	8-21, 8-11	9¼	1	Int.	10.5	389.00	
8650[7]	1	40	—	5¼	30mm	Int.	4.8	265.00	

[1]Black finish; silver, **$269.00**. [2]Rail mount. [3]Black finish; silver, **$357.00**. [4]Black; silver, **$305.00**. [5]Lighted reticle, black, rail mount; std. mount, **$314.00**; silver, std., **$329**. [6]Lighted reticle, black. [7]Red dot scope. [8]lighted reticle. [9]Adj. obj. [10]Adj. obj. [11]Matte black; silver finish **$165.00**. From Thompson/Center.

HUNTING, TARGET & VARMINT SCOPES

Maker and Model	Magn.	Field at 100 Yds. (feet)	Eye Relief (in.)	Length (in.)	Tube Dia. (in.)	W&E Adjust-ments	Weight (ozs.)	Price	Other Data
Thompson/Center (cont.)									
Muzzleloader Scopes									
8626[8]	3-9	33-11	3	10¾	1	Int.	10.1	411.00	
8658	1	60	3.8	9⅛	1	Int.	10.2	128.00	
8656[11]	1.5-5	53-16	3	11½	1	Int.	12.5	160.00	
8664[9]	6-18	18.8-6.2	3	14⅓	1	Int.	13.5	210.00	
8666[10]	4-12	26.7-9	3	12⅘	1	Int.	19.5	263.00	
TRIJICON									
Reflex	1	—	—	4.25	1.35	Int.	—	299.00	[1]Also 24mm. [2]Also 20mm, $495.00 to $595.00. [3]Advanced Combat Optical Gunsight for AR-15, M-16, with integral mount. From Trijicon, Inc.
1x16[1]	1	43.8	4.4	4.6	—	Int.	—	467.00	
1.5x16[1]	1.5	43.8	2.4	4.1	—	Int.	—	495.00-595.00	
2x16[2]	2	43.8	1.6	3.7	—	Int.	—	485.00-585.00	
2.5x20	2.5	43.8	1.4	4.2	—	Int.	—	519.00-619.00	
2.25x24	2.25	28.9	2	5.1	—	Int.	—	519.00-619.00	
3x24	3	28.9	1.4	4.8	—	Int.	—	519.00-619.00	
Variables									
2.5-10x42	2.5-10	7.4-2.3	4.3-3.3	13.4	—	Int.	—	1,276.00	
3-12x56	3-12	6.6-1.9	3.9-3.3	14.4	—	Int.	—	1,396.00	
8-24x56	8-24	—	—	—	—	Int.	—	1,700.00	
ACOG 3.5x35	3.5	29	2.4	8.0	—	Int.	14.0	1,295.00	
ACOG 4x32[3]	4	37	1.5	5.8	—	Int.	9.7	1,195.00	
UNERTL									
1" Target	6,8,10	16-10	2	21½	¾	Ext.	21	307.00	[1]Dural ¼-MOA click mounts. Hard coated lenses. Non-rotating objective lens focusing. [2]¼-MOA click mounts. [3]With target mounts. [4]With calibrated head. [5]Same as 1" Target but without objective lens focusing. [6]With new Posa mounts. [7]Range focus unit near rear of tube. Price is with Posa or standard mounts. Magnum clamp. From Unertl.
1¼" Target[1]	8,10,12,14	12-16	2	25	¾	Ext.	21	399.00	
1½" Target	10,12,14, 16,18,20	11.5-3.2	2¼	25½	¾	Ext.	31	416.00	
2" Target[2]	10,12,14, 16,18,24, 30,32,36	8	2¼	26¼	1	Ext.	44	549.00	
Varmint, 1¼"[3]	6,8,10,12	1-7	2½	19½	⅞	Ext.	26	395.00	
Ultra Varmint, 2"[4]	8,10,12,15	12.6-7	2½	24	1	Ext.	34	538.00	
Small Game[5]	3,4,6	25-17	2¼	18	¾	Ext.	16	243.00	
Programmer 200[7]	10,12,14, 16,18,20, 24,30,36	11.3-4	—	26½	1	Ext.	45	688.00	
BV-20[8]	20	8	4.4	17⅞	1	Ext.	21¼	508.00	
Tube Sight	—	—	—	17	—	Ext.	—	226.00	
U.S. OPTICS									
SN-1/TAR Fixed Power System									
9.6x	10	11.3	3.8	14.5	30mm	Int.	24	1,100.00	Prices shown are estimates; scopes built as ordered, to order; choice of reticles; choice of front or rear focal plane; extra-heavy MIL-SPEC construction; extra-long turrets; individual w&e rebound springs; up to 88mm dia. objectives; up to 50mm tubes; all lenses multi-coated. Made in U.S. by U. S. Optics.
16.2x	15	8.6	4.3	16.5	30mm	Int.	27	1,200.00	
22.4x	20	5.8	3.8	18.0	30mm	Int.	29	1,300.00	
26x	24	5.0	3.4	18.0	30mm	Int.	31	1,400.00	
31x	30	4.6	3.5	18.0	30mm	Int.	32	1,500.00	
37x	36	4.0	3.6	18.0	30mm	Int.	32	1,600.00	
42x	40	3.6	3.7	18.0	30mm	Int.	32	1,700.00	
48x	50	3.0	3.8	18.0	30mm	Int.	32	1,800.00	
Variables									
SN-2	4-22	26.8-5.8	5.4-3.8	18.0	30mm	Int.	24	1,256.00	
SN-3	1.6-8	—	4.4-4.8	18.4	30mm	Int.	36	1,010.00	
SN-4	1-4	116-31.2	4.6-4.9	18.0	30mm	Int.	35	680.00	
Fixed Power									
SN-6	4,6,8,10	—	4.2-4.8	9.2	30mm	Int.	18	655.00	
SN-8	4, 10, 20, 40	32	3.3	7.5	30mm	Int.	11.1	620.00	
WEAVER									
K2.5	2.5	35	3.7	9.5	1	Int.	7.3	150.93	Micro-Trac adjustment system with ¼-minute clicks on all T-Series. All have Dual-X reticle. One-piece aluminum tube, satin finish, nitrogen filled, multi-coated lenses, waterproof. [1]Also available in matte finish: V3, $208.29; K4, $171.91; V9, $226.86; V10, $241.15; V10 stainless, $238.42. [2]Available with Dual-X, fine crosshair or ¼-min. dot reticles. [3]4 MOA red dot; also with 12 MOA dot; comes with Weaver q.d. rings. [4]Variable 4, 8, 12 MOA red dot; comes with Weaver q.d. rings. [5]4 MOA, 12 MOA, variable 4, 8, 12 MOA $364.86; matte finish $383.11. [6]Stainless finish, $226.42. [7]Stainless, finish, $232.04. [8]Stainless finish, $287.58. [9]Gloss; matte $285.04; stainless $292.36. [10]Stainless or matte finish. [11]Matte finish $312.58. [12]Matte or stainless finish $321.54. From Weaver.
K4[1]	3.7	26.5	3.3	11.3	1	Int.	10	171.15	
K6	5.7	18.5	3.3	11.4	1	Int.	10	185.43	
V3[1]	1.1-2.8	88-32	3.9-3.7	9.2	1	Int.	8.5	192.29	
V9[1]	2.8-8.7	33-11	3.5-3.4	12.1	1	Int.	11.1	213.16	
V9x50[11]	3-9	29.4-9.9	3.6-3.0	13.1	1	Int.	14.5	310.63	
V10[1]	2.2-9.6	38.5-9.5	3.4-3.3	12.2	1	Int.	11.2	231.15	
V10x50[12]	2.3-9.7	40.2-9.2	2.9-2.8	13.75	1	Int.	15.2	310.69	
V16[2]	3.8-15.5	26.8-6.8	3.1	13.9	1	Int.	16.5	401.15	
KT15	14.6	7.5	3.2	12.9	1	Int.	14.7	364.00	
T-10 Varminter	10	9.3	3.0	15.1	1	Int.	16.7	824.02	
T-16	16	6.5	3.0	15.1	1	Int.	16.7	830.49	
T-24	24	4.4	3.0	15.1	1	Int.	16.7	837.00	
T-36	36	3.0	3.0	15.1	1	Int.	16.7	843.47	
Rimfire									
R4[10]	3.9	29	3.7	9.7	1	Int.	8.8	136.07	
RV7[10]	2.5-7	37-13	3.3	10.75	1	Int.	10.7	158.73	
Qwik-Point									
QP30[3]	1	12.6	—	5.39	30mm	Int.	5.3	235.81	
QP33[4]	1	14.4	—	5.74	33mm	Int.	6.3	383.11	

CAUTION: PRICES SHOWN ARE SUPPLIED BY THE MANUFACTURER OR IMPORTER. CHECK YOUR LOCAL GUNSHOP.

HUNTING, TARGET & VARMINT SCOPES

Maker and Model	Magn.	Field at 100 Yds. (feet)	Eye Relief (in.)	Length (in.)	Tube Dia. (in.)	W&E Adjust- ments	Weight (ozs.)	Price	Other Data
Weaver (cont.)									
QP45[5]	1	21.8	—	4.8	45mm	Int.	8.46	296.19	
Handgun									
2x28[6]	2	21	4-29	8.5	1	Int.	6.7	214.52	
VH8 2.5-8x28[9]	2.5-8	8.5-3.7	12-16	9.3	1	Int.	8.3	280.58	
4x28[7]	4	18	11.5-18	8.5	1	Int.	6.7	226.42	
1.5-4x20[8]	1.5-4	13.5-5.8	12-24, 10.5-17	8.6	1	Int.	8.1	275.68	
ZEISS									All scopes have ¼-minute click-stop adjustments. Choice of Z-Plex or fine crosshair reticles. Rubber armored objective bell, rubber eyepiece ring. Lenses have T-Star coating for highest light transmission. Z-Series scopes offered in non-rail tubes with duplex reticles only; 1" and 30mm. Black matte finish. ²Also in stainless matte finish. ³Also with illuminated reticle, $1,738.00. Bullet Drop Compensator avail. for all Z-Series scopes. Imported from Germany by Carl Zeiss Optical, Inc.
Diatal Z 6x42	6	22.9	3.2	12.7	1.02 (26mm)	Int.	13.4	917.00	
Diatal Z 8x56	8	18	3.2	13.8	1.02 (26mm)	Int.	17.6	1,092.00	
Diavari 1.25-4x24	1.25-4	105-33	3.2	11.46	30mm	Int.	17.3	1,041.00	
Diavari Z 2.5x10x48[1,2]	2.5-10	33-11.7	3.2	14.5	30mm	Int.	24	1,407.00	
Diavari C 3-9x36	3-9	36-13	3.5	11.2	1	Int.	15.2	783.00	
Diavari Z 1.5-6x42[1,2]	1.5-6	65.5-22.9	3.2	12.4	1.18 (30mm)	Int.	18.5	1,190.00	
Diavari Z 3-12x56[1,2,3]	3-12	27.6-9.9	3.2	15.3	1.18 (30mm)	Int.	25.8	1,515.00	

Hunting scopes in general are furnished with a choice of reticle—crosshairs, post with crosshairs, tapered or blunt post, or dot crosshairs, etc. The great majority of target and varmint scopes have medium or fine crosshairs but post or dot reticles may be ordered. W—Windage E—Elevation MOA—Minute of angle or 1" (approx.) at 100 yards, etc.

Laseraim G1/G1 HOT.

Bushnell HOLOsight.

Laseraim LA93 Illusion III.

Weaver V9x50 3-9x.

ADCO MiRAGE Ranger 1" Red Dot.

Simmons 4x20 Black Powder scope.

SCOPE MOUNTS

Maker, Model, Type	Adjust.	Scopes	Price
AIMPOINT	No	1"	$49.95-89.95
Laser Mounts[1]	No	1", 30mm	51.95

Mounts/rings for all Aimpoint sights and 1" scopes. For many popular revolvers, auto pistols, shotguns, military-style rifles/carbines, sporting rifles. Most require no gunsmithing. [1]Mounts Aimpoint Laser-dot below barrel; many popular handguns, military-style rifles. Contact Aimpoint.

Maker, Model, Type	Adjust.	Scopes	Price
AIMTECH			
Handguns			
AMT Auto Mag II, III	No	1"	56.99-64.95
Auto Mag IV	No	1"	64.95
Astra revolvers	No	1"	63.25
Beretta/Taurus auto	No	1"	63.25
Browning Buck Mark/Challenger II	No	1"	56.99
Browning Hi-Power	No	1"	63.25
Glock 17, 17L, 19, 22, 23	No	1"	63.25
Govt. 45 Auto	No	1"	63.25
Rossi revolvers	No	1"	63.25
Ruger Mk I, Mk II	No	1"	49.95
S&W K,L,N frame	No	1"	63.25
S&W Model 41 Target	No	1"	63.25
S&W Model 52 Target	No	1"	63.25
S&W 45, 9mm autos	No	1"	56.99
S&W 422/622/2206	No	1"	56.99
Taurus revolvers	No	1"	63.25
TZ/CZ/P9 9mm	No	1"	63.25
Rifles			
AR-15	No	1"	21.95
Browning A-Bolt	No	1"	21.95
Knight MK85	No	1"	21.95
Remington 700	No	1"	21.95
Ruger 10/22	No	1"	21.95
Savage 110G	No	1"	21.95
Winchester 70	No	1"	21.95
Winchester 94	No	1"	21.95
Shotguns			
Benelli Super 90	No	1"	40.95
Ithaca 37	No	1"	40.95
Mossberg 500	No	1"	40.95
Mossberg 835 Ultimag	No	1"	40.95
Mossberg 5500	No	1"	40.95
Remington 870/1100	No	1"	40.95
Winchester 1300/1400	No	1"	40.95

Mount scopes, lasers, electronic sights using Weaver-style base. All mounts allow use of iron sights; no gunsmithing. Available in satin black or satin stainless finish. **Partial listing shown.** Contact maker for full details. From L&S Technologies, Inc.

Maker, Model, Type	Adjust.	Scopes	Price
A.R.M.S.			
M16A1/A2/AR-15	No	Weaver-type rail	59.95
Multibase	No	Weaver-type rail	59.95
M21/14 Mount	No	—	159.00
#19 Weaver/STANAG Throw Lever Rail	No	Weaver-type rail	140.00
STANAG Rings	No	30mm	75.00
Ring Inserts	No	1", 30mm	29.00
#38 Std. Swan Sleeve[1]	No	—	150.00

[1]Avail in three lengths. From A.R.M.S., Inc.

Maker, Model, Type	Adjust.	Scopes	Price
ARMSON			
AR-15[1]	No	1"	45.00
Mini-14[2]	No	1"	66.00
H&K[3]	No	1"	82.00

[1]Fastens with one nut. [2]Models 181, 182, 183, 184, etc. [3]Claw mount. From Trijicon, Inc.

Maker, Model, Type	Adjust.	Scopes	Price
ARMSPORT			
100 Series[1]	No	1" rings. Low, med., high	10.75
104 22-cal.	No	1"	10.75
201 See-Thru	No	1"	13.00
1-Piece Base[2]	No	—	5.50
2-Piece Base[2]	No	—	2.75

[1]Weaver-type rings. [2]Weaver-type base; most poular rifles. Made in U.S. From Armsport.

Maker, Model, Type	Adjust.	Scopes	Price
B-SQUARE			
Pistols			
Beretta/Taurus 92/99[6]	—	1"	69.95
Browning Buck Mark[6]	No	1"	49.95
Colt 45 Auto	E only	1"	69.95
Colt Python/MkIV, 4",6",8"[1,6]	E	1"	59.95
Dan Wesson Clamp-On[2,6]	E	1"	59.95
Ruger 22 Auto Mono-Mount[3]	No	1"	59.95
Ruger Single-Six[4]	No	1"	59.95
Ruger Blackhawk, Super B'hwk[8]	W&E	1"	59.95
Ruger GP-100[9]	No	1"	59.95
Ruger Redhawk[8]	W&E	1"	59.95
S&W 422/2206[9]	No	1"	59.95
Taurus 66[9]	No	1"	59.95
S&W K, L, N frame[2,6]	No	1"	59.95
T/C Contender (Dovetail Base)	W&E	1"	39.95
Rifles			
Charter AR-7	No	1"	29.95
Mini-14 (dovetail/NATO Stanag)[5,6]	W&E	1"	59.95
M-94 Side Mount	W&E	1"	49.95
RWS, Beeman/FWB, Anschutz, Diana, Walther Air Rifles	E only	—	39.95
SMLE Side Mount with rings	W&E	1"	69.95
Military			
AK-47/AKS/SKS-56[10]	No	1"	59.95
AK-47, SKS-56[11]	No	1"	59.95
M1-A[7]	W&E	1"	99.95
AR-15/16[7]	W&E	1"	59.95
FN-LAR/FAL[6,7]	E only	1"	99.95
HK-91/93/94[6,7]	E only	1"	99.95
Shotguns[6]			
Ithaca 37[6]	No	1"	49.95
Mossberg 500, 712, 5500[6]	No	1"	49.95
Rem. 870/1100 (12 & 20 ga.)[6]	No	1"	49.95
Rem. 870, 1100 (and L.H.)[6]	No	1"	49.95
BSL Laser Mounts			
Scope Tube Clamp[12,13,16]	No	—	39.95
45 Auto[12,13,16]	No	—	39.95
SIG P226[12,13,16]	No	—	39.95
Beretta 92F/Taurus PT99[12,13,16]	No	—	39.95
Colt King Cobra, Python, MkV[12,13,16]	No	—	39.95
S&W L Frame[13,16]	No	—	39.95
Browning HP[12,13,16]	No	—	39.95
Glock	No	—	39.95
Star Firestar[12,13,16]	No	—	39.95
Rossi small frame revolver[12,13,16]	No	—	39.95
Taurus 85 revolver[12,13,16]	No	—	39.95
Interlock Rings			
Standard Dovetail[17]	No	1", 30mm	34.95
Vertical Split[18]	No	1", 30mm	12.95
High/View Thru[19]	No	1"	15.95
Tip-Off 3/8" Dovetail[20]	No	1", 30mm	29.95
Interlock Bases			
One-Piece[21]	No	Standard dovetail rings	9.95-10.95

[1]Clamp-on, blue finish; stainless finish $59.95. [2]Blue finish; stainless finish $59.95. [3]Clamp-on, blue; stainless finish $59.95. [4]Dovetail; stainless finish $59.95. [5]No gunsmithing, no sight removal; blue; stainless finish $79.95. [6]Weaver-style rings. Rings not included with Weaver-type bases; stainless finish add $10. [7]NATO Stanag dovetail model, $99.50. [8]Blue; stainless finish $69.95. [9]Blue; stainless finish $69.95. [10]Handguard mounts. [11]Receiver mounts. [12]Stainless finish add $10. [13]Under-barrel mount, no gunsmithing. [14]Ejector rod mount. [15]Guide rod mount. [16]Used with B-Square BSL-1 Laser Sight only. [17]With recoil key. Blue, black matte; stainless finish, $39.95. [18]Blue; stainless finish, $14.95. Blue $16.95, stainless $18.95. [19]Blue; stainless finish, $18.95. [20]Blue; stainless finish, $34.95; 30mm, blue, $39.95, stainless $44.95. [21]Most popular sporting rifles. Mounts for many shotguns, airguns, military and law enforcement guns also available. **Partial listing of mounts shown here.** Contact B-Square for more data.

B-Square makes mounts for the following military rifles: AK47/AKS, Egyptian Hakim, French MAS 1936, M91 Argentine Mauser, Model 98 Brazilian and German Mausers, Model 93, Spanish Mauser (long and short), Model 1916 Mauser, Model 38 and 96 Swedish Mausers, Model 91 Russian (round and octagon receivers), Chinese SKS 56, SMLE No. 1, Mk. III, 1903 Springfield, U.S. 30-cal. Carbine, and others. Those following replace gun's rear sight: AK47/AKS, P14/1917 Enfield, FN49, M1 Garand, M1-A/M14 (no sight removal), SMLE No. 1, Mk III/No. 4 & 5, Mk. 1, 1903/1903-A3 Springfield, Beretta AR 70 (no sight removal).

Maker, Model, Type	Adjust.	Scopes	Price
BEEMAN			
Two-Piece, Med.	No	1"	31.50
Deluxe Two-Piece, High	No	1"	33.00
Deluxe Two-Piece	No	30mm	41.00
Deluxe One-Piece	No	1"	50.00
Dampamount	No	1"	110.00

All grooved receivers and scope bases on all known air rifles and 22-cal. rimfire rifles (1/2" to 5/8"—6mm to 15mm).

Maker, Model, Type	Adjust.	Scopes	Price
BOCK			
Swing ALK[1]	W&E	1", 26mm, 30mm	349.00
Safari KEMEL[2]	W&E	1", 26mm, 30mm	149.00
Claw KEMKA[3]	W&E	1", 26mm, 30mm	224.00

CAUTION: PRICES SHOWN ARE SUPPLIED BY THE MANUFACTURER OR IMPORTER. CHECK YOU LOCAL GUNSHOP.

SCOPE MOUNTS

Maker, Model, Type	Adjust.	Scopes	Price
Bock (cont.)			
ProHunter Fixed[4]	No	1", 26mm, 30mm	95.00

[1] Q.D.; pivots right for removal. For Steyr-Mannlicher, Win. 70, Rem. 700, Mauser 98, Dakota, Sako, Sauer 80, 90. Magnum has extra-wide rings, same price. [2] Heavy-duty claw-type; reversible for front or rear removal. For Steyr-Mannlicher rifles. [3] True claw mount for bolt-action rifles. Also in extended model. For Steyr-Mannlicher, Win. 70, Rem. 700. Also avail. as Gunsmith Bases—bases not drilled or contoured—same price. [4] Extra-wide rings. Imported from Germany by GSI, Inc.

Maker, Model, Type	Adjust.	Scopes	Price
BURRIS			
Supreme (SU) One Piece (T)[1]	W only	1" split rings, 3 heights	1 piece base 27.00-34.00
Trumount (TU) Two Piece (T)	W only	1" split rings, 3 heights	2 piece base 25.00-39.00
Trumount (TU) Two Piece Ext.	W only	1" split rings	31.00
Browning 22-cal. Auto Mount[2]	No	1" split rings	21.00
1" 22-cal. Ring Mounts[3]	No	1" rings—	23.00-46.00
L.E.R. (LU) Mount Bases[4]	W only	1" split rings	25.00-66.00
L.E.R. No Drill-No Tap Bases[4,7,8]	W only	1" split rings	46.00-52.00
Extension Rings[5]	No	1" scopes	44.00-52.00
Ruger Ring Mount[6,9]	W only	1" split rings	52.00-74.00
Std. 1" Rings[9]	—	Low, medium, high heights	35.00-48.00
Zee Rings[9]	—	Fit Weaver bases; medium and high heights	33.00-46.00

[1] Most popular rifles. Universal rings, mounts fit Burris, Universal, Redfield, Leupold and Browning bases. Comparable prices. [2] Browning Standard 22 Auto rifle. [3] Grooved receivers. [4] Universal dovetail; accept Burris, Universal, Redfield, Leupold rings. For Dan Wesson, S&W, Virginian, Ruger Blackhawk, Win. 94. [5] Medium standard front, extension rear, per pair. Low standard front, extension rear, per pair. [6] Compact scopes, scopes with 2" bell, for M77R. [7] Selected rings and bases available with matte Safari or silver finish. [8] For S&W K,L,N frames, Colt Python, Dan Wesson with 6" or longer barrels. [9] Also in 30mm.

Maker, Model, Type	Adjust.	Scopes	Price
CAPE OUTFITTERS			
Quick Detachable	No	1" split rings, lever quick detachable	99.95

Double rifles; Rem. 700-721, Colt Sauer, Sauer 200, Kimber, Win. 61-63-07-100-70, Browning High Power, 22, BLR, BAR, BBR, A-Bolt; Wea. Mark V, Vanguard; Modern Muzzle Loading, Knight, Thompson/Center, CVA rifles, Dixie rifles. All steel; returns to zero. From Cape Outfitters.

Maker, Model, Type	Adjust.	Scopes	Price
CLEAR VIEW			
Universal Rings, Mod. 101[1]	No	1" split rings	21.95
Standard Model[2]	No	1" split rings	21.95
Broad View[3]	No	1"	21.95
22 Model[4]	No	3/4", 7/8", 1"	13.95
SM-94 Winchester[5]	No	1" split rings	23.95
94 EJ[6]	No	1" split rings	21.95

[1] Most rifles by using Weaver-type base; allows use of iron sights. [2] Most popular rifles; allows use of iron sights. [3] Most popular rifles; low profile, wide field of view. [4] 22 rifles with grooved receiver. [5] Side mount. [6] For Win. A.E. From Clear View Mfg.

Maker, Model, Type	Adjust.	Scopes	Price
CONETROL			
Huntur[1]	W only	1", 26mm, 26.5mm solid or split rings, 3 heights	59.88
Gunnur[2]	W only	1", 26mm, 26.5mm solid or split rings, 3 heights	79.92
Custum[3]	W only	1", 26mm, 26.5mm solid or split rings, 3 heights	99.96
One Piece Side Mount Base[4]	W only	1", 26mm, 26.5mm solid or split rings, 3 heights	—
DapTar Bases[5]	W only	1", 26mm, 26.5mm solid or split rings, 3 heights	—
Pistol Bases, 2 or 3-ring[6]	W only	1" scopes	—
Fluted Bases[7]	W only	Standard Conetrol rings	99.96
30mm Rings[8]	W only	30mm	59.88-79.92

[1] All popular rifles, including metric-drilled foreign guns. Price shown for base, two rings. Matte finish. [2] Gunnur grade has mirror-finished rings, satin-finish base. Price shown for base, two rings. [3] Custum grade has mirror-finished rings and mirror-finished, streamlined base. Price shown for base, two rings. [4] Win. 94, Krag, older split-bridge Mannlicher-Schoenauer, Mini-14, etc. Prices same as above. [5] For all popular guns with integral mounting provision, including Sako, BSA, Ithacagun, Ruger, Tikka, H&K, BRNO—$29.94-$49.98—and many others. Also for grooved-receiver rimfires and air rifles. Prices same as above. [6] For XP-100, T/C Contender, Colt SAA, Ruger Blackhawk, S&W. [7] Sculptured two-piece bases as found on fine custom rifles. Price shown is for base alone. Also available unfinished—$79.92, or finished but unblued—$89.91. [8] 30mm rings made in projectionless style, medium height only. Three-ring mount available for T/C Contender and other pistols in Conetrol's three grades. Any Conetrol mount available in stainless or Teflon for double regular cost of grade.

Maker, Model, Type	Adjust.	Scopes	Price
EAW			
Quick-Loc Mount	W&E	1", 26mm	253.00
	W&E	30mm	291.00
Magnum Fixed Mount	W&E	1", 26mm	198.00
	W&E	30mm	215.00

Fit most popular rifles. Avail. in 4 heights, 4 extensions. Reliable return to zero. Stress-free mounting. Imported by New England Custom Gun Svc.

Maker, Model, Type	Adjust.	Scopes	Price
GENTRY			
Feather-Light Rings	No	1", 30mm	75.00

One-piece of stainless or chrome moly; matte blue or gray. From David Gentry.

Maker, Model, Type	Adjust.	Scopes	Price
GRIFFIN & HOWE			
Standard Double Lever (S)	No	1" or 26mm split rings.	405.00

All popular models (Garand $255). All rings $105. Top ejection rings available. Price installed for side mount.

Maker, Model, Type	Adjust.	Scopes	Price
G. G. & G.			
Swan G-3[1]	No	Weaver-type rail	225.00
FN FAL[2]	No	Weaver-type rail	149.00
Remington 700, Win. 70	No	Weaver base	85.00
Sniper Grade Rings	No	1", 30mm	125.00
M-14 Mount	No	1", 30mm	175.00
M-16 Carry Handle Mount	No	1"	80.00

[1] Universal top claw lock. [2] Paratrooper model, $169.00. From Guns, Gear & Gadgets.

Maker, Model, Type	Adjust.	Scopes	Price
IRONSIGHTER			
Wide Ironsighter™	No	1" split rings	35.98
Ironsighter Center Fire[1]	No	1" split rings	32.95
Ironsighter S-94	No	1" split rings	39.95
Ironsighter AR-15/M-16[8]	No	1", 30mm	$103.95
Ironsighter 22-Cal.Rimfire			
Model #570[9]	No	1" split rings	32.95
Model #573[9]	No	30mm split rings	32.95
Model #722	No	1" split rings	17.75
Model #727	No	7/8" split rings	17.75
Series #700[5]	No	1" split rings	32.95
Ruger Base Mounts[6]	No	1", 30mm	83.95
Ironsighter Handguns[4]	No	1" split rings	38.95
Blackpowder Mount[7]	No	1"	32.95-76.95

[1] Most popular rifles, including Ruger Mini-14, H&R M700, and muzzleloaders. Rings have oval holes to permit use of iron sights. [2] For 1" dia. scopes. [3] For 7/8" dia. scopes. [4] For 1" dia. extended eye relief scopes. [5] 702—Browning A-Bolt; 709—Marlin 39A. [6] 732—Ruger 77/22 R&RS, No. 1, Ranch Rifle; 778 fits Ruger 77R, RS. Both 733, 778 fit Ruger integral bases. [7] Fits most popular blackpowder rifles; one model for Holden Ironsighter mounts, one for Weaver rings. [8] Model 716 with 1" #540 rings; Model 717 with 30mm #530 rings. [9] Fits mount rail on Rem. 522 Viper. Adj. rear sight is integral. Some models in stainless finish. From Ironsighter Co.

Maker, Model, Type	Adjust.	Scopes	Price
K MOUNT By KENPATABLE			
Shotgun Mount	No	1", laser or red dot device	49.95
SKS[1]	No	1"	39.95

Wrap-around design; no gunsmithing required. Models for Browning BPS, A-5 12-ga., Sweet 16, 20, Rem. 870/1100 (LTW and L.H.), S&W 916, Mossberg 500, Ithaca 37 & 51 12-ga., S&W 1000/3000, Win. 1400. [1] Requires simple modification to gun. From KenPatable Ent.

Maker, Model, Type	Adjust.	Scopes	Price
KRIS MOUNTS			
Side-Saddle[1]	No	1", 26mm split rings	12.98
Two Piece (T)[2]	No	1", 26mm split rings	8.98
One Piece (T)[3]	No	1", 26mm split rings	12.98

[1] One-piece mount for Win. 94. [2] Most popular rifles and Ruger. [3] Blackhawk revolver. Mounts have oval hole to permit use of iron sights.

Maker, Model, Type	Adjust.	Scopes	Price
KWIK-SITE			
KS-See-Thru[1]	No	1"	31.95
KS-22 See-Thru[2]	No	1"	23.95
KS-W94[3]	No	1"	39.95
Bench Rest	No	1"	31.95
KS-WEV	No	1"	31.95
KS-WEV-HIGH	No	1"	37.95
KS-T22 1"[4]	No	1"	23.95
KS-FL Flashlite[5]	No	Mini or C cell flashlight	49.95
KS-T88[6]	No	1"	11.95
KS-T89	No	30mm	14.95
KSN 22 See-Thru	No	1", 7/8"	20.95
KSN-T22	No	1", 7/8"	20.95
KSN-M16 See-Thru	No	1"	99.95
KS-202[1]	No	1"	31.95
KS-203	No	30mm	43.95
KSBP[7]	No	Intergral	76.95
KSSM[8]	No	1"	31.95

SCOPE MOUNTS

Maker, Model, Type	Adjust.	Scopes	Price
Kwik-Site (cont.)			
KSB Base Set	—	—	5.95
Combo Bases & Rings	No	1"	31.95

Bases interchangeable with Weaver bases. [1]Most rifles. Allows use of iron sights. [2]22-cal. rifles with grooved receivers. Allows use of iron sights. [3]Model 94, 94 Big Bore. No drilling or tapping. Also in adjustable model $49.95. [4]Non-see-through model for grooved receivers. [5]Allows Mag Lite or C or D, Mini Mag Lites to be mounted atop See-Thru mounts. [6]Fits any Redfield, Tasco, Weaver or universal-style Kwik-Site dovetail base. [7]Blackpowder mount with integral rings and sights. [8]Shotgun side mount. Bright blue, black matte or satin finish. Standard, high heights.

Maker, Model, Type	Adjust.	Scopes	Price
LASER AIM	No	Laser Aim	19.00-69.00

Mounts Laser Aim above or below barrel. Avail. for most popular handguns, rifles, shotguns, including militaries. From Laseraim Technologies, Inc.

Maker, Model, Type	Adjust.	Scopes	Price
LEUPOLD			
STD Bases[1]	W only	One- or two-piece bases	23.80
STD Rings[2]	—	1" super low, low, medium, high	31.40
STD Handgun mounts[3]	No	—	57.00
Dual Dovetail Bases[1,4]	No	—	23.80
Dual Dovetail Rings[9]	—	1", super low, low	31.40
Ring Mounts[5,6,7]	No	7/8", 1"	79.80
22 Rimfire[9]	No	7/8", 1"	58.20
Gunmaker Base[8]	W only	1"	16.50
Quick Release Rings	—	1", low, med., high	31.90-68.90
Quick Release Bases[10]	No	1", one- or two-piece	69.30

[1]Rev. front and rear combinations; matte finish $22.90. [2]Avail. polished, matte or silver (low, med. only) finish. [3]Base and two rings; Casull, Ruger, S&W, T/C; add $5.00 for silver finish. [4]Rem. 700, Win. 70-type actions. [5]For Ruger No. 1, 77, 77/22; interchangeable with Ruger units. [6]For dovetailed rimfire rifles. [7]Sako; high, medium, low. [8]Must be drilled, tapped for each action. [9]Most dovetail-receiver 22s. [10]BSA Monarch, Rem. 40X, 700, 721, 725, Ruger M77, S&W 1500, Weatherby Mark V, Vanguard, Win M70.

Maker, Model, Type	Adjust.	Scopes	Price
MARLIN			
One Piece QD (T)	No	1" split rings	10.10
Most Marlin lever actions.			

Maker, Model, Type	Adjust.	Scopes	Price
MILLETT			
Black Onyx Smooth	—	1", low, medium, high	31.15
Chaparral Engraved	—	1" engraved	46.15
One-Piece Bases[6]	Yes	1"	23.95
Universal Two-Piece Bases			
700 Series	W only	Two-piece bases	25.15
FN Series	W only	Two-piece bases	25.15
70 Series[1]	W only	1", two-piece bases	25.15
Angle-Loc Rings[2]	W only	1", low, medium, high	32.20-47.20
Ruger 77 Rings[3]	—	1"	47.20
Shotgun Rings[4]	—	1"	28.29
Handgun Bases, Rings[5]	—	1"	34.60-69.15
30mm Rings[7]	—	30mm	37.75-42.95
Extension Rings[8]	—	1"	35.65
See-Thru Mounts[9]	No	1"	27.95-32.95
Shotgun Mounts[10]	No	1"	49.95

[1]Rem. 40X, 700, 722, 725, Ruger 77 (round top), Weatherby, FN Mauser, FN Brownings, Colt 57, Interarms Mark X, Parker-Hale, Sako (round receiver), many others. [2]Fits Win. M70, 70XTR, 670, Browning BBR, BAR, BLR, A-Bolt, Rem. 7400/7600, Four, Six, Marlin 336, Win. 94 A.E., Sav. 110. [2]To fit Weaver-type bases. [3]Engraved. Smooth $34.60. [4]For Rem. 870, 1100; smooth. [5]Two and three-ring sets for Colt Python, Trooper, Diamondback, Peacekeeper, Dan Wesson, Ruger Redhawk, Super Redhawk. [6]Turn-in bases and Weaver-style for most popular rifles and T/C Contender, XP-100 pistols. [7]Both Weaver and turn-in styles; three heights. [8]Med. or high; ext. front—std. rear, ext. rear—std. front, ext. front—ext. rear: $40.90 for double extension. [9]Many popular rifles, Knight MK-85, T/C Hawken, Renegade, Mossberg 500 Slugster, 835 Slug. [10]For Rem. 870/1100, Win. 1200, 1300/1400, 1500, Mossberg 500. Some models available in nickel at extra cost. From Millett Sights.

Maker, Model, Type	Adjust.	Scopes	Price
OAKSHORE			
Handguns			
Browning Buck Mark	No	1"	29.00
Colt Cobra, Diamondback, Python, 1911	No	1"	38.00-52.00
Ruger 22 Auto, GP100	No	1"	33.00-49.00
S&W N Frame	No	1"	45.00-60.00
S&W 422	No	1"	35.00-38.00
Rifles			
Colt AR-15	No	1"	26.00-34.00
H&K 91, 93, 94, MP-5, G-3	No	1"	56.00
Galil	No	1"	75.00
Marlin 336 & 1800 Series	No	1"	21.00
Win. 94	No	1"	39.00
Shotguns			
Mossberg 500	No	1"	40.00
Rem. 870, 1100	No	1"	33.00-52.00
Rings	—	1", med., high	5.20-9.80

See Through offered in some models. Black or silver finish; 1" rings also avail. for 3/8" grooved receivers (See Through). From Oakshore Electronic Sights, Inc.

Maker, Model, Type	Adjust.	Scopes	Price
PEM'S			
22T Mount[1]	No	1"	17.95
The Mount[2]	Yes	1"	29.50

[1]Fit all 3/8" dovetail on rimfire rifles. [2]Base and ring set; for over 100 popular rifles; low, medium rings. From Pem's.

Maker, Model, Type	Adjust.	Scopes	Price
RAM-LINE			
Mini-14 Mount	Yes	1"	24.97

No drilling or tapping. Use std. dovetail rings. Has built-in shell deflector. Made of solid black polymer. From Ram-Line, Inc.

Maker, Model, Type	Adjust.	Scopes	Price
REDFIELD			
American Rings[6]	No	1", low, med., high	16.95
American Bases[6]	No	—	2.65-10.55
American Widefield See-Thru[7]	No	1"	16.95
JR-SR (T)[1]	W only	3/4", 1", 26mm, 30mm	JR—26.95-52.95 SR—20.95-22.95
Ring (T)[2]	No	3/4" and 1"	30.95-45.95
Three-Ring Pistol System SMP[3]	No	1" split rings (three)	56.95-62.95
Widefield See-Thru Mounts	No	1"	16.95
Ruger Rings[4]	No	1", med., high	36.95
Ruger 30mm[5]	No	1"	47.95
Midline Ext. Rings	No	1"	24.95

[1]Low, med. & high, split rings. Reversible extension front rings for 1". 2-piece bases for Sako. Colt Sauer bases $39.95. Med. Top Access JR nickel-plated, $28.95. SR two-piece ABN mount nickel-plated, $22.95. [2]Split rings for grooved 22s; 30mm, black matte $42.95.. [3]Used with MP scopes for: S&W K, L or N frame, XP-100, T/C Contender, Ruger receivers. [4]For Ruger Model 77 rifles, medium and high; medium only for M77/22. [5]For Model 77. Also in matte finish, $45.95. [6]Aluminum 22 groove mount $14.95; base and medium rings $18.95. [7]Fits American or Weaver-style base.

Maker, Model, Type	Adjust.	Scopes	Price
S&K			
Insta-Mount (T) bases and rings[1]	W only	Use S&K rings only	47.00-117.00
Conventional rings and bases[2]	W only	1" split rings	From 65.00
Skulptured Bases, Rings[2]	W only	1", 26mm, 30mm	From 65.00
Smooth Kontoured Rings[3]	Yes	1", 26mm, 30mm	90.00-120.00

[1]1903, A3, M1 Carbine, Lee Enfield #1, Mk. III, #4, #5, M1917, M98 Mauser, AR-15, AR-180, M-14, M-1, Ger. K-43, Mini-14, M1-A, Krag, AKM, Win. 94, SKS Type 56, Daewoo, H&K. [2]Most popular rifles already drilled and tapped. [3]No projections; weigh 1/2-oz. each; matte or gloss finish. Horizontally and vertically split rings, matte or high gloss.

Maker, Model, Type	Adjust.	Scopes	Price
SSK INDUSTRIES			
T'SOB	No	1"	65.00-145.00
Quick Detachable	No	1"	From 160.00

Custom installation using from two to four rings (included). For T/C Contender, most 22 auto pistols, Ruger and other S.A. revolvers, Ruger, Dan Wesson, S&W, Colt DA revolvers. Black or white finish. Uses Kimber rings in two- or three-ring sets. In blue or SSK Khrome. For T/C Contender or most popular revolvers. Standard, non-detachable model also available, from $65.00.

Maker, Model, Type	Adjust.	Scopes	Price
SAKO			
QD Dovetail	W only	1" only	70.00-155.00

Sako, or any rifle using Sako action, 3 heights available. Stoeger, importer.

Maker, Model, Type	Adjust.	Scopes	Price
SPRINGFIELD, INC.			
M1A Third Generation	No	1" or 30mm	123.00
M1A Standard	No	1" or 30mm	77.00
SAR-4800 Mount	No	—	96.00
M6 Scount Mount	No	—	29.00

Weaver-style bases. From Springfield, Inc.

Maker, Model, Type	Adjust.	Scopes	Price
TASCO			
World Class			
Universal "W" Ringmount[1]	No	1", 30mm	25.50-30.00
Ruger[2]	No	1", 30mm	31.00-73.00
22, Air Rifle[3]	No	1", 30mm	18.00-82.00
Ringsets[4]	No	1", 26mm, 30mm	39.00-66.00
Handgun Revolver	No	1"	33.50-58.00
Handgun Competition	No	1"	103.00
Traditional Ringsets	No	1"	33.00-66.00

CAUTION: PRICES SHOWN ARE SUPPLIED BY THE MANUFACTURER OR IMPORTER. CHECK YOU LOCAL GUNSHOP.

SCOPE MOUNTS

Maker, Model, Type	Adjust.	Scopes	Price
Tasco (cont.)			
See-Thru	No	1"	19.00
Bases[5]	Yes	—	24.00-61.00

[1]Steel; low, high only; also high-profile see-through; fit Tasco, Weaver, other universal bases; black gloss or satin chrome. [2]Low, high only; for Redhawk and Super, No.1, Mini-14 & Thirty, 77, 77/22; blue or stainless. [3]Low, med., high; 3/8" grooved receivers; black or satin chrome. [4]Low, med., high; black gloss, matte satin chrome; also Traditional Ringsets $31.00 (1"), $42.00 (26mm), $53.00 (30mm). [5]For popular rifles and shotguns; one-piece, two-piece, Q.D., long and short action, extension. Handgun bases have w&e adj. From Tasco.

Maker, Model, Type	Adjust.	Scopes	Price
THOMPSON/CENTER			
Contender 9741[1]	No	2½, 4 RP	20.00
Duo-Ring Mount[2]	No	1"	65.00
Weaver-Style Bases[3]	No	—	13.00
Weaver-Style Rings[4]	No	1"	29.00-41.00
Weaver-Style See-Through Rings[5]	No	1"	29.00
Quick Release System[6]	No	1"	Rings 56.00
			Base 30.00

[1]T/C rail mount scopes; all Contenders except vent. rib. [2]Attaches directly to T/C Contender bbl., no drilling/tapping; also for T/C M/L rifles, needs base adapter; blue or stainless; for M/L guns, $59.80. [3]For T/C ThunderHawk, FireHawk rifles; blue; silver, $37.00. [4]Medium and high; blue or silver finish. [5]For T/C FireHawk, ThunderHawk; blue; silver, $25.00. [6]For Contender pistol, Carbine, Scout, all M/L long guns. From Thompson/Center.

Maker, Model, Type	Adjust.	Scopes	Price
UNERTL			
¼ Click[1]	Yes	¾", 1" target scopes	Per set 165.00

[1]Unertl target or varmint scopes. Posa or standard mounts, less bases. From Unertl.

Maker, Model, Type	Adjust.	Scopes	Price
WARNE			
Deluxe Series (all steel non-Q.D. rings)			
Standard	No	1", 4 heights	95.50
		30mm, 2 heights	107.50
Sako	No	1", 4 heights	95.50
		30mm, 3 heights	107.50
Deluxe Series Rings fit Premier Series Bases			
Premier Series (all-steel Q.D. rings)			
Adjustable Double Levers	No	1", 4 heights	105.50
		26mm, 2 heights	117.50
		30mm, 3 heights	117.50
Thumb Knob	No	1", 4 heights	95.50
		26mm, 2 heights	107.50
		30mm, 3 heights	107.50
Brno 19mm	No	1", 3 heights	105.50
		30mm, 2 heights	117.50
Brno 16mm		1" 2 heights	105.50
Ruger	No	1", 4 heights	105.50
		30mm, 3 heights	117.50
Ruger M77	No	1", 3 heights	105.50
		30mm, 2 heights	117.50
Sako Medium & Long Action	No	1", 4 heights	105.50
		30mm, 3 heights	117.50
Sako Short Action	No	1", 3 heights	105.50
All-Steel One-Piece Base, ea.			32.00
All-Steel Two-Piece Base, ea.			12.50
Maxima Series (fits all Weaver-style bases)			
Permanently Attached[1]	No	1", 3 heights	31.40
		30mm, 3 heights	35.40
Adjustable Double Lever[2]	No	1", 3 heights	65.50
		30mm, 3 heights	69.50
Thumb Knob	No	1", 3 heights	55.50
		30mm, 3 heights	59.50
All-Steel Two-Piece Base, ea.			12.50

Vertically split rings with dovetail clamp, precise return to zero. Fit most popular rifles, handguns. Regular blue, matte blue, silver finish. [1]All-steel, non-q.d. rings. [2]All-steel, q.d. rings. From Warne Mfg. Co.

Maker, Model, Type	Adjust.	Scopes	Price
WEAVER			
Detachable Mounts			
Top Mount[1]	No	7/8", 1"	25.00-38.00
Side Mount[2]	No	1", 1" Long	29.00-35.00
Pivot Mount[3]	No	1"	39.00
Tip-Off Mount[4]	No	7/8", 1"	21.00-27.00
See-Thru Mount			
Traditional[5]	No	1"	16.00-23.00
Tip-Off[4]	No	1", 7/8"	14.00-16.00
Pro View[5]	No	1"	14.00-16.00
Mount Base System[6]			
Blue Finish	No	1"	75.00
Stainless Finish	No	1"	105.00
Shotgun Converta-Mount System[7]	No	1"	75.00
Rifle Mount System[8]	No	1"	33.00

[1]Nearly all modern rifles. Low, med., high. 1" extension $25.00. 1" low, med., high stainless steel $38.00. [2]Nearly all modern rifles, shotguns. [3]Most modern big bore rifles; std., high. [4]22s with 3/8" grooved receivers. [5]Most modern big bore rifles. Some in stainless finish, $20.00-21.00. [6]No drilling, tapping. For Colt Python, Trooper, 357, Officer's Model, Ruger Blackhawk & Super, Mini-14, Security-Six, 22 auto pistols, Single-Six 22, Redhawk, Blackhawk SRM 357, S&W current K, L with adj. sights. [7]For Rem. 870, 1100, 11-87, Browning A-5, BPS, Ithaca 37, 87, Beretta A303, Beretta A-390, Winchester 1200-1500, Mossberg 500. [8]For some popular sporting rifles. From Weaver.

Maker, Model, Type	Adjust.	Scopes	Price
WEIGAND			
1911 PDP4[1]	No	40mm, PDP4	69.95
1911 General Purpose[2]	No	—	59.95
Ruger Mark II[3]	No	—	49.95
3rd Generation[4]	No	—	99.95
Pro Ringless[5]	No	30mm	99.95
Stabilizer I Ringless[6,7]	No	30mm	99.95
Revolver Mount[8]	No	—	35.50
Ruger 10/22[9]	No	—	39.95

[1]For Tasco PDP4 and similar 40mm sights. [2]Weaver rail; takes any standard rings. [3]No drilling, tapping. [4]For M1911; grooved top for Weaver-style rings; requires drilling, tapping. [5]Two-piece design; for P9/EA-9, CZ-75 copies; integral rings; silver alum. finish. [6]Three-piece design; fits M1911, P9/EA-9, TZ, CZ-75 copies; silver alum. finish. [7]Stabilizer II—more forward position; for M1911, McCormick frames. [8]Frame mount. [9]Barrel mount. From Weigand Combat Handguns, Inc.

Maker, Model, Type	Adjust.	Scopes	Price
WIDEVIEW			
Premium 94 Angle Eject	No	1"	24.00
Premium See-Thru	No	1"	22.00
22 Premium See-Thru	No	¾", 1"	16.00
Universal Ring Angle Cut	No	1"	24.00
Universal Ring Straight Cut	No	1"	22.00
Solid Mounts			
Lo Ring Solid[1]	No	1"	16.00
Hi Ring Solid[1]	No	1"	16.00
SR Rings	—	1", 30mm	18.64
22 Grooved Receiver	No	1"	16.00
94 Side Mount	No	1"	26.00
Blackpowder Mounts[2]	No	1"	22.00-44.00

[1]For Weaver-type bases. Models for many popular rifles. Low ring, high ring and grooved receiver types. [2]No drilling, tapping; for T/C Renegade, Hawken, CVA, Knight Traditions guns. From Wideview Scope Mount Corp.

Maker, Model, Type	Adjust.	Scopes	Price
WILLIAMS			
Sidemount with HCO Rings[1]	No	1", split or extension rings.	74.21
Sidemount, offset rings[2]	No	Same	61.08
Sight-Thru Mounts[3]	No	1", 7/8" sleeves	18.95
Streamline Mounts	No	1" (bases form rings).	25.70
Guideline Handgun[4]	No	1" split rings.	61.75

[1]Most rifles, Br. S.M.L.E. (round rec.) $14.41 extra. [2]Most rifles including Win. 94 Big Bore. [3]Many modern rifles, including CVA Apollo, others with 1" octagon barrels. [4]No drilling, tapping required; heat treated alloy. For Ruger MkII Bull Barrel ($61.75); Streamline Top Mount for T/C Contender ($41.15), Scout Rifle, ($24.00), High Top Mount with sub-base ($51.45). From Williams Gunsight Co.

Maker, Model, Type	Adjust.	Scopes	Price
YORK			
M-1 Garand	Yes	1"	39.95

Centers scope over the action. No drilling, tapping or gunsmithing. Uses standard dovetail rings. From York M-1 Conversions.

NOTES

(S)—Side Mount (T)—Top Mount; 22mm=.866"; 25.4mm=1.024"; 26.5mm=1.045"; 30mm=1.81".

ARMS ASSOCIATIONS

UNITED STATES

ALABAMA
Alabama Gun Collectors Assn.
Secretary, P.O. Box 70965, Tuscaloosa, AL 35407

ALASKA
Alaska Gun Collectors Assn., Inc.
C.W. Floyd, Pres., 5240 Little Tree, Anchorage, AK 99507

ARIZONA
Arizona Arms Assn.
Don DeBusk, President, 4837 Bryce Ave., Glendale, AZ 85301

CALIFORNIA
California Cartridge Collectors Assn.
Rick Montgomery, 1729 Christina, Stockton, CA 95204
California Waterfowl Assn.
4630 Northgate Blvd., #150, Sacramento, CA 95834
Greater Calif. Arms & Collectors Assn.
Donald L. Bullock, 8291 Carburton St., Long Beach, CA 90808-3302
Los Angeles Gun Ctg. Collectors Assn.
F.H. Ruffra, 20810 Amie Ave., Apt. #9, Torrance, CA 90503
Stock Gun Players Assn.
6038 Appian Way, Long Beach, CA, 90803

COLORADO
Colorado Gun Collectors Assn.
L.E.(Bud) Greenwald, 2553 S. Quitman St., Denver, CO 80219/303-935-3850
Rocky Mountain Cartridge Collectors Assn.
John Roth, P.O. Box 757, Conifer, CO 80433

CONNECTICUT
Ye Connecticut Gun Guild, Inc.
Dick Fraser, P.O. Box 425, Windsor, CT 06095

FLORIDA
Unified Sportsmen of Florida
P.O. Box 6565, Tallahassee, FL 32314

GEORGIA
Georgia Arms Collectors Assn., Inc.
Michael Kindberg, President, P.O. Box 277, Alpharetta, GA 30239-0277

ILLINOIS
Illinois State Rifle Assn.
P.O. Box 637, Chatsworth, IL 60921
Mississippi Valley Gun & Cartridge Coll. Assn.
Bob Filbert, P.O. Box 61, Port Byron, IL 61275/309-523-2593
Sauk Trail Gun Collectors
Gordell M. Matson, P.O. Box 1113, Milan, IL 61264
Wabash Valley Gun Collectors Assn., Inc.
Roger L. Dorsett, 2601 Willow Rd., Urbana, IL 61801/217-384-7302

INDIANA
Indiana State Rifle & Pistol Assn.
Thos. Glancy, P.O. Box 552, Chesterton, IN 46304
Southern Indiana Gun Collectors Assn., Inc.
Sheila McClary, 309 W. Monroe St., Boonville, IN 47601/812-897-3742

IOWA
Beaver Creek Plainsmen Inc.
Steve Murphy, Secy., P.O. Box 298, Bondurant, IA 50035
Central States Gun Collectors Assn.
Avery Giles, 1104 S. 1st Ave., Marshtown, IA 50158

KANSAS
Kansas Cartridge Collectors Assn.
Bob Linder, Box 84, Plainville, KS 67663

KENTUCKY
Kentuckiana Arms Collectors Assn.
Charles Billips, President, Box 1776, Louisville, KY 40201
Kentucky Gun Collectors Assn., Inc.
Ruth Johnson, Box 64, Owensboro, KY 42302/502-729-4197

LOUISIANA
Washitaw River Renegades
Sandra Rushing, P.O. Box 256, Main St., Grayson, LA 71435

MARYLAND
Baltimore Antique Arms Assn.
Mr. Cillo, 1034 Main St., Darlington, MD 21304

MASSACHUSETTS
Bay Colony Weapons Collectors, Inc.
John Brandt, Box 111, Hingham, MA 02043
Massachusetts Arms Collectors
Bruce E. Skinner, P.O. Box 31, No. Carver, MA 02355/508-866-5259

MICHIGAN
Association for the Study and Research of .22 Caliber Rimfire Cartridges
George Kass, 4512 Nakoma Dr., Okemos, MI 48864

MINNESOTA
Sioux Empire Cartridge Collectors Assn.
Bob Cameron, 14597 Glendale Ave. SE, Prior Lake, MN 55372

MISSISSIPPI
Mississippi Gun Collectors Assn.
Jack E. Swinney, P.O. Box 16323, Hattiesburg, MS 39402

MISSOURI
Greater St. Louis Cartridge Collectors Assn.
Don MacChesney, 634 Scottsdale Rd., Kirkwood, MO 63122-1109
Mineral Belt Gun Collectors Assn.
D.F. Saunders, 1110 Cleveland Ave., Monett, MO 65708
Missouri Valley Arms Collectors Assn., Inc.
L.P Brammer II, Membership Secy., P.O. Box 33033, Kansas City, MO 64114

MONTANA
Montana Arms Collectors Assn.
Lewis E. Yearout, 308 Riverview Dr. East, Great Falls, MT 59404
Weapons Collectors Society of Montana
R.G. Schipf, Ex. Secy., 3100 Bancroft St., Missoula, MT 59801/406-728-2995

NEBRASKA
Nebraska Cartridge Collectors Club
Gary Muckel, P.O. Box 84442, Lincoln, NE 68501

NEW HAMPSHIRE
New Hampshire Arms Collectors, Inc.
James Stamatelos, Secy., P.O. Box 5, Cambridge, MA 02139

NEW JERSEY
Englishtown Benchrest Shooters Assn.
Michael Toth, 64 Cooke Ave., Carteret, NJ 07008
Jersey Shore Antique Arms Collectors
Joe Sisia, P.O. Box 100, Bayville, NJ 08721-0100
New Jersey Arms Collectors Club, Inc.
Angus Laidlaw, Vice President, 230 Valley Rd., Montclair, NJ 07042/201-746-0939

NEW YORK
Iroquois Arms Collectors Assn.
Bonnie Robinson, Show Secy., P.O. Box 142, Ransomville, NY 14131/716-791-4096
Mid-State Arms Coll. & Shooters Club
Jack Ackerman, 24 S. Mountain Terr., Binghamton, NY 13903

NORTH CAROLINA
North Carolina Gun Collectors Assn.
Jerry Ledford, 3231-7th St. Dr. NE, Hickory, NC 28601

OHIO
Ohio Gun Collectors Assn.
P.O. Box 9007, Maumee, OH 43537-9007/419-897-0861;Fax:419-897-0860
Shotshell Historical and Collectors Society
Madeline Bruemmer, 3886 Dawley Rd., Ravenna, OH 44266
The Stark Gun Collectors, Inc.
William I. Gann, 5666 Waynesburg Dr., Waynesburg, OH 44688

OKLAHOMA
Indian Territory Gun Collector's Assn.
P.O. Box 4491, Tulsa, OK 74159/918-745-9141

OREGON
Oregon Arms Collectors Assn., Inc.
Phil Bailey, P.O. Box 13000-A, Portland, OR 97213-0017/503-281-6864;off.:503-620-1024
Oregon Cartridge Collectors Assn.
Gale Stockton, 52 N.W. 2nd, Gresham, OR 97030

PENNSYLVANIA
Presque Isle Gun Collectors Assn.
James Welch, 156 E. 37 St., Erie, PA 16504

SOUTH CAROLINA
Belton Gun Club, Inc.
J.K. Phillips, 195 Phillips Dr., Belton, SC 29627
Gun Owners of South Carolina
Membership Div.: William Strozier, Secretary, P.O. Box 70, Johns Island, SC 29457-0070/803-762-3240;Fax:803-795-0711;e-mail:76053.222@compuserve.com

SOUTH DAKOTA
Dakota Territory Gun Coll. Assn., Inc.
Curt Carter, Castlewood, SD 57223

TENNESSEE
Smoky Mountain Gun Coll. Assn., Inc.
Hugh W. Yabro, President, P.O. Box 23225, Knoxville, TN 37933
Tennessee Gun Collectors Assn., Inc.
M.H. Parks, 3556 Pleasant Valley Rd., Nashville, TN 37204-3419

TEXAS
Houston Gun Collectors Assn., Inc.
P.O. Box 741429, Houston, TX 77274-1429
Texas Cartridge Collectors Assn., Inc.
Robert Mellichamp, Memb. Contact, 907 Shirkmere, Houston, TX 77008/713-869-0558
Texas Gun Collectors Assn.
Bob Eder, Pres., P.O. Box 12067, El Paso, TX 79913/915-584-8183
Texas State Rifle Assn.
4600 Greenville Ave., #292, Dallas, TX 75206/214-369-8772

WASHINGTON
Association of Cartridge Collectors on the Pacific Northwest
Robert Jardin, 14214 Meadowlark Drive KPN, Gig Harbor, WA 98329
Washington Arms Collectors, Inc.
Joyce Boss, P.O. Box 389, Renton, WA, 98057-0389/206-255-8410

WISCONSIN
Great Lakes Arms Collectors Assn., Inc.
Edward C. Warnke, 2913 Woodridge Lane, Waukesha, WI 53188
Wisconsin Gun Collectors Assn., Inc.
Lulita Zellmer, P.O. Box 181, Sussex, WI 53089

WYOMING
Wyoming Weapons Collectors
P.O. Box 284, Laramie, WY 82070/307-745-4652 or 745-9530

NATIONAL ORGANIZATIONS

Amateur Trapshooting Assn.
601 W. National Rd., Vandalia, OH 45377/513-898-4638;Fax:513-898-5472
American Airgun Field Target Assn.
5911 Cherokee Ave., Tampa, FL 33604
American Coon Hunters Assn.
Opal Johnston, P.O. Cadet, Route 1, Box 492, Old Mines, MO 63630
American Custom Gunmakers Guild
Jan Billeb, Exec. Director, P.O. Box 812, Burlington, IA 52601-0812/319-752-6114 (Phone or Fax)
American Defense Preparedness Assn.
Two Colonial Place, 2101 Wilson Blvd., Suite 400, Arlington, VA 22201-3061
American Paintball League
P.O. Box 3561, Johnson City, TN 37602/800-541-9169
American Pistolsmiths Guild
Alex B. Hamilton, Pres., 1449 Blue Crest Lane, San Antonio, TX 78232/210-494-3063
American Police Pistol & Rifle Assn.
3801 Biscayne Blvd., Miami, FL 33137
American Single Shot Rifle Assn.
Gary Staup, Secy., 709 Carolyn Dr., Delphos, OH 45833/419-692-3866
American Society of Arms Collectors
George E. Weatherly, P.O. Box 2567, Waxahachie, TX 75165
American Tactical Shooting Assn.(A.T.S.A.)
c/o Skip Gouchenour, 2600 N. Third St., Harrisburg, PA 17110/717-233-0402;Fax:717-233-5340

ARMS ASSOCIATIONS IN AMERICA AND ABROAD

Association of Firearm and Tool Mark Examiners
Lannie G. Emanuel, Secy., Southwest Institute of Forecsic Sciences, P.O. Box 35728, Dallas, TX 75235; Membership Secy., Ann D. Jones, VA Div. of Forensic Science, P.O. Box 999, Richmond, VA 23208/804-786-4706;Fax:804-371-8328

Boone & Crockett Club
250 Station Dr., Missoula, MT 59801-2753

Browning Collectors Assn.
Secretary:Scherrie L. Brennac, 2749 Keith Dr., Villa Ridge, MO 63089/314-742-0571

The Cast Bullet Assn., Inc.
Ralland J. Fortier, Membership Director, 4103 Foxcraft Dr., Traverse City, MI 49684

Citizens Committee for the Right to Keep and Bear Arms
Natl. Hq., Liberty Park, 12500 NE Tenth Pl., Bellevue, WA 98005

Colt Collectors Assn.
25000 Highland Way, Los Gatos, CA 95030

Ducks Unlimited, Inc.
Natl. Headquarters, One Waterfowl Way, Memphis, TN 38120

Fifty Caliber Shooters Assn.
11469 Olive St. Rd., Suite 50, St. Louis, MO 63141/601-475-7545;Fax:601-475-0452

Firearms Coalition
Box 6537, Silver Spring, MD 20906/301-871-3006

Firearms Engravers Guild of America
Rex C. Pedersen, Secy., 511 N. Rath Ave., Lundington, MI 49431/616-845-7695(Phone and Fax)

Foundation for North American Wild Sheep
720 Allen Ave., Cody, WY 82414-3402

Freedom Arms Collectors Assn.
P.O. Box 160302, Miami, FL 33116-0302

Garand Collectors Assn.
P.O. Box 181, Richmond, KY 40475

Golden Eagle Collectors Assn.
Chris Showler, 11144 Slate Creek Rd., Grass Valley, CA 95945

Gun Owners of America
8001 Forbes Place, Suite 102, Springfield, VA 22151/703-321-8585

Handgun Hunters International
J.D. Jones, Director, P.O. Box 357 MAG, Bloomingdale, OH 43910

Harrington & Richardson Gun Coll. Assn.
George L. Cardet, 330 S.W. 27th Ave., Suite 603, Miami, FL 33135

High Standard Collectors' Assn.
John J. Stimson, Jr., Pres., 540 W. 92nd St., Indianapolis, IN 46260

Hopkins & Allen Arms & Memorabilia Society (HAAMS)
1309 Pamela Circle, Delphos, OH 45833

International Ammunition Association, Inc.
C.R. Punnett, Secy., 8 Hillock Lane, Chadds Ford, PA 19317/610-358-1258;Fax:610-358-1560

International Benchrest Shooters
Joan Borden, RR1, Box 250BB, Springville, PA 18844/717-965-2366

International Blackpowder Hunting Assn.
P.O. Box 1180, Glenrock, WY 82637/307-436-9817

IHMSA (Intl. Handgun Metallic Silhouette Assn.)
Frank Scotto, P.O. Box 5038, Meriden, CT 06451

International Handloaders Assn.
6471 Airpark Dr., Prescott, AZ 86301/520-445-7810;Fax:520-778-5124

International Paintball Field Operators Assn.
15507 S. Normandie Ave. #487, Gardena, CA 90247/310-323-1021

IPPA (International Paintball Players Assn.)
P.O. Box 26669, San Diego, CA 92196-0669/619-695-8882;Fax:619-695-6909

Jews for the Preservation of Firearms Ownership (JPFO) 501(c)(3)
2872 S. Wentworth Ave., Milwaukee, WI 53207/414-769-0760;Fax:414-483-8435

The Mannlicher Collectors Assn.
Rev. Don L. Henry, Secy., P.O. Box 7144, Salem, OR 97303-0028

Marlin Firearms Collectors Assn., Ltd.
Dick Paterson, Secy., 407 Lincoln Bldg., 44 Main St., Champaign, IL 61820

Miniature Arms Collectors/Makers Society, Ltd.
Ralph Koebbeman, Pres., 4910 Kilburn Ave., Rockford, IL 61101/815-964-2569

M1 Carbine Collectors Assn. (M1-CCA)
P.O. Box 4895, Stateline, NV 89449

National Association of Buckskinners (NAB)
Territorial Dispatch, 4701 Marion St., Suite 324, Livestock Exchange Bldg., Denver, CO 80216

The National Association of Derringer Collectors
P.O. Box 20572, San Jose, CA 95160

National Assn. of Federally Licensed Firearms Dealers
Andrew Molchan, 2455 E. Sunrise, Ft. Lauderdale, FL 33304

National Association to Keep and Bear Arms
P.O. Box 78336, Seattle, WA 98178

National Automatic Pistol Collectors Assn.
Tom Knox, P.O. Box 15738, Tower Grove Station, St. Louis, MO 63163

National Bench Rest Shooters Assn., Inc.
Pat Ferrell, 2835 Guilford Lane, Oklahoma City, OK 73120-4404/405-842-9585

National Firearms Assn.
P.O. Box 160038, Austin, TX 78716/403-439-1094; FAX: 403-439-4091

National Muzzle Loading Rifle Assn.
Box 67, Friendship, IN 47021

National Professional Paintball League (NPPL)
540 Main St., Mount Kisco, NY 10549/914-241-7400

National Reloading Manufacturers Assn.
One Centerpointe Dr., Suite 300, Lake Oswego, OR 97035

National Rifle Assn. of America
11250 Waples Mill Rd., Fairfax, VA 22030

National Shooting Sports Foundation, Inc.
Robert T. Delfay, President, Flintlock Ridge Office Center, 11 Mile @NORMAL:Hill Rd., Newtown, CT 06470-2359/203-426-1320; FAX: 203-426-1087

National Skeet Shooting Assn.
Mike Hampton, Exec. Director, 5931 Roft Road, San Antonio, TX 78253-9261

National Sporting Clays Association
5931 Roft Road, San Antonio, TX 78253-9261/800-877-5338

National Wild Turkey Federation, Inc.
P.O. Box 530, Edgefield, SC 29824

North American Hunting Club
P.O. Box 3401, Minnetonka, MN 55343

North American Paintball Referees Association (NAPRA)
584 Cestaric Dr., Milpitas, CA 95035

North-South Skirmish Assn., Inc.
Stevan F. Meserve, Exec. Secretary, 507 N. Brighton Court, Sterling, VA 20164-3919

Remington Society of America
Leon W. Wier Jr., President, 8268 Lone Feather Ln., Las Vegas, NV 89123

Rocky Mountain Elk Foundation
P.O. Box 8249, Missoula, MT 59807-8249/406-523-4500;Fax:406-523-4581

Ruger Collector's Assn., Inc.
P.O. Box 240, Greens Farms, CT 06436

Safari Club International
Philip DeLone, Executive Dir., 4800 W. Gates Pass Rd., Tucson, AZ 85745/602-620-1220

Sako Collectors Assn., Inc.
Jim Lutes, 202 N. Locust, Whitewater, KS 67154

Second Amendment Foundation
James Madison Building, 12500 NE 10th Pl., Bellevue, WA 98005

Single-Action Shooting Society
1938 North Batavia St., Suite C, Orange, CA 92665/714-998-0209;Fax:714-998-1992

Smith & Wesson Collectors Assn.
George Linne, 2711 Miami St., St. Louis, MO 63118

The Society of American Bayonet Collectors
P.O. Box 234, East Islip, NY 11730-0234

Southern California Schuetzen Society
Dean Lillard, 34657 Ave. E., Yucaipa, CA 92399

Sporting Arms & Ammunition Manufacturers Institute (SAAMI)
Flintlock Ridge Office Center, 11 Mile Hill Rd., Newtown, CT 06470-2359/203-426-1320; FAX: 203-426-1087

Sporting Clays of America (SCA)
Ellen McCormick, Director of Membership Services, 9 Mott Ave., Suite 103, Norwalk, CT 06850/203-831-8483; FAX: 203-831-8497

The Thompson/Center Assn.
Joe Wright, President, Box 792, Northboro, MA 01532/508-845-6960

U.S. Practical Shooting Assn./IPSC
Dave Thomas, P.O. Box 811, Sedro Woolley, WA 98284/360-855-2245

U.S. Revolver Assn.
Brian J. Barer, 40 Larchmont Ave., Taunton, MA 02780/508-824-4836

U.S. Shooting Team
U.S. Olympic Shooting Center, One Olympic Plaza, Colorado Springs, CO 80909/719-578-4670

The Varmint Hunters Assn., Inc.
Box 759, Pierre, SD 57501/Member Services 800-528-4868

Weatherby Collectors Assn., Inc.
P.O. Box 128, Moira, NY 12957

The Wildcatters
P.O. Box 170, Greenville, WI 54942

Winchester Arms Collectors Assn.
Richard Berg, Executive Secy., P.O. Box 6754, Great Falls, MT 59406

The Women's Shooting Sports Foundation (WSSF)
1505 Highway 6 South, Suite 101, Houston, TX 77077

ARGENTINA

Association Argentina de Colleccionistas de Armes y Municiones
Castilla de Correas No. 28, Succursal I B, 1401 Buenos Aires, Republica Argentina

AUSTRALIA

The Arms Collector's Guild of Queensland Inc.
Ian Skennerton, P.O. Box 433, Ashmore City 4214, Queensland, Australia

Australian Cartridge Collectors Assn., Inc.
Bob Bennett, 126 Landscape Dr., E. Doncaster 3109, Victoria, Ausrtalia

Sporting Shooters Assn. of Australia, Inc.
P.O. Box 2066, Kent Town, SA 5071, Australia

CANADA
ALBERTA

Canadian Historical Arms Society
P.O. Box 901, Edmonton, Alb., Canada T5J 2L8

National Firearms Assn.
Natl. Hq: P.O. Box 1779, Edmonton, Alb., Canada T5J 2P1

BRITISH COLUMBIA

The Historical Arms Collectors of B.C. (Canada)
Harry Moon, Pres., P.O. Box 50117, South Slope RPO, Burnaby, BC V5J 5G3, Canada/604-438-0950;Fax:604-277-3646

ONTARIO

Association of Canadian Cartridge Collectors
Monica Wright, RR 1, Millgrove, ON, L0R IV0, Canada

Tri-County Antique Arms Fair
P.O. Box 122, RR #1, North Lancaster, Ont., Canada K0C 1Z0

EUROPE
BELGIUM

European Catridge Researchers Assn.
Graham Irving, 21 Rue Schaltin, 4900 Spa, Belgium/32.87.77.43.40;Fax:32.87.77.27.51

CZECHOSLOVAKIA

Spolecnost Pro Studium Naboju (Czech Cartridge Research Assn.)
JUDr. Jaroslav Bubak, Pod Homolko 1439, 26601 Beroun 2, Czech Republic

DENMARK

Aquila Dansk Jagtpatron Historic Forening (Danish Historical Cartridge Collectors Club)
Steen Elgaard Moler, Ulriksdalsvej 7, 4840 Nr. Alslev, Denmark 10045-53846218;Fax:004553846209

ENGLAND

Arms and Armour Society
Hon. Secretary A. Dove, P.O. Box 10232, London, 5W19 22D, England

Dutch Paintball Federation
Aceville Publ., Castle House 97 High Street, Colchester, Essex C01 1TH, England/011-44-206-564840

European Paintball Sports Foundation
c/o Aceville Publ., Castle House 97 High St., Colchester, Essex, C01 1TH, England

Historical Breechloading Smallarms Assn.
D.J. Penn M.A., Secy., Imperial War Museum, Lambeth Rd., London SE 1 6HZ, England.
Journal and newsletter are $21 a yr., including airmail.

National Rifle Assn.
(Great Britain) Bisley Camp, Brookwood, Woking Surrey GU24 0PB, England/01483.797777

United Kingdom Cartridge Club
Ian Southgate, 20 Millfield, Elmley Castle, Nr. Pershore, Worcestershire, WR10 3HR, England

FRANCE

Syndicat National de l'Arquebuserie du Commerce de l'Arme Historique
B.P. No. 3, 78110 Le Vesinet, France

GERMANY

Bund Deutscher Sportschützen e.v. (BDS)
Borsigallee 10, 53125 Bonn 1, Germany

Deutscher Schützenbund
Lahnstrasse 120, 65195 Wiesbaden, Germany

SPAIN

Asociacion Espanola de Colleccionistas de Cartuchos
Secretary, APDO. Correos No. 682, 50080 Zaragoza, Spain

SWEDEN

Scandinavian Ammunition Research Assn.
Box 107, 77622 Hedemora, Sweden

NEW ZEALAND

New Zealand Cartridge Collectors Club
Terry Castle, 70 Tiraumea Dr., Pakuranga, Auckland, New Zealand

New Zealand Deerstalkers Assn.
Michael Watt, P.O. Box 6514, Wellington, New Zealand

SOUTH AFRICA

Historical Firearms Soc. of South Africa
P.O. Box 145, 7725 Newlands, Republic of South Africa

Republic of South Africa Cartridge Collectors Assn.
Arno Klee, 20 Eugene St., Malanshof Randburg, Gauteng 2194, Republic of South Africa

S.A.A.C.A. (South African Arms and Ammunition Assn.)
P.O. Box 4065, Northway, Kwazulu-Natal 4065, Republic of South Africa

SAGA (S.A. Gunowners' Assn.)
P.O. Box 4065, Northway, Kwazulu-Natal 4065, Republic of South Africa

DIRECTORY OF THE ARMS TRADE

The Directory of the Arms Trade is divided into two sections to help the reader more easily find a listing. The **Product Directory** contains fifty-three product categories. Each entry is cross-referenced to the **Manufacturer's Directory,** an alphabetical listing giving the address, telephone number and, where available, the FAX number to allow faster access to the company.

DIRECTORY OF THE ARMS TRADE INDEX

PRODUCT DIRECTORY 298-312

AMMUNITION, COMMERCIAL .... .298	GUNSMITHS, HANDGUN (See Pistolsmiths)
AMMUNITION, CUSTOM .... .298	GUNSMITH SCHOOLS .... .306
AMMUNITION, FOREIGN .... .298	GUNSMITH SUPPLIES, TOOLS, SERVICES ..... .306
AMMUNITION COMPONENTS—BULLETS,	HANDGUN ACCESSORIES .... .306
POWDER, PRIMERS .... .298	HANDGUN GRIPS .... .307
ANTIQUE ARMS DEALERS .... .299	HEARING PROTECTORS .... .307
APPRAISERS—GUNS, ETC. .... .299	HOLSTERS AND LEATHER GOODS .... .307
AUCTIONEERS—GUNS, ETC .... .300	HUNTING AND CAMP GEAR, CLOTHING, ETC . . .307
BOOKS (Publishers and Dealers) .... .300	KNIVES AND KNIFEMAKER'S SUPPLIES—
BULLET AND CASE LUBRICANTS .... .300	FACTORY AND MAIL ORDER .... .308
BULLET SWAGE DIES AND TOOLS .... .300	LABELS, BOXES, CARTRIDGE HOLDERS ...... .308
CARTRIDGES FOR COLLECTORS .... .300	LOAD TESTING AND PRODUCT TESTING
CASES, CABINETS, RACKS AND SAFES—GUN .300	(Chronographing, Ballistic Studies) .... .308
CHOKE DEVICES, RECOIL ABSORBERS	MISCELLANEOUS .... .308
AND RECOIL PADS .... .300	MUZZLE-LOADING GUNS, BARRELS AND
CHRONOGRAPHS AND PRESSURE TOOLS ... .301	EQUIPMENT .... .309
CLEANING AND REFINISHING SUPPLIES ..... .301	PISTOLSMITHS .... .309
COMPUTER SOFTWARE—BALLISTICS .... .301	REBORING AND RERIFLING .... .309
CUSTOM GUNSMITHS .... .301	RELOADING TOOLS AND ACCESSORIES ..... .309
CUSTOM METALSMITHS .... .302	RESTS—BENCH, PORTABLE—AND
DECOYS .... .303	ACCESSORIES .... .310
ENGRAVERS, ENGRAVING TOOLS .... .303	RIFLE BARREL MAKERS (See also Muzzle-Loading
GAME CALLS .... .303	Guns, Barrels and Equipment) .... .310
GUN PARTS, U.S. AND FOREIGN .... .303	SCOPES, MOUNTS, ACCESSORIES, OPTICAL
GUNS, AIR .... .304	EQUIPMENT .... .310
GUNS, FOREIGN—IMPORTERS .... .304	SHOOTING/TRAINING SCHOOLS .... .311
GUNS, FOREIGN—MANUFACTURERS .... .304	SIGHTS, METALLIC .... .311
GUNS, U.S.-MADE .... .305	STOCKS (Commercial and Custom) .... .311
GUNS AND GUN PARTS, REPLICA	TARGETS, BULLET AND CLAYBIRD TRAPS .... .312
AND ANTIQUE .... .305	TAXIDERMY .... .312
GUNS, SURPLUS—PARTS AND AMMUNITION . .306	TRAP AND SKEET SHOOTER'S EQUIPMENT . . .312
GUNSMITHS, CUSTOM (See Custom Gunsmiths)	TRIGGERS, RELATED EQUIPMENT .... .312

MANUFACTURERS' DIRECTORY 313-336

PRODUCT DIRECTORY

AMMUNITION, COMMERCIAL

ACTIV Industries, Inc.
American Ammunition
Arms Corporation of the Philippines
A-Square Co., Inc.
Bergman & Williams
Black Hills Ammunition, Inc.
Blammo Ammo
Brenneke KG, Wilhelm
Buffalo Bullet Co., Inc.
Bull-X, Inc.
BulletMakers Workshop, The
California Magnum
CBC
Cor-Bon Bullet & Ammo Co.
C.W. Cartridge Co.
Daisy Mfg. Co.
Delta Frangible Ammunition, LLC
Denver Bullets, Inc.
Diana
Dynamit Nobel-RWS, Inc.
Effebi SNC, Dr. Franco Beretta
Eley Ltd.
Elite Ammunition
Estate Cartridge, Inc.
Federal Cartridge Co.
Fiocchi of America, Inc.
Gamo
Garrett Cartridges, Inc.
Gibbs Rifle Co., Inc.
Goldcoast Reloaders, Inc.
Grand Falls Bullets, Inc.
Hansen & Co.
Hansen Cartridge Co.
Hart & Son, Inc., Robert W.
Hirtenberger Aktiengesellschaft
Hornady Mfg. Co.
ICI-America
IMI
Keng's Firearms Specialty, Inc.
Kent Cartridge Mfg. Co. Ltd.
Lapua Ltd.
M&D Munitions Ltd.
Mac-1 Distributors
Magnum Research, Inc.
MagSafe Ammo Co.
MAGTECH Recreational Products, Inc.
Maionchi-L.M.I.
Markell, Inc.
Men—Metallwerk Elisenhuette, GmbH
Moreton/Fordyce Enterprises
Mullins Ammo
Naval Ordnance Works
NECO
New England Ammunition Co.
Oklahoma Ammunition Co.
Old Western Scrounger, Inc.
Omark Industries
PMC/Eldorado Cartridge Corp.
Polywad, Inc.
Pony Express Reloaders
Precision Delta Corp.
Pro Load Ammunition, Inc.
Remington Arms Co., Inc.
Rocky Fork Enterprises
Rucker Dist. Inc.
RWS
Shooting Components Marketing
Slug Group, Inc.
Spence, George W.
Star Reloading Co., Inc.
Talon Mfg. Co., Inc.
TCCI
3-D Ammunition & Bullets
3-Ten Corp.
USAC
Valor Corp.
Victory USA
Vihtavuori Oy/Kaltron-Pettibone
Voere-KGH m.b.H.
Weatherby, Inc.
Widener's Reloading & Shooting Supply, Inc.
Winchester Div., Olin Corp.
Zero Ammunition Co., Inc.
Zonie Bullets

AMMUNITION, CUSTOM

Accuracy Unlimited (Littleton, CO)
AFSCO Ammunition
American Derringer Corp.
Arms Corporation of the Philippines
A-Square Co., Inc.
Ballistica Maximus North
Berger Bullets, Ltd.
Bergman & Williams
Black Hills Ammunition, Inc.
Blue Mountain Bullets
Bruno Shooters Supply
Brynin, Milton
Buck Stix—SOS Products Co.
BulletMakers Workshop, The
Carroll Bullets
CBC
CHAA, Ltd.
Christman Jr., David
Country Armourer, The
Cubic Shot Shell Co., Inc.
Custom Tackle and Ammo
C.W. Cartridge Co.
Dakota Arms, Inc.
Dead Eye's Sport Center
DKT, Inc.
Elite Ammunition
Elko Arms
Estate Cartridge, Inc.
Freedom Arms, Inc.
Gammog, Gregory B. Gally
GDL Enterprises
Glaser Safety Slug, Inc.
Grand Falls Bullets, Inc.
Granite Custom Bullets
Heidenstrom Bullets
Hirtenberger Aktiengesellschaft
Hoelscher, Virgil
Horizons Unlimited
Hornady Mfg. Co.
Jackalope Gun Shop
Jensen Bullets
Jensen's Custom Ammunition
Jensen's Firearms Academy
Jones, J.D.
Kaswer Custom, Inc.
Keeler, R.H.
Kent Cartridge Mfg. Co. Ltd.
KJM Fabritek, Inc.
Lapua Ltd.
Lindsley Arms Cartridge Co.
Lomont Precision Bullets
MagSafe Ammo Co.
MAST Technology
McMurdo, Lynn
Men-Metallwerk Elisenhuette, GmbH
Milstor Corp.
Moreton/Fordyce Enterprises
Mullins Ammo
Naval Ordnance Works
NECO
Old Western Scrounger, Inc.
Oklahoma Ammunition Company
Parts & Surplus
Personal Protection Systems
Precision Delta Corp.
Precision Munitions, Inc.
Precision Reloading, Inc.
Professional Hunter Supplies
Rolston, Inc., Fred W.
Sandia Die & Cartridge Co.
SOS Products Co.
Specialty Gunsmithing
Spence, George W.
Spencer's Custom Guns
SSK Industries
Star Custom Bullets
State Arms Gun Co.
Stewart's Gunsmithing
Swift Bullet Co.
Talon Mfg. Co., Inc.
TCCI
3-D Ammunition & Bullets
3-Ten Corp.
Vitt/Boos
Vulpes Ventures, Inc.
Warren Muzzleloading Co., Inc.
Weaver Arms Corp. Gun Shop
Wells Custom Gunsmith, R.A.
Westley Richards & Co.
Worthy Products, Inc.
Yukon Arms Classic Ammunition
Zonie Bullets

AMMUNITION, FOREIGN

AFSCO Ammunition
Armscorp USA, Inc.
A-Square Co., Inc.
Beretta S.p.A., Pietro
B-West Imports, Inc.
BulletMakers Workshop, The
CBC
Century International Arms, Inc.
Cubic Shot Shell Co., Inc.
Dead Eye's Sport Center
Diana
DKT, Inc.
Dynamit Nobel-RWS, Inc.
Fiocchi of America, Inc.
First, Inc., Jack
Fisher Enterprises, Inc.
Fisher, R. Kermit
FN Herstal
Forgett Jr., Valmore J.
Gamo
Gibbs Rifle Co., Inc.
Hansen & Co.
Hansen Cartridge Co.
Hirtenberger Aktiengesellschaft
Hornady Mfg. Co.
IMI
IMI Services USA, Inc.
Jackalope Gun Shop
JagerSport, Ltd.
K.B.I., Inc.
Keng's Firearms Specialty, Inc.
Lapua Ltd.
MagSafe Ammo Co.
Maionchi-L.M.I.
Mandall Shooting Supplies, Inc.
MAST Technology
Merkuria Ltd.
New England Arms Co.
Oklahoma Ammunition Co.
Old Western Scrounger, Inc.
Paragon Sales & Services, Inc.
Precision Delta Corp.
R.E.T. Enterprises
Rocky Fork Enterprises
RWS
Sentinel Arms
Stoeger Industries
Southern Ammunition Co., Inc.
Spence, George W.
Stratco, Inc.
SwaroSports, Inc.
Talon Mfg. Co., Inc.
T.F.C. S.p.A.
USA Sporting Inc.
Vihtavuori Oy/Kaltron-Pettibone
Yukon Arms Classic Ammunition

AMMUNITION COMPONENTS—BULLETS, POWDER, PRIMERS, CASES

Acadian Ballistic Specialties
Accuracy Unlimited (Littleton, CO)
Accurate Arms Co., Inc.
Action Bullets, Inc.
ACTIV Industries, Inc.
Alaska Bullet Works
Alliant Techsystems
Allred Bullet Co.
Alpha LaFranck Enterprises
Arco Powder
Armfield Custom Bullets
A-Square Co., Inc.
Atlantic Rose, Inc.
Ballard Built
Barnes Bullets, Inc.
Beartooth Bullets
Beeline Custom Bullets Limited
Bell Reloading, Inc.
Belt MTN Arms
Berger Bullets, Ltd.
Bergman & Williams
Berry's Bullets
Bertram Bullet Co.
Big Bore Bullets of Alaska
Big Bore Express Ltd.
Bitterroot Bullet Co.
Black Belt Bullets
Black Hills Shooters Supply
Black Powder Products
Brenneke KG, Wilhelm
Briese Bullet Co., Inc.
Brown Co., E. Arthur
Brownells, Inc.
BRP, Inc.
Bruno Shooters Supply
Buckeye Custom Bullets
Buckskin Bullet Co.
Buffalo Arms
Buffalo Rock Shooters Supply
Bullet, Inc.
Bull-X, Inc.
Butler Enterprises
Buzztail Brass
Calhoon Varmint Bullets, James
Canyon Cartridge Corp.
Carnahan Bullets
Cascade Bullet Co., Inc.
CCI
Champion's Choice, Inc.
Cheddite France, S.A.
CheVron Bullets
C.J. Ballistics, Inc.
Clark Custom Guns, Inc.
Classic Brass
Competitor Corp., Inc.
Cook Engineering Service
Cor-Bon Bullet & Ammo Co.
Crawford Co., Inc., R.M.
Creative Cartridge Co.
Cummings Bullets
Curtis Gun Shop
Custom Bullets by Hoffman
Cutsinger Bench Rest Bullets
D&J Bullet Co. & Custom Gun Shop, Inc.
Dakota Arms, Inc.
Diamondback Supply
DKT, Inc.
Dohring Bullets
Double A Ltd.
DuPont
Eichelberger Bullets, Wm.
Elkhorn Bullets
Epps, Ellwood
Federal Cartridge Co.
Finch Custom Bullets
Fiocchi of America, Inc.
First, Inc., Jack
Forkin, Ben
Fowler Bullets
Foy Custom Bullets
Freedom Arms, Inc.
Fusilier Bullets
G&C Bullet Co., Inc.
Gander Mountain, Inc.
Gehmann, Walter
GOEX, Inc.
Golden Bear Bullets
Gonic Bullet Works
Gotz Bullets
"Gramps" Antique Cartridges
Granite Custom Bullets

PRODUCT DIRECTORY

Grayback Wildcats
Green Bay Bullets
Grier's Hard Cast Bullets
Grizzly Bullets
Group Tight Bullets
Gun City
Hammets VLD Bullets
Hardin Specialty Dist.
Harris Enterprises
Harrison Bullets
Hart & Son, Inc., Robert W.
Haselbauer Products, Jerry
Hawk, Inc.
Hawk Laboratories, Inc.
Heidenstrom Bullets
Hercules, Inc.
Hirtenberger Aktiengesellschaft
Hobson Precision Mfg. Co.
Hodgdon Powder Co., Inc.
Hornady Mfg. Co.
HT Bullets
Huntington Die Specialties
IMI
IMI Services USA, Inc.
Imperial Magnum Corp.
IMR Powder Co.
J-4, Inc.
J&D Components
J&L Superior Bullets
Jensen Bullets
Jensen's Firearms Academy
Jester Bullets
JLK Bullets
Johnson's Lage Uniwad
JRP Custom Bullets
Ka Pu Kapili
Kasmarsik Bullets
Kaswer Custom, Inc.
Keith's Bullets
Ken's Kustom Kartridge
Keng's Firearms Specialty, Inc.
Kent Cartridge Mfg. Co. Ltd.
KJM Fabritek, Inc.
KLA Enterprises
Kodiak Custom Bullets
Lapua Ltd.
Lawrence Brand Shot
Legend Products Corp.
Liberty Shooting Supplies
Lightfield Ammunition Corp., The Slug Group
Lightning Performance Innovations, Inc.
Littleton, J.F.
M&D Munitions Ltd.
Magnus Bullets
Maine Custom Bullets
Maionchi-L.M.I.
Marchmon Bullets
MarMik Inc.
Marple & Associates, Dick
MAST Technology
Master Class Bullets
McMurdo, Lynn
MEC, Inc.
Meister Bullets
Men-Metallwerk Elisenhuette, GmbH
Merkuria Ltd.
Michael's Antiques
Miller Enterprises, Inc., R.P.
Mitchell Bullets, R.F.
MI-TE Bullets
MoLoc Bullets
Montana Precision Swaging
Mt. Baldy Bullet Co.
Mulhern, Rick
Murmur Corp.
Mushroom Express Bullet Co.
Nagel's Bullets
National Bullet Co.
Naval Ordnance Works
Necromancer Industries, Inc.
Norma
North American Shooting Systems
North Devon Firearms Services
Northern Precision Custom Swaged Bullets
Nosler, Inc.
Oklahoma Ammunition Co.
Old Wagon Bullets

Old Western Scrounger, Inc.
Omark Industries
Ordnance Works, The
Pacific Rifle Co.
Page Custom Bullets
Patrick Bullets
Pattern Control
Peerless Alloy, Inc.
Petro-Explo, Inc.
Phillippi Custom Bullets, Justin
Pinetree Bullets
Polywad, Inc.
Pomeroy, Robert
Powder Valley Services
Precision Components
Precision Components and Guns
Precision Delta Corp.
Precision Munitions, Inc.
Prescott Projectile Co.
Price Bullets, Patrick W.
Professional Hunter Supplies
Rainier Ballistics Corp.
Ranger Products
Red Cedar Precision Mfg.
Redwood Bullet Works
Reloading Specialties, Inc.
Remington Arms Co., Inc.
Radical Concepts
Rifle Works & Armory
R.I.S. Co., Inc.
R.M. Precision, Inc.
Robinson H.V. Bullets
Rolston, Inc., Fred W.
Rubright Bullets
Scharch Mfg., Inc.
Schmidtman Custom Ammunition
Schneider Bullets
Schroeder Bullets
Scot Powder
Seebeck Assoc., R.E.
Shappy Bullets
Shilen Rifles, Inc.
Shooting Components Marketing
Sierra Bullets
Silhouette, The
Specialty Gunsmithing
Speer Products
Spencer's Custom Guns
Stanley Bullets
Star Custom Bullets
Stark's Bullet Mfg.
Stewart's Gunsmithing
Talon Mfg. Co., Inc.
Taracorp Industries
TCCI
TCSR
T.F.C. S.p.A.
Thompson Precision
3-D Ammunition & Bullets
TMI Products
Trico Plastics
Trophy Bonded Bullets, Inc.
True Flight Bullet Co.
USAC
Vann Custom Bullets
Vihtavuori Oy/Kaltron-Pettibone
Vincent's Shop
Vom Hoffe
Watson Trophy Match Bullets
Weatherby, Inc.
Western Nevada West Coast Bullets
White Shooting Systems, Inc.
Widener's Reloading & Shooting Supply
Williams Bullet Co., J.R.
Winchester Div., Olin Corp.
Windjammer Tournament Wads, Inc.
Winkle Bullets
Woodleigh
Worthy Products, Inc.
Wosenitz VHP, Inc.
Wyant Bullets
Wyoming Bonded Bullets
Wyoming Custom Bullets
Yukon Arms Classic Ammunition
Zero Ammunition Co., Inc.
Zonie Bullets

ANTIQUE ARMS DEALERS

Ackerman & Co.
Ad Hominem
Ahlman Guns
Antique American Firearms
Antique Arms Co.

Aplan Antiques & Art, James O.
Armoury, Inc., The
Bear Mountain Gun & Tool
Bob's Tactical Indoor Shooting Range & Gun Shop

Boggs, Wm.
British Antiques
Buckskin Machine Works
Buffalo Arms
Burgess & Son Gunsmiths, R.W.
Cabela's
Cannon's Guns
Cape Outfitters
Carlson, Douglas R.
Chadick's Ltd.
Chambers Flintlocks Ltd., Jim
Champlin Firearms, Inc.
Chuck's Gun Shop
Classic Guns, Inc.
Cole's Gun Works
D&D Gunsmiths, Ltd.
Delhi Gun House
Dixie Gun Works, Inc.
Dixon Muzzleloading Shop, Inc.
Duffy, Charles E.
Dyson & Son Ltd., Peter
Ed's Gun House
Enguix Import-Export
Fagan & Co., William
First, Inc., Jack
Fish, Marshall F.
Flayderman & Co., N.
Forgett Jr., Valmore J.
Frielich Police Equipment
Fulmer's Antique Firearms, Chet
Getz Barrel Co.
Glass, Herb
Goergen's Gun Shop, Inc.
Golden Age Arms Co.
Greenwald, Leon E. "Bud"
Gun Room, The
Gun Room Press, The
Gun Works, The
Guns Antique & Modern DBA/ Charles E. Duffy
Guncraft Sports, Inc.

APPRAISERS—GUNS, ETC.

Accuracy Gun Shop
Ahlman Guns
Antique Arms Co.
Armoury, Inc., The
Arundel Arms & Ammunition, Inc., A.
Blue Book Publications, Inc.
Bob's Tactical Indoor Shooting Range & Gun Shop
Bustani, Leo
Butterfield & Butterfield
Camilli, Lou
Cannon's Guns
Cape Outfitters
Chadick's Ltd.
Champlin Firearms, Inc.
Christie's East
Clark Custom Guns, Inc.
Clark Firearms Engraving
Classic Guns, Inc.
Clements' Custom Leathercraft, Chas
Cole's Gun Works
Colonial Repair
Corry, John
Costa, David
Custom Tackle and Ammo
D&D Gunsmiths, Ltd.
DGR Custom Rifles
Dixie Gun Works, Inc.
Dixon Muzzleloading Shop, Inc.
Duane's Gun Repair
Ed's Gun House
Epps, Ellwood
Eversull Co., Inc., K.
Fagan & Co., William
First, Inc., Jack
Fish, Marshall F.
Flayderman & Co., Inc., N.
Forgett, Valmore J., Jr.
Forty Five Ranch Enterprises
Frontier Arms Co., Inc.
Golden Age Arms Co.
Gonzalez Guns, Ramon B.
"Gramps" Antique Cartridges
Greenwald, Leon E. "Bud"
Griffin & Howe, Inc.
Groenewold, John
Gun City
Gun Room Press, The
Gun Shop, The
Gun Works, The
Guncraft Sports, Inc.
Hallowell & Co.
Hammans, Charles E.

Hallowell & Co.
Hansen & Co.
Hunkeler, A.
Johns, Bill
Kelley's
Ledbetter Airguns, Riley
LeFever Arms Co., Inc.
Lever Arms Service Ltd.
Liberty Antique Gunworks
Lock's Philadelphia Gun Exchange
Log Cabin Sport Shop
Martin's Gun Shop
Mathews & Son, Inc., George E.
Mendez, John A.
Montana Outfitters
Mountain Bear Rifle Works, Inc.
Museum of Historical Arms, Inc.
Muzzleloaders Etcetera, Inc.
Navy Arms Co.
N.C. Ordnance Co.
New England Arms Co.
Pioneer Guns
Pony Express Sport Shop, Inc.
Retting, Inc., Martin B.
S&S Firearms
Sarco, Inc.
Scott Fine Guns, Inc., Thad
Semmer, Charles
Shootin' Shack, Inc.
Steves House of Guns
Stott's Creek Armory, Inc.
Strawbridge, Victor W.
Track of the Wolf, Inc.
Vic's Gun Refinishing
Vintage Arms, Inc.
Wiest, M.C.
Winchester Sutler, Inc., The
Wood, Frank
Yearout, Lewis E.

HandiCrafts Unltd.
Hank's Gun Shop
Hansen & Co.
Hughes, Steven Dodd
Idaho Ammunition Service
Irwin, Campbell H.
Island Pond Gun Shop
Jaeger, Inc., Paul/Dunn's
Jensen's Custom Ammunition
Jonas Appraisers—Taxidermy Animals, Jack
Kelley's
Ledbetter Airguns, Riley
LeFever Arms Co., Inc.
Lever Arms Service Ltd.
Liberty Antique Gunworks
Lock's Philadelphia Gun Exchange
Mac's .45 Shop
Madis, George
Martin's Gun Shop
Montana Outfitters
Mowrey's Guns & Gunsmithing
Museum of Historical Arms, Inc.
Muzzleloaders Etcetera, Inc.
Navy Arms Co.
N.C. Ordnance Co.
New England Arms Co.
Nitex, Inc.
Orvis Co., The
Pasadena Gun Center
Pentheny de Pentheny
Perazzi USA, Inc.
Peterson Gun Shop, Inc., A.W.
Pettinger Books, Gerald
Pioneer Guns
Pony Express Sport Shop, Inc.
R.E.T. Enterprises
Retting, Inc., Martin B.
Richards, John
S&S Firearms
Safari Outfitters Ltd.
Scott Fine Guns, Inc., Thad
Shell Shack
Shootin' Shack, Inc.
Sipes Gun Shop
Sportsmen's Exchange & Western Starnes Gunmaker, Ken
Steger, James R.
Stott's Creek Armory, Inc.
Stratco, Inc.
Strawbridge, Victor W.
Thurston Sports, Inc.
Vic's Gun Refinishing
Walker Arms Co., Inc.

DIRECTORY OF THE ARMS TRADE

Wayne Firearms for Collectors and Investors, James
Wells Custom Gunsmith, R.A.
Whildin & Sons Ltd., E.H.
Wiest, M.C.
Williams Shootin' Iron Service
Winchester Sutler, Inc., The
Wood, Frank
Yearout, Lewis E.

AUCTIONEERS—GUNS, ETC.

Butterfield & Butterfield
Christie's East
Kelley's
"Little John's" Antique Arms
Sotheby's

BOOKS (Publishers and Dealers)

American Handgunner Magazine
Armory Publications
Arms & Armour Press
Arms, Peripheral Data Systems
Arms Software
Ballistic Products, Inc.
Barnes Bullets, Inc.
Blackhawk West
Blacksmith Corp.
Blacktail Mountain Books
Blue Book Publications, Inc.
Brown Co., E. Arthur
Brownell's, Inc.
Buffalo Arms
Calibre Press, Inc.
Cape Outfitters
Colonial Repair
Colorado Sutlers Arsenal
Corbin, Inc.
Crit'R Call
Cumberland States Arsenal
DBI Books
Flores Publications, Inc., J.
Golden Age Arms Co.
Gun City
Gun Hunter Books
Gun List
Gun Parts Corp., The
Gun Room Press, The
Gun Works, The
Guncraft Books
Guncraft Sports, Inc.
Gunnerman Books
Guns, (Div. of D.C. Engineering, Inc.)
GUNS Magazine
H&P Publishing
Handgun Press
Harris Publications
Hawk, Inc.
Hawk Laboratories, Inc.
Heritage/VSP Gun Books
Hodgdon Powder Co., Inc.
Home Shop Machinist, The
Hornady Mfg. Co.
Hungry Horse Books
Info-Arm
Ironside International Publishers, Inc.
King & Co.
Krause Publications, Inc.
Lane Publishing
Lapua Ltd.
Lethal Force Institute
Lyman Products Corp.
Martin Bookseller, J.
McKee Publications
MI-TE Bullets
Mountain South
New Win Publishing, Inc.
NgraveR Co., The
OK Weber, Inc.
Old Western Scrounger, Inc.
Outdoorsman's Bookstore, The
Pejsa Ballistics
Petersen Publishing Co.
Pettinger Books, Gerald
Police Bookshelf
Precision Shooting, Inc.
Reloading Specialties, Inc.
R.G.-G., Inc.
Riling Arms Books Co., Ray
Rutgers Book Center
S&S Firearms
Safari Press, Inc.
Saunders Gun & Machine Shop
Shootin' Accessories, Ltd.
Sierra Bullets
S.P.G., Inc.
Stackpole Books
Stoeger Industries
Stoeger Publishing Co.
"Su-Press-On," Inc.
Thomas, Charles C.
Trafalgar Square
Trotman, Ken
Vega Tool Co.
VSP Publishers
WAMCO—New Mexico
Wiest, M.C.
Wilderness Sound Products Ltd.
Williams Gun Sight Co.
Wolfe Publishing Co.
Wolf's Western Traders

BULLET AND CASE LUBRICANTS

Bear Reloaders
Blackhawk West
Brass-Tech Industries
Break-Free, Inc.
Brown Co., E. Arthur
Buffalo Arms
Camp-Cap Products
CFVentures
Chem-Pak, Inc.
Cooper-Woodward
Elkhorn Bullets
E-Z-Way Systems
Forster Products
Green Bay Bullets
Guardsman Products
HEBB Resources
Hollywood Engineering
Hornady Mfg. Co.
Imperial
Le Clear Industries
Lithi Bee Bullet Lube
M&N Bullet Lube
MI-TE Bullets
NECO
Paco's
RCBS
Reardon Products
Rooster Laboratories
Shay's Gunsmithing
Small Custom Mould & Bullet Co.
S.P.G., Inc.
Tamarack Products, Inc.
Warren Muzzleloading Co., Inc.
Widener's Reloading & Shooting Supply, Inc.
Young Country Arms

BULLET SWAGE DIES AND TOOLS

Brynin, Milton
Bullet Swaging Supply, Inc.
Camdex, Inc.
Corbin, Inc.
Holland's
Hollywood Engineering
Necromancer Industries, Inc.
Niemi Engineering, W.B.
North Devon Firearms Services
Rorschach Precision Products
Sport Flite Manufacturing Co.

CARTRIDGES FOR COLLECTORS

Ad Hominem
Alpha 1 Drop Zone
Buck Stix—SOS Products Co.
Cameron's
Campbell, Dick
Cole's Gun Works
Colonial Repair
Country Armourer, The
Delhi Gun House
DGR Custom Rifles
Duane's Gun Repair
Eichelberger Bullets, Wm.
Enguix Import-Export
Epps, Ellwood
First, Inc., Jack
Forty Five Ranch Enterprises
Goergen's Gun Shop, Inc.
"Gramps" Antique Cartridges
Gun Parts Corp., The
Gun Room Press, The
Idaho Ammunition Service
MAST Technology
Michael's Antiques
Montana Outfitters
Mountain Bear Rifle Works, Inc.
Pasadena Gun Center
Pioneer Guns
Samco Global Arms, Inc.
San Francisco Gun Exchange
SOS Products Co.
Ward & Van Valkenburg
Yearout, Lewis E.

CASES, CABINETS, RACKS AND SAFES—GUN

Abel Safe & File, Inc.
Alco Carrying Cases
All Rite Products, Inc.
Allen Co., Bob
Allen Co., Inc.
Allen Sportswear, Bob
Alumna Sport by Dee Zee
American Display Co.
American Security Products Co.
Americase
Ansen Enterprises
Arizona Custom Case
Arkfeld Mfg. & Dist. Co., Inc.
Armes de Chasse
Art Jewel Enterprises Ltd.
Ashby Turkey Calls
Aspen Outdoors, Inc.
Bagmaster Mfg., Inc.
Barramundi Corp.
Berry's Mfg. Inc.
Big Sky Racks, Inc.
Big Spring Enterprises "Bore Stores"
Bill's Custom Cases
Bison Studios
Black Sheep Brand
Boyt
Brauer Bros. Mfg. Co.
Brell Mar Products
Browning Arms Co.
Brunsport, Inc.
Bucheimer, J.M.
Bushmaster Hunting & Fishing
Cannon Safe, Inc.
Cascade Fabrication
Chipmunk
Clark Custom Guns, Inc.
Cobalt Mfg., Inc.
D&L Industries
Dara-Nes, Inc.
Deepeeka Exports Pvt. Ltd.
D.J. Marketing
Doskocil Mfg. Co., Inc.
DTM International, Inc.
Elk River, Inc.
English Inc., A.G.
Enhanced Presentations, Inc.
Fort Knox Security Products
Frontier Safe Co.
Galati Internationl
Galazan
GALCO International Ltd.
Granite Custom Bullets
Gun Locker
Gun-Ho Sports Cases
Gusdorf Corp.
Hafner Creations, Inc.
Hall Plastics, Inc., John
Harrison-Hurtz Enterprises, Inc.
Hastings Barrels
Homak Mfg. Co., Inc.
Hoppe's Div.
Huey Gun Cases
Hugger Hooks Co.
Hunter Co., Inc.
Impact Case Co.
Johanssons Vapentillbehor, Bert
Johnston Bros.
Jumbo Sports Products
Kalispel Case Line
Kane Products, Inc.
KK Air International
Knock on Wood Antiques
Kolpin Mfg., Inc.
Lakewood Products, Inc.
Liberty Safe
Marsh, Mike
Maximum Security Corp.
McWelco Products
Morton Booth Co.
MPC
MTM Molded Products Co., Inc.
National Security Safe Co., Inc.
NCP Products, Inc.
Necessary Concepts, Inc.
Nesci Enterprises, Inc.
Outa-Site Gun Carriers
Outdoor Connection, Inc., The
Pachmayr Ltd.
Palmer Security Products
Penguin Industries, Inc.
Perazzi USA, Inc.
Pflumm Mfg. Co.
Poburka, Philip
Powell & Son (Gunmakers) Ltd., William
Protecto Plastics
Prototech Industries, Inc.
Quality Arms, Inc.
Savana Sports, Inc.
Schulz Industries
Southern Security
Sportsman's Communicators
Sun Welding Safe Co.
Surecase Co., The
Sweet Home, Inc.
Tinks & Ben Lee Hunting Products
Waller & Son, Inc., W.
WAMCO, Inc.
Wilson Case, Inc.
Woodstream
Zanotti Armor, Inc.
Ziegel Engineering

CHOKE DEVICES, RECOIL ABSORBERS AND RECOIL PADS

Accuright
Action Products, Inc.
Ahlman Guns
Allen Co., Bob
Allen Sportswear, Bob
Answer Products Co.
Arms Ingenuity Co.
Baer Custom, Inc., Les
Baker, Stan
Bansner's Gunsmithing Specialties
Bartlett Engineering
Black Sheep Brand
Briley Mfg., Inc.
B-Square Co., Inc.
Bull Mountain Rifle Co.
C&H Research
Cape Outfitters
Cation
Chuck's Gun Shop
Clark Custom Guns, Inc.
Clearview Products
Colonial Arms, Inc.
Connecticut Shotgun Mfg. Co.
Crane Sales Co., George S.
Danuser Machine Co.
Dayson Arms Ltd.
Dever Co., Jack
Dina Arms Corporation
D-Max, Inc.
Elsen, Inc., Pete
Fabian Bros. Sporting Goods, Inc.
Gentry Custom Gunmaker, David
Graybill's Gun Shop
Great 870 Co., The
Guns, (Div. of D.C. Engineering, Inc.)
Harper, William E.
Hastings Barrels
Holland's
I.N.C., Inc.
Intermountain Arms & Tackle, Inc.
Jaeger, Inc., Paul/Dunn's
Jenkins Recoil Pads, Inc.
J.P. Enterprises, Inc.
Kick Eez
London Guns Ltd.
Lyman Instant Targets, Inc.
Lyman Products Corp.
Mag-Na-Port International, Inc.
Marble Arms
Meadow Industries
Michaels of Oregon Co.
Morrow, Bud

PRODUCT DIRECTORY

Nelson/Weather-rite, Inc.
One Of A Kind
Pachmayr Ltd.
Palsa Outdoor Products
PAST Sporting Goods, Inc.
Powell & Son (Gunmakers) Ltd.,
  William
Pro-Port Ltd.
Protektor Model

Que Industries
R.M. Precision, Inc.
Shotguns Unlimited
Spencer's Custom Guns
Stone Enterprises Ltd.
Trulock Tool
Uncle Mike's
Wise Guns, Dale

CHRONOGRAPHS AND PRESSURE TOOLS

Brown Co., E. Arthur
Canons Delcour
Chronotech
Competition Electronics, Inc.
Custom Chronograph, Inc.
D&H Precision Tooling
Hornady Mfg. Co.

Kent Cartridge Mfg. Co. Ltd.
Oehler Research, Inc.
P.A.C.T., Inc.
Shooting Chrony, Inc.
SKAN A.R.
Tepeco

CLEANING AND REFINISHING SUPPLIES

AC Dyna-tite Corp.
Acculube II, Inc.
Accupro Gun Care
ADCO International
American Gas & Chemical Co., Ltd.
Answer Products Co.
Armsport, Inc.
Atlantic Mills, Inc.
Atsko/Sno-Seal, Inc.
Barnes Bullets, Inc.
Belltown, Ltd.
Birchwood Casey
Blackhawk East
Blue and Gray Products, Inc.
Break-Free, Inc.
Bridgers Best
Brown Co., E. Arthur
Cape Outfitters
Chem-Pak, Inc.
Chopie Mfg., Inc.
Clenzoil Corp.
Colonial Arms, Inc.
CONKKO
Crane & Crane Ltd.
Creedmoor Sports, Inc.
Custom Products
D&H Prods. Co., Inc.
Dara-Nes, Inc.
Deepeeka Exports Pvt. Ltd.
Dewey Mfg. Co., Inc., J.
Du-Lite Corp.
Dutchman's Firearms, Inc., The
Dykstra, Doug
E&L Mfg., Inc.
Eezox, Inc.
Effebi SNC, Dr. Franco Beretta
Ekol Leather Care
Faith Associates, Inc.
Flitz International Ltd.
Fluoramics, Inc.
Forster Products
Frontier Products Co.
G96 Products Co., Inc.
G.B.C. Industries, Inc.
Goddard, Allen
Golden Age Arms Co.
Gozon Corp., U.S.A.
Guardsman Products
Half Moon Rifle Shop
Heatbath Corp.
Hoppe's Div.
Hornady Mfg. Co.
Hydrosorbent Products
Iosso Products
J-B Bore Cleaner
Johnston Bros.
Kellogg's Professional Products
Kent Cartridge Mfg. Co. Ltd.
Kesselring Gun Shop

Kleen-Bore, Inc.
Laurel Mountain Forge
LEM Gun Specialties, Inc.
Lewis Lead Remover, The
List Precision Engineering
LPS Laboratories, Inc.
Marble Arms
Micro Sight Co.
Minute Man High Tech Industries
Mountain View Sports, Inc.
MTM Molded Products Co., Inc.
Muscle Products Corp.
Nesci Enterprises, Inc.
Old World Oil Products
Omark Industries
Original Mink Oil, Inc.
Outers Laboratories, Div. of Blount
Ox-Yoke Originals, Inc.
P&M Sales and Service
Pachmayr Ltd.
Parker Gun Finishes
Pendleton Royal
Penguin Industries, Inc.
Precision Reloading, Inc.
Prolix® Lubricants
Pro-Shot Products, Inc.
R&S Industries Corp.
Radiator Specialty Co.
Rickard, Inc., Pete
RIG Products Co.
Rod Guide Co.
Rooster Laboratories
Rusteprufe Laboratories
Rusty Duck Premium Gun Care
  Products
Saunders Gun & Machine Shop
Shiloh Creek
Shooter's Choice
Shootin' Accessories, Ltd.
Silencio/Safety Direct
Sno-Seal, Inc.
Spencer's Custom Guns
Svon Corp.
Tag Distributors
TDP Industries, Inc.
Tetra Gun Lubricants
Texas Platers Supply Co.
T.F.C. S.p.A.
United States Products Co.
Van Gorden & Son, Inc., C.S.
Venco Industries, Inc.
Warren Muzzleloading Co., Inc.
WD-40 Co.
Wick, David E.
Williams Shootin' Iron Service
Willow Bend
Young Country Arms
Z-Coat Industrial Coatings, Inc.

COMPUTER SOFTWARE—BALLISTICS

Action Target, Inc.
AmBr Software Group Ltd.
Arms, Peripheral Data
  Systems
Arms Software
Ballistic Engineering &
  Software, Inc.
Ballistic Program Co., Inc., The
Barnes Bullets, Inc.
Beartooth Bullets
Bestload, Inc.
Blackwell, W.
Canons Delcour
Corbin, Inc.

Country Armourer, The
Data Tech Software
  Systems
Exe, Inc.
Ford, Jack
JBM Software
Jensen Bullets
J.I.T. Ltd.
JWH:Software
Kent Cartridge Mfg. Co. Ltd.
Load From A Disk
Maionchi-L.M.I.
Oehler Research, Inc.
P.A.C.T., Inc.

PC Bullet/ADC, Inc.
Pejsa Ballistics
RCBS

Sierra Bullets
Tioga Engineering Co., Inc.
Vancini, Carl

CUSTOM GUNSMITHS

A&W Repair
Acadian Ballistic Specialties
Accuracy Gun Shop
Accuracy Unlimited (Glendale, AZ)
Ace Custom 45's, Inc.
Ackerman & Co.
Ad Hominem
Adair Custom Shop, Bill
Ahlman Guns
Aldis Gunsmithing & Shooting Supply
Alpha Gunsmith Division
Alpine's Precision Gunsmithing &
  Indoor Shooting Range
Amrine's Gun Shop
Answer Products Co.
Antique Arms Co.
Armament Gunsmithing Co., Inc.
Arms Craft Gunsmithing
Arms Ingenuity Co.
Arnold Arms Co., Inc.
Arrieta, S.L.
Art's Gun & Sport Shop, Inc.
Arundel Arms & Ammunition, Inc., A.
AWC Systems Technology
Baelder, Harry
Baer Custom, Inc., Les
Bain & Davis, Inc.
Bansner's Gunsmithing Specialties
Barnes Bullets, Inc.
Barta's Gunsmithing
Baumannize Custom
Bear Arms
Bear Mountain Gun & Tool
Beaver Lodge
Behlert Precision, Inc.
Beitzinger, George
Belding's Custom Gun Shop
Bellm Contenders
Belt MTN Arms
Benchmark Guns
Bengtson Arms Co., L.
Biesen, Al
Biesen, Roger
Billeb, Stephen L.
Billings Gunsmiths, Inc.
BlackStar AccuMax Barrels
BlackStar Barrel Accurizing
Bond Custom Firearms
Borden's Accuracy
Borovnik KG, Ludwig
Brace, Larry D.
Briese Bullet Co., Inc.
Briganti & Co., A.
Briley Mfg., Inc.
Broad Creek Rifle Works
Brockman's Custom Gunsmithing
Broken Gun Ranch
Brown Precision, Inc.
Buckhorn Gun Works
Buckskin Machine Works
Budin, Dave
Bull Mountain Rifle Co.
Bullberry Barrel Works, Ltd.
Burkhart Gunsmithing, Don
C&J Enterprises, Inc.
Cache La Poudre Rifleworks
Camilli, Lou
Campbell, Dick
Cannon's Guns
Carolina Precision Rifles
Carter's Gun Shop
Caywood, Shane J.
Chambers Flintlocks Ltd., Jim
Champlin, R. MacDonald
Champlin Firearms, Inc.
Chicasaw Gun Works
Christman Jr., David
Chuck's Gun Shop
Clark Custom Guns, Inc.
Clark Firearms Engraving
Classic Arms Corp.
Classic Guns, Inc.
Cloward's Gun Shop
Cochran, Oliver
Coffin, Charles H.
Cogar's Gunsmithing
Cole's Gun Works
Coleman's Custom Repair
Colonial Repair
Colorado Gunsmithing Academy
  Lamar
Colt's Mfg. Co., Inc.

Competitive Pistol Shop, The
Conrad, C.A.
Corkys Gun Clinic
Costa, David
Cox, C. Ed
Craig Custom Ltd.
Creekside Gun Shop, Inc.
Cullity Restoration, Daniel
Cumberland Knife & Gun Works
Curtis Custom Shop
Custom Checkering Service
Custom Gun Products
Custom Gun Stocks
Custom Gunsmiths
Custom Shop, The
Cylinder & Slide, Inc.
D&D Gunsmiths, Ltd.
D&J Bullet Co. & Custom Gun
  Shop, Inc.
Dangler, Homer L.
Darlington Gun Works, Inc.
Davis, Don
Davis Service Center, Bill
Delorge, Ed
Dever Co., Jack
DGR Custom Rifles
DGS, Inc.
Dietz Gun Shop & Range, Inc.
Dilliott Gunsmithing, Inc.
Donnelly, C.P.
Dowtin Gunworks
Duane's Gun Repair
Duffy, Charles E.
Duncan's Gun Works, Inc.
Dyson & Son Ltd., Peter
Echols & Co., D'Arcy
Eckelman Gunsmithing
Eggleston, Jere D.
EGW Evolution Gun Works
Erhardt, Dennis
Eskridge Rifles, Steven Eskridge
Eversull Co., Inc., K.
Eyster Heritage Gunsmiths, Inc., Ken
Fanzoj GmbH
Ferris Firearms
First, Inc., Jack
Fish, Marshall F.
Fisher, Jerry A.
Fisher Custom Firearms
Flaig's
Fleming Firearms
Flynn's Custom Guns
Forkin, Ben
Forster, Kathy
Forster, Larry L.
Forthofer's Gunsmithing & Knifemaking
Francesca, Inc.
Francotte & Cie S.A., Auguste
Frank Custom Classic Arms, Ron
Frazier Brothers Enterprises
Frontier Arms Co., Inc.
Fullmer, Geo. M.
Gator Guns & Repair
Genecco Gun Works, K.
Gentry Custom Gunmaker, David
G.G. & G.
Gillmann, Edwin
Gilman-Mayfield, Inc.
Giron, Robert E.
Goens, Dale W.
Gonzalez Guns, Ramon B.
Goodling's Gunsmithing
Goodwin, Fred
Gordie's Gun Shop
Grace, Charles E.
Graybill's Gun Shop
Green, Roger M.
Greg Gunsmithing Repair
Griffin & Howe, Inc.
Groenewold, John
Gun Shop, The
Guns
Guns Antique & Modern DBA/
  Charles E. Duffy
Gunsite Custom Shop
Gunsite Gunsmithy
Gunsite Training Center
Gunsmithing Ltd.
Hagn Rifles & Actions, Martin
Hallberg Gunsmith, Fritz
Hamilton, Alex B.
Hammans, Charles E.

29th EDITION, 1997 **301**

DIRECTORY OF THE ARMS TRADE

Hammond Custom Guns Ltd., Guy
Hank's Gun Shop
Hanson's Gun Center, Dick
Hardison, Charles
Harold's Custom Gun Shop, Inc.
Harris Gunworks
Hart & Son, Inc., Robert W.
Hart Rifle Barrels, Inc.
Hartmann & Weiss GmbH
Hecht, Hubert J.
Heinie Specialty Products
Hendricks Gun Works
Hensler, Jerry
Hensley, Darwin
High Bridge Arms, Inc.
High Performance International
Highline Machine Co.
Hill, Loring F.
Hiptmayer, Armurier
Hiptmayer, Klaus
Hoag, James W.
Hobbie Gunsmithing, Duane A.
Hodgson, Richard
Hoehn Sales, Inc.
Hoelscher, Virgil
Hoenig & Rodman
Hofer Jagdwaffen, P.
Holland, Dick
Holland's
Hollis Gun Shop
Horst, Alan K.
Huebner, Corey O.
Hughes, Steven Dodd
Hunkeler, A.
Hyper-Single, Inc.
Imperial Magnum Corp.
Intermountain Arms & Tackle, Inc.
Irwin, Campbell H.
Island Pond Gun Shop
Ivanoff, Thomas G.
J&S Heat Treat
Jackalope Gun Shop
Jaeger, Inc., Paul/Dunn's
Jamison's Forge Works
Jarrett Rifles, Inc.
Jarvis, Inc.
Jensen's Custom Ammunition
Jim's Gun Shop
Jim's Precision
Johnston, James
Jones, J.D.
J.P. Enterprises, Inc.
Juenke, Vern
Jurras, L.E.
K-D, Inc.
KDF, Inc.
Ken's Gun Specialties
Ketchum, Jim
Kilham & Co.
Kimball, Gary
King's Gun Works
KLA Enterprises
Klein Custom Guns, Don
Kleinendorst, K.W.
Kneiper Custom Guns, Jim
Knippel, Richard
KOGOT
Kopp, Terry K.
Korzinek Riflesmith, J.
LaFrance Specialties
Lair, Sam
LaRocca Gun Works, Inc.
Lathrop's, Inc.
Laughridge, William R.
Lawson Co., Harry
Lebeau-Courally
LeFever Arms Co., Inc.
Liberty Antique Gunworks
Lind Custom Guns, Al
Linebaugh Custom Sixguns & Rifle Works
List Precision Engineering
Lock's Philadelphia Gun Exchange
Lomont Precision Bullets
London Guns Ltd.
Mac-1 Distributors
Mac's .45 Shop
Mag-Na-Port International, Inc.
Mahony, Philip Bruce
Makinson, Nicholas
Manley Shooting Supplies, Lowell
Martin's Gun Shop
Martz, John V.
Masker, Seely
Mathews & Son, Inc., George E.
Maxi-Mount
Mazur Restoration, Pete

McBros Rifle Co.
McCament, Jay
McCann's Machine & Gun Shop
McCann's Muzzle-Gun Works
McCluskey Precision Rifles
McFarland, Stan
McGowen Rifle Barrels
McKinney, R.P.
McMillan Rifle Barrels
MCS, Inc.
Mercer Custom Stocks, R.M.
Michael's Antiques
Mid-America Recreation, Inc.
Middlebrooks Custom Shop
Miller Co., David
Miller Arms, Inc.
Miller Custom
Mills Jr., Hugh B.
Mo's Competitor Supplies
Moeller, Steve
Monell Custom Guns
Moreton/Fordyce Enterprises
Morrison Custom Rifles, J.W.
Morrow, Bud
Mountain Bear Rifle Works, Inc.
Mowrey's Guns & Gunsmithing
Mullis Guncraft
Mustra's Custom Guns, Inc., Carl
NCP Products, Inc.
Nelson, Stephen
Nettestad Gun Works
New England Custom Gun Service
Newman Gunshop
Nicholson Custom
Nicklas, Ted
Nitex, Inc.
Norrell Arms, John
North American Shooting Systems
North Fork Custom Gunsmithing
Nu-Line Guns, Inc.
Oakland Custom Arms, Inc.
Old World Gunsmithing
Olson, Vic
Orvis Co., The
Ottmar, Maurice
Ozark Gun Works
P&S Gun Service
Pace Marketing, Inc.
Pagel Gun Works, Inc.
Parker Gun Finishes
Pasadena Gun Center
Paterson Gunsmithing
Pell, John T.
PEM's Mfg. Co.
Pence Precision Barrels
Penrod Precision
Pentheny de Pentheny
Perazone, Brian
Performance Specialists
Peterson Gun Shop, Inc., A.W.
Power Custom, Inc.
P.S.M.G. Gun Co.
Quality Firearms of Idaho, Inc.
Ray's Gunsmith Shop
Renfrew Guns & Supplies
Ridgetop Sporting Goods
Ries, Chuck
Rifles Inc.
Rigby & Co., John
RMS Custom Gunsmithing
Robar Co.'s, Inc., The
Roberts Products
Robinson, Don
Rocky Mountain Arms, Inc.
Rocky Mountain Rifle Works Ltd.
Rogers Gunsmithing, Bob
Romain's Custom Guns, Inc.
RPM
Rudnicky, Susan
Rupert's Gun Shop
Ryan, Chad L.
Sanders Custom Gun Service
Schiffman, Curt
Schiffman, Mike
Schiffman, Norman
Schuetzen Gun Co.
Schumakers Gun Shop, William
Schwartz Custom Guns, Wayne E.
Scott Fine Guns, Inc., Thad
Scott, Dwight
Scott, McDougall & Associates
Shaw, Inc., E.R.
Shay's Gunsmithing
Shell Shack
Shockley, Harold H.
Shooten' Haus, The
Shooter Trap, The

Shooters Supply
Shootin' Shack, Inc.
Shooting Specialties
Shotgun Shop, The
Shotguns Unlimited
Silver Ridge Gun Shop
Simmons Gun Repair, Inc.
Singletary, Kent
Sipes Gun Shop
Siskiyou Gun Works
Skeoch, Brian R.
Slezak, Jerome F.
Small Arms Mfg. Co.
Smith, Art
Smith, Sharmon
Snapp's Gunshop
Spencer Reblue Service
Spencer's Custom Guns
Spokhandguns, Inc.
Sportsmen's Exchange & Western Gun Traders, Inc.
Spradlin's
Springfield, Inc.
SSK Industries
Starnes Gunmaker, Ken
Steelman's Gun Shop
Steffens, Ron
Steger, James R.
Stiles Custom Guns
Storey, Dale A.
Stott's Creek Armory, Inc.
Strawbridge, Victor W.
Sullivan, David S.
Swampfire Shop, The
Swann, D.J.
Swenson's 45 Shop, A.D.
Swift River Gunworks, Inc.
Szweda, Robert
300 Gunsmith Service, Inc.
Talmage, William G.
Tank's Rifle Shop
Tarnhelm Supply Co., Inc.
Taylor & Robbins
Ten-Ring Precision, Inc.
Thompson, Randall

CUSTOM METALSMITHS

Adair Custom Shop, Bill
Ahlman Guns
Aldis Gunsmithing & Shooting Supply
Allen, Richard L.
Amrine's Gun Shop
Answer Products Co.
Arnold Arms Co., Inc.
Arundel Arms & Ammunition, Inc., A.
Baer Custom, Inc., Les
Bansner's Gunsmithing Specialties
Baron Technology
Bear Mountain Gun & Tool
Behlert Precision, Inc.
Beitzinger, George
Benchmark Guns
Bengtson Arms Co., L.
Biesen, Al
Billingsley & Brownell
BlackStar AccuMax Barrels
BlackStar Barrel Accurizing
Brace, Larry D.
Broad Creek Rifle Works
Brockmans Custom Gunsmithing
Brown Precision, Inc.
Buckhorn Gun Works
Bull Mountain Rifle Co.
Campbell, Dick
Carter's Gun Shop
Champlin Firearms, Inc.
Checkmate Refinishing
Classic Guns, Inc.
Colonial Repair
Colorado Gunsmithing Academy Lamar
Craftguard
Crandall Tool & Machine Co.
Cullity Restoration, Daniel
Custom Gun Products
Custom Gunsmiths
D&D Gunsmiths, Ltd.
D&H Precision Tooling
Dietz Gun Shop & Range, Inc.
Duncan's Gunworks, Inc.
Erhardt, Dennis
Eyster Heritage Gunsmiths, Inc., Ken
First, Inc., Jack
Fisher, Jerry A.
Forster, Larry L.
Francesca, Inc.
Frank Custom Classic Arms, Ron

Thurston Sports, Inc.
Time Precision, Inc.
Titus, Daniel
Tom's Gun Repair
Tooley Custom Rifles
Trevallion Gunstocks
Upper Missouri Trading Co.
USA Sporting Inc.
Van Epps, Milton
Van Horn, Gil
Van Patten, J.W.
Vest, John
Vic's Gun Refinishing
Vintage Arms, Inc.
Volquartsen Custom Ltd.
Von Minden Gunsmithing Services
Walker Arms Co., Inc.
Wardell Precision Handguns Ltd.
Weaver Arms Corp. Gun Shop
Weber & Markin Custom Gunsmiths
Weems, Cecil
Weigand Combat Handguns, Inc.
Wells, Fred F.
Wells Custom Gunsmith, R.A.
Welsh, Bud
Werth, T.W.
Wessinger Custom Guns & Engraving
West, Robert G.
Western Design
Westley Richards & Co.
Westwind Rifles, Inc.
Wichita Arms, Inc.
Wiebe, Duane
Wild West Guns
Williams Gun Sight Co.
Williams Shootin' Iron Service
Williamson Precision Gunsmithing
Wilson's Gun Shop
Winter, Robert M.
Wise Guns, Dale
Wiseman and Co., Bill
Wood, Frank
Yankee Gunsmith
Zeeryp, Russ

Fullmer, Geo. M.
Gentry Custom Gunmaker, David
Gordie's Gun Shop
Grace, Charles E.
Graybill's Gun Shop
Green, Roger M.
Griffin & Howe, Inc.
Gun Shop, The
Guns
Gunsmithing Ltd.
Hagn Rifles & Actions, Martin
Hallberg Gunsmith, Fritz
Hart & Son, Inc., Robert W.
Hecht, Hubert J.
Heilmann, Stephen
Heppler's Machining
Highline Machine Co.
Hiptmayer, Armurier
Hiptmayer, Klaus
Hoelscher, Virgil
Holland's
Hollis Gun Shop
Horst, Alan K.
Hyper-Single, Inc.
Intermountain Arms & Tackle
Ivanoff, Thomas G.
J&S Heat Treat
Jaeger, Inc., Paul/Dunn's
Jeffredo Gunsight
Johnston, James
Ken's Gun Specialties
Kilham & Co.
Klein Custom Guns, Don
Kleinendorst, K.W.
Kopp, Terry K.
Lampert, Ron
LaRocca Gun Works, Inc.
Lawson Co., Harry
Lind Custom Guns, Al
List Precision Engineering
Mac's .45 Shop
Mains Enterprises, Inc.
Makinson, Nicholas
Mazur Restoration, Pete
McCament, Jay
McFarland, Stan
Morrison Custom Rifles, J.W.
Mullis Guncraft
Nettestad Gun Works
Nicholson Custom

PRODUCT DIRECTORY

Nitex, Inc.
Noreen, Peter H.
North Fork Custom Gunsmithing
Nu-Line Guns, Inc.
Olson, Vic
Ozark Gun Works
P&S Gun Service
Pagel Gun Works, Inc.
Parker Gun Finishes
Pasadena Gun Center
Penrod Precision
Precision Metal Finishing
Precise Metalsmithing Enterprises
Precision Specialties
Rice, Keith
Rifles Inc.
Robar Co.'s, Inc., The
Rocky Mountain Arms, Inc.
Shirley Co. Gun & Riflemakers Ltd., J.A.
Simmons Gun Repair, Inc.
Sipes Gun Shop
Skeoch, Brian R.
Smith, Art
Snapp's Gunshop
Spencer's Custom Guns
Sportsmen's Exchange & Western
Gun Traders, Inc.
Steffens, Ron
Stiles Custom Guns
Stott's Creek Armory, Inc.
Strawbridge, Victor W.
Talmage, William G.
Taylor & Robbins
Thompson, Randall
Tom's Gun Repair
Van Horn, Gil
Von Minden Gunsmithing Services
Waldron, Herman
Weber & Markin Custom Gunsmiths
Wells, Fred F.
Welsh, Bud
Werth, T.W.
Wessinger Custom Guns & Engraving
West, Robert G.
Westrom, John
White Rock Tool & Die
Wiebe, Duane
Williams Gun Sight Co.
Williamson Precision Gunsmithing
Winter, Robert M.
Wise Guns, Dale
Wood, Frank
Zufall, Joseph F.
Pilkington, Scott
Piquette, Paul R.
Potts, Wayne E.
Rabeno, Martin
Reed, Dave
Reno, Wayne
Riggs, Jim
Roberts, J.J.
Rohner, Hans
Rohner, John
Rosser, Bob
Rundell's Gun Shop
Runge, Robert P.
Sampson, Roger
Schiffman, Mike
Sherwood, George
Sinclair, W.P.
Singletary, Kent
Skaggs, R.E.
Smith, Mark A.
Smith, Ron
Smokey Valley Rifles
Theis, Terry
Thiewes, George W.
Thirion Gun Engraving, Denise
Valade Engraving, Robert
Vest, John
Viramontez, Ray
Vorhes, David
Wagoner, Vernon G.
Wallace, Terry
Warenski, Julie
Warren, Kenneth W.
Weber & Markin Custom Gunsmiths
Welch, Sam
Wells, Rachel
Wessinger Custom Guns & Engraving
Willig Custom Engraving, Claus
Wood, Mel

DECOYS

A&M Waterfowl, Inc.
Baekgaard Ltd.
Boyds' Gunstock Industries, Inc.
Carry-Lite, Inc.
Deer Me Products Co.
Fair Game International
Farm Form Decoys, Inc.
Feather Flex Decoys
Flambeau Products Corp.
G&H Decoys, Inc.
Herter's Manufacturing, Inc.
Hiti-Schuch, Atelier Wilma
Klingler Woodcarving
Molin Industries
North Wind Decoy Co.
Penn's Woods Products, Inc.
Quack Decoy & Sporting Clays
Sports Innovations, Inc.
Tanglefree Industries
Waterfield Sports, Inc.
Woods Wise Products

ENGRAVERS, ENGRAVING TOOLS

Ackerman & Co.
Adair Custom Shop, Bill
Adams, John J. & Son Engravers
Adams Jr., John J.
Ahlman Guns
Alfano, Sam
Allard, Gary
Allen, Richard L.
Altamont Co.
American Pioneer Video
Anthony and George Ltd.
Baron Technology
Barraclough, John K.
Bates Engraving, Billy
Bell Originals, Inc., Sid
Bleile, C. Roger
Boessler, Erich
Bone Engraving, Ralph
Bratcher, Dan
Brooker, Dennis
Brownell Checkering Tools, W.E.
Burgess, Byron
Churchill, Winston
Clark Firearms Engraving
Collings, Ronald
Creek Side Metal & Woodcrafters
Cullity Restoration, Daniel
Cupp, Custom Engraver, Alana
Davidson, Jere
Delorge, Ed
Desquesnes, Gerald
Dixon Muzzleloading Shop, Inc.
Dolbare, Elizabeth
Drain, Mark
Dubber, Michael W.
Dyson & Son Ltd., Peter
Engraving Artistry
Evans Engraving, Robert
Fanzoj GmbH
Firearms Engraver's Guild of America
Flannery Engraving Co., Jeff W.
Floatstone Mfg. Co.
Forty Five Ranch Enterprises
Fountain Products
Francolini, Leonard
Frank Custom Classic Arms, Ron
Frank Knives
French, J.R.
Gene's Custom Guns
George, Tim
Glimm, Jerome C.
Golden Age Arms Co.
Gournet, Geoffroy
Grant, Howard V.
Griffin & Howe, Inc.
GRS Corp., Glendo
Gun Room, The
Guns
Gurney, F.R.
Gwinnell, Bryson J.
Hale/Engraver, Peter
Half Moon Rifle Shop
Hands Engraving, Barry Lee
Harris Gunworks
Harris Hand Engraving, Paul A.
Harwood, Jack O.
Hendricks, Frank E.
Hiptmayer, Armurier
Hiptmayer, Heidemarie
Hiptmayer, Klaus
Horst, Alan K.
Ingle, Ralph W.
Jaeger, Inc., Paul/Dunn's
Jantz Supply
Johns Master Engraver, Bill
Kamyk Engraving Co., Steve
Kane, Edward
Kehr, Roger
Kelly, Lance
Klingler Woodcarving
Koevenig's Engraving Service
Kudlas, John M.
Lebeau-Courally
LeFever Arms Co., Inc.
Leibowitz, Leonard
Lindsay, Steve
Lister, Weldon
Little Trees Ramble
Lutz Engraving, Ron
Mains Enterprises, Inc.
Master Engravers, Inc.
McCombs, Leo
McDonald, Dennis
McKenzie, Lynton
Mele, Frank
Mittermeier, Inc., Frank
Moschetti, Mitchell R.
Mountain States Engraving
Napoleon Bonaparte, Inc.
Nelson, Gary K.
New Orleans Jewelers Supply Co.
NgraveR Co., The
Oker's Engraving
Old Dominion Engravers
P&S Gun Service
Pedersen, C.R.
Pedersen, Rex C.
Pilgrim Pewter, Inc.

GAME CALLS

Adventure Game Calls
Arkansas Mallard Duck Calls
Ashby Turkey Calls
Bostick Wildlife Calls, Inc.
Brell Mar Products
Carter's Wildlife Calls, Inc., Garth
Cedar Hill Game Calls, Inc.
Crawford Co., Inc., R.M.
Crit'R Call
Custom Calls
D&H Prods. Co., Inc.
D-Boone Ent., Inc.
Deepeeka Exports Pvt. Ltd.
Dr. O's Products Ltd.
Duck Call Specialists
Faulhaber Wildlocker
Faulk's Game Call Co., Inc.
Flow-Rite of Tennessee, Inc.
Gander Mountain, Inc.
Green Head Game Call Co.
Hally Caller
Haydel's Game Calls, Inc.
Herter's Manufacturing, Inc.
Hunter's Specialties, Inc.
Keowee Game Calls
Kingyon, Paul L.
Knight & Hale Game Calls
Lohman Mfg. Co., Inc.
Mallardtone Game Calls
Marsh, Johnny
Moss Double Tone, Inc.
Mountain Hollow Game Calls
Oakman Turkey Calls
Olt Co., Philip S.
Penn's Woods Products, Inc.
Primos, Inc.
Quaker Boy, Inc.
Rickard, Inc., Pete
Robbins Scent, Inc.
Rocky Mountain Wildlife Products
Salter Calls, Inc., Eddie
Savana Sports, Inc.
Sceery Game Calls
Scobey Duck & Goose Calls, Glynn
Scruggs' Game Calls, Stanley
Simmons Outdoor Corp.
Sports Innovations, Inc.
Stewart Game Calls, Inc., Johnny
Sure-Shot Game Calls, Inc.
Tanglefree Industries
Tink's & Ben Lee Hunting Products
Tink's Safariland Hunting Corp.
Wellington Outdoors
Wilderness Sound Products Ltd.
Woods Wise Products
Wyant's Outdoor Products, Inc.

GUN PARTS, U.S. AND FOREIGN

Accuracy Gun Shop
Ahlman Guns
Amherst Arms
Armscorp USA, Inc.
Aro-Tek, Ltd.
Badger Shooters Supply, Inc.
Bear Mountain Gun & Tool
Bob's Gun Shop
Briese Bullet Co., Inc.
British Antiques
Bushmaster Firearms
Bustani, Leo
Cape Outfitters
Caspian Arms Ltd.
Century International Arms, Inc.
Clark Custom Guns, Inc.
Cole's Gun Works
Colonial Repair
Cylinder & Slide, Inc.
Delta Arms Ltd.
DGR Custom Rifles
Dibble, Derek A.
Dilliott Gunsmithing, Inc.
Dixie Gun Works, Inc.
Duane's Gun Repair
Duffy, Charles E.
Dyson & Son Ltd., Peter
E&L Mfg., Inc.
Elliott Inc., G.W.
EMF Co., Inc.
Enguix Import-Export
Fabian Bros. Sporting Goods, Inc.
Fleming Firearms
Forrest, Inc., Tom
Forster Products
Galati International
Goodwin, Fred
Groenewold, John
Gun Parts Corp., The
Gun Shop, The
Guns Antique & Modern DBA/Charles E. Duffy
Gun-Tec
Hastings Barrels
High Performance International
Irwin, Campbell H.
I.S.S.
Jaeger, Inc., Paul/Dunn's
Johnson's Gunsmithing, Inc., Neal G.
K&T Co.
Kimber of America, Inc.
K.K. Arms Co.
Krico Jagd-und Sportwaffen GmbH
Laughridge, William R.
List Precision Engineering
Lodewick, Walter H.
Lothar Walther Precision Tool, Inc.
L.P.A. Snc
Mac's .45 Shop
Mandall Shooting Supplies, Inc.
Markell, Inc.
Martin's Gun Shop
Martz, John V.
Mathews & Son, Inc., George E.
McCann's Machine & Gun Shop
McCormick Corp., Chip
Merkuria Ltd.
Mid-America Recreation, Inc.
Morrow, Bud
Nu-Line Guns, Inc.
Pachmayr Ltd.
Parts & Surplus
Pennsylvania Gun Parts
Perazzi USA, Inc.
Performance Specialists
Peterson Gun Shop, Inc., A.W.
Pre-Winchester 92-90-62 Parts Co.
P.S.M.G. Gun Co.
Quality Firearms of Idaho, Inc.
Quality Parts Co.
Ranch Products
Randco UK
Retting, Inc., Martin B.
Ruvel & Co., Inc.
S&S Firearms
Sabatti S.R.L.
Sarco, Inc.
Scherer

DIRECTORY OF THE ARMS TRADE

Shockley, Harold H.
Silver Ridge Gun Shop
Sipes Gun Shop
Smires, C.L.
Smith & Wesson
Southern Ammunition Co., Inc.
Southern Armory, The
Sportsmen's Exchange & Western Gun Traders, Inc.
Springfield, Inc.
Springfield Sporters, Inc.
Starr Trading Co., Jedediah
"Su-Press-On," Inc.
Swampfire Shop, The
Tank's Rifle Shop
Tarnhelm Supply Co., Inc.
Twin Pine Armory
USA Sporting Inc.
Vintage Arms, Inc.
Vintage Industries, Inc.
Volquartsen Custom Ltd.
Walker Arms Co., Inc.
Weaver Arms Corp. Gun Shop
Westfield Engineering
Williams Mfg. of Oregon
Winchester Sutler, Inc., The
Wise Guns, Dale
Wolff Co., W.C.

GUNS, AIR

Air Arms
Air Venture
Airrow
Anschutz GmbH
Arms Corporation of the Philippines
Arms United Corp.
Baikal
Beeman Precision Airguns
Benjamin/Sheridan Co.
Brass Eagle, Inc.
Brocock Ltd.
BSA Guns Ltd.
Compasseco, Ltd.
Component Concepts, Inc.
Crawford Co., Inc., R.M.
Creedmoor Sports, Inc.
Crosman Airguns
Crosman Products of Canada Ltd.
Daisy Mfg. Co.
Daystate Ltd.
Diana
Dynamit Nobel-RWS, Inc.
E.A.A. Corp.
FAS
Frankonia Jagd
FWB
Gamo
Gamo USA, Inc.
GFR Corp.
Great Lakes Airguns
GZ Paintball Sports Products
Hebard Guns, Gil
Interarms
Labanu, Inc.
List Precision Engineering
Mac-1 Distributors
Marksman Products
Maryland Paintball Supply
Merkuria Ltd.
Pardini Armi Srl
Park Rifle Co., Ltd., The
Penguin Industries, Inc.
Powell & Son (Gunmakers) Ltd., William
Precision Airgun Sales, Inc.
Precision Sales Int'l, Inc.
Ravell Ltd.
Ripley Rifles
RWS
Savana Sports, Inc.
S.G.S. Sporting Guns Srl
Shanghai Airguns, Ltd.
SKAN A.R.
Smart Parts
Sportsman Airguns, Inc.
Steyr Mannlicher AG
Stone Enterprises Ltd.
Swivel Machine Works, Inc.
Theoben Engineering
Tippman Pneumatics, Inc.
Trooper Walsh
UltraSport Arms, Inc.
Valor Corp.
Venom Arms Co.
Vortek Products
Walther GmbH, Carl
Webley and Scott Ltd.
Weihrauch KG, Hermann
Whiscombe
World Class Airguns

GUNS, FOREIGN—IMPORTERS (Manufacturers)

Accuracy International (Anschutz GmbH)
AcuSport Corporation (Anschutz GmbH)
Air Rifle Specialists (airguns)
Air Venture (airguns)
Airguns-R-Us (Falcon Pneumatic Systems; air rifles and pistols)
American Arms, Inc. (Fausti Cav. Stefano & Figlie snc; Franchi S.p.A.; Grulla Armes; Uberti, Aldo; Zabala Hermanos S.A.; blackpowder arms)
Amtec 2000, Inc. (Erma Werke GmbH)
Anics Firm, Inc. (Anics)
Armes de Chasse (Armas Azor, J.A.; AYA; Francotte & Cie S.A., Auguste)
Arms United Corp. (Gamo)
Armscorp USA, Inc.
Armsport, Inc. (airguns, blackpowder arms and shotguns)
Autumn Sales, Inc. (Blaser Jagdwaffen GmbH)
Auto-Ordnance Corp. (Techno Arms)
Beauchamp & Son, Inc. (Pedersoli, Davide & C.)
Beeman Precision Airguns (Beeman Precision Airguns; FWB; Webley & Scott Ltd.; Weihrauch KG, Hermann)
Bell's Legendary Country Wear (Miroku, B.C./Daly, Charles; Powell & Son, Ltd., William)
Beretta U.S.A. Corp. (Beretta S.p.A., Pietro)
Bohemia Arms Co. (BRNO)
British Sporting Arms
Browning Arms Co. (Browning Arms Co.)
B-West Imports, Inc.
Cabela's (Pedersoli, Davide & C.; blackpowder arms)
Cape Outfitters (Armi Sport; Bertuzzi; Pedersoli, Davide & C.; San Marco; Societa Armi Bresciane Srl.; Westley Richards & Co.; blackpowder arms)
Century International Arms, Inc. (Famas; FEG; Norinco)
Champion Shooters' Supply (Anschutz GmbH)
Champion's Choice (Anschutz GmbH; Lapua; Walther GmbH, Carl)
Chapuis USA (Chapuis Armes)
Christopher Firearms Co., Inc., E.
Cimarron Arms (Uberti, Aldo; blackpowder arms)
County Arms (I.T.S.)
CVA (blackpowder arms)
Daisy Mfg. Co. (Daisy Mfg. Co.; Gamo)
Dixie Gun Works, Inc. (Pedersoli, Davide & C.; Uberti, Aldo; blackpowder arms)
Dynamit Nobel-RWS, Inc. (Brenneke KG, Wilhelm; Diana; Gamo; Norma Precision AB; RWS)
E.A.A. Corp. (Astra-Sport, S.A.; Benelli Armi S.p.A.; Sabatti S.r.l.; Tanfoglio S.r.l., Fratelli; Weihrauch KG, Hermann)
Eagle Imports, Inc. (Bersa S.A.)
Ellett Bros. (Churchill)
EMF Co., Inc. (Dakota; Hartford; Pedersoli, Davide & C.; San Marco; Uberti, Aldo; blackpowder arms)
Euroarms of America, Inc. (blackpowder arms)
Eversull Co., Inc., K.
Fiocchi of America, Inc. (Fiocchi Munizioni S.p.A.)
First National Gun Bank Corp., The (Gamba S.p.A.-Societa Armi Bresciane Srl., Renato)
Forgett Jr., Valmore J. (Navy Arms Co.; Uberti, Aldo)
Galaxy Imports Ltd., Inc. (Laurona Armas Eibar, S.A.D.; Ugartechea S.A., Ignacio)
Gamba, USA (Societa Armi Bresciane Srl.)
Gamo USA, Inc. (Gamo)
Giacomo Sporting, Inc.
Glock, Inc. (Glock GmbH)
Great Lakes Airguns (air pistols)
Griffin & Howe (Arrieta, S.L.)
Groenewold, John (BSA Guns Ltd.; Paragon and Prometheus pellets; Webley & Scott Ltd.)
GSI, Inc. (Mauser Werke Oberndorf; Merkel Freres; Steyr; Steyr-Mannlicher AG)
G.U., Inc. (New SKB Arms Co.; SKB Arms Co.)
Gunsite Custom Shop (Accuracy International Precision Rifles)
Gunsite Training Center (Accuracy International Precision Rifles)
Gunsmithing, Inc. (Anschutz GmbH)
Hammerli USA (Hammerli Ltd.)
Harris Gunworks (Peters Stahl GmbH)
Heckler & Koch, Inc. (Benelli Armi S.p.A.; Heckler & Koch, GmbH)
Hi-Grade Imports (Arrieta, S.L.)
Imperial Magnum Corp. (Imperial Magnum Corp.)
Import Sports Inc. (Llama Gabilondo Y Cia)
Interarms (Helwan; Howa Machinery Ltd.; Interarms; Korth; Norinco; Rossi S.A., Amadeo Rua; Star Bonifacio Echeverria S.A.; Walther GmbH, Carl)
JägerSport, Ltd. (Voere-KGH m.b.H.)
Jansma, Jack J. (Arrieta, S.L.)
J.O. Arms Inc (KSN Industries, Ltd.)
K.B.I., Inc. (Armscorp USA, Inc.; Baikal; FEG; K.B.I., Inc.; Sabatti S.R.L.)
Keng's Firearms Specialty, Inc. (Lapua; Ultralux)
Kongsberg America L.L.C. (Kongsberg)
Krieghoff International, Inc. (Krieghoff Gun Co., H.)
K-Sports Imports, Inc.
Labanu, Inc. (air rifles)
London Guns Ltd. (London Guns Ltd.)
Mac-1 Distributors (Venom Arms Co.)
Magnum Research, Inc. (BRNO; CZ)
MAGTECH Recreational Products, Inc. (Magtech)
Mandall Shooting Supplies, Inc. (Arizaga; Atamec-Bretton; Cabanas; Crucelegui, Hermanos; Erma Werke GmbH; Firearms Co. Ltd./Alpine; Hammerli Ltd.; Korth; Krico Jagd-und Sportwaffen GmbH; Morini; SIG; Tanner; Ugartechea S.A., Ignacio; Zanoletti, Pietro; blackpowder arms)
Marx, Harry (FERLIB)
MEC-Gar U.S.A., Inc. (MEC-Gar s.r.l.)
Mitchell Arms, Inc. (Mitchell Arms, Inc.)
Moore & Co., Wm. Larkin (Bertuzzi; Garbi, Armas Urki; Piotti; Rizzini, Battista; Rizzini, F.LLI)
Nationwide Sports Distributors, Inc. (Daewoo Precision Industries Ltd.)
Navy Arms Co. (Navy Arms Co.;
Pedersoli, Davide & C.; Pietta; Uberti, Aldo; blackpowder and cartridge arms)
Nevada Cartridge Co. (Effebi SNC-Dr. Franco Beretta)
New England Arms Co. (Arrieta, S.L.; Bertuzzi; Bosis; Cosmi Americo & Figlio s.n.c.; Dumoulin, Ernest; Lebeau-Courally; Rizzini, Battista; Rizzini, F.LLI)
New England Custom Gun Service (AYA; EAW)
Nygord Precision Products (FAS; Morini; Pardini Armi Srl; Steyr; Steyr-Mannlicher AG; TOZ; Unique/M.A.P.F.)
OK Weber, Inc. (target rifles)
Orvis Co., Inc., The (Arrieta, S.L.)
Pachmayr Ltd.
Para-Ordnance, Inc. (Para-Ordnance Mfg., Inc.)
Paul Co., The (Norma Precision AB; Sauer)
Pelaire Products (Whiscombe)
Perazzi USA, Inc. (Perazzi m.a.p. S.p.A.)
Powell Agency, William, The (William Powell & Son [Gunmakers] Ltd.)
P.S.M.G. Gun Co. (Astra Sport, S.A.; Interarms; Star Bonifacio Echeverria S.A.; Walther GmbH, Carl)
Quality Arms, Inc. (Arrieta, S.L.)
Sarco, Inc.
Savage Arms, Inc. (Lakefield Arms Ltd.; Savage Arms, Inc.)
Schuetzen Pistol Works (Peters Stahl GmbH)
Sheridan USA, Inc., Austin
Sigarms, Inc. (Hammerli Ltd.; Sauer; SIG-Sauer)
Sile Distributors (Marocchi F.lli S.p.A.)
SKB Shotguns (SKB Arms Co.)
Sphinx USA Inc. (Sphinx Engineering SA)
Sportsman Airguns, Inc. (QB air rifles; Shanghai Airguns, Ltd.)
Springfield, Inc. (Springfield, Inc.)
Stoeger Industries (IGA; Sako Ltd.; Tikka; target pistols)
Stone Enterprises Ltd. (airguns)
Swarovski Optik North America Ltd.
Taurus Firearms, Inc. (Taurus International Firearms)
Taylor's & Co., Inc. (Armi San Marco; Armi Sport; I.A.B.; Pietta; Uberti, Aldo)
Tradewinds, Inc. (blackpowder arms)
Tristar Sporting Arms, Ltd. (Turkish made firearms)
Trooper Walsh (Venom Arms Co.)
Turkish Firearms Corp. (Turkish Firearms Corp.)
Uberti USA, Inc. (Uberti, Aldo; blackpowder arms)
USA Sporting Inc. (Armas Kemen S.A.)
Vintage Arms, Inc.
Weatherby, Inc. (Weatherby, Inc.)
Wingshooters Ltd. (Arrieta, S.L.)
World Class Airguns (Air Arms)

GUNS, FOREIGN—MANUFACTURERS (Importers)

Accuracy International Precision Rifles (Gunsite Custom Shop; Gunsite Training Center)
Air Arms (World Class Airguns)
Anics (Anics Firm, Inc.)
Anschutz GmbH (Accuracy International; AcuSport Corporation; Champion Shooters' Supply; Champion's Choice; Gunsmithing, Inc.)
Arizaga (Mandall Shooting Supplies, Inc.)
Armas Azor, J.A. (Armes de Chasse)
Armas Kemen S.A. (USA Sporting Inc.)
Armi San Marco (Taylor's & Co., Inc.)
Armi Sport (Cape Outfitters; Taylor's & Co., Inc.)
Arms Corporation of the Philippines
Armscorp USA, Inc. (K.B.I., Inc.)
Arrieta, S.L. (Griffin & Howe; Hi-Grade Imports; Jansma, Jack J.; New England Arms Co.; The Orvis Co., Inc.; Quality Arms, Inc.; Wingshooters Ltd.)
Astra Sport, S.A. (E.A.A. Corp.; P.S.M.G. Gun Co.)
Atamec Bretton (Mandall Shooting Supplies, Inc.)
ATIS Armi S.A.S.
AYA (Armes de Chasse; New England Custom Gun Service)
Baikal (K.B.I., Inc.)
Beeman Precision Airguns (Beeman Precision Airguns)
Benelli Armi S.p.A. (E.A.A. Corp.; Heckler & Koch, Inc.)
Beretta S.p.A., Pietro (Beretta U.S.A. Corp.)
Bernardelli S.p.A., Vincenzo
Bersa S.A. (Eagle Imports, Inc.)
Bertuzzi (Cape Outfitters; Moore & Co., Wm. Larkin; New England Arms Co.)
Blaser Jagdwaffen GmbH (Autumn Sales, Inc.)
Bondini Paolo (blackpowder arms)
Borovnik KG, Ludwig
Bosis (New England Arms Co.)
Brenneke KG, Wilhelm (Dynamit Nobel-RWS, Inc.)
BRNO (Bohemia Arms Co.; Magnum Research, Inc.)
Brocock Ltd.
Browning Arms Co. (Browning Arms Co.)
BSA Guns Ltd. (Groenewold, John)

304 GUNS ILLUSTRATED

PRODUCT DIRECTORY

Cabanas (Mandall Shooting Supplies, Inc.)
CBC
Chapuis Armes (Chapuis USA)
Churchill (Ellett Bros.)
Cosmi Americo & Figlio s.n.c. (New England Arms Co.)
Crucelegui, Hermanos (Mandall Shooting Supplies, Inc.)
CVA (blackpowder arms)
CZ (Magnum Research, Inc.)
Daewoo Precision Industries Ltd. (Nationwide Sports Distributors, Inc.)
Dakota (EMF Co., Inc.)
Daisy Mfg. Co. (Daisy Mfg. Co.)
Diana (Dynamit Nobel-RWS, Inc.)
Dumoulin, Ernest (New England Arms Co.)
EAW (New England Custom Gun Service)
Effebi SNC-Dr. Franco Beretta (Nevada Cartridge Co.)
Erma Werke GmbH (Amtec 2000, Inc.; Mandall Shooting Supplies, Inc.)
Fabarm S.p.A.
F.A.I.R. Techni-Mec s.n.c.
Falcon Pneumatic Systems (Airguns-R-Us)
Famas (Century International Arms, Inc.)
FAS (Nygord Precision Products)
Fausti Cav. Stefano & Figlie snc (American Arms, Inc.)
FEG (Century International Arms, Inc.; K.B.I., Inc.)
FERLIB (Marx, Harry)
Fiocchi Munizioni S.P.A. (Fiocchi of America, Inc.)
Firearms Co. Ltd./Alpine (Mandall Shooting Supplies, Inc.)
FN Herstal
Franchi S.p.A (American Arms, Inc.)
Francotte & Cie S.A., Auguste (Armes de Chasse)
FWB (Beeman Precision Airguns)
Gamba S.p.A.-Societa Armi Bresciane Srl., Renato (First National Gun Bank Corp., The)
Gamo (Arms United Corp.; Daisy Mfg. Co.; Dynamit Nobel-RWS, Inc.; Gamo USA, Inc.)
Garbi, Armas Urki (Moore & Co., Wm. Larkin)
Gaucher Armes S.A.
Glock GmbH (Glock, Inc.)
Grulla Armes (American Arms, Inc.)
Hammerli Ltd. (Hammerli USA; Mandall Shooting Supplies, Inc.; Sigarms, Inc.)
Hartford (EMF Co., Inc.)
Hartmann & Weiss GmbH
Heckler & Koch, GmbH (Heckler & Koch, Inc.)
Helwan (Interarms)
Heym GmbH & Co., Friedrich Wilh.
Holland & Holland Ltd.
Howa Machinery Ltd. (Interarms)
I.A.B. (Taylor's & Co., Inc.)
IGA (Stoeger Industries)
IMI
Imperial Magnum Corp. (Imperial Magnum Corp.)
Interarms (Interarms; P.S.M.G. Gun Co.)
I.T.S. (County Arms)
K.B.I., Inc. (K.B.I., Inc.)
Kongsberg (Kongsberg America L.L.C.)
Korth (Interarms; Mandall Shooting Supplies, Inc.)
Krico Jagd-und Sportwaffen GmbH (Mandall Shooting Supplies, Inc.)
Krieghoff Gun Co., H. (Krieghoff International, Inc.)
KSN Industries, Ltd. (J.O. Arms Inc.)
Lakefield Arms Ltd. (Savage Arms, Inc.)
Lanber Armas S.A.
Lapua (Champion's Choice; Keng's Firearms Specialty, Inc.)
Laurona Armas Eibar S.A.D. (Galaxy Imports Ltd., Inc.)
Lebeau-Courally (New England Arms Co.)
Llama Gabilondo Y Cia (Import Sports Inc.)
London Guns Ltd. (London Guns Ltd.)
Magtech (Magtech Recreational Products, Inc.)
Marocchi F.lli S.p.A. (Sile Distributors, Inc.)
Mauser Werke Oberndorf (GSI, Inc.)
MEC-Gar s.r.l. (MEC-Gar U.S.A., Inc.)
Merkel Freres (GSI, Inc.)
Miroku, B.C./Daly, Charles (Bell's Legendary Country Wear)
Mitchell Arms, Inc. (Mitchell Arms, Inc.)
Morini (Mandall Shooting Supplies; Nygord Precision Products)
Navy Arms Co. (Forgett Jr., Valmore J.; Navy Arms Co.)
New SKB Arms Co. (G.U., Inc.)
Norica, Avnda Otaola
Norinco (Century International Arms, Inc.; Interarms)
Norma Precision AB (Dynamit Nobel-RWS Inc.; The Paul Co., Inc.)
Para-Ordnance Mfg., Inc. (Para-Ordnance, Inc.)
Pardini Armi Srl. (Nygord Precision Products)
Pedersoli, Davide & C. (Beauchamp & Son, Inc.; Cabela's; Cape Outfitters; Dixie Gun Works, Inc.; EMF Co., Inc.; Navy Arms Co.)
Perazzi m.a.p. S.p.A. (Perazzi USA, Inc.)
Perugini-Visini & Co. s.r.l.
Peters Stahl GmbH (Harris Gunworks; Schuetzen Pistol Works)
Pietta (Navy Arms Co.; Taylor's & Co., Inc.)
Piotti (Moore & Co., Wm. Larkin)
Powell & Son Ltd., William (Bell's Legendary Country Wear; Powell Agency, The, William)
QB air rifles (Sportsman Airguns, Inc.)
Rigby & Co., John
Rizzini, Battista (Moore & Co., Wm. Larkin; New England Arms Co.)
Rizzini, F.LLI (Moore & Co., Wm. Larkin; New England Arms Co.)
Rossi S.A., Amadeo Rua (Interarms)
RWS (Dynamit Nobel-RWS, Inc.)
Sabatti S.R.L. (E.A.A. Corp.; K.B.I., Inc.)
Sako Ltd. (Stoeger Industries)
San Marco (Cape Outfitters; EMF Co., Inc.)
S.A.R.L. G. Granger
Sauer (Paul Co., The; Sigarms, Inc.)
Savage Arms, Inc. (Savage Arms, Inc.)
Shanghai Airguns, Ltd. (Sportsman Airguns, Inc.)
SIG (Mandall Shooting Supplies, Inc.)
SIG-Sauer (Sigarms, Inc.)
SKB Arms Co. (G.U., Inc.; SKB Shotguns)
Societa Armi Bresciane Srl. (Cape Outfitters; Gamba, USA)
Sphinx Engineering SA (Sphinx USA Inc.)
Springfield, Inc. (Springfield, Inc.)
Star Bonifacio Echeverria S.A. (Interarms; P.S.M.G. Gun Co.)
Steyr (GSI, Inc.; Nygord Precision Products)
Steyr-Mannlicher AG (GSI, Inc.; Nygord Precision Products)
Tanfoglio S.r.l., Fratelli (E.A.A. Corp.)
Tanner (Mandall Shooting Supplies, Inc.)
Taurus International Firearms (Taurus Firearms, Inc.)
Taurus S.A., Forjas
Techni-Mec
Techno Arms (Auto-Ordnance Corp.)
T.F.C. S.p.A.
Tikka (Stoeger Industries)
TOZ (Nygord Precision Products)
Turkish Firearms Corp. (Turkish Firearms Corp.)
Uberti, Aldo (American Arms, Inc.; Cimarron Arms; Dixie Gun Works, Inc.; EMF Co., Inc.; Forgett Jr., Valmore J.; Navy Arms Co.; Taylor's & Co., Inc.; Uberti USA, Inc.)
Ugartechea S.A., Ignacio (Galaxy Imports Ltd., Inc.; Mandall Shooting Supplies, Inc.)
Ultralux (Keng's Firearms Specialty, Inc.)
Unique/M.A.P.F. (Nygord Precision Products)
Venom Arms Co. (Mac-1 Distributors; Trooper Walsh)
Voere-KGH m.b.H. (JägerSport, Ltd.)
Walther GmbH, Carl (Champion's Choice; Interarms; P.S.M.G. Gun Co.)
Weatherby, Inc. (Weatherby, Inc.)
Webley & Scott Ltd. (Beeman Precision Airguns; Groenewold, John)
Weihrauch KG, Hermann (Beeman Precision Airguns; E.A.A. Corp.)
Westley Richards & Co. (Cape Outfitters)
Whiscombe (Pelaire Products)

GUNS, U.S.-MADE

A.A. Arms, Inc.
Accu-Tek
Airrow
American Arms & Ordnance, Inc.
American Arms, Inc.
American Derringer Corp.
AMT
Amtec 2000, Inc.
ArmaLite, Inc.
A-Square Co., Inc.
Auto-Ordnance Corp.
Baer Custom, Inc., Les
Barrett Firearms Mfg., Inc.
Bar-Sto Precision Machine
Beretta U.S.A. Corp.
Braverman, R.J.
Brolin Arms
Brown Co., E. Arthur
Brown Products, Inc., Ed
Browning Arms Co. (Parts & Service)
Bullberry Barrel Works, Ltd.
Bushmaster Firearms
Calico Light Weapon Systems
Century Gun Dist., Inc.
Colt's Mfg. Co., Inc.
Competitor Corp., Inc.
Connecticut Valley Classics
Connecticut Shotgun Mfg. Co.
Coonan Arms
Cooper Arms
Cumberland Arms
CVA
Dakota Arms, Inc.
Dangler, Homer L.
Davis Industries
Desert Industries, Inc.
Eagle Arms, Inc.
Emerging Technologies, Inc.
Essex Arms
Feather Industries, Inc.
Federal Engineering Corp.
FN Herstal
Freedom Arms, Inc.
Gibbs Rifle Co., Inc.
Gilbert Equipment Co., Inc.
Gonic Arms, Inc.
Gunsite Custom Shop
Gunsite Gunsmithy
H&R 1871, Inc.
Harrington & Richardson
Harris Gunworks
Hatfield Gun Co., Inc.
Hawken Shop, The
Heritage Firearms
Heritage Manufacturing, Inc.
High Standard Mfg. Co., Inc.
Hi-Point Firearms
HJS Arms, Inc.
H-S Precision, Inc.
Intratec
Jennings Firearms Inc.
Zabala, Hermanos S.A. (American Arms, Inc.)
Zanoletti, Pietro (Mandall Shooting Supplies, Inc.)
Zoli, Antonio

JS Worldwide DBA
Kahr Arms
Kelbly, Inc.
Kel-Tec CNC Industries, Inc.
Kimber of America, Inc.
Kimel Industries
K.K. Arms Co.
Knight's Mfg. Co.
LaFrance Specialties
L.A.R. Mfg., Inc.
Laseraim, Inc.
Lorcin Engineering Co., Inc.
Magnum Research, Inc.
Marlin Firearms Co.
Maverick Arms, Inc.
McBros Rifle Co.
McCann's Muzzle-Gun Works
Miller Arms, Inc.
Mitchell Arms, Inc.
MKS Supply, Inc.
M.O.A. Corp.
Montana Armory, Inc.
Mossberg & Sons, Inc., O.F.
NCP Products, Inc.
New Advantage Arms Corp.
New England Firearms
Noreen, Peter H.
North American Arms, Inc.
Nowlin Custom Mfg.
Paragon Sales & Services, Inc.
Phoenix Arms
Precision Small Arms
Quality Parts Co.
Recoilless Technologies, Inc.
Remington Arms Co., Inc.
Rifle Works & Armory
Rocky Mountain Arms, Inc.
Ruger
Seecamp Co., Inc., L.W.
Sharps Arms Co., Inc., C.
Shiloh Rifle Mfg.
Smith & Wesson
Sporting Arms Mfg., Inc.
Springfield, Inc.
Stoeger Industries
Sturm, Ruger & Co., Inc.
Sundance Industries, Inc.
Survival Arms, Inc.
Swivel Machine Works, Inc.
Tar-Hunt Custom Rifles, Inc.
Taurus Firearms, Inc.
Texas Armory
Texas Longhorn Arms, Inc.
Thompson/Center Arms
Ultra Light Arms, Inc.
U.S. Repeating Arms Co.
Weatherby, Inc.
White Shooting Systems, Inc.
Wichita Arms, Inc.
Wildey, Inc.
Wilkinson Arms

GUNS AND GUN PARTS, REPLICA AND ANTIQUE

Ahlman Guns
Armi San Paolo
Bear Mountain Gun & Tool
Beauchamp & Son, Inc.
Bob's Gun Shop
British Antiques
Buckskin Machine Works
Buffalo Arms
Burgess & Son Gunsmiths, R.W.
Cache La Poudre Rifleworks
Cape Outfitters
Century International Arms, Inc.
Chambers Flintlocks Ltd., Jim
Cogar's Gunsmithing
Cole's Gun Works
Colonial Repair
Curly Maple Stock Blanks
Dangler, Homer L.
Day & Sons, Inc., Leonard
Delhi Gun House
Delta Arms Ltd.
Dilliott Gunsmithing, Inc.
Dixie Gun Works, Inc.
Dixon Muzzleloading Shop, Inc.
Ed's Gun House
Euroarms of America, Inc.
Flintlocks, Etc.
Forgett, Valmore J., Jr.
Forster Products
Galazan
Golden Age Arms Co.
Goodwin, Fred
Groenewold, John
Gun Parts Corp., The
Gun-Tec
Hastings Barrels
Hunkeler, A.
Liberty Antique Gunworks
List Precision Engineering
Lock's Philadelphia Gun Exchange
Lucas, Edw. E.
McKinney, R.P.
Meier Works
Mountain State Muzzleloading Supplies
Munsch Gunsmithing, Tommy
Museum of Historical Arms, Inc.
Neumann GmbH
Pasadena Gun Center
Peacemaker Specialists

DIRECTORY OF THE ARMS TRADE

PEM's Mfg. Co.
P.M. Enterprises, Inc.
Pony Express Sport Shop, Inc.
Precise Metalsmithing Enterprises
Quality Firearms of Idaho, Inc.
Randco UK
Retting, Inc., Martin B.
S&S Firearms
Sarco, Inc.
Scattergun Technologies, Inc.
Schuetzen Gun Co.
Silver Ridge Gun Shop
Sipes Gun Shop

South Bend Replicas, Inc.
Southern Ammunition Co., Inc.
Stott's Creek Armory, Inc.
Taylor's & Co., Inc.
Tennessee Valley Mfg.
Tiger-Hunt
Track of the Wolf, Inc.
Uberti USA, Inc.
Vintage Industries, Inc.
Weisz Parts
Wescombe
Winchester Sutler, Inc., The

GUNS, SURPLUS—PARTS AND AMMUNITION

Ad Hominem
Armscorp USA, Inc.
Arundel Arms & Ammunition, Inc., A.
Aztec International Ltd.
Badger Shooters Supply, Inc.
Ballistica Maximus North
Bohemia Arms Co.
Bondini Paolo
Braun, M.
Century International Arms, Inc.
Chuck's Gun Shop
Cole's Gun Works
Combat Military Ordnance Ltd.
Delta Arms Ltd.
First, Inc., Jack
Flaig's
Fleming Firearms
Forgett, Valmore J., Jr.
Forrest, Inc., Tom
Fulton Armory
Galazan
Garcia National Gun Traders, Inc.
Goodwin, Fred
Gun Parts Corp., The
Hart & Son, Inc., Robert W.
Interarms
Lever Arms Service Ltd.
Lomont Precision Bullets

Moreton/Fordyce Enterprises
Mountain Bear Rifle Works, Inc.
Navy Arms Co.
Nevada Pistol Academy Inc.
Oil Rod and Gun Shop
Parts & Surplus
Pasadena Gun Center
Perazone, Brian
Quality Firearms of Idaho, Inc.
Ravell Ltd.
Retting, Inc., Martin B.
Samco Global Arms, Inc.
Sarco, Inc.
Shell Shack
Shootin' Shack, Inc.
Silver Ridge Gun Shop
Simmons Gun Repair, Inc.
Sipes Gun Shop
Southern Armory, The
Sportsmen's Exchange & Western Gun Traders, Inc.
Springfield Sporters, Inc.
Stratco, Inc.
Tarnhelm Supply Co., Inc.
T.F.C. S.p.A.
Thurston Sports, Inc.
Westfield Engineering

GUNSMITHS, CUSTOM (see Custom Gunsmiths)

GUNSMITHS, HANDGUN (see Pistolsmiths)

GUNSMITH SCHOOLS

Bull Mountain Rifle Co.
Colorado Gunsmithing Academy Lamar
Colorado School of Trades
Cylinder & Slide, Inc.
Lassen Community College, Gunsmithing Dept.
Laughridge, William R.
Mathews & Son, Inc., George E.
Modern Gun Repair School
Montgomery Community College
Murray State College
North American Correspondence Schools

Nowlin Custom Mfg.
NRI Gunsmith School
Pennsylvania Gunsmith School
Piedmont Community College
Pine Technical College
Professional Gunsmiths of America, Inc.
Southeastern Community College
Smith & Wesson
Spencer's Custom Guns
Trinidad State Junior College Gunsmithing Dept.
Weigand Combat Handguns, Inc.

GUNSMITH SUPPLIES, TOOLS, SERVICES

Actions by "T"
Aldis Gunsmithing & Shooting Supply
Auto-Ordnance Corp.
Baer Custom, Inc., Les
Bar-Sto Precision Machine
Bear Mountain Gun & Tool
Belltown, Ltd.
Belt MTN Arms
Bengtson Arms Co., L.
Biesen, Al
Biesen, Roger
Bill's Gun Repair
Blue Ridge Machinery & Tools, Inc.
Bowen Classic Arms Corp.
Break-Free, Inc.
Briley Mfg., Inc.
Brownells, Inc.
B-Square Co., Inc.
Bull Mountain Rifle Co.
Carbide Checkering Tools
Chapman Manufacturing Co.
Chem-Pak, Inc.
Choate Machine & Tool Co., Inc.
Chopie Mfg., Inc.
Chuck's Gun Shop
Clark Custom Guns, Inc.
Clenzoil Corp.
Colonial Arms, Inc.
Conetrol Scope Mounts
Craig Custom Ltd.
Cumberland Arms

Custom Checkering Service
Custom Gun Products
D&J Bullet Co. & Custom Gun Shop, Inc.
Dakota Arms, Inc.
Dan's Whetstone Co., Inc.
Dayton Traister
Dem-Bart Checkering Tools, Inc.
Dever Co., Jack
Dremel Mfg. Co.
Du-Lite Corp.
Dutchman's Firearms, Inc., The
Echols & Co., D'Arcy
EGW Evolution Gun Works
Faith Associates, Inc.
Fisher, Jerry A.
Forgreens Tool Mfg., Inc.
Forkin, Ben
Forster, Kathy
Forster Products
Frazier Brothers Enterprises
G.B.C. Industries, Inc.
Grace Metal Products, Inc.
Greider Precision
Gunline Tools
Gun-Tec
Half Moon Rifle Shop
Hastings Barrels
Henriksen Tool Co., Inc.
High Performance International
Hoelscher, Virgil

Holland's
Ivanoff, Thomas G.
J&R Engineering
J&S Heat Treat
Jantz Supply
JBM Software
JGS Precision Tool Mfg.
Kasenit Co., Inc.
KenPatable Ent., Inc.
Kimball, Gary
Kleinendorst, K.W.
Kmount
Korzinek Riflesmith, J.
Kwik Mount Corp.
LaBounty Precision Reboring
Lea Mfg. Co.
Lee Supplies, Mark
Lee's Red Ramps
List Precision Engineering
London Guns Ltd.
Mag-Na-Port International, Inc.
Mahovsky's Metalife
Marsh, Mike
MCS, Inc.
Menck, Thomas W.
Metalife Industries
Metaloy Inc.
Michael's Antiques
Millett Sights
MMC
Morrow, Bud
Mo's Competitor Supplies
N&J Sales
NCP Products, Inc.
Nowlin Custom Mfg.
Ole Frontier Gunsmith Shop
PanaVise Products, Inc.
Passive Bullet Traps, Inc.
PEM's Mfg. Co.
Perazone, Brian
Power Custom, Inc.
Practical Tools, Inc.
Precision Metal Finishing

Precision Specialties
Prolix® Lubricants
Reardon Products
Rice, Keith
Romain's Custom Guns, Inc.
Roto Carve
Royal Arms Gunstocks
Rusteprufe Laboratories
Savage Range Systems, Inc.
Scott, McDougall & Associates
Shirley Co. Gun & Riflemakers Ltd., J.A.
Shooter's Choice
Slug Group, Inc.
Smith Abrasives, Inc.
Starrett Co., L.S.
Sullivan, David S.
Talley, Dave
Texas Platers Supply
Time Precision, Inc.
Tom's Gun Repair
Tom's Gunshop
Trulock Tool
Turnbull Restoration, Doug
Van Gorden & Son, Inc., C.S.
Venco Industries, Inc.
Vintage Industries, Inc.
Washita Mountain Whetstone Co.
Weaver Arms Corp. Gun Shop
Weigand Combat Handguns, Inc.
Welsh, Bud
Westfield Engineering
Westrom, John
Westwind Rifles, Inc.
White Rock Tool & Die
Wilcox All-Pro Tools & Supply
Wild West Guns
Will-Burt Co.
Williams Gun Sight Co.
Williams Shootin' Iron Service
Willow Bend
Wilson's Gun Shop
Wise Guns, Dale

HANDGUN ACCESSORIES

A.A. Arms, Inc.
ADCO International
Adventurer's Outpost
Alpha Gunsmith Division
American Derringer Corp.
Armite Laboratories
Arms Corporation of the Philippines
Aro-Tek, Ltd.
Astra Sport, S.A.
Auto-Ordnance Corp.
Baer Custom, Inc., Les
Bar-Sto Precision Machine
Baumannize Custom
Behlert Precision, Inc.
Beretta S.p.A., Pietro
Bill's Custom Cases
Black Sheep Brand
Blue and Gray Products, Inc.
Bob's Gun Shop
Bond Custom Firearms
Bowen Classic Arms Corp.
Broken Gun Ranch
Brown Products, Inc., Ed
Brownells, Inc.
Bucheimer, J.M.
Bushmaster Firearms
Bushmaster Hunting & Fishing
Butler Creek Corp.
C3 Systems
Centaur Systems, Inc.
Central Specialties Ltd.
Clark Custom Guns, Inc.
Cobra Gunskin
Craig Custom Ltd.
D&L Industries
Dade Screw Machine Products
Delhi Gun House
Dewey Mfg. Co., Inc., J.
D.J. Marketing
Doskocil Mfg. Co., Inc
E&L Mfg., Inc.
E.A.A. Corp.
Eagle International, Inc.
EGW Evolution Gun Works
Faith Associates, Inc.
FAS
Feather Industries, Inc.
Feminine Protection, Inc.
Ferris Firearms
Fleming Firearms
Frielich Police Equipment
Galati International

GALCO International Ltd.
Glock, Inc.
Greider Precision
Gremmel Enterprises
Gun Parts Corp., The
Gun-Alert
Gun-Ho Sports Cases
Harvey, Frank
Haselbauer Products, Jerry
Hebard Guns, Gil
Heinie Specialty Products
Hill Speed Leather, Ernie
H.K.S. Products
Hoppe's Div.
Hunter Co., Inc.
Jarvis, Inc.
Jeffredo Gunsight
J.P. Enterprises, Inc.
Jumbo Sports Products
KeeCo Impressions
Keller Co., The
King's Gun Works
K.K. Arms Co.
Lakewood Products, Inc.
Lee's Red Ramps
Lem Sports, Inc.
Loch Leven Industries
Lohman Mfg. Co., Inc.
Mac's .45 Shop
Mag-Na-Port International, Inc.
Magnolia Sports, Inc.
Magnum Research, Inc.
Mahony, Philip Bruce
Mandall Shooting Supplies, Inc.
Markell Inc.
McCormick Corp., Chip
MEC-Gar S.R.L.
Merkuria Ltd.
Mid-America Guns and Ammo
Minute Man High Tech Industries
Mitchell Arms, Inc.
MTM Molded Products Co., Inc.
Mustra's Custom Guns, Inc., Carl
North American Specialties
No-Sho Mfg. Co.
Ox-Yoke Originals, Inc.
PAST Sporting Goods, Inc.
Penguin Industries, Inc.
Power Custom, Inc.
Practical Tools, Inc.
Protector Mfg. Co., Inc., The
Protektor Model

PRODUCT DIRECTORY

Quality Parts Co.
Ram-Line, Inc.
Ranch Products
Round Edge, Inc.
RPM
Slings 'N Things, Inc.
Southwind Sanctions
TacStar Industries, Inc.
TacTell, Inc.
T.F.C. S.p.A.

TMI Products
Trijicon, Inc.
Tyler Mfg.-Dist., Melvin
Valor Corp.
Vintage Industries, Inc.
Volquartsen Custom Ltd.
Weigand Combat Handguns, Inc.
Western Design
Wilson's Gun Shop

HANDGUN GRIPS

Ahrends, Kim
Ajax Custom Grips, Inc.
Altamont Co.
American Derringer Corp.
American Gripcraft
Arms Corporation of the Philippines
Art Jewel Enterprises Ltd.
Baer Custom, Inc., Les
Barami Corp.
Bear Hug Grips, Inc.
Bell Originals, Inc., Sid
Beretta S.p.A., Pietro
Bob's Gun Shop
Boone's Custom Ivory Grips, Inc.
Boyds' Gunstock Industries, Inc.
Brooks Tactical Systems
Brown Products, Inc., Ed
Clark Custom Guns, Inc.
Cobra Gunskin
Cole-Grip
Colonial Repair
Custom Firearms
Dayson Arms Ltd.
Desert Industries, Inc.
E.A.A. Corp.
Eagle Mfg. & Engineering
EMF Co., Inc.
Ferris Firearms
Fisher Custom Firearms
Fitz Pistol Grip Co.
Forrest, Inc., Tom
Harrison-Hurtz Enterprises, Inc.
Herrett's Stocks, Inc.
Hogue Grips

J.P. Enterprises, Inc.
KeeCo Impressions
Lett Custom Grips
Linebaugh Custom Sixguns & Rifle Works
Mac's .45 Shop
Mandall Shooting Supplies, Inc.
Masen Co., Inc., John
Michaels of Oregon Co.
Mid-America Guns and Ammo
Millett Sights
Monte Kristo Pistol Grip Co.
N.C. Ordnance Co.
Newell, Robert H.
North American Specialties
Pacific Rifle Co.
Pardini Armi Srl
Pilgrim Pewter, Inc.
Radical Concepts
Rosenberg & Sons, Jack A.
Roy's Custom Grips
Savana Sports, Inc.
Sile Distributors, Inc.
Smith & Wesson
Speedfeed, Inc.
Spegel, Craig
Taurus Firearms, Inc.
Triple-K Mfg. Co., Inc.
Tyler Mfg.-Dist., Melvin
Uncle Mike's
Vintage Industries, Inc.
Volquartsen Custom Ltd.
Wilson's Gun Shop

HEARING PROTECTORS

Brown Co., E. Arthur
Brown Products, Inc., Ed
Browning Arms Co.
Clark Co., Inc., David
Clark Custom Guns, Inc.
Cobra Gunskin
E-A-R, Inc.
Electronic Shooters Protection, Inc.
Faith Associates, Inc.
Flents Products Co., Inc.
Gentex Corp.
Hoppe's Div.

Kesselring Gun Shop
North American Specialties
North Specialty Products
Paterson Gunsmithing
Peltor, Inc.
Penguin Industries, Inc.
R.E.T. Enterprises
Rucker Dist. Inc.
Safesport Manufacturing Co.
Silencio/Safety Direct
Willson Safety Prods. Div.

HOLSTERS AND LEATHER GOODS

A&B Industries, Inc.
Action Products, Inc.
Aker Leather Products
Alessi Holsters, Inc.
American Sales & Kirkpatrick
Arratoonian, Andy
Bagmaster Mfg., Inc.
Baker's Leather Goods, Roy
Bandcor Industries
Bang-Bang Boutique
Barami Corp.
Bear Hug Grips, Inc.
Bianchi International, Inc.
Bill's Custom Cases
Black Sheep Brand
Blocker Holsters, Inc., Ted
Brauer Bros. Mfg. Co.
Brown, H.R.
Browning Arms Co.
Bucheimer, J.M.
Bull-X, Inc.
Bushwacker Backpack & Supply Co.
Carvajal Belts & Holsters
Cathey Enterprises, Inc.
Chace Leather Products
Churchill Glove Co., James
Cimarron Arms
Clark Custom Guns, Inc.
Clements' Custom Leathercraft, Chas
Cobra Gunskin
Cobra Sport
Colonial Repair
Counter Assault
Crawford Co., Inc., R.M.

Creedmoor Sports, Inc.
Davis Leather Co., G. Wm.
Delhi Gun House
DeSantis Holster & Leather Goods, Inc.
Desert Industries, Inc.
D-Max, Inc.
Easy Pull Outlaw Products
Ekol Leather Care
El Dorado Leather
El Paso Saddlery Co.
EMF Co., Inc.
Eutaw Co., Inc., The
F&A Inc.
Faust, Inc., T.G.
Ferdinand, Inc.
Flores Publications, Inc., J.
Fobus International Ltd.
Fury Cutlery
Gage Manufacturing
GALCO International Ltd.
Glock, Inc.
GML Products, Inc.
Gould & Goodrich
Gun Leather Limited
Gunfitters, The
Gusty Winds Corp.
Hafner Creations, Inc.
HandiCrafts Unltd.
Hebard Guns, Gil
Hellweg Ltd.
Henigson & Associates, Steve
High North Products, Inc.
Hill Speed Leather, Ernie

Holster Shop, The
Horseshoe Leather Products
Hoyt Holster Co., Inc.
Hume, Don
Hunter Co., Inc.
John's Custom Leather
Joy Enterprises
Jumbo Sports Products
Kane Products, Inc.
Keller Co., The
Kirkpatrick Leather Co.
Kolpin Mfg., Inc.
Korth
Kramer Handgun Leather, Inc.
L.A.R. Mfg., Inc.
Law Concealment Systems, Inc.
Lawrence Leather Co.
Leather Arsenal
Lone Star Gunleather
Magnolia Sports, Inc.
Markell, Inc.
Michaels of Oregon Co.
Minute Man High Tech Industries
Mixson Corp.
Nelson Combat Leather, Bruce
Noble Co., Jim
No-Sho Mfg. Co.
Null Holsters Ltd., K.L.
October Country
Ojala Holsters, Arvo
Oklahoma Leather Products, Inc.
Old West Reproductions, Inc.

Pathfinder Sports Leather
PWL Gunleather
Renegade
Ringler Custom Leather Co.
Rybka Custom Leather Equipment, Thad
Safariland Ltd., Inc.
Safety Speed Holster, Inc.
Savana Sports, Inc.
Schulz Industries
Second Chance Body Armor
Shoemaker & Sons, Inc., Tex
Silhouette Leathers
Smith Saddlery, Jesse W.
Southwind Sanctions
Sparks, Milt
Stalker, Inc.
Strong Holster Co.
Stuart, V. Pat
Tabler Marketing
Texas Longhorn Arms, Inc.
Top-Line USA Inc.
Torel, Inc.
Triple-K Mfg. Co., Inc.
Tyler Mfg.-Dist., Melvin
Uncle Mike's
Valor Corp.
Venus Industries
Viking Leathercraft, Inc.
Walt's Custom Leather
Whinnery, Walt
Wild Bill's Originals

HUNTING AND CAMP GEAR, CLOTHING, ETC.

A&M Waterfowl, Inc.
Ace Sportswear, Inc.
Action Products, Inc.
Adventure 16, Inc.
Allen Co., Bob
Allen Sportswear, Bob
Armor
Atlanta Cutlery Corp.
Baekgaard Ltd.
Bagmaster Mfg., Inc.
Barbour, Inc.
Bauer, Eddie
Bear Archery
Beaver Park Products, Inc
Better Concepts Co.
Big Beam Emergency Systems, Inc.
Boss Manufacturing Co.
Brown Manufacturing
Browning Arms Co.
Buck Stop Lure Co., Inc.
Bushmaster Hunting & Fishing
Bushnell Sports Optics Worldwide
Camp-Cap Products
Carhartt, Inc.
Catoctin Cutlery
Chippewa Shoe Co.
Churchill Glove Co., James
Clarkfield Enterprises, Inc.
Cobra Gunskin
Coghlan's Ltd.
Coleman Co., Inc.
Coulston Products, Inc.
Crawford Co., Inc., R.M.
Creedmoor Sports, Inc.
D&H Prods. Co., Inc.
Dakota Corp.
Danner Shoe Mfg. Co.
DeckSlider of Florida
Deer Me Products
Dr. O's Products Ltd.
Dunham Co.
Duofold, Inc.
Dynalite Products, Inc.
E-A-R, Inc.
Ekol Leather Care
Erickson's Mfg., Inc., C.W.
Eutaw Co., Inc., The
F&A Inc.
Flow-Rite of Tennessee, Inc.
Forrest Tool Co.
Fox River Mills, Inc.
Frankonia Jagd
G&H Decoys, Inc.
Game Winner, Inc.
Gander Mountain, Inc.
Gerber Legendary Blades
Glacier Glove
H&B Forge Co.
Hafner Creations, Inc.
Hawken Shop, The
Hinman Outfitters, Bob
Hodgman, Inc.

Houtz & Barwick
Hunter's Specialties, Inc.
K&M Industries, Inc.
Kamik Outdoor Footwear
Kolpin Mfg., Inc.
LaCrosse Footwear, Inc.
Langenberg Hat Co.
Lectro Science, Inc.
Liberty Trouser Co.
L.L. Bean
MAG Instrument, Inc.
Marathon Rubber Prods. Co., Inc.
Melton Shirt Co., Inc.
Molin Industries
Mountain Hollow Game Calls
Nelson/Weather-Rite, Inc.
North Specialty Products
Northlake Outdoor Footwear
Original Mink Oil, Inc.
Orvis Co., The
Palsa Outdoor Products
Partridge Sales Ltd., John
Pointing Dog Journal
Porta Blind, Inc.
Pro-Mark
Pyromid, Inc.
Randolph Engineering, Inc.
Ranger Mfg. Co., Inc.
Ranging, Inc.
Rattlers Brand
Red Ball
Refrigiwear, Inc.
Rocky, Shoes & Boots
Safesport Manufacturing Co.
Savana Sports, Inc.
Scansport, Inc.
Sceery Game Calls
Schaefer Shooting Sports
Servus Footwear Co.
Simmons Outdoor Corp.
Slings 'N Things, Inc.
Streamlight, Inc.
Swanndri New Zealand
10-X Products Group
Thompson, Norm
T.H.U. Enterprises, Inc.
Tink's Safariland Hunting Corp.
Torel, Inc.
TrailTimer Co.
Venus Industries
Wakina by Pic
Walker Co., B.B.
Walls Industries
Wilcox All-Pro Tools & Supply
Wilderness Sound Products Ltd.
Willson Safety Prods. Div.
Winchester Sutler, Inc., The
Wolverine Boots & Outdoor Footwear Division
Woolrich, Inc.
Wyoming Knife Corp.
Yellowstone Wilderness Supply

DIRECTORY OF THE ARMS TRADE

KNIVES AND KNIFEMAKER'S SUPPLIES
FACTORY AND MAIL ORDER

Adventure 16, Inc.
Aitor-Cuchilleria Del Norte, S.A.
All Rite Products, Inc.
American Target Knives
Aristocrat Knives
Art Jewel Enterprises Ltd.
Atlanta Cutlery Corp.
B&D Trading Co., Inc.
Barteaux Machetes, Inc.
Bell Originals, Inc., Sid
Benchmark Knives
Beretta U.S.A. Corp.
Bill's Custom Cases
Blackjack Knives, Ltd.
Boker USA, Inc.
Bowen Knife Co. Inc.
Browning Arms Co.
Buck Knives, Inc.
Buster's Custom Knives
Camillus Cutlery Co.
Case & Sons Cutlery Co., W.R.
Catoctin Cutlery
Chicago Cutlery Co.
Christopher Firearms Co., Inc., E.
Clements' Custom Leathercraft, Chas
Coast Cutlery Co.
Cold Steel, Inc.
Coleman Co., Inc.
Colonial Knife Co., Inc.
Compass Industries, Inc.
Crawford Co., Inc., R.M.
Creative Craftsman, Inc., The
Crosman Blades
Cutco Cutlery
Cutlery Shoppe
Damascus-U.S.A.
Dan's Whetstone Co., Inc.
Degen Inc.
Delhi Gun House
DeSantis Holster & Leather Goods, Inc.
Diamontd Machining Technology, Inc.
EdgeCraft Corp.
EK Knife Co.
Empire Cutlery Corp.
Eze-Lap Diamond Prods.
Forrest Tool Co.
Forthofer's Gunsmithing & Knifemaking
Fortune Products, Inc.
Frank Knives
Frost Cutlery Co.
Fury Cutlery
Gerber Legendary Blades
Gibbs Rifle Co., Inc.
Golden Age Arms Co.
Gun Room, The
Gutmann Cutlery Inc.
H&B Forge Co.
HandiCrafts Unltd.
Harrington Cutlery, Inc., Russell
Harris Publications
Hawken Shop, The
Henckels Zwillingswerk, Inc., J.A.
High North Products, Inc.
Hoppe's Div.
Hubertus Schneidwarenfabrik
Hunter Co., Inc.
Hunting Classics
Ibberson (Sheffield) Ltd., George
Imperial Schrade Corp.
Iron Mountain Knife Co.
J.A. Blades, Inc.
Jantz Supply
Jenco Sales, Inc.
Johnson Wood Products
Joy Enterprises
KA-BAR Knives
Kasenit Co., Inc.
Kershaw Knives
Knife Importers, Inc.
Koval Knives
Lamson & Goodnow Mfg. Co.
Leatherman Tool Group, Inc.
Linder Solingen Knives
L.L. Bean
Mar Knives, Inc., Al
Matthews Cutlery
Molin Industries
Murphy Co., Inc., R.
Normark Corp.
North American Specialties
Outdoor Edge Cutlery Corp.
Penguin Industries, Inc.
Pilgrim Pewter, Inc.
Plaza Cutlery, Inc.
Precise International
Queen Cutlery Co.
R&C Knives & Such
Randall-Made Knives
Russell Knives, Inc., A.G.
Safesport Manufacturing Co.
Scansport, Inc.
Schiffman, Mike
Schrimsher's Custom Knifemaker's Supply, Bob
Sheffield Knifemakers Supply, Inc.
Smith Saddlery, Jesse W.
Soque River Knives
Spyderco, Inc.
Swiss Army Knives, Inc.
T.F.C. S.p.A.
Traditions, Inc.
Tru-Balance Knife Co.
United Cutlery Corp.
Utica Cutlery Co.
Venus Industries
Walt's Custom Leather
Washita Mountain Whetstone Co.
Weber Jr., Rudolf
Wenoka/Seastyle
Western Cutlery Co.
Whinnery, Walt
Wostenholm
Wyoming Knife Corp.

LABELS, BOXES, CARTRIDGE HOLDERS

American Sales & Kirkpatrick
Ballistic Products, Inc.
Berry's Mfg. Inc.
Brown Co., E. Arthur
Cabinet Mountain Outfitters Scents & Lures
Crane & Crane Ltd.
Del Rey Products
DeSantis Holster & Leather Goods, Inc.
Fitz Pistol Grip Co.
Flambeau Products Corp.
J&J Products Co.
Kolpin Mfg., Inc.
Lakewood Products, Inc.
Liberty Shooting Supplies
Loadmaster
Midway Arms, Inc.
MTM Molded Products Co., Inc.
Pendleton Royal

LOAD TESTING AND PRODUCT TESTING,
(Chronographing, Ballistic Studies)

Ballistic Research
Bartlett, Don
Bestload, Inc.
Briese Bullet Co., Inc.
Briganti & Co., A.
Buck Stix—SOS Products Co.
CFVentures
Clerke Co., J.A.
D&H Precision Tooling
Dead Eye's Sport Center
Defense Training International, Inc.
DGR Custom Rifles
DKT, Inc.
Duane's Gun Repair
Gonzalez Guns, Ramon B.
Hank's Gun Shop
Hensler, Jerry
Hoelscher, Virgil
Jackalope Gun Shop
Jensen Bullets
Jurras, L.E.
Lomont Precision Bullets
Maionchi-L.M.I.
MAST Technology
Master Class Bullets
McCann's Machine & Gun Shop
McMurdo, Lynn
Moreton/Fordyce Enterprises
Multiplex International
Oil Rod and Gun Shop
Ransom International Corp.
RPM
Rupert's Gun Shop
SOS Products Co.
Spencer's Custom Guns
Vancini, Carl

MISCELLANEOUS

Actions, Rifle
Hall Manufacturing
Accurizing, Rifle
Richards, John
Stoney Baroque Shooters Supply
Adapters, Cartridge
Alex, Inc.
Adapters, Shotshell
PC Co.
Airgun Accessories
BSA Guns Ltd.
Airgun Repair
Airgun Repair Centre
Nationwide Airgun Repairs
Ray's Gunsmith Shop
Assault Rifle Accessories
Feather Industries, Inc.
Ram-Line, Inc.
Barrel Stress Relieving
Cryo-Accurizing
Bi-Pods
B.M.F. Activator, Inc.
Body Armor
A&B Industries, Inc.
Faust, Inc., T.G.
Second Chance Body Armor
Top-Line USA Inc.
Bore Illuminator
Flashette Co.
Bore Lights
N.C. Ordnance Co.
MDS, Inc.
Brass Catcher
Gage Manufacturing
M.A.M. Products, Inc.
Bullets, Rubber
CIDCO
Calendar, Gun Shows
Stott's Creek Printers
Cannons, Miniature Replicas
Furr Arms
R.G.-G., Inc.
Dehumidifiers
Buenger Enterprises
Hydrosorbent Products
Dryers
Peet Shoe Dryer, Inc.
E-Z Loader
Del Rey Products
Firearm Refinishers
Armoloy Co. of Ft. Worth
Firearm Restoration
Adair Custom Shop, Bill
Burgess & Son Gunsmiths, R.W.
Johns, Bill
Liberty Antique Gunworks
Mazur Restoration, Pete
Moeller, Steve
Nicholson Custom
FFL Record Keeping
Basics Information Systems, Inc.
PFRB Co.
R.E.T. Enterprises
Hunting Trips
J/B Adventures & Safaris, Inc.
Professional Hunter Specialties
Hypodermic Rifles/Pistols
Multipropulseurs
Industrial Dessicants
WAMCO—New Mexico
Insert Barrels
MCA Sports
Multi-Caliber Adapters
Lettering Restoration System
Pranger, Ed G.
Locks, Gun
Brown Manufacturing
Master Lock Co.
Magazines
Mag-Pack Corp.
Mats
Brigade Quartermasters
Military Equipment/Accessories
Alpha 1 Drop Zone
Amherst Arms
Photographers, Gun
Bilal, Mustafa
Hanusin, John
Macbean, Stan
Payne Photography, Robert
Semmer, Charles
Smith, Michael
Weyer International
White Pine Photographic Services
Pistol Barrel Maker
Bar-Sto Precision Machine
Power Tools, Rotary Flexible Shaft
Foredom Electric Co.
Saddle Rings, Studs
Silver Ridge Gun Shop
Safety Devices
P&M Sales and Service
Safeties
Harper, William E./ The Great 870 Co.
P.M. Enterprises, Inc.
Scents and Lures
Buck Stop Lure Co., Inc.
Cabinet Mountain Outfitters Scents & Lures
Dr. O's Products Ltd.
Flow-Rite of Tennessee, Inc.
Mountain Hollow Game Calls
Robbins Scent, Inc.
Tink's Safariland Hunting Corp.
Tinks & Ben Lee Hunting Products
Wellington Outdoors
Wildlife Research Center, Inc.
Scrimshaw
Boone's Custom Ivory Grips, Inc.
Dolbare, Elizabeth
Hoover, Harvey
Lovestrand, Erik
Reno, Wayne
Sherwood, George
Shooting Range Equipment
Caswell International Corp.
Passive Bullet Traps, Inc.
Savage Range Systems, Inc.
Shotgun Barrel Maker
Baker, Stan
Silencers
AWC Systems Technology
Ciener, Jonathan Arthur
DLO Mfg.
Fleming Firearms
S.C.R.C.
Sound Technology
Ward Machine
Slings and Swivels
DTM International, Inc.
High North Products, Inc.
Leather Arsenal
Pathfinder Sports Leather
Schulz Industries
Torel, Inc.
Treestands and Steps
A&J Products
Apache Products, Inc.
Brell Mar Products
Dr. O's Products Ltd.
Silent Hunter
Summit Specialties, Inc.
Trax America, Inc.
Treemaster
Warren & Sweat Mfg. Co.
Trophies
Blackinton & Co., Inc., V.H.
Ventilated Rib
Simmons Gun Repair, Inc.
Ventilation
ScanCo Environmental Systems
Video Tapes
American Pioneer Video
Calibre Press, Inc.
Eastman Products, R.T.
Foothills Video Productions, Inc.
New Historians Productions, The
Primos, Inc.
Rocky Mountain Wildlife Products
Trail Visions
Wilderness Sound Products Ltd.
Xythos-Miniature Revolver
Andres & Dworsky

Vulpes Ventures, Inc.
Wells Custom Gunsmith, R.A.
Whildin & Sons Ltd., E.H.
White Laboratory, Inc., H.P.
X-Spand Target Systems

PRODUCT DIRECTORY

MUZZLE-LOADING GUNS, BARRELS AND EQUIPMENT

Accuracy Unlimited (Littleton, CO)
Adkins, Luther
Allen Manufacturing
Anderson Manufacturing Co., Inc.
Armi San Paolo
Bauska Barrels
Beauchamp & Son, Inc.
Beaver Lodge
Bentley, John
Birdsong & Associates, W.E.
Blackhawk West
Blue and Gray Products, Inc.
Bridgers Best
Buckskin Machine Works
Burgess & Son Gunsmiths, R.W.
Butler Creek Corp.
Cache La Poudre Rifleworks
California Sights
Cape Outfitters
Cash Manufacturing Co., Inc.
CenterMark
Chambers Flintlocks, Ltd., Jim
Chopie Mfg., Inc.
Cimarron Arms
Cogar's Gunsmithing
Colonial Repair
Colt Blackpowder Arms Co.
Cousin Bob's Mountain Products
Cumberland Arms
Cumberland Knife & Gun Works
Curly Maple Stock Blanks
CVA
Dangler, Homer L.
Davis Co., R.E.
Day & Sons, Inc., Leonard
Dayton Traister
deHaas Barrels
Delhi Gun House
Desert Industries, Inc.
Dewey Mfg. Co., Inc., J.
DGS, Inc.
Dyson & Son Ltd., Peter
EMF Co., Inc.
Euroarms of America, Inc.
Eutaw Co., Inc., The
Fautheree, Andy
Feken, Dennis
Fellowes, Ted
Fire'n Five
Flintlocks, Etc.
Forster Products
Fort Hill Gunstocks
Frontier
Getz Barrel Co.
GOEX, Inc.
Golden Age Arms Co.
Gonic Arms, Inc.
Green Mountain Rifle Barrel Co., Inc.
Hastings Barrels
Hatfield Gun Co., Inc.
Hawken Shop, The
Hege Jagd-u. Sporthandels, GmbH
Hoppe's Div.
Hornady Mfg. Co.
House of Muskets, Inc., The
Hunkeler, A.
Jamison's Forge Works
Jones Co., Dale
K&M Industries, Inc.
Kennedy Firearms
Knight Rifles

Kwik-Site Co.
L&R Lock Co.
Legend Products Corp.
Log Cabin Sport Shop
Lothar Walther Precision Tool, Inc.
Lyman Products Corp.
McCann's Muzzle-Gun Works
Michaels of Oregon Co.
MMP
Modern MuzzleLoading, Inc.
Montana Armory, Inc.
Montana Precision Swaging
Mountain State Muzzleloading Supplies
Mowrey Gun Works
MSC Industrial Supply Co.
Mt. Alto Outdoor Products
Mushroom Express Bullet Co.
Muzzleloaders Etcetera, Inc.
Navy Arms Co.
North Star West
October Country
Oklahoma Leather Products, Inc.
Olson, Myron
Orion Rifle Barrel Co.
Ox-Yoke Originals, Inc.
Pacific Rifle Co.
Pedersoli, Davide & C.
Penguin Industries, Inc.
Pioneer Arms Co.
Prairie River Arms
Radical Concepts
Rusty Duck Premium Gun Care Products
R.V.I.
S&B Industries
S&S Firearms
Selsi Co., Inc.
Sharps Arms Co., Inc., C.
Shooter's Choice
Sile Distributors
Single Shot, Inc.
Sklany, Steve
Slings 'N Things, Inc.
Smokey Valley Rifles
South Bend Replicas, Inc.
Southern Bloomer Mfg. Co.
Starr Trading Co., Jedediah
Stone Mountain Arms
Storey, Dale A.
Tennessee Valley Mfg.
Thompson Bullet Lube Co.
Thompson/Center Arms
Thunder Mountain Arms
Tiger-Hunt
Track of the Wolf, Inc.
Traditions, Inc.
Treso, Inc.
UFA, Inc.
Uberti, Aldo
Uncle Mike's
Upper Missouri Trading Co.
Venco Industries, Inc.
Walters, John
Warren Muzzleloading Co., Inc.
Wescombe
White Owl Enterprises
White Shooting Systems, Inc.
Williams Gun Sight Co.
Woodworker's Supply
Young Country Arms

PISTOLSMITHS

Accuracy Gun Shop
Accuracy Unlimited (Glendale, AZ)
Ace Custom 45's, Inc.
Actions by "T"
Adair Custom Shop, Bill
Ahlman Guns
Aldis Gunsmithing & Shooting Supply
Alpha Precision, Inc.
Alpine's Precision Gunsmithing & Indoor Shooting Range
Armament Gunsmithing Co., Inc.
AWC Systems Technology
Baer Custom, Inc., Les
Bain & Davis, Inc.
Banks, Ed
Behlert Precision, Inc.
Bellm Contenders
Belt MTN Arms
Bengtson Arms Co., L.
BlackStar AccuMax Barrels
BlackStar Barrel Accurizing
Bowen Classic Arms Corp.

Campbell, Dick
Cannon's Guns
Caraville Manufacturing
Clark Custom Guns, Inc.
Colonial Repair
Colorado Gunsmithing Academy Lamar
Corkys Gun Clinic
Costa, David
Craig Custom Ltd.
Curtis Custom Shop
Custom Gunsmiths
D&L Sports
Davis Service Center, Bill
Ellicott Arms, Inc./Woods Pistolsmithing
Ferris Firearms
Fisher Custom Firearms
Forkin, Ben
Francesca, Inc.
Frank Custom Classic Arms, Ron
Frielich Police Equipment

Garthwaite, Jim
Giron, Robert E.
Gonzalez Guns, Ramon B.
Greider Precision
Gun Room Press, The
Guncraft Sports, Inc.
Guns
Gunsite Custom Shop
Gunsite Gunsmithy
Gunsite Training Center
Gunsmithing Ltd.
Hamilton, Alex B.
Hamilton, Keith
Hank's Gun Shop
Hanson's Gun Center, Dick
Hardison, Charles
Harris Gunworks
Hebard Guns, Gil
Heinie Specialty Products
High Bridge Arms, Inc.
Highline Machine Co.
Hoag, James W.
Intermountain Arms & Tackle, Inc.
Irwin, Campbell H.
Island Pond Gun Shop
Ivanoff, Thomas G.
J&S Heat Treat
Jarvis, Inc.
Jensen's Custom Ammunition
Johnston, James
Jones, J.D.
J.P. Enterprises, Inc.
Jungkind, Reeves C.
K-D, Inc.
Kaswer Custom, Inc.
Ken's Gun Specialties
Kilham & Co.
Kimball, Gary
Kopp, Terry K.
La Clinique du .45
LaFrance Specialties
LaRocca Gun Works, Inc.
Lathrop's, Inc.
Lawson, John G.
Leckie Professional Gunsmithing
Lee's Red Ramps
Linebaugh Custom Sixguns & Rifle Works
List Precision Engineering
Long, George F.
Mac's .45 Shop
Mahony, Philip Bruce
Marent, Rudolf
Martin's Gun Shop
Marvel, Alan
McCann's Machine & Gun Shop
McGowen Rifle Barrels

Middlebrooks Custom Shop
Miller Custom
Mitchell's Accuracy Shop
MJK Gunsmithing, Inc.
Mountain Bear Rifle Works, Inc.
Mullis Guncraft
Mustra's Custom Guns, Inc., Carl
Nastoff's 45 Shop, Inc., Steve
NCP Products, Inc.
North Fork Custom Gunsmithing
Novak's Inc.
Nowlin Custom Mfg.
Oglesby & Oglesby Gunmakers, Inc.
Paris, Frank J.
Pasadena Gun Center
Peacemaker Specialists
PEM's Mfg. Co.
Performance Specialists
Peterson Gun Shop, Inc., A.W.
Pierce Pistols
Plaxco, J. Michael
Precision Specialties
Randco UK
Ries, Chuck
Rim Pac Sports, Inc.
Robar Co.'s, Inc., The
Rogers Gunsmithing, Bob
Scott, McDougall & Associates
Seecamp Co., Inc., L.W.
Shooter Shop, The
Shooters Supply
Shootin' Shack, Inc.
Sight Shop, The
Singletary, Kent
Sipes Gun Shop
Springfield, Inc.
SSK Industries
Steger, James R.
Swampfire Shop, The
Swenson's 45 Shop, A.D.
300 Gunsmith Service, Inc.
Ten-Ring Precision, Inc.
Thompson, Randall
Thurston Sports, Inc.
Tom's Gun Repair
Vic's Gun Refinishing
Volquartsen Custom Ltd.
Walker Arms Co., Inc.
Walters Industries
Wardell Precision Handguns Ltd.
Weigand Combat Handguns, Inc.
Wessinger Custom Guns & Engraving
Whitestone Lumber Corp.
Wichita Arms, Inc.
Williams Gun Sight Co.
Williamson Precision Gunsmithing
Wilson's Gun Shop

REBORING AND RERIFLING

Flaig's
H&S Liner Service
Ivanoff, Thomas G.
Jackalope Gun Shop
K-D, Inc.
Kopp, Terry K.
LaBounty Precision Reboring
Matco, Inc.
Pence Precision Barrels
Redman's Rifling & Reboring
Rice, Keith

Ridgetop Sporting Goods
Shaw, Inc., E.R.
Siegrist Gun Shop
Simmons Gun Repair, Inc.
300 Gunsmith Service, Inc.
Tom's Gun Repair
Van Patten, J.W.
West, Robert G.
White Rock Tool & Die
Zufall, Joseph F.

RELOADING TOOLS AND ACCESSORIES

Action Bullets, Inc.
Advance Car Mover Co., Rowell Div.
American Products Co.
Ames Metal Products
Ammo Load, Inc.
Anderson Manufacturing Co., Inc.
Arms Corporation of the Philippines
Atlantic Rose, Inc.
Bald Eagle Precision Machine Co.
Ballistic Products, Inc.
Ballisti-Cast, Inc.
Bear Reloaders
Belltown, Ltd.
Ben's Machines
Berger Bullets, Ltd.
Berry's Mfg. Inc.
Birchwood Casey
Blue Ridge Machinery & Tools, Inc.
Brass-Tech Industries
Break-Free, Inc.
Briganti & Co., A.
Brobst, Jim
Brown Co., E. Arthur
BRP, Inc. High Performance Cast Bullets

Bruno Shooters Supply
Brynin, Milton
B-Square Co., Inc.
Buck Stix—SOS Products Co.
Buffalo Arms
Bull Mountain Rifle Co.
Bullet Swaging Supply, Inc.
Bullseye Bullets
C&D Special Products
Camdex, Inc.
Canyon Cartridge Corp.
Carbide Die & Mfg. Co., Inc.
Case Sorting System
CFVentures
C-H Tool & Die Corp.
Chem-Pak, Inc.
CheVron Case Master
Clark Custom Guns, Inc.
Claybuster Wads & Harvester Bullets
Clymer Manufacturing Co., Inc.
Coats, Mrs. Lester
Colorado Shooter's Supply
CONKKO
Cook Engineering Service

29th EDITION, 1997

DIRECTORY OF THE ARMS TRADE

Corbin, Inc.
Crouse's Country Cover
Custom Products, Neil A. Jones
Davis, Don
Davis Products, Mike
D.C.C. Enterprises
Denver Bullets, Inc.
Denver Instrument Co.
Dever Co., Jack
Dewey Mfg. Co., Inc., J.
Dillon Precision Prods., Inc.
Dropkick
Dutchman's Firearms, Inc., The
E&L Mfg., Inc.
Eagan, Donald V.
Eezox, Inc.
Engineered Accessories
Enguix Import-Export
Essex Metals
4-D Custom Die Co.
F&A Inc.
Federal Cartridge Co.
Federated-Fry
Feken, Dennis
Ferguson, Bill
First, Inc., Jack
Fitz Pistol Grip Co.
Flambeau Products Corp.
Forgett Jr., Valmore J.
Forgreens Tool Mfg., Inc.
Forster Products
Fremont Tool Works
Fry Metals
Fusilier Bullets
G&C Bullet Co., Inc.
GAR
Goddard, Allen
GOEX, Inc.
Gozon Corp., U.S.A.
Graphics Direct
Graves Co.
Green, Arthur S.
Greenwood Precision
Grizzly Bullets
Hanned Line, The
Hanned Precision
Harrell's Precision
Harris Enterprises
Harrison Bullets
Haydon Shooters' Supply, Russ
Heidenstrom Bullets
Hensley & Gibbs
Hirtenberger Aktiengesellschaft
Hobson Precision Mfg. Co.
Hoch Custom Bullet Moulds
Hoehn Sales, Inc.
Hoelscher, Virgil
Hollywood Engineering
Hondo Industries
Hornady Mfg. Co.
Howell Machine
Huntington Die Specialties
IMI Services USA, Inc.
Imperial Magnum Corp.
INTEC International, Inc.
Iosso Products
Javelina Lube Products
JGS Precision Tool Mfg.
JLK Bullets
Jonad Corp.
Jones Custom Products, Neil A.
Jones Moulds, Paul
K&M Services
K&S Mfg. Inc.
Kapro Mfg. Co., Inc.
King & Co.
KLA Enterprises
Kleen-Bore, Inc.
Lane Bullets, Inc.
LBT
Lee Precision, Inc.
Legend Products Corp.
Liberty Metals
Littleton, J.F.
Lomont Precision Bullets
Lortone, Inc.
Loweth, Richard
Luch Metal Merchants, Barbara
Lyman Instant Targets, Inc.
Lyman Products Corp.
M&D Munitions Ltd.
MA Systems
Magma Engineering Co.
MarMik Inc.
Marquart Precision Co., Inc.
MAST Technology
Master Class Bullets

Match Prep
McKillen & Heyer, Inc.
MCRW Associates Shooting Supplies
MEC, Inc.
Midway Arms, Inc.
Miller Engineering
MI-TE Bullets
MKL Service Co.
MMP
Mt. Baldy Bullet Co.
MTM Molded Products Co., Inc.
Multi-Scale Charge Ltd.
Naval Ordnance Works
Necromancer Industries, Inc.
NEI Handtools, Inc.
Niemi Engineering, W.B.
North Devon Firearms Services
Old West Bullet Moulds
Old Western Scrounger, Inc.
Omark Industries
Paco's
Pattern Control
Pedersoli, Davide & C.
Peerless Alloy, Inc.
Pend Oreille Sport Shop
Petro-Explo, Inc.
Pinetree Bullets
Plum City Ballistic Range
Policlips North America
Polywad, Inc.
Pomeroy, Robert
Ponsness/Warren
Powder Valley Services
Prairie River Arms
Precision Castings & Equipment, Inc.
Precision Reloading, Inc.
Prime Reloading
Prolix® Lubricants
Pro-Shot Products, Inc.
Protector Mfg. Co., Inc., The
Rapine Bullet Mould Mfg. Co.
Raytech
RCBS
Redding Reloading Equipment
R.E.I.
Reloading Specialties, Inc.
Rice, Keith
Riebe Co., W.J.
RIG Products
R.I.S. Co., Inc.
Roberts Products
Rochester Lead Works, Inc.
Rooster Laboratories
Rorschach Precision Products
Rosenthal, Brad and Sallie
SAECO
Sandia Die & Cartridge Co.
Saunders Gun & Machine Shop
Saville Iron Co.
Scharch Mfg., Inc.
Scot Powder Co. of Ohio, Inc.
Scott, Dwight
Seebeck Assoc., R.E.
Sierra Specialty Prod. Co.
Silhouette, The
Silver Eagle Machining
Simmons, Jerry
Sinclair International, Inc.
Skip's Machine
S.L.A.P. Industries
Small Custom Mould & Bullet Co.
SOS Products Co.
Spence, George W.
Spencer's Custom Guns
Sport Flite Manufacturing Co.
Sportsman Supply Co.
Stalwart Corp.
Star Machine Works
Stillwell, Robert
Stoney Point Products, Inc.
Talon Mfg. Co., Inc.
Tamarack Products, Inc.
Taracorp Industries
TCCI
TCSR
TDP Industries, Inc.
Tetra Gun Lubricants
Thompson Bullet Lube Co.
Timber Heirloom Products
TMI Products
TR Metals Corp.
Trammco, Inc.
Trophy Bonded Bullets, Inc.
Tru-Square Metal Prods., Inc.
TTM
Tyler Scott, Inc.
Varner's Service

Vega Tool Co.
VibraShine, Inc.
Vibra-Tek Co.
Vihtavuori Oy
Vitt/Boos
Von Minden Gunsmithing Services
Walters, John
Webster Scale Mfg. Co.
Welsh, Bud
Werner, Carl
Westfield Engineering

White Rock Tool & Die
Whitetail Design & Engineering Ltd.
Widener's Reloading &
  Shooting Supply
William's Gun Shop, Ben
Wilson, Inc., L.E.
Wise Guns, Dale
Wolf's Western Traders
Yesteryear Armory & Supply
Young Country Arms

RESTS—BENCH, PORTABLE—AND ACCESSORIES

Accuright
Adaptive Technology
Adventure 16, Inc.
Armor Metal Products
Aspen Outdoors, Inc.
Bald Eagle Precision Machine Co.
Bartlett Engineering
Browning Arms Co.
B-Square Co., Inc.
Bull Mountain Rifle Co.
Canons Delcour
Chem-Pak, Inc.
Clift Mfg., L.R.
Clift Welding Supply
Decker Shooting Products
Desert Mountain Mfg.
F&A Inc.
Greenwood Precision
Harris Engineering, Inc.
Hidalgo, Tony
Hoelscher, Virgil
Hoppe's Div.

J&J Sales
Kolpin Mfg., Inc.
Kramer Designs
Midway Arms, Inc.
Millett Sights
MJM Manufacturing
Outdoor Connection, Inc., The
PAST Sporting Goods, Inc.
Pease Accuracy, Bob
Penguin Industries, Inc.
Portus, Robert
Protektor Model
Ransom International Corp
Saville Iron Co.
Slug Group, Inc.
Stoney Point Products, Inc.
Thompson Target Technology
T.H.U. Enterprises, Inc.
Tonoloway Tack Drivers
Varner's Service
Wichita Arms, Inc.
Zanotti Armor, Inc.

RIFLE BARREL MAKERS (See also Muzzle-Loading Guns, Barrels and Equipment)

Airrow
Bain & Davis, Inc.
Bauska Barrels
BlackStar AccuMax Barrels
BlackStar Barrel Accurizing
Border Barrels Ltd.
Broad Creek Rifle Works
Brown Co., E. Arthur
Bullberry Barrel Works, Ltd.
Bustani, Leo
Canons Delcour
Carter's Gun Shop
Christensen Arms
Cincinnati Swaging
Citadel Mfg., Inc.
Clerke Co., J.A.
D&J Bullet Co. & Custom Gun
  Shop, Inc.
deHaas Barrels
Dilliott Gunsmithing, Inc.
Donnelly, C.P.
Douglas Barrels, Inc.
Gaillard Barrels
Getz Barrel Co.
Green Mountain Rifle Barrel Co., Inc.
Half Moon Rifle Shop
Harold's Custom Gun Shop, Inc.
Harris Gunworks
Hart Rifle Barrels, Inc.
Hastings Barrels
Hoelscher, Virgil
H-S Precision, Inc.
Jackalope Gun Shop
Jones, J.D.
K-D, Inc.

KOGOT
Kopp, Terry K.
Krieger Barrels, Inc.
LaBounty Precision Reboring
Lilja Precision Rifle Barrels
Lothar Walther Precision Tool, Inc.
Mac's .45 Shop
Matco, Inc.
McGowen Rifle Barrels
McMillan Rifle Barrels
Mid-America Recreation, Inc.
Nowlin Custom Mfg.
Obermeyer Rifled Barrels
Pac-Nor Barreling
Pell, John T.
Pence Precision Barrels
Rocky Mountain Rifle Works Ltd.
Rosenthal, Brad and Sallie
Sabatti S.R.L.
Schneider Rifle Barrels, Inc., Gary
Shaw, Inc., E.R.
Shilen Rifles, Inc.
Siskiyou Gun Works
Small Arms Mfg. Co.
Sonora Rifle Barrel Co.
Specialty Shooters Supply, Inc.
Springfield, Inc.
SSK Industries
Strutz Rifle Barrels, Inc., W.C.
Swivel Machine Works, Inc.
Volquartsen Custom Ltd.
Wells, Fred F.
Wilson Arms Co., The
Wiseman and Co., Bill

SCOPES, MOUNTS, ACCESSORIES, OPTICAL EQUIPMENT

Accuracy Innovations, Inc.
Ackerman, Bill
ADCO International
Adventurer's Outpost
Aimpoint, Inc.
Aimtech Mount Systems
Air Venture
Alley Supply Co.
Anderson Manufacturing Co., Inc.
Anschutz GmbH
Apel GmbH, Ernst
A.R.M.S., Inc.
Armscorp USA, Inc.
Aro-Tek, Ltd.
Baer Custom, Inc., Les
Barrett Firearms Mfg., Inc.
Bushnell Sports Optics Worldwide
Beaver Park Products, Inc.
Bohemia Arms Co.
Boonie Packer Products

Brown Co., E. Arthur
Brownells, Inc.
Browning Arms Co.
Brunton U.S.A.
B-Square Co., Inc.
Bull Mountain Rifle Co.
Burris Co., Inc.
Bushnell
Butler Creek Corp.
Celestron International
Center Lock Scope Rings
Champion's Choice, Inc.
Clark Custom Guns, Inc.
Clearview Mfg. Co., Inc.
Combat Military Ordnance Ltd.
Compass Industries, Inc.
Concept Development Corp.
Conetrol Scope Mounts
CRDC Laser Systems Group
Creedmoor Sports, Inc.

PRODUCT DIRECTORY

Custom Quality Products, Inc.
D&H Prods. Co., Inc.
D.C.C. Enterprises
Del-Sports, Inc.
DHB Products
Doctor Optic Technologies, Inc.
Eagle International, Inc.
Eagle Mfg. & Engineering
Edmund Scientific Co.
Ednar, Inc.
Eggleston, Jere D.
Emerging Technologies, Inc.
Europtik Ltd.
Excalibur Enterprises
Farr Studio, Inc.
Feather Industries, Inc.
Forster Products
From Jena
Fujinon, Inc.
Gentry Custom Gunmaker, David
G.G. & G.
Glaser Safety Slug, Inc.
Great Lakes Airguns
Guns, (Div. of D.C. Engineering, Inc.)
Hakko Co. Ltd.
Hammerli USA
Harris Gunworks
Hermann Leather Co., H.J.
Hertel & Reuss
Holland's
H-S Precision, Inc.
Ironsighter Co.
Jaeger, Inc., Paul/Dunn's
JagerSport, Ltd.
Jeffredo Gunsight
Jewell, Arnold W.
Jones, J.D.
Kahles, A Swarovski Company
Kelbly, Inc.
Keng's Firearms Specialty, Inc.
KenPatable Ent., Inc.
Kesselring Gun Shop
Kimber of America, Inc.
Kmount
Kowa Optimed, Inc.
Kris Mounts
KVH Industries, Inc.
Kwik Mount Corp.
Kwik-Site Co.
L&S Technologies, Inc.
L.A.R. Mfg., Inc.
Laser Devices, Inc.
Laseraim
LaserMax
Lectro Science, Inc.
Lee Co., T.K.
Leica USA, Inc.
Leupold & Stevens, Inc.
List Precision Engineering
Lohman Mfg. Co., Inc.
London Guns Ltd.
Mac's .45 Shop
Masen Co., Inc., John
Maxi-Mount
McCann's Machine & Gun Shop
McMillan Optical Gunsight Co.
MDS
Michaels of Oregon Co.
Military Armament Corp.
Millett Sights
Mirador Optical Corp.
Mitchell Arms, Inc.
MWG Co.
New Democracy, Inc.
New England Custom Gun Service
Nikon, Inc.
North American Specialties
Oakshore Electronic Sights, Inc.
Olympic Optical Co.
Optical Services Co.
Orchard Park Enterprise
Outdoor Connection, Inc., The
Parsons Optical Mfg. Co.
PECAR Herbert Schwarz, GmbH
PEM's Mfg. Co.
Pentax Corp.
Perazone, Brian
Precise Metalsmithing Enterprises
Precision Sport Optics
Premier Reticles
Ram-Line, Inc.
Ranch Products
Randolph Engineering, Inc.
Ranging, Inc.
Redfield, Inc.
Rice, Keith
Rocky Mountain High Sports Glasses
S&K Mfg. Co.
Saunders Gun & Machine Shop
Schmidt & Bender, Inc.
Scope Control Inc.
ScopLevel
Seattle Binocular & Scope Repair Co.
Selsi Co., Inc.
Shepherd Scope Ltd.
Sightron, Inc.
Simmons Enterprises, Ernie
Simmons Outdoor Corp.
Six Enterprises
SKAN A.R.
SKB Shotguns
Sportsmatch U.K. Ltd.
Springfield, Inc.
SSK Industries
Steyr Mannlicher AG
Stoeger Industries
SwaroSports, Inc.
Swarovski Optik North America Ltd.
Swift Instruments, Inc.
TacStar Industires, Inc.
Talley, Dave
Tank's Rifle Shop
Tasco Sales, Inc.
Tele-Optics
Thompson/Center Arms
Trijicon, Inc.
Uncle Mike's
Unertl Optical Co., Inc., John
United Binocular Co.
United States Optics Technologies, Inc.
Valor Corp.
Volquartsen Custom Ltd.
Warne Manufacturing Co.
Warren Muzzleloading Co., Inc.
WASP Shooting Systems
Weatherby, Inc.
Weaver Products
Weaver Scope Repair Service
Weigand Combat Handguns, Inc.
Westfield Engineering
White Rock Tool & Die
Wideview Scope Mount Corp.
Williams Gun Sight Co.
York M-1 Conversions
Zanotti Armor, Inc.
Zeiss Optical, Carl

SHOOTING/TRAINING SCHOOLS

Accuracy Gun Shop
Alpine Precision Gunsmithing & Indoor Shooting Range
American Small Arms Academy
Auto Arms
Bob's Tactical Indoor Shooting Range & Gun Shop
Chapman Academy of Practical Shooting
Chelsea Gun Club of New York City, Inc.
Clark Custom Guns, Inc.
CQB Training
Daisy Mfg. Co.
Defense Training International, Inc.
Dowtin Gunworks
Executive Protection Institute
Firearm Training Center, The
Firearms Academy of Seattle
G.H. Enterprises Ltd.
Gonzalez Guns, Ramon B.
Gunsite Training Center
Hank's Gun Shop
I.S.S.
Jensen's Custom Ammunition
Jensen's Firearms Acadamy
J.P. Enterprises, Inc.
McMurdo, Lynn
Mendez, John A.
Middlebrooks Custom Shop
Modern Gun School
Nevada Pistol Academy Inc.
North American Shooting Systems
North Mountain Pines Training Center
Pacific Pistolcraft
Passive Bullet Traps, Inc.
Performance Specialists
Quigley's Personal Protection Strategies, Paxton
River Road Sporting Clays
Robar Co.'s, Inc., The
SAFE
Savage Range Systems, Inc.
Shooter's World
Shooting Gallery, The
Shotgun Shop, The
Smith & Wesson
Specialty Gunsmithing

SIGHTS, METALLIC

Accura-Site
All's, The Jim J. Tembelis Co., Inc.
Alpec Team, Inc.
Andela Tool & Machine, Inc.
Anschutz GmbH
Armsport, Inc.
Aro-Tek, Ltd.
Baer Custom, Inc., Les
Bob's Gun Shop
Bo-Mar Tool & Mfg. Co.
Bond Custom Firearms
Bowen Classic Arms Corp.
Bradley Gunsight Co.
Brown Co., E. Arthur
Brown Products, Inc., Ed
Buffalo Arms
California Sights
Cape Outfitters
Champion's Choice, Inc.
C-More Systems
Colonial Repair
DHB Products
Engineered Accessories
Evans, Andrew
Evans Gunsmithing
Farr Studio, Inc.
Fautheree, Andy
GSI, Inc.
Gun Doctor, The
Gun South, Inc.
Guns, (Div. of D.C. Engineering, Inc.)
Heinie Specialty Products
Hesco-Meprolight
Innovative Weaponry, Inc.
Innovision Enterprises
Jaeger, Inc., Paul/Dunn's
Lee's Red Ramps
List Precision Engineering
Lofland, James W.
London Guns Ltd.
L.P.A. Snc
Lyman Instant Targets, Inc.
Lyman Products Corp.
Mac's .45 Shop
Marble Arms
Meier Works
Meprolight
Merit Corp.
Mid-America Recreation, Inc.
Millett Sights
Mitchell Arms, Inc.
MMC
Montana Vintage Arms
New England Custom Gun Service
North American Specialties
Novak's Inc.
Oakshore Electronic Sights, Inc.
OK Weber, Inc.
Pachmayr Ltd.
PEM's Mfg. Co.
P.M. Enterprises, Inc.
Quarton USA, Ltd. Co.
Robar Co.'s, Inc., The
RPM
Scattergun Technologies, Inc.
Shepherd Scope Ltd.
Slug Site Co.
Talley, Dave
T.F.C. S.p.A.
Trijicon, Inc.
WASP Shooting Systems
Wichita Arms, Inc.
Williams Gun Sight Co.

STOCKS (Commercial and Custom)

Accuracy Unlimited (Glendale, AZ)
Ackerman & Co.
Adair Custom Shop, Bill
Ahlman Guns
Amrine's Gun Shop
Anschutz GmbH
Arms Ingenuity Co.
Artistry In Wood
Bain & Davis, Inc.
Balickie, Joe
Bansner's Gunsmithing Specialties
Barnes Bullets, Inc.
Bartlett, Don
Beitzinger, George
Belding's Custom Gun Shop
Bell & Carlson, Inc.
Benchmark Guns
Biesen, Al
Biesen, Roger
Bob's Gun Shop
Boltin, John M.
Bowerly, Kent
Boyds' Gunstock Industries, Inc.
Burgess & Son Gunsmiths, R.W.
Brace, Larry D.
Briganti & Co., A.
Brockmans Custom Gunsmithing
Brown Co., E. Arthur
Brown Precision, Inc.
Brownell Checkering Tools, W.E.
Buckhorn Gun Works
Bull Mountain Rifle Co.
Bullberry Barrel Works, Ltd.
Burkhart Gunsmithing, Don
Burres, Jack
Butler Creek Corp.
Cali'co Hardwoods, Inc.
Camilli, Lou
Campbell, Dick
Caywood, Shane J.
Chambers Flintlocks Ltd., Jim
Champlin Firearms, Inc.
Chicasaw Gun Works
Christman Jr., David
Churchill, Winston
Clark Custom Guns, Inc.
Claro Walnut Gunstock Co.
Cloward's Gun Shop
Cochran, Oliver
Starlight Training Center, Inc.
300 Gunsmith Service, Inc.
Tactical Defense Institute
Western Missouri Shooters Alliance
Yankee Gunsmith
Yavapai Firearms Academy Ltd.
Coffin, Charles H.
Coffin, Jim
Coleman's Custom Repair
Colonial Repair
Colorado Gunsmithing Academy Lamar
Conrad, C.A.
Cooper Arms
Costa, David
Crane Sales Co., George S.
Creedmoor Sports, Inc.
Curly Maple Stock Blanks
Custom Checkering Service
Custom Gun Products
Custom Gun Stocks
Custom Riflestocks, Inc.
D&D Gunsmiths, Ltd.
D&G Presicion Duplicators
D&J Bullet Co. & Custom Gun Shop, Inc.
Dahl's Custom Stocks
Dangler, Homer L.
D.D. Custom Stocks
Desert Industries, Inc.
de Treville & Co., Stan
Dever Co., Jack
Devereaux, R.H. "Dick"
DGS, Inc.
Dilliott Gunsmithing, Inc.
Dillon, Ed
Dowtin Gunworks
Dressel Jr., Paul G.
Duane Custom Stocks, Randy
Duncan's Gunworks, Inc.
Echols & Co., D'Arcy
Eggleston, Jere D.
Erhardt, Dennis
Eversull Co., Inc., K.
Fajen, Inc., Reinhart
Farmer-Dressel, Sharon
Fibron Products, Inc.
Fisher, Jerry A.
Flaig's
Folks, Donald E.
Forster, Kathy
Forster, Larry L.
Forty Five Ranch Enterprises
Frank Custom Classic Arms, Ron
Game Haven Gunstocks

29th EDITION, 1997 **311**

DIRECTORY OF THE ARMS TRADE

Gene's Custom Guns
Gervais, Mike
Gilman-Mayfield, Inc.
Giron, Robert E.
Goens, Dale W.
Golden Age Arms Co.
Gordie's Gun Shop
Goudy Classic Stocks, Gary
Grace, Charles E.
Green, Roger M.
Greene Precision Duplicators
Greenwood Precision
Griffin & Howe, Inc.
Gun Shop, The
Guns
Guns, (Div. of D.C. Engineering, Inc.)
Gunsmithing Ltd.
Hallberg Gunsmith, Fritz
Halstead, Rick
Hanson's Gun Center, Dick
Harper's Custom Stocks
Harris Gunworks
Hart & Son, Inc., Robert W.
Hastings Barrels
Hecht, Hubert J.
Heilmann, Stephen
Hensley, Darwin
Heppler, Keith M.
Heydenberk, Warren R.
High Tech Specialties, Inc.
Hillmer Custom Gunstocks, Paul D.
Hiptmayer, Armurier
Hiptmayer, Klaus
Hoelscher, Virgil
Hoenig & Rodman
H-S Precision, Inc.
Huebner, Corey O.
Hughes, Steven Dodd
Intermountain Arms & Tackle, Inc.
Island Pond Gun Shop
Ivanoff, Thomas G.
Jackalope Gun Shop
Jaeger, Inc., Paul/Dunn's
Jamison's Forge Works
Jarrett Rifles, Inc.
Johnson Wood Products
J.P. Gunstocks, Inc.
KDF, Inc.
Keith's Custom Gunstocks
Ken's Rifle Blanks
Kilham & Co.
Klein Custom Guns, Don
Klingler Woodcarving
Knippel, Richard
Kokolus, Michael M.
Lawson Co., Harry
Lock's Philadelphia Gun Exchange
Lynn's Custom Gunstocks
Mac's .45 Shop
Marple & Associates, Dick
Masen Co., Inc., John
Mathews & Son, Inc., George E.
Mazur Restoraton, Pete
McCament, Jay
McCullough, Ken
McDonald, Dennis
McFarland, Stan
McGowen Rifle Barrels
McGuire, Bill
McKinney, R.P.
McMillan Fiberglass Stocks, Inc.
Mercer Custom Stocks, R.M.
Mid-America Recreation, Inc.
Miller Arms, Inc.
Morrison Custom Rifles, J.W.
Morrow, Bud
MPI Fiberglass Stocks
Nelson, Stephen
Nettestad Gun Works
New England Arms Co.
New England Custom Gun Service
Newman Gunshop
Nickels, Paul R.
Norman Custom Gunstocks, Jim
Oakland Custom Arms, Inc.
Oil Rod and Gun Shop
OK Weber, Inc.
Old World Gunsmithing
One Of A Kind
Or-Un
Orvis Co., The
Ottmar, Maurice
Ozark Gun Works
P&S Gun Service
Pacific Research Laboratories, Inc.
Pagel Gun Works, Inc.
Paulsen Gunstocks
Pecatonica River Longrifle
PEM's Mfg. Co.
Pentheny de Pentheny
Perazone, Brian
Perazzi USA, Inc.
R&J Gun Shop
Ram-Line, Inc.
Reagent Chemical and Research, Inc.
Reiswig, Wallace E.
Richards Micro-Fit Stocks
Rimrock Rifle Stocks
RMS Custom Gunsmithing
Robar Co.'s, Inc., The
Robinson, Don
Robinson Firearms Mfg. Ltd.
Roto Carve
Royal Arms Gunstocks
Ryan, Chad L.
Sanders Custom Gun Service
Saville Iron Co.
Schiffman, Curt
Schiffman, Mike
Schuetzen Gun Co.
Schumakers Gun Shop, William
Schwartz Custom Guns, David W.
Schwartz Custom Guns, Wayne E.
Shell Shack
Sile Distributors, Inc.
Six Enterprises
Skeoch, Brian R.
Slug Group, Inc.
Smith, Art
Smith, Sharmon
Snider Stocks, Walter S.
Speedfeed, Inc.
Speiser, Fred D.
Stiles Custom Guns
Storey, Dale A.
Strawbridge, Victor W.
Swann, D.J.
Szweda, Robert
Talmage, William G.
Taylor & Robbins
Tecnolegno S.p.A.
T.F.C. S.p.A.
Tiger-Hunt
Tirelli
Tom's Gun Repair
Tom's Gunshop
Trevallion Gunstocks
Tucker, James C.
Turkish Firearms Corp.
Tuttle, Dale
Vest, John
Vic's Gun Refinishing
Vintage Industries, Inc.
Volquartsen Custom Ltd.
Von Minden Gunsmithing Services
Walnut Factory, The
Weatherby, Inc.
Weber & Markin Custom Gunsmiths
Weems, Cecil
Wells Custom Gunsmith, R.A.
Wells, Fred F.
Wenig Custom Gunstocks, Inc.
Werth, T.W.
Wessinger Custom Guns & Engraving
West, Robert G.
Western Gunstock Mfg. Co.
Williams Gun Sight Co.
Williamson Precision Gunsmithing
Windish, Jim
Winter, Robert M.
Wright's Hardwood Gunstock Blanks
Yee, Mike
Zeeryp, Russ

TARGETS, BULLET AND CLAYBIRD TRAPS

Action Target, Inc.
American Target
American Whitetail Target Systems
A-Tech Corp.
Barsotti, Bruce
Beomat of America Inc.
Birchwood Casey
Blue and Gray Products, Inc.
Bull-X, Inc.
Caswell International Corp.
Champion Target Co.
Champion's Choice, Inc.
Cunningham Co., Eaton
Dapkus Co., Inc., J.G.
Datumtech Corp.
Dayson Arms Ltd.
D.C.C. Enterprises
Detroit-Armor Corp.
Diamond Mfg. Co.
Erickson's Mfg., Inc., C.W.
Federal Champion Target Co.
Freeman Animal Targets
G.H. Enterprises Ltd.
Gun Parts Corp., The
Hiti-Schuch, Atelier Wilma
Hunterjohn
Innovision Enterprises
Jackalope Gun Shop
JWH: Software
Kennebec Journal
Kleen-Bore, Inc.
Littler Sales Co.
Lyman Instant Targets, Inc.
Lyman Products Corp.
M&D Munitions Ltd.
MSR Targets
National Target Co.
N.B.B., Inc.
North American Shooting Systems
Nu-Teck
Outers Laboratories, Div. of Blount
Ox-Yoke Originals, Inc.
Parker Reproductions
Passive Bullet Traps, Inc.
Pease Accuracy, Bob
PlumFire Press, Inc.
Quack Decoy & Sporting Clays
Red Star Target Co.
Remington Arms Co., Inc.
River Road Sporting Clays
Rockwood Corp., Speedwell Div.
Rocky Mountain Target Co.
Savage Range Systems, Inc.
Schaefer Shooting Sports
Seligman Shooting Products
Shooters Supply
Shoot-N-C Targets
Shotgun Shop, The
Thompson Target Technology
White Flyer Targets
World of Targets
X-Spand Target Systems
Z's Metal Targets & Frames
Zriny's Metal Targets

TAXIDERMY

African Import Co.
Jonas Appraisers—Taxidermy Animals, Jack
Kulis Freeze Dry Taxidermy
Parker, Mark D.
World Trek, Inc.

TRAP AND SKEET SHOOTER'S EQUIPMENT

Allen Co., Bob
Allen Sportswear, Bob
Bagmaster Mfg., Inc.
Baker, Stan
Ballistic Products, Inc.
Beomat of America Inc.
Clymer Manufacturing Co., Inc.
Colonial Arms, Inc.
Crane & Crane Ltd.
Dayson Arms Ltd.
Dewey Mfg. Co., Inc., J.
F&A Inc.
Fiocchi of America, Inc.
Gander Mountain, Inc.
G.H. Enterprises Ltd.
Great 870 Co., The
Harper, William E.
Hastings Barrels
Hillmer Custom Gunstocks, Paul D.
Hoppe's Div.
Hunter Co., Inc.
K&T Co.
Ljutic Industries, Inc.
Lynn's Custom Gunstocks
Maionchi-L.M.I.
Meadow Industries
Moneymaker Guncraft Corp.
MTM Molded Products Co., Inc.
Noble Co., Jim
Palsa Outdoor Products
Passive Bullet Traps, Inc.
PAST Sporting Goods, Inc.
Penguin Industries, Inc.
Perazzi USA, Inc.
Pro-Port Ltd.
Protektor Model
Quack Decoy & Sporting Clays
Remington Arms Co., Inc.
Rhodeside, Inc.
Savage Range Systems, Inc.
Shootin' Accessories, Ltd.
Shooting Specialties
Shotgun Shop, The
Titus, Daniel
Trius Products, Inc.
X-Spand Target Systems

TRIGGERS, RELATED EQUIPMENT

Actions by "T"
B&D Trading Co., Inc.
Baer Custom, Inc., Les
Behlert Precision, Inc.
Bob's Gun Shop
Bond Custom Firearms
Boyds' Gunstock Industries, Inc.
Bull Mountain Rifle Co.
Canjar Co., M.H.
Cape Outfitters
Clark Custom Guns, Inc.
Dayton Traister
Electronic Trigger Systems, Inc.
Eversull Co., Inc., K.
Galati International
Gentry Custom Gunmaker, David
Guns, (Div. of D.C. Engineering, Inc.)
Hastings Barrels
Hoelscher, Virgil
Holland's
Jaeger, Inc., Paul/Dunn's
Jewell, Arnold W.
J.P. Enterprises, Inc.
List Precision Engineering
Masen Co., Inc., John
Master Lock Co.
Miller Single Trigger Mfg. Co.
OK Weber, Inc.
Pease Accuracy, Bob
PEM's Mfg. Co.
Penrod Precision
Perazone, Brian
Perazzi USA, Inc.
S&B Industries
Shilen Rifles, Inc.
Timney Mfg., Inc.
Videki

MANUFACTURERS' DIRECTORY

A

A&B Industries, Inc. (See Top-Line USA, Inc.)
A&J Products, Inc., 5791 Hall Rd., Muskegon, MI 49442-1964
A&M Waterfowl, Inc., P.O. Box 102, Ripley, TN 38063/901-635-4003; FAX: 901-635-2320
A&W Repair, 2930 Schneider Dr., Arnold, MO 63010/314-287-3725
A.A. Arms, Inc., 4811 Persimmont Ct., Monroe, NC 28110/704-289-5356, 800-935-1119; FAX: 704-289-5859
AAL Optics, Inc., 2316 NE 8th Rd., Ocala, FL 33470/904-629-3211; FAX: 904-629-1433
Abel Safe & File, Inc., 124 West Locust St., Fairbury, IL 61739/800-346-9280, 815-692-2131; FAX: 815-692-3350
A.B.S. III, 9238 St. Morritz Dr., Fern Creek, KY 40291
AC Dyna-tite Corp., 155 Kelly St., P.O. Box 0984, Elk Grove Village, IL 60007/847-593-5566; FAX: 847-593-1304
Acadian Ballistic Specialties, P.O. Box 61, Covington, LA 70434
Acculube II, Inc., 4366 Shackleford Rd., Norcross, GA 30093-2912
Accupro Gun Care, 15512-109 Ave., Surrey, BC U3R 7E8, CANADA/604-583-7807
Accuracy Den, The, 25 Bitterbrush Rd., Reno, NV 89523/702-345-0225
Accuracy Gun Shop, 7818 Wilkerson Ct., San Diego, CA 92111/619-282-8500
Accuracy Innovations, Inc., P.O. Box 376, New Paris, PA 15554/814-839-4517; FAX: 814-839-2601
Accuracy International, 9115 Trooper Trail, P.O. Box 2019, Bozeman, MT 59715/406-587-7922; FAX: 406-585-9434
Accuracy International Precision Rifles (See U.S. importer—Gunsite Training Center)
Accuracy Unlimited, 7479 S. DePew St., Littleton, CO 80123
Accuracy Unlimited, 16036 N. 49 Ave., Glendale, AZ 85306/602-978-9089; FAX: 602-978-9089
Accura-Site (See All's, The Jim Tembellis Co., Inc.)
Accurate Arms Co., Inc., 5891 Hwy. 230 West, McEwen, TN 37101/615-729-4207, 800-416-3006; FAX 615-729-4211
Accuright, RR 2 Box 397, Sebeka, MN 56477/218-472-3583
Accu-Tek, 4525 Carter Ct., Chino, CA 91710/909-627-2404; FAX: 909-627-7817
Ace Custom 45's, Inc., 1880 1/2 Upper Turtle Creek Rd., Kerrville, TX 78028/210-257-4290; FAX: 210-257-5724
Ace Sportswear, Inc., 700 Quality Rd., Fayetteville, NC 28306/919-323-1223; FAX: 919-323-5392
Ackerman & Co., 16 Cortez St., Westfield, MA 01085/413-568-8008
Ackerman, Bill (See Optical Services Co.)
Action Bullets, Inc., 1811 W. 13th Ave., Denver, CO 80204/303-595-9636; FAX: 303-595-4413
Action Products, Inc., 22 N. Mulberry St., Hagerstown, MD 21740/301-797-1414; FAX: 301-733-2073
Action Target, Inc., P.O. Box 636, Provo, UT 84603/801-377-8033; FAX: 801-377-8096
Actions by "T", Teddy Jacobson, 16315 Redwood Forest Ct., Sugar Land, TX 77478/713-277-4008
ACTIV Industries, Inc., 1000 Zigor Rd., P.O. Box 339, Kearneysville, WV 25430/304-725-0451; FAX: 304-725-2080
AcuSport Corporation, 1 Hunter Place, Bellefontaine, OH 43311-3001/513-593-7010; FAX: 513-592-5625
Ad Hominem, RR 3, Orillia, Ont. L3V 6H3, CANADA/705-689-5303
Adair Custom Shop, Bill, 2886 Westridge, Carrollton, TX 75006
Adams & Son Engravers, John J., 87 Acorn Rd., Dennis, MA 02638/508-385-7971
Adams Jr., John J., 87 Acorn Rd., Dennis, MA 02638/508-385-7971
Adaptive Technology, 939 Barnum Ave, Bridgeport, CT 06609/800-643-6735; FAX: 800-643-6735
ADCO International, 10 Cedar St., Unit 17, Woburn, MA 01801/617-935-1799; FAX: 617-935-1011
Adkins, Luther, 1292 E. McKay Rd., Shelbyville, IN 46176-9353/317-392-3795
Advance Car Mover Co., Rowell Div., P.O. Box 1, 240 N. Depot St., Juneau, WI 53039/414-386-4464; FAX: 414-386-4416
Adventure 16, Inc., 4620 Alvarado Canyon Rd., San Diego, CA 92120/619-283-6314
Adventure Game Calls, R.D. 1, Leonard Rd., Spencer, NY 14883/607-589-4611
Adventurer's Outpost, P.O. Box 70, Cottonwood, AZ 86326/800-762-7471; FAX: 602-634-8781
African Import Co., 20 Braunecker Rd., Plymouth, MA 02360/508-746-8552
AFSCO Ammunition, 731 W. Third St., P.O. Box L, Owen, WI 54460/715-229-2516
Ahlman Guns, Rt. 1, Box 20, Morristown, MN 55052/507-685-4243; FAX: 507-685-4247
Ahrends, Kim, Custom Firearms, Box 203, Clarion, IA 50525/515-532-3449; FAX: 515-532-3926
Aimpoint, Inc., 580 Herndon Parkway, Suite 500, Herndon, VA 22070/703-471-6828; FAX: 703-689-0575
Aimtech Mount Systems, P.O. Box 223, 101 Inwood Acres, Thomasville, GA 31799/912-226-4313; FAX: 912-227-0222
Air Arms, Hailsham Industrial Park, Diplocks Way, Hailsham, E. Sussex, BN27 3JF ENGLAND/011-0323-845853 (U.S. importers—Air Werks International; World Class Airguns)
Air Rifle Specialists, P.O. Box 138, 130 Holden Rd., Pine City, NY 14871-0138/607-734-7340; FAX: 607-733-3261
Air Venture, 9752 E. Flower St., Bellflower, CA 90706/310-867-6355
Airgun Repair Centre, 3227 Garden Meadows, Lawrenceburg, IN 47025/812-637-1463; FAX: 812-637-1463
Airguns-R-Us, 101 7th Ave., Columbia, TN 38401/615-381-4428; FAX: 615-381-1218
Airrow (See Swivel Machine Works, Inc.)
Aitor-Cuchilleria Del Norte, S.A., Izelaieta, 17, 48260 Ermua (Vizcaya), SPAIN/43-17-08-50; FAX: 43-17-00-01
Ajax Custom Grips, Inc., 9130 Viscount Row, Dallas, TX 75247/214-630-8893; FAX: 214-630-4942
Aker Leather Products, 2248 Main St., Suite 6, Chula Vista, CA 91911/619-423-5182; FAX: 619-423-1363
Alaska Bullet Works, P.O. Box 54, Douglas, AK 99824/907-789-3834
Alcas Cutlery Corp. (See Cutco Cutlery)
Alco Carrying Cases, 601 W. 26th St., New York, NY 10001/212-675-5820; FAX: 212-691-5935
Aldis Gunsmithing & Shooting Supply, 502 S. Montezuma St., Prescott, AZ 86303/602-445-6723; FAX: 602-445-6763
Alessi Holsters, Inc., 2465 Niagara Falls Blvd., Amherst, NY 14228-3527/716-691-5615
Alex, Inc., Box 3034, Bozeman, MT 59772/406-282-7396; FAX: 406-282-7396
Alfano, Sam, 36180 Henry Gaines Rd., Pearl River, LA 70452/504-863-3364; FAX: 504-863-7715
All's, The Jim J. Tembelis Co., Inc., 280 E. Fernau Ave., Oshkosh, WI 54901/414-426-1080; FAX: 414-426-1080
All American Lead Shot Corp., P.O. Box 224566, Dallas, TX 75062
All Rite Products, Inc., 5752 N. Silverstone Circle, Mountain Green, UT 84050/801-876-3330; 801-876-2216
Allard, Gary, Creek Side Metal & Woodcrafters, Fishers Hill, VA 22626/703-465-3903
Allen Co., Bob, 214 SW Jackson, P.O. Box 477, Des Moines, IA 50315/515-283-2191; 800-685-7020; FAX: 515-283-0779
Allen Co., Inc., 525 Burbank St., Broomfield, CO 80020/303-469-1857, 800-876-8600; FAX: 303-466-7437
Allen Mfg., 6449 Hodgson Rd., Circle Pines, MN 55014/612-429-8231
Allen, Richard L., 339 Grove Ave., Prescott, AZ 86301/602-778-1237
Allen Sportswear, Bob (See Allen Co., Bob)
Alley Supply Co., P.O. Box 848, Gardnerville, NV 89410/702-782-3800
Alliant Techsystems, Smokeless Powder Group, 200 Valley Rd., Suite 305, Mt. Arlington, NJ 07856/800-276-9337; FAX: 201-770-2528
Allred Bullet Co., 932 Evergreen Drive, Logan, UT 84321/801-752-6983
Alpec Team, Inc., 201 Ricken Backer Cir., Livermore, CA 94550/510-606-8245; FAX: 510-606-4279
Alpha 1 Drop Zone, 2121 N. Tyler, Wichita, KS 67212/316-729-0800
Alpha Gunsmith Division, 1629 Via Monserate, Fallbrook, CA 92028/619-723-9279, 619-728-2663
Alpha LaFranck Enterprises, P.O. Box 81072, Lincoln, NE 68501/402-466-3193
Alpha Precision, Inc., 2765-B Preston Rd. NE, Good Hope, GA 30641/770-267-6163
Alpine's Precision Gunsmithing & Indoor Shooting Range, 2401 Government Way, Coeur d'Alene, ID 83814/208-765-3559; FAX: 208-765-3559
Altamont Co., 901 N. Church St., P.O. Box 309, Thomasboro, IL 61878/217-643-3125, 800-626-5774; FAX: 217-643-7973
Alumna Sport by Dee Zee, 1572 NE 58th Ave., P.O. Box 3090, Des Moines, IA 50316/800-798-9899
AmBr Software Group Ltd., P.O. Box 301, Reistertown, MD 21136-0301/410-526-4106; FAX: 410-526-7212
American Ammunition, 3545 NW 71st St., Miami, FL 33147/305-835-7400; FAX: 305-694-0037
American Arms & Ordnance, Inc., P.O. Box 2691, 1303 S. College Ave., Bryan, TX 77805/409-822-4983
American Arms, Inc., 715 Armour Rd., N. Kansas City, MO 64116/816-474-3161; FAX: 816-474-1225
American Derringer Corp., 127 N. Lacy Dr., Waco, TX 76705/800-642-7817, 817-799-9111; FAX: 817-799-7935
American Display Co., 55 Cromwell St., Providence, RI 02907/401-331-2464; FAX: 401-421-1264
American Frontier Firearms Co., 40725 Brook Trails Way, Aguanga, CA 92536/909-763-0014; FAX: 909-763-0014
American Gas & Chemical Co., Ltd., 220 Pegasus Ave., Northvale, NJ 07647/201-767-7300
American Gripcraft, 3230 S. Dodge 2, Tucson, AZ 85713/602-790-1222
American Handgunner Magazine, 591 Camino de la Reina, Suite 200, San Diego, CA 92108/619-297-5350; FAX: 619-297-5353
American Pioneer Video, P.O. Box 50049, Bowling Green, KY 42102-2649/800-743-4675
American Products Co., 14729 Spring Valley Road, Morrison, IL 61270/815-772-3336; FAX: 815-772-7921
American Safe Arms, Inc., 1240 Riverview Dr., Garland, UT 84312/801-257-7472; FAX: 801-785-8156
American Sales & Kirkpatrick, P.O. Box 677, Laredo, TX 78042/210-723-6893; FAX: 210-725-0672
American Security Products Company, 11925 Pacific Ave., Fontana, CA 92337/909-685-9680, 800-421-6142; FAX: 909-685-9685
American Small Arms Academy, P.O. Box 12111, Prescott, AZ 86304/602-778-5623
American Target, 1328 S. Jason St., Denver, CO 80223/303-733-0433; FAX: 303-777-0311

29th EDITION, 1997 **313**

DIRECTORY OF THE ARMS TRADE

American Target Knives, 1030 Brownwood NW, Grand Rapids, MI 49504/616-453-1998
American Whitetail Target Systems, P.O. Box 41, 106 S. Church St., Tennyson, IN 47637/812-567-4527
Americase, P.O. Box 271, 1610 E. Main, Waxahachie, TX 75165/800-880-3629; FAX: 214-937-8373
Ames Metal Products, 4324 S. Western Blvd., Chicago, IL 60609/312-523-3230; FAX: 312-523-3854
Amherst Arms, P.O. Box 1457, Englewood, FL 34295/941-475-2020; FAX: 941-473-1212
Ammo Load, Inc., 1560 E. Edinger, Suite G, Santa Ana, CA 92705/714-558-8858; FAX: 714-569-0319
Amrine's Gun Shop, 937 La Luna, Ojai, CA 93023/805-646-2376
Amsec, 11925 Pacific Ave., Fontana, CA 92337
AMT, 6226 Santos Diaz St., Irwindale, CA 91702/818-334-6629; FAX: 818-969-5247
Amtec 2000, Inc., 84 Industrial Rowe, Gardner, MA 01440/508-632-9608; FAX: 508-632-2300
Analog Devices, Box 9106, Norwood, MA 02062
Andela Tool & Machine, Inc., RD3, Box 246, Richfield Springs, NY 13439
Anderson Manufacturing Co., Inc., 22602 53rd Ave. SE, Bothell, WA 98021/206-481-1858; FAX: 206-481-7839
Andres & Dworsky, Bergstrasse 18, A-3822 Karlstein, Thaya, Austria, EUROPE, 0 28 44-285
Angelo & Little Custom Gun Stock Blanks, P.O. Box 240046, Dell, MT 59724-0046
Anics Firm, Inc., 3 Commerce Park Square, 23200 Chagrin Blvd., Suite 240, Beechwood, OH 44122/216-292-4363, 800-550-1582; FAX: 216-292-2588
Anschutz GmbH, Postfach 1128, D-89001 Ulm, Donau, GERMANY (U.S. importers—Accuracy International; AcuSport Corporation; Champion Shooters' Supply; Champion's Choice; Gunsmithing, Inc.)
Ansen Enterprises, Inc., 1506 W. 228th St., Torrance, CA 90501-5105/310-534-1837; FAX: 310-534-3162
Answer Products Co., 1519 Westbury Drive, Davison, MI 48423/810-653-2911
Anthony and George Ltd., Rt. 1, P.O. Box 45, Evington, VA 24550/804-821-8117
Antique American Firearms (See Carlson, Douglas R.)
Antique Arms Co., 1110 Cleveland Ave., Monett, MO 65708/417-235-6501
Apache Products, Inc., 4224 Old Sterington Rd., Monroe, LA 71203/318-325-1761; FAX: 318-325-4873
Apel GmbH, Ernst, Am Kirschberg 3, D-97218 Gerbrunn, GERMANY/0 (931) 707192
Aplan Antiques & Art, James O., HC 80, Box 793-25, Piedmont, SD 57769/605-347-5016
Arcadia Machine & Tool, Inc. (See AMT)
Arco Powder, HC-Rt. 1, P.O. Box 102, County Rd. 357, Mayo, FL 32066/904-294-3882; FAX: 904-294-1498
Aristocrat Knives, 1701 W. Wernsing Ave., Effingham, IL 62401/800-953-3436; FAX: 217-347-3083
Arizaga (See U.S. importer—Mandall Shooting Supplies, Inc.)
Arizona Custom Case, 1015 S. 23rd St., Phoenix, AZ 85034/602-273-0220
Arkansas Mallard Duck Calls, Rt. Box 182, England, AR 72046/501-842-3597
Arkfeld Mfg. & Dist. Co., Inc., 1230 Monroe Ave., Norfolk, NE 68702-0054/402-371-9430; 800-533-0676
ArmaLite, Inc., P.O. Box 299, Geneseo, IL 61254/309-944-6939; FAX: 309-944-6949
Armament Gunsmithing Co., Inc., 525 Rt. 22, Hillside, NJ 07205/908-686-0960
Armas Azor, J.A. (See U.S. importer—Armes de Chasse)
Armas Kemen S.A. (See U.S. importer—USA Sporting)
Armes de Chasse, P.O. Box 827, Chadds Ford, PA 19317/610-388-1146; FAX: 610-388-1147
Armfield Custom Bullets, 4775 Caroline Drive, San Diego, CA 92115/619-582-7188; FAX: 619-287-3238
Armi San Marco (See U.S. importer—Taylor's & Co., Inc.)
Armi San Paolo, via Europa 172-A, I-25062 Concesio, 030-2751725 (BS) ITALY
Armi Sport (See U.S. importers—Cape Outfitters; Taylor's & Co., Inc.)
Armite Laboratories, 1845 Randolph St., Los Angeles, CA 90001/213-587-7768; FAX: 213-587-5075
Armoloy Co. of Ft. Worth, 204 E. Daggett St., Fort Worth, TX 76104/817-332-5604; FAX: 817-335-6517
Armor (See Buck Stop Lure Co., Inc.)
Armor Metal Products, P.O. Box 4609, Helena, MT 59604/406-442-5560
Armory Publications, P.O. Box 4206, Oceanside, CA 92052-4206/619-757-3930; FAX: 619-722-4108
Armoury, The, Rt. 202, Box 2340, New Preston, CT 06777/203-868-0001
A.R.M.S., Inc., 230 W. Center St., West Bridgewater, MA 02379-1620/508-584-7816; FAX: 508-588-8045
Arms & Armour Press, Ltd., Wellington House, 125 Strand, London WC2R 0BB ENGLAND/0171-420-5555; FAX: 0171-240-7265
Arms Corporation of the Philippines, Bo. Parang Marikina, Metro Manila, PHILIPPINES/632-941-6243, 632-941-6244; FAX: 632-942-0682
Arms Craft Gunsmithing, 1106 Linda Dr., Arroyo Grande, CA 93420/805-481-2830
Arms Ingenuity Co., P.O. Box 1, 51 Canal St., Weatogue, CT 06089/203-658-5624
Arms, Peripheral Data Systems (See Arms Software)
Arms Software, P.O. Box 1526, Lake Oswego, OR 97035/800-366-5559, 503-697-0533; FAX: 503-697-3337
Arms United Corp., 1018 Cedar St., Niles, MI 49120/616-683-6837
Armscorp USA, Inc., 4424 John Ave., Baltimore, MD 21227/410-247-6200; FAX: 410-247-6205
Armsport, Inc., 3950 NW 49th St., Miami, FL 33142/305-635-7850; FAX: 305-633-2877
Arnold Arms Co., Inc., P.O. Box 1011, Arlington, WA 98223/800-371-1011, 360-435-1011; FAX: 360-435-7304
Aro-Tek, Ltd., 206 Frontage Rd. North, Suite C, Pacific, WA 98047/206-351-2984; FAX: 206-833-4483
Arratoonian, Andy (See Horseshoe Leather Products)
Arrieta, S.L., Morkaiko, 5, Elgoibar, E-20870, SPAIN/(43) 74 31 50; FAX: (43) 74 31 54 (U.S. importers—Griffin & Howe; Hi-Grade Imports; Jansma, Jack J.; New England Arms Co.; The Orvis Co., Inc.; Quality Arms, Inc.)

Art Jewel Enterprises Ltd., Eagle Business Ctr., 460 Randy Rd., Carol Stream, IL 60188/708-260-0400
Art's Gun & Sport Shop, Inc., 6008 Hwy. Y, Hillsboro, MO 63050
Artistry in Leather (See Stuart, V. Pat)
Artistry in Wood, 134 Zimmerman Rd., Kalispell, MT 59901/406-257-9003
Arundel Arms & Ammunition, Inc., A., 24 Defense St., Annapolis, MD 21401/301-224-8683
Ashby Turkey Calls, P.O. Box 1466, Ava, MO 65608-1466/417-967-3787
Aspen Outdoors, Inc., 1059 W. Market St., York, PA 17404/717-846-0255, 800-677-4780; FAX: 717-845-7447
A-Square Co., Inc., One Industrial Park, Bedford, KY 40006-9667/502-255-7456; FAX: 502-255-7657
Astra Sport, S.A., Apartado 3, 48300 Guernica, Espagne, SPAIN/34-4-6250100; FAX: 34-4-6255186 (U.S. importer—E.A.A. Corp.; P.S.M.G. Gun Co.)
A-Tech Corp., P.O. Box 1281, Cottage Grove, OR 97424
Atamec-Bretton, 19, rue Victor Grignard, F-42026 St.-Etienne (Cedex 1) FRANCE/77-93-54-69; FAX: 33-77-93-57-98 (U.S. importer—Mandall Shooting Supplies, Inc.)
ATIS Armi S.A.S., via Gussalli 24, Zona Industriale-Loc. Fornaci, 25020 Brescia, ITALY
Atlanta Cutlery Corp., 2143 Gees Mill Rd., Box 839 CIS, Conyers, GA 30207/800-883-0300; FAX: 404-388-0246
Atlantic Mills, Inc., 1325 Washington Ave., Asbury Park, NJ 07712/800-242-7374
Atlantic Research Marketing Systems (See A.R.M.S., Inc.)
Atlantic Rose, Inc., P.O. Box 1305, Union, NJ 07083
Atsko/Sno-Seal, Inc., 2530 Russell SE, Orangeburg, SC 29115/803-531-1820; FAX: 803-531-2139
Audette, Creighton, 19 Highland Circle, Springfield, VT 05156/802-885-2331
Austin's Calls, Bill, Box 284, Kaycee, WY 82639/307-738-2552
Auto Arms, 738 Clearview, San Antonio, TX 78228/512-434-5450
Autauga Arms, Inc., 817 S. Memorial Dr., Prattville, AL 36067-5734/800-262-9563; FAX: 334-361-2961
Automatic Equipment Sales, 627 E. Railroad Ave., Salesburg, MD 21801
Auto-Ordnance Corp., Williams Lane, West Hurley, NY 12491/914-679-4190; FAX: 914-679-2698
Autumn Sales, Inc. (Blaser), 1320 Lake St., Fort Worth, TX 76103/817-335-1634; FAX: 817-338-0119
AWC Systems Technology, P.O. Box 41938, Phoenix, AZ 85080-1938/602-780-1050
AYA (See U.S. importer—Armes de Chasse; New England Custom Gun Service)
A Zone Bullets, 2039 Walter Rd., Billings, MT 59105/800-252-3111; 406-248-1961
Aztec International Ltd., P.O. Box 1384, Clarkesville, GA 30523/706-754-7263

B

B&D Trading Co., Inc., 3935 Fair Hill Rd., Fair Oaks, CA 95628/800-334-3790, 916-967-9366; FAX: 916-967-4873
B&G Bullets (See Northside Gun Shop)
Badger Shooters Supply, Inc., P.O. Box 397, Owen, WI 54460/800-424-9069; FAX: 715-229-2332
Baekgaard Ltd., 1855 Janke Dr., Northbrook, IL 60062/708-498-3040; FAX: 708-493-3106
Baelder, Harry, Alte Goennebeker Strasse 5, 24635 Rickling, GERMANY/04328-722733; FAX: 04328-722732
Baer Custom, Inc., Les, 29601 34th Ave., Hillsdale, IL 61257/309-658-2716; FAX: 309-658-2610
Bagmaster Mfg., Inc., 2731 Sutton Ave., St. Louis, MO 63143/314-781-8002; FAX: 314-781-3363
Baikal (See U.S. importer—Air Werks International; K.B.I., Inc.)
Bain & Davis, Inc., 307 E. Valley Blvd., San Gabriel, CA 91776-3522/818-573-4241, 213-283-7449
Baker, Stan, 10,000 Lake City Way, Seattle, WA 98125/206-522-4575
Baker's Leather Goods, Roy, P.O. Box 893, Magnolia, AR 71753/501-234-0344
Balaance Co., 340-39 Ave. S.E. Box 505, Calgary, AB, T2G 1X6 CANADA
Bald Eagle Precision Machine Co., 101-K Allison St., Lock Haven, PA 17745/717-748-6772; FAX: 717-748-4443
Balickie, Joe, 408 Trelawney Lane, Apex, NC 27502/919-362-5185
Ballard Built, P.O. Box 1443, Kingsville, TX 78364/512-592-0853
Ballard Industries, 10271 Lockwood Dr., Suite B, Cupertino, CA 95014/408-996-0957; FAX: 408-257-6828
Ballistic Engineering & Software, Inc., 185 N. Park Blvd., Suite 330, Lake Orion, MI 48362/313-391-1074
Ballistic Products, Inc., 20015 75th Ave. North, Hamel, MN 55340-9456/612-494-9237; FAX: 612-494-9236
Ballistic Program Co., Inc., The, 2417 N. Patterson St., Thomasville, GA 31792/912-228-5739, 800-368-0835
Ballistic Research, 1108 W. May Ave., McHenry, IL 60050/815-385-0037
Ballistica Maximus North, 107 College Park Plaza, Johnstown, PA 15904/814-266-8380
Ballisti-Cast, Inc., Box 383, Parshall, ND 58770/701-862-3324; FAX: 701-862-3331
Bandcor Industries, Div. of Man-Sew Corp., 6108 Sherwin Dr., Port Richey, FL 34668/813-848-0432
Bang-Bang Boutique (See Holster Shop, The)
Banks, Ed, 2762 Hwy. 41 N., Ft. Valley, GA 31030/912-987-4665
Bansner's Gunsmithing Specialties, 261 East Main St. Box VH, Adamstown, PA 19501/800-368-2379; FAX: 717-484-0523
Barami Corp., 6689 Orchard Lake Rd. No. 148, West Bloomfield, MI 48322/810-738-0462; FAX: 810-855-4084
Barbour, Inc., 55 Meadowbrook Dr., Milford, NH 03055/603-673-1313; FAX: 603-673-6510
Barnes Bullets, Inc., P.O. Box 215, American Fork, UT 84003/801-756-4222, 800-574-9200; FAX: 801-756-2465; WEB: http://www.itsnet.com/home/bbullets
Baron Technology, 62 Spring Hill Rd., Trumbull, CT 06611/203-452-0515; FAX: 203-452-0663
Barraclough, John K., 55 Merit Park Dr., Gardena, CA 90247/310-324-2574
Barramundi Corp., P.O. Drawer 4259, Homosassa Springs, FL 32687/904-628-0200
Barrett Firearms Manufacturer, Inc., P.O. Box 1077, Murfreesboro, TN 37133/615-896-2938; FAX: 615-896-7313

MANUFACTURERS' DIRECTORY

Barska Optics Int'l., 1765 E. Colorado Blvd., Pasadena, CA 91106/818-568-0618; FAX: 818-568-9681
Barsotti, Bruce (See River Road Sporting Clays)
Bar-Sto Precision Machine, 73377 Sullivan Rd., P.O. Box 1838, Twentynine Palms, CA 92277/619-367-2747; FAX: 619-367-2407
Barta's Gunsmithing, 10231 US Hwy. 10, Cato, WI 54206/414-732-4472
Barteaux Machete, 1916 SE 50th Ave., Portland, OR 97215-3238/503-233-5880
Bartlett, Don, P.O. Box 55, Colbert, WA 99005/509-467-5009
Bartlett Engineering, 40 South 200 East, Smithfield, UT 84335-1645/801-563-5910; FAX: 801-563-8416
Basics Information Systems, Inc., 1141 Georgia Ave., Suite 515, Wheaton, MD 20902/301-949-1070; FAX: 301-949-5326
Bates Engraving, Billy, 2302 Winthrop Dr., Decatur, AL 35603/205-355-3690
Bauer, Eddie, 15010 NE 36th St., Redmond, WA 98052
Baumannize Custom, 4784 Sunrise Hwy., Bohemia, NY 11716/800-472-4387; FAX: 516-567-0001
Baumgartner Bullets, 3011 S. Alane St., W. Valley City, UT 84120
Bausch & Lomb Sports Optics Div. (See Bushnell Sports Optics Worldwide)
Bauska Barrels, 105 9th Ave. W., Kalispell, MT 59901/406-752-7706
Bear Archery, RR 4, 4600 Southwest 41st Blvd., Gainesville, FL 32601/904-376-2327
Bear Arms, 121 Rhodes St., Jackson, SC 29831/803-471-9859
Bear Hug Grips, Inc., 17230 County Rd. 338, Buena Vista, CO 81211/800-232-7710
Bear Mountain Gun & Tool, 120 N. Plymouth, New Plymouth, ID 83655/208-278-5221; FAX: 208-278-5221
Bear Reloaders, P.O. Box 1613, Akron, OH 44309-1613/216-920-1811
Beartooth Bullets, P.O. Box 491, Dept. HLD, Dover, ID 83825-0491/208-448-1865
Beauchamp & Son, Inc., 160 Rossiter Rd., P.O. Box 181, Richmond, MA 01254/413-698-3822; FAX: 413-698-3866
Beaver Lodge (See Fellowes, Ted)
Beaver Park Products, Inc., 840 J St., Penrose, CO 81240/719-372-6744
Beeline Custom Bullets Limited, P.O. Box 85, Yarmouth, Nova Scotia CANADA B5A 4B1/902-648-3494; FAX: 902-648-0253
Beeman Precision Airguns, 5454 Argosy Dr., Huntington Beach, CA 92649/714-890-4800; FAX: 714-890-4808
BEC, Inc., 1227 W. Valley Blvd., Suite 204, Alhambra, CA 91803-2438/818-281-5751; FAX: 818-293-7073
Behlert Precision, Inc., P.O. Box 288, 7067 Easton Rd., Pipersville, PA 18947/215-766-8681, 215-766-7301; FAX: 215-766-8681
Beitzinger, George, 116-20 Atlantic Ave., Richmond Hill, NY 11419/718-847-7661
Belding's Custom Gun Shop, 10691 Sayers Rd., Munith, MI 49259/517-596-2388
Bell & Carlson, Inc., Dodge City Industrial Park/101 Allen Rd., Dodge City, KS 67801/800-634-8586, 316-225-6688; FAX: 316-225-9095
Bell Originals, Inc., Sid, 7776 Shackham Rd., Tully, NY 13159-9333/607-842-6431
Bell Reloading, Inc., 1725 Harlin Lane Rd., Villa Rica, GA 30180
Bell's Gun & Sport Shop, 3309-19 Mannheim Rd, Franklin Park, IL 60131
Bell's Legendary Country Wear, 22 Circle Dr., Bellmore, NY 11710/516-679-1158
Bellm Contenders, P.O. Box 459, Cleveland, UT 84518/801-653-2530
Belltown, Ltd., 11 Camps Rd., Kent, CT 06757/860-354-5750
Belt MTN Arms, 107 10th Ave. SW, White Sulphur Springs, MT 59645/406-586-4495
Ben's Machines, 1151 S. Cedar Ridge, Duncanville, TX 75137/214-780-1807; FAX: 214-780-0316
Benchmark Guns, 12593 S. Ave. 5 East, Yuma, AZ 85365
Benchmark Knives (See Gerber Legendary Blades)
Benelli Armi, S.p.A., Via della Stazione, 61029 Urbino, ITALY/39-722-307-1; FAX: 39-722-327427 (U.S. importers—E.A.A. Corp.; Heckler & Koch, Inc.)
Bengtson Arms Co., L., 6345-B E. Akron St., Mesa, AZ 85205/602-981-6375
Benjamin/Sheridan Co., Crossman, Rts. 5 and 20, E. Bloomfield, NY 14443/716-657-6161; FAX: 716-657-5405
Bentley, John, 128-D Watson Dr., Turtle Creek, PA 15145
Beomat of America Inc., 300 Railway Ave., Campbell, CA 95008/408-379-4829
Beretta S.p.A., Pietro, Via Beretta, 18-25063 Gardone V.T. (BS) ITALY/XX39/30-8341.1; FAX: XX39/30-8341.421 (U.S. importer—Beretta U.S.A. Corp.)
Beretta U.S.A. Corp., 17601 Beretta Drive, Accokeek, MD 20607/301-283-2191; FAX: 301-283-0435
Berger Bullets, Ltd., 5342 W. Camelback Rd., Suite 200, Glendale, AZ 85301/602-842-4001; FAX: 602-934-9083
Bergman & Williams, 2450 Losee Rd., Suite F, Las Vegas, NV 89030/702-642-1901; FAX: 702-642-1540
Bernardelli S.p.A., Vincenzo, 125 Via Matteotti, P.O. Box 74, Gardone V.T., Brescia ITALY, 25063/39-30-8912851-2-3; FAX: 39-30-8910249
Berry's Bullets, Div. of Berry's Mfg., Inc., 401 N. 3050 E., St. George, UT 84770-9004
Berry's Mfg., Inc., 401 North 3050 East St., St. George, UT 84770/801-634-1682; FAX: 801-634-1683
Bersa S.A., Gonzales Castillo 312, 1704 Ramos Mejia, ARGENTINA/541-656-2377; FAX: 541-656-2093 (U.S. importer—Eagle Imports, Inc.)
Bertram Bullet Co., P.O. Box 313, Seymour, Victoria 3660, AUSTRALIA/61-57-922912; FAX: 61-57-991650
Bertuzzi (See U.S. importers—Cape Outfitters; Moore & Co., Wm. Larkin; New England Arms Co.)
Bestload, Inc., Carl Vancini, P.O. Box 4354, Stamford, CT 06907/203-978-0796; FAX: 203-978-0796
Better Concepts Co., 663 New Castle Rd., Butler, PA 16001/412-285-9000
Beverly, Mary, 3201 Horseshoe Trail, Tallahassee, FL 32312
Bianchi International, Inc., 100 Calle Cortez, Temecula, CA 92590/909-676-5621; FAX: 909-676-6777
Biesen, Al, 5021 Rosewood, Spokane, WA 99208/509-328-9340
Biesen, Roger, 5021 W. Rosewood, Spokane, WA 99208/509-328-9340
Big Beam Emergency Systems, Inc., 290 E. Prairie St., Crystal Lake, IL 60039
Big Bear Arms & Sporting Goods, Inc., 2714 Fairmount St., Dallas, TX 75201/214-871-7061, 800-400-BEAR; FAX: 214-754-0449
Big Bore Bullets of Alaska, P.O. Box 872785, Wasilla, AK 99687/907-373-2673; FAX: 907-373-2673
Big Sky Racks, Inc., P.O. Box 729, Bozeman, MT 59771-0729/406-586-9393; FAX: 406-585-7378
Big Spring Enterprises "Bore Stores", P.O. Box 1115, Big Spring Rd., Yellville, AR 72687/501-449-5297; FAX: 501-449-4446

Bilal, Mustafa, 908 NW 50th St., Seattle, WA 98107-3634/206-782-4164
Bill's Custom Cases, P.O. Box 2, Dunsmuir, CA 96025/916-235-0177; FAX: 916-235-4959
Bill's Gun Repair, 1007 Burlington St., Mendota, IL 61342/815-539-5786
Billeb, Stephen L., 1101 N. 7th St., Burlington, IA 52601/319-753-2110
Billings Gunsmiths, Inc., 1841 Grand Ave., Billings, MT 59102/406-652-3104
Billingsley & Brownell, P.O. Box 25, Dayton, WY 82836/307-655-9344
Birchwood Casey, 7900 Fuller Rd., Eden Prairie, MN 55344/800-328-6156, 612-937-7933; FAX: 612-937-7979
Birdsong & Assoc., W.E., 1435 Monterey Rd., Florence, MS 39073-9748/601-366-8270
Bismuth Cartridge Co., 3500 Maple Ave., Suite 1650, Dallas, TX 75219/800-759-3333, 214-521-5880; FAX: 214-521-9035
Bison Studios, 1409 South Commerce St., Las Vegas, NV 89102/702-388-2891; FAX: 702-383-9967
Bitterroot Bullet Co., Box 412, Lewiston, ID 83501-0412/208-743-5635
Black Belt Bullets, Big Bore Express Ltd., 7154 W. State St., Suite 200, Boise, ID 83703
Black Hills Ammunition, Inc., P.O. Box 3090, Rapid City, SD 57709-3090/605-348-5150; FAX: 605-348-9827
Black Hills Shooters Supply, P.O. Box 4220, Rapid City, SD 57709/800-289-2506
Black Sheep Brand, 3220 W. Gentry Parkway, Tyler, TX 75702/903-592-3853; FAX: 903-592-0527
Blackhawk East, Box 2274, Loves Park, IL 61131
Blackhawk West, Box 285, Hiawatha, KS 66434
Blackinton & Co., Inc., V.H., 221 John L. Dietsch, Attleboro Falls, MA 02763-0300/508-699-4436; FAX: 508-695-5349
Blackjack Knives, Ltd., 1307 W. Wabash, Effingham, IL 62401/217-347-7700; FAX: 217-347-7737
Black Powder Products, 67 Township Rd., P.O. Box 1411, Chesapeake, OH 45619/614-867-8047
Blacksmith Corp., 830 N. Road No. 1 E., P.O. Box 1752, Chino Valley, AZ 86323/520-636-4456; FAX: 520-636-4457
BlackStar Accurizing, 11501 Brittmoore Park Drive, Houston, TX 77041/713-849-9999; FAX: 713-849-5445
BlackStar AccuMax Barrels (See BlackStar Accurizing)
BlackStar Barrel Accurizing (See BlackStar Accurizing)
Blacktail Mountain Books, 42 First Ave. W., Kalispell, MT 59901/406-257-5573
Blackwell, W. (See Load From a Disk)
Blair Engraving, J.R., P.O. Box 64, Glenrock, WY 82637/307-436-8115
Blammo Ammo, P.O. Box 1677, Seneca, SC 29679/803-882-1768
Blaser Jagdwaffen GmbH, D-88316 Isny Im Allgau, GERMANY (U.S. importer—Autumn Sales, Inc.)
Bleile, C. Roger, 5040 Ralph Ave., Cincinnati, OH 45238/513-251-0249
Blocker Holsters, Inc., Ted, Clackamas Business Park Bld. A, 14787 S.E. 82nd Dr./Clackamas, OR 97015 503-557-7757; FAX: 503-557-3771
Blount, Inc., Sporting Equipment Div., 2299 Snake River Ave., P.O. Box 856, Lewiston, ID 83501/800-627-3640, 208-746-2351; FAX: 208-799-3904
Blue and Gray Products, Inc. (See Ox-Yoke Originals, Inc.)
Blue Book Publications, Inc., One Appletree Square, Minneapolis, MN 55425/800-877-4867, 612-854-5229; FAX: 612-853-1486
Blue Mountain Bullets, HCR 77, P.O. Box 231, John Day, OR 97845/503-820-4594
Blue Ridge Machinery & Tools, Inc., P.O. Box 536-GD, Hurricane, WV 25526/800-872-6500; FAX: 304-562-5311
BMC Supply, Inc., 26051 - 179th Ave. S.E., Kent, WA 98042
B.M.F. Activator, Inc., 803 Mill Creek Run, Plantersville, TX 77363/409-894-2005, 800-527-2881
Bob's Gun Shop, P.O. Box 200, Royal, AR 71968/501-767-1970
Bob's Tactical Indoor Shooting Range & Gun Shop, 122 Lafayette Rd., Salisbury, MA 01952/508-465-5561
Boessler, Erich, Am Vogeltal 3, 97702 Munnerstadt, GERMANY/9733-9443
Boggs, Wm., 1816 Riverside Dr. C, Columbus, OH 43212/614-486-6965
Bohemia Arms Co., 17101 Los Modelos, Fountain Valley, CA 92708/619-442-7005; FAX: 619-442-7005
Boker USA, Inc., 14818 West 6th Ave., Suite 10A, Golden, CO 80401-5045/303-279-5997; FAX: 303-279-5919
Boltin, John M., P.O. Box 644, Estill, SC 29918/803-625-2185
Bo-Mar Tool & Mfg. Co., Rt. 12, Box 405, Longview, TX 75605/903-759-4784; FAX: 903-759-9141
Bonanza (See Forster Products)
Bond Custom Firearms, 8954 N. Lewis Ln., Bloomington, IN 47408/812-332-4519
Bondini Paolo, Via Sorrento, 345, San Carlo di Cesena, ITALY I-47020/0547 663 240; FAX: 0547 663 780
Bone Engraving, Ralph, 718 N. Atlanta, Owasso, OK 74055/918-272-9745
Boone Trading Co., Inc., P.O. Box BB, Brinnan, WA 98320
Boone's Custom Ivory Grips, Inc., 562 Coyote Rd., Brinnon, WA 98320/206-796-4330
Boonie Packer Products, P.O. Box 12204, Salem, OR 97309/800-477-3244, 503-581-3244; FAX: 503-581-3191
Borden's Accuracy, RD 1, Box 250BC, Springville, PA 18844/717-965-2505; FAX: 717-965-2328
Border Barrels Ltd., Riccarton Farm, Newcastleton SCOTLAND U.K. TD9 0SN
Borovnik KG, Ludwig, 9170 Ferlach, Bahnhofstrasse 7, AUSTRIA/042 27 24 42; FAX: 042 26 43 49
Bosis (See U.S. importer—New England Arms Co.)
Boss Manufacturing Co., 221 W. First St., Kewanee, IL 61443/309-852-2131, 800-447-4581; FAX: 309-852-0848
Bostick Wildlife Calls, Inc., P.O. Box 728, Estill, SC 29918/803-625-2210, 803-625-4512
Bowen Classic Arms Corp., P.O. Box 67, Louisville, TN 37777/615-984-3583
Bowen Knife Co., Inc., P.O. Box 590, Blackshear, GA 31516/912-449-4794
Bowerly, Kent, HCR Box 1903, Camp Sherman, OR 97730/541-595-6028
Bowlin, Gene, Rt. 1, Box 890, Snyder, TX 79549
Boyds' Gunstock Industries, Inc., 3rd & Main, P.O. Box 305, Geddes, SD 57342/605-337-2125; FAX: 605-337-3363
Boyt, 509 Hamilton, P.O. Drawer 668, Iowa Falls, IA 50126/515-648-4626; FAX: 515-648-2385

29TH EDITION, 1997 **315**

DIRECTORY OF THE ARMS TRADE

Brace, Larry D., 771 Blackfoot Ave., Eugene, OR 97404/503-688-1278
Bradley Gunsight Co., P.O. Box 340, Plymouth, VT 05056/860-589-0531; FAX: 860-582-6294
Brass and Bullet Alloys, P.O. Box 1238, Sierra Vista, AZ 85636/602-458-5321; FAX: 602-458-9125
Brass Eagle, Inc., 7050A Bramalea Rd., Unit 19, Mississauga, Ont. L4Z 1C7, CANADA/416-848-4844
Brass-Tech Industries, P.O. Box 521-v, Wharton, NJ 07885/201-366-8540
Bratcher, Dan, 311 Belle Air Pl., Carthage, MO 64836/417-358-1518
Brauer Bros. Mfg. Co., 2020 Delman Blvd., St. Louis, MO 63103/314-231-2864; FAX: 314-249-4952
Braun, M., 32, rue Notre-Dame, 2440 LUXEMBURG
Braverman Corp., R.J., 88 Parade Rd., Meridith, NH 03293/800-736-4867
Break-Free, Inc., P.O. Box 25020, Santa Ana, CA 92799/714-953-1900; FAX: 714-953-0402
Brell Mar Products, Inc., 113 Boyce Dr., Brookhaven, MS 39601/601-833-2050; FAX: 601-835-1817
Brenneke KG, Wilhelm, Ilmenauweg 2, 30851 Langenhagen, GERMANY/0511/97262-0; FAX: 0511/97262-62 (U.S. importer—Dynamit Nobel-RWS, Inc.)
Bretton (See Atamec-Bretton)
Bridgers Best, P.O. Box 1410, Berthoud, CO 80513
Briese Bullet Co., Inc., RR1, Box 108, Tappen, ND 58487/701-327-4578; FAX: 701-327-4579
Brigade Quartermasters, 1025 Cobb International Blvd., Dept. VH, Kennesaw, GA 30144-4300/404-428-1248, 800-241-3125; FAX: 404-426-7726
Briganti & Co., A., 475 Rt. 32, Highland Mills, NY 10930/914-928-9573
Briley Mfg., Inc., 1230 Lumpkin, Houston, TX 77043/800-331-5718, 713-932-6995; FAX: 713-932-1043
British Antiques, P.O. Box 7, Latham, NY 12110/518-783-0773
British Sporting Arms, RR1, Box 130, Millbrook, NY 12545/914-677-8303
BRNO (See U.S. importers—Bohemia Arms Co.; Magnum Research, Inc.)
Broad Creek Rifle Works, 120 Horsey Ave., Laurel, DE 19956/302-875-5446
Brobst, Jim, 299 Poplar St., Hamburg, PA 19526/215-562-2103
Brockman's Custom Gunsmithing, P.O. Box 357, Gooding, ID 83330/208-934-5050
Brocock Ltd., 43 River Street, Digbeth, Birmingham, B5 5SA ENGLAND/011-021-773-1200
Broken Gun Ranch, 10739 126 Rd., Spearville, KS 67876/316-385-2587; FAX: 316-385-2597
Brolin Arms, 2755 Thompson Creek Rd., Pomona, CA 91767/909-392-2352; FAX: 909-392-2354
Brooker, Dennis, Rt. 1, Box 12A, Derby, IA 50068/515-533-2103
Brooks Tactical Systems, 279-A Shorewood Ct., Fox Island, WA 98333/800-410-4747; FAX: 206-572-6797
Brown Co., E. Arthur, 3404 Pawnee Dr., Alexandria, MN 56308/612-762-8847
Brown, H.R. (See Silhouette Leathers)
Brown Manufacturing, P.O. Box 9219, Akron, OH 44305/800-837-GUNS
Brown Precision, Inc., 7786 Molinos Ave., Los Molinos, CA 96055/916-384-2506; FAX: 916-384-1638
Brown Products, Inc., Ed, Rt. 2, Box 492, Perry, MO 63462/573-565-3261; FAX: 573-565-2791
Brownell Checkering Tools, W.E., 9390 Twin Mountain Circle, San Diego, CA 92126/619-695-2479; FAX: 619-695-2479
Brownells, Inc., 200 S. Front St., Montezuma, IA 50171/515-623-5401; FAX: 515-623-3896
Browning Arms Co. (Gen. Offices), One Browning Place, Morgan, UT 84050/801-876-2711; FAX: 801-876-3331
Browning Arms Co. (Parts & Service), 3005 Arnold Tenbrook Rd., Arnold, MO 63010-9406/314-287-6800; FAX: 314-287-9751
BRP, Inc. High Performance Cast Bullets, 1210 Alexander Rd., Colorado Springs, CO 80909/719-633-0658
Bruno Shooters Supply, 111 N. Wyoming St., Hazleton, PA 18201/717-455-2281; FAX: 717-455-2211
Brunsport, Inc., 1131 Bayview Dr., Quincy, IL 62301/217-223-8844; FAX: 217-223-8847
Brunton U.S.A., 620 E. Monroe Ave., Riverton, WY 82501/307-856-6559; FAX: 307-856-1840
Brynin, Milton, P.O. Box 383, Yonkers, NY 10710/914-779-4333
BSA Guns Ltd., Armoury Rd. Small Heath, Birmingham, ENGLAND B11 2PX/011-021-772-8543; FAX: 011-021-773-0845
B-Square Company, Inc., P.O. Box 11281, 2708 St. Louis Ave., Ft. Worth, TX 76110/817-923-0964, 800-433-2909; FAX: 817-926-7012
Bucheimer, J.M., Jumbo Sports Products, 721 N. 20th St., St. Louis, MO 63103/314-241-1020
Buck Knives, Inc., 1900 Weld Blvd., P.O. Box 1267, El Cajon, CA 92020/619-449-1100, 800-326-2825; FAX: 619-562-5774, 800-729-2825
Buck Stix—SOS Products Co., Box 3, Neenah, WI 54956
Buck Stop Lure Co., Inc., 3600 Grow Rd. NW, P.O. Box 636, Stanton, MI 48888/517-762-5091; FAX: 517-762-5124
Buckeye Custom Bullets, 6490 Stewart Rd., Elida, OH 45807/419-641-4463
Buckhorn Gun Works, 8109 Woodland Dr., Black Hawk, SD 57718/605-787-6472
Buckskin Bullet Co., P.O. Box 1893, Cedar City, UT 84721/801-586-3286
Buckskin Machine Works, A. Hunkeler, 3235 S. 358th St., Auburn, WA 98001/206-927-5412
Budin, Dave, Main St., Margaretville, NY 12455/914-568-4103; FAX: 914-586-4105
Buenger Enterprises/Goldenrod Dehumidifier, 3600 S. Harbor Blvd., Oxnard, CA 93035/800-451-6797, 805-985-5828; FAX: 805-985-1534
Buffalo Arms, 123 S. Third, Suite 6, Sandpoint, ID 83864/208-263-6953; FAX: 208-265-2096
Buffalo Bullet Co., Inc., 12637 Los Nietos Rd., Unit A, Santa Fe Springs, CA 90670/310-944-0322; FAX: 310-944-5054
Buffalo Rock Shooters Supply, R.R. 1, Ottawa, IL 61350/815-433-2471
Bull Mountain Rifle Co., 6327 Golden West Terrace, Billings, MT 59106/406-656-0778
Bullberry Barrel Works, Ltd., 2430 W. Bullberry Ln. 67-5, Hurricane, UT 84737/801-635-9866
Bullet, Inc., 3745 Hiram Alworth Rd., Dallas, GA 30132

Bullet Swaging Supply, Inc., P.O. Box 1056, 303 McMillan Rd, West Monroe, LA 71291/318-387-7257; FAX: 318-387-7779
BulletMakers Workshop, The, RFD 1 Box 1755, Brooks, ME 04921
Bullseye Bullets, 1610 State Road 60, No. 12, Valrico, FL 33594/813-654-6563
Bull-X, Inc., 520 N. Main, Farmer City, IL 61842/309-928-2574, 800-248-3845 orders only; FAX: 309-928-2130
Burgess, Byron, P.O. Box 6853, Los Osos, CA 93412/805-528-1005
Burgess & Son Gunsmiths, R.W., P.O. Box 3364, Warner Robins, GA 31099/912-328-7487
Burkhart Gunsmithing, Don, P.O. Box 852, Rawlins, WY 82301/307-324-6007
Burnham Bros., P.O. Box 1148, Menard, TX 78659/915-396-4572; FAX: 915-396-4574
Burres, Jack, 10333 San Fernando Rd., Pacoima, CA 91331/818-899-8000
Burris Co., Inc., P.O. Box 1747, 331 E. 8th St., Greeley, CO 80631/970-356-1670; FAX: 970-356-8702
Bushmann Hunters & Safaris, P.O. Box 293088, Lewisville, TX 75029/214-317-0768
Bushmaster Firearms (See Quality Parts Co./Bushmaster Firearms)
Bushmaster Hunting & Fishing, 451 Alliance Ave., Toronto, Ont. M6N 2J1 CANADA/416-763-4040; FAX: 416-763-0623
Bushnell (See Bausch & Lomb)
Bushwacker Backpack & Supply Co. (See Counter Assault)
Bustani, Leo, P.O. Box 8125, W. Palm Beach, FL 33407/305-622-2710
Buster's Custom Knives, P.O. Box 214, Richfield, UT 84701/801-896-5319
Butler Creek Corporation, 290 Arden Dr., Belgrade, MT 59714/800-423-8327, 406-388-1356; FAX: 406-388-7204
Butler Enterprises, 834 Oberting Rd., Lawrenceburg, IN 47025/812-537-3584
Butterfield & Butterfield, 220 San Bruno Ave., San Francisco, CA 94103/415-861-7500
Buzztail Brass (See Grayback Wildcats)
B-West Imports, Inc., 2425 N. Huachuca Dr., Tucson, AZ 85745-1201/602-628-1990; FAX: 602-628-3602

C

C3 Systems, 678 Killingly St., Johnston, RI 02919
C&D Special Products (See Claybuster Wads & Harvester Bullets)
C&H Research, 115 Sunnyside Dr., Box 351, Lewis, KS 67552/316-324-5445
C&J Enterprises, Inc., 7101 Jurupa Ave., No. 12, Riverside, CA 92504/909-689-7758
Cabanas (See U.S. importer—Mandall Shooting Supplies, Inc.)
Cabela's, 812-13th Ave., Sidney, NE 69160/308-254-6644; FAX: 308-254-6669
Cabinet Mtn. Outfitters Scents & Lures, P.O. Box 766, Plains, MT 59859/406-826-3970
Cache La Poudre Rifleworks, 140 N. College, Ft. Collins, CO 80524/303-482-6913
Cadre Supply (See Parts & Surplus)
Calhoon Varmint Bullets, James, Shambo Rt., Box 304, Havre, MT 59501/406-395-4079
Calibre Press, Inc., 666 Dundee Rd., Suite 1607, Northbrook, IL 60062-2760/800-323-0037; FAX: 708-498-6869
Cali'co Hardwoods, Inc., 3580 Westwind Blvd., Santa Rosa, CA 95403/707-546-4045; FAX: 707-546-4027
Calico Light Weapon Systems, 405 E. 19th St., Bakersfield, CA 93305/805-323-1327; FAX: 805-323-7844
California Magnum, 20746 Dearborn St., Chatsworth, CA 91313/818-341-7302; FAX: 818-341-7304
California Sights (See Fautheree, Andy)
Camdex, Inc., 2330 Alger, Troy, MI 48083/810-528-2300; FAX: 810-528-0989
Cameron's, 16690 W. 11th Ave., Golden, CO 80401/303-279-7365; FAX: 303-628-5413
Camilli, Lou, 4700 Oahu Dr. NE, Albuquerque, NM 87111/505-293-5259
Camillus Cutlery Co., 54 Main St., Camillus, NY 13031/315-672-8111; FAX: 315-672-8832
Campbell, Dick, 20,000 Silver Ranch Rd., Conifer, CO 80433/303-697-0150
Camp-Cap Products, P.O. Box 173, Chesterfield, MO 63006/314-532-4340; FAX: 314-532-4340
Canjar Co., M.H., 500 E. 45th Ave., Denver, CO 80216/303-295-2638
Cannon's Guns, Box 1036, 320 Main St., Polson, MT 59860/406-887-2048
Cannon Safe, Inc., 9358 Stephens St., Pico Rivera, CA 90660/310-692-0636, 800-242-1055; FAX: 310-692-7252
Canons Delcour, Rue J.B. Cools, B-4040 Herstal, BELGIUM 32.(0)41.40.61.40; FAX: 32(0)412.40.22.88
Canyon Cartridge Corp., P.O. Box 152, Albertson, NY 11507/FAX: 516-294-8946
Cape Outfitters, 599 County Rd. 206, Cape Girardeau, MO 63701/314-335-4103; FAX: 314-335-1555
Caraville Manufacturing, P.O. Box 4545, Thousand Oaks, CA 91359/805-499-1234
Carbide Checkering Tools (See J&R Engineering)
Carbide Die & Mfg. Co., Inc., 15615 E. Arrow Hwy., Irwindale, CA 91706/818-337-2518
Carhartt, Inc., P.O. Box 600, 3 Parklane Blvd., Dearborn, MI 48121/800-358-3825, 313-271-8460; FAX: 313-271-3455
Carlson, Douglas R., Antique American Firearms, P.O. Box 71035, Dept. GD, Des Moines, IA 50325/515-224-6552
Carnahan Bullets, 17645 110th Ave. SE, Renton, WA 98055
Carolina Precision Rifles, 1200 Old Jackson Hwy., Jackson, SC 29831/803-827-2069
Carrell's Precision Firearms, 643 Clark Ave., Billings, MT 59101-1614/406-962-3593
Carroll Bullets (See Precision Reloading, Inc.)
Carry-Lite, Inc., 5203 W. Clinton Ave., Milwaukee, WI 53223/414-355-3520; FAX: 414-355-4775
Carter's Gun Shop, 225 G St., Penrose, CO 81240/719-372-6240
Carter's Wildlife Calls, Garth, Inc., P.O. Box 821, Cedar City, UT 84720/801-586-7639
Cartridge Transfer Group, Pete de Coux, 235 Oak St., Butler, PA 16001/412-282-3426
Carvajal Belts & Holsters, 422 Chestnut, San Antonio, TX 78202/210-222-1634
Cascade Arms, Inc., P.O. Box 268, Colton, Oregon 97017

MANUFACTURERS' DIRECTORY

Cascade Bullet Co., Inc., 2355 South 6th St., Klamath Falls, OR 97601/503-884-9316
Cascade Fabrication, 1090 Bailey Hill Rd. Unit A, Eugene, OR 97402/503-485-3433; FAX: 503-485-3543
Cascade Shooters, 2155 N.W. 12th St., Redwood, OR 97756
Case & Sons Cutlery Co., W.R., Owens Way, Bradford, PA 16701/814-368-4123, 800-523-6350; FAX: 814-768-5369
Case Sorting System, 12695 Cobblestone Creek Rd., Poway, CA 92064/619-486-9340
Cash Mfg. Co., Inc., P.O. Box 130, 201 S. Klein Dr., Waunakee, WI 53597-0130/608-849-5664; FAX: 608-849-5664
Caspian Arms Ltd., 14 North Main St., Hardwick, VT 05843/802-472-6454; FAX: 802-472-6709
Caswell International Corp., 1221 Marshall St. NE, Minneapolis, MN 55413-1055/612-379-2000; FAX: 612-379-2367
Catco-Ambush, Inc., P.O.Box 300, Corte Madera, CA 94926
Cathey Enterprises, Inc., P.O. Box 2202, Brownwood, TX 76804/915-643-2553; FAX: 915-643-3653
Cation, 2341 Alger St., Troy, MI 48083/810-689-0658; FAX: 810-689-7558
Catoctin Cutlery, P.O. Box 188, 17 S. Main St., Smithsburg, MD 21783/301-824-7416; FAX: 301-824-6138
Caywood, Shane J., P.O. Box 321, Minocqua, WI 54548/715-277-3866 evenings
CBC, Avenida Humberto de Campos, 3220, 09400-000 Ribeirao Pires-SP-BRAZIL/55-11-742-7500; FAX: 55-11-459-7385
C.C.G. Enterprises, 5217 E. Belknap St., Halton City, TX 76117/817-834-9554
CCI, Div. of Blount, Inc., Sporting Equipment Div., 2299 Snake River Ave.,, P.O. Box 856/Lewiston, ID 83501
800-627-3640, 208-746-2351; FAX: 208-746-2915
Cedar Hill Game Calls, Inc., Rt. 2 Box 236, Downsville, LA 71234/318-982-5632; FAX: 318-368-2245
Celestron International, P.O. Box 3578, 2835 Columbia St., Torrance, CA 90503/310-328-9560; FAX: 310-212-5835
Centaur Systems, Inc., 1602 Foothill Rd., Kalispell, MT 59901/406-755-8609; FAX: 406-755-8609
Center Lock Scope Rings, 9901 France Ct., Lakeville, MN 55044/612-461-2114
CenterMark, P.O. Box 4066, Parnassus Station, New Kensington, PA 15068/412-335-1319
Central Specialties Ltd., 1122 Silver Lake Road, Cary, IL 60013/708-639-3900; FAX: 708-639-3972
Century Gun Dist., Inc., 1467 Jason Rd., Greenfield, IN 46140/317-462-4524
Century International Arms, Inc., P.O. Box 714, St. Albans, VT 05478-0714/802-527-1252; FAX: 802-527-0470; WEB: http://www.generation.net/~century
CFVentures, 509 Harvey Dr., Bloomington, IN 47403-1715
C-H Tool & Die Corp. (See 4-D Custom Die Co.)
CHAA, Ltd., P.O. Box 565, Howell, MI 48844/800-677-8737; FAX: 313-894-6930
Chace Leather Products, 507 Alden St., Fall River, MA 02722/508-678-7556; FAX: 508-675-9666
Chadick's Ltd., P.O. Box 100, Terrell, TX 75160/214-563-7577
Chambers Flintlocks Ltd., Jim, Rt. 1, Box 513-A, Candler, NC 28715/704-667-8361
Champion Shooters' Supply, P.O. Box 303, New Albany, OH 43054/614-855-1603; FAX: 614-855-1209
Champion Target Co., 232 Industrial Parkway, Richmond, IN 47374/800-441-4971
Champion's Choice, Inc., 201 International Blvd., LaVergne, TN 37086/615-793-4066; FAX: 615-793-4070
Champlin, R. MacDonald, P.O. Box 132, Candia, NH 03034
Champlin Firearms, Inc., P.O. Box 3191, Woodring Airport, Enid, OK 73701/405-237-7388; FAX: 405-237-6922
Chapman Academy of Practical Shooting, 4350 Academy Rd., Hallsville, MO 65255/573-696-5544, 573-696-2266
Chapman Manufacturing Co., 471 New Haven Rd., P.O. Box 250, Durham, CT 06422/203-349-9228; FAX: 203-349-0084
Chapuis Armes, 21 La Gravoux, BP15, 42380 St. Bonnet-le-Chateau, FRANCE/(33)77.50.06.96 (U.S. importer—Chapuis USA)
Chapuis USA, 416 Business Park, Bedford, KY 40006
Checkmate Refinishing, 370 Champion Dr., Brooksville, FL 34601/904-799-5774
Cheddite France, S.A., 99, Route de Lyon, F-26500 Bourg-les-Valence, FRANCE/33-75-56-4545; FAX: 33-75-56-3587
Chelsea Gun Club of New York City, Inc., 237 Ovington Ave., Apt. D53, Brooklyn, NY 11209/718-836-9422, 718-833-2704
Chem-Pak, Inc., 11 Oates Ave., P.O. Box 1685, Winchester, VA 22604/800-336-9828, 703-667-1341; FAX: 703-722-3993
Cherry's Fine Guns, P.O. Box 5307, Greensboro, NC 27435-0307/919-854-4182
Chesapeake Importing & Distributing Co. (See CIDCO)
CheVron Bullets, RR1, Ottawa, IL 61350/815-433-2471
CheVron Case Master (See CheVron Bullets)
Chicago Cutlery Co., 1536 Beech St., Terre Haute, IN 47804/800-457-2665
Chicasaw Gun Works (See Cochran, Oliver)
Chipmunk (See Oregon Arms, Inc.)
Chippewa Shoe Co., P.O. Box 2521, Ft. Worth, TX 76113/817-332-4385
Choate Machine & Tool Co., Inc., P.O. Box 218, 116 Lovers Ln., Bald Knob, AR 72010/501-724-6193, 800-972-6390; FAX: 501-724-5873
Chopie Mfg., Inc., 700 Copeland Ave., LaCrosse, WI 54603/608-784-0926
Christensen Arms, 192 East 100 North, Fayette, UT 84630/801-528-7999; FAX: 801-528-7494
Christie's East, 219 E. 67th St., New York, NY 10021/212-606-0400
Christman Jr., David, 937 Lee Hedrick Rd., Colville, WA 99114/509-684-5686 days; 509-684-3314 evenings
Christopher Firearms Co., Inc., E., Route 128 & Ferry St., Miamitown, OH 45041/513-353-1321
Chronotech, 1655 Siamet Rd. Unit 6, Mississauga, Ont. L4W 1Z4 CANADA/905-625-5200; FAX: 905-625-5190
Chu Tani Ind., Inc., P.O. Box 2064, Cody, WY 82414-2064
Chuck's Gun Shop, P.O. Box 597, Waldo, FL 32694/904-468-2264
Churchill (See U.S. importer—Ellett Bros.)
Churchill, Winston, Twenty Mile Stream Rd., RFD P.O. Box 29B, Proctorsville, VT 05153/802-226-7772
Churchill Glove Co., James, P.O. Box 298, Centralia, WA 98531

CIDCO, 21480 Pacific Blvd., Sterling, VA 22170/703-444-5353
Ciener, Inc., Jonathan Arthur, 8700 Commerce St., Cape Canaveral, FL 32920/407-868-2200; FAX: 407-868-2201
Cimarron Arms, P.O. Box 906, Fredericksburg, TX 78624-0906/210-997-9090; FAX: 210-997-0802
Cincinnati Swaging, 2605 Marlington Ave., Cincinnati, OH 45208
Citadel Mfg. Inc., 5220 Gabbert Rd., Moorpark, CA 93021/805-529-7294; FAX: 805-529-7297
C.J. Ballistics, Inc., P.O. Box 132, Acme, WA 98220/206-595-5001
Clark Co., Inc., David, P.O. Box 15054, Worcester, MA 01615-0054/508-756-6216; FAX: 508-753-5827
Clark Custom Guns, Inc., 336 Shootout Lane, Princeton, LA 71067/318-949-9884; FAX: 318-949-9829
Clark Firearms Engraving, P.O. Box 80746, San Marino, CA 91118/818-287-1652
Clarkfield Enterprises, Inc., 1032 10th Ave., Clarkfield, MN 56223/612-669-7140
Claro Walnut Gunstock Co., 1235 Stanley Ave., Chico, CA 95928/916-342-5188
Classic Arms Corp., P.O. Box 106, Dunsmuir, CA 96025-0106/916-235-2000
Classic Brass, 14 Grove St., Plympton, MA 02367/FAX: 617-585-5673
Classic Guns, Inc., Frank S. Wood, 3230 Medlock Bridge Rd., Suite 110, Norcross, GA 30092/404-242-7944
Claybuster Wads & Harvester Bullets, 309 Sequoya Dr., Hopkinsville, KY 42240/800-922-6287, 800-284-1746, 502-885-8088; FAX: 502-885-1951
Clearview Mfg. Co., Inc., 413 S. Oakley St., Fordyce, AR 71742/501-352-8557; FAX: 501-352-8557
Clearview Products, 3021 N. Portland, Oklahoma City, OK 73107
Cleland's Gun Shop, Inc., 10306 Airport Hwy., Swanton, OH 43558/419-865-4713
Clements' Custom Leathercraft, Chas, 1741 Dallas St., Aurora, CO 80010-2018/303-364-0403
Clenzoil Corp., P.O. Box 80226, Sta. C, Canton, OH 44708-0226/330-833-9758; FAX: 330-833-4724
Clerke Co., J.A., P.O. Box 627, Pearblossom, CA 93553-0627/805-945-0713
Clift Mfg., L.R., 3821 Hammonton Rd., Marysville, CA 95901/916-755-3390; FAX: 916-755-3393
Clift Welding Supply & Cases, 1332-A Colusa Hwy., Yuba City, CA 95993/916-755-3390; FAX: 916-755-3393
Cloward's Gun Shop, 4023 Aurora Ave. N, Seattle, WA 98103/206-632-2072
Clymer Manufacturing Co., Inc., 1645 W. Hamlin Rd., Rochester Hills, MI 48309-1530/810-853-5555, 810-853-5627; FAX: 810-853-1530
C-More Systems, P.O. Box 1750, 7553 Gary Rd., Manassas, VA 22110/703-361-2663; FAX: 703-361-5881
Coast Cutlery Co., 609 SE Ankeny St., Portland, OR 97214/503-234-4545; FAX: 503-234-4422
Coats, Mrs. Lester, 300 Luman Rd., Space 125, Phoenix, OR 97535/503-535-1611
Cobalt Mfg., Inc., 1020 Shady Oak Dr., Denton, TX 76205/817-382-8986; FAX: 817-383-4281
Cobra Gunskin, 133-30 32nd Ave., Flushing, NY 11354/718-762-8181; FAX: 718-762-0890
Cobra Sport s.r.l., Via Caduti Nei Lager No. 1, 56020 San Romano, Montopoli v/Arno (Pi), ITALY/0039-571-450490; FAX: 0039-571-450492
Cochran, Oliver, Box 868, Shady Spring, WV 25918/304-763-3838
Coffin, Charles H., 3719 Scarlet Ave., Odessa, TX 79762/915-366-4729
Coffin, Jim, 250 Country Club Lane, Albany, OR 97321/541-928-4391
Cogar's Gunsmithing, P.O. Box 755, Houghton Lake, MI 48629/517-422-4591
Coghlan's Ltd., 121 Irene St., Winnipeg, Man., CANADA R3T 4C7/204-284-9550; FAX: 204-475-4127
Cold Steel, Inc., 2128-D Knoll Dr., Ventura, CA 93003/800-255-4716, 800-624-2363 (in CA); FAX: 805-642-9727
Cole's Gun Works, Old Bank Building, Rt. 4, Box 250, Moyock, NC 27958/919-435-2345
Cole-Grip, 16135 Cohasset St., Van Nuys, CA 91406/818-782-4424
Coleman Co., Inc., 250 N. St. Francis, Wichita, KS 67201
Coleman's Custom Repair, 4035 N. 20th Rd., Arlington, VA 22207/703-528-4486
Collings, Ronald, 1006 Cielta Linda, Vista, CA 92083
Colonial Arms, Inc., P.O. Box 636, Selma, AL 36702-0636/334-872-9455; FAX: 334-872-9540
Colonial Knife Co., Inc., P.O. Box 3327, Providence, RI 02909/401-421-1600; FAX: 401-421-2047
Colonial Repair, P.O. Box 372, Hyde Park, MA 02136-9998/617-469-4951
Colorado Gunsmithing Academy Lamar, 27533 Highway 287 South, Lamar, CO 81052/719-336-4099
Colorado School of Trades, 1575 Hoyt St., Lakewood, CO 80215/800-234-4594; FAX: 303-233-4723
Colorado Shooter's Supply, 1163 W. Paradise Way, Fruita, CO 81521/303-858-9191
Colorado Sutlers Arsenal (See Cumberland States Arsenal)
Colt Blackpowder Arms Co., 5 Centre Market Place, New York, NY 10013/212-925-2159; FAX: 212-966-4986
Colt's Mfg. Co., Inc., P.O. Box 1868, Hartford, CT 06144-1868/800-962-COLT, 203-236-6311; FAX: 203-244-1449
Combat Military Ordnance Ltd., 3900 Hopkins St., Savannah, GA 31405/912-238-1900; FAX: 912-236-7570
Companhia Brasileira de Cartuchos (See CBC)
Compass Industries, Inc., 104 East 25th St., New York, NY 10010/212-473-2614, 800-221-9904; FAX: 212-353-0826
Compasseco, Ltd., 151 Atkinson Hill Ave., Bardtown, KY 40004/502-349-0910
Competition Electronics, Inc., 3469 Precision Dr., Rockford, IL 61109/815-874-8001; FAX: 815-874-8181
Competitive Pistol Shop, The, 5233 Palmer Dr., Ft. Worth, TX 76117-2433/817-834-8479
Competitor Corp., Inc., Appleton Business Center, 30 Tricnit Road, Unit 16, New Ipswich, NH 03071-0508/603-878-3891; FAX: 603-878-3950
Component Concepts, Inc., 10240 SW Nimbus Ave., Suite L-8, Portland, OR 97223/503-684-9262; FAX: 503-620-4285
Concept Development Corp., 14715 N. 78th Way, Suite 300, Scottsdale, AZ 85260/800-472-4405; FAX: 602-948-7560
Condon, Inc., David, 109 E. Washington St., Middleburg, VA 22117/703-687-5642
Conetrol Scope Mounts, 10225 Hwy. 123 S., Seguin, TX 78155/210-379-3030, 800-CONETROL; FAX: 210-379-3030

29th EDITION, 1997 **317**

DIRECTORY OF THE ARMS TRADE

CONKKO, P.O. Box 40, Broomall, PA 19008/215-356-0711
Connecticut Shotgun Mfg. Co., P.O. Box 1692, 35 Woodland St., New Britain, CT 06051-1692/203-225-6581; FAX: 203-832-8707
Connecticut Valley Arms Co. (See CVA)
Connecticut Valley Classics, P.O. Box 2068, 12 Taylor Lane, Westport, CT 06880/203-254-3202; FAX: 203-256-1180
Conrad, C.A., 3964 Ebert St., Winston-Salem, NC 27127/919-788-5469
Continental Kite & Key (See CONKKO)
Cook Engineering Service, 891 Highbury Rd., Vermont VICT 3133 AUSTRALIA
Coonan Arms (JS Worldwide DBA), 1745 Hwy. 36 E., Maplewood, MN 55109/612-777-3156; FAX: 612-777-3683
Cooper Arms, P.O. Box 114, Stevensville, MT 59870/406-777-5534; FAX: 406-777-5228
Cooper-Woodward, 3800 Pelican Rd., Helena, MT 59601/406-458-3800
Corbin, Inc., 600 Industrial Circle, P.O. Box 2659, White City, OR 97503/541-826-5211; FAX: 541-826-8669
Cor-Bon Bullet & Ammo Co., 1311 Industry Rd., Sturgis, SD 57785/800-626-7266; FAX: 800-923-2666
Corkys Gun Clinic, 4401 Hot Springs Dr., Greeley, CO 80634-9226/970-330-0516
Corry, John, 861 Princeton Ct., Neshanic Station, NJ 08853/908-369-8019
Cosmi Americo & Figlio s.n.c., Via Flaminia 307, Ancona, ITALY I-60020/071-888208; FAX: 39-071-887008 (U.S. importer—New England Arms Co.)
Costa, David, Island Pond Gun Shop, P.O. Box 428, Cross St., Island Pond, VT 05846/802-723-4546
Coulston Products, Inc., P.O. Box 30, 201 Ferry St., Suite 212, Easton, PA 18044-0030/215-253-0167, 800-445-9927; FAX: 215-252-1511
Counter Assault, Box 4721, Missoula, MT 59806/406-728-6241; FAX: 406-728-8800
Country Armourer, The, P.O. Box .308, Ashby, MA 01431-0308/508-827-6797; FAX: 508-827-4845
County Arms, 11020 Whitman Ln., Tamarac, FL 33321/305-720-2066; FAX: 305-722-6353
Cousin Bob's Mountain Products, 7119 Ohio River Blvd., Ben Avon, PA 15202/412-766-5114; FAX: 412-766-5114
Cox, C. Ed, RD 2, Box 192, Prosperity, PA 15329/412-228-4984
CP Bullets, 340-1 Constance Dr., Warminster, PA 18974
CQB Training, P.O. Box 1739, Manchester, MO 63011
Craftguard, 3624 Logan Ave., Waterloo, IA 50703/319-232-2959; FAX: 319-234-0804
Craig Custom Ltd., Research & Development, 629 E. 10th, Hutchinson, KS 67501/316-669-0601
Crandall Tool & Machine Co., 19163 21 Mile Rd., Tustin, MI 49688/616-829-4430
Crane & Crane Ltd., 105 N. Edison Way 6, Reno, NV 89502-2355/702-856-1516; FAX: 702-856-1616
Crane Sales Co., George S., P.O. Box 385, Van Nuys, CA 91408/818-505-8337
Crawford Co., Inc., R.M., P.O. Box 277, Everett, PA 15537/814-652-6536; FAX: 814-652-9526
CRDC Laser Systems Group, 3972 Barranca Parkway, Ste. J-484, Irvine, CA 92714/714-586-1295; FAX: 714-831-4823
Creative Cartridge Co., 56 Morgan Rd., Canton, CT 06019/203-693-2529
Creative Craftsman, Inc., The, 95 Highway 29 North, P.O. Box 331, Lawrenceville, GA 30246/404-963-2112; FAX: 404-513-9488
Creedmoor Sports, Inc., P.O. Box 1040, Oceanside, CA 92051/619-757-5529
Creek Side Metal & Woodcrafters (See Allard, Gary)
Creekside Gun Shop, Inc., Main St., Holcomb, NY 14469/716-657-6338; FAX: 716-657-7900
Crit'R Call, Box 999G, La Porte, CO 80535/970-484-2768; FAX: 970-484-0807
Crosman Airguns, Rts. 5 and 20, E. Bloomfield, NY 14443/716-657-6161; FAX: 716-657-6505
Crosman Blades (See Coleman Co., Inc.)
Crosman Products of Canada Ltd., 1173 N. Service Rd. West, Oakville, Ontario, L6M 2V9 CANADA/905-827-1822
Crouse's Country Cover, P.O. Box 160, Storrs, CT 06268/860-423-8736
CRR, Inc./Marble's Inc., 420 Industrial Park, P.O. Box 111, Gladstone, MI 49837/906-428-3710; FAX: 906-428-3711
Crucelegui Hermanos (See U.S. importer—Mandall Shooting Supplies, Inc.)
Cryo-Accurizing, 1160 South Monroe, Decatur, IL 62521/217-423-3070; FAX: 217-423-2756
Cubic Shot Shell Co., Inc., 98 Fatima Dr., Campbell, OH 44405/216-755-0349; FAX: 216-755-0349
Cullity Restoration, Daniel, 209 Old County Rd., East Sandwich, MA 02537/508-888-1147
Cumberland Arms, 514 Shafer Road, Manchester, TN 37355/800-797-8414
Cumberland Knife & Gun Works, 5661 Bragg Blvd., Fayetteville, NC 28303/919-867-0009
Cumberland Mountain Arms, P.O. Box 710, Winchester, TN 37398/615-967-8414; FAX: 615-967-9199
Cumberland States Arsenal, 1124 Palmyra Road, Clarksville, TN 37040
Cummings Bullets, 1417 Esperanza Way, Escondido, CA 92027
Cunningham Co., Eaton, 607 Superior St., Kansas City, MO 64106/816-842-2600
Cupp, Alana, Custom Engraver, P.O. Box 207, Annabella, UT 84711/801-896-4834
Curly Maple Stock Blanks (See Tiger-Hunt)
Curtis Custom Shop, RR1, Box 193A, Wallingford, KY 41093/703-659-4265
Curtis Gun Shop, Dept. ST, 119 W. College, Bozeman, MT 59715/406-587-4934
Custom Barreling & Stocks, 937 Lee Hedrick Rd., Colville, WA 99114/509-684-5686 (days), 509-684-3314 (evenings)
Custom Bullets by Hoffman, 2604 Peconic Ave., Seaford, NY 11783
Custom Calls, 607 N. 5th St., Burlington, IA 52601/319-752-4465
Custom Checkering Service, Kathy Forster, 2124 SE Yamhill St., Portland, OR 97214/503-236-5874
Custom Chronograph, Inc., 5305 Reese Hill Rd., Sumas, WA 98295/360-988-7801
Custom Firearms (See Ahrends, Kim)
Custom Gun Products, 5021 W. Rosewood, Spokane, WA 99208/509-328-9340
Custom Gun Stocks, Rt. 6, P.O. Box 177, McMinnville, TN 37110/615-668-3912
Custom Gunsmiths, 4303 Friar Lane, Colorado Springs, CO 80907/719-599-3366
Custom Hunting Ammo & Arms (See CHAA, Ltd.)
Custom Products (See Jones Custom Products, Neil A.)
Custom Quality Products, Inc., 345 W. Girard Ave., P.O. Box 71129, Madison Heights, MI 48071/810-585-1616; FAX: 810-585-0644
Custom Riflestocks, Inc., Michael M. Kokolus, 7005 Herber Rd., New Tripoli, PA 18066/610-298-3013
Custom Shop, The, 890 Cochrane Crescent, Peterborough, Ont. K9H 5N3 CANADA/705-742-6693
Custom Tackle and Ammo, P.O. Box 1886, Farmington, NM 87499/505-632-3539
Cutco Cutlery, P.O. Box 810, Olean, NY 14760/716-372-3111
Cutlery Shoppe, 5461 Kendall St., Boise, ID 83706-1248/800-231-1272
Cutsinger Bench Rest Bullets, RR 8, Box 161-A, Shelbyville, IN 46176/317-729-5360
CVA, 5988 Peachtree Corners East, Norcross, GA 30071/800-251-9412; FAX: 404-242-8546
C.W. Cartridge Co., 242 Highland Ave., Kearney, NJ 07032/201-998-1030
C.W. Cartridge Co., 71 Hackensack St., Wood Ridge, NJ 07075
Cylinder & Slide, Inc., William R. Laughridge, 245 E. 4th St., Fremont, NE 68025/402-721-4277; FAX: 402-721-0263
CZ (See U.S. importer—Magnum Research, Inc.)

D

D&D Gunsmiths, Ltd., 363 E. Elmwood, Troy, MI 48083/810-583-1512; FAX: 810-583-1524
D&G Precision Duplicators (See Greene Precision Duplicators)
D&H Precision Tooling, 7522 Barnard Mill Rd., Ringwood, IL 60072/815-653-4011
D&H Prods. Co., Inc., 465 Denny Rd., Valencia, PA 16059/412-898-2840, 800-776-0281; FAX: 412-898-2013
D&J Bullet Co. & Custom Gun Shop, Inc., 426 Ferry St., Russell, KY 41169/606-836-2663; FAX: 606-836-2663
D&L Industries (See D.J. Marketing)
D&L Sports, P.O. Box 651, Gillette, WY 82717/307-686-4008
D&R Distributing, 308 S.E. Valley St., Myrtle Creek, OR 97457/503-863-6850
Dade Screw Machine Products, 2319 NW 7th Ave., Miami, FL 33127/305-573-5050
Daewoo Precision Industries Ltd., 34-3 Yeoeuido-Dong, Yeongdeungoo-GU, 15th, Fl./Seoul, KOREA (U.S. importer—Nationwide Sports Distributors)
Dahl's Custom Stocks, N2863 Schofield Rd., Lake Geneva, WI 53147/414-248-2464
Daisy Mfg. Co., P.O. Box 220, Rogers, AR 72757/501-636-1200; FAX: 501-636-1601
Dakota (See U.S. importer—EMF Co., Inc.)
Dakota Arms, Inc., HC 55, Box 326, Sturgis, SD 57785/605-347-4686; FAX: 605-347-4459
Dakota Corp., 77 Wales St., P.O. Box 543, Rutland, VT 05701/802-775-6062, 800-451-4167; FAX: 802-773-3919
Daly, Charles (See B.C. Miroku/Charles Daly)
Damascus-U.S.A., 149 Deans Farm Rd., Tyner, NC 27980/919-221-2010; FAX: 919-221-2009
Dan's Whetstone Co., Inc., 130 Timbs Place, Hot Springs, AR 71913/501-767-1616; FAX: 501-767-9598
Dangler, Homer L., Box 254, Addison, MI 49220/517-547-6745
Danner Shoe Mfg. Co., 12722 NE Airport Way, Portland, OR 97230/503-251-1100, 800-345-0430; FAX: 503-251-1119
Danuser Machine Co., 550 E. Third St., P.O. Box 368, Fulton, MO 65251/573-642-2246; FAX: 573-642-2240
Dapkus Co., Inc., J.G., Commerce Circle, P.O. Box 293, Durham, CT 06422
Dara-Nes, Inc. (See Nesci Enterprises, Inc.)
Darlington Gun Works, Inc., P.O. Box 698, 516 S. 52 Bypass, Darlington, SC 29532/803-393-3931
Data Tech Software Systems, 19312 East Eldorado Drive, Aurora, CO 80013
Datumtech Corp., 2275 Wehrle Dr., Buffalo, NY 14221
Davidson, Jere, Rt. 1, Box 132, Rustburg, VA 24588/804-821-3637
Davis, Don, 1619 Heights, Katy, TX 77493/713-391-3090
Davis Co., R.E., 3450 Pleasantville NE, Pleasantville, OH 43148/614-654-9990
Davis Industries, 15150 Sierra Bonita Ln., Chino, CA 91710/909-597-4726; FAX: 909-393-9771
Davis Leather Co., G. Wm., 3990 Valley Blvd., Unit D, Walnut, CA 91789/909-598-5620
Davis Products, Mike, 643 Loop Dr., Moses Lake, WA 98837/509-765-6178, 509-766-7281 orders only
Davis Service Center, Bill, 7221 Florin Mall Dr., Sacramento, CA 95823/916-393-4867
Day & Sons, Inc., Leonard, P.O. Box 122, Flagg Hill Rd., Heath, MA 01346/413-337-8369
Dayson Arms Ltd., P.O. Box 532, Vincennes, IN 47591/812-882-8680; FAX: 812-882-8446
Daystate Ltd., Newcastle Street, Stone, Staffs, ST15 8JU ENGLAND/01785-812473; FAX: 01785-812105
Dayton Traister, 4778 N. Monkey Hill Rd., P.O. Box 593, Oak Harbor, WA 98277/206-679-4657; FAX:206-675-1114
DBASE Consultants (See Arms, Peripheral Data Systems)
DBI Books, Division of Krause Publications, 4092 Commercial Ave., Northbrook, IL 60062/847-272-6310; FAX: 847-272-2051; For consumer orders, see Krause Publications
D-Boone Ent., Inc., 5900 Colwyn Dr., Harrisburg, PA 17109
D.C.C. Enterprises, 259 Wynburn Ave., Athens, GA 30601
D.D. Custom Stocks, R.H. "Dick" Devereaux, 5240 Mule Deer Dr., Colorado Springs, CO 80919/719-548-8468
de Coux, Pete (See Cartridge Transfer Group)
de Treville & Co., Stan, 4129 Normal St., San Diego, CA 92103/619-298-3393
Dead Eye's Sport Center, RD 1, Box 147B, Shickshinny, PA 18655/717-256-7432
Decker Shooting Products, 1729 Laguna Ave., Schofield, WI 54476/715-359-5873
DeckSlider of Florida, 27641-2 Reahard Ct., Bonita Springs, FL 33923/800-782-1474

MANUFACTURERS' DIRECTORY

Deepeeka Exports Pvt. Ltd., D-78, Saket, Meerut-250-006, INDIA/011-91-121-512889, 011-91-121-545363; FAX: 011-91-121-542988, 011-91-121-511599
Deer Me Products Co., Box 34, 1208 Park St., Anoka, MN 55303/612-421-8971; FAX: 612-422-0526
Defense Training International, Inc., 749 S. Lemay, Ste. A3-337, Ft. Collins, CO 80524/303-482-2520; FAX: 303-482-0548
Degen Inc. (See Aristocrat Knives)
deHaas Barrels, RR 3, Box 77, Ridgeway, MO 64481/816-872-6308
Del Rey Products, P.O. Box 91561, Los Angeles, CA 90009/213-823-0494
Delhi Gun House, 1374 Kashmere Gate, Delhi, INDIA 110 006/(011)237375 239116; FAX: 91-11-2917344
Delorge, Ed, 2231 Hwy. 308, Thibodaux, LA 70301/504-447-1633
Del-Sports, Inc., Box 685, Main St., Margaretville, NY 12455/914-586-4103; FAX: 914-586-4105
Delta Arms Ltd., P.O. Box 1000, Delta, VT 84624-1000
Delta Co. Ammo Bunker, 1209 16th Place, Yuma, AZ 85364/602-783-4563
Delta Enterprises, 284 Hagemann Drive, Livermore, CA 94550
Delta Frangible Ammunition, LLC, 1111 Jefferson Davis Hwy., Suite 508, Arlington, VA 22202/703-416-4928; FAX: 703-416-4934
Dem-Bart Checkering Tools, Inc., 6807 Bickford Ave., Old Hwy. 2, Snohomish, WA 98290/360-568-7356; FAX: 360-568-1798
Denver Bullets, Inc., 1811 W. 13th Ave., Denver, CO 80204/303-893-3146; FAX: 303-893-9161
Denver Instrument Co., 6542 Fig St., Arvada, CO 80004/800-321-1135, 303-431-7255; FAX: 303-423-4831
DeSantis Holster & Leather Goods, Inc., P.O. Box 2039, 149 Denton Ave., New Hyde Park, NY 11040-0701/516-354-8000; FAX: 516-354-7501
Desert Industries, Inc., P.O. Box 93443, Las Vegas, NV 89193-3443/702-597-1066; FAX: 702-871-9452
Desert Mountain Mfg., P.O. Box 2767, Columbia Falls, MT 59912/800-477-0762, 406-892-7772; FAX: 406-892-7772
Desquesnes, Gerald (See Napoleon Bonaparte, Inc.)
Detroit-Armor Corp., 720 Industrial Dr. No. 112, Cary, IL 60013/708-639-7666; FAX: 708-639-7694
Dever Co., Jack, 8590 NW 90, Oklahoma City, OK 73132/405-721-6393
Devereaux, R.H. "Dick" (See D.D. Custom Stocks)
Dewey Mfg. Co., Inc., J., P.O. Box 2014, Southbury, CT 06488/203-264-3064; FAX: 203-262-6907
DGR Custom Rifles, RR1, Box 8A, Tappen, ND 58487/701-327-8135
DGS, Inc., Dale A. Storey, 1117 E. 12th, Casper, WY 82601/307-237-2414
DHB Products, P.O. Box 3092, Alexandria, VA 22302/703-836-2648
Diamond Machining Techonology (See DMT—Diamond Machining Technology)
Diamond Mfg. Co., P.O. Box 174, Wyoming, PA 18644/800-233-9601
Diamondback Supply, 2431 Juan Tabo, Suite 163, Albuquerque, NM 87112/505-237-0068
Diana (See U.S. importer—Dynamit Nobel-RWS, Inc.)
Dibble, Derek A., 555 John Downey Dr., New Britain, CT 06051/203-224-2630
Dietz Gun Shop & Range, Inc., 421 Range Rd., New Braunfels, TX 78132/210-885-4662
Dilliott Gunsmithing, Inc., 657 Scarlett Rd., Dandridge, TN 37725/615-397-9204
Dillon, Ed, 1035 War Eagle Dr. N., Colorado Springs, CO 80919/719-598-4929; FAX: 719-598-4929
Dillon Precision Products, Inc., 8009 East Dillon's Way, Scottsdale, AZ 85260/602-948-8009, 800-762-3845; FAX: 602-998-2786
Dina Arms Corporation, P.O. Box 46, Royersford, PA 19468/610-287-0266; FAX: 610-287-0266
Division Lead Co., 7742 W. 61st Pl., Summit, IL 60502
Dixie Gun Works, Inc., Hwy. 51 South, Union City, TN 38261/901-885-0561, order 800-238-6785; FAX: 901-885-0440
Dixon Muzzleloading Shop, Inc., RD 1, Box 175, Kempton, PA 19529/610-756-6271
D.J. Marketing, 10602 Horton Ave., Downey, CA 90241/310-806-0891; FAX: 310-806-6231
DKT, Inc., 14623 Vera Drive, Union, MI 49130-9744/616-641-7120; FAX: 616-641-2015
DLO Mfg., 10807 SE Foster Ave., Arcadia, FL 33821-7304
D-Max, Inc., RR1, Box 473, Bagley, MN 56621/218-785-2278
DMT—Diamond Machining Technology, Inc., 85 Hayes Memorial Dr., Marlborough, MA 01752-1892/508-481-5944; FAX: 508-485-3924
Doctor Optic Technologies, Inc., 4695 Boulder Highway, Suite A, Las Vegas, NV 89121/800-290-3634, 702-898-7161; FAX: 702-898-3737
Dogtown Varmint Supplies, 1048 Irvine Ave. No. 333, Newport Beach, CA 92660/714-642-3997
Dohring Bullets, 100 W. 8 Mile Rd., Ferndale, MI 48220
Dolbare, Elizabeth, P.O. Box 222, Sunburst, MT 59482-0222
Donnelly, C.P., 405 Kubli Rd., Grants Pass, OR 97527/541-846-6604
Doskocil Mfg. Co., Inc., P.O. Box 1246, 4209 Barnett, Arlington, TX 76017/817-467-5116; FAX: 817-472-9810
Double A Ltd., Dept. ST, Box 11306, Minneapolis, MN 55411
Douglas Barrels, Inc., 5504 Big Tyler Rd., Charleston, WV 25313-1398/304-776-1341; FAX: 304-776-8560
Dowtin Gunworks, Rt. 4, Box 930A, Flagstaff, AZ 86001/602-779-1898
Dr. O's Products Ltd., P.O. Box 111, Niverville, NY 12130/518-784-3333; FAX: 518-784-2800
Drain, Mark, SE 3211 Kamilche Point Rd., Shelton, WA 98584/206-426-5452
Dremel Mfg. Co., 4915-21st St., Racine, WI 53406
Dressel Jr., Paul G., 209 N. 92nd Ave., Yakima, WA 98908/509-966-9233; FAX: 509-966-3365
Dri-Slide, Inc., 411 N. Darling, Fremont, MI 49412/616-924-3950
Dropkick, 1460 Washington Blvd., Williamsport, PA 17701/717-326-6561; FAX: 717-326-4950
DTM International, Inc., 40 Joslyn Rd., P.O. Box 5, Lake Orion, MI 48362/313-693-6670
Duane Custom Stocks, Randy, 110 W. North Ave., Winchester, VA 22601/703-667-9461; FAX: 703-722-3993
Duane's Gun Repair (See DGR Custom Rifles)
Dubber, Michael W., P.O. Box 312, Evansville, IN 47702/812-424-9000; FAX: 812-424-6551
Duck Call Specialists, P.O. Box 124, Jerseyville, IL 62052/618-498-9855
Duffy (See Guns Antique & Modern DBA/Charles E. Duffy)
Du-Lite Corp., Charles E., 171 River Rd., Middletown, CT 06457/203-347-2505; FAX: 203-347-9404
Dumoulin, Ernest, Rue Florent Boclinville 8-10, 13-4041 Votten, BELGIUM/41 27 78 92 (U.S. importer—New England Arms Co.)
Duncan's Gun Works, Inc., 1619 Grand Ave., San Marcos, CA 92069/619-727-0515
Dunham Co., P.O. Box 813, Brattleboro, VT 05301/802-254-2316
Dunphy, Ted, W. 5100 Winch Rd., Rathdrum, ID 83858/208-687-1399; FAX: 208-687-1399
Duofold, Inc., RD 3 Rt. 309, Valley Square Mall, Tamaqua, PA 18252/717-386-2666; FAX: 717-386-3652
DuPont (See IMR Powder Co.)
Dutchman's Firearms, Inc., The, 4143 Taylor Blvd., Louisville, KY 40215/502-366-0555
Dybala Gun Shop, P.O. Box 1024, FM 3156, Bay City, TX 77414/409-245-0866
Dykstra, Doug, 411 N. Darling, Fremont, MI 49412/616-924-3950
Dynalite Products, Inc., 215 S. Washington St., Greenfield, OH 45123/513-981-2124
Dynamit Nobel-RWS, Inc., 81 Ruckman Rd., Closter, NJ 07624/201-767-7971; FAX: 201-767-1589
Dyson & Son Ltd., Peter, 29-31 Church St., Honley Huddersfield, W. Yorkshire HD7 2AH, ENGLAND/44-1484-661062; FAX: 44-1484-663709

E

E&L Mfg., Inc., 4177 Riddle by Pass Rd., Riddle, OR 97469/541-874-2137; FAX: 541-874-3107
E.A.A. Corp., P.O. Box 1299, Sharpes, FL 32959/407-639-4842, 800-536-4442; FAX: 407-639-7006
Eagan, Donald V., P.O. Box 196, Benton, PA 17814/717-925-6134
Eagle Arms (See ArmaLite, Inc.)
Eagle Grips, Eagle Business Center, 460 Randy Rd., Carol Stream, IL 60188/800-323-6144, 708-260-0400; FAX: 708-260-0486
Eagle Imports, Inc., 1750 Brielle Ave., Unit B1, Wanamassa, NJ 07712/908-493-0333; FAX: 908-493-0301
Eagle International, Inc., 5195 W. 58th Ave., Suite 300, Arvada, CO 80002/303-426-8100; FAX: 303-426-5475
Eagle Mfg. & Engineering, 2648 Keen Dr., San Diego, CA 92139/619-479-4402; FAX: 619-472-5585
E-A-R, Inc., Div. of Cabot Safety Corp., 5457 W. 79th St., Indianapolis, IN 46268/800-327-3431; FAX: 800-488-8007
Eastman Products, R.T., P.O. Box 1531, Jackson, WY 83001/307-733-3217, 800-624-4311
Easy Pull Outlaw Products, 316 1st St. East, Polson, MT 59860/406-883-6822
EAW (See U.S. importer—New England Custom Gun Service)
Echols & Co., D'Arcy, 164 W. 580 S., Providence, UT 84332/801-753-2367
Eckelman Gunsmithing, 3125 133rd St. SW, Fort Ripley, MN 56449/218-829-3176
Ed's Gun House, Rt. 1, Box 62, Minnesota City, MN 55959/507-689-2925
Edenpine, Inc. c/o Six Enterprises, Inc., 320 D Turtle Creek Ct., San Jose, CA 95125/408-999-0201; FAX: 408-999-0216
EdgeCraft Corp., P.O. Box 3000, Limestone and Southwood Rd., Avondale, PA 19311/215-268-0500, 800-342-3255; FAX: 215-268-3545
Edmisten Co., P.O. Box 1293, Boone, NC 28607
Edmund Scientific Co., 101 E. Gloucester Pike, Barrington, NJ 08033/609-543-6250
Ednar, Inc., 2-4-8 Kayabacho, Nihonbashi, Chuo-ku, Tokyo, JAPAN 103/81(Japan)-3-3667-1651; FAX: 81-3-3661-8113
Eezox, Inc., P.O. Box 772, Waterford, CT 06385-0772/860-447-8282, 800-462-3331; FAX: 860-447-3484
Effebi SNC-Dr. Franco Beretta, via Rossa, 4, 25062 Concesio, Italy/030-2751955; FAX: 030-2180414 (U.S. importer—Nevada Cartridge Co.
Eggleston, Jere D., 400 Saluda Ave., Columbia, SC 29205/803-799-3402
EGW Evolution Gun Works, 4050 B-8 Skyron Dr., Doylestown, PA 18901/215-348-9892; FAX: 215-348-1056
Eichelberger Bullets, Wm., 158 Crossfield Rd., King of Prussia, PA 19406
EK Knife Co., c/o Blackjack Knives, Ltd., 1307 Wabash Ave., Effingham, IL 62401
Ekol Leather Care, P.O. Box 2652, West Lafayette, IN 47906/317-463-2250; FAX: 317-463-7004
El Dorado Leather, P.O. Box 2603, Tucson, AZ 85702/520-586-4791; FAX: 520-586-4791
El Paso Saddlery Co., P.O. Box 27194, El Paso, TX 79926/915-544-2233; FAX: 915-544-2535
Eldorado Cartridge Corp. (See PMC/Eldorado Cartridge Corp.)
Electro Prismatic Collimators, Inc., 1441 Manatt St., Lincoln, NE 68521
Electronic Shooters Protection, Inc., 11997 West 85th Place, Arvada, CO 80005/303-456-8964; 800-797-7791
Electronic Trigger Systems, Inc., P.O. Box 13, 230 Main St. S., Hector, MN 55342/612-848-2760
Eley Ltd., P.O. Box 705, Witton, Birmingham, B6 7UT, ENGLAND/021-356-8899; FAX: 021-331-4173
Elite Ammunition, P.O. Box 3251, Oakbrook, IL 60522/708-366-9006
Elk River, Inc., 1225 Paonia St., Colorado Springs, CO 80915/719-574-4407
Elkhorn Bullets, P.O. Box 5293, Central Point, OR 97502/541-826-7440
Elko Arms, Dr. L. Kortz, 28 rue Ecole Moderne, B-7060 Soignies, BELGIUM/(32)67-33-29-34
Ellett Bros., 267 Columbia Ave., P.O. Box 128, Chapin, SC 29036/803-345-3751, 800-845-3711; FAX: 803-345-1820
Ellicott Arms, Inc./Woods Pistolsmithing, 3840 Dahlgren Ct., Ellicott City, MD 21042/410-465-7979
Elliott Inc., G.W., 514 Burnside Ave., East Hartford, CT 06108/203-289-5741; FAX: 203-289-3137
Elsen, Inc., Pete, 1529 S. 113th St., West Allis, WI 53214
Emerging Technologies, Inc. (See Laseraim Technologies, Inc.)
EMF Co., Inc., 1900 E. Warner Ave. Suite 1-D, Santa Ana, CA 92705/714-261-6611; FAX: 714-756-0133
Empire Cutlery Corp., 12 Kruger Ct., Clifton, NJ 07013/201-472-5155; FAX: 201-779-0759

29th EDITION, 1997 **319**

DIRECTORY OF THE ARMS TRADE

Engineered Accessories, 1307 W. Wabash Ave., Effingham, IL 62401/217-347-7700; FAX: 217-347-7737
English, Inc., A.G., 708 S. 12th St., Broken Arrow, OK 74012/918-251-3399
Englishtown Sporting Goods Co., Inc., David J. Maxham, 38 Main St., Englishtown, NJ 07726/201-446-7717
Engraving Artistry, 36 Alto Rd., RFD 2, Burlington, CT 06013/203-673-6837
Enguix Import-Export, Alpujarras 58, Alzira, Valencia, SPAIN 46600/(96) 241 43 95; FAX: (96) (241 43 95) 240 21 53
Enhanced Presentations, Inc., 5929 Market St., Wilmington, NC 28405/910-799-1622; FAX: 910-799-5004
Enlow, Charles, 895 Box, Beaver, OK 73932/405-625-4487
Ensign-Bickford Co., The, 660 Hopmeadow St., Simsbury, CT 06070
EPC, 1441 Manatt St., Lincoln, NE 68521/402-476-3946
Epps, Ellwood (See "Gramps" Antique Cartridges)
Erhardt, Dennis, 3280 Green Meadow Dr., Helena, MT 59601/406-442-4533
Erickson's Mfg., C.W., Inc., 530 Garrison Ave. N.E., P.O. Box 522, Buffalo, MN 55313/612-682-3665; FAX: 612-642-4328
Erma Werke GmbH, Johan Ziegler St., 13/15/FeldiglSt., D-8060 Dachau, GERMANY (U.S. importers—Amtec 2000, Inc.; Mandall Shooting Supplies, Inc.)
Eskridge Rifles, Steven Eskridge, 218 N. Emerson, Mart, TX 76664/817-876-3544
Essex Arms, P.O. Box 345, Island Pond, VT 05846/802-723-4313
Essex Metals, 1000 Brighton St., Union, NJ 07083/800-282-8369
Estate Cartridge, Inc., 12161 FM 830, Willis, TX 77378/409-856-7277; FAX: 409-856-5486
Euber Bullets, No. Orwell Rd., Orwell, VT 05760/802-948-2621
Euroarms of America, Inc., P.O. Box 3277, Winchester, VA 22604/540-662-1863; FAX: 540-662-4464
European American Armory Corp. (See E.A.A. Corp.)
Europtik Ltd., P.O. Box 319, Dunmore, PA 18512/717-347-6049; FAX: 717-969-4330
Eutaw Co., Inc., The, P.O. Box 608, U.S. Hwy. 176 West, Holly Hill, SC 29059/803-496-3341
Evans, Andrew, 2325 NW Squire St., Albany, OR 97321/541-928-3190; FAX: 541-928-4128
Evans Engraving, Robert, 332 Vine St., Oregon City, OR 97045/503-656-5693
Evans Gunsmithing (See Evans, Andrew)
Eversull Co., Inc., K., 1 Tracemont, Boyce, LA 71409/318-793-8728; FAX: 318-793-5483
Excalibur Enterprises, P.O. Box 400, Fogelsville, PA 18051-0400/610-391-9105; FAX: 610-391-9223
Exe, Inc., 18830 Partridge Circle, Eden Prairie, MN 55346/612-944-7662
Executive Protection Institute, Rt. 2, Box 3645, Berryville, VA 22611/540-955-1128
Eyears, Roland C., 576 Binns Blvd., Columbus, OH 43204-2441
Eyster Heritage Gunsmiths, Inc., Ken, 6441 Bishop Rd., Centerburg, OH 43011/614-625-6131
Eze-Lap Diamond Prods., P.O. Box 2229, 15164 Weststate St., Westminster, CA 92683/714-847-1555; FAX: 714-897-0280
E-Z-Way Systems, P.O. Box 4310, Newark, OH 43058-4310/614-345-6645, 800-848-2072; FAX: 614-345-6600

F

F&A Inc., 50 Elm St., Richfield Springs, NY 13439/315-858-1470; FAX: 315-858-2969
Fabarm S.p.A., Via Averolda 31, 25039 Travagliato, Brescia, ITALY/030-6863629; FAX: 030-6863684 (U.S. importer—Ithaca Acquisition Corp.)
Fabian Bros. Sporting Goods, Inc., 1510 Morena Blvd., Suite "G", San Diego, CA 92110/619-275-0816; FAX: 619-276-8733
Fagan & Co., William, 22952 15 Mile Rd., Clinton Township, MI 48035/313-465-4637; FAX: 313-792-6996
Fair Game International, P.O. Box 77234-34053, Houston, TX 77234/713-941-6269
F.A.I.R. Tecni-Mec s.n.c. di Isidoro Rizzini & C., Via Gitti, 41 Zona Indu, triale/25060 Marcheno (Brescia), ITALY/030-861162-8610344; FAX: 030-8610179
Faith Associates, Inc., 1139 S. Greenville Hwy., Hendersonville, NC 28792/704-692-1916; FAX: 704-697-6827
Fajen, Inc., Reinhart, Route 1, P.O. Box 214-A, Lincoln, MO 65338/816-547-3030; FAX: 816-547-2215
Falcon Pneumatic Systems (See U.S. importer—Airguns-R-Us)
Famas (See U.S. importer—Century International Arms, Inc.)
Fanzoj GmbH, Griesgasse 1, 9170 Ferlach, AUSTRIA 9170/(43) 04227-2283; FAX: (43) 04227-2867
Far North Outfitters, Box 1252, Bethel, AK 99559
Farm Form Decoys, Inc., 1602 Biovu, P.O. Box 748, Galveston, TX 77553/409-744-0762, 409-765-6361; FAX: 409-765-8513
Farmer-Dressel, Sharon, 209 N. 92nd Ave., Yakima, WA 98908/509-966-9233; FAX: 509-966-3365
Farr Studio, Inc., 1231 Robinhood Rd., Greeneville, TN 37743/615-638-8825
Farrar Tool Co., Inc., 12150 Bloomfield Ave., Suite E, Santa Fe Springs, CA 90670/310-863-4367; FAX: 310-863-5123
FAS, Via E. Fermi, 8, 20019 Settimo Milanese, Milano, ITALY/02-3285846; FAX: 02-33500196 (U.S. importer—Nygord Precision Products)
Faulhaber Wildlocker, Dipl.-Ing. Norbert Wittasek, Seilergasse 2, A-1010 Wien, AUSTRIA/OM-43-1-5137001; FAX: OM-43-1-5137001
Faulk's Game Call Co., Inc., 616 18th St., Lake Charles, LA 70601/318-436-9726
Faust, Inc., T.G., 544 Minor St., Reading, PA 19602/610-375-8549; FAX: 610-375-4488
Fausti Cav. Stefano & Figlie snc, Via Martiri Dell Indipendenza, 70, Marcheno ITALY 25060 (U.S. importer—American Arms, Inc.)
Fautheree, Andy, P.O. Box 4607, Pagosa Springs, CO 81157/303-731-5003
Feather Flex Decoys, 1655 Swan Lake Rd., Bossier City, LA 71111/318-746-8596; FAX: 318-742-4815
Feather Industries, Inc., 37600 Liberty Dr., Trinidad, CO 81082/719-846-2699; FAX: 719-846-2644
Federal Cartridge Co., 900 Ehlen Dr., Anoka, MN 55303/612-323-2300; FAX: 612-323-2506
Federal Champion Target Co., 232 Industrial Parkway, Richmond, IN 47374/800-441-4971; FAX: 317-966-7747

Federal Engineering Corp., 1090 Bryn Mawr, Bensenville, IL 60106/708-860-1938; FAX: 708-860-2085
Federated-Fry (See Fry Metals)
FEG, Budapest, Soroksariut 158, H-1095 HUNGARY (U.S. importers—Century International Arms, Inc.; K.B.I., Inc.)
Feinwerkbau Westinger & Altenburger GmbH (See FWB)
Feken, Dennis, Rt. 2 Box 124, Perry, OK 73077/405-336-5611
Fellowes, Ted, Beaver Lodge, 9245 16th Ave. SW, Seattle, WA 98106/206-763-1698
Feminine Protection, Inc., 10514 Shady Trail, Dallas, TX 75220/214-351-4500; FAX: 214-352-4686
Ferdinand, Inc., P.O. Box 5, 201 Main St., Harrison, ID 83833/208-689-3012, 800-522-6010 (U.S.A.), 800-258-5266 (Canada); FAX: 208-689-3142
Ferguson, Bill, P.O. Box 1238, Sierra Vista, AZ 85636/520-458-5321; FAX: 520-458-9125
FERLIB, Via Costa 46, 25063 Gardone V.T. (Brescia) ITALY/30-89-12-586; FAX: 30-89-12-586 (U.S. importers—Harry Marx)
Ferris Firearms, 30115 U.S. Hwy. 281 North, Suite 158, Bulverde, TX 78163/210-980-4811
Fibron Products, Inc., P.O. Box 430, Buffalo, NY 14209-0430/716-886-2378; FAX: 716-886-2394
Finch Custom Bullets, 40204 La Rochelle, Prairieville, LA 70769
Fiocchi Munizioni s.p.a. (See U.S. importer—Fiocchi of America, Inc.)
Fiocchi of America, Inc., 5030 Fremont Rd., Ozark, MO 65721/417-725-4118, 800-721-2666; FAX: 417-725-1039
Firearm Training Center, The, 9555 Blandville Rd., West Paducah, KY 42086/502-554-5886
Firearms Academy of Seattle, P.O. Box 2814, Kirkland, WA 98083/206-820-4853
Firearms Co. Ltd./Alpine (See U.S. importer—Mandall Shooting Supplies, Inc.)
Firearms Engraver's Guild of America, 332 Vine St., Oregon City, OR 97045/503-656-5693
Firearms Safety Products, Inc. (See FSPI)
Fire'n Five, P.O. Box 11 Granite Rt., Sumpter, OR 97877
First, Inc., Jack, 1201 Turbine Dr., Rapid City, SD 57701/605-343-9544; FAX: 605-343-9420
Fish, Marshall F., Rt. 22 N., P.O. Box 2439, Westport, NY 12993/518-962-4897
Fisher, Jerry A., 553 Crane Mt. Rd., Big Fork, MT 59911/406-837-2722
Fisher Custom Firearms, 2199 S. Kittredge Way, Aurora, CO 80013/303-755-3710
Fisher Enterprises, Inc., 1071 4th Ave. S., Suite 303, Edmonds, WA 98020-4143/206-771-5382
Fisher, R. Kermit (See Fisher Enterprises, Inc.)
Fitz Pistol Grip Co., P.O. Box 610, Douglas City, CA 96024/916-778-0240
Flaig's, 2200 Evergreen Rd., Millvale, PA 15209/412-821-1717
Flambeau Products Corp., 15981 Valplast Rd., Middlefield, OH 44062/216-632-1631; FAX: 216-632-1581
Flannery Engraving Co., Jeff W., 11034 Riddles Run Rd., Union, KY 41091/606-384-3127
Flashette Co., 4725 S. Kolin Ave., Chicago, IL 60632/312-927-1302; FAX: 312-927-3083
Flayderman & Co., N., Inc., P.O. Box 2446, Ft. Lauderdale, FL 33303/305-761-8855
Fleming Firearms, 7720 E 126th St. N, Collinsville, OK 74021-7016/918-665-3624
Flents Products Co., Inc., P.O. Box 2109, Norwalk, CT 06852/203-866-2581; FAX: 203-854-9322
Flintlocks, Etc. (See Beauchamp & Son, Inc.)
Flitz International Ltd., 821 Mohr Ave., Waterford, WI 53185/414-534-5898; FAX: 414-534-2991
Floatstone Mfg. Co., 106 Powder Mill Rd., P.O. Box 765, Canton, CT 06019/203-693-1977
Flores Publications, Inc., J., P.O. Box 830131, Miami, FL 33283/305-559-4652
Fluoramics, Inc., 18 Industrial Ave., Mahwah, NJ 07430/800-922-0075, 201-825-7035
Flow-Rite of Tennessee, Inc., 107 Allen St., P.O. Box 196, Bruceton, TN 38317/901-586-2271; FAX: 901-586-2300
Flynn's Custom Guns, P.O. Box 7461, Alexandria, LA 71306/318-455-7130
FN Herstal, Voie de Liege 33, Herstal 4040, BELGIUM/(32)41.40.82.83; FAX: (32)41.40.86.79
Fobus International Ltd., Kfar Hess, ISRAEL 40692/972-9-911716; FAX: 972-9-911716
Folks, Donald E., 205 W. Lincoln St., Pontiac, IL 61764/815-844-7901
Foothills Video Productions, Inc., P.O. Box 651, Spartanburg, SC 29304/803-573-7023, 800-782-5358
Ford, Jack, 1430 Elkwood, Missouri City, TX 77489/713-499-9984
Foredom Electric Co., Rt. 6, 16 Stony Hill Rd., Bethel, CT 06801/203-792-8622
Forgett Jr., Valmore J., 689 Bergen Blvd., Ridgefield, NJ 07657/201-945-2500; FAX: 201-945-6859
Forgreens Tool Mfg., Inc., P.O. Box 990, 723 Austin St., Robert Lee, TX 76945/915-453-2800
Forkin, Ben (See Belt MTN Arms)
Forrest, Inc., Tom, P.O. Box 326, Lakeside, CA 92040/619-561-5800; FAX: 619-561-0227
Forrest Tool Co., P.O. Box 768, 44380 Gordon Lane, Mendocino, CA 95460/707-937-2141; FAX: 717-937-1817
Forster, Kathy (See Custom Checkering Service)
Forster, Larry L., P.O. Box 212, 220 First St. NE, Gwinner, ND 58040-0212/701-678-2475
Forster Products, 82 E. Lanark Ave., Lanark, IL 61046/815-493-6360; FAX: 815-493-2371
Fort Hill Gunstocks, 12807 Fort Hill Rd., Hillsboro, OH 45133/513-466-2763
Fort Knox Security Products, 1051 N. Industrial Park Rd., Orem, UT 84057/801-224-7233, 800-821-5216; FAX: 801-226-5493
Fort Worth Firearms, 2006-B Martin Luther King Fwy., Ft. Worth, TX 76104/817-536-0718; FAX: 817-535-0290
Forthofer's Gunsmithing & Knifemaking, 5535 U.S. Hwy 93S, Whitefish, MT 59937-8411/406-862-2674
Fortune Products, Inc., HC04, Box 303, Marble Falls, TX 78654/210-693-6111; FAX: 210-693-6394

MANUFACTURERS' DIRECTORY

Forty Five Ranch Enterprises, Box 1080, Miami, OK 74355-1080/918-542-5875
Fouling Shot, The, 6465 Parfet St., Arvada, CO 80004
Fountain Products, 492 Prospect Ave., West Springfield, MA 01089/413-781-4651; FAX: 413-733-8217
4-D Custom Die Co., 711 N. Sandusky St., P.O. Box 889, Mt. Vernon, OH 43050-0889/614-397-7214; FAX: 614-397-6600
4W Ammunition, Rt. 1, P.O. Box 313, Tioga, TX 76271/817-437-2458; FAX: 817-437-2228
Fowler Bullets, 806 Dogwood Dr., Gastonia, NC 28054/704-867-3259
Fox River Mills, Inc., P.O. Box 298, 227 Poplar St., Osage, IA 50461/515-732-3798; FAX: 515-732-5128
Foy Custom Bullets, 104 Wells Ave., Daleville, AL 36322
Francesca, Inc., 3115 Old Ranch Rd., San Antonio, TX 78217/512-826-2584; FAX: 512-826-8211
Franchi S.p.A., Via del Serpente, 12, 25131 Brescia, ITALY/030-3581833; FAX: 030-3581554 (U.S. importer—American Arms, Inc.)
Francolini, Leonard, 106 Powder Mill Rd., P.O. Box 765, Canton, CT 06019/203-693-1977
Francotte & Cie S.A., Auguste, rue du Trois Juin 109, 4400 Herstal-Liege, BELGIUM/41-48.13.18; FAX: 32-41-48-11-70 (U.S. importer—Armes de Chasse)
Frank Custom Classic Arms, Ron, 7131 Richland Rd., Ft. Worth, TX 76118/817-284-9300; FAX: 817-284-9300
Frank Knives, Box 984, Whitefish, MT 59937/406-862-2681; FAX: 406-862-2681
Frankonia Jagd, Hofmann & Co., D-97064 Wurzburg, GERMANY/09302-200; FAX: 09302-20200
Frazier Brothers Enterprises, 1118 N. Main St., Franklin, IN 46131/317-736-4000; FAX: 317-736-4000
Freedom Arms, Inc., P.O. Box 1776, Freedom, WY 83120/307-883-2468, 800-833-4432 (orders only); FAX: 307-883-2005
Freeman Animal Targets, 5519 East County Road, 100 South, Plainsfield, IN 46168/317-487-9482; FAX: 317-487-9671
Fremont Tool Works, 1214 Prairie, Ford, KS 67842/316-369-2327
French, J.R., 1712 Creek Ridge Ct., Irving, TX 75060/214-254-2654
Frielich Police Equipment, 211 East 21st St., New York, NY 10010/212-254-3045
From Jena (See Europtik Ltd.)
Frontier, 2910 San Bernardo, Laredo, TX 78040/210-723-5409; FAX: 210-723-1774
Frontier Arms Co., Inc., 401 W. Rio Santa Cruz, Green Valley, AZ 85614-3932
Frontier Products Co., 164 E. Longview Ave., Columbus, OH 43202/614-262-9357
Frontier Safe Co., 3201 S. Clinton St., Fort Wayne, IN 46806/219-744-7233; FAX: 219-744-6678
Frost Cutlery Co., P.O. Box 22636, Chattanooga, TN 37422/615-894-6079; FAX: 615-894-9576
Fry Metals, 4100 6th Ave., Altoona, PA 16602/814-946-1611
FSPI, 5885 Glenridge Dr. Suite 220A, Atlanta, GA 30328/404-843-2881; FAX: 404-843-0271
Fujinon, Inc., 10 High Point Dr., Wayne, NJ 07470/201-633-5600; FAX: 201-633-5216
Fullmer, Geo. M., 2499 Mavis St., Oakland, CA 94601/510-533-4193
Fulmer's Antique Firearms, Chet, P.O. Box 792, Rt. 2 Buffalo Lake, Detroit Lakes, MN 56501/218-847-7712
Fulton Armory, 8725 Bollman Place No. 1, Savage, MD 20763/301-490-9485; FAX: 301-490-9547
Furr Arms, 91 N. 970 W., Orem, UT 84057/801-226-3877; FAX: 801-226-3877
Fury Cutlery, 801 Broad Ave., Ridgefield, NJ 07657/201-943-5920; FAX: 201-943-1579
Fusilier Bullets, 10010 N. 6000 W., Highland, UT 84003/801-756-6813
FWB, Neckarstrasse 43, 78727 Oberndorf a. N., GERMANY/07423-814-0; FAX: 07423-814-89 (U.S. importer—Beeman Precision Airguns)

G

G3 & Co., 18 Old Northville Rd., New Milford, CT 06776/203-354-7500
G96 Products Co., Inc., River St. Station, P.O. Box 1684, Paterson, NJ 07544/201-684-4050; FAX: 201-684-3848
G&C Bullet Co., Inc., 8835 Thornton Rd., Stockton, CA 95209/209-477-6479; FAX: 209-477-2813
G&H Decoys, Inc., P.O. Box 1208, Hwy. 75 North, Henryetta, OK 74437/918-652-3314; FAX: 918-652-3400
Gage Manufacturing, 663 W. 7th St., San Pedro, CA 90731
Gaillard Barrels, P.O. Box 21, Pathlow, Sask., S0K 3B0 CANADA/306-752-3769; FAX: 306-752-5969
Galati International, P.O. Box 326, Catawissa, MO 63015/314-257-4837; FAX: 314-257-2268
Galaxy Imports Ltd., Inc., P.O. Box 3361, Victoria, TX 77903/512-573-4867; FAX: 512-576-9622
Galazan, P.O. Box 1692, New Britain, CT 06051-1692/203-225-6581; FAX: 203-832-8707
GALCO International Ltd., 2019 W. Quail Ave., Phoenix, AZ 85027/602-258-8295, 800-874-2526; FAX: 602-582-6854
Gamba-Societa Armi Bresciane Srl., Renato, Via Artigiani, 93, 25063 Gardone Val Trompia (BS), ITALY/30-8911640; FAX: 30-8911648 (U.S. importer—The First National Gun Bank Corp.)
Gamba, USA, P.O. Box 60452, Colorado Springs, CO 80960/719-578-1145; FAX: 719-444-0731
Game Haven Gunstocks, 13750 Shire Rd., Wolverine, MI 49799/616-525-8257
Game Winner, Inc., 2625 Cumberland Parkway, Suite 220, Atlanta, GA 30339/770-434-9210; FAX: 770-434-9215
Gammog, Gregory B. Gally, 14608 Old Gunpowder Rd., Laurel, MD 20707-3131/301-725-3838
Gamo (See U.S. importers—Daisy Mfg. Co.; Dynamit Nobel-RWS, Inc.)
Gamo USA, Inc., 3721 S.W. 47th Ave., Suite 304, Ft. Lauderdale, FL 33314
Gander Mountain, Inc., P.O. Box 128, Hwy. "W", Wilmot, WI 53192/414-862-2331,Ext. 6425
GAR, 590 McBride Avenue, West Paterson, NJ 07424/201-754-1114; FAX: 201-742-2897
Garbi, Armas Urki, 12-14, 20.600 Eibar (Guipuzcoa) SPAIN/43-11 38 73 (U.S. importer—Moore & Co., Wm. Larkin)

Garcia National Gun Traders, Inc., 225 SW 22nd Ave., Miami, FL 33135/305-642-2355
Garrett Cartridges, Inc., P.O. Box 178, Chehalis, WA 98532/360-736-0702
Garthwaite, Jim, Rt. 2, Box 310, Watsontown, PA 17777/717-538-1566
Gator Guns & Repair, 6255 Spur Hwy., Kenai, AK 99611/907-283-7947
Gaucher Armes, S.A., 46, rue Desjoyaux, 42000 Saint-Etienne, FRANCE/77 33 38 92; FAX: 77 61 95 72
G.B.C. Industries, Inc., P.O. Box 1602, Spring, TX 77373/713-350-9690; FAX: 713-350-0601
G.C.C.T., 4455 Torrance Blvd., Ste. 453, Torrance, CA 90509-2806
GDL Enterprises, 409 Le Gardeur, Slidell, LA 70460/504-649-0693
Gehmann, Walter (See Huntington Die Specialties)
Genco, P.O. Box 5704, Asheville, NC 28803
Genecco Gun Works, K., 10512 Lower Sacramento Rd., Stockton, CA 95210/209-951-0706
General Lead, Inc., 1022 Grand Ave., Phoenix, AZ 85007
Gene's Custom Guns, P.O. Box 10534, White Bear Lake, MN 55110/612-429-5105
Gentex Corp., 5 Tinkham Ave., Derry, NH 03038/603-434-0311; FAX: 603-434-3002
Gentner Bullets, 109 Woodlawn Ave., Upper Darby, PA 19082/610-352-9396
Gentry Custom Gunmaker, David, 314 N. Hoffman, Belgrade, MT 59714/406-388-GUNS
George & Roy's, 2950 NW 29th, Portland, OR 97210/503-228-5424, 800-553-3022; FAX: 503-225-9409
George, Tim, Rt. 1, P.O. Box 45, Evington, VA 24550/804-821-8117
Gerber Legendary Blades, 14200 SW 72nd Ave., Portland, OR 97223/503-639-6161, 800-950-6161; FAX: 503-684-7008
Gervais, Mike, 3804 S. Cruise Dr., Salt Lake City, UT 84109/801-277-7729
Getz Barrel Co., P.O. Box 88, Beavertown, PA 17813/717-658-7263
GFR Corp., P.O. Box 1439, New London, NH 03257-1439
G.G. & G., 3602 E. 42nd Stravenue, Tucson, AZ 85713/520-748-7167; FAX: 520-748-7583
G.H. Enterprises Ltd., Bag 10, Okotoks, Alberta T0L 1T0 CANADA/403-938-6070
Giacomo Sporting USA, 6234 Stokes Lee Center Rd., Lee Center, NY 13363
Gibbs Rifle Co., Inc., Cannon Hill Industrial Park, Rt. 2, Box 214 Hoffman, Rd./Martinsburg, WV 25401 304-274-0458; FAX: 304-274-0078
Gilbert Equipment Co., Inc., 960 Downtowner Rd., Mobile, AL 36609/205-344-3322
Gillmann, Edwin, 33 Valley View Dr., Hanover, PA 17331/717-632-1662
Gilman-Mayfield, Inc., 3279 E. Shields, Fresno, CA 93703/209-221-9415; FAX: 209-221-9419
Gilmore Sports Concepts, 5949 S. Garnett, Tulsa, OK 74146/918-250-4867; FAX: 918-250-3845
Giron, Robert E., 1328 Pocono St., Pittsburgh, PA 15218/412-731-6041
Glacier Glove, 4890 Aircenter Circle, Suite 210, Reno, NV 89502/702-825-8225; FAX: 702-825-6544
Glaser Safety Slug, Inc., P.O. Box 8223, Foster City, CA 94404-8223/800-221-3489, 415-345-7677; FAX: 415-345-8217
Glass, Herb, P.O. Box 25, Bullville, NY 10915/914-361-3021
Glimm, Jerome C., 19 S. Maryland, Conrad, MT 59425/406-278-3574
Glock GmbH, P.O. Box 50, A-2232 Deutsch Wagram, AUSTRIA (U.S. importer—Glock, Inc.)
Glock, Inc., P.O. Box 369, Smyrna, GA 30081/770-432-1202; FAX: 770-433-8719
GML Products, Inc., 394 Laredo Dr., Birmingham, AL 35226/205-979-4867
Gner's Hard Cast Bullets, 1107 11th St., LaGrande, OR 97850/503-963-8796
Goddard, Allen, 716 Medford Ave., Hayward, CA 94541/510-276-6830
Goens, Dale W., P.O. Box 224, Cedar Crest, NM 87008/505-281-5419
Goergen's Gun Shop, Inc., Rt. 2, Box 182BB, Austin, MN 55912/507-433-9280
GOEX, Inc., 1002 Springbrook Ave., Moosic, PA 18507/717-457-6724; FAX: 717-457-1130
Goldcoast Reloaders, Inc., 2421 NE 4th Ave., Pompano Beach, FL 33064/305-783-4849
Golden Age Arms Co., 115 E. High St., Ashley, OH 43003/614-747-2488
Golden Bear Bullets, 3065 Fairfax Ave., San Jose, CA 95148/408-238-9515
Gonic Arms, Inc., 134 Flagg Rd., Gonic, NH 03839/603-332-8456, 603-332-8457
Gonic Bullet Works, P.O. Box 7365, Gonic, NH 03839
Gonzalez Guns, Ramon B., P.O. Box 370, Monticello, NY 12701/914-794-4515
Goodling's Gunsmithing, R.D. 1, Box 1097, Spring Grove, PA 17362/717-225-3350
Goodwin, Fred, Silver Ridge Gun Shop, Sherman Mills, ME 04776/207-365-4451
Gordie's Gun Shop, 1401 Fulton St., Streator, IL 61364/815-672-7202
Gotz Bullets, 7313 Rogers St., Rockford, IL 61111
Goudy Classic Stocks, Gary, 263 Hedge Rd., Menlo Park, CA 94025-1711/415-322-1338
Gould & Goodrich, P.O. Box 1479, Lillington, NC 27546/910-893-2071; FAX: 910-893-4742
Gournet, Geoffroy, 820 Paxinosa Ave., Easton, PA 18042/215-559-0710
Gozon Corp., U.S.A., P.O. Box 6278, Folson, CA 95763/916-983-2026; FAX: 916-983-9500
Grace, Charles E., 6943 85.5 Rd., Trinchera, CO 81081/719-846-9435
Grace Metal Products, Inc., P.O. Box 67, Elk Rapids, MI 49629/616-264-8133
"Gramps" Antique Cartridges, Box 341, Washago, Ont. L0K 2B0 CANADA/705-689-5348
Grand Falls Bullets, Inc., P.O. Box 720, 803 Arnold Wallen Way, Stockton, MO 65785/816-229-0112
Granite Custom Bullets, Box 190, Philipsburg, MT 59858/406-859-3245
Grant, Howard V., Hiawatha 15, Woodruff, WI 54568/715-356-7146
Graphics Direct, P.O. Box 372421, Reseda, CA 91337-2421/818-344-9002
Graves Co., 1800 Andrews Ave., Pompano Beach, FL 33069/800-327-9103; FAX: 305-960-0301
Grayback Wildcats, 5306 Bryant Ave., Klamath Falls, OR 97603/541-884-1072
Graybill's Gun Shop, 1035 Ironville Pike, Columbia, PA 17512/717-684-2739
Great 870 Co., The, P.O. Box 6309, El Monte, CA 91734
Great American Gun Co., 3420 Industrial Drive, Yuba City, CA 95993/916-671-4570
Great Lakes Airguns, 6175 S. Park Ave., Hamburg, NY 14075/716-648-6666; FAX: 716-648-5279

DIRECTORY OF THE ARMS TRADE

Green, Arthur S., 485 S. Robertson Blvd., Beverly Hills, CA 90211/310-274-1283
Green Bay Bullets, 1638 Hazelwood Dr., Sobieski, WI 54171/414-826-7760
Green Genie, Box 114, Cusseta, GA 31805
Green Head Game Call Co., RR 1, Box 33, Lacon, IL 61540/309-246-2155
Green Mountain Rifle Barrel Co., Inc., P.O. Box 2670, 153 West Main St., Conway, NH 03818/603-447-1095; FAX: 603-447-1099
Green, Roger M., P.O. Box 984, 435 E. Birch, Glenrock, WY 82637/307-436-9804
Greene Precision Duplicators, M.L. Greene Engineering Services, P.O. Box, 1150/Golden, CO 80402-1150/303-279-2383
Greenwald, Leon E. "Bud", 2553 S. Quitman St., Denver, CO 80219/303-935-3850
Greenwood Precision, P.O. Box 468, Nixa, MO 65714-0468/417-725-2330
Greg Gunsmithing Repair, 3732 26th Ave. North, Robbinsdale, MN 55422/612-529-8103
Greg's Superior Products, P.O. Box 46219, Seattle, WA 98146
Greider Precision, 431 Santa Marina Ct., Escondido, CA 92029/619-480-8892
Gremmel Enterprises, 2111 Carriage Drive, Eugene, OR 97408-7537/541-302-3000
Grier's Hard Cast Bullets, 1107 11th St., LaGrande, OR 97850/503-963-8796
Griffin & Howe, Inc., 33 Claremont Rd., Bernardsville, NJ 07924/908-766-2287; FAX: 908-766-1068
Griffin & Howe, Inc., 36 W. 44th St., Suite 1011, New York, NY 10036/212-921-0980
Grifon, Inc., 58 Guinam St., Waltham, MS 02154
Grizzly Bullets, 322 Green Mountain Rd., Trout Creek, MT 59874/406-847-2627
Groenewold, John, P.O. Box 830, Mundelein, IL 60060/708-566-2365
Group Tight Bullets, 482 Comerwood Court, San Francisco, CA 94080/415-583-1550
GRS Corp., Glendo, P.O. Box 1153, 900 Overlander St., Emporia, KS 66801/316-343-1084, 800-835-3519
Grulla Armes, Apartado 453, Avda Otaloa, 12, Eiber, SPAIN (U.S. importer—American Arms, Inc.)
GSI, Inc., 108 Morrow Ave., P.O. Box 129, Trussville, AL 35173/205-655-8299; FAX: 205-655-7078
GSS Scheller (See U.S. importer—American Bullets)
GTM, 15915B E. Main St., La Puente, CA 91744
Guardsman Products, 411 N. Darling, Fremont, MI 49412/616-924-3950
Gun Accessories (See Glaser Safety Slug, Inc.)
Gun-Alert, 1010 N. Maclay Ave., San Fernando, CA 91340/818-365-0864; FAX: 818-365-1308
Gun City, 212 W. Main Ave., Bismarck, ND 58501/701-223-2304
Gun Doctor, The, 435 East Maple, Roselle, IL 60172/708-894-0668
Gun Doctor, The, P.O. Box 39242, Downey, CA 90242/310-862-3158
Gun-Ho Sports Cases, 110 E. 10th St., St. Paul, MN 55101/612-224-9491
Gun Hunter Books, Div. of Gun Hunter Trading Co., 5075 Heisig St., Beaumont, TX 77705/409-835-3006
Gun Leather Limited, 116 Lipscomb, Ft. Worth, TX 76104/817-334-0225; 800-247-0609
Gun List (See Krause Publications, Inc.)
Gun Locker, Div. of Airmold, W.R. Grace & Co.-Conn., Becker Farms Ind. Park,, P.O. Box 610/Roanoke Rapids, NC 27870/800-344-5716; FAX: 919-536-2201
Gun Parts Corp., The, 226 Williams Lane, West Hurley, NY 12491/914-679-2417; FAX: 914-679-5849
Gun Room, The, 1121 Burlington, Muncie, IN 47302/317-282-9073; FAX: 317-282-5270
Gun Room Press, The, 127 Raritan Ave., Highland Park, NJ 08904/908-545-4344; FAX: 908-545-6686
Gun Shop, The, 5550 S. 900 East, Salt Lake City, UT 84117/801-263-3633
Gun Shop, The, 62778 Spring Creek Rd., Montrose, CO 81401
Gun South, Inc. (See GSI, Inc.)
Gun-Tec, P.O. Box 8125, W. Palm Beach, FL 33407
Gun Works, The, 247 S. 2nd, Springfield, OR 97477/541-741-4118; FAX: 541-988-1097
Guncraft Books (See Guncraft Sports, Inc.)
Guncraft Sports, Inc., 10737 Dutchtown Rd., Knoxville, TN 37932/423-966-4545; FAX: 423-966-4500
Gunfitters, The, P.O. 426, Cambridge, WI 53523-0426/608-764-8128
Gunline Tools, 2950 Saturn St., Suite O, Brea, CA 92621/714-993-5100; FAX: 714-572-4128
Gunnerman Books, P.O. Box 214292, Auburn Hills, MI 48321/810-879-2779
Guns, 81 E. Streetsboro St., Hudson, OH 44236/216-650-4563
Guns Antique & Modern DBA/Charles E. Duffy, Williams Lane, West Hurley, NY 12491/914-679-2997
Guns, Div. of D.C. Engineering, Inc., 8633 Southfield Fwy., Detroit, MI 48228/313-271-7111, 800-886-7623 (orders only); FAX: 313-271-7112
GUNS Magazine, 591 Camino de la Reina, Suite 200, San Diego, CA 92108/619-297-5350; FAX: 619-297-5353
Gunsight, The, 1712 North Placentia Ave., Fullerton, CA 92631
Gunsite Custom Shop, P.O. Box 451, Paulden, AZ 86334/520-636-4104; FAX: 520-636-1236
Gunsite Gunsmithy (See Gunsite Custom Shop)
Gunsite Training Center, P.O. Box 700, Paulden, AZ 86334/520-636-4565; FAX: 520-636-1236
Gunsmith in Elk River, The, 14021 Victoria Lane, Elk River, MN 55330/612-441-7761
Gunsmithing, Inc., 208 West Buchanan St., Colorado Springs, CO 80907/719-632-3795; FAX: 719-632-3493
Gunsmithing Ltd., 57 Unquowa Rd., Fairfield, CT 06430/203-254-0436; FAX: 203-254-1535
Gurney, F.R., Box 13, Sooke, BC V0S 1N0 CANADA/604-642-5282: FAX: 604-642-7859
Gusdorf Corp., 11440 Lackland Rd., St. Louis, MO 63146/314-567-5249
Gusty Winds Corp., 2950 Bear St., Suite 120, Costa Mesa, CA 92626/714-536-3587
Gutmann Cutlery Inc., 1100 W. 45th Ave., Denver, CO 80211/303-433-6506
Gwinnell, Bryson J., P.O. Box 248C, Maple Hill Rd., Rochester, VT 05767/802-767-3664
GZ Paintball Sports Products (See GFR Corp.)

H

H&B Forge Co., Rt. 2 Geisinger Rd., Shiloh, OH 44878/419-895-1856
H&P Publishing, 7174 Hoffman Rd., San Angelo, TX 76905/915-655-5953
H&R 1871, Inc., 60 Industrial Rowe, Gardner, MA 01440/508-632-9393; FAX: 508-632-2300
H&S Liner Service, 515 E. 8th, Odessa, TX 79761/915-332-1021
Hafner Creations, Inc., P.O. Box 1987, Lake City, FL 32055/904-755-6481; FAX: 904-755-6595
Hagn Rifles & Actions, Martin, P.O. Box 444, Cranbrook, B.C. V1C 4H9, CANADA/604-489-4861
Hakko Co. Ltd., Daini-Tsunemi Bldg., 1-13-12, Narimasu, Itabashiku Tokyo 175, JAPAN/03-5997-7870/2; FAX: 81-3-5997-7840
Hale/Engraver, Peter, 800 E. Canyon Rd., Spanish Fork, UT 84660/801-798-8215
Half Moon Rifle Shop, 490 Halfmoon Rd., Columbia Falls, MT 59912/406-892-4409
Hall Manufacturing, 1801 Yellow Leaf Rd., Clanton, AL 35045/205-755-4094
Hall Plastics, Inc., John, P.O. Box 1526, Alvin, TX 77512/713-489-8709
Hallberg Gunsmith, Fritz, 33 S. Main, Payette, ID 83661/208-642-7157; FAX: 208-642-9643
Hallowell & Co., 340 W. Putnam Ave., Greenwich, CT 06830/203-869-2190; FAX: 203-869-0692
Hally Caller, 443 Wells Rd., Doylestown, PA 18901/215-345-6354
Halstead, Rick, RR4, Box 272, Miami, OK 74354/918-540-0933
Hamilton, Alex B. (See Ten-Ring Precision, Inc.)
Hamilton, Keith, P.O. Box 871, Gridley, CA 95948/916-846-2316
Hammans, Charles E., P.O. Box 788, 2022 McCracken, Stuttgart, AR 72106/501-673-1388
Hammerli USA, 19296 Oak Grove Circle, Groveland, CA 95321/209-962-5311; FAX: 209-962-5931
Hammerli Ltd., Seonerstrasse 37, CH-5600 Lenzburg, SWITZERLAND/064-50 11 44; FAX: 064-51 38 27 (U.S. importer—Hammerli USA)
Hammets VLD Bullets, P.O. Box 479, Rayville, LA 71269/318-728-2019
Hammond Custom Guns Ltd., Guy, 619 S. Pandora, Gilbert, AZ 85234/602-892-3437
Hammonds Rifles, RD 4, Box 504, Red Lion, PA 17356/717-244-7879
Handgun Press, P.O. Box 406, Glenview, IL 60025/847-657-6500; FAX: 847-724-8831
HandiCrafts Unltd. (See Clements' Custom Leathercraft, Chas)
Hands Engraving, Barry Lee, 26192 E. Shore Route, Bigfork, MT 59911/406-837-0035
Hank's Gun Shop, Box 370, 50 West 100 South, Monroe, UT 84754/801-527-4456
Hanned Line, The, P.O. Box 2387, Cupertino, CA 95015-2387
Hanned Precision (See Hanned Line, The)
Hansen & Co. (See Hansen Cartridge Co.)
Hansen Cartridge Co., 244-246 Old Post Rd., Southport, CT 06490/203-259-6222, 203-259-7337; FAX: 203-254-3832
Hanson's Gun Center, Dick, 233 Everett Dr., Colorado Springs, CO 80911
Hanusin, John, 3306 Commercial, Northbrook, IL 60062/708-564-2706
Hardin Specialty Dist., P.O. Box 338, Radcliff, KY 40159-0338/502-351-6649
Hardison, Charles, P.O. Box 356, 200 W. Baseline Rd., Lafayette, CO 80026-0356/303-666-5171
Harold's Custom Gun Shop, Inc., Broughton Rifle Barrels, Rt. 1, Box 447, Big Spring, TX 79720/915-394-4430
Harper, William E. (See Great 870 Co., The)
Harper's Custom Stocks, 928 Lombrano St., San Antonio, TX 78207/512-732-5780
Harrell's Precision, 5756 Hickory Dr., Salem, VA 24133/703-380-2683
Harrington & Richardson (See H&R 1871, Inc.)
Harrington Cutlery, Inc., Russell, Subs. of Hyde Mfg. Co., 44 River St., Southbridge, MA 01550/617-765-0201
Harris Engineering, Inc., Rt. 1, Barlow, KY 42024/502-334-3633; FAX: 502-334-3000
Harris Enterprises, P.O. Box 105, Bly, OR 97622/503-353-2625
Harris Gunworks, 3840 N. 28th Ave., Phoenix, AZ 85017-4733/602-230-1414; FAX: 602-230-1422
Harris Hand Engraving, Paul A., 10630 Janet Lee, San Antonio, TX 78230/512-391-5121
Harris Publications, 1115 Broadway, New York, NY 10010/212-807-7100; FAX: 212-627-4678
Harrison Bullets, 6437 E. Hobart St., Mesa, AZ 85205
Harrison-Hurtz Enterprises, Inc., P.O. Box 268, RR1, Wymore, NE 68466/402-645-3378; FAX: 402-645-3606
Hart & Son, Inc., Robert W., 401 Montgomery St., Nescopeck, PA 18635/717-752-3655, 800-368-3656; FAX: 717-752-1088
Hart Rifle Barrels, Inc., P.O. Box 182, 1690 Apulia Rd., Lafayette, NY 13084/315-677-9841; FAX: 315-677-9610
Hartford (See U.S. importer— EMF Co., Inc.)
Hartmann & Weiss GmbH, Rahlstedter Bahnhofstr. 47, 22143 Hamburg, GERMANY/(40) 677 55 85; FAX: (40) 677 55 92
Harvey, Frank, 218 Nightfall, Terrace, NV 89015/702-558-6998
Harwood, Jack O., 1191 S. Pendlebury Lane, Blackfoot, ID 83221/208-785-5368
Haselbauer Products, Jerry, P.O. Box 27629, Tucson, AZ 85726/602-792-1075
Hastings Barrels, 320 Court St., Clay Center, KS 67432/913-632-3169; FAX: 913-632-6554
Hatfield Gun Co., Inc., 224 N. 4th St., St. Joseph, MO 64501/816-279-8688; FAX: 816-279-2716
Hawk, Inc., 849 Hawks Bridge Rd., Salem, NJ 08079/609-299-2700; FAX: 609-299-2800
Hawk Laboratories, Inc. (See Hawk, Inc.)
Hawken Shop, The (See Dayton Traister)
Haydel's Game Calls, Inc., 5018 Hazel Jones Rd., Bossier City, LA 71111/318-746-3586, 800-HAYDELS; FAX: 318-746-3711
Haydon Shooters' Supply, Russ, 15018 Goodrich Dr. NW, Gig Harbor, WA 98329/206-857-7557
Heatbath Corp., P.O. Box 2978, Springfield, MA 01101/413-543-3381
Hebard Guns, Gil, 125-129 Public Square, Knoxville, IL 61448
HEBB Resources, P.O. Box 999, Mead, WA 99021-09996/509-466-1292
Hecht, Hubert J., Waffen-Hecht, P.O. Box 2635, Fair Oaks, CA 95628/916-966-1020

MANUFACTURERS' DIRECTORY

Heckler & Koch GmbH, P.O. Box 1329, 78722 Oberndorf, Neckar, GERMANY/49-7423179-0; FAX: 49-7423179-2406 (U.S. importer—Heckler & Koch, Inc.)
Heckler & Koch, Inc., 21480 Pacific Blvd., Sterling, VA 20166-8903/703-450-1900; FAX: 703-450-8160
Hege Jagd-u. Sporthandels, GmbH, P.O. Box 101461, W-7770 Ueberlingen a. Bodensee, GERMANY
Heidenstrom Bullets, Urds GT 1 Heroya, 3900 Porsgrunn, NORWAY
Heilmann, Stephen, P.O. Box 657, Grass Valley, CA 95945/916-272-8758
Heinie Specialty Products, 301 Oak St., Quincy, IL 62301-2500/309-543-4535; FAX: 309-543-2521
Heintz, David, 800 N. Hwy. 17, Moffat, CO 81143/719-256-4194
Hellweg Ltd., 40356 Oak Park Way, Suite H, Oakhurst, CA 93644/209-683-3030; FAX: 209-683-3422
Helwan (See U.S. importer—Interarms)
Henckels Zwillingswerk, Inc., J.A., 9 Skyline Dr., Hawthorne, NY 10532/914-592-7370
Hendricks, Frank E., Master Engravers, Inc., HC03, Box 434, Dripping Springs, TX 78620/512-858-7828
Hendricks Gun Works, 1162 Gillionville Rd., Albany, GA 31707/912-439-2003
Henigson & Associates, Steve, 2049 Kerwood Ave., Los Angeles, CA 90025/213-305-8288
Henriksen Tool Co., Inc., 8515 Wagner Creek Rd., Talent, OR 97540/541-535-2309
Hensler, Jerry, 6614 Country Field, San Antonio, TX 78240/210-690-7491
Hensley & Gibbs, Box 10, Murphy, OR 97533/541-862-2341
Hensley, Darwin, P.O. Box 329, Brightwood, OR 97011/503-622-5411
Heppler, Keith M., Keith's Custom Gunstocks, 540 Banyan Circle, Walnut Creek, CA 94598/510-934-3509; FAX: 510-934-3143
Heppler's Machining, 2240 Calle Del Mundo, Santa Clara, CA 95054/408-748-9166; FAX: 408-988-7711
Hercules, Inc. (See Alliant Techsystems, Smokeless Powder Group)
Heritage Firearms (See Heritage Manufacturing, Inc.)
Heritage Manufacturing, Inc., 4600 NW 135th St., Opa Locka, FL 33054/305-685-5966; FAX: 305-687-6721
Heritage/VSP Gun Books, P.O. Box 887, McCall, ID 83638/208-634-4104; FAX: 208-634-3101
Hermann Leather Co., H.J., Rt. 1, P.O. Box 525, Skiatook, OK 74070/918-396-1226
Herrett's Stocks, Inc., P.O. Box 741, Twin Falls, ID 83303/208-733-1498
Hertel & Reuss, Werk für Optik und Feinmechanik GmbH, Quellhofstrabe, 67/34 127 Kassel, GERMANY 0561-83006; FAX: 0561-893308
Herter's Manufacturing, Inc., 111 E. Burnett St., P.O. Box 518, Beaver Dam, WI 53916/414-887-1765; FAX: 414-887-8444
Hesco-Meprolight, 2139 Greenville Rd., LaGrange, GA 30240/706-884-7967; FAX: 706-882-4683
Heydenberk, Warren R., 1059 W. Sawmill Rd., Quakertown, PA 18951/215-538-2682
Heym GmbH & Co. KG, Friedrich Wilh, Coburger Str.8, D-97702 Muennerstadt, GERMANY
Hi-Grade Imports, 8655 Monterey Rd., Gilroy, CA 95021/408-842-9301; FAX: 408-842-2374
Hi-Point Firearms, 5990 Philadelphia Dr., Dayton, OH 45415/513-275-4991; FAX: 513-522-8330
Hickman, Jaclyn, Box 1900, Glenrock, WY 82637
Hidalgo, Tony, 12701 SW 9th Pl., Davie, FL 33325/305-476-7645
High Bridge Arms, Inc., 3185 Mission St., San Francisco, CA 94110/415-282-8358
High North Products, Inc., P.O. Box 2, Antigo, WI 54409/715-627-2331
High Performance International, 5734 W. Florist Ave., Milwaukee, WI 53218/414-466-9040
High Standard Mfg. Co., Inc., 4601 S. Pinemont, 148-B, Houston, TX 77041/713-462-4200; FAX: 713-462-6437
High Tech Specialties, Inc., P.O. Box 387R, Adamstown, PA 19501/215-484-0405, 800-231-9385
Highline Machine Co., 654 Lela Place, Grand Junction, CO 81504/970-434-4971
Hill, Loring F., 304 Cedar Rd., Elkins Park, PA 19117
Hill Speed Leather, Ernie, 4507 N. 195th Ave., Litchfield Park, AZ 85340/602-853-9222; FAX: 602-853-9235
Hillmer Custom Gunstocks, Paul D., 7251 Hudson Heights, Hudson, IA 50643/319-988-3941
Hinman Outfitters, Bob, 1217 W. Glen, Peoria, IL 61614/309-691-8132
Hiptmayer, Armurier, RR 112 750, P.O. Box 136, Eastman, Quebec J0E 1P0, CANADA/514-297-2492
Hiptmayer, Heidemarie, RR 112 750, P.O. Box 136, Eastman, Quebec J0E 1P0, CANADA/514-297-2492
Hiptmayer, Klaus, RR 112 750, P.O. Box 136, Eastman, Quebec J0E 1P0, CANADA/514-297-2492
Hirtenberger Aktiengesellschaft, Leobersdorferstrasse 31, A-2552 Hirtenberg, AUSTRIA/43(0)2256 81184; FAX: 43(0)2256 81807
HiTek International, 484 El Camino Real, Redwood City, CA 94063/415-363-1404, 800-54-NIGHT; FAX: 415-363-1408
Hiti-Schuch, Atelier Wilma, A-8863 Predlitz, Pirming Y1 AUSTRIA/0353418278
HJS Arms, Inc., P.O. Box 3711, Brownsville, TX 78523-3711/800-453-2767, 210-542-2767
H.K.S. Products, 7841 Founion Dr., Florence, KY 41042/606-342-7841, 800-354-9814; FAX: 606-342-5865
Hoag, James W., 8523 Canoga Ave., Suite C, Canoga Park, CA 91304/818-998-1510
Hobbie Gunsmithing, Duane A., 2412 Pattie Ave., Wichita, KS 67216/316-264-8166
Hobson Precision Mfg. Co., Rt. 1, Box 220-C, Brent, AL 35034/205-926-4662
Hoch Custom Bullet Moulds (See Colorado Shooter's Supply)
Hodgdon Powder Co., Inc., P.O. Box 2932, 6231 Robinson, Shawnee Mission, KS 66202/913-362-9455; FAX: 913-362-1307; WEB: http://www.unicom.net/hpc
Hodgman, Inc., 1750 Orchard Rd., Montgomery, IL 60538/708-897-7555; FAX: 708-897-7558

Hodgson, Richard, 9081 Tahoe Lane, Boulder, CO 80301
Hoehn Sales, Inc., 75 Greensburg Ct., St. Charles, MO 63304/314-441-4231
Hoelscher, Virgil, 11047 Pope Ave., Lynwood, CA 90262/310-631-8545
Hoenig & Rodman, 6521 Morton Dr., Boise, ID 83704/208-375-1116
Hofer Jagdwaffen, P., Buchsenmachermeister, Kirchgasse 24, A-9170 Ferlach, AUSTRIA/04227-3683
Hoffman New Ideas, 821 Northmoor Rd., Lake Forest, IL 60045/312-234-4075
Hogue Grips, P.O. Box 1138, Paso Robles, CA 93447/800-438-4747, 805-239-1440; FAX: 805-239-2553
Holland & Holland Ltd., 33 Bruton St., London, ENGLAND 1W1/44-171-499-4411; FAX: 44-171-408-7962
Holland, Dick, 422 NE 6th St., Newport, OR 97365/503-265-7556
Holland's, Box 69, Powers, OR 97466/503-439-5155; FAX: 503-439-5155
Hollis Gun Shop, 917 Rex St., Carlsbad, NM 88220/505-885-3782
Hollywood Engineering, 10642 Arminta St., Sun Valley, CA 91352/818-842-8376
Holster Shop, The, 720 N. Flagler Dr., Ft. Lauderdale, FL 33304/305-463-7910; FAX: 305-761-1483
Homak Mfg. Co., Inc., 3800 W. 45th St., Chicago, IL 60632/312-523-3100, FAX: 312-523-9455
Home Shop Machinist, The, Village Press Publications, P.O. Box 1810, Traverse City, MI 49685/800-447-7367; FAX: 616-946-3289
Hondo Ind., 510 S. 52nd St.,l04, Tempe, AZ 85281
Hoover, Harvey, 5750 Pearl Dr., Paradise, CA 95969-4829
Hoppe's Div., Penguin Industries, Inc., Airport Industrial Mall, Coatesville, PA 19320/610-384-6000
Horizons Unlimited, P.O. Box 426, Warm Springs, GA 31830/706-655-3603; FAX: 706-655-3603
Hornady Mfg. Co., P.O. Box 1848, Grand Island, NE 68802/800-338-3220, 308-382-1390; FAX: 308-382-5761
Horseshoe Leather Products, Andy Arratoonian, The Cottage Sharow, Ripon HG4 5BP ENGLAND/44-1765-605858
Horst, Alan K., 3221 2nd Ave. N., Great Falls, MT 59401/406-454-1831
Horton Dist. Co., Inc., Lew, 15 Walkup Dr., Westboro, MA 01581/508-366-7400; FAX: 508-366-5332
House of Muskets, Inc., The, P.O. Box 4640, Pagosa Springs, CO 81157/303-731-2295
Houtz & Barwick, P.O. Box 435, W. Church St., Elizabeth City, NC 27909/800-775-0337, 919-335-4191; FAX: 919-335-1152
Howa Machinery, Ltd., Sukaguchi, Shinkawa-cho, Nishikasugai-gun, Aichi 452, JAPAN (U.S. importer—Interarms)
Howell Machine, 815 1/2 D St., Lewiston, ID 83501/208-743-7418
Hoyt Holster Co., Inc., P.O. Box 69, Coupeville, WA 98239-0069/360-678-6640; FAX: 360-678-6549
H-S Precision, Inc., 1301 Turbine Dr., Rapid City, SD 57701/605-341-3006; FAX: 605-342-8964
HT Bullets, 244 Belleville Rd., New Bedford, MA 02745/508-999-3338
Hubertus Schneidwarenfabrik, P.O. Box 180 106, D-42626 Solingen, GERMANY/01149-212-59-19-94; FAX: 01149-212-59-19-92
Huebner, Corey O., P.O. Box 2074, Missoula, MT 59806-2074/406-721-7168
Huey Gun Cases, P.O. Box 22456, Kansas City, MO 64113/816-444-1637; FAX: 816-444-1637
Hugger Hooks Co., 3900 Easley Way, Golden, CO 80403/303-279-0600
Hughes, Steven Dodd, P.O. Box 545, Livingston, MT 59047/406-222-9377
Hume, Don, P.O. Box 351, Miami, OK 74355/918-542-6604; FAX: 918-542-4340
Hungry Horse Books, 4605 Hwy. 93 South, Whitefish, MT 59937/406-862-7997
Hunkeler, A. (See Buckskin Machine Works)
Hunter Co., Inc., 3300 W. 71st Ave., Westminster, CO 80030/303-427-4626; FAX: 303-428-3980
Hunter's Specialties, Inc., 6000 Huntington Ct. NE, Cedar Rapids, IA 52402-1268/319-395-0321; FAX: 319-395-0326
Hunterjohn, P.O. Box 477, St. Louis, MO 63166/314-531-7250
Hunting Classics Ltd., P.O. Box 2089, Gastonia, NC 28053/704-867-1307; FAX: 704-867-0491
Huntington Die Specialties, 601 Oro Dam Blvd., Oroville, CA 95965/916-534-1210; FAX: 916-534-1212
Hydrosorbent Products, P.O. Box 437, Ashley Falls, MA 01222/413-229-2967; FAX: 413-229-8743
Hyper-Single, Inc., 520 E. Beaver, Jenks, OK 74037/918-299-2391

I

I.A.B. (See U.S. importer—Taylor's & Co., Inc.)
IAI, 6226 Santos Diaz St., Irwindale, CA 91702/818-334-1200
IAR, Inc., 33171 Camino Capistrano, San Juan Capistrano, CA 92675/714-443-3642; FAX: 714-443-3647
Ibberson (Sheffield) Ltd., George, 25-31 Allen St., Sheffield, S3 7AW ENGLAND/0114-2766123; FAX: 0114-2738465
ICI-America, P.O. Box 751, Wilmington, DE 19897/302-575-3000
Idaho Ammunition Service, 2816 Mayfair Dr., Lewiston, ID 83501/208-743-0270; FAX: 208-743-4930
IGA (See U.S. importer—Stoeger Industries)
Illinois Lead Shop, 7742 W. 61st Place, Summit, IL 60501
IMI, P.O. Box 1044, Ramat Hasharon 47100, ISRAEL/972-3-5485222
IMI Services USA, Inc., 2 Wisconsin Circle, Suite 420, Chevy Chase, MD 20815/301-215-4800; FAX: 301-657-1446
Impact Case Co., P.O. Box 9912, Spokane, WA 99209-0912/800-262-3322, 509-467-3303; FAX: 509-326-5436
Imperial (See E-Z-Way Systems)
Imperial Magnum Corp., P.O. Box 249, Oroville, WA 98844/604-495-3131; FAX: 604-495-2816
Imperial Schrade Corp., 7 Schrade Ct., Box 7000, Ellenville, NY 12428/914-647-7601; FAX: 914-647-8701
Import Sports Inc., 1750 Brielle Ave., Unit B1, Wanamassa, NJ 07712/908-493-0302; FAX: 908-493-0301
IMR Powder Co., 1080 Military Turnpike, Suite 2, Plattsburgh, NY 12901/518-563-2253; FAX: 518-563-6916
I.N.C., Inc. (See Kick Eez)
Independent Machine & Gun Shop, 1416 N. Hayes, Pocatello, ID 83201

DIRECTORY OF THE ARMS TRADE

Info-Arm, P.O. Box 1262, Champlain, NY 12919
Ingle, Ralph W., 4 Missing Link, Rossville, GA 30741/404-866-5589
Innovative Weaponry, Inc., 337 Eubank NE, Albuquerque, NM 87123/800-334-3573, 505-296-4645; FAX: 505-271-2633
Innovision Enterprises, 728 Skinner Dr., Kalamazoo, MI 49001/616-382-1681; FAX: 616-382-1830
INTEC International, Inc., P.O. Box 5708, Scottsdale, AZ 85261/602-483-1708
Interarms, 10 Prince St., Alexandria, VA 22314/703-548-1400; FAX: 703-549-7826
Intercontinental Munitions Distributors, Ltd., P.O. Box 815, Beulah, ND 58523/701-948-2260; FAX: 701-948-2282
Intermountain Arms & Tackle, Inc., 1375 E. Fairview Ave., Meridian, ID 83642-1816/208-888-4911; FAX: 208-888-4381
International Shooters Service (See I.S.S.)
Intratec, 12405 SW 130th St., Miami, FL 33186/305-232-1821; FAX: 305-253-7207
Iosso Products, 1485 Lively Blvd., Elk Grove Village, IL 60007/708-437-8400; FAX: 708-437-8478
Iron Bench, 12619 Bailey Rd., Redding, CA 96003/916-241-4623
Iron Mountain Knife Co., P.O. Box 2146, Sparks, NV 89432-2146/702-356-3632; FAX: 702-356-3640
Ironside International Publishers, Inc., P.O. Box 55, 800 Slaters Lane, Alexandria, VA 22313/703-684-6111; FAX: 703-683-5486
Ironsighter Co., P.O. Box 85070, Westland, MI 48185/313-326-8731; FAX: 313-326-3378
Irwin, Campbell H., 140 Hartland Blvd., East Hartland, CT 06027/203-653-3901
Irwindale Arms, Inc. (See IAI)
Island Pond Gun Shop (See Costa, David)
Israel Military Industries Ltd. (See IMI)
I.S.S., P.O. Box 185234, Ft. Worth, TX 76181/817-595-2090
I.S.W., 106 E. Cairo Dr., Tempe, AZ 85282
I.T.S. (See U.S. importer—County Arms)
Ivanoff, Thomas G. (See Tom's Gun Repair)

J

J-4, Inc., 1700 Via Burton, Anaheim, CA 92806/714-254-8315; FAX: 714-956-4421
J&D Components, 75 East 350 North, Orem, UT 84057-4719/801-225-7007
J&J Products, Inc., 9240 Whitmore, El Monte, CA 91731/818-571-5228, 800-927-8361; FAX: 818-571-8704
J&J Sales, 1501 21st Ave. S., Great Falls, MT 59405/406-453-7549
J&L Superior Bullets (See Huntington Die Specialties)
J&R Engineering, P.O. Box 77, 200 Lyons Hill Rd., Athol, MA 01331/508-249-9241
J&R Enterprises, 4550 Scotts Valley Rd., Lakeport, CA 95453
J&S Heat Treat, 803 S. 16th St., Blue Springs, MO 64015/816-229-2149; FAX: 816-228-1135
J.A. Blades, Inc. (See Christopher Firearms Co., Inc., E.)
Jackalope Gun Shop, 1048 S. 5th St., Douglas, WY 82633/307-358-3441
Jaeger, Paul, Inc./Dunn's, P.O. Box 449, 1 Madison Ave., Grand Junction, TN 38039/901-764-6909; FAX: 901-764-6503
JagerSport, Ltd., One Wholesale Way, Cranston, RI 02920/800-962-4867, 401-944-9682; FAX: 401-946-2587
Jamison's Forge Works, 4527 Rd. 6.5 NE, Moses Lake, WA 98837/509-762-2659
Jansma, Jack J. (See Wingshooters, Ltd.)
Jantz Supply, P.O. Box 584-GD, Davis, OK 73030-0584/405-369-2316; FAX: 405-369-3082
Jarrett Rifles, Inc., 383 Brown Rd., Jackson, SC 29831/803-471-3616
Jarvis, Inc., 1123 Cherry Orchard Lane, Hamilton, MT 59840/406-961-4392
JAS, Inc., P.O. Box 0, Rosemount, MN 55068/612-890-7631
Javelina Lube Products, P.O. Box 337, San Bernardino, CA 92402/714-882-5847; FAX: 714-434-6937
J/B Adventures & Safaris, Inc., 2275 E. Arapahoe Rd. Ste. 109, Littleton, CO 80122-1521/303-771-0977
J-B Bore Cleaner, 299 Poplar St., Hamburg, PA 19526/610-562-2103
JBM, P.O. Box 3648, University Park, NM 88003
Jeffredo Gunsight, P.O. Box 669, San Marcos, CA 92079/619-728-2695
Jenco Sales, Inc., P.O. Box 1000, Manchaca, TX 78652/800-531-5301; FAX: 800-266-2373
Jenkins Recoil Pads, Inc., 5438 E. Frontage Ln., Olney, IL 62450/618-395-3416
Jennings Firearms, Inc., 17692 Cowan, Irvine, CA 92714/714-252-7621; FAX: 714-252-7626
Jensen Bullets, 86 North, 400 West, Blackfoot, ID 83221/208-785-5590
Jensen's Custom Ammunition, 5146 E. Pima, Tucson, AZ 85712/602-325-3346; FAX: 602-322-5704
Jensen's Firearms Academy, 1280 W. Prince, Tucson, AZ 85705/602-293-8516
Jester Bullets, Rt. 1 Box 27, Orienta, OK 73737
Jewell, Arnold W., 1490 Whitewater Rd., New Braunfels, TX 78132/210-620-0971
J-Gar Co., 183 Turnpike Rd., Dept. 3, Petersham, MA 01366-9604
JGS Precision Tool Mfg., 1141 S. Summer Rd., Coos Bay, OR 97420/503-267-4331; FAX:503-267-5996
Jim's Gun Shop (See Spradlin's)
Jim's Precision, Jim Ketchum, 1725 Moclips Dr., Petaluma, CA 94952/707-762-3014
J.I.T., Ltd., P.O. Box 230, Freedom, WY 83120/708-494-0937
JLK Bullets, 414 Turner Rd., Dover, AR 72837/501-331-4194
J.O. Arms Inc., 5709 Hartsdale, Houston, TX 77036/713-789-0745; FAX: 713-789-7513
Johanssons Vapentillbehor, Bert, S-430 20 Veddige, SWEDEN
John's Custom Leather, 523 S. Liberty St., Blairsville, PA 15717/412-459-6802
Johns Master Engraver, Bill, RR 4, Box 220, Fredericksburg, TX 78624-9545/210-997-6795
Johnson's Gunsmithing, Inc., Neal, 208 W. Buchanan St., Suite B, Colorado Springs, CO 80907/800-284-8671 (orders), 719-632-3795; FAX: 719-632-3493
Johnson Wood Products, RR 1, Strawberry Point, IA 52076/319-933-4930

Johnson's Lage Uniwad, P.O. Box 2302, Davenport, IA 52809/319-388-LAGE
Johnston Bros., 1889 Rt. 9, Unit 22, Toms River, NJ 08755/800-257-2595; FAX: 800-257-2534
Johnston, James (See North Fork Custom Gunsmithing)
Jonad Corp., 2091 Lakeland Ave., Lakewood, OH 44107/216-226-3161
Jonas Appraisals & Taxidermy, Jack, 1675 S. Birch, Suite 506, Denver, CO 80222/303-757-7347: FAX: 303-639-9655
Jones Co., Dale, 680 Hoffman Draw, Kila, MT 59920/406-755-4684
Jones Custom Products, Neil A., 17217 Brookhouser Road, Saegertown, PA 16433/814-763-2769; FAX: 814-763-4228
Jones Moulds, Paul, 4901 Telegraph Rd., Los Angeles, CA 90022/213-262-1510
Jones, J.D. (See SSK Industries)
Joy Enterprises (See Fury Cutlery)
J.P. Enterprises, Inc., P.O. Box 26324, Shoreview, MN 55126/612-486-9064; FAX: 612-482-0970
J.P. Gunstocks, Inc., 4508 San Miguel Ave., North Las Vegas, NV 89030/702-645-0718
JP Sales, Box 307, Anderson, TX 77830
JRP Custom Bullets, RR2-2233 Carlton Rd., Whitehall, NY 12887/802-438-5548 (p.m.), 518-282-0084 (a.m.)
JRW, 2425 Taffy Ct., Nampa, ID 83687
JS Worldwide DBA (See Coonan Arms)
Juenke, Vern, 25 Bitterbush Rd., Reno, NV 89523/702-345-0225
Jumbo Sports Products (See Bucheimer, J.M.)
Jungkind, Reeves C., 5001 Buckskin Pass, Austin, TX 78745-2841/512-442-1094
Jurras, L.E., P.O. Box 680, Washington, IN 47501/812-254-7698
JWH: Software, 6947 Haggerty Rd., Hillsboro, OH 45133/513-393-2402

K

K&M Industries, Inc., Box 66, 510 S. Main, Troy, ID 83871/208-835-2281; FAX: 208-835-5211
K&M Services, 5430 Salmon Run Rd., Dover, PA 17315/717-764-1461
K&P Gun Co., 1024 Central Ave., New Rockford, ND 58356/701-947-2248
K&S Mfg., 2611 Hwy. 40 East, Inglis, FL 34449/904-447-3571
K&T Co., Div. of T&S Industries, Inc., 1027 Skyview Dr., W. Carrollton, OH 45449/513-859-8414
KA-BAR Knives, 31100 Solon Rd., Solon, OH 44139/216-248-7000; 800-321-9316, ext. 329; FAX: 216-248-8651
Kahles, A Swarovski Company, 1 Wholesale Way, Cranston, RI 02920-5540/800-426-3089; FAX: 401-946-2587
Kahnke Gunworks, 206 West 11th St., Redwood Falls, MN 56283/507-637-2901
Kahr Arms, P.O. Box 220, 630 Route 303, Blauvelt, NY 10913/914-353-5996; FAX: 914-353-7833
Kalispel Case Line, P.O. Box 267, Cusick, WA 99119/509-445-1121
Kamik Outdoor Footwear, 554 Montee de Liesse, Montreal, Quebec, H4T 1P1 CANADA/514-341-3950; FAX: 514-341-1861
Kamyk Engraving Co., Steve, 9 Grandview Dr., Westfield, MA 01085-1810/413-568-0457
Kandel, P.O. Box 4529, Portland, OR 97208
Kane, Edward, P.O. Box 385, Ukiah, CA 95482/707-462-2937
Kane Products, Inc., 5572 Brecksville Rd., Cleveland, OH 44131/216-524-9962
Ka Pu Kapili, P.O. Box 745, Honokaa, HI 96727/808-776-1644; FAX: 808-776-1731
Kapro Mfg. Co., Inc. (See R.E.I.)
Kasenit Co., Inc., 13 Park Ave., Highland Mills, NY 10930/914-928-9595; FAX: 914-928-7292
Kasmarsik Bullets, 152 Crstler Rd., Chehalis, WA 98532
Kaswer Custom, Inc., 13 Surrey Drive, Brookfield, CT 06804/203-775-0564; FAX: 203-775-6872
K.B.I., Inc., P.O. Box 5440, Harrisburg, PA 17110-0440/717-540-8518; FAX: 717-540-8567
K-D, Inc., Box 459, 585 N. Hwy. 155, Cleveland, UT 84518/801-653-2530
KDF, Inc., 2485 Hwy. 46 N., Seguin, TX 78155/210-379-8141; FAX: 210-379-5420
KeeCo Impressions, Inc., 346 Wood Ave., North Brunswick, NJ 08902/800-468-0546
Keeler, R.H., 817 "N" St., Port Angeles, WA 98362/206-457-4702
Kehr, Roger, 2131 Agate Ct. SE, Lacy, WA 98503/360-456-0831
Keith's Bullets, 942 Twisted Oak, Algonquin, IL 60102/708-658-3520
Keith's Custom Gunstocks (See Heppler, Keith M.)
Kelbly, Inc., 7222 Dalton Fox Lake Rd., North Lawrence, OH 44666/216-683-4674; FAX: 216-683-7349
Keller Co., The, 4215 McEwen Rd., Dallas, TX 75244/214-770-8585
Kelley's, P.O. Box 125, Woburn, MA 01801/617-935-3389
Kellogg's Professional Products, 325 Pearl St., Sandusky, OH 44870/419-625-6551; FAX: 419-625-6167
Kelly, Lance, 1723 Willow Oak Dr., Edgewater, FL 32132/904-423-4933
Kel-Tec CNC Industries, Inc., P.O. Box 3427, Cocoa, FL 32924/407-631-0068; FAX: 407-631-1169
Ken's Gun Specialties, Rt. 1, Box 147, Lakeview, AR 72642/501-431-5606
Ken's Kustom Kartridges, 331 Jacobs Rd., Hubbard, OH 44425/216-534-4595
Ken's Rifle Blanks, Ken McCullough, Rt. 2, P.O. Box 85B, Weston, OR 97886/503-566-3879
Keng's Firearms Specialty, Inc., P.O. Box 44405, 875 Wharton Dr. SW, Atlanta, GA 30336/404-691-7611; FAX: 404-505-8445
Kennebec Journal, 274 Western Ave., Augusta, ME 04330/207-622-6288
Kennedy Firearms, 10 N. Market St., Muncy, PA 17756/717-546-6695
KenPatable Ent., Inc., P.O. Box 19422, Louisville, KY 40259/502-239-5447
Kent Cartridge Mfg. Co. Ltd., Unit 16, Branbridges Industrial Estate, East, Peckham/Tonbridge, Kent, TN12 5HF ENGLAND 622-872255; FAX: 622-872645
Keowee Game Calls, 608 Hwy. 25 North, Travelers Rest, SC 29690/803-834-7204
Kershaw Knives, 25300 SW Parkway Ave., Wilsonville, OR 97070/503-682-1966, 800-325-2891; FAX: 503-682-7168
Kesselring Gun Shop, 400 Hwy. 99 North, Burlington, WA 98233/206-724-3113; FAX: 206-724-7003
Ketchum, Jim (See Jim's Precision)

MANUFACTURERS' DIRECTORY

Kick Eez, P.O. Box 12767, Wichita, KS 67277/316-721-9570; FAX: 316-721-5260
Kilham & Co., Main St., P.O. Box 37, Lyme, NH 03768/603-795-4112
Kimball, Gary, 1526 N. Circle Dr., Colorado Springs, CO 80909/719-634-1274
Kimber of America, Inc., 9039 SE Jannsen Rd., Clackamas, OR 97015/503-656-1704, 800-880-2418; FAX: 503-656-5357
Kimel Industries (See A.A. Arms, Inc.)
King & Co., P.O. Box 1242, Bloomington, IL 61702/309-473-3964
King's Gun Works, 1837 W. Glenoaks Blvd., Glendale, CA 91201/818-956-6010; FAX: 818-548-8606
Kingyon, Paul L. (See Custom Calls)
Kirk Game Calls, Inc., Dennis, RD1, Box 184, Laurens, NY 13796/607-433-2710; FAX: 607-433-2711
Kirkpatrick Leather Co., 1910 San Bernardo, Laredo, TX 78040/210-723-6631; FAX: 210-725-0672
KJM Fabritek, Inc., P.O. Box 162, Marietta, GA 30061/404-426-8251
KK Air International (See Impact Case Co.)
K.K. Arms Co., Star Route Box 671, Kerrville, TX 78028/210-257-4718; FAX: 210-257-4891
KLA Enterprises, P.O. Box 2028, Eaton Park, FL 33840/941-682-2829; FAX: 941-682-2829
Kleen-Bore, Inc., 16 Industrial Pkwy., Easthampton, MA 01027/413-527-0300; FAX: 413-527-2522
Klein Custom Guns, Don, 433 Murray Park Dr., Ripon, WI 54971/414-748-2931
Kleinendorst, K.W., RR 1, Box 1500, Hop Bottom, PA 18824/717-289-4687
Klingler Woodcarving, P.O. Box 141, Thistle Hill, Cabot, VT 05647/802-426-3811
Kmount, P.O. Box 19422, Louisville, KY 40259/502-239-5447
Kneiper, James, Inc., P.O. Box 1516, Basalt, CO 81621-1516/303-963-9880
Knife Importers, Inc., P.O. Box 1000, Manchaca, TX 78652/512-282-6860
Knight & Hale Game Calls, Box 468 Industrial Park, Cadiz, KY 42211/502-924-1755; FAX: 502-924-1763
Knight Rifles (See Modern MuzzleLoading, Inc.)
Knight's Mfg. Co., 7750 9th St. SW, Vero Beach, FL 32968/407-562-5697; FAX: 407-569-2955
Knippel, Richard, 500 Gayle Ave., Apt. 213, Modesto, CA 95350-4241/209-869-1469
Knock on Wood Antiques, 355 Post Rd., Darien, CT 06820/203-655-9031
Knoell, Doug, 9737 McCardle Way, Santee, CA 92071
Kodiak Custom Bullets, 8261 Henry Circle, Anchorage, AK 99507/907-349-2282
Koevenig's Engraving Service, Box 55 Rabbit Gulch, Hill City, SD 57745
KOGOT, 410 College, Trinidad, CO 81082/719-846-9406
Kokolus, Michael M. (See Custom Riflestocks, Inc.)
Kolpin Mfg., Inc., P.O. Box 107, 205 Depot St., Fox Lake, WI 53933/414-928-3118; FAX: 414-928-3687
Kongsberg America L.L.C., P.O. Box 252, Fairfield, CT 06430/203-259-0938; FAX: 203-259-2566
Kopec Enterprises, John (See Peacemaker Specialists)
Kopp, Terry K., Route 1, Box 224F, Lexington, MO 64067/816-259-2636
Korth, Robert-Bosch-Str. 4, P.O. Box 1320, 23909 Ratzeburg, GERMANY/451-4991497; FAX: 451-4993230 (U.S. importer—Interarms; Mandall Shooting Supplies, Inc.)
Korzinek Riflesmith, J., RD 2, Box 73D, Canton, PA 17724/717-673-8512
Koval Knives, 5819 Zarley St., Suite A, New Albany, OH 43054/614-855-0777; FAX: 614-855-0945
Kowa Optimed, Inc., 20001 S. Vermont Ave., Torrance, CA 90502/310-327-1913; FAX: 310-327-4177
Kramer Designs, 36 Chokecherry Ln., Clancy, MT 59634/406-933-8658; FAX: 406-933-8658
Kramer Handgun Leather, P.O. Box 112154, Tacoma, WA 98411/206-564-6652; FAX: 206-564-1214
Krause Publications, Inc., 700 E. State St., Iola, WI 54990/715-445-2214; FAX: 715-445-4087; Consumer orders only 800-258-0929
Krico Jagd-und Sportwaffen GmbH, Nurnbergerstrasse 6, D-90602 Pyrbaum GERMANY/09180-2780; FAX: 09180-2661 (U.S. importer—Mandall Shooting Supplies, Inc.)
Krieger Barrels, Inc., N114 W18697 Clinton Dr., Germantown, WI 53022/414-255-9593; FAX: 414-255-9586
Krieghoff Gun Co., H., Boschstrasse 22, D-89079 Ulm, GERMANY/731-401820; FAX: 731-4018270 (U.S. importer—Krieghoff International, Inc.)
Krieghoff International, Inc., 7528 Easton Rd., Ottsville, PA 18942/610-847-5173; FAX: 610-847-8691
Kris Mounts, 108 Lehigh St., Johnstown, PA 15905/814-539-9751
KSN Industries, Ltd. (See U.S. importer—J.O. Arms Inc.)
K-Sports Imports, Inc., 2755 Thompson Creek Rd., Pomona, CA 91767/909-392-2345; FAX: 909-392-2354
Kudlas, John M., 622 14th St. SE, Rochester, MN 55904/507-288-5579
Kulis Freeze Dry Taxidermy, 725 Broadway Ave., Bedford, OH 44146/216-232-8352; FAX: 216-232-7305
KVH Industries, Inc., 110 Enterprise Center, Middletown, RI 02842/401-847-3327; FAX: 401-849-0045
Kwik Mount Corp., P.O. Box 19422, Louisville, KY 40259/502-239-5447
Kwik-Site Co., 5555 Treadwell, Wayne, MI 48184/313-326-1500; FAX: 313-326-4120

L

L&R Lock Co., 1137 Pocalla Rd., Sumter, SC 29150/803-775-6127
L&S Technologies, Inc. (See Aimtech Mount Systems)
La Clinique du .45, 1432 Rougemont, Chambly, Quebec, J3L 2L8 CANADA/514-658-1144
Labanu, Inc., 2201-F Fifth Ave., Ronkonkoma, NY 11779/516-467-6197; FAX: 516-981-4112
LaBounty Precision Reboring, P.O. Box 186, 7968 Silver Lk. Rd., Maple Falls, WA 98266/360-599-2047
LaCrosse Footwear, Inc., P.O. Box 1328, La Crosse, WI 54602/608-782-3020, 800-323-2668; FAX: 800-658-9444
Lady Clays, P.O. Box 457, Shawnee Mission, KS 66201/913-268-8006
LaFrance Specialties, P.O. Box 178211, San Diego, CA 92177-8211/619-293-3373
Lair, Sam, 520 E. Beaver, Jenks, OK 74037/918-299-2391
Lake Center, P.O. Box 38, St. Charles, MO 63302/314-946-7500
Lakefield Arms Ltd. (See Savage Arms, Inc.)
Lakewood Products, Inc., 275 June St., P.O. Box 230, Berlin, WI 54923/800-US-BUILT; FAX: 414-361-5058
Lampert, Ron, Rt. 1, Box 177, Guthrie, MN 56461/218-854-7345
Lamson & Goodnow Mfg. Co., 45 Conway St., Shelburne Falls, MA 03170/413-625-6331; FAX: 413-625-9816
Lanber Armas, S.A., Zubiaurre 5, Zaldibar, SPAIN 48250/34-4-6827702; FAX: 34-4-6827999
Lane Bullets, Inc., 1011 S. 10th St., Kansas City, KS 66105/913-621-6113, 800-444-7468
Lane Publishing, P.O. Box 459, Lake Hamilton, AR 71951/501-525-7514; FAX: 501-525-7519
Langenberg Hat Co., P.O. Box 1860, Washington, MO 63090/800-428-1860; FAX: 314-239-3151
Lanphert, Paul, P.O. Box 1985, Wenatchee, WA 98807
Lapua Ltd., P.O. Box 5, Lapua, FINLAND SF-62101/64-310111; FAX: 64-4388991 (U.S. importers—Champion's Choice; Keng's Firearms Specialty, Inc.
L.A.R. Mfg., Inc., 4133 W. Farm Rd., West Jordan, UT 84088/801-280-3505; FAX: 801-280-1972
LaRocca Gun Works, Inc., 51 Union Place, Worcester, MA 01608/508-754-2887; FAX: 508-754-2887
Laser Devices, Inc., 2 Harris Ct. A4, Monterey, CA 93940/408-373-0701, 800-235-2162; FAX: 408-373-0903
Laseraim, Inc. (See Emerging Technologies, Inc.)
Laseraim Arms, Inc., P.O. Box 3548, Little Rock, AR 72203/501-375-2227; FAX: 501-372-1445
Laseraim Technologies, Inc., P.O. Box 3548, Little Rock, AR 72203/501-375-2227; FAX: 501-372-1445
LaserMax, 3495 Winton Place, Bldg. B, Rochester, NY 14623/716-272-5420; FAX: 716-272-5427
Lassen Community College, Gunsmithing Dept., P.O. Box 3000, Hwy. 139, Susanville, CA 96130/916-251-8809 ext. 109 or 200; FAX: 916-257-8964
Lathrop's, Inc., 5146 E. Pima, Tucson, AZ 85712/520-881-0266, 800-875-4867; FAX: 520-322-5704
Laughridge, William R. (See Cylinder & Slide, Inc.)
Laurel Mountain Forge, P.O. Box 224C, Romeo, MI 48065/810-749-5742
Laurona Armas Eibar, S.A.L., Avenida de Otaola 25, P.O. Box 260, 20600 Eibar, SPAIN/34-43-700600; FAX: 34-43-700616 (U.S. importers—Galaxy Imports Ltd., Inc.)
Law Concealment Systems, Inc., P.O. Box 3952, Wilmington, NC 28406/919-791-6656, 800-373-0116 orders
Lawrence Brand Shot (See Precision Reloading, Inc.)
Lawrence Leather Co., P.O. Box 1479, Lillington, NC 27546/910-893-2071; FAX: 910-893-4742
Lawson Co., Harry, 3328 N. Richey Blvd., Tucson, AZ 85716/520-326-1117
Lawson, John G. (See Sight Shop, The)
LBT, HCR 62, Box 145, Moyie Springs, ID 83845/208-267-3588
Le Clear Industries (See E-Z-Way Systems)
Lea Mfg. Co., 237 E. Aurora St., Waterbury, CT 06720/203-753-5116
Lead Bullets Technology (See LBT)
Leather Arsenal, 27549 Middleton Rd., Middleton, ID 83644/208-585-6212
Leatherman Tool Group, Inc., 12106 NE Ainsworth Cir., P.O. Box 20595, Portland, OR 97294/503-253-7826; FAX: 503-253-7830
Lebeau-Courally, Rue St. Gilles, 386, 4000 Liege, BELGIUM/041-52-48-43; FAX: 32-041-52-20-08 (U.S. importer—New England Arms Co.)
Leckie Professional Gunsmithing, 546 Quarry Rd., Ottsville, PA 18942/215-847-8594
Lectro Science, Inc., 6410 W. Ridge Rd., Erie, PA 16506/814-833-6487; FAX: 814-833-0447
Ledbetter Airguns, Riley, 1804 E. Sprague St., Winston Salem, NC 27107-3521/919-784-0676
Lee Co., T.K., One Independence Plaza, Suite 520, Birmingham, AL 35209/205-913-5222
Lee Precision, Inc., 4275 Hwy. U, Hartford, WI 53027/414-673-3075
Lee Supplies, Mark, 9901 France Ct., Lakeville, MN 55044/612-461-2114
Lee's Red Ramps, 4 Kristine Ln., Silver City, NM 88061/505-538-8529
LeFever Arms Co., Inc., 6234 Stokes, Lee Center Rd., Lee Center, NY 13363/315-337-6722; FAX: 315-337-1543
Legend Products Corp., 1555 E. Flamingo Rd., Suite 404, Las Vegas, NV 89119/702-228-1808, 702-796-5778; FAX: 702-228-7484
Leibowitz, Leonard, 1205 Murrayhill Ave., Pittsburgh, PA 15217/412-361-5455
Leica USA, Inc., 156 Ludlow Ave., Northvale, NJ 07647/201-767-7500; FAX: 201-767-8666
L.E.M. Gun Specialties, Inc., The Lewis Lead Remover, P.O. Box 2855, Peachtree City, GA 30269-2024/770-487-0556
Lem Sports, Inc., P.O. Box 2107, Aurora, IL 60506/815-286-7421, 800-688-8801 (orders only)
Lenahan Family Enterprise, P.O. Box 46, Manitou Springs, CO 80829
Lethal Force Institute (See Police Bookshelf)
Lett Custom Grips, 672 Currier Rd., Hopkinton, NH 03229-2652
Leupold & Stevens, Inc., P.O. Box 688, Beaverton, OR 97075/503-646-9171; FAX: 503-526-1455
Lever Arms Service Ltd., 2131 Burrard St., Vancouver, B.C. V6J 3H7 CANADA/604-736-0004; FAX: 604-738-3503
Lewis Lead Remover, The (See LEM Gun Specialties, Inc.)
Liberty Antique Gunworks, 19 Key St., P.O. Box 183, Eastport, ME 04631/207-853-4116
Liberty Metals, 2233 East 16th St., Los Angeles, CA 90021/213-581-9171; FAX: 213-581-9351
Liberty Safe, 1060 N. Spring Creek Pl., Springville, UT 84663/800-247-5625; FAX: 801-489-6409
Liberty Shooting Supplies, P.O. Box 357, Hillsboro, OR 97123/503-640-5518
Liberty Trouser Co., 3500 6 Ave S., Birmingham, AL 35222-2406/205-251-9143
Lightfield Ammunition Corp., The Slug Group, P.O. Box 376, New Paris, PA 15554/814-839-4517; FAX: 814-839-2601
Lightning Performance Innovations, Inc., RD1 Box 555, Mohawk, NY 13407/315-866-8819, 800-242-5873; FAX: 315-866-8819
Lilja Precision Rifle Barrels, P.O. Box 372, Plains, MT 59859/406-826-3084; FAX: 406-826-3083

DIRECTORY OF THE ARMS TRADE

Lincoln, Dean, Box 1886, Farmington, NM 87401
Lind Custom Guns, Al, 7821 76th Ave. SW, Tacoma, WA 98498/206-584-6361
Linder Solingen Knives, 4401 Sentry Dr., Tucker, GA 30084/770-939-6915; FAX: 770-939-6738
Lindsay, Steve, RR 2 Cedar Hills, Kearney, NE 68847/308-236-7885
Lindsley Arms Cartridge Co., P.O. Box 757, 20 College Hill Rd., Henniker, NH 03242/603-428-3127
Linebaugh Custom Sixguns, Route 2, Box 100, Maryville, MO 64468/816-562-3031
List Precision Engineering, Unit 1, Ingley Works, 13 River Road, Barking, Essex 1G11 0HE ENGLAND/011-081-594-1686
Lister, Weldon, Route 1, P.O. Box 1517, Boerne, TX 78006/210-755-2210
Lithi Bee Bullet Lube, 1885 Dyson St., Muskegon, MI 49442/616-726-3400
"Little John's" Antique Arms, 1740 W. Laveta, Orange, CA 92668
Little Trees Ramble (See Scott Pilkington, Little Trees Ramble)
Littler Sales Co., 20815 W. Chicago, Detroit, MI 48228/313-273-6889; FAX: 313-273-1099
Littleton, J.F., 275 Pinedale Ave., Oroville, CA 95966/916-533-6084
Ljutic Industries, Inc., 732 N. 16th Ave., Suite 22, Yakima, WA 98902/509-248-0476; FAX: 509-576-8233
Llama Gabilondo Y Cia, Apartado 290, E-01080, Victoria, SPAIN (U.S. importer—Import Sports, Inc.)
L.L. Bean, 386 Main St., Freeport, ME 04032/207-865-3111
Load From A Disk, 9826 Sagedale, Houston, TX 77089/713-484-0935
Loadmaster, P.O. Box 1209, Warminster, Wilts. BA12 9XJ ENGLAND/01044 1985 218544; FAX: 01044 1985 214111
Loch Leven Industries, P.O. Box 2751, Santa Rosa, CA 95405/707-573-8735; FAX: 707-573-0369
Lock's Philadelphia Gun Exchange, 6700 Rowland Ave., Philadelphia, PA 19149/215-332-6225; FAX: 215-332-4800
Lodewick, Walter H., 2816 NE Halsey St., Portland, OR 97232/503-284-2554
Lofland, James W., 2275 Larkin Rd., Boothwyn, PA 19061/610-485-0391
Log Cabin Sport Shop, 8010 Lafayette Rd., Lodi, OH 44254/216-948-1082
Logan, Harry M., Box 745, Honokaa, HI 96727/808-776-1644
Lohman Game Call Company, 4500 Doniphan Dr., P.O. Box 220, Neosho, MO 64850/417-451-4438; FAX: 417-451-2576
Lomont Precision Bullets, RR 1, P.O. Box 34, Salmon, ID 83467/208-756-6819; FAX: 208-756-6824
London Guns Ltd., Box 3750, Santa Barbara, CA 93130/805-683-4141; FAX: 805-683-1712
Lone Star Gunleather, 1301 Brushy Bend Dr., Round Rock, TX 78681/512-255-1805
Long, George F., 1500 Rogue River Hwy., Ste. F, Grants Pass, OR 97527/541-476-7552
Lorcin Engineering Co., Inc., 10427 San Sevaine Way, Ste. A, Mira Loma, CA 91752/909-360-1406; FAX: 909-360-0623
Lortone, Inc., 2856 NW Market St., Seattle, WA 98107/206-789-3100
Lothar Walther Precision Tool, Inc., 2190 Coffee Rd., Lithonia, GA 30058/770-482-4253; Fax: 770-482-9344
Lovestrand, Erik, 206 Bent Oak Circle, Harvest, AL 35749-9334
Loweth, Richard, 29 Hedgegrow Lane, Kirby Muxloe, Leics. LE9 9BN ENGLAND
L.P.A. Snc, Via Alfieri 26, Gardone V.T., Brescia, ITALY 25063/30-891-14-81; FAX: 30-891-09-51
LPS Laboratories, Inc., 4647 Hugh Howell Rd., P.O. Box 3050, Tucker, GA 30084/404-934-7800
Lucas, Edward E., 32 Garfield Ave., East Brunswick, NJ 08816/201-251-5526
Lucas, Mike, 1631 Jessamine Rd., Lexington, SC 29073/803-356-0282
Luch Metal Merchants, Barbara, 48861 West Rd., Wixon, MI 48393/800-876-5337
Lutz Engraving, Ron, E. 1998 Smokey Valley Rd., Scandinavia, WI 54977/715-467-2674
Lyman Instant Targets, Inc. (See Lyman Products Corp.)
Lyman Products Corporation, 475 Smith Street, Middletown, CT 06457-1541/860-632-2020, 800-22-LYMAN; FAX: 860-632-1699
Lynn's Custom Gunstocks, RR 1, Brandon, IA 52210/319-474-2453

M

M&D Munitions Ltd., 127 Verdi St., Farmingdale, NY 11735/800-878-2788, 516-752-1038; FAX: 516-752-1905
M&M Engineering (See Hollywood Engineering)
M&N Bullet Lube, P.O. Box 495, 151 NE Jefferson St., Madras, OR 97741/503-255-3750
MA Systems, P.O. Box 1143, Chouteau, OK 74337/918-479-6378
Mac-1 Distributors, 13974 Van Ness Ave., Gardena, CA 90249/310-327-3582
Mac's .45 Shop, P.O. Box 2028, Seal Beach, CA 90740/310-438-5046
Macbean, Stan, 754 North 1200 West, Orem, UT 84057/801-224-6446
Madis, David, 2453 West Five Mile Pkwy., Dallas, TX 75233/214-330-7168
Madis, George, P.O. Box 545, Brownsboro, TX 75756
MAG Instrument, Inc., 1635 S. Sacramento Ave., Ontario, CA 91761/909-947-1006; FAX: 909-947-3116
Mag-Na-Port International, Inc., 41302 Executive Dr., Harrison Twp., MI 48045-1306/810-469-6727; FAX: 810-469-0425
Mag-Pack Corp., P.O. Box 846, Chesterland, OH 44026
Magma Engineering Co., P.O. Box 161, 20955 E. Ocotillo Rd., Queen Creek, AZ 85242/602-987-9008; FAX: 602-987-0148
Magnolia Sports, Inc., 211 W. Main, Magnolia, AR 71753/501-234-8410, 800-530-7816; FAX: 501-234-8117
Magnum Grips, Box 801G, Payson, AZ 85547
Magnum Power Products, Inc., P.O. Box 17768, Fountain Hills, AZ 85268
Magnum Research, Inc., 7110 University Ave. NE, Minneapolis, MN 55432/800-772-6168, 612-574-1868; FAX: 612-574-0109
Magnus Bullets, P.O. Box 239, Toney, AL 35773/205-828-5089; FAX: 205-828-7756
MagSafe Ammo Co., 2725 Friendly Grove Rd NE, Olympia, WA 98506/360-357-6383; FAX: 360-705-4715
MAGTECH Recreational Products, Inc., 5030 Paradise Rd., Suite A104, Las Vegas, NV 89119/702-736-2043; FAX: 702-736-2140
Mahony, Philip Bruce, 67 White Hollow Rd., Lime Rock, CT 06039-2418/203-435-9341

Mahovsky's Metalife, R.D. 1, Box 149a Eureka Road, Grand Valley, PA 16420/814-436-7747
Maine Custom Bullets, RFD 1, Box 1755, Brooks, ME 04921
Mains Enterprises, Inc., 3111 S. Valley View Blvd., Suite B120, Las Vegas, NV 89102-7790/702-876-6278; FAX: 702-876-1269
Maionchi-L.M.I., Via Di Coselli-Zona Industriale Di Guamo, Lucca, ITALY 55060/011 39-583 94291
Makinson, Nicholas, RR 3, Komoka, Ont. N0L 1R0 CANADA/519-471-5462
Malcolm Enterprises, 1023 E. Prien Lake Rd., Lake Charles, LA 70601
Mallardtone Game Calls, 2901 16th St., Moline, IL 61265/309-762-8089
M.A.M. Products, Inc., 153 B Cross Slope Court, Englishtown, NJ 07726/908-536-3604
Mandall Shooting Supplies, Inc., 3616 N. Scottsdale Rd., Scottsdale, AZ 85252/602-945-2553; FAX: 602-949-0734
Manley Shooting Supplies, Lowell, 3684 Pine St., Deckerville, MI 48427/313-376-3665
Manufacture D'Armes Des Pyrenees Francaises (See Unique/M.A.P.F.)
Mar Knives, Inc., Al, 5755 SW Jean Rd., Suite 101, Lake Oswego, OR 97035/503-635-9229; FAX: 503-223-0467
Marathon Rubber Prods. Co., Inc., 510 Sherman St., Wausau, WI 54401/715-845-6255
Marble Arms, P.O. Box 111, Gladstone, MI 49837/906-428-3710; FAX: 906-428-3711
Marchmon Bullets, 8191 Woodland Shore Dr., Brighton, MI 48116
Marent, Rudolf, 9711 Tiltree St., Houston, TX 77075/713-946-7028
Markell, Inc., 422 Larkfield Center 235, Santa Rosa, CA 95403/707-573-0792; FAX: 707-573-9867
Markesbery Muzzle Loaders, Inc., 7785 Foundation Dr., Ste. 6, Florence, KY 41042/800-875-0121; 606-342-2380
Marksman Products, 5482 Argosy Dr., Huntington Beach, CA 92649/714-898-7535, 800-822-8005; FAX: 714-891-0782
Marlin Firearms Co., 100 Kenna Dr., North Haven, CT 06473/203-239-5621; FAX: 203-234-7991
Marmik Inc., 2116 S. Woodland Ave., Michigan City, IN 46361-7508/219-872-7231
Marocchi F.lli SRL, Via Galileo Galilei 8, I-25068 Zanano di Sarezzo, ITALY (U.S. importers—Sile Distributors)
Marple & Associates, Dick, 21 Dartmouth St., Hooksett, NH 03106/603-627-1837; FAX: 603-627-1837
Marquart Precision Co., Inc., Rear 136 Grove Ave., Box 1740, Prescott, AZ 86302/602-445-5646
Marsh, Johnny, 1007 Drummond Dr., Nashville, TN 37211/615-833-3259
Marsh, Mike, Croft Cottage, Main St., Elton, Derbyshire DE4 2BY, ENGLAND/01629 650 669
Marshall Enterprises, 792 Canyon Rd., Redwood City, CA 94062
Martin Bookseller, J., P.O. Drawer AP, Beckley, WV 25802/304-255-4073; FAX: 304-255-4077
Martin's Gun Shop, 937 S. Sheridan Blvd., Lakewood, CO 80226/303-922-2184
Martz, John V., 8060 Lakeview Lane, Lincoln, CA 95648/916-645-2250
Marvel, Alan, 3922 Madonna Rd., Jarretsville, MD 21084/301-557-6545
Maryland Paintball Supply, 8507 Harford Rd., Parkville, MD 21234/410-882-5607
Masen Co., Inc., John, 1305 Jelmak, Grand Prairie, TX 75050/817-430-8732; FAX: 817-430-1715
Masker, Seely, 54 Woodshire S., Getzville, NY 14068/716-689-8894
MAST Technology, 4350 S. Arville, Suite 3, Las Vegas, NV 89103/702-362-5043; FAX: 702-362-9554
Master Class Bullets, 4209-D West 6th, Eugene, OR 97402/503-687-1263, 800-883-1263
Master Engravers, Inc. (See Hendricks, Frank E.)
Master Lock Co., 2600 N. 32nd St., Milwaukee, WI 53245/414-444-2800
Master Products, Inc. (See Gun-Alert/Master Products, Inc.)
Match Prep, P.O. Box 155, Tehachapi, CA 93581/805-822-5383
Matco, Inc., 1003-2nd St., N. Manchester, IN 46962/219-982-8282
Mathews & Son, Inc., George E., 10224 S. Paramount Blvd., Downey, CA 90241/310-862-6719; FAX: 310-862-6719
Matthews Cutlery, 4401 Sentry Dr., Tucker, GA 30084/770-939-6915
Mauser Werke Oberndorf Waffensysteme GmbH, Postfach 1349, 78722 Oberndorf/N. GERMANY (U.S. importer—GSI, Inc.)
Maverick Arms, Inc., 7 Grasso Ave., P.O. Box 497, North Haven, CT 06473/203-230-5300; FAX: 203-230-5420
Maxi-Mount, P.O. Box 291, Willoughby Hills, OH 44094-0291/216-944-9456; FAX: 216-944-9456
Maximum Security Corp., 32841 Calle Perfecto, San Juan Capistrano, CA 92675/714-493-3684; FAX: 714-496-7733
Mayville Engineering Co. (See MEC, Inc.)
Mazur Restoration, Pete, 13083 Drummer Way, Grass Valley, CA 95949/916-268-2412
MCA Sports, P.O. Box 8868, Palm Springs, CA 92263/619-770-2005
McBros Rifle Co., P.O. Box 86549, Phoenix, AZ 85080/602-780-2115; FAX: 602-581-3825
McCament, Jay, 1730-134th St. Ct. S., Tacoma, WA 98444/206-531-8832
McCann's Machine & Gun Shop, P.O. Box 641, Spanaway, WA 98387/206-537-6919; FAX: 206-537-6993
McCann's Muzzle-Gun Works, 14 Walton Dr., New Hope, PA 18938/215-862-2728
McCluskey Precision Rifles, 10502 14th Ave. NW, Seattle, WA 98177/206-781-2776
McCombs, Leo, 1862 White Cemetery Rd., Patriot, OH 45658/614-256-1714
McCormick Corp., Chip, 1825 Fortview Rd., Ste. 115, Austin, TX 78704/800-328-CHIP, 512-462-0004; FAX: 512-462-0009
McCullough, Ken (See Ken's Rifle Blanks)
McDonald, Dennis, 8359 Brady St., Peosta, IA 52068/319-556-7940
McFarland, Stan, 2221 Idella Ct., Grand Junction, CO 81505/303-243-4704
McGowen Rifle Barrels, 5961 Spruce Lane, St. Anne, IL 60964/815-937-9816; FAX: 815-937-4024
McGuire, Bill, 1600 N. Eastmont Ave., East Wenatchee, WA 98802/509-884-6021
McKee Publications, 121 Eatons Neck Rd., Northport, NY 11768/516-575-8850
McKenzie, Lynton, 6940 N. Alvernon Way, Tucson, AZ 85718/520-299-5090

MANUFACTURERS' DIRECTORY

McKillen & Heyer, Inc., 35535 Euclid Ave. Suite 11, Willoughby, OH 44094/216-942-2044
McKinney, R.P. (See Schuetzen Gun Co.)
McMillan Fiberglass Stocks, Inc., 21421 N. 14th Ave., Phoenix, AZ 85027/602-582-9635; FAX: 602-581-3825
McMillan Optical Gunsight Co., 28638 N. 42nd St., Cave Creek, AZ 85331/602-585-7868; FAX: 602-585-7872
McMillan Rifle Barrels, P.O. Box 3427, Bryan, TX 77805/409-690-3456; FAX: 409-690-0156
McMurdo, Lynn (See Specialty Gunsmithing)
MCRW Associates Shooting Supplies, R.R. 1 Box 1425, Sweet Valley, PA 18656/717-864-3967; FAX: 717-864-2669
MCS, Inc., 34 Delmar Dr., Brookfield, CT 06804/203-775-1013; FAX: 203-775-9462
McWelco Products, 6730 Santa Fe Ave., Hesperia, CA 92345/619-244-8876; FAX: 619-244-9398
MDS, P.O. Box 1441, Brandon, FL 33509-1441/813-653-1180; FAX: 813-684-5953
Meadow Industries, 24 Club Lane, Palmyra, VA 22963/804-589-7672; FAX: 804-589-7672
Measurement Group, Inc., Box 27777, Raleigh, NC 27611
MEC, Inc., 715 South St., Mayville, WI 53050/414-387-4500; FAX: 414-387-5802
MEC-Gar S.R.L., Via Madonnina 64, Gardone V.T., Brescia, ITALY 25063/39-30-8912687; FAX: 39-30-8910065 (U.S. importer—MEC-Gar U.S.A., Inc.)
MEC-Gar U.S.A., Inc., Box 112, 500B Monroe Turnpike, Monroe, CT 06468/203-635-8662; FAX: 203-635-8662
Meier Works, P.O. Box 423, Tijeras, NM 87059/505-281-3783
Meister Bullets (See Gander Mountain)
Mele, Frank, 201 S. Wellow Ave., Cookeville, TN 38501/615-526-4860
Melton Shirt Co., Inc., 56 Harvester Ave., Batavia, NY 14020/716-343-8750; FAX: 716-343-6887
Men-Metallwerk Elisenhuette, GmbH, P.O. Box 1263, D-56372 Nassau/Lahn, GERMANY/2604-7819
Menck, Thomas W., 5703 S. 77th St., Ralston, NE 68127-4201
Mendez, John A., P.O. Box 620984, Orlando, FL 32862/407-282-2178
Meprolight (See Hesco-Meprolight)
Mercer Custom Stocks, R.M., 216 S. Whitewater Ave., Jefferson, WI 53549/414-674-5130
Merit Corporation, Box 9044, Schenectady, NY 12309/518-346-1420
Merkel Freres, Strasse 7 October, 10, Suhl, GERMANY (U.S. importer—GSI, Inc.)
Merkuria Ltd., Argentinska 38, 17005 Praha 7, CZECH REPUBLIC/422-875117; FAX: 422-809152
Mesa Sportsmen's Assoc., L.L.C., 250 Main St., Box 854, Delta, CO 81416/970-874-4571
Metal Products Co. (See MPC)
Metalife Industries (See Mahovsky's Metalife)
Metaloy Inc., Rt. 5, Box 595, Berryville, AR 72616/501-545-3611
Michael's Antiques, Box 591, Waldoboro, ME 04572
Michaels of Oregon Co., P.O. Box 13010, Portland, OR 97213/503-255-6890; FAX: 503-255-0746
Micro Sight Co., 242 Harbor Blvd., Belmont, CA 94002/415-591-0769; FAX: 415-591-7531
Microfusion Alfa S.A., Paseo San Andres N8, P.O. Box 271, Eibar, SPAIN 20600/34-43-11-89-16; FAX: 34-43-11-40-38
Mid-America Guns and Ammo, 1205 W. Jefferson, Suite E, Effingham, IL 62401/800-820-5177
Mid-America Recreation, Inc., 1328 5th Ave., Moline, IL 61265/309-764-5089; FAX: 309-764-2722
Middlebrooks Custom Shop, 7366 Colonial Trail East, Surry, VA 23883/804-357-0881; FAX: 804-365-0442
Midway Arms, Inc., 5875 W. Van Horn Tavern Rd., Columbia, MO 65203/800-243-3220, 314-445-6363; FAX: 314-446-1018
Midwest Gun Sport, 1108 Herbert Dr., Zebulon, NC 27597/919-269-5570
Midwest Sport Distributors, Box 129, Fayette, MO 65248
Military Armament Corp., P.O. Box 120, Mt. Zion Rd., Lingleville, TX 76461/817-965-3253
Miller Arms, Inc., P.O. Box 260 Purl St., St. Onge, SD 57779/605-642-5160; FAX: 605-642-5160
Miller Co., David, 3131 E. Greenlee Rd., Tucson, AZ 85716/602-326-3117
Miller Custom, 210 E. Julia, Clinton, IL 61727/217-935-9362
Miller Enterprises, Inc., R.P., 1557 E. Main St., P.O. Box 234, Brownsburg, IN 46112/317-852-8187
Miller Single Trigger Mfg. Co., Rt. 209 Box 1275, Millersburg, PA 17061/717-692-3704
Millett Sights, 16131 Gothard St., Huntington Beach, CA 92647/714-842-5575, 800-645-5388; FAX: 714-843-5707
Mills Jr., Hugh B., 3615 Canterbury Rd., New Bern, NC 28560/919-637-4631
Milstor Corp., 80-975 E. Valley Pkwy. C-7, Indio, CA 92201/619-775-9998; FAX: 619-772-4990
Miniature Machine Co. (MMC), 2513 East Loop 820 North, Ft. Worth, TX 76118/817-595-0404; FAX: 817-595-3074
Minute Man High Tech Industries, 10611 Canyon Rd. E., Suite 151, Puyallup, WA 98373/800-233-2734
Mirador Optical Corp., P.O. Box 11614, Marina Del Rey, CA 90295-7614/310-821-5587; FAX: 310-305-0386
Miroku, B.C./Daly, Charles (See U.S. importer—Bell's Legendary Country Wear; U.S. distributor—Outdoor Sports Headquarters, Inc.)
Mitchell Arms, Inc., 3433-B. W. Harvard St., Santa Ana, CA 92704/714-957-5711; FAX: 714-957-5732
Mitchell Bullets, R.F., 430 Walnut St., Westernport, MD 21562
Mitchell's Accuracy Shop, 68 Greenridge Dr., Stafford, VA 22554/703-659-0165
MI-TE Bullets, R.R. 1 Box 230, Ellsworth, KS 67439/913-472-4575
Mittermeier, Inc., Frank, P.O. Box 2G, 3577 E. Tremont Ave., Bronx, NY 10465/718-828-3843
Mixson Corp., 7435 W. 19th Ct., Hialeah, FL 33014/305-821-5190, 800-327-0078; FAX: 305-558-9318
MJK Gunsmithing, Inc., 417 N. Huber Ct., E. Wenatchee, WA 98802/509-884-7683
MJM Mfg., 3283 Rocky Water Ln. Suite B, San Jose, CA 95148/408-270-4207
MKL Service Co., 610 S. Troy St., P.O. Box D, Royal Oak, MI 48068/810-548-5453
MKS Supply, Inc. (See Hi-Point Firearms)
MMP, Rt. 6, Box 384, Harrison, AR 72601/501-741-5019; FAX: 501-741-3104
M.O.A. Corp., 2451 Old Camden Pike, Eaton, OH 45320/513-456-3669
Modern Gun Repair School, P.O. Box 92577, Southlake, TX 76092/800-493-4114; FAX: 800-556-5112
Modern Gun School, 500 N. Kimball, Suite 105, Southlake, TX 76092/800-774-5112
Modern MuzzleLoading, Inc., 234 Airport Rd., P.O. Box 130, Centerville, IA 52544/515-856-2626; FAX: 515-856-2628
Moeller, Steve, 1213 4th St., Fulton, IL 61252/815-589-2300
Molin Industries, Tru-Nord Division, P.O. Box 365, 204 North 9th St., Brainerd, MN 56401/218-829-2870
MoLoc Bullets, P.O. Box 2810, Turlock, CA 95381-2810/209-632-1644
Monell Custom Guns, 228 Red Mills Rd., Pine Bush, NY 12566/914-744-3021
Moneymaker Guncraft Corp., 1420 Military Ave., Omaha, NE 68131/402-556-0226
Montana Armory, Inc., 100 Centennial Dr., Big Timber, MT 59011/406-932-4353
Montana Outfitters, Lewis E. Yearout, 308 Riverview Dr. E., Great Falls, MT 59404/406-761-0859
Montana Precision Swaging, P.O. Box 4746, Butte, MT 59702/406-782-7502
Montana Vintage Arms, 2354 Bear Canyon Rd., Bozeman, MT 59715
Monte Kristo Pistol Grip Co., P.O. Box 85, Whiskeytown, CA 96095/916-778-0240
Montgomery Community College, P.O. Box 787-GD, Troy, NC 27371/910-572-3691, 800-839-6222
Moore & Co., Wm. Larkin, 8727 E. Via de Commencio, Suite A, Scottsdale, AZ 85258/602-951-8913; FAX: 602-951-8913
Moreton/Fordyce Enterprises, P.O. Box 940, Saylorsburg, PA 18353/717-992-5742; FAX: 717-992-8775
Morini (See U.S. importers—Mandall Shooting Supplies, Inc.; Nygord Precision Products)
Morrison Custom Rifles, J.W., 4015 W. Sharon, Phoenix, AZ 85029/602-978-3754
Morrow, Bud, 11 Hillside Lane, Sheridan, WY 82801-9729/307-674-8360
Morton Booth Co., P.O. Box 123, Joplin, MO 64802/417-673-1962; FAX: 417-673-3642
Mo's Competitor Supplies (See MCS, Inc.)
Moschetti, Mitchell R., P.O. Box 27065, Denver, CO 80227
Moss Double Tone, Inc., P.O. Box 1112, 2101 S. Kentucky, Sedalia, MO 65301/816-827-0827
Mossberg & Sons, Inc., O.F, 7 Grasso Ave., North Haven, CT 06473/203-230-5300; FAX: 203-230-5420
Mountain Bear Rifle Works, Inc., 100 B Ruritan Rd., Sterling, VA 20164/703-430-0420; FAX: 703-430-7068
Mountain Hollow Game Calls, Box 121, Cascade, MD 21719/301-241-3282
Mountain South, P.O. Box 381, Barnwell, SC 29812/FAX: 803-259-3227
Mountain State Muzzleloading Supplies, Box 154-1, Rt. 2, Williamstown, WV 26187/304-375-7842; FAX: 304-375-3737
Mountain States Engraving, Kenneth W. Warren, P.O. Box 2842, Wenatchee, WA 98802/509-663-6123
Mountain View Sports, Inc., Box 188, Troy, NH 03465/603-357-9690; FAX: 603-357-9691
Mowrey Gun Works, P.O. Box 246, Waldron, IN 46182/317-525-6181; FAX: 317-525-9595
Mowrey's Guns & Gunsmithing, RR1, Box 82, Canajoharie, NY 13317/518-673-3483
MPC, P.O. Box 450, McMinnville, TN 37110-0450/615-473-5513; FAX: 615-473-5516
MPI Fiberglass Stocks, 5655 NW St. Helens Rd., Portland, OR 97210/503-226-1215; FAX: 503-226-2661
MSC Industrial Supply Co., 151 Sunnyside Blvd., Plainview, NY 11803-9915/516-349-0330
MSR Targets, P.O. Box 1042, West Covina, CA 91793/818-331-7840
Mt. Alto Outdoor Products, Rt. 735, Howardsville, VA 24562
Mt. Baldy Bullet Co., 12981 Old Hill City Rd., Keystone, SD 57751-6623/605-666-4725
MTM Molded Products Co., Inc., 3370 Obco Ct., Dayton, OH 45414/513-890-7461; FAX: 513-890-1747
Mulhern, Rick, Rt. 5, Box 152, Rayville, LA 71269/318-728-2688
Mullins Ammo, Rt. 2, Box 304K, Clintwood, VA 24228/703-926-6772
Mullis Guncraft, 3523 Lawyers Road E., Monroe, NC 28110/704-283-6683
Multi-Caliber Adapters (See MCA Sports)
Multipax, 8086 S. Yale, Suite 286, Tulsa, OK 74136/918-496-1999; FAX: 918-492-7465
Multiplex International, 26 S. Main St., Concord, NH 03301/FAX: 603-796-2223
Multipropulseurs, La Bertrandiere, 42580 L'Etrat, FRANCE/77 74 01 30; FAX: 77 93 19 34
Multi-Scale Charge Ltd., 3269 Niagara Falls Blvd., N. Tonawanda, NY 14120/905-566-1255; FAX: 905-276-6295
Mundy, Thomas A., 69 Robbins Road, Somerville, NJ 08876/201-722-2199
Munsch Gunsmithing, Tommy, Rt. 2, P.O. Box 248, Little Falls, MN 56345/612-632-6695
Murmur Corp., 2823 N. Westmoreland Ave., Dallas, TX 75222/214-630-5400
Murphy Co., Inc., R., 13 Groton-Harvard Rd., P.O. Box 376, Ayer, MA 01432/617-772-3481
Murray State College, 100 Faculty Dr., Tishomingo, OK 73460/405-371-2371 ext. 238, 800-342-0698
Muscle Products Corp., 112 Fennell Dr., Butler, PA 16001/800-227-7049, 412-283-0567; FAX: 412-283-8310
Museum of Historical Arms Inc., 2750 Coral Way, Suite 204, Miami, FL 33145/305-444-9199
Mushroom Express Bullet Co., 601 W. 6th St., Greenfield, IN 46140-1728/317-462-6332
Mustra's Custom Guns, Inc., Carl, 1002 Pennsylvania Ave., Palm Harbor, FL 34683/813-785-1403
Muzzleload Magnum Products (See MMP)
Muzzleloaders Etcetera, Inc., 9901 Lyndale Ave. S., Bloomington, MN 55420/612-884-1161
MWG Co., P.O. Box 971202, Miami, FL 33197/800-428-9394, 305-253-8393; FAX: 305-232-1247

DIRECTORY OF THE ARMS TRADE

N

N&J Sales, Lime Kiln Rd., Northford, CT 06472/203-484-0247
Nagel's Bullets, 9 Wilburn, Baytown, TX 77520
Napoleon Bonaparte, Inc., Gerald Desquesnes, 640 Harrison St., Santa Clara, CA 95050
Nastoff's 45 Shop, Inc., Steve, 12288 Mahoning Ave., P.O. Box 446, North Jackson, OH 44451/216-538-2977
National Bullet Co., 1585 E. 361 St., Eastlake, OH 44095/216-951-1854; FAX: 216-951-7761
National Security Safe Co., Inc., P.O. Box 39, 620 S. 380 E., American Fork, UT 84003/801-756-7706, 800-544-3829; FAX: 801-756-8043
National Target Co., 4690 Wyaconda Rd., Rockville, MD 20852/800-827-7060, 301-770-7060; FAX: 301-770-7892
Nationwide Airgun Repairs (See Airgun Repair Centre)
Nationwide Sports Distributors, Inc., 70 James Way, Southampton, PA 18966/215-322-2050, 800-355-3006; FAX: 702-358-2093
Naval Ordnance Works, Rt. 2, Box 919, Sheperdstown, WV 25443/304-876-0998
Navy Arms Co., 689 Bergen Blvd., Ridgefield, NJ 07657/201-945-2500; FAX: 201-945-6859
N.B.B., Inc., 24 Elliot Rd., Sterling, MA 01564/508-422-7538, 800-942-9444
N.C. Ordnance Co., P.O. Box 3254, Wilson, NC 27895/919-237-2440; FAX: 919-243-0927
NCP Products, Inc., 3500 12th St. N.W., Canton, OH 44708/330-456-5130: FAX: 330-456-5234
Necessary Concepts, Inc., P.O. Box 571, Deer Park, NY 11729/516-667-8509; 800-671-8881
NECO, 1316-67th St., Emeryville, CA 94608/510-450-0420; FAX: 510-450-0421
Necromancer Industries, Inc., 14 Communications Way, West Newton, PA 15089/412-872-8722
NEI Handtools, Inc., 51583 Columbia River Hwy., Scappoose, OR 97056/503-543-6776; FAX: 503-543-6799; E-MAIL: neiht@mcimail.com
Nelson Combat Leather, Bruce, P.O. Box 8691 CRB, Tucson, AZ 85738
Nelson, Gary K., 975 Terrace Dr., Oakdale, CA 95361/209-847-4590
Nelson, Stephen, 7365 NW Spring Creek Dr., Corvallis, OR 97330/541-745-5232
Nelson/Weather-Rite, Inc., 14760 Santa Fe Trail Dr., Lenexa, KS 66215/913-492-3200; FAX: 913-492-8749
Nesci Enterprises, Inc., P.O. Box 119, Summit St., East Hampton, CT 06424/860-267-2588; FAX: 860-267-2589
Nesika Bay Precision, 22239 Big Valley Rd., Poulsbo, WA 98370/206-697-3830
Nettestad Gun Works, RR 1, Box 160, Pelican Rapids, MN 56572/218-863-4301
Neumann GmbH, Am Galgenberg 6, 90575 Langenzenn, GERMANY/09101/8258; FAX: 09101/6356
Nevada Cartridge Co., 44 Montgomery St., Suite 500, San Francisco, CA 94104/415-925-9394; FAX: 415-925-9396
Nevada Pistol Academy Inc., 4610 Blue Diamond Rd., Las Vegas, NV 89139/702-897-1100
New Advantage Arms Corp., 2843 N. Alvernon Way, Tucson, AZ 85712/602-881-7444; FAX: 602-323-0949
New Democracy, Inc., 751 W. Lamar Blvd., Suite 102, Arlington, TX 76012-2010
New England Ammunition Co., 1771 Post Rd. East, Suite 223, Westport, CT 06880/203-254-8048
New England Arms Co., Box 278, Lawrence Lane, Kittery Point, ME 03905/207-439-0593; FAX: 207-439-6726
New England Custom Gun Service, 438 Willow Brook Rd., RR2, Box 122W, W. Lebanon, NH 03784/603-469-3450; FAX: 603-469-3471
New England Firearms, 60 Industrial Rowe, Gardner, MA 01440/508-632-9393; FAX: 508-632-2300
New Historians Productions, The, 131 Oak St., Royal Oak, MI 48067/313-544-7544
New Orleans Jewelers Supply Co., 206 Charters St., New Orleans, LA 70130/504-523-3839; FAX: 504-523-3836
New SKB Arms Co., C.P.O. Box 1401, Tokyo, JAPAN/81-3-3943-9550; FAX: 81-3-3943-0695
New Win Publishing, Inc., Box 5159, Clinton, NJ 08809/201-735-9701; FAX: 201-735-9703
Newark Electronics, 4801 N. Ravenswood Ave., Chicago, IL 60640
Newell, Robert H., 55 Coyote, Los Alamos, NM 87544/505-662-7135
Newman Gunshop, 119 Miller Rd., Agency, IA 52530/515-937-5775
NgraveR Co., The, 67 Wawecus Hill Rd., Bozrah, CT 06334/203-823-1533
Nic Max, Inc., 535 Midland Ave., Garfield, NJ 07026/201-546-7191; FAX: 201-546-7419
Nicholson Custom, Rt. 1, Box 176-3, Sedalia, MO 65301/816-826-8746
Nickels, Paul R., 4789 Summerhill Rd., Las Vegas, NV 89121/702-435-5318
Nicklas, Ted, 5504 Hegel Rd., Goodrich, MI 48438/810-797-4493
Niemi Engineering, W.B., Box 126 Center Road, Greensboro, VT 05841/802-533-7180 days, 802-533-7141 evenings
Nikon, Inc., 1300 Walt Whitman Rd., Melville, NY 11747/516-547-8623; FAX: 516-547-0309
Nitex, Inc., P.O. Box 1706, Uvalde, TX 78801/210-278-8843
Noble Co., Jim, 1305 Columbia St., Vancouver, WA 98660/206-695-1309
Noreen, Peter H., 5075 Buena Vista Dr., Belgrade, MT 59714/406-586-7383
Norica, Avnda Otaola, 16, Apartado 68, 20600 Eibar, SPAIN
Norin, Dave, Schrank's Smoke & Gun, 2010 Washington St., Waukegan, IL 60085/708-662-4034
Norinco, 7A, Yun Tan N Beijing, CHINA (U.S. importers—Century International Arms, Inc.; Interarms)
Norma Precision AB (See U.S. importers—Dynamit Nobel-RWS Inc.; Paul Co. Inc., The)
Norman Custom Gunstocks, Jim, 14281 Cane Rd., Valley Center, CA 92082/619-749-6252
Normark Corp., 10395 Yellow Circle Dr., Minnetonka, MN 55343-9101/612-933-7060; FAX: 612-933-0046
Norrell Arms, John, 2608 Grist Mill Rd., Little Rock, AR 72207/501-225-7864
North American Arms, Inc., 2150 South 950 East, Provo, UT 84606-6285/800-821-5783, 801-374-9990; FAX: 801-374-9998
North American Correspondence Schools, The Gun Pro School, Oak & Pawnee St., Scranton, PA 18515/717-342-7701
North American Munitions, P.O. Box 815, Beulah, ND 58523/701-948-2260; FAX: 701-948-2282
North American Shooting Systems, P.O. Box 306, Osoyoos, B.C. V0H 1V0 CANADA/604-495-3131; FAX: 604-495-2816
North American Specialties, P.O. Box 189, Baker City, OR 97814/503-523-6954
North Devon Firearms Services, 3 North St., Braunton, EX33 1AJ ENGLAND/01271 813624; FAX: 01271 813624
North Fork Custom Gunsmithing, James Johnston, 428 Del Rio Rd., Roseburg, OR 97470/503-673-4467
North Mountain Pine Training Center (See Executive Protection Institute)
North Specialty Products, 2664-B Saturn St., Brea, CA 92621/714-524-1665
North Star West, P.O. Box 488, Glencoe, CA 95232/209-293-7010
North Wind Decoy Co., 1005 N. Tower Rd., Fergus Falls, MN 56537/218-736-4378; FAX: 218-736-7060
Northern Precision Custom Swaged Bullets, 329 S. James St., Carthage, NY 13619/315-493-1711
Northlake Outdoor Footwear, P.O. Box 10, Franklin, TN 37065-0010/615-794-1556; FAX: 615-790-8005
Northside Gun Shop, 2725 NW 109th, Oklahoma City, OK 73120/405-840-2353
No-Sho Mfg. Co., 10727 Glenfield Ct., Houston, TX 77096/713-723-5332
Nosler, Inc., P.O. Box 671, Bend, OR 97709/800-285-3701, 503-382-3921; FAX: 503-388-4667
Novak's, Inc., 1206½ 30th St., P.O. Box 4045, Parkersburg, WV 26101/304-485-9295; FAX: 304-428-6722
Nowlin Custom Mfg., Rt. 1, Box 308, Claremore, OK 74017/918-342-0689; FAX: 918-342-0624
NRI Gunsmith School, 4401 Connecticut Ave. NW, Washington, D.C. 20008
Nu-Line Guns, Inc., 1053 Caulks Hill Rd., Harvester, MO 63304/314-441-4500, 314-447-4501; FAX: 314-447-5018
Null Holsters Ltd., K.L., 161 School St. NW, Hill City Station, Resaca, GA 30735/706-625-5643; FAX: 706-625-9392
Numrich Arms Corp., 203 Broadway, W. Hurley, NY 12491
Nu-Teck, 30 Industrial Park Rd., Box 37, Centerbrook, CT 06409/203-767-3573; FAX: 203-767-9137
NW Sinker and Tackle, 380 Valley Dr., Myrtle Creek, OR 97457-9717
Nygord Precision Products, P.O. Box 12578, Prescott, AZ 86304/520-717-2315; FAX: 520-717-2198

O

Oakland Custom Arms, Inc., 4690 W. Walton Blvd., Waterford, MI 48329/810-674-8261
Oakman Turkey Calls, RD 1, Box 825, Harrisonville, PA 17228/717-485-4620
Oakshore Electronic Sights, Inc., P.O. Box 4470, Ocala, FL 32678-4470/904-629-7112; FAX: 904-629-1433
Obermeyer Rifled Barrels, 23122 60th St., Bristol, WI 53104/414-843-3537; FAX: 414-843-2129
October Country, P.O. Box 969, Dept. GD, Hayden, ID 83835/208-772-2068; FAX: 208-772-9230
Oehler Research, Inc., P.O. Box 9135, Austin, TX 78766/512-327-6900, 800-531-5125; FAX: 512-327-6903
Oglesby & Oglesby Gunmakers, Inc., RR 5, Springfield, IL 62707/217-487-7100
Oil Rod and Gun Shop, 69 Oak St., East Douglas, MA 01516/508-476-3687
Ojala Holsters, Arvo, P.O. Box 98, N. Hollywood, CA 91603/503-669-1404
Oker's Engraving, 365 Bell Rd., P.O. Box 126, Shawnee, CO 80475/303-838-6042
Oklahoma Ammunition Co., 4310 W. Rogers Blvd., Skiatook, OK 74070/918-396-3187; FAX: 918-396-4270
Oklahoma Leather Products, Inc., 500 26th NW, Miami, OK 74354/918-542-6651; FAX: 918-542-6653
OK Weber, Inc., P.O. Box 7485, Eugene, OR 97401/541-747-0458; FAX: 541-747-5927
Old Dominion Engravers, 100 Progress Drive, Lynchburg, VA 24502/804-237-4450
Old Wagon Bullets, 32 Old Wagon Rd., Wilton, CT 06897
Old West Bullet Moulds, P.O. Box 519, Flora Vista, NM 87415/505-334-6970
Old West Reproductions, Inc., 446 Florence S. Loop, Florence, MT 59833/406-273-2615
Old Western Scrounger, Inc., 12924 Hwy. A-l2, Montague, CA 96064/916-459-5445; FAX: 916-459-3944
Old World Gunsmithing, 2901 SE 122nd St., Portland, OR 97236/503-760-7681
Old World Oil Products, 3827 Queen Ave. N., Minneapolis, MN 55412/612-522-5037
Ole Frontier Gunsmith Shop, 2617 Hwy. 29 S., Cantonment, FL 32533/904-477-8074
Olsen Development Lab, 111 Lakeview Ave., Blackwood, NJ 08012
Olson, Myron, 989 W. Kemp, Watertown, SD 57201/605-886-9787
Olson, Vic, 5002 Countryside Dr., Imperial, MO 63052/314-296-8086
Olt Co., Philip S., P.O. Box 550, 12662 Fifth St., Pekin, IL 61554/309-348-3633; FAX: 309-348-3300
Olympic Optical Co., P.O. Box 752377, Memphis, TN 38175-2377/901-794-3890, 800-238-7120; FAX: 901-794-0676, 800-748-1669
Omark Industries, Div. of Blount, Inc., 2299 Snake River Ave., P.O. Box 856, Lewiston, ID 83501/800-627-3640, 208-746-2351
Omega Sales, P.O. Box 1066, Mt. Clemens, MI 48043/810-469-7323; FAX: 810-469-0425
One Of A Kind, 15610 Purple Sage, San Antonio, TX 78255/512-695-3364
Op-Tec, P.O. Box L632, Langhorn, PA 19047/215-757-5037
Optical Services Co., P.O. Box 1174, Santa Teresa, NM 88008-1174/505-589-3833
Orchard Park Enterprise, P.O. Box 563, Orchard Park, NY 14227/616-656-0356
Ordnance Works, The, 2969 Pidgeon Point Road, Eureka, CA 95501/707-443-3252
Oregon Arms, Inc., P.O. Box 20, Prospect OR 97536/503-560-4040; FAX: 503-560-4041
Original Mink Oil, Inc., 10652 NE Holman, Portland, OR 97220/503-255-2814, 800-547-5895; FAX: 503-255-2487
Orion Rifle Barrel Co., RR2, 137 Cobler Village, Kalispell, MT 59901/406-257-5649
Or-Un, Tahtakale Menekse Han 18, Istanbul, TURKEY 34460/90212-522-5912; FAX: 90212-522-7973

MANUFACTURERS' DIRECTORY

Orvis Co., The, Rt. 7, Manchester, VT 05254/802-362-3622 ext. 283; FAX: 802-362-3525
Ottmar, Maurice, Box 657, 113 E. Fir, Coulee City, WA 99115/509-632-5717
Outa-Site Gun Carriers, 219 Market St., Laredo, TX 78040/210-722-4678, 800-880-9715; FAX: 210-726-4858
Outdoor Connection, Inc., The, 201 Cotton Dr., P.O. Box 7751, Waco, TX 76714-7751/800-533-6076; 817-772-5575; FAX: 817-776-3553
Outdoor Edge Cutlery Corp., 2888 Bluff St., Suite 130, Boulder, CO 80301/303-652-8212; FAX: 303-652-8238
Outdoor Enthusiast, 3784 W. Woodland, Springfield, MO 65807/417-883-9841
Outdoor Sports Headquarters, Inc., 967 Watertower Ln., West Carrollton, OH 45449/513-865-5855; FAX: 513-865-5962
Outdoorsman's Bookstore, The, Llangorse, Brecon, Powys LD3 7UE, U.K./44-1874-658-660; FAX: 44-1874-658-650
Outers Laboratories, Div. of Blount, Inc., Sporting Equipment Div., Route 2,, P.O. Box 39/Onalaska, WI 54650 608-781-5800; FAX: 608-781-0368
Ox-Yoke Originals, Inc., 34 Main St., Milo, ME 04463/800-231-8313, 207-943-7351; FAX: 207-943-2416
Ozark Gun Works, 11830 Cemetery Rd., Rogers, AR 72756/501-631-6944; FAX: 501-631-6944

P

P&M Sales and Service, 5724 Gainsborough Pl., Oak Forest, IL 60452/708-687-7149
P&S Gun Service, 2138 Old Shepardsville Rd., Louisville, KY 40218/502-456-9346
Pac-Nor Barreling, 99299 Overlook Rd., P.O. Box 6188, Brookings, OR 97415/503-469-7330; FAX: 503-469-7331
Pace Marketing, Inc., P.O. Box 2039, Stuart, FL 34995/407-871-9682; FAX: 407-871-6552
Pachmayr, Ltd., 1875 S. Mountain Ave., Monrovia, CA 91016/818-357-7771, 800-423-9704; FAX: 818-358-7251
Pacific Pistolcraft, 1810 E. Columbia Ave., Tacoma, WA 98404/206-474-5465
Pacific Precision, 755 Antelope Rd., P.O. Box 2549, White City, OR 97503/503-826-5808; FAX: 503-826-5304
Pacific Research Laboratories, Inc., 10221 S.W. 188th St., Vashon Island, WA 98070/206-463-5551; FAX: 206-463-2526
Pacific Rifle Co., 1040-D Industrial Parkway, Newberg, OR 97132/503-538-7437
Pacific Tool Co., P.O. Box 2048, Ordnance Plant Rd., Grand Island, NE 68801
Paco's (See Small Custom Mould & Bullet Co.)
P.A.C.T., Inc., P.O. Box 531525, Grand Prairie, TX 75053/214-641-0049
Page Custom Bullets, P.O. Box 25, Port Moresby Papua, NEW GUINEA
Pagel Gun Works, Inc., 1407 4th St. NW, Grand Rapids, MN 55744/218-326-3003
Paintball Consumer Reports (International Paintball Pub. Inc.), 14573-C Jefferson Davis Highway/Woodridge, VA 22191 703-491-6199
Paintball Games International Magazine (Aceville Publications), Castle House, 97 High St./Colchester, Essex, CO1 1TH ENGLAND 011-44-206-564840
Paintball Sports Magazine, 540 Main St., Mt. Kisco, NY 10549/914-241-7400
Palmer Manufacturing Co., Inc., C., P.O. Box 220, West Newton, PA 15089/412-872-8200; FAX: 412-872-8302
Palmer Security Products, 2930 N. Campbell Ave., Chicago, IL 60618/800-788-7725; FAX: 312-267-8080
Palsa Outdoor Products, P.O. Box 81336, Lincoln, NE 68501-1336/402-488-5288, 800-456-9281; FAX: 402-488-2321
PanaVise Products, Inc., 1485 Southern Way, Sparks, NV 89431/702-353-2900; FAX: 702-353-2929
Para-Ordnance Mfg., Inc., 980 Tapscott Rd., Scarborough, Ont. M1X 1E7, CANADA/416-297-7855; FAX: 416-297-1289 (U.S. importer—Para-Ordnance, Inc.)
Para-Ordnance, Inc., 1919 NE 45th St., Ft. Lauderdale, FL 33308
Paragon Sales & Services, Inc., P.O. Box 2022, Joliet, IL 60434/815-725-9212; FAX: 815-725-8974
Pardini Armi Srl, Via Italica 154, 55043 Lido Di Camaiore Lu, ITALY/584-90121; FAX: 584-90122 (U.S. importers—Nygord Precision Products)
Paris, Frank J., 17417 Pershing St., Livonia, MI 48152-3822
Park Rifle Co., Ltd., The, Unit 6a, Dartford Trade Park, Power Mill Lane, Dartford, Kent DA7 7NX/011-0322-222512 (U.S. importer—Air Werks International)
Parker Div. Reageant Chemical (See Parker Reproductions)
Parker Gun Finishes, 9337 Smokey Row Rd., Strawberry Plains, TN 37871/423-933-3286
Parker Reproductions, 124 River Rd., Middlesex, NJ 08846/908-469-0100; FAX: 908-469-9692
Parker, Mark D., 1240 Florida Ave. 7, Longmont, CO 80501/303-772-0214
Parsons Optical Mfg. Co., P.O. Box 192, Ross, OH 45061/513-867-0820; FAX: 513-867-8380
Parts & Surplus, P.O. Box 22074, Memphis, TN 38122/901-683-4007
Partridge Sales Ltd., John, Trent Meadows, Rugeley, Staffordshire, WS15 2HS ENGLAND/0889-584438
Pasadena Gun Center, 206 E. Shaw, Pasadena, TX 77506/713-472-0417; FAX: 713-472-1322
Passive Bullet Traps, Inc. (See Savage Range Systems, Inc.)
PAST Sporting Goods, Inc., P.O. Box 1035, Columbia, MO 65205/314-445-9200; FAX: 314-446-6606
Paterson Gunsmithing, 438 Main St., Paterson, NJ 07502/201-345-4100
Pathfinder Sports Leather, 2920 E. Chambers St., Phoenix, AZ 85040/602-276-0016
Patrick Bullets, P.O. Box 172, Warwick QSLD 4370 AUSTRALIA
Pattern Control, 114 N. Third St., P.O. Box 462105, Garland, TX 75046/214-494-3551; FAX: 214-272-8447
Paul Co., The, 27385 Pressonville Rd., Wellsville, KS 66092/913-883-4444; FAX: 913-883-2525
Paulsen Gunstocks, Rt. 71, Box 11, Chinook, MT 59523/406-357-3403
Payne Photography, Robert, P.O. Box 141471, Austin, TX 78714/512-272-4554

PC Bullet/ADC, Inc., 52700 NE First, Scappoose, OR 97056-3212/503-543-5088; FAX: 503-543-5990
PC Co., 5942 Secor Rd., Toledo, OH 43623/419-472-6222
Peacemaker Specialists, P.O. Box 157, Whitmore, CA 96096/916-472-3438
Pease Accuracy, Bob, P.O. Box 310787, New Braunfels, TX 78131/210-625-1342
Peasley, David, P.O. Box 604, 2067 S. Hiway 17, Alamosa, CO 81101
PECAR Herbert Schwarz, GmbH, Kreuzbergstrasse 6, 10965 Berlin, GERMANY/004930-785-7383; FAX: 004930-785-1934
Pecatonica River Longrifle, 5205 Noddingham Dr., Rockford, IL 61111/815-968-1995; FAX: 815-968-1996
Pedersen, C.R., 2717 S. Pere Marquette Hwy., Ludington, MI 49431/616-843-2061
Pedersen, Rex C., 2717 S. Pere Marquette Hwy., Ludington, MI 49431/616-843-2061
Pedersoli Davide & C., Via Artigiani 57, Gardone V.T., Brescia, ITALY 25063/030-8912402; FAX: 030-8911019 (U.S. importers—Beauchamp & Son, Inc.; Cabela's; Cape Outfitters; Dixie Gun Works; EMF Co., Inc.; Navy Arms Co.)
Peerless Alloy, Inc., 1445 Osage St., Denver, CO 80204-2439/303-825-6394, 800-253-1278
Peet Shoe Dryer, Inc., 130 S. 5th St., P.O. Box 618, St. Maries, ID 83861/208-245-2095, 800-222-PEET; FAX: 208-245-5441
Peifer Rifle Co., P.O. Box 192, Nokomis, IL 62075-0192/217-563-7050; FAX: 217-563-7060
Pejsa Ballistics, 2120 Kenwood Pkwy., Minneapolis, MN 55405/612-374-3337; FAX: 612-374-3337
Pelaire Products, 5346 Bonky Ct., W. Palm Beach, FL 33415/407-439-0691; FAX: 407-967-0052
Pell, John T. (See KOGOT)
Peltor, Inc., 41 Commercial Way, E. Providence, RI 02914/401-438-4800; FAX: 401-434-1708
PEM's Mfg. Co., 5063 Waterloo Rd., Atwater, OH 44201/216-947-3721
Pence Precision Barrels, 7567 E. 900 S., S. Whitley, IN 46787/219-839-4745
Pend Oreille Sport Shop, 3100 Hwy. 200 East, Sandpoint, ID 83864/208-263-2412
Pendleton Royal, c/o Swingler Buckland Ltd., 4/7 Highgate St., Birmingham, ENGLAND B12 0XS/44 121 440 3060, 44 121 446 5898; FAX: 44 121 446 4165
Pendleton Woolen Mills, P.O. Box 3030, 220 N.W. Broadway, Portland, OR 97208/503-226-4801
Penguin Industries, Inc., Airport Industrial Mall, Coatesville, PA 19320/610-384-6000; FAX: 610-857-5980
Penn Bullets, P.O. Box 756, Indianola, PA 15051
Penn's Woods Products, Inc., 19 W. Pittsburgh St., Delmont, PA 15626/412-468-8311; FAX: 412-468-8975
Pennsylvania Gun Parts, 1701 Mud Run Rd., York Springs, PA 17372/717-259-8010
Pennsylvania Gunsmith School, 812 Ohio River Blvd., Avalon, Pittsburgh, PA 15202/412-766-1812
Penrod Precision, 312 College Ave., P.O. Box 307, N. Manchester, IN 46962/219-982-8385
Pentax Corp., 35 Inverness Dr. E., Englewood, CO 80112/303-799-8000; FAX: 303-790-1131
Pentheny de Pentheny, 2352 Baggett Ct., Santa Rosa, CA 95401/707-573-1390; FAX: 707-573-1390
Perazone-Gunsmith, Brian, P.O. Box 275GD, Cold Spring Rd., Roxbury, NY 12474/607-326-4088; FAX: 607-326-3140
Perazzi m.a.p. S.P.A., Via Fontanelle 1/3, 1-25080 Botticino Mattina, ITALY (U.S. importer—Perazzi USA, Inc.)
Perazzi USA, Inc., 1207 S. Shamrock Ave., Monrovia, CA 91016/818-303-0068; FAX: 818-303-2081
Peregrine Sporting Arms, Inc., 14155 Brighton Rd., Brighton, CO 80601/303-654-0850
Performance Specialists, 308 Eanes School Rd., Austin, TX 78746/512-327-0119
Peripheral Data Systems (See Arms Software)
Personal Protection Systems, RD 5, Box 5027-A, Moscow, PA 18444/717-842-1766
Perugini Visini & Co. s.r.l., Via Camprelle, 126, 25080 Nuvolera (Bs.), ITALY
Peters Stahl GmbH, Stettiner Strasse 42, D-33106 Paderborn, GERMANY/05251-750025; FAX: 05251-75611 (U.S. importers—Harris Gunworks; Olympic Arms)
Petersen Publishing Co., 6420 Wilshire Blvd., Los Angeles, CA 90048/213-782-2000; FAX: 213-782-2867
Peterson Gun Shop, Inc., A.W., 4255 W. Old U.S. 441, Mt. Dora, FL 32757-3299/904-383-4258
Petro-Explo, Inc., 7650 U.S. Hwy. 287, Suite 100, Arlington, TX 76017/817-478-8888
Pettinger Books, Gerald, Rt. 2, Box 125, Russell, IA 50238/515-535-2239
Pflumm Mfg. Co., 10662 Widmer Rd., Lenexa, KS 66215/800-888-4867; FAX: 913-451-7857
PFRB Co., P.O. Box 1242, Bloomington, IL 61702/309-473-3964
Phil-Chem, Inc. (See George & Roy's)
Phillippi Custom Bullets, Justin, P.O. Box 773, Ligonier, PA 15658/412-238-9671
Phillips, Jerry, P.O. Box L632, Langhorne, PA 19047/215-757-5037
Phillips & Rodgers, 100 Hilbig, Suite C, Conroe, TX 77301/800-682-2247
Phoenix Arms, 1420 S. Archibald Ave., Ontario, CA 91761/909-947-4843; FAX: 909-947-6798
Photronic Systems Engineering Company, 6731 Via De La Reina, Bonsall, CA 92003/619-758-8000
Piedmont Community College, P.O. Box 1197, Roxboro, NC 27573/910-599-1181
Pierce Pistols, 2326 E. Hwy. 34, Newnan, GA 30263/404-253-8192
Pietta (See U.S. importers—Navy Arms Co.; Taylor's & Co., Inc.)
Pilgrim Pewter, Inc. (See Bell Originals Inc., Sid)
Pilkington, Scott, Little Trees Ramble, P.O. Box 97, Monteagle, TN 37356/615-924-3475; FAX: 615-924-3489
Pine Technical College, 1100 4th St., Pine City, MN 55063/800-521-7463; FAX: 612-629-6766

DIRECTORY OF THE ARMS TRADE

Pinetree Bullets, 133 Skeena St., Kitimat BC, CANADA V8C 1Z1/604-632-3768; FAX: 604-632-3768
Pioneer Arms Co., 355 Lawrence Rd., Broomall, PA 19008/215-356-5203
Pioneer Guns, 5228 Montgomery Rd., Norwood, OH 45212/513-631-4871
Pioneer Research, Inc., 216 Haddon Ave. Suite 102, Westmont, NJ 08108/800-257-7742; FAX: 609-858-8695
Piotti (See U.S. importer—Moore & Co., Wm. Larkin)
Piquette, Paul R., 80 Bradford Dr., Feeding Hills, MA 01030/413-781-8300, Ext. 682
Plaxco, J. Michael, Rt. 1, P.O. Box 203, Roland, AR 72135/501-868-9787
Plaza Cutlery, Inc., 3333 Bristol, 161, South Coast Plaza, Costa Mesa, CA 92626/714-549-3932
Plum City Ballistic Range, N2162 80th St., Plum City, WI 54761-8622/715-647-2539
PlumFire Press, Inc., 30-A Grove Ave., Patchogue, NY 11772-4112/800-695-7246; FAX:516-758-4071
PMC/Eldorado Cartridge Corp., P.O. Box 62508, 12801 U.S. Hwy. 95 S., Boulder City, NV 89005/702-294-0025; FAX: 702-294-0121
P.M. Enterprises, Inc., 146 Curtis Hill Rd., Chehalis, WA 98532/206-748-3743; FAX: 206-748-1802
Poburka, Philip (See Bison Studios)
Pohl, Henry A. (See Great American Gun Co.)
Pointing Dog Journal, Village Press Publications, P.O. Box 968, Dept. PGD, Traverse City, MI 49685/800-272-3246; FAX: 616-946-3289
Police Bookshelf, P.O. Box 122, Concord, NH 03301/603-224-6814; FAX: 603-226-3554
Policlips North America, 59 Douglas Crescent, Toronto, Ont. CANADA M4W 2E6/800-229-5089, 416-924-0383; FAX: 416-924-4375
Polywad, Inc., P.O. Box 7916, Macon, GA 31209/912-477-0669
Pomeroy, Robert, RR1, Box 50, E. Corinth, ME 04427/207-285-7721
Ponsness/Warren, P.O. Box 8, Rathdrum, ID 83858/208-687-2231; FAX: 208-687-2233
Pony Express Reloaders, 608 E. Co. Rd. D, Suite 3, St. Paul, MN 55117/612-483-9406; FAX: 612-483-9884
Pony Express Sport Shop, Inc., 16606 Schoenborn St., North Hills, CA 91343/818-895-1231
Porta Blind, Inc., 2700 Speedway, Wichita Falls, TX 76308/817-723-6620
Portus, Robert, 130 Ferry Rd., Grants Pass, OR 97526/503-476-4919
Potts, Wayne E., 912 Poplar St., Denver, CO 80220/303-355-5462
Powder Horn Antiques, P.O. Box 4196, Ft. Lauderdale, FL 33338/305-565-6060
Powder Horn, Inc., The, P.O. Box 114 Patty Drive, Cusseta, GA 31805/404-989-3257
Powder Valley Services, Rt. 1, Box 100, Dexter, KS 67038/316-876-5418
Powell & Son (Gunmakers) Ltd., William, 35-37 Carrs Lane, Birmingham B4 7SX ENGLAND/121-643-0689; FAX: 121-631-3504 (U.S. importer—Bell's Legendary Country Wear; The William Powell Agency)
Powell Agency, William, The, 22 Circle Dr., Bellmore, NY 11710/516-679-1158
Power Custom, Inc., RR 2, P.O. Box 756AB, Gravois Mills, MO 65037/314-372-5684
Practical Tools, Inc., Div. Behlert Precision, 7067 Easton Rd., P.O. Box 133, Pipersville, PA 18947/215-766-7301; FAX: 215-766-8681
Pragotrade, 307 Humberline Dr., Rexdale, Ontario, CANADA M9W 5V1/416-675-1322
Prairie River Arms, 1220 N. Sixth St., Princeton, IL 61356/815-875-1616, 800-445-1541; FAX: 815-875-1402
Pranger, Ed G., 1414 7th St., Anacortes, WA 98221/206-293-3488
Pre-Winchester 92-90-62 Parts Co., P.O. Box 8125, W. Palm Beach, FL 33407
Precise International, 15 Corporate Dr., Orangeburg, NY 10962/914-365-3500; FAX: 914-425-4700
Precise Metalsmithing Enterprises, 146 Curtis Hill Rd., Chehalis, WA 98532/206-748-3743; FAX: 206-748-8102
Precision, Jim, 1725 Moclip's Dr., Petaluma, CA 94952/707-762-3014
Precision Airgun Sales, Inc., 5139 Warrensville Center Rd., Maple Hts., OH 44137-1906/216-587-5005
Precision Cartridge, 176 Eastside Rd., Deer Lodge, MT 59722/800-397-3901, 406-846-3900
Precision Cast Bullets, 101 Mud Creek Lane, Ronan, MT 59864/406-676-5135
Precision Castings & Equipment, Inc., P.O. Box 326, Jasper, IN 47547-0135/812-634-9167
Precision Components, 3177 Sunrise Lake, Milford, PA 18337/717-686-4414
Precision Components and Guns, Rt. 55, P.O. Box 337, Pawling, NY 12564/914-855-3040
Precision Delta Corp., P.O. Box 128, Ruleville, MS 38771/601-756-2810; FAX: 601-756-2590
Precision Metal Finishing, John Westrom, P.O. Box 3186, Des Moines, IA 50316/515-288-8680; FAX: 515-244-3925
Precision Munitions, Inc., P.O. Box 326, Jasper, IN 47547
Precision Ordnance, 1316 E. North St., Jackson, MI 49202
Precision Reloading, Inc., P.O. Box 122, Stafford Springs, CT 06076/860-684-7979; FAX: 860-684-6788
Precision Sales International, Inc., P.O. Box 1776, Westfield, MA 01086/413-562-5055; FAX: 413-562-5056
Precision Shooting, Inc., 222 McKee St., Manchester, CT 06040/860-645-8776; FAX: 860-643-8215
Precision Small Arms, 9777 Wilshire Blvd., Suite 1005, Beverly Hills, CA 90212/310-859-4867; FAX: 310-859-2868
Precision Specialties, 131 Hendom Dr., Feeding Hills, MA 01030/413-786-3365; FAX: 413-786-3365
Precision Sport Optics, 15571 Producer Lane, Unit G, Huntington Beach, CA 92649/714-891-1309; FAX: 714-892-6920
Premier Reticles, 920 Breckinridge Lane, Winchester, VA 22601-6707/540-722-0601; FAX: 540-722-3522
Prescott Projectile Co., 1808 Meadowbrook Road, Prescott, AZ 86303
Price Bullets, Patrick W., 16520 Worthley Drive, San Lorenzo, CA 94580/510-278-1547
Preslik's Gunstocks, 4245 Keith Ln., Chico, CA 95926/916-891-8236
Prime Reloading, 30 Chiswick End, Meldreth, Royston SG8 6LZ UK/0763-260636

Primos, Inc., P.O. Box 12785, Jackson, MS 39236-2785/601-366-1288; FAX: 601-362-3274
Pro Load Ammunition, Inc., 5180 E. Seltice Way, Post Falls, ID 83854/208-773-9444; FAX: 208-773-9441
Pro-Mark, Div. of Wells Lamont, 6640 W. Touhy, Chicago, IL 60648/312-647-8200
Pro-Port Ltd., 41302 Executive Dr., Harrison Twp., MI 48045-1306/810-469-7323; FAX: 810-469-0425
Pro-Shot Products, Inc., P.O. Box 763, Taylorville, IL 62568/217-824-9133; FAX: 217-824-8861
Professional Firearms Record Book Co. (See PFRB Co.)
Professional Gunsmiths of America, Inc., Route 1, Box 224F, Lexington, MO 64067/816-259-2636
Professional Hunter Supplies (See Star Custom Bullets)
Prolix® Lubricants, P.O. Box 1348, Victorville, CA 92393/800-248-LUBE, 619-243-3129; FAX: 619-241-0148
Protecto Plastics, Div. of Penguin Ind., Airport Industrial Mall, Coatesville, PA 19320/215-384-6000
Protector Mfg. Co., Inc., The, 443 Ashwood Place, Boca Raton, FL 33431/407-394-6011
Protektor Model, 1-11 Bridge St., Galeton, PA 16922/814-435-2442
Prototech Industries, Inc., Rt. 1, Box 81, Delia, KS 66418/913-771-3571; FAX: 913-771-2531
ProWare,Inc., 15847 NE Hancock St., Portland, OR 97230/503-239-0159
P.S.M.G. Gun Co., 10 Park Ave., Arlington, MA 02174/617-646-8845; FAX: 617-646-2133
PWL Gunleather, P.O. Box 450432, Atlanta, GA 31145/404-822-1640; FAX: 404-822-1704
Pyromid, Inc., 3292 S. Highway 97, Redmond, OR 97756/503-548-1041; FAX: 503-923-1004

Q

QB air rifles (See U.S. importer—Sportsman Airguns, Inc.)
Quack Decoy & Sporting Clays, 4 Ann & Hope Way, P.O. Box 98, Cumberland, RI 02864/401-723-8202; FAX: 401-722-5910
Quaker Boy, Inc., 5455 Webster Rd., Orchard Parks, NY 14127/716-662-3979; FAX: 716-662-9426
Quality Arms, Inc., Box 19477, Dept. GD, Houston, TX 77224/713-870-8377; FAX: 713-870-8524
Quality Firearms of Idaho, Inc., 114 13th Ave. S., Nampa, ID 83651/208-466-1631
Quality Parts Co./Bushmaster Firearms, 999 Roosevelt Trail, Bldg. 3, Windham, ME 04062/800-998-7928, 207-892-2005; FAX: 207-892-8068
Quarton USA, Ltd. Co., 7042 Alamo Downs Pkwy., Suite 370, San Antonio, TX 78238-4518/800-520-8435, 210-520-8430; FAX: 210-520-8433
Quartz-Lok, 13137 N. 21st Lane, Phoenix, AZ 85029
Que Industries, Inc., P.O. Box 2471, Everett, WA 98203/800-769-6930, 206-347-9843; FAX: 206-514-3266
Queen Cutlery Co., P.O. Box 500, Franklinville, NY 14737/800-222-5233; FAX: 716-676-5535
Quigley's Personal Protection Strategies, Paxton, 9903 Santa Monica Blvd.,, 300/Beverly Hills, CA 90212 310-281-1762

R

R&C Knives & Such, P.O. Box 1047, Manteca, CA 95336/209-239-3722; FAX: 209-825-6947
R&J Gun Shop, 133 W. Main St., John Day, OR 97845/503-575-2130
R&S Industries Corp., 8255 Brentwood Industrial Dr., St. Louis, MO 63144/314-781-5400
Rabeno, Martin, 92 Spook Hole Rd., Ellenville, NY 12428/914-647-4567
Radiator Specialty Co., 1900 Wilkinson Blvd., P.O. Box 34689, Charlotte, NC 28234/800-438-6947; FAX: 800-421-9525
Radical Concepts, P.O. Box 1473, Lake Grove, OR 97035/503-538-7437
Rainier Ballistics Corp., 4500 15th St. East, Tacoma, WA 98424/800-638-8722, 206-922-7589; FAX: 206-922-7854
Ram-Line, Inc., 545 Thirty-One Rd., Grand Junction, CO 81504/303-434-4500; FAX: 303-434-4004
Ranch Products, P.O. Box 145, Malinta, OH 43535/313-277-3118; FAX: 313-565-8536
Randall-Made Knives, P.O. Box 1988, Orlando, FL 32802/407-855-8075
Randco UK, 286 Gipsy Rd., Welling, Kent DA16 1JJ, ENGLAND/44 81 303 4118
Randolph Engineering, Inc., 26 Thomas Patten Dr., Randolph, MA 02368/800-541-1405; FAX: 617-986-0337
Ranger Mfg. Co., Inc., 1536 Crescent Dr., P.O. Box 14069, Augusta, GA 30919-0069/706-738-2023; FAX: 404-738-3608
Ranger Products, 2623 Grand Blvd., Suite 209, Holiday, FL 34609/813-942-4652, 800-407-7007; FAX: 813-942-6221
Ranger Shooting Glasses, 26 Thomas Patten Dr., Randolph, MA 02368/800-541-1405; FAX: 617-986-0337
Ranging, Inc., Routes 5 & 20, East Bloomfield, NY 14443/716-657-6161; FAX: 716-657-5405
Ransom International Corp., P.O. Box 3845, 1040-A Sandretto Dr., Prescott, AZ 86302/520-778-7899; FAX: 520-778-7993; E-MAIL: ransom@primenet.com; WEB: http://www.primenet.com/~ransom
Rapine Bullet Mould Mfg. Co., 9503 Landis Lane, East Greenville, PA 18041/215-679-5413; FAX: 215-679-9795
Rattlers Brand, P.O. Box 311, 115 E. Main St., Thomaston, GA 30286/706-647-7131, 800-825-7131; FAX: 706-647-6652
Ravell Ltd., 289 Diputacion St., 08009, Barcelona SPAIN/34(3) 4874486; FAX: 34(3) 4881394
Ray's Gunsmith Shop, 3199 Elm Ave., Grand Junction, CO 81504/970-434-6162; FAX: 970-434-6162
Raytech, Div. of Lyman Products Corp., 475 Smith Street, Middletown, CT 06457-1541/860-632-2020; FAX: 860-632-1699
RCBS, Div. of Blount, Inc., Sporting Equipment Div., 605 Oro Dam Blvd., Oroville, CA 95965/800-533-5000, 916-533-5191; FAX: 916-533-1647

MANUFACTURERS' DIRECTORY

Reagent Chemical & Research, Inc. (See Calico Hardwoods, Inc.)
Reardon Products, P.O. Box 126, Morrison, IL 61270/815-772-3155
Recoilless Technologies, Inc., 3432 W. Wilshire Dr., Suite 11, Phoenix, AZ 85009/602-278-8903; FAX: 602-272-5946
Red Ball, 100 Factory St., Nashua, NH 03060/603-881-4420
Red Cedar Precision Mfg., W. 485 Spruce Dr., Brodhead, WI 53520/608-897-8416
Red Diamond Dist. Co., 1304 Snowdon Dr., Knoxville, TN 37912
Red Star Target Co., P.O. Box 275, Babb, MT 59411-0275/800-679-2917; FAX: 800-679-2918
Redding Reloading Equipment, 1097 Starr Rd., Cortland, NY 13045/607-753-3331; FAX: 607-756-8445
Redfield, Inc., 5800 E. Jewell Ave., Denver, CO 80224-2303/303-757-6411; FAX: 303-756-2338
Redman's Rifling & Reboring, 189 Nichols Rd., Omak, WA 98841/509-826-5512
Redwood Bullet Works, 3559 Bay Rd., Redwood City, CA 94063/415-367-6741
Reed, Dave, Rt. 1, Box 374, Minnesota City, MN 55959/507-689-2944
Refrigiwear, Inc., 71 Inip Dr., Inwood, Long Island, NY 11696
R.E.I., P.O. Box 88, Tallevast, FL 34270/813-755-0085
Reiswig, Wallace E. (See Claro Walnut Gunstock Co.)
Reloaders Equipment Co., 4680 High St., Ecorse, MI 48229
Reloading Specialties, Inc., Box 1130, Pine Island, MN 55463/507-356-8500; FAX: 507-356-8800
Remington Arms Co., Inc., P.O. Box 700, 870 Remington Drive, Madison, NC 27025-0700/800-243-9700
Renegade, P.O. Box 31546, Phoenix, AZ 85046/602-482-6777; FAX: 602-482-1952
Renfrew Guns & Supplies, R.R. 4, Renfrew, Ontario K7V 3Z7 CANADA/613-432-7080
Reno, Wayne, 2808 Stagestop Rd., Jefferson, CO 80456/719-836-3452
R.E.T. Enterprises, 2608 S. Chestnut, Broken Arrow, OK 74012/918-251-GUNS; FAX: 918-251-0587
Retting, Inc., Martin B., 11029 Washington, Culver City, CA 90232/213-837-2412
R.G.-G., Inc., P.O. Box 1261, Conifer, CO 80433-1261/303-697-4154; FAX: 303-697-4154
Rhodeside, Inc., 1704 Commerce Dr., Piqua, OH 45356/513-773-5781
Rice, Keith (See White Rock Tool & Die)
Richards, John, Richards Classic Oil Finish, Rt. 2, Box 325, Bedford, KY 40006/502-255-7222
Richards Micro-Fit Stocks, 8331 N. San Fernando Ave., Sun Valley, CA 91352/818-767-6097; FAX: 818-767-7121
Rickard, Inc., Pete, RD 1, Box 292, Cobleskill, NY 12043/800-282-5663; FAX: 518-234-2454
Ridgetop Sporting Goods, P.O. Box 306, 42907 Hilligoss Ln. East, Eatonville, WA 98328/360-832-6422; FAX: 360-832-6422
Riebe Co., W.J., 3434 Tucker Rd., Boise, ID 83703
Ries, Chuck, 415 Ridgecrest Dr., Grants Pass, OR 97527/503-476-5623
Rifle Works & Armory, 707 N 12 St., Cody, WY 82414/307-587-4914
Rifles Inc., 873 W. 5400 N., Cedar City, UT 84720/801-586-5996; FAX: 801-586-5996
RIG Products, 87 Coney Island Dr., Sparks, NV 89431-6334/702-331-5666; FAX: 702-331-5669
Rigby & Co., John, 66 Great Suffolk St., London SE1 0BU, ENGLAND/0171-620-0690; FAX: 0171-928-9205
Riggs, Jim, 206 Azalea, Boerne, TX 78006/210-249-8567
Riling Arms Books Co., Ray, 6844 Gorsten St., P.O. Box 18925, Philadelphia, PA 19119/215-438-2456; FAX: 215-438-5395
Rim Pac Sports, Inc., 1034 N. Soldano Ave., Azusa, CA 91702-2135
Rimrock Rifle Stocks, P.O. Box 589, Vashon Island, WA 98070/206-463-5551; FAX: 206-463-2526
Ringler Custom Leather Co., 31 Shining Mtn. Rd., Powell, WY 82435/307-645-3255
Ripley Rifles, 42 Fletcher Street, Ripley, Derbyshire, DE5 3LP ENGLAND/011-0773-748353
R.I.S. Co., Inc., 718 Timberlake Circle, Richardson, TX 75080/214-235-0933
River Road Sporting Clays, Bruce Barsotti, P.O. Box 3016, Gonzales, CA 93926/408-675-2473
Rizzini, Battista, Via 2 Giugno, 7/7Bis-25060 Marcheno (Brescia), ITALY (U.S. importers—Wm. Larkin Moore & Co.; New England Arms Co.)
Rizzini, F.LLI (See U.S. importers—Moore & Co. Wm. Larkin; New England Arms Co.)
RLCM Enterprises, 110 Hill Crest Drive, Burleson, TX 76028
R.M. Precision, Inc., Attn. Greg F. Smith Marketing, P.O. Box 210, LaVerkin, UT 84745/801-635-4656; FAX: 801-635-4430
RMS Custom Gunsmithing, 4120 N. Bitterwell, Prescott Valley, AZ 86314/520-772-7626
Robar Co.'s, Inc., The, 21438 N. 7th Ave., Suite B, Phoenix, AZ 85027/602-581-2648; FAX: 602-582-0059
Robbins Scent, Inc., P.O. Box 779, Connellsville, PA 15425/412-628-2529; FAX: 412-628-9598
Roberts/Engraver, J.J., 7808 Lake Dr., Manassas, VA 22111/703-330-0448
Roberts Products, 25328 SE Iss. Beaver Lk. Rd., Issaquah, WA 98029/206-392-8172
Robinett, R.G., P.O. Box 72, Madrid, IA 50156/515-795-2906
Robinson, Don, Pennsylvania Hse., 36 Fairfax Crescent, Southowram, Halifax, W. Yorkshire HX3 9SQ, ENGLAND/0422-364458
Robinson Firearms Mfg. Ltd., 1699 Blondeaux Crescent, Kelowna, B.C. CANADA V1Y 4J8/604-868-9596
Robinson H.V. Bullets, 3145 Church St., Zachary, LA 70791/504-654-4029
Rochester Lead Works, 76 Anderson Ave., Rochester, NY 14607/716-442-8500; FAX: 716-442-4712
Rockwood Corp., Speedwell Division, 136 Lincoln Blvd., Middlesex, NJ 08846/908-560-7171, 800-243-8274; FAX: 980-560-7475
Rocky Fork Enterprises, P.O. Box 427, 878 Battle Rd., Nolensville, TN 37135/615-941-1307
Rocky Mountain Arms, Inc., 600 S. Sunset, Unit C, Longmont, CO 80501/303-768-8522; FAX: 303-678-8766
Rocky Mountain High Sports Glasses, 8121 N. Central Park Ave., Skokie, IL 60076/708-679-1012; FAX: 708-679-0184
Rocky Mountain Rifle Works Ltd., 1707 14th St., Boulder, CO 80302/303-443-9189
Rocky Mountain Target Co., 3 Aloe Way, Leesburg, FL 34788/904-365-9598
Rocky Mountain Wildlife Products, P.O. Box 999, La Porte, CO 80535/303-484-2768; FAX: 303-223-9389
Rocky Shoes & Boots, 294 Harper St., Nelsonville, OH 45764/800-848-9452, 614-753-1951; FAX: 614-753-4024
Rod Guide Co., Box 1149, Forsyth, MO 65653/800-952-2774
Rogers Gunsmithing, Bob, P.O. Box 305, 344 S. Walnut St., Franklin Grove, IL 61031/815-456-2685; FAX: 815-288-7142
Rohner, Hans, 1148 Twin Sisters Ranch Rd., Nederland, CO 80466-9600
Rohner, John, 710 Sunshine Canyon, Boulder, CO 80302/303-444-3841
Rolston, Inc., Fred W., 210 E. Cummins St., Tecumseh, MI 49286/517-423-6002, 800-314-9061 (orders only); FAX: 517-423-6002
Romain's Custom Guns, Inc., RD 1, Whetstone Rd., Brockport, PA 15823/814-265-1948
Rooster Laboratories, P.O. Box 412514, Kansas City, MO 64141/816-474-1622; FAX: 816-474-1307
Rorschach Precision Products, P.O. Box 151613, Irving, TX 75015/214-790-3487
Rosenberg & Sons, Jack A., 12229 Cox Ln., Dallas, TX 75234/214-241-6302
Rosenthal, Brad and Sallie, 19303 Ossenfort Ct., St. Louis, MO 63038/314-273-5159; FAX: 314-273-5149
Ross & Webb (See Ross, Don)
Ross, Don, 12813 West 83 Terrace, Lenexa, KS 66215/913-492-6982
Rosser, Bob, 1824 29th Ave., Suite 24, Birmingham, AL 35209/205-870-4422
Rossi S.A., Amadeo, Rua: Amadeo Rossi, 143, Sao Leopoldo, RS, BRAZIL 93030-220/051-592-5566 (U.S. importer—Interarms)
Roto Carve, 2754 Garden Ave., Janesville, IA 50647
Round Edge, Inc., P.O. Box 723, Lansdale, PA 19446/215-361-0859
Rowe Engineering, Inc. (See R.E.I.)
Royal Arms Gunstocks, 919 8th Ave. NW, Great Falls, MT 59404/406-453-1149
Roy's Custom Grips, Rt. 3, Box 174-E, Lynchburg, VA 24504/804-993-3470
RPM, 15481 N. Twin Lakes Dr., Tucson, AZ 85737/602-825-1233; FAX: 602-825-3333
Rubright Bullets, 1008 S. Quince Rd., Walnutport, PA 18088/215-767-1339
Rucker Dist. Inc., P.O. Box 479, Terrell, TX 75160/214-563-2094
Rudnicky, Susan, 9 Water St., Arcade, NY 14009/716-492-2450
Ruger (See Sturm, Ruger & Co., Inc.)
Rundell's Gun Shop, 6198 Frances Rd., Clio, MI 48420/313-687-0559
Runge, Robert P., 94 Grove St., Ilion, NY 13357/315-894-3036
Rupert's Gun Shop, 2202 Dick Rd., Suite B, Fenwick, MI 48834/517-248-3252,
Russ, 23 William St., Addison, NY 14801/607-359-3896
Russell Knives, Inc., A.G., 1705 Hwy. 71B North, Springdale, AR 72764/501-751-7341
Rusteprufe Laboratories, 1319 Jefferson Ave., Sparta, WI 54656/608-269-4144
Rusty Duck Premium Gun Care Products, 7785 Foundation Dr., Suite 6, Florence, KY 41042/606-342-5553; FAX: 606-342-5556
Rutgers Book Center, 127 Raritan Ave., Highland Park, NJ 08904/908-545-4344; FAX: 908-545-6686
Ruvel & Co., Inc., 4128-30 W. Belmont Ave., Chicago, IL 60641/312-286-9494; FAX: 312-286-9323
R.V.I. (See Fire'n Five)
RWS (See U.S. importer—Dynamit Nobel-RWS, Inc.)
Ryan, Chad L., RR 3, Box 72, Cresco, IA 52136/319-547-4384
Rybka Custom Leather Equipment, Thad, 134 Havilah Hill, Odenville, AL 35120

S

S&B Industries, 11238 McKinley Rd., Montrose, MI 48457/810-639-5491
S&K Manufacturing Co., P.O. Box 247, Pittsfield, PA 16340/814-563-7808; FAX: 814-563-7808
S&S Firearms, 74-11 Myrtle Ave., Glendale, NY 11385/718-497-1100; FAX: 718-497-1105
Sabatti S.R.L., via Alessandro Volta 90, 25063 Gardone V.T., Brescia, ITALY/030-8912207-831312; FAX: 030-8912059 (U.S. importer—E.A.A. Corp.; K.B.I., Inc.)
SAECO (See Redding Reloading Equipment)
Saf-T-Lok, 5713 Corporate Way, Suite 100, W. Palm Beach, FL 33407
Safari Outfitters Ltd., 71 Ethan Allan Hwy., Ridgefield, CT 06877/203-544-9505
Safari Press, Inc., 15621 Chemical Lane B, Huntington Beach, CA 92649/714-894-9080; FAX: 714-894-4949
Safariland Ltd., Inc., 3120 E. Mission Blvd., P.O. Box 51478, Ontario, CA 91761/909-923-7300; FAX: 909-923-7400
SAFE, P.O. Box 864, Post Falls, ID 83854/208-773-3624
Safesport Manufacturing Co., 1100 W. 45th Ave., Denver, CO 80211/303-433-6506, 800-433-6506; FAX: 303-433-4112
Safety Speed Holster, Inc., 910 S. Vail Ave., Montebello, CA 90640/213-723-4140; FAX: 213-726-6973
Sako Ltd., P.O. Box 149, SF-11101, Riihimaki, FINLAND (U.S. importer—Stoeger Industries)
Salter Calls, Inc., Eddie, Hwy. 31 South-Brewton Industrial Park, Brewton, AL 36426/205-867-2584; FAX: 206-867-9005
Samco Global Arms, Inc., 6995 NW 43rd St., Miami, FL 33166/305-593-9782
Sampson, Roger, 430 N. Grove, Mora, MN 55051/320-679-4868
San Francisco Gun Exchange, 124 Second St., San Francisco, CA 94105/415-982-6097
San Marco (See U.S. importers—Cape Outfitters; EMF Co., Inc.)
Sanders Custom Gun Service, 2358 Tyler Lane, Louisville, KY 40205/502-454-3338
Sanders Gun and Machine Shop, 145 Delhi Road, Manchester, IA 52057
Sandia Die & Cartridge Co., 37 Atancacio Rd. NE, Albuquerque, NM 87123/505-298-5729
Sarco, Inc., 323 Union St., Stirling, NJ 07980/908-647-3800
S.A.R.L. G. Granger, 66 cours Fauriel, 42100 Saint Etienne, FRANCE/04 77 25 14 73; FAX: 04 77 38 66 99
Sauer (See U.S. importer—Paul Co., The; Sigarms, Inc.)
Saunders Gun & Machine Shop, R.R. 2, Delhi Road, Manchester, IA 52057
Savage Arms, Inc., 100 Springdale Rd., Westfield, MA 01085/413-568-7001; FAX: 413-562-7764
Savage Arms, Inc., 248 Water St., P.O. Box 1240, Lakefield, Ont. K0L 2H0, CANADA/705-652-8000; FAX: 705-652-8431

DIRECTORY OF THE ARMS TRADE

Savage Range Systems, Inc., 100 Springdale RD., Westfield, MA 01085/413-568-7001; FAX: 413-562-1152
Savana Sports, Inc., 5763 Ferrier St., Montreal, Quebec, CANADA H4P 1N3/514-739-1753; FAX: 514-739-1755
Saville Iron Co. (See Greenwood Precision)
Savino, Barbara J., P.O. Box 1104, Hardwick, VT 05843-1104
Scanco Environmental Systems, 5000 Highlands Parkway, Suite 180, Atlanta, GA 30082/404-431-0025; FAX: 404-431-0028
Scansport, Inc., P.O. Box 700, Enfield, NH 03748/603-632-7654
Scattergun Technologies Inc., 620 8th Ave. S., Nashville, TN 37203/615-254-1441; FAX: 615-254-1449; WEB: http://www.scattergun.com
Sceery Game Calls, P.O. Box 6520, Sante Fe, NM 87502/505-471-9110; FAX: 505-471-3476
Schaefer Shooting Sports, 1923 Grand Ave., Baldwin, NY 11510/516-379-4900; FAX: 516-379-6701
Scharch Mfg., Inc., 10325 Co. Rd. 120, Unit C, Salida, CO 81201/719-539-7242, 800-836-4683; FAX: 719-539-3021
Scherer, Box 250, Ewing, VA 24240/615-733-2615; FAX: 615-733-2073
Schiffman, Curt, 3017 Kevin Cr., Idaho Falls, ID 83402/208-524-4684
Schiffman, Mike, 8233 S. Crystal Springs, McCammon, ID 83250/208-254-9114
Schiffman, Norman, 3017 Kevin Cr., Idaho Falls, ID 83402/208-524-4684
Schmidtke Group, 17050 W. Salentine Dr., New Berlin, WI 53151-7349
Schmidt & Bender, Inc., Brook Rd., P.O. Box 134, Meriden, NH 03770/603-469-3565, 800-468-3450; FAX: 603-469-3471
Schmidtman Custom Ammunition, 6 Gilbert Court, Cotati, CA 94931
Schneider Bullets, 3655 West 214th St., Fairview Park, OH 44126
Schneider Rifle Barrels, Inc., Gary, 12202 N. 62nd Pl., Scottsdale, AZ 85254/602-948-2525
School of Gunsmithing, The, 6065 Roswell Rd., Atlanta, GA 30328/800-223-4542
Schrimsher's Custom Knifemaker's Supply, Bob, P.O. Box 308, Emory, TX 75440/903-473-3330; FAX: 903-473-2235
Schroeder Bullets, 1421 Thermal Ave., San Diego, CA 92154/619-423-3523
Schuetzen Gun Co., P.O. Box 272113, Fort Collins, CO 80527/970-223-3678
Schuetzen Pistol Works, 620-626 Old Pacific Hwy. SE, Olympia, WA 98513/360-459-3471; FAX: 360-491-3447
Schulz Industries, 16247 Minnesota Ave., Paramount, CA 90723/213-439-5903
Schumakers Gun Shop, William, 512 Prouty Corner Lp. A, Colville, WA 99114/509-684-4848
Schwartz Custom Guns, David W., 2505 Waller St., Eau Claire, WI 54703/715-832-1735
Schwartz Custom Guns, Wayne E., 970 E. Britton Rd., Morrice, MI 48857/517-625-4079
Scobey Duck & Goose Calls, Glynn, Rt. 3, Box 37, Newbern, TN 38059/901-643-6241
Scope Control, Inc., 5775 Co. Rd. 23 SE, Alexandria, MN 56308/612-762-7295
ScopLevel, 151 Lindbergh Ave., Suite C, Livermore, CA 94550/510-449-5052; FAX: 510-373-0861
Scot Powder, Rt.1 Box 167, McEwen, TN 37101/800-416-3006; FAX: 615-729-4211
Scot Powder Co. of Ohio, Inc., Box GD96, Only, TN 37140/615-729-4207, 800-416-3006; FAX: 615-729-4217
Scott, Dwight, 23089 Englehardt St., Clair Shores, MI 48080/313-779-4735
Scott Fine Guns, Inc., Thad, P.O. Box 412, Indianola, MS 38751/601-887-5929
Scott, McDougall & Associates, 7950 Redwood Dr., Cotati, CA 94931/707-546-2264; FAX: 707-795-1911
S.C.R.C., P.O. Box 660, Katy, TX 77492-0660/FAX: 713-578-2124
Scruggs' Game Calls, Stanley, Rt. 1, Hwy. 661, Cullen, VA 23934/804-542-4241, 800-323-4828
Seattle Binocular & Scope Repair Co., P.O. Box 46094, Seattle, WA 98146/206-932-3733
Second Chance Body Armor, P.O. Box 578, Central Lake, MI 49622/616-544-5721; FAX: 616-544-9824
Security Awareness & Firearms Education (See SAFE)
Seebeck Assoc., R.E., P.O. Box 59752, Dallas, TX 75229
Seecamp Co., Inc., L.W., P.O. Box 255, New Haven, CT 06502/203-877-3429
Seligman Shooting Products, Box 133, Seligman, AZ 86337/602-422-3607
Selsi Co., Inc., P.O. Box 10, Midland Park, NJ 07432-0010/201-935-0388; FAX: 201-935-5851
Semmer, Charles, 7885 Cyd Dr., Denver, CO 80221/303-429-6947
Sentinel Arms, P.O. Box 57, Detroit, MI 48231/313-331-1951; FAX: 313-331-1456
Serva Arms Co., Inc., RD 1, Box 483A, Greene, NY 13778/607-656-4764
Service Armament, 689 Bergen Blvd., Ridgefield, NJ 07657
Servus Footwear Co., 1136 2nd St., Rock Island, IL 61204-3610/309-786-7741; FAX: 309-786-9808
S.G.S. Sporting Guns Srl., Via Della Resistenza, 37, 20090 Buccinasco (MI) ITALY/2-45702446; FAX: 2-45702464
Shanghai Airguns, Ltd. (See U.S. importer—Sportsman Airguns, Inc.)
Shappy Bullets, 76 Milldale Ave., Plantsville, CT 06479/203-621-3704
Sharps Arms Co., Inc., C. (See Montana Armory, Inc.)
Shaw, Inc., E.R. (See Small Arms Mfg. Co.)
Shay's Gunsmithing, 931 Marvin Ave., Lebanon, PA 17042
Sheffield Knifemakers Supply, Inc., P.O. Box 741107, Orange City, FL 32774-1107/904-775-6453; FAX: 904-774-5754
Shell Shack, 113 E. Main, Laurel, MT 59044/406-628-8986
Shepherd Scope Ltd., Box 189, Waterloo, NE 68069/402-779-2424; FAX: 402-779-4010
Sheridan USA, Inc., Austin, P.O. Box 577, 36 Haddam Quarter Rd., Durham, CT 06422/203-349-1772; FAX: 203-349-1771
Sherwood, George, 46 N. River Dr., Roseburg, OR 97470/541-672-3159
Shilen Rifles, Inc., P.O. Box 1300, 205 Metro Park Blvd., Ennis, TX 75119/214-875-5318; FAX: 214-875-5402
Shiloh Creek, Box 357, Cottleville, MO 63338/314-447-2900; FAX: 314-447-2900
Shiloh Rifle Mfg., 201 Centennial Dr., Big Timber, MT 59011/406-932-4454; FAX: 406-932-5627
Shirley Co. Gun & Riflemakers Ltd., J.A., P.O. Box 368, High Wycombe, Bucks. HP13 6YN, ENGLAND/0494-446883; FAX: 0494-463685
Shockley, Harold H., 204 E. Farmington Rd., Hanna City, IL 61536/309-565-4524

Shoemaker & Sons, Inc., Tex, 714 W. Cienega Ave., San Dimas, CA 91773/909-592-2071; FAX: 909-592-2378
The Shooten' Haus, 102 W. 13th, Kearney, NE 68847/308-236-7929
Shooter Shop, The, 221 N. Main, Butte, MT 59701/406-723-3842
Shooter's Choice, 16770 Hilltop Park Place, Chagrin Falls, OH 44023/216-543-8808; FAX: 216-543-8811
Shooter's Edge, Inc., P.O.Box 769, Trinidad, CO 81082
Shooter's World, 3828 N. 28th Ave., Phoenix, AZ 85017/602-266-0170
Shooters Supply, 1120 Tieton Dr., Yakima, WA 98902/509-452-1181
Shootin' Accessories, Ltd., P.O. Box 6810, Auburn, CA 95604/916-889-2220
Shootin' Shack, Inc., 1065 Silver Beach Rd., Riviera Beach, FL 33403/407-842-0990
Shooting Chrony Inc., 3269 Niagara Falls Blvd., N. Tonawanda, NY 14120/905-276-6292; FAX: 905-276-6295
Shooting Components Marketing, P.O. Box 1069, Englewood, CO 80150/303-987-2543; FAX: 303-989-3508
Shooting Gallery, The, 8070 Southern Blvd., Boardman, OH 44512/216-726-7788
Shooting Specialties (See Titus, Daniel)
Shooting Star, 1825 Fortview Rd., Ste. 115, Austin, TX 78747/512-462-0009
Shoot-N-C Targets (See Birchwood Casey)
Shotgun Shop, The, 14145 Proctor Ave., Suite 3, Industry, CA 91746/818-855-2737; FAX: 818-855-2735
Shotguns Unlimited, 2307 Fon Du Lac Rd., Richmond, VA 23229/804-752-7115
Siegrist Gun Shop, 8754 Turtle Road, Whittemore, MI 48770
Sierra Bullets, 1400 W. Henry St., Sedalia, MO 65301/816-827-6300; FAX: 816-827-6300; WEB: http://www.sierrabullets.com
Sierra Specialty Prod. Co., 1344 Oakhurst Ave., Los Altos, CA 94024/FAX: 415-965-1536
SIG, CH-8212 Neuhausen, SWITZERLAND (U.S. importer—Mandall Shooting Supplies, Inc.)
SIG-Sauer (See U.S. importer—Sigarms, Inc.)
Sigarms, Inc., Corporate Park, Industrial Drive, Exeter, NH 03833/603-772-2302; FAX: 603-772-9082
Sight Shop, The, John G. Lawson, 1802 E. Columbia Ave., Tacoma, WA 98404/206-474-5465
Sightron, Inc., Rt. 1, Box 293, Franklinton, NC 27525/919-494-5040; FAX: 919-494-2612
Signet Metal Corp., 551 Stewart Ave., Brooklyn, NY 11222/718-384-5400; FAX: 718-388-7488
Sile Distributors, Inc., 7 Centre Market Pl., New York, NY 10013/212-925-4111; FAX: 212-925-3149
Silencio/Safety Direct, 56 Coney Island Dr., Sparks, NV 89431/800-648-1812, 702-354-4451; FAX: 702-359-1074
Silent Hunter, 1100 Newton Ave., W. Collingswood, NJ 08107/609-854-3276
Silhouette Leathers, P.O. Box 1161, Gunnison, CO 81230/303-641-6639
Silhouette, The, P.O. Box 1509, Idaho Falls, ID 83403
Silver Eagle Machining, 18007 N. 69th Ave., Glendale, AZ 85308
Silver Ridge Gun Shop (See Goodwin, Fred)
Silver-Tip Corp., RR2, Box 184, Gloster, MS 39638-9520
Simmons, Jerry, 715 Middlebury St., Goshen, IN 46526/219-533-8546
Simmons Enterprises, Ernie, 709 East Elizabethtown Rd., Manheim, PA 17545/717-664-4040
Simmons Gun Repair, Inc., 700 S. Rogers Rd., Olathe, KS 66062/913-782-3131; FAX: 913-782-4189
Simmons Outdoor Corp., 2120 Kilarney Way, Tallahassee, FL 32308/904-878-5100; FAX: 904-878-0300
Sinclair International, Inc., 2330 Wayne Haven St., Fort Wayne, IN 46803/219-493-1858; FAX: 219-493-2530
Sinclair, W.P., Box 1209, Warminster, Wiltshire BA12 9XJ, ENGLAND/01044-1985-218544; FAX: 01044-1985-214111
Single Shot, Inc. (See Montana Armory, Inc.)
Singletary, Kent, 2915 W. Ross, Phoenix, AZ 85027/602-582-4900
Sipes Gun Shop, 7415 Asher Ave., Little Rock, AR 72204/501-565-8480
Siskiyou Gun Works (See Donnelly, C.P.)
Six Enterprises, 320-D Turtle Creek Ct., San Jose, CA 95125/408-999-0201; FAX: 408-999-0216
Skaggs, R.E., P.O. Box 555, Hamilton, IN 46742/219-488-3755
SKAN A.R., 4 St. Catherines Road, Long Melford, Suffolk, CO10 9JU ENGLAND/011-0787-312942
SKB Arms Co. (See New SKB Arms Co.)
SKB Shotguns, 4325 S. 120th St., P.O. Box 37669, Omaha, NE 68137/800-752-2767; FAX: 402-330-8029
Skeoch, Brian R., P.O. Box 279, Glenrock, WY 82637/307-436-9655; FAX: 307-436-9034
Skip's Machine, 364 29 Road, Grand Junction, CO 81501/303-245-5417
Sklany, Steve, 566 Birch Grove Dr., Kalispell, MT 59901/406-755-4257
SKR Industries, POB 1382, San Angelo, TX 76902/915-658-3133
S.L.A.P. Industries, P.O. Box 1121, Parklands 2121, SOUTH AFRICA/27-11-788-0030; FAX: 27-11-788-0030
Slezak, Jerome F., 1290 Marlowe, Lakewood (Cleveland), OH 44107/216-221-1668
Slings 'N Things, Inc., 8909 Bedford Circle, Suite 11, Omaha, NE 68134/402-571-6954; FAX: 402-571-7082
Slug Group, Inc., P.O. Box 376, New Paris, PA 15554/814-839-4517; FAX: 814-839-2601
Slug Site Co., Ozark Wilds, Rt. 2, Box 158, Versailles, MO 65084/314-378-6430
Small Arms Mfg. Co., 5312 Thoms Run Rd., Bridgeville, PA 15017/412-221-4343; FAX: 412-221-4303
Small Custom Mould & Bullet Co., Box 17211, Tucson, AZ 85731
Smart Parts, 1203 Spring St., Latrobe, PA 15650/412-539-2660; FAX: 412-539-2298
Smires, C.L., 28269 Old Schoolhouse Rd., Columbus, NJ 08022/609-298-3158
Smith & Wesson, 2100 Roosevelt Ave., Springfield, MA 01102/413-781-8300; FAX: 413-731-8980
Smith, Art, 230 Main St. S., Hector, MN 55342/612-848-2760; FAX: 612-848-2760
Smith, Mark A., P.O. Box 182, Sinclair, WY 82334/307-324-7929

MANUFACTURERS' DIRECTORY

Smith, Michael, 620 Nye Circle, Chattanooga, TN 37405/615-267-8341
Smith, Ron, 5869 Straley, Ft. Worth, TX 76114/817-732-6768
Smith, Sharmon, 4545 Speas Rd., Fruitland, ID 83619/208-452-6329
Smith Abrasives, Inc., 1700 Sleepy Valley Rd., P.O. Box 5095, Hot Springs, AR 71902-5095/501-321-2244; FAX: 501-321-9232
Smith Saddlery, Jesse W., 3601 E. Boone Ave., Spokane, WA 99202-4501/509-325-0622
Smokey Valley Rifles (See Lutz Engraving, Ron E.)
Snapp's Gunshop, 6911 E. Washington Rd., Clare, MI 48617/517-386-9226
Snider Stocks, Walter S., Rt. 2 P.O. Box 147, Denton, NC 27239
Sno-Seal (See Atsko/Sno-Seal)
Societa Armi Bresciane Srl. (See U.S. importer—Cape Outfitters; Gamba, USA)
Sonora Rifle Barrel Co., 14396 D. Tuolumne Rd., Sonora, CA 95370/209-532-4139
Soque River Knives, P.O. Box 880, Clarkesville, GA 30523/706-754-8500; FAX: 706-754-7263
SOS Products Co. (See Buck Stix—SOS Products Co.)
Sotheby's, 1334 York Ave. at 72nd St., New York, NY 10021/212-606-7260
Sound Technology, P.O. Box 1132, Kodiak, AK 99615/907-486-8448
South Bend Replicas, Inc., 61650 Oak Rd., South Bend, IN 46614/219-289-4500
Southeastern Community College, 1015 S. Gear Ave., West Burlington, IA 52655/319-752-2731
Southern Ammunition Co., Inc., 4232 Meadow St., Loris, SC 29569-3124/803-756-3262; FAX: 803-756-3583
Southern Armory, The, Rt. 2, Box 134, Woodlawn, VA 24381/703-238-1343; FAX: 703-238-1453
Southern Bloomer Mfg. Co., P.O. Box 1621, Bristol, TN 37620/615-878-6660; FAX: 615-878-8761
Southern Security, 1700 Oak Hills Dr., Kingston, TN 37763/423-376-6297; 800-251-9992
Southwind Sanctions, P.O. Box 445, Aledo, TX 76008/817-441-8917
Sparks, Milt, 605 E. 44th St. No. 2, Boise, ID 83714-4800
Spartan-Realtree Products, Inc., 1390 Box Circle, Columbus, GA 31907/706-569-9101; FAX: 706-569-0042
Specialty Gunsmithing, Lynn McMurdo, P.O. Box 404, Afton, WY 83110/307-886-5535
Specialty Shooters Supply, Inc., 3325 Griffin Rd., Suite 9mm, Fort Lauderdale, FL 33317
Speedfeed, Inc., 3820 Industrial Way, Suite N, Benicia, CA 94510/707-746-1221; FAX: 707-746-1888
Speer Products, Div. of Blount, Inc., Sporting Equipment Div., P.O. Box 856, Lewiston, ID 83501/208-746-2351; FAX: 208-746-2915
Spegel, Craig, P.O. Box 3108, Bay City, OR 97107/503-377-2697
Speiser, Fred D., 2229 Dearborn, Missoula, MT 59801/406-549-8133
Spence, George W., 115 Locust St., Steele, MO 63877/314-695-4926
Spencer Reblue Service, 1820 Tupelo Trail, Holt, MI 48842/517-694-7474
Spencer's Custom Guns, Rt. 1, Box 546, Scottsville, VA 24590/804-293-6836
Spezial Waffen (See U.S. importer—American Bullets)
S.P.G., Inc., P.O. Box 761-H, Livingston, MT 59047/406-222-8416; FAX: 406-222-8416
Sphinx Engineering SA, Ch. des Grandes-Vies 2, CH-2900 Porrentruy, SWITZERLAND/41 66 66 73 81; FAX: 41 66 66 30 90 (U.S. importer—Sphinx USA Inc.)
Sphinx USA Inc., 998 N. Colony, Meriden, CT 06450/203-238-1399; FAX: 203-238-1375
Spokhandguns, Inc., 1206 Fig St., Benton City, WA 99320/509-588-5255
Sport Flite Manufacturing Co., P.O. Box 1082, Bloomfield Hills, MI 48303/810-647-3747
Sporting Arms Mfg., Inc., 801 Hall Ave., Littlefield, TX 79339/806-385-5665; FAX: 806-385-3394
Sports Innovations, Inc., P.O. Box 5181, 8505 Jacksboro Hwy., Wichita Falls, TX 76307/817-723-6015
Sportsman Airguns, Inc., 17712 Carmenita Rd., Cerritos, CA 90703-8639/800-424-7486
Sportsman Safe Mfg. Co., 6309-6311 Paramount Blvd., Long Beach, CA 90805/800-266-7150, 310-984-5445
Sportsman Supply Co., 714 East Eastwood, P.O. Box 650, Marshall, MO 65340/816-886-9393
Sportsman's Communicators, 588 Radcliffe Ave., Pacific Palisades, CA 90272/800-538-3752
Sportsmatch U.K. Ltd., 16 Summer St., Leighton Buzzard, Bedfordshire, LU7 8HT ENGLAND/01525-381638; FAX: 01525-851236
Sportsmen's Exchange & Western Gun Traders, Inc., 560 S. "C" St., Oxnard, CA 93030/805-483-1917
Spradlin's, 113 Arthur St., Pueblo, CO 81004/719-543-9462; FAX: 719-543-9465
Springfield, Inc., 420 W. Main St., Geneseo, IL 61254/309-944-5631; FAX: 309-944-3676
Springfield Sporters, Inc., RD 1, Penn Run, PA 15765/412-254-2626; FAX: 412-254-9173
Spyderco, Inc., 4565 N. Hwy. 93, P.O. Box 800, Golden, CO 80403/303-279-8383, 800-525-7770; FAX: 303-278-2229
SSK Co., 220 N. Belvidere Ave., York, PA 17404/717-854-2897
SSK Industries, 721 Woodvue Lane, Wintersville, OH 43952/614-264-0176; FAX: 614-264-2257
Stackpole Books, 5067 Ritter Rd., Mechanicsburg, PA 17055-6921/717-234-5041; FAX: 717-234-1359
Stalker, Inc., P.O. Box 21, Fishermans Wharf Rd., Malakoff, TX 75148/903-489-1010
Stalwart Corporation, 76 Imperial, Unit A, Evanston, WY 82930/307-789-7687; FAX: 307-789-7688
Stanley Bullets, 2085 Heatheridge Ln., Reno, NV 89509
Star Bonifacio Echeverria S.A., Torrekva 3, Eibar, SPAIN 20600/43-107340; FAX: 43-101524 (U.S. importer—Interarms; P.S.M.G. Gun Co.)
Star Custom Bullets, P.O. Box 608, 468 Main St., Ferndale, CA 95536/707-786-9140; FAX: 707-786-9117
Starke Bullet Company, P.O. Box 400, Cooperstown, ND 58425/701-797-3431
Starkey Labs, 6700 Washington Ave. S., Eden Prairie, MN 55344
Starkey's Gun Shop, 9430 McCombs, El Paso, TX 79924/915-751-3030
Starline, 1300 W. Henry St., Sedalia, MO 65301/816-827-6640; FAX: 816-827-6650
Star Machine Works, 418 10th Ave., San Diego, CA 92101/619-232-3216
Star Reloading Co., Inc., 5520 Rock Hampton Ct., Indianapolis, IN 46268/317-872-5840
Stark's Bullet Mfg., 2580 Monroe St., Eugene, OR 97405
Starlight Training Center, Inc., Rt. 1, P.O. Box 88, Bronaugh, MO 64728/417-843-3555
Starnes Gunmaker, Ken, 32900 SW Laurelview Rd., Hillsboro, OR 97123/503-628-0705; FAX: 503-628-6005
Starr Trading Co., Jedediah, P.O. Box 2007, Farmington Hills, MI 48333/810-683-4343; FAX: 810-683-3282
Starrett Co., L.S., 121 Crescent St., Athol, MA 01331/617-249-3551
State Arms Gun Co., 815 S. Division St., Waunakee, WI 53597/608-849-5800
Steelman's Gun Shop, 10465 Beers Rd., Swartz Creek, MI 48473/810-735-4884
Steffens, Ron, 18396 Mariposa Creek Rd., Willits, CA 95490/707-485-0873
Stegall, James B., 26 Forest Rd., Wallkill, NY 12589
Steger, James R., 1131 Dorsey Pl., Plainfield, NJ 07062
Steves House of Guns, Rt. 1, Minnesota City, MN 55959/507-689-2573
Stewart Game Calls, Johnny, Inc., P.O. Box 7954, 5100 Fort Ave., Waco, TX 76714/817-772-3261; FAX: 817-772-3670
Stewart's Gunsmithing, P.O. Box 5854, Pietersburg North 0750, Transvaal, SOUTH AFRICA/01521-89401
Steyr Mannlicher AG, Mannlicherstrasse 1, P.O.B. 1000, A-4400 Steyr, AUSTRIA/0043-7252-896-0; FAX: 0043-7252-68621 (U.S. importer—GSI, Inc.; Nygord Precision Products)
Stiles Custom Guns, RD3, Box 1605, Homer City, PA 15748/412-479-9945, 412-479-8666
Stillwell, Robert, 421 Judith Ann Dr., Schertz, TX 78154
Stoeger Industries, 5 Mansard Ct., Wayne, NJ 07470/201-872-9500, 800-631-0722; FAX: 201-872-2230
Stoeger Publishing Co. (See Stoeger Industries)
Stone Enterprises Ltd., Rt. 609, P.O. Box 335, Wicomico Church, VA 22579/804-580-5114; FAX: 804-580-8421
Stone Mountain Arms, 5988 Peachtree Corners E., Norcross, GA 30071/800-251-9412
Stoney Baroque Shooters Supply, John Richards, Rt. 2, Box 325, Bedford, KY 40006/502-255-7222
Stoney Point Products, Inc., P.O. Box 234, 1815 North Spring Street, New Ulm, MN 56073-0234/507-354-3360; FAX: 507-354-7236
Storage Tech, 1254 Morris Ave., N. Huntingdon, PA 15642/800-437-9393
Storey, Dale A. (See DGS, Inc.)
Storm, Gary, P.O. Box 5211, Richardson, TX 75083/214-385-0862
Stott's Creek Armory, Inc., RR1, Box 70, Morgantown, IN 46160/317-878-5489
Stott's Creek Printers, RR1, Box 70, Morgantown, IN 46160/317-878-5489
Stratco, Inc., P.O. Box 2270, Kalispell, MT 59901/406-755-1221; FAX: 406-755-1226
Strawbridge, Victor W., 6 Pineview Dr., Dover, NH 03820/603-742-0013
Streamlight, Inc., 1030 W. Germantown Pike, Norristown, PA 19403/215-631-0600; FAX: 610-631-0712
Strong Holster Co., 39 Grove St., Gloucester, MA 01930/508-281-3300; FAX: 508-281-6321
Strutz Rifle Barrels, Inc., W.C., P.O. Box 611, Eagle River, WI 54521/715-479-4766
Stuart, V. Pat, Rt.1, Box 447-S, Greenville, VA 24440/804-556-3845
Sturm, Ruger & Co., Inc., Lacey Place, Southport, CT 06490/203-259-4537; FAX: 203-259-2167
"Su-Press-On," Inc., P.O. Box 09161, Detroit, MI 48209/313-842-4222 7:30-11p.m. Mon-Thurs.
Sullivan, David S. (See Westwind Rifles, Inc.)
Summit Specialties, Inc., P.O. Box 786, Decatur, AL 35602/205-353-0634; FAX: 205-353-9818
Sundance Industries, Inc., 25163 W. Avenue Stanford, Valencia, CA 91355/805-257-4807
Sun Welding Safe Co., 290 Easy St. No.3, Simi Valley, CA 93065/805-584-6678, 800-729-SAFE; FAX: 805-584-6169
Surecase Co., The, 233 Wilshire Blvd., Ste. 900, Santa Monica, CA 90401/800-92ARMLOC
Sure-Shot Game Calls, Inc., P.O. Box 816, 6835 Capitol, Groves, TX 77619/409-962-1636; FAX: 409-962-5465
Survival Arms, Inc., P.O. Box 965, Orange, CT 06477/203-924-6533; FAX: 203-924-2581
Svon Corp., 280 Eliot St., Ashland, MA 01721/508-881-8852
Swampfire Shop, The (See Peterson Gun Shop, Inc., A.W.)
Swann, D.J., 5 Orsova Close, Eltham North, Vic. 3095, AUSTRALIA/03-431-0323
Swanndri New Zealand, 152 Elm Ave., Burlingame, CA 94010/415-347-6158
SwaroSports, Inc. (See JagerSport, Ltd.)
Swarovski Optik North America Ltd., One Wholesale Way, Cranston, RI 02920/401-942-3380, 800-426-3089; FAX: 401-946-2587
Sweet Home, Inc., P.O. Box 900, Orrville, OH 44667-0900
Swenson's 45 Shop, A.D., P.O. Box 606, Fallbrook, CA 92028
Swift Bullet Co., P.O. Box 27, 201 Main St., Quinter, KS 67752/913-754-3959; FAX: 913-754-2359
Swift Instruments, Inc., 952 Dorchester Ave., Boston, MA 02125/617-436-2960, 800-446-1116; FAX: 617-436-3232
Swift River Gunworks, Inc., 450 State St., Belchertown, MA 01007/413-323-4052
Swiss Army Knives, Inc., 151 Long Hill Crossroads, 37 Canal St., Shelton, CT 06484/800-243-4032
Swivel Machine Works, Inc., 11 Monitor Hill Rd., Newtown, CT 06470/203-270-6343; FAX: 203-874-9212
Szweda, Robert (See RMS Custom Gunsmithing)

T

3-D Ammunition & Bullets, 112 W. Plum St., P.O. Box J, Doniphan, NE 68832/402-845-2285, 800-255-6712; FAX: 402-845-6546
3-Ten Corp., P.O. Box 269, Feeding Hills, MA 01030/413-789-2086; FAX: 413-789-1549
10-X Products Group, 2915 Lyndon B. Johnson Freeway, Suite 133, Dallas, TX 75234/214-243-4016, 800-433-2225; FAX: 214-243-4112
300 Gunsmith Service, Inc., at Cherry Creek State Park Shooting Center,, 12500 E. Belleview Ave./Englewood, CO 80111/303-690-3300

DIRECTORY OF THE ARMS TRADE

Tabler Marketing, 2554 Lincoln Blvd., Suite 555, Marina Del Rey, CA 90291/818-755-4565; FAX: 818-755-0972
TacStar Industries, Inc., 218 Justin Drive, P.O. Box 70, Cottonwood, AZ 86326/602-639-0072; FAX: 602-634-8781
TacTell, Inc., P.O. Box 5654, Maryville, TN 37802/615-982-7855; FAX: 615-558-8294
Tactical Defense Institute, 574 Miami Bluff Ct., Loveland, OH 45140/513-677-8229
Tag Distributors, 1331 Penna. Ave., Emmaus, PA 18049/610-966-3839
Talbot QD Mounts, 2210 E. Grand Blanc Rd., Grand Blanc, MI 48439-8113/810-695-2497
Talley, Dave, P.O. Box 821, Glenrock, WY 82637/307-436-8724, 307-436-9315
Talmage, William G., 10208 N. County Rd. 425 W., Brazil, IN 47834/812-442-0804
Talon Mfg. Co., Inc., 575 Bevans Industrial Ln., Paw Paw, WV 25434/304-947-7440; FAX: 304-947-7447
Tamarack Products, Inc., P.O. Box 625, Wauconda, IL 60084/708-526-9333; FAX: 708-526-9353
Tanfoglio S.r.l., Fratelli, via Valtrompia 39, 41, 25068 Gardone V.T., Brescia, ITALY/30-8910361; FAX: 30-8910183 (U.S. importer—E.A.A. Corp.)
Tanglefree Industries, 1261 Heavenly Dr., Martinez, CA 94553/800-982-4868; FAX: 510-825-3874
Tank's Rifle Shop, P.O. Box 474, Fremont, NE 68025/402-727-1317; FAX: 402-721-2573
Tanner (See U.S. importer—Mandall Shooting Supplies, Inc.)
Taracorp Industries, Inc., 1200 Sixteenth St., Granite City, IL 62040/618-451-4400
Tar-Hunt Custom Rifles, Inc., RR3, P.O. Box 572, Bloomsburg, PA 17815-9351/717-784-6368; FAX: 717-784-6368
Tarnhelm Supply Co., Inc., 431 High St., Boscawen, NH 03303/603-796-2551; FAX: 603-796-2918
Tasco Sales, Inc., 7600 NW 26th St., Miami, FL 33156/305-591-3670; FAX: 305-592-5895
Taurus Firearms, Inc., 16175 NW 49th Ave., Miami, FL 33014/305-624-1115; FAX: 305-623-7506
Taurus International Firearms (See U.S. importer—Taurus Firearms, Inc.)
Taurus S.A., Forjas, Avenida Do Forte 511, Porto Alegre, RS BRAZIL 91360/55-51-347-4050; FAX: 55-51-347-3065
Taylor & Robbins, P.O. Box 164, Rixford, PA 16745/814-966-3233
Taylor's & Co., Inc., 304 Lenoir Dr., Winchester, VA 22603/540-722-2017; FAX: 540-722-2018
TCCI, P.O. Box 302, Phoenix, AZ 85001/602-237-3823; FAX: 602-237-3858
TCSR, 3998 Hoffman Rd., White Bear Lake, MN 55110-4626/800-328-5323; FAX: 612-429-0526
TDP Industries, Inc., 606 Airport Blvd., Doylestown, PA 18901/215-345-8687; FAX: 215-345-6057
Techni-Mec (See F.A.I.R. Tecni-Mec s.n.c. di Isidoro Rizzini & C.)
Techno Arms (See U.S. importer—Auto-Ordnance Corp.)
Tecnolegno S.p.A., Via A. Locatelli, 6, 10, 24019 Zogno, ITALY/0345-91114; FAX: 0345-93254
Tele-Optics, 5514 W. Lawrence Ave., Chicago, IL 60630/312-283-7757; FAX: 312-283-7757
Ten-Ring Precision, Inc., Alex B. Hamilton, 1449 Blue Crest Lane, San Antonio, TX 78232/210-494-3063; FAX: 210-494-3066
Tennessee Valley Mfg., P.O. Box 1175, Corinth, MS 38834/601-286-5014
Tepeco, P.O. Box 342, Friendswood, TX 77546/713-482-2702
Testing Systems, Inc., 220 Pegasus Ave., Northvale, NJ 07647
Teton Arms, Inc., P.O. Box 411, Wilson, WY 83014/307-733-3395
Tetra Gun Lubricants, 1812 Margaret Ave., Annapolis, MD 21401/410-268-6451; FAX: 410-268-8377
Texas Armory, P.O. Box 154906, Waco, TX 76715/817-867-6972
Texas Longhorn Arms, Inc., 5959 W. Loop South, Suite 424, Bellaire, TX 77401/713-660-6323; FAX: 713-660-0493
Texas Platers Supply Co., 2453 W. Five Mile Parkway, Dallas, TX 75233/214-330-7168
T.F.C. S.p.A., Via G. Marconi 118, B, Villa Carcina, Brescia 25069, ITALY/030-881271; FAX: 030-881826
Theis, Terry, P.O. Box 535, Fredericksburg, TX 78624/210-997-6778
Theoben Engineering, Stephenson Road, St. Ives, Huntingdon, Cambs., PE17 4WJ ENGLAND/011-0480-461718
Thiewes, George W., 14329 W. Parada Dr., Sun City West, AZ 85375
Things Unlimited, 235 N. Kimbau, Casper, WY 82601/307-234-5277
Thirion Gun Engraving, Denise, P.O. Box 408, Graton, CA 95444/707-829-1876
Thomas, Charles C., 2600 S. First St., Springfield, IL 62794/217-789-8980; FAX: 217-789-9130
Thompson, Norm, 18905 NW Thurman St., Portland, OR 97209
Thompson, Randall (See Highline Machine Co.)
Thompson Bullet Lube Co., P.O. Box 472343, Garland, TX 75047-2343/214-271-8063; FAX: 214-840-6743
Thompson/Center Arms, P.O. Box 5002, Rochester, NH 03866/603-332-2394; FAX: 603-332-5133
Thompson Precision, 110 Mary St., P.O. Box 251, Warren, IL 61087/815-745-3625
Thompson Target Technology, 618 Roslyn Ave., SW, Canton, OH 44710/216-453-7707; FAX: 216-478-4723
Thompson Tool Mount (See TTM)
T.H.U. Enterprises, Inc., P.O. Box 418, Lederach, PA 19450/215-256-1665; FAX: 215-256-9718
Thunder Mountain Arms, P.O. Box 593, Oak Harbor, WA 98277/206-679-4657; FAX: 206-675-1114
Thunderbird Cartridge Co., Inc. (See TCCI)
Thurston Sports, Inc., RD 3 Donovan Rd., Auburn, NY 13021/315-253-0966
Tiger-Hunt, Box 379, Beaverdale, PA 15921/814-472-5161
Tikka (See U.S. importer—Stoeger Industries)
Timber Heirloom Products, 618 Roslyn Ave. SW, Canton, OH 44710/216-453-7707; FAX: 216-478-4723
Time Precision, Inc., 640 Federal Rd., Brookfield, CT 06804/203-775-8343
Timney Mfg., Inc., 3065 W. Fairmont Ave., Phoenix, AZ 85017/602-274-2999; FAX: 602-241-0361

Tink's Safariland Hunting Corp., P.O. Box 244, 1140 Monticello Rd., Madison, GA 30650/706-342-4915; FAX: 706-342-7568
Tinks & Ben Lee Hunting Products (See Wellington Outdoors)
Tioga Engineering Co., Inc., P.O. Box 913, 13 Cone St., Wellsboro, PA 16901/717-724-3533, 717-662-3347
Tippman Pneumatics, Inc., 3518 Adams Center Rd., Fort Wayne, IN 46806/219-749-6022; FAX: 219-749-6619
Tirelli, Snc Di Tirelli Primo E.C., Via Matteotti No. 359, Gardone V.T., Brescia, ITALY 25063/030-8912819; FAX: 030-832240
Titus, Daniel, Shooting Specialties, 119 Morlyn Ave., Bryn Mawr, PA 19010-3737/215-525-8829
TMI Products (See Haselbauer Products, Jerry)
TM Stockworks, 6355 Maplecrest Rd., Fort Wayne, IN 46835/219-485-5389
Tom's Gun Repair, Thomas G. Ivanoff, 76-6 Rt. Southfork Rd., Cody, WY 82414/307-587-6949
Tom's Gunshop, 3601 Central Ave., Hot Springs, AR 71913/501-624-3856
Tomboy, Inc., P.O. Box 846, Dallas, OR 97338/503-623-8405
Tombstone Smoke`n'Deals, 3218 East Bell Road, Phoenix, AZ 85032/602-905-7013; Fax: 602-443-1998
Tonoloway Tack Drives, HCR 81, Box 100, Needmore, PA 17238
Tooley Custom Rifles, 516 Creek Meadow Dr., Gastonia, NC 28054/704-864-7525
Top-Line USA, Inc., 7920-28 Hamilton Ave., Cincinnati, OH 45231/513-522-2992, 800-346-6699; FAX: 513-522-0916
Torel, Inc., 1708 N. South St., P.O. Box 592, Yoakum, TX 77995/512-293-2341; FAX: 512-293-3413
Totally Dependable Products (See TDP Industries, Inc.)
TOZ (See U.S. importer—Nygord Precision Products)
TR Metals Corp., 1 Pavilion Ave., Riverside, NJ 08075/609-461-9000; FAX: 609-764-6340
Track of the Wolf, Inc., P.O. Box 6, Osseo, MN 55369-0006/612-424-2500; FAX: 612-424-9860
Tradewinds, Inc., P.O. Box 1191, 2339-41 Tacoma Ave. S., Tacoma, WA 98401/206-272-4887
Traditions, Inc., P.O. Box 776, 1375 Boston Post Rd., Old Saybrook, CT 06475/860-388-4656; FAX: 860-388-4657
Trafalgar Square, P.O. Box 257, N. Pomfret, VT 05053/802-457-1911
Traft Gunshop, P.O. Box 1078, Buena Vista, CO 81211
TrailTimer Co., 1992-A Suburban Ave., P.O. Box 19722, St. Paul, MN 55119/612-738-0925
Trail Visions, 5800 N. Ames Terrace, Glendale, WI 53209/414-228-1328
Trammco, 839 Gold Run Rd., Boulder, CO 80302
Trappers Trading, P.O. Box 26946, Austin, TX 78755/800-788-9334
Trax America, Inc., P.O. Box 898, 1150 Eldridge, Forrest City, AR 72335/501-633-0410, 800-232-2327; FAX: 501-633-4788
Treadlok Gun Safe, Inc., 1764 Granby St. NE, Roanoke, VA 24012/800-729-8732, 703-982-6881; FAX: 703-982-1059
Treemaster, P.O. Box 247, Guntersville, AL 35976/205-878-3597
Treso, Inc., P.O. Box 4640, Pagosa Springs, CO 81157/303-731-2295
Trevallion Gunstocks, 9 Old Mountain Rd., Cape Neddick, ME 03902/207-361-1130
Trico Plastics, 590 S. Vincent Ave., Azusa, CA 91702
Trijicon, Inc., 49385 Shafer Ave., P.O. Box 930059, Wixom, MI 48393-0059/810-960-7700; FAX: 810-960-7725
Trilux Inc., P.O. Box 24608, Winston-Salem, NC 27114/910-659-9438; FAX: 910-768-7720
Trinidad State Junior College, Gunsmithing Dept., 600 Prospect St., Trinidad, CO 81082/719-846-5631; FAX: 719-846-5667
Triple-K Mfg. Co., Inc., 2222 Commercial St., San Diego, CA 92113/619-232-2066; FAX: 619-232-7675
Tristar Sporting Arms, Ltd., 1814-16 Linn St., P.O. Box 7496, N. Kansas City, MO 64116/816-421-1400; FAX: 816-421-4182
Trius Traps, Inc., P.O. Box 25, 221 S. Miami Ave., Cleves, OH 45002/513-941-5682; FAX: 513-941-7970
Trooper Walsh, 2393 N. Edgewood St., Arlington, VA 22207
Trophy Bonded Bullets, Inc., 900 S. Loop W., Suite 190, Houston, TX 77054/713-645-4499; FAX: 713-741-6393
Trotman, Ken, 135 Ditton Walk, Unit 11, Cambridge CB5 8PY, ENGLAND/01223-211030; FAX: 01223-212317
Tru-Balance Knife Co., P.O. Box 140555, Grand Rapids, MI 49514/616-453-3679
Tru-Square Metal Prods., Inc., 640 First St. SW, P.O. Box 585, Auburn, WA 98071/206-833-2310; FAX: 206-833-2349
True Flight Bullet Co., 5581 Roosevelt St., Whitehall, PA 18052/610-262-7630; FAX: 610-262-7806
Trulock Tool, Broad St., Whigham, GA 31797/912-762-4678
TTM, 1550 Solomon Rd., Santa Maria, CA 93455/805-934-1281
Tucker, James C., P.O. Box 15485, Sacramento, CA 95851/916-923-0571
Turkish Firearms Corp., 522 W. Maple St., Allentown, PA 18101/610-821-8660; FAX: 610-821-9049
Turnbull Restoration, Inc., Doug, 6426 County Rd. 30, P.O. Box 471, Bloomfield, NY 14469/716-657-6338; WEB: http://gunshop.com/dougt.htm
Tuttle, Dale, 4046 Russell Rd., Muskegon, MI 49445/616-766-2250
Twin Pine Armory, P.O. Box 58, Hwy. 6, Adna, WA 98522/360-748-4590; FAX: 360-748-1802
Tyler Mfg.-Dist., Melvin, 1326 W. Britton Rd., Oklahoma City, OK 73114/405-842-8044, 800-654-8415
Tyler Scott, Inc., 313 Rugby Ave., Terrace Park, OH 45174/513-831-7603; FAX: 513-831-7417

U

Uberti USA, Inc., P.O. Box 469, Lakeville, CT 06039/860-435-8068; FAX: 860-435-8146
Uberti, Aldo, Casella Postale 43, I-25063 Gardone V.T., ITALY (U.S. importers—American Arms, Inc.; Cimarron Arms; Dixie Gun Works; EMF Co., Inc.; Forgett Jr., Valmore J.; Navy Arms Co; Taylor's & Co., Inc.; Uberti USA, Inc.)
UFA, Inc., 6927 E. Grandview Dr., Scottsdale, AZ 85254/800-616-2776

MANUFACTURERS' DIRECTORY

Ugartechea S.A., Ignacio, Chonta 26, Eibar, SPAIN 20600/43-121257; FAX: 43-121669 (U.S. importer—Galaxy Imports Ltd., Inc.; Mandall Shooting Supplies, Inc.)
Ultimate Accuracy, 121 John Shelton Rd., Jacksonville, AR 72076/501-985-2530
Ultra Light Arms, Inc., P.O. Box 1270, 214 Price St., Granville, WV 26505/304-599-5687; FAX: 304-599-5687
Ultralux (See U.S. importer—Keng's Firearms Specialty, Inc.)
UltraSport Arms, Inc., 1955 Norwood Ct., Racine, WI 53403/414-554-3237; FAX: 414-554-9731
Uncle Bud's, HCR 81, Box 100, Needmore, PA 17238/717-294-6000; FAX: 717-294-6005
Uncle Mike's (See Michaels of Oregon Co.)
Unertl Optical Co., Inc., John, 308 Clay Ave., P.O. Box 818, Mars, PA 16046-0818/412-625-3810
Unique/M.A.P.F., 10, Les Allees, 64700 Hendaye, FRANCE 64700/33-59 20 71 93 (U.S. importer—Nygord Precision Products)
UniTec, 1250 Bedford SW, Canton, OH 44710/216-452-4017
United Binocular Co., 9043 S. Western Ave., Chicago, IL 60620
United Cutlery Corp., 1425 United Blvd., Sevierville, TN 37876/615-428-2532, 800-548-0835; FAX: 615-428-2267
United States Ammunition Co. (See USAC)
United States Optics Technologies, Inc., 5900 Dale St., Buena Park, CA 90621/714-994-4901; FAX: 714-994-4904
United States Products Co., 518 Melwood Ave., Pittsburgh, PA 15213/412-621-2130
Upper Missouri Trading Co., 304 Harold St., Crofton, NE 68730/402-388-4844
USAC, 4500-15th St. East, Tacoma, WA 98424/206-922-7589
U.S.A. Magazines, Inc., P.O. Box 39115, Downey, CA 90241/800-872-2577
USA Sporting Inc., 1330 N. Glassell, Unit M, Orange, CA 92667/714-538-3109, 800-538-3109; FAX: 714-538-1334
U.S. Patent Fire Arms, No. 25-55 Van Dyke Ave., Hartford, CT 06106/800-877-2832; FAX: 800-644-7265
U.S. Repeating Arms Co., Inc., 275 Winchester Ave., Morgan, UT 84050-9333/801-876-3440; FAX: 801-876-3737
Utica Cutlery Co., 820 Noyes St., Utica, NY 13503/315-733-4663; FAX: 315-733-6602
Uvalde Machine & Tool, P.O. Box 1604, Uvalde, TX 78802

V

Valade Engraving, Robert, 931 3rd Ave., Seaside, OR 97138/503-738-7672
Valmet (See Tikka/U.S. importer—Stoeger Industries)
Valor Corp., 5555 NW 36th Ave., Miami, FL 33142/305-633-0127; FAX: 305-634-4536
Van Epps, Milton, Rt. 69-A, Parish, NY 13131/315-625-7251
Van Gorden & Son, Inc., C.S., 1815 Main St., Bloomer, WI 54724/715-568-2612
Van Horn, Gil, P.O. Box 207, Llano, CA 93544
Van Patten, J.W., P.O. Box 145, Foster Hill, Milford, PA 18337/717-296-7069
Vancini, Carl (See Bestload, Inc.)
Vann Custom Bullets, 330 Grandview Ave., Novato, CA 94947
Varner's Service, 102 Shaffer Rd., Antwerp, OH 45813/419-258-8631
Vega Tool Co., c/o T.R. Ross, 4865 Tanglewood Ct., Boulder, CO 80301/303-530-0174
Venco Industries, Inc. (See Shooter's Choice)
Venom Arms Co., Unit 1, Gun Garrel Industrial Centre, Hayseech, Cradley, Heath/West Midlands B64 7JZ ENGLAND 011-021-501-3794 (U.S. importers—Mac-1 Distributors, Trooper Walsh)
Venus Industries, P.O. Box 246, Sialkot-1, PAKISTAN/FAX: 92 432 85579
Verney-Carron, B.P. 72, 54 Boulevard Thiers, 42002 St. Etienne Cedex 1, FRANCE/33-77791500; FAX: 33-77790702
Vest, John, P.O. Box 1552, Susanville, CA 96130/916-257-7228
VibraShine, Inc., P.O. Box 577, Taylorsville, MS 39168/601-785-9854; FAX: 601-785-9874
Vibra-Tek Co., 1844 Arroya Rd., Colorado Springs, CO 80906/719-634-8611; FAX: 719-634-6886
Vic's Gun Refinishing, 6 Pineview Dr., Dover, NH 03820-6422/603-742-0013
Victory USA, P.O. Box 1021, Pine Bush, NY 12566/914-744-2060; FAX: 914-744-5181
Vihtavuori Oy, FIN-41330 Vihtavuori, FINLAND/358-41-3779211; FAX: 358-41-3771643
Vihtavuori Oy/Kaltron-Pettibone, 1241 Ellis St., Bensenville, IL 60106/708-350-1116; FAX: 708-350-1606
Viking Leathercraft, Inc., 1579A Jayken Way, Chula Vista, CA 91911/800-262-6666; FAX: 619-429-8268
Viking Video Productions, P.O. Box 251, Roseburg, OR 97470
Vincent's Shop, 210 Antoinette, Fairbanks, AK 99701
Vintage Arms, Inc., 6003 Saddle Horse, Fairfax, VA 22030/703-968-0779; FAX: 703-968-0780
Vintage Industries, Inc., 781 Big Tree Dr., Longwood, FL 32750/407-831-8949; FAX: 407-831-5346
VIP Products, 488 East 17th St., Ste. A-101, Costa Mesa, CA 92627/714-722-5986
Viramontez, Ray, 601 Springfield Dr., Albany, GA 31707/912-432-9683
Visible Impact Targets, Rts. 5 & 20, E. Bloomfield, NY 14443/716-657-6161; FAX: 716-657-5405
Vitt/Boos, 2178 Nichols Ave., Stratford, CT 06497/203-375-6859
Voere-KGH m.b.H., P.O. Box 416, A-6333 Kufstein, Tirol, AUSTRIA/0043-5372-62547; FAX: 0043-5372-65752 (U.S. importers—JagerSport, Ltd.)
Volquartsen Custom Ltd., 24276 240th Street, P.O. Box 271, Carroll, IA 51401/712-792-4238; FAX: 712-792-2542; E-MAIL: vcl@netins.net
Vom Hofe (See Old Western Scrounger, Inc., The)
Von Minden Gunsmithing Services, 2403 SW 39 Terrace, Cape Coral, FL 33914/813-542-8946
Vorhes, David, 3042 Beecham St., Napa, CA 94558/707-226-9116
Vortek Products, Inc., P.O. Box 871181, Canton, MI 48187-6181/313-397-5656; FAX:313-397-5656
VSP Publishers (See Heritage/VSP Gun Books)
Vulpes Ventures, Inc., Fox Cartridge Division, P.O. Box 1363, Bolingbrook, IL 60440-7363/708-759-1229

W

Wagoner, Vernon G., 2325 E. Encanto, Mesa, AZ 85213/602-835-1307
Wakina by Pic, 24813 Alderbrook Dr., Santa Clarita, CA 91321/800-295-8194
Waldron, Herman, Box 475, 80 N. 17th St., Pomeroy, WA 99347/509-843-1404
Walker Arms Co., Inc., 499 County Rd. 820, Selma, AL 36701/334-872-6231
Walker Mfg., Inc., 8296 S. Channel, Harsen's Island, MI 48028
Walker Co., B.B., P.O. Box 1167, 414 E. Dixie Dr., Asheboro, NC 27203/910-625-1380; FAX: 910-625-8125
Wallace, Terry, 385 San Marino, Vallejo, CA 94589/707-642-7041
Waller & Son, Inc., W., 59 Stoney Brook Road, Grandtham, NH 03753/603-863-4177; WEB: http://shooter.com
Walls Industries, Inc., P.O. Box 98, 1905 N. Main, Cleburne, TX 76031/817-645-4366; FAX: 817-645-7946
Walnut Factory, The, 235 West Rd. No. 1, Portsmouth, NH 03801/603-436-2225; FAX: 603-433-7003
Walt's Custom Leather, Walt Whinnery, 1947 Meadow Creek Dr., Louisville, KY 40218/502-458-4361
Walters Industries, 6226 Park Lane, Dallas, TX 75225/214-691-6973
Walters, John, 500 N. Avery Dr., Moore, OK 73160/405-799-0376
Walther GmbH, Carl, B.P. 4325, D-89033 Ulm, GERMANY (U.S. importer—Champion's Choice; Interarms; P.S.M.G. Gun Co.)
WAMCO, Inc., Mingo Loop, P.O. Box 337, Oquossoc, ME 04964-0337/207-864-3344
WAMCO—New Mexico, P.O. Box 205, Peralta, NM 87042-0205/505-869-0826
Ward & Van Valkenburg, 114 32nd Ave. N., Fargo, ND 58102/701-232-2351
Ward Machine, 5620 Lexington Rd., Corpus Christi, TX 78412/512-992-1221
Wardell Precision Handguns Ltd., 48851 N. Fig Springs Rd., New River, AZ 85027-8513/602-465-7995
Warenski, Julie, 590 E. 500 N., Richfield, UT 84701/801-896-5319; FAX: 801-896-5319
Warne Manufacturing Co., 9039 SE Jannsen Rd., Clackamas, OR 97015/503-657-5590, 800-683-5590; FAX: 503-657-5695
Warren & Sweat Mfg. Co., P.O. Box 350440, Grand Island, FL 32784/904-669-3166; FAX: 904-669-7272
Warren Muzzleloading Co., Inc., Hwy. 21 North, P.O. Box 100, Ozone, AR 72854/501-292-3268
Warren, Kenneth W. (See Mountain States Engraving)
Washita Mountain Whetstone Co., P.O. Box 378, Lake Hamilton, AR 71951/501-525-3914
WASP Shooting Systems, Rt. 1, Box 147, Lakeview, AR 72642/501-431-5606
Waterfield Sports, Inc., 13611 Country Lane, Burnsville, MN 55337/612-435-8531
Watson Bros., 39 Redcross Way, London Bridge, London, United Kingdom, SE1 1HG/FAX: 44-171-403-3367
Watson Trophy Match Bullets, 2404 Wade Hampton Blvd., Greenville, SC 29615/803-244-7948
Watsontown Machine & Tool Co., 309 Dickson Ave., Watsontown, PA 17777/717-538-3533
Wayne Firearms for Collectors and Investors, James, 2608 N. Laurent, Victoria, TX 77901/512-578-1258; FAX: 512-578-3559
Wayne Specialty Services, 260 Waterford Drive, Florissant, MO 63033/413-831-7083
WD-40 Co., 1061 Cudahy Pl., San Diego, CA 92110/619-275-1400; FAX: 619-275-5823
Weatherby, Inc., 3100 El Camino Real, Atascadero, CA 93422/805-466-1767, 800-227-2016, 800-334-4423 (Calif.); FAX: 805-466-2527
Weaver Arms Corp. Gun Shop, RR 3, P.O. Box 266, Bloomfield, MO 63825-9528
Weaver Products, Div. of Blount, Inc., Sporting Equipment Div., P.O. Box 39, Onalaska, WI 54650/800-648-9624, 608-781-5800; FAX: 608-781-0368
Weaver Scope Repair Service, 1121 Larry Mahan Dr., Suite B, El Paso, TX 79925/915-593-1005
Webb, Bill, 6504 North Bellefontaine, Kansas City, MO 64119/816-453-7431
Weber & Markin Custom Gunsmiths, 4-1691 Powick Rd., Kelowna, B.C. CANADA V1X 4L1/604-762-7575; FAX: 604-861-3655
Weber Jr., Rudolf, P.O. Box 160106, D-5650 Solingen, GERMANY/0212-592136
Webley and Scott Ltd., Frankley Industrial Park, Tay Rd., Rubery, Rednal, Birmingham B45 0PA, ENGLAND/011-021-453-1864; FAX: 021-457-7846 (U.S. importer—Beeman Precision Airguns; Groenewold, Inc.)
Webster Scale Mfg. Co., P.O. Box 188, Sebring, FL 33870/813-385-6362
Weems, Cecil, P.O. Box 657, Mineral Wells, TX 76067/817-325-1462
Weigand Combat Handguns, Inc., P.O. Box 239, Crestwood Industrial Park, Mountain Top, PA 18707/717-474-9804; FAX: 717-474-9987
Weihrauch KG, Hermann, Industriestrasse 11, 8744 Mellrichstadt, GERMANY/09776-497-498 (U.S. importers—Beeman Precision Airguns; E.A.A. Corp.)
Weisz Parts, P.O. Box 20038, Columbus, OH 43220-0038/614-45-70-500; FAX: 614-846-8585
Welch, Sam, CVSR 2110, Moab, UT 84532/801-259-8131
Wellington Outdoors, P.O. Box 244, 1140 Monticello Rd., Madison, GA 30650/706-342-4915; FAX: 706-342-7568
Wells Creek Knife & Gun Works, 32956 State Hwy. 38, Scottsburg, OR 97473/503-587-4202
Wells Custom Gunsmith, R.A., 3452 1st Ave., Racine, WI 53402/414-639-5223
Wells, Fred F., Wells Sport Store, 110 N. Summit St., Prescott, AZ 86301/520-445-3655
Wells, Rachel, 110 N. Summit St., Prescott, AZ 86301/520-445-3655
Welsh, Bud, 80 New Road, E. Amherst, NY 14051/716-688-6344
Wenig Custom Gunstocks, Inc., 103 N. Market St., P.O. Box 249, Lincoln, MO 65338/816-547-3334; FAX: 816-547-2881
Wenoka/Seastyle, P.O. Box 10969, Riviera Beach, FL 33419/407-845-6155; FAX: 407-842-4247
Werner, Carl, P.O. Box 492, Littleton, CO 80160
Werth, T.W., 1203 Woodlawn Rd., Lincoln, IL 62656/217-732-1300
Wescombe, P.O. Box 488, Glencoe, CA 95232/209-293-7010
Wessinger Custom Guns & Engraving, 268 Limestone Rd., Chapin, SC 29036/803-345-5677

DIRECTORY OF THE ARMS TRADE

West, Jack L., 1220 W. Fifth, P.O. Box 427, Arlington, OR 97812
West, Robert G., 3973 Pam St., Eugene, OR 97402/541-344-3700
Western Cutlery (See Camillus Cutlery Co.)
Western Design (See Alpha Gunsmith Division)
Western Gunstock Mfg. Co., 550 Valencia School Rd., Aptos, CA 95003/408-688-5884
Western Missouri Shooters Alliance, P.O. Box 11144, Kansas City, MO 64119/816-597-3950; FAX: 816-229-7350
Western Munitions (See North American Munitions)
Western Nevada West Coast Bullets, 2307 W. Washington St., Carson City, NV 89703/702-246-3941; FAX: 702-246-0836
Westfield Engineering, 6823 Watcher St., Commerce, CA 90040/FAX: 213-928-8270
Westley Richards & Co., 40 Grange Rd., Birmingham, ENGLAND B29 6AR/010-214722953 (U.S. importer—Cape Outfitters)
Westrom, John (See Precision Metal Finishing)
Westwind Rifles, Inc., David S. Sullivan, P.O. Box 261, 640 Briggs St., Erie, CO 80516/303-828-3823
Weyer International, 2740 Nebraska Ave., Toledo, OH 43607/419-534-2020; FAX: 419-534-2697
Whildin & Sons Ltd., E.H., RR2, Box 119, Tamaqua, PA 18252/717-668-6743; FAX: 717-668-6745
Whinnery, Walt (See Walt's Custom Leather)
Whiscombe (See U.S. importer—Pelaire Products)
White Flyer Targets, 124 River Road, Middlesex, NJ 08846/908-469-0100, 602-972-7528 (Export); FAX: 908-469-9692, 602-530-3360 (Export)
White Laboratory, Inc., H.P., 3114 Scarboro Rd., Street, MD 21154/410-838-6550; FAX: 410-838-2802
White Owl Enterprises, 2583 Flag Rd., Abilene, KS 67410/913-263-2613; FAX: 913-263-2613
White Pine Photographic Services, Hwy. 60, General Delivery, Wilno, Ontario K0J 2N0 CANADA/613-756-3452
White Rock Tool & Die, 6400 N. Brighton Ave., Kansas City, MO 64119/816-454-0478
White Shooting Systems, Inc., 25 E. Hwy. 40, Box 330-12, Roosevelt, UT 84066/801-722-3085, 800-213-1315; FAX: 801-722-3054
Whitehead, James D., 204 Cappucino Way, Sacramento, CA 95838
Whitestone Lumber Corp., 148-02 14th Ave., Whitestone, NY 11357/718-746-4400; FAX: 718-767-1748
Whitetail Design & Engineering Ltd., 9421 E. Mannsiding Rd., Clare, MI 48617/517-386-3932
Whits Shooting Stuff, Box 1340, Cody, WY 82414
Wichita Arms, Inc., 923 E. Gilbert, P.O. Box 11371, Wichita, KS 67211/316-265-0661; FAX: 316-265-0760
Wick, David E., 1504 Michigan Ave., Columbus, IN 47201/812-376-6960
Widener's Reloading & Shooting Supply, Inc., P.O. Box 3009 CRS, Johnson City, TN 37602/615-282-6786; FAX: 615-282-6651
Wideview Scope Mount Corp., 13535 S. Hwy. 16, Rapid City, SD 57701/605-341-3220; FAX: 605-341-9142
Wiebe, Duane, 33604 Palm Dr., Burlington, WI 53105-9260
Wiest, M.C., 10737 Dutchtown Rd., Knoxville, TN 37932/423-966-4545
Wilcox All-Pro Tools & Supply, 4880 147th St., Montezuma, IA 50171/515-623-3138; FAX: 515-623-3104
Wild Bill's Originals, P.O. Box 13037, Burton, WA 98013/206-463-5738
Wild West Guns, 7521 Old Seward Hwy, Unit A, Anchorage, AK 99518/907-344-4500; FAX: 907-344-4005
Wilderness Sound Products Ltd., 4015 Main St. A, Springfield, OR 97478/503-741-0263, 800-437-0006; FAX: 503-741-7648
Wildey, Inc., P.O. Box 475, Brookfield, CT 06804/203-355-9000; FAX: 203-354-7759
Wildlife Research Center, Inc., 4345 157th Ave. NW, Anoka, MN 55304/612-427-3350, 800-USE-LURE; FAX: 612-427-8354
Wilkinson Arms, 26884 Pearl Rd., Parma, ID 83660/208-722-6771; FAX: 208-722-5197
Will-Burt Co., 169 S. Main, Orrville, OH 44667
William's Gun Shop, Ben, 1151 S. Cedar Ridge, Duncanville, TX 75137/214-780-1807
Williams Bullet Co., J.R., 2008 Tucker Rd., Perry, GA 31069/912-987-0274
Williams Gun Sight Co., 7389 Lapeer Rd., Box 329, Davison, MI 48423/810-653-2131, 800-530-9028; FAX: 810-658-2140
Williams Mfg. of Oregon, 110 East B St., Drain, OR 97435/541-836-7461; FAX: 541-836-7245
Williams Shootin' Iron Service, The Lynx-Line, 8857 Bennett Hill Rd., Central Lake, MI 49622/616-544-6615
Williamson Precision Gunsmithing, 117 W. Pipeline, Hurst, TX 76053/817-285-0064
Willig Custom Engraving, Claus, D-97422 Schweinfurt, Siedlerweg 17, GERMANY/01149-9721-41446; FAX: 01149-9721-44413
Willow Bend, P.O. Box 203, Chelmsford, MA 01824/508-256-8508; FAX: 508-256-8508
Willson Safety Prods. Div., P.O. Box 622, Reading, PA 19603-0622/610-376-6161; FAX: 610-371-7725
Wilson Arms Co., The, 63 Leetes Island Rd., Branford, CT 06405/203-488-7297; FAX: 203-488-0135
Wilson Case, Inc., P.O. Box 1106, Hastings, NE 68902-1106/800-322-5493; FAX: 402-463-5276
Wilson, Inc., L.E., Box 324, 404 Pioneer Ave., Cashmere, WA 98815/509-782-1328
Wilson's Gun Shop, Box 578, Rt. 3, Berryville, AR 72616/501-545-3618; FAX: 501-545-3310
Winchester (See U.S. Repeating Arms Co., Inc.)
Winchester Div., Olin Corp., 427 N. Shamrock, E. Alton, IL 62024/618-258-3566; FAX: 618-258-3599
Winchester Press (See New Win Publishing, Inc.)
Winchester Sutler, Inc., The, 270 Shadow Brook Lane, Winchester, VA 22603/540-888-3595; FAX: 540-888-4632
Windish, Jim, 2510 Dawn Dr., Alexandria, VA 22306/703-765-1994
Windjammer Tournament Wads, Inc., 750 W. Hampden Ave. Suite 170, Englewood, CO 80110/303-781-6329
Wingshooters Ltd., 4320 Kalamazoo Ave., Grand Rapids, MI 49508/616-455-7810; FAX: 616-455-5212
Wingshooting Adventures, 4320 Kalamazoo Ave. SE, Grand Rapids, MI 49507/616-455-7810; FAX: 616-455-5212
Winkle Bullets, R.R. 1 Box 316, Heyworth, IL 61745
Winter, Robert M., P.O. Box 484, Menno, SD 57045/605-387-5322
Wise Guns, Dale, 333 W. Olmos Dr., San Antonio, TX 78212/210-828-3388
Wiseman and Co., Bill, P.O. Box 3427, Bryan, TX 77805/409-690-3456; FAX: 409-690-0156
Wolf's Western Traders, 40 E. Works, No. 3F, Sheridan, WY 82801/307-674-5352
Wolfe Publishing Co., 6471 Airpark Dr., Prescott, AZ 86301/602-445-7810, 800-899-7810; FAX: 602-778-5124
Wolff Co., W.C., P.O. Box 458, Newtown Square, PA 19073/610-359-9600, 800-545-0077
Wolverine Footwear Group, 9341 Courtland Dr. NE, Rockford, MI 49351/616-866-5500; FAX: 616-866-5658
Wood, Frank (See Classic Guns, Inc.)
Wood, Mel, P.O. Box 1255, Sierra Vista, AZ 85636/602-455-5541
Woodleigh (See Huntington Die Specialties)
Woods Wise Products, P.O. Box 681552, 2200 Bowman Rd., Franklin, TN 37068/800-735-8182; FAX: 615-726-2637
Woodstream, P.O. Box 327, Lititz, PA 17543/717-626-2125; FAX: 717-626-1912
Woodworker's Supply, 1108 North Glenn Rd., Casper, WY 82601/307-237-5354
Woolrich Inc., Mill St., Woolrich, PA 17701/800-995-1299; FAX: 717-769-6234/6259
World of Targets (See Birchwood Casey)
World Class Airguns, 2736 Morningstar Dr., Indianapolis, IN 46229/317-897-5548
World Trek, Inc., 7170 Turkey Creek Rd., Pueblo, CO 81007-1046/719-546-2121; FAX: 719-543-6886
Worthy Products, Inc., RR 1, P.O. Box 213, Martville, NY 13111/315-324-5298
Wosenitz VHP, Inc., Box 741, Dania, FL 33004/305-923-3748; FAX: 305-925-2217
Wostenholm (See Ibberson [Sheffield] Ltd., George)
Wright's Hardwood Gunstock Blanks, 8540 SE Kane Rd., Gresham, OR 97080/503-666-1705
Wyant Bullets, Gen. Del., Swan Lake, MT 59911
Wyant's Outdoor Products, Inc., P.O. Box B, Broadway, VA 22815
Wyoming Bonded Bullets, Box 91, Sheridan, WY 82801/307-674-8091
Wyoming Custom Bullets, 1626 21st St., Cody, WY 82414
Wyoming Knife Corp., 101 Commerce Dr., Ft. Collins, CO 80524/303-224-3454

X, Y

X-Spand Target Systems, 26-10th St. SE, Medicine Hat, AB T1A 1P7 CANADA/403-526-7997; FAX: 403-528-2362
Yankee Gunsmith, 2901 Deer Flat Dr., Copperas Cove, TX 76522/817-547-8433
Yavapai College, 1100 E. Sheldon St., Prescott, AZ 86301/602-776-2359; FAX: 602-776-2193
Yavapai Firearms Academy Ltd., P.O. Box 27290, Prescott Valley, AZ 86312/520-772-8262
Yearout, Lewis E. (See Montana Outfitters)
Yee, Mike, 29927 56 Pl. S., Auburn, WA 98001/206-839-3991
Yellowstone Wilderness Supply, P.O. Box 129, W. Yellowstone, MT 59758/406-646-7613
Yesteryear Armory & Supply, P.O. Box 408, Carthage, TN 37030
York M-1 Conversions, 803 Mill Creek Run, Plantersville, TX 77363/800-527-2881, 713-477-8442
Young, Paul A., RR 1 Box 694, Blowing Rock, NC 28605-9746
Young Country Arms, P.O. Box 3615, Simi Valley, CA 93093
Yukon Arms Classic Ammunition, 1916 Brooks, P.O. Box 223, Missoula, MT 59801/406-543-9614

Z

Z's Metal Targets & Frames, P.O. Box 78, South Newbury, NH 03255/603-938-2826
Zabala Hermanos S.A., P.O. Box 97, Eibar, SPAIN 20600/43-768085, 43-768076; FAX: 34-43-768201 (U.S. importer—American Arms, Inc.)
Zanoletti, Pietro, Via Monte Gugielpo, 4, I-25063 Gardone V.T., ITALY (U.S. importer—Mandall Shooting Supplies, Inc.)
Zanotti Armor, Inc., 123 W. Lone Tree Rd., Cedar Falls, IA 50613/319-232-9650
Z-Coat Industrial Coatings, Inc., 3375 U.S. Hwy. 98 S. No. A, Lakeland, FL 33803-8365/813-665-1734
ZDF Import/Export Inc., 2975 South 300 West, Salt Lake City, UT 84115/801-485-1012; FAX: 801-484-4363
Zeeryp, Russ, 1601 Foard Dr., Lynn Ross Manor, Morristown, TN 37814/615-586-2357
Zeiss Optical, Carl, 1015 Commerce St., Petersburg, VA 23803/804-861-0033, 800-388-2984; FAX: 804-733-4024
Zero Ammunition Co., Inc., 1601 22nd St. SE, P.O. Box 1188, Cullman, AL 35056-1188/800-545-9376; FAX: 205-739-4683
Ziegel Engineering, 2108 Lomina Ave., Long Beach, CA 90815/310-596-9481; FAX: 310-598-4734
Zim's Inc., 4370 S. 3rd West, Salt Lake City, UT 84107/801-268-2505
Zoli, Antonio, Via Zanardelli 39, Casier Postal 21, I-25063 Gardone V.T., ITALY
Zonie Bullets, 790 N. Lake Havasu Ave., Suite 26, Lake Havasu City, AZ 86403/520-680-6303; FAX: 520-680-6201
Zriny's Metal Targets (See Z's Metal Targets & Frames)
Zufall, Joseph F., P.O. Box 304, Golden, CO 80402-0304